The Voucher Worth £1

May be redeemed in accordance
with the conditions overleaf at any of the
establishments whose gazetteer entry shows the
symbol £

The Voucher Worth £1

May be redeemed in accordance
with the conditions overleaf at any of the
establishments whose gazetteer entry shows the
symbol £

The Voucher Worth £1

May be redeemed in accordance
with the conditions overleaf at any of the
establishments whose gazetteer entry shows the
symbol £

The Voucher Worth £1

May be redeemed in accordance
with the conditions overleaf at any of the
establishments whose gazetteer entry shows the
symbol £

The Voucher Worth £1

May be redeemed in accordance
with the conditions overleaf at any of the
establishments whose gazetteer entry shows the
symbol £

The Voucher Worth £1

May be redeemed in accordance
with the conditions overleaf at any of the
establishments whose gazetteer entry shows the
symbol £

Conditions

A COPY OF AA INSPECTED BED AND BREAKFAST IN
BRITAIN AND IRELAND 1992 MUST BE PRODUCED WITH
THIS VOUCHER.
ONLY ONE VOUCHER PER PERSON OR PARTY ACCEPTED.
NOT REDEEMABLE FOR CASH. NO CHANGE GIVEN.
THE VOUCHER WILL NOT BE VALID AFTER 31ST
DECEMBER 1992.
USE OF THE VOUCHER WILL ONLY BE ACCEPTED
AGAINST ACCOMMODATION AT FULL TARIFF RATES.

Conditions

A COPY OF AA INSPECTED BED AND BREAKFAST IN
BRITAIN AND IRELAND 1992 MUST BE PRODUCED WITH
THIS VOUCHER.
ONLY ONE VOUCHER PER PERSON OR PARTY ACCEPTED.
NOT REDEEMABLE FOR CASH. NO CHANGE GIVEN.
THE VOUCHER WILL NOT BE VALID AFTER 31ST
DECEMBER 1992.
USE OF THE VOUCHER WILL ONLY BE ACCEPTED
AGAINST ACCOMMODATION AT FULL TARIFF RATES.

Conditions

A COPY OF AA INSPECTED BED AND BREAKFAST IN
BRITAIN AND IRELAND 1992 MUST BE PRODUCED WITH
THIS VOUCHER.
ONLY ONE VOUCHER PER PERSON OR PARTY ACCEPTED.
NOT REDEEMABLE FOR CASH. NO CHANGE GIVEN.
THE VOUCHER WILL NOT BE VALID AFTER 31ST
DECEMBER 1992.
USE OF THE VOUCHER WILL ONLY BE ACCEPTED
AGAINST ACCOMMODATION AT FULL TARIFF RATES.

Conditions

A COPY OF AA INSPECTED BED AND BREAKFAST IN
BRITAIN AND IRELAND 1992 MUST BE PRODUCED WITH
THIS VOUCHER.
ONLY ONE VOUCHER PER PERSON OR PARTY ACCEPTED.
NOT REDEEMABLE FOR CASH. NO CHANGE GIVEN.
THE VOUCHER WILL NOT BE VALID AFTER 31ST
DECEMBER 1992.
USE OF THE VOUCHER WILL ONLY BE ACCEPTED
AGAINST ACCOMMODATION AT FULL TARIFF RATES.

Conditions

A COPY OF AA INSPECTED BED AND BREAKFAST IN
BRITAIN AND IRELAND 1992 MUST BE PRODUCED WITH
THIS VOUCHER.
ONLY ONE VOUCHER PER PERSON OR PARTY ACCEPTED.
NOT REDEEMABLE FOR CASH. NO CHANGE GIVEN.
THE VOUCHER WILL NOT BE VALID AFTER 31ST
DECEMBER 1992.
USE OF THE VOUCHER WILL ONLY BE ACCEPTED
AGAINST ACCOMMODATION AT FULL TARIFF RATES.

Conditions

A COPY OF AA INSPECTED BED AND BREAKFAST IN
BRITAIN AND IRELAND 1992 MUST BE PRODUCED WITH
THIS VOUCHER.
ONLY ONE VOUCHER PER PERSON OR PARTY ACCEPTED.
NOT REDEEMABLE FOR CASH. NO CHANGE GIVEN.
THE VOUCHER WILL NOT BE VALID AFTER 31ST
DECEMBER 1992.
USE OF THE VOUCHER WILL ONLY BE ACCEPTED
AGAINST ACCOMMODATION AT FULL TARIFF RATES.

AA

INSPECTED
BED AND
BREAKFAST
in
BRITAIN
AND IRELAND
1992

PRODUCED BY THE PUBLISHING DIVISION OF THE AUTOMOBILE
ASSOCIATION

DIRECTORY: compiled by the AA's Research Unit, Information Control, in co-
operation with AA Hotels Services, and generated by the AA's Establishment
Database.

MAPS: prepared by the Cartographic Department of the Automobile Association
© The Automobile Association 1991
COVER DESIGN: The Paul Hampson Partnership
COVER PHOTOGRAPHY: Gordon Hammond ABIPP, Southampton
COLOUR SUPPLEMENT DESIGN: Neil Roebuck Design

HEAD OF ADVERTISEMENT SALES: Christopher Heard Tel: (0256) 20123
ADVERTISEMENT PRODUCTION: Karen Weeks Tel: (0256) 20123
Typeset and printed by William Clowes Ltd, Beccles, Suffolk.
Colour supplement printed by J B Shears & Sons Ltd, Basingstoke, Hampshire.

Contents

INTRODUCTION

❖ ──────────────────────────────── ❖

STAYING IN A BED AND BREAKFAST ESTABLISHMENT is an option many holidaymakers choose, not just because it is less expensive than a hotel, but because they receive a much more personal service. Good home cooking, extra touches to the comfort of the rooms and, of course value for money, all combine to make your holiday special. For those who want more than the anonymity of a large hotel, a guesthouse, farmhouse or inn can offer a refreshing alternative. And this year's guide provides details of more than 2,800 such establishments. At each of the establishments we list all over Britain and Ireland, you can be assured of good value for money and high standards of service, because AA Inspectors visit regularly and we update our information every year.

The AA Inspected Bed and Breakfast guide has assisted holidaymakers for many years, but for 1992 it has been extended to include Ireland, too. While we have not been able to award symbols for quality to Republic of Ireland establishments, they have all been inspected, and all have achieved the necessary requirements for inclusion in the guide.

Other new features include an entertaining article on the changing face of bed and breakfast. We all have fixed images in our minds of dark lodgings, formidable landladies, no privacy, and lumpy porridge, or worse! But bed and breakfast today can mean many different things - a cheerful weekend in an historic inn, a gourmet break, or a week on a working farm, for example. Denise Laing looks at a few of the choices offered to holidaymakers today, and gives her verdict.

We also feature the Best Newcomer Awards, in which we choose from all of the establishments new to the AA classification scheme this year, the seven that we think offer the highest standards of comfort and hospitality for their particular ratings.

All establishments in Britain are rated for quality, and receive between one and four Q awards. Details of these are provided on page 24. Those whose standards are exceptionally good are also highlighted in the directory under the heading 'SELECTED' and the entries are enclosed in a tinted panel. A full list of these places is given on pages 25-28. They have been chosen by our Inspectors as offering standards of cooking, accommodation and hospitality that are well above the normal requirements for an AA listing. In all, only 234 establishments have been awarded the distinction this year.

A warm welcome
awaits you
at

St Johns Lodge

Lake Road,
Windermere LA23 2EQ
Telephone: (05394) 43078

Situated mid-way between
Windermere and Bowness.
Just ten minutes walk to
all amenities.
St Johns Lodge offers you 14 Bedrooms with private facilities, colour TV and
hospitality tray. Some have four poster beds, lace canopies or coronets. Several
ground floor bedrooms. Dining room accommodates residents bar.
Traditional English fare is supplied by chef/proprietor. Private parking.
For colour brochure and details of off-season breaks
please telephone Windermere (05394) 43078.

Ideally situated mid-way between Bowness and Windermere, within easy walking
distance of both villages and backed by woodland.
All bedrooms have en suite facilities, tea/coffee making facilities and colour
television. Licensed. Traditional English home cooking. Evening meal optional.
Some ground floor bedrooms.
Special Off-Season Breaks or Weekly Terms available.
Same ownership for last 10 years.

HAWKSMOOR

Lake Road, Windermere, Cumbria LA23 2EQ
Telephone: 05394 42110

For room availability or brochure
please telephone
Windermere
(05394) 42110

Large Private
Car Park

WHAT IS A GUESTHOUSE?

❖————————❖

The term 'guesthouse' can lead to some confusion, particularly when many include the word 'hotel' in their name. For our purposes, we include small and private hotels in this category when they cannot offer all the services required for our star classification system.

This is not to say that guesthouses are inferior to hotels, just that they are different - and many offer a very high standard of accommodation. It is not unusual to be offered en suite bathrooms, for instance, or to find a colour television in your room. It is true that some guesthouses will only offer a set meal in the evening, but many provide a varied and interesting menu, and a standard of service that one would expect of a good restaurant. At the other end of the scale, some guesthouses offer bed and breakfast only, and it would also be wise to check if there are any restrictions to your access to the house, particularly late in the morning and during the afternoon.

Guesthouses in the London section of the book are all small hotels. Of course, London prices tend to be higher than those in the provinces, but those that we list offer cost-conscious accommodation, although normally only bed and breakfast is provided. To allow for all eventualities, we have also included a few which provide a full meal service and the charges for these will naturally be higher.

STAYING AT A FARMHOUSE

❖————————❖

Farmhouse accommodation has a special quality, and is particularly noted for being inexpensive and cosy, with a high standard of good home-cooking. Those listed in our book are generally working farms, and some farmers are happy to allow visitors to look around, or even to help feed the animals. However, we must stress that the modern farm is a potentially dangerous place, especially where machinery and chemicals are concerned, and visitors must be prepared to exercise care, particularly if they bring children. Never leave children unsupervised around the farm. Sometimes, guest accommodation is run as a separate concern from the farm on which it stands, and visitors are discouraged from venturing on to the working land. In other cases, the land has been sold off. Although the directory entry states the acreage and the type of farming carried out, it is advisable to check when booking to make sure that your requirements are met. As with guesthouses, standards will vary considerably, and are often far above what one would expect. Some of our farmhouses are grand ex-manor houses furnished with antiques and offering a stylish way of life, others will offer more basic accommodation. All of the farmhouses are listed under town or village names, but

obviously many will be some distance from other habitation. Proprietors will, of course, give directions when you book, and we publish a six-figure map reference against the directory entry which can be used in conjunction with Ordnance Survey maps.

❖ ———————————————— ❖

Whatever the type of establishment, there are certain requirements common to all, including a well-maintained exterior, clean and hygienic kitchens; good standards of furnishing; friendly and courteous service; access to the premises at reasonable times; the use of a telephone; and a full English or Irish breakfast. Bedrooms should be equipped with comfortable beds, a wardrobe, a bedside cabinet, a washbasin with soap, towel, mirror and shaver socket and at least a carpet beside the bed. There should not be an extra charge for the use of baths or lavatories, and heating should be unmetered.

NB Where an establishment shows the central heating symbol, it does not necessarily mean that central heating will be available all year round. Some places only use it in winter, and then at their own discretion.

INNS

❖ ———————————————— ❖

We all know what we can expect to find in a traditional inn - a cosy bar, a convivial atmosphere, good beer and pub food. Nevertheless, we have a few criteria which must be met. Breakfast is a must of course, in a suitable breakfast room, and the inn should also serve at least light meals during licensing hours. Our inn category may also include a number of small, fully licensed hotels, and the character of the properties will vary according to whether they are pretty country inns or larger establishments in towns. Again, it is important to check details before you book.

Moonraker House

40 Alcester Road, Stratford-upon-Avon CV37 9DB Telephone (0789) 299346 or 267115 Fax (0789) 295504

* ALL rooms have en-suite bathrooms, tea and coffee making facilities, colour TV, clock radios and fitted hairdryers.

SHAKESPEARE'S TOWN

* There are also extra special rooms with four poster beds, lounge area and garden patio (non-smoking).

* Enjoy an excellent English breakfast prepared with care by the resident proprietors, Mauveen and Mike Spencer.

👑 👑 👑
COMMENDED

* ALL rooms are elegantly decorated and designed with your comfort in mind.

* Five minutes' walk from town centre.

* CAR PARK (open and garage).

* Ideal centre for exploring the Cotswolds, Shakespeare's countryside, Warwick Castle and Shakespeare Theatres.

STRATFORD-UPON-AVON

AA QQQ   MinOtels   Les Routiers

AN UNEXPECTED PLEASURE

Mention the great British Bed and Breakfast and most people instantly conjure up a memory - funny, pleasant or dreadful - of their own experiences. Almost everyone, with the possible exception of the Rothschilds and the Royal Family, has stayed in one at sometime or another, and their stories are often hilarious.

My own most forgettable Bed and Breakfast was a house filled with notices telling you to "Close the door quietly behind you", and "Don't flush the toilets after 9.30pm". Bath water and cooked breakfasts were not part of the deal: all plugs had been removed, and when we rose as planned to catch the early morning ferry, yet another notice instructed us to help ourselves to tea, toast and cereal. There was not so much as a sizzling sausage in sight, let alone the slumbering mistress of the house.

Some stories are more endearing. One friend staying in a small Borders town was woken at 5am to the sounds of someone going berserk in the kitchen. She crept down to breakfast, to be cheerfully greeted by a hostess with suspiciously floury-looking elbows who had been up since dawn cooking everything from oatcakes, to the mandatory bacon and eggs. My friend was the only guest and politeness obliged her to eat the lot.

So is a room for the night and a big enough breakfast to fuel you for the day all you can expect? Is the choice simply between 'cheap and cheerful' or 'cheap and ghastly'? Not at all, to judge by the results of this survey of six very different types of Bed and Breakfast up and down the country. You will find standards of comfort and hospitality you thought had long since vanished, and often the sort of house-party atmosphere and sumptuous cooking, including really lavish evening meals, that makes a holiday memorable for the right reasons.

Book yourself into *Wigham*, the environmentally friendly farmhouse home of Stephen and Lesley Chilcott in the wilds of Devon, and you'll forget forever any preconceived notions you harboured. Staying in this lovely old longhouse outside Morchard Bishop is more like spending a weekend with civilised friends, and the feeling is reinforced by the relaxed dinner party atmosphere in the evening. Guests all gather around the long dining table in a convivial manner, and at least one of the Chilcotts shares the meal and the conversation. By the end of the evening people are usually on very friendly terms with each other, although some groups gel less well than others.

Forget net curtains, candlewick bedspreads and forbidding landladies. Instead the charming Chilcotts show you to one of their five tastefully decorated double bedrooms, each with large en suite bathroom nestling in the eaves, colour television and video recorder. The pretty rooms are named after their individual colour schemes, and the honeymoon suite comes complete with hand carved four poster bed. Living rooms are spacious and comfortable, and huge fires make winter nights warm and cosy. There is even a snooker room.

The Chilcotts farm 30 acres of lush Devon land, and most of their produce ends up on the table. Once guests see the menu they generally choose to eat in, and are likely to be offered fresh young lamb or a joint of beef from animals that only recently roamed within yards of the house. Fruit and vegetables are picked daily, and the milk, yogurt, clotted cream and home-made ice cream all come from the Channel Island cow.

A typical meal might consist of a delicious soup, fillet steak in wine with cream and mushrooms, colourful arrays of vegetables, a choice of sweets and a cheese board. Although Stephen Chilcott is currently chasing the coveted Soil Association's organic farming symbol - only awarded after two years free of pesticides, fungicides and fertilisers - and the house is a no-smoking one, other signs of the modern-day health freak are completely lacking. Instead the emphasis is on good rich country cooking, and the hearty puddings with lashings of thick yellow cream are rarely refused.

People return again and again to the peace and hospitality offered at this 16th-century house and it's easy to see why. It offers a glimpse of a way of life that many people dream of, and a short stay is not long enough to expose its rigours. Relaxing beside the outdoor swimming pool with a Pimms within reach, the countryside spread out below and the wonderful smells of cooking wafting past on the air, it is easy to imagine that the minimum effort is required to keep the whole idyll going. In fact, the Chilcotts both work very hard at making the running of their business look effortless, and to provide for the townies who flock there an escape from urban life.

The atmosphere at the *Arden Hotel* in one of Bath's most gracefully Georgian streets could hardly be more different. Here the elegant 18th-century surroundings provide the perfect stopping place for up-market business people and the many smart tourists who visit this famous spa city. The owner is Jacqueline Newbigin, an immaculate lady who doesn't look as if she would recognise a hair curler if she saw one.

All ten bedrooms in this town house are beautifully decorated, and fitted out with the sort of solid reproduction oak furniture that breathes quality and craftsmanship from every pore. Sweeping Austrian drapes grace the windows, and each room has a spacious en suite bathroom. There is not a duvet to be seen but every bed is made up with expensive sheets and the finest soft wool blankets. Apparently duvets are never found in the best hotels.

Mrs Newbigin has run the Arden for 10 years, but it is only in the last few years after a serious fire that she has been able to renovate it to such a high standard. What she aims to provide is excellent service in a rather grand setting, and she doesn't stint on the number of staff she employs. She believes that it is the personal touch that makes many people choose the Arden in preference to the larger hotels, and judging by the comments in the visitor's book the guests agree.

But there is another surprise which one might not necessarily associate with bed and breakfast, even if it is set in a Grade 1 listed building in this stylish city. Below the stone entrance to the hotel on Great Pulteney Street is Florizel's, a superb new restaurant which is already receiving rave reviews. Here chef Lawrence Benson, late of London's Capital Hotel, Genevieve's and Otter's, creates dishes which are admired and appreciated by tourists and regulars alike.

For business visitors especially who don't relish the thought of going out in the evening for a meal, the restaurant is a godsend. They can relax in their rooms at the end of the working day, or carry on into the evening if they choose. Lights in the bedrooms are bright enough to work by, there is room to spread papers, and Mrs Newbigin provides the use of fax machines and a secretarial service if needed.

Not quite what one might expect from a Bed and Breakfast, perhaps, but then neither is helping with the haymaking or feeding the animals at the farm belonging to Geoffrey and Jackie Cook. The Cooks have been offering bed and breakfast accommodation in their 16th-century farmhouse since 1987, and many of the holiday makers who come to unwind and help on the farm return year after year, eventually becoming good friends.

Wallace Farm, Dinton is set in the Vale of Aylesbury, an excellent touring area within easy reach of Oxford, the Cotswolds and London. Guests were originally invited as a means of supplementing a sometimes precarious farming income, but the family have taken to it like ducks to water and wouldn't think of putting up the closed signs. Bed and Breakfasts vary as much as the people who run them, and the entrepreneurial urge which encourages someone to open their home to strangers often shows itself in a warm, relaxed, eager to please way that is sometimes lacking in larger hotels.

The usual friendly, enquiring farm dogs greet visitors in the courtyard where a short but very wide front door opens into a flagstoned

century is the occasional sighting of a tractor.

At the *Orotava Hotel* in Llandudno, the owner Mrs Jennifer Hall takes a personal pride in making her guests feel cosseted and cared for. The only rules and regulations in this establishment apply to the girls who help in the kitchen and dining room, and if tablecloths are found to be less than clean and crisp, or cutlery not quite lined up in perfect parallel lines, they soon hear about it.

The guests at this seaside Bed and Breakfast, whose gardens lead directly onto the beach, are thoroughly spoiled, and it is no coincidence that 80 per cent of them return. The majority are retired and elderly people, and Mrs Hall has made catering for them into an art form. She offers good plain cooking with plenty of home-made soups, fresh vegetables and sliced meats. The elderly are not so fond of chewing chops, cutlets and steaks as younger guests might be, but they relish their sweets, and bread and butter pudding is always greeted with an anticipatory murmur.

Nearly all of the eight bedrooms are en suite, and some of them have sea views to add to the relaxed holiday atmosphere. Dinner is served in a pleasant dining room, also overlooking the sea, and the attractively panelled lounge is the work of Mr Hall, a local builder. Having a husband with such a useful trade comes in very handy, and there is never any trouble getting jobs done around the house. The last two en suite facilities are soon to be installed.

Mrs Hall is very critical when she stays in a hotel herself. She feels that guests are not always treated as well as they should be, and admires places where staff are cheerful and friendly, and the surroundings comfortable. When newcomers arrive at the Orotava they are welcomed like the old friends they often become, and offered tea and scones as soon as they have had a chance to freshen up. She believes that more people are attracted to smaller hotels and bed and breakfasts nowadays because they get better attention, and she clearly practises what she preaches.

hall. You know at once that nobody will mind if you forget to take your muddy wellies off. A typical farmhouse breakfast is served at the huge polished walnut table in the large open-plan kitchen, under exposed beams beside an inglenook fireplace complete with bread ovens. In the sitting room, literally thousands of books mean that rainy days must be almost longed for. Geoffrey Cook genuinely means it when he says people are welcome to read or browse, and there is no sign that he has hidden the best editions away.

The farm is the sort of old-fashioned spread that children love to draw. Heavy horses plough the fields alongside their modern mechanical counterparts, and pull the loaded carts at haymaking time in the late summer. There are rare breeds of cattle and sheep as well as the more common varieties, ducks and geese on the ponds, numerous dogs and cats, and all of their various offspring at the appropriate times of the year. Free range chickens see to the job of producing a continuous supply of fresh breakfast eggs. In January the lambing starts, and there is shearing and dipping in June and July. Guests can help wherever they like, but haymaking remains the most popular farming activity and Geoffrey is rarely short of helpers.

The accommodation here is in three spacious and comfortable bedrooms, one with en suite facilities and two with shared use of a bathroom. The low level bedroom windows overlook the lovely lawned gardens or the farm itself, and the only reminder that this is the 20th

The *Drunken Duck Inn* at Ambleside is another place whose owners are clear about what their customers want, and know exactly how to provide it. Peter and Stephanie Barton might have been tempted to turn their 16th-century property into a country house hotel with the knowledge that its position in 60 acres of magnificent lakeland countryside would guarantee its success. But they were certain that an old world, traditional pub offering food and bedrooms was what was needed, and they have never looked back.

Nothing much has been altered in the old bar and its snug for many years, and in here local green slate blends beautifully with seasoned timbers and open log fires. There are no pinball machines and no juke boxes, and the beer is the kind of real ale the aficionados campaign for, and serious drinkers travel miles to sample. Such an ancient place is bound to have a history, and the name comes complete with its own legend. Rumour has it that a Victorian owner discovered her flock of ducks to be dead, and being a lady who did not like waste, she decided to prepare them for the oven. In the middle of being plucked they

revived, and she realised that a barrel of fine beer had seeped into their feeding ditch, leaving them in a highly inebriated state. Hence what was once Barngates Inn became the Drunken Duck.

Such a juicy legend has not been allowed to go to waste, and teeshirts, aprons and other items bearing its details have been sold in large numbers from behind the bar. In the summertime the popularity of this traditional inn in its isolated crossroad setting overlooking Lake Windermere, makes everyone thankful that there are gardens to spread into. Anyone staying here might expect a lot of crowds and noise to ruin their peace, but the rooms are delightfully private. They all have a cottagey feel with their patchwork quilts, exposed beams, antiques and old prints on the walls. Twentieth century comforts have not been neglected either, and all rooms come with en suite bathrooms, televisions, telephones, hairdryers and facilities for making hot drinks. Another nice touch is that each room is named after a former owner of the inn.

The extensive grounds offer trout fishing

in two tarns, shooting and wonderful walking country, and the food at either end of the day provides enough fuel to get the most out of all the available activities. Breakfasts are the kind that make you think you will never be able to get up from the table. After a day out exploring the fells, the healthiest appetites are satisfied with huge helpings of such meals as beefsteak and kidney pie, followed by sticky toffee pudding. Nobody goes hungry at the Drunken Duck.

The same can be said for anyone lucky enough to dine at Lin Scrannage's Bed and Breakfast in Broadway, one of England's prettiest Cotswold villages. Lin is a former chef from Manchester, and when she took over as landlady in charge of eight double rooms in this most touristy of areas last year, she knew that cooking breakfast would not be enough to satisfy her. Not that her breakfasts are exactly run of the mill. Along with the usual full English and its may variations on a theme, Lin offers a champagne breakfast with home-made brioche filled with smoked salmon and scrambled eggs. It comes at a little extra, naturally, and it probably just the thing to entice honeymooners out into the open. But not exactly what you might expect to find outside the menus of top class hotels.

Dinners at the *Small Talk Lodge* are just as unexpected. Starters like aubergine souffle with tomato and basil sauce, baked spinach custards with cumin-flavoured hollandaise and leek and mustard soup hint at the quality of the cooking, and Lin's culinary skills are amply demonstrated by what follows. Breast of chicken with lime and tarragon, filo parcels of spinach, ricotta and almonds, and mushroom, walnut and cream cheese strudel with watercress sauce are just some of the delights in store.

Nowhere will you find red meat, but there is plenty of fish, free range poultry, fresh pasta and vegetables. Factory farming and hormones are out, but puddings are in, and they might include poached pear filled with bitter chocolate, served with vanilla cream and pistachios, or gooseberry and mint pie with clotted cream.

Lin left the restaurant which she ran with two friends because she wanted to go solo, and was seeking more contact with people than working in a kitchen allows. To keep costs down and make a new success of her business, she has taken her solo act as far as she can. Apart from some help with cleaning the rooms, and an occasional assistant when the dining room is full, she does virtually everything by herself. She only cooks dinner when people ask in advance, and as her restaurant licence prohibits offering the superb food to the public, she isn't tied to the kitchen every night.

The business was fairly run down when she took it over last July, and she has enjoyed building it up and lifting its look. There is still some way to go with the decor, and the dining room may look plain when you consider the wonderful food that she serves there, but its superb situation just behind the historic Lygon Arms should ensure plenty of guests.

The six places described here are only a small selection of the many outstanding Bed and Breakfast places just waiting to be discovered within the pages of this guide. A good starting place would be the list of 'selected' entries on pp25-28.

Symbols and Abbreviations

ENGLISH	FRANÇAIS	DEUTSCH

ENGLISH

- 🛏💷 Bed and breakfast for £13 or under
- Ⓠ Quality assessment (see p. 24)
- ☎ Telephone number
- ⇄ Private bath and WC
- ☗ Private shower and WC
- ✗ Bedrooms set aside for non-smokers
- ✖ No dogs
- ® Tea/coffee-making facilities in bedrooms
- ✻ 1991 prices
- 🕮 Full central heating
- P Parking for cars
- P̸ No parking on premises
- 🚗 Garage accommodation for ... cars
- 🚌 Coach parties not accepted
- ⚭ Special facilities for children (see p. 31)
- ⊡ Indoor swimming pool
- ⊴ Outdoor swimming pool
- ▶9▶18 9-hole or 18-hole golf course
- ♟ Tennis court(s)
- ◢ Fishing
- ∪ Riding stables on premises

- sB&B Single room including breakfast per person per night
- dB&B Double room (2 persons sharing a room) including breakfast per night
- WB&B Weekly terms, bed and breakfast, per person
- WBDi Weekly terms bed, breakfast and evening meal, per person
- alc A la carte
- CTV Colour television
- Etr Easter
- fb Family bedroom
- fr From
- hc Number of bedrooms with hot and cold water
- LDO Time last dinner can be ordered
- Lic Licensed
- mdnt Midnight
- nc No children. nc ... yrs, no children under ... years of age
- rm Letting bedrooms in main building
- rs Restricted service
- TV Black and white television

- ⊡ Credit cards (p. 31)
- £ Voucher scheme (p. 29)
- → Entry continued overleaf

FRANÇAIS

- 🛏💷 Chambre et petit déjeuner pour moins de £13
- Ⓠ Symbole AA d'évaluation qualitative (voir p. 24)
- ☎ Numéro de téléphone
- ⇄ Salle de bain privée avec WC
- ☗ Douche privée et WC
- ✗ Chambres réservées aux non-fumeurs
- ✖ Chiens interdits
- ® Possibilité de faire le thé/le café dans les chambres
- ✻ Prix 1991
- 🕮 Chauffage central intégral
- P Stationnement pour voitures
- P̸ Pas de stationnement sur place
- 🚗 Garage pour ... voitures
- 🚌 Groups en autocar pas reçus
- ⚭ Facilités spéciales pour enfants – (voir p. 31)
- ⊡ Piscine à l'intérieur
- ⊴ Piscine à l'extérieur
- ▶9▶18 Terrain de golf à 9 ou 18 trous
- ♟ Court(s) de tennis
- ◢ Pêche
- ∪ Ecuries d'équitation sur les lieux

- sB&B Chambre à un lit et petit déjeuner par personne et par nuit
- dB&B Chambre à deux lits (2 personnes à une chambre) avec petit déjeuner par nuit
- WB&B Prix par semaine et par personne, chambre et petit déjeuner inclus
- WBDi Prix par semaine et par personne, chambre, petit déjeuner et diner inclus
- alc A la carte
- CTV TV en couleurs
- Etr Pâques
- fb Chambre de famille
- fr A partir de
- hc Nombre de chambres avec eau chaude et froide
- LDO Le dîner est à commander avant cette heure
- Lic Licence de boissons
- mdnt Minuit
- nc Enfants pas admis. nc ... ans, enfants au-dessous de ... ans pas admis
- rm Nombre de chambres dans le bâtiment principal
- rs Service réduit
- TV TV en noir et blanc

- ⊡ Cartes de crédit (p. 31)
- £ Bons (p. 29)
- → Suite au verso

DEUTSCH

- 🛏💷 Bett mit Frühstück für unter £13
- Ⓠ AA Katagorisierung der Qualität (siehe S. 24)
- ☎ Telefonnummer
- ⇄ Privatbadezimmer mit WC
- ☗ Privatdusche mit WC
- ✗ Zimmer für Nichtraucher
- ✖ Hundeverbot
- ® Tee/Kaffeemöglichkeiten im Zimmer
- ✻ 1991 Preise
- 🕮 Vollfernheizung
- P Parkplatz
- P̸ Kein Parkplatz
- 🚗 Garagen für ... Autos
- 🚌 Reisebusgesellschaften nicht aufgenommen
- ⚭ Sonderdienstleistungen für Kinder – (siehe S. 31)
- ⊡ Hallenbad
- ⊴ Freibad
- ▶9▶18 Golfplatz mit 9 oder 18 löcher
- ♟ Tennisplatz (Platze)
- ◢ Angeln
- ∪ Reitstall an Ort und Stelle

- sB&B Übernachtung in einem Einzelzimmer mit Frühstück pro Person
- dB&B Doppelzimmer (2 Personer in einem Zimmer) mit Frühstück pro Nacht
- WB&B Wochenpreis pro Person, Übernachtung mit Frühstück
- WBDi Wochenpreis pro Person, Übernachtung mit Frühstück und Abendessen
- alc A la carte
- CTV Farbfernsehen
- Etr Ostern
- fb Familienzimmer
- fr Von
- hc Zimmer mit Warm- und Kaltwasser
- LDO Letzte Bestellzeit für Abendessen
- Lic Ausschank alkoolischer Getränke
- mdnt Mitternacht
- nc Kinder nicht willkommen. nc .. Jahren, Kinder unter .. Jahren nicht willkommen
- rm Zimmeranzahl im Hauptgebäude
- rs Beschränkte Dienstleistungen
- TV Schwarzweissfernsehen

- ⊡ Kreditkarten (p. 31)
- £ Gutschein (p. 29)
- → Fortsetzung umseitig

15

Symbols and Abbreviations

ITALIANO

🛏🍴	Camera e prima colazione a meno di 13 sterline
Ⓠ	Simbolo di valutazione qualitativa della AA (vedi p. 24)
☎	Numero telefonica
🛁	Bagno e servizi privati
♠	Doccia e servizi privati
⚥	Camere per non fumatori
🐕	Proibito ai cani
Ⓡ	Attrezzatura per fare il té o il caffé nelle camere
✳	Prezzi del 1991
⚒	Riscaldemento centrale in tutte le camere
P	Parcheggio macchine
⚡	Senza parcheggio sul posto
🚗	Garage per . . . macchine
🚌	Non si accettano comitive in gita turistica
🧸	Attrezzature speciali per í bambini – (vedi p. 31)
▣	Piscina coperta
⌇	Piscina scoperta
▶9▶18	Campo da golf a 9 o 18 buche
🎾	Campo(i) da tennis
🎣	Pesca
☊	Scuola d'equitazione sul posto
sB&B	Prezzo di una camera singola con la colazione compresa (per notte)
dB&B	Prezzo di una camera doppia (2 persone per camera) con la colazione compresa (per notte)
WB&B	Tariffe settimanali per persona, camera e prima colazione
WBDi	Tariffe settimanali per persona, sono compresi la camera, la prima colazione e il pranzo
alc	Alla carta
CTV	Televisione a colori
Etr	Pasqua
fb	Camera familiare
fr	Da
hc	Numero di camera con acqua calda e fredda
LDO	Ora in cui si accettano le ultime ordinazioni
Lic	Autorizzato alla vendita alcolici
mdnt	Mezzanotte
nc	Proibito ai bambini. nc . . . anni, proibito ai bambini sottoi . . . anni
rm	Numero di camere nell' edificio principale
rs	Servizio limitato
TV	Televisione in bianco e nero
①	Carte di credito (p. 31)
ⓔ	Documento di riduzione (p. 29)
→	La lista delle voci continua a tergo

ESPAÑOL

🛏🍴	Cama y desaguno a menos de 13 libras esterlinas
Ⓠ	Simbolo de evaluación calitativa de la AA (Véase p. 24)
☎	Numero de teléfono
🛁	Baño y servicios en cada habitación
♠	Ducha y servicios en cada habitación
⚥	Habitaciones reservados para los no fumadores
🐕	Se prohibe a los porros
Ⓡ	Facilidades para hacer el té o el café en los habitaciones
✳	Precios de 1991
⚒	Calafacción central
P	Aparcamiento para automóviles
⚡	No poder estacionarse junto al establecimiento
🚗	Garage o espacio cubierto para . . . automóviles
🚌	No se aceptan los grupos de viajeros en coches de linea
🧸	Facilidades especialies para los niños (p. 31)
▣	Piscina cubierta
⌇	Piscina descubierta
▶9▶18	Campo de golf de 9 o 18 hoyos
🎾	Cancha(s) de tenis
🎣	Pesca
☊	Escuela hípica
sB&B	Precio por noche de una habitación individual con desayuno incluido
dB&B	Precio por noche de una habitación para dos personas (2 personas compartiendo una habitación) con desayuno incluido
WB&B	Tarifas semanales cama y desayuno
WBDi	Tarifas semanales, el precio incluye a la cama, al desayuna y a la comida
alc	A la carta
CTV	Televisión en colores
Etr	Pascua de Resurrección
fb	Habitación familiar
fr	De
hc	Número de habitaciones con agua fría y caliente
LDO	Últimas ordenes
Lic	Con licencia para vender bebidas alcóholicas
mdnt	Medianoche
nc	Se prohibe la entrada a los niños. nc . . . años, se prohibe la entrada a los niños de menos de . . . añoc
rm	Número de habitaciones del edifico principal
rs	Servicio limitado
TV	Televisión en blanco y negro
①	Tarjetas de crédito (p. 31)
ⓔ	Documento de rehaja (p. 29)
→	La lista continúa a la vuelta

BEST NEWCOMER AWARDS

Every year the AA receives hundreds of new applications from guesthouses, farmhouses and inns, and we ask our inspectors to choose the best of the newcomers in each area of the country for the Best Newcomer of the Year Awards. When considering somewhere for an award the inspectors look for something very special in the way of hospitality and friendliness as well as the expected high standards of comfort and cleanliness. The seven places described in the following pages all made an outstanding impression for the warmth of welcome the owners extended to their guests and the care they took to make everyone feel truly at home throughout their stay.

SOUTH OF ENGLAND
SWALE COTTAGE
Penshurst, Kent

Swale Cottage is a skilfully converted 18th-century barn, peacefully situated overlooking the delightful countryside of the Weald of Kent.

Nothing is too much trouble for proprietor Cynthia Dakin who takes great pleasure in anticipating her guests' needs - greeting them when they first arrive, helping them to and showing them around their rooms, offering a cup of tea, and recommending and making reservations for dinner at nearby restaurants. Later in the evening she will turn down their beds, even slipping a hot water bottle between the sheets on those chillier evenings, and providing many other little touches that ensure guests' stay will be really special.

The lounge is one of those rooms that manages to combine attractive and stylish decor with all the comforts of home and

many of the paintings of local countryside and places of interest on display here have been done by Cynthia herself.

Bedrooms too - just three of them, prettily decorated and decked out with fresh flowers - are individually and tastefully furnished. All have en suite facilities and all are thoughtfully equipped with TV, radio alarm and so on as well as having extras like mineral water, tissues and cotton wool, moisturising cream and so on.

Although this is just a bed and breakfast establishment and an evening meal is not provided, the breakfast served at the elegant communal dining table is very good indeed.

Swale Cottage is a lovely guesthouse in which outstanding and genuine hospitality can be found. It is also an excellent centre for exploring the many places of interest nearby such as Hever Castle, Knowle Park, Chartwell - once the home of Sir Winston Churchill - Leeds Castle, Royal Tunbridge Wells and much more besides.

SOUTH-WEST OF ENGLAND
BRADFORD OLD WINDMILL
Bradford-upon-Avon, Wiltshire

Peter and Priscilla Roberts have always had a passion for old buildings that is reflected in their choice of home; their first residence was a one-time slaughterhouse, the second a converted pub and their third and present home, which they run as a guesthouse with a difference, is a restored 19th-century windmill overlooking the picturesque old town of Bradford-upon-Avon.

Realising that people enjoy staying in unusual buildings, the Roberts gathered together the details of around 40 other interesting bed and breakfast establishments all over the country and set up Distinctly Different - a company to market them, and they run this business in conjunction with their own guesthouse at the Old Windmill.

Simply and attractively decorated throughout and with lots of plants, ornaments and books, this guesthouse in the round, with its large log fire in the lounge in winter makes a very comfortable place to stay for vegetarians and non-smokers.

The well equipped bedrooms (also, not surprisingly, mostly round!) are prettily decorated and furnished with old pine furniture and have a country cottage feel about them.

Delicious vegetarian meals are served in this guesthouse and guests sit down together at the large old pine table in the dining room. The evening meal, served around 8pm, features a set menu such as thick home-made soup of beans, followed by vegetable curry with Basmati rice, dahl, raita, four or so side dishes and nan bread with curd cheese and cream cheese for dessert - at a cost of £15. The Bradford Old Windmill breakfast was described by our inspector as "outstanding".

Central England
Brookfield on Longhill
Buxton, Derbyshire

"A thoroughly miserable day was brightened by my stay here," reported our inspector after his visit to this small country house set in 10 acres of grounds in the heart of Derbyshire's beautiful Peak District, just a mile from Buxton.

Partners Roger Handley and Brian Brooke, their families and staff make guests welcome from the moment they first arrive.

All guests are met and greeted, taken to their rooms, invited downstairs for a cup of tea and cake, offered drinks in the library before dinner, offered a nightcap when they retire to bed - and so on. And this level of care is maintained until checkout time and the last goodbyes are said.

As befits a country house, the public areas - the splendid entrance hall with its lovely staircase, the library and drawing room, the two dining rooms and conservatory - are all furnished in keeping with the period of the house and everywhere there are interesting prints, pretty ornaments and local craft as well as masses of books, magazines and games for guests' entertainment. The bedrooms are equally well furnished and atmospheric as well as being thoughtfully equipped.

The restaurant, which is open to non-residents on Fridays, Saturdays and Sundays has an interesting and extensive menu further supplemented by daily specials and is fast becoming popular for the quality of its food and wine. Breakfast too is excellent, offering fresh fish as well as all the usual breakfast ingredients.

Outside there are acres of gardens and woodland for guests to roam in with access to heather-clad moors for walking. There is also a riding school in the grounds.

NORTH OF ENGLAND
THE OLD RECTORY
Bolton Gate, Cumbria

Very much a private home taking guests, the Old Rectory at Bolton Gate dates back to the 15th century with other parts added on since.

Overlooking beautiful lakeland scenery, this lovely house with its low beams, stone walls and roaring log fires in winter, is the home of Anthony and Kathleen Peacock who manage to provide the sort of welcome and ongoing care and attention that makes guests feel like part of the family almost immediately.

There are two attractive lounges - one with television and one without - superbly furnished and a low beamed, 17th-century dining room with a wood-burning stove where an imaginative five-course dinner is served up to guests all seated at one table - house-party style. Our inspector enthused about his 'superb' game soup, the smoked salmon cream with Hollandaise sauce, the beef in orange and sweet stout, delicious syllabub and the cheese that were offered on the evening that he was there.

There are three guest bedrooms at the Old Rectory, two en suite, all of which are tastefully decorated and have good facilities as well as having lots of little unexpected extras like fruit, books and magazines, comfortable bath robes for guests to wear and so on.It is this extra touch of care and attention that makes this guest house so special.

A lovely house to stay in, the Old Rectory also offers excellent walking, fishing and sailing nearby as well as many places of interest to visit such as Carlisle - the county town - Cockermouth, Keswick, Solway Firth to name just a few.

WALES
BORTHWNOG HALL
COUNTRY HOUSE HOTEL
Bontddu, Dolgellau, Gwynedd

Borthwnog Hall is a lovely and elegant 17th-century country house perfectly situated to offer stunning views in almost every direction; to the east is the high peak of Aran Mawddwy, to the west far-reaching views of the Mawddach River as far as Barmouth Bridge and to the south across the river to the massive Cader Idris mountain range beyond. And as if that isn't enough, the grounds of the hall adjoin Garth Gell an RSPB nature reserve.

Within the elegant walls of this country house, Vicki and Derek Hawes and their family have created a comfortable and cosy home - complete with open fires in the winter - in which to welcome their visitors. And their three guest bedrooms - all en suite and well equipped - are individually furnished in keeping with the rest of the house.

In the intimate restaurant, which is also open to non-residents if space permits, Vicki Hawes has created an imaginative menu that features dishes like Sicilian fish soup for starter, followed by herb-stuffed chicken and for dessert perhaps hazlenut pavlova - with coffee served in the lovely sitting room.

Perhaps the most unusual feature of the house is its library gallery in which original paintings and limited edition prints, mostly of local scenes, as well as pottery by local artists are displayed for sale. It has become quite an attraction for passing motorists.

There is no shortage of things to do in this area, which is ideally placed for exploring Snowdonia National Park and mid Wales. The nature reserve is a haven for bird watchers, there's wind-surfing and canoeing on the estuary and golf at Dolgellau or Royal St Davids at Harlech.

SCOTLAND
DOWER HOUSE
Muir of Ord, Highland

Set in three acres of lovely grounds, between the rivers Beauly and Conon, just a mile from Muir of Ord lies the Dower House. Skilfully converted to its present form around 1800, the Dower House is all that remains of Highland House, once the baronial seat of the Mackenzie-Gillanders.

Today it is very much the home of Robyn and Mena Aitchison, who have given it the informal and relaxing atmosphere that makes people feel that they are guests joining a private house party rather than paying visitors in a formal hotel.

Although the public rooms are not large they are beautifully furnished in traditional style - the lounge has comfy, easy chairs and a chintzy sofa, an open fire for the winter and lots of books on the

shelves for visitors to read.

The five double bedrooms are all prettily decorated and furnished in period, and are well equipped with lots of personal touches. Each has a private bathroom with a cast iron bath.

While Mena looks after guests' every need in the front of the house, the period-style dining room is the domain of Robyn. He is a really talented chef who believes in using good, fresh ingredients and his short fixed-price, four-course menu provides imaginative and well chosen dishes that will please the most discerning of palates. Truffled, creamed free-range eggs in a light pastry garnished with truffles, followed by a delightful and tangy cream of chicory soup, prawns in Ricard sauce with excellent vegetables and a tasty, caramel steamed pudding to finish off the meal, is the sort of menu that can be expected by guests staying

here. Breakfast too is very good.

This is a part of the country that has something to amuse everyone - lovely beaches, beautiful countryside, castles, gardens, museums and distilleries to visit - and a welcoming haven to return to in the evenings.

NORTHERN IRELAND
WHITE GABLES
Bushmills, Portballintrae

"Natural hospitality of the very best kind" was the way our inspector summed up his visit to this delightful guesthouse situated on the A2 enjoying dramatic views over the Antrim coastline.

The proprietors Mr and Mrs Johnston like to greet all their guests personally and, after showing guests to their rooms, invite them to take tea and very good home-made cake downstairs in the lounge.

The house is attractively decorated and furnished throughout but the lounge, prettily decked out with flowers and ornaments and with open fires for the chillier evenings, is particularly home-like and relaxing. As well as a colour TV, video and piano - which guests are invited to play - the lounge also boasts a powerful telescope that enables visitors to pinpoint details along the coast or across the sea of the Isles of Islay.

The four bedrooms (three with en suite bathrooms) are attractive, comfortable and very thoughtfully equipped, and also command fine views.

The Johnstons do their utmost to make guests feel at home, and Mrs Johnston produces excellent meals, including an award-winning Irish breakfast guaranteed to set guests up for a day of exploring the many interesting places nearby; from the adjacent Dunluce Castle to Bushmills Distillery and, of course, the Giant's Causeway.

The friendly, attentive atmosphere created by the proprietors is undoubtedly the reason why so many of their guests make return visits - so reservations should be made well in advance.

Quality Assessment

Quality assessment is now made for all the establishments listed in the directory except for those in the Republic of Ireland. It is made on a subjective basis, following each inspection, to indicate the overall quality of the facilities and services provided by each establishment.

The quality assessment is shown as follows:

FALMOUTH Cornwall Map **2** SX25

⟐ **GH** Ⓠ Ⓠ **Ram Hotel** High Road XY21 1AB
☎(05036) 4321 Plan 9 C2

FH Ⓠ Ⓠ Ⓠ Mr & Mrs J Smith **Homestead** DX8 1WY (SX261567)
☎(05036) 3421

Each establishment receives from one to four symbols in ascending order of merit, denoting:

A simple establishment with clean, modest accommodation and adequate bathroom facilities.

A sound establishment offering a higher standard of accommodation in terms of furnishing, decor and comfort; likely to have some en suite facilities.

Ⓠ Ⓠ Ⓠ

A well-appointed establishment offering superior accommodation with comfortable public areas. En suite facilities may be provided.

Ⓠ Ⓠ Ⓠ Ⓠ

SELECTED

The very best of AA-listed establishments, offering excellent standards of accommodation, a high degree of comfort, good food and hospitable, caring hosts. Many provide a high proportion of en suite facilities.

This year **229** places have been awarded the `Selected' distinction, and their directory entries are highlighted by means of a tinted panel. A full list of these establishments will be found overleaf.

"Selected" Guesthouses, Farmhouses and Inns

The county index which follows is a list of all the guesthouses, farmhouses and inns - 229 in all - which have been awarded the AA's highest quality rating of 4 **Q** symbols and the designation 'S E L E C T E D'. You will find full details of each in the directory and the entries are highlighted by means of a tinted panel.

ENGLAND

AVON

Bath	GH	Laura Place Hotel
Bath	GH	Leighton House
Bath	GH	Paradise House
Bath	GH	Somerset House Hotel & Restaurant
Bath	GH	Old School House
Bath	GH	Underhill Lodge
Bath	GH	Arden Hotel
Bath	GH	Haydon House

CHESHIRE

Chester	GH	Redland Private Hotel

CORNWALL & ISLES OF SCILLY

Crackington Haven	FH	Manor Farm
Crackington Haven	FH	Trevigue
Fowey	GH	Carnethic House
Looe	GH	Harescombe Lodge
Pelynt	FH	Trenderway Farm
Penryn	GH	Prospect House
St Just in Roseland	GH	Rose-da-Mar Hotel
St Marys	GH	Carnwethers Country House
St Marys	GH	Brantwood Hotel

COUNTY DURHAM

Firtree	GH	Greenhead County House Hotel

CUMBRIA

Ambleside	GH	Grey Friar Lodge Country House Hotel
Ambleside	GH	Rothay Garth Hotel
Ambleside	GH	Rydal Lodge
Borrodale	GH	Greenbank
Buttermere	GH	Pickett Howe
Caldbeck	GH	High Greenrigg House
Catlowdy	FH	Bessiestown Farm
Cockermouth	GH	Low Hall Country Guest House
Coniston	GH	Coniston Lodge Hotel
Grange over Sands		
Kendal	GH	Greenacres
Kendal	GH	Lane Head Country House Hotel
Keswick	GH	Applethwaite Country House Hotel
Kirkcambeck	FH	Cracop Farm
Kirkby Lonsdale	GH	Cobwebs Country House
Kirkby Lonsdale	GH	Hipping Hall
Kirkoswald	GH	Prospect Hill Hotel
Kirkby Stephen	GH	The Town Head House
Mealsgate	GH	The Old Rectory
Penruddock	FH	Highgate Farm
Near Sawrey	GH	Ees Wyke Country House
Near Sawrey	GH	The Garth
Windermere	GH	The Hawksmoor Guest House

DERBYSHIRE

Bakewell	GH	Merlin House Country House Hotel
Buxton	GH	Brookfield on Longhill
Shottle	FH	Dannah Farm

DEVON

Bickington	FH	East Burne Farm
Bovey Tracey	FH	Willmead Farm
Colyford	GH	Swallows Eaves Hotel
Colyton	GH	Old Bakehouse
Croyde	GH	Whiteleaf at Croyde
Dartington	INN	Cott Inn
Dartmouth	GH	Captains House
Dartmouth	GH	Ford House
Feniton	GH	Colestocks House Guest House
Holne	FH	Wellpritton Farm
Kingston	GH	Trebles Cottage Hotel
Lynmouth	GH	Countisbury Lodge Hotel
Lynton	GH	Waterloo House Hotel
Morchard Bishop	FH	Wigham
Mortehoe	GH	Sunnycliffe Hotel
Teignmouth	GH	Thomas Luny House
Tiverton	FH	Lower Collipriest Farm
Torquay	GH	Glenorleigh Hotel
Totnes	GH	Lyssers
Totnes	GH	Old Forge at Totnes
West Down	GH	The Long House

DORSET

Beaminster	GH	Hams Plot
Bournemouth	GH	Cliff House Hotel
Chideock	GH	Betchworth House Hotel
Corfe Castle	GH	The Old Rectory
Horton	GH	Northill House
Wareham	FH	Redcliffe Farm
Wimborne Minster	GH	Beechleas

ESSEX

Southend-on-Sea	GH	Ilfracombe House

GLOUCESTERSHIRE

Cheltenham	GH	Lypiatt House
Clearwell	FH	Tudor Farmhouse
Laverton	GH	Leasow House
Tetbury	GH	Tavern House
Willersey	GH	Old Rectory

GREATER MANCHESTER

Altrincham	GH	Ash Farm

HAMPSHIRE

Hayling Island	GH	Cockle Warren Cottage Hotel
Lyndhurst	GH	Knightwood Lodge
Ringwood	GH	Little Forest Lodge Hotel
Winchester	INN	The Wykeham Arms

HEREFORD & WORCESTER

Bishampton	FH	Nightingale Farm
Bredwardine	GH	Bredwardine Hall
Hanley Castle	GH	Old Parsonage Farm
Hereford	GH	Hermitage Manor
Leominster	GH	Withenfield
Ruckhall	INN	The Ancient Camp Inn
Ullingswick	GH	The Steppes
Vowchurch	GH	The Croft Country House
Whitney-on-Wye	INN	The Rhydspence Inn

KENT

Canterbury	GH	Thanington Hotel
Chartham	GH	Thruxted Oast
Penshurst	GH	Swale Cottage
Royal Tunbridge Wells	GH	Danehurst House

LANCASHIRE

Blackpool	GH	Sunray Private Hotel
Capernwray	FH	New Capernwray Farm
Harrop Fold	FH	Harrop Fold Country Farmhouse Hotel
Lancaster	GH	Edenbreck House
Slaidburn	GH	Parrock Head Farm House Hotel
Thornton	GH	The Victorian House

LINCOLNSHIRE

Lincoln	GH	D'Isney Place Hotel
Sturton by Stow	FH	The Village Farm

LONDON (GREATER)

(Postal Districts)

SE3	GH	Vanbrugh
W14	GH	Aston Court Hotel
W2	GH	Byron Hotel
W2	GH	Pembridge Court

NORFOLK

Barney	GH	The Old Brick Kilns
Kings Lynn	GH	Russet House Hotel

NORTHUMBERLAND

Alnmouth	GH	Marine House Private Hotel

Haltwhistle	FH	Broomshaw Hill Farm
Haydon Bridge	GH	Langley Castle
Housesteads	FH	Beggar Bog Farm
Kirkwhelpington	FH	Shieldhall
Rothbury	GH	Orchard Guest House

OXFORDSHIRE

Chislehampton	INN	The Coach & Horses
Kidlington	GH	Bowood House
Kingston	FH	Fallowfields Bagpuize
Lew	FH	The Farmhouse Hotel & Restaurant
Milton-under-Wychwood	GH	Hillborough Hotel
Oxford	GH	Cotswold House
Oxford	GH	Tilbury Lodge Private Hotel
Thame	FH	Upper Green Farm
Woolstone	INN	The White Horse

SHROPSHIRE

Church Stretton	FH	Rectory Farm
Diddlebury	GH	The Glebe
Middleton Priors	GH	Middleton Lodge

SOMERSET

Beercrocombe	FH	Frog Street Farm
Beercrocombe	FH	Whittles Farm
Bruton	GH	Fryerning
Crewkerne	GH	Broadview
Glastonbury	FH	Berewell Farm Country Guest House
Kilve	INN	The Hood Arms
Langport	GH	Hillards Farm
Minehead	GH	Marston Lodge
Somerton	GH	The Lynch Country House
Taunton	GH	Meryan House Hotel
Wells	GH	Coach House

STAFFORDSHIRE

| Cheddleton | GH | Choir Cottage & Choir House |

SUFFOLK

Gislingham	GH	The Old Guildhall
Higham	GH	The Old Vicarage
Needham Market	GH	Pipp's Ford Farm

SUSSEX (EAST)

| Brighton | GH | Adelaide Hotel |

Hastings & St Leonards	GH	Parkside House
Hove	GH	Claremont House
Rye	GH	Holloway House
Rye	GH	Jeakes House
Rye	GH	The Old Vicarage Hotel & Restaurant
Uckfield	GH	Hooke Hall
Uckfield	GH	South Paddock
Winchelsea	GH	The Country House at Winchelsea

SUSSEX (WEST)

Bepton	GH	The Park House Hotel
Billingshurst	FH	Old Wharf
Rogate	FH	Mizzards Farm
Sutton	INN	White Horse

WARWICKSHIRE

Hatton	GH	Northleigh House
Lower Brailes	GH	Feldon House
Shrewley	GH	Shrewley House

WIGHT, ISLE OF

Sandown	GH	Braemar
Sandown	GH	St Catherine's Hotel
Shanklin	GH	Chine Lodge
Shanklin	GH	Osborne House

WILTSHIRE

Alderton	FH	Manor Farm
Bradford on Avon	GH	Bradford Old Windmill
Bradford on Avon	GH	Widbrook Grange
Burbage	GH	The Old Vicarage
Nettleton	GH	Fosse Farmhouse Country Hotel

YORKSHIRE (NORTH)

Harrogate	GH	Alexa House and Stable Cottages
Kirbymoorside	GH	Appletree Court
Patrick Brompton	GH	Elmfield House
Raskelf	GH	Old Farmhouse Country Hotel
Richmond	FH	Whashton Springs Farm
Scotch Corner	INN	Vintage Hotel
Starbotton	GH	Hilltop Country Guest House
Whitby	GH	Dunsley Hall
York	GH	Grasmead House Hotel

WALES

CLWYD

Llanfair Dyffryn Clwyd	GH	Eyarth Station
St Asaph	FH	Bach-y-Craig

DYFED

Carew	GH	Old Stable Cottage
Gwuan Valley	FH	Tregynon Country Farmhouse Hotel
New Quay	GH	Park Hall
Solva	FH	Lochmeyler Farm

GWENT

Abergavenny	GH	Llanwenarth House

GWYNEDD

Aberdovey	GH	Morlan Guesthouse
Betws-y-Coed	GH	Tan-Y-Foel
Bontddu	GH	Borthwnog Hall
Harlech	GH	Castle Cottage Hotel
LLanddeiniolen	FH	Ty'n Rhos Farm
LLandudno	GH	Craiglands Private Hotel
Llanfachreth	GH	Ty Isaf Guest House
Rhoscolyn	GH	The Old Rectory

POWYS

Penybont	GH	Ffaldau Country House & Restaurant
Sennybridge	FH	Brynfedwen Farm

WEST GLAMORGAN

Swansea	GH	Tredillon House

GUERNSEY

St Peter Port	GH	Midhurst House

JERSEY

St Aubin	GH	The Panorama
St Helier	GH	Almorah Hotel

SCOTLAND

BORDERS

Jedburgh	GH	The Spinney
West Linton	GH	Medwyn House

CENTRAL

Brig O'Turk	GH	Dundarroch
Callander	GH	Arran Lodge

DUMFRIES & GALLOWAY

Kirkbean	GH	Cavens House
Moffat	GH	Gilbert House
Twynholm	GH	Fresh Fields

FIFE

Anstruther	GH	The Spindrift

GRAMPIAN

Aberdeen	GH	Cedars Private Hotel
Ballater	GH	Moorside Guesthouse
Bridge of Marnoch	GH	The Old Manse of Marnoch
Keith	FH	The Haughs
Forres	GH	Parkmount House Hotel

HIGHLAND

Boat of Garten	GH	Heathbank House
Carrbridge	GH	Fairwinds Hotel
Contin	GH	Contin House
Gairloch	GH	Horisdale House
Grantown-on- Spey	GH	Culdearn House
Grantown-on- Spey	GH	Garden Park
Invernesss	GH	Culduthel Lodge
Kirkhill	GH	Moniack View
Muir of Ord	GH	The Dower House
Rogart	FH	Rovie Farm

LOTHIAN

Edinburgh	GH	Dorstan Private Hotel
Edinburgh	GH	The Lodge Hotel

STRATHCLYDE

Abington	FH	Netherton Farm
Ayr	GH	Brenalde Lodge
Connel	GH	Loch Etive Hotel
Machrihanish	GH	Ardell House

TAYSIDE

Blairgowrie	GH	Rosebank House
Brechin	FH	Blibberhill Farm
Pitlochry	GH	Dundarave House

Your stay - what you need to know

BOOKING

Book as early as possible, particularly if accommodation is required during the peak holiday period _ from the beginning of June to the end of September, plus public holidays and, in some parts of Scotland, during the skiing season).

Although it is possible for chance callers to find a night's accommodation, it is by no means a certainty, especially at peak holiday times and in the popular areas, so to be certain of obtaining the accommodation you require, it is always advisable to book as far in advance as possible. Some establishments will also require a deposit on booking.

We have tried to provide as much information as possible about the establishments in our directory, but if you should require further information before deciding to book, you should write to the establishment concerned. Do remember to enclose a stamped addressed envelope, or an international reply-paid coupon if writing from overseas, and please quote this publication in any enquiry.

It is regretted that the AA cannot at the present time undertake to make any reservations.

CANCELLATION

If you later find that you must cancel your visit, let the proprietor know at once, because if the room you booked cannot be re-let, you may be held legally responsible for partial payment. Whether it is a matter of losing your deposit, or of being liable for compensation, you should seriously consider taking out cancellation insurance, such as AA Travelsure.

COMPLAINTS

AA members who have any cause to complain are urged to do so on the spot. This should provide an opportunity for the proprietor to correct matters. If a personal approach fails, AA members should inform the AA Head Office at Basingstoke.

FIRE PRECAUTIONS

Many of the establishments listed in the Guide are subject to the requirements of the Fire Precautions Act of 1971. As far as we can discover, every establishment in this book has applied for, and not been refused, a fire certificate.

The Fire Precautions Act does not apply to Ireland (see page 407), the Channel Islands, or the Isle of Man, which exercise their own rules regarding fire precautions for hotels.

FOOD AND DRINK

If you intend to take dinner at an establishment, note that sometimes the meal must be ordered in advance of the actual meal time. In some cases, this may be at breakfast time, or even on the previous evening. If you have booked on bed, breakfast and evening meal terms, you may find that the tariff includes a set menu, but you can usually order from the _ la carte menu, if there is one, and pay a supplement.

On Sundays, many establishments serve the main meal at midday, and provide only a cold supper in the evening.

In some parts of Britain, particularly in Scotland, high tea (ie a savoury dish followed by bread and butter, scones, cakes, etc) is sometimes served instead of dinner, which may, however, be available on request. The last time at which high tea or dinner may be ordered on weekdays is shown, but this may be varied at weekends.

LICENCES

The directory entry will show whether or not the establishment is licensed to serve alcoholic drinks. Many places in the guesthouse category hold a residential or restaurant license only, but all inns hold a full licence. Licensed premises are not obliged to remain open throughout the permitted hours, and they may do so only when they expect reasonable trade.

Note that in establishments which have registered clubs, club membership does not come into effect, nor can a drink be bought, until 48 hours after joining.

MONEY-OFF VOUCHER SCHEME

In the front of this book you will find six £1 vouchers which can be redeemed against your bill for accommodation at any of the establishments which show the £ symbol in the directory.

Only one voucher may be presented for one room bill irrespective of the number of nights stayed. You must show your copy of the 1992 Guide in order to claim the discount and it is advisable to do this when you check in at reception. The vouchers are not valid if you are already benefitting from a discount under some other scheme, or from special off-peak rates.

The voucher scheme is not applicable in the Republic of Ireland.

PAYMENT

Most proprietors will only accept cheques in payment of accounts if notice is given and some form of identification (preferably a cheque card) is produced. If a hotel accepts credit or charge cards, this is shown in its directory entry (see page 32 for details).

PRICES

It should be noted that daily terms quoted throughout this publication show minimum and maximum prices for both one (sb&b) and two persons (db&b) and include a full breakfast. If dinner is also included this will be indicated in parenthesis _ (incl dinner). Weekly terms, where available, show minimum and maximum prices per person, which take into account minimum double occupancy and maximum single occupancy, where appropriate, and may include the price of an evening meal (WBDi).

The Hotel Industry Voluntary Code of Booking Practice was revised in 1986, and the AA

encourages its use in appropriate establishments. Its prime object is to ensure that the customer is clear about the precise services and facilities s/he is buying and what price will have to be paid, before entering into a contractually binding agreement. If the price has not been previously confirmed in writing, the guest should be handed a card at the time of registration, stipulating the total obligatory charge. The Tourism (Sleeping Accommodation Price Display) Order 1977 compels hotels, motels, guesthouses, farmhouses, inns and self-catering accommodation with four or more letting bedrooms to display in entrance halls the minimum and maximum prices charged for each category of room. This order complements the Voluntary Code of Booking Practice. The tariffs quoted in the directory of this book may be affected in the coming year by inflation, variations in the rate of VAT and many other factors.

You should always confirm the current prices before making a booking. Those given in this book have been provided by proprietors in good faith, and must be accepted as indications rather than firm quotations.

In some cases, proprietors have been unable to provide us with their 1992 charges, but to give you a rough guide we publish the 1991 price, prefixed with an asterisk (*). It is also a good idea to ascertain all that is included in the price. Weekly terms can vary according to the meals that are included. It is possible, at the height of the season, that some establishments will offer accommodation only on a weekly basis - often Saturday to Saturday - and this, too, is indicated in the directory. We cannot indicate whether or not you are able to arrive mid-week, so if this is your intention, do check when making your reservation. Where information about 1992 prices is not given, you are requested to make enquiries direct.

VAT is payable, in the United Kingdom and in the Isle of Man, on both basic prices and any service. VAT does not apply in the Channel Islands. With this exception, prices quoted in the Guide are inclusive of VAT (and service where applicable).

Prices for the Republic of Ireland are shown in Irish punts. At the time of going to press, the exchange rate is 1.07 Punts = £1.00 Sterling.

HOW TO USE THE GUIDE

The directory lists place-names alphabetically throughout England, Scotland and Wales, the Isle of Man and the Channel Islands.

Establishments on islands are listed under the appropriate island heading. The example of an entry is to help you find your way through the directory. All the abbreviations and symbols are explained on pages 15 and 16.

SAMPLE ENTRIES (Fictitious)

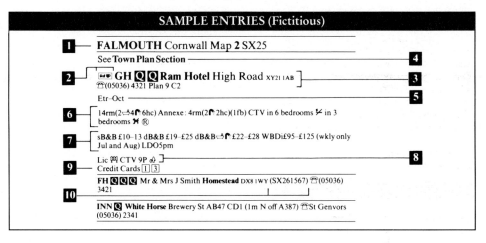

1 — **FALMOUTH** Cornwall Map **2** SX25
See Town Plan Section ———————————————————— **4**

2 ⌐ ☎☞ **GH** Ⓠ Ⓠ **Ram Hotel** High Road XY21 1AB ¬ **3**
☎(05036) 4321 Plan 9 C2

Etr–Oct ———————————————————————————————— **5**

6 ⌐14rm(2⌂4🐾6hc) Annexe: 4rm(2🐾2hc)(1fb) CTV in 6 bedrooms ✂ in 3
⌐bedrooms 🐕 Ⓡ

7 ⌐sB&B £10–13 dB&B £19–£25 dB&B⌂3🐾£22–£28 WBDi£95–£125 (wkly only
⌐Jul and Aug) LDO5pm

Lic 🎵 CTV 9P ☜ ┘ ———————————————————— **8**
9 Credit Cards ① ③

10 FH Ⓠ Ⓠ Ⓠ Mr & Mrs J Smith **Homestead** DX8 1WY (SX261567) ☎(05036)
3421

INN Ⓠ **White Horse** Brewery St AB47 CD1 (1m N off A387) ☎St Genvors
(05036) 2341

---

1 **Towns** (including London) are listed in strict alphabetical order followed by the county or region. This is the administrative county, or region, and not necessarily part of the correct postal address. Towns on islands (not connected to the mainland by a bridge) are listed under the island name. With Scottish regions or islands, the old county name follows in italics. The map reference denotes first the map number, then the grid reference. To find the location on the atlas, first find the appropriate square (indicated by two letters), then read the 1st figure across and the 2nd figure vertically.

2 This symbol indicates that the establishment expects to provide bed and breakfast for under £13 per person, per night during 1992, but remember that circumstances can change during the currency of the Guide.

3 **Establishment name**, address, postal code and telephone number. When an establishment's name is shown in the particulars have not been confirmed by the proprietor. Guesthouses are identified by the letters GH, Farmhouses by FH, Inns by INN and Town and Country by T&C- this is also the order in which they are listed beneath the town headings.

All establishments are now rated for quality on a scale of one to four, except those in the Republic of Ireland where the scheme has not yet been implemented. This is denoted by the letter Q. See page 24 for a full explanation.

The telephone exchange (STD code) is usually that of the town heading. Where it differs from the town heading the exchange is given after the symbol, and before the dialling code and number. In some areas, numbers are likely to be changed during the currency of this book. In case of difficulty, check with the operator.

4 **Town Plans** There are street plans of some major towns and resorts at the end of the directory. If there is a town plan, each establishment is given a key number and located on the plan. The London street plans, however, appear next to the London entries in the directory.

5 **Opening details** Unless otherwise stated, the establishments are open all year, but where dates are shown they are inclusive: eg 'Apr-Oct' indicates that the establishment is open from the beginning of April to the end of October. Although some places are open all year, they may offer a restricted service during the less busy months, and we indicate this is the gazetteer by using the rs abbreviation. This may mean that there is a reduction in meals served and/or accommodation available, and where not indicated in the text, you should telephone in advance to find out the nature of the restriction.

6 **Accommodation details** The first figure shows the number of letting bedrooms. Where rooms have en suite bath or shower and wc or hot and cold water (hc), the number precedes the appropriate symbol.

Annexe - bedrooms available in an annexe are shown. Their standard is acceptable, but facilities may not be the same as in the main building, and it is advisable to check the nature of the accommodation and tariff before making a reservation.

⊬ - number of bedrooms for non-smokers.

fb - family bedrooms.

CTV/TV - colour or black and white television available in lounge. This may also mean televisions permanently in bedrooms or available on request from the management. Check when making reservations.

✘ - no dogs allowed in bedrooms. Some establishments may restrict the size of dogs permitted and the rooms into which they may be taken. Establishments which do not normally accept dogs may accept guide dogs. Generally, dogs are not allowed in the dining room. Check when booking the conditions under which pets are accepted.

7 **Prices** Bed and breakfast per person/two persons, per night and per person, per week (inclusive of dinner at times). For full explanation see page 30. Prices given have been provided by the proprietor in good faith, and are indications rather than firm quotations. Some establishments offer free accommodation

to children provided they share the parents' room. Check current prices before booking. See also page 30.

8 **Facilities** For key to symbols see pages 15 and 16.

🚌- no coaches. This information is published in good faith from details supplied by the establishments concerned. Inns, however, have well-defined legal obligations towards travellers, and any member with cause for complaint should take this up with the proprietor or the local licensing authority.

nc - establishments listed accommodate children of all ages unless a minimum age is given (eg nc4yrs), but they may not necessarily be able to provide special facilites. nc by itself indicates 'no children'. For very young children, check before booking about such provisions as cots and high chairs, and any reductions made.

👶- establishments with special facilities for children, which will include babysitting service or baby intercom system, playroom or playground, laundry facilities, drying and ironing facilities, cots, high chairs and special meals.

Note - disabled people may be accommodated, and where this is the case reference to this may be made in the description. Further details for disabled people will be found in the AA's Guide for the Disabled Traveller available from AA shops, free to members, £3.50 to non-members. Intending guests with any form of disability should notify proprietors, so that arrangements can be made to minimise difficulties, particularly in the event of an emergency.

9 **Payment details** (the following cards or discount vouchers may be accepted, but check current details when booking)

1 - Access/Eurocard/Mastercard

2 - American Express

3 - Barclaycard/Visa

5 - Diners

£ - Establishment accepts AA Money-Off Vouchers as detailed on page 30.

10 **Ordnance Survey Map Reference** This is shown for farmhouse entries only. As they are often in remote areas, we provide a six-figure map reference which can be used with Ordnance Survey maps.

Follow the Country Code

Enjoy the countryside and respect its life and work.

Leave livestock, crops and machinery alone.

Guard against all risk of fire.

Take your litter home.

Fasten all gates.

Help to keep all water clean.

Keep your dogs under close control.

Protect wildlife, plants and trees.

Keep to public paths across farmland.

Take special care on country roads.

Use gates and stiles to cross fences, hedges and walls.

Make no unnecessary noise.

ABBOTS BICKINGTON Devon Map **02** SS31

⌨▣ FH ◗◗ Mrs E Bellew **Court Barton** *(SS384133)*
EX22 7LQ ☎Milton Damerel(040926) 214
May-Oct
This elegant stone-built farmhouse offers spacious bedrooms and comfortable public rooms. Guests will enjoy home cooking and a warm welcome on this 650-acre mixed farm.
4hc (1fb) ⑧ ✗ sB&B£12-£13 dB&B£24-£26 WBDi£90-£95
LDO 5pm
◫ CTV 10P nc3yrs ✔ rough shooting 640 acres arable beef sheep ⑤

ABBOTS BROMLEY Staffordshire Map **07** SK02

FH ◗◗ Mrs M K Hollins **Marsh** *(SK069261)* WS15 3EJ
☎Burton-on-Trent(0283) 840323
Closed Xmas
A deceptively large, busy farm with rooms to let, situated one mile north of the village. The owner also caters for coach parties requiring lunches or teas, but resident guests are not forgotten.
2hc (1fb) in 1 bedroom ⑧ sB&B£14-£16 dB&B£25-£27
WB&B£84-£98 LDO 5pm
◫ CTV 6P 87 acres mixed ⑤

ABERAERON Dyfed Map **02** SN46

GH ◗◗ **Moldavia** 7 & 8 Bellevue Ter SA46 0BB
☎(0545) 570107
3rm(1⇨♠2hc) (1fb)✂in 1 bedroom ✳ sB&B£13.50-£16
dB&Bfr£27 dB&B⇨♠fr£32 WB&B£94.50-£112
◫ CTV 3P ♨

ABERDEEN Grampian *Aberdeenshire* Map **15** NJ90

GH ◗◗◗ **Bimini** 69 Constitution St AB2 1ET
☎(0224) 646912
Situated in the east end with convenient access to the beach and recreational facilities, this small family-run guesthouse has a friendly informal atmosphere and offers compact but comfortable and well equipped accommodation.
7hc (1fb)✂in all bedrooms CTV in all bedrooms ⑧
✗ (ex guide dogs) ✳ sB&B£15-£19 dB&B£26-£30
◫ CTV 7P
Credit Cards ❑ ❑ ⑤

GH ◗◗ **Broomfield Private Hotel** 15 Balmoral Place AB1 6HR
☎(0224) 588758
Closed 1-23 Jan
Situated in a residential area of the town's west end, this family-run guesthouse caters for both the commercial and tourist markets. It has a friendly atmosphere and offers comfortable, good value accommodation with modern facilities.
8hc ⑧ ✳ sB&B£16.50-£20 dB&B£27-£30
◫ CTV 10P ♨
Credit Cards ❑ ❑ ⑤

SELECTED

GH ◗◗◗◗ **Cedars Private Hotel** 339 Great Western
Rd AB1 6NW ☎(0224) 583225
Situated in the west end, within easy reach of the city centre and the ring route, this friendly, personally run hotel provides clean, comfortable and well equipped bed and breakfast accommodation. The bright, cheerful bedrooms are compact but well furnished, some with private bathrooms, others with showers; additional en suite facilities are planned. Hearty breakfasts are served in the smart dining room, which features a beautiful ornate ceiling.
13rm(5⇨♠8hc) (2fb) CTV in all bedrooms ⑧
✗ (ex guide dogs) ✳ sB&B⇨♠£34-£38 dB&B⇨♠£44-£50 WB&B£224-£252
◫ 13P training/keep fit area

Credit Cards ❑ ❑ ❑

GH ◗◗◗ **Corner House Hotel** 385 Great Western Rd
AB1 6NY ☎(0224) 313063
Situated in the west end with convenient access to the ring road, this family run hotel is a popular base for the businessman and tourist alike. It is efficiently run by the enthusiastic owners, who maintain a high standard of cleanliness throughout. Bedrooms are individually furnished and well equipped, all with private bathrooms, and there is a comfortable lounge and restaurant.
17⇨♠ CTV in all bedrooms ⑧ sB&B⇨♠£35-£45
dB&B⇨♠£45-£55 WB&B£160-£260 WBDi£220-£320
LDO 8.30pm
Lic ◫ CTV 12P
Credit Cards ❑ ❑ ⑤

GH ◗◗◗ **Craiglynn Hotel** 36 Fonthill Rd AB1 2UJ
☎(0224) 584050 FAX (0224) 584050
This impressive granite Victorian house within easy reach of the city centre is constantly being upgraded and offers attractive well equipped bedrooms (no smoking requested), a choice of comfortable lounges and a panelled dining room serving well prepared meals.
9rm(6⇨♠3hc) (2fb)✂in all bedrooms CTV in all bedrooms ✗
sB&B£30-£34 sB&B⇨♠£41-£49 dB&B£43 dB&B⇨♠£55
LDO 7.30pm
Lic ◫ CTV 7P
Credit Cards ❑ ❑ ❑ ❑ ⑤

GH ◗◗◗ **Fourways** 435 Great Western Rd AB1 6NJ
☎(0224) 310218
Situated in the west, and beside the ring road, this well maintained family-run guesthouse is popular with visiting businessmen and holidaymakers alike. It has an attractive lounge where the atmosphere is friendly and relaxed, and the comfortable bedrooms are well equipped.
7rm(6⇨♠1hc) (2fb) CTV in all bedrooms ⑧
✗ (ex guide dogs) sB&B⇨♠£20-£25 dB&B⇨♠£32-£34
◫ CTV 7P ⑤

GH ◗◗ **Klibreck** 410 Great Western Rd AB1 6NR
☎(0224) 316115
Closed Xmas & New Year
A small family-run guesthouse on the main Deeside road, close to the ring road. Good value bed and breakfast accommodation is provided, and there is a friendly atmosphere. Smoking is not permitted.
6hc (1fb)✂in all bedrooms ⑧ ✗ ✳ sB&Bfr£16 dB&Bfr£26
LDO 3pm
◫ CTV 3P ⑤

GH ◗◗◗ **Open Hearth** 349 Holburn St AB1 6DQ
☎(0224) 596888
This efficiently run guesthouse is situated in a residential area and offers convenient access to both the ring road and the city centre. It has a friendly atmosphere and provides comfortable, modern accommodation and good value.
11hc (2fb) CTV in all bedrooms ⑧ ✳ sB&Bfr£18 dB&Bfr£28
◫ CTV 5P

GH ◗ **Strathboyne** 26 Abergeldie Ter AB1 6EE
☎(0224) 593400
Situated in a quiet residential area south of the city centre, this small guesthouse, suitable for both holidaymakers and business guests alike, has a friendly atmosphere and offers good value traditional comforts.
6hc (2fb) CTV in all bedrooms ⑧ sB&B£13.50-£14 dB&B£25-£26 LDO 3.30pm
◫ CTV ✗ ⑤

ABERDOVEY Gwynedd Map **06** SN69

GH QQQ **Brodawel** Tywyn Rd, Brodawel LL35 0SA
☎(0654) 767347
Closed Jan-Feb
This small, privately-owned hotel provides very well equipped accommodation and a choice of lounges for smokers and non-smokers. It is situated on the edge of the town and enjoys views across the golf course. The hotel has its own car park and is fronted by pleasant gardens.
6⇨🛏 (1fb)⊁in 3 bedrooms CTV in all bedrooms ® ✱ dB&B⇨🛏£34-£36 WB&B£109 WBDi£172 LDO noon
Lic ᵐ CTV 8P nc6yrs

GH QQ **Cartref** LL35 0NR ☎(0654) 767273
The resident owners of this attractive detached house provide a warm welcome and all round home comforts.
7rm(1⇨3🛏 3hc) (2fb) CTV in 4 bedrooms ® LDO 5pm
ᵐ CTV 8P

SELECTED

GH QQQQ **Morlan** LL35 0SE ☎(0654) 767706
A small, single-storeyed personally run guesthouse situated north of the town in an elevated position, with excellent views of Cardigan Bay, across the golf course. Furnished and decorated to a high standard throughout, it provides very well equipped bedrooms with private bathrooms, each with French windows giving direct access to the pleasant garden. Additional benefits include a private car park and the availablity of golf concessions at the nearby championship course.
4rm(1⇨3🛏) ⊁in all bedrooms CTV in all bedrooms ®
✯ (ex guide dogs) ✱ dB&B⇨🛏£36-£40 WB&B£119-£140
WBDi£196-£224 LDO 2pm
Lic ᵐ CTV 10P 🛋 nc16yrs £

ABERFELDY Tayside *Perthshire* Map **14** NN84

GH QQ **Caber-Feidh** 56 Dunkeld St PH15 2AF ☎(0887) 20342
A modernised stone house situated on the main road at the east end of the town. Tha accommodation is pleasant and comfortable, and both high tea and dinner are available. This friendly, personally run guesthouse offers good value.
6hc (2fb) ® LDO 8.45pm
Lic ᵐ CTV 5P

ABERGAVENNY Gwent Map **03** SO21

GH QQ **Belchamps** 1 Holywell Rd NP7 5LP ☎(0873) 3204
due to change to 853204
Just off the A40, near the Gavenny river and a short walk from the town centre, this simple, family-run guesthouse provides comfortable accommodation suitable for both tourists and local business people.
5hc (3fb) CTV in all bedrooms ® ✯ (ex guide dogs) ✱ sB&B£14-£16 dB&B£28-£32 WB&B£84-£98 WBDi£132-£146 LDO 7pm
ᵐ CTV 5P £

SELECTED

GH QQQQ **Llanwenarth House** Govilon NP7 9SF
☎Gilwern(0873) 830289
rs Jan-Feb
An imposing 16th-century mansion, carefully restored by the resident proprietors, set in wood and parkland within the Brecon Beacons National Park. Cooking here has an excellent reputation, and there is a spacious, elegantly furnished drawing room with a cheerful log fire. Bedrooms are mostly large, with tasteful décor and period furniture. They are well equipped with modern comforts and afford glorious views over the Vale of Usk.

5rm(3⇨2🛏) (1fb) CTV in all bedrooms ® dB&B⇨🛏£61-£70 LDO 6.30pm
Lic ᵐ 6P nc10yrs

FH QQ Mrs D Miles **Great Lwynfranc** *(SO327193)*
Llanvihangel Crucorney NP7 8EN (off A465 3m N)
☎Crucorney(0873) 890418
Mar-Nov
Enjoying an elevated position well back from the A465 north of the town, with excellent views of the countryside, this pleasant farmhouse has comfortable, traditional accommodation and the Miles family offer warm hospitality.
3hc (1fb) ®
ᵐ CTV 10P 154 acres mixed £

FH QQQ Mrs J Nicholls **Newcourt** *(SO317165)* Mardy
NP7 8AU ☎(0873) 2300 due to change to 852300
Closed Xmas wk
There are fine views of Sugar Loaf Mountain from this 16th-century stone-built farmhouse. Two comfortable lounges are available for guests, and bedrooms are very comfortably furnished; smoking is not permitted.
3⇨🛏 ⊁in all bedrooms CTV in all bedrooms ®
✯ (ex guide dogs) ✱ sB&B⇨🛏£20-£25 dB&B⇨🛏£35-£40
WB&B£117.50-£140
ᵐ CTV 10P nc10yrs snooker 160 acres arable beef £

INN Q **The Great George** Cross St NP7 5ER
☎(0873) 854230 or (0831) 107862 FAX (0873) 79261
In the centre of a busy market town, this 16th-century inn provides good, simple bar and restaurant facilities. Bedrooms are modestly furnished, but equipped with modern comforts.
3hc (1fb) CTV in all bedrooms ® ✯ ✱ sB&B£25 dB&B£38 ✱
Lunch £1.50-£7
ᵐ 50P
Credit Cards ①

ABERPORTH Dyfed Map **02** SN25

GH QQ **Ffynonwen Country** SA43 2HT ☎(0239) 810312
Just outside the town, between Aberporth and the A487, this converted farmhouse provides extensive public rooms, and is well used locally for functions and parties. Bedrooms are comfortable and well equipped and there is a spacious lounge as well as a popular bar.
7rm(3⇨1🛏 3hc) (3fb) ✱ sB&B£14.50 sB&B⇨🛏£16.50 dB&B£29 dB&B⇨🛏£33 WB&B£91.35-£103.95
WBDi£129.15-£141.75
Lic ᵐ 30P games room

ABERSOCH Gwynedd Map **06** SH32

GH QQ **Ty Draw** Lon Sarn Bach LL53 7EL ☎(075881) 2647
Etr-end Sep
A short walk from the village, this sparkling, well maintained guesthouse is located in the Lôn Sarn Bach area. Run by Jean and Peter Collins for many years, it provides comfortable bedrooms and a relaxing lounge for residents.
7hc ⊁in 2 bedrooms ✯ (ex guide dogs) ✱ sB&B£11-£16 dB&B£22-£32
CTV 10P 🚲

ABERYSTWYTH Dyfed Map **06** SN58

GH QQQ **Glyn-Garth** South Rd SY23 1JS ☎(0970) 615050
Closed 1 wk Xmas rs Oct-Etr
A double-fronted Victorian terraced house, close to the beach, harbour and castle, and only a short walk from the town centre. Bedrooms are well equipped and bright, and there is a cosy bar and comfortable lounge.

10rm(3➪3♠4hc) (3fb)✂in 5 bedrooms CTV in all bedrooms
® ✖ ✱ sB&B£15-£16 dB&B£30-£32 dB&B➪♠£38-£40
Lic ∰ CTV 4🐾 (£2 per night) nc7yrs ⓔ

GH ⓠⓠ *Llety Gwyn Hotel* Llanbadarn Fawr SY23 3SX (1m E
A44) ☎(0970) 623965
Closed 25-26 Dec
*Situated in a residential area on the eastern outskirts of the town,
this family-run hotel has the benefit of a fully equipped
gymnasium, sauna and solarium as well as extensive public areas.*
8rm(4♠4hc) Annexe 6rm(1➪3♠2hc) (3fb) CTV in all
bedrooms ® LDO 5pm
Lic ∰ CTV 50P snooker sauna solarium gymnasium
Credit Cards ①③

GH ⓠⓠ **Plas Antaron** Penparcau SY23 1SF ☎(0970) 611550
*Situated just south of the town, close to the city centre on the A487
Aberaeron road, this large family-run guesthouse provides
spacious, well equipped bedrooms with modern facilities, and a
range of public rooms including a popular function room.*
12rm(8♠4hc) (1fb) CTV in all bedrooms ® dB&B£25
dB&B♠£35 WB&B£87.50-£122.50 WBDi£129.50-£164.50
LDO noon
Lic ∰ CTV 40P pool table
Credit Cards ①③ⓔ

GH ⓠ **Shangri-La** 36 Portland St SY23 2DX ☎(0970) 617659
Closed 25 & 26 Dec
*This small, mid-terrace Victorian house is close to both the
seafront and shopping centre. Simple accommodation is provided,
but no car parking, and this may pose a problem in busy periods.*
6hc (3fb) TV in all bedrooms ® ✱ sB&B£12 dB&B£22
∰ CTV ✗ ⓔ

INN ⓠⓠ **Talbot Hotel** Market St SY23 1DL ☎(0970) 612575
*Very near the town centre, the Talbot has bright and cosy
bedrooms. There is a small well-furnished restaurant and a good
range of food.*
15rm(13➪♠) (4fb) CTV in all bedrooms ® ✖ (ex guide dogs)
LDO 9.30pm
CTV
Credit Cards ①③

ABINGDON Oxfordshire Map **04** SU49

INN ⓠⓠⓠ **Barley Mow Hotel** Clifton Hampden OX14 3EH
(through village on road to Didcot) (Berni/Chef & Brewer)
☎Clifton Hampden(086730) 7847
*A traditional, thatched country inn in the sleepy village of Clifton
Hampden (through the village towards Didcot). Extremely
popular at lunch time, the cosy bars are full of character, and there
is a wide and varied choice of fresh, home-made food.
The bedrooms are pretty and very well equipped with modern
facilities.*
4rm(1♠3hc) CTV in all bedrooms ® ✖ (ex guide dogs)
sB&B£36 dB&B£56 Bar Lunch £2.95-£5.50alc LDO 9.30pm
∰ 250P
Credit Cards ①②③⑤

ABINGTON Strathclyde *Lanarkshire* Map **11** NS92

▨▨ **FH** ⓠⓠ Mrs M L Hodge **Craighead** *(NS914236)*
ML12 6SQ ☎Crawford(08642) 356
May-Oct
*Run by friendly and enthusiastic hosts, this farm is set amid rolling
hills on the bank of the River Duneaton. The farm lies 3/4 mile
along the Crawfordjohn road (unclassified), turn off the A74, 1
mile north of its junction with the A73.*
3rm(2hc) ® ✖ (ex guide dogs) sB&B£12.50-£13.50 dB&B£25-
£27 LDO 5pm
∰ CTV 6P 4🐾 ✔ 600 acres mixed ⓔ

SELECTED

FH ⓠⓠⓠⓠ Mrs J Hyslop **Netherton** *(NS908254)*
ML12 6RU (on unclass road joining A74 & A73)
☎Crawford(08642) 321
*A splendidly proportioned house conveniently situated just off
the A74 to the north of Abington. Formerly a shooting lodge,
built in 1896, there are 3 rooms availalbe to let, all spacious
and comfortably furnished, with delicate cornices and
impressive woodwork. The owner, Mrs Hyslop, serves her fine
cuisine in the splendid, traditional dining room, making use of
fresh local produce such as venison, salmon and lamb, and
meals are served farmhouse style around a communal table.
High standards of housekeeping are maintained throughout,
and although guests have a choice of lounges in which to relax,
it is preferred that smoking is confined to outdoors.*
3rm(1➪♠2hc) ✂in all bedrooms ® ✖ ✱ dB&Bfr£26
dB&B➪♠£32-£38 LDO 4pm
∰ CTV 3P ✔ 3000 acres beef sheep ⓔ

ACASTER MALBIS North Yorkshire Map **08** SE54

INN ⓠⓠⓠ *Ship* YO2 1XB ☎York(0904) 705609 & 703888
*This 17th-century coaching house is delightfully situated
overlooking the banks of the River Ouse, yet within 4 miles of the
centre of York. Bedrooms are individually decorated with cheerful
co-ordinated fabrics and sturdy pine furniture. The cosy beamed
bar and restaurant provide congenial surroundings for substantial
meals.*
8rm(2➪6♠) ✂in all bedrooms CTV in all bedrooms ®
✖ (ex guide dogs) LDO 9.30pm
∰ 60P ✔ river cruises private moorings
Credit Cards ①③
See advertisement under YORK

ACHARACLE Highland *Argyllshire* Map **13** NM66

FH QQ Mrs M Macaulay *Dalilea House* (*NM735693*)
PH36 4JX ☎Salen(096785) 253
Etr-Oct
Delightfully situated on the shore of Loch Shiel, this fine turreted 15th-century farmhouse is an ideal base for the touring holidaymaker. It offers genuine Highland hospitality with traditional comforts and provides enjoyable farmhouse (including vegetarian) fare.
6rm(4🌂2hc)(1fb) ® LDO 7pm
Lic ♥ 8P ✦ canoes 1300 acres beef fish sheep

AIRDRIE Strathclyde *Lanarkshire* Map **11** NS76

GH Q **Rosslee** 107 Forrest St ML6 7AR ☎(0236) 65865
A detached house sitting back from the main road on the eastern side of Airdrie, this guesthouse caters for both the commercial and tourist trade, and is run by enthusiastic owners.
6rm(2🌂4hc)(2fb) CTV in 4 bedrooms TV in 2 bedrooms ®
sB&B£15-£17.50 dB&B£30-£35 dB&B🌂£36-£42 WB&B£105-£147 WBDi£150-£190 LDO 7pm
Lic ♥ CTV 8P £

ALBURY Surrey Map **04** TQ04

INN QQQ *Drummond Arms* The Street GU5 9AG
☎Shere(048641) 2039
A delightful inn set in a picturesque village. The 7 bedrooms, all en suite, are prettily appointed and provide high standards of comfort. A full à la carte menu is served in the restaurant, or lighter meals can be chosen from the interesting bar snack menu. The garden, where the ducks roam freely, can be enjoyed in summer.
7⇋🌂 CTV in all bedrooms ✖ (ex guide dogs) LDO 10pm
♥ 30P nc10yrs
Credit Cards ①③

ALDEBURGH Suffolk Map **05** TM45

GH QQQ *Cotmandene* 6 Park Ln IP15 5HL ☎(0728) 453775
An attractive double-fronted red-brick and flintstone Victorian villa in a residential area : on approaching the town, turn right immediately before Uplands Hotel and then first left. Bedrooms are well equipped, some with private bathrooms. The high standard of cleanliness is complimented by the interior design, particularly in relation to soft furnishings and décor.
7rm(2⇋2🌂3hc)(2fb) TV in all bedrooms ® ✖ (ex guide dogs) LDO 7.30pm
♥ CTV ✗
Credit Cards ①③

ALDERTON Wiltshire Map **03** ST88

FH QQQQ Mrs V Lippiatt *Manor* (*ST840831*)
SN14 6NL ☎Malmesbury(0666) 840271
Apr-Oct
A large, Cotswold stone farmhouse situated in a peaceful village midway between Acton Turville and Luckington. Bedrooms are pretty and tastefully furnished, and all three are well equipped with modern facilities. The elegant drawing room has no television so guests can relax, talk or read, and there is an open fire in the winter. A hearty full English breakfast is taken around a large table in the dining room, with a wide variety cooked and served by farmer's wife Victoria Lippiatt.
3rm(2⇋🌂1hc) CTV in all bedrooms ® ✖ ✱
sB&B⇋🌂£20-£25 dB&B⇋🌂£40-£45
♥ CTV 10P nc12yrs 600 acres arable beef £
See advertisement under MALMESBURY

ALKMONTON Derbyshire Map **07** SK13

FH QQQ Mr A Harris **Dairy House** (*SK198367*) DE6 3DG
☎Great Cubley(0335) 330359
Closed Xmas
Mr and Mrs Harris provide a friendly welcome and stay at their comfortably modernised 16th-century farmhouse, which is found three miles up Woodyard Lane after turning off the A50 at Foston.
7rm(1⇋2🌂4hc)(1fb)⚡in all bedrooms ® ✖ (ex guide dogs)
✱ sB&B£14.50 dB&B£29 dB&B⇋🌂£35 WB&B£97.50-£115.50 WBDi£155-£175 LDO 8pm
Lic ♥ CTV 8P nc5yrs ✦ bowls croquet 82 acres stock

ALMONDSBURY Avon Map **03** ST68

GH QQQ **Abbots Way** Abbots Way, Gloucester Rd BS12 4JB
☎(0454) 613134
Situated on the A38, 2 miles north of Junction 16 on the M5, this large modern house is set in 12 acres and has fine views of the surrounding countryside. Bedrooms are comfortable and well furnished, and the spacious conservatory/dining room is a delightful setting in which to enjoy the delicious breakfasts.
5rm(1⇋🌂4hc)(1fb) ✱ sB&B£16 dB&B£32 dB&B⇋🌂£40
♥ CTV 10P
Credit Cards ①③£

ALNMOUTH Northumberland Map **12** NU21

GH QQQ **Blue Dolphins** 11 Riverside Rd NE66 2SO
☎Alnwick(0665) 830893
Overlooking the mouth of the River Aln, this is a spacious, warm and friendly guesthouse with a lovely home-from-home feel to it. Bedrooms are especially well furnished and a delightful lounge is provided.
5rm(2⇋3🌂)⚡in all bedrooms CTV in all bedrooms ® ✱
sB&B⇋🌂£20-£22 dB&B⇋🌂£40-£44 WB&B£143-£157
5P £

GH QQQQ **Marine House Private Hotel** 1 Marine Dr
NE66 2RW ☎Alnwick(0665) 830349
A delightful listed building standing at the edge of the village and overlooking the golf links with views over the bay. Bedrooms have been carefully and individually decorated, and the accommodation throughout is inviting and comfortable. There is an attractive lounge overlooking the links, and the games room makes this an ideal hotel for families. An interesting table d'hôte menu is changed daily, and all dishes are freshly prepared from good quality local produce. The Inkster family offer warm and friendly service to guests.
10⇋🌂 Annexe 1🌂 (4fb) dB&B⇋🌂£68-£74 (incl dinner)
WBDi£235-£256 LDO 4pm
Lic ♥ CTV 12P £

ALNWICK Northumberland Map **12** NU11

GH QQ **Aln House** South Rd NE66 2NZ ☎(0665) 602265
A comfortably furnished Victorian house situated in its own grounds on the edge of the historic town. The resident owners offer a warm and friendly welcome.
8rm(3⇋5hc)(3fb) TV in 1 bedroom ® sB&Bfr£14
dB&Bfr£28 dB&B⇋🌂fr£34
Lic ♥ CTV 8P nc3yrs

🏠✖ GH QQ **Aydon House** South Rd NE66 2NT
☎(0665) 602218
This semidetached Victorian house is situated on the main road leading from the town centre and offers a good standard of accommodation and service.
10rm(4⇋5🌂6hc)(4fb) CTV in all bedrooms sB&B£12-£16
dB&B£24-£32 dB&B⇋🌂£30-£36 WB&B£75-£95 WBDi£120-£140 LDO 5pm
Lic ♥ 12P

GH Ⓠ Ⓠ **Bondgate House Hotel** Bondgate Without NE66 1PN
☎(0665) 602025 FAX (0665) 602554
*A well furnished and comfortable house dating back almost 250
years. The bedrooms are well equipped, a good range of food is
provided in the attractive dining room and a comfortable lounge is
available for residents. Bondgate House is family-owned and run
and is situated on the southern approach to the town centre.*
8rm(3♠5hc) (3fb) CTV in all bedrooms ® ✗ (ex guide dogs)
dB&B£30-£32 dB&B♠£32-£34 WB&B£105-£112 WBDifr£133
LDO 4.30pm
Lic ⑪ CTV 8P Ⓔ

ALTON Hampshire Map **04** SU73

INN Ⓠ Ⓠ **White Hart** London Rd, Holybourne GU34 6EX
☎(0420) 87654
*This hotel has attractive, comfortable bedrooms with colour
televisions. Tea and coffee are always available on the landing.
Barbecues are enjoyed in the pleasant garden, and freshly
prepared meals are available in the bar and restaurant.*
4hc CTV in all bedrooms ® ✗ (ex guide dogs) Lunch £1.50-
£7.95alc Dinner £1.50-£10alc LDO 10pm
⑪ 40P
Credit Cards 1 3

ALTRINCHAM Greater Manchester Map **07** SJ78

SELECTED

GH Ⓠ Ⓠ Ⓠ Ⓠ **Ash Farm** Park Ln, Little Bollington
WA14 4TJ ☎061-929 9290
Closed Xmas
*International snooker star David Taylor and his wife bought
this former 19th-century farmhouse in a derelict state, and
they have painstakingly and tastefully restored and
modernised it to provide very good quality, extremely well
equipped accommodation. Janice Taylor is an accomplished
cook and prepares good wholesome dishes, served in very
generous portions; breakfast is a veritable feast. The house is
situated in the village of Little Bollington, next to a delightful
old pub; surrounded by farmland, it is in a refreshingly
peaceful location. However, the M56 is only two miles away,
the M6 less than six miles, Manchester International Airport
is six miles away and the city centre 10 miles. The house is
reached via the A56 Altrincham-Lymm road. Facilities
include a superb snooker room.*
2⇔♠ (2fb) CTV in all bedrooms ® ✗ (ex guide dogs) ✱
sB&B⇔♠£30-£40 dB&B⇔♠£40-£50 WB&Bfr£230
WBDifr£300 LDO 9.30pm
Lic ⑪ 4P nc9yrs snooker
Credit Cards 1 2 3 5

GH Ⓠ *Bollin Hotel* 58 Manchester Rd WA14 4PJ
☎061-928 2390
*Conveniently situated on the A56 and close to the town centre, this
friendly commercial guesthouse offers modestly furnished but
neatly maintained accommodation at reasonable rates.*
10rm (2fb) ®
⑪ CTV 10P

ALYTH Tayside *Perthshire* Map **15** NO25

INN Ⓠ Ⓠ *Losset* Losset Rd PH11 8BT ☎(08283) 2393
*Dating back to 1730, this small family-run inn is situated close to
the town centre and is a popular venue for locals and visitors alike.
It has a friendly atmosphere and public areas have a rustic feel,
while the compact, well equipped bedrooms offer practical modern
appointments.*
3♠ CTV in all bedrooms ® LDO 9pm
⑪ 10P

AMBLESIDE Cumbria Map **07** NY30

GH Ⓠ Ⓠ Ⓠ **Compston House Hotel** Compston Rd LA22 9DJ
☎(05394) 32305
*This comfortable guesthouse, under the personal supervision of the
proprietors, Ann and Graham Smith, occupies a corner site in the
centre of Ambleside. Every bedroom now has en suite facilities, a
colour television and tea-making facilities.*
8♠ (1fb)✂in 2 bedrooms CTV in all bedrooms ®
✗ (ex guide dogs) ✱ dB&B♠£31-£51 WB&B£108.50-£178.50
LDO 5pm
Lic ⑪ ✗ nc5yrs

GH Ⓠ Ⓠ Ⓠ **Gables Private Hotel** Compston Rd LA22 9DJ
☎(05394) 33272
Closed Dec rs Jan & Feb
*Close to the church in a central position, this long-established
family-run hotel is designed to provide all rooms with en
suite facilities, colour TV and tea-making facilities. There is also a
private car park.*
13⇔♠ (4fb) CTV in all bedrooms ® sB&B⇔♠£18.25-£22
dB&B⇔♠£36.50-£44 WB&Bfr£127.75 WBDifr£203
LDO 5pm
Lic ⑪ CTV 10P

SELECTED

GH Ⓠ Ⓠ Ⓠ Ⓠ **Grey Friar Lodge Country House Hotel**
Brathay LA22 9NE (1m W off A593) ☎(05394) 33158
Mar-Oct
*This delightful Victorian vicarage is situated in its own well
tended gardens and woodland alongside the A593, one mile
west of Ambleside. A traditional lakeland country house, it is
furnished with antiques, books and bric-a-brac, and is
extemely comfortable. The bedrooms are well appointed, and
many have lovely views of Brathay River and valley. Family* ▶

**Marine House
Private Hotel**
ALNMOUTH, NORTHUMBERLAND NE66 2RW
Telephone: Alnmouth (0665) 830349

RUNNERS UP FOR AA Best Family Holiday in Britain 1984
and Northumbria Tourist Board, Holiday Hosts Award 1985.
Relax in the friendly atmosphere of this 200-year-old recently
modernised Granary of considerable charm, overlooking the
golf links and beautiful beaches. 10 comfortable bedrooms, all
with ensuite facilities. Traditional home cooking. Cocktail Bar
and Games Room. Spacious lounge with colour TV. Children
and pets welcome. Two adjacent self-catering cottages. Sheila
and Gordon Inkster.
SPECIAL GOLFING BREAKS AND FAMILY HOLIDAY
PRICES PLUS SPECIAL INTEREST WEEK-ENDS.

owned and run, first-class service is provided by the hospitable owners. A four-course set dinner is offered, with traditional home cooking, in charming surroundings; the lakeland breakfast is also highly recommended.

8⇨♠ ⌇in all bedrooms CTV in all bedrooms ® ✕
sB&B⇨♠£31-£43 (incl dinner) WBDif£215-£275
LDO 7.30pm
Lic ♨ 12P nc12yrs ⓔ

GH Q Q **Hillsdale Hotel** Church St LA22 0BT ☎(05394) 33174
An attractive small Lakeland-stone terraced house situated in the town centre. The accommodation is very well maintained, and includes a comfortable lounge and a nicely appointed dining room; the hotel has a residential licence.
8rm(1⇨7hc) CTV in all bedrooms ® ✕ sB&Bf£20-£25
dB&B£30-£36 dB&B⇨£37-£38
♨ ⨍

GH Q Q Q **Lyndhurst Hotel** Wansfell Rd LA22 0EG
☎(05394) 32421
A small, friendly, family-run hotel built of lakeland stone, conveniently situated only a short walk from the town centre. Bedrooms are attractively decorated, with a four-poster bed and all have private bathrooms, TV, radio and tea and coffee-making facilities. There is also a cosy bar and imaginative home-cooked meals are served in the dining room. Outside there is a small garden and a private car park.
6♠ Annexe 2♠ (3fb)⌇in 1 bedroom CTV in all bedrooms ®
✕ dB&B♠£35-£48 WB&B£125-£160 WBDif£180-£230
LDO 8pm
Lic ♨ 8P ⓔ

GH Q Q Q **Riverside Lodge Country House** Rothay Bridge
LA22 0EH ☎(05394) 34208
This charming early-Georgian house is reached by a footbridge over the River Rothay, yet is only a short walk from the town centre. A high standard of accommodation is provided, and all the bedrooms have private bathrooms. Public areas are full of charm and character, and outside three acres of grounds create a peaceful atmosphere.
5rm(3⇨2♠) (1fb) CTV in all bedrooms ® ✕ ✳
sB&B⇨♠£25-£40 dB&B⇨♠£45-£55 WB&B£155-£175
Lic ♨ 20P ✔
Credit Cards ① ③ ⓔ

SELECTED

GH Q Q Q Q **Rothay Garth Hotel** Rothay Rd LA22 0EE
☎(05394) 32217 FAX (05394) 34400
An attractive and well maintained family-run hotel, situated in well tended gardens on the edge of the village. A feature of the hotel is the elegant restaurant, where a 5-course fixed-price menu is available for both residents and non-residents. The bedrooms are individually furnished and decorated to a high standard; they are also particularly well equipped and have private bathrooms. There is a very comfortable lounge and a cocktail bar, and most helpful and courteous.
16rm(14⇨♠2hc)(3fb)⌇in 12 bedrooms CTV in all bedrooms ® LDO 8pm
Lic ♨ CTV 17P
Credit Cards ① ② ③ ⑤ ⓔ

SELECTED

GH Q Q Q Q **Rydal Lodge Hotel** LA22 9LR (2m NW
A590) ☎(05394) 33208
Closed 7 Jan-4 Feb
This charming country house stands beside the River Rothay, just north of Ambleside on the A591. It provides very well

maintained accommodation and a relaxed, hospitable atmosphere. Dinner is cooked by the proprietor using top quality fresh ingredients, and is served in the attractive dining room. The very comfortable drawing room upstairs overlooks the pleasant gardens, the river and surrounding fells; there are other, smaller lounges downstairs. Parts of the house date back to the early 1600s when is was a coaching inn; it has also been associated with William Wordsworth. There is ample car parking space.
8rm(2♠6hc) (1fb) LDO 7pm
Lic CTV 12P ✔
Credit Cards ① ③

GH Q Q Q **Rysdale Hotel** Rothay Rd LA22 0EE ☎(05394) 32140
An attractive, end-of-terrace Victorian house overlooking a bowling green towards the church, situated conveniently close to the town centre, has splendid views of surrounding fells from front-facing rooms. The hotel is now under new management.
9rm(1⇨5♠3hc) (2fb)⌇in all bedrooms CTV in all bedrooms
® ✕ (ex guide dogs) sB&B£16.50-£19.50 dB&B£33-£35
dB&B⇨♠£39-£47 WB&B£110-£153 WBDif£173-£216
LDO 10am
Lic ♨ CTV 2P nc8yrs
Credit Cards ① ③ ⓔ

GH Q Q **Smallwood Hotel** Compston Rd LA22 9DJ
☎(05394) 32330
A spacious detached house close to the town centre, with car parking at the rear. The accommodation is comfortable, with an attractive lounge and pretty dining room, where appetizing home-cooked meals are served.
13rm(3⇨♠10hc) Annexe 1⇨ (3fb) CTV in 8 bedrooms ®
sB&B£18-£26 dB&B£34-£40 dB&B⇨♠£36-£40 WB&B£120-
£126 WBDif£170-£186 LDO 6pm
Lic ♨ CTV 13P ⓔ

See advertisement on page 43

GH Q **Thrang House** Compston Rd LA22 9DJ ☎(05394) 32112
Mar-Dec
A small, slate-built friendly guesthouse serving good, hearty breakfasts. Centrally situated, there are fine views over a miniature golf course and tennis courts to the fells behind.
6rm(2♠4hc) CTV in all bedrooms ® ✕ sB&B£16-£20
dB&B£30-£40 dB&B♠£36-£44 LDO 6pm
♨ 5P nc9yrs

INN Q Q Q **Drunken Duck** Barngates LA22 0NG
☎Hawkshead(09666) 347
This popular country inn is situated on a crossroads about 3 miles from Ambleside, with delightful views of the surrounding fells with Windermere Lake in the distance. A daily changing blackboard menu offers a wide choice of bar meals, which are also served outside in summer. A small, very attractive dining room for residents has recently been opened in which mainly traditional English food is served: reservations are strongly advised, even for residents. Bedrooms are very well equipped, each with private bathrooms, telephone, TV and tea-making facilities.
8⇨ Annexe 2♠ CTV in all bedrooms ® ✳ sB&B⇨♠£40
dB&B⇨♠£54-£67 ✳ Bar Lunch £4.50-£5.25 LDO 8.45pm
♨ 40P ✔
Credit Cards ① ③

ANCASTER Lincolnshire Map **08** SK94

FH Q Mrs F Mival **Woodlands** *(SK966437)* West Willoughby
NG32 3SH (off the A153 between Sleaford and Grantham, 1m
W of Ancaster) ☎Loveden(0400) 30340
Etr-Oct
A charming traditional farmhouse located on the A153 in the village of West Willoughby, one mile west of Ancaster. Set well back from the main road and surrounded by arable and

▶

pasture land, the house is simply but comfortably furnished and the proprietor is friendly.
2hc (1fb) TV in all bedrooms ® ✱ sB&B£12-£15 dB&B£22-£28
WB&Bfr£70
🏠 CTV 3P 12 acres mixed ⓔ

ANDOVER Hampshire Map **04** SU34

GH 🅠🅠 **Istana** 4 Eversfield Close, off The Avenue SP10 3EN
🕿(0264) 351454
A modern, detached brick-built house in a quiet residential area. The neatly presented bedrooms are comfortable and well equipped; smoking is not permitted. The walled garden is a sun trap in the summer, complemented by the small swimming pool.
3hc (1fb)✗in all bedrooms CTV in all bedrooms ®
✖ (ex guide dogs) sB&Bfr£15 dB&Bfr£33 LDO 5.30pm
🏠 CTV 10P 1🏊 ⌕

ANNAN Dumfries & Galloway *Dumfriesshire* Map **11** NY16

GH 🅠🅠🅠 **Northfield House** Eaglesfield Rd DG12 5ll
🕿(0461) 202851
Closed Xmas & New Year
3⇨🏠 ✗in 2 bedrooms CTV in all bedrooms ®
✖ (ex guide dogs) ✱ sB&B⇨🏠fr£36 dB&B⇨🏠fr£52
LDO 7.30pm
🏠 8P nc12yrs croquet lawn

GH 🅠🅠 **Ravenswood Private Hotel** St Johns Rd DG12 6AW
🕿(0461) 202158
This neat establishment is well cared for and is managed by the friendly proprietress. The bedrooms are spacious and comfortable, and the home-cooked dinner offers a choice of dishes.
8hc (2fb) ® ✖ (ex guide dogs) sB&B£15.50 dB&B£28
LDO 8pm
Lic 🏠 CTV 🅿 ⓔ

ANSTRUTHER Fife Map **12** NO50

SELECTED

GH 🅠🅠🅠🅠 **The Spindrift** Pittenweem Rd KY10 3DT
🕿(0333) 310573
This three-storeyed house was completely renovated in 1990 by the owners. It occupies a dominant position on the left hand side of the road on entering the town from the west, being the first house. There is a spacious, comfortable lounge and a nice bright dining room with cane furniture. The eight bedrooms located on the first two floors are furnished and decorated in bright and cheerful style with many thoughtful extras, and some rooms have a sea view. There are two family rooms and one has an interconnecting door. On the top floor is the 'Captain's room', effectively wood lined, with a view towards the harbour. An attractive menu provides a choice for each course.
8⇨🏠 (3fb)✗in all bedrooms CTV in all bedrooms ® ✱
sB&B⇨🏠£30 dB&B⇨🏠£53 LDO 7pm
Lic 🏠 CTV 10P
Credit Cards 3

INN 🅠 **The Royal Hotel** 20 Rodger St KY10 3DU
🕿(0333) 310581 FAX (0333) 310270
Cosy bedrooms are offered in this quaint village inn, that is family owned and run. A courteous, friendly service is provided, and lunch and dinner offer very good value for money, with freshly cooked dishes.
11rm(2⇨7🏠2hc) (1fb) CTV in 6 bedrooms ®
✖ (ex guide dogs) sB&B£16-£20 sB&B⇨🏠£21-£25
dB&Bfr£32 dB&B⇨🏠fr£42 WB&B£100-£130 WBDi£145-£175 Lunch £2.50-£6alc High tea £3.95-£4.24 Dinner £5-£11alc
LDO 9pm

🏠 CTV 6P
Credit Cards 1 2 3 5 ⓔ

ANSTY Wiltshire Map **03** ST92

INN 🅠🅠🅠 **Maypole** SP3 5PY 🕿Tisbury(0747) 870607 &
871227
A pretty country inn located next to the village pond, with a stream flowing by, enjoying much local support. Bedrooms are very prettily decorated and well equipped. The public areas are attractive and busy without being uncomfortably full; each dining section is cosy and pleasantly furnished. The food is home cooked, and there is a cheery, friendly atmosphere.
3⇨🏠 CTV in all bedrooms ® ✖ (ex guide dogs) ✱ sB&B⇨£20-£23 dB&B⇨£35-£50 WB&Bfr£130 WBDifr£200 ✱ Lunch £9-£18alc Dinner £9-£18alc LDO 9.30pm
CTV 50P nc12yrs
Credit Cards 1 3

APPLEBY-IN-WESTMORLAND Cumbria Map **12** NY62

GH 🅠🅠 **Bongate House** Bongate CA16 6UE
🕿Appleby(07683) 51245
Closed Xmas and New Year
A detached Georgian house standing in an acre of garden on the approach to the town from Brough and Scotch Corner. The accommodation includes well equipped bedrooms with tea and coffee-making facilities, a comfortable lounge with TV and a cosy residents' bar. Ample car-parking space is also provided.
8rm(1⇨4🏠3hc) (4fb) ® ✖ (ex guide dogs) sB&B£15
dB&B£30 dB&B⇨🏠£36 WB&B£90-£120 WBDi£140-£160
LDO 6pm
Lic 🏠 CTV 8P 2⌕ nc7yrs croquet & putting lawn ⓔ

ARBROATH Tayside *Angus* Map **12** NO64

GH 🅠 **Kingsley** 29 Market Gate DD11 1AU 🕿(0241) 73933
Situated close to the bustling fishing harbour, with convenient access to the town centre, this family-run guesthouse has a friendly atmosphere and offers simple, good-value accommodation.
14hc (8fb) ® ✱ sB&B£13.50-£14.50 dB&B£25 WB&B£85-£90
WBDi£105-£115 LDO 7.30pm
Lic 🏠 CTV 4P snooker solarium childrens play ground ⓔ

ARDBRECKNISH Strathclyde *Argyllshire* Map **10** NN02

FH 🅠🅠🅠 **Rockhill** *(NN072219)* PA33 1BH
🕿Kilchrenan(08663) 218
May-Sep
This 17th-century stone-built cottage-style country house sits in its own attractive gardens on the south side of Loch Awe. Reached by a single track from the village, this secluded farm enjoys splendid views and is full of character. The lounge is well stocked with books and games, and the small, neat dining room offers an honesty drinks counter. The bedrooms are simply decorated and furnished, but thoughtfully equipped; two ground-floor rooms are reached from the kitchen area.
5rm(1⇨🏠4hc) (3fb) CTV in all bedrooms ®
✖ (ex guide dogs) ✱ dB&B£56-£70 dB&B⇨🏠£76-£86 (incl dinner) WBDi£175-£240 LDO 7pm
Lic 8P nc8yrs ⏎ 200 acres horses sheep

ARDERSIER Highland *Inverness-shire* Map **14** NH85

FH 🅠🅠🅠 Mrs L E MacBean **Milton-of-Gollanfield**
(NH809534) Gollanfield IV1 2QT 🕿(0667) 62207 due to change to 462207
May-Nov
A warm welcome awaits guests at Mrs MacBean's Victorian farmhouse which stands in its garden just off the A96 about 5 miles west of Nairn. It is an ideal base for the tourist, offering traditional comforts and enjoyable home cooking.
3hc ✗in all bedrooms ® ✖ (ex guide dogs) ✱ dB&B£24-£30
CTV P 360 acres mixed arable beef sheep

43

ARDGAY Highland *Sutherland* Map **14** NH58

GH |Q||Q||Q| **Ardgay House** IV24 3DH ☎(08632) 345
rs 16 Dec-Jan
*Conveniently situated beside the A9, this attractive detached
Victorian house has been considerably altered and upgraded to
provide comfortable and well equipped tourist accommodation.*
6rm(4⇨♠2hc) (2fb) CTV in all bedrooms ®
✖ (ex guide dogs) sB&B£14-£20 sB&B⇨♠£14-£20 dB&B£24-
£28 dB&B⇨♠£32-£36 LDO 7pm
Lic ⬛ 9P £

GH |Q||Q| **Croit Mairi** Kincardine Hill IV24 3DJ ☎(08632) 504
*Well signposted from the A9 to the east of the village, this modern
detached guesthouse is situated in an elevated position and enjoys
lovely views of the Kyle of Sutherland and Dornoch Firth. Meals
are served in the spacious lounge- dining room and some table
sharing may be necessary.*
5hc (2fb)⸝in all bedrooms ® ✖ (ex guide dogs) LDO 6pm
⬛ CTV 10P nc3yrs
Credit Cards ①③

ARRAN, ISLE OF Strathclyde *Buteshire* Map **10**

BRODICK Map **10** NS03

GH |Q||Q||Q| **Allandale** KD27 8BJ ☎(0770) 2278
Closed Nov-Dec
*Enjoying an elevated position to the south of Brodick, this friendly
house is surrounded by gardens and offers a good standard of
accommodation in well-equipped bedrooms. There is a most
comfortable lounge in which to relax.*
4rm(2⇨2♠) Annexe 2⇨ (1fb) CTV in all bedrooms ®
sB&B⇨♠£16-£20 dB&B⇨♠£32-£40 WB&B£105-£120
WBDif£160-£180 LDO 6pm
Lic ⬛ 12P

GH |Q||Q||Q| **Tuathair House** Shore Rd KA27 8AJ ☎(0770) 2214
*Non-smokers are especially welcome at Chris and Howard Wood's
lovely seafront home. Tastefully appointed throughout, it offers
comfortable, well-equipped bedrooms and an attractive relaxing
lounge.*
4♠ ⸝in all bedrooms CTV in all bedrooms ®
✖ (ex guide dogs) ✳ dB&B♠fr£34 WB&Bfr£115 WBDifr£168
⬛ 4P nc

LOCHRANZA Map **10** NR95

GH |Q| *Kincardine Lodge* KA27 8HL ☎(077083) 267
Apr-Oct
*Conveniently placed for the Claonaig ferry, this guesthouse has
pleasant views of the bay and castle. The bedrooms are fairly
spacious and modestly furnished and there are 2 traditional
lounges, 1 with TV. The house features an attractive wooden
staircase.*
7hc (4fb) ®
CTV 6P

ARROCHAR Strathclyde *Dunbartonshire* Map **10** NN20

GH |Q||Q||Q| *Mansefield Country House* G83 7AG ☎(03012) 282
*A fine Victorian house set in its own gardens well back from the
Helensburgh road, overlooking Loch Long. The bedrooms are
thoughtfully equipped, and there is a comfortable lounge and a
pleasant dining room with an attractive fireplace ; dinner is served
every night except Sunday.*
5hc (1fb)⸝in all bedrooms CTV in 3 bedrooms TV in 2
bedrooms ® LDO 6pm
⬛ CTV 8P

Book as early as possible for busy holiday periods.

ARUNDEL West Sussex Map **04** TQ00

GH |Q||Q| **Arden** 4 Queens Ln BN18 9JN ☎(0903) 882544
Closed 10 Dec-1 Feb
*This friendly hotel is quietly situated off the main road but is
within easy walking distance of the castle and town centre. The
bedrooms are freshly decorated, neat and well-equipped, and the
attractive breakfast room has pine furniture.*
8rm(2♠6hc) (1fb) CTV in all bedrooms ® ✖ (ex guide dogs)
dB&B£28-£32 dB&B♠£32-£36
⬛ 4P nc2yrs

GH |Q||Q| **Bridge House** 18 Queen St BN18 9JG
☎(0903) 882142 & 882779
Closed Xmas wk
*With views of the castle, the river and the South Downs, this 18th-
century house has a friendly atmosphere. The choice of rooms
includes family accommodation, and annexe rooms in the 16th-
century cottage. The dining area is non-smoking.*
12rm(5⇨♠7hc) Annexe 3⇨♠ (6fb) CTV in all bedrooms ®
sB&B£17-£20 sB&B⇨♠£24-£28 dB&B£28-£36
dB&B⇨♠£34-£40 LDO 8pm
Lic ⬛ CTV 9P 4🐾
Credit Cards ①③

INN |Q||Q| **Swan Hotel** High St BN18 9AG ☎(0903) 882314
FAX (0798) 831716
*This is a popular and lively free house with real ale and a good
selection of homemade dishes, served in the bar and restaurant,
sometimes with live entertainment. The bedrooms are modern and
well-equipped, all having private facilities.*
13rm(11⇨2♠) CTV in all bedrooms ® ✖ (ex guide dogs)
sB&B⇨♠fr£45 dB&B⇨♠fr£60 Lunch £6-£9 Dinner
fr£9&alc LDO 9.30pm
⬛
Credit Cards ①②③⑤£

ASHBOURNE Derbyshire
See **Waterhouses**

ASHBURTON Devon Map **03** SX76
See also **Bickington**
GH |Q||Q||Q| **Gages Mill** Buckfastleigh Rd TQ13 7JW
☎(0364) 52391
mid Mar-mid Nov
*A former 16th-century wool mill attractively set within an acre of
gardens ; surrounded by open countryside, on the edge of Dartmoor
National Park, it is very convenient for the A38. Carefully
converted to retain its original character, the bedrooms are cosy,
spotlessly clean and brightly decorated, and public rooms are
comfortable and traditionally furnished. Fresh home cooking is
provided by Mrs Cox, and service is friendly and informal.*
8⇨♠ (1fb) ® ✖ ✖ dB&B⇨♠£32-£39 WB&B£112-£122.50
WBDif£168-£185.50 LDO 3pm
Lic ⬛ CTV 10P nc5yrs

FH |Q| Mrs H Young **Bremridge** *(SX785701)* Woodland
TQ13 7JX (2m E unclass towards Denbury) ☎(0364) 52426
Closed Dec & Jan
5rm(1⇨4hc) (3fb) sB&B£14.50-£16.50 sB&B⇨♠£14.50-£16.50
dB&B£29-£33 dB&B⇨♠£29-£33 WB&B£85-£95 WBDif£95-
£110 LDO 6pm
⬛ CTV 6P ♧ 8 acres mixed £

ASHFORD Kent Map **05** TR04

GH |Q||Q||Q| **Croft Hotel** Canterbury Rd, Kennington
TN25 4DU ☎(0233) 622140
*Spacious, family-style, modern accommodation set in 2 acres of
well kept grounds combines with a choice of well equipped
bedrooms in the main house. A bar and tastefully furnished
lounge augment the cosy Croft Restaurant, which serves
moderately priced à la carte dishes and grills. All the garden*

rooms have generous and very comfortable sitting areas, which provide real home comforts for the tourist and business guest. Service is supervised by the very helpful and agreeable resident proprietors, Mr and Mrs John Ellerington.

15⇨♠ Annexe 13⇨♠ (3fb) CTV in all bedrooms ® ✱ sB&B⇨♠£35-£45 dB&B⇨♠£43-£47 LDO 8pm
Lic ♨ CTV 30P croquet
Credit Cards 1 3

GH Q Downsview Willesborough Rd, Kennington TN24 9QP ☎(0233) 621953
This old fashioned and well managed guesthouse is set in an acre of grounds. The best bedrooms are in the new extension, whilst the others are more simply furnished but still well equipped. The dining room overlooks the rose garden, and is augmented by the lounge and bar facilities.
21rm(4⇨17♠) (6fb) CTV in all bedrooms ® ✱ sB&B⇨♠£32-£35 dB&B⇨♠£45-£56 LDO 8.30pm
Lic ♨ CTV 25P pool table putting green
Credit Cards 1 2 3 5 £

ASHOVER Derbyshire Map **08** SK36

FH QQ Mr J A Wootton **Old School** *(SK323654)*
Uppertown s45 0JF ☎Chesterfield(0246) 590813
Mar-Oct
With all rooms on the ground floor, this modern stone-built farmhouse is ideal for young children and elderly guests. Surrounded by farmland it stands on the opposite side of the A632 from the village Ashover.
4hc (2fb)✂in all bedrooms CTV in all bedrooms ✖ ✱ sB&B£12-£14 dB&B£24-£28 WB&B£84-£98 WBDi£126-£140 LDO 9.30am
♨ CTV 10P 45 acres poultry & sheep

ASHTON-UNDER-LYNE Greater Manchester Map **07** SJ99

GH QQQ Welbeck House Hotel 324 Katherine St OL6 7BD ☎061-344 0751 FAX 061-343 4278
This privately owned small hotel, situated in a residential area close to the town centre, offers well-maintained accommodation and good off-street parking. The modern bedrooms, although generally compact, are comfortably furnished and well-equipped.
8⇨♠ (2fb) CTV in all bedrooms ® ✱ sB&B⇨♠£30-£40 dB&B⇨♠£45-£55 LDO 8pm
Lic ♨ CTV 12P games room
Credit Cards 1 2 3 5 £

ASTBURY Cheshire Map **07** SJ86

INN Q *Egerton Arms Hotel* CW12 4RQ
☎Congleton(02602) 73946
This village inn lies south of Congleton on the A34. A choice of meals is available, including a children's and a vegetarian menu, and to the rear are a small garden area and a large car park.
7hc CTV in all bedrooms ® LDO 9.30pm
♨ CTV 100P
Credit Cards 3 5

ASTON Staffordshire Map **07** SJ74

GH QQ Larksfield Country Accommodation Stoniford Ln TF9 4JB ☎Pipe Gate(063081) 7069
A modern farmhouse in a peaceful rural setting conveniently positioned for the main Shropshire, Staffordshire and Cheshire tourist area. Expert shotgun tuition is available.
7rm(5♠2hc) (4fb) CTV in all bedrooms ® ✱ sB&B£17-£18 dB&B£32-£34 dB&B♠£36
♨ CTV 10P nc12yrs ♪ clay pigeon shooting pitch & putt
Credit Cards 3 £

£ Remember to use the money-off vouchers.

ASTON MUNSLOW Shropshire Map 07 SO58

GH Q Q Q **Chadstone** SY7 9ER ☎Munslow(058476) 675
Mar-Oct
A modern dormer-style bungalow in a small hamlet on the B4368 near the Craven Arms pub. It offers neat rooms and the elegant dining room has panoramic views of the countryside. The resident proprietors are genuinely hospitable and provide attentive service.
5rm(2⇨🌂3hc) ⤢in all bedrooms CTV in 1 bedroom ® ✖ ✱ sB&Bfr£20 dB&Bfr£36 dB&B⇨🌂fr£40 LDO 7pm
卿 CTV 6P nc12yrs ⓔ

ATTLEBOROUGH Norfolk Map 05 TM09

INN Q **Griffin Hotel** Church St NR17 2AH ☎(0953) 452149
Situated in the town centre, this inn offers simple accommodation, with many of its 16th-century characteristics retained. The convivial atmosphere complements the popular bar meals. Car parking is available to the rear through the narrow courtyard.
8hc CTV in 4 bedrooms TV in 3 bedrooms ® LDO 10pm
20P

AUCHTERMUCHTY Fife Map 11 NO21

FH Q Q Q Mr I Steven **Ardchoille** *(NO248096)* Dunshalt KY14 7EY ☎(0337) 28414
Closed Xmas & New Year
Just 1 mile from Auchtermuchty on the B936, this modern farmhouse has thoughtfully equipped bedrooms. Meals are served around a communal dining table, and the good food is complemented by genuine hospitality.
3rm(2🌂1hc) (1fb) CTV in all bedrooms ® ✖ (ex guide dogs) ✱ sB&B🌂fr£40 dB&B🌂£50-£54 LDO 6pm
卿 CTV 8P ∪ 2 acres horses

AUDLEY Staffordshire Map 07 SJ75

FH Q Q Q Mrs E E Oulton **Domvilles** *(SJ776516)* Barthomley Rd ST7 8HT ☎Stoke-on-Trent(0782) 720378
Closed 25 Dec
This large farmhouse is beautifully furnished and immaculately maintained. The gardens and farmyard are also well tended, and guests are offered friendly service and comfortable accommodation. To find the house, leave the M6 at junction 16, follow signs to Barthomley, turn left at the White Lion Inn to Audley.
5rm(4⇨🌂1hc) (2fb)⤢in 3 bedrooms CTV in all bedrooms ®
✖ (ex guide dogs) ✱ sB&B£18-£20 sB&B⇨🌂fr£18
dB&B⇨🌂£30-£32 WB&Bfr£210 WBDifr£266 LDO 6pm
CTV 8P table tennis 225 acres dairy mixed
See advertisement under STOKE-ON-TRENT

AUSTWICK North Yorkshire Map 07 SD76

FH Q Q Mrs M Hird **Rawlinshaw** *(SD781673)* LA2 8DD ☎Settle(07292) 3214
Etr-Sep
200-year-old farmhouse, set in attractive countryside.
2hc (1fb) ® ✖ (ex guide dogs)
卿 CTV 10P ∪ 206 acres beef dairy horses sheep

AVIEMORE Highland *Inverness-shire* Map 14 NH81

GH Q Q Q **Corrour House** Inverdruie PH22 1QH ☎(0479) 810220
Closed Nov-26 Dec
Stone-built house standing in tree-studded grounds half a mile east of Aviemore on B970.
8rm(3⇨4🌂1hc) (2fb) CTV in all bedrooms ® sB&B⇨🌂£25-£31 dB&B⇨🌂£44-£56 WB&B£140-£180 WBDi£215-£265
LDO 8pm
Lic 卿 CTV 15P nc1yr
Credit Cards ① ③

GH Q Q Q **Craiglea** Grampian Rd PH22 1RH ☎(0479) 810210
A friendly and informal family-run guesthouse offering good value bed and breakfast accommodation. It is situated beside the main road convenient for the Aviemore Centre facilities.
11rm(1🌂10hc) (4fb) ® ✱ sB&B£14-£15 dB&B£28-£30 dB&B🌂£29-£31 WB&B£90-£100
CTV 12P sauna ⓔ

GH Q Q **Ravenscraig** Grampian Rd PH22 1RP ☎(0479) 810278
Situated on the main street, just north of the Aviemore Centre, this friendly family-run guesthouse offers good value bed and breakfast accommodation. Bedrooms are compact, modern and well furnished in traditional style; most, including those in the annexe, have private bathrooms.
6🌂 Annexe 6🌂 (2fb) CTV in all bedrooms ® sB&B🌂£15-£17.50 dB&B🌂£30-£35 WB&B£105-£122.50
卿 CTV 12P ⓔ

AXBRIDGE Somerset Map 03 ST45

FH Q Mr L F Dimmock **Manor** *(ST420549)* Cross BS26 2ED ☎(0934) 732577
Closed Xmas
A period farmhouse situated at the junction of the A38 and the A371 roads. Accommodation is simple and rustic, being a proper working sheep farm. Substantial traditional meals – mainly roasts – are always popular, and the proprietors offer a high standard of hospitality.
7rm(2hc) (2fb) ® LDO 5pm
CTV 10P 250 acres beef horses sheep

AYR Strathclyde *Ayrshire* Map 10 NS32

GH Q Q **Arrandale Hotel** 2-4 Cassillis St KA7 1DW ☎(0292) 289959
rs Winter
Used by both tourists and commercial travellers, this is a friendly, family-run hotel. There are nice bedrooms and en suite facilities, and a comfortable lounge. The dining room has a residents' bar.
13rm(1⇨2🌂10hc) (6fb) CTV in all bedrooms
✖ (ex guide dogs) ✱ sB&B£15-£21 sB&B⇨🌂£26-£28 dB&B£28-£30 dB&B⇨🌂£40 WB&B£90-£125 WBDi£125-£160 LDO 3pm
Lic 卿 CTV 🅿 ⓔ

SELECTED

GH Q Q Q Q **Brenalder Lodge** 39 Dunure, Doonfoot KA7 4HR ☎(0292) 43939
rs during props holiday
There is a warm welcome at this attractive modern house, just south of Ayr on the A719. The 5 bedrooms are well equipped and furnished in a pretty, modern style. The dining room and lounge, shared with proprietors Brenda and Albert Taylor, are filled with personal momentos. Dinner, available with 24 hours notice, is excellent value and should satisfy the heartiest appetite. No smoking except in the lounge.
5⇨🌂 (1fb)⤢in all bedrooms CTV in all bedrooms ® ✱ sB&B⇨🌂£35-£42 dB&B⇨🌂£42-£56 WB&B£147-£196 WBDi£241.50-£290.50 LDO 24hrs prior
卿 CTV 9P nc7yrs ⓔ

GH Q Q **Dargill** 7 Queens Ter KA7 1DU ☎(0292) 261955
Cheery modern bedrooms, a cosy dining room and an attractive, comfortable lounge are provided by a compact terraced hotel located between sea and town centre.
4hc (2fb) CTV in all bedrooms ® LDO 2pm
卿 CTV nc3yrs ⓔ

GH QQ **The Parkhouse Hotel** 1A Ballantine Dr KA7 2RG
☎(0292) 264151
This period house is set in a residential area on the south side of the town. There are public shower rooms for guests' use.
7hc (2fb) CTV in all bedrooms ® ✗
Lic ™ CTV ⁄P

GH QQ ***Windsor Hotel*** 6 Alloway Place KA7 2AA
☎(0292) 264689
This attractive terraced guesthouse is situated just a short distance from the centre of town. The bedrooms are bright and comfortable, and most have en suite facilities.
10rm(7⇌↱2hc) (4fb) CTV in all bedrooms ® LDO 6pm
™ CTV ⁄P

FH Q Mr & Mrs A Stevenson ***Trees*** *(NS386186)* KA6 6EW
☎(0292) 570270
Closed Xmas & New Year
A whitewashed farmhouse sitting in a sheltered position on high ground offering good quality accommodation at modest prices. Approaching from the by-pass along the A70, turn right after quarter of a mile; the road to the farm is two miles along that unclassified road on the right.
3hc (1fb) ✗ LDO 3pm
™ CTV 6P 75 acres grazing

AYTON, GREAT North Yorkshire Map **08** NZ51

INN QQ **Royal Oak Hotel** High Green TS9 6BW
☎(0642) 722361 FAX (0642) 724047
A cosy owner-run village inn, offering friendly service and a popular range of catering – morning coffee, lunch and dinner.
5⇌↱ CTV in all bedrooms ® ✱ sB&B⇌↱£25-£35 dB&B⇌↱£35-£45 ✱ LDO 9.15pm
™ ⁄P
Credit Cards 1 3

BABELL Clwyd Map **07** SJ17

FH QQ Mrs M L Williams **Bryn Glas** *(SJ155737)* CH8 7PZ
☎Caerwys(0352) 720493
Feb-Nov
This dormer-style bungalow is located opposite the Black Lion Inn, next to the original farmhouse and buildings, and is surrounded by farmland. It offers 2 nicely maintained rooms which are equipped with black and white TV and tea making facilities.
2hc (1fb) ⚞ in all bedrooms TV in all bedrooms ® ✱ sB&Bfr£15 dB&Bfr£25
™ CTV 2P pony trekking 40 acres beef mixed sheep Ⓔ

BAKEWELL Derbyshire Map **08** SK26

GH QQ **Cliffe House Hotel** Monsal Head DE4 1NL
☎Great Longstone(0629) 640376
Pleasant house at the head of Monsal Dale.
10rm(5⇌5↱) (3fb) CTV in all bedrooms ® ✗ (ex guide dogs) sB&B⇌↱£27-£37 dB&B⇌↱£37-£41 WB&B£125-£134 WBDi£180-£190 LDO 10am
Lic ™ CTV 14P
Credit Cards 1 3 Ⓔ

See advertisement on page 49

SELECTED

GH QQQQ **Merlin House Country Hotel** Ashford Ln, Monsal Head DE4 1NL ☎Great Longstone(062987) 475 due to change to (0629) 640475
Mar-Oct
A small guesthouse in a lovely rural location at Monsal Head in the Peak District. The well tended lawns, shrubs and trees provide an attractive view from the pleasant dining room and conservatory sun lounge. The well proportioned rooms are immaculately kept, and the proprietors are a genuinely ▶

Brenalder Lodge

39 DUNURE ROAD, DOONFOOT, AYR
SCOTLAND KA7 4HR
Telephone: 0292 43939
QQQQ Selected

Brenalder Lodge is situated with a panoramic view of the Carrick Hills, and overlooking the Firth of Clyde, providing an ideal base for touring the Burns Country.

All bedrooms offer you a high standard of accommodation with en suite facilities, colour television, tea and coffee making facilities.

A delicious four course breakfast is served in our new conservatory styled dining room and there is all day access to our lodge, with ample private parking.

Manor Farm

CROSS, Nr. AXBRIDGE, SOMERSET
Incorporating CIRCLE 'D' RIDING CENTRE

Tel: Axbridge (0934) 732577

A working beef and sheep farm (250 acres) adjoining the beautiful Mendip Hills. 400 year old building, once a stage-coaching inn. Central for touring. Children and pets welcome. Free Somerset cider served with evening meal. All rooms have tea/coffee making facilities.

hospitable couple who make every effort to ensure their guests have an enjoyable stay.
6rm(1⇨3♠2hc)® ✖ sB&B⇨♠♠£22-£26 dB&B⇨♠♠£40-£48 WB&B£140-£154
🍴 CTV 6P nc

BALA Gwynedd Map **06** SH93

GH Q **Frondderw** Stryd-y-Fron LL23 7YD ☎(0678) 520301
Mar-Nov
This charming period mansion dates back to 1680, and from its elevated position on the western outskirts of town, it commands lovely views of the Berwyn mountains and the lake. The accommodation is fairly simple, but some rooms have en suite facilities.
8rm(1⇨1♠6hc) (3fb) ® ✖ (ex guide dogs) ✳ sB&B£11-£12 sB&B⇨♠£15-£16 dB&B£22-£24 dB&B⇨♠£26-£30 WB&B£73.50-£108.50 WBDi£126-£161 LDO 5pm
Lic 🍴 CTV 10P £

GH Q **Plas Teg** Tegid St LL23 7EN ☎(0678) 520268
This large, stone semidetached 19th-century house is situated close to the town centre and has its own private car park. The accommodation is spacious but rather simple and dated.
6hc (5fb) ® LDO 5pm
Lic CTV 12P

FH QQ Mrs E Jones **Eirianfa** *(SH967394)* Sarnau LL23 7LH (4m N on A494) ☎Llandderfel(06783) 389
Mar-Nov
This modern farmhouse is in an isolated position overlooking the Berwyn Mountains. The bedrooms are neat and well furnished and a friendly family atmosphere prevails.
3hc (1fb) ® ✖ sB&B£15-£16 dB&B£26-£28
🍴 CTV 4P ✔ 150 acres mixed £

BALLACHULISH Highland *Argyllshire* Map **14** NN05

GH QQQ **Ballachulish House** Ballachulish House PA39 4JX ☎(08552) 266
A historic 18th-century house set in two acres of grounds. Public rooms have log fires, and there is an honesty bar in the attractive lounge. Bedrooms are comfortably appointed with elegant antiques, and various thoughtful amenities are provided. The dinner menu regularly features game and local shellfish.
4⇨♠ (2fb)✔in all bedrooms ® ✳ sB&B⇨♠£30-£40 dB&B⇨♠£40-£70 LDO 6pm
Lic 10P

GH QQQ **Fern Villa** East Laroch PA39 4JE ☎(08552) 393
Closed Xmas & New Year
Mr and Mrs Clement have recently completed a major upgrading programme at their lovely granite-built Victorian home which is situated in the centre of the village. The house is tastefully furnished throughout and the bedrooms, though compact, all have en suite facilities and offer the expected comforts. It should be noted that this is a no-smoking establishment.
5⇨♠ ✔in all bedrooms ® ✖ (ex guide dogs) ✳ dB&B⇨♠£46-£50 (incl dinner) WBDi£150-£165 LDO 6.30pm
Lic 🍴 CTV 5P nc16yrs

GH QQQ **Lyn-Leven** White St PA39 4JW ☎(08552) 392
Closed Xmas
This friendly, family-run guesthouse is a modern bungalow just off the A82 on the western fringe of the village, with magnificent views of Loch Leven and the Glencoe mountains. It has a welcoming atmosphere and offers comfortable accommodation.
8rm(7♠1hc) Annexe 5⇨♠ (1fb) CTV in 8 bedrooms ®
LDO 8pm
Lic 🍴 12P

BALLATER Grampian *Aberdeenshire* Map **15** NO39

SELECTED

GH QQQQ **Moorside** Braemar Rd AB3 5RL ☎(03397) 55492
Apr-Nov
This granite stone former church manse has been sympathetically restored and stands on the main road west of the town. The bright, airy bedrooms, some of which are quite spacious, are complemented by a vast dining room and lounge. It has a welcoming atmosphere and offers enjoyable home cooking.
9rm(3⇨6♠) (3fb) CTV in all bedrooms ®
✖ (ex guide dogs) sB&B⇨♠fr£24 dB&B⇨♠fr£32 WB&Bfr£104
Lic 🍴 10P
Credit Cards [1][3]

GH QQQ **Morvada** Braemar Rd AB3 5RL ☎(03397) 55501
27 Apr-7 Oct
This former Victorian church manse has been sympathetically restored and sits on the main road not far from the village centre, on the west side. Enthusiastically run and spotlessly maintained, it offers bright well equipped bedrooms, a comfortable lounge and an attractive little dining room together with enjoyable home cooking.
7rm(6♠1hc) CTV in all bedrooms ® LDO 6pm
Lic 🍴 7P

GH QQ **Netherley** 2 Netherley Place AB35 5QE ☎(03397) 55792
Closed Nov-Jan rs Feb
Conveniently situated beside the village green, this friendly family-run guesthouse is a popular base for tourists and golfers alike. It offers a relaxed atmosphere together with enjoyable home cooking and good value accommodation.
9rm(4⇨♠5hc) (3fb) CTV in 4 bedrooms ® sB&B£15-£17 dB&B£26-£30 dB&B⇨♠£32-£36 WB&B£84-£104 WBDi£136-£156 LDO 5pm
CTV ✗ nc4yrs £

BALLOCH Strathclyde *Dumbartonshire* Map **10** NX39

GH QQQ **Arbor Lodge** Old Luss Rd G83 8QW ☎Alexandria(0389) 56233 FAX (0389) 58988
This modern, well maintained purpose-built establishment is only 400 yards from the main Loch Lomond road on the edge of the town. Arbor Lodge is totally non-smoking.
3♠ CTV in all bedrooms ® ✖ (ex guide dogs) ✳ dB&B♠£36-£40
🍴 8P £

BALQUHIDDER Central *Perthshire* Map **11** NN52

INN QQ **Monachyle Mhor** FK19 8NZ (4mSW) ☎Strathyre(08774) 622
Apart from the occasional house, this 17th-century, fully licensed farmhouse lies in splendid isolation at the head of Loch Voil. It is reached by a four-mile single track road which meanders along the lochside west of the village. The house retains much of its original character, particularly the bedrooms, where the en suite facilities are the only modern concession. Good Scottish country cooking can be taken in the original dining room around an old refectory table or at individual tables in the small conservatory. The tiny bar is the focal point of the house and its popularity combined with the service of meals to non-residents give the atmosphere of a country inn.
4⇨♠ ® ✖ (ex guide dogs) ✳ dB&B⇨♠£37-£40 WB&B£126-£140 WBDi£200-£220 ✳ Lunch £5-£12.50alc High tea £6-£12 Dinner £10.50-£16
🍴 CTV 12P nc10yrs ✔

BAMPTON Devon Map **03** SS92

GH Q Q *Courtyard Hotel & Restaurant* 19 Fore St EX16 9ND
☎(0398) 331536
Closed Xmas & New Year
An attractive stone building enjoying a central location in the town.
Rooms are simple but well equipped with modern facilities, whilst
public rooms are in keeping with the original style of the property.
The busy restaurant is open to non-residents, and offers an à la
carte menu.
6rm(2⇨1↑3hc)(1fb) CTV in all bedrooms ® ✠ LDO 9pm
Lic ™ CTV 35P
Credit Cards 1 2 3 5

INN Q Q Q **Exeter** Tiverton Rd EX16 9DY ☎(0398) 331345
This ancient country inn has 8 bedrooms with en suite facilities and
all modern conveniences. Food is available in the bar and more
formal restaurant. Salmon and trout fishing and clay pigeon
shooting are available as well as stabling for guests' horses.
8rm(4⇨3↑1hc) CTV in all bedrooms ® ✠ (ex guide dogs)
sB&B⇨↑£24.95 dB&B⇨↑£45 LDO 9pm
™ 50P ✔ ∪ clay pigeon & game shooting
Credit Cards 1 3 £

BAMPTON Oxfordshire Map **04** SP30

INN Q Q **Talbot Hotel** Market Square OX8 2HA
☎Bampton Castle(0993) 850326
In the heart of the pretty Cotswold village, this inn offers modern,
well equipped bedrooms, along with cosy traditional public areas.
Extensive meal times and a varied choice of table d'hôte, à la carte
and bar snack menus ensure that guests won't go hungry.
6rm(5↑1hc) CTV in all bedrooms ® ✠ (ex guide dogs) ✳
sB&Bfr£28 sB&B↑£32 dB&B↑£50 ✳ Lunch £6.50&alc
Dinner £6.50&alc LDO 10pm

▶

⊞

Credit Cards 1 3

BANBURY Oxfordshire Map **04** SP44

See also Charlton (Northants)

GH Q Q **Belmont** 34 Crouch St OX16 9PR ☎(0295) 262308
A large, brightly painted guesthouse in a quiet side street near the town centre. The bedrooms are comfortable, freshly decorated and equipped with modern facilities, although some tend to be rather compact. Public areas are nicely furnished and there is a small bar where guests may enjoy a drink and a chat.
8rm(5♠3hc) (1fb) CTV in all bedrooms ® ✻ sB&B£18-£25
sB&B♠£22-£25 dB&B£25-£32 dB&B♠£32
Lic ⊞ 6P 1⇔ nc7yrs
Credit Cards 1 3

GH Q Q Q **La Madonette Country** OX15 6AA (3m W off
B4035) ☎(0295) 730212
Closed Xmas & New Year
This converted 17th-century former millers' house is set in traditional Cotswold surroundings boardered by the mill stream. Patti Ritter offers a warm welcome and the bedrooms are well equipped and comfortably furnished. There is a charming dining room and small reception/lounge in addition to the garden and outdoor swimming pool.
6⇩♠ (1fb) CTV in all bedrooms ® ✻ (ex guide dogs) ✻
sB&B⇩♠£32-£37.50 dB&B⇩♠£45-£55
Lic ⊞ CTV 20P ⩘(heated)
Credit Cards 1 3

BANTHAM Devon Map **03** SX64

INN Q Q Q **Sloop** TQ7 3AJ ☎Kingsbridge(0548) 560489 & 560215
Dating back to the 16th-century, this inn was originally a farmhouse and was owned by a famous smuggler. Situated in the village centre close to the beach, the property retains its character, with many original features. Bedrooms are spotlessly clean, comfortably furnished and equipped with a good range of modern facilities and en suite bathrooms. The popular bar is full of character and there is a panelled family restaurant where a comprehensive range of imaginative home-cooked food is available, including a good choice of fresh fish, shellfish and rich puddings.
5rm(4⇩1hc) (2fb) CTV in all bedrooms ® ✻ dB&B£39-£47
dB&B⇩£44-£49 WBDi£230-£260 ✻ Lunch £6.60-£15alc
Dinner £6.60-£15alc LDO 10pm
⊞ 35P ⓛ

BARDON MILL Northumberland Map **12** NY76

INN Q Q **The Bowes** NE47 7HY ☎Hexham(0434) 344267
Closed Xmas
A late-Victorian pub situated in the village centre just off the A69. The bedrooms are comfortable and warm, and the bar areas have retained the original character and atmosphere.
5rm(2♠3hc) (1fb) ® LDO 8.45pm
⊞ CTV 6P
Credit Cards 1 2 3 5

BARMOUTH Gwynedd Map **06** SH61

GH Q Q **Cranbourne Hotel** 9 Marine Pde LL42 1NA
☎(0341) 280202
This small family-run hotel is situated on the promenade, overlooking Cardigan Bay and the beach. The accommodation is modest but well maintained and many of the bedrooms have en suite facilities.
10rm(8⇩♠2hc) (6fb) CTV in all bedrooms ® ✈ ✻
sB&B£17.50 dB&B£37 dB&B⇩♠£42 LDO 5pm
Lic ⊞ CTV 4P (85p per day)
Credit Cards 1 3 ⓛ

GH Q Q *Morwendon* LLanaber LL42 1RR ☎(0341) 280566
Closed Jan-Mar rs Oct-Dec
This large detached house, 1.5 miles north of Barmouth on the A496 coast road, enjoys good sea views. There is a private car park and every bedroom has an en suite shower and toilet.
6♠ (3fb) CTV in all bedrooms ® ✈ (ex guide dogs) (wkly only
Jul & Aug) LDO 5pm
Lic ⊞ CTV 7P

FH Q Q Mr P Thompson *Llwyndu (SH599185)* Llwyndu
LL42 1RR ☎(0341) 280144
Closed Dec-Jan
Situated on a 4-acre smallholding, 2.5 miles north of Barmouth on A496, this stone-built farmhouse dates back to 1610 and retains much of the original character. Three bedrooms in the main house have en suite facilities and the early part of 1991 will see the completion of 4 additional rooms, also with en suite facilities, in a converted barn.
4rm(2⇩1♠) (2fb)✂in all bedrooms ® ✈ (wkly only Jul &
Aug) LDO 6.30pm
Lic ⊞ CTV 10P 4 acres non-working

INN Q *Tal-y-Don* St Anne's Square LL42 1DL ☎(0341) 280508
Situated in the town centre, this is a small public house providing simple accommodation. It also offers a choice of 3 bars and a beer garden to the rear.
7hc (3fb) CTV in all bedrooms ® ✈
⊞ CTV ⚲

BARNARD CASTLE Co Durham Map **12** NZ01

FH Q R & Mrs D M Lowson **West Roods** *(NZ022141)*
Boldron DL12 9SW ☎Teesdale(0833) 690116
Mar-Dec
Surrounded by meadows and stone walls, this farm is 2.5 miles East from Bowes and West off the A66 dual carriageway. It is signposted 'Lamb Hill', 'West Roods' and 'Roods House'. Two of the traditional bedrooms have en suite facilities and there are plenty of books, games and information.
3rm(2♠1hc) (1fb)✂in all bedrooms CTV in all bedrooms ®
✈ (ex guide dogs) ✻ sB&B£15-£20 dB&B♠£30-£40
WB&B£100-£130 LDO 6pm
⊞ 6P 58 acres dairy
Credit Cards 1 2 3 ⓛ

INN Q Q Q **The Fox and Hounds Country Inn & Restaurant**
Cotherstone DL12 9PF ☎Teesdale(0833) 50241 & 50811
3⇩♠ CTV in all bedrooms ® ✈ (ex guide dogs)
sB&B⇩♠£35-£37.50 dB&B⇩♠£45-£50 Lunch £9.50-
£11alc Dinner £15-£20&alc LDO 9pm
⊞ CTV 30P nc9yrs
Credit Cards 1 3 ⓛ

BARNEY Norfolk Map **09** TF93

GH Q Q Q Q **The Old Brick Kilns** Little Barney
NR21 0NL ☎Thursford(0328) 878305
The building, as its name implies, has been converted and now offers attractive en suite accommodation, together with an elegant lounge and dining room. Evening meals are served around a huge dining table, overlooking the garden. The proprietor Tessa Gent is an excellent hostess, offering good food and warm hospitality. The guesthouse is situated northeast of Fakenham, off the A148 towards Barney, then follow caravan site signs to Little Barney, a narrow lane which leads to the brick kilns.
3rm(1⇩2♠) CTV in all bedrooms ® ✈ (ex guide dogs)
sB&B⇩♠£19-£20 dB&B⇩♠£38-£40 WB&B£120-£126
WBDi£207-£250 LDO 10am
Lic ⊞ CTV 10P

BARNSTAPLE Devon Map **02** SS53

🖼️👜 GH 🅀🅀 *Cresta* 26 Sticklepath Hill EX31 2BU
☎(0271) 74022
Closed Xmas

This small guesthouse is next to the main Barnstaple to Bideford road, 1 mile from the centre of Barnstaple. The accommodation is simple in style, with a bright, cosy lounge, and the benefit of on-site parking.

5rm(1�štanding4hc) Annexe 1⇨ (1fb) CTV in all bedrooms ® ✖
sB&B£13-£15 sB&B⇨🌡£18-£20 dB&B£24-£28
dB&B⇨🌡£26-£30 WB&B£70-£84
🍽️ CTV 6P nc £

GH 🅀🅀🅀 *Yeo Dale Hotel* Pilton Bridge EX31 1PG
☎(0271) 42954

A family-run hotel, just off the town centre and within easy reach of the hospital. Major alterations have been carried out over the last year and now fine bedrooms offer en suite facilities, colour television, central heating and radio alarm clocks. The friendly proprietors create a relaxed atmosphere and home-cooked dishes are featured on the table d'hôte menu.

10rm(1⇨4🌡5hc) (3fb) CTV in all bedrooms ® ✳
sB&B£14.50-£16.50 sB&B⇨🌡£22.50-£25.50 dB&B£30.50
dB&B⇨🌡£38.75-£45 WB&B£101.50-£178.50 WBDi£154-£231 LDO 5pm
Lic 🍽️ CTV ✗
Credit Cards ①②③£

FH 🅀🅀 Mr & Mrs J Dallyn *Rowden Barton (SS538306)*
Roundswell EX31 3NP (2m SW B3232) ☎(0271) 44365

Mr and Mrs Dallyn provide true farmhouse hospitality at their small modern home, which enjoys views across rolling countryside. With a choice of lounges, bright cosy bedrooms and wholesome home cooking, this is a convenient retreat for tourists.

2rm ✁in all bedrooms ® ✖ (ex guide dogs) sB&B£14
dB&B£28 WB&B£90 WBDi£140
🍽️ CTV P 90 acres beef sheep £

BASINGSTOKE Hampshire Map **04** SU65

GH 🅀🅀 *May's Bounty Hotel* 12 Fairfields Rd RG21 3DR
☎(0256) 471300

Friendly, well-run accommodation, close to all amenities.

11🌡 (2fb) CTV in all bedrooms ® ✖ (ex guide dogs)
LDO 8pm
Lic 🍽️ CTV 16P
Credit Cards ①③

BASSENTHWAITE Cumbria Map **11** NY23

GH 🅀🅀🅀 *Ravenstone Hotel* CA12 4QG
☎Bassenthwaite Lake(07687) 76240
Mar-Oct

A fine period house situated in an elevated position above the A591, with beautiful views over Bassenthwaite Lake. Personally supervised by the resident owners, Ravenstone offers more facilities than usual, with spacious, relaxing lounges, a cosy bar, a pleasant dining room and a full size billiard table in the games room. Bedrooms are spacious and well equipped, most with fine views of the surrounding countryside.

14⇨🌡 (3fb) CTV in all bedrooms ® ✳ sB&B⇨🌡£32-£34
dB&B⇨🌡£64-£68 (incl dinner) WB&B£175-£189 WBDi£217-£231 LDO 6pm
Lic 🍽️ 25P ⚲ snooker

Every effort is made to provide accurate information, but details can change after we go to print. It is advisable to check prices etc. before you make a firm booking.

BATH Avon Map **03** ST76
See Town Plan Section
See also Keynsham and Timsbury

SELECTED

GH 🅀🅀🅀🅀 *Arden Hotel* 73 Great Pulteney St BA2 4DL
☎(0225) 466601 & 330039 FAX (0225) 465548
Closed mid Dec-2 Jan

This Grade I listed building is set in a delightful row of Georgian town houses, and is only a short walk from the city centre. The house is beautifully furnished and decorated in keeping with the style of the building. Some bedrooms are spacious and have good quality French furniture, each with private bathroom and excellent facilities. Imaginative food is produced in the basement Florizel's restaurant, which is highly recommended.

10⇨🌡 (2fb) CTV in all bedrooms ® ✖ (ex guide dogs)
Lic 🍽️ CTV ✗
Credit Cards ①③

See advertisement on page 53

GH 🅀 *Arney* 99 Wells Rd BA2 3AN ☎(0225) 310020
A Victorian terraced house one mile from the city centre on the A36 Wells road. Value for money bed and breakfast accommodation is offered in clean, simple surroundings.
7rm(1🌡6hc) (3fb) ✳ sB&B£18-£20 dB&B£28-£30
🍽️ CTV ✗ £

GH 🅀🅀 *Ashley Villa Hotel* 26 Newbridge Rd BA1 3JZ
☎(0225) 421683
Closed 2 wks Xmas

▶

Situated on the A4 west of the town, this large Victorian villa has been refurbished by the hosts, Mr and Mrs Kitcher, to offer good bed and breakfast accommodation. A patio garden and outdoor heated swimming pool are also provided.
14rm(4⇨10♪) (3fb) CTV in all bedrooms ® sB&B⇨♪£35-£39 dB&B⇨♪£45-£59
Lic ™ CTV 10P ⚊(heated)
Credit Cards [1][3] ⓔ

GH Ⓠ Astor House 14 Oldfield Rd BA2 3ND ☎(0225) 429134
Apr-Oct
Particularly popular with foreign visitors, this establishment is set in a pleasant residential area convenient for the city centre. The accommodation here is simple and functional.
7hc ® ✘ (ex guide dogs) ✱ dB&B£28-£30
™ CTV 4P nc7yrs ⓔ

GH ⓆⓆ Avon Hotel 9 Bathwick St BA2 6NX
☎(0225) 446176 & 422226 FAX (0225) 447452
Closed 25 & 26 Dec
A spacious semi-detached Georgian house situated parallel to Great Pulteney Street, close to the centre of the city. Bedrooms are spacious and well equipped, and there is ample parking in a large private car park.
12♪ (5fb)⚊in 2 bedrooms CTV in all bedrooms ®
sB&B♪£29-£35 dB&B♪£39-£58 WB&B£234-£270
Lic ™ CTV 20P
Credit Cards [1][2][3][5] ⓔ

See advertisement on page 55

GH ⓆⓆⓆ The Bath Tasburgh Warminster Rd, Bathampton
BA2 6SH ☎(0225) 425096
Sympathetically restored, this Victorian house is surrounded by 7 acres of gardens and grounds and has some fine views. The high standard of accommodation is maintained by owners who offer warm hospitality to their guests.
13rm(12⇨♪1hc) (4fb)⚊in 2 bedrooms CTV in all bedrooms
® ✘ sB&B£32-£34 sB&B⇨♪£39-£46 dB&B£44-£46
dB&B⇨♪£55-£60 WB&B£147-£300
Lic ™ CTV 15P croquet
Credit Cards [1][2][3][5] ⓔ

GH ⓆⓆⓆ Bloomfield House 146 Bloomfield House BA2 2AS
☎(0225) 420105 FAX (0225) 481958
Standing on the southern outskirts of Bath and enjoying excellent views of the city, this charming old house has been extensively and tastefully restored to its former elegance by proprietors Titos Argyris and John Pascoe. It is now a personally run, small hotel with well equipped accommodation. The house also contains two apartments which are available for letting as self-catering accommodation.
5⇨♪ (1fb)⚊in 3 bedrooms CTV in all bedrooms ®
✘ (ex guide dogs) ✱ sB&B⇨♪£35-£40 dB&B⇨♪£40-£50
™ 9P
Credit Cards [1][3]

GH ⓆⓆⓆ Brompton House Hotel St John's Rd BA2 6PT
☎(0225) 420972 & 448423
Closed Xmas & New Year
This Georgian house, formerly a rectory, has fine walled gardens, a good car park and enjoys a central situation in the town. The bedrooms at Brompton House are very well equipped and the public areas are comfortable, bright and attractive.
12rm(1⇨11♪) (1fb) CTV in all bedrooms ® ✘
sB&B⇨♪£28-£38 dB&B⇨♪£55-£59
Lic ™ 12P
Credit Cards [1][3] ⓔ

Visit your local AA Shop.

GH Ⓠ Ⓠ Ⓠ *Carfax Hotel* Great Pulteney St BA2 4BS
☎(0225) 462089 FAX (0225) 443257
*Formally three Regency houses on the famous Great Pulteney
Street, close to the town centre, this unlicensed hotel offers modern
bedrooms, many with good en suite facilities, and bright public
rooms.*
39rm(34⇨♠5hc) (3fb)✄in 5 bedrooms CTV in all bedrooms
Ⓡ ✖ (ex guide dogs) LDO 7.50pm
lift ⁴⁴ 13P 4🅰 (£2 per day) ቆ
Credit Cards ①②③

GH Ⓠ Ⓠ Ⓠ *Cedar Lodge* 13 Lambridge, London Rd BA1 6BJ
☎(0225) 423468
Closed 24-27 Dec
*Situated 50 yards west of the A46 junction on the A4 (London
road), this fine double-bowed Georgian house has been restored
over the past 20 years by Derek and Maria Beckett, and retains
many original features including fine cornices, stained glass and
Adam fireplaces. The 3 bedrooms are spacious, very comfortable
and furnished with quality furniture. This is a non-smoking
establishment.*
3rm(1♠2hc) (1fb)✄in all bedrooms CTV in all bedrooms
✖ (ex guide dogs)
⁴⁴ CTV 6P ቆ Ʊ

GH Ⓠ Ⓠ Ⓠ **Cheriton House** 9 Upper Oldfield Park BA2 3JX
☎(0225) 429862
Closed Xmas & New Year
*A large semi-detached Victorian villa situated south of the city
centre in a residential area off the A367 Wells road, with some fine
views over the city. Carefully restored and modernised, it now
provides intimate and comfortable public areas and well equipped
bedrooms with private bathrooms.*
9rm(2⇨7♠) CTV in all bedrooms Ⓡ ✖ (ex guide dogs) ✳
sB&B⇨♠£32-£38 dB&B⇨♠£45-£55
⁴⁴ 9P nc
Credit Cards ①③ £

GH Ⓠ Ⓠ Ⓠ **Dorian House** 1 Upper Oldfield Park BA2 3JX
☎(0225) 426336
*A large Bath stone house situated just off the A367, with views of
the city and surrounding hills. The charming proprietors are
constantly improving the hotel, and the accommodation is
comfortable, well equipped and attractively furnished and
decorated. The cosy lounge provides a selection of tourist
information, and there is a small licensed bar in the evenings.*
7rm(4⇨3♠) (2fb) CTV in all bedrooms Ⓡ ✖ (ex guide dogs)
✳ sB&B⇨♠£34-£42 dB&B⇨♠£47-£65
Lic ⁴⁴ 8P 2🅰
Credit Cards ①②③⑤ £

GH Ⓠ Ⓠ Ⓠ **Dorset Villa** 14 Newbridge Rd BA1 3JZ
☎(0225) 425975
*West of the city on the main A4 road, this small hotel has been
refurbished recently and provides well-furnished accommodation
with good facilities.*
7rm(5♠2hc) (1fb) CTV in all bedrooms sB&B£26-£28
sB&B♠£31-£33 dB&B£36-£38 dB&B♠£41-£43 WB&B£178-
£199 LDO 9pm
Lic ⁴⁴ CTV 6P
Credit Cards ①③ £

GH Ⓠ Ⓠ Ⓠ **Eagle House** Church St, Bathford BA1 7RS (3m
NE A363) ☎(0225) 859946
Closed 23-30 Dec
*Set in delightful Bathford, this lovely Georgian house stands in
spacious, attractive gardens. Owners John and Rosamund Napier
provide a warm and friendly welcome and well-equipped
accommodation. By spring 1990, 2 self-catering units in a cottage
will be available.*
6⇨♠ Annexe 2⇨♠ (2fb) CTV in all bedrooms Ⓡ
sB&B⇨♠£28-£36.75 dB&B⇨♠£41-£58 WB&Bfr£140
Lic ⁴⁴ 10P croquet lawn £

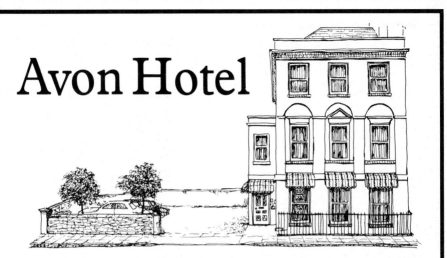

GH 🔲🔲🔲 *Edgar Hotel* 64 Gt Pulteney St BA2 4DN
☎(0225) 420619

Situated in the centre of Great Pulteney Street, this Regency town house has been modernised to offer comfortable and well equipped bed and breakfast accommodation close to the city centre.

14🟏 (1fb) CTV in all bedrooms ® 🟏
Lic ⬛ CTV 🅿

GH 🔲🔲 **Gainsborough Hotel** Weston Ln BA1 4AB
☎(0225) 311380
Closed 1 wk Xmas
16rm(12⇨4🟏) (2fb) CTV in all bedrooms ® 🟏
sB&B⇨🟏£25-£38 dB&B⇨🟏£45-£58
Lic ⬛ 18P
Credit Cards 1 2 3

GH 🔲🔲 **Grove Lodge** 11 Lambridge, London Rd BA1 6BJ
☎(0225) 310860

Situated on London Road, the A4, 1 mile from the city centre, this strictly non-smoking, fine detached Regency house offers spacious bedrooms on a room and breakfast basis only. There are some good pictures and pieces of furniture.

8hc (2fb)⦰in all bedrooms CTV in all bedrooms
🟏 (ex guide dogs) ✳ sB&B£22-£24 dB&B£40-£45
Lic 🅿 £

SELECTED

GH 🔲🔲🔲🔲 **Haydon House** 9 Bloomfield Park BA2 2BY
☎(0225) 444919 427351 FAX (0225) 469020

A delightful small, semidetached Edwardian house with pretty gardens, tucked away in a quiet residential area off the A367. The accommodation is attractive, with each room individually decorated and furnished, with good quality soft furnishings. Rooms are exceptionally well equipped with some thoughtful extras. Public areas are elegant and comfortable, and include a charming sitting room overlooking the rear garden, and a small writing room. Breakfast is the only meal provided, which is served in the dining room around a communal table, and this includes such delicacies as porridge with whisky and scrambled egg with salmon. Personal involvement including thoughtful extra services by the proprietors ensure a relaxing stay here. Smoking is prohibited.

4rm(3🟏) ⦰in all bedrooms CTV in all bedrooms ® 🟏
sB&B🟏£35-£40 dB&B🟏£48-£60
⬛ nc6yrs
Credit Cards 1 3 £

GH 🔲🔲🔲 **Highways House** 143 Wells Rd BA2 3AL
☎(0225) 421238
Closed 24-27 Dec

Enthusiastically run, this small hotel is in a residential area and offers a warm welcome to guests. High standards are maintained throughout, and a particularly comfortable lounge is provided.

7rm(6⇨🟏 1hc) CTV in all bedrooms ® 🟏 (ex guide dogs)
sB&B£30-£36 dB&B⇨🟏£46-£56
⬛ 8P nc5yrs
Credit Cards 1 3 £

GH 🔲🔲🔲 **Kennard Hotel** 11 Henrietta St BA2 6LL
☎(0225) 310472

Situated close to Pulteney Bridge, this period terrace house offers modern, well-equipped bedrooms, many with good en suite shower facilities. The bright and attractive breakfast room has a garden theme.

12rm(9🟏 3hc) (2fb) CTV in all bedrooms ® sB&B£25-£35
dB&B£35-£40 dB&B🟏£40-£55
⬛ 🅿
Credit Cards 1 2 3 £

SELECTED

GH 🔲🔲🔲🔲 **Laura Place Hotel** 3 Laura Place, Great Pulteney St BA2 4BH ☎(0225) 463815
Mar-21 Dec

This beautifully preserved former Georgian town house has been very carefully restored, and retains a wealth of charm and elegance. It is tastefully decorated and furnished throughout, with co-ordinated soft furnishings, to a very high standard. The bedrooms are a good size and very well equipped ; the majority have en suite facilities. It is conveniently located at the city end of the famous Great Pulteney Street.

9rm(7⇨🟏 2hc) (1fb) CTV in all bedrooms ®
🟏 (ex guide dogs) ✳ sB&Bfr£25 sB&B⇨🟏fr£50
dB&Bfr£50 dB&B⇨🟏£60-£80
⬛ 10P (£5 per week) nc11yrs
Credit Cards 1 2 3 £

SELECTED

GH 🔲🔲🔲🔲 **Leighton House** 139 Wells Rd BA2 3AL
☎(0225) 314769
rs May-Oct

This large Victorian house offers quality bed and breakfast facilities close to the city centre. The bedrooms are well equipped with modern en suite facilities and lots of extras. in addition to the spacious dining room, there is a cosy and comfortable lounge. David and Kathleen Slape are charming and attentive hosts who create the impression that one is an honoured personal guest.

7⇨🟏 (2fb) CTV in all bedrooms ® ✳ dB&B⇨🟏£52-£60
WB&B£168-£196 WBDi£233-£250 LDO 2pm
Lic ⬛ 7P
Credit Cards 1 3 £

GH 🔲🔲 **Millers Hotel** 69 Great Pulteney St BA2 4DL
☎(0225) 465798
Closed Xmas wk

Situated on the renowned Great Pulteney Street, Millers Hotel offers simply appointed bed and breakfast accommodation close to all amenities.

14rm(6⇨🟏 8hc) (3fb) CTV in 8 bedrooms 🟏 (ex guide dogs)
✳ sB&B£23-£25 sB&B⇨🟏£36-£38 dB&B£34-£38
dB&B⇨🟏£45-£52
Lic ⬛ CTV 🅿 £

GH 🔲🔲🔲 **Oldfields** 102 Wells Rd BA2 3AL ☎(0225) 317984

This detached Victorian house has a well-kept garden and is tastefully furnished and decorated throughout. High standards are maintained and a relaxed, friendly atmosphere prevails.

14rm(1⇨7🟏 6hc) CTV in all bedrooms ® 🟏 (ex guide dogs)
dB&B£37-£45 dB&B⇨🟏£50-£52
⬛ 10P
Credit Cards 1 3

SELECTED

GH 🔲🔲🔲🔲 **Old School House** Church St, Bathford
BA1 7RR (3m NE on A363) ☎(0225) 859593

This former Victorian school has been tastefully converted into a non-smoking, private hotel, offering very comfortable bedrooms with en suite bathrooms and many extras. A warm and relaxing atmosphere is provided in the very well-furnished public areas.

4⇨🟏 ⦰in all bedrooms CTV in all bedrooms ® 🟏
sB&B⇨🟏£40 dB&B⇨🟏£58-£62 WB&B£175-£185
WBDi£300-£310 LDO Noon
Lic ⬛ CTV 6P nc10yrs
Credit Cards 1 3

GH Q Q Q **Orchard House Hotel** Warminster Rd (A36), Bathampton BA2 6XG ☎(0225) 466115

A modern, purpose-built, stone-faced hotel providing good commercial-style accommodation, situated on the A36 Warminster road, two miles from the city centre. The bedrooms are identical, all well furnished and decorated with pretty colour schemes, with an excellent array of modern facilities; rooms close to the road are triple glazed and air conditioned. Public areas are somewhat limited: an open-plan foyer area offers some seating, and there is a pleasant dining room. Additional facilities include a sauna and solarium.

14⇨♪ (3fb) CTV in all bedrooms ® sB&B⇨♪£39-£47.50 dB&B⇨♪£49-£58.50 LDO 7.45pm
Lic ∰ 16P sauna solarium
Credit Cards 1 2 3 5 £

GH Q **Oxford Private Hotel** 5 Oxford Row Lansdown Rd BA1 2QN ☎(0225) 314039

Situated close to the centre of the town, in a Regency terrace on Lansdowne Road, this establishment offers convenient bed and breakfast accommodation.

11rm(4♪ 7hc) (3fb) CTV in 7 bedrooms ® ✖ ✱ sB&B£17-£20 dB&B♪£34-£38 LDO 10pm
Lic ∰ ✗ nc5yrs

GH Q Q Q Q **Paradise House Hotel** Holloway BA2 4PX ☎(0225) 317723 FAX (0225) 482005
Closed 20-28 Dec

This delightful house dates back to the 1720s and is situated in a quiet cul-de-sac with a very well tended spacious walled garden, and magnificent views across the city. The proprietors have extensively and tastefully restored the house to provide very high quality, well equipped accommodation, whilst retaining many original features. The spacious bedrooms are comfortably furnished, with excellent colour co-ordination in décor and soft furnishings; most have good en suite facilities.

9rm(6⇨1♪2hc) (1fb) CTV in all bedrooms ® ✖ sB&B£38-£45 sB&B⇨♪£46-£60 dB&B£45-£52 dB&B⇨♪£52-£65 WB&B£145-£205
∰ 2P 3🐾 (£2 per night) nc10yrs croquet lawn
Credit Cards 1 2 3 £

GH Q Q **Parkside** 11 Marlborough Ln BA1 2NQ ☎(0225) 429444
Closed Xmas wk

Standing on the edge of Victoria Park, this Edwardian property offers easy access to the city centre. The rooms are spacious and comfortable, and the resident proprietors provide a pleasant atmosphere and a warm welcome.

5hc (3fb)⚥in all bedrooms CTV in all bedrooms ® ✱ sB&B£25-£29 dB&B£34-£36 dB&B£42-£44 WB&Bfr£157.50 WBDifr£220.50 LDO 5pm
∰ CTV 2P nc5yrs

GH Q Q Q **Hotel St Clair** 1 Crescent Gdns, Upper Bristol Rd BA1 2NA ☎(0225) 425543

This spacious, semi-detached Victorian villa is on the Bristol Road, near Royal Crescent. The hosts, Mr and Mrs Codd, provide friendly services, in addition to the modern, well-equipped bedrooms, and the cosy dining room.

10rm(2♪8hc) (1fb) CTV in all bedrooms ® ✖ (ex guide dogs) sB&B£20-£25 sB&B♪£26-£32 dB&B£32-£36 dB&B♪£38-£45 WB&Bfr£110
Lic ∰ ✗ nc3yrs
Credit Cards 1 3 £

GH Q Q Q Q **Somerset House Hotel & Restaurant** 35 Bathwick Hill BA2 6LD ☎(0225) 466451

A fine period house situated in an elevated position on Bathwick Hill at its junction with Cleveland Way. Many original features have been retained, including fine moulded cornices and open fireplaces. The accommodation is attractively decorated and comfortably furnished, with good facilities and some thoughtful finishing touches. There is a choice of sitting rooms in either the first floor drawing room or the ground floor library/music room. The attractive basement dining room features the original hearth ovens, and imaginative well cooked food is offered. The hotel operates a no-smoking policy throughout.

10⇨♪ (5fb) CTV in all bedrooms ® sB&B⇨♪£46.45 dB&B⇨♪£92.90 (incl dinner) WBDif£302 LDO 6.30pm
Lic ∰ CTV 12P nc10yrs
Credit Cards 1 2 3 £

GH Q Q Q **Sydney Gardens Hotel** Sydney Rd BA2 6NT ☎(0225) 464818 & 445362
Closed 22-26 Dec & 1-23 Jan

Situated on Sydney Gardens at the southern end of Pulteney Street, this large early-Victorian house has been tastefully modernised by proprietors Stanley and Diane Smithson, while retaining many original features such as fine moulding and tiled fireplaces. Bedrooms are comfortable and very well equipped, and although a room and breakfast establishment only, there is a comfortable guest lounge. Smoking is not permitted.

6⇨♪ ⚥in all bedrooms CTV in all bedrooms ® ✱ sB&B⇨♪£50-£63 dB&B⇨♪£59-£69
∰ 6P nc4yrs
Credit Cards 1 3

GH Q Q Q Q *Underhill Lodge* Warminster Rd, Bathampton BA2 6XQ ☎(0225) 464992
rs Xmas wk

Two miles from the city centre, on the Warminster Road at Bathampton, this Victorian stone villa has been carefully restored by the present owners. The bedrooms are furnished and equipped to a high standard with private bathrooms, and there is a wide variety of Eastern artefacts displayed throughout the interior. Meals are served by the owners at one large table: drinks are served before dinner, which is carefully cooked to order. There is a separate room for those who wish to smoke, as the habit is discouraged in other areas.

4⇨♪ ⚥in all bedrooms CTV in all bedrooms ® ✖ LDO noon
Lic ∰ 10P nc10yrs
Credit Cards 1 3

GH Q Q Q **Villa Magdala Private Hotel** Henrietta Rd BA2 6LX ☎(0225) 466329
Feb-Dec

This beautifully maintained house, converted from two early Victorian houses is situated 100 yards from Great Pulteney Street. Many of the original features are retained, including the fine Italian-style staircase and the moulded cornices. Bedrooms are comfortably furnished and very well equipped, and the house stands in attractive grounds and has the additional advantage of private parking.

17rm(13⇨4♪) (3fb) CTV in all bedrooms ® ✖ sB&B⇨♪£42 dB&B⇨♪£56-£70
∰ 13P 2🐾 (£3 per night)
Credit Cards 1 3

See advertisement on page 61

Underhill Lodge

COMMENDED

Warminster Road, Bathampton, Bath, Avon
Telephone: 0225 464992

Country valley views add serenity to this distinctive comfortable Lodge within 2 miles of Bath centre. Fashionable hotel standard en-suite rooms with king sized beds, colour TV and tea/coffee facility plus direct dial telephone. A separate smoking room/bar is provided, other areas non smoking. Our guests agree that Underhill provides more an experience than simply accommodation. Friendly personal service from June & Don Mather. Ample parking.

THE OXFORD HOTEL

5 Oxford Row, Lansdown Road, Bath BA1 2QN Avon.
Telephone: Bath (STD 0225) 314039

An 18th Century House-Hotel in the City Centre (near the Assembly rooms). Most rooms with TV & coffee/tea making facilities.

Proprietress: Diana Thomas

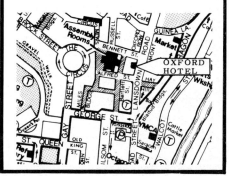

Hotel St. Clair

1 Crescent Gardens,
Upper Bristol Road,
Bath BA1 2NA
Telephone: (0225) 425543

A spacious semi detached Victorian villa situated immediately by the Royal Crescent and a level 5 minutes walk from the City Centre. This small hotel is run by the proprietors who offer a personal service and a high standard of comfortable accommodation. All rooms have colour television and tea/coffee making facilities. Some rooms en suite. A traditional English breakfast is served.

English Tourist Board
APPROVED

The Old School HOUSE
BATHFORD
PRIVATE HOTEL

Situated in a conservation area overlooking the beautiful Avon valley, the Old School House offers high quality accommodation with private bathroom and all facilities. Candle-lit dinners and log fires in an informal and friendly atmosphere.
Residential licence. Special breaks October-March. Brochure available.
A Non-Smoking House
The Old School House Church Street
Bathford BATH Avon BA1 7RR
Telephone: Bath (0225) 859593

| English Tourist Board COMMENDED | ETB Commended | AA QQQQ selected |

GH QQ ***Waltons*** 17 Crescent Gardens, Upper Bristol Rd BA1 2NA ☎(0225) 426528
This is an uncomplicated guesthouse, popular with commercial guests and tourists alike. It is situated close to the Victoria Park, and is only a few minutes from the city centre. The rooms are simply furnished, providing a relaxing atmosphere.
15hc (3fb)
ɱ CTV Ᵽ

GH QQQ Wentworth House Hotel 106 Bloomfield Rd BA2 2AP ☎(0225) 339193
Closed mid Dec-mid Jan
Under the personal supervision of owners, Mr and Mrs Kitching, this large guesthouse offers thoughtfully equipped rooms, well maintained and comfortable throughout. There is a lounge bar and the dining room has a conservatory which overlooks the outdoor swimming pool.
20rm(16⇌⋒4hc) (2fb) CTV in all bedrooms ® ✱ sB&B£22-£23 sB&B⇌⋒£32-£35 dB&B£36-£40 dB&B⇌⋒£50-£55 LDO 4.30pm
Lic ɱ 20P ≋
Credit Cards 1 3

INN QQ Chequers 50 Rivers St BA1 2QA ☎(0225) 424246
Situated in a residential area close to the Royal Crescent, this Georgian house provides attractive open-plan bars and comfortable, well-equipped bedrooms.
4hc (1fb) CTV in all bedrooms ® ✗ (ex guide dogs) ✱ sB&B£15-£17.50 dB&B£30-£35 ✱ LDO 9.45pm
ɱ Ᵽ
Credit Cards 1 2 3 5

INN QQ County Hotel 18-19 Pulteney Rd BA2 4DN ☎(0225) 425003 & 466493
Closed 25 & 26 Dec
Situated close to the town centre, this spacious, detached stone hotel offers modern, well-equipped bedrooms and bright, attractive public areas. Bar snacks are available at lunchtime, and more substantial meals are offered during the evenings in the restaurant.
22rm(1⇌11⋒10hc) (5fb) CTV in all bedrooms ® ✱ sB&B£30-£32.50 sB&B⇌⋒£47.50-£50 dB&B£50-£55 dB&B⇌⋒£55-£57.50 ✱
ɱ CTV 60P
Credit Cards 1 3

BATTLE East Sussex Map **05** TQ71

GH QQQ Netherfield Hall Netherfield TN33 9PQ (3 m NW of B2096) ☎(04246) 4450
This attractive coach house has been adapted to offer pleasant, comfortable accommodation, and is situated in a pleasant village surrounded by woodlands. As Mr Blake deals in giftwear, there is a large selection of pictures and china to choose from as a souvenir. The house has a family atmosphere and pleasant, informal style.
4rm(2⋒2hc) Annexe 1⋒ TV in 2 bedrooms ® dB&B⋒£30-£45 WB&B£150-£180
ɱ CTV 6P Ⓔ

GH QQ ***Priory House*** 17 High St TN33 0EA ☎(04246) 3366
This small hotel dates back, in parts, to pre-Tudor days and provides traditionally furnished and comfortable rooms, most of which are en suite. Ideally situated in the High Street of this historic town, the simple restaurant offers a good selection of home cooked dishes, and there is a cosy bar/lounge.
6rm(2⇌3⋒1hc) (3fb) TV in all bedrooms ® ✗ (ex guide dogs) LDO 9pm
Lic ɱ
Credit Cards 1 3

FH QQQ Paul & Alison Slater **Little Hemingfold Farmhouse Hotel** *(TQ774149)* Telham TN33 0TT (2.5m SE on N side of A2100) ☎(04246) 4338
This delightful farmhouse hotel is set in 40 acres of woodland and walks and benefits from its own trout lake and grass tennis court. The coach house bedrooms are individually decorated in a cosy, cottage style, surrounding the leafy courtyard; the rooms are particularly well equipped, and some have original wood-burning stoves. A four-course meal is served in the style of a dinner party, but a separate table can be requested. Coffee is served in the comfortable lounge with its welcoming log fire. The owners also specialise in house parties for 24 people.
4rm(3⇌1hc) Annexe 9rm(7⇌) CTV in all bedrooms ® sB&B⇌£30-£40 dB&B⇌£60-£75 WB&B£175-£200 WBDi£245-£260 LDO 7pm
Lic ɱ 30P ⚑ 18 ℘(grass) J boules swimming in lake 40 acres mixed
Credit Cards 1 3 Ⓔ

INN QQQ Abbey Hotel 84 High St TN33 0AQ ☎Hastings(04246) 2755
8rm(3⇌5⋒) CTV in all bedrooms ® ✱ sB&B⇌⋒fr£35.50 dB&B⇌⋒fr£49.50 ✱ Bar Lunch £2.50-£5.50alc Dinner £10-£15alc LDO 9.30pm
ɱ
Credit Cards 1 3

BEAMINSTER Dorset Map **03** ST40

SELECTED

GH QQQQ Hams Plot Bridport Rd DT8 3LU ☎(0308) 862979
Apr-Oct
An interesting Regency house with some earlier parts in an attractive walled garden containing a hard tennis court, croquet lawn and swimming pool. Bedrooms are spacious, furnished with antiques and comfortable chairs and (mostly) large bathrooms. In addition to the dining room there are 2 splendid lounges, the cool, formal sitting room and the cosy, cluttered library.
3rm(2⇌1⋒) ® ✗ sB&B⇌⋒£36 dB&B⇌⋒£54
Lic ɱ CTV 7P nc10yrs ≋ ℘(hard)croquet

BEAMISH Co Durham Map **12** NZ25

GH QQ ***Coppy Lodge*** Coppy Farm, Beamish Lodge DH6 0RQ ☎Stanley(0207) 231479
This converted cow byre and dairy is now an attractive guesthouse, situated amongst riding stables in Beamish Park, close to the golf club and the Open Air Museum. Bedrooms are modern and well appointed, with private bathrooms and colour TV. There is a small bar, which also contains a billiard table.
6rm(2⇌4⋒) TV available ® LDO 9pm
Lic ɱ 40P ∪ snooker

BEARWOOD West Midlands Map **07** SP08

GH QQ Bearwood Court Hotel 360-366 Bearwood Rd B66 4ET ☎021-429 9731 021-429 6880 FAX 021-429 6175
The Doyle family are friendly hosts and are sure to make guests welcome at their hotel, situated on a busy road within easy reach of the city centre. The accommodation varies in size and furnishings, but is well maintained throughout.
24rm(20⇌⋒4hc) (2fb) CTV in all bedrooms ® ✗ (ex guide dogs) sB&B£22-£28 sB&B⇌⋒£28-£30 dB&B£33-£42 dB&B⇌⋒£42 LDO 6pm
Lic ɱ CTV 24P
Credit Cards 1 3 Ⓔ

'Selected' establishments, which have the highest quality award, are highlighted by a tinted panel. For a full list of these establishments, consult the Contents page.

BEATTOCK Dumfries & Galloway *Dumfriesshire* Map **11**
NT00

FH 🇶🇶 Mr & Mrs Bell *Cogrie's (NY106974)* DG10 9PP (3m S
off A74) ☎ Johnstone Bridge(05764) 320
Mar-Nov
*Although this farm has direct access from the A47, visitors will be
impressed by the peaceful location of this house. Attractive,
comfortable accommodation is complemented by a very hospitable
proprietress.*
4hc (3fb)⊁in all bedrooms ® ✱ LDO 6pm
💷 CTV 6P 275 acres dairy mixed

BEAULY Highland *Inverness-shire* Map **14** NH54

GH 🇶🇶 **Arkton Hotel** Westend IV4 7BT ☎(0463) 782388
*Good value, practical accommodation is offered at this personally
run, licensed guesthouse which is conveniently situated in the
centre of the village near the square.*
8hc (1fb) ® sB&B£15-£25 dB&B£30-£32 WB&B£105-£140
WBDi£170-£182 LDO 8pm
Lic 💷 CTV 8P £

GH 🇶🇶🇶 **Chrialdon Hotel** Station Rd IV4 7EH
☎ Inverness(0463) 782336
*This substantial, sandstone house has bedrooms furnished in a
pleasing blend of traditional and modern styles and two lounges in
which to relax.*
7rm(1⇨2♠4hc) (2fb) CTV in all bedrooms ®
✱ (ex guide dogs) ✱ sB&B£16-£17.75 dB&B£32-£35
dB&B⇨♠£40-£46 LDO 7.30pm
Lic 💷 CTV 15P

£ Remember to use the money-off vouchers.

⚅⚄ GH ⓠⓠⓠ Heathmount Station Rd IV4 7EQ
☎(0463) 782411
Closed Xmas & New Year
This detached, double-fronted Victorian villa stands back from the
main road close to the town centre, and offers comfortable,
traditional accommodation which is kept very clean and is well
maintained.
5hc (2fb) CTV in all bedrooms ® sB&B£13-£14 dB&B£26-£28
WB&B£82-£90
⌗ CTV 5P

BEAUMARIS Gwynedd Map **06** SH67

GH ⓠⓠ Sea View 10 West End LL58 8BG ☎(0248) 810384
Closed Xmas
This small, simple but very well maintained and friendly
guesthouse is situated on the western outskirts of the town, and
enjoys panoramic views of Snowdonia, across the Menai Straits.
Smoking is not allowed.
6hc ⌦in all bedrooms ✖ sB&B£16 dB&B£30 LDO 2pm
CTV 5P nc10yrs

BEDALE North Yorkshire Map **08** SE28

See also Hunton and Patrick Brompton
FH ⓠⓠⓠ Mrs D I Knox **Blairgowrie Country House**
(SE241921) Crakehall DL8 1JZ ☎Richmond(0748) 811377
Closed Xmas & New Year
A charming country house in a tranquil setting, with a neat garden.
It has recently been modernised, but great care has been taken to
ensure improvements are in keeping with the style of the house, and
accommodation is attractive and comfortable. The house is located
north of Crakehall village: follow signs for Hackford at the
bridge; after one mile turn right for Langthorne, and Blairgowrie
is a few hundred yards along on the right.
2rm(1⚄1hc) ⌦in all bedrooms ® ✖ ✱ sB&B⚄£20
dB&B⚄£30 dB&B⚄fr£30 WB&B⚄fr£210
⌗ CTV 6P nc10yrs ✐ 3 acres small holding

BEDFORD Bedfordshire Map **04** TL04

GH ⓠⓠ Bedford Oak House 33 Shakespeare Rd MK40 2DX
☎(0234) 266972
A sympathetically extended 1930's house set back from a
residential link road near the centre of town offering bed and
breakfast accommodation. The entrance hall and breakfast room
feature period wood panelling, complemented by plates, ornaments
and books. The bedrooms are bright, simply furnished and well
equipped, and located on the ground and first floors (a couple are
reached through the car park).
15rm(9⚄6hc) (1fb) CTV in all bedrooms ✖ (ex guide dogs) ✱
sB&B£22-£25 sB&B⚄£29-£32 dB&B£32-£35 dB&B⚄£36-£40
⌗ CTV 17P
Credit Cards ①②③④

GH ⓠⓠ Clarendon House Hotel 25/27 Ampthill Rd MK42 9JP
☎(0234) 266054
Closed 24 Dec-2 Jan
A small private hotel on the A6 south of the town centre. The
accommodation is on three floors: room sizes vary, but all are neat
and nicely equipped. Downstairs there is a cheerful open-plan
lounge and breakfast room.
17rm(13⚄4hc) CTV in all bedrooms ® ✖ (ex guide dogs)
sB&B£21.50-£33.50 sB&B⚄£21.50-£33.50 dB&B£32-£35 dB&B⚄£35.50-£43
LDO 7.45pm
Lic ⌗ CTV 15P
Credit Cards ①②③⑤④

GH ⓠⓠ Hertford House Hotel 57 De Parys Av MK40 2TR
☎(0234) 50007 & 54470
Closed 24 Dec-2 Jan
An Edwardian villa in a tree-lined avenue near the town centre.
Bedrooms are on three floors and vary in size; they are in good
decorative order, in mixed furnishing styles. There is a comfortable

lounge on the ground floor with a gas coal fire. Outside there is a
new gravel car park, together with the garden and patio.
16rm(5⚄2⚄9hc) (2fb) CTV in all bedrooms ® ✱
sB&B£27.50-£29.50 sB&B⚄£32.50-£36.50 dB&B£37.50-
£42.50 dB&B⚄⚄£45-£48.50 WB&B£150-£180
⌗ CTV 4P
Credit Cards ①②③⑤

GH ⓠⓠⓠ *Kimbolton Hotel* 78 Clapham Rd MK41 7PN
☎(0234) 54854
Closed 25-31 Dec
A large, detached Victorian house set in its own grounds, situated
on the A6 just north of the town centre. It has recently been
refurbished, and now provides full en suite facilities for the
bedrooms. A limited menu is offered in the dining room, and there
is a lounge and a well stocked bar.
14rm(3⚄11⚄) CTV in all bedrooms ® ✖ LDO 8.30pm
Lic ⌗ CTV 15P nc3yrs
Credit Cards ①②③

BEEDON Berkshire Map **04** SU47

FH ⓠⓠⓠ Mrs Diana Ryder **Langley Hall** *(SU496765)*
RG16 8SD ☎Chieveley(0635) 248222
It is advisable to ask for directions to this redbrick country house
attached to a working farm. The comfortable drawing room and
breakfast room both enjoy garden views, and are attractively
decorated with ornaments, pictures and plants. Upstairs are 2
spacious family rooms which have period furniture and are well
equipped.
2hc (2fb)⌦in all bedrooms CTV in all bedrooms ®
✖ (ex guide dogs) ✱ sB&Bfr£20
⌗ CTV P ⌂ ℘(grass)600 acres mixed

BEER Devon Map **03** SY28

GH ⓠ *Bay View* Fore St EX12 3EE ☎Seaton(0297) 20489
Etr-mid Nov
Property at the end of the village overlooking the beach and sea.
6hc (1fb) ®
⌗ CTV ℘ nc5yrs

BEERCROCOMBE Somerset Map **03** ST32

SELECTED

FH ⓠⓠⓠⓠ Mrs V A Cole *Frog Street Farm*
(ST317197) Frog St TA3 6AF
☎Hatch Beauchamp(0823) 480430
Mar-Nov
This attractive, wistaria-clad Somerset longhouse dates back
to 1436, and is part of a working farm of 160 acres; it was
voted Farmhouse of the Year in 1988. The 3 bedrooms are
attractively decorated with co-ordinating furnishings and
private bathrooms. The dining room provides the focal point of
the farmhouse, where the owner serves wonderful home-made
food; a set dinner is offered and guests eat at individual
tables: all the meat served is organically produced. There is
an outdoor pool in the sheltered garden, making this a
convenient base for Taunton and the M5. To find the
farmhouse, follow the narrow lanes from Curry Mallet into
Beercrocombe and turn right at the village grassy triangle,
into more narrow lanes.
3rm(2⚄1⚄) ® ✖ LDO 2pm
⌗ CTV P nc11yrs ⌂(heated) 160 acres dairy mixed stud

This is one of many guidebooks pubished by
the AA. The full range is available at any
AA Shop or good bookshop.

SELECTED

FH ⓆⓆ Ⓠ Ⓠ Mr & Mrs Mitchem **Whittles** *(ST324194)*
TA3 6AH ☎Hatch Beauchamp(0823) 480301
mid Feb-Oct
John and Clare Mitchem welcome guests to their Victorian, ivy-clad farmhouse amidst 200 acres of dairy and beef farmland. Dinner is served on three evenings, the emphasis being on fresh food cooked by Mrs Mitchem. Served in the cosy rear dining room, guests are asked to help themselves from the honesty bar. Breakfast is served in the front-facing breakfast room with guests eating around a large table. The comfortable drawing room is available for guests. The three ensuite rooms are attractively decorated, and large bottles of toiletries are available in the bathrooms. Rooms have convenient, large 'zip and link' beds, colour televisions and tea-making facilities. There are pretty floral displays around the house. Smoking is not permitted in the bedrooms.
3⇨ CTV in all bedrooms Ⓡ ✖ ✱ sB&B⇨£25-£27
dB&B⇨£38-£40 WB&B£130-£189 WBDi£228-£287
LDO 6.30pm(previous day)
Lic ⁜ 4P nc12yrs 200 acres beef dairy

BEESTON Nottinghamshire Map **08** SK53

GH Ⓠ **Brackley House Hotel** 31 Elm Av NG9 1BU
☎Nottingham(0602) 251787
Closed Xmas & New Year
A continental atmosphere prevails at this well-furnished guesthouse set in a quiet side road. Good, all-round facilities are provided.
15rm(12⇨♣3hc) (1fb) CTV in all bedrooms Ⓡ ✖
LDO 8.15pm
Lic ⁜ CTV 15P nc9yrs ⇨(heated) sauna
Credit Cards ①②③

GH Ⓠ **Fairhaven Private Hotel** 19 Meadow Rd NG9 1JP
☎Nottingham(0602) 227509
Closed 25-26 Dec
A clean, modest hotel on the edge of the town situated close to Beeston station. There is a really comfortable lounge in which to relax and watch television.
10rm(1♣9hc) (1fb) CTV in 1 bedroom Ⓡ ✖ sB&B£18-£21.50
dB&B£28-£30 dB&B♣£38-£40 WB&B£126 WBDi£154
LDO 2pm
Lic ⁜ CTV 12P ⓔ

BELL BUSK North Yorkshire Map **07** SD95

GH ⓆⓆ **Tudor House** BD23 4DT ☎Airton(07293) 301
mid Feb-mid Nov
This delightful house was once the railway station. Cleverly converted, Tudor House offers a good standard of comfort and pleasant hospitality.
4rm(1♣3hc) (1fb)⤢ in all bedrooms Ⓡ ✖ (ex guide dogs) ✱ sB&Bfr£15
dB&B£27-£29 dB&B♣fr£32 WB&B£85-£100 WBDi£148-£163
Lic ⁜ CTV 6P games room ⓔ

BELLINGHAM Northumberland Map **12** NY88

GH ⓆⓆⓆ **Westfield House** NE48 2DP
☎Hexham(0434) 220340
Mar-Nov
A well furnished country house now a comfortable small hotel personally owned and run. Bedrooms are very well furnished, and good home cooking is provided. it is situated within the village, close to the Pennine Way and surrounded by beautiful countryside. Smoking is not permitted.
5rm(2♣3hc) (1fb)⤢ in all bedrooms Ⓡ ✖ (ex guide dogs) ✱
sB&Bfr£25 sB&B♣fr£35 dB&Bfr£34 dB&B♣fr£48
WB&B£106-£159 WBDi£190-£243 LDO noon
⁜ CTV 10P ⓔ

BELPER Derbyshire
See also Shottle
GH ⓆⓆ **The Hollins** 45 Belper Ln DE5 2UQ ☎(0773) 823955
2hc ⤢ in all bedrooms CTV in all bedrooms Ⓡ
✖ (ex guide dogs)
⁜ 1P nc4yrs

BELTON Leicestershire Map **04** SK80

FH ⓆⓆⓆ Mrs S L Renner **Old Rectory** *(SK814008)*
LE15 9LE ☎Belton In Rutland(057286) 279
Lovely old house incorporating a rural museum, craft shop, a miniature farm and a children's play area.
1♣ Annexe 6♣ CTV in 4 bedrooms Ⓡ LDO 9.30pm
Lic lift ⁜ CTV 6P 6🐾 ₰ 30 acres pastural

BEPTON (NEAR MIDHURST) West Sussex Map **04** SU81

SELECTED

GH ⓆⓆⓆⓆ **The Park House Hotel** GU29 0JB
☎Midhurst(073081) 2880 FAX (073081) 5643
The main section of this delightful country hotel dates back to the 1600s, and the charm and tranquility of the hotel is enhanced by extensive, beautiful rural views and well-kept gardens which include grass tennis courts, croquet and an outdoor swimming pool. The bedrooms are tastefully decorated and, in many cases, furnished with antiques. Modern facilities are provided to add to the guests' comfort and relaxation. There is a spacious and elegant drawing room, charming dining room and separate hospitality lounge. Service is willing and friendly.
10rm(8⇨2♣) Annexe 2⇨ CTV in 10 bedrooms Ⓡ
sB&B⇨♣£47-£48.30 dB&B⇨♣£82.25-£84.50 LDO noon
Lic ⁜ CTV 25P ⇨(heated) ₰(grass)croquet putting
▶

SHOTTLE HALL FARM GUEST HOUSE
Winner Guesthouse of the Year 1982, Midland Region

BELPER, DERBYSHIRE DE5 2EB
Telephone: Cowers Lane (0773) 550203 or 550276

Situated amid 340 acres of farmland in Derbyshire's picturesque Ecclesbourne Valley, Shottle Hall Farm Guest House is part of a large working farm.
The layout and the decor of the house have been planned specifically for the benefit of guests and the facilities provided compare well with those of good quality hotels. Personal touch is very much in evidence and proprietors Philip and Phyllis Matthews look after their guests as they would old friends.
Seven double bedrooms and two single bedrooms. Also ground floor suite suitable for limited disability. One dining room, one breakfast room. Residents lounge. Games room with colour TV and Snooker Table (not full size). Table and residential licence. Two acres of grounds for use of guests. All rooms have tea making facilities.
See gazetteer entry under Shottle.

Credit Cards [1] [3]
See advertisement under MIDHURST

BERKELEY Gloucestershire Map **03** ST69

FH QQQ Mrs B A Evans ***Greenacres*** *(ST713008)* Breadstone GL13 9HF (2m W off A38) ☎Dursley(0453) 810348
Closed 4 Dec-2 Jan
A modern farmhouse which combines charm and cosiness with a high standard of modern comfort and facilities. Spotlessly clean throughout, the bedrooms are prettily decorated in soft colours with rich co-ordinating fabrics and bright pine furnishings, and are equipped with tea-making facilities and an abundance of reading material and personal touches. Bright modern ensuites add to the comfort. The attractive breakfast room overlooks the garden, and the house, from its elevated position, boasts commanding views over the Cotswolds and beyond to the Welsh hills. Personally run by Mrs Evans, this farmhouse is well sited for both Bristol and Gloucester, and is conveniently located for touring the Cotswolds.
3rm(1⇌2♠) ⊁in all bedrooms ® ✗
🎹 CTV 10P nc10yrs snooker 47 acres horse breeding

BERRYNARBOR Devon Map **02** SS54

GH QQQ The Lodge Country House Hotel EX34 9SG (Berrynarbor 1.5m W of A399) ☎Combe Martin(0271) 883246
Closed Xmas
7rm(2⇌3♠2hc) (2fb) CTV in all bedrooms ® ✱ sB&B£15-£18 dB&B£30-£36 dB&B⇌♠£36-£42 WB&B£90-£108 WBDi£132-£159 LDO 6pm
Lic 🎹 8P nc2yrs 9 hole putting £

BETTISCOMBE Dorset Map **03** ST39

GH QQQ *Marshwood Manor* DT6 5NS
☎Bridport(0308) 68442
Mar-Nov
A 19th-century country manor house set in 10 acres of well-kept grounds which include a heated pool, croquet and a putting green. Spacious, well furnished bedrooms are very clean and comfortable, and many rooms have views of the Marshwood Vale. The lounge is an elegant and well proportioned room, with Chinese rugs and log fires, and home-cooked food using local produce is served in the dining room.
8rm(5⇌♠3hc) (5fb) CTV in all bedrooms ®
Lic 🎹 15P ⩯croquet putting

BETWS-Y-COED Gwynedd Map **06** SH75

GH Q Bryn Llewelyn Holyhead Rd LL24 0BN ☎(0690) 710601
A small family-run guesthouse in the centre of the village, with ample parking; it is a good base for touring the Snowdonia National Park, with the beaches at Llandudno within a half hour drive. Bedrooms are neat and tidy, and there is a comfortable lounge.
7hc (3fb) ® ✱ sB&B£11-£15 dB&B£22-£30 WB&B£70-£105
🎹 CTV 8P £

GH QQQ The Ferns LL24 0AN ☎(0690) 710587
On the A5 close to the village centre, this well-maintained house provides modern accommodation, some bedrooms having en suite facilities. The Ferns has the advantage of its own car park.
7♠ (2fb) CTV in all bedrooms ® sB&B♠fr£18 dB&B♠£28-£34 WB&B£98-£119 WBDi£147-£168 LDO breakfast
Lic 🎹 CTV 6P nc4yrs £

GH Q Summer Hill Non Smokers Guesthouse Coedcynhelier Rd LL24 0BL ☎(0690) 710306
This large, detached, stone-built house dates back to 1874 and is situated in an elevated position close to River Llugwy. The shops and other amenities of this popular village are within a few minutes' walk. Family-owned and run, it provides modest accommodation suitable for climbers, walkers and other tourists visiting this part of Snowdonia. The hotel has the advantage of having its own private car park.
7hc (1fb)⊁in all bedrooms ® ✱ sB&Bfr£12.50 dB&Bfr£23 WB&Bfr£80.50 WBDifr£129.50
Lic 🎹 CTV 6P

SELECTED

GH QQQQ Tan-y-Foel Capel Garmon LL26 0RE 3m SE ☎(0690) 710507 FAX (0690) 710681
A combination of many attributes make Tan-y-Foel rather special, not least the genuine warmth and hospitality of the proprietors. Once a farmhouse, the building is very old and has been sympathetically converted to include modern amenities while losing none of its charm and character. Facilities include a converted heated swimming pool and a snooker room with a full-size table. Quite remote and quietly located, yet within a few minute's drive of Betwys- y-Coed.
7⇌♠ ⊁in all bedrooms ® ✱ sB&B⇌♠£46.50 dB&B⇌♠£73 WB&B£255.50 WBDi£320.50-£334.50 LDO 6.30pm
Lic 🎹 16P 1🚗 nc⊡(heated) snooker
Credit Cards [1] [2] [3]

GH QQQ Tyn-Y-Celyn Llanwrst Rd LL24 0HD
☎(0690) 710202 FAX (0690) 710800
Situated just north of Betwys-y-Coed, on the A470, this is a small but well-maintained, family-run hotel. The bedrooms are well equipped and all have en suite facilities.
8rm(2⇌6♠) (2fb) CTV in all bedrooms ® dB&B⇌♠£32-£40
Lic 🎹 CTV 10P £

BEXHILL East Sussex Map **05** TQ70

GH QQ The Arosa 6 Albert Rd TN40 1DG
☎(0424) 212574 & 732004
A warm welcome is offered by the proprietors of this hotel, which is conveniently situated for the shops, the seafront and the centre of town. Pleasant accommodation is provided, as well as home-style cooking and personal service.
9rm(2⇌♠7hc) (1fb) CTV in all bedrooms ®
✗ (ex guide dogs) sB&B£13-£16.50 sB&B⇌♠£17-£20 dB&B£22-£27 dB&B⇌♠£32-£37 WB&B£67.50-£120 WBDi£105-£157.50 LDO noon
🎹 CTV ℙ
Credit Cards [1] [3] £

BEYTON Suffolk Map **05** TL96

FH QQ Mrs E Nicholson **The Grange** *(TL940632)* Tostock Rd IP30 9AG ☎(0359) 70184
Centrally located towards the village green, this farmhouse stands in its own well-maintained grounds. It offers a peaceful retreat with spacious, comfortable rooms, one, with en suite facilities, enjoying ground floor access. This is a no-smoking establishment.
2rm(1⇌1♠) Annexe 1⇌ ⊁in all bedrooms CTV in 2 bedrooms ® ✗ sB&B⇌♠fr£17 dB&B⇌♠fr£34 LDO By arrangement
🎹 CTV 5P 4 acres non-working

BICKINGTON (NEAR ASHBURTON) Devon Map **03** SX77

SELECTED

FH QQQQ Mrs E A Ross **East Burne** *(SX799711)* TQ12 6PA ☎Bickington(0626) 821496
Closed Xmas & New Year
A Grade II listed medieval hall house situated in a peaceful, unspoilt valley only a mile from the A38. The bedrooms are well decorated and comfortable, with a host of reading material provided. The house is full of character, with exposed

beams, stone walls and open fireplaces; several of the barns outside have been sympathetically converted to provide self-catering accommodation. A cobbled courtyard leads to a secluded garden with a heated, well fenced outdoor swimming pool. The owners provide bed and breakfast only, but are happy to advise of local places to eat.
3rm(2♠1hc) ⌇in all bedrooms ® ✕ (ex guide dogs) sB&Bfr£15 sB&B♠fr£15 dB&Bfr£30 dB&B♠fr£30 WB&Bfr£95
CTV 8P ⌂(heated) 40 acres sheep horses

FH **Q Q** Mrs J Birkenhead *Gale Farm (SX795716)* TQ12 6PG
☎Bickington(0626) 821273
A most attractive Devonshire farmhouse, dating back to the 16th century, in a peaceful, rural setting. Three bedrooms offer comfortable, spacious accommodation and the use of two bathrooms. An elegant drawing room is available for guests' use and breakfast is served in the separate dining room.
3rm(1hc) CTV in 1 bedroom TV in 1 bedroom ® LDO 5pm
CTV 4P sauna 5 acres

BIDEFORD Devon Map **02** SS42

See also Westward Ho!
GH **Q** **Kumba** Chudleigh Rd, East-the-Water EX39 4AR
☎(0237) 471526
An Edwardian property in an elevated position with views across the river. There is a relaxed atmosphere created by Mr and Mrs Doughty, and the accommodation is cosy with many of the proprietors' pieces decorating the public areas.
9rm(1⌇3♠5hc) (5fb)⌇in 2 bedrooms CTV in 7 bedrooms ®
sB&B£15-£20 sB&B⌇♠£16-£21 dB&B£26-£28
dB&B⌇♠£30-£33 WB&B£85-£110
Lic CTV 14P 2🏌 ⚓ putting green ⑤

Kumba
GUEST HOUSE
Chudleigh Road, East-The-Water, Bideford,
N Devon EX39 4AR. Telephone: (0237) 471526

A homely welcome awaits you. Situated in peaceful grounds and overlooks town and quay. Ideally situated for touring North Devon. Ample parking. Mid week bookings. En suite rooms. Family, double, twin & four poster rooms. Tea/coffee making facilities, colour TV, **B&B from £13pp.** Open all year. Traditional English or vegetarian breakfast served. Children and pets welcome.
English Tourist Board 2 crowns

TY'N-Y-CELYN HOUSE

Betws-Y-Coed
Llanrwst Road (A470), Gwynedd, LL24 0HD
Tel: 0690 710202 Fax: 0690 710800

This spacious Victorian Guest House overlooks picturesque village of Betws-y-Coed and has beautiful scenic views of the Llugwy Valley. There are eight bedrooms completely and tastefully re-furnished. Each one has CTV, beverage makers, central heating, en-suite facilities, etc.

You are assured of a warm welcome by Maureen and Clive Muskus, comfortable accommodation and robust breakfast.

Green Acres Farm
Breadstone, Berkeley, Glos
Tel: Dursley (0453) 810348

New Cotswold stone built house set in beautiful Berkeley Vale twixt Cotswolds & River Severn. Beautiful views. Tastefully furnished. Every convenience, warm welcome. Ideal for touring Cotswolds, Forest of Dean and Bath. Visit Berkeley Castle, Severnvale Wild Fowl, Gloucester Waterways Museum. Horse riding can be arranged. Many good eating places in the area. Cottage also available.

GH Ⓠ Ⓠ **Mount Private Hotel** Northdown Rd EX39 3LP
☎(0237) 473748
*A small Georgian house in a semi-walled garden close to the town.
The bedrooms are comfortable and some have en suite facilities.
The public rooms are elegant and tastefully decorated and
furnished. Home cooked dishes are offered on the limited choice
menu, and the warm welcome from the resident proprietors is
memorable.*
8rm(1⇌4♠3hc) (2fb)⊁in all bedrooms ® ⴼ (ex guide dogs)
✱ sB&B£18.50-£20.50 sB&B⇌♠£22.50-£26 dB&B£34-£36
dB&B⇌♠£40-£41 WB&B£130-£168 WBDi£170-£225
LDO 5pm
Lic ⴼ CTV 4P nc5yrs
Credit Cards ①③Ⓔ

See advertisement on page 67

GH Ⓠ Ⓠ Ⓠ *Pines at Eastleigh* Old Barnstaple Rd, Eastleigh
EX39 4PA (3m E off A39 at East-the-Water)
☎Instow(0271) 860561
*Originally an 18th-century farmhouse, this small family-run hotel
is set in a secluded location with 7 acres of grounds, on the edge of
the village, approximately four miles from Bideford. Bedrooms,
some of which have recently been converted from the outbuildings,
are well equipped, each with small but modern private bathrooms.
There is a comfortable lounge with an additional sun lounge bar,
and a bright, traditional dining room, where a choice of home-
cooked meals is available.*
6rm(1⇌2♠3hc) Annexe 2♠ (3fb) ® LDO 5pm
Lic ⴼ CTV 12P Art courses
Credit Cards ①③

BILLINGSHURST West Sussex Map 04 TQ02

GH Ⓠ *Newstead Hall* Adversane RH14 9JH ☎(0403) 783196 &
784734
*Situated in a pleasant district with good access, this older style
house has a new wing with bedrooms offering modern
accommodation. It also has a lounge, small bar and restaurant.*
17⇌♠ CTV in all bedrooms ® ⴼ (ex guide dogs) LDO 9pm
Lic ⴼ 26P
Credit Cards ①②③⑤

SELECTED

FH Ⓠ Ⓠ Ⓠ Ⓠ Mrs M Mitchell *Old Wharf* (TQ070256)
Wharf Farm, Newbridge RH14 0JG ☎(0403) 784096
*This converted warehouse was built in 1839 and has been
elegantly modernised into a charming canalside home, with its
original features retained. Bedrooms are all individually
furnished and decorated and well equipped with all modern
comforts. There is a small breakfast room and a delightful
sitting room with an inglenook fireplace and French doors
opening out on to the canalside. There is a no-smoking policy
throughout.*
4⇌♠ ⊁in all bedrooms CTV in all bedrooms ® ⴼ
ⴼ CTV 6P nc12yrs ✔ 200 acres beef sheep
Credit Cards ①②③

BINGLEY West Yorkshire Map 07 SE13

GH Ⓠ Ⓠ Ⓠ **Hall Bank Private Hotel** Beck Ln BD16 4DD
☎Bradford(0274) 565296
Closed Xmas
*A pleasant family-owned and run hotel situated in an elevated
position on the side of the Aire Valley in a quiet residential area. It
is well furnished throughout, with good facilities in the bedrooms,
all of which are en suite. Public rooms include a comfortable
lounge, a games room and a sun lounge.*
10rm(9⇌♠1hc) CTV in all bedrooms ® ⴼ
sB&B♠£40 dB&B⇌♠£52 WB&B£150-£230 WBDi£210-
£350 LDO 7.30pm
Lic ⴼ CTV 20P nc4yrs games room Ⓔ

BIRKENHEAD Merseyside Map 07 SJ38

GH Ⓠ Ⓠ **Gronwen** 11 Willowbank Rd, Devonshire Park
L42 7JU ☎051-652 8306
*Situated in a quiet residential street close to Tranmere Rovers
football ground and the Glenda Jackson Theatre, this small
friendly guesthouse offers clean, comfortable accommodation with
a home-like feel.*
5hc (1fb) CTV in all bedrooms ® ✱ sB&Bfr£15 dB&Bfr£28
WB&Bfr£98 WBDifr£143 LDO 7.30pm
ⴼ CTV ⴹ

GH Ⓠ Ⓠ *Shrewsbury Lodge Hotel* 31 Shrewsbury Rd, Oxton
L43 2JB ☎(051652) 4029
*A detached Victorian house in a corner position in the residential
area of Oxton, Shrewsbury Lodge offers comfortable
accommodation. Although bedrooms are modestly furnished, a
wing of ten modern rooms is expected to be completed before the
end of 1991.*
8rm(6♠2hc) (3fb)⊁in all bedrooms CTV in all bedrooms ®
ⴼ CTV
Credit Cards ①

BIRMINGHAM West Midlands Map 07 SP08

See Town Plan Section
See also Bearwood & Blackheath
GH Ⓠ **Awentsbury Hotel** 21 Serpentine Rd, Selly Park
B29 7HU ☎021-472 1258 FAX 021-428 1527
*Standing in a quiet residential area close to the university,
Awentsbury has bedrooms which are simply furnished with good
facilities.*
16rm(5♠11hc) (2fb) CTV in all bedrooms ® sB&B£24-£34
sB&B♠£34 dB&B£39 dB&B♠£47 WB&B£151-£207.90
WBDi£179-£235.90 LDO 6pm
ⴼ 13P
Credit Cards ①③Ⓔ

GH Ⓠ Ⓠ **Beech House Hotel** 21 Gravelly Hill North,
Erdington B23 6BT ☎021-373 0620
Closed Xmas & New Year 2 wks
*A privately owned hotel in a convenient location, close to
'Spaghetti Junction' on the M6, and popular with visitors to the
NEC. The emphasis is on personal service provided by the
proprietor. Bedrooms are comfortable, and there are two lounges,
one non-smoking and the other with a TV.*
9rm(4⇌♠5hc) (2fb) CTV in 4 bedrooms ® sB&B£26-£28
sB&B⇌♠£33-£35 dB&B£40-£43 dB&B⇌♠£47-£50
WB&B£182-£196 WBDi£252-£266 LDO noon
ⴼ CTV 10P nc5yrs
Credit Cards ①③

GH Ⓠ Ⓠ Ⓠ *Bridge House Hotel* 49 Sherbourne Rd, Acocks
Green B27 6DX ☎021-706 5900
Closed Xmas & New Year
*With easy access to the airport and National Exhibition Centre,
this hotel has rooms with modern facilities. The Hopwood family
have this year added a 'Movie Bar' as part of their improvements.*
30rm(2⇌28♠) CTV in all bedrooms ® ⴼ LDO 8.30pm
Lic ⴼ CTV 48P
Credit Cards ①②③

GH Ⓠ Ⓠ **Cape Race Hotel** 929 Chester Rd, Erdington B24 OHJ
☎021-373 3085
*Conveniently placed for access to the M5, M6, NEC and the city
centre, this hotel has its own outdoor swimming pool and tennis
court. The rooms, although limited for space, are well equipped
and the proprietors' personal service is assured.*
9rm(7♠2hc) CTV in all bedrooms ® ⴼ (ex guide dogs) ✱
sB&B♠£25-£28 sB&B♠£29 dB&B♠£40-£44 LDO 8.30pm
Lic ⴼ CTV 15P ⇌(heated) ⴹ(hard)
Credit Cards ①③Ⓔ

GH QQ **Heath Lodge Hotel** Coleshill Road, Marston Green
B37 7HT ☎021-779 2218
This hotel, located 1.5 miles from the NEC and airport, has easy access to the Midlands motorway network. Some of the rooms and shower rooms are compact, but there is a comfortable television lounge and a small bar.
12rm(6🚿6hc) (2fb) CTV in all bedrooms ® sB&B£27.50-£30 sB&B🚿£35-£39 dB&B£38-£40 dB&B🚿£46-£49 LDO 8.30pm
Lic 🅿 CTV 15P
Credit Cards ① ② ③ ⓔ

See advertisement on page 69

GH QQ **Lyndhurst Hotel** 135 Kingsbury Road, Erdington
B24 8QT ☎021-373 5695
A privately owned guesthouse, popular with commercial visitors, just 10 minutes from the city centre and well within half a mile away. Rooms vary, some are quite compact and they are modestly furnished, but Mr and Mrs Williams continue to improve facilities with the addition of more en suite shower rooms this year.
14rm(1⇔11🚿2hc) (3fb)✂in 5 bedrooms CTV in all bedrooms
® ✖ (ex guide dogs) sB&B£29.95-£31.50 sB&B⇔🚿£36.50-
£38.50 dB&B⇔🚿£49.95-£52.50 WB&B£175-£215
LDO 8.15pm
Lic 🅿 CTV 15P
Credit Cards ① ② ③ ⑤ ⓔ

See advertisement on page 69

Visit your local AA Shop.

THE MOUNT HOTEL

Northdown Road
BIDEFORD EX39 3LP
Tel: (0237) 473748

Guestaccom.
Members WCTB

A warm welcome and good food await you at our charming Georgian Hotel. Secluded garden. Parking. Short walk to Town Centre. TV. Centrally Heated. En-Suite rooms. Tea/Coffee facilities. Bedrooms non-smoking.

Explore beautiful N Devon and Tarka Country. Safe beaches, walking and other activities nearby.

Personally run by Mike and Janet Taylor.

Henaford Manor Farm
Welcombe, Nr Bideford
N. Devon EX39 6HE
Tel: Morwenstow (028883) 252

Situated just 8 miles north of Bude, the farmhouse offers a very high standard of accommodation and service with excellent food. All rooms are comfortable and tastefully furnished and still retain their character with exposed beams, large fireplaces and natural wood. Although a working dairy and sheep farm of 220 acres children are able to feed and see many different animals. There is also a games room and the garden has a swing. An ideal place to relax with many walks or short drives to the surrounding countryside and pretty villages. Dogs welcome but must be kept in the car or stable. Short breaks available except July & August.

Cape Race Hotel

929 Chester Road · Erdington
Birmingham B24 0HJ
Telephone + Fax 021 373 3085
Proprietors Phillip & Jill Jones

Hotel run personally by resident proprietors. All bedrooms with colour TV, phones and tea/coffee making facilities. Most rooms with shower & toilet en suite. Central Heating. Licensed Bar. Ample free car parking. Tennis court and outdoor pool in large garden. NEC and City Centre ten minutes, M6 junc 5 & 6 2 miles. Special weekly and weekend rates.

GH QQ ***Robin Hood Lodge Hotel*** 142 Robin Hood Ln, Hall Green B28 0JX ☎021-778 5307
A predominantly commercial hotel situated on the A4040 with easy access to the city centre, National Exhibition Centre and airport. Well equipped accommodation is offered in both the main house and nearby annexe.
7rm(1⇌2↑4hc) (1fb) CTV in all bedrooms ® LDO 7.30pm
Lic ꟿ CTV 11P
Credit Cards 1 3 5

GH Q **Rollason Wood Hotel** 130 Wood End Road, Erdington B24 8BJ ☎021-373 1230
35rm(1⇌10↑24hc) (4fb) CTV in all bedrooms ®
sB&B£17.30-£24.75 sB&B⇌↑£26.50-£36 dB&B£29.70-£43.35 dB&B⇌↑£41.80-£52.25 WB&B£122.25-£210.75 LDO 8.30pm
Lic ꟿ CTV 35P games room
Credit Cards 1 2 3 5

GH Q ***Tri-Star Hotel*** Coventry Road, Elmdon B26 3QR ☎021-782 1010 & 021-782 6131
Conveniently situated on the A45, midway between the NEC and airport, this privately owned guesthouse has simple and well-maintained accommodation.
15rm(2↑13hc) (3fb) CTV in all bedrooms ® ✗ LDO 8pm
Lic ꟿ CTV 25P pool table
Credit Cards 3

GH QQ **Willow Tree Hotel** 759 Chester Rd, Erdington B24 0BY ☎021-373 6388 & 384 7721
rs Xmas
This is a pleasant guesthouse enjoying easy access to the town centre. The accommodation is well kept, with a good array of modern facilities. The house has a friendly atmosphere created by the hospitable proprietor.
7rm(5↑2hc) (2fb) CTV in all bedrooms ® ✗ (ex guide dogs) ✱ sB&Bfr£24.70 sB&B↑£35.25 dB&B↑£54.05 LDO 8pm
Lic ꟿ CTV 7P
Credit Cards 1 3 £

BISHAMPTON Hereford & Worcester Map **03** SO95

SELECTED

FH QQQQ Mrs H K Robertson **Nightingale Hotel** *(SO988512)* WR10 2NH ☎Evesham(0386) 82521 & 82384
This mock-Tudor farmhouse was chosen as the Midlands 'Best Newcomer' for the 1988/89 season, and the hospitality of the owners, combined with the exceptional comfort of their home, has ensured that guests return regularly. The small restaurant is now established as a favourite for locals, due to the very competent standard of cooking. Good, local, English produce is used; the one exception of local items is the prime black Angus beef which is obtained regularly from Scotland. The comfortable accommodation is attractively furnished, with good facilities, and there are 2 lounge areas, with excellent seating, complemented by fresh flowers, magazines and books. The farmhouse is suitable for tourists and business travellers alike, and small meetings can be accommodated.
4⇌↑ (1fb) CTV in all bedrooms ® ✗ sB&B⇌↑£32 dB&B⇌↑£45 WB&B£200 (wkly only Oct-Mar) LDO 9pm
Lic ꟿ 30P nc6yrs ► 18 U snooker 200 acres arable
Credit Cards 1 3

BISHOP'S CLEEVE Gloucestershire Map **03** SO92

GH Q **The Old Manor House** 43 Station Rd GL52 4HH ☎(024267) 4127
6hc (3fb) ® ✗ ✱ sB&B£15.50-£18.50 dB&Bfr£29
CTV 8P U

BISHOP'S STORTFORD Hertfordshire Map **05** TL42

GH QQQ **Cottage** 71 Birchanger Ln, Birchanger CM23 5QA ☎(0279) 812349
A charming 17th-century Grade II listed cottage which has been carefully modernised to retain its character. Set in a quiet rural location yet close to Bishop's Stortford, the accommodation is attractively decorated and furnished and well equipped. The panelled lounge is comfortable, and the delightful conservatory/dining room overlooks the garden.
10rm(8↑1hc) ⊁in all bedrooms CTV in all bedrooms ® ✗ (ex guide dogs) sB&B£22-£28 sB&B↑£32 dB&B↑£45 WB&Bfr£133 WBDifr£203 LDO 9.30am
Lic ꟿ 10P croquet
Credit Cards 1 £

BISHOPSTON West Glamorgan Map **02** SS58

See also Langland Bay and Mumbles
GH QQQ ***Winston Hotel*** 11 Church Ln, Bishopston Valley SA3 3JC ☎(044128) 2074
Closed 24-29 Dec
This modern hotel is situated in a peaceful and secluded wooded valley, and it is run by the very friendly Clarke family. Bedrooms are comfortable and the public rooms are spacious and include the use of an indoor swimming pool and a snooker table.
14rm(3↑3hc) Annexe 5rm(4⇌1↑) (2fb) CTV in 5 bedrooms ® LDO 10.30am
Lic ꟿ CTV 20P ▭(heated) snooker sauna solarium
Credit Cards 1 3
See advertisement under SWANSEA

£ Remember to use the money-off vouchers.

Willow Tree
HOTEL
759 CHESTER ROAD, ERDINGTON,
BIRMINGHAM B24 0BY
Telephone: 021-373 6388
PROPRIETORS: LES & VERNA GRIFFITHS

A family run Hotel of character. Convenient to city centre, NEC, Airport, Trains & Motorway M6 Junction 5 & 6. All rooms have: direct dial telephone, colour television, video channel, hostess trays, radio, trouser press, iron and hair dryer. Most rooms have shower & toilet ensuite. Centrally heated throughout, residential bar, restaurant, lounge, large mature garden, car park.

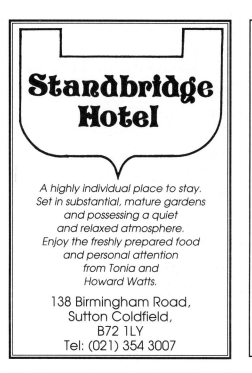

BLACKHEATH West Midlands Map 07 SO98

GH 🔲🔲 **Highfield House Hotel** Holly Rd, Rowley Regis
B65 0BH ☎021-559 1066
Closed Xmas
Mr and Mrs Pedlar make guests welcome at this predominantly commercial guesthouse, which has easy access to motorways and Black Country business centres. It is located at Blackheath, which is also known as Rowley Regis.The rooms are modestly furnished but well kept, and light snacks are always available.
14rm(2⇄🥾12hc) CTV in all bedrooms ® ✖ (ex guide dogs) ✱
sB&B£24-£28 sB&B⇄🥾£35 dB&B£38-£46 dB&B⇄🥾£46-£51
Lic 🍴 CTV 12P nc5yrs
Credit Cards 1 3 £

BLACKPOOL Lancashire Map 07 SD33

See **Town Plan Section**

GH 🔲🔲 **Arosa Hotel** 18-20 Empress Dr FY2 9SA
☎(0253) 52555
Apr-Nov & Xmas
In a residential area close to the seafront, this friendly hotel offers pleasant, well maintained accommodation.
21rm(4⇄17🥾) (7fb) CTV in all bedrooms ® ✱
sB&B⇄🥾£18-£25 dB&B⇄🥾£36-£50 LDO 4pm
Lic 🍴 CTV 7P

GH 🔲🔲 **Ashcroft Private Hotel** 42 King Edward Av FY2 9TA
☎(0253) 51538
Situated close to the promenade among other similar hotels, the Ashcroft offers well maintained accommodation and a congenial atmosphere.
10hc (3fb) ® ✖ (ex guide dogs) ✱ sB&B£15-£17 dB&B£30-£34
WB&B£99-£110 WBDi£123-£151 LDO 2pm
Lic 🍴 CTV 3P 1🎱
Credit Cards 1 3 £

GH 🔲🔲 **Berwick Private Hotel** 23 King Edward Av FY2 9TA
☎(0253) 51496
Closed 29 Dec-11 Jan
The Berwick is a well maintained hotel situated in a side road leading off the North Promenade. Some of the bedrooms have en suite facilities and there is a small, but comfortable lounge.
8rm(6🥾2hc) ® sB&B£13.50-£16 dB&B£27-£32
dB&B🥾£29-£34 (incl dinner) WB&B£81.50-£91 WBDi£94.50-£101.50 LDO 3pm
Lic 🍴 CTV 4P nc3yrs

GH 🔲🔲 **Brooklands Hotel** 28-30 King Edward Av FY2 9TA
☎(0253) 51479
Situated close to Queen's Promenade, this friendly, family-run small hotel offers well maintained accommodation which includes a neat dining room and a comfortable lounge with a small bar.
18rm(9🥾9hc) (3fb) CTV in all bedrooms ® ✖ (ex guide dogs)
sB&B£15-£15.50 sB&B🥾£17-£17.50 dB&B£30-£31
dB&B🥾£34-£35 WB&B£105-£108.50 WBDi£110-£130
LDO 3.30pm
Lic 🍴 5P £

GH 🔲🔲🔲 **Burlees Hotel** 40 Knowle Av FY2 9TQ
☎(0253) 54535
Feb-Nov
In a quiet residential area a short walk from Queens Promenade, this friendly small hotel has excellent en suite shower and WC facilities and maintains a high standard of cleanliness throughout.
10rm(7🥾3hc) (2fb) CTV in 7 bedrooms ® ✖ sB&B£15.60-£18
sB&B🥾£18.65-£21.30 dB&B£31.20-£36 dB&B🥾£37.30-£42.60
WB&B£103.60-£139 WBDi£148.45-£185 LDO 4pm
Lic 🍴 CTV 5P 1🎱
Credit Cards 1 3 £

GH 🔲🔲 **Cliff Head Hotel** 174 Queens Promenade, Bispham
FY2 9JN ☎(0253) 591086
Cosy public rooms and well equipped bedrooms with en suite facilities are features of this well maintained private hotel, situated at the northern end of Queens Promenade.
7rm(3⇄4🥾) (1fb) CTV in all bedrooms ® sB&B⇄🥾£14.50-£17.50 dB&B⇄🥾£29-£35 WB&B£96.50-£116.50 WBDi£113-£135 LDO 5.30pm
Lic 🍴 CTV 3P £

GH 🔲🔲 **Cliftonville Hotel** 14 Empress Dr, Northshore
FY2 9SE ☎(0253) 51052
Etr-Nov
This guesthouse is situated just off the promenade in Blackpool. All the bedrooms have en suite facilities as well as tea-making equipment. Cliftonville is fully centrally heated and there is a comfortable lounge bar and a spacious dining room with seperate tables.
19🥾 (8fb) ® ✖ ✱ sB&B🥾£15.50-£18.50 dB&B🥾£31-£37
WB&B£97-£124 WBDi£112-£137
Lic lift 🍴 CTV 2P
Credit Cards 1 3

GH 🔲🔲 **Denely Private Hotel** 15 King Edward Av FY2 9TA
☎(0253) 52757
A friendly establishment close to the North Promenade. Some of the bedrooms have en suite facilities, all are centrally heated and have tea-making facilities. The dining room is nicely appointed and there is a comfortable lounge at the front of the hotel.
9rm(2🥾7hc) (2fb) ® ✖ ✱ sB&B£13.50-£15.50 sB&B🥾£16.50-£19 dB&B£27-£31 dB&B🥾£54.50-£62 WB&B£94.50-£108.50
WBDi£122.50-£150.50 LDO 3.30pm
🍴 CTV 6P £

GH 🔲🔲 *Derwent Private Hotel* 8 Gynn Av FY1 2LD
☎(0253) 55194
Mar-3 Nov
Situated in a quiet street, close to the seafront, this friendly small hotel offers compact, well-maintained accommodation at very reasonable prices.
12rm(4🥾8hc) (2fb) ® ✖ (ex guide dogs) LDO 2pm
Lic 🍴 CTV 4P

GH 🔲🔲 *The Garville Hotel* 3 Beaufort Av, Bispham FY2 9HQ
(2m N) ☎(0253) 51004
Pleasant, family-run guesthouse close to the seafront.
7rm(2⇄5hc) (2fb)⊬in all bedrooms CTV in 5 bedrooms ®
LDO 1pm
Lic 🍴 CTV 5P

GH 🔲🔲🔲 **Hartshead Hotel** 17 King Edward Av FY2 9TA
☎(0253) 53133 & 57111
Closed end Nov-2 wk Dec
Situated 200 yards from the North Shore and within easy reach of the town centre, this small, friendly hotel offers comfortable lounges and well equipped bedrooms, all with en suite facilities, colour TV, direct-dial telephones, radios and tea-making equipment.
10rm(1⇄9🥾) (3fb)⊬in all bedrooms CTV in all bedrooms ®
✖ (ex guide dogs) sB&B⇄🥾£16-£26 dB&B⇄🥾£32-£42
WB&B£100-£132 WBDi£116-£149 LDO 2pm
Lic 🍴 CTV 7P nc3yrs £

GH 🔲🔲 **Inglewood Hotel** 18 Holmfield Rd FY2 9TB
☎(0253) 51668
A pleasant small hotel offering very good value for money, situated on a quiet side road on the North Shore, close to the sea. The house is comfortable and well furnished throughout, and service is friendly.
10🥾 (2fb) CTV in all bedrooms ® ✖ (ex guide dogs) ✱
sB&B🥾£14.50-£21 dB&B🥾£29-£42 WB&B£101.50-£119
WBDi£105-£130 LDO 10am
Lic 🍴 CTV nc2yrs £

GH ⓆⒺⓆ *Lynstead Private Hotel* 40 King Edward Av
FY2 9TA ☎(0253) 51050
Closed 1st 2 wks Jan
The tramcar bar is the outstanding feature of this very well maintained private hotel, featuring a mock-up of a tram cab, and a wealth of photographs and models. All the bedrooms have full en suite facilities, and a 5-course meal is served in the attractive dining room.
10➡ (4fb) Ⓡ ✖ (ex guide dogs) LDO 3pm
Lic lift ⊞ CTV ⋗ nc3yrs

See advertisement on page 73

◻◖ GH ⒺⒺⓆ **Lynwood** 38 Osborne Rd FY4 1HQ
☎(0253) 44628
Closed Xmas & New Year
An immaculate little guesthouse providing very good value for money, with well equipped bedrooms, most with en suite facilities, a comfortable lounge, and an attractive dining room in which good home cooking can be enjoyed. Situated close to the south shore and the Sandcastle Centre.
8rm(1⇌5➡2hc) (1fb) CTV in all bedrooms Ⓡ ✖ sB&B£13-£15 sB&B⇌➡£16-£19 dB&B⇌➡£28-£30 WB&B£90-£105 WBDi£112-£126 LDO breakfast
⊞ ⋗
Credit Cards ① ② ③ Ⓔ

See advertisement on page 73

GH ⒺⓆ **Motel Mimosa** 24A Lonsdale Rd FY1 6EE
☎(0253) 41906
Closed Xmas
This is a modern establishment situated close to the promenade and the central pier. It offers comfortable bedrooms to which breakfast is delivered.
15⇌➡ (3fb) CTV in all bedrooms Ⓡ ✳ sB&B⇌➡£25-£35 dB&B⇌➡£30-£40 WB&B120-£150 LDO 8.30pm

▶

Denely Private Hotel

15 King Edward Avenue, Blackpool FY2 9TA
Telephone: Blackpool (0253) 52757

Situated close to Queens Promenade, cliffs and Gynn Square with easy access to centre of town, station and amenities.

The hotel offers you every modern convenience including full central heating. Tea/coffee facilities, hair dryers, H&C and shaving point in all rooms. Ensuites available also ironing facilities on request. Visitors lounge with colour TV. Spacious non smoking dining room. Excellent cuisine.

Resident Proprietress: Mrs Pauline Davis.

HARTSHEAD HOTEL

RESIDENTIAL LICENCE
PROPRIETORS:
LOUISE CANTLAY & FAMILY
17 King Edward Avenue, Blackpool, North Shore FY2 9TA. Tel: 0253 53133 Guests: 0253 57111

The Hartshead is adjacent to Queens Promenade, North Shore. 300 yards from the sea and within easy access to town centre and golf club. A family run hotel with a first-class reputation for hospitality, excellent cuisine and value. 10 comfortably furnished bedrooms all ensuite having colour TV, radio/intercom, telephone, tea/coffee facilities. Full central heating, car park. The Hartshead is open all year round.

Burlees Hotel

40, Knowle Avenue, Blackpool FY2 9TQ
Tel: (0253) 54535
Proprietors: Mike and Linda Lawrence

Friendly, family run hotel situated off Queen's Promenade in peaceful residential area.

★ Ideal for holidays, business or conference delegates
★ Easy access to town centre and amenities
★ Unrestricted car parking, some on premises
★ Comfort and excellent cuisine assured
★ Central heating throughout
★ Most rooms en-suite
★ All rooms with tea/coffee making facilities and colour T.V.
★ Licensed to residents
★ Low seasons rates Feb to May. Over 55's May and June

Blackpool

Lic ™ CTV 13P 2🏠
Credit Cards 1 3 £

GH Q Q The New Esplanade Hotel 551 New South
Promenade FY4 1NF ☎(0253) 41646
Etr-Nov & Xmas/New Year
*This private hotel overlooks the promenade and the sea, and is
situated close to the pleasure beach and Sandcastle Centre. Most
bedrooms have sea views, and the public rooms include an
attractive bar, games room and a small TV lounge. A large car
park is a welcome facility.*
15rm(5🟊10hc) (3fb) CTV in 5 bedrooms ® ✠ sB&B£13-£20
dB&B£26-£40 dB&B🟊£33-£48 WB&B£91-£140 WBDi£140-
£165 LDO 2pm
Lic ™ CTV 20P games room
Credit Cards 1 3 £

GH Q Q North Mount Private Hotel 22 King Edward Av
FY2 9TD ☎(0253) 55937
*A charming, guesthouse standing in peaceful surroundings on
Blackpool's North Shore.*
8hc (1fb) ® ✠ sB&B£12.50-£15.50 dB&B£25-£31 WB&B£87-
£105 WBDi£110-£130 LDO 3pm
Lic ™ CTV 1P £

GH Q Q The Old Coach House 50 Dean St FY4 1BP
☎(0253) 44330
rs Nov-Mar
*Although the façade of this detached house is Tudor in style, it was
built in 1851 and its appearance is unique in this area. Good sized,
very well equipped bedrooms, all with private bathrooms, are a
feature, as are the well tended gardens. Situated near the South
Pier, the guesthouse is within easy reach of some of Blackpool's
many amenities.*
5🟊 (2fb) CTV in all bedrooms ® ✠ (ex guide dogs) ✻
sB&B🟊£18.50-£20.50 dB&B🟊£35-£39 WB&B£122.50-£136.50
WBDi£150.50-£164.50 (wkly only 24-28 Dec) LDO 2pm
™ 10P
Credit Cards 1 3 £

GH Q Q Rewa Private Hotel 561 New South Prom FY2 9TB
☎(0253) 42463
Apr-Oct
*A family-run, licensed, private hotel on the seafront close to the
south pier and leisure complex. It is very clean and well
maintained, and offers a wide range of services.*
19rm(1↩7🟊11hc) (3fb) CTV in 9 bedrooms ® ✠
Lic ™ CTV 12P
Credit Cards 3

GH Q Sunny Cliff 98 Queens Promenade, Northshore FY2 9NS
☎(0253) 51155
Etr-9 Nov & 4 days Xmas
*Sunny Cliff enjoys a quiet seafront location with easy access to all
amenities, and offers unpretentious, well-maintained
accommodation.*
12hc (4fb) ® ✠ sB&B£13.50-£14.30 dB&B£27-£29
WBDi£114.45-£124 LDO 5pm
Lic CTV 8P £

SELECTED

GH Q Q Q Q Sunray Private Hotel 42 Knowle Av,
Queens Promenade FY2 9TQ ☎(0253) 51937
Closed 15 Dec-5 Jan
*Situated in a quiet residential area off the North shore, yet
only a short walk from the town centre and seafront, this small
hotel was built in 1935. Substantial modernisation has taken
place since then, and all rooms now have private bathrooms,
TV, radio, telephone and tea-making facilites. There is a
comfortable lounge well stocked with books, magazines and
games, and an attactive dining room where traditional English*

---

*dinner is served at 5pm each evening to enable guests to see
the shows in good time.*
9rm(1↩8🟊) (2fb) CTV in all bedrooms ® sB&B↩🟊£22-
£31 dB&B↩🟊£44-£62 WB&B£139-£172 WBDi£200-£248
LDO 3pm
™ CTV 6P
Credit Cards 1 3 £

GH Q Q Surrey House Hotel 9 Northumberland Av FY2 9SB
☎(0253) 51743
Apr-Oct rs Mar & early Nov
*Just off Queens Promenade to the north of the town, this small and
friendly private hotel offers comfortable, centrally heated
accommodation in congenial surroundings.*
12rm(2↩9🟊1hc) (2fb)↙in 1 bedroom ® ✻ sB&B£12.50-
£17.50 sB&B↩🟊£12.50-£17.50 dB&B£25-£35 dB&B↩🟊£25-
£35 WB&B£87.50-£12.50 WBDi£112-£172.50 LDO 4.30pm
™ CTV 6P 1🏠 (£1) nc3mths table tennis pool table £

GH Q Q Westmorland Hotel 256 Queens Promenade FY2 9HB
☎(0253) 54974
*Located in a select area of the promenade, this canopied, licensed
hotel is situated on the North Shore with many of its rooms
overlooking the sea. The majority also have en suite facilities, and
all have colour TV, radio and tea-making facilities. There is a lift
to all floors.*
17rm(13↩🟊4hc) (6fb) CTV in all bedrooms ® LDO 7pm
Lic lift ™ CTV 6P
Credit Cards 1 3

See advertisement on page 75

GH Q Q **Woodleigh Private Hotel** 32 King Edward Av, North Shore FY2 9TA ☎(0253) 593624

Mar-Oct

This well-maintained, friendly guesthouse is close to the Queen's Promenade and offers comfortable, pleasant accommodation. Some bedrooms are fairly compact, and guests may need to share tables in the dining room.

10rm(7♠3hc) (3fb) CTV in all bedrooms ® ✕ sB&B£14.50-£18 dB&B£29-£36 dB&B♠£34-£40.70 WB&B£88.50-£93 WBDi£106-£122 LDO 2pm

 CTV ⚡

BLACKWOOD Gwent Map **03** ST19

INN Q Q **Plas** Gordon Rd NP2 1D ☎(0495) 224674

Originally a farmhouse, this family-run inn stands above the town and has good views of the valley. Bedrooms are attractive and well equipped, and the bars are full of character, with stone walls and an inglenook fireplace.

6rm(4♠2hc) (1fb) CTV in 6 bedrooms ® LDO 9.45pm

 50P

Credit Cards ① ③ ⑤

BLAGDON Avon Map **03** ST55

INN Q Q Q **Seymour Arms** Bath Rd BS18 6TH ☎(0761) 62279

Situated in the heart of the village, on the main Bath road, this Victorian inn has been completely refurbished to provide attractive open-plan public areas and pretty bedrooms, many with good en suite facilities.

4rm(3♠1hc) (1fb) CTV in all bedrooms ® ✕ (ex guide dogs) ✱ sB&B£17 sB&B♠£22 dB&B♠£30 ✱ Lunch £6-£12alc Dinner £6-£12alc LDO 9.30pm

 30P nc5yrs ⓔ

BLAIRGOWRIE Tayside *Perthshire* Map **11** NO14

GH Q Q **Ivybank House** Boat Brae, Rattray PH10 7BH ☎(0250) 3056

This substantial Victorian house is set in its own grounds near the town centre. It offers comfortable, well equipped accommodation, and there is a floodlit tennis court for guests' use.

6hc (2fb) CTV in all bedrooms ® LDO 6pm

 CTV 6P ℘(hard)

GH Q Q **The Laurels** Golf Course Rd, Rosemount PH10 6LH ☎(0250) 4920

Closed Dec

A detached stone house lying off the A93 on the southern outskirts of town, close to the golf course, which has been converted into a bright, modern guesthouse. There is a comfortable lounge, and the evening meal offers a good choice of dishes.

6hc ® ✕ ✱ sB&B£14-£19 dB&B£26-£28 WB&Bfr£91 WBDifr£140

Lic CTV 6P

Credit Cards ① ② ③ ⑤

Lic CTV 12P nc9yrs ⓔ

BLAKENEY Gloucestershire

See **Lydney**

BLANDFORD FORUM Dorset Map **03** ST80

GH Q Q Q **Fairfield House** Church Rd DT11 8UB ☎(0258) 456756 FAX (0258) 480053

An attractive Georgian house with a large garden in the centre of the village, off the A354. Recently converted bedrooms retain much charm whilst incorporating many modern facilities. The lounge provides books, games and local information, and there is an elegant dining room where guests generally share one large table.

5♠♠ (1fb)⚡in 4 bedrooms CTV in all bedrooms ®
✕ (ex guide dogs) sB&B£28-£33 sB&B♠£30-£36 dB&B♠£45-£53 WB&B£210-£252 WBDi£260-£292 LDO 6pm

Lic 10P nc7yrs

Credit Cards ① ② ③ ⓔ

See advertisement on page 77

BLEDINGTON Gloucestershire Map **04** SP22

INN Q Q Q **Kings Head Inn & Restaurant** The Green OX7 6HD ☎Kingham(0608) 658365

This delightful 15th-century inn looks out over the quiet village green, complete with brooks and ducks. Comfortable, well-appointed bedrooms (all en suite) are popular, as is the restaurant. Imaginatively prepared food is offered in a wide choice of daily dishes, all reasonably priced and very tasty.

6♠ (2fb)⚡in 3 bedrooms CTV in all bedrooms ®
✕ (ex guide dogs) ✱ sB&B♠£27-£30 dB&B♠£49-£55 ✱ Bar Lunch £2.95-£6.50 Dinner fr£5.95&alc LDO 9.45pm

 CTV 70P ⓔ

BLICKLING Norfolk Map **09** TG12

INN Q Q Q *Buckinghamshire Arms Hotel* Blickling, Aylsham
NR11 6NF ☎Aylsham(0263) 732133
*This 17th-century inn, part of the Blickling Estate, is very close to
the historic Hall which is owned by the National Trust.
Authentically furnished and unspoilt, there is a well appointed
quarry-tiled restaurant, together with a snug and a cosy bar with a
wood-burning stove, where bar meals are served. Two of the three
bedrooms have tester beds, and each is comfortably furnished in
keeping with the era. There is also an attractive garden and ample
car parking.*
3hc (1fb) CTV in all bedrooms ® ✖ (ex guide dogs)
LDO 9.30pm
80P ✔
Credit Cards [1] [3]

BOAT OF GARTEN Highland *Inverness-shire* Map **14** NH91

SELECTED

GH Q Q Q Q **Heathbank House** PH24 3BD
☎(047983) 234
Closed Nov & Dec
*A comfortably appointed Victorian house set in its own
peaceful garden. Every care has been taken to preserve the
original charm and character of the house, despite
considerable refurbishment. Each of the delightful bedrooms
has been individually decorated to a high standard, and every
room has an abundance of interesting and imaginative bric-a-
brac. The comfortable lounge has a log fire, and in the
candlelit dining room the emphasis is on good food,
imaginatively prepared from fresh local produce.*
8rm(4↑4hc) (2fb)⊬in all bedrooms ® ✖ (ex guide dogs)
sB&Bfr£16 dB&Bfr£32 dB&B↑fr£40 LDO 5pm
⅏ CTV 8P

BODEDERN Gwynedd Map **06** SH38

INN Q **Crown Hotel** LL65 3TU ☎Valley(0407) 740734
*A warm friendly village inn, conveniently situated on the A5109,
near the ferry terminal at Holyhead and within easy reach of the
A5. Well furnished, it has a pleasant atmosphere, and a good
selection of meals is available.*
5hc (2fb) CTV in all bedrooms ® sB&B£14-£15 dB&B£28-£30
WB&B£75-£80 Lunch £4.55-£6.50 LDO 9.45pm
⅏ 50P ℰ

BODENHAM Hereford & Worcester Map **03** SO55

FH Q Q Q Mr & Mrs P J Edwards **Maund Court** *(SO561505)*
HR1 3JA ☎(056884) 282
Closed mid Dec-mid Jan
*Situated on the A417 east of Leominster, Maud Court Farm is an
ideal base from which to explore this lovely countryside. The
proprietors thoughtfully provide guests with maps and tourist
information. Rooms are comfortable and well equipped, each
different in style and furnishings. There is an outdoor swimming
pool for the more energetic, or guests can enjoy a game of croquet
on the lawn.*
4rm(3⇨1↑) CTV in all bedrooms ® sB&B⇨↑£15-£16
dB&B⇨↑£30 WB&B£100-£105
⅏ CTV 6P ⌇(heated) croquet 130 acres mixed

BODLE STREET GREEN East Sussex Map **05** TQ61

FH Q Q Mr & Mrs P Gentry **Stud** *(TQ652144)* BN27 4RJ
☎Herstmonceux(0323) 833201
Closed Xmas
*A farmhouse, set in 70 acres of land, providing simple
accommodation, a comfortable residents' lounge and good
hospitality.*

3rm(1↑2hc) ⊬in all bedrooms ® ✖ ✳ sB&Bfr£22
sB&B↑fr£22 dB&Bfr£34 dB&B↑fr£34 WB&B£105-£140
⅏ CTV 3P 70 acres cattle sheep

BODMIN Cornwall & Isles of Scilly Map **02** SX06

See also Mount
FH Q Q Q Mrs P A Smith **Treffry** *(SW073637)* PL30 5AF
☎(0208) 74405
Closed Xmas rs 20 Oct-18 Mar
*A 16th-century stone and slate farmhouse set in mature gardens
adjoining National Trust property, and part of a working dairy
farm. Bedrooms are comfortable, well equipped and attractively
decorated. Fresh, home-cooked meals are provided using home
grown produce; award winning self-catering accommodation is
also available.*
3rm(2↑1hc) ⊬in all bedrooms CTV in all bedrooms ®
✖ (ex guide dogs) sB&B£17.50 dB&B↑£35 WB&B£115
WBDi£170 (wkly only Jul & Aug) LDO noon
⅏ CTV 4P nc3yrs 200 acres dairy ℰ

BOLLINGTON Cheshire Map **07** SJ97

INN Q **Turners Arms Hotel** 1 Ingersley Rd SK10 5RE
☎(0625) 573864
*Standing on the edge of the town, this inn offers meals every day of
the week, including a competitively-priced, traditional Sunday
lunch. Value for money is certainly one of the proprietor's
priorities.*
8rm(2⇨3↑3hc) (2fb) CTV in all bedrooms ® ✳ sB&B£20-£25
sB&B⇨↑£35-£45 dB&B£40-£45 dB&B⇨↑£45-£55 ✳ Lunch
£8-£10alc Dinner £8-£12.50alc LDO 9.30pm
⅏ 2P 1☂ pool darts
Credit Cards [1] [3] ℰ

BO'NESS Central *West Lothian* Map **11** NS98

FH Q Q Q Mrs A Kirk **Kinglass** *(NT006803)* Borrowstoun
Rd EH51 9RW ☎(0506) 822861 & 824185
*Situated high above the town to the south and commanding
outstanding views across the Firth of Forth, this farmhouse is
popular with business people and tourists alike. Bedrooms are well
equipped, and there is an attractive dining room and a comfortable
lounge. Service is friendly and informal, combined with good home
cooking.*
6rm(1↑5hc) (1fb) CTV in all bedrooms ® ✳ sB&B£13.75-£19
sB&B↑fr£25 dB&Bfr£27.50 dB&B↑fr£43 LDO 5.30pm
Lic ⅏ CTV 20P 120 acres arable ℰ

BONSALL Derbyshire Map **08** SK25

GH Q Q **Sycamore** 76 High St, Town Head DE4 2AA
☎Wirksworth(0629) 823903
*Guests can relax on the front lawn of this 18th-century house which
enjoys an elevated position overlooking the village. There is a
choice of meals in the evening and prepared lunches are available.*
7rm(1↑6hc) (1fb) CTV in all bedrooms ® LDO 5pm
Lic ⅏ CTV 7P
See advertisement under MATLOCK

GH Q Q **Town Head Farmhouse** 70 High St DE4 2AR
☎Wirksworth(0629) 823762
*Tastefully converted and modernised in keeping with its 18th-
century character, this house and its outbuildings are built around
a small cottage garden and sited at the top of the town.*
6↑ CTV in all bedrooms ® LDO noon
Lic ⅏ CTV 8P nc10 yrs
See advertisement under MATLOCK

This guide is updated annually – make sure you
use an up-to-date edition.

BONTDDU Gwynedd Map **06** SH61

SELECTED

GH ◑◑◑◑ *Borthwnog Hall Hotel* LL40 2TT
☎(034149) 271
Closed Xmas

This 17th-century Regency house is set in beautiful grounds overlooking the Mawddach Estuary to the massive Cader Idris mountain range. Public rooms are comfortable and elegant, and bedrooms are all individually furnished and decorated in the style of the house. There is an intimate restaurant with imaginative menus, and coffee is served in the very ornate sitting room, which has a log fire. The house features a library art gallery, with original paintings, limited edition prints and local pottery. This is an ideal location for bird watchers, with water-loving birds in the front of the hotel, and the steep, wild slopes of Garth Gell, an RSPB nature reserve.

3⇄3♠ CTV in all bedrooms ®
Lic ⅏ 6P
Credit Cards ① ③

BORDON Hampshire Map **04** SU73

GH ◑◑◑ **St Lucia House Country Club** Lindford Rd
GU35 0LL ☎(0420) 472584

An exceptionally well presented and equipped bedroom in a separate south-facing building, quietly located but convenient for the garrison town. The original red brick Victorian building stands in 2 acres of lawns surrounded by woods, and is run as a country club (private membership) with discos at weekends.

Annexe 6⇄3♠ CTV in all bedrooms ® ✖ ✱ sB&B⇄3♠£40
dB&B⇄3♠£40-£50 WB&B£280-£300
Lic ⅏ 30P
Credit Cards ① ③ ⑤ ⑥

BOROUGHBRIDGE North Yorkshire Map **08** SE36

INN ◑◑◑ *The Crown* Roecliffe YO5 9LY ☎(0423) 322578
FAX (0423) 324060

An attractive, family-run, traditional inn with excellent, spacious, modern bedrooms, all with en suite facilities, situated in the unspoilt village of Roecliffe, two miles west of Boroughbridge. Renowned for its home-cooked bar meals and its à la carte restaurant, the Crown is open for dinner and Sunday lunch, and can also cater for conference parties, weddings and such like in the Coach House function room, situated at the rear.

6⇄♠ CTV in all bedrooms ® LDO 9.30pm
⅏ 70P ✦
Credit Cards ① ③

BORROWDALE Cumbria Map **11** NY21

GH ◑◑ *The Grange* CA12 5UQ ☎(07687) 77251
19 Mar-Oct

An attractive old lakeland farmhouse, situated in the delightful hamlet of Grange in the beautiful Borrowdale valley. Welcoming in appearance, with sizeable bedrooms, a comfortable lounge and characterful dining room, The Grange offers warmth and hospitality in an area of outstanding natural beauty.

7rm(1⇄6hc) (1fb) ® ✖ (ex guide dogs)
⅏ 8P

SELECTED

GH ◑◑◑◑ **Greenbank** CA12 5UY ☎(07687) 77215
Closed 5-30 Jan & 6-26 Dec

A lovely Borrowdale stone building standing in its own grounds in the beautiful Borrowdale valley. The house is very well furnished and offers spacious en suite bedrooms, together with two delightful lounges, both ▶

*with log fires. An excellent four-course dinner is provided
every evening.*
10rm(9⇨1♠) (1fb)⊁in all bedrooms ® ✶
sB&B⇨♠£30.50 dB&B⇨♠£61-£67 WB&B£112-£133
WBDi£185.50-£206.50 LDO 5pm
Lic ▥ CTV 15P ⓔ

GH QQ **Mary Mount Hotel** CA12 5UU (Stakis)
☎Keswick(07687) 77223 Telex no 64305 FAX (07687) 77343
Mar-Oct
*Under the same management as the nearby Lodore Swiss Hotel,
this small hotel stands near the peaceful lake. The en suite
bedrooms are well equipped and there is a cosy bar, a comfortable
lounge and spacious dining room.*
7⇨♠ Annexe 6⇨ CTV in all bedrooms ® ✶
sB&B⇨♠£33.50-£37.50 dB&B⇨♠£50-£58 WB&B£234.50-
£262.50
Lic ▥ 40P
Credit Cards ①②③⑤
See advertisement under KESWICK

BORTH Dyfed Map **06** SN68

GH QQ **Glanmor Hotel** Princess St SY24 5JP ☎(0970) 871689
*This small hotel stands opposite the seafront with a safe, sandy
beach, a few yards from the local golf club. Run by the very
friendly Elliott family, the bedrooms are neat and comfortable and
there is a cosy bar for residents.*
7rm(2♠5hc) (3fb) CTV in 4 bedrooms ® sB&B£16 dB&B£32
dB&B♠£32 WB&B£112 WBDi£164.50 LDO 5pm
Lic CTV 10P 2🖼 ⓔ

BOSCASTLE Cornwall & Isles of Scilly Map **02** SX09

GH QQ *Belvedere House* Tintagel Rd PL35 0AB
☎(0840) 250683
rs Nov-Mar
*A large Victorian stone house in the upper part of the village,
reputed to have been built by Thomas Hardy. Bedrooms are all
spacious, well equipped and furnished in keeping with the age of
the building ; there is a ground floor bedroom available. Dinner is
served in the conservatory dining room, and lunches and cream
teas are available. There is ample car parking.*
5⇨♠ (5fb) CTV in all bedrooms ® LDO 9pm
Lic ▥ CTV 10P ⚗

Credit Cards ①③

GH QQ **Lower Meadows House** Penally Hill PL35 0HF
☎(0840) 250570
*A detached modern house located next to the main village car
park, with views of the Valency valley. The simply furnished
bedrooms are on the ground floor. Meals are served all day and
cater for vegans, vegetarians and children as well as snacks and a
full à la carte menu. Children and pets are welcome.*
5hc (2fb)⊁in 1 bedroom sB&B£14-£30 dB&B£25-£38
WB&B£82.50-£110.50 LDO 9.30pm
Lic ▥ CTV ✗

Credit Cards ①③ ⓔ

🖼📺**GH** QQ **Melbourne House** New Rd PL35 0DH
☎(0840) 250650
*A charming Victorian house in a commanding position overlooking
the Jordan valley and village. Tastefully restored, its character has
been retained, and the en suite bedrooms are comfortable and the
well furnished drawing room has an open fire, and in the simply
appointed dining room imaginative meals are served using fresh
local produce.*
6rm(1⇨2♠3hc) CTV in all bedrooms ® sB&B£12-£14
dB&B£24-£28 dB&B♠£30-£34 WB&B£84-£119
WBDi£129-£164 LDO 6pm

Lic ▥ 8P nc
Credit Cards ①③ ⓔ

GH QQQ **Old Coach House** Tintagel Rd PL35 0AS
☎(0840) 250398
Closed 23 Dec-2 Jan rs Nov-Mar
*This 300-year-old coaching inn has been skilfully converted to
provide modern facilities, whilst retaining the original character.
Bedrooms are well equipped and furnished and include 2 ground
floor rooms designed with the disabled in mind. The rear
conservatory dining room has views over a wooded valley, and
there is a cosy lounge. The owners have recently purchased the
adjoining property, and are building additional en suite rooms.
There is parking on site.*
6rm(1⇨5♠) (1fb) CTV in all bedrooms ® ✶ (ex guide dogs)
sB&B⇨♠£15-£22 dB&B⇨♠£30-£44 WB&B£84-£139
WBDi£150-£205 LDO 11am
Lic ▥ 7P nc6yrs
Credit Cards ①②③

GH QQQ **St Christophers Country House Hotel** High St
PL35 0BD ☎(0840) 250412
Mar-Oct & Xmas
*Set on a steep hill in a residential area, this family-run hotel has
warm, comfortable bedrooms and a dining room where home-
cooked meals, in generous portions, are served. After dinner, guests
can relax in the lounge.*
9rm(7♠2hc) CTV in 2 bedrooms ® sB&B£15-£16 sB&B♠£17-
£18 dB&B£30-£32 dB&B♠£34-£36 WB&B£105-£126
WBDi£148-£167 LDO 8pm
Lic ▥ CTV 8P nc12yrs
Credit Cards ①③ ⓔ

GH QQ **Tolcarne Hotel** Tintagel Rd PL35 0AS
☎(0840) 250654
Etr-Oct
*A substantial Victorian stone house with spectacular views of the
Headland. Bedrooms are well equipped and comfortable. Home-
cooked dinners are served nightly and provide good value for
money, and guests are made to feel very welcome by the owners.*
9rm(8⇨♠1hc) (1fb) CTV in all bedrooms ® ✶ sB&B£16-£21
sB&B⇨♠£19-£21 dB&B⇨♠£32-£38 WBDi£158-£167
LDO 5.30pm
Lic ▥ CTV 15P croquet
Credit Cards ①②③

BOSTON SPA West Yorkshire Map **08** SE44

INN QQQ *The Royal Hotel* 182 High St LS23 7AY
☎(0937) 842142
*A comfortable hotel in the centre of the village, very convenient for
the A1. Bedrooms are especially well furnished, and there is a good
range of food available in either the bar or the carvery restaurant.*
13⇨♠ CTV in all bedrooms ® ✶ (ex guide dogs) LDO 10pm
▥ 60P
Credit Cards ①②③⑤

BOURNEMOUTH Dorset Map **04** SZ09

See Town Plan Section
See also Christchurch and Poole
GH Q **Albemarle Private Hotel** BH2 5PH ☎(0202) 551351
*Close to the International Centre, shops and sea, this terraced
Victorian house offers simply furnished, compact bedrooms, a
comfortable lounge and neat dining room.*
12rm(5♠7hc) (3fb) CTV in all bedrooms ® ✶ (ex guide dogs)
✶ sB&B£14-£18 sB&B♠£16.50-£20.50 dB&B£28-£36
dB&B♠£33-£41 WB&B£84-£123 WBDi£120-£159 LDO 11am
Lic ▥ CTV ✗
Credit Cards ①③ ⓔ

GH 🇶🇶 **Alum Bay Hotel** 19 Burnaby Rd BH4 8JF
☎(0202) 761034
A few minutes' walk from Alum Chine and the beach, this Victorian house with its resident proprietors, offers well-equipped, comfortable bedrooms.
12rm(2⇨5🟦5hc) (4fb) CTV in all bedrooms ® sB&B£17-£20.50 sB&B⇨🟦£19.50-£23 dB&B£30-£37 dB&B⇨🟦£35-£42 WB&B£90-£111 WBDi£129-£162 LDO noon
Lic ஊ CTV 10P
Credit Cards 1 3 £

See advertisement on page 81

GH 🇶🇶🇶 *Alum Grange Hotel* 1 Burnaby Rd, Alum Chine
BH4 8JF ☎(0202) 761195
A well run hotel with enthusiastic and welcoming proprietors. The bedrooms are freshly decorated and have modern facilities. There is a bar and sun lounge as well as a smart dining room where a short à la carte menu supplements the daily table d'hote.
14rm(4⇨6🟦4hc) (5fb) CTV in all bedrooms ® LDO noon
Lic ஊ CTV 10P
Credit Cards 3

GH 🇶🇶🇶 **Amitie** 1247 Christchurch Rd BH7 6BP
☎(0202) 427255
A small, friendly guesthouse well situated between Christchurch and Bournemouth, near the shops and sea. The bedrooms have been refurbished to a high standard, with good quality beds, and are neat and very well equipped.
8rm(2⇨2🟦4hc) (2fb) CTV in all bedrooms ®
✈ (ex guide dogs) ✳ sB&B£12-£16 sB&B⇨🟦£13.50-£17 dB&B£24-£30 dB&B⇨🟦£27-£32 WB&B£84-£92
ஊ 8P nc3yrs £

Book as early as possible for busy holiday periods.

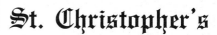

Bournemouth

GH Q Q **Braemar Private Hotel** 30 Glen Rd BH5 1HS
☎(0202) 396054
Mar-Oct
*A well established, gabled hotel, quietly situated in a pleasant
residential area near Boscombe Pier. Simple, seaside family
accommodation is provided by the Whitehurst family, with many
of their guests returning every year.*
10rm(1⇔5ℕ4hc) (4fb) CTV in all bedrooms ® ⌘ ✳
sB&B£16-£20 sB&B⇔ℕ£18.50-£22.50 dB&B£32-£40
dB&B⇔ℕ£37-£45 (incl dinner) WBDi£110-£150 (wkly only
Jul & Aug) LDO 6pm
Lic ⴲ CTV 6P

GH Q Q **Carisbrooke Hotel** BH2 5NT ☎(0202) 290432
Telex no 310499
Feb-Dec
*A modern hotel conveniently located for the shops with well
equipped bedrooms and an attractive dining room. It caters mainly
for family holidays.*
22rm(19⇔ℕ3hc) (6fb) CTV in all bedrooms ®
⌘ (ex guide dogs) sB&B£22-£27 sB&B⇔ℕ£30-£35
dB&B⇔ℕ£54-£64 WB&B£150-£180 WBDi£165-£190
LDO 7pm
Lic ⴲ CTV 18P
Credit Cards ① ② ③ ⓔ

SELECTED

GH Q Q Q Q *Cliff House Hotel* 113 Alumhurst Rd
BH4 8HS ☎(0202) 763003
Mar-Nov & Xmas
*This spacious guesthouse sits high above the sea at Alum
Chine, and some rooms have private balconies from which
guests can enjoy spectacular sea views. The large light rooms
are spotlessly clean and well furnished, and bedrooms are also
spacious, with private bathrooms and tea and coffee-making
facilities. The licensed restaurant serves a good choice of main
courses and desserts if ordered in advance, and private
parking is provided at the rear.*
12rm(2⇔9ℕ1hc) (4fb) CTV in all bedrooms ® ⌘
LDO 6.30pm
Lic lift ⴲ 12P nc7yrs snooker

GH Q Q **Cransley Private Hotel** 11 Knyveton Rd BH1 3QG
☎(0202) 290067
Apr-Oct
*This detached house is in a quiet location and has a neat garden
and parking space. Well-equipped bedrooms are complemented by
a comfortable lounge and dining room.*
12rm(10⇔ℕ2hc) (2fb) CTV in all bedrooms ® ✳ sB&B£13-
£24 sB&B⇔ℕ£15-£24 dB&B£26-£48 dB&B⇔ℕ£30-£48
WB&B£75-£110 WBDi£100-£149
Lic CTV 10P
Credit Cards ① ③ ⓔ

GH Q Q Q *Croham Hurst Hotel* 9 Durley Rd South BH2 5JH
☎(0202) 552353
Closed Jan
*The attractive public rooms at Croham Hurst include the luxury of
an air-conditioned dining room. There are lounges and a bar
where evening entertainment is sometimes provided. Some bedrms
have modern furnishings, while the traditionally furnished rooms
are more spacious. Resident proprietors Mr and Mrs Brown make
thier guests very welcome.*
40⇔ℕ (7fb) CTV in all bedrooms ® ⌘ LDO 7.15pm
Lic lift ⴲ 20P
Credit Cards ① ③

Visit your local AA Shop.

GH Q Q **Derwent House** 36 Hamilton Rd BH1 4EH
☎(0202) 309102
*This detached Victorian house is conveniently placed for shopping
in Boscombe. The bedrooms are freshly decorated and some have
their own, modern, bathrooms. There is a small TV lounge and a
separate, larger bar/lounge.*
9rm(4ℕ5hc) (3fb) CTV in all bedrooms ® sB&B£14-£16
sB&Bℕ£16-£18 dB&B£28-£36 dB&Bℕ£32-£40 WB&B£80-
£110 WBDi£110-£130 LDO 5pm
Lic ⴲ CTV 10P
Credit Cards ① ③ ⓔ

GH Q Q Q **Golden Sands Hotel** BH4 8HR ☎(0202) 763832
Mar-Oct & Xmas
*Close to Alum Chine, this well maintained and nicely presented
guesthouse offers bright and clean bedrooms, reasonably equipped
in addition to a comfortable, traditional lounge and dining
room. A home-cooked evening meal is offered and the resident
proprietors take pride in running this small hotel.*
11⇔ℕ (2fb) CTV in all bedrooms ® ⌘ (ex guide dogs)
sB&B⇔ℕ£20.40-£26.40 dB&B⇔ℕ£40.80-£46.80
WB&B£112-£143 WBDi£135-£178 LDO 4pm
Lic ⴲ 10P nc3yrs

GH Q Q **Hawaiian Hotel** 4 Glen Rd BH5 1HR ☎(0202) 393234
mid Apr-Oct
*A well established hotel where an older clientèle return year after
year to enjoy the quiet atmosphere and genial company of the
resident proprietors.*
12rm(8⇔ℕ4hc) (3fb) CTV in all bedrooms ®
⌘ (ex guide dogs) ✳ sB&B£17-£19 sB&B⇔ℕ£19-£22
dB&B£34-£38 dB&B⇔ℕ£38-£44 WB&Bfr£112 WBDifr£142
LDO 6pm
Lic ⴲ CTV 7P

GH Q Q Q **Highclere Hotel** 15 Burnaby Rd BH4 8JF
☎(0202) 761350
Apr-Sep
*A neat, well maintained Victorian hotel near the sea. Bedrooms
are freshly decorated and well cared for, with good private
bathrooms. A choice of dishes for each course of every meal is
offered, and families on holiday with children are encouraged.
Alum Chine and the beach are within an easy walk.*
9rm(4⇔5ℕ) (5fb) CTV in all bedrooms ® sB&B⇔ℕ£21.50-
£23.50 dB&B⇔ℕ£43-£47 WB&B£140.50-£161.50 WBDi£145-
£164 LDO 4pm
Lic ⴲ CTV 7P nc3yrs ♨
Credit Cards ① ② ③ ⓔ

GH Q Q Q **Holmcroft Hotel** 5 Earle Rd BH4 8JQ
☎(0202) 761289
*Close to Alum Chine, this well presented, neat hotel is owned by
young, friendly proprietors. Bedrooms are bright, clean and well
equipped, whilst public areas are comfortably laid out, with plenty
of green plants and personal ornaments giving the hotel a warm,
welcoming feel. A home-cooked evening meal is offered in an
attractive dining room.*
19⇔ℕ (3fb) CTV in all bedrooms ® sB&B⇔ℕ£27.50-£33
dB&B⇔ℕ£55-£66 (incl dinner) WB&B£126-£157.50
WBDi£157-£178 LDO 5pm
Lic ⴲ CTV 13P
Credit Cards ① ③ ⓔ

GH Q Q **Kelmor Lodge** 30 Stourcliffe Av, Southbourne
BH6 3PT ☎(0202) 424061
*In a pleasant residential area close to the sea, this small family
hotel has cosy bedrooms, a lounge and a nicely appointed dining
room.*
8rm(2⇔ℕ6hc) (1fb) CTV in all bedrooms ® ⌘ ✳
sB&B£12.25-£15 dB&B£22.50-£28 dB&B⇔ℕ£25.50-£31 (incl
dinner) WB&B£76-£95 WBDi£101-£119 (wkly only Aug)
LDO 9am
Lic ⴲ CTV 6P nc8yrs
Credit Cards ③

GH Q Q Q *Linwood House Hotel* BH5 1ND ☎(0202) 397818
Mar-Oct
A detached house with a neat garden, in a quiet residential area near the beach and Boscombe. Bedrooms are simply furnished but are cosy, clean and well kept. There is a spacious comfortable lounge and the smart dining room has a small bar.
10rm(5↑5hc) (2fb) CTV in 3 bedrooms TV in 1 bedroom ® ✗ (wkly only mid Jun-mid Sep)
Lic ♨ CTV 7P nc6yrs

GH Q Q Q *Lynthwaite Hotel* 10 Owls Rd BH5 1AF
☎(0202) 398015
This Victorian villa, with a first floor lounge and balcony, is situated close to the shops and the sea. The newly decorated and furnished bedrooms are of a high standard, offering both comfort and modern facilities.
14rm(10⇌1↑3hc) (3fb) CTV in all bedrooms ® ✗
sB&B£13.50-£17 sB&B⇌↑£16.50-£21 dB&B£27-£34
dB&B⇌↑£34-£42 WB&B£99-£129 WBDi£139-£168
LDO 5pm
Lic ♨ CTV 17P nc3yrs
Credit Cards ① ② ③ ⓔ

GH Q *Mae-Mar Private Hotel* 91/95 West Hill Rd BH2 5PQ
☎(0202) 553167
In the heart of West Cliff hotel area.
43rm(2⇌24↑17hc) (12fb) CTV in all bedrooms ®
LDO 5.30pm
Lic lift ♨ CTV
Credit Cards ① ③

✉🖙 **GH** Q Q *Mayfield Private Hotel* 46 Frances Rd BH1 3SA
☎(0202) 551839
Closed Dec
A small, well established, personally run hotel catering for a regular clientèle. The bedrooms have modern furnishings and are well equipped, and public rooms are comfortable. The Mayfield ▶

Highclere Hotel

- All bedrooms have en suite facilities ⅄BHRA
- Private telephones all bedrooms
- Colour TV/radio all bedrooms
- Licensed   **AA** Listed
- Children very welcome over the age of three
- Free tea making facilities all bedrooms
- 4 minutes walk to the beach
- Children's sunny playroom with toy box
- Ample free parking ■ Garden with play area
- Sea views

English Tourist Board **COMMENDED** ♛♛♛

Terms: Half Board from £145 per week inclusive
Delicious choice of menu for all meals
Brochure from: David and Averil Baldwin
15 Burnaby Road, Bournemouth BH14 8JF
Telephone: (0202) 761350

Bournemouth

easily distinguished by its abundant hanging baskets and garden gnomes.
8rm(4♠4hc) (1fb) CTV in all bedrooms ® sB&B£12-£15 dB&B£24-£35 dB&B♠£29-£35 WB&B£70-£80 WBDi£94-£117 (wkly only 2wks-Jul/Aug) LDO 9am
Lic ⁿ CTV 5P nc7yrs ©

GH |Q||Q||Q| Naseby-Nye Hotel Byron Rd BH5 1JD
☎(0202) 394079
A large, detached, brick-built house with neat, colourful gardens, close to the cliff top and Boscombe promenade. The two lounges are comfortable and well furnished, with antiques and fresh flowers. The dining room is spacious and houses a small bar. Bedrooms are old-fashioned but clean and comfortable, and the owners continue to welcome guests returning year after year for the peace and tranquillity their home provides.
13rm(3⇌10hc) (1fb) LDO 7pm
Lic ⁿ CTV 12P nc5yrs

GH |Q||Q| New Dorchester Hotel 64 Lansdowne Rd North
BH1 1RS ☎(0202) 551271
Closed 24 Dec-4 Jan
A Victorian villa with a garden and parking, not far from the town centre. Public rooms are smart and comfortable. Bedrooms vary in size with some smaller single rooms, but beds are comfortable.
7rm(3⇌1♠3hc) CTV in all bedrooms ® ✈ ✳ sB&B£15-£17 sB&B⇌♠£23-£27 dB&B⇌♠£30-£37 WB&B£90-£112 WBDi£140-£162 LDO 6pm
Lic ⁿ 10P nc12yrs
Credit Cards [1][2][3][5]

GH |Q||Q| Newfield Private Hotel 29 Burnaby Rd BH4 8JF
☎(0202) 762724
A cheerful holiday guesthouse close to Alum Chine and the beach. Inexpensively furnished bedrooms are complemented by the nicely decorated lounge and dining room.
12rm(1⇌5♠6hc) (3fb) CTV in all bedrooms ®
Lic ⁿ CTV 4P

|✈✈| GH |Q| Norland Private Hotel 6 Westby Rd BH5 1HD
☎(0202) 396729
A semi-detached Victorian house situated close to Boscombe's shopping centre. Inexpensive, comfortable accommodation is provided : bedrooms are small but well maintained and freshly decorated. The lounge is spacious and has a TV, and the dining room has a bar.
9rm(3⇌♠6hc) (2fb) CTV in all bedrooms ® sB&B£13-£17 dB&B£26-£34 dB&B⇌♠£30-£38 WB&B£85-£110 WBDi£105-£130 LDO 4.30pm
Lic ⁿ CTV 8P ©

GH |Q||Q| Northover Private Hotel 10 Earle Rd BH4 8JQ
☎(0202) 767349
Apr-Oct & Xmas
Not far from Alum Chine, this small, family-run hotel has simply furnished bedrooms, some with en suite facilities. The public lounge is comfortable and drinks may be ordered from reception.
10rm(6♠4hc) (6fb) ® ✳ sB&B£16-£20 sB&B♠£18-£24 dB&B£32-£40 dB&B♠£36-£48 WB&B£98-£120 WBDi£140-£170 LDO 5pm
Lic ⁿ CTV 11P nc3yrs ©

GH |Q||Q| Oak Hall Private Hotel 9 Wilfred Rd BH5 1ND
☎(0202) 395062
Nov-1 Oct
This detached house is in a pleasant area of the resort, between the shops and the popular sandy beaches. Its modern facilities are combined with a traditional style of comfort offered by the hospitable proprietors.
13rm(1⇌8♠4hc) (2fb) CTV in all bedrooms ® (wkly only mid Jun-end Aug) LDO 3pm
Lic ⁿ CTV 9P
Credit Cards [1][3]

GH |Q||Q| St John's Lodge Hotel 10 St Swithun's Rd South
BH1 3RQ ☎(0202) 290677
A family-run hotel in a central location close to the railway and bus stations, and within walking distance of the Chine and pier. Bedrooms vary in size and are simply furnished but freshly decorated, and some have private bathrooms. Public rooms are pleasant, with a spacious dining room and a cocktail bar.
15rm(5♠10hc) (2fb) CTV in all bedrooms ® ✈ LDO 4pm
Lic ⁿ CTV 14P sauna jacuzzi
Credit Cards [1][3]

GH |Q||Q| Sea-Dene Hotel 10 Burnaby Rd BH4 8JF
☎(0202) 761372
Mar-Oct & Xmas
A small, friendly hotel close to the beach at Alum Chine, with forecourt parking. Bedrooms are neat and clean and there is a comfortable lounge. The good quality home cooking entices guests to return.
7rm(5♠2hc) (3fb) CTV in all bedrooms ® ✈ (ex guide dogs) ✳ sB&B£13-£16 dB&B£26-£32 dB&B♠£32-£36 WB&B£84-£119 WBDi£128-£155 (wkly only mid Jul-mid Sep) LDO 6.30pm
Lic ⁿ CTV 4P nc3yrs
Credit Cards [1][3]

GH |Q||Q||Q| Silver Trees Hotel BH3 7AL ☎(0202) 556040
An elegant Victorian house in neatly manicured gardens offering outstanding comfort. The attractive lounge and dining room are both well furnished and spacious bedrooms provide quality beds and deep armchairs. Resident proprietors Jo and Bill Smith create an informal and hospitable atmosphere.
8rm(5♠3hc) (2fb)⤴in 4 bedrooms CTV in all bedrooms ✈ dB&B£38-£40 dB&B♠£40-£42
ⁿ 10P nc3yrs
Credit Cards [1][3]

GH |Q||Q| Hotel Sorrento 16 Owls Rd BH5 1AG
☎(0202) 394019
rs Xmas
Situated half way between the Boscombe shopping area and the pier, this holiday hotel has an informal, relaxed atmosphere. A smart bar, TV lounge and attractive restaurant complement the bedrooms, which vary in size.
17rm(12⇌5hc) (5fb) CTV in all bedrooms ® sB&B£14-£19 sB&B⇌♠£16.50-£21.50 dB&B£28-£38 dB&B⇌♠£33-£43 WB&B£83-£135.50 WBDi£125-£177.50 LDO 6pm
Lic ⁿ CTV 19P nc2yrs solarium gymnasium
Credit Cards [1][3] ©

GH |Q||Q||Q| Tudor Grange Hotel BH1 3EE ☎(0202) 291472 & 291463
Mar-Dec
Mr and Mrs Heeley's mock-Tudor house, set in pleasant gardens, has panelled public rooms and ornate moulded ceilings. There is a lounge, bar and dining room. The comfortable bedrooms have well-maintained modern facilities.
12rm(11⇌1hc) (4fb) CTV in all bedrooms ® ✳ sB&B£21-£25.25 sB&B⇌♠£23.50-£27.75 dB&B£42-£50.50 dB&B⇌♠£47-£55.50 WB&B£133-£174 WBDi£180-£221 LDO 7pm
Lic ⁿ CTV 11P
Credit Cards [1][3]

GH |Q||Q||Q| Valberg Hotel 1a Wollstonecraft Rd BH5 1JQ
☎(0202) 394644
An unusual looking house with a Spanish style exterior, quietly situated in a pleasant area close to the sea and shops. Clean and freshly decorated bedrooms provide en suite facilities together with comfortable beds ; the top 2 bedrooms have access to a large balcony. The lounge and dining room , with a small bar, overlook the attractive garden.

10☎ (2fb) CTV in all bedrooms ® ✗ ✳ dB&B☎£30-£40
WB&B£90-£120 WBDi£139-£169 LDO 12pm
Lic ⑭ CTV 9P nc4yrs

GH ⓠⓠⓠ Weavers Hotel 14 Wilfred Rd BH5 1ND
☎(0202) 397871
Apr-Oct
*This is a well presented 1920s detached house, freshly decorated
throughout and with high standards of house keeping. There is a
small quiet lounge in addition to the smart bar lounge and light
spacious dining room. Bedrooms vary a little in size but most have
modern fully tiled showers. Situated in a tree- lined street in a
pleasant residential area, it is close to Boscombe's shops and beach.*
7rm(6☎1hc) (1fb) CTV in all bedrooms ® ✗ sB&B£18.50-£20
dB&B☎£37-£40 (incl dinner) WB&B£100-£130 WBDi£125-
£135 (wkly only mid May-mid Sep) LDO 5pm
Lic ⑭ 7P nc7yrs ⓔ

GH ⓠⓠⓠ West Dene Private Hotel 117 Alumhurst Rd
BH4 8HS ☎(0202) 764843
Mar-Oct
*Set at the foot of Alum Chine, this well-presented private hotel
overlooks the sea and has nicely equipped, modern bedrooms.*
17rm(5⇄7☎5hc) (4fb) CTV in 15 bedrooms ® ✗ ✳ sB&B£23
dB&B£46 dB&B⇄☎£53 WB&B£138-£159 WBDi£183-£225
LDO 3.30pm
Lic ⑭ CTV 17P nc4yrs
Credit Cards ①②③⑤

GH ⓠⓠ Woodford Court Hotel 19-21 Studland Rd BH4 8HZ
☎(0202) 764907 FAX (0202) 761214
Mar-Nov & 21-31 Dec
*This family-managed establishment is in a residential area near
Alum Chine. With the recent purchase of the adjacent property the
hotel now has en suite bedrooms and busy public lounges and bars.*
35rm(8⇄18☎9hc) (11fb) CTV in all bedrooms ® sB&B£17-
£21 sB&B⇄☎£17-£21 dB&B£34-£42 dB&B⇄☎£34-£42
WB&B£117.50-£139 WBDi£147-£188 LDO 6.15pm
Lic ⑭ CTV 18P nc2yrs
Credit Cards ①②③ⓔ

GH ⓠⓠ Woodlands Hotel 28 Percy Rd, Boscombe BH5 1JG
☎(0202) 396499
*A pretty house in a quiet residential area quite close to the sea with
individually decorated bedrooms. The dining room and bar have
recently been refurbished and there is a cosy lounge.*
11rm(5☎6hc) (3fb) CTV in all bedrooms ® sB&B£15.50-£19
sB&B☎£18.50-£24.50 dB&B£31-£36 dB&B☎£36-£41
WB&B£105-£140 WBDi£145-£195 LDO 6.15pm
Lic ⑭ CTV 7P
Credit Cards ①③ ⓔ

GH ⓠⓠⓠ Wood Lodge Hotel 10 Manor Rd BH1 3EY
☎(0202) 290891
Etr-Oct
*Peaceful and elegant house opposite East Cliff with attentive
service and good accommodation.*
15rm(7⇄7☎1hc) (5fb) CTV in all bedrooms ® LDO 6pm
Lic ⑭ CTV 12P 9 hole putting green
Credit Cards ①③

BOVEY TRACEY Devon Map **03** SX87

GH ⓠ Blenheim Hotel Brimley Rd TQ13 9DH ☎(0626) 832422
rs 25 & 26 Dec
*This fine detached Victorian house is situated within its own
secluded grounds and gardens on the outskirts of the village. There
is a choice of comfortable lounges and the bedrooms are simply
appointed and bright.*
5hc (1fb) CTV in 4 bedrooms sB&B£19.50-£21 dB&B£39-£42
WB&B£120-£130 WBDi£195-£210 LDO 7.30pm
Lic ⑭ CTV 8P ⓔ

FH ⓠⓠⓠⓠ Mrs H Roberts **Willmead** *(SX795812)*
TQ13 9NP ☎Lustleigh(06477) 214
Closed Xmas & New Year
*A private road through meadows leads to a fairytale setting on
the edge of Dartmoor and this delightful thatched and oak-
beamed 14th-century farmhouse. Inglenook fireplaces and a
minstrel's gallery are features of the house, and resident
proprietor Mrs Roberts has carefully decorated and furnished
the comfortable lounge and well equipped bedrooms in keeping
with its character. Guests eat at one antique table in the dining
room, where breakfast only is served, and they are requested
not to smoke. There is a distinct feeling of peace about
Willmead and a warm welcome is assured.*
3rm(1☎2hc) ✗in all bedrooms ✗ ✳ dB&B£38
dB&B☎£43 WB&Bfr£133
⑭ CTV P nc10yrs 32 acres beef

BOWNESS-ON-WINDERMERE Cumbria

See **Windermere**

BRADFORD West Yorkshire Map **07** SE13

GH ⓠⓠ Maple Hill Hotel 3 Park Dr, Heaton BD9 4DP
☎(0274) 544061 FAX (0274) 481154
*Set in a quiet residential area about 2 miles from the city centre,
this well furnished Victorian house offers good home comforts and
service.*
12rm(2☎10hc) (1fb)✗in 1 bedroom CTV in all bedrooms ®
sB&Bfr£33.60 sB&B☎fr£40.06 dB&Bfr£46.53
dB&B☎fr£52.99 WB&B£235.20-£280.42 WBDi£319.20-
£364.42
Lic ⑭ 20P 2🎱 half size snooker table
Credit Cards ①③ ⓔ

Silver Trees
Touring Hotel
**57 Wimborne Road,
Bournemouth, BH3 7AL.**
Telephone: Bournemouth (0202) 556040

At Silver Trees we offer bed and breakfast luxury for the guest
who wants that little extra comfort whilst away from home.
Our charming Victorian period house with its elegantly
furnished bedrooms, residents lounge and dining room com-
pliments the warmth of the welcome and hospitality extended
to your guest. Our comfortable double and twin bedded
rooms have ensuite facilities, central heating and colour
television. For that special occasion or extended stay we also
offer a private suite, which includes a double bedroom and
your own sitting room. Early morning tea, evening snacks and
refreshments served in your room are available on request.
Mini-breaks available – Parking for ten cars. **Resident Proprietors: Joanna and Bill Smith.**

FH Q Q Q Mr & Mrs Priestley **Brow Top** *(SD112310)*
Baldwin Lanem, Clayton BD14 6PS ☎(0274) 882178
Closed Xmas
*A delightfully converted barn and cottage set in open countryside,
only 15 minutes from Bradford city centre. Bedrooms have lovely
soft furnishings, and the guesthouse is full of character.*
3⇆ (1fb) CTV in all bedrooms ® ✗ (ex guide dogs)
sB&B⇆£18 dB&B⇆£28
♥♥ CTV 4P 300 acres beef dairy

INN Q Q **New Beehive** 171 Westgate BD1 3AA
☎(0274) 721784
*This popular and busy pub is situated just on the edge of the city
centre. Bedrooms are pleasantly furnished and offer good value for
money. There is a good range of bar meals, and ample car parking
is available.*
7rm(1⇆6♠) (2fb) CTV in all bedrooms ® ✗ (ex guide dogs)
✳ sB&B⇆no♠£18-£26 ✳ Lunch fr£5 Dinner fr£5 LDO 8.30pm
♥♥ 20P
Credit Cards ③

BRADFORD ON AVON Wiltshire Map 03 ST86

SELECTED

GH Q Q Q Q **Bradford Old Windmill** 4 Masons Ln
BA15 1QN ☎(0225) 866842
*A former windmill built in 1806 which has been lovingly
restored. The four bedrooms are delightful, decorated in
country style with old pine furniture; one has a round bed,
another a water bed. The comfortable lounge has a large log
fire and no TV; the dining room is furnished with stripped pine
and a communal table. Dinner is served at 8pm, only by prior
arrangement, on certain nights; the set menu offers ethnic
vegetarian food and might include dishes from the Gambia,
Mexico or the Caribbean. Breakfast ranges from English,
American or continental and is carefully prepared and
beautifully presented. Smoking is not permittted in this
unusual home which provides a wealth of books and objets
d'art to interest guests.*
4rm(1⇆2♠1hc) (2fb)✄in all bedrooms CTV in all
bedrooms ® ✗ ✳ sB&B£27-£30 sB&B⇆♠£37-£50
dB&B£34-£40 dB&B⇆♠£54-£59 WB&B£120-£190
LDO previous day
♥♥ 4P nc5yrs ⓔ

SELECTED

GH Q Q Q Q **Widbrook Grange** Trowbridge Rd
BA15 1UH ☎(02216) 3173 & 2899 FAX (02216) 2890
Closed Xmas & New Year
*An attractive 18th-century farmhouse, one mile from the town
on the Trowbridge road, yet set in rolling countryside. The
house is impressive and very comfortable, with attractively
furnished bedrooms, complemented by thoughtful extras and
period furnishings; some of the bedrooms are outside in a
recently converted stable block.*
4rm(3⇆♠1hc) Annexe 11⇆♠ (2fb)✄in 4 bedrooms
CTV in all bedrooms ® ✗ ✳ sB&Bfr£25 dB&B⇆♠£55-
£75 LDO noon (not Fri, Sat or Sun)
Lic ♥♥ 50P 10☜
Credit Cards ① ② ③ ⓔ

Q is for quality. For a full explanation of this AA quality
award, consult the Contents page.

BRAEMAR Grampian *Aberdeenshire* Map 15 NO19

GH Q **Callater Lodge Hotel** 9 Glenshee Rd AB3 5YQ
☎(03397) 41275
Closed mid Oct-26 Dec
*This family-run hotel offers the holidaymaker good value and
practical accommodation. It is set in its own grounds on the edge of
the village, overlooking the surrounding hills.*
9rm(2♠7hc) (1fb) ® LDO 7pm
Lic ♥♥ CTV 14P
Credit Cards ① ③

BRAITHWAITE Cumbria Map 11 NY22

GH Q Q Q **Maple Bank** CA12 5RY ☎(07687) 78229
Closed mid Nov-mid Dec
*A double-fronted, detached Edwardian country house situated in
attractive gardens, with fine views towards Skiddaw. Bedrooms
are attractively decorated, comfortable and well appointed, with
private bathrooms. The house is located just off the A66: turn at
the sign to Thornthwaite Gallery, then turn right and it is on the
left hand side.*
7♠ (1fb) CTV in all bedrooms ® ✗ LDO 4pm
♥♥ CTV 10P nc8yrs
See advertisement under KESWICK

BRAMBER West Sussex Map 04 TQ11

INN Q **The Castle Hotel** The Street BN4 3WE
☎Steyning(0903) 812102 & 815993
Closed Xmas & 26 Dec
*This is a popular and lively village inn which offers a good
standard of bar food and also has an à la carte restaurant. The
accommodation is functional and in keeping with the style.*
8rm(3♠5hc) (2fb) CTV in 5 bedrooms ® ✗ (ex guide dogs)
LDO 9.45pm
♥♥ 30P 2☜ ⌂
Credit Cards ③
See advertisement under STEYNING

BRAMLEY South Yorkshire Map 08 SK49

GH Q Q Q **Stonecroft** Main St, S66 0SF (4m E of Rotherham)
☎Rotherham(0709) 540922
*Standing in walled gardens, this ivy-clad house is comfortable and
well furnished with antiques. The tasteful accommodation includes
well-appointed bedrooms.*
4rm(1⇆♠3hc) Annexe 5⇆ (1fb) CTV in all bedrooms ®
sB&B£20-£24 sB&B⇆♠£24-£29 dB&B£30-£35
dB&B⇆♠£35-£39
Lic ♥♥ CTV 10P ⓔ

BRAMPTON Cumbria Map 12 NY56

See also Castle Carrock and Kirkcambeck
GH Q Q **Oakwood Park Hotel** Longtown Rd CA8 2AP
☎(06977) 2436
*A Victorian country house situated amongst parkland just off the
A6071, only a short distance from the town centre. Bedrooms all
have private bathrooms and colour TV. The comfortable lounge
has an open fire, and there is a library bar in which cocktails are
served.*
4rm(1⇆3♠) (1fb)✄in all bedrooms CTV in all bedrooms ®
✗ (ex guide dogs) ✳ sB&B⇆♠£23.50 dB&B⇆♠£33
WB&B£99 WBDi£159 LDO 8pm
Lic ♥♥ CTV 7P ♪(hard)
Credit Cards ① ③

INN Q Q Q **The Blacksmiths Arms** Talkin Village CA8 1LE
☎(06977) 3452
*Situated two miles south east of Brampton, this charming inn,
under the supervision of proprietors Pat and Tom Bagshaw, has
well appointed and attractively decorated bedrooms, all with full
en suite facilities. Good home-cooked meals are served.*

5rm(3⇄2♠) CTV in all bedrooms ® ✖ (ex guide dogs)
LDO 9pm
12P games room
Credit Cards ①③

BRAMSHAW Hampshire Map **04** SU21
INN ⓆⓆ **Bramble Hill Hotel** SO43 7JG
☎Southampton(0703) 813165
Etr or 1 Apr-15 Jan
12rm(7⇄5♠5hc) (3fb) CTV in 9 bedrooms TV in 1 bedroom ®
✳ sB&B£35-£55 sB&B⇄♠£45-£55 dB&B£30-£60
dB&B⇄♠£70-£90 WB&B£220-£285 WBDi£285-£345 ✳
Lunch £6.95-£10&alc Dinner £10-£15&alc LDO 9pm
📖 CTV 70P
Credit Cards ①③

BRANDON Co Durham Map **12** NZ23
INN ⓆⒸ **Bay Horse** DH7 8ST ☎091-378 0498
Off the A690 3 miles from Durham, this traditional stone-built inn
has modern bedrooms in an annexe to the rear. Each has en suite
facilities, TV, telephone and beverage facilities. Bar meals are
served, including Yorkshire pudding with a variety of fillings.
Annexe 4♠ ✕in all bedrooms CTV in all bedrooms ® ✳
sB&B♠£26 dB&B♠£35 ✳ Lunch £1.50-£5.50 Dinner £1.50-
£5.50 LDO 9.30pm
📖 15P
Credit Cards ① Ⓔ
See advertisement under DURHAM

See the regional maps of popular holiday
areas at the back of the book.

TALKIN VILLAGE, BRAMPTON, CUMBRIA
Telephone: BRAMPTON 3452

The Blacksmith's Arms offers all the hospitality
and comforts of a traditional Country Inn.
Enjoy tasty meals served in our bar lounges or
linger over dinner in our well-appointed
restaurant.
We also have five lovely bedrooms all en suite
and offering every comfort.
We guarantee the hospitality you would expect
from a family concern and we can assure you
of a pleasant and comfortable stay.
Peacefully situated in the beautiful village of
Talkin, the Inn is convenient for the Borders,
Hadrian's Wall and the Lake District. Good Golf
course, pony trekking, walking and other
country pursuits nearby.
Personally managed by proprietors Pat and Tom
Bagshaw.

CALLATER LODGE

Braemar, Aberdeenshire AB3 5YQ
Telephone: Braemar (03397) 41275

A small comfortable hotel situated in grounds of over one
acre on the south side of Braemar, with accommodation for
18 persons. All rooms have pleasant views of surrounding
hills, hot & cold water, electric fires, razor sockets, tea &
coffee making facilities and comfortable beds. Some rooms with
private facilities. An ideal centre for climbing, fishing, touring
ski-ing, hang-gliding and an 18-hole golf course nearby. Glenshee
Ski Centre — nine miles and Balmoral — eight miles. Ample
car parking.
Under the personal supervision of the proprietors – Mr
& Mrs W J O Rose.

Widbrook Grange

Trowbridge Road, Bradford-on-Avon
Wiltshire, BA15 1UH
Tel: 02216 4750 & 3173   Fax: 02216 2890

John and Pauline Price extend a warm welcome
to their elegant, peaceful Georgian home in
eleven secluded acres. The house and courtyard
rooms, and the Manvers Suite for conferences,
have been lovingly restored and exquisitely
decorated and furnished with antiques, the
board-meeting room offering an oak table with
twenty-one oak carver chairs, and adjoining
Victorian conservatory.

BRANSGORE Hampshire Map **04** SZ19

GH **Q Q Q** **Tothill House** off Forest Rd ☎(0425) 74414
4rm(1⇨2🛏1hc) ⊁in all bedrooms TV in all bedrooms ®
🏃 (ex guide dogs) ✳ sB&B⇨🛏£20-£25 dB&B⇨🛏£40-£50
WBDi£100-£135
🍽 10P nc18yrs

BRAUNTON Devon Map **02** SS43

GH **Q Q Q** **Alexander Brookdale Hotel** 62 South St EX33 2AN
☎(0271) 812075
*This family-run guesthouse offers excellent value for money, with
prettily decorated bedrooms and cosy public rooms. Mr and Mrs
Sargeant are congenial hosts who upgrade the hotel every season.*
8hc (2fb)⊁in all bedrooms CTV in all bedrooms ®
🏃 (ex guide dogs) sB&B£16-£19 dB&B£30-£36 LDO 11am
Lic 🍽 CTV 9P 2☎ nc8yrs
Credit Cards ②£

FH **Q Q Q** Mr & Mrs Barnes **Denham Farm & Country House**
(SS480404) North Buckland EX33 1HY
☎Croyde(0271) 890297
Closed 18-28 Dec
*This characterful farmhouse has been recently refurbished to
provide bright, well equipped bedrooms with TV and tea-making
facilities and modern en suite bath and shower rooms. Good home-
cooked meals are offered in the informal restaurant. Set in a quiet
village location, this provides a good touring base for north Devon,
with a Championship golf course nearby.*
10⇨🛏 (2fb) CTV in all bedrooms ® 🏃 (ex guide dogs) ✳
dB&B⇨🛏fr£39 WB&Bfr£130 WBDifr£185 (wkly only 18 Jul-
30 Aug) LDO 6pm
Lic CTV 8P 3☎ ♪(grass)160 acres beef

BRECHIN Tayside *Angus* Map **15** NO56

SELECTED

FH **Q Q Q Q** Mrs M Stewart **Blibberhill** *(NO553568)*
DD9 6TH (5m WSW off B9134) ☎Aberlemno(030783) 225
*Peacefully set in the Vale of Strathmore about a mile off the
B9143, Mrs Stewart's delightful 18th-century farmhouse
offers guests a warm welcome. Well maintained tastefully
furnished bedrooms have good modern facilities and a choice
of comfortable lounges includes an attractive sun porch. Good
home cooking is served at the communal dining room table.*
3rm(2⇨🛏1hc) ⊁in all bedrooms ® 🏃 (ex guide dogs) ✳
sB&Bfr£13 dB&Bfr£24 dB&B⇨🛏fr£27
🍽 CTV 4P 300 acres arable beef mixed £

BRECON Powys Map **03** SO02

GH **Q Q** **Beacons** 16 Bridge St LD3 8AH ☎(0874) 623339
*A Georgian house situated a short walk from the town centre and
near the River Usk. The accommodation is comfortable, and there
is a small cellar bar for residents and a new coffee shop serving
snacks and light meals.*
10rm(7⇨🛏 3hc) (2fb) CTV in all bedrooms ® sB&Bfr£15
sB&B⇨🛏fr£17.50 dB&Bfr£30 dB&B⇨🛏fr£35 WB&B£90-
£105 WBDi£139-£154 LDO 7pm
Lic 🍽 CTV 12P
Credit Cards ① ② ③ £

GH **Q Q Q** **The Coach** Orchard St, Llanfaes LD3 8AN
☎(0874) 623803
Closed 22 Dec-7 Jan
*Originally an early 19th-century inn, this friendly guesthouse
provides pretty, comfortable and very well equipped bedrooms.
Carefully modernised, it has a pleasant lounge for residents, and is
conveniently located opposite Christ College.*

6⇨🛏 (2fb) CTV in all bedrooms ® 🏃 (ex guide dogs) ✳
dB&B⇨🛏£32-£35 LDO 7pm
Lic 🍽 5P £

GH **Q Q** **Flag & Castle** 11 Orchard St, Llanfaes LD3 8AN
☎(0874) 625860
*Once a busy hostelry, this is now a cosy guesthouse run by the
friendly Mrs Jones. It lies on the western side of the town. Diners
use a communal table in the open-plan lounge/dining room.*
6rm(1🛏5hc) (1fb) ® sB&B£13.50-£15 dB&B£25-£28
dB&B🛏£28-£32 WB&B£85-£105
Lic 🍽 CTV 2P £

BREDWARDINE Hereford & Worcester Map **03** SO34

SELECTED

GH **Q Q Q Q** **Bredwardine Hall** HR3 6DB
☎Moccas(09817) 596
Mar-Nov
*An imposing stone-built mid-19th-century manor house,
peacefully situated in its own wooded grounds. The River Wye
and the Golden Valley are both close, making this an ideal
base from which to explore the beautiful surrounding
countryside. The accommodation is spacious, with bright,
fresh décor and a good range of modern facilities. The
comfortable lounge overlooks the garden, and there is a
courtesy bar in the dining room.*
5rm(3⇨🛏1hc) CTV in all bedrooms ®
🏃 (ex guide dogs) sB&B⇨🛏£27-£29 dB&B⇨🛏£42-£46
WB&B£142-£156 WBDi£215.50-£229.50 LDO 4.30pm
Lic 🍽 7P nc10yrs £
See advertisement under HEREFORD

BRENDON Devon Map **03** SS74

GH **Q** **Brendon House** EX35 6PS ☎(05987) 206
2 Mar-mid Nov
*Set in Exmoor's beautiful Lyn Valley, this house offers
comfortable and attractive accommodation which is ideal for
guests touring the North Devon coast. Cream teas are served in the
season.*
5rm(1⇨3🛏1hc) (1fb) ® sB&B⇨🛏£17-£19 dB&Bfr£32
dB&B⇨🛏£34-£38 WB&B£109-£125 WBDi£172-£186
LDO 5pm
Lic 🍽 CTV 5P £

FH **Q** Mrs C A South **Farley Water** *(SS744464)* EX35 6LQ
☎(05987) 272
May-Sep
*Peacefully situated on the edge of Exmoor, this farmhouse offers
comfortable accommodation and a friendly atmosphere.*
4rm(3hc) (2fb)
223 acres beef sheep

BRENT ELEIGH Suffolk Map **05** TL94

FH **Q Q Q** Mrs J P Gage **Street** *(TL945476)* CO10 9NU
☎Lavenham(0787) 247271
Closed Dec-mid Feb
*Set at the heart of the village, with access from the A114
Lavenham/Hadleigh road, this 16th-century timbered farmhouse
and its well-maintained walled garden are surrounded by 143
acres of arable land. Rooms are furnished individually and
exceptionally well with period antique pieces, the lounge featuring
an inglenook fireplace, and a particularly hospitable proprietor
offers a warm welcome to guests.*
4rm(1⇨1🛏1hc) ® 🏃 sB&Bfr£16 dB&Bfr£32 dB&B⇨🛏£35-
£36 WB&Bfr£235
🍽 CTV 4P nc9yrs 143 acres arable £

BRIDESTOWE Devon Map **02** SX58

FH ⓠⓠ Mrs J E Down **Little Bidlake** *(SX494887)* EX20 4NS
☎(083786) 233
Etr-Oct
Neat, clean and efficient farmhouse adjacent to A30 between Bridestowe and Launceston.
2hc ⚲in all bedrooms ⓡ ✖ (ex guide dogs) sB&Bfr£15 dB&Bfr£25 WB&Bfr£80 WBDifr£120 LDO 7.30pm
🎮 CTV P ⏌ putting 150 acres beef dairy mixed £

FH ⓠⓠ Mrs M Hockridge **Week** *(SX519913)* EX20 4HZ
☎(083786) 221
Large friendly 17th-century stone-built farmhouse set in peaceful Devon countryside.
6rm(3⌂3hc) (4fb) CTV in 3 bedrooms ⓡ ✳ sB&B£13.50-£15 dB&B£28-£30 dB&B⌂£32.50-£34 LDO 5pm
🎮 CTV 10P 180 acres dairy sheep
Credit Cards ② £

BRIDGE OF MARNOCH Grampian *Aberdeenshire* Map **15** NJ55

SELECTED

GH ⓠⓠⓠⓠ **Old Manse of Marnoch** AB54 5RS (off B9117 10m N of Huntly) ☎Aberchirder(0466) 780873
Set in three acres of secluded grounds beside the River Deveron, this lovely Georgian manor house has been sympathetically refurbished by its caring owners Patrick and Karen Carter to provide a high standard of comfort. Individually decorated and furnished bedrooms are thoughtfully equipped and the attractive lounge invites relaxation. An imaginative four-course dinner is served at the communal dining room table and the breakfast menu is notable for its extensive choice.
5rm(2⌂1⌂2hc) ⓡ sB&Bfr£30 sB&B⌂⌂fr£44 dB&Bfr£40 dB&B⌂⌂fr£54 LDO 8pm
Lic 🎮 CTV 6P nc12yrs £

BRIDGWATER Somerset Map **03** ST33

GH ⓠⓠ **Brookland Hotel** 56 North St TA6 3PN
☎(0278) 423263
A comfortable guesthouse prominently positioned on the Minehead road out of town, within walking distance of the town centre. It offers simply appointed bedrooms with TV and tea-making facilities. There is a small dining room with a bar, and a comfortable lounge.
8rm(3⌂5hc) (1fb) CTV in all bedrooms ⓡ ✳ sB&B£20 sB&B⌂£32.50 dB&B£35 dB&B⌂£42.50 WB&B£120-£195 WBDi£172.50-£247.50 LDO 7pm
Lic 🎮 CTV 10P
Credit Cards ①②③

BRIDGNORTH Shropshire Map **07** SO79

GH ⓠⓠ **Severn Arms Hotel** Underhill St, Low Town WV16 4BB ☎(0746) 764616
Closed 23 Dec-2 Jan
A comfortable family hotel, this tall, terraced house is close to the bridge at Low Town. Popular with anglers and their families, it is equally suitable for commercial visitors.
9rm(2⌂3⌂4hc) (5fb) CTV in 5 bedrooms TV in 2 bedrooms ⓡ LDO 7pm
Lic 🎮 CTV ⏌
Credit Cards ①③

This guide is updated annually – make sure you use an up-to-date edition.

INN ⓠ *Kings Head Hotel* Whitburn St WV16 4QN
☎(0746) 762141
Retaining many of its original 17th-century features, this town centre inn has well-equipped bedrooms. Bar meals are served here and there is a small dining room available for guests who prefer a little more privacy.
5hc (3fb) CTV in all bedrooms ⓡ ✖ (ex guide dogs) LDO 8pm
🎮 8P

BRIDLINGTON Humberside Map **08** TA16

GH ⓠⓠ **Bay Ridge Hotel** Summerfield Rd YO15 3LF
☎(0262) 673425
Spacious, well-designed conversion of two semi-detached houses, close to South Bay.
14rm(6⌂6⌂2hc) (5fb) CTV in all bedrooms ⓡ sB&B£19.50-£21.50 dB&B⌂⌂£39-£43 (incl dinner) WB&B£105-£110 WBDi£128-£135 LDO 5.45pm
Lic 🎮 CTV 6P 2🚗 (£2 per day) bar billiards library
Credit Cards ①③ £

GH ⓠⓠⓠ *Langdon Hotel* Pembroke Ter YO15 3BX
☎(0262) 673065
This hotel is centrally placed in a quiet position on the south side of the town, and enjoys views of the sea. It has spacious lounges, a small, snug bar and well-equipped comfortable accommodation. Guests are cared for by friendly staff.
20rm(11⌂9hc) (8fb) CTV in all bedrooms ⓡ ✖ (ex guide dogs) LDO 5pm
Lic lift 🎮

GH ⓠⓠⓠ *Southdowne Hotel* South Marine Dr YO15 3NS
☎(0262) 673270
A pleasant house standing on the seafront, to the south of the bay. Friendly proprietors aim to provide good home cooking, with comfortable and clean accomodation.
▶

Middleton Priors,
Bridgnorth,
Shropshire WV16 6UR.
Tel: 074634 228 or 675.

Historically the Shropshire hunting and shooting lodge of the Howard family. The original building dates back to the 17th century and is set in 20 acres of beautiful rural Shropshire countryside overlooking Brown Clee hill.

The Lodge offers 2 double bedrooms with bathrooms en suite, one featuring a 4-poster bed, and 1 twin bedroom with shower. All rooms have tea and coffee making facilities and both full English or continental breakfasts are available.

There are many places of historical interest as well as areas of breath-taking beauty within easy reach of the Lodge, and nearby towns providing interesting features in which to while away the day.

12rm(8↱4hc) (2fb) TV in 1 bedroom ® ✘ LDO 5.30pm
Lic 🍽 CTV 10P

BRIDPORT Dorset Map **03** SY49

See also Bettiscombe, Chideock & Nettlecombe

GH QQQ Bridge House 115 East St DT6 3LB ☎(0308) 23371
An early 18th-century house near the centre of town, with low beamed ceilings and plenty of character. Accommodation is comfortable and well appointed, and the cellar restaurant serves fresh, skillfully prepared dishes including some local fish.
10⇨↱ (4fb) CTV in all bedrooms ® sB&B⇨↱£26-£30 dB&B⇨↱£43-£47 WB&B£140-£190 WBDi£195-£230 LDO 9pm
Lic 🍽 15P
Credit Cards [1] [2] [3]

GH QQQ Britmead House 154 West Bay Rd DT6 4EG ☎(0308) 22941
Pleasantly situated between the small historic market town of Bridport and the quaint harbour of West Bay, this is a particularly clean and neat house where bedrooms provide many additional items such as hairdryers and electric blankets. Proprietors Mr and Mrs Walker are proud of their reputation for providing superb meals. Menus change daily, and dishes are prepared from fresh local produce.
7rm(6⇨↱1hc) (1fb) CTV in all bedrooms ® sB&B£20.40-£25 sB&B⇨↱£25-£29 dB&B£31.50-£37 dB&B⇨↱£40.80-£44 WB&B£103.25-£140 WBDi£174.65-£217 LDO 6pm
Lic 🍽 8P
Credit Cards [1] [2] [3] [5] (£)

BRIGHTON & HOVE East Sussex Map **04** TQ30

See **Town Plan Section**
See also Rottingdean

SELECTED

GH QQQQ Adelaide Hotel 51 Regency Square BN1 2FF ☎Brighton(0273) 205286 FAX (0273) 220904
Closed 23-30 Dec
A charming Regency building set in this prestigious square close to the seafront. The bedrooms are tastefully furnished, and exceptionally well maintained and equipped. There is an elegant lounge to the front, and dinner is served by request in the cosy basement dining room. Alternatively a range of light snacks can be served in your room.
12⇨↱ (1fb) CTV in all bedrooms ® ✘ sB&B⇨↱£36-£62 dB&B⇨↱£55-£75 LDO 5pm
Lic 🍽 P̸
Credit Cards [1] [2] [3] [5] (£)

GH QQQ Allendale Hotel 3 New Steine BN2 1PB ☎Brighton(0273) 672994 & 675436 FAX (0273) 602603
Set on a pleasant garden square, close to the seafront and local amenities, this charming Regency house offers well-equipped, modern accommodation. Completely refurbished to offer thoughtfully appointed rooms, a ground floor dining room and an adjoining, cosy lounge.
13rm(5↱8hc) (5fb) CTV in all bedrooms ® ✘ (ex guide dogs) sB&B£27 sB&B↱£30 dB&B£38-£44 dB&B↱£54-£64 WB&B£120-£200 WBDi£190-£270 LDO 6pm
Lic 🍽 P̸ nc8yrs
Credit Cards [1] [2] [3] [5] (£)

GH QQQ Ambassador Hotel 22 New Steine BN2 1PD ☎Brighton(0273) 676869
Conveniently situated close to the seafront, Palace Pier and within walking distance of the town, this hotel has bedrooms with modern facilities, all of which are en suite. There is also a TV lounge.
9rm(2⇨7↱) (4fb) CTV in all bedrooms ® ✘ *
sB&B⇨↱£23-£30 dB&B⇨↱£40-£54
Lic 🍽 CTV P̸
Credit Cards [1] [2] [3] [5] (£)

GH QQ Amblecliff Hotel 35 Upper Rock Gardens BN2 1QF ☎Brighton(0273) 681161 & 676945
The friendly proprietors here offer a hospitable atmosphere which complements the well-maintained and modern accommodation. There is also a snug television lounge, and the dining room offers a good selection of meals.
11rm(7⇨↱4hc) ⊘in 3 bedrooms CTV in all bedrooms ® ✘ (ex guide dogs) sB&B£16-£20 dB&B£32-£40 dB&B⇨↱£40-£50 WB&B£96-£150
Lic 🍽 CTV 3P (£1.50-£2) nc4yrs
Credit Cards [1] [2] [3] (£)

GH QQQ Arlanda Hotel 20 New Steine BN2 1PD ☎Brighton(0273) 699300
This family-run, charming Regency-style hotel stands on a garden square and is close to the local amenities. Well-equipped modern accommodation is offered, together with a pleasant, well-appointed dining room and adjoining lounge with a piano.
12rm(2⇨10↱) (4fb) CTV in all bedrooms ® ✘ (ex guide dogs) * sB&B⇨↱£28-£32 dB&B⇨↱£46-£62 WB&B£190-£215 LDO 4pm
Lic 🍽 P̸
Credit Cards [1] [2] [3] [5] (£)

GH QQQ Ascott House Hotel 21 New Steine, Marine Pde BN2 1PD ☎Brighton(0273) 688085 FAX (0273) 623733
This appealing hotel is close to the seafront and town. Every effort has been made to ensure guests' comfort and the bedrooms are well-equipped with modern conveniences. There is also a comfortable lounge and small bar.
12rm(9↱3hc) (8fb) CTV in all bedrooms ® ✘ sB&B£25-£35 sB&B↱£35-£40 dB&B£48-£50 dB&B↱£54-£66
Lic 🍽 P̸ nc3yrs
Credit Cards [1] [2] [3] [5]

GH QQ Cavalaire House 34 Upper Rock Gardens, Kemptown BN2 1QF ☎Brighton(0273) 696899
Closed Xmas-mid Jan
Within walking distance of the beach and local amenities, this pleasant Victorian hotel offers neat, well-kept accommodation with modern facilities. There is a small cosy lounge and a pleasant breakfast room.
9rm(3↱3hc) (2fb) CTV in all bedrooms ® * sB&B£16-£19 dB&B£28-£33 dB&B↱£34-£42
🍽 P̸ nc9yrs

SELECTED

GH QQQQ Claremont House Second Av BN3 2LL ☎Brighton(0273) 735161
A small, Victorian family-run hotel in a quiet residential area close to the seafront. Well appointed, it retains many original features, and the standard of hospitality and service is notable. Bedrooms vary in size, but they are tastefully appointed and well equipped; some baths have the additional luxury of a jacuzzi. A short menu of mainly English dishes is served in the attractive dining room.
12⇨↱ (2fb) CTV in all bedrooms ® * sB&B⇨↱£33-£45 dB&B⇨↱£46-£68 LDO 10pm
Lic 🍽 CTV P̸ ♿
Credit Cards [1] [2] [3] [5] (£)

GH QQ Cornerways Private Hotel 18-20 Caburn Rd BN3 6EF ☎Brighton(0273) 731882
A large Victorian corner house, Cornerways, offers a variety of accommodation, mostly furnished in traditional style. There is a small bar, cosy TV lounge and a traditional dining room.

10rm(1🪶9hc) (2fb) CTV in 2 bedrooms ⑧ ✳ sB&B£15-£16 dB&B£30-£32 dB&B🪶£35-£37 WB&B£95-£102 WBDi£130-£150 LDO 2pm
Lic 🍽 CTV 🅿

GH ⓠⓠ Croft Hotel 24 Palmeira Av BN3 3GB
☎Brighton(0273) 732860
Only a short walk from the seafront, the Croft is situated in a quiet residential area. The bedrooms are simply furnished but offer adequate comfort and many modern conveniences. There is a small lounge in the basement and the pleasant dining room leads out to the garden.
10hc (2fb) CTV in all bedrooms ⑧ sB&B£22-£24 dB&B£38-£41
Lic 🍽 CTV 🅿 ⓔ

GH ⓠⓠⓠ George IV Hotel 34 Regency Square BN1 2FJ
☎Brighton(0273) 21196
This newly converted guesthouse is situated in Regency square, which overlooks the sea. Bedrooms are equipped to the highest standards and are bright and comfortable; there are also 2 charming rooms with 4 poster beds and sea views. There is a small but pretty dining room, and a lounge area for the use of guests.
10⇨🪶 (2fb) CTV in all bedrooms ⑧ ✳ sB&B⇨🪶£30-£40 dB&B⇨🪶£45-£65 LDO by arrangement
Lic lift 🍽 nc3yrs
Credit Cards ①②③⑤ ⓔ

GH ⓠⓠⓠ Gullivers 10 New Steine BN2 1PB
☎Brighton(0273) 695415
Situated in a quiet square just off the seafront is this pleasant Regency hotel. The attractive bedrooms are comfortable, well equipped and some have private bathrooms. The friendly owners extend a warm welcome.
9rm(5🪶4hc) (3fb) CTV in all bedrooms ⑧ sB&B£20-£22 sB&B🪶£34 dB&B£38-£40 dB&B🪶£48-£54
🍽
Credit Cards ①②③ ⓔ

GH ⓠⓠ Kempton House Hotel 33/34 Marine Pde BN2 1TR
☎Brighton(0273) 570248
Two seafront Regency houses have been combined to provide bedrooms with modern facilities, and a pleasant bar and dining room. Kempton House is close to the Palace Pier and other amenities.
13rm(12🪶1hc) (4fb) CTV in all bedrooms ⑧ sB&B£28-£38 sB&B🪶£35-£38 dB&B£36-£44 dB&B🪶£44-£52 WB&B£132-£156 WBDi£202-£226 LDO 9am
Lic 🍽
Credit Cards ①②③⑤ ⓔ

See advertisement on page 91

GH ⓠⓠ *Malvern Hotel* 33 Regency Square BN1 2GG
☎Brighton(0273) 24302
A well maintained guesthouse which offers comfortable rooms equipped with most modern conveniences including en suite facilities. There is a small residents' bar and a pleasant lounge.
12🪶 CTV in all bedrooms ⑧ ✖
Lic 🍽
Credit Cards ①②③⑤

🚐🖦 GH ⓠⓠ Marina House Hotel 8 Charlotte St, Marine Pde BN2 1AG ☎Brighton(0273) 605349 & 679484
FAX (0273) 605349
A single-fronted Victorian mid-terrace building just off the Marine Parade and a short walk to all the town's tourist and conference venues. The well equipped bedrooms are situated on four floors and are simply furnished. In the lower ground floor dining room, English, Indian, Chinese and vegetarian meals are available by prior arrangement.
10rm(7🪶3hc) (2fb) CTV in all bedrooms ⑧ ✖ sB&B£12.50-£19 dB&B🪶£25-£39 WB&B£72-£120 WBDi£135-£183 LDO 4pm ▶

Lic 🏤 CTV
Credit Cards ① ② ③ ⑤

GH QQQ **New Steine Hotel** 12a New Steine, Marine Pde
BN2 1PB ☎Brighton(0273) 681546
mid Mar-mid Dec rs Xmas & New Year
This attractive Regency-style house has been refurbished to offer a
good standard of accommodation. The caring proprietors offer
genuine hospitality and the hotel is conveniently located for the
beach and amenities.
11rm(4🚻7hc) (2fb) CTV in all bedrooms ® ✻ sB&B£15-£17
sB&B🚻£25 dB&B£32-£34 dB&B🚻£36-£42
🏤 CTV 🅿 nc8yrs ⓔ

GH QQQ **Paskins Hotel** 19 Charlotte St BN2 1AG
☎Brighton(0273) 601203 FAX (0273) 621973
A mid-terrace Georgian building situated close to the seafront and
the town centre. The bedrooms vary in size but most of them have
en suite facilities and all are attractively decorated and
exceptionally well equipped. There is a small residents' bar where
snacks are available in the evening.
19rm(16🚻3hc) (2fb) CTV in all bedrooms ® sB&Bfr£19
sB&B🖘🚻£25-£30 dB&B£30-£38 dB&B🖘🚻£42-£55
WB&B£90-£180 LDO 5.30pm
Lic 🏤
Credit Cards ① ③ ⓔ

GH QQQ **Pier View Hotel** 28 New Steine BN2 1PD
☎Brighton(0273) 605310
10rm(7🚻3hc) (3fb) CTV in all bedrooms ® ✗ (ex guide dogs)
✻ sB&B£20-£21 sB&B🚻£25 dB&B£36 dB&B🚻£40-£50
LDO 5pm
🏤 CTV
Credit Cards ① ② ③ ⓔ

GH QQ **Prince Regent Hotel** 29 Regency Square BN1 2FH
☎Brighton(0273) 29962 FAX (0273) 748162
rs closed Xmas Eve & New Years Eve
This elegant hotel, overlooking the sea, offers a range of bedrooms
to suit every taste. Some are spacious and ornately decorated in
the Regency style, while others are bright and compact. All have en
suite facilities and are well equipped. Breakfast is served in the
basement dining room and there is a small residents' bar.
20rm(2🖘18🚻) 🍴in 1 bedroom CTV in all bedrooms ®
✗ (ex guide dogs) sB&B🖘🚻£30-£40 dB&B🖘🚻£50-£80
Lic 🏤 CTV 🅿 nc12yrs
Credit Cards ① ③ ⑤ ⓔ

GH Q *Regency Hotel* 28 Regency Square BN1 2FH
☎Brighton(0273) 202690 FAX (0273) 220438
A small hotel offering a variety of simply furnished rooms, all well
equipped, and most with en suite facilities. There is an elegant
dining room with adjoining lounge and a small bar.
14rm(1🖘10🚻3hc) (1fb) CTV in all bedrooms ®
✗ (ex guide dogs) LDO noon
Lic 🏤 CTV 🅿
Credit Cards ① ② ③ ⑤

GH QQ **Sea Breeze** 12a Upper Rock Gardens, Kemptown
BN2 1QE ☎Brighton(0273) 602608 FAX (0273) 607166
Close to the town centre and seafront, this small guesthouse offers
a range of tastefully decorated bedrooms, including one with a
four-poster bed. All have private bathrooms and are well equipped
although compact.
7🚻 CTV in all bedrooms ® ✻ sB&B🚻£23-£28 dB&B🚻£36-
£56
🏤 🅿 nc8yrs
Credit Cards ① ② ③

GH QQ *Sutherland Hotel* 9-10 Regency Square BN1 2FG
☎Brighton(0273) 27055
Situated close to all Brighton's amenities, this small hotel offers a
variety of well equipped bedrooms, most of which have their own
bathrooms; some rooms may be considered to be compact. There is

a lift to all floors, a quiet and comfortable lounge and dinner is
served in the dining room on request.
26rm(20🖘🚻6hc) (2fb) CTV in all bedrooms ®
✗ (ex guide dogs) LDO 9pm
Lic lift 🏤 🅿
Credit Cards ① ② ③ ⑤

See advertisement on page 93

GH QQQ **Trouville Hotel** 11 New Steine, Marine Pde
BN2 1PB ☎Brighton(0273) 697384
Closed Jan
Located close to the seafront, and within walking distance of the
centre of the town, this is a well-maintained hotel offering
attractive accommodation, including a cosy lounge and a nicely
appointed dining room.
9rm(2🚻7hc) (2fb) CTV in all bedrooms ® ✗ sB&B£18
dB&B£30-£35 dB&B🚻£42-£46
Lic 🏤 CTV
Credit Cards ① ② ③

GH QQQ **Twenty One** 21 Charlotte St, Marine Pde BN2 1AG
☎Brighton(0273) 686450
The bedrooms of this establishment, which is close to the beach,
include a pleasant room with a separate sitting room on the lower
ground floor which overlooks the ivy-clad courtyard, and a
charming room with a four-poster bed on a higher floor. Meals
other than breakfast must be ordered in advance.
6rm(5🚻1hc) CTV in all bedrooms ® ✗ (ex guide dogs) ✻
sB&B🚻£55 dB&B🚻£46-£68 LDO 9am
Lic 🏤 🅿 nc9yrs
Credit Cards ① ② ③ ⓔ

ⓔ Remember to use the money-off vouchers.

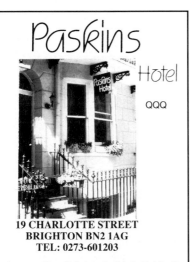

BRIG O'TURK Central *Perthshire* Map **11** NN50

SELECTED

GH QQQQ **Dundarroch** Trossachs FK17 8HT
☎Trossachs(08776) 200
rs Dec-Feb

Quietly situated in the heart of the Trossachs, this charming country house combines first class facilities with superior appointments. The individually decorated en suite bedrooms are comfortably furnished and thoughtfully equipped with a wide range of useful accessories. Public rooms are tastefully furnished with paintings and fine antiques; the attractive lounge has a natural stone wall and a large Victorian fireplace with a wood-burning stove. The breakfast room enjoys a spectacular view of Ben Venue. For the evening meal, special arrangements exist at the Byrs Inn, a characterful Victorian bar and restaurant, close to the house. Dundarroch is located at Brig O'Turk, six miles from Callander on the A821 Aberfoyle road.

3⇨🐾 CTV in all bedrooms ® 🏃 (ex guide dogs) ✳
sB&B⇨🐾£29.65-£35 dB&B⇨🐾£45-£49 WB&Bfr£155
LDO 8.45pm
🍴6P nc3mths 🍴 ⓔ

BRIGSTEER (NEAR KENDAL) Cumbria Map **07** SD48

FH QQ Mrs B Gardner *Barrowfield (SD484908)* LA8 8BJ
☎Crosthwaite(04488) 336
Apr-Oct

This Elizabethan farmhouse, situated on a dairy farm just north of the village, is surrounded by fields and woods. It is found by taking the Kendal road from the village, and then a Forestry Commission road at the hill's top.

3rm(2hc) (1fb) 🏃
🍴 CTV 6P 180 acres dairy sheep

BRISTOL Avon Map **03** ST57

See Town Plan Section
See also Redhill (Avon)

GH QQ *Alandale Hotel* Tyndall's Park Rd, Clifton BS8 1PG
☎(0272) 735407
Closed 2wks Xmas

Centrally situated in Clifton, close to the university, this guesthouse offers functional accommodation, popular with commercial travellers. A comfortable lounge and a small bar are available for residents' use.

17rm(5⇨12🐾) CTV in all bedrooms ® sB&B⇨🐾£26-£38
dB&B⇨🐾£38-£48
Lic 🍴 10P
Credit Cards [1][3] ⓔ

GH QQ **Alcove** 508-510 Fishponds Rd, Fishponds BS16 3DT
☎(0272) 653886

Situated north east of the city, close to the M32 yet offering easy access to the centre, a friendly, pleasant guesthouse provides well-kept and comfortable accommodation with some modern facilities.

9rm(2🐾7hc) (2fb) CTV in all bedrooms ® 🏃 (ex guide dogs)
✳ sB&B£18-£25 dB&B£33-£39 dB&B🐾£36-£42 (wkly only all year) LDO 4pm
Lic 🍴 CTV 8P 1🍴 ⓔ

GH QQ *Birkdale Hotel* 11 Ashgrove Road, Redland BS6 6LY
☎(0272) 733635 & 736332 FAX (0272) 739964
Closed Xmas wk

Situated off Whiteladies road a mile from the city centre, this hotel is unusual in that the majority of its bedrooms are situated in separate houses near by and the main building is used for food and drink services. The spacious lounge-bar is comfortable and the bedrooms are well equipped with modern en suite facilities.

42rm(34⇨8🐾) CTV in all bedrooms ® LDO 8pm

Lic 🍴 16P snooker
Credit Cards [1][3]

GH Q **Chesterfield Hotel** 3 Westbourne Place, Clifton BS8 1LX
☎(0272) 734606 Telex no 449075
Closed Xmas

Situated on the edge of Clifton, this nice terraced house provides low-cost, comfortable accommodation, ideal for the businessman. Evening meals are available at a nearby sister hotel.

13hc (2fb) CTV in all bedrooms ®
🍴 🏃
Credit Cards [1][2][3][5]

GH QQQ **Downlands** 33 Henleaze Gardens, Henleaze
BS9 4HH ☎(0272) 621639

A short drive from the city centre, Downlands is situated in a pleasant residential area. Rooms are well decorated and furnished; the house is comfortable and friendly.

10hc (1fb) CTV in all bedrooms ® sB&Bfr£20 dB&Bfr£36
🍴 🏃 ⓔ

GH Q **Oakfield Hotel** 52-54 Oakfield Rd, Clifton BS8 2BG
☎(0272) 735556
Closed 23 Dec-1-Jan

This simple guesthouse offers well-kept, functional accommodation, and is particularly popular with commercial clients. Early morning tea, and hot drinks and biscuits in the evening are thoughtfully provided.

27hc (4fb) CTV in all bedrooms ® ✳ sB&B£25-£27 dB&B£35-£37 WB&B£175 WBDi£210 LDO 7pm
🍴 CTV 4P 2🍴

GH QQ **Rowan Lodge** 41 Gloucester Rd North, Filton Park
BS7 0SN ☎(0272) 312170
Closed Xmas & New Year

A large detached house on the junction of the A38 and Bronksea Road in the suburb of Filton. Rooms are quite spacious and cheerfully decorated, and there is a car park at the rear.

6rm(3🐾3hc) (2fb) CTV in all bedrooms ✳ sB&Bfr£22
sB&B🐾fr£30 dB&Bfr£35 dB&B🐾fr£40
🍴 8P
Credit Cards [1][3]

GH QQQ *Seeleys Hotel* 17-27 St Pauls Rd, Clifton BS8 1LX
☎(0272) 738544 FAX (0272) 732406
Closed Xmas wk

This large hotel offers accommodation with excellent modern facilities, many rooms having spa or air baths. Jacuzzi, sauna and steam baths are available in the small health centre, and the lively basement restaurant features live entertainment 3 times a week.

53rm(14⇨29🐾10hc) Annexe 10rm(6⇨🐾4hc) (20fb) CTV in all bedrooms ® 🏃 (ex guide dogs) LDO 10.30pm
Lic 🍴 13P 22🍴 🏊 sauna solarium gymnasium
Credit Cards [1][2][3]

GH QQ **Washington Hotel** 11-15 St Pauls Rd, Clifton BS8 1LX
☎(0272) 733980 Telex no 449075
Closed 23 Dec-3 Jan

The car park belonging to this large, unlicensed private hotel is a particular bonus in this area. The rooms are modern and well equipped but public areas are limited.

46rm(34⇨🐾12hc) (5fb) CTV in all bedrooms ® sB&Bfr£29
sB&B⇨🐾fr£45 dB&Bfr£46 dB&B⇨🐾fr£59
Lic 🍴 20P
Credit Cards [1][2][3][5] ⓔ

GH QQQ **Westbury Park Hotel** 37 Westbury Rd, Westbury-on-Trym BS9 3AU ☎(0272) 620465 FAX (0272) 628607

9rm(2⇨3🐾4hc) (1fb) CTV in all bedrooms ® 🏃 ✳ sB&B£25-£30 sB&B⇨🐾£33.50-£38.50 dB&B£36-£40 dB&B⇨🐾£43-£48.50 WB&B£116-£220 WBDi£188-£292 (wkly only all year) LDO 8.30pm
Lic 🍴 CTV 4P
Credit Cards [1][3] ⓔ

93

BRIXHAM Devon Map **03** SX95

See **Town Plan Section**
GH ⓠⓠⓠ **Harbour Side** 65 Berry Head Rd TQ5 9AA
☎(0803) 858899
Friendly guesthouse overlooking harbour and coastline.
5rm(1♪4hc)(2fb) CTV in all bedrooms ⓡ ✱ (ex guide dogs)
sB&B£14.50-£16 dB&B£27-£31 dB&B♪£31-£33
WB&B£94.50-£110 WBDi£150-£166 LDO 10am
CTV ✗ ⓔ

GH ⓠⓠ **Raddicombe Lodge** 105 Kingswear Rd TQ5 0EX
☎(0803) 882125
14 Apr-14 Oct
8rm(3♪5hc)(2fb) CTV in all bedrooms ⓡ ✱ sB&B£15-£22.80
sB&B♪£18.10-£26.60 dB&B£30-£36.40 dB&B♪£36.20-£42.60
WB&B£105-£137.20
CTV 9P
Credit Cards 1 3 ⓔ

GH ⓠⓠ **Ranscombe House Hotel** Ranscombe Rd TQ5 9UP
☎(0803) 882337
This detached property dates back to 1743 and is within walking
distance of the harbour. The well-equipped bedrooms have en suite
facilities and the restaurant offers an interesting à la carte menu.
Guests receive a warm welcome and good service here.
9↩♪ (2fb) CTV in all bedrooms ⓡ ✱ (ex guide dogs)
sB&B↩♪£21-£29 dB&B↩♪£42-£58 LDO 7pm
Lic ⅏ 16P
Credit Cards 1 2 3 ⓔ

GH ⓠⓠⓠ **Sampford House** 59 King St TQ5 9TH
☎(0803) 857761
Mar-Oct
This family-run terraced property enjoys an elevated position
providing views of the inner harbour. The cosy bedrooms are
furnished to make good use of the available space. Sampford
House provides dinner on request and has no private parking.
6hc (2fb) CTV in 5 bedrooms TV in 1 bedroom ⓡ ✳ sB&B£14-
£18 dB&B£28-£36
⅏ CTV ⓔ

GH ⓠⓠⓠ **Woodlands** Parkham Rd TQ5 9BU
☎(0803) 852040
Apr-Oct
Overlooking the town and harbour, this attractive Victorian house
provides quality bed and breakfast accommodation for non-
smokers. Mr and Mrs Doling offer modern facilities and, after
living in Holland, make this hotel especially popular with Dutch
tourists. The guesthouse is 'no smoking' throughout.
5♪ (1fb)⅍in all bedrooms CTV in all bedrooms ⓡ ✱
sB&B♪£17.50-£18.50 dB&B♪£34-£37 WB&B£105-£116
⅏ 4P
Credit Cards 1 3 ⓔ

BROAD HAVEN (NEAR HAVERFORDWEST) Dyfed
Map **02** SM81

GH ⓠⓠ **Broad Haven Hotel** SA62 3JN
☎Haverfordwest(0437) 781366
This large family holiday hotel stands opposite the sandy beach of
the small resort. Bedrooms are modestly furnished but provide
modern facilities, and most are en suite. The bars are popular with
tourists and locals, and there are extensive leisure facilities
including an outdoor pool.
39rm(34↩♪5hc)(7fb) CTV in all bedrooms ⓡ sB&B£19.55-
£20.82 sB&B↩♪£23-£29.50 dB&B£30.60-£38.25
dB&B↩♪£36-£45 WB&B£119-£160.50 WBDi£167-£205
LDO 9pm
Lic 100P ⌇(heated) solarium table tennis
Credit Cards 1 2 3 ⓔ
See advertisement under **HAVERFORDWEST**

BROADSTAIRS Kent Map **05** TR36

GH ⓠⓠⓠ **Bay Tree Hotel** 12 Eastern Esplanade CT10 1DR
☎Thanet(0843) 62502
An attractive Victorian house with tastefully modernised
accommodation. The bedrooms are comfortable and well
maintained, with en suite facilities and most have magnificent sea
views; one room has its own balcony. There is a comfortable
combined bar-lounge and an attractive separate dining room. Car
parking is provided at the rear, and service is friendly and helpful.
11↩♪ CTV in all bedrooms ⓡ ✱ (ex guide dogs)
sB&B↩♪£18.50-£20 dB&B↩♪£37-£40 WB&B£112-£120
WBDi£159-£170 LDO 4pm
Lic ⅏ 12P nc10yrs
Credit Cards 1 3 ⓔ

GH ⓠⓠ **Devonhurst Hotel** Eastern Esplanade CT10 1DR
☎Thanet(0843) 63010
A friendly, family-run hotel overlooking the sea. Bedrooms have
been skilfully upgraded, and are furnished and equipped to the
same high standard, with double glazing and pretty, individual
décor. The comfortable lounge/sitting area has a balcony with
stunning views of the sea and coastline: a feature which 2 of the
bedrooms share.
9♪ (1fb) CTV in all bedrooms ⓡ ✱ (ex guide dogs)
dB&B♪£38-£44 WB&B£120-£135 WBDi£148-£168 LDO 6pm
Lic ⅏ ✗ nc5yrs
Credit Cards 1 2 3 ⓔ

GH ⓠ **East Horndon Private Hotel** 4 Eastern Esplanade
CT10 1DP ☎Thanet(0843) 68306
A small, old-fashioned licensed hotel facing the sea, in a quiet
position 5 minutes walk from the town centre. There is a cosy bar/
lounge, dining room and adequately furnished and well equipped
bedrooms, with some new en suite facilities. Service is helpful and
friendly.
11rm(4↩♪4hc) CTV in 9 bedrooms TV in 1 bedroom ⓡ ✳
sB&Bfr£15 dB&Bfr£30 dB&B↩♪fr£33 WB&Bfr£115
WBDifr£145
Lic ⅏ ✗
Credit Cards 1 3

BROADWAY Hereford & Worcester Map **04** SP03

SELECTED

GH ⓠⓠⓠⓠ **Leasow House** WR12 7NA
☎Stanton(038673) 526 FAX (038673) 596
(For full entry see Laverton)

GH ⓠⓠⓠ **Milestone House Hotel** 122 High St WR12 7AJ
☎(0386) 853432
Closed 24 Dec-Jan
Comfortable, well equipped accommodation is combined here with
Luigi's Backyard Restaurant, where the chef/proprietor offers a
tempting range of mostly Italian dishes. A small bar caters for both
diners and residents, and there is an attractive little garden at the
rear, which is pretty in summer.
4rm(2↩♪2♪)(1fb) CTV in all bedrooms ⓡ ✱ (ex guide dogs)
✳ dB&B↩♪£42.50-£49.50 LDO 9.30pm
Lic ⅏ 8P
Credit Cards 1 2 3

SELECTED

GH ⓠⓠⓠⓠ **Old Rectory** Church St WR12 7PN
☎(0386) 853729
(For full entry see Willersey)

GH QQ **Olive Branch Guest House** 78 High St WR12 7AJ
☎(0386) 853440
Closed 24-31 Dec
The rooms in this fine 16th-century house are situated above both a
grocery shop and an antique shop. To the rear is a secluded garden
and a large car park.
9rm(7↑2hc)(2fb) CTV in all bedrooms ® ✻ (ex guide dogs)
✻ sB&B£16.50-£18 dB&B↑£35 WB&B£119 WBDi£170
LDO 7.30pm
CTV 9P
Credit Cards ②ⓔ

GH QQQ **Small Talk Lodge** 32 High St WR12 7DP
☎Evesham(0386) 858953
A small, centrally situated hotel, set back from the High Street,
with its own car park. Bedrooms are comfortable and well
equipped with modern facilities. The small, attractive dining room
forms the heart of the hotel, and the proprietor prepares
imaginative and mouthwatering menus.
8rm(6⇨↑2hc)(1fb) CTV in all bedrooms ®
✻ (ex guide dogs) sB&Bfr£17.50 sB&B⇨↑fr£17.50
dB&B£34-£42 dB&B⇨↑£37-£50
Lic CTV 8P nc5yrs
Credit Cards ①③ⓔ

GH QQ **Whiteacres** Station Rd WR12 7DE ☎(0386) 852320
Mar-Oct
Situated within walking distance of the village, this guesthouse has
its own car park. Accommodation is well maintained and
comfortable and all rooms have private bathrooms. The dining
room overlooks the rear garden, and there is a residents' lounge.
6⇨↑ CTV in all bedrooms ® ✻ (ex guide dogs)
dB&B⇨↑£38-£40 WB&B£120-£126
⑭ 6P nc

BRODICK

See **ARRAN, ISLE OF**

BROMLEY Greater London London plan **4** F2 (pages 221-
227)

GH QQ **Glendevon House** 80 Southborough Rd, Bickley
BR1 2EN (2m E off A22) ☎081-467 2183
Mrs Dignam offers a cheery welcome at her converted Victorian
house in a quiet residential road near Bickley station.
Accommodation is simple and clean.
11rm(3⇨↑8hc)(2fb) CTV in 8 bedrooms ® ✻ sB&B£19.75-
£28.75 sB&B⇨↑£28.75 dB&B£35.75 dB&B⇨↑£41
LDO 9pm
⑭ CTV 7P
Credit Cards ①③ⓔ

BROMPTON REGIS Somerset Map **03** SS93

FH Q Mrs G Payne *Lower Holworthy (SS978308)* TA22 9NY
☎(03987) 244
Closed Xmas
Small 18th-century hill farm overlooking and bordering
Wimbleball Lake in Exmoor National Park.
3rm(2hc) ® ✻ (ex guide dogs)
⑭ CTV 6P 200 acres beef sheep

BROMSGROVE Hereford & Worcester Map **07** SO97

INN Q *The Forest* 290 Birmingham Rd B61 0XO
☎(0527) 72063
Closed Xmas
The Forest Inn is situated on the A38 at its junction with the M42
motorway. The accommodation is modest and some rooms are
quite compact, though the addition of some en suite facilities is
planned.
9hc CTV in all bedrooms ® LDO 9.15pm

▶

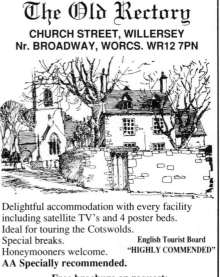

70P
Credit Cards 1 2 3

BRONLLYS Powys Map **03** SO13

GH QQ *Beacons Edge Country Hotel* Pontithel LD3 0RY
☎Brecon(0874) 711182
A family run hotel situated alongside the A438 Brecon to Hereford road. The restaurant offers a good choice of food and is popular locally, and the bedrooms, although on the small side, are comfortably appointed.
7rm(1⇄6♠)(1fb) CTV in all bedrooms ® LDO 9.30pm
Lic ⬛ 24P
Credit Cards 1 3

BRORA Highland *Sutherlandshire* Map **14** NC90

GH QQ *Lynwood* Golf Rd KW9 6QS ☎(0408) 21226
Closed Jan & Feb
Comfortably appointed throughout, this guesthouse has its own garden overlooking the harbour, and offers convenient access to the golf course; special golfing packages are available. It has a friendly atmosphere and provides well equipped accommodation, with one bedroom suitable for disabled use. To create a friendly atmosphere, guests normally share a communal table at meals.
3hc Annexe 1♠ (1fb)↙in all bedrooms CTV in all bedrooms
® sB&B£15-£20 dB&B£30-£40 dB&B♠£36-£40 WB&B£99-£119 WBDi£149-£172
⬛ CTV 4P ⓔ

BROUGH Cumbria Map **12** NY71

FH QQQ Mrs J M Atkinson **Augill House** *(NY814148)*
CA17 4DX ☎(07683) 41305
Closed Xmas & New Year
Situated just off the southern end of the bypass, this attractive Georgian house is run by a friendly proprietress and offers comfortable accommodation.
1⇄♠ Annexe 2⇄♠ CTV in all bedrooms ® dB&B⇄♠£30
LDO 4pm
⬛ CTV 6P nc12yrs 40 acres mixed ⓔ

BRUTON Somerset Map **03** ST63

SELECTED

GH QQQQ *Fryerning* Frome Road, Burrowfield
BA10 0HH ☎(0749) 812343
A charming late-Victorian stone house with a covered, glazed veranda overlooking the well tended garden. Bedrooms are spacious and well furnished, and there is a comfortable and attractive lounge with plenty of books. Dinner is served to residents only by reservation: a set menu is offered and represents excellent value for money, with all ingredients local and fresh; home-made jams and marmalade are specialities.
3⇄♠ CTV in 2 bedrooms TV in 1 bedroom ®
sB&B⇄♠£21.50 dB&B⇄♠£38 WB&B£133-£150.50
WBDi£172.50-£210 LDO noon
Lic ⬛ CTV 6P nc9yrs

BRYNGWYN Powys Map **03** SO14

FH Q Mrs H E A Nicholls **Newhouse** *(SO169485)* LD2 3JT
☎Painscastle(04975) 671
200-year-old, two-storey, stone-built farmhouse in rolling countryside.
2hc ↙in all bedrooms ® ✶ (ex guide dogs) ✻ sB&Bfr£14
dB&Bfr£24
⬛ CTV 3P nc11yrs ◢ pony treking 150 acres beef sheep

BUCKFAST Devon Map **03** SX76

GH QQ *Furzeleigh Mill Country Hotel* Dart Bridge TQ11 0JP
☎Buckfastleigh(0364) 43476
This 16th-century mill house has been converted into a pleasant, small hotel with comfortable public rooms including a restaurant offering a table d'hôte menu with interesting home-cooked dishes; the cosy lounge has an informal residents' bar. The compact bedrooms are bright and simply styled and furnished; they are equipped with TV and tea and coffee-making facilities, and many have en suite bathrooms. Located in a pleasant rural spot mid-way between Exeter and Plymouth, the hotel is conveniently close to the A38, providing a good base for touring South Devon and Dartmoor National Park.
15rm(13⇄♠2hc)(2fb) CTV in all bedrooms ® LDO 8pm
Lic ⬛ CTV 32P ⚬
Credit Cards 1 2 3

BUCKFASTLEIGH Devon Map **03** SX76

GH QQQ *Dartbridge Manor* 20 Dartbridge Rd TQ11 0DZ
☎(0364) 43575
Conveniently situated close to the A38 Exeter to Plymouth road, this 400-year-old property has been sympathetically restored and offers spotlessly clean, warm bedrooms, individually styled with soft co-ordinated fabrics, brass beds and assorted Victoriana. The residents' lounge is richly furnished and hearty breakfasts are taken in the pine-furnished dining room.
10⇄♠ (2fb) ✻
⬛ CTV 30P ◢

BUDE Cornwall & Isles of Scilly Map **02** SS20

GH Q *Atlantic Beach Hotel* 25 Downs View EX23 8RG
☎(0288) 353431
This terraced house, set close to the sea, and overlooking the golf course and Downs, offers fresh, modern accommodation suitable for family holidays. There is a small bar and lounge, as well as a pretty dining room.
9rm(5♠4hc)(3fb) CTV in all bedrooms ® ✶ (ex guide dogs)
✻ sB&B£13.50-£17.50 sB&B♠£16-£20 dB&B£27-£35
dB&B♠£32-£40 LDO 6.30pm
Lic ⬛ CTV 4P
Credit Cards 1 2 3 ⓔ

GH QQQ **Cliff Hotel** Maer Down, Crooklets Beach
EX23 8NG ☎(0288) 353110
Apr-Oct
The purpose-built hotel stands in an elevated position, surrounded by grounds which include a putting green, tennis court and children's play area; an indoor heated pool, spa bath and solarium are also available for guests' use. All bedrooms have en suite bathrooms and the restaurant features imaginative, home-cooked meals.
15⇄ (12fb) CTV in all bedrooms ✶ dB&B⇄£39-£53
WB&B£135-£170 WBDi£165-£200 LDO 6pm
Lic CTV 15P 1🛆 ⬜(heated) ♪ (hard)solarium indoor spa pool
putting ⓔ

GH QQQ *Corisande Hotel* 24 Downs View EX23 8RG
☎(0288) 353474
Closed Xmas
Close to the beach and overlooking the golf course, this family-run hotel has comfortable bedrooms with good facilities. A variety of home-cooked food is served in the dining room by friendly proprietors.
9rm(5♠4hc)(2fb) CTV in all bedrooms ® LDO 5.30pm
Lic ⬛ 3P nc3yrs
Credit Cards 1 3

Visit your local AA Shop.

GH Q Q Q **Dorset House Hotel** 47 Killerton Rd EX23 8EN
☎(0288) 352665
*This attractive licensed hotel with its wood-panelled walls, retains
much of its original charm. The bedrooms are of ample size, and
have good bath and shower facilities, and the public rooms are
complemented by a bar and pool room.*
6rm(1⇨5hc) (2fb)⊁in all bedrooms ® ✠ sB&B£16-£21
dB&B£32-£42 WB&B£96-£118 WBDi£118-£150 LDO 6.30pm
Lic ꝶ CTV 6P games room
Credit Cards 1 3 £

⊯⊮**GH** Q **Links View** 13 Morwenna Ter EX23 8BU
☎(0288) 352561
Closed Dec
*Enjoying an elevated position overlooking the Downs, this hotel
offers compact accommodation with cosy public rooms and well-
furnished and equipped bedrooms.*
7hc (2fb) CTV in all bedrooms ® ✠ (ex guide dogs) sB&B£13-
£14 dB&B£26-£28 WB&B£84-£90
Lic ꝶ CTV 2P 1🏕 £

⊯⊮**GH** Q Q **Pencarrol** 21 Downs View EX23 8RF
☎(0288) 352478
Closed Dec rs Jan-Mar & Nov
*A friendly guesthouse in a quiet location overlooking the golf
course, and a short walk from Crooklets Beach. Bedrooms,
including two on the ground floor, are light and airy and well
presented. There is a comfortable first-floor lounge and the
ground-floor dining room serves home-cooked food.*
8rm(2🌢6hc) (1fb) CTV in 2 bedrooms ® ✠ (ex guide dogs)
sB&B£12.50-£17 dB&B£25-£30 dB&B🌢£29-£34 WB&B£76-
£113 WBDi£114-£141 LDO 5pm
ꝶ CTV 1🏕 £

FH Q Q Mrs S Trewin **Lower Northcott** *(SS215087)* Poughill
EX23 7EL ☎(0288) 352350
Closed Dec
*Standing in 470 acres with views over countryside and coastline,
this Georgian farmhouse has a secure garden with swings and
young animals, and guests can take tours around the farm.
Families are well catered for with spacious bedrooms.*
5rm(1⇨2🌢2hc) (3fb) ® ✠ (ex guide dogs) sB&Bfr£14
dB&Bfr£28 dB&B🌢fr£28 WB&Bfr£98 WBDifr£135 (wkly
only Jul-Aug) LDO 6.30pm
ꝶ CTV 4P 470 acres arable beef dairy sheep

BUDLEIGH SALTERTON Devon Map 03 SY08

GH Q Q Q *Copperfields* 7 Upper Stoneborough Ln EX9 6SZ
☎(03954) 3430
Etr-Sep
*This delightful Victorian house is set in a quiet location just five
minutes' walk from the sea and town centre. Whilst retaining its
original charm, Copperfields offers modern-day comfort, including
bright bedrooms with en suite showers, lavatory and television.*
6rm(3🌢3hc) (1fb) CTV in all bedrooms ® LDO 5pm
Lic ꝶ 8P nc9yrs

GH Q Q Q **Long Range Hotel** Vale's Rd EX9 6HS
☎(03954) 3321
Apr-Oct rs Nov-Mar
*This modern detached building within attractive gardens, is 15
minutes' walk from the town centre and seafront. After major
refurbishment, 6 of the 7 bedrooms have en suite facilities and all
are well equipped. All areas are tastefully decorated, and the sun
lounge offers access to the lounge garden. A choice of evening meal
is provided, and owners Mr and Mrs Griffin are always available
to give guests their personal attention.*
7rm(2⇨4🌢1hc) (1fb) CTV in all bedrooms ® ✠ ✳
sB&B⇨£21 dB&B⇨£42 WB&B£132 WBDi£195
LDO 7pm
Lic ꝶ CTV 8P 2🏕 nc4yrs £

Dorset House
Licensed Hotel

Resident Proprietors: Eric and Lorna Hatch

Killerton Road, Bude, Cornwall EX23 8EN
Telephone: Bude (0288) 352665

**We would like to welcome you to our charming detached
hotel of character, quietly situated, convenient to shops,
beaches and golf course. It is with some pride we welcome
back so many familiar faces every year.**

Sunroom, snooker, darts, table tennis, colour TV, lounge,
separate dining tables. All rooms H/C, shaver points,
tea/coffee makers, some en suite. Full central heating. Bar.
Private car park. Garden.

B&B from £16.00, children at reduced prices.

OPEN ALL YEAR

BEACH HOUSE HOTEL
Widemouth Bay, Bude, Cornwall EX23 0AW
*A delightful private hotel in own grounds. Ideally situated
in an unrivalled position in Widemouth Bay.*

● Your nearest hotel to the beach and the only hotel on Widemouth Bay foreshore
● Good Cornish recipes personally prepared by Cornish Proprietress and chef (son)
● Separate colour TV Lounge
● Rooms individually with private shower/toilet/sun balcony/tea making facilities
● Ground floor bedrooms/Honeymoon Suite
● Games Room ● Reduced rates for children sharing parents rooms ● Own car park
● Heating in all rooms ● No service charge ● Resident Proprietors for 25 years
● Wetsuits and Surfboards available

Write or phone for Colour Brochure Mr & Mrs R Wilkins.
Tel: Widemouth Bay (0288361) 256. Terms: Dinner, Room
and Breakfast £23.50 daily, £145 weekly per person
inclusive of VAT.

GH QQ **Willowmead** 12 Little Knowle EX9 6QS
☎(03954) 3115
6rm(4♠2hc) ® sB&B£16-£17 sB&B♠£18-£19 dB&B♠£32-
£36 WBDi£140-£155
♚ CTV 6P nc5yrs

BUNESSAN

See **MULL, ISLE OF**

BURBAGE Wiltshire Map **04** SU26

SELECTED

GH QQQQ **The Old Vicarage** SN8 3AG
☎Marlborough(0672) 810494
Feb-18 Dec
*A delightful brick and flint Victorian former vicarage dating
from 1853, set in its own well tended grounds in the village of
Burbage, between Hungerford and Marlborough. Each of the
three bedrooms has been tastefully decorated and furnished
with style; they are thoughtfully stocked with a selection of
amenities including hot or cold beverages, home-made biscuits
and truffles, books and magazines and fresh flowers and fruit.
The drawing room is bright and pretty, with a log fire and
comfortable seating. Guests dine together round a large
polished antique table in the candlelit dining room; drinks are
served before dinner in the drawing room. The menu is a
surprise until guests are seated at 8.0pm, and dishes are full-
flavoured and well presented, using only the finest, freshest
produce. Breakfast is informal, with a good choice of cooked
and continental-style dishes. The proprietors are a charming,
friendly couple, and the atmosphere is warm and welcoming.*
3⇄♠ ⊀in all bedrooms CTV in all bedrooms ®
✖ (ex guide dogs) sB&B⇄£32-£40 dB&B⇄£55-£65
LDO 6pm
♚ CTV 10P nc18yrs
Credit Cards 1 3 £

BURFORD Oxfordshire Map **04** SP21

GH QQQ **Andrews Hotel** High St OX18 4QA ☎(099382) 3151
FAX (099382) 3240
Closed 5 Jan-4 Feb & Xmas
*An attractive Cotswold stone building, parts of which date from the
16th century. Since purchasing the hotel, Mr Gibbons has
renovated the bedrooms and the public areas. Bedrooms are pretty
and comfortable and all have very smart en suite facilities. Public
areas are cosy and attractive. The small dining room where
tempting cream teas and home baking are served is particularly
popular with both residents and locals.*
10⇄♠ ⊀in all bedrooms CTV in all bedrooms ®
✖ (ex guide dogs) * sB&B⇄♠£45-£50 dB&B⇄♠£50-£85
Lic ♚ CTV ⨍
Credit Cards 1 2 3 5

GH QQQ **Elm Farm House** Meadow Ln, Fulbrook OX8 4BW
☎(0993) 823611
Closed 16 Dec-Jan
*A Cotswold stone house dating back in parts to the Jacobean era
situated at the end of a quiet lane in the pretty village of Fulbrook,
close to Burford. Bedrooms have been refurbished by the resident
proprietors and are comfortable and well equipped. Public areas
are attractive and include a small bar.*
7rm(2⇄2♠3hc) (2fb)⊀in all bedrooms CTV in all bedrooms
® ✖ sB&B£29.50-£34.50 sB&B⇄£34.50 dB&B£41
dB&B⇄♠£43-£57 WB&B£140-£234.50 WBDi£245-£339.50
LDO 10am
Lic ♚ CTV 10P nc1-10yrs
Credit Cards 1 2 3

BURNSALL North Yorkshire Map **07** SE06

GH Q **Manor House** BD23 6BW ☎(075672) 231
Closed Jan
Small, private hotel whose gardens run down to River Wharfe.
7hc (2fb) ✖ LDO 5pm
Lic ♚ CTV 7P ✈ Ü solarium

BURRELTON Tayside *Perthshire* Map **11** NO23

INN QQQ **Burrelton Park** High St PH13 9NX ☎(08287) 206
*A small, welcoming family-run hotel situated beside the main road
in the centre of the village, appealing to the business traveller as
well as touring holidaymakers. It has a friendly bar, an attractive à
la carte restaurant, and the bedrooms, though compact, are
comfortably appointed in the modern style.*
6⇄♠ CTV ® ♚ 40P
Credit Cards 1 3

BURROWBRIDGE Somerset Map **03** ST32

GH Q **The Old Bakery** TA7 ORB ☎(082369) 234
Mar-24 Dec
*A warm and friendly welcome is to be had at this family-run
guesthouse. Standing on the A361, halfway between Street and
Taunton, it offers comfortable, simply appointed accommodation
and an extensive menu.*
6rm(1⇄5hc) (2fb)⊀in all bedrooms ✖ (ex guide dogs) *
sB&B£12.50-£13.50 dB&B£25-£27 dB&B⇄£27-£31
LDO 9.30pm
Lic ♚ CTV 8P
Credit Cards 1 3

BURTON BRADSTOCK Dorset Map **03** SY48

GH QQQ **Common Knapp House** Coast Rd DT6 4RJ
☎(0308) 897428
Closed Dec-Jan
*This modern house is on the coast road and has spacious, well
equipped bedrooms with en suite showers. There is a cosy bar
lounge with books and games and a spacious dining room. This is a
'no smoking' house.*
12rm(9♠3hc) (1fb)⊀in all bedrooms CTV in 9 bedrooms ®
✖ (ex guide dogs) sB&B£22 dB&B£46 dB&B♠£48-£52
WB&Bfr£160 WBDifr£230 LDO 4pm
Lic ♚ 12P nc4yrs

BURTON UPON TRENT Staffordshire Map **08** SK22

GH QQQ **Delter Hotel** 5 Derby Rd DE14 1RU
☎(0283) 35115
*A fully modernised house situated on the edge of town, on the busy
Derby road. The bedrooms are bright and clean, and in the small
basement bar snacks are served in the evening.*
5rm(1⇄4♠) CTV in all bedrooms ® ✖ (ex guide dogs) *
sB&B⇄♠£28 dB&B⇄♠£38 LDO 9pm
Lic ♚ CTV 6P
Credit Cards 1 3 £

GH Q **Edgecote Hotel** 179 Ashby Rd DE15 OLB
☎Burton on Trent(0283) 68966
*This family-run hotel is a large, detached house situated on the
edge of the town on the A50, Ashby road. It has a well maintained
rear garden and an oak-panelled dining room.*
12rm(1♠11hc) (3fb)⊀in all bedrooms CTV in all bedrooms ®
sB&B£18-£25 sB&B♠£25-£30 dB&B£33-£36 dB&B♠£38-£45
LDO 7.30pm
Lic ♚ CTV 6P 2🚗
Credit Cards 1 3 £

Book as early as possible for busy holiday periods.

BURWASH East Sussex Map **05** TQ62

FH Ⓠ Ⓠ Mrs E Sirrell **Woodlands** *(TQ656242)* TN19 7LA
☎(0435) 882794
Etr-Oct
Remotely situated and surrounded by woodland, this 16th-century cottage-style farmhouse has functional modern bedrooms and a breakfast room. There is a private track access from the main road. This farmhouse offers very good value for money.
4rm(1🅵 1hc) 🇽 ✳ sB&B£13-£16 dB&Bfr£26 dB&B🅵fr£33 LDO am
🆖 CTV 4P 55 acres mixed

INN Ⓠ *Admiral Vernon* Etchingham Rd TN19 7BJ
☎(0435) 882230
This cosy old fasioned 'free house' offers home cooking, and good views over the Rother Valley. The rear garden is delightful.
5rm(2🅵 2fb) CTV in 1 bedroom TV in 4 bedrooms Ⓡ LDO 8.15pm
🆖 CTV 30P 2🛎 nc9yrs

BURY ST EDMUNDS Suffolk Map **05** TL86

See also Beyton
GH Ⓠ Ⓠ Ⓠ **The Chantry Hotel** 8 Sparhawk St IP33 1RY
☎(0284) 767427 FAX (0284) 760946
rs wknds
A listed 16th century terraced building situated a few minutes' walk from the Abbey, south of the town centre. This substantial, professionally run private hotel offers good quality, well equipped accommodation, with a pleasant bar lounge, a restaurant and a variety of bedrooms, the best of which are in the Tudor annexe; all the rooms have good modern en suite facilities.
14rm(5🅵 9🅵) Annexe 3🅵 (1fb) CTV in all bedrooms Ⓡ
sB&B🅵£35-£39 dB&B🅵£44-£49 LDO 6.45pm
Lic 🆖 16P
Credit Cards ①③£

GH Ⓠ Ⓠ Ⓠ **Dunston House Hotel** 8 Springfield Rd IP33 3AN
☎(0284) 767981
A delightful guesthouse located just off the ring road, the A1302 to Newmarket, yet in a quiet residential street. The accommodation has some en suite facilities and is well equipped for the commerical and leisure user, there is a comfortable lounge and dining rom. All very well cared for and warm.
11rm(6🅵 5hc) Annexe 6rm(2🅵 4hc) (5fb) CTV in all bedrooms
Ⓡ 🇽 ✳ sB&B£16-£20 sB&B🅵£25-£30 dB&B£32-£34
dB&B🅵£34-£38 WB&B£112-£140 WBDi£122-£150
LDO 10pm previous day
Lic 🆖 CTV 12P £

GH Ⓠ Ⓠ Ⓠ **The Olde White Hart Hotel** 35 Southgate St
IP33 2AZ ☎(0284) 755547
Easily found if approached from the most easterly exit of the A45, this inn near the town centre was originally an 11th-century chapel beside the river Linnet before being converted into a Tudor public house and then an 18th-century maltings. Most of the original buildings still remain and have been converted into a small luxury hotel. The accommodation is in good order with every modern facility, including en suite rooms.
10🅵 (2fb) CTV in all bedrooms Ⓡ 🇽 (ex guide dogs) ✳
sB&B🅵£35-£39.50 dB&B🅵£45-£49.50
Lic 🆖 10P
Credit Cards ①②③£

BUTLEIGH Somerset Map **03** ST53

FH Ⓠ Ⓠ Mrs Atkinson **Court Lodge** *(ST517339)* BA6 8SA
☎Baltonsborough(0458) 50575
This pretty house nestles in secluded gardens in the village of Butleigh and has commanding views of the surrounding countryside. The rooms have traditional style and charm, and substantial breakfasts are served in the bright dining room.
2rm TV available ✳ sB&Bfr£10.50 dB&Bfr£21
🆖 CTV 4P 110 acres beef £

FH Q Q Q Mrs J M Gillam **Dower House** *(ST517333)*
BA6 8TG ☎Baltonsborough(0458) 50354
Feb-Nov
Attractive 18th-century farmhouse with friendly atmosphere.
3rm(1⇨2hc) (1fb) ® ✖ (ex guide dogs) ✱ sB&Bfr£15.50
dB&Bfr£28 dB&B⇨frf£34 LDO 4.30pm
🍴 CTV 6P 80 acres non-working ⓔ

BUTTERMERE Cumbria Map **11** NY11

SELECTED

GH Q Q Q Q **Pickett Howe** Brackenthwaite, Buttermere
Valley CA13 9UY ☎Cockermouth(0900) 85444
Closed Dec-Jan exs Xmas & New Year
*A luxury guesthouse converted from a Cumbrian Long House,
parts of which date from 1650. It stands in 15 acres of pasture
at the foot of Whiteside Fell, just off the B5289 Lorton
Buttermere road, with beautiful views of the fells and
surrounding countryside. Bedrooms are exceptionally well
appointed, all en suite with many other beams, a stone
chimney breast and Victorian bedsteads, slate floors, oak
beams and mullioned windows. Owners David and Dani
Edwards provides a warm, hospitable atmosphere, and Dani's
delicious 5-course dinners are recommended. Breakfast is
exceptional, ranging from a traditional farmhouse meal to
simple beans on toast.*
4⇨♠ ✌in all bedrooms CTV in all bedrooms ® ✖ ✱
dB&B⇨♠£86-£94 (incl dinner) WB&B£196 WBDif£301
Lic 10P nc10yrs
Credit Cards ① ② ③

BUXTON Derbyshire Map **07** SK07

SELECTED

GH Q Q Q Q **Brookfield On Longhill** Brookfield Hall,
Long Hill SK17 6SU ☎(0298) 24151
*A Victorian retreat, just over a mile from Buxton, in 10 acres
of gardens and woodlands amid beautiful Peak District
countryside. Brookfield Hall is a quality small country hotel
with period furnishings and antique pieces, but modern
facilities and hospitable service. The restaurant is fast
becoming popular for its interesting menus and good food and
wines.*
4⇨♠ CTV in all bedrooms ® sB&B⇨♠£41-£45
dB&B⇨♠£61.50-£67.50 LDO 10.30pm
Lic 🍴 CTV 35P ∪
Credit Cards ① ② ③ ⓔ

GH Q Q *Buxton Lodge Private Hotel* 28 London Rd SK17 9NX
☎(0298) 23522
*This modern hotel is close to the town centre, on the main road out
of Buxton towards Ashbourne. Families are encouraged and a
children's room is provided. On summer evenings barbecues are
held in the rear gardens.*
7rm(3♠4hc) (1fb) CTV in all bedrooms ® LDO 4pm
Lic 🍴 CTV 5P ♨
Credit Cards ③

GH Q Q *Buxton View* 74 Corbar Rd SK17 6RJ ☎(0298) 79222
Mar-Nov
*Standing on the north side of the town, this well-equipped, stone-
built house is in a quiet residential area with commanding views
over the town.*
5⇨♠ (1fb)✌in all bedrooms CTV in all bedrooms ® ✱
sB&B⇨♠£20 dB&B⇨♠£35 WB&B£110-£126 WBDif£173-
£189 LDO 9am
🍴 CTV 5P 2☻

GH Q **Griff** 2 Compton Rd SK17 9DN ☎(0298) 23628
*A busy house set in a residential area of the town, Griff offers fully
equipped bedrooms and has parking facilities.*
5hc (1fb) CTV in all bedrooms ® ✱ sB&B£12-£13 dB&B£24-
£26 LDO noon
🍴 CTV 5P

GH Q **Hawthorn Farm** Fairfield Rd SK17 7ED ☎(0298) 23230
Apr-Oct
*This charming, fully converted farmhouse and its outbuildings are
fronted by well-kept gardens and lawns, and stand on the outskirts
of Buxton.*
5hc Annexe 6rm(4♠2hc) (1fb) ® sB&B£15.50-£16.50
dB&B£31-£33 dB&B♠£38-£40
🍴 CTV 12P 2☻ ⓔ

GH Q **Kingscroft** 10 Green Ln SK17 9DP ☎(0298) 22757
Mar-Dec
Large, stone-built town house in a surburban area.
7hc (2fb)✌in 2 bedrooms CTV in all bedrooms ® dB&B£36-
£38 (incl dinner) WB&B£90 WBDif£120 LDO 5pm
Lic 🍴 CTV 9P 2☻ nc5yrs ⓔ

GH Q **The Old Manse Private Hotel** 6 Clifton Rd, Silverlands
SK17 6QL ☎(0298) 25638
Closed Xmas & New Year
*Close to the town centre this stone-built semi-detached house
provides simple accommodation with a comfortable atmosphere
and the advantage of having it's own small car park.*
8rm(4♠4hc) (2fb) ® sB&B£14-£15 dB&B£28-£30 dB&B♠£33-
£35 WBDif£150-£168 LDO 5pm
Lic 🍴 CTV 4P nc2yrs ⓔ

GH Q **Roseleigh Private Hotel** 19 Broad Walk SK17 6JR
☎(0298) 24904
Closed Xmas-Jan rs Feb & Dec
*Roseleigh has an enviable position overlooking the Pavilion
Gardens and lake. Small and comfortable, the hotel has vehicular
access via Hartington Road as Broadwalk is for pedestrians only.*
13rm(9⇨♠4hc) (1fb) CTV in all bedrooms ® ✱ sB&B£16-
£16.50 dB&B£32-£33 dB&B⇨♠£38-£40 WBDif£185-£192
LDO 5pm
Lic CTV 12P

GH Q Q **Swanleigh** 7 Grange Rd SK17 6NH ☎(0298) 24588
*Centrally situated in a quiet residential area, this semi-detached
house offers attractive, well-equipped rooms and bright,
comfortable public rooms. The friendly proprietors give personal
and professional service.*
7hc (1fb) TV in all bedrooms ® ✖ (ex guide dogs) ✱
sB&B£15-£17 dB&B£30-£34 WB&B£100-£107
🍴 CTV 6P

GH Q Q **Templeton** 13 Compton Rd SK17 9DN ☎(0298) 25275
rs Nov-Etr
*A semi-detached house in a quiet residential area, Templeton
provides bright, warm and well-equipped accommodation close to
the town centre. Good home-cooked meals are provided and there
is ample parking space.*
6rm(2♠4hc) (2fb) CTV in 4 bedrooms ® ✖ ✱ sB&B£19-
£21.50 dB&B£27-£31 dB&B♠£32-£36 WB&B£87-£105
WBDif£132-£147 LDO noon
Lic 🍴 CTV 6P nc14yrs ⓔ

GH Q Q Q **Thorn Heyes Private Hotel** 137 London Rd
SK17 9NW ☎(0298) 23539
Closed last 2 wks Nov & Jan
*Set in large attractive gardens, this Victorian house provides guests
with almost every convenience they require on holiday. Mrs Green
prepares the meals, and her husband has a store of local
knowledge, having lived in Buxton all his life.*
8♠ Annexe 3rm(1⇨2♠) (2fb) CTV in all bedrooms ® ✱
sB&B⇨♠£20-£38 dB&B⇨♠frf£40 WB&Bfr£136
WBDifrf£200 LDO 6pm

Lic 🕮 12P nc14yrs
Credit Cards ①③

GH Ⓠ Ⓠ Ⓠ **Westminster Hotel** 21 Broadwalk SK17 6JT
☎(0298) 23929
Feb-Nov & Xmas
*Set in a quiet residential area with views of the lake in the Pavillion
Gardens, this friendly hotel provides well equipped
accommodation. Because Broad Walk is closed to traffic the hotel
is approached via Hartington Road.*
12rm(5⇨7↾⇩) CTV in all bedrooms Ⓡ ✗ (ex guide dogs)
dB&B⇨↾⇩£40-£42 WB&Bfr£140 WBDifr£180 LDO 3pm
Lic 🕮 14P
Credit Cards ①②③ⓔ

FH Ⓠ Ⓠ Ⓠ Mrs M A Mackenzie **Staden Grange** *(SK075717)*
Staden Ln SK17 9RZ (1.5m SE off A515) ☎(0298) 24965
FAX (0298) 72067
*Don't be put off by the approach to this spacious farm, as once
through the industrial estate, you will be in a very rural district.
Superior accommodation is offered here, as well as a caravan site
and self-catering accommodation.*
14⇨↾⇩ (4fb) CTV in all bedrooms Ⓡ sB&B⇨↾⇩fr£25
dB&B⇨↾⇩fr£43 LDO 4pm
Lic 🕮 CTV 30P ✔ Ⓤ sauna spa pool 250 acres beef/sheep ⓔ

BYFORD Hereford & Worcester Map **03** SO34

GH Ⓠ Ⓠ **Old Rectory** HR4 7LD ☎Bridge Sollars(098122) 218
Etr-Nov
3rm(1↾⇩2hc) (1fb)⤢in all bedrooms CTV in 2 bedrooms
✗ (ex guide dogs) sB&B£15-£20 sB&B↾⇩£20-£30 dB&B£24-
£27 dB&B↾⇩£28-£33 WB&B£77-£91 LDO previous day
🕮 6P ⓔ

BYRNESS Northumberland Map **12** NT70

FH Ⓠ Ⓠ Mrs A Anderson **Blakehope Burnhaugh** *(NT783002)*
Otterburn NE19 1SW (1.5m along A68 towards Rochester)
☎Otterburn(0830) 20267
*A pleasant farmhouse located in a beautiful forest setting. The
house is very comfortable and a good standard of hospitality is
provided by the resident owners.*
3hc (1fb) Ⓡ sB&B£14 dB&B£26 LDO 4pm
🕮 CTV 5P 3🐏 150 acres beef ⓔ

CADNAM Hampshire Map **04** SU21

FH Ⓠ Ⓠ Ⓠ Mrs A M Dawe **Budds** *(SU310139)* Winsor Rd,
Winsor SO4 2HN ☎Southampton(0703) 812381
Apr-Oct
*A delightful thatched farmhouse dating from the 17th century.
Mrs Dawes extends a warm and friendly welcome to her guests
and ensures their comfort throughout their stay. Bedrooms are
spacious and pretty, and in the lounge a log fire burns in cold
weather. Personal bric-a-brac adds to the charm of this
comfortable home.*
2hc (1fb)⤢in all bedrooms ✗ (ex guide dogs) ✳ dB&B£30-£32
WB&B£105-£112
🕮 CTV 3P 200 acres beef dairy

FH Ⓠ Ⓠ Ⓠ Mrs A Dawe **Kents** *(SU315139)* Winsor Rd,
Winsor SO4 2HN ☎Southampton(0703) 813497
Apr-Oct
*A 16th-century thatched farmhouse renovated to provide 2
attractive and comfortable bedrooms for bed and breakfast
accommodation. Set in well tended cottage gardens and
surrounded by its own pastureland, the farmhouse offers
comfortable cottage décor, with oak beams and an inglenook
fireplace. There is a pleasant lounge where guests are joined by the
friendly owners, who can recommend one of the many New Forest
pubs or restaurants.*
2rm(1⇨1↾⇩) (1fb)⤢in all bedrooms ✗ dB&B⇨↾⇩fr£28
🕮 CTV 4P nc2yrs 200 acres beef dairy

CAERNARFON Gwynedd Map **06** SH46
See also Llanddeiniolen

GH Ⓠ Ⓠ Ⓠ **Caer Menai** 15 Church St LL55 1SW ☎(0286) 2612
Mar-Dec
*This small family-run hotel is situated in a quiet road, close to the
town walls and within a short walk of both the castle and the
harbour. It is impeccably maintained and provides good quality,
well equipped accommodation.*
7rm(3↾⇩4hc) (2fb)⤢in 3 bedrooms CTV in all bedrooms Ⓡ
✗ (ex guide dogs) sB&B£15.50-£16.50 sB&B↾⇩£20-£21
dB&B£27-£29 dB&B↾⇩£32-£36
CTV ✗ solarium ⓔ

GH Ⓠ **Menai View Hotel** North Rd LL55 1BD ☎(0286) 4602
*This small family-run hotel is situated on the A487, just north of
the town, and overlooks the Menai Straits. The accommodation is
simple, but all bedrooms are equipped with colour televisions and
central heating.*
7rm(2↾⇩5hc) (4fb) CTV in all bedrooms Ⓡ sB&Bfr£14
dB&Bfr£25 dB&B↾⇩fr£29 WB&B£80-£95 WBDi£120-£140
LDO 8pm
Lic 🕮 CTV ✗ ⓔ

FH Ⓠ Ⓠ Ⓠ Mr & Mrs D Mackinnon **Plas Tirion** *(SH524628)*
Llanrug LL55 4PY (Llanrug 3m E A4086) ☎(0286) 673190
May-Sep
*This delightfully furnished farmhouse offers home comforts and
accommodation of a high standard, with a very pleasant lounge.
Good service is provided and a stay here is excellent value for
money.*
3↾⇩ (1fb) CTV in 2 bedrooms Ⓡ ✗ LDO midday
Lic 🕮 CTV 6P ॐ rough shooting 450 acres mixed

𝔅uxton 𝔏odge 𝔥otel

28 London Road, Buxton, Derbyshire SK17 9NX
Telephone: (0298) 23522
Proprietors: Tony and Veronica Sellors

A Small family run hotel offering a homely,
comfortable and pleasant stay in the old spa
town of Buxton. Close to all the local amenities
and within the beautiful Peak District with all
it's attractions.

Rooms include en suite, basic and a family suite.
All of which contain -

* Hot and cold water
* Tea and coffee making facilities
* Colour tele-text T.Vs.
* Radio alarm
* Electric shaver point and power sockets
* Bed-side lamps
* Heating

Evening meals from our 'home style' menu.
Residential licence and bar lounge.
Bar meals and snacks.
The hotel has a full fire certificate.
Forecourt parking.

CALDBECK Cumbria Map **11** NY33

SELECTED
GH ⓠⓠⓠⓠ **High Greenrigg House** CA7 8HD
☎(06998) 430
Mar-Oct
This 17th-century farmhouse is situated 3 miles west of the
village, off the B5299, and is delightfully isolated, with
splendid views of Caldbeck Fells. Carefully restored, there is
much of interest throughout the house, including a stone
flagged floor and original fireplace. Bedrooms are mostly pine
furnished and have modern facilities. There is a television
lounge where guests can make themselves hot drinks, and
beneath the bar there are facilities for table tennis, darts and
snooker. Dinner is served in the attractive dining room, which
has views over the garden and surrounding fells.
8rm(6⇨3♠2hc) (1fb) in all bedrooms ✱ sB&B£19.50
sB&B⇨♠£25 dB&B⇨♠£39 WB&B£117-£150 LDO 5pm
Lic ⑭ CTV 8P ⓔ

FH ⓠⓠⓠ Mrs D H Coulthard *Friar Hall (NY324399)*
CA7 8DS ☎(06998) 633
Mar-Oct
Spacious bedrooms and a comfortable lounge are features of this
warm, friendly farmhouse, parts of which date back to the 12th
century. It is part of a dairy and sheep farm in the village centre
and overlooks the river.
3hc (2fb) ✖ (ex guide dogs)
CTV 3P 140 acres dairy mixed sheep

CALLANDER Central *Perthshire* Map **11** NN60
GH ⓠⓠ **Abbotsford Lodge** Stirling Rd FK17 8DA
☎(0877) 30066
A popular base for a touring holiday, this friendly guesthouse is
conveniently situated on the edge of the town. The bedrooms
provide traditional comforts.
19rm(4⇨3♠12hc) (7fb) ⓡ ✱ sB&Bfr£18.25 dB&Bfr£28.50
dB&B⇨♠fr£35.50 WB&Bfr£159.50 LDO 7pm
Lic ⑭ CTV 20P ⓔ

GH ⓠⓠ **Annfield** 18 North Church St FK17 8EG
☎(0877) 30204
Attractive stone-built house on a quiet street in the town centre.
8rm(2♠6hc) (2fb) ⓡ sB&Bfr£13 dB&Bfr£26 dB&B♠fr£30
WB&Bfr£91
⑭ CTV 9P nc10yrs ⓔ

GH ⓠⓠⓠ **Arden House** Bracklinn Rd FK17 8EQ
☎(0877) 30235
Feb-Nov
Attractive stone house standing on hillside close to golf course,
formerly used in the making of Dr Finlay's Casebook.
8⇨♠ (3fb) in all bedrooms ⓡ dB&B⇨♠£32-£36
WBDi£150-£165 LDO 7pm
⑭ CTV 12P ⚬ putting green ⓔ

SELECTED
GH ⓠⓠⓠⓠ **Arran Lodge** Leny Rd FK17 8AJ
☎(0877) 30976
Closed 16 Jan-14 Feb
A lovely spacious bungalow with a large rear garden
extending to the banks of the River Leny. The house is
beautifully furnished in all areas, with a spacious comfortable
lounge and an elegantly furnished dining room. The three
bedrooms are very comfortable and have top quality
furnishings; one has a four-poster bed. Robert and Pasqua
Moore are always on hand, caring for their guests' comfort
and well being.

3rm(2⇨1♠) in all bedrooms CTV in all bedrooms ⓡ
✖ (ex guide dogs) ✱ sB&B⇨♠£24-£28 dB&B⇨♠£34-
£38 LDO 8.30pm
⑭ CTV 5P ♪

GH ⓠⓠⓠ **Brook Linn Country House** Leny Feus FK17 8AU
☎(0877) 30103
Etr-Oct
Set in its own grounds overlooking the town, this attractive
Victorian house is comfortably appointed and has a country-house
atmosphere.
7rm(5♠2hc) (2fb) in all bedrooms CTV in all bedrooms ⓡ
sB&B♠£16-£18 dB&B♠£36-£40 WB&B£112-£126
WBDi£182-£196 LDO 4pm
Lic ⑭ 10P

GH ⓠ *Greenbank* 143 Main St FK17 8BH ☎(0877) 30296
Pleasant house standing in the main street.
6hc (2fb) CTV in 1 bedroom TV in 1 bedroom LDO 6pm
Lic ⑭ CTV 5P

GH ⓠⓠⓠ **Highland House Hotel** South Church St FK17 8BN
☎(0877) 30269
Closed Dec-Jan
Dee Shirley's Scottish cooking is a feature of this cosy little hotel,
just off the main street in the town centre. There is an attractive
lounge as well as a small bar for residents and diners.
9rm(7⇨3♠2hc) (2fb) in all bedrooms CTV in all bedrooms ⓡ
sB&B£17-£25 sB&B⇨♠£19-£35 dB&B£34-£44
dB&B⇨♠£38-£50 WB&B£105-£130 WBDi£199-£265
LDO 7pm
Lic ⑭ CTV ♪
Credit Cards ①②③ ⓔ

GH ⓠⓠ **Rock Villa** 1 Bracklinn Rd FK17 8EH ☎(0877) 30331
mid Mar-mid Nov
This guesthouse stands in its own gardens close to the town centre,
the bedrooms here are simple and comfortable. There is a
traditional-style lounge and home-cooked meals are provided in
the bright, airy dining room.
6rm(2♠4hc) (1fb) CTV in 2 bedrooms ⓡ ✱ sB&B£14.50-£15
dB&B£26-£29 dB&B♠£32-£36 LDO 4.30pm
⑭ CTV 7P

CAMBRIDGE Cambridgeshire Map **05** TL45
GH ⓠⓠ **Assisi** 193 Cherry Hinton Rd CB1 4BX
☎(0223) 211466 & 246648
Closed 15 Dec-5 Jan
Close to the city centre, with off-street parking, this newly
converted guesthouse has good quality en suite facilities, an open-
plan breakfast/dining room and lounge and an attractive reception/
lobby.
8rm(7⇨♠1hc) (1fb) CTV in all bedrooms ✖ ✱ sB&B£19-£26
sB&B⇨♠£26 dB&B⇨♠£32-£36 LDO 7.30pm
⑭ CTV 12P
Credit Cards ①②③ ⓔ

GH ⓠⓠ **Bon Accord House** 20 St Margarets Square CB1 4AP
☎(0223) 411188 & 246568
Closed Xmas & New Year
Situated in a quiet residential cul-de-sac off Cherry Hinton Road.
Mr and Mrs Northrop provide comfortable accommodation which
is well maintained and equipped. There is a large dining room and
a small, comfortable lounge. The guesthouse is 'no smoking'
throughout.
12rm(1♠11hc) (1fb) in all bedrooms CTV in all bedrooms ⓡ
✖ ✱ sB&B£18.50-£21 sB&B♠£26-£30 dB&B£31-£36
dB&B♠£36-£46
⑭ 12P 2⇦
Credit Cards ①③ ⓔ

GH Q Q **Cristina's** 47 St. Andrews Rd CB4 1DL
☎(0223) 65855 & 327700
This well maintained, friendly guesthouse is located at the end of a row of terraced houses. The accommodation is modern, and most bedrooms have their own bathrooms. There is also a comfortable lounge. The guesthouse provides bed and breakfast only, but has the advantage of its own private car park. It is situated north of the city centre, within easy reach of the A45, via the A1309.
6rm(4♪2hc) (2fb) CTV in all bedrooms ℝ � ✻ sB&B£22-£24 dB&B£32-£34 dB&B♪£38-£40
♨ CTV 8P ⓔ

See advertisement on page 105

GH Q Q *Fairways* 141-143 Cherry Hinton Rd CB1 4BX
☎(0223) 246063 FAX (0223) 212093
Closed 24-26 Dec
This friendly, family-run guesthouse is popular with commercial guests and tourists. The accommodation is well equipped with some en suite facilities. Fairways is situated on a main road, close to the city centre, and has off-street parking.
14rm(8♪6hc) (2fb)⤴in 2 bedrooms CTV in all bedrooms ℝ
� (ex guide dogs)
Lic ♨ 20P pool table

See advertisement on page 105

GH Q Q *Hamilton Hotel* 156 Chesterton Rd CB4 1DA
☎(0223) 65664
A professionally run guesthouse situated within walking distance of the town with a car park to the rear. Public areas are very smart and the bedrooms are well equipped but tend to be compact. Hamilton Lodge is well cared for with good standards of cleanliness.
10rm(5♪5hc) (3fb) CTV in all bedrooms ℝ ✘ LDO noon
Lic ♨ 10P nc4yrs
Credit Cards ③

►

GH QQQ *Helen Hotel* 167-169 Hills Rd CB2 2RJ
☎(0223) 246465 FAX (0223) 214406
Closed 15 Dec-5 Jan
Situated in a residential area south of the city (B1307), this friendly, caring establishment is run by Gino Agodino and his wife. Homemade dishes are served in the dining room which overlooks the garden, and off-street parking is available.
23rm(20⇨3♠3hc) Annexe 6rm(5♠1hc) (4fb) CTV in all bedrooms LDO 7.30pm
Lic ⁽ᵐ⁾ CTV 20P
Credit Cards ⬜1 ⬜3

GH QQQ **Lensfield Hotel** 53 Lensfield Rd CB2 1EN
☎(0223) 355017 Telex no 818183 FAX (0223) 312022
Closed 2wks Xmas
The Paschalis family run this friendly hotel which stands on the ring road, a few minutes' walk from the city centre, with a large public car park to the rear. The accommodation is very well equipped and comfortable.
36rm(2⇨18♠16hc) (4fb) CTV in all bedrooms ® ⅓ ✻
sB&B£32 sB&B⇨♠£42 dB&B⇨♠£55-£65 LDO 8.45pm
Lic ⁽ᵐ⁾ CTV 5P 2🐾
Credit Cards ⬜1 ⬜2 ⬜3 ⬜5

GH QQQ *Number Eleven* 11 Glisson Rd CB1 2HA
☎(0223) 461142
Off Hills Road (but more easily found via Tennison Road), this establishment is close to the city centre and offers a quiet and elegant retreat, with comfortable and well-furnished and decorated rooms. Breakfast is taken in the drawing room around a large oval table.
5rm(1⇨2♠2hc) (1fb) CTV in all bedrooms ®
⅓ (ex guide dogs)
🅿

GH QQQ **Sorrento Hotel** 196 Cherry Hinton Rd CB1 4AN
☎(0223) 243533 FAX (0223) 213463
A friendly family-run guesthouse with well equipped accommodation, mostly with en suite facilities, and a good standard of cleanliness is maintained. Public areas are spacious and include a well stocked bar and a no-smoking lounge. A good car park is provided for guests.
24rm(5⇨19♠) (5fb) CTV in all bedrooms ® sB&B⇨♠£35-£50 dB&B⇨♠£50-£60 LDO 8.30pm
Lic ⁽ᵐ⁾ CTV 25P petanque terraine
Credit Cards ⬜1 ⬜2 ⬜3 ⬜5 ⓔ

GH QQQ **Suffolk House Private Hotel** 69 Milton Rd
CB4 1XA ☎(0223) 352016
Standing on the A1134 in a residential area north of the city centre, Suffolk House offers refurbished en suite accommodation, which is most attractive. Mrs Cuthbert is a friendly host, and provides a buffet-style breakfast.
8♠ (3fb) CTV in all bedrooms ® ⅓ ✻ sB&B♠£40
dB&B♠£50-£55
Lic ⁽ᵐ⁾ CTV 11P nc4yrs
Credit Cards ⬜1 ⬜3

See advertisement on page 107

CAMPBELTOWN *Argyllshire* Strathclyde Map **10** NR72

GH QQQ **Ballegreggan House** Ballegreggan Rd PA28 6NN
☎Campbeltown(0586) 52062
Considerable renovations and improvements have been carried out at this impressive mansion house, which is set on a hill just outside the town and offers a fine outlook over Campbeltown Loch. The house has been tastefully decorated throughout and is comfortably furnished. At peak periods it may be necessary to share a dining table; it should be noted that smoking is not encouraged in the bedrooms.

6rm(3♠3hc) (1fb)⅟in all bedrooms ® ✻ sB&B£16-£19
sB&B♠£20-£23 dB&B£32 dB&B♠£40 LDO 6pm
⁽ᵐ⁾ CTV 8P ✓ ⓔ

CANTERBURY Kent Map **05** TR15

GH Q **Castle Court** 8 Castle St CT1 2QF ☎(0227) 463441
12hc (1fb) sB&B£16-£20 dB&B£30-£34
⁽ᵐ⁾ CTV 2P
Credit Cards ⬜1 ⬜3 ⓔ

GH QQ **Cathedral Gate Hotel** 36 Burgate CT1 2HA
☎(0227) 464381 FAX (0227) 462800
12rm(2⇨8hc) (4fb) CTV in all bedrooms ® ✻ sB&Bfr£19
sB&B⇨♠fr£35 dB&Bfr£35 dB&B⇨♠fr£52 LDO 9pm
Lic ⁽ᵐ⁾ 12P (£2 per night)
Credit Cards ⬜1 ⬜2 ⬜3 ⬜5

GH QQQ **Ebury Hotel** New Dover Rd CT1 3DX
☎(0227) 768433 FAX (0227) 459187
Closed 25 Dec-14 Jan
This charming Victorian hotel offers well-equipped accommodation of a high standard. The delightful, spacious lounge houses a display of clocks, and the elegant restaurant serves English food. Guests have the use of the recently opened indoor pool and spa.
15⇨♠ (6fb) CTV in all bedrooms ® sB&B⇨♠£39-£41
dB&B⇨♠£58.50-£62.50 WBDif£215-£230 LDO 8.30pm
Lic ⁽ᵐ⁾ CTV 20P 1🐾 (£2) ▣(heated)
Credit Cards ⬜1 ⬜2 ⬜3 ⓔ

GH QQQ **Ersham Lodge** 12 New Dover Rd CT1 3AP
☎(0227) 463174 FAX (0227) 455482
Apr-Dec
An attractive ivy-clad, Tudor beamed hotel conveniently located, with good forecourt parking. Very well equipped bedrooms are individually furnished with antiques, and offer good facilities, ▶

SORRENTO HOTEL

196 Cherryhinton Road, Cambridge CB1 4AN
Telephone: 0223 243533

A medium size family managed hotel offering a comfortable and friendly service. Situated approx 1½ miles from City Centre. All bedrooms with en suite facilities, television and telephone.
Relax in our licensed bar or television lounge where coffee/tea and snacks are served. Our pleasant restaurant offers a variety of English, French and Italian cuisine. Private car park at rear.

complemented by particularly good standards of housekeeping. The breakfast room is a no-smoking area, and there is a sitting area with a bar. Service from the French proprietors is personal and helpful.
14rm(2⇌11↱1hc) (2fb) CTV in all bedrooms
✗ (ex guide dogs) ✱ sB&B⇌↱£29-£37 dB&B⇌↱£39-£56
Lic ⊞ 11P 1⌂ (£3)
Credit Cards [1] [2] [3] £

GH QQ Highfield Hotel Summer Hill, Harbledown CT2 8NH
☏(0227) 462772
Feb-Nov
Georgian-style country house, family-run and providing value for money.
8rm(3↱5hc) Ⓡ ✗ sB&B£24-£28 dB&B£34-£41 dB&B↱£44-£52
Lic ⊞ 12P nc5yrs
Credit Cards [1] [3]

GH QQQ Magnolia House 36 St Dunstan's Ter CT2 8AX
☏(0227) 765121
This small, cosy guesthouse is in a quiet and pleasant residential area close to the Westgate Towers. Family-run, the accommodation is comfortable and well maintained.
6⇌↱ ⊘in all bedrooms CTV in 3 bedrooms TV in 1 bedroom
Ⓡ ✗ sB&B⇌↱£28-£32 dB&B⇌↱£42-£48
⊞ CTV 4P
Credit Cards [1] [2] [3]

GH QQ Pointers Hotel 1 London Rd CT2 8LR
☏(0227) 456846 FAX (0227) 457076
Closed Xmas & New Year
This elegant Georgian house, close to the centre of Canterbury, offers a range of comfortable public rooms including a small residents' bar overseen by the friendly proprietor. All the bedrooms are spacious, bright and airy, with good modern facilities. Pointers offers good standards of accommodation with a choice of an evening meal in relaxed surroundings.
14rm(10⇌↱4hc) (2fb) CTV in all bedrooms Ⓡ sB&Bfr£30 sB&B⇌↱fr£35 dB&Bfr£42 dB&B⇌↱fr£50 WB&Bfr£147 WBDifr£203 LDO 8.15pm
Lic ⊞ 10P
Credit Cards [1] [2] [3] [5] £

SELECTED

GH QQQQ Thanington Hotel 140 Wincheap CT1 3RY
☏(0227) 453227
Built around 1800, this house has lots of distinctive architectural features. The accommodation has been tastefully furnished and particularly well equipped, with every modern convenience. Breakfast is served in the elegant dining room and guests can relax in the lounge or garden room. Mr and Mrs Jenkins provide personal service and pay close attention to detail, making this a perfect venue for relaxation and comfort.
10⇌ (2fb) CTV in all bedrooms Ⓡ sB&B⇌£40-£48 dB&B⇌£55-£62
⊞ CTV 8P 2⌂
Credit Cards [1] [3] £

SELECTED

GH QQQQ Thruxted Oast Mystole, Chartham CT4 7BX
☏(0227) 730080
Closed Xmas
An original five-bay square kilned oast and barn built in 1791 and skilfully converted to provide a family home, luxury guest accommodation and a picture farming business. Situated in an area of outstanding natural beauty, the accommodation is spacious and provides every conceivable amenity. The enchanting bedrooms are exceedingly well equipped, and there is a very comfortable lounge and drawing room. Breakfast is served in a large farmhouse- style open-plan kitchen at a communal table.
3↱ ⊘in all bedrooms CTV in all bedrooms Ⓡ
✗ (ex guide dogs) ✱ sB&B↱fr£58 dB&B↱fr£68
⊞ 8P nc8yrs croquet lawn
Credit Cards [1] [2] [3] [5] £

INN QQQ The Pilgrims Hotel 18 The Friars CT1 2AS
☏(0227) 464531
15⇌↱ (1fb) CTV in all bedrooms Ⓡ ✱ sB&B⇌↱fr£40 dB&B⇌↱£50-£70 ✱ Lunch £3.95-£4.50&alc Dinner £3.95-£4.50&alc LDO 11pm
⊞
Credit Cards [1] [2] [3] [5]

See advertisement on page 109

CAPUTH Tayside *Perthshire* Map **11** NO04

FH QQ Mrs R Smith ***Stralochy*** *(NO086413)* PH1 4LQ
☏(073871) 250
May-Oct
Approached by a rough track, this small farmhouse has lovely views of the surrounding countryside. Providing a welcoming atmosphere and traditional comforts, Stralochy offers good value for money.
2rm Ⓡ ✗ LDO 4pm
CTV 2P 239 acres arable beef sheep

POINTERS HOTEL

1 London Road, Canterbury
Tel. 0227-456846

Situated only a few minutes' walk from the City Centre and Cathedral and close to the University.

Pointers is a family-run Georgian hotel offering home-produced English meals.

All bedrooms have either bath or shower and each is equipped with colour television, radio, direct-dial telephone and tea and coffee making facilities.

Private car park.

*M*AGNOLIA *H*OUSE

36 St Dunstan's Terrace, Canterbury, Kent CT2 8AX
Telephone: (0227) 765121

COMMENDED

This friendly, family run Georgian house, set in a quiet street, just a few minutes walk from the Westgate Towers and the City centre, with its magnificent Cathedral is ideally situated for the University and touring the Kentish coast and countryside. Enjoy our en suite facilities, varied and delicious breakfasts and relax in the beautiful walled garden. Car parking.

⊨ THE SUFFOLK HOUSE ⊨
private hotel

Small family run hotel. 15 minutes' walk from the city centre and Colleges. All rooms are en suite and have colour TV and tea and coffee making facilities. Pleasant secluded garden. Hotel car park.

69 Milton Road, Cambridge CB4 1XA
Tel: (0223) 352016

CARDIFF South Glamorgan Map **03** ST17

GH Q Q *Balkan Hotel* 144 Newport Rd CF2 1DJ
☎(0222) 463673
This hotel, situated on the main Newport road, is convenient for both the city centre and the Broadway shopping complex. Accommodation is clean and bright, and the hotel has been run by the same friendly family for many years.
14rm(5♠9hc) (3fb) CTV in 13 bedrooms ® ⊁ LDO 7pm
🛏 CTV 18P
Credit Cards ①②

GH Q Q Q **Clare Court Hotel** 46/48 Clare Rd CF1 7QP
☎(0222) 344839
Closed Xmas Day & Boxing Day
This family-run hotel is situated within walking distance of the city centre. The bedrooms are spacious and well equipped, and there is a comfortable lounge and small bar.
9➪♠ (2fb) CTV in all bedrooms ® ⊁ (ex guide dogs)
sB&B➪♠£25-£27 dB&B➪♠£34-£40 WB&B£130-£157
WBDi£175-£200 LDO 7.45pm
Lic 🛏 CTV ⊁
Credit Cards ①②③④

GH Q Q **Courtfield** 101 Cathedral Rd CF1 9PH
☎(0222) 227701
16rm(4♠7hc) (3fb) CTV in all bedrooms ® sB&B£23-£25
sB&B♠£30-£35 dB&B£35-£40 dB&B♠£45-£50 LDO 8.30pm
Lic lift 🛏 2P 1🏠
Credit Cards ①②③⑤

GH Q Q Q **Ferrier's (Alva) Hotel** 130/132 Cathedral Rd
CF1 9LQ ☎(0222) 383413
Closed 2wks Xmas & New Year
A very well maintained private hotel situated near Sophia Gardens, a few minutes walk from the city centre. Bedrooms are all well equipped and bright, and there is a comfortable residents' lounge and a cosy bar.
26rm(6➪♠20hc) (4fb) CTV in all bedrooms ® sB&B£23-£27
sB&B➪♠£34 dB&B£40-£42 dB&B➪♠£46 LDO 7.45pm
Lic 🛏 CTV 10P
Credit Cards ①②③⑤

GH Q Q **Tane's Hotel** 148 Newport Rd CF2 1DJ
☎(0222) 491755 & 493898
On the busy Newport Road and within walking distance of the city centre, this family-run guesthouse provides good clean accommodation. The bedrooms are all equipped with colour televisions and there is a comfortable residents' lounge.
9hc (1fb) CTV in all bedrooms ® ⊁ LDO 7pm
Lic 🛏 CTV 10P nc6yrs
Credit Cards ②③④

CARDIGAN Dyfed Map **02** SN14

◧♥**GH** Q Q Q **Brynhyfryd** Gwbert Rd SA43 1AE
☎(0239) 612861
A well maintained guesthouse overlooking the George V Recreational Grounds, a short walk from the town centre. Bedrooms, all well equipped, are bright and cheery and there is a very comfortable lounge for residents.
7rm(2♠5hc) (2fb) CTV in all bedrooms ® ⊁ (ex guide dogs)
sB&B£13-£14 dB&B£26-£28 dB&B♠£30-£32 WBDi£130-£140
LDO 7.30pm
🛏 CTV ④

GH Q Q Q **Highbury** Pendre SA43 1JU ☎(0239) 613403
Set in the heart of this small market town, the hotel has recently been extended, and it provides comfortable and well equipped bedrooms. A new conservatory/restaurant has been added, serving a good range of food.
6rm(3♠3hc) CTV in all bedrooms ®
Lic 🛏 ⊁
Credit Cards ①③

GH Q Q Q **Maes-A-Mor** Gwbert Rd SA43 1AE
☎(0239) 614929
Just a short walk from the town centre on the Gwbert road, this very pleasant small guesthouse has 3 en suite and well equipped pretty bedrooms, a comfortable and cosy lounge and an attractive dining room.
3♠ (2fb)⊁in all bedrooms CTV in all bedrooms ®
dB&B♠£25-£32 WB&B£87.50-£105 WBDi£143-£161
LDO 4pm
🛏 CTV 4P ♨ ④

CARDROSS Strathclyde *Dunbartonshire* Map **10** NS37

GH Q Q Q **Kirkton House** Darleith Rd G82 5EZ (0.5m N of village) ☎(0389) 841951 FAX (0389) 841868
Tastefully converted, this farmhouse stands in a quiet rural setting high above the village, with fine panoramic views southwards across the Firth of Clyde. Bedrooms are most thoughtfully equipped, and all have direct dial telephones.
6rm(4➪♠2hc) (3fb) CTV in all bedrooms ® sB&B£21-£26
sB&B➪♠£27.50-£32.50 dB&B£37 dB&B➪♠£49
WB&B£116.55 WBDi£201.60 LDO 7pm
Lic 🛏 CTV 12P ♨ ∪
Credit Cards ①③④
See advertisement under HELENSBURGH

GH Q Q **Westlade** Darleith Rd G82 5PG ☎(0389) 841007
A traditional private house offering bed and breakfast in a modern extension. The house is set 300 yards off the main road on the edge of a residential area, with a small garden to the rear, and overlooking a wooded glen. There are two very nice bedrooms with modern showers, and a lounge where breakfast is served. The owners are friendly and enthusiastic.
2hc (1fb) ® dB&B£26 WB&Bfr£82
🛏 CTV 3P ④

CAREW Dyfed Map **02** SN00

SELECTED

GH Q Q Q Q **Old Stable Cottage** 3 Picton Ter SA70 8SL
☎(0646) 651889
Feb-20 Dec
A character cottage that has had close links with Carew Castle, only a short walk away. It is found by leaving the A477, signed to the castle, turn right at the Carew Inn and the cottage is in the centre of a row of houses on the right hand side of the lane. There are 3 lounges, one part of a conservatory where breakfast is served. Evening meals are available by prior arrangement; they are prepared by Joyce Fielder using fresh local produce, and husband Lionel helps to serve them. Bedrooms, reached by a unusual iron spiral staircase, are prettily furnished in a country style with exposed natural beams and en suite facilities. The Fielders make their guests feel at home, and are not deterred when guests stray into their domain – a dream of a country kitchen.
2➪♠ (1fb)⊁in all bedrooms CTV in all bedrooms ®
⊁ (ex guide dogs) ✻ sB&B➪♠£25 dB&B➪♠£45
WB&B£157.50 WBDi£252 LDO 7pm
🛏 2P nc5yrs

CARLISLE Cumbria Map **11** NY45

See also Catlowdy

GH Q Q **Angus Hotel** 14 Scotland Rd CA3 9DG
☎(0228) 23546
rs 24-31Dec
This well maintained guesthouse is situated on the A7, just north of the city centre. Some bedrooms have private bathrooms, and there is a free public car park nearby.
11rm(6♠5hc) (4fb)⊁in 6 bedrooms CTV in 1 bedroom ®
sB&Bfr£20 sB&B♠£28 dB&Bfr£31 dB&B♠£42 LDO 7.45pm

▶

ST·Y·NYLL HOUSE

Situated with lovely views of the Vale of Glamorgan, 7 miles Cardiff, 4 miles M4 - close to Welsh Folk Museum. Relax in lovely country house own extensive grounds, plenty of parking. Licensed. Central heating, colour TV, tea/coffee all rooms. Personal supervision resident owners Paul and Monica Renwick. Welsh Tourist Board approved.

St Brides-Super-Ely, South Glamorgan CF5 6EZ Tel: (0446) 760209

The Albany Hotel

M4 junction 33

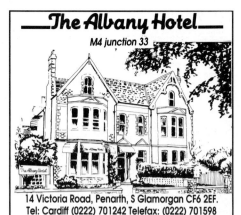

14 Victoria Road, Penarth, S Glamorgan CF6 2EF. Tel: Cardiff (0222) 701242 Telefax: (0222) 701598

Ideally situated in quiet Victorian tree lined surroundings in this attractive coastal resort 3 miles from Cardiff. Only minutes walk away from station, shopping centre, excellent restaurants, breathtaking cliff walks, elegant promenade and pier.

Home of the 'Waverley'. Reasonable rates from £20.00pp. Comfortable rooms, many en suite. All with colour TV, satellite, video channel, room phone, clock radio and tea/coffee facilities. Licensed, extensive menu, full fire certificate and parking. You will find us friendly, convenient, comfortable as well as inexpensive.

FERRIER'S HOTEL

132 Cathedral Road, Cardiff, CF1 9LQ
Tel: (0222) 383413

Ferrier's Hotel is a family-managed hotel set in a Victorian Conservation area and yet within walking distance of the city centre. 26 bedrooms, including 7 on the ground floor. All rooms tastefully furnished and have hot and cold water, central heating, radio, colour TV, tea & coffee making facilities and direct dial telephone. Many rooms with private shower and many en suite. Reasonably priced à la carte menu available Monday to Thursday. Light refreshments are available in the Cane Lounge and well stocked Bar. Residents' Lounge with colour TV. Full fire certificate. Car Park, locked at night.

The Pilgrims Hotel

Canterbury's new quaint hotel. Completely refurbished whilst retaining historical roman wall. Very tastefully decorated throughout. Situated opposite the Marlowe Theatre and five minutes walk from the Cathedral. The Restaurant/Bar gives a warm welcome to all Pilgrims. An atmosphere of care awaits you.

Quoted "luxury elegance charm, history and location blend to make The Pilgrims Hotel, Caterbury – one of Kent's finest" seeing is believing – give us a call for more information.

THE PILGRIMS HOTEL

18 THE FRIARS : CANTERBURY : CT1 2AS

Telephone: 0227 464537
Fax: 0227 762514

Lic ♔ CTV 8🍽
Credit Cards ① ③

GH ⓠⓠ Crossroads House Brisco CA4 0QZ ☎(0228) 28994
Closed Xmas & New Year
A bright, fresh, clean and well maintained guesthouse with a very comfortable lounge, situated three quarters of a mile from junction 42 of the M6, signposted for Dalston. Converted from two 19th-century estate workers' cottages, now totally modernised; a Roman well located beneath the main staircase is an interesting feature of the property.
5hc (1fb)⊁in all bedrooms TV in 2 bedrooms sB&B£16.50-£22 dB&B£30-£33 LDO 10am
Lic ♔ CTV 6P ⓔ

GH ⓠⓠ East View 110 Warwick Rd CA1 1JU ☎(0228) 22112
Follow the road into Carlisle from junction 43 of the M6 and in 1.5 miles you will find East View occupying a corner site. The bedrooms are compact but nicely fitted and all have en suite facilities, colour television and tea- making equipment.
9♠ (3fb) CTV in all bedrooms ⓡ ✳ sB&B♠fr£18 dB&B♠fr£30
♔ 4P

GH ⓠⓠ *Kenilworth Hotel* 34 Lazonby Ter CA1 2PZ ☎(0228) 26179
A small, spotlessly clean and very well maintained, family-run guesthouse with secure parking for 5 cars. The house, situated two miles from junction 42 of the M6, is an end-of-terrace Victorian property with colourful flower borders at the front.
6hc (2fb) ⓡ
♔ CTV 5P

FH ⓠⓠ Mr A J Westmorland **Blackwell** *(NY387512)*
Blackwell CA2 4SH ☎(0228) 24073
A neat and compact family-run dairy farm situated 2 miles south of Carlisle, close to the race course. The accommodation is clean, nicely decorated and well maintained, and includes a cosy lounge for residents. To find the guesthouse, leave the M6 at Junction 42; from the south take the first exit signposted to Dalston; from the north take the fourth exit. After about 3 miles, at Durdar, turn right at the Black Lion and continue past the race course to the White Ox. Turn left into Lowry street and the farm is on the right.
2rm ✖ (ex guide dogs) ✳ sB&B£12 dB&B£24 WB&B£80
CTV 4P ⚷ 120 acres dairy mixed

CARMARTHEN Dyfed Map 02 SN42

See also Cwmduad & Llanfynydd

FH ⓠⓠⓠ Mrs J Willmott **Cwmtwrch Farm Hotel & Four Seasons Restaurant** *(SN497220)* Nantgaredig SA32 7NY (5mE)
☎Nantgaredig(0267) 290238
A very pleasant early 19th-century Welsh stone farmhouse with modern pine-furnished bedrooms, offering good, comfortable accommodation. Converted outbuildings provide a separate bar and restaurant, which attract much local custom.
6rm(3⇉3♠) (2fb) CTV in 3 bedrooms ⓡ sB&B⇉♠£28-£32 dB&B⇉♠£38-£38 WB&B£126-£196 WBDi£220-£290 LDO 9pm
Lic ♔ CTV 20P 30 acres sheep ⓔ

CARNFORTH Lancashire Map 07 SD47

GH ⓠⓠⓠⓠ New Capernwray Farm Capernwray LA6 1AD ☎(0524) 734284
A charming 300-year-old stone-built farmhouse set in beautifully kept gardens surrounded by open countryside. This is the home of genial hosts Peter and Sally Townend and guests will enjoy the relaxed, informal atmosphere as well as the excellent 4-course dinners prepared daily by Mrs Townend, served at a communal table in the tiny candlelit

dining room – once the farm's dairy. No choice is offered, but the cooking is outstanding, and while there is no drinks licence, guests are encouraged to serve themselves to as much as they like. Each of the 3 bedrooms is well equipped and beautifully furnished. There are lots of thoughtful touches including books, sewing kits, toiletries and writing materials.
3rm(1⇉) ⊁in all bedrooms CTV in all bedrooms ⓡ sB&B⇉£36-£39 dB&B⇉£52-£58 LDO 5pm
♔ 4P nc10yrs clay pigeon shooting arranged
Credit Cards ① ③ ⓔ

CARRADALE Strathclyde *Argyllshire* Map 10 NR83

GH ⓠⓠ Ashbank Hotel PA28 6RY ☎(05833) 650
An attractive dining room and cosy bar/lounge with wood-panelled walls (for residents and diners only) are features of this friendly little hotel close to the village golf course.
6rm(3♠3hc) (1fb) TV in 1 bedroom ⓡ
Lic ♔ 8P

GH ⓠⓠ Dunvalanree Portrigh Bay PA28 6SE ☎(05833) 226
Etr-Nov
A fine Edwardian house at the end of a small row in the hamlet of Port Righ. Overlooking the bay, its attractive gardens stretch almost down to the shore, while Carradale Bay, with its mile of silver sands, is within walking distance, as are the village and golf course. Much of the house's character has been retained and developed by the charming and enthusiastic owner.
14hc (3fb) ⓡ sB&B£15 dB&B£30 WB&B£105 WBDi£154
Lic CTV 10P ▶ 9

CARRBRIDGE Highland *Inverness-shire* Map 14 NH92

GH ⓠⓠⓠ Carrmoor Carr Rd PH23 3AD ☎(047984) 244
A charming little house where you will get a warm welcome from the owners, with bright airy cottage-style bedrooms and comfortable lounge in which to relax. The recently refurbished dining room serves good home-cooked meals.
5rm(1♠4hc) (3fb)⊁in all bedrooms ⓡ ✳ dB&B£25-£27 dB&B♠£27-£29 WB&B£87.50-£94.50 WBDi£154-£164 LDO 5.30pm
Lic ♔ CTV 5P ⓔ

GH ⓠⓠⓠⓠ Fairwinds Hotel PH23 3AA ☎(047984) 240
Closed 2 Nov-14 Dec
Set in a secluded position standing some 200 yards back from the road in the centre of the village, this stone-built former manse has been sympathetically modernised and extended. Surrounded by 6 acres of grounds, with a small loch and a backdrop of mature pine woods, it provides superior accommodation, with friendly and attentive service. The well appointed bedrooms are bright and cheery, with pine furniture and private bathrooms. Public rooms are well furnished, and traditional Scottish meals are served in the neat dining room overlooking the garden.
5⇉♠ CTV in all bedrooms ⓡ ✖ sB&B⇉♠£22-£24 dB&B⇉♠£40-£50 WB&B£133-£168 WBDi£202-£234 LDO 4pm
Lic ♔ 8P nc12yrs
Credit Cards ① ③ ⓔ

GH ⓠⓠⓠ Feith Mhor Country House Station Rd PH23 3AP ☎(047984) 621
Closed 16 Nov-19 Dec
A comfortable and nicely-appointed country guesthouse. Situated half a mile west of Carrbridge station.

6rm(3⇔3♙) (1fb) CTV in all bedrooms ® sB&B⇔♙£29-£32
dB&B⇔♙£58-£64 (incl dinner) WB&B£133-£154 WBDi£194-
£215 LDO 6.45pm
Lic ⊠ 8P nc10yrs

CARRONBRIDGE Central *Stirlingshire*

See **Denny**

CASTLE CARROCK Cumbria Map **12** NY55

FH Q B W Robinson Gelt Hall *(NY542554)* CA4 9LT
☎Hayton(0228) 70260
Simple, neat accommodation is provided by this friendly little
village centre farmhouse. Guests can enjoy a true farm atmosphere
at this sheep and dairy farm.
3rm(1⇔⅜) (1fb) ✖ LDO 5pm
⊠ CTV 6P 1🐄 250 acres beef dairy sheep ⓔ

CASTLE CARY Somerset Map **03** ST63

INN Q Q Q The George Hotel Market Place BA7 7AH
☎(0963) 50761
In the heart of this historic market town, this old coaching inn,
dating in parts from 1470, offers a warm, friendly and informal
atmosphere, along with cosy and smart public areas. Bedrooms are
gradually being refurbished in a pretty and individual style, and
each is well equipped with modern facilities. In addition to
extensive bar menus and daily blackboard specials, the smart
dining room offers an interesting, fixed-price menu. The charming
hosts remain very involved in the day to day running of the inn.
12⇔♙ Annexe 4⇔♙ (1fb) CTV in all bedrooms ®
sB&B⇔♙£42-£46 dB&B⇔♙£57-£65 Lunch £8.50 Dinner
£13.50-£16 LDO 9.30pm
⊠ 10P
Credit Cards ① ③

CASTLE DONINGTON Leicestershire Map **08** SK42

GH Q Q *The Four Poster* 73 Clapgun St DE7 2LF
☎Derby(0332) 810335 & 812418
Tastefully restored and modernised old ivy-clad house in a quiet
street.
7rm(3⇔♙4hc) Annexe 4hc ✗in 7 bedrooms CTV in all
bedrooms ®
⊠ CTV 18P 4🐄

GH Q Q Park Farmhouse Hotel Melbourne Rd, Isley Walton
DE7 2RN ☎Derby(0332) 862409
Closed Xmas & New Year
8rm(3⇔3♙2hc) (2fb) CTV in all bedrooms ® sB&B£32-£33
sB&B⇔♙£39.50-£43 dB&B£42-£45 dB&B⇔♙£52-£55
WB&B£156 LDO 8pm
Lic ⊠ 20P
Credit Cards ① ② ③ ⑤ ⓔ

INN Q Q Le Chevalier Bistro Restaurant 2 Borough St
DE7 2LA ☎Derby(0332) 812005 & 812106 FAX (0322) 811372
Locals and businessmen find the food and friendly atmosphere at
this popular little Bistro worth the visit. The bedrooms have their
own entrance via a courtyard where guests can enjoy a pre-dinner
drink or after dinner coffee.
4⇔♙ (1fb) CTV in all bedrooms ® ✖ (ex guide dogs) ✳
sB&B⇔♙£30 dB&B⇔♙£38 ✳ Dinner £14.95&alc
LDO 10.30pm
⊠ CTV 100P 2🐄 pool table
Credit Cards ① ② ③ ⑤ ⓔ

Every effort is made to provide accurate
information, but details can change after we go to
print. It is advisable to check prices etc. before
you make a firm booking.

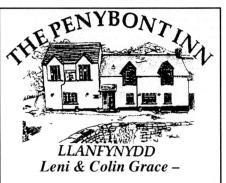

Castle Douglas - Channel Islands (Guernsey)

CASTLE DOUGLAS Dumfries & Galloway
Kirkcudbrightshire Map **11** NX76

GH 〇〇〇 **Rose Cottage** Gelston DG7 1SH ☎(0556) 2513
Feb-Oct

*In a rural setting, 2 miles from the town centre on the B736, this
delightful whitewashed cottage is as quaint inside as it appears
outside. The accommodation is all on the ground floor, and is neat,
cosy and most inviting.*

3rm(1⇌🛁2hc) Annexe 2hc (1fb) TV in 3 bedrooms ® ✻
sB&B£13-£16 dB&B£26 dB&B⇌🛁£31 WBDif135-£152.50
LDO 5pm
🏵 CTV 15P £

CATLOWDY Cumbria Map **12** NY47

SELECTED

FH 〇〇〇〇 Mr & Mrs J Sisson **Bessiestown**
(NY457768) CA6 5QP ☎Nicholforest(022877) 219 due to
change to (0228) 577219

*A small beef and sheep rearing farm situated in the
countryside just off the B6318 in the centre of this tiny village,
not far from the Scottish border. The bedrooms are
exceptionally attractive, all with en suite facilities, and several
extra touches. There is a cosy TV lounge and an elegant bar
lounge. The owner serves delicious traditional home cooking in
the pretty, beamed dining room. Across the courtyard guests
can take advantage of the large indoor heated swimming pool,
and there is an attractive garden at the front of the house.*

5⇌🛁 ✻in all bedrooms ® ✖ (ex guide dogs)
sB&B⇌🛁fr£26 dB&B⇌🛁fr£42 WB&Bfr£140
WBDifr£215 (wkly only mid Jul-end Aug) LDO 4pm
Lic 🏵 CTV 10P ⊠(heated) games room 80 acres beef
sheep £

FH 〇〇 Mr & Mrs Lawson **Craigburn** *(NY474761)* CA6 5QP
☎Nicholforest(022877) 214 due to change to (0228) 577214
Closed Dec

*This family farmhouse is situated in a secluded location on a 250-
acre working farm. All bedrooms have en suite facilities. There are
comfortable lounges and a residents' bar, as well as an attractive
dining room in which the owner's delicious home cooking can be
sampled. Craigburn is a mile off the B6318 in Catlowdy village
and is clearly signed.*

7rm(4⇌3🛁) (3fb) ® sB&B⇌🛁£21-£23 dB&B⇌🛁£32-£36
WB&B£112-£126 WBDi£163.80-£176.40 LDO 5.30pm
Lic 🏵 CTV 20P ♨ snooker 250 acres beef mixed sheep £

CHAGFORD Devon Map **03** SX78

GH 〇〇〇 **Bly House** Nattadon Hill TQ13 8BW
☎(0647) 432404
Closed 8 Nov-Dec

*Situated in a quiet position, Bly House makes an excellent base for
exploring the national park. Every room is furnished with beautiful
pictures and objets d'art, bedrooms being spacious, with en suite
facilities, colour television and tea and coffee-making equipment.*

6⇌ CTV in all bedrooms ® sB&B⇌fr£27 dB&B⇌£42-£44
WB&Bfr£147
🏵 CTV 10P nc9yrs croquet £

GH 〇〇 **Glendarah** TQ13 8BZ ☎(0647) 433270
Mar-Dec

*A stable has been converted to provide 1 of the 7 bedrooms of this
attractive guesthouse. It is tastefully decorated with a lounge and
dining room, and Mr and Mrs Willett extend a warm welcome to
the guests.*

7hc Annexe 1⇌🛁 (2fb) CTV in 1 bedroom ® ✖ (ex guide dogs)
sB&B£15 dB&B£30 dB&B⇌🛁£39 WB&B£98-£129.50
LDO 6.30pm
Lic 🏵 CTV 9P ♨ £

CHANNEL ISLANDS Map **16**

GUERNSEY

GRANDES ROCQUES

GH 〇〇〇 *La Galaad Hotel* Rue des Francais
☎Guernsey(0481) 57233
27 Mar-Oct

*Set in a quiet residential area, close to the impressive 'Grandes
Rocques' and the rugged seafront, this guesthouse offers nicely
appointed, comfortable bedrooms, and spacious public rooms with
an attractive dining room and a small residents' bar.*

12rm(2⇌10🛁) (4fb) CTV in all bedrooms ® ✖ LDO 9.30am
Lic 🏵 14P

ST MARTINS

GH 〇〇〇 **Hotel La Michelle** Les Hubits
☎Guernsey(0481) 38065 FAX (0481) 39492
Apr-Oct

*A smartly presented private hotel quietly located in a residential
area, not far from the town centre and airport. Bedrooms are all
very well equipped and stylishly furnished with quality and comfort
in mind. Public areas are also attractive and comfortable, and an
evening meal is offered.*

13⇌🛁 (5fb) CTV in all bedrooms ® ✖ (ex guide dogs) ✻
dB&B⇌🛁£44-£60 (incl dinner) WB&B£133-£189 WBDi£154-
£210 LDO 6.45pm
Lic 🏵 CTV 13P nc4yrs

ST PETER PORT

GH 〇〇〇 **Marine Hotel** Well Rd ☎Guernsey(0481) 724978
*Situated just a short distance from the North Esplanade in a one-
way street, this family-run private hotel offers clean, comfortable
accommodation which is constantly being improved. Bedrooms are
modestly equipped, spotlessly clean and all are en suite. Breakfast
only is served, but the resident proprietors can suggest reasonable
local restaurants for the benefit of guests.*

11⇌🛁 (3fb) ® ✖ (ex guide dogs) sB&B⇌🛁£13.75-£22.50
dB&B⇌🛁£27-£42 WB&B£96.25-£147
Lic 🏵 CTV ⚡

SELECTED

GH 〇〇〇〇 **Midhurst House** Candie Rd
☎Guernsey(0481) 724391
mid Apr-mid Oct

*A charming Regency house not far from the centre of town.
Lovingly restored, the hotel combines elegance and comfort in
the bedrooms, four of which are in the main house, and the rest
in a cottage in the pretty, country garden. Public areas include
a bright lounge area with a domed conservatory skylight,
which creates an indoor garden atrium atmosphere. The
proprietor offers an excellent standard of cooking, using top
quality fresh local produce.*

5rm(2⇌3🛁) Annexe 3🛁 (1fb) CTV in all bedrooms ® ✖
sB&B⇌🛁£30-£35 dB&B⇌🛁£46-£56 WB&B£181-£196
WBDi£210-£245 LDO 6.45pm
Lic 🏵 1🅿 nc8yrs

GH 〇〇〇 **Les Ozouets Lodge** Ozouets Rd
☎Guernsey(0481) 721288
Mar-Oct

*A private hotel dating back to 1903, situated in a quiet residential
area, away from the town centre. Run by the chef-patron, it offers
excellent cooking complemented by a well chosen wine list. A*

simple table d'hôte menu and a more imaginative à la carte menu are available to guests and a limited number of non-residents also . The house is grandly furnished downstairs, with handsome antiques and attractive soft furnishings. Bedrooms are comfortable and well presented, with modern facilities. The gardens are outstanding and include bowling and putting greens, and a tennis court.

13rm(5⇨8♠) Annexe 1⇨♠ (3fb) CTV in all bedrooms ® ⊁ ✱ sB&B⇨♠£35 dB&B⇨♠£39-£58 (incl dinner) WB&B£115.50-£147 WBDi£136.50-£203 LDO 7.45pm
Lic ℙℚ 20P nc5yrs ♪(grass)bowling green putting green petanques
Credit Cards ①③

ST SAMPSON

GH ℚℚ Ann-Dawn Private Hotel Route des Capelles
☎Guernsey(0481) 725606
Etr-Oct
Located in a quiet, residential street, some distance from the town and harbour, this guesthouse is surrounded by landscaped gardens. Bedrooms are freshly decorated, simply appointed and reasonably equipped, and housekeeping standards are good. In addition to breakfast, an evening meal is offered, and guests may also enjoy drinks from the residents' bar.
14rm(3⇨9♠) CTV in all bedrooms ® ⊁ ✱ sB&B£19.25-£24.75 sB&B⇨♠£21.25-£26.75 dB&B⇨♠£38.50-£53.50 (incl dinner) WBDi£134.75-£187.25 LDO 5pm
Lic ℙℚ 12P nc12yrs
Credit Cards ①③ £

JERSEY

GOREY

GH ℚℚ Royal Bay Hotel ☎Jersey(0534) 53318
May-Oct
A long-established family-run hotel near the beach and Royal Jersey golf course, in a picturesque village. The accommodation comprises traditionally furnished and old fashioned, spacious bedrooms, a panelled dining room, a sun lounge as well as a TV lounge and a popular bar.
16⇨♠ (2fb) LDO 9.30am
Lic ℙℚ CTV 11P nc6yrs

GREVE DE LECQ BAY

GH ℚℚℚ Des Pierres (on B65 near beach)
☎Jersey(0534) 81858 FAX (0534) 85273
Apr-Nov
This guesthouse is situated on top of a hill overlooking the pretty bay and offers modern, smartly decorated bedrooms, some of which have superb sea views; all rooms have good en suite facilities. There is a basement bar and dining room, and the daily choice of fresh home-cooked dishes is displayed on a blackboard in the pretty dining area. The resident proprietors have owned the guesthouse for the past 11 years, and now enjoy a loyal returning clientèle who appreciate the relaxed atmosphere.
14rm(7⇨7♠) (3fb) CTV in all bedrooms ® ⊁ sB&B⇨♠£19-£26 dB&B⇨♠£20-£23 WB&B£133-£182 WBDi£182-£231 LDO 8pm
Lic ℙℚ CTV 13P
Credit Cards ①③ £

GROUVILLE

GH ℚℚℚ Lavender Villa Hotel Rue A Don
☎Jersey(0534) 54937
Mar-Nov
A well maintained, family-run hotel adjoining the Royal Jersey golf course, and only a short walk to the beach. Bedrooms are modern and bright, each with private bathrooms, and there are two 'luxury standard' bedrooms. A cosy bar augments the popular simple dining room, and service is available all day. There is a

separate 'no-smoking' lounge, and leisure facilities include an outdoor swimming pool. Ample car parking is provided.
21rm(10⇨11♠) (3fb) CTV in all bedrooms ® ⊁ LDO 7.15pm
Lic ℙℚ CTV 20P nc3yrs ⌂

ST AUBIN

GH ℚℚ Bryn-y-Mor Route de la Haule ☎Jersey(0534) 20295
Telex no 4192638
This small cosy hotel is in a prime position overlooking St Aubins Bay. It offers bright, modestly appointed bedrooms with modern equipment and pleasant public rooms. Predominantly English cuisine is served with traditional set menus in the wood-panelled dining room.
14rm(11⇨♠3hc) (4fb) CTV in all bedrooms LDO 7pm
Lic 6P ♿
Credit Cards ①②③

SELECTED

GH ℚℚℚℚ The Panorama JE3 8BR
☎Jersey(0534) 42429 FAX (0534) 45940
Etr-Xmas
Set high above the town, with its own Terrace Tea Garden, this hotel has views across the bay from most of the bedrooms. Rooms are individually decorated and custom fitted and equipped with every possible amenity. The comfortable, traditional lounge features a 200-year-old carved fireplace, and there is a breakfast room in the basement. Afternoon teas are served in the conservatory 'Terrace Tea Pot' garden, and service is attentive and enthusiastic. Car parking can be difficult, and the steps up to the terrace will keep you very fit!
17⇨♠ (2fb) CTV in all bedrooms ® ⊁ sB&B⇨♠£20-£34 dB&B⇨♠£35-£57 (wkly only Sat Jun-Sep)
ℙℚ ⊁ nc10yrs Tea garden
▶

Credit Cards 1 2 3 5 £

ST HELIER

SELECTED

GH QQQQ Almorah Hotel Lower Kings Cliff
☎Jersey(0534) 21648 FAX (0534) 68600
*This listed terraced house was built in 1841 and is situated in
an elevated position above the town centre, in a quiet
residential crescent. Bedrooms have been much improved and
are still being refurbished; each is nicely decorated and very
well appointed with modern facilities. The lounge area is
notable for its oak panelling, polished floors and comfortable,
pretty seating. There is also a tiny bar area leading through
into a Breton-style dining room, where a five-course menu is
offered daily, using good quality, fresh produce. The most
outstanding aspect of this small hotel is the superb hospitality,
combined with good service and a relaxed, informal
atmosphere.*
16rm(13⇨3↟) (4fb) CTV in all bedrooms ®
✖ (ex guide dogs) LDO 6.30pm
Lic ♛ CTV 10P
Credit Cards 1 2 3 5

GH QQQ Cliff Court Hotel St Andrews Rd, First Tower
☎(0534) 34919
14 Apr-29 Oct
*This hotel is in a quiet location overlooking St Aubins Bay, and
provides extensive accommodation; some bedrooms have sea
views, and most have private bathrooms. The combined bar/lounge
augments the large, bright dining room, and there is a professional
Portuguese chef. Outside, the small but secluded terrace and
swimming pool provide an enjoyable sun trap. Service is under the
personal supervision of the resident proprietors.*
16rm(15⇨1hc) (4fb) ® ✖ (ex guide dogs) LDO 7.30pm
Lic ♛ CTV 14P ⌿(heated)
Credit Cards 3

GH QQQ Cornucopia Hotel & Restaurant Mont Pinel
☎Jersey(0534) 32646
*Enjoying a fine location overlooking rural farmland, this modern
and skilfully extended family-run hotel offers a choice of bedrooms
and very good leisure facilities. Improvements continue with the
remaining private bathrooms being upgraded. The owners provide
traditional comfort and friendly levels of service which have been
associated with this hotel for over 20 years.*
15rm(4⇨11↟) (2fb) CTV in all bedrooms ® ✳
sB&B⇨↟fr£23.75 dB&B⇨↟fr£38.50 WB&Bfr£134
WBDifr£183 LDO 2.30pm
Lic ♛ 21P ⌿(heated) solarium gymnasium games room
jacuzzi turkish bath
Credit Cards 1 2 3 £

GH QQ Millbrook House Rue de Trachy JE2 3JN
☎Jersey(0534) 33036
27 Apr-7 Oct
*This Georgian and Colonial-style house is set in 10 acres of
mature, and in many parts, wild gardens, 500 yards from the
beach. A quiet, family-run hotel, it offers bright, well equipped
bedrooms and cosy, traditional lounges. A peaceful country-house
atmosphere prevails, complemented by wholesome home cooking.*
24rm(18⇨6hc) (2fb) CTV in all bedrooms ® ✖
sB&B⇨↟£25-£35 dB&B⇨↟£50-£70 (incl dinner)
WBDif£175-£245 LDO 7pm
Lic lift CTV 20P
Credit Cards 2 £

GH QQQ Runnymede Court Hotel 46/52 Roseville St
JE2 4PN ☎Jersey(0534) 20044 FAX (0534) 27880
mid Feb-mid Dec
*Conveniently positioned, this established and popular hotel has
been extensively refurbished to offer a choice of comfortable,
bright, well equipped bedrooms with a good range of facilities;
some of the rooms are situated around a rear central garden. The
public rooms are well furnished, spacious and comfortable and
include a bar, lounge and large dining room. The beach and
shopping centre are within easy reach.*
57⇨↟ (6fb) CTV in all bedrooms ® ✖ (ex guide dogs)
sB&B⇨↟£22-£32 dB&B⇨↟£34-£64 (incl dinner)
WBDif£154-£224 (wkly only 15 Jun-5 Oct) LDO 7.15pm
Lic lift ♛ CTV ⌿ nc3yrs
Credit Cards 1 2 3

TRINITY

GH QQQ Highfield Country Hotel Route du Ebenezer
JF3 5DS ☎Jersey(0534) 62194 FAX (0534) 65342
30 Mar-30 Oct
*This bright, spacious hotel, pleasantly situated in a country
location, stands in an acre of grounds which include a swimming
pool. Bedrooms are pretty and well equipped with modern facilities
and private bathrooms. There is a comfortable bar and lounge to
complement the well appointed dining room. Ground floor self-
catering apartments are also available.*
25rm(14⇨11↟) (4fb) CTV in all bedrooms ® ✖ LDO 7.45pm
Lic ♛ 25P ⌿
Credit Cards 1 2 3 5

CHARD Somerset Map 03 ST30

🅿♿ **GH QQQ Watermead** 83 High St TA20 1QT
☎(0460) 62834
*This is a small and friendly guesthouse with good-sized,
comfortable bedrooms that are nicely equipped. The simple and
honest cooking is served in the spacious dining room.*
9rm(6↟3hc) ⚥in 3 bedrooms CTV in all bedrooms ®
sB&B£12.50-£13.50 sB&B↟£15-£20 dB&B↟£30-£32
WB&B£80-£100 LDO noon
Lic ♛ CTV 9P 2♨ ♨ ❧

CHARFIELD Gloucestershire Map 03 ST79

INN QQ Huntingford Mill Hotel GL12 8EX
☎Dursley(0453) 843431
*Situated one mile from the village in a quiet river setting, this was
the last working flour mill in Gloucestershire. Carefully converted
to retain the original character, bedrooms are simply appointed
and well equipped. There is also a spacious restaurant specialising
in North American dishes, and over two miles of private fishing is
available to resident guests.*
5hc (1fb) CTV in all bedrooms ® ✖ (ex guide dogs) sB&B£20-
£25 dB&B£30-£35 WB&B£140-£175 WBDif£220-£255.65
Lunch £11.95&alc Dinner £11.95&alc LDO 10pm
♛ CTV 25P ✔
Credit Cards 1 3

CHARING Kent Map 05 TQ94

FH QQQ Mrs P Pym Barnfield *(TQ924477)* TN27 0BN
☎(023371) 2421
*Built around 1415 and furnished throughout with antiques, this
ancient farmhouse has a comfortable sitting room with plenty of
books. Good leisure facilities are available along with a barn for
functions. Ordnance Survey map 189 is recommended for location
details.*
5rm(4hc) (1fb)⚥in all bedrooms ® ✖ sB&Bfr£17.50
dB&B£35-£39 WB&B£105-£117 WBDif£178.50-£190.50
LDO 5pm
♛ CTV 100P 1♨ ♪(hard)500 acres arable sheep £

CHARLTON Northamptonshire Map **04** SP53

GH Q Q *Home Farm* Main St OX17 3DR
☎Banbury(0295) 811683
Set in half an acre of walled garden, Colonel and Mrs Grove-White's cottage-style farmhouse offers two country bedrooms, each with private bathrooms and one with a small lounge. The accommodation is reached by a winding staircase. A third bedroom is in a building across the courtyard, which can also be let as a self-catering unit.
2⇨₃♠ Annexe 1⇨₃♠ ⊁in 2 bedrooms CTV in all bedrooms ®
CTV 3P nc12yrs

CHARLWOOD Surrey For accommodation details see under
Gatwick Airport

CHARMOUTH Dorset Map **03** SY39

GH Q Q Q **Newlands House** Stonebarrow Ln DT6 6RA
☎(0297) 60212
Mar-Oct
This converted 16th-century farmhouse stands on the edge of the village, close to the beach. Bedrooms have attractive co-ordinated soft furnishings and comfortable beds, and public rooms are convivial and well furnished, featuring some of the original beams and brickwork. Smoking is only permitted in the bar lounge.
12rm(11⇨₃♠1hc) (2fb)⊁in all bedrooms CTV in all bedrooms
® sB&B£18.10-£20.75 sB&B⇨₃♠£19.60-£22.25
dB&B⇨₃♠£39.20-£44.50 WB&B£123.50-£140.25
WBDi£185.90-£202.60 LDO noon
Lic ₩ CTV 12P nc6yrs ⓔ

CHEDDAR Somerset Map **03** ST45

FH Q Mrs C A Ladd **Tor** *(ST473513)* Nyland BS27 3UD
☎(0934) 743710
Three miles south of Cheddar, a 1.5-mile single-track unclassified road leads to this recently built farmhouse overlooking the Somerset Levels. Simple family accommodation is offered.
8rm(3⇨₃♠2hc) (1fb)⊁in all bedrooms ® ✖ sB&Bfr£16
dB&B£27-£31 dB&B⇨₃♠£34 WB&B£94.45-£113 LDO 6pm
Lic ₩ CTV 10P ✔ 33 acres mixed ⓔ

CHEDDLETON Staffordshire Map **07** SJ95

SELECTED

GH Q Q Q Q **Choir Cottage and Choir House** Ostlers Ln
ST13 7HS ☎Churnet Side(0538) 360561
This guesthouse was originally two cottages, one stone built and over 300 years old, with four-poster beds in two rooms; the other cottage is modern and has a small conservatory lounge with a view of the pretty alpine and shrub garden. Set on the edge of the village, the delightful gardens overlook lovely countryside, and the service is very friendly. Breakfast is served in the pine-furnished dining room, and evening meals by prior arrangement. Smoking is discouraged in the bedrooms.
2rm(1⇨₃1♠) Annexe 2♠ ⊁in 2 bedrooms CTV in all
bedrooms ® ✖ sB&B⇨₃♠£30-£35 dB&B⇨₃♠£40-£42
WB&B£130-£150 LDO 24hrs notice
₩ 5P nc4yrs

CHELMSFORD Essex Map **05** TL70

GH Q Q **Beechcroft Private Hotel** 211 New London Rd
CM2 0AJ ☎(0245) 352462
Closed Xmas & New Year
A pleasant, family-run guesthouse offering Bed and Breakfast. Bedrooms are on three floors, and come in various shapes and sizes, although all are clean and nicely decorated; eight have en suite showers, and several have colour TV. Downstairs there are two lounges: one with a TV, the other with armchairs. ▶

Millbrook House

**RUE DE TRACHY, ST. HELIER,
JERSEY, C.I.**
Tel (0534) 33036 Fax (0534) 24317
Quiet family run hotel in 10 acres of ground, 200 yards from road, offering every comfort in an informal country house atmosphere.
No disco, no cabaret, no swimming pool — to ensure peace and quiet.
27 bedrooms all with private facilities, most with central heating and views to extensive gardens and to sea.
Large car park.

Almorah Hotel

1 Almorah Crescent, Lower Kings Cliff, St Helier
Jersey, Channel Islands.
Telephone: 0534 21648   Fax: 0534 68600

Relax in comfort and style in one of the finest lounges in Jersey. The Almorah Hotel built around 1841 is situated in an elevated position above the town of St Helier with magnificent views over the town. The hotel is family run by the resident proprietors. All rooms are fully en suite with all facilities. A full Jersey breakfast can be enjoyed in the olde world Breton styled dining room also a delicious five cours evening meal complemented by a selection of fine wines, available from the traditional granite cellar.

20rm(8↑12hc)(2fb) CTV in 17 bedrooms ® sB&B£25.75-
£27.30 sB&B↑£32.95-£36.70 dB&B£41.65-£43.75
dB&B↑fr£52.30
🍴 CTV 15P
Credit Cards 1 3

GH ロロロ Boswell House Hotel 118-120 Springfield Rd
CM2 6LF ☎(0245) 287587
Closed 10 days Xmas
*The friendly and enthusiastic proprietors offer efficient service at
this well well-managed hotel, which is a tastefully renovated
Victorian building. A cosy bar complements the bedrooms which
are freshly decorated and well equipped, with pine furnishings
enhancing the warm atmosphere.*
13rm(9⇨4↑)(2fb)⊁in 7 bedrooms CTV in all bedrooms ®
★ (ex guide dogs) ✱ sB&B⇨↑£36-£40 dB&B⇨↑£52-£58
WB&B£273-£301 WBDi£336-£364 LDO 8.30pm
Lic 🍴 CTV 15P
Credit Cards 1 2 3 5 ④

GH ロロロ Snows Oaklands Hotel 240 Springfield Rd
CM2 6BP ☎(0245) 352004
*Situated north of the city off the A12, this attractive detached
house has a well kept garden, with a pond and small aviary.
Bedrooms come in various shapes and sizes, are well maintained
and offer most facilities. Public areas are traditionally furnished in
an informal style, with a magnificent clock collection owned by the
proprietor. Bar snacks (soups and sandwiches) are available
during lunch time and for a limited period in the evening.*
14rm(13⇨↑1hc)(3fb) CTV in all bedrooms ®
★ (ex guide dogs) ✱ sB&B£36-£41 sB&B⇨↑£36-£41
dB&B⇨↑£41-£51 LDO 8pm
Lic 🍴 CTV 14P ④

GH ロロ *Tanunda Hotel* 219 New London Rd CM2 0AJ
☎(0245) 354295
Closed 2wks Xmas
*A fairly large commercial guesthouse, run in a business-like
fashion. Bedrooms are well equipped, many with private bathrooms
and colour TV, and all have direct dial telephones. There is a TV
lounge and a smaller sun lounge overlooking the garden.*
20rm(2⇨9↑9hc) CTV in 12 bedrooms ® LDO 7.25pm
Lic 🍴 CTV 20P

CHELTENHAM Gloucestershire Map 03 SO92

See also Bishop's Cleeve
GH ロロ Abbey Hotel 16 Bath Pde GL53 7HN ☎(0242) 516053
Telex no 513034
*Situated behind Stanford Park and close to the town centre, this
former early Victorian terraced house has been carefully
modernised to provide attractive well-equipped bedrooms and cosy
public areas.*
11rm(7↑1hc)(1fb) CTV in all bedrooms ® ✱ sB&B£22-£26
sB&B↑£30-£32 dB&B£44-£48 dB&B↑£50-£54 WB&B£170-
£210 WBDi£226-£270 LDO 8pm
Lic 🍴 ✗ ♨
Credit Cards 1 3 ④

GH ロロロ Allards Hotel Shurdington Rd GL51 5XA
☎(0242) 862498 FAX (0242) 863017
*Guests are assured of a warm welcome at this elegant, period villa,
personally run by Mr and Mrs Castle. Accommodation is spacious
and attractive, and the house is situated about two miles from the
town centre.*
12⇨↑ (2fb) CTV in all bedrooms ® ★ sB&B⇨↑£26-£28
dB&B⇨↑£46-£48 WB&B£150-£160 WBDi£220-£250
LDO 8pm
Lic 🍴 20P 1🐾
Credit Cards 1 3 ④

GH ロロ Askham Court Hotel Pittville Circus Rd GL52 2PZ
☎(0242) 525547
rs Xmas
*This hotel is an early Victorian house, located within walking
distance of the town centre. The bedrooms are spacious, many with
en suite facilities. The large public areas retain many original
features, such as moulded cornices and fireplaces.*
18rm(4⇨7↑7hc)(3fb) CTV in 11 bedrooms ® LDO 6.30pm
Lic 🍴 CTV 20P

GH ロロ Beaumont House Hotel 56 Shurdington Rd GL53 0JE
☎(0242) 245986
*A listed Victorian house with picturesque garden, and spacious
attractive bedrooms, close to town centre.*
18rm(6⇨11↑1hc)(3fb) CTV in all bedrooms ® sB&B£17-£19
sB&B⇨↑£25-£40 dB&B⇨↑£45-£60 WB&B£119-£262.50
WBDi£194.25-£336 LDO 8pm
Lic 🍴 CTV 20P 1🐾
Credit Cards 1 3 ④

GH ロロロ Beechworth Lawn Hotel 133 Hales Rd GL52 6ST
☎(0242) 522583
*This spacious Victorian house, located half a mile from the town
centre on Broadway Road, has been modernised by the hosts, Mr
and Mrs Brian Toombs. It provides comfortable and well equipped
accommodation whilst retaining much of its character.*
7rm(3↑4hc)(2fb) CTV in all bedrooms ® sB&B£17-£20
sB&B↑£25-£40 dB&B⇨↑£37-£40 WB&B£110-
£160 WBDi£147-£198 LDO 2pm
🍴 CTV 10P ④

GH ロロ Hallery House 48 Shurdington Rd GL53 0JE
☎(0242) 578450 FAX (0242) 529730
*An attractive detached Regency house and grounds, set back from
the main A46 road to Stroud, within walking distance of the town
centre. The continual efforts of the proprietors have turned this into
a very attractive and well furnished small private hotel with all the
modern facilities. The restaurant provides a good menu.*
16rm(10⇨↑6hc)(1fb)⊁in 2 bedrooms CTV in all bedrooms
® sB&B£22-£25 sB&B⇨↑£30-£37 dB&B£35-£40
dB&B⇨↑£45-£60 WB&B£135-£250 WBDi£210-£330
LDO 8.00pm
Lic 🍴 20P
Credit Cards 1 2 3 ④

GH ロロロ Hannaford's 20 Evesham Rd GL52 2AB
☎(0242) 515181
*A particularly well kept terraced town house on the A435 just
north of the town. The attractive new bar, in addition to the lounge,
is much appreciated by guests. The bedrooms, while modestly
furnished, are spacious, well equipped and provided with
comfortable chairs. Redecoration is in progress.*
10rm(9⇨↑1hc)(1fb) CTV in all bedrooms ® ★ sB&B£21-
£25 sB&B⇨↑£32-£40 dB&B⇨↑£45-£58 LDO 9.30am
Lic 🍴 CTV ✗
Credit Cards 1 3 ④

GH ロロロ Hollington House Hotel 115 Hales Rd GL52 6ST
☎(0242) 519718 FAX (0242) 570280
*Situated half a mile from the town centre, this large Cotswold
stone Victorian house has 9 spacious bedrooms with en suite
facilities, beverages and colour television, as well as a comfortable
lounge and bar. Juergen and Annette Berg provide friendly service
in a pleasant and relaxed atmosphere. Good food is offered at
breakfast and dinner with a choice of menu.*
9rm(8↑1hc)(2fb) CTV in all bedrooms ® ★ ✱ sB&B£20-£25
sB&B↑£30-£40 dB&B↑£40-£60 WB&B£140-£210
WBDi£210-£280 LDO 5pm
Lic 🍴 12P nc3yrs
Credit Cards 1 2 3 ④

See advertisement on page 119

Hallery House

**48 Shurdington Road, Cheltenham
Spa, Gloucestershire GL53 0JE
Tel: 0242-578450 Fax: 0242 549730**

Steve and Angie welcome you to their lovely Victoria home offering
★ Comfortable rooms with hot drinks tray – majority en-suite
★ Colour TV with satellite in all rooms
★ Excellent traditional English or Continental breakfast
★ Excellent standard of food and we cater for all diets
★ Direct dial telephones   ★ Pets and children very welcome
★ Large car park

Three times winner of Spa award for customer comfort, excellent food and exceptional hygiene standards. Hallery House is of architectural interest and is situated on the main A46. It is a short walk from Cheltenham centre with all the attractions this beautiful town has to offer. Brochures available.

Amex, Visa and Mastercard accepted.

Beaumont House — HOTEL — AA LISTED

A warm friendly team welcomes you to this charming detached, listed Victorian building set in peaceful, picturesque gardens. On the A46, minutes from town centre. All rooms have colour TV with satellite movie channel, hot drinks tray and telephone with radio alarm. En suite available. Our Chef provides our Restaurant with freshly prepared food and a choice from an imaginative daily menu. Licensed bar and private car park.

Conferences and parties catered for.

**56 Shurdlington Road, Cheltenham, Glos.
Tel: (0242) 245986**

Beechworth Lawn Hotel

**133 Hales Road, Cheltenham, Glos.
Telephone: 0242 - 522583**

Near the centre and conveniently situated for all amenities, Betty & Brian Toombs offer you 24hr access to their carefully modernised, well appointed hotel, set in conifer and shrub gardens. All rooms have colour TV, beverages, hair dryer etc, en suite facilities available. Large comfortable lounge, easy off street parking, traditional English food. A relaxed atmosphere and friendly service is assured.

ABBEY HOTEL

Elegance and taste are the hallmarks which characterise the ambience of the Abbey Hotel, a Regency-style hotel situated in the centre of Cheltenham.

Although only 3 minutes walk from the town centre, the hotel borders Sandford Park and is situated in a peaceful and quiet area.

**14/16 Bath Parade, Cheltenham GL53 7HN
Tel: (0242) 516053 Fax: (0242) 513034**

GH 🇶🇶 **Ivy Dene** 145 Hewlett Rd GL52 6TS
☎(0242) 521726 & 521776
Situated close to the town centre on the way to Prestbury, this Victorian house has been greatly modernised. It offers well equipped and maintained bedrooms and comfortable public areas. The accommodation is on a room and breakfast basis only.
9hc (2fb) CTV in all bedrooms ® ✱ sB&B£14-£15 dB&B£28-£30
🍴 CTV 8P £

GH 🇶🇶 **Knowle House** 89 Leckhampton Rd GL53 0BS
☎(0242) 516091
Closed 24-27 Dec
This is a spacious Edwardian house situated approximately one mile from the town centre. It offers bed and breakfast in modern rooms, and has the additional benefit of a lounge for residents.
5hc (1fb) ® ✱ sB&B£13.50-£15.50 dB&B£27-£31
🍴 CTV 6P £

GH 🇶🇶 *Leeswood Hotel* 14 Montpelier Dr GL50 1TX
☎(0242) 524813
A Victorian semi-detached house situated opposite the Eagle Star headquarters building and a short walk from Montpellier centre. Good value bed and breakfast facilities are offered in modestly appointed bedrooms.
7hc CTV in all bedrooms ®
CTV 6P

SELECTED

GH 🇶🇶🇶🇶 **Lypiatt House** Lypiatt Rd GL50 2QW
☎(0242) 224994 FAX (0242) 224996
Closed 22 Dec-2 Jan
This charming Victorian house is set in pleasant grounds in the Montpellier area of town. It has been very carefully restored and modernised, and its previous elegance has been retained. Bedrooms are comfortably furnished and well equipped and all have en suite bathrooms. There is a spacious, impressive drawing room and a new conservatory lounge bar is a recent addition. Breakfast is served in the attractive basement dining room, and light suppers are available to residents. This was a previous winner for Central England of the AA's Best Newcomer Award.
10rm(9⇄1↑) CTV in all bedrooms ® ✕ sB&B⇄↑£42-£60 dB&B⇄↑£58-£70 LDO 2pm
Lic 🍴 14P nc12yrs
Credit Cards 1 3 £

GH 🇶🇶🇶 **Milton House** 12 Royal Pde, Bayshill Rd
GL50 3AY ☎(0242) 582601 FAX (0242) 222326
An elegant, Regency house set in the imposing terrace of Royal Parade, with direct rear access to Montpellier. Under careful restoration by the owners, this fine house now offers spacious, comfortable bedrooms and attractive public rooms, with many of the original features retained.
9rm(1⇄8↑) (4fb)⊬in 6 bedrooms CTV in all bedrooms ✕ sB&B⇄↑£35-£50 dB&B⇄↑£50-£65 LDO 9am
Lic 🍴 CTV 5P
Credit Cards 1 2 3 £

GH 🇶🇶🇶 **North Hall Hotel** Pittville Circus Rd GL52 2PZ
☎(0242) 520589 FAX (0242) 261953
Closed Xmas
This hotel, situated in the Pittville district close to the town centre, is an elegant early-Victorian detached house. It offers comfortable and well-equipped bedrooms, and attractive public rooms, many of which still retain the original features.
20rm(6⇄7↑7hc) (1fb) CTV in all bedrooms ® sB&Bfr£19.75 sB&B⇄↑£29.75-£33 dB&Bfr£33 dB&B⇄↑fr£46 WB&B£138.25-£208.25 WBDif£181.50-£241.50 LDO 7.15pm
Lic 🍴 CTV 20P
Credit Cards 1 3 £

GH 🇶🇶🇶 **Regency House Hotel** 50 Clarence Square
GL50 4JR ☎(0242) 582718
Closed Xmas & New Year
The Regency is situated north of the town, just off the Evesham Road (A435), overlooking a leafy square. Under new ownership, it offers comfortable, well equipped accommodation which is mainly en suite. An elegantly furnished drawing room is a particularly pleasing feature.
8rm(1⇄7↑) (1fb) CTV in all bedrooms ® ✱ sB&B⇄↑£25 dB&B⇄↑£40 LDO am
Lic 🍴 3P
Credit Cards 1 3

GH 🇶🇶🇶 *Stretton Lodge* Western Rd GL50 3RN
☎(0242) 528724 & 570771
Situated in a quiet residential area, convenient for the railway station, this large semidetached early-Victorian house has been carefully modernised by owners Mr and Mrs Price to provide good, modern hotel facilities, whilst retaining much of the original charm, especially within the comfortable public areas with their moulded cornices and open marble fireplaces. Bedrooms are of a good size and, in additional to en suite facilities, offer extras including mini bars and trouser presses with a personal ironing board.
9⇄↑ (3fb)⊬in 5 bedrooms CTV in all bedrooms ®
✕ (ex guide dogs) LDO noon
Lic 🍴 CTV 6P
Credit Cards 1 2 3

GH 🇶🇶🇶 **Willoughby** 1 Suffolk Square GL50 2DR
☎(0242) 522798
Closed Xmas & New Year
Located within the Montpellier District and occupying a prominent position on the Square, this fine late Georgian Cotswold stone house offers spacious and well equipped bedrooms, while retaining many of its original features.
10rm(5↑5hc) (1fb) CTV in all bedrooms ® ✱ sB&B£23-£30 sB&B↑£26.50-£35 dB&B£44-£42.50 dB&B↑£45-£50 LDO 4pm
🍴 CTV 10P

GH 🇶🇶 *Wishmoor* 147 Hales Rd GL52 6TD ☎(0242) 238504
A large turn-of-the-century semidetached house on the B4075 (just off the A40 a mile from the town centre). Spacious bedrooms are modestly furnished and comfortable, with an above average standard of cleanliness. Décor throughout enhances the original features, and guests can enjoy a comfy, quiet lounge.
10rm(4↑6hc) (1fb)⊬in 1 bedroom CTV in all bedrooms ®
✕ (ex guide dogs) sB&B£17-£20 sB&B↑£25-£30 dB&B£32-£35 dB&B↑£44-£50 WB&B£119-£175 WBDif£182-£238 LDO noon
🍴 10P
Credit Cards 1 3 £

CHEPSTOW Gwent
See Tintern

CHERITON FITZPAINE Devon Map 03 SS80

▣◗ **FH** 🇶🇶 Mrs D M Lock **Brindiwell** (*SS896079*)
EX17 4HR ☎(0363) 866357
Period farmhouse with oak beams and panelling on the side of a valley with views of the Exe Valley and Dartmoor.
4rm(1hc) (1fb)⊬in 1 bedroom CTV in 1 bedroom ®
✕ (ex guide dogs) sB&Bfr£12 dB&Bfr£24 WB&Bfr£75 WBDifr£110 LDO 5pm
CTV 4P 1🐄 120 acres sheep £

CHESTER Cheshire Map 07 SJ46

GH 🇶🇶 **Bawnpark Hotel** 10 Hoole Rd, Hoole CH2 3NH
☎(0244) 324971
This large, semi-detached Victorian residence has a rear car park, and stands on the outskirts of Chester. The cheerfully decorated bedrooms have many amenities expected at a hotel.

▶

Raglan Road, Tintern, Nr Chepstow, Gwent NP6 6TH

Telephone: 0291 689652

Valley House is a fine Georgian residence situated in the tranquil Angidy Valley within a mile of Tintern Abbey.
★ Charming, comfortable en suite rooms with colour TV and tea/coffee facilities.
★ Enjoy hearty breakfasts in our dining room with its unique arched stone ceiling.
★ Take forest walks straight from our doorsteps or relax by the log fire in our peaceful lounge.

IVYDENE HOUSE

145 Hewlett Road, Cheltenham, Glos GL52 6TS
Telephone: (0242) 521726/521776

A charming corner house in its own grounds, situated in a good residential area and within walking distance to town. Recommended for its warm friendly atmosphere, comfort and cleanliness. Comfortable lounge with colour TV and dining room with separate tables. All bedrooms with colour TV and tea making facilities. Full central heating.
Free car park and garage available

THE COLESBOURNE INN

This traditional Cotswold coaching inn offers the highest standards in food, accommodation and beers.
ETB 3 crown commended
AA QQQ Egon Ronay Les Routiers

· 10 en-suite bedrooms ·
A la carte restaurant · Bar meals · Ales from the wood ·
Large car park · Garden/patio
Families welcome ·
Traditional Sunday lunch
Situated on the A435
Cheltenham-Cirencester
Colesbourne Inn, Colesbourne,
Nr. Cheltenham,
Gloucestershire GL53 9NP.
**Telephone Coberley (024287) 376
Fax (024287) 397**

THE HOLLINGTON HOUSE HOTEL

**115 HALES ROAD, CHELTENHAM,
GLOUCESTERSHIRE GL52 6ST
TEL: (0242) 519718 FAX: (0242) 570280**

A detached late Victorian house with a large garden and ample parking just a few minutes from the town centre.

Guests will enjoy the pleasant, relaxed atmosphere and the proprietors personal attention.

There are 9 spacious bedrooms with en-suite facilities, in-room beverages, colour television. A comfortable lounge bar.

Good food is offered at breakfast and dinner with a choice of menu.

"A WARM WELCOME AWAITS YOU"

5⇔ (2fb) CTV in all bedrooms ® ✳ dB&B⇔£32-£38
🍴 CTV 12P
Credit Cards ⊡ ⊡ £

GH Ⓠ Ⓠ Ⓠ **Chester Court Hotel** 48 Hoole Rd (A56) CH2 3NL
☏(0244) 320779 & 311098 FAX (0244) 344795
Closed 24 Dec-5 Jan
*A well run guesthouse on the edge of town with many of the
attributes of a hotel. The house has a lot of character and the
bedrooms are supplemented by a tastefully designed annexe within
the grounds.*
8rm(1⇔4⎰ 3hc) Annexe 12rm(6⇔6⎰) (2fb) CTV in all
bedrooms ® ✳ sB&B£30 sB&B⇔⎰£38 dB&B£38
dB&B⇔⎰£48 WB&B£133-£266 WBDi£206.50-£339.50
LDO 8pm
Lic 🍴 25P
Credit Cards ⊡ ⊡ ⊡ ⊡ £

GH Ⓠ **Devonia** 33-35 Hoole Rd CH2 3NH ☏(0244) 322236
*A family-run guesthouse a mile from the city centre on the A56.
Catering for tourists and business people, it offers good value for
money and the advantage of private parking.*
10hc (6fb) CTV in all bedrooms ® ✳ sB&B£17.50-£20
dB&B£27.50-£32.50 LDO 4pm
Lic 🍴 CTV 15P £

GH Ⓠ Ⓠ **Eaton Hotel** 29 City Rd CH1 3AE ☏(0244) 320840
*Adjacent to the Shropshire Union Canal, the hotel has well
equipped bedrooms and is close to the city centre.*
22rm(6⇔7⎰9hc) (3fb) CTV in all bedrooms ® sB&B£30
sB&B⇔⎰£38 dB&Bfr£45 dB&B⇔⎰fr£54 WB&B£150-£266
WBDi£203-£300 LDO 8pm
Lic 🍴 8P 1🚗
Credit Cards ⊡ ⊡ ⊡ ⊡ £

GH Ⓠ Ⓠ **Egerton Lodge Hotel** 57 Hoole Rd, Hoole CH2 3NJ
☏(0244) 320712
Closed 19 Dec-3 Jan
*An attractive mid-terrace Victorian house situated on the A56
leading to the city centre. Bedrooms are compact but attractive
and well equipped, and parking facilities are provided.*
4rm(3⎰1hc) (3fb) CTV in all bedrooms ® ✘ ✳ sB&B£17.50-
£19.50 sB&B⎰£17.50-£19.50 dB&B⎰£27-£32
5P nc3yrs
Credit Cards ⊡ ⊡ ⊡ £

GH Ⓠ Ⓠ *Eversley Hotel* 9 Eversley Park CH2 2AJ
☏(0244) 373744
Closed 24 Dec-2 Jan
*A fully modernised hotel on the outskirts of Chester, reached by
taking the A5116 Liverpool road due north of the town centre. The
proprietors are friendly and keen to make guests comfortable.*
11rm(4⇔5⎰2hc) (3fb) CTV in all bedrooms ® ✘ LDO 8pm
Lic 🍴 CTV 17P 🔵
Credit Cards ⊡ ⊡

GH Ⓠ *Gables* 5 Vicarage Rd, Hoole CH2 3HZ ☏(0244) 323969
*This end-terrace Victorian house is in a quiet residential area just
off the Hoole road leading to the town. Limited parking space is
available but street parking is permitted.*
7hc (4fb) CTV in all bedrooms ®
CTV 7P
Credit Cards ⊡

GH Ⓠ Ⓠ **Gloster Lodge Hotel** 44 Hoole Rd, Hoole CH2 3NL
☏(0244) 348410 & 320231
Closed 24-31 Dec
*A well run family hotel on the edge of the town centre, opposite All
Saints Church. The bedrooms are well furnished and have many
amenities normally found at larger establishments.*

5⇔⎰ Annexe 3⇔⎰ (2fb) CTV in all bedrooms ® ✳
sB&B⇔⎰£30-£36.50 dB&B⇔⎰⎰fr£36.50 WB&Bfr£115
WBDifr£148 LDO 8pm
Lic 🍴 9P
Credit Cards ⊡ ⊡

GH Ⓠ Ⓠ Ⓠ **Green Gables** 11 Eversley Park CH2 2AJ
☏(0244) 372243 FAX (0244) 376352
*A semi-detached, Victorian gabled house, beautifully furnished
and decorated, located in a quiet residential area just off the
Liverpool road out of the city. All the bedrooms are well appointed,
with telephone, TV and tea-making facilities. There is a very
comfortable lounge, and a small, modern breakfast room.*
4rm(3⎰1hc) (1fb) CTV in all bedrooms ® ✘ (ex guide dogs)
sB&B⇔⎰£22-£25 dB&B⎰£35-£37 LDO 9.30pm
🍴 CTV 8P 3🚗

GH Ⓠ Ⓠ **Hamilton Court** 5-7 Hamilton St CH2 3JG
☏(0244) 345387
Closed Xmas wk
*A well appointed, hospitable hotel converted from 2 gabled houses,
just off the A56, a mile from the city centre. Evening meals are
available by prior booking, and parking can also be arranged.*
12rm(6⎰6hc) (5fb) CTV in all bedrooms ® sB&Bfr£14.50
dB&Bfr£29 dB&B⎰fr£34 LDO 6.30pm
Lic 🍴 CTV 8P 10🚗
Credit Cards ⊡ ⊡ £

SELECTED

GH Ⓠ Ⓠ Ⓠ Ⓠ **Redland Private Hotel** 64 Hough Green
CH4 8JY ☏(0244) 671024
*Situated on the edge of town on the busy A549, this private
house has been painstakingly restored to its former glory by
the owners. Bedrooms are spacious and thoughtfully furnished
and 3 rooms have 4-poster beds, 1 dating back to the Jacobean
era. The interior has been likened to that of a baronial hall; a
small courtesy bar has been installed on the staircase and a
further room added, making this a popular choice for visitors
to Chester.*
13⇔⎰ (3fb) CTV in all bedrooms ® sB&B⇔⎰£35-£40
dB&B⇔⎰£45-£60
Lic 🍴 10P 2🚗 sauna solarium £

GH Ⓠ **The Riverside Hotel** 22 City Walls, Duke St, Off Lower
Bridge St CH1 1SB ☏(0244) 326580 & 325278
FAX (0244) 311567
Well-furnished modern hotel on city walls next to the River Dee.
13⇔⎰ (2fb)✂in 1 bedroom CTV in all bedrooms ® ✳
sB&B⇔⎰£32-£38 dB&B⇔⎰£45-£60 LDO 9pm
Lic 🍴 CTV 25P
Credit Cards ⊡ ⊡ ⊡

GH Ⓠ Ⓠ **Riverside Recorder Hotel** 19 City Walls CH1 1SB
☏(0244) 311498 FAX (0244) 311567
*Situated on the Roman city wall at the top of the Recorder Steps,
this comfortable guesthouse, with views over the River Dee,
provides many facilities in its well appointed bedrooms, some of
which have four-poster beds.*
10⇔⎰ (2fb) CTV in all bedrooms ® ✳ sB&B⇔⎰£30-£38
dB&B⇔⎰£42-£53 LDO 9pm
Lic 🍴 CTV 15P

'Selected' establishments, which have the highest
quality award, are highlighted by a tinted panel.
For a full list of these establishments, consult the
Contents page.

CHIDEOCK Dorset Map **03** SY49

SELECTED
GH Ⓠ Ⓠ Ⓠ Ⓠ **Betchworth House Hotel** DT6 6JW
☎(0297) 89478
Mar-Oct
*An attractive stone cottage with a flower-filled garden and car
parking across the road. The bedrooms are freshly decorated
and pretty with co-ordinating soft furnishings. Modern
showers and WCs are available in some rooms, while others
share a spacious general bathroom. There is a very
comfortable lounge with deep settees and armchairs, and a
cosy dining room for breakfast. In the summer a set cream tea
is served in the garden.*
6rm(3🌂3hc)(1fb) Ⓡ ✗ (ex guide dogs) sB&B£20-£22
dB&B£36-£40 dB&B🌂£40-£44 WB&B£122.50-£150.50
Lic 🎪 CTV 15P nc7yrs Ⓔ

CHILHAM Kent Map **05** TR05

INN Ⓠ Ⓠ Ⓠ **Woolpack** High St CT4 8DL
☎Canterbury(0227) 730208 FAX (0227) 731053
5⇌ Annexe 10🌂 (3fb) Ⓡ ✱ sB&B⇌🌂fr£43.50
dB&B⇌🌂fr£56.50 ✱ Lunch £8-£12alc Dinner £10-£15alc
LDO 10pm
🎪 CTV 30P
Credit Cards ①③

CHINNOR Oxfordshire Map **04** SP70

FH Ⓠ Ⓠ Ⓠ Mr & Mrs Steel *Chinnor Hill Manor* (SU762994)
OX9 4BG ☎Kingston Blount(0844) 51469
*A large farmhouse set on top of Chinnor Hill, surrounded by 15
acres of well kept grounds. Bedrooms in this charming house are
comfortable, spacious and nicely appointed. The public rooms are* ▶

𝕽𝖎𝖛𝖊𝖗𝖘𝖎𝖉𝖊 𝕳𝖔𝖙𝖊𝖑

22 City Walls off Lower Bridge Street, Chester CH1 1SB
Telephone: (0244) 326580 & 325278

The Riverside Hotel and Recorder Building are situated in a peaceful location on the historic City Walls of Chester with views from
most rooms overlooking the River Dee.
There is a total of 23 bedrooms all with en-suite facilities, colour
television, tea/coffee facilities, direct dial telephone and hairdryer.
There are a number of 4 poster bedded rooms and a deluxe room
with a balcony. A large private car park is to the rear of the Hotel
with access from Duke Street via Lower Bridge Street.
Edgards Restaurant provides an elegant Georgian setting where
fresh food of the highest quality is served and naturally there is a
licensed bar.

𝕰𝖛𝖊𝖗𝖘𝖑𝖊𝖞 𝕳𝖔𝖙𝖊𝖑

9 Eversley Park,
Chester, CH2 2AJ
Telephone: (0244) 373744

Attractive Victorian residence with all
modern facilities, relaxing atmosphere
and good food. All rooms are
en suite and have TV, telephone,
tea/coffee. Hotel has its own car park.

Proprietors:
Bryn and Barbara Povey

Devonia
Guest House

33-35 Hoole Road
Chester
Cheshire
CH2 3NH

Tel: 0244 322236

attractive, and the proprietors are happy to share their home and leisure facilities with guests, which include a heated outdoor pool and grass tennis court.

3rm
ᵐᵐ CTV P 2🐾 ᴸ(heated) ℛ(grass)15 acres horses

CHIPPENHAM Wiltshire Map 03 ST97

GH Ⓠ Ⓠ Ⓠ *Oxford Hotel* 32/36 Langley Rd SN15 1BX
☎(0249) 652542
A small privately owned and personally run hotel with an attractive and comfortable bar and conservatory lounge. Bedrooms are very well equipped, many with en suite facilities.
13rm(7�క6hc) (1fb) CTV in all bedrooms Ⓡ LDO 5.30pm
Lic ᵐᵐ 9P
Credit Cards ① ② ③

CHIPPING CAMPDEN Gloucestershire Map 04 SP13

GH Ⓠ Ⓠ Ⓠ *The Malt House* Broad Campden GL55 6UU
☎Evesham(0386) 840295
Closed 23 Dec-1 Jan rs Sun
Just a mile from Chipping Campden in the picturesque village of Broad Campden, this comfortable guesthouse was once a row of cottages. The Malt House is lovingly cared for and very clean. Each bedroom is unique, but with the same period character as the gorgeous lounge which overlooks a walled garden. Dinner is also available.
3rm(2ᴸ1hc) CTV in all bedrooms Ⓡ ✕ (ex guide dogs)
LDO noon
Lic ᵐᵐ 8P nc12yrs

CHIPPING ONGAR Essex Map 05 TL50

GH Ⓠ Ⓠ *Stanford Rivers Hall* Stanford Rivers CM5 9QG
☎Ongar(0277) 362997
This solid Georgian house lies behind the church next to farm buildings, in a rural setting. Guests have the use of a spacious lounge with comfortable armchairs and a log burning stove, and a fine breakfast room with exposed timbers and brickwork and a communal table. Bedrooms are on the first floor and are reached by a spiral staircase ; they are attractively decorated and vary in size.
4rm(1ᴸ3🌂) ⊬in all bedrooms CTV in all bedrooms Ⓡ ✕ ✳
sB&Bᴸ🌂£25-£30 dB&Bᴸ🌂£38-£45 WB&B£165-£200
ᵐᵐ 12P

CHISELBOROUGH Somerset Map 03 ST41

FH Ⓠ Ⓠ Mrs E Holloway **Manor** *(ST468151)* TA14 6TQ
☎(0935) 881203
Apr-Oct
This Ham stone house with leaded windows has comfortable bedrooms, some with antique furniture and easy chairs. The large lounge has a log fire, and freshly prepared meals are taken around the large dining table.
4hc (1fb) CTV in all bedrooms Ⓡ ✕ ✳ sB&B£16-£18
dB&B£32-£36
ᵐᵐ CTV 4P ⏴ 450 acres mixed Ⓔ

CHISELDON Wiltshire Map 04 SU17

FH Ⓠ Ⓠ M Hughes **Parsonage** *(SU185799)* SN4 0NJ
☎Swindon(0793) 740204
This 16th-century building is situated at one end of the village high street, backing on to the church and grounds. Some of the bedrooms are ensuite, each being reasonably spacious, simply decorated, comfortable and well kept. Public areas are attractive and include a cosy lounge with an open fire and a dining room with a polished trestle table. The gardens are well tended with neat lawns, and views are rural.
4rm(2ᴸ🌂) Ⓡ sB&B£20-£25 sB&Bᴸ🌂£25-£27.50
dB&Bᴸ🌂£40-£50
Lic ᵐᵐ CTV 8P 2🐾 ∪ 400 acres arable

CHISLEHAMPTON Oxfordshire Map 04 SU59

SELECTED

INN Ⓠ Ⓠ Ⓠ Ⓠ **Coach & Horses** Stadhampton Rd
OX9 7UX ☎Stadhampton(0865) 890255 Telex no 83602
This 16th-century stone-built inn stands beside the B480, just 7 miles from Oxford. Bedrooms are situated in a modern annexe and have recently been refurbished : each is nicely decorated, comfortably furnished and very well equipped with private bathrooms. The public areas, in the original main building, are cosy and inviting, with exposed stone work, oak beams and roaring log fires. The popular restaurant offers extensive à la carte and table d'hôte menus comprising home-cooked, nicely presented dishes from quality produce. Staff and management are courteous, polite and friendly.
9ᴸ🌂 CTV in all bedrooms Ⓡ ✕ (ex guide dogs) ✳
sB&Bᴸ🌂£37-£55.50 dB&Bᴸ🌂£52-£72.50 WB&B£196-£314 WBDi£285.50-£404 ✳ Lunch fr£12.50&alc Dinner fr£12.50&alc LDO 10pm
42P
Credit Cards ① ② ③ ⑤ Ⓔ

CHOLDERTON Wiltshire Map 04 SU24

GH Ⓠ Ⓠ Ⓠ **Cholderton Country Hotel** Parkhouse Corner
SP4 0EG ☎(098064) 484 & 487
Closed Xmas & New Year
14ᴸ🌂 (2fb) CTV in all bedrooms Ⓡ ✕ (ex guide dogs)
sB&Bᴸ🌂£34-£38 dB&Bᴸ🌂£44-£48 WB&B£214 WBDi£284
(wkly only Oct-Mar) LDO 8.30pm
Lic ᵐᵐ CTV 25P
Credit Cards ① ② ③ ⑤ Ⓔ

CHOLMONDELEY Cheshire Map 07 SJ55

GH Ⓠ Ⓠ Ⓠ **The Cholmondeley Arms** SY14 8BT
☎(0829) 720300
Once a village school, situated on the A49, this inn now offers an excellent range of home-prepared bar meals in the bar/dining area amongst the old wooden benches and ink-stained school desks which lend a touch of nostalgia to the atmosphere. The adjacent school house provides, in contrast, modern, well decorated and equipped bedrooms with private bathrooms.
4🌂 (1fb) CTV in all bedrooms Ⓡ ✳ sB&B🌂fr£30
dB&B🌂fr£40 LDO 10pm
Lic ᵐᵐ
Credit Cards ① ③ Ⓔ

CHRISTCHURCH Dorset Map 04 SZ19

See also Bournemouth
GH Ⓠ **Belvedere Hotel** 59 Barrack Rd BH23 1PD
☎(0202) 485978
Large Victorian hotel on main Christchurch to Bournemouth road.
8hc (3fb) CTV in 7 bedrooms Ⓡ ✳ sB&B£16-£18 dB&B£30-£34 WB&B£110-£115 LDO 4pm
Lic ᵐᵐ CTV 12P

CHURCH STOKE Powys Map 07 SO29

FH Ⓠ Ⓠ Mrs C Richards **The Drewin** *(SO261905)* SY15 6TW
☎(05885) 325
Apr-Oct
A Border farmhouse with beams and inglenook fireplace. There are fine views of surrounding countryside, and Offa's Dyke footpath runs through the farm.
2hc (1fb) CTV in 1 bedroom TV in 1 bedroom Ⓡ
✕ (ex guide dogs) LDO 7pm
ᵐᵐ CTV 6P ♨ games room 102 acres mixed

CHURCH STRETTON Shropshire Map **07** SO49

GH Ⓠ Ⓠ Ⓠ **Belvedere** Burway Rd SY6 6DP ☎(0694) 722232
The recent improvements to this large detached house include a large, split-level lounge and two en suite rooms. All the bedrooms have fine countryside views.
12rm(6↑6hc)(2fb) ® sB&Bf£18-£20 sB&Bf↑£20-£22 dB&Bf£36 dB&Bf↑£40 WB&Bf£113.40-£126 WBDif£169.40-£182 LDO 6pm
Lic ⦿ CTV 9P 1🐾
Credit Cards ① ③ £

FH Ⓠ Ⓠ Mrs J C Inglis **Hope Bowdler Hall** *(SO478925)* Hope Bowdler SY6 7DD (1m E B4371) ☎(0694) 722041
Apr-Oct rs Mar-Nov
Set on the edge of the tiny village of Hope Bowdler and surrounded by hills, this 17th-century manor house has been modernised to a very high standard. It is 'no smoking' throughout.
3hc ✗in all bedrooms ✗ sB&Bf£15-£17.50 dB&Bfrf£30
⦿ 6P nc12yrs ♬(hard)22 acres sheep woodland

FH Ⓠ Ⓠ Ⓠ Mrs C J Hotchkiss **Olde Hall** *(SO509926)* Wall-under-Heywood SY6 7DU ☎Longville(06943) 253 due to change to (0694) 771253
Feb-Nov
Beautifully preserved Elizabethan farmhouse with cruck timbers and a fine Jacobean staircase.
3hc (1fb) CTV in all bedrooms ® ✗ sB&Bf£14.50-£16 dB&Bf£29-£32 WB&Bf£95
⦿ CTV 6P 275 acres dairy £

SELECTED

FH Ⓠ Ⓠ Ⓠ Ⓠ Mrs J A Davies **Rectory** *(SO452985)* Woolstaston SY6 6NN (3.5m off B4370 at All Stretton) ☎Leebotwood(06945) 306 due to change to (0694) 751306
Mar-Nov
An Elizabethan half-timbered farmhouse beside the Long Mynd in the village of Woolstaston; to find it, turn off the A49 at the Pound Inn, Leebotwood, signed to the village; at the village green take the right fork and the farm is the first on the right. Standing on a hill, the house has panoramic views across countryside to the Wrekin. The interior is full of character and has been furnished with good quality period artefacts. The divided lounge area features a copper-canopied fireplace, and barns have been converted into a gallery- style TV lounge. The spacious bedrooms are spotlessly clean, with rural views and festooned with fresh flowers. The dining room is at the far end of the house, through the kitchen, where a hearty English breakfast is prepared.
3⇌ TV available ✗ dB&B⇌£32 WB&Bf£112
⦿ CTV 10P nc12yrs 170 acres beef

CIRENCESTER Gloucestershire Map **04** SP00

GH Ⓠ Ⓠ **La Ronde Hotel** 52-54 Ashcroft Rd GL7 1QX ☎(0285) 654611 & 652216
Situated in the centre of the town, this hotel offers well equipped en suite bedrooms and cosy public areas that include a good dining room where a range of imaginative and well cooked dishes are served.
10⇌↑ (2fb) CTV in all bedrooms ® sB&B⇌↑£30-£43.50 dB&B⇌↑£43.50-£52.50 LDO 9pm
Lic ⦿ 9P
Credit Cards ① ③ £

GH Ⓠ Ⓠ Ⓠ **Wimborne House** 91 Victoria Rd GL7 1ES ☎(0285) 653890
This friendly guesthouse caters for non-smokers only. Just 5 minutes walk from the town centre, it offers well-equipped rooms, together with private parking and gardens to the front and rear.

5⇌↑ (1fb)✗in all bedrooms CTV in all bedrooms ® ✗ sB&B⇌↑£20-£30 dB&B⇌↑£28-£40 LDO 4pm
⦿ 8P nc5yrs £

INN Ⓠ Ⓠ Ⓠ **Eliot Arms** Clark's Hay, South Cerney GL7 5UA ☎(0285) 860215
Set in the charming hamlet of South Cerney, this stone-built inn has attractive open plan public rooms, a cosy dining area and very attractive and well equipped en suite bedrooms.
9⇌↑ (1fb) CTV in all bedrooms ® sB&B⇌↑£28-£30 dB&B⇌↑£40-£45 Lunch £3.95-£9.95alc Dinner £3.95-£9.95alc LDO 10pm
⦿ 28P ♬
Credit Cards ① ③ £

CLACTON-ON-SEA Essex Map **05** TM11

GH Ⓠ Ⓠ Ⓠ **Chudleigh Hotel** Agate Rd CO15 1RA ☎(0255) 425407
Closed 15 Dec-6 Jan
A small family-run guesthouse, conveniently situated near the seafront, pier and shopping centre. Bedrooms are tastefully furnished and well equipped, providing comfortable accommodation, some with private bathrooms.
12rm(11⇌↑)(3fb) CTV in all bedrooms ® ✱ sB&Bf£20-£21 sB&B⇌↑£25 dB&B⇌↑£45 WB&Bf£162-£165 WBDif£197-£200 LDO 7pm
Lic ⦿ 7P nc2yrs
Credit Cards ① ② ③ ⑤ £

See advertisement on page 125

GH Ⓠ Ⓠ Ⓠ **Sandrock Hotel** 1 Penfold Rd CO15 1JN ☎(0255) 428215
A detached Edwardian house just 50 yards from the seafront, with off-street parking. Bedrooms are well equipped and comfortable, with good en suite facilities, and some have sea views. A small, ▶

freshly prepared menu is offered, and the proprietors work hard to ensure a high standard of cleanliness.
7♠ (3fb) CTV in all bedrooms ® dB&B♠fr£47 WB&Bfr£145 WBDifr£185 LDO 6pm
Lic ₩ 6P
Credit Cards ①③

CLAPHAM North Yorkshire Map **07** SD76

INN Q *The Flying Horseshoe* LA2 8ES ☎(04685) 229
Set in beautiful countryside, this stone-built inn is located opposite the railway station, just over a mile west of the village. The bedrooms are comfortable and all have private bathrooms. An extensive menu is offered in the nicely decorated dining room.
5rm(1↪4♠) CTV in all bedrooms ® ✖ (ex guide dogs) LDO 10.30pm
₩ 50P 2☎ ♪

CLAVERDON Warwickshire Map **04** SP16

GH QQ Woodside Country House Langley Rd CV35 8PJ (0.75m S of B4095) ☎(092684) 2446
Closed Xmas wk
3hc (1fb) CTV in 1 bedroom TV in 1 bedroom ® ✱ sB&B£14-£19 dB&B£28-£32 WB&B£95-£109 WBDi£185.50-£196.50 LDO 2pm
₩ CTV 12P 1☎ ♨ ♪(hard)croquet £

CLAYTON-LE-WOODS Lancashire Map **07** SD52

GH QQQ Brook House Hotel 662 Preston Rd PR6 7EH ☎Preston(0772) 36403
Beside the A6 at Clayton-le-Woods, a mile from the M6 and M61, this 19th-century house has been carefully modernised to provide comfortable, well equipped accommodation, with a high standard of housekeeping.
20rm(15↪5hc) (3fb) CTV in 12 bedrooms ®
✖ (ex guide dogs) sB&B£22 sB&B↪♠£30 dB&B£34 dB&B↪♠£42 LDO 8.30pm
Lic ₩ CTV 25P
Credit Cards ①③ £

CLEARWELL Gloucestershire Map **03** SO50

SELECTED

GH QQQQ Tudor Farmhouse Hotel GL16 8JS ☎Dean(0594) 33046 FAX (0594) 37093
A listed Tudor farmhouse, in the heart of the fascinating village of Clearwell, which has been lovingly restored by the present owners. Rooms in the main house are reached by an oak spiral staircase, whilst less mobile residents can be accommodated in the converted cottages in the grounds at the rear of the house. The bedrooms are very individual, with good en suite facilities, yet the charm and character of this old house has been successfully retained. The restaurant is extremely popular and the food is imaginative and wholesome: reservations are advisable as a result, especially at weekends.
6↪♠ Annexe 3↪♠ CTV in all bedrooms ® ✱
sB&B↪♠£42.50-£49 dB&B↪♠£49-£65 LDO 9pm
Lic ₩ 15P 2☎ nc8yrs
Credit Cards ①②③ £

CLEETHORPES Humberside Map **08** TA30

GH QQ Mallow View 9-11 Albert Rd DN35 8LX ☎(0472) 691297
Three terraced houses, close to the seafront and town centre, are combined to form this guesthouse. There is a small reception lounge, a separate bar lounge and a cosy dining room. The bedrooms are compact and nicely equipped.

16rm(1♠15hc) (1fb) CTV in 15 bedrooms ® LDO 7pm
Lic ₩ CTV ✗ £

CLIFTONVILLE Kent

See **Margate**

CLITHEROE Lancashire Map **07** SD74

GH QQQ Brooklyn 32 Pimlico Rd BB7 2AH ☎(0200) 28268
An immaculate Victorian town house situated in a quiet residential area just east of the town centre. Most of the comfortable bedrooms have private bathrooms and are tastefully furnished and decorated, each with colour TV and tea-making facilities; 4 of the rooms are located in a small house immediately opposite, which has a comfortable separate lounge.
4rm(2♠2hc) Annexe 4♠ CTV in all bedrooms ®
✖ (ex guide dogs) ✱ sB&B£18 sB&B♠£19 dB&B£34 dB&B♠£37 WB&B£119-£132 WBDi£178.50-£191.50 LDO 10am
Lic ₩ CTV 1☎
Credit Cards ①③ £

CLOUGHTON North Yorkshire Map **08** TA09

[符]**GH Q Cober Hill** Newlands Rd YO13 0AR ☎Scarborough(0723) 870310
Set in 6.5 acres, this large guesthouse offers very good value for money. It is 6 miles north of Scarborough and specialises in group activity holidays, with comfortable accommodation in simple style, and ample lounges.
48hc Annexe 31rm(17↪14♠) (13fb) ® sB&B£13-£20 sB&B↪♠£16-£25 dB&B£26-£40 dB&B↪♠£32-£50 WB&B£70-£150 WBDi£125-£190 LDO 7pm
Lic ₩ 60P ♪(hard)bowling green croquet table-tennis
See advertisement under SCARBOROUGH

CLOVELLY Devon Map **02** SS32

FH QQQ Mrs E Symons *Burnstone (SS325233)* Higher Clovelly EX39 5RX ☎(02373) 219
This attractive 17th-century Devon longhouse retains many original features and is tastefully decorated and furnished. Guests will find bed and breakfast accommodation here, together with a warm welcome.
2hc (2fb) ®
₩ CTV 3P 500 acres dairy sheep mixed
Credit Cards ③

CLUNTON Shropshire Map **07** SO38

[符]**FH QQ** Mrs J Williams *Hurst Mill (SO318811)* SY7 0JA ☎Clun(05884) 224
Surrounded by woods and almost encircled by the river Clun, this hospitable farm offers warm accommodation and home cooked meals. Children and dogs are also made welcome.
3rm(2hc) (1fb)⤳in 1 bedroom CTV in 1 bedroom TV in 1 bedroom ® sB&B£12-£14 dB&B£24-£28 LDO 6.30pm
CTV 4P 2☎ ♪ 2 ponies 100 acres mixed £

COCKERMOUTH Cumbria Map **11** NY13

SELECTED

GH QQQQ Low Hall Country Brandlingill CA13 0RE (3m S on unclass off A5086) ☎(0900) 826654
Mar-Nov
David and Dani Edwards have successfully blended old and new at their 17th-century farmhouse, to retain throughout an atmosphere of warmth and relaxation. Mrs Edwards serves delicious dinners, with the menu changing daily, to include many traditional Lakeland dishes, seasonal items, dishes from other countries and even other centuries! Low Hall is ideally

---

located for touring anywhere in the Lake District or even further afield.

6rm(1⇨5♠) ⌇in all bedrooms ® ✖ (ex guide dogs) ✱
dB&B⇨♠£46-£49 WB&B£154-£157.50 WBDi£238-£248
LDO 7.30pm
Lic ∭ CTV 10P nc10yrs
Credit Cards 1 3

GH QQQ Sundawn Carlisle Rd, Bridekirk CA13 0PA
☎(0900) 822384
A private house situated in an elevated position on the A595, just over a mile from the town centre, with splendid views of the Cumbrian mountains and fells. Bedrooms are very well appointed and comfortable, two with private bathrooms.
4rm(2⇨♠) ®
∭

CODSALL Staffordshire Map 07 SJ80

FH QQQ Mrs D E Moreton **Moors Farm & Country Restaurant** *(SJ859048)* Chillington Ln WV8 1QH
☎(09074) 2330 due to change to (0902) 842330
A busy working farm in an isolated position which is well known in the area for both its accommodation and the restaurant. There is a choice of menus including an interesting vegetarian selection; booking is essential.
6rm(2♠4hc) (3fb) CTV in all bedrooms ® ✖ ✱ sB&B£20-£22
sB&B♠£24-£26 dB&B£34-£36 dB&B♠£42-£44 WB&B£140-£145 WBDi£176-£235 LDO 6pm
Lic ∭ CTV 20P nc4yrs 100 acres mixed

COLCHESTER Essex Map 05 TL92

GH QQ Four Sevens 28 Inglis Rd CO3 3HU ☎(0206) 46093
This guesthouse provides simple, cheerful accommodation with well equipped, spacious bedrooms, some with private bathrooms. It is located in a quiet residential area, near the town centre: down the Maldon road, 2nd on the right then 1st left.
6rm(2♠4hc) (1fb) CTV in all bedrooms ® ✖ ✱ sB&B£25-£30
sB&B♠£30-£35 dB&B£32-£34 dB&B♠£36-£38
∭

GH QQ 14 Roman Road 14 Roman Rd CO1 1UR
☎(0206) 577905
Closed 23-31 Dec
A semidetached house near the town centre with a cheerful red front door. The three bedrooms are spick and span, well appointed and comfortable. Breakfast is served in the kitchen at a large pine table, and there is a small neat garden outside by the original Roman wall.
3rm(1⇨) ⌇in all bedrooms CTV in all bedrooms ® ✖ ✱
sB&B£18 sB&B⇨£22 dB&B£28 dB&B⇨£32
1P

GH QQ Tarquins 26 Inglis Rd CO3 3HU ☎(0206) 579508
FAX 579508
6rm(2♠4hc) (4fb) CTV in all bedrooms ® ✱ sB&B£20-£22
sB&B♠£30 dB&B£30 dB&B♠£38 WB&B£120-£180
WBDi£169-£229 LDO 10am
∭ CTV 1P nc5yrs

COLEFORD Gloucestershire Map 03 SO51

FH Q Mrs Sylvia Davis **Lower Tump** *(SO588160)* Eastbach, English Bicknor GL16 7EU ☎Dean(0594) 60253
Set in a lovely position close to the beautiful Forest of Dean, this farmhouse provides simply appointed accommodation.
2rm(1⇨1♠) (1fb) CTV in all bedrooms ®
∭ 10P 150 acres mixed

Visit your local AA Shop.

COLESBOURNE Gloucestershire Map 03 SO91

INN QQQ Colesbourne GL53 9NP
☎Coberley(024287) 376 & 396 FAX (024287) 397
A Cotswold stone former coaching inn situated in the village centre, providing friendly service and good food, with real ale from the wood in the bars. Bedrooms are situated in the former stables, which have been converted to provide comfortable, well equipped accommodation, and all rooms have private bath or shower.
Annexe 10rm(6⇨4♠) CTV in all bedrooms ® ✱
dB&B⇨♠£50-£55 ✱ Lunch £8-£15alc High tea £2.25-£4.95alc Dinner £9-£18alc LDO 10pm
70P
Credit Cards 1 2 3 5 £
See advertisement under CHELTENHAM

COLNE Lancashire Map 07 SD84

FH QQQ Mrs C Mitson **Higher Wanless** *(SD873413)* Red Ln BB8 7JP ☎(0282) 865301
Closed Dec
Overlooking the Leeds-Liverpool canal, close to Barrowford, this farm is within easy reach of 'Pendle Witch' and 'Brontë' country. Mrs Mitson gives a warm welcome and provides a relaxed atmosphere in which guests can unwind. One of the two bedrooms is en suite; both are spacious, comfortable and very well equipped. A wholesome home cooked meal is available on request.
2rm(1♠1hc) (2fb) CTV in 1 bedroom ® sB&B£17-£23
sB&B♠£20-£23 dB&B£32-£40 dB&B♠£36-£44 WB&B£125
WBDifr£185 LDO 9am
∭ CTV 4P nc3yrs 25 acres Shire horses, sheep £

£ Remember to use the money-off vouchers.

COLWYN BAY Clwyd Map **06** SH87

GH Q Alwyn House Hotel 4 Upper Promenade LL28 4BS ☎(0492) 532004

This terraced property is located close to the seafront. The simple but pleasant, well maintained accommodation is equally suitable for holidaymakers and commercial travellers, and is popular with local actors.

9hc (5fb) CTV in 8 bedrooms ® ✱ sB&Bfr£15 dB&Bfr£26 LDO 6pm

Lic ♨ ⚑ solarium £

GH Q Briar Lea 44 Greenfield Rd LL29 8EW ☎(0492) 530052

This semidetached Victorian house has been extensively renovated and converted into a small, personally run, friendy guesthouse. It is conveniently located for the town centre and the access road to the A55 expressway, and it has a private car park.

4hc (1fb) CTV in all bedrooms dB&B£20-£22 WB&B£70-£84 WBDi£105-£119

CTV 6P £

GH QQQ Cabin Hill Private Hotel College Avenue, Rhos-on-Sea LL28 4NT ☎(0492) 544568 & 874642

Mar-Nov

This modernised Edwardian house, now a personally run private hotel, is situated in a quiet road, close to Rhos-on-Sea promenade. The accommodation is very well maintained and quite well equipped, the majority of rooms having en suite facilities.

10rm(7↱3hc) (2fb) CTV in all bedrooms ® ✖ sB&Bfr£16.35 sB&B↱fr£20 dB&Bfr£29.50 dB&B↱fr£36.50 WBDi£123.50-£141 LDO 5pm

Lic ♨ CTV 6P nc3yrs £

GH Q Grosvenor Hotel 106-108 Abergele Rd LL29 7PS ☎(0492) 530798 & 531586

A double-fronted house on the main road close to the town centre, the Grosvenor Hotel provides simple accommodation suitable for both tourists and commercial visitors.

18rm(2⇌16hc) (8fb) CTV in 7 bedrooms TV in 3 bedrooms ® sB&B£15.90-£16.90 dB&B£31.80-£33.80 dB&B⇌£36.30-£38.30 WB&B£89-£93 WBDi£122-£129 LDO 7pm

Lic CTV 16P pool table darts

Credit Cards [3]

GH QQ Northwood Hotel 47 Rhos Rd, Rhos-on-Sea LL28 4RS ☎(0492) 549931

This large detached house, now a private hotel, is situated about a quarter of a mile from the Rhos-on-Sea shops and promenade. Northwood provides nicely maintained and quite well equipped accommodation, equally suitable for both holidaymakers and commercial visitors.

12rm(1⇌10↱1hc) (3fb) CTV in all bedrooms ® ✱ sB&B£21 sB&B⇌↱£23 dB&B£42 dB&B⇌↱£46 WB&B£100-£105 WBDi£132-£145 LDO 6.15pm

Lic ♨ CTV 11P

Credit Cards [1] [3] £

COLYFORD Devon Map **03** SY29

SELECTED

GH QQQQ Swallows Eaves Hotel Swan Hill Rd EX13 6QJ ☎Colyton(0297) 53184

One of the favourite small hotels of several of our inspectors, Swallows Eaves never fails to please. Jane Beck with her husband John is the driving force, and they are very congenial hosts. The creeper-clad, former gentleman's residence is squeaky clean throughout and, nicely set back in its own small grounds and gardens, it is the ideal retreat. The emphasis here is on a warm welcome and hospitable service. Tastefully decorated bedrooms provide an abundance of creature comforts, public rooms are bright and unpretentious, and quality fresh cooking is served in the pretty little dining room.

8⇌↱ ⊬in 4 bedrooms CTV in all bedrooms ® ✖ (ex guide dogs) sB&B⇌↱£32-£39 dB&B⇌↱£50-£62 WB&B£150-£195 WBDi£250-£290 LDO 8pm

Lic ♨ 10P nc14yrs

Credit Cards [2] £

COLYTON Devon Map **03** SY29

SELECTED

GH QQQQ *Old Bakehouse* Lower Church St EX13 6ND ☎(0297) 52518

Dating back to the 17th century, this former bakery stands in the centre of Colyton and has been carefully converted to offer accommodation of character with stone walls, beams and open fireplaces. All rooms have en suite facilities and a colour television. The varied menu offers freshly cooked food, painstakingly prepared, and personal service is provided by the resident proprietors and their staff who make guests feel at home.

6rm(5⇌1↱) (1fb) CTV in all bedrooms ® LDO 9.30pm

Lic ♨ 8P

Credit Cards [3]

COMBE MARTIN Devon Map **02** SS54

See also Berrynarbor

GH QQQ Channel Vista EX34 0AT ☎(0271) 883514

Etr-Oct & Xmas

This charming Edwardian house is only 150 yards from the picturesque cove. The resident proprietors provide home cooking and friendly service in comfortable accommodation with good facilities.

7rm(2⇌5↱) (3fb) CTV in 3 bedrooms ® ✖ (ex guide dogs) ✱ dB&B⇌↱£32-£36 WB&B£110-£120 WBDi£122.50-£143.50 LDO 3pm

Lic ♨ CTV 9P nc3yrs

Credit Cards [1] [2] [3]

GH Q *The Woodlands* 2 The Woodlands EX34 0AT ☎(0271) 882769

Mar-Oct

Close to the sheltered cove and village centre, this small, friendly guesthouse is on the edge of Exmoor National Park.

8hc (2fb) ✖ LDO 5pm

Lic CTV 8P nc2yrs

Credit Cards [3]

COMRIE Tayside *Perthshire* Map **11** NN72

GH Q *Mossgiel* Burrell St PH6 2JP ☎(0764) 70567

Etr-Oct

This small friendly guesthouse is situated on the main road at the west end of the town. Offering good value, it is a popular base for the touring holidaymaker.

6hc TV in 1 bedroom LDO 5.30pm

♨ CTV 6P nc5yrs

CONISHOLME Lincolnshire Map **09** TF39

GH QQQ *Wickham House* Church Ln LN11 7LX ☎North Somercotes(0507) 358465

Closed Xmas & New Year

This tasteful conversion of 3 19th-century cottages set amidst beautiful gardens is situated in a small, peaceful village beside the B1031. Bedrooms are comfortable and well equipped, complemented by an abundance of fresh flowers, and there is a spacious lounge and a small library. Fresh, competently prepared set evening meals are available.

4rm(2⇌2♠) CTV in all bedrooms ® ✖ (ex guide dogs)
LDO noon
⑭ 4P nc8yrs

CONISTON Cumbria Map **07** SD39

SELECTED

GH Ⓠ Ⓠ Ⓠ Ⓠ **Coniston Lodge Hotel** Sunny Brow
LA21 8HH ☎(05394) 41201
rs Sun & Mon pm
Just through the village on a peaceful side road at the foot of the Old Man of Coniston, this delightful private hotel offers accommodation of the very highest standard. The 6 spacious bedrooms are well equipped and beautifully decorated and furnished. The lounge and dining room are most attractive in country cottage style. Excellent English and local dishes are served for dinner, and a full Lakeland breakfast in the morning. There is a garden and covered parking is provided. This is a warm and hospitable hotel, under the personal supervision of resident proprietors Anthony and Elizabeth Robinson. It is a non-smoking establishment.
6⇌♠ ✄in all bedrooms CTV in all bedrooms ®
✖ (ex guide dogs) sB&B⇌♠£31.50-£39 dB&B⇌♠£63-£70 LDO 7.30pm
Lic ⑭ 3P 6🍴 nc10yrs
Credit Cards ①③ ⑤

CONNEL Strathclyde *Argyllshire* Map **10** NM93

GH Ⓠ Ⓠ Ⓠ **Ards House** PA37 1PT ☎(063171) 255
Mar-Nov rs 1-23 Dec
This welcoming, family-run licensed guesthouse is situated at the west end of the village on the Oban road and enjoys a magnificent outlook over the Firth of Lorne to the Morvern Hills. The attractive sitting room is comfortably furnished, and a well prepared five-course set dinner is served in the cosy dining room. Bedrooms are gradually being upgraded, and several have private bathrooms; front-facing rooms offer splendid loch views.
8rm(5⇌♠3hc) ® ✖ ❊ sB&Bfr£23 dB&Bfr£41
dB&B⇌♠fr£46 WB&B£129.15-£144.90 WBDi£199.15-£214.90 LDO 6pm
Lic ⑭ CTV 12P nc12yrs
Credit Cards ①③
See advertisement under OBAN

SELECTED

GH Ⓠ Ⓠ Ⓠ Ⓠ **Loch Etive Hotel** Main St PA37 1PH
☎(063171) 400
Etr-10 Oct
This delightful small private hotel is run by the owners with enthusiasm. The bedrooms are nicely decorated and well equipped, and there is a small lounge and open-plan dining room, where a choice of dishes is served at both dinner and breakfast. The hotel nestles beside a small river in a quiet part of the village, well off the A85 and is well located for touring the beautiful west coast of Scotland.
6rm(4⇌♠2hc) (2fb) CTV in all bedrooms ® sB&B£21
sB&B⇌♠£24.50 dB&B£35 dB&B⇌♠£42 WB&B£147
WBDi£198.45 LDO 6.30pm
Lic ⑭ 7P ⑤
See advertisement under OBAN

✉✈**GH** Ⓠ Ⓠ **Ronebhal** PA37 1PJ ☎(063171) 310
Apr-Oct
This well maintained and attractively decorated detached Victorian house looks out on to Loch Etive and the Connel Bridge.
6rm(3♠2hc) (1fb) ® sB&B£12-£16 dB&B£14-£20
dB&B♠£14-£25

---

⑭ CTV 6P nc5yrs
Credit Cards ①③

CONSTANTINE Cornwall & Isles of Scilly Map **02** SW72

INN Ⓠ Ⓠ Ⓠ **Trengilly Wartha** Nancenoy TR11 5RP
☎Falmouth(0326) 40332
Enjoying a peaceful rural setting, this traditional-style country inn has simple, comfortable accommodation and a friendly atmosphere. Traditional English cooking is prepared by the chef/proprietor.
6rm(5⇌♠1hc) CTV in all bedrooms ® sB&B£32-£42
sB&B⇌♠£38-£46 dB&B£39-£48 dB&B⇌♠£47-£58
WB&B£123-£155 WBDi£182-£250 Bar Lunch £2.50-£10alc
Dinner £16-£18alc LDO 9.30pm
⑭ 55P ♨
Credit Cards ①②③ ⑤
See advertisement under FALMOUTH

CONTIN Highland *Ross-shire* Map **14** NH45

SELECTED

GH Ⓠ Ⓠ Ⓠ Ⓠ **Contin House** IV14 9EB
☎Stathpeffer(0977) 21920 FAX (0997) 21841
Mar-Oct rs Dec-Feb
This former manse sits in its own grounds, complete with summer house and pond, surrounded by pastureland, close to the River Blackwater on the southern fringe of the village. It is run in the style of a small, select, but unpretentious country house, and is tastefully furnished throughout. There are two lounges, both with log fires, and one has an honesty bar. Bedrooms are generally spacious and thoughtfully equipped. Five-course dinners using fresh produce and vegetables from ▶

the garden are a feature, and the guesthouse is popular with fishing parties during the season.
5⇄↑ CTV in all bedrooms ® dB&B⇄↑£48-£59.50 (incl dinner) WBDi£300-£355
Lic ♨ CTV 20P nc8yrs croquet
Credit Cards ⊡ ③ ⓔ

CONWY Gwynedd Map **06** SH77

See also Roewen
GH QQ **Bryn Derwen** Woodlands LL32 8LT
☎Aberconwy(0492) 596134
Closed 15 Dec-Feb
This large semidetached Victorian house, now a small personally run hotel, is situated on the southern edge of this historic town, on the B5106. From its elevated position there are views of the town walls and the surrounding mountains. The accommodation is comfortable and well maintained, and there is a small car park.
6rm(1⇄↑4hc) (2fb) ® ✱ sB&B£10.50-£15 dB&Bfr£24
dB&B⇄↑fr£30 LDO noon
CTV 6P ⓔ

GH QQ **The Old Ship** Lancaster Square LL32 8DE
☎Aberconwy(0492) 596445
This small cosy guesthouse dates back some four hundred years, and retains a lot of its original character. Situated in the town centre it is conveniently close to the railway station and has parking facilities nearby.
6rm(2↑4hc) (3fb)⤸in 2 bedrooms CTV in all bedrooms ® ✱
sB&B£13.50-£15 dB&B£27-£30 dB&B↑£35-£38
Lic ♨ CTV ⫝̸

GH Q **Sunnybanks** Woodlands, Llanwrst Rd LL32 8LT
☎Aberconwy(0492) 593845
This large semidetached house is situated on the B5106, on the outskirts of Conwy. It provides simple but clean accommodation and has the advantage of its own car park.
7rm(2↑5hc) (2fb) CTV in all bedrooms ® sB&B£14.50-£18.50
sB&B↑£16.50-£20.50 dB&B£25-£28 dB&B↑£30-£36
WB&B£82-£120 WBDi£130-£160 LDO 8.30pm
Lic ♨ CTV 8P 1☕ ⓔ

COOKLEY Suffolk Map **05** TM37

FH QQQ Mr & Mrs A T Veasy **Green** *(TM337772)* IP19 0LH
☎Linstead(098685) 209
Apr-Nov
This old farmhouse is best approached from Linstead Parva, and is just past the church. In 12 acres of land with outbuildings and duck ponds, Green Farm is comfortable and full of character, and Mrs Veasy is a charming hostess.
3hc ® ✖ (ex guide dogs) LDO 3pm
CTV 3P nc8yrs 12 acres non-working

COOMBE BISSETT Wiltshire Map **04** SU12

FH QQ A Shering **Swaynes Firs** *(SU068221)* Grimsdyke
SP5 5RF ☎Martin Cross(072589) 240
This modern farmhouse is situated 7 miles from Salisbury on the A354 Salisbury to Blandford road. The bedrooms are neat and comfortable with modern facilities, and the public rooms are cosy and nicely decorated. Mr Shering, the proprietor, is jolly and welcoming and the atmosphere is a warm one.
3↑ (1fb) CTV in all bedrooms ® dB&B↑£30-£34
WB&B£105-£112
♨ CTV 6P 11 acres beef, horses, poultry ⓔ

COPMANTHORPE North Yorkshire Map **08** SE54

GH QQ **Duke of Connaught Hotel** Copmanthorpe Grange
YO2 3TN ☎Appleton Roebuck(090484) 318
Closed Xmas wk
Nicely converted former stables in open rural surroundings.

14rm(2⇄12↑) (2fb)⤸in 4 bedrooms CTV in all bedrooms ®
✖ (ex guide dogs) sB&B⇄↑£25-£29 dB&B⇄↑£40-£46
LDO 6pm
Lic ♨ 40P ⓔ

CORBRIDGE Northumberland Map **12** NY96

FH QQQ Mr & Mrs T Jones **Low Barns** *(NY009641)*
Thornbrough NE45 5LX ☎(043463) 2408
A delightfully furnished house situated close to the town centre, in a rural location. The bedrooms are well furnished and equipped, service is warm and friendly, and there is good home cooking.
5rm(3↑2hc) (2fb) CTV in all bedrooms ®
✖ (ex guide dogs) ✱ sB&B£25 sB&B⇄↑£30 dB&B£33
dB&B⇄↑£40 WB&B£126 WBDi£210 LDO 6pm
♨ 5P 2 acres cattle hens sheep smallholding ⓔ

CORFE CASTLE Dorset Map **03** SY98

SELECTED

GH QQQQ *The Old Rectory* Church Knowle BH20 5NG
☎(0929) 480695
Mar-Nov
This fine early-Victorian former rectory is situated in the small village of Church Knowle, on an unclassified road, just over a mile from Corfe Castle. Standing in 3 acres of grounds and lawned garden, it looks directly on to the Purbeck Hills. Furnished with antiques, an elegant country-house atmosphere prevails, complemented by a log fire in the small lounge. The three bedrooms are individually furnished in different styles, served by a general bath and shower and stocked with several thoughtful extras. Breakfast is cooked to order and served around a large communal mahogony table in the dining room.
3hc (1fb)⤸in all bedrooms CTV in all bedrooms ® ✖
♨ 5P

CORTACHY Tayside *Angus* Map **15** NO35

FH QQ Mrs Joan Grant **Cullew** *(NO387609)* DD8 4QP
☎(05754) 242
Apr-Oct
Set in a secluded position at the south end of a picturesque Glen Clova, this substantial stone-built farmhouse offers traditional hospitality and comfortable accommodation.
2rm (1fb)⤸in all bedrooms CTV in 1 bedroom
✖ (ex guide dogs) ✱ sB&B£11-£12.50 dB&B£22-£24
WB&B£77-£84
♨ CTV 3P fishing permits 850 acres arable mixed ⓔ

CORWEN Clwyd Map **06** SJ04

🏨🔽 **GH** Q **Coleg-y-Groes** LL21 0AU ☎(0490) 2169
Closed 24-27 Dec
This row of former 18th-century alms houses is quietly located behind the church, close to both the town centre and the A5. Now a Christian guesthouse, it provides modest but clean accommodation.
6hc (2fb)⤸in all bedrooms ® sB&B£12.50-£15.50 dB&B£25-
£31 WB&Bfr£85 WBDifr£130.50 LDO previous evening
♨ CTV 6P ⓔ

🏨🔽 **GH** QQ **Corwen Court Private Hotel** London Rd
LL21 0DP ☎(0490) 2854
Mar-Nov rs Dec-Feb
This former Victorian police station and courthouse was converted into a small private hotel in 1983. Some of the original cells are now bedrooms. It stands on the main A5 in the centre of town.
10rm(4⇄5↑6hc) sB&B£12-£13 dB&B£24-£26 dB&B⇄↑£24-
£26 WB&B£79.80-£86.40 WBDi£119.70-£133 LDO 6pm
♨ CTV ⫝̸

COTHERIDGE Hereford & Worcester Map **03** SO75

FH 🇶🇶 Mr & Mrs V A Rogers *Little Lightwood* *(SP798554)* WR6 5LT (3m W of Worcester on A44) ☎(090566) 236 Feb-Nov
A charming farmhouse located just off the A44, three miles west of Worcester, turning up Lightwood Lane from the main road at Cotheridge. Set in open countryside and specialising in dairy farming, the farm now produces its own farmhouse cheese. The bedrooms are prettily furnished and comfortable, and there is a cosy lounge available for guests. Family owned and run, it offers warm and friendly service.
3hc (1fb)⊁in all bedrooms Ⓡ ✗ LDO 10am
📺 CTV 6P 60 acres dairy

COUNTISBURY (NEAR LYNTON) Devon Map **03** SS74

FH 🇶🇶🇶 Mrs R Pile **Coombe** *(SS766489)* EX35 6NF
☎Brendon(05987) 236
Apr-Oct rs Nov & Dec
Dating back to the 17th century, this stone-built farmhouse is part of a sheep farm lying within the Exmoor National Park. The comfortable accommodation and genuine hospitality make it an ideal centre for touring the North Devon coastline.
5rm(2🐾3hc) (2fb) Ⓡ ✗ (ex guide dogs) ✻ dB&B£30-£35 dB&B🐾£35-£40 WB&B£98-£125 WBDi£173-£199 LDO 5pm
Lic 📺 CTV 6P 365 acres sheep

COVENTRY West Midlands Map **04** SP37

GH 🇶 **Ashleigh House** 17 Park Rd CV1 2LH ☎(0203) 23804
Closed Xmas
A privately owned and run guesthouse situated in a quiet cul-de-sac, close to the town centre and the railway station. The addition of en suite facilities has improved the accommodation; however furnishings are modest and the rooms compact. There is an attractive dining room with its own small bar, and car parking is available at the rear.
10rm(2🐾2hc) (5fb) CTV in all bedrooms Ⓡ ✗ ✻ sB&B£15-£18 sB&B🐾£20-£23 dB&B£26-£28 dB&B🐾£28-£32 LDO 8.45pm
Lic 📺 CTV 12P Ⓔ

GH 🇶 **Croft Hotel** 23 Stoke Green, Off Binley Rd CV3 1FP
☎(0203) 457846
A friendly hotel situated off the Rugby road, just over one mile from the town centre. Rooms are steadily improving with redecoration and the addition of private bathrooms. There is a comfortable TV lounge for guests, and a bar, complete with pool table.
12rm(4🐾6hc) (1fb) CTV in 6 bedrooms Ⓡ ✻ sB&Bfr£25 sB&B🐾£29.50-£34 dB&Bfr£42 dB&B🐾£46-£54 LDO 8.30pm
Lic 📺 CTV 20P pool table
Credit Cards 1 3

GH 🇶 **Fairlight** 14 Regent St CV1 3EP ☎(0203) 224215
Closed 24 Dec-2 Jan
Situated in a residential area close to the station and town centre, this terraced property provides simple value-for-money accommodation. The resident proprietors are eager to make guests feel at home, and maintain a friendly, relaxed atmosphere.
12rm(1🐾11hc) (1fb) CTV in 11 bedrooms Ⓡ sB&B£14-£15 dB&Bfr£28 dB&B🐾£34
📺 CTV 6P Ⓔ

GH 🇶🇶 **Hearsall Lodge Hotel** 1 Broad Ln CV5 7AA
☎(0203) 674543
A friendly hotel close to the common and town centre. Hearsall Lodge has been recently extended and offers good accommodation with excellent facilities.
13hc (2fb) CTV in all bedrooms Ⓡ LDO 7.30pm
Lic 📺 CTV 13P
Credit Cards 1 3 Ⓔ

COWDENBEATH Fife Map **11** NT19

GH 🇶 *Struan Bank Hotel* 74 Perth Rd KY4 9BG
☎(0383) 511057
A small, family-run commercial hotel on the north side of the town. Accommodation is modest, but there is a nice lounge with a bar which is used mainly by residents and diners.
8hc Ⓡ ✗ LDO 6pm
Lic 📺 CTV 8P

CRACKINGTON HAVEN Cornwall & Isles of Scilly Map **02** SX19

SELECTED

FH 🇶🇶🇶🇶 Mrs M Knight **Manor** *(SX159962)*
EX23 0JW ☎St Gennys(08403) 304
A delightful 12th-century manor house with splendid views, set in a quiet location, with well tended gardens. Bedrooms are comfortable and pleasingly decorated and furnished. There is an elegant, spacious sitting room, and across the cobbled yard is a games room with a full sized billiard table and table tennis table. Knight's Cordon Bleu style of cooking always proves popular. The wine list is reasonably priced, and there is an honesty bar; smoking is not permitted.
4rm(2⇌2hc) Annexe 2🐾 ⊁in all bedrooms ✗ sB&B⇌🐾£25-£28 dB&B⇌🐾£50-£60 WBDifr£245 LDO 5pm
Lic 📺 CTV 6P nc18yrs snooker table tennis 40 acres beef

See advertisement on page 131

Book as early as possible for busy holiday periods.

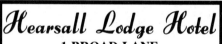

SELECTED

FH Ⓠ Ⓠ Ⓠ Ⓠ Mrs J Crocker **Trevigue** *(SX136951)*
EX23 0LQ ☎St Gennys(08403) 418
Mar-Sep
This 16th-century stone farmhouse is set around a cobbled courtyard, amidst 500 acres of National Trust headland between Crackington Haven and Boscastle, and is signed from the Boscastle road. It offers breath-taking views of glorious coastal scenery. The comfortable bedrooms have antique furnishings but with modern facilities, and the cosy lounge has a fire and books to borrow. Mrs Crocker specialises in imaginative home cooking, and there is a well chosen, reasonably priced wine list. Across the courtyard is an information centre and a charming beamed tea room, serving home-made light lunches and cream teas.
4rm(2⇨2♠) CTV in 2 bedrooms Ⓡ ✗ ✱ sB&B⇨♠£21-£24 dB&B⇨♠£34-£46 LDO 5pm
Lic CTV 20P nc12yrs 500 acres dairy mixed Ⓔ

INN Ⓠ Ⓠ **Coombe Barton** EX23 0JG ☎St Gennys(08403) 345
Mar-Oct rs Nov-Feb
7rm(3⇨4hc) (1fb) CTV in 3 bedrooms Ⓡ ✱ sB&B£17.50-£19.50 dB&B£35-£39 dB&B⇨£43-£49 WB&B£135-£154 ✱
Lunch £2.75-£9alc Dinner £3.50-£12.25alc LDO 9.30pm
🍴 40P
Credit Cards ② Ⓔ

CRAIL Fife Map **12** NO60

GH Ⓠ Ⓠ Ⓠ **Caiplie** 51-53 High St KY10 3RA ☎(0333) 50564
Mar-Sep Closed Dec-Jan rs Oct-Nov & Feb-1 Mar
Genuine hospitality and enjoyable food are the noteworthy features of this small, comfortable licensed guesthouse which is situated in the centre of the village within easy walking distance of the fishing harbour. The menu offers Scottish and continental dishes which are competently prepared from fresh local produce and may include prime beef, fish or crab. Bedrooms are warm, clean and comfortably furnished, and there is a cosy lounge on the first floor for a quiet drink in a relaxed atmosphere.
7hc (1fb) Ⓡ LDO 4pm
Lic 🍴 CTV ⓟ

CRANBROOK Kent Map **05** TQ73

GH Ⓠ Ⓠ Ⓠ **Hancocks** Tilsden Ln TN17 3PH ☎(0580) 714645
A well preserved timber-framed listed building, extended in the latter half of the 16th century, and surrounded by farmland. Bedrooms are furnished with antiques, one with a four-poster bed, and they are well equipped with many thoughtful extras. The lounge combines with the breakfast room, and features an inglenook fireplace, log-burning stove and beams.
3rm(1♠2hc) ✗in all bedrooms CTV in 1 bedroom Ⓡ ✱
dB&Bfr£28 dB&B♠fr£36 WB&Bfr£85 WBDifr£155
LDO 2pm
🍴 CTV 3P

CRASTER Northumberland Map **12** NU22

INN Ⓠ Ⓠ Ⓠ **Cottage** Dunstan Village NE66 3SZ
☎Embleton(066576) 658
Nestling in a copse in the tiny hamlet of Dunston, this friendly inn has comfortable accommodation and a cheerful conservatory lounge. The menus in the bar and elegant restaurant, which are open to non-residents, offer an interesting selection of good value dishes.
17rm(10⇨7hc) (2fb) CTV in 10 bedrooms Ⓡ
✗ (ex guide dogs) LDO 9.30pm
🍴 32P
Credit Cards ① ③

CRAVEN ARMS Shropshire Map **07** SO48

FH Ⓠ Ⓠ Mrs C Morgan **Strefford Hall** *(SO444856)* Strefford
SY7 8DE ☎(0588) 672383
Closed Xmas & New Year
This imposing stone-built Victorian farmhouse stands on a 350-acre mixed farm, just off the busy A49. The spacious bedrooms are comfortable and very clean and all have interesting views. There is a separate dining room where traditional three-course roast dinners are served. Smoking is not permitted.
3rm(2♠1hc) ✗in all bedrooms Ⓡ dB&B♠fr£32 WB&Bfr£105 WBDifr£164.50 LDO 6pm
CTV 3P 350 acres arable beef sheep Ⓔ

CRAWLEY West Sussex For accommodation details see **Gatwick Airport**

CREDITON Devon Map **03** SS80

FH Ⓠ Ⓠ Mr & Mrs M Pennington **Woolsgrove** *(SS793028)*
Sandford EX17 4PJ ☎Copplestone(0363) 84246
Feb-Nov
17th-century farmhouse overlooking grassland. Three miles north west on unclassified road and 1 mile north of A377.
3hc (2fb) Ⓑ ✗ (ex guide dogs) ✱ sB&Bfr£15 dB&Bfr£28
LDO 6pm
CTV 4P 150 acres mixed Ⓔ

CREWE Cheshire Map **07** SJ75

FH Ⓠ Ⓠ Mrs Diana Edwards **Balterley Hall** *(SJ765499)*
Balterley CW2 5QG ☎(0270) 820206
Closed Xmas
An imposing brick and sandstone house which is reached by turning down the lane opposite the village church. Evening meals can be served by prior arrangement, and a warm welcome is assured.
3rm(1♠2hc) (1fb) CTV in all bedrooms Ⓡ ✱ sB&Bfr£16
dB&B£26-£29 dB&B♠fr£32 LDO noon
CTV 6P 240 acres arable mixed
Credit Cards ③ Ⓔ

CREWKERNE Somerset Map **03** ST40

SELECTED

GH Ⓠ Ⓠ Ⓠ Ⓠ **Broadview** 43 East St TA18 7AG
☎(0460) 73424
A small, southfacing colonial style bungalow standing in well tended landscaped gardens with views over the town. The entrance is through a sunny porch leading to a small dining hall where guests eat together around a communal table. The new lounge is very comfortable and has an array of indoor plants and a collection of colourful caged birds. The bedrooms are carefully decorated and furnished and are exceptionally well equipped, with private bathrooms. A subtantial home-cooked set dinner is served by prior arrangement, making this guesthouse superb value for money. Smoking is not allowed in public rooms.
3⇨♠ CTV in all bedrooms Ⓡ sB&B⇨♠£25
dB&B⇨♠£33 WB&B£115.50 WBDi£175 LDO 9am
🍴 3P 2🚗

CRIANLARICH Central *Perthshire* Map **10** NN32

GH Ⓠ Ⓠ Ⓠ **Glenardran Guest House** FK20 8QS ☎(08383) 236
Standing on the eastern fringe of the village, overlooking Ben More, this friendly, family-run guesthouse offers pleasant, comfortable accommodation.
6hc (1fb) ✗in all bedrooms CTV in all bedrooms Ⓡ ✱
sB&Bfr£18 dB&Bfr£32 WB&B£112-£126 WBDi£175-£189
LDO 6pm

Lic 🏠 6P
Credit Cards 1 3

CRICCIETH Gwynedd Map **06** SH43

GH Q Q Glyn-Y-Coed Private Hotel Portmadoc Rd LL52 0HL
☎(0766) 522870 FAX (0766) 523341
Closed Xmas & New Year
*This family-run, friendly guesthouse is situated on the A497 just
east of the town centre and is within a short walk of the beach and
castle. All bedrooms have private bathrooms, and some have sea
views.*
10rm(3⇨7🗨) (5fb) CTV in all bedrooms ® sB&B⇨🗨£17-£20
dB&B⇨🗨£34-£40 WB&B£115-£138 WBDi£180-£208
LDO 4pm
Lic 🏠 CTV 14P ♨ ⓔ

GH Q Q Min-y-Gaer Private Hotel Porthmadog Rd LL52 0HP
☎(0766) 522151
Mar-Oct
*Close to the beach and Castle this semidetatched house is situated
on the A497 east of the town centre. All but one of the bedrooms is
equipped with en suite shower and toilet.*
10rm(9🗨1hc) (3fb) CTV in all bedrooms ® sB&B£15-£16.50
sB&B🗨£17-£18.50 dB&B£30-£33 dB&B🗨£34-£37
WB&B£100-£123 WBDi£153-£173 LDO 4pm
Lic 🏠 CTV 12P ♨
Credit Cards 1 2 3 ⓔ

GH Q Mor Heli Hotel Marine Ter LL52 0EF ☎(0766) 522878
Apr-Sep rs Mar & Oct
*One of a pair of similar adjoining large terraced houses under the
same ownership, situated on the seafront, close to the castle with
good views across Cardigan Bay. Bedrooms are simple but quite
well maintained, and two of the rooms have en suite bathrooms and
some have colour televisions.*

▶

TREVIGUE FARM
Crackington Haven

English Tourist Board

A superb 16th century farmhouse on a 500-
acre dairy and beef farm with 2½ miles of
spectacular coast-line. All bedrooms en-suite
with tea-making facilities, two with colour TV.
Beautifully appointed, tranquil sitting rooms
with great emphasis placed on imaginative
cuisine. An ideal location for touring Cornwall
and Devon. Children over 12 years most
welcome. Licensed.

**Janet Crocker, Trevigue, Crackington Haven,
Bude, Cornwall EX23 0LQ.
Phone: St. Gennys (08403) 418**
*National Winner of the
Best Newcomer Award 1989/90*

𝕸𝖆𝖓𝖔𝖗 𝕱𝖆𝖗𝖒   𝕮𝖗𝖆𝖈𝖐𝖎𝖓𝖌𝖙𝖔𝖓 𝕳𝖆𝖛𝖊𝖓, 𝕹. 𝕮𝖔𝖗𝖓𝖜𝖆𝖑𝖑

Welcome to our beautiful, secluded Domesday listed Manor House one mile from sea.
Once held by the Earl of Montain, half brother to William the Conqueror, the Manor has
since been tastefully restored and adapted to provide an elegant peaceful setting,
surrounded by landscaped gardens and rolling hills. We offer charming accommodation
with private facilities. Dining here is considered the highlight of the day. The games room
includes a full sized snooker table. Regret no children and no smoking in the house.

Mrs M. Knight   Tel St Gennys (08403) 304

10rm(2⇄8hc) (2fb) CTV in 4 bedrooms LDO 5pm
Lic CTV ⨍

GH Ⓠ *Neptune Hotel* Marine Ter LL52 0EF ☎(0766) 522794
Apr-Sep
This large terraced house adjoining Mor Heli Hotel, and under the
same ownership, is situated on the seafront, close to the castle with
good views across Cardigan Bay. The accommodation is modest
but quite well maintained. A few rooms are equipped with en suite
facilities and some also have colour TV.
10rm(1⇄3♠6hc) (2fb) CTV in 4 bedrooms LDO 5pm
Lic CTV ⨍

CRICKHOWELL Powys Map 03 SO21

GH ⓆⓆⓆ *Dragon House Hotel* High St NP8 1BE
☎(0873) 810362
This town centre hotel has been carefully converted and extended
to provide very attractive and well equipped bedrooms. The bar
and lounge are both cosy and comfortable and good food, including
vegetarian meals, is available.
14rm(6⇄♠8hc) Annexe 3⇄♠ (3fb)⫠in 5 bedrooms CTV in
9 bedrooms Ⓡ ✖ (ex guide dogs) LDO 8.30pm
Lic ▥ CTV 15P
Credit Cards ①③

CRICKLADE Wiltshire Map 04 SU09

GH ⓆⓆⓆ *Chelworth Hotel* Upper Chelworth SN6 6HD
☎Swindon(0793) 750440
Closed mid Dec-mid Jan
This 16th-century farmhouse has been thoughtfully extended and
refurbished to provide tastefully furnished, fresh and bright
bedrooms, most of which have private bathrooms with smart,
modern facilities and equipment. Public areas are traditional in
style, with a well stocked games room and a full-sized pool table.
There is a cosy residents' lounge, and a small dining room where
home- cooked evening meals are available.
7rm(6♠1hc) (1fb)⫠in 2 bedrooms CTV in 6 bedrooms Ⓡ
✖ (ex guide dogs) ✱ sB&B£28-£32 sB&B♠£35-£40 dB&B£38-
£40 dB&B♠£50-£55 WB&B£200-£300 LDO 7pm
Lic ▥ CTV 10P

CRIEFF Tayside *Perthshire* Map 11 NN82

GH ⓆⓆ *Comely Bank* 32 Burrel St PH7 4DT ☎(0764) 3409
Situated in a residential area near the town centre, this small
family-run licensed guesthouse has a friendly atmosphere, and
offers good value tourist accommodation.
5hc (1fb) LDO 7.30pm
Lic ▥ CTV

GH ⓆⓆⓆ *Heatherville* 29-31 Burrell St PH7 4DT
☎(0764) 2825
Closed Dec-Jan
This small family-run guesthouse is situated not far from the town
centre. It has a friendly atmosphere and offers good value for
money and comfortable holiday accommodation.
5rm(1♠4hc) (2fb) Ⓡ ✱ dB&B£25-£27 dB&B♠£30-£32
WB&B£82.50-£89.50 WBDi£131.50-£138.50 LDO noon
Lic ▥ CTV 5P Ⓛ

CROESGOCH Dyfed Map 02 SM83

FH ⓆⓆ Mrs A Charles **Torbant** *(SM845307)* SA62 5JN
☎(0348) 831276
rs Oct-Etr
This busy working farm provides spacious public rooms and a
function suite. The farmhouse dates back to the 17th century and
stands just off the A487.
6rm(2⇄1♠3hc) (2fb) Ⓡ ✖ (ex guide dogs) ✱ sB&B£14-£17.50
dB&B£28-£35 dB&B⇄♠£30-£37 WB&B£95-£120
WBDi£125-£150 LDO 6pm

Lic ▥ CTV 40P 110 acres dairy Ⓛ
See advertisement under ST DAVID'S

CROMER Norfolk Map 09 TG24

GH Ⓠ **Chellow Dene** 23 MacDonald Rd NR27 9AP
☎(0263) 513251
Mar-Oct
This pleasant guesthouse in a street leading down to the seafront is
only a short walk from the town centre. Mr and Mrs Leach offer
traditional hospitality and the bedrooms are airy and comfortable.
7hc (2fb) CTV in all bedrooms Ⓡ ✱ sB&Bfr£15 dB&Bfr£30
WBDifr£105 LDO 5pm
Lic ▥ CTV 6P

GH ⓆⓆⓆ *Morden House* 20 Cliff Av NR27 0AN
☎(0263) 513396
Closed 3-4wks Spring/Autumn
Within walking distance of the shops and seafront, this detached
house has generally spacious bedrooms, which are light and airy.
Mr and Mrs Votier are jovial, caring hosts, and offer an evening
menu of homemade dishes. This is an excellent place to stay.
7rm(3♠4hc) (2fb) Ⓡ ✖ (ex guide dogs) LDO 5pm
Lic ▥ CTV 3P

GH ⓆⓆ **Sandcliff Private Hotel** Runton Rd NR27 9AS
☎(0263) 512888
Feb-10 Dec
Catering for both tourists and commercial visitors, this hotel is only
a few minutes' walk from the town centre. Many rooms offer sea
views, as well as some en suite facilities. The nicely furnished
lounge and dining room complement the bar.
24rm(9⇄10♠5hc) (10fb) CTV in 15 bedrooms Ⓡ sB&B£21.60
dB&B£39.40-£43.20 dB&B⇄♠£43.20-£45 WB&B£140-£160
WBDi£165 LDO 6pm
Lic CTV 10P

GH ⓆⓆⓆ **Westgate Lodge Private Hotel** 10 MacDonald Rd
NR27 9AP ☎(0263) 512840
Mar-29 Nov
Close to the cliff top road and promenade, this exceptionally well-
maintained house has an attractive restaurant, small, cosy bar and
well equipped accommodation, with en suite facilities. Mr and Mrs
Robson ensure guests of a relaxing stay.
11♠ (4fb) CTV in all bedrooms Ⓡ ✖ dB&B♠fr£45
WBDi£171-£186 LDO 7pm
Lic ▥ 14P nc3yrs

CROMHALL Avon Map 03 ST69

FH ⓆⓆ Mrs S Scolding **Varley** *(ST699905)* Talbots End
GL12 8AJ ☎Chipping Sodbury(0454) 294065
Etr-Sep
Tucked away just outside the small village of Cromhall, this stone
clad farmhouse provides a good standard of accommodation in
attractively decorated rooms.
4hc (3fb)⫠in all bedrooms Ⓡ ✖ ✱ sB&B£15-£16 dB&B£28-
£30 WB&B£98
▥ CTV 5P 75 acres dairy

CROSTHWAITE Cumbria Map 07 SD49

GH ⓆⓆⓆ **Crosthwaite House** LA8 8BP ☎(04488) 264
mid Mar-mid Nov
Enjoying an elevated position overlooking the Lythe Valley, this
charming Georgian house has well appointed rooms with their own
facilities.
6♠ CTV in 3 bedrooms Ⓡ sB&B♠£20-£22 dB&B♠£40-£44
WB&B£140-£154 WBDi£200-£220 LDO 5pm
Lic ▥ CTV 10P 2🐾
See advertisement under KENDAL

CROYDE Devon Map **02** SS43

GH QQQ **Moorsands House Hotel** Moor Ln EX33 1NP
☎(0271) 890781
Apr-Oct
Within walking distance of the beaches and village centre, this Victorian house provides two comfortable lounges, one with a bar and the other with TV. Most of the bedrooms have en suite facilities and simple, home cooked meals are offered.
8♪ (3fb) CTV in all bedrooms ® sB&Bftℛ£20-£23
dB&Bfℛ£34-£40 WB&B£105-£147 WBDi£165-£207 LDO 6pm
Lic ♘ CTV 8P nc3yrs
Credit Cards 1 3 £

SELECTED

GH QQQQ **Whiteleaf At Croyde** EX33 1PN
☎(0271) 890266
An attractive 1930s house, set in pretty grounds and gardens, offering high standards of accommodation and commendable food. Spotlessly clean throughout, the bedrooms are individually decorated and well equipped for tourists or business guests alike. There is a cosy lounge and a bright dining room where David Wallington's cooking can be enjoyed. Dishes such as poached gold medal black pudding or potato gnocchi are followed by traditional steak and kidney pie or crusted rabbit casserole, and there are rich home-made puddings to finish.
5⇨♪ (1fb) CTV in all bedrooms ® ✳ sB&B⇨♪£29-£32
dB&B⇨♪£48-£54 WB&B£168-£189 WBDi£255-£260
LDO 8.15pm
Lic ♘ 10P
Credit Cards 1 2 3 £

CROYDON Greater London London plan **4** D1 (pages 221-227)

GH QQ **Kirkdale Hotel** 22 St Peter's Rd CR0 1HD
☎081-688 5898 FAX 081-680 6001
Closed 2 wks Xmas
The Wallingfords continue to extend and improve their friendly, well maintained Victorian house, which is situated in a residential area of the town. New bedrooms with en suite facilities have been added. Rooms are rather compact but are well equipped, smart and clean. Downstairs there is a comfortable lounge and a bright breakfast room.
19rm(12♪7hc) CTV in all bedrooms ® ✱ (ex guide dogs) ✳
sB&B£23-£26 sB&Bfℛ£32-£36 dB&B£37-£40 dB&Bfℛ£45-£50
Lic ♘ CTV 12P
Credit Cards 1 3 £

GH QQQ **Markington Hotel** 9 Haling Park Rd CR2 6NG
☎081-681 6494 FAX 081-688 6494
4 Jan-16 Dec rs Xmas
The Markington comprises several houses in a residential street which have been converted into a comfortable and well run hotel. Not surprisingly, rooms vary in size and accessiblility, but they are all cheerful, well appointed and equipped with all modern amenities. There is a friendly atmosphere which centres on the warmly decorated bar, and high standards of housekeeping and maintenance are observed.
21rm(5⇨15♪1hc) (2fb)⊁in 4 bedrooms CTV in all bedrooms ® ✱ ✳ sB&B⇨♪£35-£52 dB&B£40-£48 dB&B⇨♪£45-£65
LDO 8.30pm
Lic ♘ CTV 18P
Credit Cards 1 2 3 £

GH QQ **Oakwood Hotel** 69 Outram Rd CR0 6XJ
☎081-654 2835
rs Xmas & Boxing Day

A Victorian house in a residential street run for many years by Mrs Delve. The bedrooms, which vary in size, are all well equipped, traditionally furnished and have en suite facilities. Downstairs there is a lounge with a pool table and a colourful dining room/bar.
17rm(10⇨7♪) (3fb) CTV in all bedrooms ® LDO 8pm
Lic ♘ CTV 7P sauna solarium
Credit Cards 1 2 3 5

CUCKNEY Nottinghamshire Map **08** SK57

FH QQ Mrs J M Ibbotson *Blue Barn* (*SK539713*) NG20 9JD
☎Mansfield(0623) 742248
Closed Xmas Eve & Xmas Day
Although within easy reach of all the country's attractions, this farm is quite isolated and is reached by a private lane off the A616 out of Cuckney. As well as the comfortable rooms in the house, there is a self-catering cottage in the grounds.
3hc (1fb) ® ✱ (ex guide dogs)
♘ CTV 6P 2🏌 250 acres arable beef mixed

CULLODEN MOOR Highland *Inverness-shire* Map **14** NH74

FH QQ Mrs E M C Alexander *Culdoich* (*NH755435*) IV1 2EP
☎Inverness(0463) 790268
Etr-Oct
Situated just off the Daviot to Cawdor road, this traditional farmhouse, built a year after the Battle of Culloden, offers home-from-home accommodation in clean and pleasant surroundings.
2hc (1fb) ® ✱ ✱ dB&Bfr£26 LDO 5pm
CTV P 200 acres mixed £

CULLOMPTON Devon Map **03** ST00

GH QQQ **Rullands** Rull Ln EX15 1N ☎(0884) 33356
5rm(4⇨♪1hc) (1fb)⊁in all bedrooms CTV in all bedrooms ®
✱ sB&Bfr£25 dB&B⇨♪fr£45 LDO 9.30pm
Lic ♘ 20P nc12yrs 𝒫(hard)
Credit Cards 1 3

INN QQQ **The Manor House** 2/4 Fore St EX15 1JL
☎Tiverton(0884) 32281
9⇨♪ (1fb) CTV in all bedrooms ® ✱ (ex guide dogs) ✳
sB&B⇨♪£35 dB&B⇨♪£42.50 ✱ Lunch £8.95 Dinner £14.95
LDO 10pm
♘ 50P
Credit Cards 1 3

See advertisement on page 135

CULMINGTON Shropshire Map **07** SO48

GH QQ *Seifton Court* Culmington SY8 2DG
☎Seifton(058473) 214
3rm(2♪1hc) (1fb)⊁in all bedrooms CTV in 2 bedrooms TV in 1 bedroom ® ✱ (ex guide dogs) LDO 9am
Lic ♘ CTV 6P fishing can be arranged

CWMBRAN Gwent Map **03** ST29

FH QQ Mrs B Watkins *Glebe* (*ST325965*) Croes Y Ceiliog
NP44 2DE (1.5m E unclass towards Llandedveth village)
☎Tredunnock(063349) 251 & 242
Closed 21 Dec-7 Jan
Popular with guests using the Irish ferries, due to its proximity to the M4, this modern bungalow stands in picturesque surroundings and provides comfortable accommodation together with warm hospitality.
3hc (1fb)⊁in all bedrooms ✱ ✳ sB&Bfr£15 dB&Bfr£29
♘ CTV 6P 100 acres beef dairy

Q is for quality. For a full explanation of this AA quality award, consult the Contents page.

CWMDUAD Dyfed Map **02** SN33

[icons]GH [Q][Q][Q] Neuadd-Wen SA33 6XJ
☎Cynwyl Elfed(026787) 438
Situated alongside the A484 road, this family-run guesthouse and restaurant lies in a peaceful wooded valley. Most bedrooms now have en suite facilities and there are two lounges available for residents.
7rm(6⇔3♠1hc) (2fb) CTV in all bedrooms sB&B⇔3♠£12-£14.50 dB&B⇔3♠£24-£29 WB&B£72-£82 WBDi£99-£120 LDO 9.30pm
Lic ⋈ CTV 12P
Credit Cards [1][3] ⓔ

DALMALLY Strathclyde *Argyllshire*

See **Ardbrecknish**

DARLINGTON Co Durham Map **08** NZ21

GH [Q][Q] Woodland 63 Woodland Rd DL3 7BQ
☎(0325) 461908
A Victorian terraced house situated on the A68, just out of the town, and within easy reach of the A1(M). The conventional bedrooms all have TV, with double-glazed windows on the front rooms, and there is a very comfortable lounge.
8rm(1⇔7hc) (2fb) CTV in all bedrooms sB&Bfr£16.50 sB&B⇔fr£25 dB&Bfr£29 dB&B⇔fr£35
⋈ CTV ⓔ

FH [Q][Q][Q] Mr & Mrs D & A Armstrong Clow Beck House
(NZ281100) Monk End Farm, Croft on Tees DL2 2SW
☎(0325) 721075
All facilities at this modern farmhouse are of the highest standard. Meals are taken round the single table in the dining room. Heather and David Armstrong provide a warm welcome to their home, which is set in open countryside in Croft on Tees, just south of Darlington.
3rm(1♠2hc) ® ✖ sB&B£25 sB&B♠£35 dB&B£35 dB&B♠£45
⋈ CTV 8P ✔ 90 acres mixed

DARTINGTON Devon Map **03** SX76

SELECTED

INN [Q][Q][Q][Q] Cott TQ9 6HE ☎Totnes(0803) 863777
FAX (0803) 866629
This delightful rambling, thatched inn dates back to 1324, and offers wholesome cooking and a good choice of real ale, wines and farmhouse cider. Privately owned, it is staffed by a team of locals who provide friendly service throughout, and there is a welcoming atmosphere complemented by beamed ceilings, flagstoned floors and log fires. There is a popular, lively bar and a cosy restaurant providing a range of home-made, traditional dishes. The six cosy, spotlessly clean bedrooms are pretty and well furnished and equipped, but the accommodation is not really suitable for families with small children. The inn is ideally positioned for touring the South Hams of Devon, with Dartington Hall and the Cider Press Centre also nearby.
6rm(5⇔3♠1hc) ⤢in all bedrooms CTV in all bedrooms ®
✖ (ex guide dogs) ✲ dB&B£60-£62.50 dB&B⇔3♠£65-£67.50 ✲ Lunch £8.95-£12alc Dinner £16.75-£21alc
LDO 9pm
50P nc10yrs
Credit Cards [1][2][3]

DARTMOUTH Devon Map **03** SX84

SELECTED

GH [Q][Q][Q][Q] Captains House 18 Clarence St TQ6 9NW
☎(0803) 832133
A charming listed Georgian house built in 1780, in a quiet location yet close to the shops, harbour and River Dart. Personally run by the enthusiastic owners, it offers a high quality bed and breakfast service. Bedrooms are spotlessly clean, comfortable and well furnished and combining character with modern facilities and several extra personal touches. Superb English breakfasts using fresh local produce can be enjoyed in the dining room or bedroom. Although there is no car parking on site, local car parks are nearby, and the guesthouse is within walking distance of the ferry and quayside.
5rm(3⇔2♠) CTV in all bedrooms ® sB&B⇔3♠£22-£25 dB&B⇔3♠£32-£40 WB&B£100-£126
⋈ nc5yrs
Credit Cards [2]

SELECTED

GH [Q][Q][Q][Q] Ford House 44 Victoria Rd TQ6 9DX
☎(0803) 834047
Mar-Dec
A restored Regency house situated within 500 yards of Dartmouth's historic harbour and quayside. Two of the three bedrooms are on a lower garden floor level, and are individually styled and nicely furnished, with attractive décor and a selection of antiques and objets d'art. The rooms are all well equipped and have bright en suite bathrooms. There is a cosy lounge and an adjacent dining room with a large mahogany communal table. Menus change daily and offer fresh local produce with the accent on fish; a range of vegetarian dishes is also available. The hotel is unlicensed but will arrange local delivery or guests can provide their own drinks.
3⇔♠ CTV in all bedrooms ® ✲ sB&B⇔3♠£32.50 dB&B⇔3♠£35-£39 WB&B£140 WBDi£245 LDO noon
⋈ 3P 1☎
Credit Cards [1][3] ⓔ

GH [Q][Q] Sunny Banks 1 Vicarage Hill TQ6 9EN
☎(0803) 832766
Recently extended to provide ten comfortable bedrooms together with a small lounge and dining room, this family establishment provides a set meal, and is within walking distance of the river front and town centre.
10rm(2⇔3♠2♠6hc) (2fb)⤢in 2 bedrooms CTV in all bedrooms ® LDO 7.30pm
Lic ⋈ CTV 3P 1☎ (£2 per night)

DAVIOT Highland *Inverness-shire* Map **14** NH73

FH [Q][Q] Mrs E M MacPherson Lairgandour *(NH720376)*
IV1 2XH ☎(046385) 207
Apr-Sep
A warm Highland welcome awaits guests at this large farmhouse at the end of a long drive off the B9154 close to its junction with the A9. Bedrooms are individually decorated and although modestly furnished are well maintained and kept very clean.
5hc (3fb) ®
⋈ CTV P 1000 acres beef mixed sheep

Street plans of certain towns and cities
will be found in a separate section
at the back of the book.

Visit your local AA Shop.

DAWLISH Devon Map **03** SX97

GH 🅠 *Mimosa* 11 Barton Ter EX7 9QH ☎(0626) 863283
Close to the town centre and beaches, this holiday guesthouse is family run.
9rm(1♠)(4fb) ✱ LDO 3pm
Lic 🕮 CTV 4P nc3yrs

GH 🅠🅠 *Walton House* Plantation Ter EX7 9DR
☎(0626) 862760
Apr-Oct
Recent refurbishment has emphasized the beauty of this Nash-style Edwardian house. The comfortable, well-equipped bedrooms have quality en suite facilities. With its attractive small garden, Walton House overlooks the town and is close to the beach.
6rm(2⇄4♠)(1fb) CTV in all bedrooms ® ✱ (ex guide dogs)
6P
Credit Cards 1 3

DEBDEN GREEN Essex Map **05** TL53

FH 🅠 Mrs K M Low **Wychbars** *(TL579320)* CB11 3NA
☎Bishops Stortford(0279) 850362
Ask for directions from the hospitable proprietor, Mrs Low, as this 200-year-old whitewashed farmhouse is hidden in an attractive copse at the end of a long unmade lane. Accommodation comprises two simply furnished bedrooms sharing a shower room.
2rm CTV in all bedrooms ® ✱ dB&B£30-£32
lift 🕮 CTV 10P 600 acres arable non-working ⓔ

DENBIGH Clwyd Map **06** SJ06

GH 🅠 *Cayo* 74 Vale St LL16 2BW ☎(0745) 812686
Closed Xmas
This mid-Victorian house is situated just south of the town centre. The accommodation is simple but well maintained, and represents good value for money. There is street parking nearby.
5hc (2fb) ✱ sB&B£12-£15 dB&B£24-£30 WB&B£84-£105
LDO 2pm
Lic 🕮 CTV ✗
Credit Cards 1 3 ⓔ

DENNY Central *Stirlingshire* Map **11** NS88

FH 🅠🅠 Mrs J Morton *Lochend* *(NS759856)* Carronbridge
FK6 5JJ ☎(0324) 822778
rs Oct-Apr
Friendly and comfortable, this traditional farmhouse enjoys a secluded, scenic setting. Take the B818 west from Denny for 4 miles, then turn right at Carronbridge Hotel onto an unclassified road for two miles.
2hc CTV in 1 bedroom ® ✱ LDO 1pm
🕮 CTV P nc3yrs 650 acres sheep

FH 🅠🅠🅠 Mr & Mrs Steel *The Topps* *(NS757843)* Fintry Rd
FK6 5JF ☎(0324) 822471
Secluded amid beautiful rolling countryside, this tastefully appointed modern bungalow offers comfortable accommodation with a friendly atmosphere. The Topps is found 4 miles west of Denny on the B818.
8rm(1⇄7♠)(1fb)✗in all bedrooms CTV in all bedrooms ®
LDO 5pm
Lic 🕮 CTV 12P ♪ 300 acres cashmere goats sheep
See advertisement under STIRLING

DENT Cumbria Map **07** SD78

INN 🅠 *George & Dragon* Main St LA10 5QL ☎(05875) 256
Centrally situated in Dent village, among cobblestone streets, on the edge of the Yorkshire Dales. The dining room is attractive with a stone wall, lace cloths and candles. Bedrooms are sizeable and each have television and tea-making facilities. Bar meals are served at lunch time and during the evening in addition to dinner in the restaurant.

▶

The Gott Inn
Dartington, Devon Tel (0803) 863777

Fully Licensed since AD 1320, this fine thatched Inn is Internationally renowned for its historic atmosphere and standard of food and accommodation. A wide variety of traditional fare is served buffet-style at lunchtime whilst the evenings see a transformation to an English menu featuring interestingly prepared fresh local produce, served by waitresses. The six comfortable cottage style bedrooms, most en suite, guarantee a sound nights sleep and the breakfast is an experience not to be missed. Ideally situated to Dartington Hall, Dartmoor and the coast. The Cott is the perfect base for your holiday or two day break. (special terms available).

Manor House Hotel

2/4 Fore St., Cullompton, Devon EX15 1JL
Telephone: (0884) 32281
Fax: (0884) 38344

The Manor House is within comfortable driving distance of Exeter, the coast and Dartmoor and Exmoor National Parks.

Our nine bedrooms, each with bathroom, colour TV and telephone are superbly appointed. The restaurant, carvery, lounge and bars at the Manor House provide the food, atmosphere and service that only the very best traditional country inns can deliver.

9rm(3♪6hc) (2fb) CTV in all bedrooms ® LDO 9pm
₪ 14P pony trekking
Credit Cards ①③

DERBY Derbyshire Map **08** SK33

GH Ⓠ Dalby House Hotel 100 Radbourne St, off Windmill
Hill Ln DE3 3BU ☎(0332) 42353
*Lovely old house in residential area. Popular with tourists and
business travellers.*
9hc (2fb) CTV in all bedrooms ® sB&B£17.50-£18.50
dB&B£33-£35 LDO 4pm
₪ CTV 9P 1☎ ₳ £

GH Ⓠ Ⓠ Georgian House Hotel 32/34 Ashbourne Rd DE3 3AD
☎(0332) 49806
*Beautifully maintained house offering a high standard of
accommodation.*
20rm(2⇨8♪10hc) (5fb) CTV in all bedrooms ® sB&B£23
sB&B⇨♪£35-£40 dB&B£37 dB&B⇨♪£45-£55 LDO 9.30pm
Lic ₪ CTV 24P ₳ £

GH Ⓠ Rangemoor Hotel 67 Macklin St DE1 1LF
☎(0332) 47252
Simple accommodation in a terraced house near town centre.
12hc Annexe 8hc (3fb) CTV in all bedrooms ® ✹ ✱ sB&B£22-
£24 dB&B£34-£36
₪ CTV 18P 2☎
Credit Cards ①③

GH Ⓠ *Rollz Hotel* 684-8 Osmaston Rd DE2 8GT (on A514 2m
S) ☎(0332) 41026
*Two miles south of the city centre, on the A514, this large, well-
maintained house provides simple and comfortable accomodation.*
14hc (1fb) ® ✹ (ex guide dogs) LDO 9pm
Lic ₪ CTV 4☎

DEVIL'S BRIDGE Dyfed Map **06** SN77

FH Ⓠ Ⓠ Mrs E E Lewis **Erwbarfe** *(SN749784)* SY23 3JR
☎Ponterwyd(097085) 251
Etr-Oct
*This traditional stone-built farmhouse is very much a working
farm, situated just off the A4120, on the Ponterwyd side of the
village. There are two cosy bedrooms and a modern, comfortable
lounge.*
2hc ® ✹ ✱ dB&B£26-£30 WB&B£88-£100 WBDi£125-£130
LDO 4pm
₪ CTV 4P 400 acres beef sheep working farm

DEVIZES Wiltshire Map **04** SU06

GH Ⓠ Ⓠ *Long Street House* 27 Long St SN10 1NW
☎(0380) 724245
*A timber-framed house dating back to the 1700's, with a Georgian
frontage added later, situated a short walk from the centre of
town. The house has been nicely renovated, and bedrooms are
comfortable and well furnished. Some of the rooms are small, but
each is comfortable despite the size. The proprietors are friendly
and eager to extend their home, with plans to add more bedrooms
in the vast basement.*
7rm(5⇨♪2hc) ⅙in all bedrooms CTV in all bedrooms ®
✹ (ex guide dogs)
₪ CTV 7P

GH Ⓠ Ⓠ Pinecroft Potterne Rd SN10 5DA ☎(0380) 721433
FAX (0380) 728368
*This substantial semidetached stone house is conveniently situated
close to the town centre. The bedrooms are simply furnished and
breakfast is taken around a large table. Smoking in bedrooms is
discouraged.*
4rm(1⇨3♪) (1fb)⅙in 3 bedrooms CTV in all bedrooms ® ✹
✱ sB&B⇨♪£20-£24 dB&B⇨♪£34-£36 WB&B£75-£100

₪ 6P 1☎ ₳
Credit Cards ①②③

GH Ⓠ Ⓠ Ⓠ Rathlin Wick Ln SN10 5DP ☎(0380) 721999
*Quietly situated in a residential area, close to the town centre, this
1920's house has been tastefully renovated with flair and style by
the resident proprietors. Each of the 4 bedrooms has an individual
style and is furnished with antiques, pretty prints, lace and knick-
knacks. The public rooms have an Edwardian air about them and
the lounge, although small, is cosy and comfortable.*
4♪ ⅙in 2 bedrooms CTV in all bedrooms ® ✹ sB&B♪£20
dB&B♪£34 LDO 6pm
₪ 4P £

DIBDEN Hampshire Map **04** SU40

GH Ⓠ Ⓠ Ⓠ Dale Farm Manor Rd, Applemore Hill SO4 5TJ
☎Southampton(0703) 849632
Closed Xmas
*Do not be discouraged by the approach to Dale Farm, up a bumpy
drive and through a riding school. This 18th-century former
farmhouse is set in well tended gardens on the edge of the New
Forest. The modern bedrooms are cosy and fresh home-cooking is
served in the pine-furnished lounge/diner.*
6hc (2fb) TV in 1 bedroom ® ✹ (ex guide dogs) sB&B£14-
£17.50 dB&B£28-£32 WB&B£80-£100 WBDi£140-£150
LDO 11am
₪ CTV 20P ₳ ♪ ∪ £

DIDDLEBURY Shropshire Map **07** SO58

SELECTED

GH Ⓠ Ⓠ Ⓠ Ⓠ The Glebe SY7 9DH
☎Munslow(058476) 221
Mar-Oct (closed 10 days early Jun)
*A magnificent Elizabethan farmhouse, with oak beams,
panelling and flagstones combining sympathetically with
modern facilities and comforts. There is a spacious lounge,
quaint bar and very attractive dining room, gleaming with
polished copper and brass; evening meals are served by prior
arrangement only. Bedrooms are all individually furnished in
keeping with the farm's character.*
3♪ Annexe 3rm(1♪2hc) CTV in 5 bedrooms ®
✹ (ex guide dogs) sB&B£20-£24 dB&B£36-£40
dB&B♪£40-£52 LDO by arrangement
Lic ₪ CTV 10P 2☎ nc8yrs

DINTON Buckinghamshire Map **04** SP71

FH Ⓠ Ⓠ Ⓠ Mrs J M W Cook **Wallace** *(SP770110)* HP17 8UF
☎Aylesbury(0296) 748660 FAX (0296) 748851
*An attractive 16th-century farmhouse on the edge of a peaceful
village. Bedrooms are spacious and some have private bathrooms.
Breakfast is served in the farmhouse kitchen at one large table,
under exposed beams beside the inglenook fireplace, complete with
bread ovens. Many animals of rare breeds are kept at the farm.*
3rm(2⇨♪) (1fb) ✹ (ex guide dogs) sB&B⇨♪fr£28
dB&Bfr£34 dB&B⇨♪fr£36
₪ CTV 6P ♪ 150 acres beef cattle & sheep
Credit Cards ①③£

DIRLETON Lothian *East Lothian* Map **12** NT58

INN Ⓠ *Castle* EH39 5EP ☎(062085) 221
Closed 21 Dec-5 Jan rs Nov-Apr
*Popular with golfing parties, this simply decorated, family-run inn
overlooks the village green and its ruined namesake across the
road. Real ale is served, and there is a pleasant garden at the rear.*
4rm(3⇨1♪) Annexe 4hc ® LDO 8.30pm
₪ CTV 20P
Credit Cards ①②③

The Castle Inn

Dirleton, East Lothian
Telephone: (062 085) 221

Overlooking the green of one of Scotland's most beautiful 'heirloom' villages and situated in an area surrounded by many well known golf courses – North Berwick, Muirfield, Gullane and Luffness. The Castle Inn offers golfing parties of up to 16 accommodation in a happy, friendly atmosphere. All the bedrooms are centrally heated and have private bathrooms. Relax in the small lounge in front of the television or enjoy a glass of real ale with a bar lunch or supper.
For further information please contact Douglas Stewart.

THE GEORGIAN HOUSE HOTEL **DERBY**

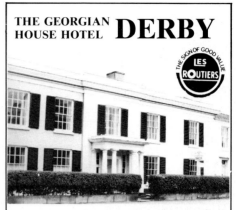

34, Ashbourne Road, (0332) 49806

The country style hotel in the town. Beautiful Georgian Architecture, in a grade II listed building. Built circa 1765, the **HOTEL** is set in a conservation area of the city's West End.
★ Table d'hôte & A la Carte menu

Licensed Bar   Garden & Car Park

Lovely Georgian farmhouse set amidst beautiful countryside. The ideal base for touring Derbyshire, or for business in the area. Superb licensed dining room.

All rooms private facilities.

EMTB 3 crowns commended   AA Selected

JOAN AND MARTIN SLACK
Dannah Farm, Bowmans Lane
Shottle, Nr. Belper
Derbyshire DE5 2DR
Tel: 0773 550273 or 550630

See Gazetteer under Shottle

DALBY HOUSE HOTEL
100 Radbourne Street,
off Windmill Hill Lane, Derby

Family run hotel in very quiet residential area. Convenient for Town Centre also Peak District and local historical buildings. Central heating — Guests lounge — Ample private parking area — Colour TV and tea/coffee facilities in all bedrooms.

Personal attention from resident proprietors Norman and Catherine Taylor.
TEL: (0332) 42353

DOCKLOW Hereford & Worcester Map **03** SO55

FH Q Mrs M R M Brooke *Nicholson* *(SO584581)* HR6 0SL
☎Steens Bridge(056882) 269
Closed Xmas & New Year
This 17th-century stone farmhouse is in a peaceful and picturesque area, 5.5 miles east of Leominster. It is reached by way of a long private road from the A44. The accommodation is simple but comfortable.
2rm(1hc) (1fb) ® LDO before 2pm
🍴 CTV P ♪ snooker 200 acres dairy mixed
Credit Cards ①③

DOLGELLAU Gwynedd Map **06** SH71

FH Q Q Mr & Mrs D I Jones **Fronolau Farm Restaurant**
Tabor LL40 2PS ☎(0341) 422361
This stone-built farmhouse, approximately 300 years old, is situated in pleasant countryside to the north of Cader Idris and is some 2 miles from Dolgellau. Facilities include a large cottage-style restaurant, where guests can choose from a wide range of dishes, and there is also a small pleasant bar and a spacious comfortable lounge with a solid fuel stove.
4hc (2fb) CTV in all bedrooms ® ✳ sB&B£14.50 dB&B£25
LDO 10pm
Lic 30P ⚗ 40 acres sheep

FH Q Q Mrs E W Price **Glyn** *(SH704178)* LL40 1YA
☎(0341) 422286
Mar-Nov
Situated approximately one mile west of Dolgellau this traditional three hundred year old farmhouse commands good views over the Mawddach Estuary from its elevated position amidst wooded hills.
4hc (2fb) TV in 3 bedrooms ® ✳ sB&Bfr£13.50 dB&Bfr£75 LDO previous day
🍴 CTV 6P 150 acres mixed £

FH Q Mrs C Tudor Owen **Rhedyncochion** *(SH773207)*
Llanfachreth LL40 2DL (3m NE unclass)
☎Rhydymain(0341) 41600
Etr-Oct
This small traditional stone-built farmhouse is in an isolated situation, up in the hills, approximately 3 miles northeast of Dolgellau. The one letting bedroom provides simple but comfortable accommodation.
2rm(1hc) (1fb) ✖ (ex guide dogs) ✳ sB&Bfr£11.50 LDO 10yrs
🍴 CTV P 120 acres mixed £

DONCASTER South Yorkshire Map **08** SE50

GH Q Q **Almel Hotel** 20 Christchurch Rd DN1 2QL
☎(0302) 365230 FAX (0302) 341434
Three town houses, close to the town centre, have been converted and modernised to form a comfortable and friendly hotel. There is a well fitted lounge bar and an attractive, pine-clad dining room.
30rm(24⇨🏠6hc) (1fb) CTV in all bedrooms ® sB&B£19-£22
sB&B⇨£25-£27 dB&B£32-£34 dB&B⇨🏠£36-£38
LDO 8pm
Lic 🍴 CTV 8P
Credit Cards ①②③

DORCHESTER Dorset Map **03** SY69

See also Evershot & Winterbourne Abbas
GH Q Q Q **Westwood House Hotel** 29 High West St DT1 1UP
☎(0305) 268018
7rm(5⇨🏠2hc) (1fb) CTV in all bedrooms ® ✳ sB&Bfr£25
dB&Bfr£38 dB&B⇨🏠fr£44 WB&Bfr£150
Lic 🍴 CTV
Credit Cards ①③

DORNOCH Highland *Sutherland* Map **14** NH78

GH Q Q Q *Evelix* IV25 3RE ☎(0862) 810271
Mar-Oct
A Jacobean farmhouse, peacefully situated at the end of a long private lane off the A9 and surrounded by a well kept garden. Bedrooms are comfortable and well equipped, and meals, available on request, are served around a communal dining table. Smoking is not permitted.
3hc ⚞in all bedrooms CTV in all bedrooms ® ✖ LDO 4pm
🍴 CTV 4P nc6yrs

DORSINGTON Warwickshire Map **04** SP14

FH Q Q Mrs M J Walters **Church** *(SP132495)* CV37 8AX
☎Stratford-on-Avon(0789) 720471 & (0831) 504194
Situated in the heart of this pretty village 6.5 miles from Stratford-upon- Avon, this 18th-century house offers comfortable and well equipped accommodation including four en suite bedrooms in a tasteful conversion of the former stable block.
3hc Annexe 4⇨🏠 (2fb)⚞in all bedrooms CTV in 4 bedrooms
® ✖ (ex guide dogs) ✳ dB&B£25-£27 dB&B⇨🏠£30-£32
🍴 CTV 12P 3🐾 127 acres mixed

DOUGLAS

See MAN, ISLE OF

DOVER Kent Map **05** TR34

GH Q **Beulah House** 94 Crabble Hill, London Rd CT17 0SA
☎(0304) 824615
Rooms, though compact, are cosy, and there are limited lounge facilities. There are extensive lawns and garden to the rear of the house, giving it an open aspect.
8hc (3fb) CTV in 1 bedroom ✖ (ex guide dogs) ✳ sB&B£18-£20 dB&B£34-£36 WB&B£112
🍴 CTV 8P 2🐾 (£2 per night)

🚗➡ GH Q Q Q **Castle House** 10 Castle Hill Rd CT16 1QW
☎(0304) 201656 FAX (0304) 210197
Closed Dec
Close to the castle, town centre and ferry ports, this friendly, family run hotel has pretty bedrooms and a small cosy lounge together with an attractive dining room.
6rm(3🏠3hc) (1fb) CTV in all bedrooms ® ✖ sB&B£12-£19
dB&B£24-£36 dB&B🏠£26-£38
Lic 🍴 3P 2🐾 (£2.50) nc10yrs
Credit Cards ①③

GH Q Q **Dell** 233 Folkestone Rd CT17 9SL ☎(0304) 202422
This is a pleasant establishment in a Victorian terraced house, which offers pretty and well-maintained accommodation, in addition to a friendly atmosphere. Breakfast is served in the nicely appointed dining room which extends from the lounge.
6hc (3fb) ® ✖ (ex guide dogs) ✳ sB&B£15-£17 dB&B£24-£29
🍴 CTV 6P £

GH Q Q **Gateway Hovertel** Snargate St CT17 9BZ
☎(0304) 205479
Closed 23 Dec-Feb
Close to the ferry and hover ports, this family-run hotel offers modestly appointed rooms, all with en suite facilities.
27rm(4⇨23🏠) (7fb) CTV in all bedrooms ✖ (ex guide dogs)
sB&B⇨🏠£25-£30 dB&B⇨🏠£40-£45 LDO 7pm
Lic 🍴 CTV 24P 2🐾
Credit Cards ①③ £

GH Q Q Q **Number One** 1 Castle St CT16 1QH
☎(0304) 202007
Delightfully Victorian in style, this hotel offers a warm welcome and accommodation equipped for every need. Full breakfast is served in the bedrooms as required, and 'early riser' trays are available for those catching an early ferry.

5rm(3⟡2hc)(3fb) CTV in all bedrooms ® ✖ dB&B£28-£32 dB&B⟡£30-£36
♨ 2P 4🛏 (£2) ⓔ

GH ⓆⓆⓆ Peverall House Hotel 28 Park Av CT16 1HD
☎(0304) 202573 & 205088
Comfortable, well appointed accommodation and a cheerful, pleasant welcome.
6rm(2⟡4hc)(2fb) CTV in all bedrooms ® ✖ ✳ sB&B£15-£17 dB&B£28-£30 dB&B⟡£34-£36 WB&B£102 WBDi£144 LDO noon
Lic ♨ CTV 8P ⓔ

GH ⓆⓆⓆ St Martins 17 Castle Hill Rd CT16 1QW
☎(0304) 205938
Closed Xmas
This charming Victorian house stands on the leas of Dover Castle and is ideally situated for the town and seaports. The pretty bedrooms are complemented by a pleasant lower ground floor dining room and a comfortable lounge.
8hc (2fb) CTV in all bedrooms ® ✖ sB&B£20-£25 dB&B£20-£40
Lic ♨ 1🛏 (£2 per night)

GH ⓆⓆⓆ Walletts Court Manor West Cliffe, St Margarets-at-Cliffe CT15 6EW (1.5m NE of A2/A258 junct, off B2058)
☎(0304) 852424 FAX (0304) 853430
Closed 24-27 Dec
A restored Jacobean farmhouse, situated on the white cliffs of Dover, three miles from the harbour. Bedrooms are individually furnished with antiques, and several have separate sitting rooms; there is also an annexe in a converted barn. Notable features include the elegant and spacious lounge, inglenook fireplaces, and carved oak staircase and a Meeting Room in the cellar. The restaurant opens for dinner Monday to Saturday, and reservations are recommended.

▶

Rectory House

Fore Street, Evershot, Dorset DT2 0JW
Telephone: (093583) 273

An 18th century listed building of great charm, situated in this quiet and unspoilt Dorset village in an area of outstanding natural beauty made famous by Thomas Hardy's 'Tess of the D'Urbevilles'. Utmost comfort, with lovely centrally heated bedrooms each with en suite bathroom, colour TV, tea & coffee making facilities. Superb home cooking using fresh local produce. Relax in the separate lounges with log fire during the winter months. Nearby many beautiful walks and places of interest to visit. Open all year except Christmas and New Year. Sorry no pets.

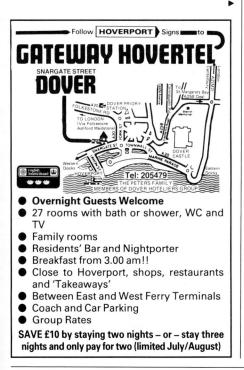

GATEWAY HOVERTEL
DOVER

● Follow **HOVERPORT** Signs to
SNARGATE STREET

Tel: 205479
THE PETERS FAMILY
MEMBERS OF DOVER HOTELIERS GROUP

● **Overnight Guests Welcome**
● 27 rooms with bath or shower, WC and TV
● Family rooms
● Residents' Bar and Nightporter
● Breakfast from 3.00 am!!
● Close to Hoverport, shops, restaurants and 'Takeaways'
● Between East and West Ferry Terminals
● Coach and Car Parking
● Group Rates

SAVE £10 by staying two nights – or – stay three nights and only pay for two (limited July/August)

CHURCHVIEW GUEST HOUSE
WINTERBOURNE ABBAS, DORCHESTER, DORSET DT2 9LS

This 300-year-old Guesthouse, noted for its warm, friendly hospitality and delicious home cooking is located in a small village 5 miles west of Dorchester. Set in a designated area of outstanding natural beauty, Churchview makes an ideal touring base. All our comfortable rooms have tea making facilities and central heating, some en-suite. There are two lounges, one set aside for non-smokers, an attractive period dining room and well-stocked bar. Evening meal, bed and breakfast from £25.00.

For further details please contact Michael and Jane Deller. ☎ (0305) 889296

3⇨🐾 Annexe 4⇨🐾 (1fb) CTV in all bedrooms ® ✖
sB&B⇨🐾£38-£50 dB&B⇨🐾£45-£60 LDO 8.30pm
Lic ﷽ 16P 10🚗 ♪(hard)games room
Credit Cards ①③

DOWNHAM MARKET Norfolk Map 05 TF60

GH ◖Q◗◖Q◗ Crosskeys Riverside Hotel Hilgay PE38 0LN
☎(0366) 387777
*Standing in lovely gardens on the banks of the River Wissey, next
to the A11, Crosskeys has been converted from 17th-century
buildings to offer a high standard of accommodation. All rooms
have en suite facilities and are very comfortable. Mr and Mrs
Bulmer are the caring hosts.*
3⇨ Annexe 2⇨ CTV in all bedrooms ® ✳ sB&B⇨£33.50
dB&B⇨£48 WB&B£144-£197.50 WBDi£193-£274.50
LDO 8pm
Lic ﷽ 10P ✈
Credit Cards ①③

DOWNTON Wiltshire Map 04 SU12

GH ◖Q◗◖Q◗ Warren 15 High St SP5 3PG ☎(0725) 20263
Closed 15 Dec-15 Jan
*A charming period house dating back in parts to the 15th century
and located in a quiet village between Salisbury and the New
Forest. The bedrooms are comfortable, well appointed and
tastefully furnished; many contain original features, including an
impressive wood panelled room with an ornate antique bed. There
are 2 lounges: 1 with TV and the other is quiet and leads through
into a breakfast room; all the rooms are nicely furnished with
antiques, complemented by fresh flowers.*
6rm(2⇨🐾4hc)(1fb) ® ✳ dB&B£35-£38 dB&B⇨🐾£38-£40
﷽ CTV 8P nc5yrs ⓔ
See advertisement under SALISBURY

DROXFORD Hampshire Map 04 SU61

GH ◖Q◗ Coach House Motel Brockbridge SO3 1QT
☎(0489) 877812
*Annexe accommodation in a converted stable block is comfortable
and well equipped here, a few yards from The Hurdles Public
House. Restaurant and bar meals are served and there is a pine-
furnished breakfast room.*
8rm(6⇨2🐾) CTV in all bedrooms ® ✖ (ex guide dogs)
﷽ 12P
Credit Cards ①②③⑤

DRUMNADROCHIT Highland *Inverness-shire* Map 14 NH52

INN ◖Q◗ Lewiston Arms Hotel Lewiston IV3 6UN ☎(04562) 225
*A comfortable and cosy old inn with a friendly relaxed atmosphere
and a reputation for good food.*
5rm(1⇨4🐾) Annexe 4🐾 CTV in all bedrooms ®
sB&B⇨🐾£22.50-£25 dB&B⇨🐾£45-£50 Bar Lunch £2.50-
£5alc Dinner £9-£15alc LDO 8.30pm
﷽ 30P
Credit Cards ③ ⓔ

DUDDINGTON Northants Map 04 SK90

INN ◖Q◗◖Q◗ Royal Oak Hotel High St PE9 3QE
☎Stamford(0780) 83267
6⇨🐾 (2fb) CTV in all bedrooms ® ✳ sB&B⇨🐾£28.50-£32
dB&B⇨🐾£40-£45 ✳ Lunch £2.25-£9.90&alc Dinner £2.25-
£9.90&alc LDO 9.30pm
﷽ 75P
Credit Cards ①③

DULVERTON Somerset

See **Oakford**

DUMBARTON Strathclyde

See **Cardross**

DUNBAR Lothian *East Lothian* Map 12 NT67

GH ◖Q◗◖Q◗ Marine 7 Marine Rd EH42 1AR ☎(0368) 63315
*A friendly, comfortable, seaside guesthouse in a quiet, residential
area on the west side of town.*
10hc (3fb) LDO 4pm
﷽ CTV 🅿

GH ◖Q◗◖Q◗ Overcliffe 11 Bayswell Park EH42 1AE
☎(0368) 64004
*A compact but nicely maintained house in a residential area on the
west side of town.*
5hc (2fb) CTV in all bedrooms ® ✳ dB&Bfr£28 LDO 5pm
Lic ﷽ CTV 🅿

GH ◖Q◗◖Q◗ St Beys 2 Bayswell Rd EH42 1AB ☎(0368) 63571
Feb-Dec
*Overlooking the sea and close to the town centre, this friendly hotel
is in a residential area and has comfortable bedrooms with many
little extras. The first floor lounge takes advantage of the views.*
6hc (3fb) CTV in all bedrooms ® LDO 6pm
﷽ CTV 🅿
Credit Cards ③

GH ◖Q◗ St Helens Queens Rd EH42 1LN ☎(0368) 63716
Closed Dec-7 Jan
*A terraced period house on the main road on the eastern side of
town, run by a retired couple, and spotlessly maintained.*
7rm(1⇨🐾6hc)(1fb)⤺in all bedrooms ® ✳ sB&B£14
dB&B£26-£28 dB&B⇨🐾£30
﷽ CTV 4P

GH ◖Q◗◖Q◗ Springfield Edinburgh Rd EH42 1NH
☎(0368) 62502
Mar-Oct
*Spacious, comfortable accommodation is offered at this attractive
stone-built house. The resident proprietors provide home cooked
dinners and attentive service.*
5hc (2fb) ® sB&B£16 dB&B£30
WB&B£105 WBDi£154 LDO 5pm
Lic ﷽ CTV 7P
Credit Cards ①③

DUNDEE Tayside *Angus* Map 11 NO43

GH ◖Q◗◖Q◗ Beach House Hotel 22 Esplanade, Broughty Ferry
DD5 2EQ ☎(0382) 76614 FAX (0382) 480241
*Beach House is pleasantly situated just outside Dundee, opposite a
sandy beach and overlooking the River Tay. Home cooking,
snacks and a wholesome breakfast are just some of the features to
recommend it. Bedrooms are very well appointed and mostly en
suite, though space is restricted in some. The recently refurbished
lounge is spacious and comfortable; it has a sea view, and is
supplied with a good selection of books.*
5⇨🐾 (2fb) CTV in all bedrooms ® ✳ sB&B⇨🐾£40.50-£47
dB&B⇨🐾£49.50-£54 LDO 9pm
Lic ﷽ 1🚗
Credit Cards ①③

DUNKELD Tayside *Perthshire* Map 11 NO04

GH ◖Q◗◖Q◗ Waterbury PH8 0BG ☎(03502) 324
*A popular base for the touring holidaymaker, this guesthouse offers
traditional comforts and good value for money. It stands in the
centre of Birnam just south of Dunkeld.*
6hc (2fb) ® LDO 7pm
Lic ﷽ CTV 6P

DUNLOP Strathclyde *Ayrshire* Map **10** NS44

FH QQ Mr & Mrs R B Wilson **Struther** *(NS412496)*
Newmill Rd KA3 4BA ☎Stewarton(0560) 84946
Closed 2wks spring & autumn rs Sun & Mon
This substantial period farmhouse sits on the edge of the village,
300 yards from the railway station. It is run in the style of a
country house and is a popular venue for dinner for non-residents.
Bedrooms are comfortable and generally quite spacious.
5hc (2fb) sB&Bfr£14 dB&Bfr£28 WB&Bfr£90 WBDifr£160
LDO 8.30pm
🕮 CTV 16P 10 acres non-working ⓔ
See advertisement under STEWARTON

DUNOON Strathclyde *Argyllshire* Map **10** NS17

GH QQQ **Cedars Hotel** 51 Alexandra Pde, East Bay
PA23 8AF ☎(0369) 2425 & 2066 FAX (0369) 6964
This small family-run hotel stands on the promenade and has well
appointed and equipped bedrooms, several of which enjoy
attractive views over the Firth of Clyde. A warm and friendly
welcome is assured here, where the hotel offers sporting and leisure
facilities and formal gardens. The scenery is magnificent and there
is much wildlife in the area, and this makes an excellent touring
centre.
12rm(3⇔9↿) (1fb) CTV in all bedrooms ⓡ ✖ (ex guide dogs)
sB&B⇔↿£24.50-£29.50 dB&B⇔↿£38-£44 WBDi£193-£213
LDO 7.30pm
Lic 🕮 ⅀
Credit Cards ① ② ③ ⑤ ⓔ

Book as early as possible for busy holiday periods.

DUNSTER Somerset

See **Minehead & Roadwater**

DUNURE Strathclyde *Ayrshire* Map **10** NS21

FH 🅀🅀🅀 Mrs R J Reid **Lagg** *(NS281166)* KA7 4LE
☎(029250) 647
May-Oct
Lying just off the main road a mile north of the village, the elevated position of this farmhouse provides fine views of the rugged coastline and out to sea. The house is attractive and well maintained with a tasteful lounge and a dining room with individual tables.
3hc ® ✱ dB&B£24-£30
🍴 CTV 6P 480 acres dairy sheep

DUNVEGAN

See **SKYE, ISLE OF**

DURHAM Co Durham Map **12** NZ24

See also **Haswell Plough**
GH 🅀🅀 **Lothlorien** 48/49 Front St, Witton Gilbert DH7 6SY
☎091-371 0067
Set in the village of Witton Gilbert, 3 miles north west of Durham, this charming guesthouse is 200 years old. A cooking range from an old miner's house is a feature of the comfortable lounge, and there is a small dining room.
4hc ® ✱ sB&B£15 dB&B£30 WB&B£105 WBDi£157.50
LDO 7.30pm
🍴 CTV 3P

INN 🅀 *Croxdale* Croxdale DH6 5HX (3m S A167)
☎Spennymoor(0388) 815727
A traditional roadside inn situated just off the A167, three miles south of Durham. Bedrooms in the main building are spacious, with four small rooms in the converted stone house at the rear, and they are all well equipped. There are also comfortable bars, and a restaurant.
9rm(1⇄4↑4hc) Annexe 4↑ (1fb) CTV in all bedrooms ®
LDO 10pm
🍴 30P
Credit Cards 1 3

DURSLEY Gloucestershire Map **03** ST79

FH 🅀🅀🅀 Mr & Mrs St John Mildmay **Drakestone House**
(ST734977) Stinchcombe GL11 6AS (2.5m W off B4060)
☎(0453) 542140
Apr-Oct
Situated between Dursley and Wooton-under-Edge on the B4060, this fine country house retains many original features, which have been enhanced by the fine antiques and objects collected by hosts Hugh and Crystal St John Mildmay during their many years overseas.
3rm(1hc) ⅍in all bedrooms ✱ ✱ sB&B£23 dB&B£36
WB&B£126 WBDi£213.50 LDO previous day
🍴 6P 10 acres sheep ©

DYFFRYN ARDUDWY Gwynedd Map **06** SH52

GH 🅀🅀🅀 *Bryntirion Country House* LL44 2HX
☎Ardudwy(03416) 770
This small family-run hotel lies in over 3 acres of woodland just off the A496 north of the village. Bedrooms are very comfortable; there is a bar for residents and a relaxing lounge with views over Cardigan Bay.
4rm(3⇄3↑1hc) (1fb) ® ✱ LDO 9.15pm
Lic 🍴 CTV 10P nc5yrs

DYLIFE Powys Map **06** SN89

INN 🅀🅀 **Star** SY19 7BW ☎Llanbrynmair(06503) 345
This remote inn stands in wild and rugged countryside in the mountains of mid Wales between Llanidloes and Machynlleth.

Bedrooms are modestly appointed, but the bars are full of character with slate floors and log fires, and a good range of reasonably priced food is available. It is a good centre for touring and the inn has its own pony trekking centre.
7rm(2⇄5hc) (1fb) ® sB&B£15-£16 sB&B⇄£15-£16
dB&B£30-£32 dB&B⇄£30-£32 Lunch £2.50-£7.95 Dinner £3-£7.95 LDO 10.30pm
🍴 CTV 30P ∪ boat hire pony trekking ©

DYMCHURCH Kent Map **05** TR12

GH 🅀🅀 *Chantry Hotel* Sycamore Gardens TN29 0LA
☎(0303) 873137
Enjoying a fine beach location, this hotel has bedrooms with interconnecting rooms for children. A four-course meal is served in the basement restaurant, with a choice selection of wines. Children are provided with a large garden with swings, well away from the roads.
6rm(5⇄3↑1hc) (5fb) CTV in all bedrooms ® LDO 8.30pm
Lic 🍴 CTV 9P
Credit Cards 1 3

GH 🅀🅀 *Waterside* 15 Hythe Rd TN29 0LN ☎(0303) 872253
Closed Xmas
Standing on the main road into Dymchurch, this pretty detached building has views over pleasant rural countryside. The accommodation includes neat bedrooms and a small cosy lounge bar.
7rm(5hc) (1fb) CTV in 3 bedrooms TV in 3 bedrooms ® ✱ ✱
sB&Bfr£14 dB&Bfr£26 dB&Bfr£28
Lic 🍴 CTV 9P

EARDISLAND Hereford & Worcester Map **03** SO45

FH 🅀🅀 Miss M Johnson **The Elms** *(SO418584)* HR6 9BN
☎Pembridge(05447) 405
This small, renovated farmhouse is set in the centre of the village and offers special interest holidays, such as photography or needlecraft. Guests are reminded that no smoking is permitted in the house.
4hc ⅍in all bedrooms ✱ LDO noon
6P nc10yrs 32 acres stock rearing

EASINGWOLD North Yorkshire Map **08** SE56

GH 🅀🅀 *Roseberry View* Easingwold Rd, Stillington YO6 1LR
☎(0347) 810795
3rm(1↑2hc) ⅍in 2 bedrooms CTV in all bedrooms ®
✱ (ex guide dogs) ✱ dB&B£24-£26 dB&B↑£30-£32
WB&B£82-£106
🍴 5P

EASTBOURNE East Sussex Map **05** TV69

See **Town Plan Section**
GH 🅀🅀🅀 **Bay Lodge Hotel** 61 & 62 Royal Pde BN22 7AQ
☎(0323) 32515
Mar-Oct
This attractive double-fronted Victorian house overlooks the sea and has neatly appointed, comfortable accommodation and a cosy bar. There are pleasant sun lounges for smokers and non-smokers, and good home cooking is provided.
12rm(5⇄4↑3hc) CTV in all bedrooms ® ✱ (ex guide dogs) ✱
sB&B£14-£19 dB&B£28-£38 dB&B⇄↑£28-£44 WB&B£75-£128 WBDi£117-£170 (wkly only Jul & Aug) LDO 6pm
Lic 🍴 CTV ✗ nc7yrs
Credit Cards 1 3 ©

GH 🅀🅀🅀 **Beachy Rise** 20 Beachy Head Rd BN20 7QN
☎(0323) 639171
This friendly establishment has been carefully refurbished and offers accommodation of a good standard with a non-smoking dining room and a comfortable, well appointed lounge. Set in a quiet residential area, it is close to local amenities.

6rm(2⇨4↟) CTV in all bedrooms ® ✘ (ex guide dogs)
dB&B⇨↟£40-£50 WB&B£130-£150 WBDi£185-£205
LDO noon
Lic ⌻ ℱ
Credit Cards ① ③ ⓔ

GH ⓠⓠ **Bourne House Private Hotel** 16 Bourne St BN21 3ER
☎(0323) 21981
*Quietly located but close to the seafront, this pleasant house is run
by the friendly owner, Mrs Barnes, who is renowned for her
breakfasts and home cooking. The bedrooms are modest but there
is a cosy lounge and a bar/dining room. Parking is limited in this
area.*
10rm(1⇨4↟5hc) (1fb) CTV in all bedrooms ® ✳ sB&Bfr£14
dB&Bfr£28 dB&B⇨↟fr£32 WB&B£84-£125 WBDi£105-£160
LDO noon
Lic ⌻ CTV ℱ
Credit Cards ① ③ ⓔ

GH ⓠⓠⓠ **Chalk Farm Hotel & Restaurant** Coopers Hill,
Willingdon BN20 9JD (2m NNE) ☎(0323) 503800
*This cosy, cottage-style flint-built farmhouse dates back to the
17th century and overlooks the Sussex Downs. The beamed
bedrooms retain their original character with traditional furniture
and brick fireplaces, whilst offering all modern facilities. The
attractive restaurant offers a full à la carte menu, and there is also
a bar, comfortable lounge and a pretty garden.*
9rm(2⇨5↟2hc) (1fb) CTV in all bedrooms ® sB&B£30-£32
dB&B£60-£64 dB&B⇨↟£66-£70 WB&B£190-£210
WBDi£250-£285 LDO 9pm
Lic ⌻ CTV 30P
Credit Cards ① ③ ⑤

ⓔ Remember to use the money-off vouchers.

GH Q Q Q **Far End Hotel** 139 Royal Pde BN22 7LH
☎(0323) 25666
Apr-Oct
This relaxing, family-run guesthouse stands beside Princes Park within easy reach of the seafront amenities. The bright, modern, comfortable bedrooms are complemented by a lounge and residential bar.
10rm(4♪6hc) CTV in all bedrooms ® sB&B£16.50-£17 dB&B£33-£34 dB&B♪£40-£41 WB&B£101-£115 WBDi£157-£175 LDO 1pm
Lic ♥ CTV 8P nc4yrs

GH Q Q Q *Flamingo Private Hotel* 20 Enys Rd BN21 2DN
☎(0323) 21654
Closed Nov
An attractive, detached period house in a peaceful residential area with unrestricted street parking. Guests can enjoy a drink in the spacious bar/lounge, and there is a small sun lounge which overlooks an attractive garden. Bedrooms are all en suite and offer a good standard of comfort; dinner is available by prior arrangement in the dining room, which is non-smoking.
12rm(5✲7♪) CTV in all bedrooms ® ✖ (ex guide dogs) LDO 4.30pm
Lic ♥ ✗ nc8yrs
Credit Cards 1 3

GH Q Q Q **Hotel Mandalay** 16 Trinity Trees BN21 3LE
☎(0323) 29222
An attractive town centre hotel with its own car park at the rear. The recently refurbished bedrooms offer a good standard of comfort and are well equipped. The fully licensed restaurant Gatsby's has an adjoining bar, and service is friendly and welcoming.
13rm(3✲10♪) (1fb) CTV in all bedrooms ®
✖ (ex guide dogs) ✳ sB&B✲♪£23-£25 dB&B✲♪£46-£50 WB&B£145-£160 WBDi£200-£220 LDO 9pm
Lic ♥ 15P
Credit Cards 1 3 £

GH Q Q **Mowbray Hotel** Lascelles Tce BN21 4BJ
☎(0323) 20012
Apr-Dec
A well maintained hotel situated close to the seafront, theatres and Winter Gardens. Some bedrooms are compact but all are freshly decorated. There is a residents' lounge, basement dining room where dinner is served and a lift to all floors.
15rm(6♪9hc) CTV in all bedrooms ® sB&Bfr£20 dB&Bfr£40 dB&B♪fr£48 WB&B£120-£138 WBDi£160-£178 LDO 5.30pm
lift CTV nc6yrs
Credit Cards 1 3

GH Q Q Q *Saffrons Hotel* 30-32 Jevington Gardens BN21 4HN
☎(0323) 25539
Etr-Oct
This friendly hotel, situated quite close to the town centre and sea front, has undergone some major improvements to offer a good standard of modern accommodation. The attractive lower ground floor restaurant and bar may be reached by a lift.
25rm(7✲6♪12hc) (2fb) CTV in all bedrooms ® LDO 7pm
Lic CTV ✗
Credit Cards 1 3

GH Q Q **Stirling House Hotel** 5-7 Cavendish Place BN21 3EJ
☎(0323) 32263
Closed 1st wk Nov, last wk Jan & 1st wk Feb
A well maintained house with a pretty frontage situated close to the seafront. The bedrooms are compact but well equipped, and many have en suite facilities. There is a lounge and cosy bar, and dinner is available to guests.
20rm(11♪9hc) (1fb) CTV in all bedrooms ®
✖ (ex guide dogs) sB&B£16-£17 dB&B£32-£34 dB&B♪£36-£38 WB&B£106-£120 WBDi£114-£145 LDO 9am
Lic CTV ✗ nc10yrs £

EAST CALDER Lothian *Midlothian* Map **11** NT06

FH Q Q Mr & Mrs D R Scott **Whitecroft** *(NT095682)*
EH53 0ET ☎Midcalder(0506) 881810 FAX (0506) 884327
A large, detached bungalow sitting by the roadside just east of the village on the B7015. Attached to a smallholding, the house enjoys fine views northwards across the Forth Valley and offers compact accommodation and a comfortable lounge. There is also a farm shop which is run by the friendly owners.
3hc (1fb)✲in all bedrooms ® ✖ ✳ sB&B£18 dB&Bfr£28 WB&Bfr£98
♥ CTV 8P 5 acres mixed beef sheep £
See advertisement under EDINBURGH

EAST GRINSTEAD West Sussex Map **05** TQ33

GH Q Q **Cranfield Lodge Hotel** Maypole Rd RH19 1HW
☎(0342) 321251 & 410371
Set in a residential area, close to all local amenities, this guesthouse has a well kept garden and a small car park. There is a pleasant residents' bar, a comfortable lounge and a dining room where an evening meal is served on request. Bedrooms vary in size, with rather small annexe rooms, but the accommodation is all well maintained and equipped.
11rm(4♪7hc) Annexe 9rm(1✲6♪2hc) (1fb) CTV in all bedrooms ® ✳ sB&B£24-£28 sB&B✲♪£36 dB&B£40-£42 dB&B✲♪£46-£48 LDO 8pm
Lic ♥ CTV 11P
Credit Cards 1 2 3 £

EASTLING Kent Map **05** TQ95

INN Q Q Q **Carpenters Arms** The Street ME13 0AZ
☎(079589) 234
3✲♪ Annexe 3✲♪ CTV in 3 bedrooms ® ✖ ✳ sB&B✲♪£30 dB&B✲♪£38-£40 WB&B£105-£160 ✳ Lunch £10&alc Dinner £10&alc LDO 10pm
♥ 20P nc10yrs
Credit Cards 1 2 3

EBBERSTON North Yorkshire Map **08** SE88

GH Q Q **Foxholm Hotel** YO13 9NJ (on B1258)
☎Scarborough(0723) 859550
Mar-Nov & Xmas
Small, family-run country hotel in a peaceful setting. York, the moors, dales and sea are all within easy reach.
9rm(2✲4♪3hc) (1fb) ® sB&B✲♪£31-£34 dB&B£56-£62 dB&B✲♪£60-£68 (incl dinner) WBDi£195-£232 LDO 7pm
Lic ♥ CTV 12P 2🐾 £

EDINBURGH Lothian *Midlothian* Map **11** NT27

See **Town Plan Section**
GH Q Q **Adam Hotel** 19 Lansdowne Crescent EH12 5EH
☎031-337 1148
This elegant Georgian house is set in a quiet location, and yet is convenient for the main road. The warm, traditional bedrooms each have a colour television set.
9hc (2fb) CTV in all bedrooms ✖ (ex guide dogs) ✳ sB&B£17 dB&B£32-£34
Lic ♥ CTV £

GH Q Q Q *The Adria Hotel* 11-12 Royal Ter EH7 5AB
☎031-556 7875
Closed Nov-Dec
Part of a Georgian terrace close to Princes Street. Spacious, well-decorated accommodation.
28rm(2✲4♪22hc) (7fb) ® ✖
♥ CTV ✗

Book as early as possible for busy holiday periods.

GH Q Q Q **Allison House** 15/17 Mayfield Gardens EH9 2AX
☎031-667 8049
A guesthouse converted from 2 terraced houses, to the south of the city centre. Bedrooms are thoughtfully appointed, service is friendly and menus are good value.
24rm(22↑2hc) (10fb) CTV in all bedrooms ®
✖ (ex guide dogs) sB&B£22-£24 sB&B↑£28-£34 dB&B£32-£44 dB&B↑£40-£55 WB&B£100-£200 LDO 7.30pm
Lic ⊞ 12P
Credit Cards ①③ £

GH Q Q Q **Ashdene House** 23 Fountainhall Rd EH9 2LN
☎031-667 6026
Closed Xmas-New Year & 2 wks winter
The well appointed bedrooms at this very comfortable house have colour TVs, hairdryers and telephones.
5rm(4↑1hc) (2fb) CTV in all bedrooms ® ✖ (ex guide dogs)
✻ dB&B£30-£36 dB&B↑£34-£40
⊞ 3P nc2yrs

GH Q Q **Avenue Hotel** 4 Murrayfield EH12 6AX
☎031-346 7270
Part of a Victorian terrace, this friendly, family-run guesthouse offers spacious, comfortable accommodation. It is located to the west of the city with easy access to the A8.
9rm(1⇨5↑3hc) (3fb) CTV in all bedrooms ®
⊞ ₽

GH Q **Ben Doran** 11 Mayfield Gardens EH9 2AX
☎031-667 8488
Closed 20-27 Dec
Neat, well maintained accommodation is offered at this comfortable guesthouse which is part of a terraced row of houses.
9rm(1⇨3↑5hc) (5fb) CTV in all bedrooms ® ✻ sB&B£15-£18
sB&B⇨↑£20-£30 dB&B£26-£32 dB&B⇨↑£32-£37
⊞ 6P 2❀

GH Q **Boisdale Hotel** 9 Coates Gardens EH12 5LB
☎031-337 1134
This pleasant terraced house is close to the city's West End, and is a comfortable establishment, where the breakfasts are enjoyable and the service friendly. Bedrooms have recently been refurbished and there are neat bath and shower rooms.
11rm(5⇨6↑) (6fb) CTV in all bedrooms ® ✻ sB&B⇨↑£20-£30 dB&B⇨↑£40-£60 LDO 7pm
Lic ⊞ CTV ₽

GH Q Q **Bonnington** 202 Ferry Rd EH6 4NW ☎031-554 7610
Situated in the northern suburbs, this friendly, family-run guesthouse offers neat, simple accommodation.
6rm(1↑5hc) (3fb) CTV in all bedrooms ® sB&B£20-£25
dB&B£33-£36 dB&B↑£40-£44 LDO 10am
⊞ CTV 9P £

GH Q Q Q **Brunswick Hotel** 7 Brunswick St EH7 5JB
☎031-556 1238
An attractively appointed and comfortable guesthouse situated close to the city centre. It offers a high standard of housekeeping, with pleasant bedrooms, all with bright, compact shower rooms.
10↑ (1fb) CTV in all bedrooms ® ✖ sB&B↑£20-£30
dB&B↑£38-£54
⊞ nc2yrs
Credit Cards ①②③ £

GH Q Q Q **Buchan Hotel** 3 Coates Gardens EH12 5LG
☎031-337 1045
Charming and well maintained, this Victorian guesthouse is set in a residential area close to the city centre. The attractive accommodation is complemented by the warm and personal attention of the owners.
11rm(2↑9hc) (6fb) CTV in all bedrooms ®
⊞ CTV ₽

SELECTED

GH QQQQ **Dorstan Private Hotel** 7 Priestfield Rd
EH16 5HJ ☎031-667 6721
Closed 23 Dec-8 Jan
Situated in a residential area on the south side of the city, this spacious private hotel is family run and spotlessly maintained. All the bedrooms are well equipped, complete with telephones, TV and beverage-making facilities, and those in the original part of the house have tastefully fitted furnishings; it is hoped those in the extension will be refurbished in a similar fashion. The menu of freshly cooked dishes changes daily, and the proprietors offer attentive, caring service.
14rm(12⇦➧🏠2hc)(2fb) CTV in all bedrooms ®
🏋 (ex guide dogs) sB&B£17-£19 sB&B⇦➧🏠£25-£27
dB&B£36-£40 dB&B⇦➧🏠£44-£48 LDO 3pm
🍴 8P
Credit Cards ①③£

GH QQ **Dunstane House** 4 West Coates EH12 5TQ
☎031-337 6169
Closed Xmas-4 Jan
An elegant house dating back to the mid-1800s. Accommodation throughout is spacious and comfortable.
15hc (5fb) CTV in all bedrooms ®
Lic 🍴 CTV 10P
Credit Cards ②③

GH QQ **Ellesmere House** 11 Glengyle Ter EH3 9LN
☎031-229 4823
Overlooking open parkland and within walking distance of the city centre, this small, friendly guesthouse enjoys a superb location.
6hc (2fb) CTV in all bedrooms ® 🏋 (ex guide dogs) ✳
sB&B£14-£18 dB&B£28-£36 WB&B£98-£126
🍴 CTV ✗ £

GH QQ **Galloway** 22 Dean Park Crescent EH4 1PH
☎031-332 3672
A handsome Victorian terraced house with comfortable, well equipped bedrooms, some of which have private bathrooms. There is a small snug lounge and a spacious dining room, where tables are sometimes shared at breakfast time.
10rm(6⇦➧🏠4hc) (6fb) CTV in all bedrooms ® sB&B£18-£28
sB&B⇦➧🏠£25-£35 dB&B£30-£32 dB&B⇦➧🏠£32-£40
WB&Bfr£90
🍴£

GH Q **Glenisla Hotel** 12 Lygon Rd EH16 5QB ☎031-667 4877
FAX 031-667 4098
A most attractive semidetached sandstone house located in a residential area on the south side of the city. The proprietors have improved the catering facilities, and refurbishment is a constant process.
7rm(4🏠3hc) (2fb) sB&B£20.50-£22.50 sB&B🏠£25-£27
dB&B£38-£40 dB&B🏠£45-£48 LDO 8.15pm
Lic 🍴 CTV 6P 1🏎
Credit Cards ①③£

GH QQQ **Glenora Hotel** 14 Rosebery Crescent EH12 5JY
☎031-337 1186
An attractively decorated and furnished compact hotel with well-equipped bedrooms.
10🏠 (2fb) CTV in all bedrooms ® 🏋
Lic 🍴 CTV
Credit Cards ①③

GH QQQ **Greenside Hotel** 9 Royal Ter EH7 5AB
☎031-557 0022
Closed Nov-Dec
Forming part of a fine Regency terraced row, this spacious house is elegant, spotlessly clean and well maintained. The bedrooms vary in size and style, with the original master rooms being particularly large. There is a quiet terraced garden to the rear.

12rm(6⇦➧🏠6hc) (3fb) sB&B£22.50-£30.50 sB&B⇦➧🏠£24.50-£30.50 dB&B£41-£45 dB&B⇦➧🏠£45-£51
🍴 CTV ✗

GH Q **Grosvenor** 1 Grosvenor Gardens EH12 5JU
☎031-337 4143 FAX 031-346 8732
A Victorian town house, managed by the friendly resident proprietor, currently being refurbished.
8⇦➧🏠 (3fb) CTV in all bedrooms ® 🏋 (ex guide dogs) ✳
sB&B⇦➧🏠£26-£30 dB&B⇦➧🏠£52-£60
🍴 ✗
Credit Cards ①②③

GH Q **Halcyon Hotel** 8 Royal Ter EH7 5AB ☎031-556 1033 &
031-556 1032
Part of a fine Georgian terrace close to the city centre, the upper floors of this establishment offer fine views across the city to the Firth of Forth. The accommodation is simply equipped but pleasant, and some bedrooms have showers.
16hc (6fb) ® ✳ sB&B£22-£25 dB&B£21-£27
🍴 CTV ✗ ✗(hard)

GH Q **A Haven** 180 Ferry Rd EH6 4MS ☎031-554 6559
Situated close to the town centre, this small guesthouse offers cosy accommodation and friendly service.
10rm(4🏠6hc) (4fb) CTV in all bedrooms ® sB&B£20-£23
dB&B£32-£39 dB&B🏠£42-£56
Lic 🍴 CTV 6P £

GH QQ **Heriott Park** 256 Ferry Rd EH5 3AN ☎031-552 6628
Smart, recently converted house on main road, north part of the city.
6rm(2🏠4hc) (4fb) CTV in all bedrooms ® ✳ sB&B£16-£20
dB&B£24-£30 dB&B🏠£34-£40
Lic 🍴 CTV P

GH QQQ **International** 37 Mayfield Gardens EH9 2BX
☎031-667 2511
Managed by the friendly resident proprietors, this guesthouse has comfortable and spacious bedrooms. Intending guests will be well looked after.
7⇦➧🏠 (3fb) CTV in all bedrooms ® 🏋 (ex guide dogs) ✳
sB&B⇦➧🏠£15-£25 dB&B⇦➧🏠£30-£50 WB&B£90-£150
🍴 3P £

GH QQ **Kariba** 10 Granville Ter EH10 4PQ ☎031-229 3773
Small and cosy guesthouse.
9rm(2🏠7hc) (2fb) CTV in all bedrooms ®
🍴 CTV 4P

See advertisement on page 149

GH QQ **Kingsley** 30 Craigmillar Park, Newington EH16 5PS
☎031-667 8439
Mrs Hogg offers clean, well-maintained standards at Kingsley Guest House. The bedrooms, some with shower cabinets, are bright and cheery, and for a relaxing end to the day, the lounge has comfortable sofas and chairs.
7hc (3fb) CTV in all bedrooms ® 🏋
🍴 CTV 7P nc6yrs

See advertisement on page 149

GH Q **Kirtle House** 8 Minto St EH9 1RG ☎031-667 2813
This neat, compact house, located on the south side of the city, offers modest standards of accommodation. There are en suite facilities available, as well as TVs with a BSB channel in the bedrooms. The dining room and lounge are combined.
7rm(4🏠3hc) (4fb) CTV in all bedrooms ® 🏋 ✳ dB&B£30-£36
dB&B🏠£32-£38
🍴 CTV 5P nc4yrs

GH [Q][Q] **Lindsay** 108 Polwarth Ter EH11 1NN ☎031-337 1580
Comfortable neatly appointed house with a relaxed and friendly atmosphere.
8rm(1♠7hc) (2fb) CTV in all bedrooms ® ✱ sB&B£17.50
dB&B£35 dB&B♠£40
⁗ 6P
Credit Cards [1][2][3]

SELECTED

GH [Q][Q][Q][Q] **The Lodge Hotel** 6 Hampton Ter, West
Coates EH12 5JD ☎031-337 3682
A Georgian mansion on the A8 just west of the city centre, transformed by the proprietors into a small, elegant town house hotel. Bedrooms are tastefully decorated and furnished, with good quality en suite shower rooms. There is a small cocktail lounge for residents in addition to the main lounge, and a patio outside. Dinner is a set three course meal with the emphasis on fresh produce, and is very good value. The hotel is in an ideal location and is spotlessly maintained throughout.
10♠ ⅟in 6 bedrooms CTV in all bedrooms ® ✘ ✱
sB&B♠£40-£50 dB&B♠£54-£75 LDO 7pm
Lic ⁗ 10P ⚙
Credit Cards [1][3] ⓔ

GH [Q][Q] *Marchhall Hotel* 14-16 Marchhall Crescent EH16 5HL
☎031-667 2743 FAX 031-662 0777
This comfortable guesthouse is situated in a pleasant residential area close to swimming pool and University buildings. The attractive lounge bar is open to non-residents.
13rm(2♠11hc) (3fb) CTV in all bedrooms ® LDO 3pm
Lic ⁗ CTV ⚐
Credit Cards [1][3]

GH [Q][Q] **Mardale** 11 Hartington Place EH10 4LF
☎031-229 2693
Located in a quiet residential area, close to the town centre, this small guesthouse offers cosy, attractive bedrooms and friendly service.
6hc (3fb) CTV in all bedrooms ® ✱ sB&B£13-£16 dB&B£26-£32
⁗ ⓔ

GH [Q][Q][Q] **Meadows** 17 Glengyle Ter EH3 9LN
☎031-229 9559 FAX 031-557 0563
Closed 18-28 Dec
Set in a terraced row overlooking Bruntsfield Links, this attractive house is well run and has some character. All the public areas, including the main entrance, are 'below stairs'; breakfast is taken in the bright, airy dining room around 2 large tables. A good standard of housekeeping prevails in the bedrooms, which are comfortable and thoughtfully equipped.
7rm(5♠2hc) (3fb) CTV in all bedrooms ® ✱ sB&Bfr£19
sB&B♠£35 dB&Bfr£36 dB&B♠£45-£47
⁗
Credit Cards [1][3] ⓔ

GH [Q][Q][Q] *The Newington* 18 Newington Rd EH9 1QS
☎031-667 3356
A house of character and appeal, well appointed and thoughtfully equipped.
8rm(3♠5hc) (1fb) CTV in all bedrooms ®
Lic ⁗ 3P

GH [Q][Q][Q] **Parklands** 20 Mayfield Gardens EH9 2BZ
☎031-667 7184
An exceptionally well maintained establishment, Parklands forms part of a terraced row south of the city centre. The bedrooms are comfortable, reflecting high standards of housekeeping. The cosy lounge is combined with the breakfast room.

6rm(5♠1hc) (1fb) ® ✘ (ex guide dogs) dB&B£34-£40
dB&B♠£36-£42
⁗ CTV ⚐ ⓔ

GH [Q][Q] **Park View Villa** 254 Ferry Rd EH5 3AN
☎031-552 3456
Situated on the northern side of the city, guests at this friendly, comfortable guesthouse look out across the main road to playing fields, and can also enjoy good views of the Edinburgh skyline. There is ample car parking space, and the owners will arrange sightseeing tours of the city.
7rm(3♠4hc) (4fb) CTV in all bedrooms ® ✘ (ex guide dogs)
sB&Bfr£20 sB&B♠fr£28 dB&Bfr£32 dB&B♠fr£40
⁗ CTV
Credit Cards [1][3]

GH [Q][Q] **Ravensdown** 248 Ferry Rd EH5 3AN ☎031-552 5438
Comfortable, well appointed house with views over the city and its imposing castle.
7hc (5fb) CTV in all bedrooms ® ✘ ✱ sB&B£18-£25
dB&B£26-£34
Lic ⁗ CTV 4P ⓔ

GH [Q][Q][Q] **Ravensnuek** 11 Blacket Av EH9 1RR
☎031-667 5347
Very comfortable, attractive accommodation is complemented here by the courteous service from the friendly resident proprietors.
6hc (2fb) ® ✘ ✱ sB&B£18-£22 dB&B£30-£40
⁗ CTV

GH [Q][Q] **Rowan** 13 Glenorchy Ter EH9 2DQ ☎031-667 2463
This stone-built, semidetached house is situated in a quiet side road to the south of the city. It offers a good all round standard of accommodation, and the service provided by the resident owners is friendly.
9rm(1♠8hc) (2fb) ✱ sB&B£16-£18 dB&B£30-£34 dB&B♠£36-£40
⁗ CTV P

GH [Q][Q] *St Margaret's* 18 Craigmillar Park EH16 5PS
☎031-667 2202
Apr-Dec
Well-appointed Victorian house with individually decorated bedrooms, on main road south of the city centre.
8hc (3fb) CTV in all bedrooms ® ✘
⁗ CTV 6P

GH [Q][Q][Q] **Salisbury Hotel** 45 Salisbury Rd EH16 5AA
☎031-667 1264
Closed Xmas-New Year
Situated between the A68 and A7 on the south side of the city, this conversion of two adjoining Georgian town house offers bright, modern and comfortable bedrooms which are neatly decorated and generally well proportioned.
12rm(9⇨♠3hc) (3fb) CTV in all bedrooms ® sB&B⇨♠£18-£22 dB&B⇨♠£32-£44 WB&B£108-£154
Lic ⁗ CTV 12P ⓔ

GH [Q] **Sherwood** 42 Minto St EH9 2BR ☎031-667 1200
Closed Xmas & New Year
A friendly terraced house south of the city centre catering essentiallly for the budget bed and breakfast market. Facilities are modest and functional, but the guesthouse is well maintained and spotlessly clean. Payment is requested on arrival.
6hc (3fb) CTV in all bedrooms ® dB&B£22-£34
⁗ 3P ⓔ

GH [Q][Q][Q] **Southdown** 20 Craigmillar Park EH16 5PS
☎031-667 2410
This substantial, Victorian terraced house offers well-appointed rooms with showers, and very comfortable public areas. The service is friendly and breakfasts are enjoyable, with homemade preserves a speciality.

►

6hc (2fb) TV in all bedrooms ® ✖ (ex guide dogs) ✱
sB&B£20-£25 dB&B£30-£36
🍴 CTV 7P

GH Ⓠ Ⓠ Ⓠ **Stra'ven** 3 Brunstane Rd North, Joppa EH15 2DL
☎031-669 5580

*Close to the beach, this handsome stone-built house offers
attractive, modern bedrooms, a comfortable first floor lounge and
friendly service from the owners.*

7⇨♠ CTV in all bedrooms ® ✖ (ex guide dogs) ✱
sB&B⇨♠£15-£18 dB&B⇨♠£30-£36
🍴 CTV ⅌

GH Ⓠ Ⓠ **Stuart House** 12 East Claremont St EH7 4JP
☎031-557 9030 FAX 031-557 0563
Closed 18-27 Dec

*Situated north of the city, in a residential terraced row of town
houses, this pretty and comfortable house is run by Gloria Stuart.
The well appointed bedrooms all have their own en suite facilities,
except a small single room which has exclusive use of the
bathroom. Breakfast is served at two communal tables in the large
front-facing room on the ground floor, and there is also a small
lounge area. A strict no-smoking policy is enforced.*

7rm(6⇨♠ 1hc) (1fb) TV in all bedrooms CTV in all bedrooms ®
✖ sB&B£20-£26 sB&B⇨♠£35-£45 dB&B⇨♠£43-£52
LDO 9pm
🍴
Credit Cards ①③

GH Ⓠ Ⓠ Ⓠ **Thrums Private Hotel** 14 Minto St, Newington
EH9 1RQ ☎031-667 5545
Closed Xmas & New Year

*Good value lunch and dinner menus offer a choice of dishes at this
attractive, spacious house. The bedrooms are provided with many
extras not normally found in the smaller hotel.*

7rm(6♠ 1hc) Annexe 8rm(3⇨4♠ 1hc) CTV in all
bedrooms ® sB&B£28-£32 sB&B⇨♠£32-£40 dB&B£46-£50
dB&B⇨♠£52-£64 WB&B£196-£224 LDO 7.45pm
Lic 🍴 12P ⓛ

💳♥️🐕 **GH** Ⓠ **Tiree** 26 Craigmillar Park EH16 5PS
☎031-667 7477

Tidy, well decorated house with good bedroom facilities.

7rm(4♠ 3hc) (2fb) CTV in all bedrooms ® sB&B£12-£16
dB&B£25-£30 dB&B♠£30-£40
🍴 7P

ELIE Fife Map **12** NO40

GH Ⓠ Ⓠ **The Elms** 14 Park Place KY9 1DH ☎(0333) 330404
Apr-Sep

*A fine detached period house set back from the road, with well
tended walled gardens to the rear. Bedrooms vary in size and are
individually decorated and fitted. The comfortable lounge is on the
1st floor and there is a spacious dining room.*

7rm(1⇨3♠ 3hc) (3fb) CTV in 4 bedrooms ® ✱ sB&B£21-£40
dB&B⇨♠£32 dB&B♠£44 WBDi£165-£205 LDO 6.30pm
Lic 🍴 CTV ⅌ nc12yrs ⓛ

ELTERWATER Cumbria Map **07** NY30

INN Ⓠ Ⓠ Ⓠ **Britannia** LA22 9HP ☎Langdale(09667) 210 &
382 FAX (09667) 311
Closed 25 & 26 Dec

9rm(6♠ 3hc) CTV in all bedrooms ® ✱ dB&B£42-£51
dB&B♠£48-£58 WB&B£136.50-£192.50 WBDi£245-£299.25
✱ Bar Lunch £5.15-£8.15alc Dinner £15.50-£17.50
LDO 7.30pm
🍴 10P 🐎
Credit Cards ①③ ⓛ

Visit your local AA Shop.

ELY Cambridgeshire Map **05** TL58

GH Ⓠ **Castle Lodge Hotel** 50 New Barns Rd CB7 4PW
☎(0353) 662276

*This family-owned and run hotel is situated in a residential area,
yet is within walking distance of the cathedral and town centre.
The public areas are quite comfortable, clean and well maintained,
and there is a well stocked bar. Rooms on the 1st floor are simply
furnished, some with private bathrooms; the 2nd-floor rooms are
quite basic and due for renovation.*

10rm(1⇨2♠ 7hc) (1fb) CTV in all bedrooms ®
✖ (ex guide dogs) ✱ sB&B£21-£30 sB&B⇨♠£35 dB&B£42
dB&B⇨♠£45-£50 WB&Bfr£140 WBDifr£195 LDO 7.30pm
Lic 🍴 8P
Credit Cards ①③

EMSWORTH Hampshire Map **04** SU70

GH Ⓠ Ⓠ **Jingles Hotel** 77 Horndean Rd PO10 7PU
☎(0243) 373755

*Just north of the town centre, this comfortable small hotel is
privately owned and has compact, adequately appointed bedrooms.
The pleasant staff create a friendly, informal atmosphere.*

13rm(5♠ 8hc) CTV in all bedrooms ® sB&B£21
sB&B♠£29.50 dB&B£39 dB&B♠£46 WB&B£133-£186.50
WBDi£192.50-£246 (wkly only Oct-Mar) LDO 7pm
Lic 🍴 CTV 14P
Credit Cards ①③ ⓛ

GH Ⓠ Ⓠ **Merry Hall Hotel** 73 Horndean Rd PO10 7PU
☎(0243) 372424
Closed 25 Dec-3 Jan

*An attractive well-appointed hotel with large garden. Ideally
situated for yachting centres.*

10rm(7⇨3♠) (2fb) CTV in all bedrooms ® ✖ sB&B⇨♠£28-
£32 dB&B⇨♠£45-£52 (wkly only Nov-Apr) LDO 7.30pm
Lic 🍴 CTV 12P putting green
Credit Cards ①③ ⓛ

GH Ⓠ Ⓠ *Queensgate Hotel* 80 Havant Rd PO10 7LH
☎(0243) 371960 & 377766

*Most of the bedrooms of this comfortable guesthouse are equipped
with showers. Mrs Nasir cooks delicious Indian dishes using
recipes from the royal kitchens of northern India's great Mogul
emperors.*

10hc (1fb) CTV in 9 bedrooms ® LDO 6pm
Lic 🍴 CTV 12P
Credit Cards ①②③⑤

EPSOM Surrey Map **04** TQ26

GH Ⓠ Ⓠ *Epsom Downs Hotel* 9 Longdown Rd KT17 3PT
☎(0372) 740643

*This charming hotel is located in a peaceful residential area, with
bedroom accommodation which is modern and well equipped. In
addition to the pleasant bar, there is a comfortable lounge and an
attractive dining room.*

17rm(14⇨3hc) CTV in all bedrooms ® LDO 8.30pm
Lic 🍴 CTV 25P 🐎
Credit Cards ①②③⑤

ERLESTOKE Wiltshire Map **03** ST95

FH Ⓠ Ⓠ Ⓠ Mrs P Hampton **Longwater Park** *(ST966541)*
Lower Rd SN10 5UE ☎Devizes(0380) 830095
Closed Xmas & New Year

*A modern farmhouse overlooking a lake and open country, just off
the B3098, signed from the village post office. The bedrooms are of
a good size and have many extras such as electric blankets,
toiletries and sewing kits. There is a newly built conservatory in
addition to the TV lounge and the dining room with its single long
table, and Mrs Hampton's collection of blue and white china is
displayed throughout.*

3⇌🐾 (1fb) CTV in all bedrooms ® sB&B⇌🐾£20-£22
dB&B⇌🐾£36 WB&B£120 WBDi£180 LDO 5pm
Lic ♨ CTV 6P ✔ 166 acres beef waterfowl organic ⓔ

ETTINGTON Warwickshire Map **04** SP24

FH ⓠⓠ Mrs B J Wakeham **Whitfield** *(SP265506)* Warwick
Rd CV37 7PN ☏Stratford on Avon(0789) 740260
Closed Dec
*Situated on the A429 just north of the A422 roundabout, this
spacious house offers comfortable bedrooms and an attractive
dining room with pretty table appointments including hand-
embroidered cloths. The Wakeham family are charming and
attentive hosts.*
3rm(1🐾2hc) (1fb) ® ✖ (ex guide dogs) sB&B£14-£15
dB&B£24-£26 dB&B🐾£29-£30
♨ CTV 3P 220 acres mixed ⓔ

EVERSHOT Dorset Map **03** ST50

GH ⓠⓠⓠ Rectory House Fore St DT2 0JW ☏(093583) 273
Closed Xmas
*An attractive old stone house on the main street of this pretty
Dorset village. The 4 rooms in the stable conversion are
comfortable and well equipped, while the rooms in the main house
are larger and have vast bathrooms. The dining room, with antique
linen cloths on polished tables, offers a daily set menu providing
large portions of fresh, home-made food.*
6⇌🐾 CTV in all bedrooms ® ✖ (ex guide dogs) ✱
sB&B⇌🐾£50 dB&B⇌🐾£60 WB&B£180 WBDi£250
LDO 6.30pm
Lic ♨ TV 6P ncl2yrs
Credit Cards ①③ⓔ
See advertisement under DORCHESTER

WHITECROFT FARM
East Calder, near Edinburgh
½ mile from East Calder on B7015

Large bungalow on small farm with attractive views.
Surrounded by farmland for only 10 miles from
Edinburgh City Centre. Ideal base for touring, golfing,
sightseeing, etc. 5 miles Airport & Ingliston; 4 miles
M8/M9 motorways; 5 miles City By-pass. Scottish
Tourist Board 2 crowns Commended. Fire Certificate.

Mrs Scott helps her husband run a farm shop yet still
finds time to provide guests with early morning tea in
bed. Full Scottish breakfast with home and local
produce – even whisky marmalade. Sorry, no smoking.

Tel: Midcalder (0506) 881810 Fax: 884327

Tiree Guest House
26, CRAIGMILLAR PARK, EDINBURGH
EH16 5PS. Telephone: 031-667 7477

Situated on the South side of Edinburgh, ten
minutes from Princes Street, on main bus
route to the City centre. Edinburgh University, Holyrood Palace, Commonwealth Pool,
Shopping Centre and restaurants close by.
Comfortable rooms with shower and toilet en-
suite and shower only. All rooms have colour
TVs, tea/coffee making facilities, central heating. Private parking available. Full Scottish
breakfast.
Small groups welcomed at reduced rates.
**Write or telephone for further details to
Mrs N Alexander**

STRA'VEN
GUEST HOUSE
3 Brunstane Road North, Joppa,
Edinburgh EH15 2DL
Telephone: 031-669 5580

A warm welcome awaits you at STRA'VEN.
Situated in a quiet cul-de-sac adjoining the
beach.
15 minutes by bus to the City centre. All our
bedrooms are centrally heated with en suite
facilities, tea and coffee making and colour
television.

Proprietors: David & Betty Johnston

EVESHAM Hereford & Worcester Map **04** SP04

GH QQQ **Lyncroft** 80 Greenhill WR11 4NH ☎(0386) 442252
Feb-Nov
The accommodation at Lyncroft is comfortable and well equipped
with an attractive dining room and comfortable lounge. Mrs.
McLean is friendly and helpful and is sure to make guests
welcome.
5rm(1⇨4♠) CTV in all bedrooms ® ⊁ sB&B⇨♠£20-£25
dB&B⇨♠£32-£40
⑪ 10P nc5yrs ⓔ

EXBOURNE Devon Map **02** SS60

FH QQQ Mrs S J Allain *Stapleford (SS580039)* EX20 3RA
☎(083785) 277
Closed Dec & New Year
This 17th-century longhouse, in a peaceful location with views of
north Devon, has been modernised to offer a high standard of
comfort. The menus offer home produced food and a warm,
friendly welcome is assured.
2rm(1hc) ® ⊁ LDO 5pm
CTV 4P 2🛋 nc12yrs ⚓ games room croquet lawn 80 acres
sheep

EXETER Devon Map **03** SX99

See **Town Plan Section**
GH Q *Braeside* 21 New North Rd EX4 4HF ☎(0392) 56875
Closed 25-26 Dec
7rm(3♠4hc) (1fb) CTV in all bedrooms ® LDO 4pm
⑪ ⊬

GH QQQ **Hotel Gledhills** 32 Alphington Rd EX2 8HN
☎(0392) 430469 & 71439
Closed 2 wks Xmas
This conveniently positioned, traditional small hotel is close to the
city, station and M5 and represents very good value for money.
Significant upgrading and refurbishment by the hospitable and
conscientious owners has resulted in very comfortable bedrooms,
brightly decorated and well equipped, with fully tiled en suite
bathrooms. The accommodation throughout is immaculately clean.
12rm(9♠3hc) (3fb) CTV in all bedrooms ® ⊁ sB&B£18
sB&B♠£25 dB&B♠£39-£41 LDO 8pm
Lic ⑪ CTV 11P 2🛋
Credit Cards ① ③

GH QQ **Park View Hotel** 8 Howell Rd EX4 4LG
☎(0392) 71772 & 53047
Closed Xmas
This bed and breakfast establishment is within walking distance of
the station and city centre. The bedrooms have good facilities
including colour TV and direct dial telephones, and some have en
suite shower rooms.
10rm(2⇨2♠6hc) Annexe 5rm(3♠2hc) (2fb)⊬in 1 bedroom
CTV in all bedrooms ® ⊁ (ex guide dogs) ✱ sB&B£18-£22
sB&B♠fr£30 dB&Bfr£36 dB&B⇨♠£42-£45
⑪ CTV 6P
Credit Cards ① ③ ⓔ

GH QQ **Sunnymede** 24 New North Rd EX4 4HF
☎(0392) 73844
Closed 24 Dec-1 Jan
A Georgian house conveniently located for the city, which has been
refurbished and provides bright, well equipped bedrooms, a cosy
lounge and a breakfast room, in a welcoming atmosphere.
9rm(5♠4hc) (1fb) CTV in all bedrooms ⊁ ✱ sB&B£16-£20
sB&B♠fr£20 dB&B♠£28-£30 LDO 9pm
⑪ CTV ⊬

ⓔ Remember to use the money-off vouchers.

GH Q **Telstar Hotel** 77 St Davids Hill EX4 4DW
☎(0392) 72466
Closed 2 wks Xmas
Friendly, family-run guesthouse with cosy bedrooms. Close to
colleges and central station.
9hc (1fb) ® ✱ sB&B£12-£15 dB&B£23-£30
⑪ CTV 5P ⓔ

GH QQ **Trees Mini Hotel** 2 Queen's Crescent, York Rd
EX4 6AY ☎(0392) 59531
Comfortable accommodation and a relaxed atmosphere are found
at this semidetached house which stands opposite the park and
close to the city centre.
10rm(1⇨9hc) (1fb) CTV in all bedrooms ® ⊁ ✱ sB&Bfr£15
dB&Bfr£26 dB&B⇨♠fr£34 LDO 10am
⑪ CTV 1🛋
Credit Cards ① ③ ⓔ

GH Q **Trenance House Hotel** 1 Queen's Crescent, York Rd
EX4 6AY ☎(0392) 73277
Closed Xmas
This family guesthouse has compact bedrooms which are simply
furnished, and comfortable public rooms. It is conveniently sited
for the city.
15rm(1⇨2♠12hc) (2fb) CTV in all bedrooms ® ✱ sB&B£17-
£18 sB&B⇨♠£23 dB&B£25-£30 dB&B⇨♠£33 WB&B£119-
£161 WBDif168-£216 LDO noon
⑪ CTV 7P
Credit Cards ① ③

EXMOUTH Devon Map **03** SY08

GH QQ *Blenheim* 39 Morton Rd EX8 1BA ☎(0395) 264230
Closed 24-26 Dec
A small, modestly appointed and personally run guesthouse
conveniently positioned close to the seafront.
6hc (2fb) CTV in all bedrooms ® ⊁ (ex guide dogs)
LDO 4.30pm
Lic ⑪ CTV 1P
Credit Cards ① ③

GH QQQ **Carlton Lodge Hotel** Carlton Hill EX8 2AJ
☎(0395) 263314
A pleasant, small hotel just off the seafront offering friendly service
in a relaxed atmosphere, with good car parking on site. Bedrooms,
whilst not spacious, are bright and very well equipped, most with a
private bathroom. There is a popular bar and a cosy little steak
restaurant, with a good range of value-for-money dishes available
in both.
6rm(2⇨2♠2hc) (3fb) CTV in all bedrooms ® LDO 9pm
Lic ⑪ 14P
Credit Cards ① ③ ⓔ

FAIRBOURNE Gwynedd Map **06** SH61

GH Q **Sea View** Friog LL38 2NX ☎(0341) 250388
Closed 24-26 Dec
A large stone-built house dating back to 1750, now a privately
owned and run guesthouse. It provides simple but nicely
maintained accommodation, and is surrounded by pleasant
gardens. The house is situated on the A493, in the hamlet of Friog,
nine miles southwest of Dolgellau; the picturesque mountains and
sandy beaches are within a few minutes' walk.
6hc (2fb)⊬in 1 bedroom CTV in all bedrooms ® ⊁ ✱
sB&B£14.50-£15 dB&B£29-£30 WB&B£87-£90 LDO 8pm
Lic ⑪ CTV ⊬ ⓔ

FAKENHAM Norfolk Map **09** TF92

See also Barney

GH QQ **Lowfields Hotel** Hayes Ln NR21 9EP ☎(0328) 855432

A modern guesthouse with a traditional Norfolk look in a quiet residential corner of the town. Surrounded by its own 4 acres of woodland and gardens, it is also within easy reach of the River Wensum. To find the hotel from the roundabout junction of the A148 and A1065, follow the town centre sign, take the first right after the Shell garage down Sandy Lane, then the third turn on the left.

10rm(2⇔8↱) CTV in all bedrooms ® ✗ (ex guide dogs) ✱ sB&B⇔↱£20-£28 dB&B⇔↱£30-£36 WB&B£105-£126 WBDi£130-£160 LDO 5.30pm

Lic 𝍖 12P

FALFIELD Avon Map **03** ST69

GH QQ **Green Farm** GL12 8DL ☎(0454) 260319

This large guesthouse is situated half a mile north of M5 junction 14 on the A38. Formerly the principal house to a large farm, parts of which date back to the 16th century, it has a rural atmosphere with stone floors, exposed beams and open fires. The bedrooms vary in size and are modestly appointed, and the well tended gardens include a tennis court and outdoor swimming pool.

8rm(1⇔7hc) ® ✱ sB&B£16-£27 sB&B⇔fr£27 dB&Bfr£25 dB&B⇔fr£35 LDO 8.30pm

𝍖 CTV 10P ⛱ 🎾(hard)

FALMOUTH Cornwall & Isles of Scilly Map **02** SW83

See **Town Plan Section**

GH QQQ **Cotswold House Hotel** 49 Melvill Rd TR11 4DF ☎(0326) 312077

Personally run for many years by its resident owners, this modern hotel is situated between the beaches and town centre. Public rooms include a well stocked cocktail bar and a comfortable lounge. Most of the cheerful bedrooms have private bathrooms, and housekeeping standards are high.

10rm(8⇔↱2hc) (2fb) CTV in all bedrooms ® ✗ ✱ sB&B£18.50 dB&B£35 dB&B⇔↱£37-£37.50 WB&B£110-£125 WBDi£140-£155 LDO 7pm

Lic 10P nc4yrs

GH QQQ **Gyllyngvase House Hotel** Gyllyngvase Rd TR11 4DJ ☎(0326) 312956

Mar-Oct

This privately-owned hotel, close to the centre of town and the seafront, is run by the charming French proprietor and his English wife. Quite compact bedrooms are comfortable with a pretty, fresh décor. They are each well equipped, with modern facilities including direct dial telephones. Lounge areas are spacious and comfortable, overlooking the rear garden and enjoying the afternoon sunshine. Housekeeping is of a high standard, and the home- cooked evening meals are enjoyed by many returning guests.

15rm(12⇔↱3hc) (2fb) CTV in all bedrooms ® ✱ sB&B£18 sB&B⇔↱£20-£32 dB&B⇔↱£40 WBDi£165-£180 LDO 7pm

Lic 𝍖 CTV 15P £

GH QQQ **Penmere** "Rosehill", Mylor Bridge TR11 5LZ ☎(0326) 74470

A traditional Cornish house standing in attractive gardens, with delightful views over Mylor Bridge Creek. There is a bright, comfortable lounge and breakfast room. The bedrooms have pretty fabrics, pine furniture and some Victorian fireplaces, and are named after local areas. For the benefit of watersport enthusiasts, the owner teaches at the nearby sailing school.

6rm(4⇔↱2hc) (2fb) CTV in all bedrooms ® ✗ (ex guide dogs) sB&B£18.50-£22 sB&B⇔↱£22-£25.50 dB&Bfr£37 dB&B⇔↱fr£44

𝍖 7P £

GH QQQ **Penty Bryn Hotel** 10 Melvill Rd TR11 4AS ☎(0326) 314988

Etr-Oct

This small family-run hotel is conveniently located for both the centre of town and the seafront. Bedrooms are nicely presented, well maintained with modern facilities in each and some enjoy good sea views. A traditional lounge area is complemented by a cosy bar and breakfast room. This honest guesthouse is personally run by the friendly and warm resident proprietor, Mrs Jane Wearne.

7rm(5↱2hc) (3fb) CTV in all bedrooms ® ✱ sB&B£15.50 dB&B£31 dB&B↱£31

Lic 𝍖 CTV 2P 1🚗

Credit Cards [1] [3]

GH QQQ **Rathgowry Hotel** Gyllyngvase Hill TR11 4DN ☎(0326) 313482

Apr-Oct

A spacious Edwardian house, quietly situated within easy walking distance of the town centre and beach. Bedrooms are bright, well maintained and comfortable, and 4 have sea views. There is a well appointed bar with a residential licence, a pleasant lounge and attractive dining room. The resident proprietors offer helpful and friendly service, and forecourt parking is provided.

10rm(2⇔8↱) (4fb) CTV in all bedrooms ® sB&B⇔↱£14-£22 dB&B⇔↱£28-£44 WB&B£87-£127 WBDi£115-£155 LDO 5pm

Lic 𝍖 10P £

GH QQQ ***Westcott Hotel*** Gyllyngvase Hill TR11 4DN ☎(0326) 311309

3 Jan-Oct rs Jan-Mar

Friendly, attentive service is provided by conscientious owners of this cosy hotel. Standing in a quiet position, with views of the bay, it offers bright bedrooms, most with en suite facilities.

▶

11rm(4⌣4♠3hc) (2fb) CTV in all bedrooms ® ⋈
LDO 6.30pm
♨ CTV 9P nc2yrs

FALSTONE Northumberland Map **12** NY78

INN Q Q Q **Pheasant** Stannersburn NE48 1DD
☎Bellingham(0434) 240382
*A lovely old inn full of character and charm situated in open
countryside close to Kielder Water. A good range of food is served
in the bar or in the attractive dining room. Service is friendly and
attentive.*
Annexe 10rm(5♠5hc) (1fb)⊁in all bedrooms CTV in 5
bedrooms ® ✱ sB&B£20-£32 dB&B£36-£40 dB&B♠£48-£54
WB&B£113.40-£201.60 WBDi£208.60-£296.80 ✱ Lunch £8.50-
£10.50&alc Dinner £11.60-£18.50alc LDO 8.50pm
♨ 40P pool room darts ⓔ

FAREHAM Hampshire Map **04** SU50

GH Q Q Q **Avenue House Hotel** 22 The Avenue PO14 1NS
☎(0329) 232175
13⌣♠ (3fb) CTV in all bedrooms ® ✱ sB&B⌣♠£29-£39.50
dB&B⌣♠£44-£48
♨ 13P
Credit Cards [1] [2] [3]

GH Q **Catisfield Hotel** Catisfield Ln, Catisfield PO15 5NN (2m
W A27) ☎Titchfield(0329) 41851 FAX (0329) 41851
*Occupying the first and second floors above Catisfield Wine Stores
in a quiet residential area, with green belt to the rear, this hotel
offers well equipped and simply furnished bedrooms.*
20rm(16⌣2♠2hc) (7fb) CTV in all bedrooms ® ✱
sB&B15.50-£17 sB&B⌣♠£22.50-£25 dB&B£25-£30
dB&B⌣♠£35-£40 LDO 6pm
Lic ♨ CTV 100P ⓔ

FARINGDON Oxfordshire Map **04** SU29

GH Q Q Q **Faringdon Hotel** Market Place SN7 7HL
☎(0367) 240536
*A substantial hotel with a smart exterior offering well equipped
bedrooms with modern facilities including satellite television. In
addition to accommodation in the main building there are five
bedrooms in the cottage-style annexe. The public areas are rather
limited, but nevertheless pleasantly furnished. The hotel enjoys an
international and commercial clientèle.*
17rm(11⌣6♠) Annexe 5rm(1⌣4♠) (3fb) CTV in all
bedrooms ® sB&B⌣♠£44 dB&B⌣♠£54 LDO 9pm
Lic ♨ 5P
Credit Cards [1] [2] [3] [5] ⓔ

GH Q Q Q **Westbrook House** 18 Gravel Walk SN7 7JW
☎(0367) 241820
3⌣♠ (1fb) CTV in 1 bedroom ® ⋈ (ex guide dogs) ✱
sB&B⌣♠£18 dB&B⌣♠£30 WB&B£100
♨ CTV 5P

FARMBOROUGH Avon Map **03** ST66

GH Q Q Q **Streets Hotel** The Street BA3 1AR
☎Timsbury(0761) 71452
Closed 23 Dec-1 Jan
*An attractive 17th-century house set in a picturesque village, this
small private hotel offers some of its accommodation in a converted
coaching house. Rooms are well furnished and decorated and have
some good modern facilities. An acre of garden is the perfect
setting for the swimming pool.*
3⌣♠ Annexe 5⌣♠ CTV in all bedrooms ® ⋈ ✱
sB&B⌣♠£42-£48 dB&B⌣♠£50-£58 LDO 8.50pm
Lic ♨ CTV 8P nc6yrs ≏(heated) solarium

FARNHAM Surrey Map **04** SU84

INN Q **The Eldon Hotel** 43 Frensham Rd, Lower Bourne
GU10 3PZ ☎Frensham(025125) 2745 FAX (025125) 5129
*Popular, privately-managed hotel with modern, well-equipped
bedrooms, good leisure facilities plus restaurant.*
14rm(12⌣♠2hc) (2fb) CTV in all bedrooms ® ✱ sB&B£30-
£36 sB&B⌣♠£36-£48 dB&B⌣♠£40-£58 ✱ Lunch £2.50-£12
Dinner £7.50-£15 LDO 9.30pm
♨ CTV 65P squash sauna solarium gymnasium pool tables
Credit Cards [1] [2] [3]

FAR SAWREY Cumbria Map **07** SD39

GH Q Q Q **West Vale Country** LA22 0LQ
☎Windermere(09662) 2817 due to change to (05394) 42817
Mar-Oct
*A family-run country guesthouse with well proportioned,
comfortable bedrooms, ample lounges and a nicely positioned
dining room with views over green fields towards Grizedale Forest.
West Vale is very well maintained throughout.*
8rm(7♠1hc) (3fb) ® ⋈ (ex guide dogs) sB&B£16 sB&B♠£19
dB&B£32 dB&B♠£38 WB&B£112-£133 WBDi£161-£182
LDO 4pm
Lic ♨ CTV 8P nc7yrs ⓔ

FAVERSHAM Kent Map **05** TR06

INN Q **White Horse** The Street, Boughton ME13 9AX
☎Canterbury(0227) 751343 FAX (0227) 751090
13rm(7⌣6♠) (2fb) CTV in all bedrooms ® ✱
sB&B⌣♠fr£43.50 dB&B⌣♠fr£56.50 ✱ Lunch £15-£20alc
Dinner £15-£20alc LDO 9.30pm
♨ 35P
Credit Cards [1] [2] [3] [5]

FAZELEY Staffordshire Map **04** SK20

GH Q **Buxton Hotel** 65 Coleshill St B78 3RG
☎Tamworth(0827) 285805 & 284842
Closed 25-26 Dec rs 1 Jan
*A commercial, inexpensive hotel on the A4091, just off the A5 and
very close to Drayton Manor Park. A large house with an oak
panelled bar and a snooker table in the lounge.*
15rm(4⌣9♠) (4fb) CTV in all bedrooms ® sB&B£23-£30
sB&B⌣♠£28.75-£30.95 dB&B£32-£40 dB&B⌣♠£36.95-£42
LDO 8.45pm
Lic ♨ CTV 16P
Credit Cards [1] [3] ⓔ

FELINDRE (NEAR SWANSEA) West Glamorgan Map **02**
SN60

FH Q Q Q Mr F Jones *Coynant* *(SN648070)* SA5 7PU (4m N
of Felindre off unclass rd linking M4 j unc 46 and Ammanford)
☎Ammanford(0269) 595640 & 592064
*Rather isolated and reached by a gated concrete road, this
comfortably appointed and family-run farmhouse is well worth the
journey. It is set in spectacular countryside, with pursuits such as
fishing and pony riding available to guests, children particularly
may enjoy feeding the farm pets.*
5rm(3⌣♠2hc) (2fb) CTV in all bedrooms ®
⋈ (ex guide dogs) (wkly only Jul-Aug) LDO 7pm
Lic ♨ 10P ⏌ ∪ games room 150 acres mixed

FILEY North Yorkshire Map **08** TA18

GH Q Q **Abbots Leigh** 7 Rutland St YO14 9JA
☎Scarborough(0723) 513334
*This delightful small guesthouse is set in a quiet side road close to
the Esplanade. Bedrooms, although not spacious, are attractively
decorated, comfortably furnished and particularly clean and well
maintained.*

6⟜ (3fb)⅄in all bedrooms CTV in all bedrooms ®
✖ (ex guide dogs) sB&B⟜£18-£26 dB&B⟜£30
WB&B£95-£164 WBDi£139-£208 LDO 4pm
Lic ♒ 4P
Credit Cards ①③ ⓔ

GH ⓠⓠ Downcliffe Hotel The Beach YO14 9LA
☎Scarborough(0723) 513310
Apr-Oct
*This detached hotel on the seafront offers a special welcome to
families.*
17rm(1⟜6⟜10hc) (9fb) CTV in all bedrooms ® ✳
sB&B£19.50-£22.50 sB&B⟜£22.50-£26.50 dB&B£40-£46
dB&B⟜£42-£48 LDO 6pm
Lic ♒ CTV 8P 2⊜
Credit Cards ①③ ⓔ

GH ⓠⓠ Seafield Hotel 9/11 Rutland St YO14 9JA
☎Scarborough(0723) 513715
*Improvements continue to be made to this family-run private hotel
situated in a quiet road of Victorian terraced houses just off the
Esplanade. It offers pleasant, if compact, bedrooms, a small lounge
bar and an attractive dining room.*
13rm(3⟜6⟜4hc) (7fb) CTV in all bedrooms ® ✖ LDO 4pm
Lic ♒ CTV 8P

FIR TREE Co Durham Map 12 NZ13

SELECTED

GH ⓠⓠⓠⓠ Greenhead Country House Hotel DL15 8BL
☎Bishop Auckland(0388) 763143
*In a delightful rural setting just off the A68, this attractive
whitewashed hotel provides comfortable, inviting
accommodation. The pretty bedrooms are bright, spacious and
well appointed. Beamed ceilings are featured in the lounge
and bar which are separated by a chunky stone chimney
breast and stone arches. The dining room is equally attractive.
Resident proprietors Ann and Paul Birbeck spent a great deal
of time and effort converting the listed building to offer
modern facilities, while taking care to retain the character and
atmosphere of the place.*
8⟜ (1fb) CTV in 7 bedrooms ® ✖ (ex guide dogs)
sB&B£30-£35 dB&B⟜£40-£45 WB&B£200-£245
LDO 5pm
Lic ♒ CTV 18P 2⊜ (£2 per night) nc13yrs
Credit Cards ①③

FLAX BOURTON Avon Map 03 ST56

INN ⓠⓠⓠ Jubilee Main Rd BS19 3QX ☎(0275) 462741
Closed 25 Dec evening
*Located on the A370, at the edge of the village, this inn offers three
comfortable bedrooms and a spacious, relaxing residents' lounge.
The public areas have character, and the food offered is cooked
with both skill and imagination.*
3hc ✳ sB&B£24 ✳ Lunch £7.25-£13alc Dinner £7.25-£13alc
LDO 10pm
CTV 51P nc14yrs

FOLKESTONE Kent Map 05 TR23

GH ⓠⓠⓠ Belmonte Private Hotel 30 Castle Hill Av
CT20 2RE ☎(0303) 54470 FAX (0303) 50568
*Pleasant accommodation and a warm welcome are to be found at
this large, attractive Victorian house. The attractive dining room is
complemented by a conservatory area and a cosy, relaxing lounge.
Plants and dried flowers abound here.*
9rm(1⟜4⟜4hc) (1fb) CTV in all bedrooms ® sB&Bfr£22
sB&B⟜fr£26 dB&Bfr£44 dB&B⟜fr£48 WB&B£132-
£156 WBDi£228-£252 LDO 5pm
Lic ♒ 4P
Credit Cards ①②③⑤ ⓔ

FONTMELL MAGNA Dorset Map **03** ST81

GH 🅠🅠 *Estyard House Hotel* SP7 0PB ☎(0747) 811460
Closed Nov-Dec
This attractive house has large gardens which supply many of the fruits and vegetables which are served for dinner. Mr and Mrs Jones cater for an older clientele, and offer a comfortable lounge with books and games. The 6 comfortable bedrooms share one bathroom and two toilets. This is a non-smoking house.
6hc ⊁in all bedrooms ✗ LDO 7pm
⊞ 8P nc10yrs

FORDOUN Grampian *Kincardineshire* Map **15** NO77

FH 🅠🅠🅠 Mrs M Anderson *Ringwood (NO743774)* AB3 1JS
(1.5m off A94 on B966) ☎Auchenblae(05612) 313
Apr-Oct
Set in its own delightful garden amid gentle rolling countryside, this small modernised hotel has much charm and character, and offers excellent value bed and breakfast accommodation. The house is tastefully decorated and well furnished throughout and Mrs Anderson's breakfasts are hearty and wholesome.
4hc (1fb) ® ✗
⊞ CTV 4P 16 acres arable

FORGANDENNY Tayside *Perthshire* Map **11** NO01

FH 🅠🅠🅠 Mrs M Fotheringham *Craighall (NO081176)*
PH2 9DF (0.5m W off B935 Bridge of Earn-Forteviot Rd)
☎Bridge of Earn(0738) 812415
A comfortably furnished farmhouse set amidst peaceful rural countryside just off the B935 west of the village. The house has a relaxed atmosphere and provides good value bed and breakfast accommodation.
3rm(2🅝1hc) (1fb)⊁in all bedrooms ® ✗ sB&Bfr£15
sB&B🅝fr£20 dB&Bfr£25 dB&B🅝fr£30 WB&Bfr£87.50
WBDifr£150.50 LDO 9pm
⊞ CTV 4P ✈ 1000 acres beef mixed sheep ⓔ

FORRES Grampian *Morayshire* Map **14** NJ05

SELECTED

GH 🅠🅠🅠🅠 **Parkmount House Hotel** St Leonards Rd
IV36 0DW ☎(0309) 73312
Closed Xmas & New Year
A charming mid 19th-century town house, with well-kept gardens, has been tastefully converted to offer comfortable, modern accommodation. Bedrooms are bright, spacious and well equipped, all with private bathrooms, and there is a cosy sitting room. A choice of simple, home-cooked dishes is offered in the neatly furnished dining room. Self-drive car hire is available, and there is a warm, friendly atmosphere, ensuring guests of an enjoyable stay.
8⇨🅝 (1fb)⊁in 1 bedroom CTV in all bedrooms ® ✱
sB&B⇨🅝£29-£33 dB&B⇨🅝£43-£50 LDO 5pm
Lic ⊞ 25P ⚘ ▸ 18 special rate car hire is available to guests
Credit Cards 🏧 🏧 ⓔ

FORT WILLIAM Highland *Inverness-shire* Map **14** NN17

GH 🅠🅠 **Benview** Belford Rd PH33 6ER ☎(0397) 702966
Mar-Nov
Situated beside the A82 just north of the town centre, this comfortably appointed family-run guesthouse is a popular base for the visiting holidaymaker. It has a friendly atmosphere and there are two lounges where guests can relax in comfort. The well maintained bedrooms, some with en suite facilities, all have radios and tea-making facilities.

13rm(3⇨3🅝7hc) CTV in 6 bedrooms ® ✗ (ex guide dogs) ✱
sB&B£16-£18 dB&B£32-£36 dB&B⇨🅝£35-£40 WB&B£112-£140 WBDi£160-£189 LDO 5pm
⊞ CTV 20P ⓔ

GH 🅠🅠 **Glenlochy** Nevis Bridge PH33 6PF ☎(0397) 702909
Situated beside the A82 near the entrance to Glen Nevis, this friendly family-run guesthouse stands in its own grounds opposite the distillery. It has been fully modernised and offers good value bed and breakfast accommodation, and is an ideal base for touring and hillwalking.
10rm(8⇨2hc) (2fb)⊁in 2 bedrooms ® ✗ (ex guide dogs)
dB&B£26-£36 dB&B🅝£30-£50 WB&B£91-£140
⊞ CTV 12P ⓔ

GH 🅠🅠 **Guisachan** Alma Rd PH33 6HA ☎(0397) 703797
Closed 23 Dec-3 Jan
This guesthouse with a comfortable lounge and an attractive dining room enjoys an elevated position which affords fine views across the town and Loch Linnhe.
13rm(2⇨9🅝2hc) (3fb) CTV in 8 bedrooms ® ✗ ✱ sB&B£16-£20 sB&B⇨🅝£18-£24 dB&B£34-£38 dB&B⇨🅝£36-£48
LDO 5.30pm
Lic ⊞ CTV 15P

GH 🅠🅠🅠 **Lochview** Heathercroft, Argyll Rd PH33 6RE
☎(0397) 703149
Etr-Oct
A former crofthouse has been modernised and extended to create this comfortably appointed guesthouse which is situated on the hillside above the town, with panoramic views of Loch Linnhe. Smoking is not permitted.
8⇨🅝 ⊁in all bedrooms CTV in all bedrooms ® ✗
dB&B⇨🅝£34-£40
⊞ 8P

GH 🅠🅠 **Orchy Villa** Alma Rd PH33 6HA ☎(0397) 702445
This friendly and well cared for family-run holiday guesthouse is set in an elevated position above the town and offers good value bed and breakfast accommodation.
6hc (4fb)⊁in all bedrooms ® ✗
⊞ CTV 6P

GH 🅠🅠 **Rhu Mhor** Alma Rd PH33 6BP ☎(0397) 702213
Etr-Sep
Many guests return year after year to this well established, family-run guesthouse, situated in a quiet residential area above the town. It has a welcoming atmosphere and offers traditional services and comforts.
7hc (2fb) sB&B£11.75-£12.50 dB&B£23.50-£25 LDO 5pm
⊞ CTV 7P ⓔ

FOVANT Wiltshire Map **04** SU02

INN 🅠🅠 **Cross Keys** SP3 5JH ☎(072270) 284
A coaching inn dating from the 1500s, but mostly built in 1845, nestling in the village of Fovant beneath the military emblems. Public areas are particularly cosy with roaring log fires and friendly proprietors behind the bar. Bedrooms are compact, comfortable and simply appointed. The atmosphere is charming, and the home-made dishes are popular with diners.
4hc (1fb) ✗ (ex guide dogs) ✱ sB&B£17.50 dB&B£35
WB&Bfr£115 ✱ Lunch £7-£16.50alc Dinner £7-£16.50alc
LDO 9pm
⊞ CTV 30P
Credit Cards 🏧 🏧 ⓔ

FOWEY Cornwall & Isles of Scilly Map **02** SX15

GH 🅠🅠 **Ashley House Hotel** 14 Esplanade PL23 1BJ
☎(0726) 832310
Etr-Oct
On a narrow one-way street, close to the seafront, this small private hotel offers bright, sunny bedrooms, comfortably furnished and with some modern facilities. Cosy public areas are

complemented by a small garden and a first-floor sun terrace. A home-cooked evening meal is offered.

6rm(3⇨1♠2hc) (6fb) CTV in all bedrooms ®
✻ (ex guide dogs) ✳ sB&B£20-£25 dB&B⇨♠£40-£50
LDO 6pm
Lic ♨ CTV ✗
Credit Cards ①③

SELECTED

GH ⓆⓆⓆⓆ **Carnethic House** Lambs Barn PL23 1HQ
☎(0726) 833336
Closed Dec-Jan
An elegant Regency manor house surrounded by award-winning gardens, the pride and joy of the proprietor of this smart, comfortable private hotel. The owners have restored and modernised the house and bedrooms are freshly decorated and well furnished and equipped. Public areas are similarly well appointed and offer comfortable, pleasant surroundings. The home-made food is reputed to be very good, and many guests return time and time again. The house is run along the lines of a house party and is extremely popular: early bookings are strongly advised.
8rm(5♠) (2fb) CTV in all bedrooms ®
✻ (ex guide dogs) ✳ sB&B£30-£35 sB&B♠£40-£45
dB&B£40-£45 dB&B♠£45-£55 WB&B£140-£185
WBDi£210-£255 LDO 8pm
Lic ♨ 20P ⚓ ⌒(heated) ✗(grass)badminton, putting, pool table & short tennis
Credit Cards ①②③⑤ⓔ

GH ⓆⓆⓆ **Wheelhouse** 60 Esplanade PL23 1JA
☎(0726) 832452
Mar-Oct rs Nov-Feb
A Victorian terraced house set in an elevated position, with splendid panoramic views over the estuary. Bedrooms are well equipped and individually furnished, and there is a bright, traditional lounge and an attractive front garden.
6hc (1fb) CTV in 4 bedrooms ® ✻ sB&B£14-£16.50 dB&B£28-£33 WB&B£98-£115.50 WBDi£158-£175.50 LDO noon
Lic ♨ CTV ✗ ⓔ

INN ⓆⓆⓆ **King of Prussia** Town Quay PL23 1AT (St Austell Brewery) ☎St Austell(0726) 832450
Dating back to 1765, this inn is linked with a notorious local smuggler. Situated in the quiet village, the inn attracts both locals and tourists; the port itself is full of character and charm, with narrow streets and brightly painted houses. The bedrooms have all recently been superbly refurbished and offer good modern facilities and magnificent sea views over the estuary and quay. The public areas include a basement restaurant, and the young landlord is a sociable and friendly host.
6⇨♠ (4fb)✗in all bedrooms CTV in all bedrooms ®
✻ (ex guide dogs) ✳ sB&B⇨♠fr£25.65 dB&B⇨♠fr£39.90
WB&Bfr£120 ✳ Lunch £1-£7.95 Dinner £1-£7.95 LDO 9.30pm
♨
Credit Cards ①②③

FOWNHOPE Hereford & Worcester Map 03 SO53

GH ⓆⓆⓆ **Bowens Country House** HR1 4PS ☎(0432) 860430
Closed New Year
This beautifully preserved 17th-century house is set on the edge of the village in its own attractive grounds. The comfortable, well equipped accommodation includes two rooms which have been specifically designed and equipped for disabled guests and wheelchairs.
8rm(3⇨♠5hc) Annexe 4⇨♠ (2fb) CTV in all bedrooms ®
✻ (ex guide dogs) ✳ sB&Bfr£19.25 sB&B⇨♠fr£25.50
dB&Bfr£38.50 dB&B⇨♠fr£41 WB&Bfr£116 WBDifr£194.75
LDO 8pm

Lic ♨ 15P nc10yrs ✗(grass)putting
Credit Cards ①③ⓔ
See advertisement on page 159

FOYERS Highland *Invernesshire* Map 14 NH42

GH ⓆⓆⓆ **Foyers Bay House** Lochness IV1 2YB
☎Gorthleck(04563) 624 FAX (04563) 337
Set in 4 acres of grounds overlooking Loch Ness, this lovely Victorian house has been sympathetically refurbished to provide excellent accommodation. Bedrooms, all with private bathrooms, are comfortably appointed and well equipped, and the attractive conservatory café/restaurant overlooking the loch offers snacks and meals all day.
3⇨♠ CTV in all bedrooms ® ✻ (ex guide dogs) ✳
sB&B⇨♠£17.50-£25 dB&B⇨♠£30-£40 WBDi£129.50-£168
LDO 7.30pm
♨ CTV 6P
Credit Cards ①③ⓔ

FRANT East Sussex Map 05 TQ53

GH ⓆⓆⓆ **The Old Parsonage** Frant TN3 9DX ☎(089275) 773
This former rectory dates from 1820 and has been beautifully restored and furnished by the new proprietors, Tony and Mary Dakin. Public rooms capture the atmosphere of earlier times when two Canadian prime ministers were entertained on pilgrimages to the grave of Colonel By who is buried in the churchyard. Bedrooms are spacious and comfortable with a host of extras.
3⇨♠ CTV in all bedrooms ✻ sB&B⇨♠£34-£37
dB&B⇨♠£45-£49
♨ CTV 12P ⓔ

Lambs Barn · Fowey · Cornwall
Tel: (0726) 833336
David & Trisha Hogg

This delightful Regency house, situated in tranquil countryside close to the sea at Fowey, provides gracious accommodation and excellent food. Licensed bar & heated outdoor swimming pool. 1½ acres mature gardens. AA selected in 1991. For FREE brochure write or telephone

Ashley Courtenay Recommended

FRASERBURGH Grampian *Aberdeenshire* Map **15** NJ96

INN Q *Ban-Car* High St AB43 4XL ☎Lonmay(0346)32578
This small family-run roadside inn stands beside the A952 between Peterhead and Fraserburgh. It enjoys a good local reputation for the imaginative food served in the smart little à la carte restaurant. Accommodation is simple and practical.

FRESHWATER

See **WIGHT, ISLE OF**

FRINTON-ON-SEA Essex Map **05** TM21

GH Q **Forde** 18 Queens Rd CO13 9BL ☎(0255) 674758
Closed Dec
A very clean and tidy traditional seaside guesthouse run by friendly proprietors. Facilities are limited, but bedrooms and public areas are comfortable.
6hc (1fb) ✳ sB&B£17.50 dB&B£28 WB&B£96.50
卿 CTV 1P nc5yrs ⓔ

FROGMORE Devon Map **03** SX74

INN QQ **Globe** TQ7 2NR ☎Kingsbridge(0548) 531351
In a rural location 3 miles from Kingsbridge on the A379 Dartmouth road, the Globe is in an excellent position from which to tour this picturesque part of south Devon. Bedrooms are gradually being upgraded and are clean and comfortable. The bars are characterful, the restaurant caters for family budgets and there are many facilities for children.
6rm(2✿4hc) (1fb) CTV in all bedrooms ⓡ sB&Bfr£17 sB&B✿fr£19 dB&Bfr£30 dB&B✿fr£34 WB&Bfr£100 Lunch £4-£12 Dinner £4-£12 LDO 9.30pm
卿 CTV 20P
Credit Cards ①③
See advertisement under KINGSBRIDGE

GAIRLOCH Highland *Ross & Cromarty* Map **14** NG87

GH QQ **Bain's House** Strath IV21 2BZ ☎(0445) 2472
A neat and compact guesthouse located on the main street of this small coastal town.
5hc (1fb) ✳ dB&Bfr£25
卿 CTV 6P sea angling

GH QQQ **Birchwood** IV21 2AH ☎(0445) 2011
Apr-mid Oct
Set in its own elevated grounds overlooking old Gairloch harbour, this friendly and efficiently run holiday guesthouse is tastefully furnished throughout and offers comfortable bed and breakfast accommodation.
6✿ (1fb)✂in all bedrooms ⓡ ✳ dB&B✿£44-£48 WB&B£154-£168
卿 CTV 7P

SELECTED

GH QQQQ **Horisdale House** Strath IV21 2DA
☎(0445) 2151
May-Sep
An attractive modern villa set in its own garden, with delightful views over the bay, located just off the B8021. Bedrooms are airy and well furnished, and the lounge has a welcoming open fire. Many guests return year after year to enjoy the welcoming hospitality and imaginatively prepared food which is served in the pleasant dining room. Non-smokers are especially welcome, and it provides an excellent base from which to explore Wester Ross.
6hc (1fb)✂in all bedrooms ⓡ ✖ sB&Bfr£15 dB&Bfr£28 LDO 9am
卿 10P nc7yrs

GALSTON Strathclyde *Ayrshire* Map **11** NS53

FH QQ Mrs J Bone **Auchencloigh** *(NS535320)* KA4 8NP (5m S off B7037-Scorn Rd) ☎(0563) 820567
Apr-Oct
This well maintained farmhouse sits amidst rolling countryside, with views on clear days of the Ayrshire coast and the Isle of Arran. Mrs Bone is a cheerful and enthusiastic hostess.
2rm (1fb)✂in all bedrooms ⓡ ✖ ✳ sB&B£11.50-£14 dB&B£23-£28 WB&B£80-£98 LDO 4pm
卿 CTV 4P 4✿ sauna 240 acres beef mixed sheep

GARBOLDISHAM Norfolk Map **05** TM08

GH QQQ **Ingleneuk Lodge** Hopton Rd IP22 2RQ
☎(095381) 541
rs Xmas
Modern bungalow set in 10 acres of quiet wooded countryside.
11rm(10✿✿hc) (2fb)✂in all bedrooms CTV in all bedrooms ⓡ sB&B£20-£29 sB&B✿✿£29-£32 dB&B£32.50 dB&B✿✿£45 WB&B£107-£147 WBDi£189-£232 LDO 1pm
Lic 卿 20P
Credit Cards ①②③

GARGRAVE North Yorkshire Map **07** SD95

GH QQ **Kirk Syke** 19 High St BD23 3RA
☎Skipton(0756) 749356
Closed 16 Dec-2 Jan
Situated in the middle of the village beside the main A65 road, this friendly, small, family-run guesthouse offers comfortable and well maintained accommodation. Most rooms have modern en suite facilities, and rooms in the annexe have attractive tiled floors.
6rm(3✿3hc) Annexe 6✿✿✿ CTV in all bedrooms ⓡ ✖ sB&B£25 sB&B✿✿£27 dB&B£40 dB&B✿✿£42 WB&B£140-£180 WBDi£215-£257 LDO 10am
Lic 卿 CTV 12P nc5yrs
Credit Cards ①③

GARSTANG Lancashire Map **07** SD44

FH QQ Mrs J Higginson **Clay Lane Head** *(SD490474)* Cabus, Preston PR3 1WL (2m N on A6) ☎(09952) 3132
Mar-23 Dec
Two miles north of Garstang, this ivy-clad farmhouse stands in front of meadowland on the A6 at Cabus.
3hc ⓡ ✖ (ex guide dogs) ✳ sB&B£16 dB&B£25 WB&B£84
CTV 4P 1✿ 30 acres beef

GATEHOUSE OF FLEET Dumfries & Galloway *Kirkcudbrightshire* Map **11** NX55

GH QQ **Bobbin** 36 High St DG7 2HP ☎(0557) 814229
A neat, well maintained little guesthouse, part of a terraced row in the High Street. The bright accommodation is comfortable, and good value home-cooked dinners are provided; there is also a coffee shop featuring home baking.
7rm(1✿6hc) (3fb) ⓡ LDO 5pm
卿 CTV 8P
Credit Cards ①③

GATWICK AIRPORT (LONDON) West Sussex Map **04** TQ24

GH QQ **Barnwood Hotel** Balcombe Rd, Pound Hill RH10 7RU
☎Crawley(0293) 882709 Telex no 877005
Closed Xmas-New Years Day
A popular family-run hotel on the B2036 south of Gatwick airport. Bedrooms are gradually being upgraded and completely refurbished to a high standard, the best are now on the ground floor. A combined bar and lounge augment the smallish Barn Restaurant. Reception facilities are available 24 hours a day. There are 2 conference rooms and good car parking facilities.

35⇆🐾 (3fb) CTV in all bedrooms ® ✖ (ex guide dogs) ✱
sB&B⇆🐾£40-£50 dB&B⇆🐾£45-£60 LDO 9pm
Lic ◫ 50P
Credit Cards 1 2 3 5

GH Q Q Q **Chalet** 77 Massetts Rd RH6 7EB
☎Horley(0293) 821666 FAX (0293) 821619
6rm(4🐾2hc) Annexe 1🐾 CTV in 6 bedrooms ®
✖ (ex guide dogs) ✱ sB&Bfr£22 sB&B🐾fr£28 dB&B🐾fr£38
◫ CTV 12P
Credit Cards 1 3

GH Q Q Q **Gainsborough Lodge** 39 Massetts Rd RH6 7DT (2m
NE of airport adjacent A23) ☎Horley(0293) 783982
*Gainsborough Lodge is situated close to Horley town centre and
only 1 1/2 miles from Gatwick Airport. Some of the bedrooms are
compact but all have en suite facilities and modern conveniences.
There is a cosy lounge and a garden which guests may use.*
13rm(3⇆10🐾) (3fb) CTV in all bedrooms ® ✖
◫ 16P
Credit Cards 1 3

See advertisement on page 161

GH Q Q **Gatwick Skylodge** London Rd, County Oak
RH11 0PF (2m S of airport on A23) ☎Crawley(0293) 544511
Telex no 878307
Closed 25-29 Dec
*A purpose-built hotel situated close to the airport. The bedrooms
are all well equipped and have en suite facilities. Dinner is
available to guests and there is also an open-plan bar/lounge. Ideal
for a one-night stay.*
51⇆ (7fb) CTV in all bedrooms ® ✖ (ex guide dogs)
LDO 9.15pm
Lic ◫ 60P (£2.35 nightly)
Credit Cards 1 2 3 £

GH |Q||Q||Q| **The Lawn** 30 Massetts Rd RH6 7DE
☎Horley(0293) 775751
Closed Xmas
*A charming Victorian house situated close to Horley town centre.
The bedrooms are bright, well maintained and some feature
original Victorian fireplaces. The owners, Mr and Mrs Stock,
make guests feel really welcome.*
7rm(4♠3hc) CTV in all bedrooms ® dB&B£35 dB&B♠£42
♥♥♥ 10P
Credit Cards |1| |3| £

GH |Q||Q||Q| **Little Foxes** Ifield Woods, Ifield Rd RH11 0JY
☎Crawley(0293) 552430
*A modern bungalow set in 5 acres of grounds, close to the airport.
The spacious bedrooms are well equipped and offer a high degree
of comfort. Breakfast is served in the large dining room and there
is an adjoining lounge. Guests benefit from a courtesy coach
service, free parking for up to 14 days and 24-hour service is
readily available.*
13rm(10⇨♠3hc) (2fb) CTV in all bedrooms ® ⊁ ✱
sB&B⇨♠£45 dB&B£55 dB&B⇨♠£65
♥♥♥ 150P
Credit Cards |1| |2| |3| £

GH |Q||Q| **Massetts Lodge** 28 Massets Rd RH6 7DE
☎Crawley(0293) 782738
*This small, friendly establishment has cosy bedrooms, well
equipped with colour TV, coffee facilities and modern en suites.
Convenient for Gatwick airport, it has limited public areas and a
pleasant dining room.*
8rm(5⇨♠3hc) (2fb) CTV in all bedrooms ®
⊁ (ex guide dogs) sB&B£23 sB&B⇨♠£33 dB&B£35
dB&B⇨♠£41 LDO 7.45pm
♥♥♥ 10P ⊇(heated)
Credit Cards |1| |2| |3| £

GH |Q||Q| **Rosemead** 19 Church Rd RH6 7EY
☎Horley(0293) 784965 FAX (0293) 820438
*A small, family bed and breakfast guesthouse, with freshly
decorated bedrooms and a sound standard of housekeeping.
Breakfast is served in a cheerful dining room.*
6hc (2fb) CTV in all bedrooms ® sB&B£18-£21 dB&B£32-£35
♥♥♥ 10P
Credit Cards |1| |3| £

GH |Q||Q||Q| **Vulcan Lodge** 27 Massetts Rd RH6 7DQ
☎Horley(0293) 771522
*A former farmhouse dating from the late 17th century offers easy
access to both town centre and airport from its very secluded
location off the main road. Individually furnished bedrooms have
been beautifully decorated with style and imagination, and a
comfortable lounge supplements the 'no-smoking' breakfast room.
Forecourt car parking is available, friendly staff provide relaxed
service and the atmosphere is welcoming.*
4rm(3♠1hc) CTV in all bedrooms ® ⊁ ✱ sB&Bfr£22
sB&B♠frf29.50 dB&B♠£38-£40
♥♥♥ 10P (charged)

GH |Q||Q| **Woodlands** 42 Massetts Rd RH6 7DS
☎Horley(0293) 782994 & 776358
*The cosy, well-furnished and equipped accommodation at this
small guesthouse is ideal for travellers using Gatwick Airport. It
has a friendly atmosphere and offers bed and breakfast.*
5♠ (2fb)⊁in all bedrooms CTV in all bedrooms ® ⊁ ✱
sB&B♠frf26 dB&B♠frf36
♥♥♥ 20P (£10 per wk) 2☂ (£15 per wk) nc5yrs £

GAYHURST Buckinghamshire Map **04** SP84

FH |Q||Q| Mrs K Adams **Mill** *(SP852454)* MK16 8LT (1m S off
B526 unclass rd to Haversham)
☎Newport Pagnell(0908) 611489
*A beautiful 17th-century farmhouse, three miles from Newport
Pagnell; the River Ouse runs through the grounds, and fishing is*

*available. Bedrooms are comfortable and all have wash hand
basins and TV. The lounge/dining room is comfortable and the
atmosphere is informal.*
3rm(1⇨♠2hc) (1fb)⊁in 1 bedroom CTV in all bedrooms ®
sB&B£15-£18 sB&B⇨♠£15-£18 dB&B£30-£35
dB&B⇨♠£30-£35 LDO 4pm
♥♥♥ CTV 10P 3☂ ℛ(hard)➜ ∪ 550 acres mixed £

GIGGLESWICK North Yorkshire Map **07** SD86

INN |Q||Q| **Black Horse Hotel** Church St BD24 0BE
☎Settle(0729) 822506
*A secluded village inn dating back to 1663 with well furnished
bedrooms and good home-cooking.*
3rm(1⇨♠2♠) ® ⊁ sB&B⇨♠frf24 dB&B⇨♠frf40 Lunch
£5.50-£8.50alc Dinner £5.50-£10.50alc LDO 8.45pm
♥♥♥ CTV 20P
Credit Cards |1| |3| |5|

GILWERN Gwent Map **03** SO21

FH |Q||Q||Q| Mr B L Harris **The Wenallt** *(SO245138)* NP7 0HP
(Three quarters of a mile S of A465 Gilwern by pass)
☎(0873) 830694
*This 16th-century Welsh longhouse has lovely views of the Usk
Valley. Spacious comfortable bedrooms are provided together with
good public rooms.*
3rm(1⇨♠2hc) Annexe 4rm(1⇨♠3♠) ® ⊁ (ex guide dogs) ✱
sB&B£14.69-£17.62 sB&B⇨♠£21.15 dB&B£29.37
dB&B⇨♠£35.25 WB&B£94.59-£115.15 WBDi£148.05-
£168.62 LDO 6pm
Lic ♥♥♥ CTV 10P 50 acres sheep £

161

GISLINGHAM Suffolk Map **05** TM07

SELECTED

GH QQQQ The Old Guildhall Mill St IP23 8JT
☎Mellis(0379) 783361
Closed Jan
A timber-framed 15th-century guildhall in the centre of the village. While modern facilities have been provided, the distinctive thatched roof and the original features inside have been carefully maintained. Immaculate throughout, reflecting the high standards of proprietors Mr and Mrs Tranter, rooms are all en suite and have comfortable armchairs; there is a small dining room, spacious lounge and a well equipped bar.
3⇌ CTV in all bedrooms Ⓡ sB&B⇌£40 dB&B⇌£50 WB&B£150 WBDi£200 LDO 6pm
Lic 🍽 5P

GLAN-YR-AFON (NEAR CORWEN) Gwynedd Map **06** SJ04

FH Q Mrs G B Jones ***Llawr-Bettws*** *(SJ016424)* Bala Rd
☎Maerdy(049081) 224
This stone-built farmhouse dates back to 1918 and is situated close to the A494 Bala road, about 2 miles south of its junction with the A5, at Druid. It offers simple but sound accommodation and a friendly atmosphere.
4hc (2fb) ✗ LDO 7pm
CTV 3P 18 acres mixed beef sheep

GLASBURY Powys Map **03** SO13

FH QQ Mrs B Eckley ***Fforddfawr*** *(SO192398)* HR3 5PT
☎(04974) 332
Apr-Oct
On the B4350 Brecon road just 3 miles west of Hay-on-Wye, this 17th-century stone-built farmhouse is bordered by the river Wye. Very much a working farm, there are spacious lounges and comfortable bedrooms.
2hc Ⓡ ✗
CTV 4P 280 acres mixed

GLASGOW Strathclyde *Lanarkshire* Map **11** NS56

GH QQQ ***Dalmeny Hotel*** 62 St Andrews Dr, Nithsdale Cross G41 5EZ ☎041-427 1106 & 6288
Closed 1 wk New Year
The bedrooms are comfortable and thoughfully equipped at this small, family-run hotel, situated in a residential area on the city's southern side. The attractive public rooms, including a restaurant open to non-residents, highlight the house's period features.
8rm(2⇌1↱5hc) CTV in all bedrooms Ⓡ
Lic 🍽 CTV 20P
Credit Cards [1] [2] [3]

GH QQ ***Kelvin Private Hotel*** 15 Buckingham Ter, Hillhead G12 8EB ☎041-339 7143
A terraced house just off the main road on the north west side of the city, close to the Botanical Gardens. Enthusiastically managed, it is popular with visiting business people.
15hc (3fb) CTV in all bedrooms Ⓡ
🍽 5P

Street plans of certain towns and cities will be found in a separate section at the back of the book.

GLASTONBURY Somerset Map **03** ST53

SELECTED

FH QQQQ Mrs J I Nurse **Berewall Farm Country Guest House** *(ST516375)* Cinnamon Ln BA6 8LL
☎(0458) 31451 due to change to 831451
Don't expect antiques or old masters at this farmhouse, south of Glastonbury Tor with glorious views over the surrounding countryside. The bedrooms are simply furnished, all en suite, with colour TV and tea-making facilities. Mrs Nurse cooks and a choice is offered and ordered from a blackboard in the lounge. Guests may bring their own horses; Mrs Nurse owns about 6 which can be hired. Rides can be arranged to suit ability, and an outdoor pool and hard tennis court are available to guests.
9⇌↱ (3fb) CTV in all bedrooms Ⓡ ✗ (ex guide dogs) ✱ sB&B⇌↱fr£21 dB&B⇌↱fr£37 WBDifr£175
LDO 7.30pm
Lic 🍽 12P ⩍ 𝒫(hard) U 30 acres grazing
Credit Cards [1] [2] [3]

FH QQQ Mrs H T Tinney **Cradlebridge** *(ST477385)* BA16 9SD ☎(0458) 31827 due to change to 831827
Closed Xmas
Under the expert care of Mrs Tinney, the accommodation here is in a purpose-built bungalow next to the farmhouse. The two lovely bedrooms have en suite facilities and each has a sitting area and patio.
2↱ Annexe 3hc (2fb) CTV in 2 bedrooms Ⓡ ✗ sB&B£17.50-£20 sB&B↱£17.50-£20 dB&B£30-£35 dB&B↱£30-£35 WB&B£180-£210
🍽 6P 200 acres dairy Ⓔ

GLENCOE Highland *Argyllshire* Map **14** NN15

GH QQ Scorrybreac PA39 4HT ☎Ballachulish(08552) 354
This friendly, family-run guesthouse is set in its own peaceful garden above the village and enjoys a beautiful outlook over Loch Leven. It offers good value accommodation and is a popular base for tourists and climbers alike. This is a no-smoking establishment.
5hc (2fb)⊁in all bedrooms CTV in 1 bedroom TV in 1 bedroom Ⓡ ✱ sB&B£13-£15 dB&B£24-£26 WB&B£70-£77 WBDi£110-£120 LDO 10am
🍽 CTV 8P Ⓔ

GLENMAVIS Strathclyde *Lanarkshire* Map **11** NS76

FH Q Mrs M Dunbar ***Braidenhill*** *(NS742673)* ML6 0PJ
☎Glenboig(0236) 872319
The friendly, welcoming attention of Mrs Dunbar awaits guests at her 300-year-old farmhouse. The comfortable, modest accommodation includes a lounge and dining-room.
3hc (1fb) Ⓡ ✗
🍽 CTV 4P 50 acres arable mixed

GLOUCESTER Gloucestershire Map **03** SO81

GH Q Claremont 135 Stroud Rd GL1 5LJ ☎(0452) 529540 & 529270
This Edwardian terraced house situated on the Stroud road, close to the city centre, offers bed and breakfast in well equipped bedrooms which are fitted with double glazing and central heating. Mrs Powell has built up a regular clientèle during her 23 years in the city.
7hc (2fb) CTV in all bedrooms Ⓡ ✗ ✱ sB&B£12-£15.50 dB&B£24-£27 WB&Bfr£84
🍽 CTV 6P Ⓔ

Visit your local AA Shop.

GH Q Lulworth 12 Midland Rd GL1 4UF ☎(0452) 21881 due to change to 821881
Situated 100 yards from the leisure centre, this Victorian semidetached house offers a good bed and breakfast service in modestly appointed but well equipped bedrooms, and at reasonable prices.
8rm(1⇨1♠6hc)(2fb) CTV in all bedrooms ® ✱
sB&B⇨♠£15-£20 dB&B£28-£32 dB&B⇨♠£32-£34
♚ CTV 14P

GOATHLAND North Yorkshire Map **08** NZ80

GH Q Q Q Heatherdene Hotel YO22 5AN
☎Whitby(0947) 86334
Apr-Dec
Situated on the fringe of the unspoilt village, this spacious house offers comfortable accommodation, with fine views over the moors.
6rm(2⇨2♠2hc)(3fb)⚡in 1 bedroom CTV in all bedrooms ®
LDO 4pm
Lic ♚ CTV 10P solarium

GOREY

See **JERSEY under CHANNEL ISLANDS**

GORRAN HAVEN Cornwall & Isles of Scilly Map **02** SX04

INN Q Q Llawnroc PL26 6NU ☎Mevagissey(0726) 843461
Closed Xmas & Boxing Day
A solid stone-built inn standing in its own grounds with views over the peaceful village and bay. There is a choice of 2 comfortable bars or the garden in which to enjoy a drink. Overnight guests find well equipped spacious bedrooms in a modern extension, and they have the use of a private lounge.
6rm(3⇨3♠)(2fb) CTV in all bedrooms ® ✖ (ex guide dogs)
sB&B⇨♠£20-£26 dB&B⇨♠£32-£44 WB&B£112-£140 Bar
Lunch £4.60-£8.35 Dinner £5.30-£11.90&alc LDO 9.30pm
♚ CTV 40P table tennis pool
Credit Cards ① ② ③ ⑤ ⓔ
See advertisement under MEVAGISSEY

GRAMPOUND Cornwall & Isles of Scilly Map **02** SW94

⟨⟩ GH Q Q Perran House Fore St TR2 4RS
☎St Austell(0726) 882066
There is a cheery welcome at this semidetached house beside the A390. Bedrooms are compact but well presented and equipped. Visitors can enjoy a cream tea here in the summer, on the patio when it is fine, otherwise indoors with a chance to admire John Sharman's collection of diecast model cars.
5rm(2⇨1♠2hc)(1fb)⚡in all bedrooms CTV in all bedrooms
® ✖ (ex guide dogs) sB&B£12-£14 dB&B£24-£28
dB&B⇨♠£26-£33 WB&B£80-£110
♚ 8P
Credit Cards ① ③ ⓔ

GRANDES ROCQUES

See **GUERNSEY under CHANNEL ISLANDS**

GRANGE-OVER-SANDS Cumbria Map **07** SD47

GH Q Q Q *Elton Private Hotel* Windermere Rd LA11 6EQ
☎(05395) 32838
A short distance from the shops and railway station, this family-run house has very well appointed bedrooms, most with en suite facilities, and all with colour television and tea-making facilities. There is a cosy first floor lounge and a comfortable dining room.
7rm(5⇨3♠2hc)(3fb) CTV in all bedrooms ® ✖ LDO 2pm
Lic ♚ CTV ✗

Street plans of certain towns and cities
will be found in a separate section
at the back of the book.

SELECTED

GH [Q][Q][Q][Q] **Greenacres** Lindale LA11 6LP (2m N)
☎(05395) 34578
Closed 15 Nov-Dec
*A charming 19th-century cottage, tastefully modernised and
extended, providing accommodation of a very high standard.
It is situated in the village of Lindale on the B5277, about two
miles from the town. The attractive bedrooms all have private
bathrooms, colour TV and tea-making facilities. There is a
very comfortable lounge, and a small conservatory adjoining
the cosy dining room. Parking facilities are provided.*
5rm(4⇌1♠) Annexe 1⇌ (1fb) CTV in all bedrooms ® ✹
sB&B⇌♠£25-£30 dB&B⇌♠£38-£48 WB&B£193-£210
WBDi£266.50-£283.50 LDO 3pm
Lic 🕮 CTV 6P ②

GRANTOWN-ON-SPEY Highland *Morayshire* Map **14** NJ02

SELECTED

GH [Q][Q][Q][Q] **Culdearn House** Woodlands Ter PH26 3JU
☎(0479) 2106
Feb-Oct
*Set in a quiet residential area on the southern fringe of the
town, this delightful Victorian house has been substantially
refurbished by the resident owners. A distinctly Scottish
atmosphere prevails, with welcoming log fires in winter. The
tastefully appointed sitting room is the ideal setting for a quiet
drink and convivial conversation. A 3-course dinner is served,
offering well prepared traditional Scottish fare based on fresh
local produce such as lamb, beef, venison, salmon and trout,
with a modestly priced wine list. Bedrooms, all with private
bathrooms, are bright, airy, well equipped and offer
impeccable standards of housekeeping and maintenance.*
9rm(2⇌7♠) (1fb) CTV in all bedrooms ®
✹ (ex guide dogs) sB&B⇌♠£35-£45 dB&B⇌♠£70-£90
(incl dinner) WBDi£229-£285 LDO 6pm
Lic 🕮 9P
Credit Cards [1][3] ②

GH [Q][Q][Q] **Dar-Il-Hena** Grant Rd PH26 3LA ☎(0479) 2929
Etr-Oct
*This charming Victorian house stands in its own extensive grounds,
enjoying an elevated position in a quiet residential road close to the
centre of town. Wood panelling is a feature of the spacious,
comfortable accommodation, and good home cooking is provided.*
7hc (3fb) ® ✳ sB&Bfr£14 dB&Bfr£28 WBDifr£140
🕮 CTV 10P ♨

GH [Q][Q] *Dunallan* Woodside Av PH26 3JN ☎(0479) 2140
May-Nov
*A welcoming atmosphere prevails at this family-run guesthouse
situated in a residential area. It offers traditional services and
comforts, and provides good value accommodation.*
6hc (2fb)⊁in 3 bedrooms ® ✹ (ex guide dogs) LDO 4pm
🕮 CTV 5P

SELECTED

GH [Q][Q][Q][Q] **Garden Park** Woodside Av PH26 3JN
☎(0479) 3235
*Set in its own attractive gardens in a quiet residential area
close to the town centre, this delightful Victorian house has
been sympathetically extended and modernised to provide
comfortable accommodation. Bedrooms, although compact,
are bright and cheerful with en suite facilities and many rooms
have lovely views over pine forests to the Cromdale hills.
There are 2 comfortable lounges, one with TV and the other*

---

*well stocked with books. Enjoyable home cooking using fresh
ingredients is served in the smart dining room.*
5rm(2⇌3♠) ® ✹ sB&B⇌♠£24.20-£27
dB&B⇌♠£35.80-£38 WB&B£117.60-£123.30
WBDi£168.90-£178.50 LDO 5pm
Lic 🕮 CTV 8P nc12yrs

GH [Q][Q][Q] **Kinross House** Woodside Av PH26 3JR
☎(0479) 2042
Mar-Oct
*This attractive Victorian house is situated in a quiet residential
area within easy reach of the town centre and the River Spey. It
has a friendly atmosphere and provides comfortable
accommodation with well equipped bedrooms, some of which have
en suite facilities. A no-smoking policy prevails.*
7rm(4♠3hc) (2fb)⊁in all bedrooms CTV in all bedrooms ®
✹ (ex guide dogs) sB&B£16.50-£19 dB&B£31-£36
dB&B♠£37-£42 WB&B£108.50-£147 WBDi£175-£213
LDO 4pm
Lic 🕮 6P nc7yrs ②

GH [Q][Q] **Pines Hotel** Woodside Av PH26 3JR ☎(0479) 2092
*Situated in a peaceful residential area, this small family-run
guesthouse offers good value practical accommodation to the
touring holidaymaker.*
9rm(2♠7hc) (3fb) CTV in all bedrooms ® sB&Bfr£14
dB&Bfr£28 dB&B♠fr£36 WBDifr£150 LDO 3pm
Lic 🕮 9P ②

GH [Q][Q] **Umaria** Woodlands Ter PH26 3JU ☎(0479) 2104
Closed Nov-Dec
*A well maintained Victorian house set in its own garden at the
southern edge of the town. It has a relaxed atmosphere and offers
comfortable appointments and good home cooking.*
8hc (3fb)⊁in all bedrooms ® sB&B£18 dB&B£32-£36
WB&B£105-£110 WBDi£150-£160 LDO 4.30pm
Lic 🕮 CTV 9P croquet ②

GRASMERE Cumbria Map **11** NY30

GH [Q][Q][Q] **Bridge House Hotel** Stock Ln LA22 9SN
☎(09665) 425 due to change to (05394) 35425
mid Mar-mid Nov
*An attractive, family-owned detached house set in its own gardens
right in the centre of the village, by the 13th-century church, its
grounds bordering on to the River Rothay. The house is well
furnished throughout ; all the bedrooms are comfortable, most with
private bathrooms. A five-course evening meal is available in the
pleasant dining room, and there is a comfortable lounge.*
12rm(10⇌♠2hc) CTV in all bedrooms ® ✹ sB&B⇌♠£37-
£42 dB&B⇌♠£74-£84 (incl dinner) WBDi£210-£265
LDO 7pm
Lic 🕮 20P nc5yrs
Credit Cards [1][3]

GH [Q][Q] **Lake View** Lake View Dr LA22 9TD ☎(09665) 384
due to change to (05394) 35384
Mar-Nov rs Dec-Feb
*This small guesthouse, positioned close to the village centre yet
overlooking meadowland towards the lake and fells, has a friendly
and relaxing atmosphere and also gardens in which to enjoy the
peaceful surroundings.*
6rm(3♠3hc) ® sB&B£21-£25 dB&B£42-£50 dB&B♠£50
WB&B£140-£169 WBDi£207-£226 LDO noon
CTV 11P nc12yrs

GH [Q][Q][Q] **Raise View** Whitebridge LA22 9RQ ☎(09665) 215
due to change to (05394) 353215
Apr-Oct
*This attractive and immaculate Lakeland house is situated on the
edge of the village and enjoys delightful views of the surrounding
countryside. It is reached by turning off at the Swan Hotel on the
A591.*

6rm(4♪2hc)(1fb) ® ⋈ ✳ dB&Bfr£13 dB&B♪fr£15
뻬 CTV 6P nc5yrs

GRASSINGTON North Yorkshire Map **07** SE06

GH Q Q Q **Ashfield House Hotel** BD23 5AE ☎(0756) 752584
early Feb-Oct
*A charming 17th-century house situated in a secluded location, just
off the village square. The house is full of character and charm,
and although centrally heated, it also features wood-burning fires
in its two comfortable, beamed lounges. Bedrooms are attractively
decorated and well furnished with antique-style furniture. Most
bedrooms have modern en suite facilities and all have colour TV.
The small dining room, in which excellent home-cooked dinners
can be sampled, is very attractively appointed, with polished
wooden tables and fresh flowers. Spacious lawns and gardens at
the rear can be used by guests, and there are also private car-
parking facilities.*
7rm(5♪2hc) CTV in all bedrooms ® ⋈ ✳ dB&B£45
dB&B♪£46-£53 WBDi£208-£235 LDO 5.30pm
Lic 뻬 7P nc5yrs

GH Q Q **The Lodge** 8 Wood Ln BD23 5LU ☎(0756) 752518
Mar-Oct rs Dec
*The Lodge is a pleasant family-owned and run guesthouse just a
short walk from the centre of the village.*
8rm(1⇋7hc)(1fb) TV in 1 bedroom ® LDO 2pm
뻬 CTV 7P

GRAVESEND Kent Map **05** TQ67

GH Q Q **The Cromer** 194 Parrock St DA12 1EW
☎(0474) 361935
Closed 24 Dec-2 Jan
*This friendly, Victorian-style establishment has well maintained
accommodation and a delightful, well appointed dining room.
There is also a cosy, comfortable lounge.*
11rm(1⇋10hc)(3fb) CTV in all bedrooms ⋈
뻬 CTV 15P nc9yrs
Credit Cards ③

GH Q Q Q **Overcliffe Hotel** 15-16 The Overcliffe DA11 0EF
☎(0474) 322131 Telex no 965117 FAX (0474) 536737
*This well run hotel offers a good standard of well equipped
accommodation which is nicely appointed annexe rooms.
There is a pleasant restaurant and bar.*
19♪ Annexe 10⇋♪ (1fb) CTV in all bedrooms ® ✳
sB&B⇋♪£56-£60 dB&B⇋♪£64-£70 LDO 9.30pm
Lic 뻬 45P
Credit Cards ① ② ③ ⑤

GREAT Placenames incorporating the word 'Great', such as
Gt Yarmouth, will be found under the actual placename, ie
Yarmouth.

GREENGAIRS Strathclyde *Lanarkshire* Map **11** NS77

FH Q Q Mrs E C Hunter **Easter Glentore** *(NS813717)*
ML6 7TJ (on B803) ☎(023683) 243
*Situated six miles northeast of Airdrie on the B803, this small but
well maintained farmhouse lies amidst open countryside, with fine
views of the Trossachs mountains to the north on clear days. The
proprietor is cheerful and enthusiastic, and the house is nicely
decorated.*
2hc (1fb) ® ⋈ ✳ sB&B£14.50-£16.50 dB&B£27-£30
WB&Bfr£85 WBDifr£135.50 LDO 2pm
뻬 CTV 6P nc3yrs 245 acres beef sheep ⑤

GREENHEAD Northumberland Map **12** NY66

FH 🅠🅠 Mrs P Staff **Holmhead** *(NY659661)* Hadrians Wall
CA6 7HY ☎Brampton(06977) 47402
Closed 19 Dec-9 Jan
*A traditional Northumbrian farmhouse situated on the Roman
wall, reached by a long, gated road and overlooked by the
crumbling ruin of Thirlwall Castle. The house is comfortably
furnished, and there is an excellent selection of breakfast dishes.*
4🐾 (1fb)⚡in all bedrooms ⑧ 💢 ✱ dB&B🐾£39.50
WB&B£117 WBDi£225.50 LDO 3pm
Lic ⁂ CTV 6P ✦ table tennis 300 acres breeding sheep cattle
Credit Cards ①②③ ⓔ

GRETNA (WITH GRETNA GREEN) Dumfries & Galloway
Dumfriesshire Map **11** NY36

GH 🅠🅠🅠 **The Beeches** Loanworth Rd CA6 5EP
☎Gretna(0461) 37448
Closed 8 Dec-14 Jan
*In a peaceful location on the fringe of the town, overlooking the
Solway Firth, this converted farmhouse offers attractive bedrooms
and an inviting lounge/dine room. The Beeches is a totally non-smoking
house.*
2🐾 (1fb)⚡in all bedrooms CTV in all bedrooms ⑧ 💢
dB&B🐾£27-£32 WB&B£94-£110
⁂ CTV 4P nc10yrs

GH 🅠 **Greenlaw** CA6 5DU ☎Gretna(0461) 38361
*Situated between Gretna and Gretna Green, within walking
distance of the Old Smithy, this red-brick detached house offers
compact, fresh accommodation and a friendly welcome.*
8hc (1fb) CTV in 6 bedrooms ⑧ ✱ sB&B£14 dB&B£24
⁂ CTV 12P 1🐾 ⓔ

GH 🅠🅠 **Surrone House** Annan Rd CA6 5DL
☎Gretna(0461) 38341
*Managed by the friendly resident proprietors, this small hotel
offers well appointed bedrooms, comfortable lounges and good
value evening meals.*
6rm(5⇨🐾1hc) (4fb) CTV in all bedrooms ⑧ LDO 8pm
Lic ⁂ CTV 16P

GREVE DE LECQ BAY
See **JERSEY under CHANNEL ISLANDS**

GRINDON Staffordshire Map **07** SK05

GH 🅠🅠🅠 **Porch Farmhouse** ST13 7IP ☎Onecote(05388) 545
*Overlooking the Manifold valley, this charming 400-year-old stone
cottage provides a warm welcome and home-cooked country fayre.
The proprietors are keen walkers and have many guidebooks to
peruse in the comfortable lounge.*
3rm(2🐾1hc) CTV in all bedrooms ⑧
3P nc5yrs

GROUVILLE
See **JERSEY under CHANNEL ISLANDS**

GUERNSEY
See **CHANNEL ISLANDS**

GUILDFORD Surrey Map **04** SU94

GH 🅠🅠 **Blanes Court Hotel** Albury Rd GU1 2BT
☎(0483) 573171 FAX (0483) 32780
Closed 1wk Xmas
*Located in a residential area with parking to the front and an
attractive conservatory and garden to the rear. The bedrooms vary
in size and décor but are equipped with modern facilities, most with
private bathrooms.*
20rm(4⇨🐾10🐾6hc) (3fb) CTV in all bedrooms ⑧ ✱ sB&B£25-
£30 sB&B⇨🐾£40-£50 dB&B£45 dB&B⇨🐾£55-£60
WB&Bfr£180

Lic ⁂ CTV 22P
Credit Cards ①②③ ⓔ

GH 🅠🅠 **Quinns Hotel** 78 Epsom Rd GU1 2BX ☎(0483) 60422
Telex no 859754 FAX (0483) 578551
*Situated close to the town centre, this guesthouse provides modest
but well equipped rooms, a comfortable lounge and ample car
parking.*
10rm(7⇨🐾3hc) (2fb) CTV in all bedrooms ⑧ 💢 ✱ sB&B£38-
£48 sB&B⇨🐾£48-£56 dB&B£57-£68 dB&B⇨🐾£68-£72
LDO 6pm
⁂ CTV 14P
Credit Cards ①②③⑤ ⓔ

GUNNISLAKE Cornwall & Isles of Scilly Map **02** SX47

GH 🅠🅠🅠 **Hingston House Country Hotel** St Anns Chapel
PL18 9HB ☎Tavistock(0822) 832468
*A late-Georgian house surrounded by well kept gardens in an
elevated position affording breathtaking views of the Tamar
Valley. Bedrooms are comfortable, if simply furnished and
decorated, and most have private bathrooms. The spacious lounge
is full of character and well stocked with books and board games.
There is also a cosy bar, and a set meal is served in the restaurant.*
10rm(8🐾2hc) (1fb) CTV in all bedrooms ⑧ ✱ sB&B£22.50-
£24.50 sB&B🐾£28-£30 dB&B£37-£41 dB&B🐾£46-£50
WB&B£129.50-£196 WBDi£220.50-£287 LDO 7pm
Lic ⁂ CTV 12P croquet, putting green
Credit Cards ①③ ⓔ

GWAUN VALLEY Dyfed Map **02** SN03

FH 🅠🅠🅠🅠 Mr P Heard & Mrs M J Heard **Tregynon
Country Farmhouse Hotel** *(SN054345)* SA65 9TU (4m E of
Pontfaen, off unclass road joining B 4313)
☎Newport(0239) 820531 FAX (0239) 820808
Closed 2wks winter
*This secluded 16th-century farmhouse situated in the
picturesque Gwaun Valley has been carefully converted to
provide very comfortable accommodation. The older
bedrooms in the main house are somewhat small, but the 5
stable rooms are spacious and furnished to a high standard
with pine. The restaurant enjoys an excellent local reputation,
with wholefood and vegetarian dishes much in evidence.*
3🐾 Annexe 5⇨ (4fb) CTV in all bedrooms ⑧ 💢
dB&B⇨🐾£44-£57 WB&B£154-£199.50 WBDi£230-£275
LDO 6pm
Lic ⁂ 20P 10 acres sheep
Credit Cards ①③

HADDINGTON Lothian *East Lothian* Map **12** NT57

FH 🅠🅠 Mrs K Kerr **Barney Mains** *(NT523764)* Barney
Mains EH41 3SA (off A1, 1m S of Haddington)
☎Athelstaneford(062088) 310 FAX (062088) 639
Apr-Oct
*This large period farmhouse sits in an elevated position well off the
A1 east of Haddington and commands fine panoramic views in all
directions, particularly northwards towards the Firth of Forth. The
bedrooms are large and airy, there is a comfortable lounge and a
dining room where breakfast is taken around a communal table.*
3rm ⚡in all bedrooms ⑧ 💢 (ex guide dogs) ✱ sB&B£15-£20
dB&B£24-£36 WB&B£84-£121
CTV 8P 580 acres arable beef sheep

See the regional maps of popular holiday
areas at the back of the book.

HADLEIGH Suffolk Map **05** TM04

GH Q Q **Odds & Ends** 131 High St IP7 5EJ
☎Ipswich(0473) 822032
A 16th-century town house with Victorian additions and a walled garden in the centre of Hadleigh. The restaurant, spread over 3 rooms, is full of charm and character, with an open fire range, flagstone floors and harmonious furnishings, serving freshly made appetising meals. There are comfortably furnished bedrooms on the first floor with a further 3 through the garden which cater well for the disabled.
6rm(2⇔4hc) Annexe 3♠ CTV in all bedrooms ® sB&B£18-£20 sB&B⇔♠£28-£32 dB&B£32-£36 dB&B⇔♠£35-£40 LDO 5.30pm
♨ 3P nc8yrs
Credit Cards 1 3 £

HALFORD Warwickshire Map **04** SP24

INN Q Q **Halford Bridge** Fosse Way CV36 5BN
☎Stratford on Avon(0789) 740382
This spacious Cotswold stone road-house, situated on the A429, offers pretty, well equipped bedrooms and public areas that have character. A wide choice of food is available in either the bars or the dining room.
6hc (1fb) CTV in all bedrooms ® ✖ (ex guide dogs) ✱
sB&B£17.50-£35 dB&B£35 ✱ Lunch £6.50-£13.50alc Dinner £7.25-£14.75alc LDO 9pm
50P
Credit Cards 1 3

This guide is updated annually – make sure you use an up-to-date edition.

Surrone House

ANNAN ROAD, GRETNA
Tel: 0461-38341

Situated in the country village of Gretna. All bedrooms have their own private bathroom and TV and are very comfortable and QUIET. Catering for breakfast and evening meals, all our produce is home grown and freshly prepared. Many facilities available locally, while the English Lakes – South West Scotland – The Borders – Kielder Forest and Dam make excellent day visits.

Quinns Hotel
Guildford's Country House Hotel

78 Epsom Road, Guildford, Surrey GU1 2BX
Tel: (0483) 60422 Telex: 859754 MHANCO Fax: (0483) 578551

This is a small, select hotel where the resident proprietors ensure a high standard of personal service. The satisfaction of our guests is of paramount importance to us. The restful atmosphere will result in a pleasant and relaxed stay in Guildford. All the bedrooms are comfortable and individually decorated, each with colour TV and direct dial telephone, many are en suite. Ideal for London's Gatwick and Heathrow airports via the M25 or direct rail link from Guildford to Gatwick and rail/bus to Heathrow.

Blanes Court Hotel

Albury Road, *off Epsom Road,* Guildford, Surrey
Telephone: (0483) 573171

Quietly situated, elegant accommodation with mostly en suite facilities. Convenient for Gatwick and Heathrow airports via M25. Direct rail link from Guildford to Gatwick and rail bus to Heathrow. Lovely sun room and garden with cosy bar. Ample parking.

HALLWORTHY Cornwall & Isles of Scilly Map **02** SX18

INN Q **Wilsey Down** PL32 9SH ☎(08406) 205
This fully licensed free house stands on the A395, 10 miles from Launceston. The accommodation is comfortable and bar meals are served.
6hc (2fb)⊁in all bedrooms TV in 1 bedroom ® ✹ ✳
sB&B£15.30 dB&B£31 WB&B£107 ✳ Lunch £8-£10alc Dinner £15-£20alc
CTV 10P nc12yrs pool table darts ⓛ

HALSTOCK Dorset Map **03** ST50

See also Yeovil
GH QQQ **Halstock Mill** BA22 9SJ
☎Corscombe(0935) 891278
Closed Dec
An attractive 17th-century cornmill, quietly situated in 10 acres of garden and paddocks. Tastefully converted, it now provides individually furnished bedrooms, all with en suite facilities. The lounge and dining room retain many original features including beams and fireplaces. Fresh local produce and some home-grown fruit and vegetables are served at dinner.
4� CTV in all bedrooms ® sB&B➪fr£22 dB&B➪£40-£44 WB&Bfr£126 WBDifr£212 LDO am
Lic ♨ 20P nc5yrs
Credit Cards ① ② ③ ⓛ

HALTWHISTLE Northumberland Map **12** NY76

GH QQ **Ashcroft** NE49 0DA ☎(0434) 320213
Closed 23 Dec-2 Jan
A large comfortable house with good furnishings, situated on the edge of the village. The accommodation is spacious, and friendly service is provided by the resident owners.
6hc (3fb)⊁in all bedrooms ✹ ✳ dB&B£26-£30
♨ CTV 15P croquet lawn ⓛ

FH QQ Mrs J I Laidlow **Ald White Craig** *(NY713649)*
Shield Hill NE49 9NW ☎(0434) 320565
This is an attractive and comfortable farmhouse with very pleasant bedrooms and a cosy lounge. A good standard of hospitality is provided by the resident owner.
3rm(1➪2🐾) ⊁in all bedrooms CTV in all bedrooms ®
✹ (ex guide dogs) dB&B➪🐾fr£37
♨ 3P nc60 acres stock rearing rare breeds ⓛ

SELECTED

FH QQQQ Mrs J Brown **Broomshaw Hill** *(NY706654)*
Willia Rd NE49 9NP ☎(0434) 320866
Apr-Oct
A delightful stone-built farmhouse along a country lane to the north side of the village, beautifully furnished and very comfortable. There are three pretty bedrooms with good facilities, and the lounge is a perfect place in which to relax. A warm and friendly welcome is extended by the owner, Mrs Brown.
3hc (1fb) CTV in all bedrooms ® dB&B£28-£30
WB&B£95-£100 WBDi£140-£145 LDO 10am
♨ CTV 4P 2🐾 7 acres livestock horses ⓛ

HALWELL Devon Map **03** SX75

GH Q **Stanborough Hundred Hotel** TQ9 7JG
☎East Allington(054852) 236
20 Mar-15 Oct
This charming, small hotel stands in sheltered gardens in an elevated position between Totnes and Kingsbridge, near a Bronze Age campsite. A friendly welcome awaits the visitor, who will enjoy splendid views of Dartmoor and the coast.

5rm(3➪2hc) (2fb) CTV in all bedrooms ® ✹ (ex guide dogs)
sB&B£19.50 dB&B£39 dB&B➪£45 WB&B£115 WBDi£180
LDO 6.30pm
Lic ♨ CTV 10P nc5yrs ⓛ

HAMPTON-IN-ARDEN West Midlands Map **04** SP28

GH QQ **Cottage** Kenilworth Rd B92 0LW
☎Hampton In Arden(06755) 2323
Guests are made very welcome at this friendly guesthouse within easy reach of the M6. Rooms are generally compact, but very attractively decorated and furnished with some thoughtful finishing touches.
7rm(2➪🐾5hc) (1fb) CTV in all bedrooms ® ✳ sB&B£16-£18
sB&B➪🐾£24-£25 dB&B£32-£36 dB&B➪🐾£36-£40
WB&B£105-£150
♨ CTV 14P ⓛ

HAMSTERLEY Co Durham Map **12** NZ13

GH QQQ **Grove House** Hamsterley Forest DL13 1NL
☎Witton-Le-Wear(038888) 203
Closed Aug & Xmas & New Year
Situated in the heart of Hamsterley Forest, this charming house, once a shooting lodge, will appeal to those seeking peace and tranquillity and will appeal to lovers of wildlife. Now the home of Helene and Russell Close, Grove House offers comfortable, attractive accommodation in which to relax. From Hamsterley Village follow the signs to Hamsterley Forest and Redburn, and then take the forest road for about 3 miles to Grove House.
4hc ⊁in all bedrooms ® ✹ LDO 7.30pm
♨ CTV 8P nc6yrs ⓛ

HANLEY CASTLE Hereford & Worcester Map **03** SO84

SELECTED

GH QQQQ **Old Parsonage Farm** WR8 0BU
☎Hanley Swan(0684) 310124
Closed 11 Dec-2 Feb
Old Parsonage farm is an 18th-century guesthouse which treats visitors as guests of the family. Surrounded by beautiful countryside it is situated close to many places of interest. Accommodation is spacious and comfortable with en suite facilities and two delightful sitting rooms. Ann Addison's meals are a highlight of the stay and as Tony Addison runs his own wine business, there is an interesting and extensive wine list.
3➪ (1fb) TV in 1 bedroom ✹ sB&B➪£28.50
dB&B➪£40-£45 WB&B£140-£157.50 WBDi£235-£250
Lic ♨ CTV 6P 1🐾 nc8yrs
Credit Cards ② ⓛ

HANMER Clwyd Map **07** SJ44

FH Q C Sumner & F Williams-Lee **Buck** *(SJ435424)* SY14 7LX
☎(094874) 339
This 16th-century, timber-framed farmhouse stands on the A525, midway between Wrexham and Whitchurch, amid eight acres of gardens and woodland. The cuisine served here reflects the international travels of the proprietors.
4hc (1fb)⊁in all bedrooms ✹ (ex guide dogs) LDO previous day
♨ CTV 12P 8 acres non-working

HARBERTON Devon Map **03** SX75

GH QQQ **Ford Farm** TQ9 7SJ ☎Totnes(0803) 863539
A 17th-century house ideally suited to the tourist, with 3 comfortable bedrooms (all in an en suite shower), individually decorated and furnished on traditional lines. The proprietor (a Master Sommelier) and his wife are experienced restauranteurs, and have created a cosy little retreat with rural style which blends

nicely with the pretty village setting. The comfortable lounge is full of character, and the beamed dining room has an open fire and hearty full English breakfasts are served. There is a private car park and a small secluded garden with a stream.

3rm(1🌣2hc) sB&Bfr£18 dB&B£34-£37 dB&Bſ£36-£40 ₪ CTV 6P nc12yrs £

HARLECH Gwynedd Map **06** SH53

SELECTED

GH 🔲🔲🔲🔲 **Castle Cottage Hotel** Pen Llech LL46 2YL ☎(0766) 780479

A quaint little hotel, only a stone's throw from the famous castle and recently taken over by new owners, offers small but comfortable cottage-style bedrooms and modern en suite accommodation, all provided with such thoughtful extras as bowls of fresh fruit. Two relaxing lounges contain colour televisions and a supply of books, while the restaurant is a feature in its own right – the chef/proprietor making good use of fresh local produce in a range of imaginative and very attractively presented dishes. A good base for touring North Wales, the hotel is also convenient for the local championship golf course.

6rm(4🌣ſ2hc) ® ✻ sB&Bfr£19 dB&Bſ꘠ſfr£41 LDO 9pm Lic ₪ CTV Credit Cards 1 3 £

GH 🔲🔲🔲 *Gwrach Ynys Country* Ynys, Talsarnau LL47 6TS ☎(0766) 780742 Feb-Nov

Beautifully restored Edwardian country house situated in own grounds, close to Harlech.

7rm(1🌣5ſ1hc) (2fb) CTV in all bedrooms ® LDO noon ₪ CTV 10P

FH 🔲 Mrs E A Jones **Tyddyn Gwynt** *(SH601302)* LL46 2TH (2.5m off B4573 (A496)) ☎(0766) 780298

A traditional farmhouse, Tyddyn Gwynt is approximately 2.5 miles south east of Harlech and surrounded by spectacular mountain scenery. The accommodation is pleasant and well maintained.

4rm(3hc) (1fb) ® ✻ sB&Bfr£12 dB&Bfr£24 LDO 7pm CTV 6P 3 acres small holding £

INN 🔲 *Rum Hole Hotel* Ffordd Newydd LL46 2UB ☎(0766) 780477 Closed 23 Dec-2 Jan

This family-run hostelry is situated on the A496 close to the castle and St David's Golf Course, and the inn is understandably popular with golfers. The bedrooms are quite well equipped and several have en suite facilities. Bed and breakfast only, with the option of bar meals.

8rm(2🌣3ſ3hc) (5fb) CTV in all bedrooms ® ✻ (ex guide dogs) LDO 9.30pm CTV 25P

HARROGATE North Yorkshire Map **08** SE35

GH 🔲🔲🔲 **Acacia Lodge** 21 Ripon Rd HG1 2JL ☎(0423) 560752 Closed Xmas & New Year

Situated within a short walk of the town centre, this comfortable guesthouse offers bed and breakfast in well maintained accommodation, combined with a warm and friendly atmosphere.

5rm(1🌣4ſ) (1fb) CTV in all bedrooms ® ✻ (ex guide dogs) ✻ sB&Bſfr£25 dB&Bſfr£42 ₪ CTV 6P 1🖤

SELECTED

GH 🔲🔲🔲🔲 **Alexa House & Stable Cottages** 26 Ripon Rd HG1 2JJ ☎(0423) 501988 FAX (0423) 504086

Built in 1830 for Baron de Ferrier, this attractive house is now a short walk from the town centre, and the conference and exhibition centres. All bedrooms are attractive and well equipped with many extras. Some are situated in a converted stable block. There is also a spacious dining room and cosy bar lounge. Hosts Roberta and John Block enjoy welcoming guests to their home, and are eager to ensure a comfortable and memorable stay. Whilst dinners are not normally served, they are offered on Winter Breaks.

9rm(2🌣5ſ2hc) Annexe 4ſ (1fb) CTV in all bedrooms ® ✻ sB&Bfr£21 sB&Bſfr£23 dB&B🌣ſ£46 WB&Bfr£145 Lic ₪ CTV 14P Credit Cards 1 3 £

GH 🔲 *Argyll House* 80 Kings Rd HG1 5JX ☎(0423) 562408

Situated close to the exhibition centre and within easy walking distance of the town centre, this attractive Victorian terraced house caters mostly for the business market, and its simply furnished bedrooms are well equipped with modern facilities.

6hc (1fb) ® LDO 4pm ₪ CTV 6P

GH 🔲🔲🔲 **Ashley House Hotel** 36-40 Franklin Rd HG1 5EE ☎(0423) 507474 & 560858

Situated in a residential area close to the Conference and Exhibition centre, this attractive small hotel has been converted from three town houses. Bedrooms are individually decorated with attractive fabrics, and although they vary in size, all are well equipped and maintained. Public areas include two lounges, a spacious attractive dining room and a cosy bar.

17rm(11🌣ſ6hc) (2fb) CTV in all bedrooms ® sB&B£23.50-£32 sB&B🌣ſ£32-£33 dB&B£40-£41 dB&B🌣ſ£50-£55 WB&B£150-£195 WBDi£220-£265 LDO noon Lic ₪ CTV 6P Credit Cards 1 3 £

GH 🔲🔲🔲 **Ashwood House** 7 Spring Grove HG1 2HS ☎(0423) 560081 Closed 24 Dec-1 Jan

Just off the Ripon road and close to the town centre and all amenities, this comfortable guesthouse offers attractive well equipped accommodation.

10rm(8🌣ſ2hc) (2fb)✎in 1 bedroom CTV in all bedrooms ® ✻ ✻ sB&B£19 sB&B🌣ſ£26 dB&B£38 dB&B🌣ſ£40-£44 WB&B£133-£154 Lic ₪ CTV 5P £

See advertisement on page 171

GH 🔲🔲 **The Dales Hotel** 101 Valley Dr HG2 0JP ☎(0423) 507248

This friendly guesthouse stands opposite the beautiful Valley Gardens close to the town centre. Mrs Burton is a welcoming hostess and provides very well equipped, pretty bedrooms and a comfortable lounge.

8rm(3ſ5hc) (2fb) CTV in all bedrooms ® sB&B£20-£22 dB&B£36-£38 dB&Bſ£42 LDO 9am Lic ₪ CTV 1P Credit Cards 1 3 £

GH 🔲🔲🔲 **Delaine Hotel** 17 Ripon Rd HG1 2JL ☎(0423) 567974

Rupert and Marian Viner are the friendly hosts at this hotel which is on the A61 Ripon road. It has comfortable, attractive bedrooms, a lovely lounge and a small bar. A home cooked meal is available upon request.

9rm(1🌣6ſ2hc) Annexe 2rm(1🌣1ſ) (2fb)✎in 3 bedrooms CTV in all bedrooms ® ✻ ✻ sB&B£25-£30 sB&B🌣ſ£30-£35 dB&B🌣ſ£44-£50

▶

Lic 🍴 CTV 12P
Credit Cards [1] [3] ⓔ

GH Q Gillmore Hotel 98 Kings Rd HG1 5HH ☎(0423) 503699
Situated within easy reach of the conference centre, this converted and extended terraced property has been under the same ownership since 1967, and offers furnctional but well maintained accommodation.
22rm(2⇨4♠16hc) (8fb) CTV in 9 bedrooms ® LDO 4pm
Lic 🍴 CTV 20P snooker

GH QQ Glenayr 19 Franklin Mount HG1 5EJ
☎(0423) 504259
Conveniently located for the town centre and the Exhibition Centre, in a peaceful tree-lined avenue, this guesthouse offers neat accommodation and friendly service.
6rm(5♠1hc) CTV in all bedrooms ® ✱ (ex guide dogs) ✱
sB&B£16.50-£17.50 dB&B♠£40-£44 WB&B£115-£140
WBDi£175-£210 LDO 4.30pm
Lic 🍴 3P
Credit Cards [1] [2] [3] ⓔ

GH QQ Knox Mill House Knox Mill Ln, Killinghall
HG3 2AE ☎(0423) 560650
Set in a delightful, peaceful location, yet only one mile north of Harrogate town centre, this former miller's residence, built around 1785, is adjacent to Knox Mill, with its original waterwheel and millrack, on the banks of an attractive stream, with meadows and open countryside beyond. The bedrooms, all of which face south, are attractively decorated, comfortable and very well maintained, and a feature downstairs, as well as the spacious lounge, is a tiny alcoved library with shelves of books for guests to read. The hotel is just off the A61, Ripon Road.
3rm(2♠1hc) ® ✱ dB&B£30 dB&B♠£34
🍴 CTV 4P ⓔ

GH QQ Lamont House 12 St Mary's Walk HG2 0LW
☎(0423) 567143
Closed Xmas
This detached house with a pretty front garden is situated in a quiet residential area close to the town centre. Family-owned and run, it offers comfortable accommodation with well maintained bedrooms, some with private bathrooms which are particularly attractive.
9rm(2♠7hc) (2fb) CTV in all bedrooms ® sB&Bfr£18
sB&B♠fr£30 dB&Bfr£30 dB&B♠fr£50
Lic 🍴 CTV
Credit Cards [1] ⓔ

GH QQ Prince's Hotel 7 Granby Rd HG1 4ST
☎(0423) 883469
This listed building is part of an imposing Victorian terrace quietly situated just off the A59 and overlooking the famous parkland known as The Stray. Many of the individually styled, comfortable bedrooms are furnished with antiques ; some rooms without en suite bathrooms have showers.
8rm(2⇨4hc) (4fb)⊬in 1 bedroom CTV in all bedrooms ®
✱ ✱ sB&B⇨♠fr£18 dB&B⇨♠£33-£50 LDO 9am
Lic 🍴 CTV ⍾ nc3yrs

GH QQ The Richmond 56 Dragon View, Skipton Rd
HG1 4DG ☎(0423) 530612
Set just off the A59 at the northern tip of the Stray, the Richmond is comfortable and friendly, with a cosy lounge and well appointed bedrooms.
6rm(5♠1hc) (1fb) CTV in all bedrooms ® ✱ (ex guide dogs)
✱ sB&B£18 sB&B♠£18 dB&B♠£36
🍴 CTV 3P ⓔ

GH QQ Roan 90 Kings Rd HG1 5JX ☎(0423) 503087
Closed 25-26 Dec
This attractively converted Victorian town house is situated close to the town's conference and exhibition centre. The compact bedrooms are well kept and comfortable, and there is a cosy lounge with a colour television for guests' use.

7rm(3♠4hc) (1fb) ® ✱ ✱ sB&Bfr£17 dB&Bfr£32
dB&B♠fr£36 LDO 4.30pm
🍴 CTV ⍾ nc7yrs ⓔ

GH QQQ Scotia House Hotel 66/68 Kings Rd HG1 5JR
☎(0423) 504361 FAX (0423) 526578
Immediately opposite the conference centre, this small family-run hotel has a lounge, cocktail bar and well appointed dining room. Most bedrooms are en suite and are all well furnished, comfortable and well equipped.
14rm(1⇨10♠3hc) (1fb)⊬in 6 bedrooms CTV in all bedrooms
® sB&Bfr£24 sB&B⇨♠fr£27.50 dB&Bfr£48 dB&B⇨♠fr£55
LDO 6pm
Lic 🍴 CTV 8P nc7yrs
Credit Cards [1] [3] ⓔ

GH Q Shelbourne 78 Kings Rd HG1 5JX ☎(0423) 504390
An unpretentious guesthouse, conveniently situated opposite the Exhibition Centre, which offers friendly service.
7hc (2fb) ® LDO noon
Lic 🍴 CTV 1P

GH QQQ Stoney Lea 13 Spring Grove HG1 2HS
☎(0423) 501524
Closed Xmas & New Year
A well furnished and comfortable guesthouse situated in a quiet cul de sac, close to the conference centre. Bedrooms are of a high standard and have good facilities.
7⇨♠ CTV in all bedrooms ® ✱ (ex guide dogs)
sB&B⇨♠£22-£25 dB&B⇨♠£38 WB&B£133-£175
🍴 CTV 3P nc4yrs ⓔ

GH QQQ Wharfedale House 28 Harlow Moor Dr HG2 0JY
☎(0423) 522233
Hospitable hosts Tricia and Howard Quinn have made Wharfedale House into a most welcoming small hotel. Situated in a quiet area overlooking Valley Gardens it provides comfortable, well equipped accommodation and good home cooking.
8rm(1⇨7♠) (2fb) CTV in all bedrooms ® ✱ sB&B⇨♠£25
dB&B⇨♠£46 WB&B£138-£150 LDO 4pm
Lic 🍴 3P ⓔ

HARROP FOLD Lancashire Map **07** SD74

Q is for quality. For a full explanation of this AA quality award, consult the Contents page.

HARROW Greater London London plan **4** B5 (pages 221-227)

GH 🅀 Central Hotel 6 Hindes Rd HA1 1SJ ☎081-427 0893
Ideally situated in a residential area near the town centre, this converted Edwardian house offers accommodation on 3 floors. Rooms are simply furnished and vary in size : some are reached through the kitchen. The hotel is under the personal supervision of the owners.
10rm(3♪7hc) (3fb) CTV in all bedrooms ® ⊁
৩৩ CTV 12P
Credit Cards 1️⃣ 3️⃣

GH 🅀🅀 Crescent Lodge Hotel 58/62 Welldon Crescent
HA1 1QR ☎081-863 5491 & 081-863 5163 FAX 081-427 5965
A small family run commercial hotel in a quiet residential crescent. Bedrooms come in different sizes, are cheerfully decorated, well equipped and show high standards of housekeeping. Downstairs there is a bright breakfast room overlooking the garden, and a bar/ lounge with deep, comfortable sofas.
21rm(12♪9hc) (2fb) CTV in all bedrooms ®
⊁ (ex guide dogs) sB&B£30-£35 sB&B♪£43-£45 dB&B£45-£48 dB&B♪£55-£60 WB&B£210-£300 WBDi£308-£380
LDO 8.30pm
Lic ৩৩ CTV 8P 1🎁 (£2 per night) ⋒
Credit Cards 1️⃣ 3️⃣ £️

GH 🅀 Hindes Hotel 8 Hindes Rd HA1 1SJ ☎081-427 7468
Owner-run, the Hindes is located in a residential street near the town centre. The bedrooms, on 3 floors, are compact and simply furnished. There is a bright television lounge and an open-plan kitchen and breakfast room.
13rm(1♪12hc) (2fb) CTV in all bedrooms ® ⊁ ✻ sB&B£28-£29 dB&B£38-£39 dB&B♪£48-£49
৩৩ CTV 5P
Credit Cards 1️⃣ 2️⃣ 3️⃣ £️

HARTFIELD East Sussex Map **05** TQ43

FH 🅀🅀🅀 Mrs C Cooper **Bolebroke Watermill** *(TQ481373)*
Perry Hill, Edenbridge Rd TN7 4JP (off B2026 1m N of Hartfield) ☎(0892) 770425
Mar-Nov
This charming and quite unique watermill is set in 6.5 acres of secluded woodlands, with an ancient history dating back to King William in 1086. The tools and machinery are still much in evidence. The bedrooms are reached by very steep staircases and are hence completely unsuitable for anybody with restricted mobility. The bedrooms are comfortable and well appointed, and all have private facilities. There is a comfortable lounge, and dinner, available by prior arrangement, is served in the adjoining mill house.
2⇨♪ Annexe 2⇨♪ ⊁in all bedrooms CTV in all bedrooms ® ⊁ sB&B⇨♪£40-£53 dB&B⇨♪£45-£58 LDO 10am
৩৩ CTV 16P nc7yrs supervised rough shooting 6 acres smallholding
Credit Cards 1️⃣ 2️⃣ 3️⃣

HARTLAND Devon Map **02** SS22

GH 🅀🅀 Fosfelle EX39 6EF ☎(0237) 441273
Well kept gardens surround this 17th-century manor which now offers comfortable accommodation. The spacious bar and TV lounge are popular with non-residents for coffee and afternoon tea. Resident proprietors provide simple home cooked meals and personal service.
7rm(1⇨1♪5hc) (2fb) CTV in 3 bedrooms TV in 2 bedrooms
® ⊁ sB&B£16-£19 dB&B£32-£36 dB&B⇨♪£35-£40
WB&B£95-£125 WBDi£140-£180 LDO 9pm
Lic ৩৩ CTV 20P ⋒ ⋗ snooker
Credit Cards 1️⃣ 3️⃣ £️

HASELEY KNOB Warwickshire Map **04** SP27

GH 🅀🅀🅀 Croft CV35 7NL ☎(0926) 484447
This modern conversion of a former farmhouse, situated half a mile north of the A41 Fiveways roundabout on the A4177 and 5 miles northwest of Warwick city centre, offers comfortable, spacious bedrooms and bright, attractive public areas including a conservatory dining room overlooking the well tended gardens.
4rm(2♪2hc) (2fb)⊁in 3 bedrooms CTV in all bedrooms ®
LDO 2pm
৩৩ CTV 6P
See advertisement under WARWICK

HASTINGS & ST LEONARDS East Sussex Map **05** TQ80

📧💌GH 🅀🅀 Argyle 32 Cambridge Gardens TN34 1EN
☎(0424) 421294
Closed Xmas
A mid-terrace house situated close to the railway station and shops. The bedrooms are fresh, well maintained and comfortable. There is a small residents' TV lounge, and a modest dining room in the basement.
8rm(3♪5hc) (1fb) ® ⊁ sB&Bfr£13 sB&B♪fr£20 dB&Bfr£24
dB&B♪fr£30 WB&Bfr£77
৩৩ CTV ⅌ nc4yrs

GH 🅀 Bryn-y-Mor 12 Godwin Rd TN35 5JR
☎Hastings(0424) 722744 FAX (0424) 445933
The atmosphere of a past era is recreated in this Victorian house which overlooks the Bourne Valley from a quiet residential area. Bedrooms, though provided with most modern facilities, are ornately furnished in period style, the shared bathroom is elegant and the small characterful library is supplemented by a conservatory with bar and full-sized billiard table. Two self-catering apartments are also available.
3rm(1♪2hc) CTV in all bedrooms ® ⊁ ✻ sB&Bfr£25
sB&B♪fr£25 dB&Bfr£38 dB&B♪fr£38 WB&Bfr£114
LDO 4.30pm
Lic ৩৩ CTV ⇨(heated) snooker

GH 🅀🅀🅀 Eagle House Pevensey Rd TN38 0JZ
☎(0424) 430535 & 441273
Set in a peaceful situation, this friendly privately-run Victorian hotel benefits from its own car park and an attractive garden to the rear. The bedrooms, most of which are spacious, are exceptionally well equipped and offer a good standard of comfort. There is an elegant bar and a beautifully furnished restaurant where dinner is served, personally supervised by the friendly owners.
23rm(20⇨♪3hc) (2fb) CTV in all bedrooms ® sB&B£29
sB&B⇨♪£33 dB&B£39 dB&B⇨♪£47 WB&B£299
WBDi£417 LDO 8.30pm
Lic ৩৩ 13P
Credit Cards 1️⃣ 2️⃣ 3️⃣ 5️⃣ £️

GH 🅀 Gainsborough Hotel 5 Carlisle Pde TN34 1JG
☎(0424) 434010
Closed 24-26 Dec
Situated on the seafront, this family-run guesthouse offers simply furnished bedrooms, some of which have en suite facilities. There is a pleasant dining room and an adjoining bar/lounge. Car parking may prove difficult.
12rm(3⇨5♪4hc) (3fb) CTV in all bedrooms ® ✻ sB&B£15-£18 sB&B⇨♪£18-£21 dB&B£30-£36 dB&B⇨♪£36-£42
WB&B£98-£133 WBDi£157-£199.50 LDO 4.30pm
Lic ৩৩ £️

Every effort is made to provide accurate information, but details can change after we go to print. It is advisable to check prices etc. before you make a firm booking.

SELECTED

GH ◪◪◪◪ **Parkside House** 59 Lower Park Rd
TN34 2LD ☎Hastings(0424) 433096
High up overlooking Alexandra Park, this elegant Victorian house retains its original architectural features. Resident proprietors Janet and Brian Kent provide a warm welcome for their guests, many of whom are return visitors. Freshly decorated bedrooms have pretty fabrics and a multitude of extras, from children's toys and ducks in the bath to hot water bottles and hair tongs. There is a comfortable lounge and a small conservatory as well as a spacious dining room, elegantly appointed with lace cloths and good silver. A set, fixed-price dinner is served by prior arrangement. Food is freshly prepared and alternative dishes are available on request. Mrs Kent goes out of her way to accommodate guests' wishes.
4rm(3♠1hc) (1fb)✠in all bedrooms CTV in all bedrooms
® ♺ (ex guide dogs) ✻ sB&B£20-£35 sB&B♠£25-£35
dB&B£32-£40 dB&B♠£34-£40 WB&B£110-£135
WBDi£160-£180 LDO 3pm
Lic ♨ CTV ✗ £

GH ◪◪ **The Ridge Guest House & Restaurant** 361 The Ridge
TN34 2RD ☎Hastings(0424) 754240 & 753607
A family-run guesthouse set in an elevated position in a residential area, close to the new Conquest Hospital. It offers a range of purpose-built bedrooms which are basically furnished, but all have modern en suite facilities; a further six rooms are presently being built. The dining room doubles as a fish and chips restaurant at weekends, and there is a small bar and a simply furnished lounge.
11♠ (2fb) CTV in all bedrooms ® ♺ ✻ sB&B♠£18
dB&B♠£30 WB&B£70-£90 WBDi£110-£130 LDO 9.15pm
♨ CTV 40P
Credit Cards ①②

GH ◪◪◪ **Tower Hotel** 28 Tower Rd West TN38 0RG
☎(0424) 427217
This welcoming Victorian hotel, half a mile from the seafront and convenient for local amenities, has comfortable and individually decorated bedrooms. There is a lounge and a cosy bar, soon to include a new conservatory.
10rm(8➘♠2hc) (2fb) CTV in all bedrooms ® sB&B£18-£21
sB&B➘♠£21.50-£30 dB&B£36-£41 dB&B➘♠£43-£48
WB&B£108-£126 WBDi£164-£182 LDO 4pm
Lic ♨ CTV ✗ £

GH ◪◪ **Waldorf Hotel** 4 Carlisle Pde TN34 1JG
☎(0424) 422185
This friendly, family-run hotel is conveniently located for all amenities and has a prime seafront situation. There is a pleasant dining room and adjoining lounge with a bar. Many of the neat bedrooms have good sea views.
12rm(3➘1♠8hc) (3fb) CTV in all bedrooms ® ♺
LDO 11.30am
Lic CTV ✗

FH ◪◪◪ Mrs B Yorke **Filsham Farmhouse** *(TQ784096)* 111
Harley Shute Rd TN38 8BY ☎(0424) 433109
Closed Xmas & New Year
Now in a residential area, this listed Sussex farmhouse offers a wealth of rural charm, in addition to pretty bedrooms richly furnished with antiques, combined with television, central heating and tea and coffee-making facilities. One bedroom has private facilities as well.
3rm ✠in all bedrooms CTV in all bedrooms ® ♺ sB&B£15-£20 dB&B£25-£35 WB&B£175-£210
♨ CTV 4P 1 acres non-working £

INN ◪◪◪ *Highlands* 1 Boscobel Rd TN38 0LU
☎Hastings(0424) 420299
Quietly situated on a steep hillside behind the Royal Victorian Hotel, this friendly, well-managed inn has modern, well-equipped bedrooms, a small old-fashioned lounge, public bar and a good restaurant. Craig O'Brien, the young chef, uses fresh ingredients in his cooking for the à la carte and table d'hôte menus. Fish is his speciality.
9➘♠ (1fb) CTV in all bedrooms ® ♺ (ex guide dogs)
LDO 9.30pm
♨ CTV 8P
Credit Cards ①③

HASWELL PLOUGH Co Durham Map **12** NZ34

GH ◪ **The Gables** Front St DH6 2EW ☎091-526 2982
This is a licensed property situated on the B1283, 6 miles east of Durham. The bar and the dining room are particularly attractive, and there are ample car parking facilities.
5hc (3fb) CTV in all bedrooms ® ✻ sB&B£24-£27 dB&B£36-£40 LDO 9.30pm
Lic ♨ 20P £

HATHERSAGE Derbyshire Map **08** SK28

FH ◪◪◪ Mrs T C Wain *Highlow Hall* *(SK219802)* S30 1AX
☎Hope Valley(0433) 50393
mid Mar-Oct
Surrounded by farmland, this 16th-century manor house stands in the heart of the Peak District National Park and has superb views of the countryside. It is found by taking the B6001 to Bakewell and then following signs to Abney.
6hc (2fb) ®
Lic CTV 12P 900 acres mixed sheep

HATTON Warwickshire Map **04** SP26

SELECTED

GH ◨◨◨◨ **Northleigh House** Five Ways Rd CV35 7HZ
☎Warwick(0926) 484203
Closed 15 Dec-4 Jan
Tucked away in the countryside, Northleigh House can be a little awkward to find, but if you take the Shewsbury/ Claverton signed road at the roundabout junction of the A4141 and the A4177, and follow it for half a mile, you should find this delightful little house. Sylvia Fenwick is a most caring and enthusiastic proprietress, nothing is too much trouble and standards are kept very high, especially the housekeeping. The 6 bedrooms, where guests are requested not to smoke, are individually furnished and supplied with helpful extras.
6⇨Ⓝ ⊬in all bedrooms CTV in all bedrooms ⓡ
sB&B⇨Ⓝ£28-£36 dB&B⇨Ⓝ£40-£52
⑩ CTV 8P ⓔ
See advertisement under **WARWICK**

HAVANT Hampshire
See **Emsworth**

HAVERFORDWEST Dyfed
See **Broad Haven**

HAVERIGG Cumbria Map **07** SD17

GH ◨◨◨ **Dunelm Cottage** Main St LA18 4EX
☎Millom(0229) 770097
Closed Jan
Two charming cottages have been converted into one tastefully decorated to provide 3 bedrooms, a cosy lounge with TV, and a small dining room with one large table. A free public car park is opposite.
3hc ⓡ ✻ dB&B£47-£50 (incl dinner) WB&Bfr£120
WBDifr£165 LDO 6.30pm
⑩ CTV ⊬ nc10yrs

HAWES North Yorkshire Map **07** SD88

GH ◨◨◨ **Steppe Haugh** Town Head DL8 3RJ
☎Wensleydale(0969) 667645
A 17th-century stone-built house standing on the edge of the village. Managed by the charming resident proprietors, it offers small and cosy bedrooms with lovely views, an inviting spacious lounge with a log fire and colour TV, and an attractive dining room.
6rm(2Ⓝ4hc) CTV in 2 bedrooms ⓡ ✻ dB&B£30
dB&BⓃ£40 WB&B£105 WBDi£192.50 LDO 5pm
Lic ⑩ CTV 8P nc10yrs

HAWKSHEAD Cumbria Map **07** SD39

GH ◨◨ **Greenbank Country House Hotel** Main St LA22 0NS
☎(09666) 497 due to change to (05394) 36497
Originally a 17th-century farmhouse, Greenbank is now an attractive and comfortable small hotel, under the personal supervision of the resident owners. It is situated just on the edge of picturesque Hawkshead village, with ample parking on the premises.
10rm(2Ⓝ8hc) (1fb) ⓡ LDO 4.30pm
Lic ⑩ CTV 12P

GH ◨◨ **Ivy House** LA22 0NS ☎(09666) 204 due to change to (05394) 36204
28 Mar-2 Nov
An attractive Georgian house situated in the centre of the village, with car parking at the rear. There are 6 bedrooms in the main house and 5 in an adjoining annexe ; 6 rooms have private bathrooms.

6rm(3⇨3Ⓝ) Annexe 5hc (3fb) ⓡ ✻ sB&B£23-£27.50
sB&B⇨Ⓝ£26.50-£30.50 dB&B£46-£55 dB&B⇨Ⓝ£53-£61
(incl dinner) WB&B£147-£157.50 WBDi£161-£192.50
LDO 6pm
Lic ⑩ CTV 14P ⚓ bicycles & windsurfers available ⓔ

GH ◨◨◨ **Rough Close Country House** LA22 0QF
☎(09666) 370 due to change to (05394) 36370
Apr-Oct rs Mar
A charming country house situated in most attractive gardens about a mile south of Hawkshead on the west side of Esthwaite Water. Bedrooms are comfortably furnished, there is a spacious lounge and a small residents' bar.
5⇨Ⓝ ⊬in all bedrooms ⓡ ✖ (ex guide dogs) dB&B⇨Ⓝ£65
(incl dinner) WB&B£157.50 WBDi£217 LDO 7pm
Lic ⑩ CTV 10P nc5yrs
Credit Cards ①③ⓔ

INN ◨ **Kings Arms Hotel** LA22 0NZ ☎(09666) 372 due to change to (05394) 36372
A 16th-century inn situated in the centre of the village, overlooking the square. The 8 well decorated bedrooms all have TV and tea-making facilities, some have telephones and 4 have private bathrooms. A wide range of bar meals is served in the oak-beamed bar along with real ale, and an à la carte menu is available in the dining room in the evenings.
8rm(4Ⓝ4hc) (2fb) CTV in all bedrooms ⓡ LDO 9pm
⑩
Credit Cards ①③

INN ◨◨ **Red Lion** The Square LA22 0HB ☎(09666) 213 due to change to (05394) 36213
Closed Xmas Day
A 15th-century coaching inn situated at the northern end of the village. All the bedrooms have en suite facilities, colour television and tea-making equipment.
8Ⓝ (2fb) CTV in all bedrooms ⓡ ✖ LDO 9pm
⑩ 8P
Credit Cards ①③

HAWORTH West Yorkshire Map **07** SE03

GH ◨◨ **Ferncliffe Hotel** Hebden Rd BD22 8RS
☎(0535) 643405
A small, comfortable family-owned and run hotel in an elevated position overlooking the valley and village. There is a good range of home-cooked meals available in the cosy restaurant.
6Ⓝ (1fb) CTV in all bedrooms ⓡ ✻ sB&BⓃ£21-£25
dB&BⓃ£42-£50 WB&B£147-£175 WBDi£210-£238
LDO 8.30pm
Lic ⑩ CTV 12P
Credit Cards ③

HAYDON BRIDGE Northumberland Map **12** NY86

SELECTED

GH ◨◨◨◨ **Langley Castle** Langley-on-Tyne NE4 5LU
☎(0434) 688888
A splendidly modernised castle dating back to 1350, and now a very comfortable hotel. Each of the 8 spacious bedrooms has been beautifully furnished and carefully designed to retain and complement their unique style, with luxurious bathrooms to match, including jacuzzi baths. The 1st floor lounge is quite superbly furnished and very elegant and comfortable, and there is an extensive à la carte menu available in the intimate restaurant.
8⇨ (3fb) CTV in all bedrooms ⓡ ✻ sB&B⇨£42-£89
dB&B⇨£58-£110 LDO 9pm
Lic lift ⑩ CTV 50P
Credit Cards ①②③⑤

HAYFIELD Derbyshire Map **07** SK08

INN **Q** *Sportsman* Kinder Rd SK12 5EL
☎New Mills(0663) 742118
Traditional country inn, with well-furnished, modern bedrooms, in valley of the River Set on the approach to Kinder Scout.
7rm(5♠2hc)(1fb) CTV in all bedrooms ® LDO 9.30pm
卿 20P
Credit Cards 1 3

HAYLING ISLAND Hampshire Map **04** SZ79

SELECTED

GH **Q Q Q Q** **Cockle Warren Cottage Hotel** 36 Seafront
PO11 9HL ☎(0705) 464961
The owners designed this house about 12 years ago in the style of a tile-hung Sussex farmhouse. Bedrooms are comfortable, attractively decorated and well equipped; two face the sea and have four-poster beds. Mrs Skelton's excellent French country cooking, produced from fresh ingredients, is served in a cool, tiled conservatory, and portions are generous. There is a walled pool at the rear of the house available for guests.
4⇨♠ Annexe 1⇨♠ ⊁in all bedrooms CTV in all bedrooms ✖ (ex guide dogs) sB&B⇨♠£35-£45
dB&B⇨♠£48-£68 LDO 4.30pm
Lic 卿 7P 2🚗 nc10yrs ⊜(heated) ▶18
Credit Cards 1 3 £

GH **Q Q Q** **The Rook Hollow Hotel** 84 Church Rd PO11 0NX
☎(0705) 467080 & 469620
Wendy Prior creates a friendly, relaxed atmosphere, and provides attentive service at this centrally situated Edwardian building. The bedrooms are comfortable and well equipped.
▶

FOR QUALITY ACCOMMODATION AT A REASONABLE PRICE . . .

GARTH GUEST HOUSE

NEAR SAWREY, AMBLESIDE, CUMBRIA LA22 0JZ

Visit THE GARTH a beautiful Victorian Country House set in two acres of gardens, overlooking Esthwaite Lake to the Coniston & Langdale mountains. Whilst retaining much of its Victorian charm and elegance THE GARTH offers up-to-date facilities to ensure the comfort of our guests. Two en-suite rooms have 4-poster beds for the romantically inclined. Log fired lounge, tastefully furnished. High standards throughout. Delicious imaginative home cooking. Table Licence.
AMPLE PARKING - PETS BY PRIOR ARRANGEMENT

Phone for brochure
Personal attention from resident owners:
Pat & Walter Sommerville
HAWKSHEAD (096-66-373)

Ees Wyke
· COUNTRY HOUSE ·

Blessed with a beautiful, tranquil setting amidst rolling hills and overlooking the peaceful, Esthwaite Water, this impressive Georgian house has uninterrupted views from all bedrooms of the lake, mountains, forest and fells.

Once the holiday home of Beatrix Potter, and only 5 mins walk from "Hill Top", her Lakeland farmhouse, Ees Wyke now offers accommodation of a high standard, a growing reputation for first class cuisine, and welcoming hospitality.

An ideal base for touring, walking or just relaxing surrounded by the beauty of Cumbria.

**Near Sawrey, Hawkshead,
Cumbria LA22 0JZ
Telephone: Hawkshead (09666) 393**

PEMBROKESHIRE

BROAD HAVEN HOTEL
Nr. Haverfordwest, Dyfed SA62 3JN
Tel: (0437) 781366
Comfortable hotel with all facilities and good food situated in the Pembrokeshire National Park just 50 yards from the water's edge amid some of Britain's finest coastal scenery. Special 2 night breaks including D, B&B in en-suite bedrooms. Pets welcome.
Please write or phone for details.

A MEMBER OF
CONSORT HOTELS

6rm(3♪3hc) ⚲in 1 bedroom CTV in all bedrooms ®
sB&B£20-£23 sB&B♪£33-£43 dB&B£33-£37 dB&B♪£40-£50
LDO 9pm
Lic ♚ CTV 9P
Credit Cards ① ③ ⑤ ⓔ

HAY-ON-WYE Powys Map **03** SO24

GH 🇶🇶🇶 **York House** Hardwick Rd, Cusop HR3 5QX (1m
SE in England) ☎(0497) 820705
rs Xmas
*This fine stone house is set in an acre of peaceful gardens and is
only a short walk from the town centre on the Peterchurch road.
The bedrooms are all pretty and comfortable, and there is a
pleasant lounge; several of the original fireplaces remain, adding
to the character of the house.*
5rm(3♪2hc)(2fb)⚲in all bedrooms CTV in all bedrooms ®
sB&B£16.50-£21.25 sB&B⇨♪£27.50 dB&B£33-£35.50
dB&B⇨♪£39-£43 WB&B£103.95-£135.45 WBDi£168.53-
£200.03 LDO 5pm
♚ 8P nc8yrs
Credit Cards ① ③ ⓔ

HEASLEY MILL Devon Map **03** SS73

GH 🇶🇶 **Heasley House** EX36 3LE
☎North Molton(05984) 213
Closed Feb
*A Georgian-style building, full of atmosphere and furnished with
antiques, Heasley House overlooks a mill stream.*
8rm(2⇨3♪3hc) sB&Bfr£29.95 sB&B⇨♪fr£31.45
dB&Bfr£59.90 dB&B⇨♪fr£62.90 (incl dinner) WB&B£125-
£135 WBDi£199-£209 LDO 5pm
Lic ♚ CTV 11P
Credit Cards ① ③ ⓔ

HEATHROW AIRPORT Greater London London plan **4** A3
(pages 221-227)

See also Slough

GH 🇶🇶 *The Cottage* 150 High St, Cranford TW5 9PD
☎081-897 1815
*Set in a quiet cul-de-sac off Cranford High Street, The Cottage
offers clean, comfortable and well maintained accommodation on
ground and first floors. There is an informal and relaxed
atmosphere under Mrs Parry's personal supervision.*
6hc (1fb) CTV in all bedrooms ✖ (ex guide dogs)
♚ 20P

HEBDEN BRIDGE West Yorkshire Map **07** SD92

GH 🇶🇶🇶 **Redacre Mill** Redacre, Mytholmroyd HX7 5DQ
☎Halifax(0422) 885563
Closed Dec-Jan
*A lovingly converted mill standing beside the tranquil Rochdale
canal, in Calderdale. Bedrooms are exceptionally well furnished
and equipped, and the resident owners offer a warm Yorkshire
welcome to all their guests.*
5rm(2⇨3♪)(1fb)⚲in all bedrooms CTV in all bedrooms ®
✖ (ex guide dogs) ✳ sB&B⇨♪£30 dB&B⇨♪£40-£45
WB&B£140-£200 WBDi£195-£245 LDO 8pm
Lic ♚ 8P
Credit Cards ① ③ ⓔ

HELENSBURGH Strathclyde *Dunbartonshire*

See Cardross

HELMSLEY North Yorkshire Map **08** SE68

GH 🇶🇶 *Beaconsfield* Bondgate YO6 5BW ☎(0439) 71346
*A small guesthouse set back from the main Scarborough road,
close to the centre of this attractive market town. Comfortable and
well maintained, it provides bed and breakfast and pleasantly
decorated bedrooms, with TV and tea/coffee-making facilities.*

6hc CTV in all bedrooms ® ✖
♚ 8P nc12yrs

HELSTON Cornwall & Isles of Scilly Map **02** SW62

FH 🇶🇶 Iris White **Little Pengwedna** *(SW638318)* Little
Pengwedna Farm TR13 0BA ☎Leedstown(0736) 850649
Etr-Oct
*A friendly farmhouse with bright, well decorated bedrooms and
modern facilities. There is a traditional lounge and dining room. It
is located about four miles outside Helston on the B3303
Camborne road, and provides a good touring base for south west
Cornwall.*
3hc ⚲in all bedrooms ® ✖ (ex guide dogs) ✳ dB&B£24-£25
WB&Bfr£84 LDO 9am
CTV 6P 74 acres cattle

HENFIELD West Sussex Map **04** TQ21

FH 🇶🇶 Mrs M Wilkin **Great Wapses** *(TQ242192)* Wineham
BN5 9BJ ☎(0273) 492544
*This appealing farmhouse is about half a mile off the road in lovely
surroundings. Dating back to the 16th century, with a Georgian
extension, the house has spacious rooms with private facilities.*
3rm(2⇨1♪)(1fb) CTV in all bedrooms ® ✳ sB&B⇨♪£22-
£24 dB&B⇨♪£34-£36 WB&B£119-£168
♚ 7P ♟(hard)33 acres mixed
Credit Cards ② ⓔ

HENLEY-IN-ARDEN Warwickshire Map **07** SP16

GH 🇶🇶🇶 **Ashleigh House** Whitley Hill B95 5DL
☎(0564) 792315 FAX (0564) 794133
*A large extended Edwardian house situated east of the town centre
on the A4095 Warwick road. Much of its original charm has been
retained, enhanced by the antique furniture in the public rooms and
the fine collection of miniatures by the owner which are on display
throughout the house. Bedrooms are comfortable and very well
equipped. The hotel is in a peaceful area, surrounded by interesting
gardens.*
6rm(2⇨4♪) Annexe 4♪ CTV in all bedrooms ®
✖ (ex guide dogs) sB&B⇨♪£39-£50 dB&B⇨♪£49-£60
♚ 11P nc14yrs
Credit Cards ① ③

HENLEY-ON-THAMES Oxfordshire Map **04** SU78

See also Nettlebed

GH 🇶 *Flohr's Hotel & Restaurant* Northfield End RG9 2JG
☎(0491) 573412
*A listed Georgian town house dating back to 1750, just 5 minutes'
walk from the town centre. Bedrooms are bright and simply
furnished with individual décor and TV. A choice of interesting
dishes is available from the table d'hôte menu in the formal
restaurant which has character and quality.*
9rm(1⇨2♪6hc) (4fb) CTV in all bedrooms ® LDO 10pm
Lic ♚ CTV 6P
Credit Cards ① ② ③ ⑤

HENSTRIDGE Somerset Map **03** ST71

FH 🇶🇶🇶 Mrs P J Doggrell **Toomer** *(ST708192)*
Templecombe BA8 0PH ☎Templecombe(0963) 250237
*200-year-old, stone-built farmhouse with large, walled garden with
an Elizabethan dovecote. 1.5 miles west then south off A30.*
3rm(1♪2hc) (2fb) CTV in all bedrooms ® ✖ (ex guide dogs)
✳ sB&B£13.50-£15 dB&B£25-£30 dB&B♪fr£30
♚ CTV 6P ✈ 400 acres arable dairy ⓔ

HEREFORD Hereford & Worcester Map **03** SO54

See also Bodenham & Little Dewchurch

BREDWARDINE HALL

Mr & Mrs Jancey,
**Bredwardine Hall, Bredwardine,
Nr Hereford HR3 6DB Moccas (09817) 596**

The Hall is a charming 19th-century Manor House with immense character and literary interest standing in secluded wooded gardens, providing elegant well appointed accommodation; five delightful bedrooms; spacious en-suite bathrooms; full central heating; tea/coffee facilities; colour TV's; ample parking. Excellent food and wine; relaxed friendly atmosphere; personal service. Situated in the tranquil unspoiled Wye Valley; 7 miles Hay-on-Wye; 12 miles Hereford. Sorry no pets or children under 10.

GH QQ Ferncroft Hotel 144 Ledbury Rd HR1 2TB ☏(0432) 265538
Closed mid Dec-2 Jan
Standing in pleasant gardens in a residential area, yet conveniently close to the town centre, Ferncroft provides comfortable accommodation and is suitable for tourists and commercial visitors.
11rm(6↱5hc) (2fb) CTV in all bedrooms Ⓡ ✗ sB&B£22 sB&B↱£27.50 dB&B£37 dB&B↱£45 LDO 6.30pm
Lic ⓟ CTV 8P
Credit Cards [1] [3]

SELECTED

GH QQQQ *Hermitage Manor* Canon Pyon HR4 8NR (3.5m NW off A4110 towards Canon Pyon) ☏(0432) 760317
Mar-mid Dec
An impressive manor house set in 11 acres overlooking beautiful countryside and fruit orchards. There are 3 separate lounge areas, including a very impressive oak-panelled entrance hall, a non-smoking lounge and a smaller TV lounge. A sweeping staircase leads to the spacious, traditionally decorated bedrooms, all of which are en suite. A substantial English breakfast is served, but dinner is not available.
3rm(2⇨1↱) Ⓡ ✗
ⓟ CTV 12P 2🚗 nc9yrs

GH Q Hopbine Hotel Roman Rd HR1 1LE ☏(0432) 268722
A predominantly commercial guesthouse on the A4103, on the northern outskirts of the city. Accommodation is compact and modest but well equipped. It is popular due to the friendly, welcoming atmosphere created by the proprietors.
10rm(3⇨7hc) (1fb) CTV in all bedrooms Ⓡ ✱ sB&B£17-£21 sB&B⇨£21-£25 dB&B£28-£32 dB&B⇨£32-£36 WB&B£98-£126 WBDi£157.50-£186 LDO before noon
Lic CTV 20P £

GH QQ *White Lodge Hotel* 50 Ledbury Rd HR1 2SY ☏(0432) 273382
Closed Xmas
Situated on the A368, this small private hotel is only a short walk from the town centre. The rooms are comfortable and well equipped, and the attractive dining room has a very impressive, carved mantlepiece.
7⇨↱ CTV in all bedrooms Ⓡ ✗ LDO 5.30pm
Lic ⓟ CTV 14P

FH QQ Mrs R A Price **Dinedor Court** *(SO545368)* Dinedor HR2 6LG (3m SE B4399) ☏Holme Lacy(0432) 870481
Etr-4 Nov
Situated on the B4399, just three miles from Hereford in an idyllic setting, here is an ideal base from which to explore the beautiful countryside. A long drive leads to the 16th-century farmhouse, with its comfortable accommodation, well kept gardens and access to the River Wye.
3rm(2hc) (1fb) Ⓡ sB&B£15-£18 dB&B£28-£32 WB&B£98-£112
CTV 6P 200 acres mixed

FH Q Mrs M J Barrell **Orchard** *(SO575384)* Mordiford HR1 4EJ (Mordiford 3m E off B4224) ☏Holme Lacey(0432) 870253
Closed Xmas
Comfortable accommodation is provided at this 17th-century, stone-built farmhouse, which is set in a quiet location with fine views of the surrounding countryside.
3hc ⊬in all bedrooms Ⓡ ✱ sB&Bfr£16 dB&B£28-£30
LDO 7pm
Lic ⓟ CTV P nc10yrs ⤴ 57 acres cattle mixed
Credit Cards [2] £

FH QQQ Mr & Mrs D E Jones **Sink Green** *(SO542377)* Rotherwas HR2 6LE ☏Holme Lacy(0432) 870223
Etr-Oct rs Nov-Etr
A delightful 16th-century farmhouse, situated on the B4399 in beautiful countryside, overlooking the River Wye, yet only three miles from the city centre. Bedrooms have been completely refurbished to offer excellent accommodation and are attractively decorated, with some lovely antiques; all rooms have neat, modern en suite facilities. The spacious, comfortable lounge has a log fire and piano. Breakfast is served at the communal table in the dining room, which features a flagstone floor.
3rm(2⇨1↱) ⊬in all bedrooms CTV in all bedrooms Ⓡ ✗ (ex guide dogs) ✱ dB&B⇨↱£30-£38
ⓟ CTV 10P 180 acres beef sheep

HERMITAGE Dorset

See **Holnest**

HERSTMONCEUX East Sussex Map 05 TQ61

GH QQ Cleavers Lyng Country Hotel Church Rd BN27 1QJ ☏(0323) 833131
Closed 24 Dec-1 Jan
A charming 16th-century house set in its own attractive grounds. The bedrooms are traditionally furnished but provide adequate comfort. There is a cosy lounge and the beamed dining room, with a log fire in cold weather, is full of character.
8hc Ⓡ ✱ sB&B£17.25-£17.95 dB&B£34.50-£35.90 WB&B£115-£120 WBDi£172.50-£182.50 LDO 6pm
Lic ⓟ CTV 15P £

HEXHAM Northumberland Map 12 NY96

GH QQ Westbrooke Hotel Allendale Rd NE46 2DE ☏(0434) 603818
A detached house set in a pleasant residential area on the edge of the town on the Allendale road. The bedrooms are adequately furnished and there is a public bar as part of the hotel.
11rm(5↱6hc) (2fb)⊬in 2 bedrooms CTV in all bedrooms Ⓡ
Lic CTV 3P snooker
Credit Cards [1] [3]

FH QQQ Elizabeth Anne Courage **Rye Hill** *(NY958580)* Slaley NE47 0AH (5m S, off B6306) ☏Slaley(0434) 673259
A lovely farmhouse set in the countryside near to the village of Slaley. Bedrooms are well equipped and comfortable, and you are assured of a warm welcome from Mrs Courage.
6⇨↱ (2fb)⊬in all bedrooms CTV in all bedrooms Ⓡ ✱ sB&B⇨↱fr£18.50 dB&B⇨↱fr£33 WB&Bfr£104 WBDifr£158 LDO 6pm
Lic ⓟ CTV 6P games room 30 acres sheep £

HEYSHAM Lancashire Map 07 SD46

GH QQ Carr-Garth Bailey Ln LA3 2PS ☏(0524) 51175 due to change to 851175
Etr-mid Oct
Set within its walled garden in a quiet residential area, this small hotel offers comfortable accommodation.
8hc (2fb) Ⓡ sB&Bfr£13 dB&Bfr£23 WB&Bfr£74 WBDifr£97 LDO 4pm
CTV 8P

HIGHAM Suffolk Map 05 TM03

GH QQQ The Bauble Higham CO7 6LA ☏Colchester(0206) 37254
This charming cottage lies in a rural setting in Constable country, so check for directions. Bed and breakfast accommodation is offered, with three pretty bedrooms of good size and well equipped for guests' needs. Downstairs there is a delightful sitting room with comfortable armchairs and an open fire, and the breakfast room has a communal polished table; both rooms are complemented by lovely pictures, ornaments and antiques. Outside, the delightful garden offers tennis and swimming.

3hc CTV in all bedrooms ® ✕ ✳ sB&B£20-£25 dB&B£35-£45
📠 5P nc12yrs ⌂(heated) ♪(hard) ©

GH ⓠⓠⓠⓠ **The Old Vicarage** CO7 6JY ☎(020637) 248
*The vicarage has an Elizabethan/Tudor exterior, dating back
to the 15th century, with more recent Victorian and Georgian
additions. Set in a picturesque village next to the church, the
house is situated south of Ipswich, 1.5 miles from the A12. It is
furnished with notable period and antique pieces,
complemented by floral arrangements. The bedrooms are light
and spacious, offering a high degree of comfort. Delightful
gardens lead down to the river Brett.*
3rm(2⇆1hc) (1fb) CTV in all bedrooms ® ✳ sB&B£20-
£25 sB&B⇆£28-£34 dB&B£36-£40 dB&B⇆£44-£50
📠 CTV 10P ⌂ ♪(hard)🚣 boats ©

HIGH CATTON North Yorkshire Map **08** SE75

FH ⓠⓠ Mr & Mrs Foster **High Catton Grange** *(SE128541)*
YO4 1EP ☎Stamford Bridge(0759) 71374
Closed Xmas & New Year
*One mile east of High Catton crossroads towards Pocklington, this
farmhouse is part of a mixed farm. There is a well-maintained
garden and a large duckpond to the rear, and the accommodation
is of a good standard.*
3rm(1hc) (1fb) ✳ sB&Bfr£15 dB&Bfr£26
📠 CTV 6P 🐄 300 acres arable beef dairy sheep ©

HIGH WYCOMBE Buckinghamshire Map **04** SU89

GH ⓠ *Amersham Hill* 52 Amersham Hill HP13 6PQ
☎(0494) 20635
Closed Xmas & New Year
Small, friendly place in which to stay.
8rm(1↰7hc) CTV in all bedrooms ® ✕
📠 CTV 9P

GH ⓠⓠⓠ *Clifton Lodge Hotel* 210 West Wycombe Rd
HP12 3AR ☎(0494) 440095 & 29062
rs 25 & 26 Dec
*In 7 years Jane and Brian Taylor have developed their guesthouse
on the A40 into a comfortable and well run private hotel. They
have extended the bar and the dining room into an attractive
conservatory. Bedrooms vary, but all are well equipped and
maintained, and have good modern fitted furniture.*
31rm(12⇆7↰12hc) (2fb) CTV in all bedrooms ®
✕ (ex guide dogs) LDO 8.45pm
Lic 📠 CTV 28P sauna jacuzzi
Credit Cards ① ② ③ ⑤

HIMBLETON Hereford & Worcester Map **03** SO95

FH ⓠⓠ Mrs P Havard **Phepson** *(SO941599)* WR9 7JZ
☎(090569) 205
Closed Xmas & New Year
*The rooms in this 17th-century farmhouse are quite simple in
furnishings and décor. The Granary annexe provides en suite
rooms of good quality. Set in the heart of the country, yet only 5
miles from the M5 motorway.*
3hc Annexe 2⇆ (1fb) CTV in 2 bedrooms ® sB&Bfr£17
sB&B⇆£19-£20 dB&B£28-£30 dB&B⇆£32-£35
📠 CTV 6P 170 acres beef sheep ©

HINCKLEY Leicestershire Map **04** SP49

GH ⓠⓠⓠ *Ambion Court Hotel* The Green, Dadlington
CV13 6JB ☎(0455) 212292 FAX (0455) 213141
*About 2 miles north of Hinckley, this small hotel is set in a quiet
village overlooking the green. Comfortably appointed public rooms
and bedrooms (all with en suite facilities) are clean and well
maintained.*

▶

Clifton Lodge Hotel

210 West Wycombe Road,
High Wycombe, Bucks HP12 3AR
Telephone: 0494 440095 & 29062

Situated on the A40 West Wycombe approximately one
mile from the M40 London to Oxford motorway and
close to the centre of historic High Wycombe, the
principal town of the Chilterns. Ideal for touring the
Thames Valley, Oxford, Cotswold etc. There are ample
car parking facilities and pleasant gardens. Good
English breakfast, lunches and dinner available. All
rooms have central heating, wash basin, colour TV and
direct dial telephone. Small functions catered for.
Licensed.
**Under the personal supervision of the resident
proprietors Jane & Brian Taylor**

CWM CRAIG FARM
Little Dewchurch, Hereford HR2 6PS.
Tel: (0432) 840250   B + B Accommodation

Spacious Georgian farmhouse, surrounded by superb unspoilt
countryside. Situated between the Cathedral City of Hereford
and Ross-on Wye just a few minutes drive from the Wye Valley,
ideal base for touring Forest of Dean, Golden Valley, Malverns etc.

Accommodation which is fully centrally heated consists of 1
double, 1 double/triple, 1 family bedrooms all with H&C and
shaver points and tea/coffee facilities. Shower room and
bathroom with shower. Lounge, separate dining room both
with colour TV. A full English breakfast is served.

Access to accommodation all day. Open all year. Regret no
pets. There are excellent eating out Inns within the vicinity.

**English Tourist Board
COMMENDED**
♨ ♨

Proprietor: Mrs Gladys Lee
ETB – Classification 2 crowns   *AA listed*

2⌐ Annexe 5rm(1⇌4⌐) CTV in all bedrooms ®
LDO 8.30pm
Lic ♨ CTV 8P nc5yrs
Credit Cards [1] [3]

HINTON CHARTERHOUSE Avon Map **03** ST75

GH QQQ Green Lane House 1 Green Ln BA3 6BL
☎Limpley Stoke(0225) 723631
Feb-Nov rs Dec-Jan
John and Lucille Baxter have tastefully converted this property, which was once two early 18th-century cottages, into a cosy and comfortable guest house situated close to the village centre.
4rm(2⌐2hc) ® ✗ sB&B£24-£30 sB&B⌐£31-£35 dB&B£36-£40 dB&B⌐£42-£57 WB&B£113.40-£220.50
♨ CTV 1P 2🚗
Credit Cards [1] [2] [3] £

HITCHAM Suffolk Map **05** TL95

FH Q Mrs B Elsden **Wetherden Hall** *(TL971509)* IP7 7PZ
☎Bildeston(0449) 740412
Mar-Oct
Part Tudor-style farmhouse close to the ruins of a former hall, offering friendly accommodation. 1 mile west of unclassified road to Kettlebaston.
3rm (1fb) ✗ ✱ sB&B£14-£16 dB&B£26-£28 WB&B£72-£78
♨ CTV 6P nc9yrs ✓ 300 acres mixed £

HITCHIN Hertfordshire Map **04** TL12

GH QQQ Firs Hotel 83 Bedford Rd SG5 2TY
☎(0462) 422322
rs 25 Dec-2 Jan
This pleasant family-run hotel is situated close to the town centre and offers varied accommodation. There are some modern, spacious bedrooms, others are more compact, but all are well equipped. There is a comfortable lounge bar, and the 'Ristorante Classico' offers Italian cuisine in the evenings. Extensive car parking is available at the rear of the hotel.
30rm(24⇌⌐6hc) (2fb) CTV in all bedrooms ® ✱ sB&B£31 sB&B⇌⌐£37-£49 dB&B£48 dB&B⇌⌐£54-£59 LDO 9.30pm
Lic ♨ CTV 30P
Credit Cards [1] [2] [3] [5]

HOARWITHY Hereford & Worcester Map **03** SO52

FH QQ Mrs C Probert ***The Old Mill*** *(SO546294)* HR2 6QH
☎Carey(043270) 602
Small, white, cottage-style farmhouse in village centre with a traditional country garden at the front of the house.
6hc ⊬in 1 bedroom LDO 7pm
CTV 6P

HOLBEACH Lincolnshire Map **09** TF32

GH QQQ Pipwell Manor Washway Rd, Saracens Head PE12 8AL ☎(0406) 23119
This detached period farmhouse is surrounded by gardens and arable farmland, and is located just off the A17 at Saracens Head. There are four bedrooms and two bathrooms, but no en suite facilities; this is more than compensated for by the quality and comfort of the country-style furnishings, chosen with deliberate care to enhance the period façade. Public rooms include an elegant dining room and light, sunny lounge.
4rm(1hc) ⊬in all bedrooms ® ✗ sB&B£17 dB&B£30 dB&B£34
♨ CTV 4P £

See the regional maps of popular holiday areas at the back of the book.

HOLLYBUSH Strathclyde *Ayrshire* Map **10** NS31

FH QQ Mrs A Woodburn **Boreland** *(NS400139)* KA6 7ED
☎Patna(0292) 531228
Jun-Sep
Two-storeyed farmhouse with roughcast exterior, situated on the banks of the River Doon. West off A713 south of village.
3rm (2fb) ® ✗ ✱ sB&B£13-£15 dB&B£24-£28
♨ CTV 6P 190 acres dairy £

HOLMFIRTH West Yorkshire Map **07** SE10

INN QQ White Horse Scholes Road, Jackson Bridge HD7 7HF ☎(0484) 683940
Closed 24-25 Dec & 31 Jan
This typical Yorkshire pub is featured in the television programme 'The Last Of The Summer Wine', and offers a characteristic Yorkshire welcome and atmosphere. It is located two miles from Holmfirth, just off the A616 at Jacksons Bridge. Bedrooms are well equipped, and there is a good range of bar meals.
5hc (3fb) CTV in 2 bedrooms TV in 3 bedrooms ®
✗ (ex guide dogs) sB&B£20 dB&B£34 Lunch £3.80-£9alc Dinner £3.80-£9alc LDO 9.30pm
♨ 12P 2🚗 £

HOLNE Devon Map **03** SX76

SELECTED

FH QQQQ Mrs S Townsend **Wellpritton** *(SX716704)* TQ13 7RX ☎Poundsgate(03643) 273
Closed 25-26 Dec
A peacefully situated, well maintained farmhouse on the edge of Dartmoor, within easy reach of the south coast of Devon and many other places of interest. The bedrooms have been furnished with comfort in mind with many thoughtful extras. There is a cosy lounge, and a set meal of home-cooked farmhouse dishes is served in the dining room. The warm welcome and hospitality of Sue and Jim Townsend make for a memorable stay.
4rm(1⇌2⌐1hc) (2fb)⊬in all bedrooms ®
✗ (ex guide dogs) sB&B£15-£16 sB&B⇌⌐£15-£16 dB&B£30-£32 dB&B⇌⌐£30-£32 WB&B£105 WBDi£139 (wkly only Jul-Aug) LDO 4pm
♨ CTV 6P ⇌games room with snooker table tennis & skittles 15 acres mixed £

INN QQ *Church House* TQ13 7SJ ☎Poundsgate(03643) 208
An inn of great character standing in the centre of this moorland village, Church House has comfortable bedrooms with en suite facilities and colour TV. The bars have a cheerful atmosphere and interesting home cooked dishes are included on the menus.
7rm(1⇌3⌐3hc) (1fb) CTV in all bedrooms ® LDO 9pm
♨ 5P
Credit Cards [1] [3]

HOLNEST Dorset Map **03** ST60

FH QQ Mrs J Mayo **Almshouse** *(ST651082)* Hermitage DT9 6HA (S off A352 on unclass road towards Hermitage)
☎(096321) 296 due to change to (0963) 210296
Mar-Oct
Set in the peaceful rural surroundings of a large dairy farm, this comfortable house provides simple, clean accommodation and extends a warm welcome to guests.
3hc ® ✗ ✱ dB&Bfr£27
CTV 4P 140 acres dairy £

Book as early as possible for busy holiday periods.

HOLSWORTHY Devon Map **02** SS30

GH [Q][Q] **Coles Mill** EX22 6LX ☎(0409) 253313
Mar-mid Oct
The lounge and dining room of this attractive 18th-century mill still retain some original features. Just out of Holsworthy's centre, the accommodation includes 5 well equipped bedrooms and guests will enjoy home cooked meals and a warm welcome.
5♪ TV in all bedrooms ® ✖ (ex guide dogs) sB&B♪£16-£18.50 dB&B♪£28-£31 WB&B£95.50-£106.50
Lic CTV 12P nc6yrs

FH [Q][Q] Mr & Mrs E Cornish **Leworthy** *(SS323012)* EX22 6SJ ☎(0409) 253488
This low, white-fronted farmhouse has an attractive garden facing open country.
10rm(3♪7hc) (5fb) ® ✖ (ex guide dogs) ✳ sB&B£15-£18 sB&B♪£16.50-£20 dB&B£30-£36 dB&B♪£33-£40 WB&B£80-£100 WBDi£150-£180 LDO 6pm
Lic CTV 20P 2🍴 ♨ ♪(hard)⤢ ♃ badminton skittles archery shooting pitch & putt 235 acres mixed ⓔ

HOLT Norfolk Map **09** TG03

GH [Q][Q][Q] **Lawns Private Hotel** Station Rd NR25 6BS ☎(0263) 713390
Quietly situated just away from the town centre, The Lawns was built around 1800 as a Georgian farmhouse, and subsequently used as a dormitory for the adjacent public school; it became a hotel in 1966. The accommodation has been attractively refurbished with Laura Ashley soft furnishings and good en suite facilities. There is an elegant dining room, a cosy bar and a large comfortable lounge.
11⇨♪ (2fb)⤢in all bedrooms CTV in all bedrooms ® ✳ sB&B⇨♪fr£33 dB&B⇨♪fr£55 WB&Bfr£175 WBDifr£280 LDO 8.30pm
Lic ♥ 12P
Credit Cards [1][2][3][5] ⓔ

HOLYHEAD Gwynedd Map **06** SH28

GH [Q][Q][Q] **Hendre** Porth-Y-Felin Rd LL65 1AH ☎(0407) 762929
Closed 25-26 Dec
This large detached house was built in 1927 and has been tastefully converted into a small, personally run hotel. The accommodation is comfortable and well equipped; one of the three bedrooms has a private bathroom. It is conveniently situated for access to the ferry terminal, and only a short walk from the promenade.
3rm(1⇨2hc) CTV in all bedrooms ® ✳ sB&Bfr£12 sB&B⇨fr£15 dB&Bfr£24 dB&B⇨fr£30 LDO 3pm
♥ CTV 6P

GH [Q][Q] **Offaly** 20 Walthew Av LL65 1AF ☎(0407) 762426
This small, privately owned and personally run detached guesthouse is close to the harbour and conveniently placed for the ferry terminal. It provides well maintained accommodation.
5rm(1♪4hc) (2fb) ® ✖ ✳ sB&B£10-£13 sB&B♪£12-£14 dB&B£20-£24 dB&B♪£24-£26 LDO 3pm
♥ CTV 3P (charged)

⟷D GH [Q][Q] **Wavecrest** 93 Newry St LL65 1HU ☎(0407) 763637
This small guesthouse is personally run by young proprietors and is conveniently located for the harbour, ferry terminal and town centre. Street parking presents no problem.
4hc (1fb) CTV in all bedrooms ® sB&B£12-£14 dB&B£22-£26 WB&B£75-£85 WBDi£110-£125 LDO 3pm
♥ CTV 1P ⓔ

Visit your local AA Shop.

HOLYWELL Clwyd Map **07** SJ17

FH [Q][Q][Q] Mrs M D Jones **Green Hill** *(SJ186776)* CH8 7QF ☎(0352) 713270
Mar-Nov
Situated on a 120-acre mixed and dairy farm on the outskirts of town, this farmhouse has excellent views across the Dee Estuary to the Wirral. Parts of this charming old house date back to the late 15th century and it has a wealth of character, which is enhanced by exposed wall and ceiling timbers.
3rm(1⇨2hc) (1fb) ® ✖ ✳ sB&Bfr£12.50 dB&Bfr£25 dB&B⇨fr£29 LDO 9am
CTV 6P snooker table childrens play area 120 acres dairy mixed ⓔ

See advertisement on page 183

HONITON Devon Map **03** ST10

See also Feniton

⟷D FH [Q][Q] Mrs I J Underdown **Roebuck** *(ST147001)* EX14 0PB (western end of Honiton-by-pass) ☎(0404) 42225
Comfortable farmhouse accommodation is provided in this farmhouse situated in a dominant position on the western end of the Honiton bypass. Bed and breakfast only is provided in a warm atmosphere. Tea-making facilities and colour TV are available in bedrooms on request.
4rm(3hc) (1fb) CTV in 1 bedroom ® sB&B£12-£12.50
♥ CTV P 180 acres dairy mixed ⓔ

INN [Q][Q][Q] *The Heathfield* Walnut Rd EX14 8UG ☎(0404) 45321 or 45322
In an unlikely situation in a residential area, the Heathfield Inn is an attractive thatched-roofed building dating back to the 16th century. The rooms are well appointed and provide excellent facilities, there is a comfortable bar and a varied bar/dining room menu is offered. The inn also has a small conference room and a provisions store.

▶

ambion court hotel

The Green, Dadlington, Nuneaton CV13 6JB
Telephone: (0455) 212292
Fax: (0455) 213141

Charming, modernised Victorian farmhouse overlooking Dadlington's village green, 2 miles north of Hinckley, central for Leicester, Coventry and NEC and convenient for M1 and M6. Each room is comfortably furnished with en-suite bathroom, hospitality tray, colour TV, radio and telephone. There is a lounge, cocktail bar and a restaurant offering traditional British fare. Business facilities include a small conference room and fax. Ambion Court offers comfort, hospitality and exceptional tranquillity for tourists and business people alike.

Personally managed by proprietor John Walliker
See gazetteer under Hinckley

5⇨♠ CTV in all bedrooms ® ✗ (ex guide dogs) LDO 10pm
⑭ 50P nc14yrs pool table skittle alley
Credit Cards ①②③

INN Ⓠ Ⓠ Ⓠ **Monkton Court** Monkton EX14 9QH (2m E A30)
☎(0404) 42309
*This roadside inn has seen quite a transformation since its change
of ownership. The Taylors have furnished and equipped the
property well with bright modern-styled bedrooms, complete with
en suite facilities. The cosy bar and restaurant offer a good range
of wholesome food. The Monkton Court Inn is a friendly,
personally run establishment conveniently situated adjacent to the
A30.*
8rm(2⇨4♠2hc)(1fb) CTV in all bedrooms ®
✗ (ex guide dogs) sB&Bf22-£25 sB&B⇨♠£32-£35
dB&Bf39.50-£45 dB&B⇨♠£49.50-£55 WB&Bf147.50-£135
WBDif165-£239 Lunch £6-£10alc Dinner £10&alc
LDO 9.30pm
⑭ 100P
Credit Cards ①③

HOOK Hampshire Map **04** SU75

GH Ⓠ Ⓠ **Oaklea** London Rd RG27 9LA ☎(0256) 762673
*A detached red-brick Victorian house on the outskirts of Hook
with a large well tended garden. Bedrooms are simply furnished,
and there is a relaxed, friendly atmosphere complemented by good
home cooking.*
10rm(4♠6hc)(1fb)⊬in 4 bedrooms CTV in 5 bedrooms ® ✳
sB&Bf23 sB&Bf♠£36 dB&Bf32 dB&Bf♠£47 WB&Bf161-£252
WBDif232.75-£323.75 LDO noon
Lic CTV 11P £
See advertisement under BASINGSTOKE

HOPE COVE Devon Map **03** SX63

GH Ⓠ Ⓠ **Fern Lodge** TQ7 3HF ☎Kingsbridge(0548) 561326
Apr-Sep rs Mar
*Enjoying views of the sea and countryside, this modern detached
house is in an elevated position, 3 minutes walk from the sea. It
provides comfortable bedrooms, peaceful public rooms together
with interesting menus and friendly service.*
5rm(1⇨4♠) Annexe 3hc (2fb) ® LDO 5pm
Lic ⑭ CTV 8P 1🏖 nc3yrs ♿

HOPTON Derbyshire Map **08** SK25

GH Ⓠ Ⓠ Ⓠ **Henmore Grange** DE4 4DF
☎Carsington(062985) 420
*Standing in a natural butterfly garden of 2.5 acres, this charming
house has been fully extended and now incorporates a popular
restaurant serving English fruit wines and afternoon cream teas.*
14rm(12⇨♠2hc)(4fb) ® ✳ sB&Bf22 sB&B⇨♠£31
dB&Bfrf40 dB&B⇨♠£56 WB&Bf200-£217 WBDif270-£287
LDO 6pm
Lic ⑭ CTV 14P
Credit Cards ② £

HORLEY Surrey For accommodation details see under
Gatwick Airport, London

HORSFORD Norfolk Map **09** TG11

GH Ⓠ Ⓠ Ⓠ **Church Farm** Church St NR10 3DB
☎Norwich(0603) 898020 & 898582
*Conveniently located for Norwich airport, Church Farm
Guesthouse is a very well maintained and clean establishment with
modern public rooms and bedrooms, all of which have en suite
showers.*
6♠ (3fb) CTV in all bedrooms ® ✗ (ex guide dogs) ✳
sB&Bf♠£17-£20 dB&Bf♠£30-£36
⑭ CTV 20P £

HORSHAM West Sussex Map **04** TQ13

GH Ⓠ Ⓠ Ⓠ *Blatchford House* 52 Kings Rd RH13 5PR
☎(0403) 65317
Closed Xmas
*This converted Georgian house offers comfortable bedrooms with
modern shower rooms. Proprietor-run, a warm welcome is
extended to all guests at Blatchford House which is popular with
business people and tourists alike.*
11♠ CTV in all bedrooms ®
⑭ 14P
Credit Cards ① ③

GH Ⓠ Ⓠ Ⓠ **Horsham Wimblehurst Hotel** 6 Wimblehurst Rd
RH12 2ED ☎(0403) 62319 FAX (0403) 211212
*Quietly situated in mature grounds, this fine Victorian residence
has been skilfully modernised to provide well-equipped, compact
bedrooms, two lounges and a comfortable dining-room. Location
directions are advisable.*
14rm(11⇨♠2hc) (2fb)⊬in all bedrooms CTV in all bedrooms
® ✗ (ex guide dogs) ✳ sB&Bfrf37.50 sB&B⇨♠£39.50-
£49.50 dB&Bf44.50-£49.50 dB&B⇨♠£49.50-£59.50
LDO 6.45pm
⑭ CTV 14P
Credit Cards ① ② ③ £

HORSHAM ST FAITH Norfolk Map **09** TG21

GH Ⓠ Ⓠ Ⓠ **Elm Farm Chalet Hotel** Norwich Rd NR10 3HH
☎Norwich(0603) 898366
rs 25-26 Dec
*Set in the middle of this picturesque village, this former farmhouse
has well equipped, comfortable barn conversions with a lovely
lounge. The Parker family extend a warm welcome to all their
guests.*
Annexe 21rm(19⇨♠) (2fb)⊬in 8 bedrooms CTV in all
bedrooms ® ✗ (ex guide dogs) sB&B⇨♠£25.50-£33.75
sB&B⇨♠£25.50-£33.75 dB&B⇨♠£43.25-£50.50
WB&Bf171.50-£229.25 WBDif243.50-£301.25 LDO 6.30pm
Lic ⑭ CTV 20P
Credit Cards ① ② ③ £

HORSMONDEN Kent Map **05** TQ74

FH Ⓠ Mrs S M Russell *Pullens (TQ689389)* Lamberhurst Rd
TN12 8ED ☎Brenchley(089272) 2241
Mar-Nov
*This attractive timbered farmhouse has an abundance of charm
and character. Bedrooms are spacious and the large lounge/dining
room offers unpretentious comfort.*
3hc (1fb)⊬in all bedrooms ® ✗ sB&Bf23-£25 dB&Bf32-£35
⑭ CTV 3P ⚓ 10 acres non-working

HORTON Dorset Map **04** SU00

SELECTED

GH Ⓠ Ⓠ Ⓠ Ⓠ **Northill House** BH21 7HL
☎Witchampton(0258) 840407
Closed 20 Dec-mid Feb
*An attractive 19th-century farmhouse with good views of the
surrounding countryside. Bedrooms in the main house have
been carefully modernised to provide comfortable, practical
accommodation. The more modern rooms situated outside
include a room equipped for handicapped guests; all
bedrooms have private bathrooms and a variety of extras. A
set dinner is served at 7.30pm in the spacious dining room,
which has a conservatory extension. Local produce is much in
evidence, including home-made bread and shortbread. There
is an elegant lounge and a cosy bar with a log fire.*
9rm(7⇨2♠) (1fb) CTV in all bedrooms ®
✗ (ex guide dogs) sB&B⇨♠£32 dB&B⇨♠£58
WB&Bf182.70-£201.60 WBDif261.45-£280.35 LDO 7pm

Lic 🏮 9P nc8yrs
Credit Cards ①②③
See advertisement under WIMBORNE MINSTER

INN Ⓠ Ⓠ Ⓠ *Horton* Cranborne Rd BH21 5AD
☎Witchampton(0258) 840252
A large, detached 17th-century inn on hill top crossroads with sweeping views of open farmland. Bedrooms are spacious and well proportioned, comfortable and well equipped. The restaurant serves à la carte food, and informal meals are available in the bar, which has an open fire; the food is home-made and fresh.
5rm(2⇌3hc) ⊬in 1 bedroom CTV in all bedrooms Ⓡ
⊁ (ex guide dogs) LDO 10pm
🏮 100P
Credit Cards ① ③

HORTON-CUM-STUDLEY Oxfordshire Map **04** SP51

FH Ⓠ Ⓠ Ⓠ Mrs J R Hicks **Studley** *(SP615126)* OX9 1BP
☎Stanton St John(086735) 286
This smart farmhouse is ideally situated for people preferring a rural setting, but needing access to major routes and the town centre. It is signposted Horton-cum-Studley 4.5 miles on the Headington roundabout, on the Oxford ring road, and is seven miles from the M40. Bedrooms are pretty and comfortable, with en suite facilities planned, if not already installed. The proprietors are anxious to provide a good service, and offer guests a warm welcome; smoking is not permitted.
3rm(2⇌🌢) ⊬in all bedrooms CTV in 2 bedrooms ⊁ ✳
sB&B£18-£22 sB&B⇌🌢£27-£32 dB&B£35-£40
dB&B⇌🌢£40-£45
🏮 CTV 6P nc12yrs 50 acres arable
Credit Cards ① ③ Ⓔ

Blatchford House

A Grade II Listed Georgian Guest House conveniently situated for the station and town centre and, only 20 minutes from Gatwick. 11 spacious, centrally heated bedrooms all fully ensuite and with colour TV. Ample car parking. Incorporating Figure Shapers toning salon.
Open year round with limited service at Christmas.

Write for brochure: **Blatchford House, 52 Kings Rd., Horsham, Sussex RH13 5PR. Tel: (0403) 65317.**

HORTON IN RIBBLESDALE North Yorkshire Map **07** SD87

INN QQ Crown Hotel BD24 0HF ☎(07296) 209 due to change to (0729) 860209

A good range of home cooked bar meals is available at this popular village inn. On fine days, you can eat in the pleasant garden. Dinner is served in the attractive dining room.

10rm(2↱3hc) (4fb) ® sB&B£16.75-£19.85 dB&B£33.50-£39.70 dB&B↱£44-£48 WB&B£120.50-£142 WBDi£187.50-£206.50 LDO 6.30pm
🛋 CTV 15P (£)

HOUNSLOW Greater London London plan **4** B3 (pages 221-227)

GH QQ Shalimar Hotel 215-221 Staines Rd TW3 3JJ ☎081-577 7070 & 081-572 2816 FAX 081-569 6789

The Shalimar provides useful accommodation, with simply decorated but well equipped bedrooms, some overlooking the main road, some the garden. The spacious open-plan bar/lounge has recently been attractively extended.

31rm(22↱9hc) (7fb) CTV in all bedrooms ® ✗ sB&B↱£34-£38 dB&B£44-£48 dB&B↱£44-£48 LDO noon
Lic 🛋 CTV 8P
Credit Cards [1] [2] [3] [5] (£)

HOUSESTEADS Northumberland Map **12** NY87

SELECTED

FH QQQQ Mrs B Huddleston **Beggar Bog** *(NY797686)* NE47 6NN ☎Haydon Bridge(0434) 344320

Standing beside the Roman military road (now the B6318) which runs beside Hadrian's Wall, this farm overlooks Housesteads Roman Fort. The farmhouse has been sympathetically restored and offers a high standard of comfort and service. Bedrooms are well equipped with several thoughtful extras, and the charming first-floor lounge provides an excellent place to relax.

3hc (1fb) ✗ sB&B£20-£22 dB&B£32-£34 LDO 5pm
🛋 CTV 6P 2🚗 38 acres stock (£)

HOVE East Sussex

See **Brighton & Hove**

HUDDERSFIELD West Yorkshire Map **07** SE11

GH QQ Elm Crest 2 Queens Rd, Edgerton HD2 2AG ☎(0484) 530990 FAX (0484) 516227

An impressive stone-built house standing in its own grounds in a pleasant residential area, convenient for the M62 and the town centre. Bedrooms are well furnished, and good friendly service is provided.

8rm(3↱5hc) (2fb)⚟in all bedrooms CTV in all bedrooms ✗ sB&B£21-£25 sB&B↱£31-£40 dB&B£40-£60 dB&B↱£55-£65 WB&B£200-£280
🛋 CTV 12P nc5yrs
Credit Cards [1] [2] [3] (£)

HUGHLEY Shropshire Map **07** SO59

FH QQ Mrs E Bosworth **Mill** *(SO565978)* SY5 6NT ☎Brockton(074636) 645

Lovely old house in pleasant rural area beneath Wenlock Edge.

2↱ (1fb) CTV in 1 bedroom ✗ sB&B↱£18-£25 dB&B↱£30-£40
CTV 6P ✓ U own riding centre 250 acres beef (£)

(£) Remember to use the money-off vouchers.

HULL Humberside Map **08** TA02

GH QQ Earlesmere Hotel 76/78 Sunny Bank, Spring Bank West HU3 1LQ ☎(0482) 41977 Telex no 592729 FAX (0482) 473714

Closed Xmas rs wknds

This small, privately owned hotel is a mile northwest of the city centre, just off Spring Bank West. It provides sound, well maintained accommodation and is popular with commercial guests.

15rm(7↱8hc) (4fb) CTV in all bedrooms ® ✱ sB&Bfr£19.97 sB&B↱fr£27.02 dB&B↱fr£41.12 WB&Bfr£140 WBDifr£200 LDO 6pm
Lic 🛋 CTV P̸
Credit Cards [1] [3] (£)

HUNGERFORD Berkshire Map **04** SU36

GH QQQ Marshgate Cottage Hotel Marsh Ln RG17 0QX ☎(0488) 682307 FAX (0488) 685475

Closed 25 Dec-Jan

A delightful 17th-century thatched cottage overlooking the Kennet & Avon Canal and the Marsh common land. A sympathetically designed extension provides a cosy lounge, bar/dining room and pretty, well equipped bedrooms. The friendly proprietors offer a personal welcome and serve imaginative meals with their unique style of hospitality.

9rm(1⇌6↱2hc) (2fb)⚟in 3 bedrooms CTV in all bedrooms ® ✗ (ex guide dogs) sB&Bfr£25.25 sB&B⇌↱fr£35.50 dB&B⇌↱fr£48.50 LDO 7.30pm
Lic 🛋 7P 2🚗 nc5yrs bike hire
Credit Cards [1] [2] [3] (£)

HUNSTANTON Norfolk Map **09** TF64

GH QQQ Claremont 35 Greevegate PE36 6AF ☎(0485) 533171

A detached house a few minute's walk from both shops and seafront. The guesthouse has been totally refurbished with thought and care. Each bedroom is individually decorated in a pretty cottage style, and some rooms are larger and furnished with armchairs or sofas; en suite facilities are good and well maintained. Public rooms include a cheerful dining room, separate lounge and a small bar.

7rm(4⇌3↱) (1fb)⚟in all bedrooms CTV in all bedrooms ® ✱ sB&B⇌↱£18-£22 dB&B⇌↱£32-£44 WB&B£112-£140 WBDi£163-£191 LDO 6pm
Lic 🛋 CTV 3P
Credit Cards [1] [3]

GH QQQ Pinewood Hotel 26 Northgate PE36 6AP ☎(0485) 533068

Closed Xmas

Popular with commercial and leisure users, the Pinewood offers well furnished accommodation and a relaxed, informal atmosphere. The restaurant uses fresh ingredients in a simple à la carte menu supplemented by specials of the day.

8rm(4↱4hc) (4fb)⚟in 2 bedrooms CTV in all bedrooms ® sB&B£18.50-£25 sB&B↱£20-£25 dB&B£37-£44 dB&B↱£40-£44 WB&Bfr£120 WBDifr£165 LDO 9pm
Lic 🛋 6P
Credit Cards [1] [3] (£)

GH QQQ Sutton House Hotel 24 Northgate PE36 6AP ☎(0485) 532552

A large, stone-built house in an elevated, peaceful location, with fine sea views from most of the bedrooms and the first floor lounge. Most bedrooms have private bathrooms, and there is a variety of dishes on the well chosen menu.

7rm(5⇌↱2hc) (2fb) CTV in all bedrooms ® sB&B£20-£27 sB&B⇌↱£25-£32 dB&B£36-£44 dB&B⇌↱£40-£50 WB&B£140-£200 WBDi£175-£245 LDO 7.30pm
Lic 🛋 CTV 5P
Credit Cards [1] [3] (£)

HUNTON North Yorkshire Map **07** SE19

INN Q Q Q **The Countryman's** DL8 1PY
☎Bedale(0677) 50554
*This charming stone-built village inn dates from the late 17th
century, and features a beamed ceiling, stone fireplace and an
interesting collection of over 100 teapots. Bedrooms are most
attractive and stylishly decorated, and although compact, are
comfortably furnished with thoughtful extras. A residents' lounge
has been recently added, and accommodation is well maintained,
with excellent standards of housekeeping throughout.*
6rm(1⇨5🛏) 🚭in all bedrooms CTV in all bedrooms ⓇＨ✳
sB&B⇨🛏fr£25 dB&B⇨🛏£38-£40 ✳ Bar Lunch £4-£6alc
Dinner £4.50-£11.50alc LDO 9.30pm
🍴 20P nc14yrs ▶9 pool table
Credit Cards ①③£
See advertisement under LEYBURN

HURSLEY Hampshire Map **04** SU42

INN Q **Kings Head Hotel** SO21 2JW
☎Winchester(0962) 75208
Closed Xmas Day
*This large, sprawling public house provides clean, good value-for-
money accommodation. A fairly extensive bar menu is available
and is popular at lunch times, generating a lively atmosphere.*
5hc (1fb) Ⓡ Ｈ (ex guide dogs) ✳ sB&Bfr£17.50 dB&Bfr£35 ✳
Bar Lunch fr£2alc Dinner fr£2.50alc LDO 9.30pm
🍴 CTV 30P nc1yr
Credit Cards ①③

HUTTON-LE-HOLE North Yorkshire Map **08** SE79

GH Q Q Q **The Barn Hotel** YO6 6UA
☎Lastingham(07515) 311
Mar-Oct
*A converted barn set in the centre of this picturesque village,
overlooking the green. The interior has been attractively renovated
while maintaining the character, with stone walls, flagged floors
and beamed ceilings. There is a busy coffee shop, and guests may
dine in the attractive small restaurant. Bedrooms are small but
comfortable.*
8rm(3⇨🛏5hc) TV available Ⓡ Ｈ✳ sB&B£18 dB&B£35
LDO 10am
Lic 🍴 15P nc12yrs
Credit Cards ①③£

HYDE Greater Manchester Map **07** SJ99

FH Q Q Q Mr & Mrs I Walsh **Needhams** *(SJ968925)*
Uplands Rd, Werneth Low, Gee Cross SK14 3AQ
☎061-368 4610 FAX 061-367 9106
*Situated at the end of a long farm track off Werneth Low road and
surrounded by open countryside, this 16th-century farmhouse has
been modernised to provide well equipped, if rather compact,
accommodation. A courtesy service to and from the airport is
available on request.*
6rm(5🛏1hc) (1fb) CTV in all bedrooms Ⓡ✳ sB&B£16.50-£20
sB&B🛏£20-£22 dB&Bfr£34 dB&B🛏£36-£40 LDO 9.30pm
Lic 🍴 CTV 12P 2🛏 ▶9 ᴗ 30 acres beef £

FH Q Q Mrs M G Sidebottom *Shire Cottage Ernocroft*
(SJ982910) Marple Bridge SK6 5NT ☎Glossop(0457) 866536
*Situated in an elevated position up a small lane off the A626
between Marple and Glossop, this modern bungalow enjoys lovely
views over the surrounding countryside. The bedrooms are
attractively appointed if not overly spacious.*
4rm(1🛏3hc) (1fb)🚭in 2 bedrooms CTV in all bedrooms Ⓡ
🍴 CTV 6P ♠ 180 acres mixed

Book as early as possible for busy holiday periods.

ILFORD Greater London London plan **4** F4 (pages 221-227)

GH Q Q **Cranbrook Hotel** 24 Coventry Rd IG1 4QR
☎081-554 6544 & 4765 FAX 081-518 1463
*Conveniently situated a few minutes from the town centre, this
hotel has bedrooms on 3 floors: simply furnished, they are well
maintained and equipped, in varying sizes. The combined dining
room and bar has a pool table.*
16rm(13🛏3hc) (7fb) CTV in all bedrooms Ⓡ✳ sB&B£25.02
sB&B🛏£35.25 dB&B£35.76 dB&B🛏£45.98 WB&B£160-£175
WBDi£210-£245 LDO 7.30pm
Lic 🍴 CTV 11P 2🛏
Credit Cards ①②③£
See advertisement under LONDON

GH Q Q **Park Hotel** 327 Cranbrook Rd IG1 4UE
☎081-554 9616 & 7187 FAX 081-518 2700
*The Park Hotel is a converted detached house situated on a main
road within a residential area, twenty minutes by train to London.
Bedrooms are on ground floor and first floor levels and vary in size
and style, some being simple modern units and others with older
furniture.*
21rm(6⇨8🛏7hc) (3fb) CTV in all bedrooms Ⓡ✳
sB&Bfr£27.50 sB&B⇨🛏£32.50-£36.50 dB&B£35-£38
dB&B⇨🛏£42.50-£46.50 LDO 8pm
Lic 🍴 CTV 23P
Credit Cards ①③

'Selected' establishments, which have the highest
quality award, are highlighted by a tinted panel.
For a full list of these establishments, consult the
Contents page.

HUTTON-LE-HOLE
NR, KIRKBY MOORSIDE
N. YORKS YO6 6UA
Tel: 07515 311

Stay in one of the prettiest villages in
the North Yorkshire Moors National
Park. Ideally situated for visiting the
many interesting places in the vicinity. Lunches and evening meals available. Licensed. Ample private car
parking.

ILFRACOMBE Devon Map **02** SS54

See **Town Plan Section**
See also **West Down**

GH Ⓠ *Avenue Private Hotel* Greenclose Rd EX34 8BT
☎(0271) 863767
22rm(4⇄5♠13hc) (4fb) ® ✖ (ex guide dogs) LDO 6.45pm
Lic ⅏ CTV P
Credit Cards ①③

GH ⓆⓆⓆ *Avoncourt Hotel* 6 Torrs Walk Av EX34 8AU
☎(0271) 862543
Mar-Oct & Xmas
A small modern-style, family-run hotel in an elevated position overlooking the town and sea beyond. Avoncourt is designed and run with the holidaymaker very much in mind. The accommodation is brightly decorated, soundly equipped and furnished with a good range of en suite facilities.
13rm(6⇄7hc) (3fb) ® LDO 6pm
Lic CTV 10P
Credit Cards ③

GH ⓆⓆ *Cairngorm Hotel* 43 St Brannocks Rd EX34 8EH
☎(0271) 863911
Feb-Nov
8⇄ (3fb) CTV in all bedrooms ® LDO 6.30pm
Lic ⅏ 10P
Credit Cards ①③

GH ⓆⓆ *Cavendish Hotel* 9-10 Larkstone Ter EX34 9NU
☎(0271) 863994
Etr-Oct
This family hotel enjoys an elevated position with panoramic views. The bedrooms are comfortable and the service friendly.
23rm(15♠8hc) (5fb) CTV in all bedrooms ® sB&B£16.50-£20 dB&B£27-£33 dB&B♠£33-£40 WB&B£104-£126 WBDi£105-£150 LDO 5pm
Lic CTV 20P snooker
Credit Cards ①②③

⌨✈ GH Ⓠ *Chalfont Private Hotel* 21 Church Rd EX34 8BZ
☎(0271) 862224
Feb-Nov rs 1 Dec-31 Jan
Close to the beach and town centre, this family-run establishment offers bright bedrooms and warm, comfortable public rooms, together with personal service.
8rm(6♠2hc) (2fb) ® sB&B£12-£13.75 sB&B♠£14-£15.75 dB&B£24-£27.50 dB&B♠£28-£31.50 WB&B£82.50-£94.50 WBDi£92-£144 LDO 4pm
Lic ⅏ CTV ⚹
Credit Cards ①③

GH ⓆⓆ *Collingdale Hotel* Larkstone Ter EX34 9NU
☎(0271) 863770
Mar-Oct
This family-run guesthouse enjoys an elevated position with fine sea views. It is close to the town centre, all amenities and beaches.
9rm(3♠6hc) (6fb) ® ✖ sB&B£25 dB&B£40 dB&B♠£45 (incl dinner) WB&B£105 WBDi£130 (wkly only Mar-Oct) LDO 5.30pm
Lic CTV ⚹

GH Ⓠ *Cresta Private Hotel* Torrs Park EX34 8AY
☎(0271) 863742
mid May-Sep
24rm(15♠9hc) (10fb) TV available ® LDO 6.30pm
Lic lift ⅏ CTV 30P putting green
Credit Cards ①

GH ⓆⓆ *Dedes Hotel* 1-3 The Promenade EX34 9BD
☎(0271) 862545
rs 23-26 Dec

17rm(10⇄2♠) (6fb) CTV in all bedrooms ® sB&B£16-£18.50 sB&B⇄♠£21-£23.50 dB&B£30-£40 dB&B⇄♠£35-£45 WB&B£105-£140 WBDi£154-£196 LDO 9.45pm
Lic CTV 6P
Credit Cards ①②③⑤ Ⓔ

⌨✈ GH Ⓠ *Earlsdale Hotel* 51 St Brannocks Rd EX34 8EQ
☎(0271) 862496
This family-run establishment is close to all the amenities of the town, and guests will receive friendly service. Earlsdale has a lively bar.
10rm(5♠5hc) (4fb) CTV in 5 bedrooms ✖ (ex guide dogs) sB&B£11-£13.50 sB&B♠£12.50-£15 dB&B£22-£27 dB&B♠£44-£54 (incl dinner) WB&B£75-£80 WBDi£121.50-£128.50 LDO 6.30pm
Lic ⅏ CTV 10P table board games Ⓔ

GH ⓆⓆ *Lympstone Private Hotel* Cross Park EX34 8BJ
☎(0271) 863038
Mar-Oct rs Mar-May
15rm(9♠6hc) (4fb) CTV in all bedrooms ® ✳ sB&B£14-£16 sB&B♠£14.50-£16.50 dB&B£28-£32 dB&B♠£32-£36 WB&B£91-£112 LDO 4.30pm
Lic CTV 10P Ⓔ

GH ⓆⓆⓆ *Merlin Court Hotel* Torrs Park EX34 8AY
☎(0271) 862697
Mar-Nov
14rm(2⇄9♠3hc) (4fb) CTV in all bedrooms ® ✖ sB&B£20 sB&B⇄♠£22 dB&B£40 dB&B⇄♠£44 WB&B£140-£154 WBDi£173-£186 LDO 5pm
Lic ⅏ 14P skittle alley
Credit Cards ①③ Ⓔ

GH ⓆⓆ *Southcliffe Hotel* Torrs Park EX34 8AZ
☎(0271) 862958
Spring BH-17 Sep rs Mar-Apr
A small family-run hotel offering friendly service and attractive bedrooms.
13♠ (8fb) ® ✖ WBDi£161-£169 LDO 6pm
Lic CTV 12P ⚘ games room childrens play area & room Ⓔ

GH ⓆⓆⓆ *South Tor Hotel* Torrs Park EX34 8AZ
☎(0271) 863750
Etr-Oct
This Victorian house is situated in a quiet location half a mile from the town centre and beaches. Bedrooms are comfortable and have en suite facilities. Public areas provide attractive surroundings in which to relax; a stone well is near the pool and skittle room on the lower ground floor. Mr and Mrs Moor extend a warm welcome to all guests, and provide a choice of table d'hôte menus.
12♠ (3fb) ® ✖ LDO 6pm
Lic ⅏ CTV 14P nc6yrs snooker games room

GH ⓆⓆ *Strathmore Private Hotel* 57 St Brannocks Rd EX34 8EQ ☎(0271) 862248
This attractive, tall Victorian house is gradually being restored to its former style and charm under new ownership, and friendly, personal service is provided by the owner and local staff. Bedrooms are well equipped and furnished, with small private bathrooms; there is a cosy bar, a comfortable lounge and a bright dining room where interesting menus are served. Limited car parking on site is available.
9rm(2⇄6♠1hc) (2fb) CTV in all bedrooms ® ✳ sB&B£14-£18.50 sB&B⇄♠£16-£20.50 dB&B£28-£33 dB&B⇄♠£32-£41 WB&B£90-£117 WBDi£135-£165 LDO 5pm
Lic ⅏ 7P
Credit Cards ①②③⑤ Ⓔ

GH ⓆⓆⓆ *Varley House* 13 Chambercombe Ter, Chambercombe Park EX34 9QW ☎(0271) 863927
mid Mar-Oct
A well proportioned house in a quiet residential area, only a short stroll from the harbour and town centre. The bedrooms are

tastefully decorated, comfortably furnished and spotlessly clean, and they all have en suite bathrooms, TV and tea-making facilities. There is a table d'hôte menu offering a choice of dishes, and orders are taken in advance to ensure all food is freshly prepared. After dinner, guests can relax in the cosy lounge where a host of books and games have been provided. Some rooms have sea views, and the guesthouse has its own garden and car park.

9rm(8⇆🌂1hc) (3fb) CTV in all bedrooms ® sB&B£16-£17 dB&B⇆🌂£35-£37 WBDi£160-£170 LDO 5.30pm
Lic ♨ CTV 7P nc5yrs
Credit Cards 1 3 £

GH Q Q Q **Westwell Hall Hotel** Torrs Park EX34 8AZ
🕾(0271) 862792
An elegant, detached Victorian property with lovely views of the town and coastline, Westwell Hall has spacious bedrooms with en suite facilities. Within the intimate dining room, imaginative home cooked meals are served, and a warm welcome awaits all guests.
9⇆🌂 (1fb) CTV in all bedrooms ® sB&B⇆🌂£20-£30 dB&B⇆🌂£40-£60 (incl dinner) WB&B£140 WBDi£175-£185 LDO 7pm
Lic ♨ 14P nc6yrs snooker croquet table tennis
Credit Cards 3 £

ILKLEY West Yorkshire Map **07** SE14

GH Q Q **Moorview House Hotel** 104 Skipton Rd LS29 9HE
🕾(0943) 600156
A spacious and well furnished house situated on the Skipton road, just on the edge of town, set back from the road in its own grounds. There are some fine views of the moor and river from the rear of the house. Good all round comforts and service are offered, and the bedrooms are comfortable.
11rm(1⇆8🌂2hc) (6fb) CTV in 10 bedrooms TV in 1 bedroom ® ✱ ✱ sB&B£26-£30 sB&B⇆🌂£34-£40 dB&B£30-£36 dB&B⇆🌂£45-£50 WB&B£105-£185 LDO 5pm
Lic ♨ CTV 12P £

INGLEBY GREENHOW North Yorkshire Map **08** NZ50

FH Q Q Q Mrs M Bloom **Manor House** *(NZ586056)* TS9 6RB
🕾Great Ayton(0642) 722384
Closed 21-29 Dec
This working farm provides comfortable accommodation in the superb setting of the North Yorkshire National Park. Ideal for walking, the farm also provides rough shooting, and stabling and grazing for visitors bringing their own horses. Visitors enjoy the good cooking here and dinner is served by candlelight. Price per night includes a 3-course dinner. Dogs may be accepted by prior arrangement.
3hc ⅟₂in all bedrooms ® ✈ dB&B£57-£60 (incl dinner) WBDi£189-£200 LDO 5pm
Lic ♨ CTV 40P 10🐎 nc12yrs ✔ rough shooting & stabling for guest horses 164 acres mixed

---

INGLETON North Yorkshire Map **07** SD67

GH Q Q **Langber Country** LA6 3DT 🕾(05242) 41587
Closed 24 Dec-1 Jan
A large, detached property in open countryside. Occupies an elevated position situated in a quiet country lane about 1m south of Ingleton village. Turn off A65 at 'Masons Arms'.
7rm(2⇆1🌂4hc) (3fb)⅟₂in all bedrooms ® ✱ sB&B£13.50-£16 dB&B£26-£31 dB&B⇆🌂£31-£37 WB&B£84-£99 WBDi£116-£132 LDO 5.15pm
♨ CTV 6P ⬮ £

GH Q Q Q **Oakroyd Hotel** Main St LA6 3HJ 🕾(05242) 41258
Peter and Ann Hudson are a charming, hospitable couple who enjoy looking after guests at this attractive former rectory. Peter cooks good wholesome meals. The bedrooms are comfortable and simply equipped and there is also a lounge and residents' bar.

7rm(6🌂1hc) (2fb) CTV in all bedrooms ® ✈ (ex guide dogs) sB&B£20-£28 dB&B🌂£42-£48 LDO 5.30pm
Lic ♨ CTV 7P nc11yrs £

GH Q Q Q **Pines Country House Hotel** LA6 3HN
🕾(05242) 41252
A charming guesthouse with a relaxed atmosphere situated on the A65 just outside the picturesque village of Ingleton. The four bedrooms are all comfortable, with lovely views over the surrounding countryside. Wholesome, home-cooked meals are served in the pleasant conservatory dining room, and there is a comfortable lounge, well stocked with reading material and information on the locality.
4⇆🌂 (1fb) CTV in all bedrooms ® sB&B⇆🌂£20-£25 dB&B⇆🌂£32-£36 WB&B£112-£126 WBDi£178-£192 LDO 6pm
Lic ♨ CTV 14P 2🐎 (£2 per night)

GH Q Q Q **Springfield Private Hotel** Main St LA6 3HJ
🕾(05242) 41280
Jan-Oct
Jack and Kathleen Thornton have run this charming late-Victorian guesthouse close to the village centre for over 20 years. Bedrooms have good facilities, the lounge is attractive and home-cooking is served in the cosy dining room.
5🌂 (3fb) CTV in all bedrooms ® sB&B🌂£17-£18 dB&B🌂£34-£36 WB&B£102-£117.50 WBDi£155-£170 LDO 5pm
Lic ♨ CTV 12P £

INGLEWHITE Lancashire Map **07** SD54

🚗➧ **FH** Q Q Mrs R Rhodes **Park Head** *(SD542395)* Bilsborrow Ln PR3 2LN 🕾Brock(0995) 40352
A 200-year-old farmhouse with well furnished bedrooms and oak beams. It is situated on a working farm in rural Lancashire, but within easy reach of the A6 and motorway junctions. ▶

Licensed

1-3 The Promenade, Ilfracombe, EX34 9BD
Tel: 0271 862545
Overlooking the sea!

Inglewhite - Inverness

3hc (1fb) CTV in all bedrooms ® ✗ sB&Bfr£12 dB&Bfr£24 WB&Bfr£80
🍴 10P 255 acres dairy ⓔ

INSTOW Devon Map **02** SS43

GH |Q||Q| **Anchorage Hotel** The Quay EX39 4HX
☎(0271) 860655
Mar-Dec
Private hotel on quay, facing river and beach. Excellent views.
17rm(2⇌15↑) (6fb) CTV in 2 bedrooms ® sB&B⇌↑£33.75-£36.50 dB&B⇌↑£67.50-£73 (incl dinner) LDO 9.30pm
Lic 🍴 CTV 18P
Credit Cards [1] [3] ⓔ

INVERGARRY Highland *Inverness-shire* Map **14** NH30

GH |Q||Q||Q| **Craigard** PH35 4HG ☎(08093) 258
Situated just west of the village on the main route to the Isle of Skye ferry, this hospitable family-run licensed guesthouse is an ideal touring base for the visiting holidaymaker. It has a friendly, relaxed atmosphere and offers a choice of lounges together with comfortable and neatly appointed accommodation.
7hc ® ✗ (ex guide dogs) ✳ sB&B£14.50-£15 dB&B£29-£30 WB&B£101.50-£105 WBDi£168-£175 LDO 4.30pm
Lic CTV 10P

GH |Q| **Faichem Lodge** PH35 4HG ☎(08093) 314
Mar-Oct
4hc (1fb)⊁in all bedrooms ® dB&B£24-£25 LDO 4pm
🍴 CTV 5P

GH |Q||Q| **Forest Lodge** South Laggan PH34 4EA (3m SW A82)
☎(08093) 219
Set back from the A82, three miles to the south of Invergarry, this modern guesthouse offers comfortable and clean accommodation. The friendly proprietors have collected a considerable amount of information about the locality to ensure that their guests make the most of their stay.
7rm(5↑2hc) (2fb) ® ✗ sB&B↑fr£20 dB&B↑fr£30 WB&Bfr£98 WBDifr£145 LDO 6.30pm
🍴 CTV 10P

INVERKEITHING Fife Map **11** NT18

GH |Q||Q||Q| **Forth Craig Private Hotel** 90 Hope St KY11 1LL
☎(0383) 418440
A bright, modern, purpose-built small hotel overlooking the Forth, very close to the road bridge. Bedrooms are compact but well appointed, and it is popular with business people.
5↑ CTV in all bedrooms ® sB&B↑fr£19 dB&B↑fr£32 LDO 6pm
Lic 🍴 8P
Credit Cards [1] [3] ⓔ

INVERNESS Highland *Inverness-shire* Map **14** NH64

See **Town Plan Section**
GH |Q||Q||Q| **Aberfeldy Lodge** 11 Southside Rd IV2 3BG
☎(0463) 231120
Set in a residential area, not far from the town centre, this friendly, family-run guesthouse offers traditional hospitality and sound, modern appointments. As well as an attractive dining room, it has two cosy lounges, one of which is for non-smokers. The spacious bedrooms, all with ensuite facilities, are comfortably furnished and well equipped.
9↑ (4fb) CTV in all bedrooms ® ✗ dB&B↑£36-£42 WBDi£210-£231 LDO 4pm
🍴 9P

Visit your local AA Shop.

GH |Q||Q| **Ardmuir House** 16 Ness Bank IV2 4SF
☎(0463) 231151
Good progress is being made with refurbishment of the Georgian house which overlooks the River Ness close to the town centre. It has a relaxed atmosphere, and the bedrooms, all with en suite facilities, are comfortable and well equipped.
11↑ (2fb) CTV in all bedrooms ® sB&B↑£25-£30 dB&B↑£40-£48 WB&B£140-£168 WBDi£182-£215 LDO 7pm
Lic 🍴 4P ⓔ

GH |Q||Q| **Ardnacoille House** 1A Annfield Rd IV2 3HP
☎(0463) 233451
Apr-Oct
Situated in a residential area, this personally run attractive Victorian house offers good value bed and breakfast accommodation.
6hc (2fb) ✗ ✳ sB&Bfr£15 dB&Bfr£28
🍴 CTV 8P nc7yrs

GH |Q||Q| **Brae Ness Hotel** 17 Ness Bank IV2 4SF
☎(0463) 712266
Etr-15 Nov
Ideally situated on the river front within a few minutes' walk of the town centre, this small family-run private hotel is a popular base for the visiting holidaymaker. It has a friendly atmosphere and the well equipped bedrooms are gradually being upgraded with modern décor and fabrics being used to good effect.
10rm(9⇌↑1hc) (2fb)⊁in 4 bedrooms CTV in all bedrooms ® ✳ sB&B⇌↑£26-£30 dB&B⇌↑£34-£53 WBDi£197-£240 LDO 7pm
Lic 🍴 6P 2🐾 ⓔ

GH |Q||Q||Q| **Craigside** 4 Gordon Ter IV2 3HD ☎(0463) 231576
A family-run bed and breakfast establishment in an elevated position close to the centre of Inverness. Bedrooms are compact but well appointed, and the comfortable lounge offers fine panoramic views.
6rm(4⇌↑2hc) CTV in all bedrooms ® ✗ (ex guide dogs) ✳ sB&B⇌↑fr£20 dB&Bfr£26 dB&B⇌↑fr£32 WB&B£170-£200
🍴 4P nc9yrs ⓔ

See advertisement on page 191

GH |Q||Q| **Four Winds** 42 Old Edinburgh Rd IV2 3PG
☎(0463) 230397
Closed Xmas wk & New Year
This fine Victorian house is set in its own well maintained garden in a residential area. Family-owned and run, it offers well equipped bedrooms, some with private bathrooms, and an attractive first-floor lounge.
7rm(4↑3hc) (2fb) CTV in all bedrooms ® sB&B£16 sB&B↑£16 dB&B£30 dB&B↑£32 WB&B£100
🍴 16P ⓔ

GH ⓠⓠ **Leinster Lodge** 27 Southside Rd IV2 4XA
☎(0463) 233311
Closed Xmas & New Year
Situated in a residential area, this friendly family-run guesthouse
offers comfortable, good value bed and breakfast accommodation.
6rm(1⋔5hc) (2fb) ® ✱ sB&B£12.50-£13 dB&B£25-£26
WB&B£87.50-£91
⚏ CTV 8P £

See advertisement on page 191

GH ⓠⓠ **Murellan** Drumchardine IV5 7PX ☎(0463) 83679
Mar-Oct
This comfortable, detached house is situated seven miles west of
Inverness, just off the A862 near the village of Inchmore. It offers
good value holiday accommodation; breakfast is served at the
communal table in the neatly appointed dining room.
3rm(1⋔2hc) (1fb)⚲in 2 bedrooms dB&B£22 dB&B⋔£25
WB&B£71-£78
⚏ 3P £

GH ⓠⓠⓠ *The Old Rectory* 9 Southside Rd IV2 3BG
☎(0463) 220969
Closed 21 Dec-5 Jan
Situated in a residential area, this small, welcoming family-run
guesthouse has been tastefully upgraded to provide a high
standard of comfort and appointments. It has a relaxed
atmosphere, and smoking is not encouraged anywhere in the house.
4rm(2⋔2hc) (1fb)⚲in all bedrooms ® ✖ (ex guide dogs)
⚏ CTV 5P nc7yrs

GH ⓠⓠⓠ *Riverside House Hotel* 8 Ness Bank IV2 4SF
☎(0463) 231052
Situated on the east bank of the River Ness just a short walk from
the town centre, this well run holiday guesthouse is constantly
being improved. The tastefully appointed day rooms are ▶

complemented by comfortable, well equipped bedrooms and the atmosphere is relaxed and friendly.

11rm(5⇨5🌂1hc)(3fb) CTV in all bedrooms ⓇLDO 7pm
Lic 🏴 CTV 🅟

GH 🆀🆀🆀 *St Ann's Hotel* 37 Harrowden Rd IV3 5QN
🕾(0463) 236157
A stone-built Victorian house situated in a quiet west end residential area. Bedrooms are modern and well equipped, and the house is comfortably appointed throughout.

6rm(5⇨🌂1hc)(3fb) CTV in all bedrooms Ⓡ LDO 3.30pm
Lic 🏴 CTV 3P

GH 🆀🆀🆀 Villa Fontana 13 Bishops Rd IV3 5SB
🕾(0463) 232999
Situated in a quiet residential area close to the Eden Court Theatre and the River Ness, this detached Victorian villa provides tastefully decorated bed and breakfast accommodation and a friendly welcome.

4hc (2fb) CTV in all bedrooms Ⓡ sB&B£14-£15 dB&B£26-£28 (wkly only Nov-1 Mar)
🏴 4P Ⓔ

GH 🆀🆀 *Windsor House Hotel* 22 Ness Bank IV2 4SF
🕾(0463) 233715
This small personally-run private hotel beside the banks of the River Mess is conveniently situated for the town's amenities. Popular with commercial and leisure users alike, Windsor House offers good-value accommodation in well equipped bedrooms.

18rm(15⇨🌂3hc) CTV in all bedrooms Ⓡ ✖ (ex guide dogs)
Lic 🏴

INN 🆀🆀 Heathmount Kingsmills Rd IV2 3JU
🕾(0463) 235877
Closed 31 Dec-2 Jan
Situated in a residential area near the town centre, this is a popular venue for locals and visitors alike. The atmosphere is friendly, and it offers a choice of bars together with good value commercial accommodation.

5⇨🌂 (1fb) CTV in all bedrooms Ⓡ ✱ sB&B⇨🌂£35.50
dB&B⇨🌂£44.50 LDO 9.15pm
🏴 20P solarium
Credit Cards ①③

INN 🆀🆀 Smithton Hotel Smithton IV1 2NL 🕾(0463) 791999
This friendly, family-run hotel stands on the edge of the village, just over three miles east of Inverness off the A96. Modern and well furnished , it offers a choice of bars and well equipped, pine-furnished bedrooms, all of which have en suite facilities.

10rm(2⇨8🌂) (1fb) CTV in all bedrooms Ⓡ ✖ (ex guide dogs)
LDO 8.30pm
CTV 50P pool tables
Credit Cards ①③

IPSWICH Suffolk Map **05** TM14

GH 🆀🆀🆀 Bentley Tower Hotel 172 Norwich Rd IP1 2PY
🕾(0473) 212142
Closed 24 Dec-4 Jan
An imposing Victorian detached building set back from the A1156 on an arterial route just outside the city centre, with a car park at the front. Bedrooms are en suite, well equipped and comfortable, and the high-ceilinged public rooms are elegant, light and spacious.

11🌂 (2fb) CTV in all bedrooms Ⓡ ✖ ✱ sB&B🌂£30-£40
dB&B🌂£40-£48 WB&B£210-£280 LDO 8.45pm
Lic 🏴 12P
Credit Cards ①③

GH 🆀🆀🆀 Highview House Hotel 56 Belstead Rd IP2 8BE
🕾(0473) 601620 & 688659
A commercial, family-owned guesthouse situated in a quiet area of the city above the railway station. Bedrooms are very well equipped and a high standard of cleanliness is maintained. Dinner is provided with a small simple à la carte menu in a pleasant dining

room, which leads into a sitting area with a full-sized metered snooker table.

11rm(7⇨🌂4hc) (1fb) CTV in all bedrooms Ⓡ ✱ sB&B£30
sB&B⇨🌂£35 dB&B⇨🌂£45 LDO 7.30pm
Lic 🏴 CTV 15P
Credit Cards ①③

See advertisement on page 193

ISLE OF Places incorporating the words 'Isle of' or 'Isle' will be found under the actual name, eg Isle of Wight is listed under Wight, Isle of.

ISLEWORTH Greater London London plan **4** B3 (pages 000-000)

GH 🆀🆀 Kingswood Hotel 33 Woodlands Rd TW7 6NR
🕾081-560 5614
14rm(5⇨9hc) (3fb) CTV in 10 bedrooms Ⓡ ✖
Lic 🏴 CTV 5P nc8yrs Ⓔ

IVER HEATH Buckinghamshire Map **04** TQ08

GH 🆀🆀 Bridgettine Convent Fulmer Common Rd SL0 0NR
🕾Fulmer(0753) 662073 & 662645
A small, gracious Tudor-style building in well kept gardens, run as a guesthouse by an order of Sisters from the house of St Bridget in Rome. Attached to the private convent, the chapel and library are open to guests. The accommodation is simple but spotlessly clean, and an atmosphere of peace and tranquility prevails.

13hc (3fb) ✖ ✱ sB&Bfr£18 LDO 2pm
🏴 CTV

This guide is updated annually – make sure you use an up-to-date edition.

JACOBSTOWE Devon Map **02** SS50

FH Ⓠ Ⓠ Mrs J King **Higher Cadham** *(SS585026)* EX20 3RB
☎Exbourne(083785) 647
Mar-Oct rs Nov & Feb
Well-decorated and comfortably furnished 16th-century
farmhouse. Ideal base for touring.
4hc (1fb) ® ⅀ ✻ sB&B£11.50-£12 dB&B£22-£24 WB&B£68-
£70 WBDi£110 (wkly only Aug) LDO 5pm
Lic ⊯ CTV 6P nc3yrs ✔ games room 139 acres beef sheep Ⓔ

JEDBURGH Borders *Roxburghshire* Map **12** NT62

GH Ⓠ Ⓠ **Ferniehirst Mill Lodge** TD8 6PQ ☎(0835) 63279
This modern, purpose-built lodge is situated 3 miles south of the
town off the A68, in a secluded location beside the river. It offers
friendly service, home-cooked dinners, a comfortable spacious
lounge and neat, if compact, bedrooms.
11rm(5⇨3♐︎3hc) ® sB&B⇨3♐︎£20 dB&B⇨3♐︎£40
WB&B£133 WBDi£216 LDO 8pm
Lic ⊯ 10P ✔ ∪
Credit Cards ①③ Ⓔ

GH Ⓠ Ⓠ Ⓠ '**Froylehurst**' Friars TD8 6BN ☎(0835) 62477
Mar-Nov
A handsome Victorian house set above its own gardens, with views
across town to the countryside. Accommodation is spacious,
comfortable and well maintained. To find the house, leave the
Market Place by Exchange Street, take the first right into Friars
and the third drive on the left.
5hc (3fb) CTV in all bedrooms ® ✻ sB&B£15.50-£16.50
dB&B£26-£30
⊯ CTV 5P nc5yrs

GH Ⓠ Ⓠ Ⓠ **Kenmore Bank Hotel** Oxnam Rd TD8 6JJ
☎(0835) 62369
In an elevated situation just off the A68, this detached house has
attractive views over the gardens and river to the town and abbey.
Bedrooms are compact, but quaint and inviting, and the dinner
menu offers a good choice of dishes. Conveniently placed for the
town centre, the guesthouse provides a good base from which to
explore the historic border country.
6⇨3♐︎ (2fb) CTV in all bedrooms ® ✻ (ex guide dogs) ✻
sB&B⇨3♐︎£16.50-£27 dB&B⇨3♐︎£33-£38 WB&B£104-£120
WBDi£195-£211 LDO 8pm
Lic 6P ✔
Credit Cards ①③ Ⓔ

SELECTED

GH Ⓠ Ⓠ Ⓠ Ⓠ **The Spinney** Langlee TD8 6PB (2m S on
A68) ☎(0835) 63525
Mar-Oct
Situated on the A68, two miles south of Jedburgh, this
delightful house stands within its own well tended gardens,
screened from the road and traffic noise. Originally two
country cottages, public rooms are well appointed and
comfortable, and the bedrooms are nicely decorated. A warm
welcome from the friendly resident proprietors makes this a
congenial place to stay.
3rm(2♐︎) ® ✻ (ex guide dogs) ✻ dB&B♐︎fr£32
⊯ CTV P

GH Ⓠ Ⓠ Ⓠ **Willow Court** Willow Court, The Friars TD8 6BN
☎(0835) 63702
3rm(2⇨3♐︎1hc) ✻in all bedrooms ® ✻ sB&Bfr£19.50
sB&B⇨3♐︎fr£19.50 dB&Bfr£28 dB&B⇨3♐︎fr£30 LDO 5.30pm
⊯ CTV 4P ๑

Ⓔ Remember to use the money-off vouchers.

JERSEY

See **CHANNEL ISLANDS**

KEITH Grampian *Banffshire* Map **15** NJ45

SELECTED

FH Ⓠ Ⓠ Ⓠ Ⓠ Mrs J Jackson **The Haughs** *(NJ416515)*
AB5 3QN (1m from Keith off A96) ☎(05422) 2238
Apr-Oct
Situated west of the village, this welcoming traditional
Scottish farmhouse enjoys lovely views over the garden and
gently rolling countryside. Bedrooms are comfortable and well
equipped, some with private bathrooms. There is a pleasant
lounge, and enjoyable farmhouse fare is served in the bright
dining room.
4rm(3⇨3♐︎1hc) (1fb)✻in all bedrooms CTV in all
bedrooms ® ✻ (ex guide dogs) ✻ dB&B£25-£28
dB&B⇨3♐︎£30-£32 LDO 3pm
⊯ 10P 2๑ 165 acres beef mixed sheep Ⓔ

KELMSCOT Oxfordshire Map **04** SU29

FH Ⓠ Ⓠ Mrs A Amor **Manor Farm** *(SU253995)* GL7 3HJ
☎Faringdon(0367) 52620
A warm and friendly atmosphere is offered at this farmhouse, well
run along informal lines by Mrs Amor, set in an arable and dairy
farm. Each of the two bedrooms are spacious and reasonably
equipped, suitable for families but a comfortable choice for
business travellers too. Situated 10-12 miles from the M4 (exit
15), it enjoys a quiet setting but is close to major routes and larger
towns such as Oxford, Lechlade and Swindon.
2hc (2fb)✻in all bedrooms ® ✻ ✻ sB&Bfr£18 dB&Bfr£32
LDO noon
⊯ CTV 4P 315 acres arable dairy Ⓔ

KENDAL Cumbria Map **07** SD59

See also Brigsteer
GH Ⓠ Ⓠ Ⓠ **Higher House Farm** Oxenholme Ln, Natland
LA9 7QH ☎Sedgwick(05395) 61177
3rm(1⇨1♐︎) (1fb)✻in all bedrooms CTV in 1 bedroom ®
✻ (ex guide dogs) ✻ sB&B⇨3♐︎fr£21 dB&B⇨3♐︎fr£33
⊯ CTV 9P

SELECTED

GH Ⓠ Ⓠ Ⓠ Ⓠ **Lane Head Country House Hotel**
Helsington LA9 5RJ (0.5m S off A6) ☎(0539) 731283 &
721023
Closed Nov
This delightful 17th-century house is situated in an elevated
position in rural surroundings, just outside Kendal. Only a few
minutes from Junction 36 of the M6, follow the A591 ; it is
well signposted. Bedrooms are comfortable, spacious and very
tastefully furnished and decorated ; all have private
bathrooms and are very well equipped. The elegant lounge
overlooks the well tended gardens and nearby fells. A three or
four-course set menu is served each evening in the attractively
appointed dining room, and the hotel is licensed.
7rm(4⇨3♐︎) (1fb) CTV in all bedrooms ®
✻ (ex guide dogs) sB&B⇨3♐︎£35-£40 dB&B⇨3♐︎£50-£60
LDO 5pm
Lic ⊯ 10P nc5yrs
Credit Cards ①③ Ⓔ

GH Ⓠ Ⓠ Ⓠ **Martindales** 9-11 Sandes Av LA9 4LL
☎(0539) 724028
An extremely well maintained and tastefully decorated licensed
guesthouse, with full en suite facilities in each of its well equipped
bedrooms. Martindales is situated close to the town centre and the ▶

193

bus and railway stations, at the exit of the A6 and A685 roads from the town.
8♠ (1fb) CTV in all bedrooms ℝ 🛏 (ex guide dogs) ✳ sB&B♠£27-£28.50 dB&B♠£38-£40 WB&B£189-£199.50 LDO 1pm
Lic ⬜ 6P 1🐾 nc

FH Q Mrs S Beaty **Garnett House** *(SD500959)* Burneside
LA9 5SF ☎(0539) 724542
Closed Xmas & New Year
Good food and a convivial atmosphere are highly rated at this 15th-century house on the edge of the farmyard; at Burnside, just off the A591, two miles from Kendal. Visitors are welcome to take an interest in the many farming activities going on around them, with dairy cows, sheep and young stock a particular attraction.
5hc (2fb) CTV in all bedrooms ℝ 🛏 dB&B£24-£26 WB&B£80-£87 LDO 5pm
CTV 6P 750 acres dairy sheep £

FH Q Q Mrs J Ellis **Gateside** *(NY494955)* Windermere Rd
LA9 5SE ☎(0539) 722036
This attractive, white-painted farmhouse is situated 2 miles from Kendal on the A591 towards Windermere. The bedrooms all have a colour television and tea-making facilities, and there is a cosy lounge and an attractive dining room.
4hc (1fb) CTV in all bedrooms ℝ ✳ sB&Bfr£14 dB&Bfr£25 LDO 4.30pm
⬜ 6P 280 acres dairy sheep £

FH Q Q Mrs E M Gardner **Natland Mill Beck** *(SD520907)*
LA9 7LH (1m from Kendal on A65) ☎(0539) 721122
Mar-Oct
A very comfortable lounge and attractive bedrooms are features of this farmhouse situated about a mile from Kendal just off the A65. The dining room, with individual tables, is also tastefully decorated and furnished, and there is a secluded garden at the front of the house.
3rm(2hc) ℝ 🛏 ✳ sB&B£12.50-£13.50 dB&B£25-£30
⬜ CTV 3P 100 acres dairy £

KENILWORTH Warwickshire Map **04** SP27

GH Q Q Q **Abbey** 41 Station Rd CV8 1JD ☎(0926) 512707
A guesthouse in a residential road just off the High Street, where the hospitable owners provide personal service and clean, well maintained accommodation. The small, comfortable lounge is equipped with a selection of good books and board games. A popular place with both commercial and leisure guests.
7rm(2♠ 5hc) (1fb) CTV in all bedrooms ℝ 🛏 (ex guide dogs) ✳ sB&B£17.50 dB&B£31 dB&B♠£37 LDO 7pm
Lic ⬜ CTV

GH Q Q Q **Castle Laurels Hotel** 22 Castle Rd CV8 7NG
☎(0926) 56179 FAX (0926) 54954
Closed 24 Dec-2 Jan
Overlooking the castle and Abbey Fields, this spacious Victorian house has been carefully modernised to improve the facilities whilst retaining many of the original features, such as the floor tiling and stained glass. Bedrooms vary in size and are all well equipped, with private bathrooms. Warm hospitality and a good selection of food and wines make this a popular place to stay for business or pleasure.
12♠ (1fb) ✂in all bedrooms CTV in all bedrooms ℝ 🛏 (ex guide dogs) ✳ sB&B♠£25.50-£27.50 dB&B♠£41-£45 WB&B£178.50-£192.50 LDO 7.30pm
Lic ⬜ CTV 14P
Credit Cards 1 3 5 £

GH Q Q Q **Ferndale** 45 Priory Rd CV8 1LL ☎(0926) 53214
A large, semidetached Edwardian house set in a quiet residential area close to the town centre. Extensively refurbished, it now provides bright, attractive public areas and comfortable, well equipped bedrooms, many with good en suite facilities.

8⇨♠ (2fb) CTV in all bedrooms ℝ ✳ sB&B⇨♠£17-£18 dB&B⇨♠£34-£36 LDO 4pm
Lic ⬜ CTV 8P £

GH Q Q Q **Hollyhurst** 47 Priory Rd CV8 1LL ☎(0926) 53882
Situated in a residential area close to the town centre, this large semidetached Edwardian house offers clean, well equipped bedrooms and comfortable public areas. Service is friendly and attentive.
8rm(3♠ 5hc) (2fb) CTV in all bedrooms ℝ sB&B£15 sB&B♠£18 dB&B£30 dB&B♠£36 WB&B£100-£120 WBDi£160-£200 LDO noon
Lic ⬜ CTV 9P £

KESWICK Cumbria Map **11** NY22
See **Town Plan Section**
GH Q Q Q **Acorn House Hotel** Ambleside Rd CA12 4DL
☎(07687) 72553
Feb-Nov
Spacious bedrooms, traditional furniture and comfortable public rooms are just some of the features of this friendly Georgian house situated only two minutes from the town centre. Very well maintained throughout with full central heating, Acorn House is just the place to relax after a strenuous day touring the Lake District.
10rm(9⇨♠ 1hc) (4fb)✂in all bedrooms CTV in all bedrooms ℝ 🛏 (ex guide dogs) dB&B⇨♠£35-£50 WB&Bfr£125
Lic ⬜ CTV 9P 1🐾 nc5yrs
Credit Cards 1 3

GH Q Q **Allerdale House** 1 Eskin St CA12 4DH
☎(07687) 73891
The bedrooms of this Lakeland slate house all have en suite facilities, and the tastefully furnished, comfortable lounge and dining room really catch the eye. The neat and colourful flower borders are appealing.
6⇨♠ (2fb)✂in all bedrooms CTV in all bedrooms ℝ sB&B⇨♠£19-£26.50 dB&B⇨♠£38-£53 (incl dinner) WB&B£133 WBDi£185.50 LDO 4.30pm
Lic ⬜ 2P 4🐾 nc5yrs
Credit Cards 1 3

GH Q Q Q Q **Applethwaite Country House Hotel**
Applethwaite CA12 4PL ☎(07687) 72413
Feb-Nov
Formerly known as The Gales Country House Hotel, this private hotel is now under new ownership, but the style has not changed, with the emphasis on friendly hospitality. This splendid Victorian house stands in magnificent gardens with panoramic views over Derwent Water and the Borrowdale Valley. Public areas include a cosy bar, an elegant drawing room and the Garden Room with an attractive tented ceiling. Most of the individually designed bedrooms have private bathrooms, and enjoyable 4-course dinners are provided in the attractive dining room. Bowls, putting and croquet are available on the lawns. The hotel is situated about 1.5 miles from Keswick. Approach from the east via the A66 to a large roundabout, then take the third exit A591 and turn immediately right, signed to Underscar.
14rm(7⇨5♠ 2hc) (4fb) CTV in all bedrooms ℝ 🛏 sB&B⇨♠£27-£30 dB&B⇨♠£54-£60 WB&B£175 WBDi£247.50 LDO 6.45pm
Lic ⬜ CTV 10P bowling green putting croquet lawn
Credit Cards 1 3 £

This guide is updated annually – make sure you use an up-to-date edition.

GH Ⓠ Brierholme 21 Bank St CA12 5JZ ☎(07687) 72938
This pleasant, family-run Victorian house is on the end of a terrace close to the town centre. Most of the bedrooms have en suite facilities, colour TV and tea-making facilites. A selection of inexpensive wines is available.
6rm(5⇨♠1hc)(2fb) CTV in all bedrooms Ⓡ dB&B£32-£38 dB&B⇨♠£34-£40 LDO 3pm
Lic ♔ 6P

GH ⓆⓆⓆ Charnwood 6 Eskin St CA12 4DH (0.5m S off A6)
☎(07687) 74111
rs Nov-Mar wknds only
Conveniently situated not too far from the town centre, Charnwood is a very well maintained guesthouse. Bedrooms are comfortable and well appointed, and fine Victorian fireplaces are a feature of both the lounge and dining room. There is a small but attractive patio and front garden.
6♠(2fb) CTV in all bedrooms Ⓡ ✠ dB&B♠£34-£35
WBDi£165-£170 LDO 4pm
Lic ♔ nc5yrs Ⓔ

GH ⓆⓆⓆ Claremont House Chestnut Hill CA12 4LT
☎(07687) 72089
Situated on the A591, a mile from the town towards Windermere, this establishment was once a lodge for a manor house. It has well appointed, pretty bedrooms, and serves 5-course dinners.
5⇨♠(1fb)Ⓡ ✠ sB&B⇨♠£24 dB&B⇨♠£48-£52
WB&B£240 WBDi£338 LDO 4pm
Lic ♔ CTV 8P

See advertisement on page 197

GH ⓆⓆⓆ Clarence House 14 Eskin St CA12 4DQ
☎(07687) 73186
This Victorian house is situated within easy walking distance of the town centre, and is in an ideal position for touring the northern lakes. Very clean and well maintained, most of the bedrooms have ▶

private bathrooms and all have TV. Good home cooking can be sampled in the attractive dining room, and there is also a comfortable residents' lounge. Smoking is not permitted here.
8rm(7⚐ 1hc) (3fb)⊬in all bedrooms CTV in all bedrooms ⊁ (ex guide dogs) ✱ sB&Bfr£14.50 dB&B⚐fr£34 LDO 3pm
Lic 𝍋 CTV ⊭

GH QQQ Dalegarth House Country Hotel Portinscale CA12 5RQ ☎(07687) 72817
Spacious, comfortable lounges and very well appointed en suite bedrooms feature at this hotel which commands fine views of Derwentwater. 6-course dinners are served in the dining room each evening.
6rm(3⇌3⚐) ⊬in all bedrooms CTV in all bedrooms Ⓡ ⊁ (ex guide dogs) sB&B⇌⚐£34.80-£37 dB&B⇌⚐£65.60-£70 (incl dinner) WB&B£143.50-£155 WBDi£215-£230
LDO 5.30pm
Lic 𝍋 CTV 12P nc5yrs
Credit Cards 1 3 Ⓔ

GH QQQ Fell House 28 Stanger St CA12 5JU ☎(07687) 72669
Situated close to the town centre, this attractive Victorian terraced house offers very well-maintained accommodation. A friendly atmosphere prevails throughout.
6rm(2⚐ 4hc) (1fb) CTV in all bedrooms Ⓡ ⊁ (ex guide dogs) sB&B£13-£14.25 dB&B£24-£26.50 dB&B⚐£29.50-£32.50 WB&B£78-£106.50
𝍋 CTV 4P

GH Q Foye House 23 Eskin St CA12 4DQ ☎(07687) 73288
A mid-terraced Victorian house situated within easy reach of the town centre. The accommodation is clean and well maintained, and bedrooms all have TV and tea-making facilities. Smoking is not permitted here.
7hc (2fb)⊬in all bedrooms CTV in all bedrooms Ⓡ ✱ sB&B£12-£15 dB&B£24-£28 WB&B£85-£90 WBDi£127-£140
LDO 4pm
Lic 𝍋 ⊭ Ⓔ

GH QQQ Greystones Ambleside Rd CA12 4DP ☎(07687) 73108
Closed 1-27 Dec
A charming, spacious end-of-terrace house with an attractive garden, situated in a peaceful location but not far from the town centre. Bedrooms are very well equipped and decorated, all with private bathrooms, and some have fine views of the surrounding fells. There is a very comfortable lounge and a well appointed dining room in which imaginative home cooking is served. Enthusiastically managed, and with a friendly and relaxing atmosphere, Greystones provides an ideal base for touring or walking.
9⇌⚐ (2fb) CTV in all bedrooms Ⓡ ⊁ (ex guide dogs) ✱ sB&B⚐£19.50-£21.50 dB&B⇌⚐£35-£38 WB&B£122.50 WBDi£182.50 LDO 2pm
Lic 𝍋 7P 2🚗 nc8yrs Ⓔ

GH QQ Hazeldene Hotel The Heads CA12 5ER ☎(07687) 72106
Mar-Nov
This family-run hotel, incorporating the adjoining Burleigh Mead Hotel, stands in an elevated position to the south of the town and enjoys beautiful views down the Borrowdale Valley from its lounges and many of its bedrooms. The bedrooms are well equipped and the majority have en suite facilities.
22rm(16⚐ 6hc) (5fb) CTV in all bedrooms Ⓡ sB&B£19-£22 sB&B⚐£21-£24 dB&B£38-£44 dB&B⚐£42-£48 WB&B£127-£160 WBDi£218-£251 LDO 4pm
Lic 𝍋 CTV 18P Ⓔ

GH QQQ Holmwood House The Heads CA12 5ER ☎(07687) 73301
mid Mar-mid Nov
This well-appointed Victorian house has views towards Derwentwater and the Borrowdale Valley. The bedrooms are comfortable, and guests can enjoy the beautiful view from the first floor lounge.
7hc (1fb) ⊁ (ex guide dogs) ✱ sB&B£15.50-£17 dB&B£31-£34 WB&B£105.50 WBDi£161.50 LDO 2pm
Lic 𝍋 CTV 3P nc5yrs

GH QQ Leonards Field 3 Leonards St CA12 4EJ ☎(07687) 74170
Closed 23 Dec-Jan
An attractive, compact, friendly and very well maintained guesthouse, not far from the centre of town. Leonards Field offers a high standard of comfort, and cleanliness is evident throughout. Colourful flower baskets and window box displays are an attractive feature of the summer months.
8rm(3⚐ 5hc) (1fb) CTV in all bedrooms Ⓡ ✱ sB&B£14-£15 dB&B⚐£27-£32 WB&B£94.50-£112 WBDi£143.50-£161
LDO 4.30pm
Lic 𝍋 nc3yrs

GH QQ Lincoln House Stanger St CA12 5JU ☎(07687) 72597
Enjoying an elevated position, not far from the centre of town, this semidetached Victorian house has views of the surrounding fells from every bedroom.
6hc (1fb) CTV in 3 bedrooms Ⓡ ✱ sB&B£13-£15 dB&B£26-£28 WB&B£91-£105 LDO 3pm
Lic 𝍋 CTV 5P Ⓔ

GH QQ Lynwood 12 Ambleside Rd CA12 4DL ☎(07687) 72081
A large Victorian house providing very well maintained, comfortable accommodation. Nearly all bedrooms have en suite facilities, and each room has a television, tea-making equipment and central heating. There is a lounge, well appointed dining room and a small, attractive front garden.
7rm(6⚐ 1hc) (2fb)⊬in all bedrooms CTV in all bedrooms Ⓡ ⊁ sB&B£15.50 dB&B⚐£36-£40 WB&B£108.50-£140 WBDi£168-£199.50 LDO 2pm
Lic 𝍋 ⊭
Credit Cards 1 3 Ⓔ

GH QQQ Ravensworth Private Hotel 29 Station St CA12 5HH ☎(07687) 72476
Closed 7-31 Jan rs Feb
A charming family-run hotel in a central situation, comfortable, relaxing and very well maintained. The bedrooms are tastefully decorated and furnished, most of them with en suite facilities, and there is a delightful, spacious first-floor lounge.
8rm(1⇌7⚐) (2fb) CTV in all bedrooms Ⓡ ⊁ (ex guide dogs) sB&B⇌⚐£27.50-£32 dB&B⇌⚐£38-£43 WB&B£130-£140 WBDi£195-£200 LDO 6pm
Lic 𝍋 CTV 5P nc6yrs
Credit Cards 1 3

GH QQ Richmond House 37-39 Eskin St CA12 4DG ☎(07687) 73965
Closed Xmas
A comfortable guesthouse set in a residential area close to town centre.
10rm(6⚐ 4hc) (1fb)⊬in all bedrooms CTV in all bedrooms Ⓡ ⊁ (ex guide dogs) ✱ sB&B£13-£14 dB&B£26-£30 dB&B⚐£31-£33 WB&Bfr£135 WBDifr£150 LDO 5pm
Lic 𝍋 CTV ⊭ nc8yrs
Credit Cards 1 3 Ⓔ

GH QQQ Rickerby Grange Portinscale CA12 5RH ☎(07687) 72344
Closed 23-28 Dec
The new proprietors of this well maintained property assure a warm and relaxing atmosphere. There is a spacious, well appointed restaurant, and the bedrooms are well equipped, most having en suite facilities.

▶

Mary Mount Country House

—————— HOTEL ——————

Borrowdale, Keswick CA12 5UU
Tel: (07687) 77223 Telex: 64305

Mary Mount is situated in its own gardens near Lake Derwentwater. Accommodation is in both the main house and the picturesque Four Oaks cottage, and all have private facilities, tea, coffee, and colour T.V. There is also ample parking for guests. 200 yards away is Lodore Swiss with Restaurant and facilities available for our Guests including tennis, squash, sauna, beauty salon, swimming pools.

Accommodation is from £27.00 per person/night in a double/twin room and from £27.00 for a single room and full English Breakfast.
(Some lake views available)

This hotel is approx 3 miles outside Keswick on the B5289 in the Borrowdale Valley.

Manager/Manageress:
Gary & Ann Hawthorne

Lynwood Guest House

12 Ambleside Road, Keswick-on-Derwentwater, Cumbria CA12 4DL
Telephone: Keswick (07687) 72081

Situated on the quieter side of Keswick just 800 yards from Derwentwater and 350 yards from the town centre, we offer personal service and comfortable accommodation in this beautiful Victorian house. All of our bedrooms except the single are fully en-suite and all have a colour TV, radio, tea/coffee facilities and a hairdryer. Quality home cooking and fine wines may be enjoyed in the friendly atmosphere of our dining room. We can cater for special diets and provide wholesome packed lunches. Ample street parking is available nearby.
NON-SMOKERS ONLY.   COMMENDED

Maple Bank

Braithwaite Keswick, Cumbria, CA12 5RY

A delightfully friendly country guest house with magnificent unrivalled views of the Skiddaw range. We offer exceptionally comfortable en-suite bedrooms. Delicious food with an original touch is served in our pretty dining room overlooking the Derwent Valley.

Licensed – ample parking – open four seasons

Telephone: 07687 78229

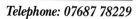

English Tourist Board

Claremont House

Chestnut Hill, Keswick, Cumbria CA12 4LT
Telephone: (07687) 72089

Claremont House is a 150 year old, former lodge house offering very pretty bedrooms with lace canopied beds and en suite facilities. Food here is our priority with a reputation over the years for consistently high quality. Vegetarians are also catered for and very welcome.

14rm(1⇆10↿3hc) (3fb) CTV in all bedrooms ® sB&Bfr£20 sB&B⇆↿fr£23.50 dB&Bfr£40 dB&B⇆↿fr£47 WB&B£128-£153 WBDi£198-£219.50 LDO 5pm
Lic ⁍ CTV 20P ⓔ

GH ⓠⓠⓠ Skiddaw Grove Hotel Vicarage Hill CA12 5QB
☎(07687) 73324
This comfortable, detached period house is peacefully situated on the edge of the town, in well tended gardens, and has a swimming pool to the rear. It commands fine views of Skiddaw, and is easily reached from the A66 bypass.
10rm(5⇆2↿3hc) ® ✗ (ex guide dogs) ✱ sB&B£14-£15 dB&B£28-£30 dB&B⇆↿£33-£35 WB&B£98-£115.50 WBDi£152-£169.50 LDO 4.30pm
Lic ⁍ CTV 11P ⬏ ⓔ

▣▶ GH ⓠⓠ Squirrel Lodge 43 Eskin St CA12 4DG
☎(07687) 73091
A small but well maintained guesthouse with pleasant bedrooms, an attractive dining room and a cosy lounge on the first floor.
7hc ⅍in all bedrooms CTV in all bedrooms ®
✗ (ex guide dogs) sB&B£12-£13 dB&B£24-£26 LDO 5pm
Lic ⁍ ℱ
Credit Cards ①②③ ⓔ

GH ⓠⓠⓠ Stonegarth 2 Eskin St CA12 4DH ☎(07687) 72436
Stonegarth is a family-run guesthouse with well-equipped bedrooms, an attractive dining room and a comfortable lounge. There is also a private car park. The Victorian building itself is of special architectural interest.
9rm(4⇆3↿2hc) (3fb) CTV in all bedrooms ®
✗ (ex guide dogs) sB&Bfr£15.50 dB&B⇆↿fr£37 WBDi£178 LDO 6pm
Lic ⁍ 9P ⓔ

GH ⓠⓠ Sunnyside 25 Southey St CA12 4EF ☎(07687) 72446
Closed 15 Dec-15 Feb rs 15 Nov-15 Dec
Within walking distance of the town centre in a residential area, this deceptively spacious house is under the personal supervision of the resident proprietors.
8hc (2fb) CTV in all bedrooms ® ✗ (ex guide dogs)
⁍ 8P
Credit Cards ①③

GH ⓠⓠ Swiss Court 25 Bank St CA12 5JZ ☎(07687) 72637
Conveniently located in a central position close to all the local amenities, the Swiss Court provides a good standard of accommodation.
7hc ✗
⁍ CTV 3P nc6yrs

GH ⓠⓠ Thornleigh 23 Bank St CA12 5JZ ☎(07687) 72863
Friendly and welcoming, this centrally situated guesthouse has well appointed en suite bedrooms, a comfortable first floor lounge and attractive little dining room. The pretty frontage, with flowers and walls makes Thornleigh particularly inviting.
6⇆↿in 2 bedrooms CTV in all bedrooms ®
dB&B⇆↿£36-£40 LDO 4.30pm
⁍ 3P nc14yrs
Credit Cards ①③ ⓔ

GH ⓠⓠ Twa Dogs Penrith Rd CA12 4JU ☎(07687) 72599
Clean, attractive and tastefully decorated bedrooms are a feature of this relatively modern inn, built on the site of a much older pub which takes its name from the poem 'The Twa Dogs' by Robert Burns. It offers an attractive dining room on the first floor, while a spacious bar provides meals on the ground floor.
5hc (2fb) CTV in all bedrooms ✗ (ex guide dogs) dB&Bfr£36 LDO 8.15pm
Lic ⁍ 20P nc5yrs games room ⓔ

KETTERING Northamptonshire Map **04** SP87

GH ⓠⓠ Headlands Private Hotel 49-51 Headlands NN15 7ET
☎(0536) 524624 FAX (0536) 83367
Particularly popular with commercial visitors to the area, this private hotel is in a residential area close to the town centre. The accommodation is well equipped and maintained : some single rooms are compact. There is an attractive dining room and a comfortable guest lounge.
13rm(2⇆4↿7hc) (3fb) CTV in all bedrooms ® ✱
sB&B£17.50-£18.50 sB&B⇆↿£28.50-£30.50 dB&B£30-£32 dB&B⇆↿£35-£38 WB&B£126.50 LDO 5pm
⁍ 10P
Credit Cards ①③ ⓔ

KETTLEWELL North Yorkshire Map **07** SD97

GH ⓠⓠⓠ Dale House BD23 5QZ ☎(075676) 836
Charming, stone-built village house close to the River Wharfe.
8rm(3⇆5↿) CTV in all bedrooms ® LDO 8.15pm
Lic ⁍ ℱ nc8yrs
Credit Cards ①③

GH ⓠⓠⓠ Langcliffe House BD23 5RJ ☎(075676) 243
Closed Jan
Charming, relaxed house on the edge of the village.
6rm(2⇆2↿2hc) Annexe 1⇆↿ (1fb) CTV in all bedrooms ®
sB&Bfr£26.50 sB&B⇆↿fr£28 dB&Bfr£43 dB&B⇆↿fr£46 WB&Bfr£149 WBDifr£210 LDO 7pm
Lic ⁍ 7P
Credit Cards ①③ ⓔ

KEXBY North Yorkshire Map **08** SE75

FH ⓠⓠ Mrs K R Daniel Ivy House *(SE691511)* YO4 5LQ
☎York(0904) 489368
Situated on the A1079 York-Hull road, this attractive farmhouse offers comfortable, neat bedrooms and cosy public rooms, with a friendly owner.
3hc (1fb) CTV in all bedrooms ✗ ✱ sB&B£15 dB&B£25-£26
⁍ CTV 5P 132 acres mixed ⓔ

KEYNSHAM Avon Map **03** ST66

GH ⓠⓠⓠ Grasmere Court Hotel 22/24 Bath Rd BS18 1SN
☎Bristol(0272) 862662
Situated on the edge of the town, this hotel has been totally refurbished to a good standard. It offers public areas of quality, and well equipped bedrooms, many of which have good, modern en suite facilities.
16⇆↿ (3fb)⅍in all bedrooms CTV in all bedrooms ® ✗
sB&B⇆↿£33-£49 dB&B⇆↿£44-£62 LDO 7.30pm
Lic ⁍ CTV 18P 1🏠 ⬏
Credit Cards ①③ ⓔ

FH ⓠ Mrs L Sparkes Uplands *(ST663664)* Wellsway BS18 2SY
☎Bristol(0272) 865764 & 865159
Closed Dec
Conveniently situated for touring this beautiful part of the country, this 19th-century stone farmhouse has simple accommodation with large, airy rooms. Mrs Sparkes is providing bed and breakfast this year.
9rm(2↿7hc) (4fb) CTV in all bedrooms ® ✗
⁍ CTV 20P 200 acres dairy

KIDDERMINSTER Hereford & Worcester Map **07** SO87

GH ⓠⓠⓠ Cedars Hotel Mason Rd DY11 6AL
☎(0562) 515595
Closed 25-31 Dec
Close to the A442, just north of the town centre, this well maintained private hotel provides good quality, well equipped accommodation. Small conferences can be accommodated.

20rm(1⇨19↑) (6fb)✗in 4 bedrooms CTV in all bedrooms ®
✱ sB&B⇨↑£32.70-£46 dB&B⇨↑£44.50-£57 LDO 8.30pm
Lic ⫟ 23P
Credit Cards ① ② ③ ⑤

KIDLINGTON Oxfordshire Map **04** SP41

SELECTED

GH Ⓠ Ⓠ Ⓠ Ⓠ **Bowood House** 238 Oxford Rd OX5 1EB
☎Oxford(0865) 842288
Closed 24 Dec-1 Jan
This hotel is situated parallel to the busy Banbury road, in the quieter slip road signposted 'Garden City'. Many of the bedrooms are located in the rear, garden wing, which is connected to the main building by a covered walkway. Rooms here are slightly larger than those in the main hotel, but they are all well decorated, comfortably furnished and offer good facilities. The public areas include a small, well appointed bar and a bright, spacious dining room, where table d'hôte or à la carte menus are offered. The hotel is professionally run by the resident proprietors with enthusiasm and enjoyment.
10rm(8⇨↑2hc) Annexe 12⇨↑ (4fb) CTV in all
bedrooms ® ⋈ ✱ sB&B£25-£35 sB&B⇨↑£35-£45
dB&B⇨↑£55-£65 LDO 8.30pm
Lic ⫟ 25P
Credit Cards ① ③
See advertisement on page 201 and also under
OXFORD

Ⓠ is for quality. For a full explanation of this AA quality
award, consult the Contents page.

Rickerby Grange

PORTINSCALE, KESWICK, CUMBRIA,
CA12 5RH
Tel: KESWICK (07687) 72344
Licensed accommodation
Resident Proprietors: Gordon and Marian Turnbull

Delightfully situated in the quiet village of
Portinscale ¾ mile west of Keswick. A licensed
residence with pretty garden and ample private
parking. You will find first class facilities in a friendly
and relaxed atmosphere. Imaginative home cooked
meals served in an attractive but informal dining
room. Most rooms with full en-suite facilities. A cosy
bar and lounge complete the picture.
Four poster available. Surfing, boating, gardens and
walks close by. Colour brochure sent with pleasure.

Sunnyside Guest House

25 Southey Street,
Keswick-on-Derwentwater, Cumbria
Telephone: (07687) 72446

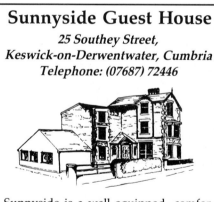

Sunnyside is a well equipped, comfortable Guest House. All rooms have tea
and coffee making facilities, colour TV,
central heating, hot & cold basins and
shaver points. Guest's Lounge. Car
park serving all guests. A few hundred
yards from the Town Centre. Well
noted for our full traditional English
breakfast. Packed lunches if required.

Bill and Anne will welcome you.

The Old Rectory

Boltongate, Cumbria CA5 1DA.
Tel: 09657 647

The Old Rectory is the home of Mr and Mrs
Anthony Peacock and dates from the early 15th
century. The three bedrooms situated in the 19th
century addition to the house are spacious and
tastefully decorated. The imaginative cuisine,
using all fresh ingredients and herbs from the
garden, is served in the 17th century dining room
with its stone walls and oak beams.

There are many places of interest nearby, with
walking, fishing and sailing all available in the
area.

Children over 14 welcome.

KILBARCHAN Strathclyde *Renfrewshire* Map **10** NS46

GH |Q||Q| *Ashburn* Milliken Park Rd PA10 2DB ☎(05057) 5477
A detached Victorian house, Kilbarchan has oak panelled stairways and hall and attractive stained glass windows. It has well equipped bedrooms and there is a children's play area within the acre of grounds.
6rm(2🌣4hc) (3fb) CTV in all bedrooms ⓡ LDO 11am
Lic ⁽ᵐ⁾ CTV 8P
Credit Cards ⑤

KILBURN North Yorkshire Map **08** SE57

INN |Q||Q||Q| Forresters Arms Hotel YO6 4AH
☎Coxwold(03476) 386
Next door to the 'Mouseman' furniture workshops, this 12th-century inn is run by the friendly Cussons family. Home cooked food is served in the bars and restaurant, and the pretty en suite bedrooms are well equipped.
8🖚 (2fb) CTV in all bedrooms ⓡ LDO 9.30pm
⁽ᵐ⁾ 40P
Credit Cards ① ③

KILLIECRANKIE Tayside *Perthshire* Map **14** NN96

GH |Q||Q| Dalnasgadh House PH16 5LN ☎Pitlochry(0796) 3237
due to change to 473237
Etr-Oct
Set in 2 acres of well tended grounds, this attractive Victorian house is an ideal base for the touring holidaymaker seeking peaceful relaxation. The house offers traditional comforts and Mrs McDougall maintains high standards throughout.
5hc 🖔in all bedrooms ⓡ 🗶 (ex guide dogs) ❊ dB&B£30-£35
⁽ᵐ⁾ CTV 10P nc
See advertisement under PITLOCHRY

KILMUN Strathclyde *Argyllshire* Map **10** NS18

GH |Q||Q| Fern Grove Fern Grove PA23 8SB ☎(036984) 334
Guests receive a particularly warm welcome from the enthusiastic and friendly owners of this small guesthouse. Well cooked meals based on fresh local produce are carefully prepared by Mrs Murray, and served by her husband in the pleasant restaurant overlooking Holy Loch.
3🖚🌣 (1fb)🖔in all bedrooms CTV in all bedrooms ⓡ
🗶 (ex guide dogs) dB&B🖚🌣£36-£50 WB&B£100-£130
LDO 9pm
Lic ⁽ᵐ⁾ 5P Argyll safaris
Credit Cards ① ② ③ ⑤ ⓔ

KILVE Somerset Map **03** ST14

SELECTED

INN |Q||Q||Q||Q| Hood Arms TA5 1EA
☎Holford(027874) 210
Closed 25 Dec
Dating back to the 17th century and reputedly connected with smuggling, this popular inn stands beside the A39 between Bridgwater and Minehead. The 5 well appointed bedrooms are individually furnished and decorated and equipped with many thoughtful extras; most are en suite. An extensive range of bar meals is served, and there is a grill menu available in the restaurant from Wednesday to Saturday nights. There is a delightful patio and walled garden for use in the summer, making this an ideal centre for touring the Quantocks and Exmoor.
5🖚 CTV in all bedrooms ⓡ sB&B🖚£35-£40 dB&B🖚£60-£66 WB&B£220-£252 WBDi£290-£330 Lunch £4.25-£10alc Dinner £8-£14alc LDO 10pm
⁽ᵐ⁾ 12P nc7yrs
Credit Cards ① ③ ⓔ

KINCRAIG Highland *Inverness-shire* Map **14** NH80

GH |Q||Q| *March House* Lagganlia, Feshie Bridge PH21 1NG
☎(05404) 388
Closed 21 Oct-26 Dec
In picturesque Glen Feshie 2 miles east of the village, this family-run guesthouse is an ideal base for the touring holidaymaker, with a range of outdoor pursuits in the vicinity. It has a relaxed atmosphere and offers good value accommodation.
6rm(5🖚🌣🌓1hc) (1fb)🖔in all bedrooms ⓡ LDO 6pm
⁽ᵐ⁾ 8P

KINGHAM Oxfordshire Map **04** SP22

GH |Q||Q||Q| *Conygree Gate* Church St OX7 6YA
☎(0608) 658389
Closed 25 Dec-Jan
A former farmhouse built of sturdy Cotswold stone, parts of which date from 1648, set in the sleepy village of Kingham. The bedrooms and public areas have been renovated and decorated with flair by resident proprietors Mr and Mrs Sykes. Bedrooms are prettily papered with co-ordinating Laura Ashley and Liberty prints, and are well equipped with modern facilities. The public rooms have a cosy country feel and retain original features, such as a large newly discovered fireplace in the residents' lounge.
8rm(1🖚5🌓2hc) (2fb) CTV in all bedrooms ⓡ LDO 5pm
Lic ⁽ᵐ⁾ 12P 2🏵
Credit Cards ① ③

KINGHORN Fife Map **11** NT28

INN |Q||Q||Q| *Long Boat* 107 Pettycur Rd KY3 9RU
☎(0592) 890625
An attractive large modern villa overlooking the Firth of Forth, decorated and furnished to the highest standard. Bedrooms are pretty and well appointed, and there is a comfortable lounge and lounge bar. In addition, there is a formal restaurant and an inviting wine bar, which offers good value menus.
6🌓🌓 CTV in all bedrooms ⓡ LDO 9.30pm
⁽ᵐ⁾ CTV 10P
Credit Cards ① ② ③ ⑤

KINGSBRIDGE Devon Map **03** SX74

GH |Q||Q||Q| *Ashleigh House* Ashleigh Rd, Westville TQ7 1HB
☎(0548) 852893
rs Nov-Mar
A small, friendly guesthouse conveniently positioned on the outskirts of town and providing a good base for touring the South Hams and coastline. Bedrooms are bright and well furnished and equipped, and there is an attractive sun lounge. Mr and Mrs Taylor are genial hosts: Michael is a professional Toast Master and Master of Ceremonies, and he and his wife provide good food and a relaxed atmosphere.
8rm(3🌓4hc) (1fb)🖔in all bedrooms ⓡ sB&B£14.50-£15.50 dB&B🌓£34-£36 WB&Bfr£146.50 WBDifr£153 LDO 4pm
Lic CTV 5P nc5yrs
Credit Cards ① ③ ⓔ

KINGSDOWN Kent Map **05** TR34

GH |Q||Q||Q| *Blencathra Country* Kingsdown Hill CT14 8EA
☎Deal(0304) 373725
Quietly situated, with a pleasant garden, this well maintained modern country guesthouse has been steadily upgraded by the new proprietors. Bedrooms are traditionally furnished and brightly decorated, and the lounge is spacious and very comfortable. Service is helpful and friendly.
7rm(3🌓4hc) (3fb) CTV in all bedrooms ⓡ 🗶 (ex guide dogs)
sB&B£16-£17 sB&B🌓£18 dB&B£34-£36 dB&B🌓£36-£38
Lic CTV 7P croquet lawn

KINGSEY Buckinghamshire Map **04** SP70

FH QQQ Mr & Mrs N M D Hooper **Foxhill** *(SP748066)*
HP17 8LZ ☎Haddenham(0844) 291650
Feb-Nov
A substantial, listed 17th-century farmhouse of enormous
character near the Oxfordshire borders. Bedrooms are spacious
and all have TV, and there is a delightful garden with an outdoor
pool available during the warmer months. The farmhouse provides
bed and breakfast, and smoking is not permitted.
3hc ⊁in all bedrooms CTV in all bedrooms ®
✖ (ex guide dogs) ✻ dB&B£32-£36 WB&B£112-£126
♨ CTV 40P nc5yrs ⌇(heated) 4 acres non-working Ⓔ

KINGSGATE Kent Map **05** TR37

GH QQ *Marylands Hotel* Marine Dr CT10 3LG
☎Thanet(0843) 61259
Apr-Oct
This small privately owned hotel has a warm, friendly atmosphere
and simple, comfortable accommodation. Overlooking the sea, it
has easy access to the beach.
9rm(1⇔5↟3hc) (3fb) CTV in 6 bedrooms ® LDO noon
Lic CTV 12P snooker

KING'S LYNN Norfolk Map **09** TF62

GH QQQ **Fairlight Lodge** 79 Goodwins Rd PE30 5PE
☎(0553) 762234
Closed 24-26 Dec
A mellow brick Victorian detached house with well tended
gardens. Pretty furnishings complement comfortable and well laid
out bedrooms which are mostly en suite. The guesthouse is
professionally run and spotlessly clean; to find it from the
roundabout at the A10/A17 at King's Lynn, follow signs to the
town centre, and at the first mini roundabout take the last exit
along Vancouver road, and the house is in the middle of this road,
which changes its name four times.
6rm(4↟2hc) (1fb) CTV in all bedrooms ® sB&B£16-£20
sB&B↟£16-£20 dB&B£24 dB&B↟£30
♨ CTV 8P

GH QQ **Guanock Hotel** South Gate PE30 5JG
☎(0553) 772959
A well run commercial guesthouse situated on the edge of the town
centre: from the A47, follow signs to the town centre, and the
house is on the right just after the roundabout. The modest
accommodation is neat and well presented, with a small bar, games
room and a dining room. A set meal or bar meals are obtainable
during the evening. Car parking is available to the rear at an extra
charge, by arrangement.
17hc (5fb) CTV in all bedrooms ® ✖ (ex guide dogs) ✻
sB&B£22-£24 dB&B£32-£34 LDO 5pm
Lic ♨ 12🏂 (£1 per day) pool room
Credit Cards ① ② ③ Ⓔ

GH QQ **Havana** 117 Gaywood Rd PE30 2PU ☎(0553) 772331
Closed Xmas
A family-run guesthouse situated on the main road on the outskirts
of town, with off-street parking. The friendly proprietors provide
comfortable, clean and simple accommodation; some rooms have
private bathrooms and some are on the ground floor to the rear.
7rm(2↟5hc) (1fb)⊁in 1 bedroom CTV in all bedrooms ® ✖
✻ sB&B£15-£16 dB&B£25-£26 dB&B↟£30-£32
♨ CTV 8P Ⓔ

GH Q **Maranatha** 115 Gaywood Rd PE30 2PU
☎(0553) 774596
Recently refurbished, this simple family run guesthouse offers well
equipped accommodation and simple good value. It is situated on
the outskirts of the town centre, on a road which leads eventually to
the B1145.

▶

6rm(1⌐ 5hc) (2fb) CTV in all bedrooms ® ✱ sB&B£12-£15 dB&B£20-£24 dB&B⌐ £24-£30 LDO 6pm
Lic 🍴 CTV 12P £

SELECTED

GH QQQQ Russet House Hotel Vancouver Ave, 53 Goodwins Rd PE30 5PE ☎(0553) 773098
Closed Xmas & New Year
A detached, Victorian house situated in a quiet residential area at the junction of Tennyson and Goodwin roads, set in secluded gardens, with ample parking. The bedrooms are immaculate and full of character; 1 has a 4-poster bed and all have private bathrooms. The restaurant is elegantly furnished, and the bar has an open fire. The high standard and warmth of hospitality and comfort provided by the proprietors is reflected in the hotel's popularity with visitors and business people alike.
12rm(8⇌4⌐) (1fb)⊬in 1 bedroom CTV in all bedrooms ® ✗ (ex guide dogs) ✱ sB&B⇌⌐ £34.50-£39 dB&B⇌⌐ £45.50-£65 LDO 7.30pm
Lic 🍴 14P
Credit Cards 1 2 3 5

FH QQ Mr N Olesen **Lodge** *(TF824172)* Castle Acre PE32 2BS ☎Castle Acre(0760) 755206
A substantial, low, white farmhouse surrounded by outbuildings forming a courtyard. Simple, comfortable accommodation is provided in light, spacious rooms, and there is a pleasant lounge and dining room. The farm is located on an unclassified track midway between Castle Clene and Rougham, in a tranquil, secluded setting.
3rm(2⇌1hc) (1fb) CTV in all bedrooms ® ✗ (ex guide dogs) ✱ sB&B£18 sB&B⇌£19 dB&B£30 dB&B⇌£32 WB&B£105-£112 WBDi£172-£182 LDO 5pm
🍴 CTV 20P 1000 acres mixed £

KINGSTON Devon Map **02** SX64

SELECTED

GH QQQQ *Trebles Cottage Hotel* TQ7 4PT ☎Bigbury-on-Sea(0548) 810268
This small, comfortable and personally managed hotel has its own woodland gardens and is set in an unspoilt village in this rural part of southwest Devon. Bedrooms are spotlessly clean and brightly decorated in pleasing colours and fabrics and are well equipped. There is a comfortable lounge, a cosy honesty bar and a small dining room where traditional home cooking features daily.
5⇌ CTV in all bedrooms ® LDO 4pm
Lic 🍴 10P nc12yrs
Credit Cards 1 3

KINGSTON BAGPUIZE Oxfordshire Map **04** SU49

SELECTED

FH QQQQ Mrs A Y Crowther **Fallowfields** *(SU393979)* Southmoor OX13 5BH ☎Longworth(0865) 820416 Telex no 83388 FAX (0865) 820629
Apr-Sep rs Wed
Dating back over 300 years, this handsome country house, with its magnificent Victorian façade, is set in 12 acres of lovely, well kept gardens. The spacious bedrooms are comfortable, stylishly furnished and well appointed. Public areas are also spacious and elegant, and an evening meal is offered, cooked by the charming owner.
4⇌⌐ CTV in all bedrooms ® sB&B⇌⌐ fr£26.50 dB&B⇌⌐ fr£60.50 WB&Bfr£211.75 WBDifr£318.25 LDO 6.30pm
Lic 🍴 CTV 15P nc10yrs ⛀(heated) 🎾(hard)table tennis croquet 12 acres sheep
Credit Cards 1 3

KINGSTON UPON THAMES Greater London, London plan **4** B2 pages 224-225

GH QQQ Chase Lodge 10 Park Rd, Hampton Wick KT1 4AS ☎081-943 1862
5⇌⌐ Annexe 4rm(2⌐) (1fb)⊬in 1 bedroom CTV in all bedrooms ® ✱ sB&B£26-£30 sB&B⇌⌐ £35-£42 dB&B£35-£40 dB&B⇌⌐ £46-£51 LDO 9pm
🍴 CTV 1🚗 (charged)
Credit Cards 1 2 3

KINGSWELLS Grampian *Aberdeenshire* Map **15** NJ80

FH QQQ Mrs M Mann ***Bellfield*** *(NJ868055)* AB1 8PX ☎Aberdeen(0224) 740239
Closed Dec
Set in gentle rolling countryside just four miles west of Aberdeen beside the A944, this traditional farmhouse has been tastefully modernised and provides comfortable excellent value accommodation, with an attractive lounge, thoughtfully equipped cheerful bedrooms and a friendly atmosphere.
3hc (2fb) CTV in 1 bedroom
🍴 CTV 200 acres arable beef

KINGUSSIE Highland *Inverness-shire* Map **14** NH70

GH QQ Craig An Darach High St ☎(0540) 661235
Closed Nov-Dec
This family-run guesthouse is set in an elevated position in 3 acres of grounds overlooking the Spey Valley. It has a friendly atmosphere and offers good value bed and breakfast accommodation. Smoking is not permitted throughout the house.
6rm(3⇌⌐) (1fb)⊬in all bedrooms ® ✱ sB&B£14 dB&B£24 dB&B⇌⌐ £28
🍴 CTV 6P £

GH QQ Homewood Lodge Newtonmore Rd PH21 1HD ☎(0540) 661507
Closed Xmas
This friendly, family-run guesthouse stands just south of the town in an elevated position above the Newtonmore road, with commanding views over the Spey Valley. Bedrooms are spacious and comfortable, and menus are varied and offer interesting home-cooked dishes featuring traditional local fare. Smoking is not permitted.
4⌐ (2fb)⊬in all bedrooms ® ✱ sB&B⌐ £22.50 dB&B⌐ £39.50 WB&B£138.25-£157.50 WBDi£225.75-£245.50 LDO 9pm
Lic 🍴 CTV 6P £

GH QQ Sonnhalde East Ter PH21 1JS ☎(0540) 661266
Closed Nov & Dec
This large sturdy Victorian house is situated in an elevated position above the High street, and enjoys a splendid outlook over the Spey valley. It has a friendly atmosphere, and is comfortably appointed throughout. A special Wildwatch package is available: details on request.
8hc (3fb)⊬in all bedrooms CTV in 1 bedroom sB&B£14-£15.50 dB&B£28-£31 WB&B£90-£100 WBDifr£150 LDO 2pm
🍴 CTV 8P £

See the regional maps of popular holiday areas at the back of the book.

KINVER Staffordshire Map **07** SO88

INN Q Q Q *Kinfayre Restaurant* 41 High St DY7 6HF
☎(0384) 872565 FAX (0384) 877724
*A fully modernised inn situated in the heart of the village, with well
equipped bedrooms in a separate building. Evenings are busy here
with the skittle alley, but peace and quiet can be found in the
private gardens which have a heated pool for resident's use only.*
11♪ (1fb) CTV in all bedrooms ® ✖ (ex guide dogs)
LDO 10pm
♨ CTV 17P ⟰(heated)

KIRKBEAN Dumfries & Galloway *Dumfriesshire* Map **11**
NX95

SELECTED

GH Q Q Q Q *Cavens House* DG2 8AA ☎(038788) 234
*A converted mansion in a peaceful location with a long drive
lined with rhododendrons and azaleas and surrounded by 11
acres of attractive gardens and woodland on the Solway
Coast. Well maintained, it offers comfortable and spacious
accommodation and enjoyable home-made dinners which are
freshly cooked and provide good value. Besides interesting
and enjoyable walks through the grounds, there is a small
putting green and games room, and in the sitting room a piano,
board games, books and an honesty bar.*
6rm(4⟶2♪) (1fb) CTV in all bedrooms ® ✱
sB&B⟶♪£30 dB&B⟶♪£44-£48 LDO 7pm
Lic ♨ CTV 10P putting green
Credit Cards ① ③ ④

KIRKBY LONSDALE Cumbria Map **07** SD67

GH Q Q Q *Abbot Hall* LA6 2AB ☎(05242) 71406
Mar-Oct
*A charming 17th-century farmhouse, full of character with oak
beams, low ceilings, flagstone floors and open fires. Bedrooms all
have private bathrooms, including three new rooms in the cottage
next door. Home-cooked meals are served on an impressive
antique oak table. Situated just a short walk from the town centre,
there is ample parking provided, including stabling if required.*
4♪ Annexe 3♪ (1fb)⊁in all bedrooms CTV in 3 bedrooms ®
✖ (ex guide dogs) LDO 6pm
♨ CTV 10P nc12yrs

SELECTED

GH Q Q Q Q *Cobwebs Country House* Leck, Cowan
Bridge LA6 2HZ ☎Kirby Lonsdale(05242) 72141
Mar-Dec rs Sun
*A charming Victorian house with an excellent restaurant
situated at Cowan Bridge, off the A68 2 miles southeast of
Kirkby Lonsdale, turn off at the sign for Leck. In its own
landscaped gardens, surrounded by open countryside,
Cobwebs has 5 delightful bedrooms, all individually decorated
and furnished in Victorian style, but with every modern
facility and many thoughtful extras. There are 2 lounges
where pre-dinner drinks are served, and an attractively
appointed conservatory restaurant where tempting 4-course
dinners are provided. The friendly hosts, Yvonne does the cooking and Paul looks
after front of house.*
5⟶♪ CTV in all bedrooms ® ✖ sB&B⟶♪fr£40
dB&B⟶♪fr£60 WB&Bfr£210 WBDifr£385 LDO 7.30pm
Lic ♨ 20P nc12yrs ♪
Credit Cards ① ③ ④

Book as early as possible for busy holiday periods.

SELECTED

GH Q Q Q Q *Hipping Hall Hotel* Cowan Bridge LA6 2JJ
☎(05242) 71187 FAX (05242) 72452
Mar-Nov
*An elegant country house, parts of which date back to the 17th
century, set in 4 acres of beautiful walled gardens and grounds
beside the A65, 3 miles east of Kirkby Lonsdale. There are 5
handsome bedrooms in the main house, all with excellent en
suite bathrooms, and in an adjacent building there are 2
versatile cottage apartments. A feature of the house is the
Great Hall with its timbered ceiling and minstrel's gallery,
here guests dine together at one table, relaxing afterwards in
the sumptuous Great Hall lounge or the equally comfortable
television lounge. This is a very hospitable and relaxing house,
and the food is excellent.*
7rm(6⟶1♪) CTV in all bedrooms ® dB&B⟶♪£69
WBDifr£325 LDO 6.30pm
Lic ♨ CTV 12P nc12yrs croquet
Credit Cards ① ③

KIRKBYMOORSIDE North Yorkshire Map **08** SE68

SELECTED

GH Q Q Q Q *Appletree Court* Town Farm, 9 High
Market Place YO6 6AT ☎(0751) 31536
*A charming little guesthouse centrally situated in the quaint
market town of Kirkby Moorside. Once a working farm, the
original character of the building has been preserved, and the
accommodation is warm and comfortable, complemented by
the sincere and caring hospitality of the owners. Bedrooms are
thoughtfully designed and individually decorated with many* ▶

Russet House Hotel

Tel. King's Lynn (0553) 773098 ♔ ♔ ♔

*One of the nicest old houses in one of the most historic
Towns in England. Set in beautiful secluded gardens a
short walk from Town Centre and River Ouse. Four poster
suite. Pretty en suite rooms with TV and courtesy Tea/
Coffee.*

Cosy little bar – roaring fire in winter!

*Elegant Dining Room – good food. Ample room to park
your car.*

*Rae & Barry Muddle (we try not to live up to our
name!)*
*Vancouver Ave/Goodwins Road, King's Lynn Norfolk
PE30 5PE*

personal touches including some beautiful embroidery and tapestry made by the proprietor's wife. The charming, pretty lounge is well stocked with books and flowers and overlooks the walled garden. Traditional farmhouse meals are provided, including a wholesome English breakfast.
6rm(4⇔2hc) (2fb)⊁in all bedrooms CTV in all bedrooms ✗ ✳ sB&B⇔♠fr£20 dB&B⇔♠fr£40 WB&Bfr£133 LDO noon
⊞ 2P nc12yrs

KIRKBY STEPHEN Cumbria Map **12** NY70

SELECTED

GH ⓆⓆⓆⓆ **The Town Head House** High St CA17 4SH
☎(07683) 71044 FAX (07683) 72128
An elegant house beside the A685 as it approaches the town centre from Tebay. Although its style is Victorian, parts are said to date from 1724. The 6 well equipped bedrooms are spacious and tastefully furnished and 2 have 4-poster beds. There are 2 very comfortable lounges with open fires and plenty of books and games, and a first-floor writing room. Fresh flowers are much in evidence throughout. Delicious 3 or 4-course meals are served each evening in the attractively appointed dining room, and many notable wines are kept in an intriguing wall safe. This is a delightful house with ample parking and a secluded garden at the rear.
6⇔♠ ⊁in 2 bedrooms CTV in all bedrooms ®
sB&B⇔♠£39.50-£46.50 dB&B⇔♠£60.50-£72
WB&B£230-£270 WBDi£350-£390 LDO 4pm
Lic ⊞ 8P 1🐾 nc12yrs
Credit Cards ①③ ⓔ

KIRKCAMBECK Cumbria Map **12** NY56

SELECTED

FH ⓆⓆⓆⓆ Mrs M Stobart **Cracrop** *(NY521697)*
CA8 2BW ☎Roadhead(06978) 245
Jan-Nov
A working farm of over 400 acres of arable and pastureland, a pedigree Ayrshire milking herd, a small Charolais herd and 500 breeding ewes, as well as other farm and domestic animals. The house, adjacent to farm buildings and many of the farm's activities, dates back to 1847, but has been carefully modernised. The 3 well equipped bedrooms each have en suite facilities; there is a comfortable lounge, a dining room, games room and a spa bath and sauna. Outside is a pleasant garden and there are a number of farm trails. Cracrop is just off the B6318, 7 miles from Brampton, signed from Kirkcambeck.
3♠ (2fb)⊁in all bedrooms CTV in all bedrooms ®
✗ (ex guide dogs) ✳ sB&B♠£17 dB&B♠£30
WB&Bfr£100 LDO 1pm
⊞ CTV 3P sauna 425 acres arable beef dairy mixed sheep
Credit Cards ②

KIRKHILL Highland *Inverness-shire* Map **14** NH54

SELECTED

GH ⓆⓆⓆⓆ **Moniack View** IV5 7PQ
☎Drumchardine(046383) 757
Apr-Oct
Set in its own garden with lovely views of the tree-covered hills above Moniack, Mrs Munroe's delightful modern bungalow offers superior tourist accommodation. The cosy bedrooms are tastefully decorated and well furnished, there is a comfortable

lounge and an attractive dining room where hearty breakfasts are served at the communal table.
3hc ✗ ✳ sB&B£15-£20
⊞ CTV 3P nc12yrs ⓔ

FH ⓆⓆⓆ Mrs C Munro **Wester Moniack** *(NH551438)*
IV5 7PQ ☎Drumchardine(046383) 237
Situated beside the Moniack Castle Wineries, this traditional farmhouse offers attractive, well decorated accommodation at very reasonable prices. The 2 bedrooms are small but comfortable, and there is a pleasant lounge. Home-cooked meals are served in farmhouse fashion around a communal table in the small dining room.
2hc (1fb) ✳ sB&B£13-£15 dB&B£24-£26 WB&B£84-£90 WBDi£126-£133 LDO 8pm
⊞ CTV 4P 600 acres arable beef mixed sheep ⓔ

KIRKMUIRHILL Strathclyde *Lanarkshire* Map **11** NS74

⊞➤FH Ⓠ Mrs I H McInally **Dykecroft** *(NS776419)*
ML11 0JQ ☎Lesmahagow(0555) 892226
A modern bungalow situated 1.5 miles west of Kirkmuirhill on the A726 Strathaven road, set amidst open farmland. Compact and cosy accommodation is provided, with modest standards but a friendly environment.
3rm ® sB&B£12-£14 dB&B£24-£25 WB&B£80-£84
⊞ CTV 4P 60 acres sheep ⓔ

KIRKOSWALD Cumbria Map **12** NY54

SELECTED

GH ⓆⓆⓆⓆ **Prospect Hill Hotel** CA10 1ER
☎Lazonby(076883) 500
Closed 24-26 Dec
The hotel has been converted from a group of 18th-century farm buildings by the present owners, and recently 2 more rooms, one ideal for a family, have been opened in a former coach house. Bedrooms are individually furnished and decorated: several have brass bedsteads and stone walls. The beamed and flagstoned bar features old farm implements, and there are many interesting antiques and bric-a-brac throughout the hotel. The dining room is an attractive modern addition, where à la carte dinners are served each evening; provision is made for vegetarians and young people. The hotel is set in open countryside, about one mile north of the village off the B6413.
10rm(4⇔♠6hc) (1fb) CTV in 2 bedrooms ® ✗
sB&Bfr£20 sB&B⇔♠fr£44 dB&Bfr£45 dB&B⇔♠fr£57
LDO 8.45pm
Lic ⊞ CTV 30P 1🐾 (£2) croquet clock golf barbecue patio
Credit Cards ①②③ ⓔ
See advertisement under PENRITH

KIRKWHELPINGTON Northumberland Map **12** NY98

SELECTED

FH ⓆⓆⓆⓆ Mrs C Robinson-Gay **Shieldhall**
(NZ026827) Wallington, Cambo NE16 4AQ (0.75m E of B6342/A696 jct) ☎Otterburn(0830) 40387
rs Nov-Feb
This delightful stone-built house enjoys a tranquil setting although it is situated only 300 yards along the B6342 from its junction with the A696. Bedrooms are set around a courtyard and are well furnished with good quality reproduction pieces made on the premises by the owner. In the main house there is a dining room featuring a wealth of bric-a-brac, as well as an impressive lounge, with a separate TV lounge also available.

6rm(5⇊🏠1hc) (1fb) ⑧ ✗ (ex guide dogs) dB&B⇊🏠£36-£39 WB&B£122.50-£136.50 WBDi£189-£203 LDO 10am Lic 🍽 CTV 10P croquet 10 acres horses

---

KIRTLING Cambridgeshire Map **05** TL65

FH Ⓠ Ⓠ Mrs C A Bailey **Hill** *(TL685585)* CB8 9HQ
☎Newmarket(0638) 730253
Situated midway between Saxon Street and the village of Kirtling, this is a traditional 16th-century farmhouse with a modern exterior, surrounded by arable and pasture farmland. Accommodation is comfortable and clean and the public rooms include a lounge and dining room with open log fires and a games room.
3rm(2🏠1hc) CTV in 1 bedroom ⑧ LDO 8.30pm
Lic 🍽 CTV 15P games room 500 acres arable Ⓔ
See advertisement under NEWMARKET

KIRTON Nottinghamshire Map **08** SK66

GH Ⓠ Ⓠ *Old Rectory* Main St NG22 9LP
☎Mansfield(0623) 861540 Telex no 378505
Closed Xmas & New Year
This attractive detached Georgian house stands in well-maintained grounds in a rural setting between Ollerton and Tuxford.
10rm(2🏠8hc) (1fb) ✗ (ex guide dogs) LDO 7pm
Lic CTV 18P
Credit Cards ①③

KNARESBOROUGH North Yorkshire Map **08** SE35

GH Ⓠ Ⓠ Ⓠ **Newton House Hotel** 5/7 York Place HG5 0AD
☎Harrogate(0423) 863539 FAX (0423) 869614
Closed 25 & 26 Dec
Len and Jackie Cohen make charming hosts at this lovely Grade II listed building that they have carefully restored. The house has been decorated throughout in rich prints and stripped pine, complemented by arrangements of dried flowers. Rooms are very well equipped, and have mini bars, colour televisions and radio alarms.
10rm(3⇊7🏠) Annexe 2rm(1⇊1🏠) (3fb) CTV in all bedrooms ⑧ ✳ sB&B⇊🏠fr£30 dB&B⇊🏠£50-£60 LDO by arrangment
Lic 🍽 CTV 8P
Credit Cards ①②③Ⓔ
See advertisement under HARROGATE

GH Ⓠ Ⓠ Ⓠ **The Villa** The Vill Hotel, 47 Kirkgate HG5 8BZ
☎Harrogate(0423) 865370
A short walk from the historic market square, The Villa overlooks the River Nidd. Four bedrooms are en suite and all are very well equipped. A pretty conservatory breakfast room overlooks the patio, and friendly Mrs Nicholson provides breakfast only.
6rm(4🏠2hc) (1fb) CTV in all bedrooms ⑧ sB&B£16.50 dB&Bfr£36 dB&B🏠fr£40
🍽 CTV ✗

INN Ⓠ Ⓠ *Mitre Hotel* Station Rd HG5 9AA
☎Harrogate(0423) 863589
9rm(4⇊5🏠) CTV in all bedrooms ⑧ ✗ (ex guide dogs) LDO 10pm
🍽 CTV
Credit Cards ①②③⑤

KNIGHTON Powys Map **07** SO27

FH Ⓠ Ⓠ R Watkins *Heartsease (SO343725)* LD7 1LU
☎Bucknell(05474) 220
Apr-Oct
Standing on the A4113 east of the town, this Georgian stone-built farmhouse offers spacious accommodation, and guests can use the conservatory as well as the large lounge.
3rm(1⇊1hc) (1fb) LDO 9am

▶

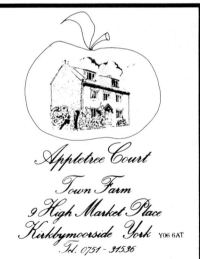

꿮 CTV 6P 3🏕 ✒ snooker 800 acres mixed
Credit Cards ③

KNOWLE West Midlands Map 07 SP17

GH ⓆⓆ **Ivy House** Warwick Rd, Heronfield B93 0EB
☎(0564) 770247
A comfortable guesthouse just outside Knowle with convenient access to the M42 and NEC. Rooms are well furnished and equipped, although some are small.
8↿ CTV in all bedrooms Ⓡ sB&B↿£20-£28 dB&B↿£36-£44
꿮 CTV 20P Ⓔ

KNUTSFORD Cheshire Map 07 SJ77

GH ⓆⓆ *Pickmere House* Park Ln, Pickmere WA16 0JX
☎(0565) 893433
Closed Xmas
Recently modernised, this 3-storeyed Georgian farmhouse is in the heart of the village. No smoking is allowed here. The lounge areas are comfortable and the bedrooms have most modern amenities.
9rm(5↿2hc) (3fb)⊬in all bedrooms CTV in all bedrooms Ⓡ
꿮 CTV 9P

LACOCK Wiltshire Map 03 ST96

GH ⓆⓆⓆ **At the Sign of the Angel** 6 Church St SN15 2LA
☎Chippenham(0249) 730230 FAX (0249) 730527
Closed 23 Dec-5 Jan
This traditional English inn dates back to the 16th century, and has been well run by the Levis family with old-fashioned hospitality since 1953. The dining rooms and lounge are beamed and wood panelled, with creaky floorboards and log fires adding to the charm. Bedrooms are furnished with French and English antiques but are also very well equipped with modern facilities.
6↩ Annexe 4↩ (1fb) CTV in all bedrooms Ⓡ sB&B↩£70
dB&B↩£93 LDO 8.15pm
Lic 꿮 P 1🏕 nc10yrs
Credit Cards ① ② ③

LADYBANK Fife Map 11 NO30

GH ⓆⓆⓆ **Redlands Country Lodge** KY7 7SH ☎(0337) 31091
Closed last wk Feb-1st wk Mar
A splendid pine-clad lodge with smart, well-appointed bedrooms and lounge. Meals are taken in the attractive stone-built house surrounded by a pretty garden and patio.
4↿ CTV in all bedrooms Ⓡ ✖ LDO 5pm
Lic 꿮 6P ✒ Ⓔ

LAMBERHURST Kent Map 05 TQ63

INN ⓆⓆ **George & Dragon** High St TN3 8DQ
☎(0892) 890277
Closed 26-27 Dec
An 18th-century timbered inn situated on the A21 offering comfortable, old fashioned accommodation. The chef prides himself on his cooking, using only fresh, good quality ingredients, and the blackboard menu, the à la carte menu and the restaurant offer a varied choice to suit all tastes. Car parking is easy, and more en suite bedrooms are planned.
6rm(2↩4hc) (2fb) CTV in all bedrooms Ⓡ
✖ (ex guide dogs) ✱ sB&B£22-£29.50 sB&B↩↿fr£29.50
dB&B£32.50 dB&B↩↿£39.50-£45 ✱ Lunch £5.50-£14.95alc
Dinner £5.50-£14.95alc LDO 9.30pm
꿮 30P
Credit Cards ① ② ③ ⑤ Ⓔ

This is one of many guidebooks pubished by
the AA. The full range is available at any
AA Shop or good bookshop.

LANCASTER Lancashire Map 07 SD46

SELECTED

GH ⓆⓆⓆⓆ **Edenbreck House** Sunnyside Ln LA1 5ED
☎(0524) 32464
Peacefully situated on the edge of town, with an open rural aspect, Edenbreck was built as a family residence in 1985. Despite its modern origin, the style is that of a Victorian house, combining the comfort and spaciousness of that era with excellent contemporary facilities. The bedrooms are individually designed, each with private bathrooms, colour TV and tea and coffee making facilities. Breakfast offers a wide choice of dishes which guests are invited to order before retiring. When arriving by car, it is best approached from the railway station along Westbourne Road, then into Ashford Avenue, thence to Sunnyside Lane. The house stands in landscaped gardens at the end of the lane.
5rm(4↩1↿) CTV in all bedrooms Ⓡ ✱ dB&B↩↿£35-£50
꿮 6P
Credit Cards ① ③ Ⓔ

GH ⓆⓆⓆ **Lancaster Town House** 11/12 Newton Ter, Caton
Rd LA1 3PB ☎(0524) 65527
This small bed and breakfast establishment offers pleasant well-maintained accommodation. With friendly proprietors, it is on the town centre road from junction 34 of the M6.
6rm(3↩3↿) (2fb) CTV in all bedrooms Ⓡ ✖ (ex guide dogs)
sB&B↩↿fr£22 dB&B↩↿fr£34.50
꿮 nc4yrs

LANCING West Sussex Map 04 TQ10

INN ⓆⓆⓆ *Sussex Pad Hotel* Old Shoreham Rd BN15 0RH
☎Shoreham(0273) 454647
Closed Xmas & New Years Day
Nestling at the foot of the South Downs looking across the Adur Valley, this friendly free house has a spacious bar and a well-appointed restaurant which serves good food, including fresh sea food, and has a good wine list. The hotel offers spacious, modern accommodation.
6↩↿ (1fb) CTV in all bedrooms Ⓡ LDO 10pm
꿮 150P
Credit Cards ① ② ③ ⑤

LANGDALE, GREAT Cumbria Map 11 NY20

GH ⓆⓆⓆ **Long House** LA22 9JS ☎Langdale(09667) 222
Feb-Nov rs Nov, Feb & Mar
A very attractive 17th-century cottage set in 2 acres of well tended gardens in the beautiful Langdale valley, located about one and a half miles past Chapel Stile on the right. The three bedrooms all have en suite bathrooms and tea and coffee-making facilities and are prettily decorated throughout. Downstairs there are two cosy lounges, with oak beams and an open fire.
3↩ ⊬in all bedrooms Ⓡ ✖ (ex guide dogs) ✱ dB&B↩£39-£43 WBDi£195-£215 (wkly only Jun-Sep) LDO 11am
꿮 CTV 6P nc9yrs
Credit Cards ① ③

LANGLAND BAY West Glamorgan Map 02 SS68

See also Bishopston and Mumbles
GH ⓆⓆⓆ **Wittemberg Hotel** SA3 4QN
☎Swansea(0792) 369696
Closed 24 Dec-4 Jan
The sea is just a short walk away from this family run holiday hotel, set in a quiet area of the town. In an ideal centre from which to tour the Gower, the hotel provides bright, well equipped accommodation.

12rm(10🔥2hc) (2fb)💀in 5 bedrooms CTV in all bedrooms ®
🔥 ✱ sB&B🔥£30-£35 dB&B£40 dB&B🔥£45 WB&B£130-£150
WBDi£180-£210 LDO 7pm
Lic ⊞ CTV 11P nc5yrs
Credit Cards 1 3 ©

LANGPORT Somerset Map **03** ST42

SELECTED

GH Q Q Q Q **Hillards** High St, Curry Rivel TA10 0EY
☎(0458) 251737
*A delightful Grade II listed farmhouse, once a working farm,
now being lovingly restored by the owners. Beamed ceilings
and a wealth of wood panelling are complemented by fine
antique furniture and beautiful drapes. There are 2 sitting
rooms, one with TV, and outside a colourful courtyard to sit
and enjoy warm summer evenings. Bedrooms are furnished to
a high standard and range from the master suite, complete
with large whirlpool bath, to 2 charming annexe rooms with
panelling hiding the en suite facilities, and some rooms without
private bathrooms, but all with individual charm. Four further
en suite rooms are planned for 1992, and Bargain Breaks are
being introduced during winter 1991/92. Dinner will also be
served for the first time here, providing good imaginative
English cooking using top quality local ingredients.*
4rm(1⇨🔥3hc) Annexe 2⇨🔥 💀in all bedrooms
🔥 (ex guide dogs) ✱ sB&B£15-£40 sB&B⇨🔥£30-£40
dB&B£30-£35 dB&B⇨🔥£44-£50 WB&B£135-£300
⊞ CTV 25P nc ©
See advertisement inside back cover

LANLIVERY Cornwall & Isles of Scilly Map **02** SX05

FH Q Q Q Mrs A Worne *Yondertown (SX066571)* Trethevy
PL24 2SA ☎Par(072681) 7747
Feb-Oct
*Surrounded by farmland and countryside, this delightful converted
stone barn has comfortable bedrooms, and an elegant sitting room.
A relaxing atmosphere prevails here.*
2rm(1hc) (1fb)💀in all bedrooms CTV in all bedrooms ® 🔥
⊞ CTV P nc11yrs 7 acres non-working with livestock

LARGS Strathclyde *Ayrshire* Map **10** NS25

GH Q *Carlton* 10 Aubery Crescent KA30 8PR ☎(0475) 672313
Apr-Oct
*This stone-built, neat terraced house stands on the seafront
overlooking the Firth of Clyde, with views out to the Isle of
Cumbrae and Bute beyond. The bedrooms are pleasant and simply
appointed, and there is a comfortable first-floor lounge.*
6hc (2fb) ®
⊞ CTV 6P

FH Q Q Mrs M Watson **South Whittlieburn** *(NS218632)*
Brisbane Glen KA30 8SN ☎(0475) 675881
Mar-Nov
*This small, friendly farmhouse sits in the beautiful Brisbane Glen,
only two miles from the centre of Largs. All bedrooms are bright
and airy, and have glorious views of the surrounding countryside.*
3rm(1⇨🔥2hc) (1fb) CTV in all bedrooms ® sB&Bfr£14
sB&B⇨🔥£18.50 dB&Bfr£27 dB&B⇨🔥£35
⊞ CTV 10P 155 acres sheep

LATHERON Highland *Caithness* Map **15** ND13

▨▶ **FH** Q Q Mrs C B Sinclair **Upper Latheron** *(ND195352)*
KW5 6DT ☎(05934) 224
May-Oct
*A traditional two-storeyed farmhouse in an elevated position
enjoying fine views across the North Sea. Situated south of the
village off the A9, it offers good value tourist accommodation and
is also a popular pony trekking centre.*

3rm (1fb)💀in 2 bedrooms TV in 1 bedroom 🔥 (ex guide dogs)
sB&B£12-£14 dB&B£22-£24
CTV 6P ∪ 200 acres arable beef mixed sheep ©

LAUNCESTON Cornwall & Isles of Scilly Map **02** SX38

FH Q Q Q Mrs Margaret Smith **Hurdon** *(SX333828)*
PL15 9LS ☎(0566) 772955
May-Oct
*An 18th-century stone-built farmhouse on the edge of the town,
with easy access to Bodmin Moor and Dartmoor and both the
north and south Cornish coasts. The bedrooms are tastefully
decorated, and most now have private bathrooms. There is a
comfortable lounge, and traditional farmhouse meals are available
six nights a week in the dining room.*
6rm(4⇨2hc) (1fb) 🔥 (ex guide dogs) ✱ sB&B£13-£14
sB&B⇨£16.50-£17 dB&B£26-£28 dB&B⇨£33-£34
WB&B£90-£100 WBDi£125-£140 LDO 4.30pm
CTV 10P 400 acres mixed ©

LAURENCEKIRK Grampian *Kincardineshire* Map **15** NO77

INN Q Q The **Alma Hotel** Alma Place AB30 1AL
☎(05617) 744
3rm(2🔥1hc) (1fb) CTV in all bedrooms ® ✱ sB&Bfr£15
sB&B🔥fr£18 dB&Bfr£24 dB&B🔥fr£30 WB&B£105-£126 ✱
Lunch fr£3 High tea fr£5 Dinner fr£7 LDO 8.30pm
⊞ CTV 4P 1🎱
Credit Cards 1 3

Street plans of certain towns and cities
will be found in a separate section
at the back of the book.

**Park Lane, Pickmere, Knutsford,
Cheshire WA16 0JX
Telephone: (0565) 893433
(0831) 384460**

Pickmere House is a listed Georgian
Country House built in 1772. It is
ideally situated 2 miles west of junction
19, M6 just off the B5391 in a rural
area close to Tatton Park and giving
swift easy access to Manchester,
Ringway Airport, Runcorn, Warrington,
Chester and Liverpool. German and
French spoken. Most rooms are en-
suite. Non smokers only.

LAVERTON Gloucestershire Map **04** SP03

SELECTED

GH ⓠⓠⓠⓠ **Leasow House** WR12 7NA (2m SW of Broadway off A46) ☎Stanton(038673) 526 FAX (038673) 596

This early 17th-century Cotswold stone farmhouse is situated southwest of Broadway off the A4632 (signposted Worminston and Dumbleton, it is the first farm on the right). Bedrooms are very modern and well equipped, all with en suite facilities, yet the character of the farmhouse has been retained. The comfortable library has a wide range of books and guides, together with a civilised tray of sherries. Two new bedrooms have recently been added, and these share a mini kitchen and comfortable lounge.

5⇨♠ Annexe 4rm(2⇨2♠) (2fb) CTV in all bedrooms ® sB&B⇨♠£38-£50 dB&B⇨♠£43-£55
₪ 10P
Credit Cards ① ② ③ ④
See advertisement under BROADWAY

LAXTON Nottinghamshire Map **08** SK76

FH ⓠ Mrs L S Rose *Moorgate (SK726665)* NG22 0NU ☎Tuxford(0777) 870274
Closed Xmas Day
This small, family-run mixed farm stands on the edge of the medieval village of Laxton, and is found by following the signs to Moorhouse.
3rm (1fb)⤢in all bedrooms ✖ (ex guide dogs) LDO 8.30pm CTV 6P 145 acres mixed

---

LEAMINGTON SPA (ROYAL) Warwickshire Map **04** SP36

GH ⓠⓠ **Buckland Lodge Hotel** 35 Avenue Rd CV31 3PG ☎(0926) 423843
This long-established guesthouse, an attractive white stucco Victorian property, offering reliable standards and well equipped bedrooms, is successfully aimed at the commercial user. It is situated south of the town centre – within walking distance – on the inner orbital road in the direction of the M40 south access, and is convenient for the railway station.
10rm(6⇨4hc) (2fb) CTV in all bedrooms ® ✳ sB&B£21-£25 sB&B⇨£32-£35 dB&B£36-£42 dB&B⇨£42-£46 LDO noon
Lic ₪ 16P
Credit Cards ① ② ③ ⑤ ④

GH ⓠⓠ **Charnwood** 47 Avenue Rd CV31 3PF ☎(0926) 831074
Closed 23 Dec-1 Jan
Close to the town centre, this late Victorian semidetached house offers modern, well equipped, pretty bedrooms and a comfortable and attractive dining room.
6rm(1⇨1♠4hc) (1fb) CTV in all bedrooms ® ✖ sB&B£14-£16 sB&B⇨♠£25-£38 dB&B£29-£30 dB&B⇨♠£34-£38 WB&B£98-£133 WBDi£143.50-£178.50 LDO 4pm
₪ CTV 5P
Credit Cards ① ③ ④

GH ⓠⓠⓠ **Coverdale Private Hotel** 8 Portland St CV32 5HE ☎(0926) 330400 FAX (0926) 833388
An attractive and well sited Georgian town house, off Regent Street, offering a high level of comfort and facilities, appealing to commercial and leisure guests alike. Sensitively modernised, accommodation is now almost all en suite.
8rm(2⇨4♠2hc) (2fb) CTV in all bedrooms ® sB&B⇨♠£26-£31 dB&B⇨♠£36-£41
₪ 3P
Credit Cards ① ③ ④

GH ⓠⓠⓠ **Flowerdale House** 58 Warwick New Rd CV32 6AA ☎(0926) 426002
This Victorian house has been beautifully converted and is situated on the old Warwick road on the boundary of Leamington. Well maintained and comfortable, it provides a high standard of accommodation with well equipped bedrooms. The conservatory, used for breakfast in the summer months, opens on to a delightful walled garden.
6rm(4⇨2♠) (1fb) CTV in all bedrooms ® ✖ (ex guide dogs) sB&B⇨♠£19-£24 dB&B⇨♠£33-£39
Lic ₪ 6P
Credit Cards ① ③ ④

GH ⓠⓠ **Glendower** 8 Warwick Place CV32 5BJ ☎(0926) 422784
This is a late Victorian end-of-terrace house, situated on the old Warwick road. The bedrooms are modern and well equipped, while the spacious public rooms retain many original features.
9rm(2⇨7hc) (3fb) ® sB&B£15 dB&B£30 dB&B⇨£36
₪ CTV ✗

GH ⓠⓠ **Guys Cliffe Guesthouse** 157 Rugby Rd, Milverton CV32 6DJ ☎Leamington Spa(0926) 336217
An end-of-terrace Victorian property situated on the Rugby road, a short drive from the town centre. Accommodation is generally quite spacious, and two ground-floor rooms have good en suite facilities. Public areas are limited, with only a small dining room where breakfast is served.
7rm(2♠5hc) (1fb) CTV in all bedrooms ® ✖ (ex guide dogs) ✳ sB&B£12.50-£17.50 dB&B£25-£31 dB&B♠£36-£40
₪ 4P ④

GH ⓠⓠⓠ **Milverton House Hotel** 1 Milverton Ter CV32 5BE ☎(0926) 428335
On the corner of Warwick Place and Milverton Terrace, this Victorian house retains the splendour of its era and offers a particularly good level of comfort, in the well equipped bedrooms and the spacious lounge and dining room. There is a noticeably high standard of care and cleanliness.
11rm(3⇨4♠4hc) (1fb) CTV in all bedrooms ® ✖ (ex guide dogs) LDO 5pm
Lic ₪ 5P
Credit Cards ① ③

GH ⓠⓠⓠ **York House Hotel** 9 York Rd CV31 3PR ☎(0926) 424671
Closed 24-31 Dec
Close to the main shopping centre and overlooking the Royal Pump Room and the River Leam, this imposing Victorian house offers quality public rooms and well equipped bedrooms, some with good en suite facilities.
8rm(4⇨♠4hc) (2fb) CTV in all bedrooms ® LDO 7.30pm
Lic ₪ 3P
Credit Cards ① ② ③

FH ⓠⓠⓠ Mrs R Gibbs **Hill** *(SP343637)* Lewis Rd, Radford Semele CV31 1UX ☎(0926) 337571
Closed Xmas & New Year
Situated at the end of Lewis Road off the A425 at Radford Semele, this cosy farmhouse offers pretty co-ordinated bedrooms, some with modern en suite shower facilities and comfortable public areas, including a separate television lounge. Children are especially welcome.
6rm(3♠3hc) (1fb)⤢in all bedrooms ® ✖ ✳ sB&Bfr£15 sB&B♠£17 dB&Bfr£26 dB&B♠£32
₪ CTV 6P 4☻ ✿ 350 acres arable beef mixed sheep ④

LEEDS West Yorkshire Map **08** SE33

GH ⓠⓠⓠ **Aragon Hotel** 250 Stainbeck Lane, Meanwood LS7 2PS ☎(0532) 759306
Closed Xmas
A well furnished and comfortable hotel offering a high standard of accommodation. Bedrooms have very good facilities, and there is a

cosy lounge, small cocktail bar and a bright, fresh dining room; facilities also include a small conference room. The hotel is set in a very pleasant residential area 2 miles from the city centre, within its own well kept grounds.
14rm(8⇄2♠4hc) (1fb) CTV in all bedrooms ® sB&B£25.79 sB&B⇄♠£37.30 dB&B£39.24 dB&B⇄♠£49 LDO 6pm
Lic ⁿⁿ 25P
Credit Cards ① ② ③ ⑤ ⑤

GH ◐ Ash Mount Hotel 22 Wetherby Road, Oakwood LS8 2QD ☎(0532) 658164
Closed Xmas wk
An attractive stone-built detached house standing in its own grounds, with a car park to the rear. Comfortable and pleasantly furnished, its resident owners offer friendly service.
12rm(5♠7hc) (1fb) CTV in all bedrooms ® ✳ sB&Bfr£20 sB&B♠£30 dB&B♠£33 dB&B♠£39 LDO am
Lic ⁿⁿ CTV 10P ⑤

GH ◐ Highfield Hotel 79 Cardigan Road, Headingley LS6 1EB
☎(0532) 752193
A large semidetached house standing well back from the main road, close to the Yorkshire county cricket ground. Bedrooms are modern with good furnishings. Family-owned and run, this guesthouse offers good service.
10hc (1fb) ® LDO 7pm
ⁿⁿ CTV 7P

GH ◐◐◐ Trafford House Hotel 18 Cardigan Road, Headingley LS6 3AG ☎(0532) 752034 FAX (0532) 756637
Closed Xmas
A small, comfortable guesthouse situated close to the county cricket ground. The accommodation is well furnished and bedrooms offer good facilities. Friendly service is provided by the resident owners.
18rm(4♠14hc) (4fb) CTV in all bedrooms ®
✄ (ex guide dogs) sB&B£20-£25 sB&B♠£35-£40 dB&B£30-£35 dB&B♠£50-£55 WB&B£105-£130 LDO noon
Lic ⁿⁿ CTV 30P
Credit Cards ① ③ ⑤

LEEK Staffordshire Map **07** SJ95

GH ◐ Peak Weavers Hotel King St ST13 5NW ☎(0538) 383729
Once a convent, this large Georgian house with well kept front gardens stands in a side street minutes from the town centre, backing on to the Catholic church.
11rm(3⇄1♠7hc) (2fb) TV in all bedrooms ®
✄ (ex guide dogs) LDO 8.30pm
Lic ⁿⁿ CTV 8P 4🚗
Credit Cards ① ② ③

INN ◐◐ Abbey Abbey Green Rd ST13 8SA ☎(0538) 382865
Located off the A523 Leek-Macclesfield road, this tall, sandstone-built inn is found by following the signs off to Meerbrook. The letting rooms are in an annexe, created from a converted barn, and they have most modern facilities.
Annexe 7♠ CTV in all bedrooms ® ✄ (ex guide dogs) ✳ sB&B♠£24.50 dB&B♠£38 ✳ Lunch £4.80-£7.15 Dinner £5.50-£9.60 LDO 8pm
ⁿⁿ 60P nc14yrs
Credit Cards ① ② ③ ⑤

LEICESTER Leicestershire Map **04** SK50

GH ◐◐ Burlington Hotel Elmfield Av LE2 1RB
☎(0533) 705112 FAX (0533) 704207
Closed Xmas
16rm(4⇄7♠5hc) (1fb) CTV in all bedrooms ® ✄ sB&B£20-£23 sB&B♠£30 dB&B£33 dB&B⇄♠£38 LDO 8pm
Lic ⁿⁿ CTV 23P
Credit Cards ① ③ ⑤

GH ◐ Croft Hotel 3 Stanley Rd LE2 1RF ☎(0533) 703220 FAX (0533) 706067
This large, detached Victorian house is to be found just off the A6, one mile south of the city centre. Catering mainly for commercial guests it provides simple and comfortable accommodation.
26rm(6⇄♠20hc) (1fb) CTV in all bedrooms ®
✄ (ex guide dogs) sB&B£22-£25 sB&B⇄♠£32-£35 dB&B£32-£35 dB&B⇄♠£36-£40 WB&B£154-£174 WBDi£210-£230 LDO 5pm
Lic ⁿⁿ CTV 26P
Credit Cards ① ③ ⑤

GH ◐ Daval Hotel 292 London Road, Stoneygate LE2 2AG
☎(0533) 708234
Popular with commercial guests, this large house stands at the end of a Victorian terrace, 1 mile south of the city centre, on the A6.
14rm(1⇄13hc) (2fb) CTV in all bedrooms ✳ sB&Bfr£22 sB&B⇄fr£35 dB&Bfr£32 dB&B⇄fr£40 LDO 7pm
Lic ⁿⁿ CTV 20P
Credit Cards ① ⑤

GH ◐◐ Scotia Hotel 10 Westcotes Dr LE3 0QR
☎(0533) 549200
This popular, value-for-money hotel offers comfortable accommodation and is convenient for access to the M1/M69 junction and city centre. Six bedrooms are located in an annexe across the road from the main house.
10hc Annexe 6hc (2fb) CTV in all bedrooms ® ✳ sB&B£20 dB&B£36 WB&B£140 LDO 9pm
Lic ⁿⁿ 5P

GH ◐◐ The Stanfre House Hotel 265 London Rd LE2 3BE
☎(0533) 704294
Closed 24 Dec-2 Jan
This simple, well maintained and friendly guesthouse stands on the A6 approximately one mile south of the city centre. Particularly popular with commercial guests, it is equally suitable for holidaymakers.
12hc (1fb) ✳ sB&B£19 dB&B£30
Lic ⁿⁿ CTV 6P

GH ◐ Stoneycroft Hotel 5/7 Elmfield Av LE2 1RB
☎(0533) 707605 FAX (0533) 706067
In a residential area just a few minutes from city centre, the hotel is large with a high proportion of single rooms.
46rm(25⇄♠21hc) (4fb) CTV in all bedrooms ®
✄ (ex guide dogs) sB&B£22-£25 sB&B⇄♠£32-£35 dB&B£32-£35 dB&B⇄♠£36-£40 WB&B£154-£174 WBDi£210-£230 LDO 9pm
Lic ⁿⁿ CTV 20P pool table
Credit Cards ① ③ ⑤

LEIGH Hereford & Worcester Map **03** SO75

FH ◐◐ Mrs F S Stewart **Leigh Court** *(SO784535)* WR6 5LB
☎Leigh Sinton(0886) 32275
28 Mar-6 Oct
Set in a quiet, rural area, this beautifully preserved example of a 17th-century farmhouse offers simple and spacious accommodation, a billiard room and a library. Next to the farm is a cruck-built tithe barn.
3rm(1♠2hc) ® dB&B£36 dB&B♠£42 WB&Bfr£112 WBDifr£172 LDO 9am
ⁿⁿ CTV 6P ⚓ billiard room library 270 acres arable sheep ⑤

LELANT Cornwall & Isles of Scilly Map **02** SW53

INN ◐◐◐ Badger TR26 3JT ☎Hayle(0723) 752181
A very popular and well appointed pub, ideally situated for weekend breaks and close to St Ives Bay. Most of the modern and very well equipped bedrooms have private bathrooms, and downstairs there are two bars and a conservatory restaurant. A good selection of beers is available including real ale, together with bar meals and various snacks.

▶

6⇨♠ CTV in all bedrooms ® ✖ (ex guide dogs) ✳
sB&B⇨♠£25-£35 dB&B⇨♠£39-£45 WB&B£175-£210 ✳
Lunch £9-£18&alc Dinner £8-£14&alc LDO 10.15pm
⑭ 100P nc6yrs
Credit Cards ①

LEOMINSTER Hereford & Worcester Map **03** SO45

See also Bodenham

GH Ⓠ **Knapp House** Luston HR6 0DB (2.5m N on B4361)
☎(0568) 615705
2hc (1fb) TV in 1 bedroom ® ✳ sB&Bfr£15 dB&Bfr£30
LDO 5pm
⑭ CTV 4P

SELECTED

GH ⓆⓆⓆⓆ **Withenfield** South St HR6 8JN
☎(0568) 612011
A beautiful, well proportioned Georgian house with Victorian additions situated on the B4316 (formerly the A49), just south of the town centre but within easy walking distance of the shops. The spacious rooms have been carefully decorated and furnished, many with antiques, and 1 room has a 4- poster bed. All bedrooms have excellent en suite facilities with good quality fittings and many thoughtful extras. The delightful drawing room is large, light and sunny, with comfortable sofas, a marble fireplace and a grand piano.
4⇨♠in all bedrooms CTV in all bedrooms ®
✖ (ex guide dogs) sB&B⇨♠£39 dB&B⇨♠£56
WB&B£171.50 WBDi£294 LDO 8.30pm
Lic ⑭ 6P
Credit Cards ①③ ⓔ

FH ⓆⓆ Mr & Mrs Black **Wharton Bank** *(SO508556)*
HR6 0NX ☎(0568) 612575
This stone-built, hill-top farmhouse, which dates back to the 18th century, is surrounded by attractive Herefordshire countryside.
4rm(1⇨3hc) ® ✖ (ex guide dogs) ✳ sB&B£14-£20 dB&B£28-£50 dB&B⇨£32-£52
⑭ CTV 8P 2♨ nc3yrs ≙ ♪(grass)174 acres dairy ⓔ

LERWICK

See **SHETLAND**

LEVENS Cumbria Map **07** SD48

INN ⓆⓆⓆ **Gilpin Bridge Hotel & Restaurant** Bridge End
LA8 8EP ☎(044852) 206
Just off the A590, this popular inn has well furnished bedrooms and attractive bars. A good range of food is available in bar and restaurant.
10rm(6⇨4♠) CTV in all bedrooms ® ✖ (ex guide dogs)
sB&B⇨♠£30 dB&B⇨♠£46-£55 Bar Lunch £5.50-£12alc
Dinner £7.50-£14alc LDO 9pm
⑭ 100P pool table darts board
Credit Cards ①③ ⓔ

LEW Oxfordshire Map **04** SP30

SELECTED

FH ⓆⓆⓆⓆ Mrs M J Rouse **The Farmhouse Hotel & Restaurant** *(SP322059)* University Farm OX18 2AU
☎Bampton Castle(0993) 850297 & 851480 Telex no 83243
Closed Xmas & New Year rs Sun
This delightful 17th-century farmhouse, hidden behind Cotswold-stone farm buildings, is in a secluded position, situated on the A4095 Bampton road. Tastefully and sympathetically modernised to a high standard by the Rouse family, each room has been individually furnished and

---

decorated to retain much of the original charm, and all are well equipped with modern facilities. Original features include oak-beamed ceilings and inglenook fireplaces; the popular, cosy restaurant is filled with dried flower arrangements, and there is an attractive conservatory extension, used mostly as a breakfast room. The restaurant offers simple, home-cooked dishes and delicious puddings in a warm, hospitable atmosphere.
6⇨♠ (2fb)⚹in all bedrooms CTV in all bedrooms ®
✖ (ex guide dogs) ✳ sB&B⇨♠fr£35 dB&B⇨♠fr£47
WB&Bfr£161 WBDifr£248 LDO 7.30pm
Lic ⑭ 25P nc5yrs 216 acres dairy
Credit Cards ①③

LEWDOWN Devon Map **02** SX48

◨▮♥ **FH** ⓆⓆⓆ Mrs M E Horn **Venn Mill** *(SX484885)*
EX20 4EB ☎Bridestowe(083786) 288
Etr-Oct
This large modern bungalow is set in peaceful surroundings with river fishing and private trout lake. It is 400 yards from the A30.
3rm(2hc) (1fb) CTV in 1 bedroom ® ✖ sB&B£13-£15
dB&B£26-£30 LDO 4pm
CTV 4P 4♨ ♪ 160 acres beef dairy sheep ⓔ

LEWIS, ISLE OF Western Isles *Ross & Cromarty* Map **13**

STORNOWAY Map **13** NB43

GH ⓆⓆ **Ardlonan** 29 Saint Francis St PA87 2PH
☎(0851) 703482
Closed Xmas & New Year
A pleasantly-appointed house just off town centre. Communal breakfast tables.
5hc (1fb)⚹in all bedrooms CTV in 1 bedroom TV in 2 bedrooms ✖ sB&B£15 dB&B£30
⑭ CTV ⓔ

LEYBURN North Yorkshire Map **07** SE19

GH Ⓠ **Eastfield Lodge Private Hotel** 1 St Matthews Ter
DL8 5EL ☎Wensleydale(0969) 23196
An unpretentious guesthouse on the outskirts of this Dales town, providing spacious bedrooms, a comfortable lounge with a bar for guests and an attractive dining room.
8hc (2fb) CTV in all bedrooms ® dB&B£28-£34 LDO 8.30pm
Lic ⑭ 10P
Credit Cards ①③ ⓔ

LICHFIELD Staffordshire Map **07** SK10

GH ⓆⓆ **Coppers End** Walsall Rd, Muckley Corner WS14 0BG
☎Brownhills(0543) 372910
This one-time police station now has bright, cheerful accommodation with two bedrooms on the ground floor and a large rear garden. It is situated 3 miles south of Lichfield on the A461.
6rm(1♠5hc) CTV in all bedrooms ® ✳ sB&B£19-£21
sB&B♠£26 dB&B£32-£34 dB&B♠fr£40 WB&B£100-£120
WBDi£156-£176 LDO noon
Lic ⑭ CTV 10P 2♨ (£1)
Credit Cards ①③ ⓔ

GH ⓆⓆⓆ **The Oakleigh House Hotel** 25 St Chads Rd
WS13 7LZ ☎(0543) 262688
rs Sun evening & Mon
The bedrooms in this small private hotel are excellently decorated and furnished, with good modern facilities. Some rooms are in the adjoining annexe. An attractive conservatory houses a well appointed restaurant, and the residents' meal is offered, as well as an à la carte menu with some unusual and enjoyable dishes.
10rm(4⇨4♠2hc) CTV in all bedrooms ® ✖ (ex guide dogs)
sB&B⇨♠fr£33 dB&Bfr£49 dB&B⇨♠fr£53.50 LDO 9.30pm
Lic ⑭ 20P nc5yrs
Credit Cards ①③

LIFTON Devon Map **02** SX38

GH QQ **Mayfield House** PL16 0AN ☎(0566) 84401
A detached house in good-sized gardens off main A30, Mayfield provides a friendly, informal atmosphere, and good food.
4hc (2fb)⊁in all bedrooms CTV in all bedrooms ®
✖ (ex guide dogs) ✳ sB&B£15.50 dB&B£29 WB&B£94.50
LDO 4.30pm
Lic 9P 1🏖 ๛
Credit Cards ②

GH QQQ *Thatched Cottage Country Hotel & Restaurant*
Sprytown PL16 0AY ☎(0566) 84224
Set within colourful and peaceful gardens, only 100 metres from the A30, this attractive 16th-century thatched cottage houses two restaurant areas and a comfortable lounge with open fire. Morning coffee, light lunches and delicious afternoon teas are served. An imaginative à la carte menu is served at dinner, and changes monthly. The four ensuite rooms are in a barn conversion in the garden; each is comfortable, simply furnished and well equipped. The resident proprietors provide a friendly welcome.
4🏠 (2fb) CTV in all bedrooms ® ✖ LDO 9.30pm
Lic ℳ CTV 10P nc2yrs

LIGHTHORNE Warwickshire Map **04** SP35

FH QQ **Mrs J Stanton Redlands** *(SP334570)* Banbury Rd
CV35 0AH (on A41, 5m S of Warwick)
☎Warwick(0926) 651241
Closed Xmas
A long drive leads from the A41 to this carefully preserved 16th-century house. The pretty gardens and open-air swimming pool are available to guests, and Mrs Stanton cooks wholesome dishes using home grown produce where possible.
3rm(1⇨2hc) (1fb)⊁in all bedrooms ✖ (ex guide dogs)
ℳ CTV 6P ⌂100 acres arable ④
See advertisement under WARWICK

LINCOLN Lincolnshire Map **08** SK97

GH Q **Brierley House Hotel** 54 South Park LN5 8ER
☎(0522) 526945 & 522945
On a quiet avenue overlooking South Park, south of the city centre, this professionally run hotel offers rooms which are generally well proportioned with some en suite facilities. There is a comfortable lounge and the dining room has a small bar. Brierley House successfully caters for both commercial and weekend visitors to the city.
11rm(2⇨4🏠 5hc) CTV in 10 bedrooms TV in 1 bedroom ® ✖
sB&B£18-£25 sB&B⇨🏠£18-£25 dB&B£36-£40 dB&B⇨🏠£40
LDO Breakfast
Lic ℳ CTV adjacent 18 hole golf course ④

SELECTED

GH QQQQ **D'Isney Place Hotel** Eastgate LN2 4AA
☎(0522) 538881 FAX (0522) 511321
A Georgian town house adjacent to the Minster with a pay and display car park across the road. In the absence of any public areas, the bedrooms, most of which are spacious, have been furnished comfortably in period style. Antiques are set off against lavish fabrics, with which some beds are canopied, and all rooms have modern facilities and excellent en suites. An ample and well presented breakfast is served in the bedrooms.
18rm(15⇨3🏠) (2fb) CTV in all bedrooms ®
sB&B⇨🏠£40-£53.50 dB&B⇨🏠£63-£72
ℳ 7P
Credit Cards ①②③⑤

GH QQQ *Ferncliffe House Hotel* 2 St Catherines LN5 8LY
☎(0522) 522618
Closed 24 Dec-2 Jan
▶

The Countryman's Inn

Hunton, Nr. Bedale, North Yorkshire.
Telephone: (0677) 50554

Ideally situated to visit the Yorkshire Dales and Herriot country. Family owned Inn with home cooking and home comforts. The Inn has been completely refurbished but still maintains its character with beamed ceilings and open log fire. All 6 bedrooms are furnished to a high standard and are all ensuite with central heating, television, tea and coffee making facilities.

A warm welcome all year round awaits you from David and Pauline Robinson.

The Farmhouse Hotel & Restaurant

University Farm, Lew, Bampton, Oxford OX8 2AU
Tel: Bampton Castle (0993) 850297

A warm and friendly welcome awaits you at this tastefully modernised 17th-century farmhouse. Situated on the A4095 twixt Bampton and Witney. We are in an ideal position for touring The Cotswolds and visiting Oxford – city of spires. Superb country cooking, homemade bread and preserves. Oak beamed restaurants. Sitting room with inglenook fireplace. Tastefully furnished bedrooms with bathrooms/shower rooms en suite and Colour T.V. Honeymoon suite. Ground floor rooms with facilities for disabled guests. Central heating. Large garden with sun terrace.
Award winner 1980

This guesthouse, once a substantial family home, is situated just on the outskirts of the city centre, with a large private car park with access from Crossclyffe Hill, A15. Its Victorian origins are evident in the high ceilings and spacious bedrooms, which are individually and attractively furnished with comfort in mind. The lounge has a splendid fireplace with an open fire, and there is a separate dining room.

5rm(2♠3hc) (2fb) CTV in all bedrooms ® LDO 9pm
Lic 8P
Credit Cards ① ② ③

GH **Q Q Q** **Minster Lodge Hotel** 3 Church Ln LN2 1QJ
☎(0522) 513220 FAX (0522) 513220
Very good accommodation is available at the delightful small hotel. Exeptionally clean and well maintained bedrooms offer a good range of facilities, and all have quality bathrooms. A good choice is available at breakfast, which is served in the attractive dining room.

6⇄♠ (2fb) CTV in all bedrooms ® ✹ (ex guide dogs) ✱
sB&B⇄♠£43.50 dB&B⇄♠£48
Lic ♨ CTV 6P
Credit Cards ① ② ③ ⓔ

GH **Q Q Q** **Tennyson Hotel** 7 South Park LN5 8EN
☎(0522) 521624 & 513684
Situated towards the city centre on the inner southern ring road, this extremely well kept and comfortable guesthouse offers bedrooms which are comfortably fitted and furnished and benefit from good, modern en suite facilities. Proprietors Mr and Mrs Saggiorato also provide an à la carte menu in the dining room.

8rm(2⇄6♠) (1fb) CTV in all bedrooms ® ✹ sB&B⇄♠£26-£28 dB&B⇄♠£37-£41 LDO 7.45pm
Lic ♨ 8P
Credit Cards ① ② ③ ⓔ

LINLITHGOW Lothian *West Lothian* Map **11** NS97

FH **Q Q** Mrs A Hay **Belsyde House** *(NS976755)* Lanark Rd
EH49 6QE ☎(0506) 842098
Closed Xmas
Situated 1.5 miles south west of the A706, this well maintained Georgian farmhouse is located in tree-studded grounds above town.

4rm(1♠3hc) (1fb) CTV in all bedrooms ® ✹ (ex guide dogs)
✱ sB&Bfr£14 dB&Bfr£28 dB&B♠fr£34 LDO noon
♨ CTV 10P 106 acres beef sheep ⓔ

LISKEARD Cornwall & Isles of Scilly Map **02** SX26

GH **Q Q** **Elnor** 1 Russell St PL14 4BP ☎(0579) 42472
Closed Xmas
Proprietors Nancy and Gordon Strudwick provide a warm welcome at this 19th-century town house, which is close to the town centre and the railway station. The bedrooms are bright, with modern furnishings, complemented by a cosy television lounge.

9rm(4♠5hc) (1fb) ® ✹ sB&Bfr£14 sB&B♠£17 dB&Bfr£28
dB&B♠£34 WB&B£91-£112 WBDi£154-£175 LDO 5pm
Lic ♨ CTV 6P ⓔ

FH **Q Q Q** Mrs S Rowe **Tregondale** *(SX294643)* Menheniot
PL14 3RG (E of Liskeard 1.5m N of A38) ☎(0579) 42407
Easily located 1½ miles off the A390 at Merrymeet, this Cornish farmhouse has been sympathetically modernised, yet retains its charm and character. The bedrooms are bright and tastefully decorated and furnished. Public rooms are shared with the family, and traditional farmhouse fare is served in the dining room around a large table.

3rm(1⇄♠2hc) (1fb) ® ✹ ✱ sB&B£15-£18 dB&B£25-£28
dB&B⇄♠£30-£35 WB&B£97.50-£120 WBDi£147-£160
LDO 6pm
CTV 3P shooting pony rides 180 acres arable beef mixed sheep
ⓔ

LITTLE DEWCHURCH Hereford & Worcester Map **03**
SO53

FH **Q Q** Mrs G Lee **Cwm Craig** *(SO535322)* HR2 6PS
☎Carey(0432) 840250
A large Georgian farmhouse located midway between Ross-on-Wye and Hereford, providing a good base for touring the Wye and Golden valleys. Spacious and comfortable accommodation includes a games room with a snooker table.

3hc (1fb) ® ✹ (ex guide dogs) ✱ sB&B£13-£14 dB&B£24-£26
WB&B£84
♨ CTV 5P 190 acres arable beef ⓔ
See advertisement under HEREFORD

LITTLE MILL Gwent Map **03** SO30

FH **Q Q Q** Mrs A Bradley **Pentwyn** *(SO325035)* NP4 0HQ (off
A472, 0.5m E of junct with A4042) ☎(049528) 249
Etr-Oct rs Dec & Jan
This 16th-century, traditional Welsh longhouse provides bright, modern bedrooms and a large, comfortable lounge. It is set in large gardens and lawns which also contain a swimming pool.

4rm(2♠2hc) (1fb) ® ✹ sB&Bfr£17.50 sB&B♠fr£21
dB&Bfr£25 dB&B♠fr£32 LDO 6pm
Lic ♨ CTV nc4yrs ⌇(heated) table tennis 120 acres ⓔ

LITTLE PETHERICK Cornwall & Isles of Scilly Map **02**
SW97

GH **Q Q Q** **The Old Mill Country House Hotel** PL27 7QT
☎Rumford(0841) 540388
Mar-Oct rs Nov-Etr
This 16th century corn mill has been skillfully converted, is set in its own gardens next to a stream, and features a water wheel. Bedrooms have been individually furnished, retaining much of the original character. Public areas include a spacious beamed dining/ sitting area, 2 lounges, 1 with TV, and a sunny slate-paved patio outside. There is a choice of menus for dinner, with alternative à la carte dishes available if ordered after breakfast, and served at 7pm.

6rm(1⇄4♠1hc) ⚤in 1 bedroom ® ✹ (ex guide dogs)
sB&B£28-£36 sB&B⇄♠£35-£45 dB&B£40 dB&B⇄♠£50
WB&B£140-£175 WBDi£207-£242 LDO 6pm
Lic ♨ CTV 10P nc14yrs ⓔ

LITTON Derbyshire Map **07** SK17

⌂⛰FH **Q Q** Mrs A Barnsley **Dale House** *(SK160750)*
SK17 8QL ☎Tideswell(0298) 871309
Closed Xmas
Situated on the outskirts of the village, this is a simple Edwardian stone farmhouse. To the front is a mature garden, and the farmyard is nearby, while rolling hillsides and grazing sheep abound. The hostess is warm and caring.

3rm(1hc) (1fb) ✹ sB&Bfr£12.50 dB&Bfr£25 WB&Bfr£87.50
♨ CTV 6P nc5yrs 51 acres sheep ⓔ

LIVERPOOL Merseyside Map **07** SJ39

GH **Q Q** **Aachen Hotel** 91 Mount Pleasant L3 5TB
☎051-709 3477 & 1126
rs 20 Dec-7 Jan
Convenient for the centre of the city and close to the Roman Catholic Cathedral, this long established and friendly private hotel offers generally compact accommodation. Everywhere is kept spotlessly clean and the bedrooms are particularly well equipped and furnished with attractive fabrics.

17rm(1♠6♠10hc) (6fb) CTV in all bedrooms ®
✹ (ex guide dogs) sB&B£20-£28 sB&B⇄♠£28 dB&B£34-£41
dB&B⇄♠£42 WB&B£140-£196 WBDi£180.25-£236.25
LDO 8.30pm
Lic ♨ CTV P (charged) ⚓ (charged) pool room
Credit Cards ① ② ③ ⑤ ⓔ

GH 🛈 *New Manx Hotel* 39 Catherine St L8 7NE
☎051-708 6171
Close to the Anglican cathedral, this friendly and unpretentious bed and breakfast establishment offers reasonably priced accommodation which is popular with students and theatre people – whose photographs adorn the dining room walls.
11hc (2fb) CTV in all bedrooms ®
₪ 20P
Credit Cards [1] [2] [3] [5]

LIZARD Cornwall & Isles of Scilly Map **02** SW71

GH 🛈🛈🛈 **The Caerthillian** TR12 7NQ ☎(0326) 290019
15 Mar-24 Dec rs Feb-14 Mar
This Victorian property is full of character and has recently been upgraded and refurbished. Situated in the centre of the Lizard, it is operated very much as 'a restaurant with rooms' rather than a traditional guesthouse. Worthy home-cooked dishes feature regularly in the elegant restaurant, and service is hospitable. There is a cosy bar lounge on the ground floor, and bedrooms are compact but bright and comfortable.
5rm(2⇔͚3hc) CTV in all bedrooms ® ✖ (ex guide dogs)
LDO 9pm
Lic ₪ 3P nc12yrs
Credit Cards [1] [3]

GH 🛈🛈 **Mounts Bay House Hotel** Penmenner Rd TR12 7NP
☎(0326) 290305 & 290393
Closed Nov
A friendly Victorian guesthouse set on the edge of the village with glorious unrestricted views across the fields to Kynance Cove. Bedrooms are traditionally furnished and spotlessly clean. Public rooms are comfortable, and guests are well cared for.
7hc (1fb) ® sB&Bf16.50-£22 dB&Bf33-£44 WB&Bf103.50-£142 WBDif170-£208.50 LDO 6.30pm
▶

Tennyson Hotel
7 South Park, South Park Avenue, Lincoln,
Telephone: (0522) 521624

A first class hotel ½ mile from City Centre near South Park Common and golf courses. All rooms en-suite, radio, colour TV, hair dryer, tea making facilities, licensed restaurant, lounge, car park. Good food. Bargain breaks. A perfect base for visiting picturesque Lincolnshire.
Access/Visa/Amex accepted.
Personally supervised by
Resident Proprietors
Lino and Maybelle Saggiorato

Belsyde Farm

Belsyde, Linlithgow,
West Lothian EH49 6QE
Telephone: (0506) 842098
2 miles south of Linlithgow on the A706. Standing above the Union Canal, Belsyde has outstanding views over the Forth estuary to the Ochil Hills. The house titles date back to 1788, when the land belonged to the Dukes of Hamilton, whose crest appears on the west wall of the house. Set in just over 100 acres, Belsyde is readily accessible to all parts of central Scotland, by road and by rail. Edinburgh Aiport is just 25 minutes drive away.

Halfway Farm,
Motel and Guest House
Swinderby, Lincoln LN6 9HN
Telephone: Swinderby (052 286) 749

This elegant Georgian farmhouse clad in Virginia creeper provides excellent accommodation in 18 rooms split between the main house and the single-storey outbuildings, modernised to a high standard providing character rooms at a reasonable price. Car parking is unlimited. Full English breakfast is served in the farmhouse.

Lic ⍩ CTV 10P
Credit Cards 1 3 £

⌂⛟ GH ◖◗ **Parc Brawse House** Penmenner Rd TR12 7NR
☎(0326) 290466
Closed Dec-Jan rs Nov & Feb
A comfortable house of character, set back in its own grounds, with commanding views out to sea across farmland. Friendly service is provided by the owners, whose pleasantly refurbished house provides a good base for touring south Cornwall.
6rm(2⋔4hc) (1fb) ® sB&B£11-£16 dB&Bfr£22 dB&B⋔£30-£34 WB&B£77-£108.50 WBDi£133-£164.50 LDO 5.30pm
Lic CTV 6P
Credit Cards 1 3

GH ◖◗◗ **Penmenner House Hotel** Penmenner Rd TR12 7NR
☎(0326) 290370
This hotel has been transformed into a very comfortable and welcoming retreat. Standing in its own grounds, Penmenner House has panoramic views of the coastline and lighthouse. The excellent accommodation is complemented by fine home cooking using fresh local produce.
8rm(5⋔3hc) (2fb) CTV in all bedrooms ® ✕ (ex guide dogs)
✱ sB&Bfr£21.45 sB&B⋔fr£23.50 dB&Bfr£38.90
dB&B⋔fr£42.90 WB&Bfr£139.65 WBDifr£204.05 LDO 6pm
Lic ⍩ CTV 10P
Credit Cards 1 3 £

LLANBEDR Gwynedd Map 06 SH52

INN ◖◗◗ **Victoria** LL45 2LD (Frederic Robinson)
☎(034123) 213
This busy and popular stone-built former coaching inn dates back to the 17th century and is situated in the pleasant village of Llanbedr. All of the attractively decorated and well furnished bedrooms are well equipped including en suite facilities.
5⇔⋔ CTV in all bedrooms ® sB&B⇔⋔£24 dB&B⇔⋔£45
Lunch £7.95-£9.95 High tea £1.75-£6.50alc Dinner £7.95-£10.50 LDO 9.30pm
⍩ CTV 75P 7⛟
Credit Cards 1 3

LLANBERIS Gwynedd Map 06 SH56

GH ◖◗ *Lake View Hotel* Tan-y-Pant LL55 4EL
☎(0286) 870422
Lake view is an old stone-built property which has recently been much extended and stands on the western edge of Llanberis, overlooking the lake. All about one of the well-equipped bedrooms have en suite facilities and the cottage style restaurant is popular with non-residents.
10rm(9⋔1hc) (3fb) CTV in all bedrooms ® ✕ (ex guide dogs)
LDO 9.30pm
Lic ⍩ CTV 10P
Credit Cards 1 3

LLANDDEINIOLEN Gwynedd Map 06 SH56

FH ◖◗◗ Mr & Mrs Pierce *Ty-Mawr* (SH553664) LL55 3AD
☎Port Dinorwic(0248) 670147
This very well maintained, modernised farmhouse dates back to 1760 and is quietly located on the B4366, from where there are good views of the Snowdonia mountains. The bedrooms are well equipped and all have en suite facilities.
4rm(1⇔3⋔) (1fb)⚲in 1 bedroom CTV in 1 bedroom ®
✕ (ex guide dogs) LDO 6pm
⍩ CTV 20P 87 acres beef sheep

This is one of many guidebooks pubished by
the AA. The full range is available at any
AA Shop or good bookshop.

SELECTED

FH ◖◗◗◗◗ Mrs Kettle **Ty'n-Rhos** (SH548672) Seion
LL55 3AE ☎Port Dinorwic(0248) 670489
Closed 20 Dec-6 Jan
Little remains of the original late 17th-century farmhouse which occupied this site. Considerable alterations and extensions have been carried out in recent times to provide a large modern house with very good quality, well equipped accommodation. Situated in a quiet rural area, Ty'n-Rhos commands good views of the surrounding countryside. Caernarfon, Llanberis, Snowdon and Anglessey are all within a few minutes' drive.
11⇔⋔ (3fb) CTV in all bedrooms ® ✕ (ex guide dogs) ✱
sB&B⇔⋔£28.50-£30 dB&B⇔⋔£42-£56 WB&B£140-£170 WBDi£226-£256 LDO 6.30pm
Lic ⍩ 12P nc5yrs ✔ 72 acres mixed
Credit Cards 1 £

LLANDEILO Dyfed Map 02 SN62

GH ◖◗◗ *Brynawel* 19 New Rd SA19 6DD ☎(0558) 822925
rs 25 & 26 Dec
This family-run hotel has been recently modernised and offers good quality accommodation with well equipped bedrooms. A wide range of food is served in the popular restaurant. Brynawel stands on the A40.
5rm(2⇔1⋔2hc) (1fb) CTV in all bedrooms ®
✕ (ex guide dogs) LDO 5pm
Lic ⍩ 6P
Credit Cards 1 3

FH ◖◗ Mrs R du Feu **Goetre Hall** (SN641179) Trapp
SA19 6TS ☎Ammanford(0269) 850619
A well maintained farmhouse with pretty bedrooms and a spacious, comfortable lounge. South of the town take the Trapp road off the A483 at Derwydd. Turn left after the telephone box after roughly a mile, and left again after 400 yards.
2hc CTV in all bedrooms ® ✕ (ex guide dogs) ✱ sB&B£13.50
dB&B£25 WB&B£75
⍩ CTV 6P 6 acres non working £

LLANDELOY Dyfed Map 02 SM82

GH ◖◗◗ *Upper Vanley Farmhouse* SA62 6LJ
☎Croesgoch(0348) 831418
Mar-Oct
7rm(6⇔3⋔1hc) (6fb) CTV in all bedrooms ® (wkly only Jun-Aug) LDO 4pm
Lic ⍩ CTV 15P

LLANDOGO Gwent Map 03 SO50

GH ◖ *Brown's Hotel & Restaurant* NP5 4TW
☎Dean(0594) 530262
Feb-Nov
Set alongside the A466 in the beautiful Wye Valley, this modestly furnished guesthouse also has a shop and café providing snacks and teas all day.
7rm(1⋔6hc) LDO 7.30pm
Lic CTV 20P nc

INN ◖◗◗ **The Sloop** NP5 4TW ☎Dean(0594) 530291
This roadside inn stands beside a river ; once a mill, it has fine views of the Wye Valley. The bedrooms are modern, well furnished and comfortable, and the bars are cosy. A wide range of bar food is offered.
4⇔⋔ CTV in all bedrooms ® sB&B⇔⋔£27.50
dB&B⇔⋔£39.50-£46 Lunch fr£6.20&alc High tea fr£6.20&alc
Dinner fr£6.20&alc LDO 10pm
⍩ 40P nc9yrs
Credit Cards 1 2 3 £

LLANDOVERY Dyfed Map **03** SN73

GH Q Q **Llwyncelyn** SA20 0EP ☎(0550) 20566
Closed Xmas
Just west of the town, alongside the river and the A40, this
spotlessly clean and comfortable guesthouse has some lovely views.
Run by the Griffiths family for many years, the accommodation
includes a residents' lounge, separate dining room and neat
bedrooms.
6hc (3fb) ® ✷ (ex guide dogs) sB&B£17-£20 dB&B£30-£32
WB&B£84-£95.20 WBDi£161-£172.20 LDO 7.30pm
Lic ▦ CTV 12P ✔ ⓔ

LLANDRINDOD WELLS Powys Map **03** SO06

See also Penybont
GH Q Q **Griffin Lodge Hotel** Temple St LD1 5HF
☎(0597) 822432
The friendly and experienced Jones family run this Victorian
house, situated in the town centre, providing a spacious and
comfortable lounge and dining room, and well equipped bedrooms.
8rm(5♠3hc) CTV in 5 bedrooms TV in 3 bedrooms ® ✳
sB&B£18-£22 sB&B♠£22-£23 dB&B£32-£34 dB&B♠£40
WB&B£96-£120 WBDi£155.50-£179.50 LDO 7.30pm
Lic ▦ CTV 8P
Credit Cards ①③ ⓔ

GH Q Q Q **Guidfa House** Crossgates LD1 6RF
☎Penybont(059787) 241 FAX (059787) 875
A country guesthouse just 3 miles north of this spa town at the
junction of the A483 with the A44. Bedrooms are neat and well
appointed, and there is a large residents' lounge with a small
dispenser bar. New owners have just taken over and many
improvements are planned.
6rm(3⇄♠3hc) (4fb) CTV in all bedrooms ® sB&B£20.50-£34
sB&B⇄♠£34 dB&B£39-£44 dB&B⇄♠fr£44 WB&B£117-
£204 WBDi£192-£279
Lic ▦ 10P
Credit Cards ①③ ⓔ

GH Q Q **The Kincoed** Temple St LD1 5HF ☎(0597) 822656
FAX (0597) 824660
Near the centre of this mid-Wales spa town, the guesthouse offers
clean and bright bedrooms all well equipped with modern facilities,
some of which are en suite. There is a small bar and the attractive
restaurant is also popular locally.
10rm(1⇄4♠5hc) (3fb) CTV in all bedrooms ® ✳ sB&B£13.50
sB&B⇄♠£17-£18.50 dB&B£27-£30 dB&B⇄♠£32-£36
WB&B£81-£108 WBDi£135-£162 LDO 9.30pm
Lic ▦ 10P
Credit Cards ①③

GH Q Q **Ty-Cerrig** Tremont Rd LD1 5EB ☎(0597) 822704
9hc (2fb)⚥in all bedrooms CTV in all ® ✳
sB&B£13 dB&B£26 WB&B£91 LDO 9pm
Lic ▦ CTV 10P ⓔ

FH Q Q Mrs S A Evans *Highbury (SO044628)* Lanyre
LD1 6EA (1m W off A4081) ☎(0597) 822716
Apr-Sep
3rm(2hc) (1fb) ® ✷ LDO 3pm
▦ CTV 3P 1🐎 20 acres sheep

FH Q Q Mrs R Jones *Holly (SJ045593)* Howey LD1 5PP
(Howey 2m S A483) ☎(0597) 822402
Apr-Nov
At Howey, just off the A483, this stone farmhouse has three cosy
bedrooms, and a comfortable lounge. The Jones family are very
friendly hosts.
3rm(1♠2hc) (1fb) ® ✷ ✳ dB&B£26-£32 WB&Bfr£91
WBDi£125-£140 LDO 5pm
▦ CTV 4P 70 acres beef sheep

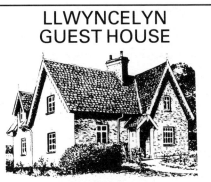

FH 🅠🅠🅠 Mr & Mrs R Bufton **Three Wells** *(SO062586)* Chapel Rd, Howey LD1 5PB (Howey 2m S A483 then unclass rd, E 1m) ☎(0597) 824427 & 822484

Three Wells stands east of the A483 at Howey and overlooks a duck pond. An excellent standard of accommodation is maintained and the Bufton family have run this relaxing 'Farm Hotel' for many years. Good food is served and fishing is available.

14⇨🏾 CTV in all bedrooms Ⓡ ✖ sB&B⇨🏾£16-£17 dB&B⇨🏾£30-£34 WB&B£100-£130 WBDi£150-£175 LDO 6pm
Lic lift 🏵 CTV 20P nc10yrs ✔ ○ 50 acres beef mixed sheep

LLANDUDNO Gwynedd Map **06** SH78

See **Town Plan Section** During the currency of this publication Llandudno telephone numbers are liable to change.

GH 🅠🅠 **Beach Cove** 8 Church Walks LL30 2HD ☎(0492) 879638
Closed Xmas

This small, well maintained, personally run guesthouse is located within a few hundred yards of the pier, and is also conveniently close to most amenities in the town. There is no car park, but street parking can usually be found without difficulty. The guesthouse is equally popular with tourists and commercial visitors.

7rm(3🏾4hc) (2fb) CTV in all bedrooms Ⓡ ✖ (ex guide dogs) ✳ sB&B£11.50 dB&B£22 dB&B🏾£27 WB&B£70-£88 WBDi£105-£125 LDO 5.30pm
🏵 CTV

◪▬ **GH** 🅠🅠 **Brannock Private Hotel** 36 St Davids Rd LL30 2UH ☎(0492) 877483
Closed Xmas & New Year

This small, well maintained, family-run hotel is situated in a quiet road convenient for access to the town centre and beaches and has the additional advantage of its own small car park.

8rm(3🏾5hc) (1fb) CTV in all bedrooms Ⓡ sB&B£13-£15 sB&B£15-£17 dB&B£26-£30 dB&B🏾£30-£34 WB&B£84-£98 WBDi£98-£112 LDO 5pm
🏵 5P nc3yrs
Credit Cards ❑1❑ ❑3❑ Ⓔ

GH 🅠🅠🅠 **Brigstock Private Hotel** 1 St David's Close LL30 2UG ☎(0492) 876416

Quietly situated, this friendly establishment has its own car park and is within easy reach of the town centre and other amenities. The accommodation is comfortable and well equipped, including several en suite facilities, and is well maintained throughout.

10rm(2⇨2🏾6hc) (2fb)⌫in all bedrooms CTV in all bedrooms Ⓡ ✖ sB&B£14-£17 dB&B£28-£34 dB&B⇨🏾£32-£38 WB&B£93-£114 WBDi£135-£156 LDO 5.30pm
Lic 🏵 CTV 7P nc4yrs Ⓔ

GH 🅠🅠 **Britannia Hotel** Promenade, 15 Craig-y-Don Pde LL30 1BG ☎(0492) 877185
Closed Dec

This small family-run hotel is situated on the promenade and enjoys good views of the bay. The accommodation is nicely maintained and many of the bedrooms have en suite facilities.

9rm(7⇨🏾2hc) (5fb) CTV in all bedrooms Ⓡ ✖ (ex guide dogs) dB&Bfr£24 dB&B⇨🏾£29-£30 WBDi£117.25-£135 LDO 5pm
🏵

GH 🅠🅠 *Bryn Rosa* 16 Abbey Rd LL30 2EA ☎(0492) 878215

Ths small, privately owned, friendly hotel is conveniently situated for access to the town centre and promenade. Several of the bedrooms have en suite facilities, and it is well maintained, with a cosy atmosphere.

7rm(2🏾5hc) (2fb) CTV in all bedrooms Ⓡ LDO 4.30pm
🏵 CTV 4P nc2yrs
Credit Cards ❑1❑ ❑3❑

GH 🅠🅠🅠 **Buile Hill Private Hotel** 46 St Mary's Rd LL30 2UE ☎(0492) 876972
Mar-Nov

This large, well maintained private hotel is centrally situated and provides easy access to the centre of the town and other amenities. Several of the bedrooms here are equipped with en suite facilities.

13rm(3⇨4🏾6hc) Ⓡ ✳ sB&B£14-£16 dB&B£28-£30 dB&B⇨🏾£40-£46 WB&B£100-£130 WBDi£120-£160 LDO 4pm
Lic 🏵 CTV 6P nc5yrs Ⓔ

GH 🅠🅠 *Capri Hotel* 70 Church Walks LL30 2HG ☎(0492) 879177

Situated in a quiet side street this pleasant guesthouse offers convenient accommodation, with easy access to the shops, the pier, the beach and other amenities.

8hc (7fb) Ⓡ LDO 4.30pm
Lic 🏵 CTV 3P nc3yrs

GH 🅠🅠 **Carmel Private Hotel** 17 Craig-y-Don Pde, Promenade LL30 1BG ☎(0492) 877643
Etr-Oct rs Apr

Situated on the seafront, this large end-terraced house is nicely maintained throughout and provides well-equipped accommodation with the advantage of its own small car park.

10rm(5🏾5hc) (3fb) CTV in all bedrooms Ⓡ ✳ sB&B£12.50-£13 dB&B£25-£26 dB&B🏾£31-£32 WB&B£87.50-£91 WBDi£122.50-£126 LDO noon
🏵 CTV 6P nc4yrs

GH 🅠🅠 **Hotel Carmen** Carmen Sylva Rd, Craig-y-Don LL30 1LZ ☎(0492) 876361

Situated approximately one hundred yards from the promenade, this small family-run private hotel is convenient for the town centre and other amenities. The bedrooms are well equipped and many have en suite facilities.

18rm(12⇨6hc) (5fb) CTV in 15 bedrooms Ⓡ ✳ sB&B£16.50 sB&B⇨🏾£20-£21.50 dB&B⇨🏾£35-£39 LDO 6pm
Lic 🏵 CTV Ⓔ

GH 🅠🅠🅠 **Cornerways Hotel** 2 St Davids Place LL30 2UG ☎(0492) 877334
Mar-mid Dec

New owners in 1989 have noticeably improved this very pleasant, small private hotel, which is centrally situated in a quiet side road, convenient for most of the town's amenities. The bedrooms are well furnished and equipped, each with a private bathroom. The hotel also has a small private car park.

6rm(5⇨1🏾) CTV in all bedrooms Ⓡ ✖ (ex guide dogs) ✳ sB&B⇨🏾£29.50-£30.50 dB&B⇨🏾£50-£52 (incl dinner) WB&B£126-£168 WBDi£171.50-£213.50 LDO 4pm
Lic 🏵 5P nc

SELECTED

GH 🅠🅠🅠🅠 **Craiglands Private Hotel** 7 Carmen Sylva Rd, Craig-y-Don LL30 1LZ ☎(0492) 875090
Mar-Nov

This large detached gabled house is situated in a residential road at the eastern end of town, close to the promenade and shops. Privately owned and personally run, it offers impeccably maintained accommodation and the attractive bedrooms are quite well equipped, each with a private bathroom. There is a comfortable lounge and a pleasant dining room, where good home cooking using fresh produce is served. Although unlicensed, guests may bring their own wine by prior arrangement. A warm and friendly welcome is assured, and the hotel has a regular patronage from guests who return year after year.

6🏾 (1fb) CTV in all bedrooms Ⓡ ✳ sB&B🏾£17.40-£19.90 dB&B🏾£35-£39.80 (incl dinner) WB&B£105 WBDi£125-£135 LDO 4pm

---

🎮 CTV nc4yrs

GH Ⓠ Ⓠ Ⓠ **Cranberry House** 12 Abbey Rd LL30 2EA
☎(0492) 879760
Apr-7 Oct
Good quality accommodation is offered at this charming Victorian house. Conveniently situated for access to the town centre and amenities, it has the advantage of its own car park. Cranberry house caters for non-smokers only.
6rm(2⇨3↑3hc) (2fb)⤢in all bedrooms CTV in 3 bedrooms Ⓡ
✖ (ex guide dogs) ✳ sB&B£13-£15 dB&B£25-£30
dB&B⇨3↑£30-£36 LDO noon
🎮 CTV 4P nc4yrs
Credit Cards ①③ Ⓔ

GH Ⓠ Ⓠ **Granby** Deganwy Av LL30 2DD ☎(0492) 876095
Apr-Oct
Bright, well-appointed guesthouse in quiet, residential area.
7rm(5↑2hc) (4fb) CTV in all bedrooms Ⓡ ✖ ✳ sB&B£19-
£19.95 dB&B£37 dB&B↑£40-£40 (incl dinner) WB&Bfr£112
WBDifr£140 LDO 4.30pm
Lic CTV 6P
Credit Cards ①③ Ⓔ

GH Ⓠ Ⓠ **Heath House Hotel** Central Promenade LL30 1AT
☎(0492) 876538 FAX (0492) 860307
Privately owned, this hotel has well equipped bedrooms, several with en suite facilities. It enjoys a position on the promenade overlooking the bay.
22rm(12⇨10hc) (14fb) CTV in all bedrooms Ⓡ
✖ (ex guide dogs) ✳ sB&B£20-£25 sB&B⇨£30-£35 dB&B£36-
£38 dB&B⇨£44-£50 WB&B£108-£150 WBDi£157-£199
LDO 4pm
Lic 🎮 CTV 1P cabaret twice wkly in season (May-Sep) Ⓔ

GH Ⓠ Ⓠ Ⓠ **Hên Dy Hotel** 10 North Pde LL30 2LP
☎(0492) 876184
rs Nov-Mar
This small, well maintained and privately owned hotel is situated at the northern end of the promenade, opposite the pier and overlooking the bay. The shops and other amenities are within easy reach.
12rm(2⇨2↑8hc) (3fb) CTV in all bedrooms Ⓡ ✳
sB&B£16.50-£22.50 sB&B⇨↑£18.50-£22.50 dB&B£33
dB&B⇨↑£37 WB&B£105-£119 WBDi£155-£169
LDO 5.30pm
Lic 🎮 CTV nc5yrs
Credit Cards ①③ Ⓔ

GH Ⓠ Ⓠ Ⓠ **Hollybank** 9 St Davids Place LL30 2UG
☎(0492) 878521
Etr-mid Oct
This comfortable, attractive and well maintained private hotel provides good quality, well equipped accommodation. Located in a quiet road convenient for the town centre, it also has a small car park.
7⇨3↑ (3fb) CTV in all bedrooms Ⓡ ✳ dB&B⇨3↑£28-£32
WB&B£91-£105 WBDi£130-£144 LDO 6.30pm
Lic 🎮 5P
Credit Cards ①③

GH Ⓠ Ⓠ **Kinmel Private Hotel** 12 Mostyn Crescent LL30 1AR
☎(0492) 876171
Etr-Sep
This privately owned, friendly hotel stands on the promenade overlooking the bay and beach. Many rooms have en suite facilities.
16rm(9⇨1↑6hc) (1fb) CTV in all bedrooms Ⓡ sB&B£18
sB&B⇨↑£23 dB&B⇨↑£38 WB&B£122-£130 WBDi£152-
£162.50 LDO 5.30pm
▶

🏵 **Hollybank** ♛♛♛
QQQ   9 ST DAVIDS PLACE, LLANDUDNO   COMMENDED
GWYNEDD LL30 2UG
TEL: (0492) 878521

Refurbished popular family hotel in elegant Edwardian house. Centrally situated on level quiet road. Close to every amenity. Lockable off-street car park, central heating, payphone, fire certificate. All bedrooms are spacious and airy with en-suite, colour TV, clock radio and drinks facilities. Residential licence. Tasteful lounge. Enjoy a choice of menu with generous portions in our sunny non-smoking dining room. OAP and childrens reductions. Hollybank is warm, friendly and welcoming.
Please send SAE for brochure to:
ROSEMARY ANTROBUS

Three Wells Farm

🏵 CHAPEL ROAD, HOWEY, ♛♛
AWARD
LLANDRINDOD WELLS, POWYS LD1 5PB
Tel; (0597) 822484

Welcome to our licensed farm guest house overlooking fishing lake in beautiful countryside. Ideal for exploring the "Heart of Wales". 12 bedrooms all with TV, tea/coffee making, direct dial telephone and en suite shower/bath. Centrally heated. Lift. Good food, spacious dining room. Lounge. TV room, sun lounge, 2 bars, four guest suites with own lounges, also one room with a four poster bed. Working farm with plenty of farm animals and wildlife. FHG Diploma WTB farmhouse award.
Your Hosts: Ron, Margaret & Sarah Bufton

Llandudno

Lic ⑭ 𝒫 snooker games room pool
Credit Cards ① ② ③ ⑤

GH Ⓠ Ⓠ Ⓠ **Mayfair Private Hotel** 4 Abbey Rd LL30 2EA
☎(0492) 876170
Mar-Oct
*Set in a residential area near the sea and shops, this family-run
hotel offers comfortable accommodation.*
12rm(9⇨3↑3hc) (7fb) CTV in all bedrooms Ⓡ sB&B£15-£18
dB&B£30-£36 dB&B⇨↑£32.80-£39 WB&B£107.60-£123
WBDi£153.75-£175 LDO 6pm
Lic ⑭ CTV 3P ⑤

GH Ⓠ *Mayfield* 19 Curzon Rd, Craig-y-Don LL30 1TB
☎(0492) 877427
Etr-Sep
*This small, simple family-run guesthouse is located in a quiet side
street on the eastern outskirts of the town. The seafront is a few
minutes' walk away and there is no private parking available.*
8hc (5fb) CTV in all bedrooms Ⓡ LDO 6pm
Lic CTV

GH Ⓠ Ⓠ *Minion Private Hotel* 21-23 Carmen Sylva Rd
LL30 1EQ ☎(0492) 877740
Etr-mid Oct
*A detached Edwardian house situated at the eastern end of the
town in a quiet residential area, within a short walk of the
promenade. Privately owned and personally run, the
accommodation is well maintained and the majority of bedrooms
have en suite facilities.*
14rm(4⇨6↑4hc) (4fb) Ⓡ LDO 4pm
Lic CTV 8P

GH Ⓠ Ⓠ **Montclare Hotel** North Pde LL30 2LP
☎(0492) 877061
Mar-Oct
*This tall, terraced, privately owned hotel offers quite well equipped
accommodation, and most of the bedrooms have private
bathrooms. It is conveniently situated close to the main shopping
area, the pier and other amenities.*
15rm(3⇨12↑) (6fb) CTV in all bedrooms Ⓡ
✖ (ex guide dogs) LDO 3pm
Lic ⑭ 4P ⑤

GH Ⓠ Ⓠ **Oak Alyn** Deganwy Av LL30 2YB ☎(0492) 860320
mid Feb-Nov rs Feb
13rm(4⇨9↑) (1fb) CTV in all bedrooms Ⓡ
sB&B⇨↑frf16.50 dB&B⇨↑frf33
Lic CTV 16P
Credit Cards ① ③

GH Ⓠ Ⓠ Ⓠ **Orotava Private Hotel** 105 Glan-Y-Mor Rd,
Penrhyn Bay LL30 3PH ☎(0492) 549780
*This small privately owned and personally run hotel is situated on
the eastern outskirts of Llandudno, on the edge of Penrhyn Bay,
with access to the seafront from the garden. The accommodation is
of a high standard: some bedrooms have private bathrooms and
many have sea views. There is a small private car park.*
6rm(3⇨3↑) ✂in all bedrooms CTV in all bedrooms Ⓡ ✖
sB&B⇨↑frf16.50 dB&B⇨↑frf33 WB&Bfrf161
WBDifrf206.50 LDO 8pm
Lic ⑭ CTV 8P nc15yrs
Credit Cards ① ③

GH Ⓠ **Rosaire Private Hotel** 2 St Seiriols Rd LL30 2YY
☎(0492) 877677
Mar-Oct
*This is a small, family-run hotel, which is located in a quiet road. It
provides convenient access to the town centre and to both shores.*
10rm(4↑6hc) (3fb) Ⓡ ✻ sB&B£14-£15 dB&B£25-£27
dB&B↑£29-£33 WB&B£85-£95 WBDi£120-£130 LDO 4pm
Lic ⑭ CTV 6P nc3yrs ⑤

⊠✈ GH Ⓠ Ⓠ Ⓠ **St Hilary Hotel** 16 Promenade, Craig-y-
Don LL30 1BG ☎(0492) 875551
Jan-Nov rs Oct-Spring BH
*This Victorian, family-run terraced hotel is situated on the
seafront, at the eastern end of the town, not far from the main
shopping area. Refurbished in 1991, the accommodation is well
appointed and impeccably maintained; most of the bedrooms now
have private bathrooms.*
11rm(8↑3hc) (8fb) CTV in all bedrooms Ⓡ ✖ (ex guide dogs)
sB&B£12.50-£21.50 sB&B↑£15.25-£27 dB&B£25
dB&B↑£30.50 WB&B£87.50-£106.75 WBDi£120.75-£140
LDO 5.30pm
Lic ⑭ CTV 𝒫
Credit Cards ① ③ ⑤

GH Ⓠ Ⓠ *Stratford Hotel* Promenade, Craig-y-Don LL30 1BG
☎(0492) 877962
*This small, privately owned and personally run hotel is situated on
the promenade, overlooking the bay. The bedrooms are modern
and well furnished, many with private bathrooms.*
10rm(4↑6hc) (6fb) CTV in all bedrooms Ⓡ
Lic ⑭ CTV 𝒫
Credit Cards ① ③

GH Ⓠ Ⓠ **Sunnyside Private Hotel** Llewelyn Av LL30 2ER
☎(0492) 877150
Etr-Oct & Xmas
*Set between Great Orme and the town centre, a few minutes from
the seafront, this guesthouse offers well kept bright rooms, some
with en suite facilities. The bar and lounge areas are attractive and
relaxing.*
26rm(4⇨8↑14hc) (4fb) CTV in 18 bedrooms TV in 1
bedroom Ⓡ LDO 7.30pm
Lic ⑭ CTV

GH Ⓠ Ⓠ *Thorpe House* 3 St Davids Rd LL30 2UL
☎(0492) 877089
Closed Xmas
*This nicely maintained, small, personally run hotel is conveniently
situated for access to the town centre and other amenities. Some
rooms have en suite facilities, and the guesthouse is well furnished
and comfortable.*
10rm(1↑9hc) (4fb) ✖
⑭ CTV 𝒫

GH Ⓠ Ⓠ **Warwick Hotel** 56 Church Walks LL30 2HL
☎(0492) 876823
*Standing on the lower slopes of the Great Orme, this large house is
a few minutes' walk from the promenade, pier and other amenities.
Many of the well equipped rooms have en suite facilities. On-street
parking is available.*
16rm(8⇨5↑3hc) (9fb) CTV in all bedrooms Ⓡ sB&B£16.50-
£18.50 sB&B⇨↑£18.50-£20.50 dB&B£33-£37 dB&B⇨↑£37-
£41 WB&B£99-£111 WBDi£132-£159 LDO 6.45pm
Lic ⑭ CTV 𝒫 ⑤

GH Ⓠ Ⓠ **Wedgewood Hotel** 6 Deganwy Av LL30 2YB
☎(0492) 878016
Etr-Dec
*This is a friendly, family-run hotel which provides well equipped
accommodation, many of the bedrooms having en suite facilities. It
is centrally situated, and has easy access to the town's amenities.*
11rm(2⇨7↑2hc) (1fb) CTV in all bedrooms Ⓡ dB&Bfrf40
dB&B↑frf45 (incl dinner) WB&Bfrf119 WBDifrf157
LDO 3pm
Lic ⑭ CTV 7P ⑤

GH Ⓠ Ⓠ **The Wilton Hotel** South Pde LL30 2LN
☎(0492) 876086 & 878343
Feb-Nov
*Well maintained and privately owned, this small hotel is close to
the shops, river and beach. The accommodation is well equipped,
most of the bedrooms having en suite facilities.*

14rm(7⇨5♠2hc) (7fb) CTV in all bedrooms ⓇsB&B⇨♠£18-£20 dB&B£36-£40 dB&B⇨♠£36-£40 WB&B£128-£138 WBDi£155-£165 LDO 4.30pm
Lic ♪ ⓔ

LLANEGRYN Gwynedd Map **06** SH50

FH Ⓠ Ⓠ Ⓠ Mrs Griffiths *Bryn Gwyn Country Farm House*
(SH610060) LL36 9UF ☎Tywyn(0654) 711771
Closed Jan-Feb
*A lovely old house dating back to 1730, set in 4 acres of gardens
and paddocks within the Snowdonia National Park,
approximately seven miles north of Aberdovey. Accommodation is
simple but well maintained, and there is a cosy lounge and snooker
table in a converted garage.*
5rm(1⇨1♠3hc) (1fb)⊁in 3 bedrooms CTV in 1 bedroom TV
in 1 bedroom Ⓡ ✖ (ex guide dogs) LDO 7.30am
🍴 CTV 7P ₰ bicycles 4 acres non-working

LLANFACHRETH Gwynedd Map **06** SH72

SELECTED

GH Ⓠ Ⓠ Ⓠ Ⓠ **Ty Isaf** LL40 2EA
☎Dolgellau(0341) 423261
*This traditional, stone-built Welsh longhouse dates back to
1624 and is situated in a small and peaceful village,
surrounded by the magnificent scenery of the Snowdonia
National Park. It has been extensively and tastefully
renovated to provide good quality, well equipped
accommodation, yet retains much of its original charm and
character. The standard of service and warm hospitality of the
proprietors is one of the reasons for the increasing popularity
of this guesthouse.*
3⇨♠ ⊁in all bedrooms Ⓡ ✳ sB&B⇨♠£20-£30
dB&B⇨♠£40 WB&B£140 WBDi£210 LDO 6pm
CTV 3P 1🐾 nc13yrs ⓔ

LLANFAIR CAEREINION Powys Map **06** SJ10

FH Ⓠ Ⓠ Mrs J Cornes *Cwmllwynog (SJ071065)* SY21 0HF
☎(0938) 810791
Etr-Sep
*This 17th-century farmhouse with its exposed beams and
inglenook fireplace is just off the B4385. It offers a warm welcome
and traditional home cooking using local produce wherever
possible.*
3rm(1♠1hc) CTV in 2 bedrooms Ⓡ ✖ ✳ dB&Bfr£24
dB&B♠fr£28 LDO 4pm
🍴 CTV 3P 105 acres dairy ⓔ

LLANFAIR DYFFRYN CLWYD Clwyd Map **06** SJ15

FH Ⓠ Ⓠ Mrs E Jones *Llanbenwch (SJ137533)* LL15 2SH
☎Ruthin(08242) 2340
Mar-Sep
*This small traditional farmhouse is set in a 40-acre farm, situated
on the A525, in picturesque countryside. The well maintained
accommodation has been modernised, yet retains its original
character. Meals are provided from home- grown or local produce.*
3hc (1fb) TV in all bedrooms Ⓡ ✖ LDO 5pm
🍴 CTV P nc5yrs 40 acres mixed ⓔ

LLANFIHANGEL-YNG-NGWYNFA Powys Map **06** SJ01

FH Ⓠ Ⓠ Ⓠ Mrs E Jenkins *Cyfie (SJ085147)* SY22 5JE (2m S
on unclass road off B4382) ☎Llanfyllin(069184) 451
*This 17th-century beamed farmhouse is situated in lovely
countryside amid the Welsh hills. All of the bedrooms are very
comfortable; one has its own lounge, and public rooms are of high
quality with guests enjoying good Welsh food.*

3rm(2⇨1♠) (1fb) CTV in 2 bedrooms Ⓡ ✖ ✳ sB&B⇨♠£29
dB&B⇨♠£47-£59 (incl dinner) WBDi£138-£168
LDO 7.30pm
🍴 CTV 6P 2🐾 180 acres mixed

LLANFYNYDD Dyfed Map **02** SN52

INN Ⓠ Ⓠ Ⓠ *Penybont* SA32 7TG ☎Dryslwyn(0558) 668292
*This very pleasant family-run country inn is situated 5 miles north
of the A40 at Clothi Bridge. Bedrooms are well furnished and
equipped, each with private bathrooms. A la carte meals are served
in the attractive restaurant, and there is a popular carvery
available at weekends.*
8⇨♠ (2fb) CTV in all bedrooms Ⓡ LDO 9pm
🍴 CTV 50P
Credit Cards ① ③
See advertisement under CARMARTHEN

LLANGOLLEN Clwyd Map **07** SJ24

FH Ⓠ Ⓠ Mrs A Kenrick *Rhydonnen Ucha Rhewl (SJ174429)*
Rhewl LL20 7AJ ☎(0978) 860153
Etr-Nov
*Large, stone-built, 3-storeyed farmhouse, pleasantly situated with
shooting on farm and trout fishing on River Dee (permit).*
4hc (2fb) LDO 3pm
🍴 CTV P 125 acres dairy

LLANGURIG Powys Map **06** SN98

GH Ⓠ Ⓠ Ⓠ **Old Vicarage** SY18 6RN ☎(05515) 280
Mar-Oct
*Run by the very friendly Rollings family, this pleasant guesthouse
lies in a cul-de-sac just off the main road. The modern bedrooms
are well equipped and two comfortable lounges are available for
guests' use.*
5rm(2⇨2♠1hc) (2fb)⊁in all bedrooms CTV in 2 bedrooms
TV in 1 bedroom Ⓡ sB&B£15-£16 dB&B⇨♠£35-£40
WB&B£122.50-£140 WBDi£175-£195 LDO 7pm
Lic 🍴 CTV 8P nc4yrs ⓔ

LLANON Dyfed Map **02** SN50

INN Ⓠ Ⓠ Ⓠ *Plas Morfa Hotel & Restaurant* Plas Morfa
SY23 5LX ☎(0974) 202415
8⇨♠ (2fb) CTV in all bedrooms Ⓡ ✳ sB&B⇨♠£18.50-£25
dB&B⇨♠£37-£50 WB&B£100-£128 WBDi£150-£178 ✳
Lunch fr£7.50 High tea fr£1.50alc Dinner fr£8&alc
LDO 9.30pm
🍴 40P

LLANRHYSTUD Dyfed Map **06** SN56

FH Ⓠ Ⓠ Ⓠ Mrs T T Mizen *Pen-Y-Castell (SN539684)*
SY23 5BZ ☎Nebo(0974) 272622
*Just 2.5 miles from the A487 coast road and signposted off the
B4337, this delightful modernised farmhouse overlooks the lovely
Cardigan Bay, and also has its own lake. The family-run
accommodation is pretty and comfortable.*
6⇨♠ (1fb)⊁in all bedrooms CTV in 3 bedrooms Ⓡ
✖ (ex guide dogs) sB&B⇨♠£22-£24 dB&B⇨♠£44-£46
WB&B£160 WBDi£226 LDO 6pm
Lic 🍴 CTV 10P 2🐾 ♩ boating lake pitch & putt 35 acres beef
sheep ⓔ

LLANSANTFFRAID-YM-MECHAIN Powys Map **07** SJ22

FH Ⓠ Ⓠ Mrs M E Jones *Glanvyrnwy (SJ229202)* SY22 6SU
☎Llansantffraid(0691) 828258
*This cosy farmhouse is set in very pretty lawns and gardens with an
abundance of seasonal blossoms. It lies on the Llanymywech side
of the village and provides bright and cheerful bedrooms.*
2hc Ⓡ ✖ (ex guide dogs)
CTV 3P nc3yrs 42 acres beef

LLANSILIN Clwyd Map **07** SJ22

FH Ⓠ Ⓠ Ⓠ Mrs B Jones & Mrs A Gallagher **Bwlch-Y-Rhiw** *(ST226298)* SY10 7PT ☎(069170) 261
Mar-Nov
Set in lovely border country with beautiful rural views, this early 19th-century farmhouse is very well furnished and offers spacious and comfortable accommodation.
3⇨🌂 (1fb) CTV in all bedrooms Ⓡ ✖ (ex guide dogs) sB&B⇨🌂fr£24 dB&B⇨🌂fr£32 WB&Bfr£105
🏵 4P nc8yrs ✔ 120 acres sheep Ⓔ

LLANVAIR DISCOED Gwent Map **03** ST49

FH Ⓠ Ⓠ Mr & Mrs Price **Great Llanmellyn** *(SO456923)* NP6 6LU ☎Shirenewton(02917) 210
Apr-Oct
This 14th-century farmhouse is just over a mile from the A48 road between Newport and Chepstow. Family run, it is full of character and the accommodation is spacious and comfortable.
2rm(1🌂1hc) (2fb) Ⓡ ✖ (ex guide dogs) dB&B£30 dB&B🌂£32 WB&B£90
🏵 CTV 3P 250 acres dairy mixed Ⓔ

LLANWDDYN Powys Map **06** SJ01

FH Ⓠ Ⓠ R B & H A Parry **Tynymaes** *(SJ048183)* SY10 0NN ☎(069173) 216
May-29 Sep
Situated just a few miles from Lake Vyrnwy this cosy farmhouse, run by the Parry family offers a warm welcome. The lounge is spacious and comfortable and the bedrooms are bright and cheerful.
3hc (1fb) Ⓡ ✖ ✱ dB&B£24-£26 WB&B£90 WBDi£125 LDO 5pm
🏵 CTV 4P 420 acres beef sheep Ⓔ

LLANWRIN Powys Map **06** SH70

FH Ⓠ Ⓠ Ⓠ Mrs R J Hughes **Mathafarn** *(SN812055)* Cemmaes Rd SY20 8QJ ☎Cemmaes Road(0650) 511226
Set in the beautiful Dovey Valley, this ivy-clad house dates back to 1628. Henry VII is said to have stayed here en route to the Battle of Bosworth. Today's guests will find comfortable accommodation provided by the friendly Hughes family.
3rm(1⇨2hc) Ⓡ ✖ (ex guide dogs) sB&B£14-£15 dB&B⇨£30
🏵 CTV 3P 600 acres beef sheep Ⓔ

LLANWRTYD WELLS Powys Map **03** SN84

GH Ⓠ Ⓠ Ⓠ **Lasswade Country House Hotel** LD5 4RW ☎(05913) 515 FAX (05913) 611
This Edwardian country house set in a lovely rural location provides very comfortable accommodation. Bedrooms are particularly well equipped with modest facilities, and there is a spacious lounge. Visitors may have to move one of three cats from their favourite arm chair in the lounge, or be cajoled by the Remy the Great Dane into having his tummy scratched.
7rm(2⇨4🌂1hc) CTV in all bedrooms Ⓡ ✱ sB&B⇨🌂£31.50-£34 dB&B⇨🌂£48-£53 WB&B£164.50 WBDi£252 LDO 8pm
Lic 🏵 12P
Credit Cards ①②③Ⓔ

LOCHINVER Highland *Sutherland* Map **14** NC02

GH Ⓠ Ⓠ **Ardglas** IV27 4LI ☎(05714) 257
Feb-Nov
A popular holiday guesthouse set on the hill with a lovely view of the bay and the harbour. It offers comfortable, compact but good value bed and breakfast accommodation, with a relaxed atmosphere.
8hc (2fb)⊁in all bedrooms CTV in 1 bedroom Ⓡ
🏵 CTV 12P

GH Ⓠ Ⓠ Ⓠ **Drumbeg House** Drumbeg IV27 4NW ☎Drumbeg(05713) 209
This warmly welcoming Victorian house is set in 3 acres of secluded grounds, just north of the village, and is an ideal base for those seeking peaceful relaxation. To help create a friendly atmosphere, guests normally share a communal table at dinner and breakfast.
3🌂 ⊁in all bedrooms Ⓡ ✖ ✱ dB&B🌂£60-£70 (incl dinner) LDO 7pm
🏵 CTV 6P nc14yrs

LOCHRANZA
See **ARRAN, ISLE OF**

LOCHWINNOCH Strathclyde *Renfrewshire* Map **10** NS35

FH Ⓠ Ⓠ Mrs A Mackie **High Belltrees** *(NS377584)* PA12 4JN (situated 1m off the A737 to Largs road) ☎(0505) 842376
A friendly, cheery environment awaits the visitor to this farmhouse which enjoys an elevated position looking out across the valley and Castle Semple Loch. There are some nice spacious bedrooms, which will be particularly attractive to birdwatchers as the loch has an RSPB sanctuary.
4rm(3hc) (2fb) CTV in all bedrooms Ⓡ ✖ (ex guide dogs) ✱ sB&B£14-£16 dB&B£25-£27 WB&B£95-£98
🏵 CTV 6P 220 acres dairy mixed sheep

LOCKERBIE Dumfries & Galloway *Dumfriesshire* Map **11** NY18

GH Ⓠ Ⓠ Ⓠ **Rosehill** Carlisle Rd DG11 2DR ☎(05762) 2378
A neat, comfortable house offering spacious accommodation, Rosehill Guesthouse is situated on the main street with easy access to the A74.
5hc (3fb) CTV in all bedrooms Ⓡ sB&B£14-£15 dB&B£26-£28
🏵 CTV 5P

SHORT WALKS ~TO~ COUNTRY PUBS

One hundred of England's best pubs are included, each at the half-way stage of a pleasant country walk. The round trip will average around five miles and the guide gives full directions for walkers, together with things to see on the way, places of interest nearby and, most important of all, a fine country pub to break the journey and enjoy a good bar meal and a pint of real ale.

Available at good bookshops and AA Centres

Another great guide from the AA

London
Plan 1

1 Bryanston Court (W1)
2 Camelot Hotel (W2)
3 Hotel Concorde (W1)
4 Edward Lear Hotel (W1)

5 Georgian House Hotel (W1)
6 Hart House Hotel (W1)
7 Kingsway Hotel (W2)
8 Mitre House Hotel (W2)
9 Park Lodge Hotel (W2)

Details of the establishments shown on this map can be found under the *London Postal District* which follows the establishment name.

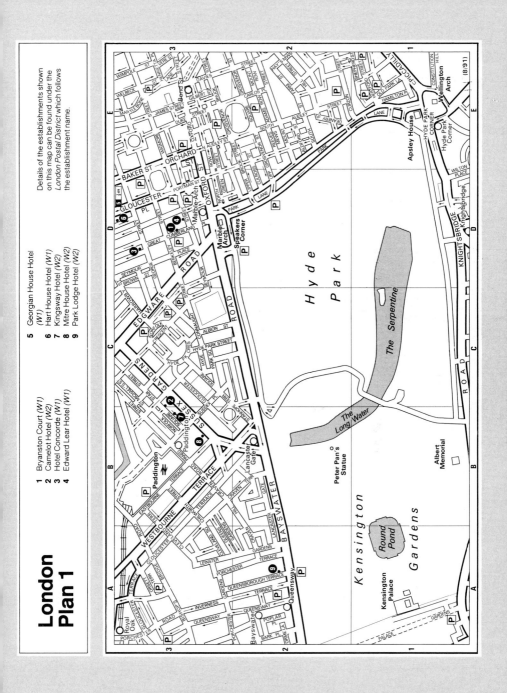

London
Plan 2

Details of the establishments shown on this map can be found under the *London Postal District* which follows the establishment name.

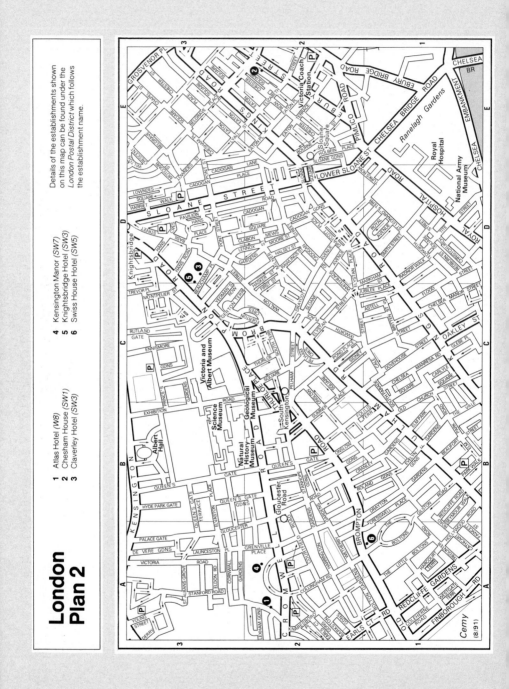

London
Plan 3

Details of the establishments shown on this map can be found under the *London Postal District* which follows the establishment name.

1 Winchester Hotel (*SW1*) **2** Windermere Hotel (*SW1*)

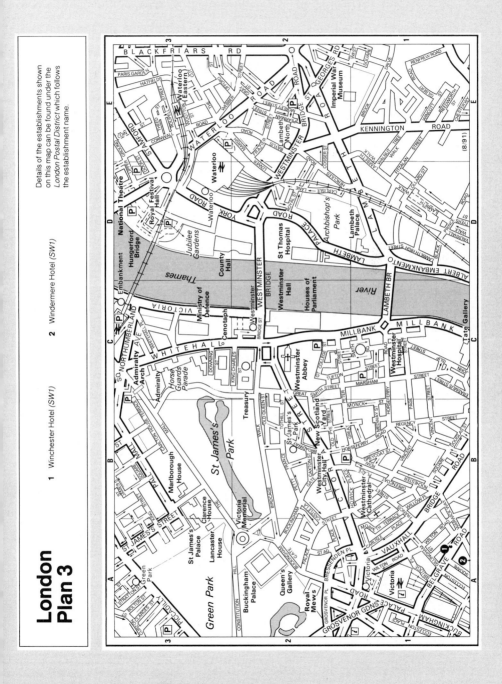

London
Plan 4

The placenames highlighted by a **dot** are locations of AA listed establishments outside the Central London Plan area (Plans 1–3). Some of these fall within the London Postal District area and can therefore be found in the gazetteer under **London** in postal district order (see London Postal District map on following page). Others outside the London Postal District area can therefore be found under their respective placenames in the main gazetteer.

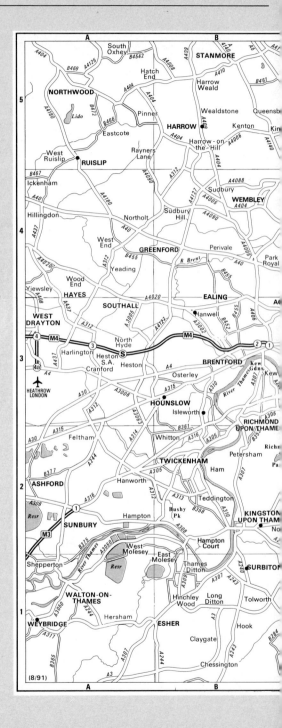

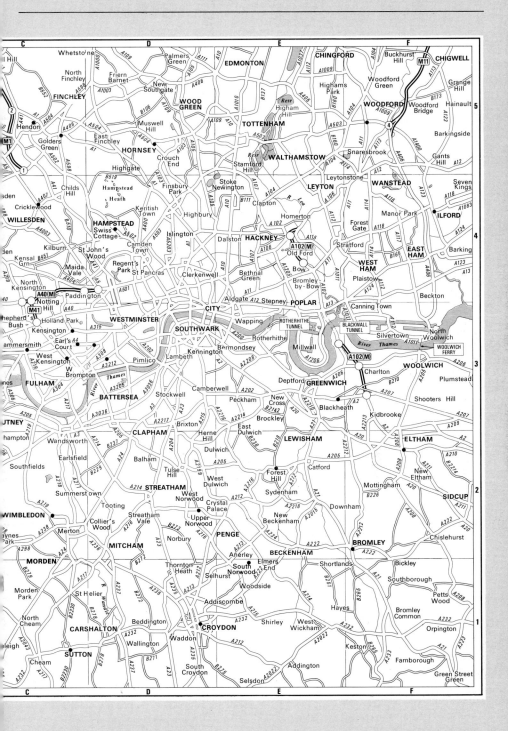

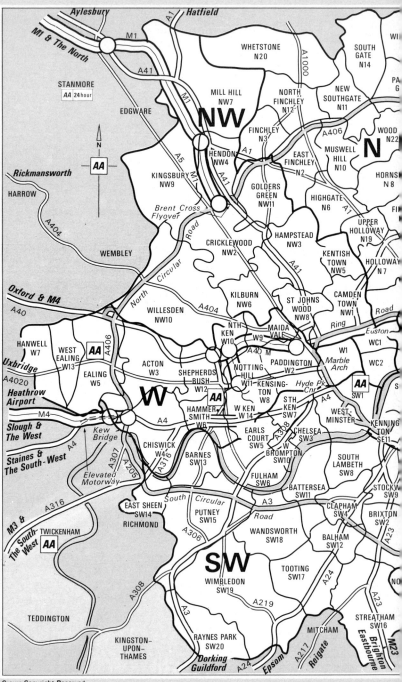

Crown Copyright Reserved

London Postal Districts and ways in and out of London

London Postal Area Boundary	
London Postal District Boundaries	
Main Roads into and out of London	
Signposted North and South Circular Roads & Ring Road	
Other Main Roads	
Service Centre	**AA**

Scale of Miles

0 1 2 3 4

(5/90) © The Automobile Association

LONDON Greater London Map **04**

See plans 1-4 pages 221-225. A map of the London postal area appears on pages 226-227.
Places within the London postal area are listed below in postal district order commencing East then North, South and West, with a brief indication of the area covered. Detailed plans **1-3** show the locations of AA-listed hotels within Central London and are indicated by a number. Plan **4** highlights the districts. **Other places within the county of London are listed under their respective placenames and are also keyed to this plan or the main map section.**

E18 SOUTH WOODFORD London plan **4** F5

GH Q Q **Grove Hill Hotel** 38 Grove Hill, South Woodford
E18 2JG ☎081-989 3344 FAX 081-530 5286
This popular and well-managed small hotel has compact, well-maintained rooms, each with radio and TV. Generous breakfasts are inclusive and served daily.
21rm(10⇆2♪9hc) (2fb) CTV in all bedrooms ® ✳ sB&Bfr£25 sB&B⇆♪£38 dB&B£44 dB&B⇆♪£53
Lic 鬥 CTV 8P 4🐾
Credit Cards ①②③⓵

N8 HORNSEY London plan **4** D5

GH Q Q **Aber Hotel** 89 Crouch Hill N8 9EG ☎081-340 2847 FAX 081-340 2847
This small, family-run hotel offers warm and friendly service. It is situated in a busy residential area within easy reach of the city centre.
9hc (4fb) ✖ sB&B£20-£22 dB&B£35-£38 WB&Bfr£110
鬥 CTV
Credit Cards ①③⓵

GH Q Q Q **White Lodge Hotel** 1 Church Ln, Hornsey N8 7BU ☎081-348 9765
A private family-run guesthouse which has been skilfully extended and provides modern, well designed bedrooms, double glazing and a comfortable front lounge for guests. Full English breakfast is available on request at an extra charge.
18rm(6♪12hc) (4fb) CTV in all bedrooms ®
✖ (ex guide dogs) ✳ sB&B£20-£22 dB&B£30-£32 dB&B♪£36-£38 LDO at breakfast
鬥 CTV ♪
Credit Cards ①③⓵

NW2 CRICKLEWOOD London plan **4** C4

GH Q Q **Clearview House** 161 Fordwych Rd NW2 3NG ☎081-452 9773
This peaceful, family run guesthouse is situated in a quiet residential area. The accommodation here is comfortable, and each bedroom is well equipped.
6hc (1fb) CTV in 1 bedroom TV in 5 bedrooms
✖ (ex guide dogs) ✳ sB&Bfr£13 dB&Bfr£26 WB&Bfr£80
鬥 CTV ♪ nc5yrs ⓵

GH Q *The Garth Hotel* 64-76 Hendon Way NW2 2NL ☎081-455 4742 FAX 081-455 4744
Situated on the busy Hendon Way, this commercial hotel has nicely appointed bedrooms and functional public areas. It is at present being refurbished to provide additional bedrooms.
53rm(30⇆10♪)(9fb) CTV in all bedrooms ® LDO 11pm
Lic 鬥 CTV 58P
Credit Cards ①②③⑤

NW3 HAMPSTEAD London plan **4** D4

GH Q Q *Seaford Lodge* 2 Fellows Rd, Hampstead NW3 3LP ☎071-722 5032
Close to Regents Park, this guesthouse has well equipped modern bedrooms with en suite facilities, some ideal for family use. The proprietors personally supervise the running of Seaford House.

15⇆♪ (1fb) CTV in all bedrooms ® LDO noon
鬥 3P 2🐾
Credit Cards ①③⑤

NW4 HENDON London plan **4** C5

GH Q Q Q *Peacehaven Hotel* 94 Audley Rd, Hendon Central NW4 3HB ☎081-202 9758 & 081-202 1225
Modern, bright bedrooms, all with colour TV and many with en suite facilities. A bright yellow breakfast room overlooking a landscaped garden, reflects the cheerful disposition of the proprietor.
13rm(7⇆2♪4hc) CTV in all bedrooms ® ✖ (ex guide dogs)
鬥 2P
Credit Cards ①②③⑤

See advertisement on page 231

NW11 GOLDERS GREEN London plan **4** C5

GH Q Q Q **Anchor Hotel** 10 West Heatt Dr, Golders Green NW11 ☎081-458 8764 FAX 081-455 3204
12rm(9♪) (2fb) CTV in all bedrooms ✳ sB&Bfr£26 sB&B♪£28-£30 dB&B£38-£40 dB&B♪£45-£49 (wkly only 3 Jan-3 Mar)
鬥 CTV 6P 3🐾

GH Q Q **Croft Court Hotel** 44 Ravenscroft Av, Golders Green NW11 8AY ☎081-458 3331 FAX 081-455 9175
A small, personally run Kosher hotel with modern, well furnished and equipped bedrooms, each with private bathrooms. There is a bright, dual dining room/lounge, and the hotel is situated in a convenient location in a residential area just off the Finchley road.
20⇆♪ (4fb) CTV in all bedrooms ® ✖
鬥 CTV 3P
Credit Cards ①②③

ABER HOTEL

A quiet family run hotel with a warm and friendly atmosphere. Situated in a pleasant residential area of North London and within easy access of the city centre by public transport. Also, we are on a direct route via the Piccadilly line Underground from Heathrow Airport to Finsbury Park.

All rooms are centrally heated. There is a lounge for guests with CTV. Included in our realistic prices is a full English breakfast. Unrestricted parking outside hotel.

**89, Crouch Hill, Hornsey, London N8 9EG.
Telephone/Fax. No: 081-340-2847**

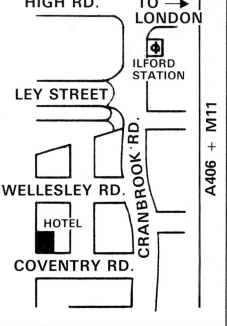

SE3 BLACKHEATH London plan **4** E3

GH **Q Q** **Stonehall House Hotel** 35-37 Westcombe Park Rd
SE3 7RE ☎081-858 8706
*An old fashioned, long-established guesthouse in a convenient,
quiet location providing relatively easy access to all the travel
services. The accommodation comprises a choice of functional but
well equipped bedrooms which have recently been improved under
helpful and efficient management.*
27rm(1⇌10♠16hc)(10fb) CTV in all bedrooms sB&Bfr£23
sB&B⇌♠£28-£29 dB&Bfr£34 dB&B⇌♠£38-£40
♨ CTV ⚡
Credit Cards ① ③ ⓔ

SELECTED

GH **Q Q Q Q** **Vanbrugh Hotel** 21/23 St Johns Park
SE3 7TD ☎081-853 4051
*This Victorian villa in a quiet Blackheath residential street
has been skilfully and sympathetically converted into a very
comfortable hotel offering bed and breakfast. Bedrooms are
on 3 floors (there is a lift) and are spacious, modern and
tastefully furnished. Guests are also offered a TV lounge, car
parking, a well designed garden, a hearty cooked breakfast
and a friendly welcome.*
30⇌♠ CTV in all bedrooms ® ✻ (ex guide dogs) ✻
sB&B⇌♠£59-£64 dB&B⇌♠£82-£110 LDO 9.15pm
Lic lift ♨ CTV 16P
Credit Cards ① ② ③ ⓔ

SE9 ELTHAM London plan **4** F4

GH **Q Q Q** *Yardley Court Private Hotel* 18 Court Rd SE9
☎081-850 1850
*This small privately managed hotel has comfortable bedrooms with
showers and modern furnishings. The generous English breakfasts
are freshly cooked.*
9rm(6♠3hc)(1fb) CTV in all bedrooms ® ✻ (ex guide dogs)
♨ 8P
Credit Cards ① ③

SE19 NORWOOD London plan **4** D2

GH **Q Q** **Crystal Palace Tower Hotel** 114 Church Rd SE19 2UB
☎081-653 0176
*Large Victorian house, close to all amenities and with easy access
to central London. Spacious, comfortable bedrooms, compact
lounge and basement dining room. Car parking on hotel forecourt.*
11rm(2⇌3♠6hc)(4fb) CTV in 3 bedrooms TV in 8 bedrooms
® ✻ sB&B£21 sB&B⇌♠£25 dB&B£32 dB&B⇌♠£36
♨ CTV 10P
Credit Cards ① ③ ⑤ ⓔ

SE25 SOUTH NORWOOD London plan **4** E1

GH **Q Q Q** **Norwood Lodge** 17-19 South Norwood Hill, South
Norwood SE25 6AA ☎081-653 3962
*A small, modern hotel, very comfortable and well equipped.
Bedrooms are well furnished, and there is a quiet lounge and a
breakfast room in the basement. An attractive lawned rear garden,
with easy access and ample parking make this an agreeable place
to stay, with extensive, friendly service.*
19⇌♠ (1fb) CTV in all bedrooms ® ✻ sB&B⇌♠£35-£50
dB&B⇌♠£45-£60 WB&B£210-£245 WBDi£262.50-£297.50
LDO 7.30pm
Lic ♨ CTV 16P 1🐾
Credit Cards ① ② ③ ⑤ ⓔ

Book as early as possible for busy holiday periods.

SW1 WESTMINSTER London plan **4** D3

GH **Q Q** **Belgrave House** 28-32 Belgrave Rd, Victoria
SW1V 1RG ☎071-828 1563 & 071-834 8620
*This imposing 4-storeyed terraced house is ideally situated for
Victoria. It offers reasonably priced accommodation, with the
bedrooms having been recently refurbished.*
46rm(2⇌4♠40hc)(8fb)✂in 25 bedrooms ✻
♨ CTV ⚡ ⓔ

GH **Q Q** **Chesham House** 64-66 Ebury St, Belgravia SW1N 9QD
☎071-730 8513 Telex no 946797 FAX 071-730 3267
23hc (3fb) CTV in all bedrooms ✻ ✻ sB&B£28-£30 dB&B£43-
£45
♨ ⚡
Credit Cards ① ② ③ ⑤

GH **Q Q** **Winchester Hotel** 12 Belgrave Rd SW1
☎071-828 2972 Telex no 269674 FAX 071-828 5191
Closed 23-29 Dec
*A high standard of accommodation is offered here with nicely
appointed rooms with en suite facilities. Breakfast is served in the
pleasant lower ground floor dining room.*
18⇌♠ (2fb) CTV in all bedrooms ✻ ✻ sB&B⇌♠£58
dB&B⇌♠£58
♨ ⚡ nc10yrs

GH **Q Q** **Windermere Hotel** 142/144 Warwick Way, Victoria
SW1V 4JE ☎071-834 5163 & 071-834 5480 Telex no 94017182
FAX 071-630 8831
*This friendly hotel offers pleasant accommodation in nicely
equipped modern rooms. Windermere is within easy reach of
central London.*
23rm(19⇌♠4hc)(7fb) CTV in all bedrooms
✻ (ex guide dogs) sB&B£30-£38 sB&B⇌♠£38-£49 dB&B£40-
£49 dB&B⇌♠£56-£79 LDO 9.30pm

▶

Lic ⁽ᵐ⁾ CTV ✗
Credit Cards ① ② ③

SW3 CHELSEA London plan **4** D3

GH Ⓠ Ⓠ Ⓠ *Claverley House* 13-14 Beaufort Gardens,
Knightsbridge SW3 ☎071-589 8541
*This delightful, elegant hotel has a warm atmosphere and
comfortable rooms. Guests can relax in the leather Chesterfield
sofas in the reading room. The pretty breakfast room is on the
lower ground floor.*
36rm(25⇨11hc) (2fb) CTV in all bedrooms ✖
lift ⁽ᵐ⁾ ✗
Credit Cards ③

GH Ⓠ Ⓠ Ⓠ *Knightsbridge Hotel* 10 Beaufort Gardens SW3 1PT
☎071-589 9271
*The charm and elegance of the Victorian era shows in the
architecture of this terraced hotel. Attractive and equipped with
modern conveniences, and with a pleasant breakfast room on the
lower ground floor, the hotel benefits from a convenient location.*
20rm(4⇨5♠11hc) (4fb) CTV in all bedrooms Ⓡ ✖
LDO 9.30pm
Lic ⁽ᵐ⁾ ✗
Credit Cards ① ② ③

SW5 EARLS COURT London plan **4** C3

GH Ⓠ Ⓠ *Swiss House Hotel* 171 Old Brompton Rd, South
Kensington SW5 0AN ☎071-373 2769 FAX 071-373 4983
16rm(10⇨♠6hc) (7fb) CTV in 15 bedrooms TV in 1 bedroom
✱ sB&B£27.50 sB&B⇨♠£31 dB&B£41.80 dB&B⇨♠£49.50
WB&B£173-£277 LDO 9pm
⁽ᵐ⁾ CTV
Credit Cards ① ③

SW7 SOUTH KENSINGTON London plan **4** D3

GH Ⓠ Ⓠ *Kensington Manor* 8 Emperors Gate SW7 4HH
☎071-370 7516 Telex no 925975 FAX 071-373 3163
*This small, friendly hotel offers pleasant bedrooms with limited
public areas. Standing in a quiet terrace, it is conveniently placed
for transport to the West End.*
15rm(14⇨♠1hc) (2fb) CTV in all bedrooms Ⓡ
✖ (ex guide dogs) ✱ sB&B£52-£59.95 sB&B⇨♠£69.95-£76.50
dB&B£72-£82 dB&B⇨♠£82-£94
Lic ⁽ᵐ⁾ ✗
Credit Cards ① ② ③ ⑤ Ⓔ

SW19 WIMBLEDON London plan **4** C2

GH Ⓠ Ⓠ *Kings Lodge* 5 Kings Rd SW19 8PJ ☎081-545 0191
FAX 081-545 0381
Closed Xmas
7rm(2⇨5♠) (2fb) CTV in all bedrooms Ⓡ ✖ (ex guide dogs)
(wkly only last wk Jun/1st wk Jul) LDO 9pm
⁽ᵐ⁾ CTV 2P 2⊜
Credit Cards ① ② ③ ⑤

GH Ⓠ Ⓠ *Trochee Hotel* 21 Malcolm Rd SW19 4AS
☎081-946 1579 & 3924 FAX 081-785 4058
*A warm and comfortable atmosphere is found in this hotel.
Situated in a quiet residential area, it is ideally located for all local
amenities, and for easy access to both central London and the
countryside.*
17hc (2fb) CTV in all bedrooms Ⓡ ✖ (ex guide dogs) sB&B£35
dB&B£50
⁽ᵐ⁾ CTV 3P
Credit Cards ① ③ Ⓔ

GH Ⓠ Ⓠ *Wimbledon Hotel* 78 Worple Rd SW19 4HZ
☎081-946 9265
*This small, family-run hotel offers a cosy and friendly atmosphere.
It is ideally situated, being only a ten minute walk from the main
street and the station.*

14rm(3⇨2♠9hc) (6fb)⊬in 8 bedrooms CTV in all bedrooms
Ⓡ ✖ ✱ sB&B£39-£42 sB&B⇨♠£42-£48 dB&B£51-£54
dB&B⇨♠£54-£58
⁽ᵐ⁾ CTV 10P
Credit Cards ① ③

GH Ⓠ Ⓠ Ⓠ *Worcester House* 38 Alwyne Rd SW19 7AE
☎081-946 1300 FAX 081-785 4058
*All the bedrooms at this hotel have en suite facilities and are
equipped with radio, colour TV, direct dial telephone, hairdryer
and beverage facilites. A pleasant atmosphere prevails, and
Worcester House is a few minutes walk from the village centre.*
9♠ (1fb) CTV in all bedrooms Ⓡ ✖ ✱ sB&B♠£42.50-£49.50
dB&B♠£56.50-£59.50
⁽ᵐ⁾ ✗
Credit Cards ① ③ ⑤ Ⓔ

W1 WEST END London plan **4** D3/4

GH Ⓠ Ⓠ *Bryanston Court* 60 Great Cumberland Place W1
(Best Western) ☎071-262 3141 Telex no 262076
*An ideal location for business or pleasure, this long-established
family-run hotel provides generally good standards of service.
There is a choice of bedrooms with compact showers, a cosy, well
furnished bar, lobby lounge and small breakfast room. Light
refreshments are available throughout the day and there is a 24-
hour reception service. Car parking can be a problem but there is
an NCP car park near by.*
54rm(4⇨50♠) (3fb) CTV in all bedrooms Ⓡ ✖ ✱
sB&B⇨♠frf65 dB&B⇨♠frf80 LDO 10pm
Lic lift ⁽ᵐ⁾ 2⊜ (£15 per day)
Credit Cards ① ② ③ ⑤

GH Ⓠ Ⓠ *Hotel Concorde* 50 Great Cumberland Place
W1H 7FD ☎071-402 6169 Telex no 262076
Closed 23 Dec-1 Jan
*Adjoining the Bryanston Court hotel which the Theodore family
also manage, this useful hotel provides good value and a choice of
modern, traditionally furnished and very well equipped bedrooms.
A cosy bar is open throughout the day, and there is a comfortable
front lounge and a tastefully furnished breakfast room; easy
access is provided by a lift to all floors. Bath and shower rooms are
currently being refurbished, and the hotel provides the ideal central
location. Parking can be difficult, but there is an NCP car park
nearby.*
28rm(5⇨23♠) (1fb) CTV in all bedrooms Ⓡ ✖ ✱
sB&B⇨♠frf55 dB&B⇨♠frf68
Lic lift ⁽ᵐ⁾ CTV 2⊜ (£15 per day)
Credit Cards ① ② ③ ⑤

GH Ⓠ *Edward Lear Hotel* 28-30 Seymour St W1
☎071-402 5401
*Named after the artist and writer, Edward Lear, who lived here
from 1812-1888, this conveniently located rambling house offers
good basic accommodation on 6 floors. Some of the bedrooms have
recently been redecorated and some have private bathrooms.
Service is friendly and well managed, providing overall good value
with functional basic facilities, some of which are rather old-
fashioned, but improved by modern amenities such as TV, direct
dial telephones and early morning tea making provisions.*
30rm(5♠25hc) (3fb) CTV in all bedrooms Ⓡ ✖
CTV ✗
Credit Cards ③

See advertisement on page 235

GH Ⓠ Ⓠ *Georgian House Hotel* 87 Gloucester Place, Baker St
W1H 3PG ☎071-935 2211 Telex no 266079 FAX 071-486 7535
*Despite its central location, the pleasantly appointed bedrooms at
this well managed and friendly small hotel are very quiet, with
good modern facilities. A continental buffet-style breakfast is
served in the basement dining room, and there is a lift available to
all floors.*
19rm(14⇨5♠) (3fb) CTV in all bedrooms Ⓡ ✖
sB&B⇨♠£45-£50 dB&B⇨♠£60-£65 (wkly only Nov-Mar)

▶

Lic lift ♨ ⚲ nc5yrs
Credit Cards ①②③ⓔ

GH Ⓠ Hart House Hotel 51 Gloucester Place, Portman Sq
W1H 3PE ☎071-935 2288
*A long-established family-run terraced house on 5 floors offering
bed and breakfast. Bedrooms are slowly being upgraded to a good
standard and all now include TV, radio, telephone and tea and
coffee making facilities. The basement breakfast room is a little
confined, but overall the general level of comfort is quite agreeable.
Car parking is very difficult, but there is good bus access to all
local amenities.*
15rm(7⇨🌂8hc) (4fb) CTV in all bedrooms Ⓡ ✖ sB&B£35-
£40 sB&B⇨🌂£40-£45 dB&B£50-£55 dB&B⇨🌂£60-£70
♨ CTV ⚲
Credit Cards ①②③ⓔ

GH Ⓠ Montagu House 3 Montagu Place, Baker St W1H 1RG
☎071-935 4632 & 071-486 1443
*With new ownership this year, this conveniently situated
guesthouse near Marble Arch, is currently being upgraded.*
18rm(1🌂17hc) (4fb) CTV in all bedrooms Ⓡ ✖
♨ CTV ⚲
Credit Cards ①③ ⓔ

W2 BAYSWATER, PADDINGTON London plan 4 C/D3/4

SELECTED

GH ⓆⓆⓆⓆ Byron Hotel 36-38 Queensborough Ter
W2 3SH ☎071-243 0987 Telex no 263431
*A highly recommended, conveniently situated bed and
breakfast hotel. Designed to recreate the style and elegance of
Victorian times, the accommodation has been equipped to the
highest standard. Bedrooms range from luxurious to compact,
but all have good en suite facilities. There is a comfortable
sitting room and a small penthouse conference room with
business services, and air conditioning is provided throughout.
Parking is very difficult and taxis are recommended.*
42⇨🌂 (2fb)✂in 10 bedrooms CTV in all bedrooms Ⓡ
✖ (ex guide dogs) ✳ sB&B⇨🌂£70 dB&B⇨🌂£80-£90
LDO 8pm
Lic lift ♨ CTV ⚲
Credit Cards ①②③⑤ⓔ

GH ⓆⓆⓆ Camelot Hotel 45-47 Norfolk Square W2 1RX
☎071-723 9118 & 071-262 1980 Telex no 268312
FAX 071-402 3412
*Friendly hotel providing modern facilities in a range of
accommodation.*
44rm(36⇨🌂8hc) (8fb) CTV in all bedrooms Ⓡ
✖ (ex guide dogs) sB&B£36.50-£44 sB&B⇨🌂£53
dB&B⇨🌂£72
lift ♨ CTV ⚲
Credit Cards ①③ ⓔ

GH ⓆⓆⓆ Kingsway Hotel 27 Norfolk Square, Hyde Park
W2 1RX ☎071-723 7784 & 071-723 5569 FAX 071-723 7317
33rm(30⇨🌂3hc) (4fb) CTV in all bedrooms Ⓡ
✖ (ex guide dogs) ✳ sB&B£22-£28 sB&B⇨🌂£30-£42
dB&B£35-£42 dB&B⇨🌂£42-£52 WB&B£140-£266
lift ♨ CTV
Credit Cards ①②③⑤

GH ⓆⓆ Mitre House Hotel 178-184 Sussex Gardens, Hyde
Park W2 1TU ☎071-723 8040 Telex no 914113
FAX 071-402 0990
*This family-run licensed hotel is ideally situated in the heart of
town. At the time of inspection, half of the house was closed due to
the addition of full en suite facilities to all bedrooms, as well as the
colour TVs, radios and direct dial telephones. There is a lift to all
floors, a TV lounge and free parking on the forecourt.*

70rm(64⇨🌂6hc) (3fb) CTV in all bedrooms ✖ sB&Bfr£55
sB&B⇨🌂£55-£60 dB&B⇨🌂£65-£70
Lic lift ♨ CTV 25P jacuzzi
Credit Cards ①②③⑤

See advertisement on page 237

GH ⓆⓆⓆ Mornington Hotel 12 Lancaster Gate W2 3LG
(Best Western) ☎071-262 7361 Telex no 24281
FAX 071-706 1028
Closed 23 Dec-1 Jan
*Consistently good standards of accommodation are provided by
this competently managed hotel, under the same ownership as the
Mornington in Stockholm and set in a reasonably quiet part of
London close to Hyde Park. Well furnished and equipped
Swedish-style bedrooms with modular bathrooms complement
public areas which include a reception lobby, a wood-panelled
library bar and a basement breakfast room featuring an excellent
self-service continental breakfast buffet.*
68⇨🌂 (6fb) CTV in all bedrooms sB&B⇨🌂fr£75
dB&B⇨🌂£86-£103
Lic lift ♨ ⚲ sauna
Credit Cards ①②③⑤ⓔ

GH ⓆⓆ Norfolk Towers Hotel 34 Norfolk Place W2 1QW
☎071-262 3123 Telex no 268583
*Charming and tastefully restored, this Victorian house is well
equipped to meet the needs of businessmen, travellers and tourists,
with en suite accommodation. Hot and cold meals are served in the
'Cad's wine bar' and there is also a lounge bar.*
85⇨🌂 (3fb) CTV in all bedrooms ✖ (ex guide dogs)
sB&B⇨🌂fr£65 dB&B⇨🌂fr£85 LDO 10pm
Lic lift ♨ ⚲
Credit Cards ①②③⑤

GH 🅠🅠 **Park Lodge Hotel** 73 Queensborough Ter,
Bayswater W2 3SU ☎071-229 6424
29rm(2⇄27👁)(2fb) CTV in all bedrooms ✱ (ex guide dogs)
✱ sB&B⇄👁fr£30 dB&B⇄👁fr£45 (wkly only Nov-Feb)
🅫
Credit Cards 1 2 3 5

GH 🅠🅠 **Parkwood Hotel** 4 Stanhope Place W2 2HB
☎071-402 2241
This elegant, 4-storeyed, terraced house has comfortable, well-appointed bedrooms and a friendly, informal atmosphere. It is conveniently close to the West End.
18rm(12⇄👁6hc)(5fb)🗡in 3 bedrooms CTV in all bedrooms
Ⓡ ✱ (ex guide dogs) ✱ sB&Bfr£39.75 sB&B⇄👁fr£55
dB&Bfr£54.50 dB&B⇄👁fr£64.50
🅫 CTV ✗
Credit Cards 1 3 ⓔ

SELECTED

GH 🅠🅠🅠🅠 **Pembridge Court Hotel** 34 Pembridge
Gardens W2 4DX ☎071-229 9977 Telex no 298363
This privately owned, gracious 19th-century town house is situated just off a most architecturally attractive square. Skilfully extended, it has been tastefully furnished with style and elegance, and retains much of the original character. Bedrooms are generously furnished and extensively equipped: the best and most spacious in the main building, the others are up a separate staircase and more compact, but still prettily furnished, with en suite showers. The charming lounge has recently been refurbished, and the Caps restaurant features a collection of framed caps, with freshly prepared traditional fare, and a selection of hot and spicy Thai dishes on a short menu. Service and hospitality from this long-standing team is warm, spontaneous and attentive.
17⇄👁 Annexe 8⇄👁 (4fb) CTV in all bedrooms ✱
sB&B⇄👁£76-£99 dB&B⇄👁£96-£117.50 LDO 11.15pm
Lic lift 🅫 2🎗
Credit Cards 1 2 3 5

GH 🅠🅠 **Slavia Hotel** 2 Pembridge Square W2 4EW
☎071-727 1316 Telex no 917458 FAX 071-229 0803
Set in one of the most attractive squares in this part of London, this hotel provides a choice of well equipped bedrooms, of which the best are on the 3rd floor. There is a cosy front lounge, formal reception facilities, and an unusual 'Yugoslavian style' breakfast room. Service is very friendly and helpful. Local public transport gives good access to central London.
31👁 (8fb) ✱ sB&B👁£30-£45 dB&B👁£40-£60
Lic lift 🅫 CTV 1P (£6 per day)
Credit Cards 1 2 3 5 ⓔ

W4 CHISWICK London plan **4** C3

GH 🅠🅠🅠 **Chiswick Hotel** 73 Chiswick High Rd W4 2LS
☎081-994 1712 FAX 081-742 2585
Ideally situated for central London and Heathrow Airport, this hotel offers attractive accommodation and good service. The restaurant has a residential bar and the standard of cooking is high.
30rm(13⇄17👁)(5fb) CTV in all bedrooms Ⓡ ✱
sB&B⇄👁fr£55 dB&B⇄👁fr£72.50 LDO 8.30pm
Lic 🅫 CTV 15P sauna solarium jacuzzi
Credit Cards 1 2 3 5 ⓔ

W6 HAMMERSMITH London plan **4** C3

GH 🅠🅠 *Hotel West Six* 99 Shepherd Bush Rd W6
☎071-603 0948 Telex no 929120 FAX 9029445
This imposing 3-storeyed terrace house has well appointed en suite bedrooms and serves continental breakfasts.
12👁 (2fb) CTV in all bedrooms Ⓡ ✱ (ex guide dogs)

🅫 ✗
Credit Cards 1 2 3

W7 HANWELL London plan **4** B3

GH 🅠🅠 **Wellmeadow** 24 Wellmeadow Rd W7 2AL
☎081-567 7294
Quietly situated in a residential area of west London, this charming little guesthouse has 4 individually furnished bedrooms. Breakfast is served in the kitchen at a communal dining table which complements the relaxed and informal atmosphere generated by the resident proprietors.
4hc 🗡in all bedrooms CTV in all bedrooms Ⓡ ✱ ✱ sB&B£35-£38 dB&Bfr£50 LDO noon
🅫 CTV
Credit Cards 1 2 3

W8 KENSINGTON London plan **4** C3

GH 🅠🅠 **Apollo Hotel** 18-22 Lexham Gardens W8 5JE
☎071-835 1133 & 071-373 3236 Telex no 264189
FAX 071-370 4853
Closed 24 Dec-1 Jan
The proprietor of this well managed hotel continues to offer friendly service and well-equipped accommodation. Many rooms have en suite facilities, and the public areas are to be upgraded this year.
59rm(40⇄10👁9hc)(4fb) CTV in all bedrooms
✱ (ex guide dogs) ✱ sB&B£30 sB&B⇄👁£46 dB&B⇄👁£56
Lic lift 🅫 CTV ✗
Credit Cards 1 2 3 5 ⓔ

GH 🅠🅠 **Atlas Hotel** 24-30 Lexham Gardens W8 5JE
☎071-373 7873 & 071-835 1155 Telex no 264189
FAX 071-370 4853
Closed 24 Dec-1 Jan
Well situated and offering good value for money, this hotel has traditionally furnished rooms, many with en suite facilities, and all well equipped. There is also a small bar and separate lounge. The sister hotel, the Apollo, is next door.
64rm(15⇄30👁19hc)(7fb) CTV in all bedrooms
✱ (ex guide dogs) ✱ sB&B£30 sB&B⇄👁£46 dB&B⇄👁£56
Lic lift 🅫 CTV ✗
Credit Cards 1 2 3 5 ⓔ

GH 🅠🅠 **Observatory House Hotel** 37 Hornton St W8 7NR
☎071-937-1577 & 071-937 6353 Telex no 914972
Delightfully situated in a quiet area a stroll away from Kensington High Street, this hotel offers bedrooms with private bath/shower, direct dial telephone, colour TV and other modern facilities. Tastefully designed, the rooms are to be refurbished this year.
24rm(7⇄17👁)(5fb) CTV in all bedrooms Ⓡ
✱ (ex guide dogs) sB&B⇄👁£49.90-£64.90 dB&B⇄👁£69.90-£84.90 WB&B£250-£300
Lic 🅫 ✗
Credit Cards 1 2 3 5 ⓔ

W14 WEST KENSINGTON London plan **4** C3

SELECTED

GH 🅠🅠🅠🅠 *Aston Court Hotel* 25/27 Matheson Rd
W14 8SN ☎071-602 9954 Telex no 919208
FAX 071-371 1338
Equipped to very high standards, the hotel is tastefully decorated and provides 24-hour room service and many thoughtful extras. The bedrooms vary in shape and size, but have good quality co-ordinated furnishings. The lobby reception extends into a bar sitting area where a cordial bar counter service can be obtained. Breakfast is served in a small conservatory extension, and there is a lift to all floors. Car parking is very difficult, and a taxi is recommended in this excellent value-for-money hotel.
▶

29rm(10⊷19↑) (3fb) CTV in all bedrooms ®
✖ (ex guide dogs)
Lic lift ㎖ CTV ♪
Credit Cards ① ② ③ ⑤

GH Ⓠ Ⓠ Ⓠ **Avonmore Hotel** 66 Avonmore Rd W14 8RS
☎071-603 4296 & 3121 Telex no 945922 FAX 071-603 4035
This delightful little terraced guesthouse is ideally situated for the Exhibition Centre at Olympia. Completely upgraded, it offers modern, comfortable and well equipped bedrooms with good en suite facilities. Light refreshments are available throughout the day, and there is a breakfast room in the basement. Parking can be extremely difficult.
9rm(4↑2hc) (3fb) CTV in all bedrooms ✖ ⚹ sB&B£33-£38
sB&B↑£40-£45 dB&B£48-£49 dB&B↑£56.40-£58
WB&B£150
Lic ㎖ CTV ♪

GH Ⓠ **Centaur Hotel** 21 Avonmore Rd W14 8RP
☎071-602 3857 & 071-603 5973
Small and family-run, this hotel has nicely equipped, simple accommodation with radio alarms and direct dial telephones. Ideally situated for Olympia and Earls Court, the Centaur Hotel is in a residential area with street parking.
12hc (4fb) CTV in all bedrooms ✖
㎖

WC1 BLOOMSBURY, HOLBORN London plan **4 D4**

GH Ⓠ Ⓠ **Mentone Hotel** 54-55 Cartwright Gardens WC1H 9EL
☎071-387 3927 & 071-388 4671
A long-established family-run guesthouse benefiting from a central London location. There is a choice of old-fashioned, traditionally furnished bedrooms located on several floors, the best of which have been upgraded with en suite showers. The accommodation represents good value for this part of London, and includes a full traditional cooked English breakfast.
27rm(11↑16hc) (10fb) CTV in all bedrooms ✖ (wkly only Dec-Feb)
㎖ ♪ ♪(hard)

LONGLEAT Wiltshire Map **03** ST84

FH Ⓠ Ⓠ Ⓠ **Mrs J Crossman Stalls** *(ST806439)* BA12 7NE
☎Maiden Bradley(0985) 844323
A detached house built of Bath stone, originally the home farm for Longleat House. The proprietor Mrs Crossman has run the farmhouse for many years, and enjoys a regular, returning clientèle. Bedrooms are comfortable and there is a large and well stocked playroom, and swings and slides for children, who are very welcome. The well kept garden has a sun terrace and stream. The farmhouse is difficult to find: turn left at the White Hart pub, continue for 2 miles down the lane, past a 'no through road' sign, and the farm is on the right.
3hc ✖ ⚹ sB&B£14-£15 dB&B£28-£30
㎖ CTV 6P table tennis table childrens play area 350 acres dairy

FH Ⓠ Ⓠ Ⓠ **Mrs M A Cottle Sturford Mead** *(ST834456)*
BA12 7QU ☎Westbury(0373) 832213
This farmhouse is very close to Longleat House, and enjoys views over pretty National Trust countryside. Accommodation is comfortable, spacious and very well maintained, each with private facilities. Public areas are simple in style, with a small breakfast room leading into a cosy lounge area. Whilst the farm enjoys a rural setting, it is located very close to the A36 and direct routes to major towns.
3rm(2⊷↑1hc) CTV in all bedrooms ® ✖ (ex guide dogs)
dB&B£28-£32 dB&B⊷↑£32-£34
㎖ CTV 10P 5 acres pig

LONGSDON Staffordshire Map **07** SJ95

FH Ⓠ Ⓠ Ⓠ Mr & Mrs M M Robinson **Bank End** *(SJ953541)*
Old Leek Rd ST9 9QJ (0.5m SW off A53) ☎Leek(0538) 383638
Closed Xmas wk
The bedrooms of this busy and popular farm are above average in standard, all having been converted from stables or barns; activities available include fishing, riding and swimming (in summer).
9rm(6⊷↑2hc) (3fb) CTV in all bedrooms ® ⚹ sB&B£22.50-£30 sB&B⊷↑£22.50-£30 dB&B£40-£44 dB&B⊷↑£40-£44
LDO 8pm
Lic ㎖ CTV 10P ▤(heated) ♪ 62 acres beef

LONGTOWN Cumbria Map **11** NY36

FH Ⓠ Ⓠ Mr & Mrs Elwen **New Pallyards** *(NY469713)*
Hethersgill CA6 6HZ (5.5 m E off the A6071 Brampton-Longtown road, take unclass road.)
☎Nicholforest(022877) 308 due to change to (0228) 577308
Situated five miles east of Longtown on the Stapleford road in a lovely rural location, New Pallyards is a modern, well furnished farmhouse. There is a comfortable lounge and the bedrooms are delightful and spacious. The welcome is warm and friendly.
5rm(2⊷↑1↑2hc) (2fb) CTV in 2 bedrooms TV in 1 bedroom ®
⚹ sB&B£16-£18 sB&B⊷↑£16-£18 dB&B£32-£36
dB&B⊷↑£32-£36 WB&B£100-£110 WBDi£150-£170
LDO 8pm
㎖ CTV 8P 1🅿 ⚹ ♪ Ս bowls, putting 65 acres beef mixed sheep ⓔ

LOOE Cornwall & Isles of Scilly Map **02** SX25 During the currency of this publication Looe telephone numbers are liable to change.

See also Widesgates

SELECTED

GH Ⓠ Ⓠ Ⓠ Ⓠ **Harescombe Lodge** Watergate PL13 2NE
☎(05036) 3158 due to change to (0503) 263158
A former shooting lodge, dating from 1760, in an outstanding situation hidden by woodland beside the River Looe, about 1.5 miles northwest of Looe off the A387 towards Polperro. Quaint, cosy bedrooms are brightly decorated and filled with antique furniture. Each has a smart en suite facility and a country view. The charming proprietors, Jane and Barry Wynn, are hospitable, cheerful hosts. An excellent breakfast is served and a fresh home-cooked evening meal is available.
3rm(2⊷↑1↑) ® ✖ (ex guide dogs) ⚹ dB&B⊷↑£29-£37
LDO 4pm
㎖ CTV 4P nc12yrs ⓔ

🔲🔲 **GH** Ⓠ **'Kantara'** 7 Trelawney Ter PL13 2AG
☎(05036) 2093
This pre-war mid-terrace house on the outskirts of the town provides simple family-run accommodation which is equally suitable for tourist or businessman; guests enjoy a hearty breakfast, and a relaxed atmosphere is created by the friendly, caring proprietor.
6hc (3fb) CTV in all bedrooms ® sB&B£12-£15 dB&B£24-£30
WB&B£80-£100 WBDi£125-£145 LDO 5pm
CTV 1P 2🅿
Credit Cards ① ③ ⓔ

GH Ⓠ Ⓠ **Ogunquit** Portuan Rd, Hannafore PL13 2DW
☎(05036) 3105
A private hotel in an elevated position in Hannafore, West Looe, close to the seafront. It offers neatly presented bedrooms with fresh décor and simple furnishings. Public areas are comfortably appointed, sunny and bright, with superb views.

▶

5rm(1♠4hc) (2fb) ✱ sB&B£16-£18 dB&B£27-£30 dB&B♠£36-
£40
⑭ CTV ⚥

GH 🆀🆀🆀 *Panorama Hotel* Hannafore Rd PL13 2DE
☎(05036) 2123 due to change to (0536) 262123
Mar-Oct
A family run hotel in an elevated position affording glorious views
of the estuary and across the bay. The bedrooms have been
completely refurbished, and provide co-ordinating cottage style
decor and spotless en suite facilities ; some rooms have balconies.
The lounge and bar are positioned to enjoy the breathtaking views,
and there is a choice of home -cooked dishes in the relaxed
atmosphere of the dining room.
10rm(1⇔5♠4hc) CTV in all bedrooms ® LDO 6.30pm
Lic CTV 7P
Credit Cards 1 3

GH 🆀🆀🆀 *St Aubyns* Marine Dr, Hannafore, West Looe
PL13 2DH ☎(05036) 4351 due to change to (0536) 264351
Etr-end Oct
The Maher family offer bed and breakfast accommodation and a
warm welcome at the Victorian house which has beautiful sea
views. The bedrooms are spacious and the lounge is elegantly
furnished.
8rm(2⇔3♠6hc) (5fb) CTV in 4 bedrooms ® ⋈ ✱ sB&Bfr£18
dB&Bfr£36 dB&B⇔3♠fr£50 WB&Bfr£119
CTV 4P £

FH 🆀🆀 Mr & Mrs Hembrow **Tregoad Farm Hotel**
(SX272560) St Martins PL13 1PB ☎(05036) 2718
Etr-Oct
This farmhouse dates back over 120 years and is set in pretty, well
kept gardens with a rural surrounding, situated on the B3253 St
Martin's Road, only two miles from the town centre. Bedrooms are
simply furnished and neatly presented, many with superb views
across the fields and out to sea. Public areas are comfortably
appointed, and the farmer's wife offers evening meals.
6hc (4fb) CTV in all bedrooms ® sB&B£15-£20 dB&B£25-£36
LDO 4pm
Lic CTV 15P ⋗ 60 acres dairy sheep beef

LOUGHBOROUGH Leicestershire Map **08** SK51

GH 🆀 *De Montfort Hotel* 88 Leicester Rd LE11 2AQ
☎(0509) 216061
9hc (1fb) CTV in all bedrooms ® ✱ sB&B£19 dB&B£32
WB&B£129.50 LDO 4pm
Lic ⑭ CTV
Credit Cards 1 3 £

GH 🆀🆀🆀 **Garendon Park Hotel** 92 Leicester Rd LE11 2AQ
☎(0509) 236557
The friendly proprietors of the Garendon Park Hotel offer a
personal service and make every effort to meet the guests' needs.
The bedrooms are light and cheerful, as are the public rooms. The
lounge is comfortable and provides books, games and satellite T.V.
9hc (2fb) CTV in all bedrooms ® ✱ sB&B£22.50-£25
dB&B£30-£40 LDO 8pm
Lic ⑭ CTV
Credit Cards 1 3 £

GH 🆀 *Sunnyside Hotel* 5 The Coneries LE11 1DZ
☎(0509) 216217
Ideally suited for business people and within walking distance of
the town centre, this family-run hotel has well-equipped, compact
bedrooms, with colour TV and tea and coffee making facilities.
11hc CTV in 10 bedrooms ® ⋈ LDO 4pm
⑭ CTV 8P 3🐾 nc5yrs
Credit Cards 1 3

LOW CATTON Humberside Map **08** SE75

GH 🆀🆀🆀 **Derwent Lodge** YO4 1EA
☎Stamford Bridge(0759) 71468
Feb-Nov
Only 15 minutes' drive from York, this period house retains its
character with oak beams and York stone fireplaces. The
bedrooms offer modern facilities and most have en suite shower
rooms.
6rm(4♠2hc) (1fb)⚥in all bedrooms CTV in all bedrooms ®
dB&B£37 dB&B♠£41 WB&B£119.50-£133.60 WBDi£185.50-
£199.50 LDO 4pm
Lic ⑭ 8P nc8yrs £

LOWER BRAILES Warwickshire Map **04** SP33

SELECTED

GH 🆀🆀🆀🆀 **Feldon House** OX15 5HW
☎Brailes(060885) 580
Closed 2 wks in Autumn
Located just a short drive from Shipston on the A4035, the
house is set back from the road in its own attractive grounds
by the village church. The car park is in a narrow track
opposite the George hotel. Accommodation is split between the
main house and the coach house ; the latter has spacious,
comfortable rooms and both have en suite facilities. Rooms in
the main house are attractively decorated and furnished and
each has a private, but not en suite bathroom ; all bedrooms
have an excellent range of thoughtful facilities. There are two
lounge areas, both are comfortable, with open fires and some
lovely antiques. Breakfast is served in the main dining room
around a large communal table, and there is also a
conservatory dining area.
2⇔3♠ CTV in all bedrooms ® ⋈ (ex guide dogs)
sB&B⇔3♠£30-£44 dB&B⇔3♠£42-£56 WB&B£147-£196
WBDi£263.50-£312.50
Lic ⑭ 9P nc11yrs croquet lawn
Credit Cards 1 3 £

LOWER BEEDING West Sussex Map **04** TQ22

FH 🆀🆀🆀 Mr J Christian **Brookfield Farm Hotel**
(TQ214285) Winterpit Ln, Plummers Plain RH13 5LU
☎(0403) 891568
Enjoying attractive, peaceful surroundings, this hotel offers a
wealth of activities : an outdoor pool and play area for children and
its own lake for boating and fishing. The accommodation is well
equipped and there is a bar and a choice of restaurants.
20⇔3♠ (2fb) CTV in all bedrooms LDO 9.30pm
Lic ⑭ CTV 100P ▶ ⋗ games room putting 300 acres mixed
Credit Cards 1 2 3
See advertisement under HORSHAM

LOWESTOFT Suffolk Map **05** TM59

GH 🆀🆀🆀 *Albany Hotel* 400 London Rd South NR33 0BQ
☎(0502) 574394
Mr and Mrs Kelly provide a well-cared for house, situated just a
few minutes' walk from both the shopping centre and the beach.
The spacious rooms have some en suite facilities, and are
complemented by attractive public areas.
7rm(3⇔3♠4hc) (3fb) CTV in all bedrooms ®
⋈ (ex guide dogs) ✱ sB&B£16 sB&B⇔3♠fr£22 dB&Bfr£28
dB&B⇔3♠fr£34 WB&Bfr£102 WBDifr£151 LDO 1pm
Lic ⑭ CTV 2P
Credit Cards 1 3 £

GH 🆀🆀 *Amity* 396 London Rd South NR33 0BQ
☎(0502) 572586
Closed Xmas & New Year

A large detached Victorian house situated on the main town road, a short distance from the sea front, easily distinguished by its red painted brickwork. Bedrooms are well equipped, some with private bathrooms, and there is a pleasant lounge/bar and games room.
12rm(6♠6hc) (3fb) CTV in all bedrooms ⓡ ✱ sB&Bfr£16 sB&B♠fr£22.50 dB&Bfr£30 dB&B♠fr£34 WB&Bfr£90 WBDifr£130 LDO 2pm
Lic ⚑ CTV ⚐ solarium games room
Credit Cards ①②③

GH ⓠⓠⓠ Cornerways 12 Kensington Rd, London Rd South, Parefield NR33 0HY ☎(0502) 567821 FAX (0502) 585336
Less than a mile from the town centre, this hotel has well equipped accommodation, mostly with en suite facilities, in spacious rooms. Off-street parking is available.
10rm(7⇨8♠2hc) (2fb)⚏in 1 bedroom CTV in all bedrooms ⓡ ✖ (ex guide dogs) LDO 8.30pm
Lic ⚑ CTV 9P ⚙
Credit Cards ①②③

GH ⓠⓠ Fairways 398 London Rd South NR33 0BQ
☎(0502) 572659
Mr and Mrs Shuard offer simple, well maintained acoommodation at this guesthouse, and they ensure their visitors are provided with hospitality and comfort.
7rm(3⇨8♠4hc) (4fb) CTV in all bedrooms ⓡ sB&Bfr£16 sB&B⇨8♠frf21 dB&Bfr£32 dB&B⇨8♠frf37 WB&Bfr£105 WBDifr£130 LDO 4pm
Lic ⚑ CTV 3P
Credit Cards ①②③④

GH ⓠⓠ Kingsleigh 44 Marine Pde NR33 0QN
☎(0502) 572513
Closed Xmas
A friendly guesthouse, adjacent to the town's harbour and overlooking the sea. Accommodation is very well maintained and freshly decorated. Guests are sure to receive a warm welcome.
6hc (2fb) CTV in all bedrooms ⓡ ✱ sB&B£16-£18 dB&B£28-£30 WB&B£98-£105
⚑ 6P nc3yrs ④

GH ⓠⓠⓠ Rockville House 6 Pakefield Rd NR33 0HS
☎(0502) 581011 or 574891
A friendly hotel, suitable for business people or tourists, located just off London Road South approaching Lowestoft from Ipswich, immediately after the no entry sign on the right. This is a well run establishment offering good quality accommodation and a fair array of modern facilities, and the comfortable, book-lined lounge is a good place to relax.
8rm(2⇨8①♠5hc) CTV in all bedrooms ⓡ ✖ (ex guide dogs) sB&Bfr£20 sB&B⇨8♠frf£32.25 dB&Bfr£34.50 dB&B⇨8♠frf41.50 WB&Bfr£102.50 WBDifr£165 LDO 10am
Lic ⚑ nc12yrs beach hut
Credit Cards ①③④

GH ⓠⓠⓠ Somerton House 7 Kirkley Cliff NR33 0BY
☎(0502) 565665
Located south of Lowestoft, on the seafront, this guesthouse has commanding views to complement its brightly decorated and well-equipped comfortable rooms. There is a comfortable lounge with a well-stocked bar and a varied evening menu.
8rm(3♠5hc) (4fb) CTV in all bedrooms ⓡ ✱ sB&B£19-£22 sB&B♠£25-£28 dB&B£32-£35 dB&B♠£38-£41 WB&B£115-£130 WBDifr£160 LDO 5pm
Lic ⚑ CTV 1P
Credit Cards ①③④

This guide is updated annually – make sure you use an up-to-date edition.

LOW ROW North Yorkshire Map **07** SD99

GH ⓠⓠⓠ Peat Gate Head DL11 6PP
☎Richmond(0748) 86388
This charming house enjoys superb views over the river Swale and surrounding countryside. The accommodation is full of character, and the friendly proprietor takes great pride in his home cooking.
6rm(3♠3hc) ⚏in all bedrooms ⓡ ✖ LDO 5.30pm
Lic ⚑ CTV ⚐

LUDGVAN Cornwall & Isles of Scilly Map **02** SW53

FH ⓠ Mrs A R Blewett **Menwidden** *(SW502337)* TR20 8BN
☎Penzance(0736) 740415
Closed Dec-Jan
A small, family farmhouse in a convenient location with extensive rural and sea views across to St Michael's Mount and the southwest tip of Cornwall. While most bedrooms are without wash basins, all are bright and comfortably furnished, and there is a cosy lounge and traditional dining room.
6rm(1hc) (2fb) dB&Bfr£24 WB&Bfr£80 WBDifr£112 (wkly only Aug) LDO 1pm
CTV 6P 40 acres dairy/market gardening
Credit Cards ②

LUDLOW Shropshire Map **07** SO57

GH ⓠⓠ Cecil Sheet Rd SY8 1LR ☎(0584) 872442
26 Jan-20 Dec
A chalet-style guesthouse with very attractive floral displays at the entrance in summer, situated east of the town just off the bypass. Cecil Guesthouse offers clean, modern accommodation.
10rm(3♠7hc) (1fb)⚏in all bedrooms CTV in 3 bedrooms ⓡ sB&B£16 dB&B£32 dB&B♠£38 WB&B£112-£133 WBDi£166-£187 LDO 9am

▶

TREGOAD FARM HOTEL
St Martins, Looe.
Telephone: Looe (05036) 2718

A family run hotel in a dairy farm environment with scenic views to the sea. All rooms have hot & cold water plus a tea making service for your convenience. Plus colour TV.
Good food guaranteed.
Fully licensed bar - colour TV lounge.
Within easy reach: good safe beaches, golf course, tennis, bowls, water sports. Central location for touring and shopping.
Proprietors: Mr & Mrs K J Hembrow

Lic 💯 CTV 10P 1🛏
Credit Cards ①②③ £

GH QQQ **No. 28** Lower Broad St SY8 1PQ ☎(0584) 876996
*A half-timbered town house within walking distance of the castle
and town centre. This very well run small guesthouse is personally
supervised by experienced hoteliers, and it has much to offer its
guests including a small courtyard garden.*
2rm(1⇨1🏠) CTV in all bedrooms ® sB&B⇨🏠£32-£38
dB&B⇨🏠£57-£62 (incl dinner) WBDi£195-£250
LDO 8.30pm
Lic 💯 🅿 £

LUMSDEN Grampian *Aberdeenshire* Map 15 NJ42

FH Q Mrs June Roberts *Boghead (NJ482224)* Lumsden
AB5 4LE ☎(04646) 735
*A traditional northern farmhouse with a friendly atmosphere and
comfortable accommodation.*
2hc (1fb)⤢in all bedrooms
CTV 125 acres beef

LUTON Bedfordshire Map 04 TL02

GH QQ **Ambassador Hotel** 31 Lansdowne Rd LU8 1EE
☎(0582) 31411 or 451656
Closed Xmas
*A Victorian detached house situated just off the A6, a mile from
the town centre, in a quiet residential area. Bedrooms are well
equipped and all have private bathrooms. There is a well stocked
bar and a pool table in the lounge.*
14🏠 CTV in all bedrooms ® ✱ sB&B£30-£49 sB&B🏠£35-
£56.40 dB&B🏠£39-£72.45 LDO 8.45pm
Lic 💯 CTV 20P pool table
Credit Cards ①③ £

GH QQ **Arlington Hotel** 137 New Bedford Rd LU3 1LF
☎(0582) 419614 FAX (0582) 459047
Closed 25-26 Dec
*A detached commercial guesthouse set back from the A6 towards
the ring road, with a large car park to the rear. The
accommodation is clean, well maintained and quite well equipped,
many of the rooms with private bathrooms. The restaurant offers a
limited menu for evening meals, and there is a small bar.*
19rm(2⇨17🏠) (3fb) CTV in all bedrooms ®
✱ (ex guide dogs) ✱ sB&B£25-£48.90 dB&B⇨🏠£51.90-
£51.90 LDO 8.30pm
Lic 💯 25P
Credit Cards ①②③⑤ £

GH QQ **Humberstone Hotel** 618 Dunstable Rd LU4 8RT
☎(0582) 574399
*A commercial guesthouse located on the A6, two miles west of the
town centre, which has been extended and modernised. There is a
comfortable lounge, well stocked bar and an attractive dining room
offering an à la carte menu appealing to most tastes.*
9hc Annexe 12rm(2⇨10🏠) (4fb) CTV in all bedrooms ®
✱ (ex guide dogs) LDO 5.30pm
Lic 💯 35P
Credit Cards ①②③⑤

LUTTERWORTH Leicestershire
See **Shearsby**

LYDFORD Devon Map 02 SX58

INN QQ **Dartmoor** EX20 4AY (on A386 between Tavistock &
Okehampton) ☎(082282) 221
Closed Xmas Day
*This friendly, family-run inn, much upgraded and improved since
the recent change in ownership, provides welcoming bars, a cosy
little restaurant and bright, comfortable bedrooms for guests. Its
convenient position gives easy access to the National Park.*

3⇨ CTV in all bedrooms ® ✱ ✱ sB&B⇨🏠£25 dB&B⇨🏠£40 ✱
Lunch £1.50-£5alc Dinner £1.50-£6alc LDO 9.55pm
💯 50P nc14yrs
Credit Cards ①③⑤

LYDNEY Gloucestershire Map 03 SO60

GH QQQ **Lower Viney Country Guesthouse** Viney Hill
GL15 4LT (2.5m from Lydney on A48 on unclassed road)
☎Dean(0594) 516000
*A charming, cottage-style guesthouse just outside the village of
Blakeney, off the A48. It has been sympathetically extended and
the rooms are quite spacious, many with lovely views of the
surrounding countryside. There are 2 lounges and an interesting
garden in which to relax. Guests are requested not to smoke.*
6🏠 CTV in 4 bedrooms ® ✱ (ex guide dogs) ✱ sB&B🏠fr£26
dB&B🏠fr£36 LDO 1pm
Lic 💯 CTV 10P
Credit Cards ①③ £
See advertisement under Blakeney

LYME REGIS Dorset Map 03 SY39

GH Q **Coverdale** Woodmead Rd DT7 3AB ☎(0297) 442882
Mar-Oct
*Situated in a residential area, this well kept house has a cheerful
dining room and comfortable television lounge.*
8rm(3🏠5hc) (3fb) ® ✱ (ex guide dogs) ✱ sB&B£12.50-£15
dB&B£23-£28 dB&B🏠£28-£33 WB&B£75-£110.50
WBDi£131-£148.50 LDO 4pm
💯 CTV 12P nc3yrs

GH QQQ **White House** 47 Silver St DT7 3HR
☎(0297) 443420
Apr-Oct
*An 18th-century merchant's house converted to a neat and very
clean hotel. Bedrooms have modern furnishings including good
beds as well as all the usual facilities. There is a spacious,
comfortable lounge and freshly decorated breakfast room. Real
coffee is served at breakfast and there is a price reduction when
continental breakfast is taken.*
7rm(1⇨6🏠) CTV in all bedrooms ® dB&B⇨🏠£38
WB&B£112-£119
💯 7P nc10yrs £

LYMINGTON Hampshire Map 04 SZ39

GH QQ **Albany House** Highfield SO41 9GB ☎(0590) 671900
Closed 2wks in winter
*A centrally situated 3-storey Regency house with a walled garden
overlooking the municipal gardens. The delightful double aspect
lounge is charmingly furnished. Imaginative menus appear nightly
at dinner, bedrooms are comfortable, and Wendy Gallagher and
her family are hospitable hosts.*
4rm(2⇨2hc) (2fb) CTV in all bedrooms ® sB&B£18.50
dB&B£37 dB&B⇨🏠£41-£48 WB&B£129.50-£168 WBDi£196-
£234.50 LDO 7pm
💯 CTV 4P £

LYNDHURST Hampshire Map 04 SU30

SELECTED

GH QQQQ **Knightwood Lodge** Southampton Rd
SO43 7BU ☎(0703) 282502 FAX (0703) 283730
Closed Xmas Day
*Knightwood Lodge overlooks open heathland on the
Southampton Road, and provides a sauna and steam room –
exceptional leisure facilities for a small hotel. Bedrooms are
well equipped and attractively co-ordinated, and include a
four-poster room in pine and lace. Evening meals are served in
the cosy bar and breakfast in the well appointed dining room.*

12⇨🐾 (2fb) CTV in all bedrooms ® ✗ (ex guide dogs) ✳
sB&B⇨🐾£26.50-£32 dB&B⇨🐾£40-£50 WB&B£130-
£175 WBDi£180-£245 LDO 8pm
Lic ♨ 14P nc3yrs sauna solarium turkish steam room
Credit Cards ① ② ③ ⑤ £

See advertisement on page 245

GH ⓆⓆⓆ **Ormonde House** Southampton Rd SO43 7BT
☎(0703) 282806 FAX (0703) 283775
*A detached Edwardian house well set back from the A35 to
Southampton, on the outskirts of Lyndhurst, overlooking
moorland. Bedrooms vary in standard : the majority are charming,
with co-ordinated décor, and well equipped. A bistro- style menu is
offered at dinner, and service is friendly and helpful.*
15rm(11⇨4🐾) (1fb) CTV in all bedrooms ® sB&B⇨🐾£25-
£35 dB&B⇨🐾£35-£44 LDO 7.45pm
Lic ♨ 15P
Credit Cards ① ③ £

See advertisement on page 245

GH ⓆⓆⓆ **Whitemoor House Hotel** Southampton Rd
SO43 7BU ☎(0703) 282186
Closed Xmas
*On the edge of the town on the Southampton road overlooking
open heathland, the accommodation is spotlessly clean and well
equipped. Mr and Mrs Lewis have run Whitemore for 12 years
and they are a friendly couple who take a great pride in welcoming
guests to their small hotel.*
5rm(1⇨4🐾) (2fb) CTV in all bedrooms ® ✗ (ex guide dogs)
sB&B⇨🐾£25-£30 dB&B⇨🐾£38-£45 WB&B£120-£140
Lic ♨ CTV 8P 🅿 18
Credit Cards ① ③ £

See advertisement on page 245

LYNMOUTH Devon Map **03** SS74

See **Town Plan Section**

See also **Lynton**

SELECTED

GH ⓆⓆ Ⓠ Ⓠ **Countisbury Lodge Hotel** Tors Park
EX35 6NB ☎Lynton(0598) 52388

*A new recipient of our Selected award last year, and
deservedly so, for Mr and Mrs Hollinshead take great pride in
their small country house style retreat, which is neatly tucked
away in a wooded spot with commanding views.
Sympathetically restored, the former vicarage retains much of
its original charm and provides cosy, spotless bedrooms,
individually decorated and equipped with bright en suites and
a good range of creature comforts. The public rooms are small
but richly furnished and the tiny dispenser bar is built into the
rock face. Generous and wholesome home cooking by Mrs
Hollinshead is always well received.*

6rm(3⇌3↑)(1fb) Ⓡ ✱ dB&B⇌↑£54-£63 (incl dinner)
WB&B£138.50 WBDi£190 (wkly only Xmas) LDO 5pm
Lic ♥♥ CTV 8P
Credit Cards ①③

GH Ⓠ Ⓠ Ⓠ **East Lyn House** 17 Watersmeet Rd EX35 6EP
☎Lynton(0598) 52540

*Neatly tucked away in a riverside spot within walking distance of
the picturesque harbour, and a good base for touring Exmoor and
the North Devon coast. Significant upgrading has resulted in very
comfortable bedrooms, especially on the top floor. Cosy public
rooms and a very personal, friendly style of operation by
conscientious owners, Mr and Mrs Price, create a pleasant
relaxing atmosphere.*

8rm(5⇌3↑3hc)(2fb)✂in 2 bedrooms CTV in all bedrooms Ⓡ
sB&B⇌↑£25-£27 dB&B⇌↑£40-£44 WBDi£200-£220
LDO 8.00pm
Lic ♥♥ 5P 8🚗 nc8yrs
Credit Cards ①③ⓔ

GH Ⓠ Ⓠ Ⓠ **The Heatherville** Tors Park EX35 6NB
☎Lynton(0598) 52327

*This south-facing, stone-built house is a small family-run holiday
guesthouse, tucked away in a secluded spot with commanding
views out to sea. It offers spotlessly clean, bright bedrooms which
are nicely decorated and furnished. There is a cosy, comfortable
lounge and a small bar, with traditional wholesome meals from the
set menu. A recent change of ownership has reslted in some
upgrading and improvements.*

9rm(1⇌4↑4hc)(1fb) CTV in 1 bedroom Ⓡ dB&Bfr£40
dB&B⇌↑fr£44 WB&B£137-£151 WBDi£188-£202
LDO 5.30pm
Lic ♥♥ CTV 9P nc7yrs

INN Ⓠ Ⓠ Ⓠ **The Village Inn** Lynmouth St EX35 6EH
☎Lynton(0598) 52354

6⇌↑ (1fb)✂in 2 bedrooms CTV in all bedrooms Ⓡ
🇽 (ex guide dogs) ✱ dB&B⇌↑£35-£50 WB&B£100-£150
WBDi£168-£215 LDO 9.30pm
♥♥ ✗ nc
Credit Cards ①③

LYNTON Devon Map **03** SS74

See **Town Plan Section**

See also **Lynmouth**

GH Ⓠ Ⓠ Ⓠ **Alford House Hotel** Alford Ter EX35 6AT
☎(0598) 52359

*A warm welcome awaits guests at this 1840s house which
overlooks Lynton and the sea beyond. The cosy en suite rooms are
brightly decorated and some have four-poster beds. Prompt
informal service is offered in the well stocked bar and public areas.*

8rm(1⇌6↑1hc) CTV in all bedrooms Ⓡ 🇽 (ex guide dogs)
sB&B£20-£25 dB&B⇌↑£40-£50 WB&B£135-£160
WBDi£175-£205 LDO 7.30pm
Lic ♥♥ CTV ✗ nc9yrs
Credit Cards ①③

GH Ⓠ Ⓠ **Gable Lodge Hotel** Lee Rd EX35 6BS ☎(0598) 52367

*A recent change of ownership does not appear to have changed the
style and comfort of this small, pleasing property, though some
encouraging upgrading has begun. The house is spotlessly clean
with bright bedrooms, nicely styled and comfortably furnished, and
there is a personal atmosphere about the public rooms. In an
elevated position with a pretty garden, Gable Lodge is conveniently
located for exploring the Exmoor and North Devon coast.*

9rm(2⇌4↑3hc)(1fb) CTV in all bedrooms Ⓡ ✱ sB&B£17.50-
£19.50 sB&B⇌↑£19.50 dB&B£35-£39 dB&B⇌↑£39
WB&B£110-£135 WBDi£182-£196 LDO 5.30pm
Lic ♥♥ 8P
Credit Cards ①③

GH Ⓠ Ⓠ Ⓠ **Hazeldene** 27 Lee Rd EX35 6BP ☎(0598) 52364
Closed mid Nov-28 Dec

*Standing on the edge of the town centre, this small hotel promotes
a good standard throughout. The accommodation provides modern
facilities and is an ideal base from which to tour Exmoor and the
north Devon coast.*

9⇌↑ (2fb) CTV in all bedrooms Ⓡ sB&B⇌↑£20-£25
dB&B⇌↑£35-£40 WB&B£119-£133 WBDi£185-£198
LDO 5pm
Lic ♥♥ CTV 8P nc5yrs
Credit Cards ①②③ⓔ

Visit your local AA Shop.

HAZELDENE
Lee Rd, Lynton, Devon EX35 6BP

Charming small Victorian hotel with a first class
reputation for delicious food and a warm friendly
atmosphere. Delightful bedrooms with full
en-suite facilities, colour television, radio, hairdryer & beverage facilities. Two inviting lounges.
Candle-lit dining room with small bar. Full
central heating. Private parking. Pets welcome.
WCTB 3 Crowns. Brochure, sample menu &
tariff on request from Derek and Hazel Blight.

Telephone Lynton (0598) 52364

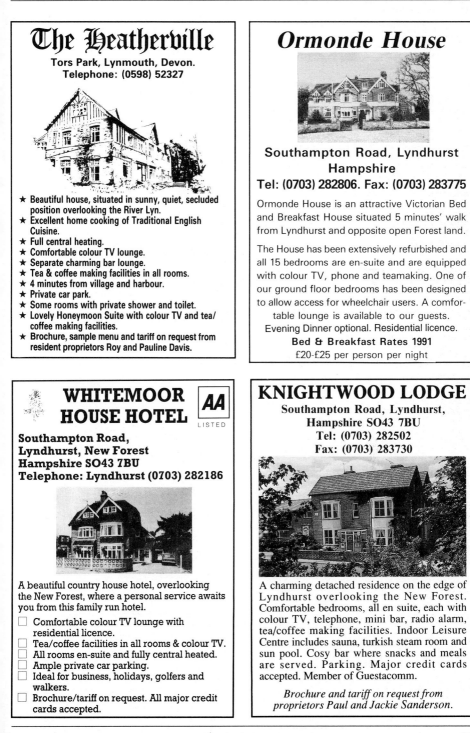
245

GH 🅠🅠🅠 **Ingleside Hotel** Lee Rd EX35 6HW ☎(0598) 52223
Mar-Oct
7rm(4⇄3🎇) (2fb) CTV in all bedrooms ® ✖ sB&B⇄🎇£24-
£26 dB&B⇄🎇£44-£48 WB&B£147-£161 WBDi£224-£238
LDO 5.30pm
Lic ⅏ 10P nc5yrs
Credit Cards 1️⃣ 3️⃣ £

GH 🅠🅠 **Mayfair Hotel** Lynway EX35 6AY ☎(0598) 53227
*Set on a hillside with commanding views of Exmoor and its
coastline, this family-run establishment provides good home
cooked food and friendly service.*
9rm(5⇄2🎇2hc) (1fb) CTV in all bedrooms ® sB&B£23-£25
dB&B£40-£44 dB&B⇄🎇£46-£50 WB&B£135-£156
WBDi£189-£210 LDO 5pm
Lic ⅏ 10P
Credit Cards 1️⃣ 2️⃣ 3️⃣ £

GH 🅠 **Retreat** 1 Park Gardens, Lydiate Ln EX35 6DF
☎(0598) 53526
*This small, friendly guesthouse offers pleasant, spotlessly clean
accommodation. While the public rooms are compact, the welcome
by the caring owners is big. Good value for money.*
6hc (2fb) ® ✳ sB&B£13-£15 dB&B£26-£30 WB&B£86.50-£100
WBDi£133-£153 LDO 5pm
⅏ CTV 3P

🗨️🖳 **GH** 🅠🅠🅠 **St Vincent** Castle Hill EX35 6JA
☎(0598) 52244
Apr-Oct
*This charming period house fronted with a pretty cottage garden, is
conveniently close to the centre of Lynton, and next door to the
Exmoor Museum. A Grade II listed building, with some parts
dating back over 300 years, the hotel has many delightful features,
including a splendid Regency spiral staircase, and a flagstone floor
in the residents' bar. Bedrooms are bright and spotlessly clean, and
public rooms are cosy and have a cheerful atmosphere. The menu
offers good home cooking.*
6rm(1⇄1🎇4hc) (2fb) ® ✖ sB&B£13-£14 dB&B£26-£28
dB&B⇄🎇£31-£33 WB&B£57.50-£112 WBDi£140-£166
LDO 4pm
Lic CTV 3P £

GH 🅠 *Valley House Hotel* Lynbridge Rd EX35 6BD
☎(0598) 52285
*Quietly secluded in an elevated position with commanding views
over Lynton, the coast and woodland, this Victorian, chalet style
property is personally owned and managed.*
8rm(4🎇4hc) (2fb) CTV in 5 bedrooms ® LDO 6pm
Lic ⅏ CTV 8P
Credit Cards 1️⃣ 2️⃣ 3️⃣

SELECTED

GH 🅠🅠🅠🅠 **Waterloo House Hotel** Lydiate Ln
EX35 6AJ ☎(0598) 53391
*Neatly tucked away yet still conveniently positioned for the
village centre, Mr and Mrs Mountis's cosy house combines
19th-century charm with modern comforts. One of the oldest
lodging houses in Lynton, it has been transformed into a
gracious hotel with bright, well equipped accommodation.
There is a separate lounge for non-smokers, and wholesome
cooking is served in the elegant dining room. Spotlessly clean
throughout, this congenial retreat offers excellent value for
money and makes an ideal base for touring Exmoor National
Park and the North Devon countryside and coast.*
10rm(3⇄4🎇3hc) (1fb)✂in 2 bedrooms CTV in all
bedrooms ® ✳ sB&Bfr£16.50 sB&B⇄🎇fr£22 dB&Bfr£30
dB&B⇄🎇£43-£47 WB&B£95-£129 WBDi£155-£189
LDO 7pm
Lic ⅏ CTV 3P £

🗨️🖳**GH** 🅠🅠 **Cullerne Hotel** 55 Lightburne Av, St Annes on
Sea FY8 1JE ☎St Annes(0253) 721753
*A small, neat, well maintained licenced hotel, situated in a quiet
road just off the Inner Promenade, close to the seafront. The
bedrooms all have colour TV and tea-making facilities, and there
is a comfortable lounge, a cosy bar and an attractively appointed
dining room. Forecourt parking is also available.*
6hc (2fb) CTV in all bedrooms ® ✖ sB&B£13 dB&B£26
WB&B£91 WBDi£104 LDO noon
Lic ⅏ CTV 4P £

GH 🅠🅠🅠 **Endsleigh Private Hotel** 315 Clifton Dr South
FY8 1HN ☎St Annes(0253) 725622
*A very well maintained property, situated close to the shops and
the seafront. All the bedrooms have been very well appointed with
en suite facilities, colour TV, radio and tea-making facilities.
There is an attractive dining room with individual tables, and a
comfortable lounge.*
15⇄🎇 (3fb) CTV in all bedrooms ® ✖ ✳ sB&B⇄🎇£18.50
dB&B⇄🎇£37 WB&B£117 WBDi£135-£145 LDO 4pm
Lic ⅏ 8P

GH 🅠 **Lyndhurst Private Hotel** 338 Clifton Dr North FY8 2PB
☎St Annes(0253) 724343
*This is a family-run guesthouse which offers spacious
accommodation. It is situated close to both the town centre and the
sea.*
12rm(1⇄3🎇8hc) (4fb) CTV in 4 bedrooms ® LDO noon
CTV 11P £

GH 🅠🅠🅠 **Strathmore Hotel** 305 Clifton Dr South FY8 1HN
☎St Annes(0253) 725478
*The young proprietors continue to make improvements to this
property which is a few minutes walk from the shops and seafront.
The bedrooms vary in size and are very well maintained.*
10rm(2⇄3🎇5hc) CTV in all bedrooms ® ✖ sB&B£17-£22
sB&B⇄🎇£19-£22 dB&B£34-£44 dB&B⇄🎇£38-£44
WB&B£105-£140 WBDi£126-£140 LDO 5pm
Lic ⅏ 10P nc9yrs

GH 🅠🅠🅠 **Crofton Hotel** Crompton Rd SK11 8DS
☎(0625) 434113
7rm(2⇄5🎇) CTV in all bedrooms ® ✖ sB&B⇄🎇fr£39.95
dB&B⇄🎇fr£56.95 LDO 8.45pm
Lic ⅏ 8P
Credit Cards 1️⃣ 2️⃣ 3️⃣ £

GH 🅠🅠 **Moorhayes House Hotel** 27 Manchester Rd SK10 2JJ
☎(0625) 433228
*A large private house on the outskirts of the town with tiered front
parking areas. Clean, light modern bedrooms offer good facilities
for business people. The house is on the A523 Stockport road out of
the town.*
9rm(5🎇4hc) CTV in all bedrooms ® sB&B£26-£29
sB&B🎇£37 dB&B£42 dB&B🎇£48
⅏ 15P £

FH 🅠🅠 Mrs Anne Read **Hardingland** *(SJ958725)*
Macclesfield Forest SK11 0ND ☎(0625) 425759
Mar-Nov
*A remotely situated farmhouse in the Peak National Park,
overlooking Teggs Nose Country Park. The rooms are tastefully
furnished, and the owner is renowned for her cuisine : dinners here
have more than a hint of France in the cooking.*
3rm(1⇄) ✂in all bedrooms ® ✳ dB&B£30 dB&B⇄🎇£35
WB&B£105-£122.50 WBDi£168-£185.50 LDO 9am
⅏ CTV 3P nc16yrs 17 acres smallholding beef sheep

MACHRIHANISH Strathclyde *Argyllshire* Map **10** NR62

SELECTED

GH Q Q Q Q **Ardell House** PA28 6PT ☎(058681) 235
Closed Xmas & New Year rs Nov-Feb
This fine detached Victorian house is in a wonderful setting, in
its own garden overlooking the golf course, with views of the
sea and the distant islands of Islay and Jura. Bedrooms vary
in size and style from the spacious master bedrooms to the
more compact, but equally well equipped chalet rooms in the
annexe, which are much in demand. There is a cosy lounge
upstairs with a self-service honesty bar, and imaginative Taste
of Scotland dishes are served in the attractive dining room.
The atmosphere is friendly and relaxed, with many visiting
golfers and tourists returning every year to David and Jill
Baxter's welcoming home.
7rm(1⇌5♠1hc) Annexe 3♠ (1fb) CTV in all bedrooms ®
dB&B⇌♠£40-£50 WB&B£150-£170
Lic ∰ 12P ⓕ

MACHYNLLETH Powys Map **06** SH70

GH Q Q **Maenllwyd** Newtown Rd SY20 8EY ☎(0654) 702928
Built in the last century, this large detached manse stands opposite
the cottage hospital. It provides comfortable accommodation with
a friendly atmosphere.
5hc (2fb) CTV in all bedrooms ® ✱ sB&B£16-£18 dB&B£26-
£30 LDO 1pm
∰ CTV 10P
Credit Cards 1 2 3 ⓕ

FH Q Mr & Mrs D Timms **Rhiwlwyfen** *(SH761983)* Forge
SY20 8RP ☎(0654) 702683
Apr-Oct rs Oct-Apr
This remote 17th-century farmhouse is comfortably furnished.
Guests can enjoy a peaceful stay and beautiful surroundings.
3rm (2fb) ® ✈ (ex guide dogs) ✱ sB&B£12.50-£14 dB&B£25-
£28 WBDi£130-£140 LDO 8pm
∰ CTV 6P 100 acres beef sheep ⓕ

INN Q Q Q **The White Lion Hotel** Heol Pentrerhedyn
SY20 8ND ☎(0654) 703455
In the centre of the busy market town near the famous 'Clock' this
former coaching inn provides attractive pine furnished bedrooms
and a comfortable bar. A good range of food is available and all of
the staff are friendly and helpful.
9rm(4⇌♠5hc) (2fb) CTV in all bedrooms ® ✱ sB&B£20
sB&B⇌♠£30 dB&B£37 dB&B⇌♠£52 WBDi£180-£220
LDO 9pm
∰ CTV 45P
Credit Cards 1 2 3 5

MAIDSTONE Kent Map **05** TQ75

GH Q Q Q **Rock House Hotel** 102 Tonbridge Rd ME16 8SL
☎(0622) 751616
Closed 24 Dec-1 Jan
Situated just away from the centre of Maidstone, this guesthouse
offers modern accommodation at reasonable prices. Bedrooms vary
in size, but all have good facilities and are well maintained. Of
particular note is the overall high standard of cleanliness. With its
small, cosy lounge and pretty dining room, Rock House is a
pleasant place to stay.
12hc (2fb) CTV in all bedrooms ® ✈ sB&B£26-£33 dB&B£34-
£42 WB&B£120-£150
∰ CTV 7P nc1yr
Credit Cards 1 3 ⓕ

ⓕ Remember to use the money-off vouchers.

GH Q Q **Willington Court** Willington St ME15 8JW
☎(0622) 38885
4rm(2⇌♠2hc) (3fb)✁in all bedrooms ® ✈ (ex guide dogs) ✱
sB&B£15-£17 sB&B⇌♠£21-£23 dB&B£30 dB&B⇌♠£34-£38
WB&B£90-£150
∰ CTV 6P nc7yrs
Credit Cards 1 3

MALDON Essex Map **05** TL80

INN Q Q *Swan Hotel* Maldon High St CM9 7EP
☎(0621) 53170
A popular inn near the centre of town. Recently completely
refurbished, it now offers a smart open-plan bar and dining area,
and some bright, simply furnished bedrooms with good facilities.
6hc (2fb)✁in 1 bedroom CTV in 1 bedroom TV in 5 bedrooms
✈ LDO 9pm
∰ CTV 30P 1🐾
Credit Cards 1 2 3 5

MALHAM North Yorkshire Map **07** SD96

GH Q Q Q **Sparth House Hotel** BD23 4DA
☎Airton(07293) 315 due to change to (0729) 830315
Set in this picturesque Dales village, Sparth House dates back to
1664, and retains many original features. Some bedrooms are
spacious, while those in the new wing are more compact. The
imaginative, traditional meals are the highlight of a stay here.
10rm(4⇌♠6hc)✁in all bedrooms CTV in 4 bedrooms ®
✈ (ex guide dogs) sB&B£19 dB&B£34 dB&B⇌♠£45
WBDi£174.50-£207 LDO 5pm
Lic ∰ CTV 7P table-tennis darts ⓕ

INGLESIDE HOTEL
Lee Road, Lynton. Tel: (0598) 52223

Since 1972 Clive and Lesley Horn have been offering a
warm welcome to their guests at Ingleside, which is set
high in its own grounds overlooking the village. The
standards are very high which you'd probably expect
from a family who pride themselves on their
accommodation and cuisine. Enjoy good food and wine
from the imaginative menu.

All bedrooms have a bath or shower and w.c. en-suite,
colour TV and beverage facilities. Ample safe car
parking is always available in hotel grounds.

Send for free brochure with sample menus or telephone
for personal service.

MALMESBURY Wiltshire Map **03** ST98

FH Ⓠ Ⓠ Ⓠ Mrs R Eavis **Manor** *(ST922837)* Corston
SN16 0HF ☎(0666) 822148
A comfortable Cotswold stone farmhouse, close to the A429, in the village of Corston. Each bedroom has an individual style and is tastefully decorated, with modern facilities provided. Due to its location close to the larger towns of Bath, Chippenham and Swindon, the farmhouse attracts many business people who prefer to stay out of the bustle of the towns, but close enough to travel to their work easily.
5rm(1⇨3♪4hc) (2fb)⊁in 2 bedrooms ® ✖ sB&B£14-£18
dB&B£28-£32 dB&B⇨3♪£32-£36
⊞ CTV 8P 436 acres arable dairy
Credit Cards ① ② ③ ④

▣ **FH** Ⓠ Mrs E G Edwards **Stonehill** *(SU986894)*
Charlton SN16 9DY (1m E) ☎(0666) 823310
Part of a busy working farm and very much a home, this grey stone house offers simply furnished, comfortable bedrooms, one with en suite shower and WC, and those without wash basins share a general bath and shower with separate WC. There is a combined lounge and dining room with colour television and an open fire in winter.
3rm(1♪) (1fb) ® sB&B£13-£17 sB&B♪£16.50-£20 dB&B£26-£30 dB&B♪£33-£36 WB&B£90-£112
⊞ CTV 4P 180 acres dairy sheep ④

MALVERN Hereford & Worcester Map **03** SO74

GH Ⓠ Ⓠ Ⓠ **Sidney House Hotel** 40 Worcester Rd WR14 4AA
☎(0684) 574994
rs Xmas & New Year
A Grade II listed house dating from 1823, standing in an elevated position on the A449 just west of the town centre. The accommodation can be compact, but is attractively furnished and well equipped; some rooms enjoy superb views across the Vale of Evesham. There is a comfortable lounge with an honesty bar, and the proprietors are hospitable hosts.
8rm(5♪3hc) (2fb) CTV in all bedrooms ® sB&B£20-£25
sB&B♪£30-£35 dB&B£39 dB&B♪£44-£49 LDO 3pm
Lic ⊞ CTV 9P
Credit Cards ① ② ③ ④

FH Ⓠ Ⓠ Mrs S Stringer **Cowleigh Park** *(SO767475)* Cowleigh
Rd WR13 5HJ ☎(0684) 566750
A fully modernised half-timbered farmhouse dating back in parts to the 13th century, located just off the A4103 Hereford-Worcester road, found by following signs to Cowleigh on the B4219. Part of a smallholding, it has a rural setting complete with a duck pond and poultry. A holiday cottage accommodating 6 people is also available in the grounds. The rooms are well furnished, comfortable and simply equipped; smoking is discouraged in the bedrooms.
3rm(1♪2hc) CTV in all bedrooms sB&B£24-£26 sB&B♪£27-£29 dB&B£35-£37 dB&B♪£37-£40 WB&B£110-£183
WBDi£176.50-£242.50 LDO 11am
⊞ 6P nc5yrs 2 acres smallholding ④

MAN, ISLE OF Map **06**

DOUGLAS Map **06** SC37

▣▼ **GH** Ⓠ **Ainsdale Guest House** 2 Empire Terrace, Central
Prom ☎(0624) 676695
Apr-Sep
Ainsdale is a personally-run guesthouse with basic facilities situated just behind the seafront in a good central position.
16hc (2fb) CTV in 1 bedroom TV in 4 bedrooms ® sB&B£13-£14 dB&B£26-£28 WB&B£91-£98 WBDi£112-£115.50 (wkly only winter) LDO 6pm
CTV ⅌ ④

GH Ⓠ Ⓠ **Edelweiss** Queens Promenade ☎(0624) 675115
FAX (0624) 673194
Set back from the main promenade, this family-run private hotel continues to be improved. The well equipped bedrooms are comfortably furnished and all have private bathrooms. There are two dining rooms: one is open to non-residents.
20rm(3⇨17♪) (3fb) CTV in all bedrooms ®
sB&B⇨♪fr£38.76 dB&B⇨♪fr£68.12 (incl dinner)
WB&Bfr£164.41 WBDifr£238.44 LDO 9pm
Lic lift ⊞ CTV ⅌ solarium
Credit Cards ① ③ ⑤ ④
See advertisement in colour supplement.

GH Ⓠ **Hydro Hotel** Queen's Promanade ☎(0624) 676870
This large, privately owned Edwardian seafront hotel offers a modest but improving standard of accommodation, and caters for tour groups and large parties. Recently redecorated public areas offer a choice of bars, one of which usually provides live entertainment, and a spacious dining room.
60rm(11⇨20♪29hc) (17fb) CTV in all bedrooms ®
✖ (ex guide dogs) sB&B£20.50-£21 sB&B⇨♪£27-£27.50
dB&B£37-£38 dB&B⇨♪£42-£43 WB&B£143.50-£147
WBDi£189-£197.50 LDO 7pm
Lic lift ⊞ solarium pool table darts
Credit Cards ① ③ ⑤

GH Ⓠ **Rosslyn Guest House** 3 Empire Ter, Central
Promenade ☎(0624) 676056
Closed 29 Nov-2 Jan
Situated just behind the seafront near the casino, this well maintained terraced property offers compact and modest accommodation which includes a cosy bar and small first-floor TV lounge.
16rm(4⇨4♪8hc) (3fb) CTV in 5 bedrooms ®
✖ (ex guide dogs) sB&B£16-£21 sB&B⇨♪fr£25 dB&Bfr£32
dB&B⇨♪fr£52 WB&Bfr£122 WBDifr£175
Lic ⊞ CTV ⅌ ④

GH Ⓠ **Rutland Hotel** Queen's Promenade ☎(0624) 621218
Etr-Oct
Situated on the seafront, this large family-run private hotel offers friendly service and improving standards of accommodation, with well furnished bedrooms, many of which have en suite facilities. Entertainment is provided in the basement 'Champs' bar.
86rm(55⇨25♪6hc) (20fb) CTV in all bedrooms ®
LDO 7.30pm
Lic lift CTV ⅌
Credit Cards ① ③

PORT ERIN Map **06** SC16

GH Ⓠ Ⓠ **Regent House** The Promenade ☎(0624) 833454
This small, friendly Victorian guesthouse overlooking the bay has been tastefully modernised to provide comfortable accommodation and bedrooms are well appointed, many with en suite facilities. Vegetarian dishes are always offered as an alternative at dinner. Smoking is not permitted.
8rm(6⇨♪2hc) ⊁in all bedrooms CTV in all bedrooms ® ✖
LDO 6.30pm
⊞ ⅌

PORT ST MARY Map **06** SC16

GH Ⓠ **Mallmore Private Hotel** The Promenade
☎(0624) 833179
May-6 Oct
This long-established private hotel overlooking the sea offers traditional standards of hospitality and good home cooking. Simple bedrooms are modestly furnished and equipped, but there are five comfortable lounges with splendid views over the bay.
43hc (10fb) ® ✖ ✳ sB&Bfr£12.75 dB&Bfr£25 WBDifr£136
LDO 6.45pm
CTV ⅌ snooker
Credit Cards ① ② ③ ⑤

MANCHESTER Greater Manchester Map **07** SJ89

GH Q Q Ebor Hotel 402 Wilbraham Rd, Chorlton Cum Hardy M21 1UH ☎061-881 1911 & 061-881 4855
Closed Xmas

A Victorian detached house situated beside the A6010, three miles from the city centre, offering easy access to both the airport and motorway network. Well maintained and comfortable accommodation is provided, and there is a TV lounge and a separate bar.

16rm(1↱15hc) (3fb) CTV in all bedrooms Ⓡ ✗ sB&B£22-£28 sB&B↱£28 dB&B£33-£38 dB&B↱fr£38 WB&B£140-£180 WBDi£178-£218 LDO 5pm
Lic 🍸 CTV 20P 🚗 nc4yrs darts Ⓔ

GH Q Q Horizon Hotel 69 Palatine Road, West Didsbury M20 9LJ ☎061-445 4705

A semidetached Victorian house, now a commercial private hotel, conveniently situated for both the A63 and M56, only 10 minutes from both the city centre and the airport. Bedrooms are well equipped and nicely decorated, although on the small side. Parking facilities are good.

18rm(5⇌13↱) (1fb) CTV in all bedrooms Ⓡ
✗ (ex guide dogs) sB&B⇌↱£24-£27 dB&B⇌↱£36-£42 WB&B£144 LDO 5pm
Lic 🍸 CTV 20P nc9yrs
Credit Cards 1 2 3

See advertisement on page 251

GH Q Kempton House Hotel 400 Wilbraham Rd, Chorlton-Cum-Hardy M21 1UH ☎061-881 8766
Closed 25 & 26 Dec

A late-Victorian semidetached house set back from the A6010 and well placed for the airport and the city centre. The accommodation is generally compact and modestly furnished, but improvements ▶

continue to be made at this friendly, mainly commercial private hotel.
14rm(3♠11hc) CTV in 12 bedrooms TV in 1 bedroom ⓡ ✖ (ex guide dogs) ✳ sB&B£20.50-£25 sB&B♠£25 dB&B£29.50 dB&B♠£35 LDO 5pm
Lic ⁜ CTV 9P
Credit Cards ① ③ ⓔ

GH ⓠⓠ New Central Hotel 144-146 Heywood St, Cheetham
M8 7PD ☎061-205 2169
Situated in a quiet residential area just off the A665 at Cheetham, this well maintained commercial hotel offers modest but clean accommodation ; there is a comfortable lounge and a small bar in which to relax.
10hc CTV in all bedrooms ⓡ ✖ (ex guide dogs) ✳ sB&Bfr£21 dB&Bfr£33.50 LDO 7.30pm
Lic ⁜ CTV 10P ⓔ

GH ⓠⓠⓠ West Lynne Hotel 16 Middleton Rd, Crumpsall
M8 6DS ☎061-721 4866 & 061-721 4922
Sound standards of accommodation are offered at this family-owned hotel situated on the A576 midway between junction 18 on the M62 and the city centre. Bedrooms are well equipped and the public areas attractively decorated.
12⇄ (2fb) CTV in all bedrooms ⓡ ✖ (ex guide dogs)
Lic ⁜ 15P
Credit Cards ① ③

MAPPOWDER Dorset Map **03** ST70

FH ⓠ Mrs A K Williamson-Jones **Boywood** *(ST733078)*
Sturminster Newton DT10 2EQ (1.5m N toward Hazelbury Bryan) ☎Hazelbury Bryan(0258) 817416
This traditional farmhouse is part of a dairy farm set in peaceful, rural surroundings. The simple accommodation offered is comfortable.
3rm ✖
⁜ CTV P ⊠(heated) ♪(hard)17 acres beef poultry

MARGARET RODING (NEAR GREAT DUNMOW) Essex
Map **05** TL51

FH ⓠⓠ Mr & Mrs J Matthews **Greys Farm** *(TL604112)*
Greys Farm, Ongar Rd CM6 1QR ☎Good Easter(024531) 509
Check for directions to this comfortable farmhouse in a rural setting. There are beamed breakfast and sitting rooms downstairs, three simple, bright and clean bedrooms above, and a cheerful welcome from Joyce and Geoffrey Matthews.
3rm(2hc) ⤢in all bedrooms ✖ sB&Bfr£16 dB&Bfr£30
⁜ CTV 3P nc10yrs 340 acres arable beef sheep

MARGATE Kent Map **05** TR37

GH ⓠⓠ *Beachcomber Hotel* 3-4 Royal Esplanade, Westbrook
CT9 5DL ☎Thanet(0843) 221616
This licensed hotel enjoys a good reputation for its cooking, which is complemented by the use of fresh ingredients and the involvement of proprietors Mr and Mrs Philip McGovern. Overlooking the sea, it offers well maintained, simply furnished rooms and pleasant public areas.
15hc (3fb) ✖ LDO 1pm
Lic ⁜ CTV 1P

GH ⓠⓠ Charnwood Private Hotel 20-22 Canterbury Rd
CT9 5BW ☎Thanet(0843) 224158
Old-fashioned, traditional accommodation under new and friendly management.
8hc (4fb) ⓡ ✖ sB&B£14-£18 dB&B£26-£34 WB&B£85-£100 WBDi£110-£125 LDO 4pm
Lic ⁜ CTV ♪
Credit Cards ① ③ ⓔ

GH ⓠⓠⓠ The Greswolde Hotel 20 Surrey Road, Cliftonville
CT9 2LA ☎Thanet(0843) 223956
6rm(1⇄5♠) (2fb) CTV in all bedrooms ⓡ sB&B⇄♠£20 dB&B⇄♠£32
Lic ⁜ ♪
Credit Cards ① ③ ⓔ

GH ⓠ The Malvern 29 Eastern Esplanade, Cliftonville
CT9 2HL ☎Thanet(0843) 290192
A terraced house, opposite Walpole Bay, on 6 floors with a cosy lounge and basement breakfast room. The bedrooms are adequately furnished and the majority have generous en suite showers. The Malvern overlooks the sea, promenade and bandstand and is close to all the local amenities.
10rm(8♠1fb) CTV in all bedrooms ⓡ ✖ sB&B£17-£20 sB&B♠£25-£36 dB&B£30-£33 dB&B♠£33-£36 WB&B£85-£99 LDO noon
Lic ⁜ ♪
Credit Cards ① ② ③ ⑤ ⓔ

GH ⓠⓠ Westbrook Bay House 12 Royal Esplanade,
Westbrook CT9 5DW ☎Thanet(0843) 292700
The proprietors of this hotel offer a warm welcome. Bedrooms are well equipped and some have marvellous sea views. There is a comfortable, well appointed lounge and an attractive dining room which incorporates a small bar.
11rm(3♠8hc) (4fb) CTV in 10 bedrooms ⓡ ✖ (ex guide dogs) sB&Bfr£15 dB&Bfr£30 dB&B♠fr£34 WB&Bfr£77 WBDifr£94 LDO 4.30pm
Lic ⁜ CTV ⓔ

MARKET DRAYTON Shropshire Map **07** SJ63

FH ⓠⓠⓠ Mr J M Thomas **Stoke Manor** *(SH646279)* Stoke-on-Tern TF9 2DU ☎Hodnet(063084) 222
Closed Dec
This lovely old farmhouse is run by the Thomas family who provide a cellar bar and warm, comfortable bedrooms. A collection of vintage farm implements and a site of archaeological interest make this a memorable place to stay.
3⇄♠ (1fb)⤢in all bedrooms CTV in all bedrooms ⓡ ✖ (ex guide dogs) ✳ sB&B⇄♠£22-£25 dB&B⇄♠£40-£44
Lic ⁜ 20P ✔ vintage tractor collection 250 acres arable ⓔ

MARKINCH Fife Map **11** NO20

INN ⓠⓠⓠ Town House Hotel 1 High St KY7 6OQ
☎Glenrothes(0592) 758459
4rm(3⇄♠1hc) CTV in all bedrooms ⓡ ✳ sB&Bfr£28 sB&B⇄♠fr£38 dB&B⇄♠fr£48 WB&Bfr£240 ✳ Lunch £7.25-£15.25 Dinner £8.50-£16.75 LDO 9pm
⁜
Credit Cards ① ② ③ ⑤

MARKSBURY Avon Map **03** TL66

GH ⓠⓠ Wansdyke Cottage Crosspost Ln BA2 9HE
☎Bath(0225) 873674
A late 18th-century stone cottage situated on the A39/B3116 crossroads south of Bath. The accommodation is comfortable, and there is a private lounge dining room available for guests. There are no hand basins in the bedrooms, but sufficient are provided within the general facilities.
4rm(1⇄♠) ⓡ ✳ sB&B£12.50-£16.50 dB&B£25-£30 dB&B⇄♠£25-£30 LDO 6pm
⁜ CTV 4P ⓔ

MARLBOROUGH Wiltshire Map **04** SU16

See also Burbage
GH ⓠⓠ Merlin Hotel High St SN8 1LW ☎(0672) 512151
This guesthouse is situated on the south side of the famous High Street, beside a popular wine bar frequented by locals. Most bedrooms have private bathrooms and are well equipped ; a few are

rather compact, but they all have bright, simple décor. Breakfast and home-made dinners are served in the dining room.

15rm(13⇨3♠2hc) Annexe 1♠ (1fb) CTV in all bedrooms ® ✱ sB&Bfr£35 sB&B⇨3♠£40 dB&Bfr£45 dB&B⇨3♠£50 LDO 9.30pm
Lic ♒ ⅌
Credit Cards 1 3 £

MARSHFIELD Avon Map 03 ST77

INN Q Q Q *Lord Nelson Inn & Carriages Restaurant* SN14 8LP
☎Bath(0225) 891820
This inn is 250 years old, with many original features – look down the porthole in the bar to view the well – and specialises in fish dishes but also has an imaginative vegetarian menu. Meals are taken in the old stables, transformed into a lamplit, cobbled Victorian Street. The accommodation is well equipped and village memorabilia abound.
3⇨3♠ (1fb) CTV in all bedrooms ® ✖ (ex guide dogs) LDO 9.30pm
♒
Credit Cards 1 3

MARTON Warwickshire Map 04 SP46

FH Q Q Q Mrs P Dronfield *Marton Fields (SP402680)*
CV23 9RS ☎(0926) 632410
Closed Xmas
Approaching Marton on the A423 from Southam/Banbury, take the first left into North Street which opens into Church Street. Follow this road to the end fork and bear left. Marton Fields, an attractive red-brick period farmhouse set in delightful gardens, is a mile from the church. Mixed arable/sheep farmland leads to the river Itchen, accessible to visitors. The house is comfortable and well kept by Mrs Dronfield, a charming host and a talented artist. A good breakfast is offered with home-baked bread.
4hc ⚥in all bedrooms ® ✖ (ex guide dogs) LDO 6pm
♒ CTV 10P ⚬ ✦ croquet lawn painting holidays 240 acres arable beef mixed sheep

MARY TAVY Devon Map 02 SX57

FH Q Q Q Mrs B Anning **Wringworthy** *(SX500773)* PL19 9LT
☎(0822) 810434
Apr-Oct
This delightful farmhouse has a dining room which is full of character with flagged floors and a traditional long table. The adjacent lounge is cosy. Bright bedrooms offer comfort and views over the countryside.
3rm (1fb)⚥in all bedrooms CTV in all bedrooms ®
✖ (ex guide dogs) ✱ sB&B£14-£20 dB&B£28
♒ CTV 3P 80 acres beef sheep

MASHAM North Yorkshire Map 08 SE28

GH Q Q Q **Bank Villa** HG4 4DB ☎Ripon(0765) 689605
Mar-Oct
A well established, popular guesthouse offering personal service from the resident proprietors, quaint bedrooms and comfortable lounges. Dinner can be especially recommended.
7hc sB&B£20 dB&B£32 WB&B£107.50-£130 WBDi£200-£220 LDO noon
Lic ♒ CTV 7P nc5yrs

MATLOCK Derbyshire Map 08 SK36

GH Q Q Q **Lane End House** Green Ln, Tansley DE4 5FJ
☎(0629) 583981
A small Georgian farmhouse situated in the quiet village of Tansley, on the outskirts of Matlock ; just behind the village green, with well tended gardens, it is an ideal base from which to explore the surrounding Peak District. Bedrooms have been carefully decorated and furnished, with many thoughtful extras provided ; all the rooms have pleasant views over the countryside. A carefully ▶

Westbrook Bay House

12 Royal Esplanade, Westbrook, Margate, Kent. Tel. 0843-292700

AA
LISTED   LICENSED BAR

Situated in prime position. Overlooking beautiful sandy bay with safe bathing. Highly recommended for excellent food and friendly atmosphere. Reduced rates for children under 12yrs sharing parents room. All rooms with tea making facilities, clock radio and TV. Some rooms en-suite, some with showers. Winter Weekend Breaks. 16 miles from Canterbury. Own Keys – Fire Certificate Issued. TV Lounge. Resident proprietors Maureen and Ken Richardson.

horizon hotel

69 Palatine Road, West Didsbury, Manchester M20
Telephone: 061-445 4705

A newly opened hotel, offering superb accommodation and providing a relaxed carefree atmosphere. 10 minutes from Manchester City Centre and Manchester international airport. All rooms have shower and/or bathroom, telephone, colour TV, tea/coffee making facilities and central heating. Conference facilities. Special disabled suite. Residents TV lounge. Restaurant with bar. Large car park.

planned 4-course home-made dinner is served, after which guests can relax in either of 2 comfortable lounges. A no-smoking policy is requested.
2rm(1⇔🅟1hc) ⊬in all bedrooms CTV in all bedrooms ® ✳
sB&B⇔🅟£26-£27.50 dB&B⇔🅟£38-£42 WB&B£118-£137
WBDi£195-£220
Lic 🍴 5P nc12yrs
Credit Cards ①③

FH ⓠⓠ Mrs M Brailsford **Farley** *(SK294622)* Farley DE4 5LR
🕾(0629) 582533
Closed Xmas & New Year
This busy working farm, set high in the Derbyshire hills, has bright warm bedrooms, and a cheery welcome awaits guests from Mrs Brailsford and her dogs!
3hc (2fb) CTV in all bedrooms CTV in 1 bedroom ® sB&B£13.50
dB&B£27 WB&B£94.50 WBDi£129.50 LDO 5pm
🍴 CTV 8P ∪ 275 acres arable beef dairy ⓔ

FH ⓠⓠⓠ M Haynes **Packhorse** *(SK323617)* Tansley
DE4 5LF (2m NE of Matlock off A632 at Tansley)
🕾(0629) 582781
Lovely countryside forms a backdrop to Mrs Haynes's lovingly maintained gardens, and the farmhouse accommodation has splendid views.
5hc (3fb) ® ✕ ✳ sB&Bfr£14 dB&Bfr£28
🍴 CTV 20P nc3yrs 40 acres mixed

FH ⓠⓠ Mrs Janet Hole **Wayside** *(SK324630)* Matlock Moor
DE4 5LF 🕾(0629) 582967
Closed Xmas & New Year
At Matlock Moor, 2 miles from the town centre, this working farm offers fine views. Cattle byres stand next to the 17th-century farmhouse. A conservatory is soon to provide an attractive dining room to complement the comfortable, simple accommodation.
6hc (2fb) ✕
🍴 CTV 8P 60 acres dairy

MAWGAN PORTH Cornwall & Isles of Scilly Map 02 SW86

GH ⓠⓠⓠ **White Lodge Hotel** TR8 4BN
🕾St Mawgan(0637) 860512
Mar-Nov & Xmas
A large, detached house situated in an elevated position with glorious views over the beach and cliffs of the bay. The bedrooms are well equipped and in the process of being refurbished. There is a good selection of dishes to choose from at dinner, and the atmosphere is relaxed and friendly.
16rm(11⇔🅟5hc) (7fb) CTV in all bedrooms ® sB&B£15.50-
£18.50 sB&B⇔🅟£18.50-£21.50 dB&B£31-£37 dB&B⇔🅟£37-
£43 WB&B£105-£126 WBDi£145-£175 (wkly only Jun-Aug & Xmas) LDO 7.30pm
Lic CTV 17P ⚬∿ games room
Credit Cards ①②③ⓔ

MAYFIELD East Sussex Map 05 TQ52

INN ⓠⓠⓠ **The Rose & Crown** Fletching St TN20 6TE
🕾(0435) 872200
3⇔🅟 CTV in all bedrooms ® ✕ (ex guide dogs) ✳
sB&B⇔🅟£44.50 dB&B⇔🅟£61 WB&B£182-£290
WBDi£217-£325 ✳ Lunch fr£1.95alc Dinner £3.95-£10.95alc
LDO 9.30pm
🍴 14P nc7yrs

MAYFIELD Staffordshire Map 07 SK14

INN ⓠ **Queen's Arms** DE6 2HH 🕾Ashbourne(0335) 42271
Standing close to a busy junction, this lively house offers darts and pool, and live entertainment at weekends. Needless to say, it is well-supported by the locals.

4hc (2fb) CTV in all bedrooms ® ✕ (ex guide dogs) ✳
sB&B£19.50-£25 dB&B£25-£33 WB&B£77-£87.50 WBDi£105-
£115.50 ✳ LDO 6.30pm
🍴 20P pool table

MEALSGATE Cumbria Map 11 NY24

SELECTED

GH ⓠⓠⓠⓠ **The Old Rectory** Boltongate CA5 1DA
🕾Low Ireby(09657) 647
Closed early Dec-late Jan
A spacious house of character dating back in parts to the 15th century. It is reached from Keswick via the A591 to the Castle Inn and then turn right through Ireby to Boltongate. The three beautifully furnished bedrooms are spacious and have good facilities. Public rooms include two lounges and a Tudor-style dining room with stone walls and a long wooden table creating an intimate atmosphere, together with oak beams and roaring log fires in winter. The set five-course dinner is really something special to enjoy.
3rm(2🅟1hc) ® ✕ (ex guide dogs) ✳ dB&B🅟£29-£32
LDO 6pm
Lic 🍴 CTV 10P nc14yrs
Credit Cards ①③ⓔ
See advertisement under KESWICK

MELKSHAM Wiltshire Map 03 ST96

GH ⓠⓠ **Longhope** 9 Beanacre Rd SN12 7AG 🕾(0225) 706737
An attractive Victorian Bath stone house with a garden on the A350 towards Chippenham. The spacious and comfortable lounge and dining room, together with well equipped bedrooms, make the Longhope a popular place with business people and tourists alike.
7rm(1⇔5🅟1hc) (2fb) CTV in all bedrooms ® ✳
sB&B⇔🅟£18 dB&B⇔🅟£33 WB&B£98 WBDi£142
LDO 4pm
🍴 CTV 12P

GH ⓠⓠ **Regency Hotel** 10-12 Spa Rd SN12 7NS
🕾(0225) 702971 & 705772
A small hotel, part of which is listed, dating from 1830. The bedrooms are well equipped with all the modern facilities suitable for business people, and there is a small bar and smart dining room open to non-residents.
10rm(2⇔4🅟2hc) (1fb) CTV in all bedrooms ® sB&B£20-£25
sB&B⇔🅟£30-£36 dB&B£40-£46 dB&B⇔🅟£40-£46
LDO 10pm
Lic 🍴 P
Credit Cards ①②③⑤ⓔ

MELROSE Borders *Roxburghshire* Map 12 NT53

GH ⓠⓠⓠ **Dunfermline House** Buccleuch St TD6 9LB
🕾(089682) 2148
Standing close to Melrose Abbey in this attractive border town, this charming Victorian house has décor and furnishings of quality. Scottish home cooking and hospitality are provided by the friendly owners.
5🅟 ⊬in all bedrooms CTV in all bedrooms ® ✕ ✳
sB&B🅟£19 dB&B🅟£38 LDO 5pm
🍴 ⓔ

MELTON MOWBRAY Leicestershire Map 08 SK71

GH ⓠ **Westbourne House Hotel** 11A-15 Nottingham Rd
LE13 0NP 🕾(0664) 63556 & 69456
Closed Xmas
16hc (1fb) CTV in all bedrooms ✳ sB&B£18-£19.50
dB&B£31.50-£35.50 LDO 7.30pm
Lic 🍴 CTV 20P ⓔ

MENDHAM Suffolk Map **05** TM28

FH QQ Mrs J E Holden **Weston House** *(TM292828)* IP20 0PB
☎St Cross(098682) 206
Mar-Nov
A charming 16th century white painted farmhouse adjacent to the farmyard, in a completely rural setting. The accommodation is simple and comfortable, with an attractive verandah and conservatory. To find the farmhouse, take the unclassified road to St Cross from the crossroads in the centre of Mendham.
3hc (1fb) ® sB&Bfr£15 dB&Bfr£26 WB&Bfr£80
WBDifr£132.50 LDO 2pm
⋈ CTV 6P 300 acres arable beef mixed
Credit Cards ⟨2⟩ ⓔ

MERE Wiltshire Map **03** ST83

GH QQQ **Chetcombe House Hotel** Chetcombe Rd BA12 6AZ
☎(0747) 860219
Closed 1-20 Feb
This large country house hotel stands adjacent to the A303, amidst an acre of gardens. The main bedrooms are south-facing with outstanding views, and all are nicely decorated and well equipped. A comfortable dining room and traditional English lounge with open fires all contribute to a warm, friendly atmosphere.
5⇔3♠ (1fb)✂in all bedrooms CTV in all bedrooms ® ✱
sB&B⇔♠fr£27 dB&B⇔♠fr£46 WB&Bfr£142.50
WBDifr£212 LDO 7pm
Lic ⋈ 10P
Credit Cards ⟨1⟩ ⟨2⟩ ⟨3⟩

INN QQ **Talbot Hotel** The Square BA12 6DR ☎(0747) 860427
This family-owned inn, situated in the heart of the country town of Mere, dates back to the 1580s. Bedrooms are gradually being refurbished and modern facilities upgraded and improved. The public bars have character and charm and some original 16th-century features remain. In addition to extensive bar snacks, there is also a varied table d'hôte lunch and dinner menu. The dining room is nicely appointed and comfortable. The proprietors Mr and Mrs Aylett remain very involved in the day to day running of the hotel.
7rm(4⇔3♠) (3fb) CTV in all bedrooms ® ✱
sB&B⇔♠fr£28.61 dB&B⇔♠fr£47 WBDifr£152.50 (wkly only Xmas & Etr) ✱ Lunch £5.95-£13.50 High tea fr£2 Dinner £10.75-£16.75 LDO 9pm
⋈ 22P
Credit Cards ⟨1⟩ ⟨2⟩ ⟨3⟩

MERIDEN West Midlands Map **04** SP28

GH QQ **Meriden Hotel** Main Rd CV7 7NH ☎(0676) 22005
FAX (0676) 23744
A friendly guesthouse situated just off the A45, close to the centre of England. The rooms can be compact, but all have bright, fresh décor and are exceptionally well equipped.
13rm(5⇔8♠) (1fb) CTV in all bedrooms ® sB&B⇔♠£38.80-£64.65 dB&B⇔♠£64.65 LDO 9pm
Lic ⋈ CTV 15P
Credit Cards ⟨1⟩ ⟨3⟩

MERTHYR TYDFIL Mid Glamorgan Map **03** SO00

GH QQQ **Llwyn On** Cwmtaf CF48 2HS ☎(0685) 4384
Just 4 miles north of Llwyn Onn, on the A470 road, overlooking the reservoir, this completely modernised guesthouse provides excellent facilities. The bedrooms are all pine furnished and well equipped and a relaxing lounge is provided for residents.
4rm(2⇔♠2hc) CTV in all bedrooms ® ✖ (ex guide dogs) ✱
sB&Bfr£15 dB&Bfr£30 dB&B⇔♠fr£35
⋈ 4P ⓔ

MERTON Devon Map **02** SS51

GH QQ **Merton House** EX20 3DR ☎Beaford(08053) 364
Apr-Oct
This Georgian residence stands in its own grounds and has a grass tennis court.
5rm(2⇔3hc) (1fb) ® ✱ sB&B£18-£20 dB&B£36-£40
dB&B⇔£40-£50 (incl dinner) LDO 10am
Lic ⋈ CTV 8P ⊿ℛ(grass)snooker putting green table tennis

MEVAGISSEY Cornwall & Isles of Scilly Map **02** SX04

GH QQQ **Headlands Hotel** Polkirt Hill PL26 6UX
☎(0726) 843453
Mar-Oct & Xmas
This family-run, licensed private hotel enjoys superb views out across the bay – the panoramic views are undoubtedly some of the best in Cornwall. Bedrooms are freshly decorated and are steadily being improved. They are furnished and equipped in a modern style. Public areas are bright and are complemented by a small, cordial bar. A home-cooked evening meal, prepared by proprietor Mrs Grist using fresh, local quality produce, may also be enjoyed by guests.
14rm(8♠6hc) (3fb) CTV in 8 bedrooms sB&B£15.50-£19.50
sB&B♠£19.50-£23.50 dB&B£31-£39 dB&B♠£39-£47
WB&B£98.50-£154.50 WBDif£175.50-£231.50 LDO 7.30pm
Lic ⋈ CTV 11P ⓔ

GH QQQ **Mevagissey House** Vicarage Hill PL26 6SZ
☎(0726) 842427
Mar-Oct
This 18th-century vicarage is perched on a hillside in four acres of grounds. Well-equipped bedrooms, a sitting room with lovely views, and a candlelit dining room combine with extensive service and wholesome English cooking to provide a relaxing place in which to stay.

▶

6rm(1⇌3ᘁ2hc) (2fb) CTV in all bedrooms ®
✱ (ex guide dogs) sB&B£22-£24 sB&B⇌ᘁ£24-£27 dB&B£34-
£38 dB&B⇌ᘁ£38-£44 WB&B£112-£147 WBDi£203-£224
LDO 5pm
Lic ᖰ 12P nc7yrs
Credit Cards 1 3 £

GH QQQ Tremarne Polkirt PL26 6UY ☎(0726) 842213
Mar-Nov
*This small family-run hotel is steadily being upgraded and
improved by the young, enthusiastic owners. Quietly situated along
a private road, some rooms overlook the bay and most are bright
and sunny. Bedrooms are furnished in a modern style, with pretty
co-ordinating décor and soft furnishings. The public areas are
nicely appointed and comfortable, and the hotel is run in a friendly
and informal manner.*
14rm(4⇌10ᘁ) (2fb) CTV in all bedrooms ® ✱
sB&B⇌ᘁ£24.50-£28 dB&B⇌ᘁ£41-£48 (incl dinner)
WB&B£140-£164.50 WBDi£182-£224 LDO 5pm
Lic ᖰ 14P nc3yrs ⌷(heated)
Credit Cards 1 2 3 £

FH QQQ Mrs L Hennah **Kerryanna** *(SX008453)* Treleaven
Farm PL26 6RZ ☎(0726) 843558
Mar-Oct
*Linda Hennah's guesthouse is situated on a working farm
overlooking the village. The bedrooms are well furnished, most
with showers. It has a comfortable lounge, dining room and bar.
No pets.*
6rm(5⇌8ᘁ 1hc) (2fb) CTV in all bedrooms ® ✱
dB&B⇌ᘁfr£58 (incl dinner) WB&B£133-£154 WBDi£180-
£195 (wkly only Jul & Aug) LDO 5pm
Lic ᖰ 7P nc5yrs ⌷(heated) games room putting green 200
acres arable beef

FH QQQ Mrs A Hennah **Treleaven** *(SX008454)* PL26 6RZ
☎(0726) 842413
Closed 15 Dec-7 Jan
*This modern farmhouse has bright, well-equipped bedrooms with
en suite facilities, some having panoramic views. The lounge has a
woodburning stove, adding to the comfortable and relaxing
atmosphere. There is a swimming pool and ample car parking.*
6ᘁ (1fb) CTV in all bedrooms ® ✱ LDO 8pm
Lic ᖰ CTV 6P ⌷(heated) games room, putting green 200
acres mixed
Credit Cards 1 3

INN QQ *The Ship* Fore St PL26 6UQ (St Austell Brewery)
☎(0726) 843324
*Follow the winding streets to the heart of the village to find this
historic fisherman's inn. Downstairs you will find a popular and
lively bar of great character with a flagstone floor and ships' wood
panelling. On the 2 floors above are a dozen modernised bedrooms.*
6hc (2fb) CTV in all bedrooms ® LDO 8.30pm
ᖰ ℙ

MIDDLETON PRIORS Shropshire Map 07 SO69

SELECTED

GH QQQQ Middleton Lodge WV16 6UR (1m NE on
unclass rd) ☎Ditton Priors(074634) 228 or 675
Closed Xmas
*This large, beautifully preserved 17th century house was once
the hunting lodge of the Howard family. It is set within 20
acres of grounds in one of the most picturesque parts of
Shropshire, and the ancient towns of Ludlow and Bridgnorth
are within a short drive. Now a privately owned and
personally run guesthouse, it provides spacious, well equipped,
good quality accommodation and is tastefully furnished and
decorated to a high standard throughout, with many original
features retained.*

3rm(2⇌1ᘁ) CTV in all bedrooms ® ✱ (ex guide dogs) ✱
sB&Bfr£20 sB&B⇌ᘁ£25 dB&B⇌ᘁ£35-£45
ᖰ CTV 4P nc5yrs
See advertisement under BRIDGNORTH

MIDDLEWICH Cheshire Map 07 SJ76

FH QQ Mrs S Moss **Forge Mill** *(SJ704624)* Warmingham
CW10 0HQ ☎Warmingham(027077) 204
*A spacious attractive Victorian farmhouse on the edge of the
village of Warmingham (a map is supplied when booking).
Standing in an acre of mature gardens, the 2 bedrooms have lovely
views of the surrounding countryside, and are comfortable and
attractively decorated. There is a lounge and a cosy dining room
where evening meals can be served by prior arrangement.*
2hc ✱ (ex guide dogs) sB&B£15-£16.50 dB&B£28-£30
WB&Bfr£98
ᖰ CTV 10P ℙ(grass)150 acres mixed £

MIDHURST West Sussex
See **Bepton** and **Rogate**

MILBORNE PORT Somerset Map 03 ST61

FH QQ Mrs P T Tizzard **Venn** *(ST684183)* DT9 5RA
☎(0963) 250208
*Attractive accommodation in a modern house, set back off main
road on Shaftesbury side of village.*
3rm(2hc) (2fb) CTV in all bedrooms ® ✱
ᖰ CTV P ⌷ 375 acres dairy

MILTON COMMON Oxfordshire Map **04** SP60

INN [Q][Q] **Three Pigeons** OX9 2NS
☎Great Milton(0844) 279247
This small country inn is conveniently located close to major motorway links and is only yards from the M40, exit 7. The three bedrooms are comfortable and well equipped, providing value for money. Congenial bars, with a varied bar snack menu, prove popular with locals and visitors alike.
3⇨🖘 (1fb) CTV in all bedrooms ® ✖ LDO 10pm
🏳 CTV 20P
Credit Cards [1] [2] [3] [5]

MILTON KEYNES Buckinghamshire Map **04** SP83

See **Gayhurst, Newport Pagnell, Salford** and **Whaddon**

MILTON-UNDER-WYCHWOOD Oxfordshire Map **04** SP21

SELECTED

GH [Q][Q][Q][Q] **Hillborough Hotel** The Green OX7 6JH (off A424 Burton-Stow village centre)
☎Shipton-under-Wychwood(0993) 830501
Closed Jan
This delightful hotel overlooks the village green and offers a peaceful and relaxing atmosphere. Bedrooms have been tastefully furnished and are well equipped, each with good, modern en suite facilities; there are also 3 family bedrooms in an adjacent cottage, which are spacious and very comfortable. Public areas include a charming conservatory full of plants and comfortable seats and a bar area offering a varied and extensive menu, whilst the recently extended dining room offers a wider menu and is also open to non-residents.
6rm(5⇨1🖘) Annexe 3⇨ CTV in all bedrooms ® ✻
sB&B⇨🖘£39 dB&B⇨🖘£53-£55 WB&B£166.50-£173.50
Lic 🏳 15P ⚫ croquet
Credit Cards [1] [3] (£)
See advertisement under OXFORD

MINEHEAD Somerset Map **03** SS94

See **Town Plan Section**
GH [Q][Q][Q] *Alcombe House Hotel* Alcombe TA24 6BG
☎(0643) 705130
Mar-Oct rs Mar-Etr
This Grade II listed Georgian house is conveniently located for Exmoor and the medieval village of Dunster, with its National Trust castle. The six bedrooms are comfortable, and all are ensuite and have TV and tea-making facilities. The elegant sitting room is comfortably furnished, with a small bar, and a simple table d'hôte menu is served in the dining room: pre-ordering is encouraged.
6rm(5⇨1🖘) CTV in all bedrooms ® LDO 7.30pm
Lic 7P nc12yrs
Credit Cards [1] [3]

GH [Q][Q] **Avill House** Townsend Rd TA24 5RG
☎(0643) 704370
Etr-mid Oct
A Victorian three-storeyed mid-terrace house, notable in the summer for its colourful red and white floral display. It is conveniently located a short walk from the town and seafront. Bedrooms are comfortable and neatly furnished and decorated. A choice of food is available at dinner.
9rm(2🖘7hc) (4fb) CTV in all bedrooms ® ✖ ✻ sB&B£15-£15.50 dB&B£25-£28 dB&B🖘£32-£33 LDO 3pm
Lic CTV 9P nc5yrs

GH [Q][Q] **Bactonleigh Private Hotel** 20 Tregonwell Rd
TA24 5DU ☎(0643) 702147
This small privately owned guesthouse is in a quiet residential area and provides adequately appointed, well maintained accommodation. Nicely prepared simple English food is served.
▶

8rm(1🐾7hc) (1fb) ✱ sB&B£14-£15 dB&B£28-£30 dB&B🐾£33-£35 WB&Bfr£94.50 WBDifr£140 LDO 5pm
Lic 🍴 CTV 8P £

GH QQQ **Gascony Hotel** The Avenue TA24 5BB
☎(0643) 705939
Mar-Oct
Friendly and efficient Victorian house in a prime position, offering well equipped bedrooms of a good size. Spacious dining room serves home cooked meals.
13⇌🐾 (2fb) CTV in all bedrooms ® sB&B⇌🐾£20.50-£22.50 dB&B⇌🐾£41-£45 WBDi£144-£158 LDO 5.30pm
Lic 🍴 15P nc5yrs
Credit Cards 1 3 £

GH QQQ **Marshfield Hotel** Tregonwell Rd TA24 5DU
☎(0643) 702517
Mar-Nov
Marshfield stands on level ground close to the shops and sea, and offers a smartly furnished dining room, TV lounge and sun lounge bar. The bedrooms are comfortable and well equipped.
12rm(2⇌6🐾4hc) (1fb) ® ✱ sB&Bfr£15.50 sB&B⇌🐾fr£19.50 dB&Bfr£31 dB&B⇌🐾fr£35 WB&Bfr£93 WBDifr£136 LDO 6.30pm
Lic 🍴 CTV 7P

SELECTED

GH QQQQ **Marston Lodge Hotel** St Michaels Rd
TA24 5JP ☎(0643) 702510
Closed 7 Nov-20 Dec & 30 Dec-7 Feb rs 20-30 Dec
An attractive detached property standing high above the town, with a well kept terraced garden, affording panoramic views of the bay and surrounding countryside. Recently refurbished, the hotel now offers spacious, spotlessly clean and well equipped bedrooms, with private bathrooms and TV. The comfortable public areas include a quiet lounge, bar/lounge and in the adjacent dining room a choice of home-cooked dishes is available on the table d'hôte menu.
12rm(4⇌8🐾) CTV in all bedrooms ® ✱ sB&B⇌🐾£30-£34 dB&B⇌🐾£60-£68 (incl dinner) WB&B£142-£156 WBDi£208-£222 LDO 7pm
Lic 🍴 7P nc10yrs
Credit Cards 1 3 £

GH QQQ **Mayfair Hotel** 25 The Avenue TA24 5AY
☎(0643) 702719
Mar-Nov rs Feb
Enjoying a central location between the shops and the sea, Mayfair has cheerful accommodation and modern, well equipped bedrooms. Some rooms are in a house across the road, equally well furnished, though all meals are served in the main building.
16rm(5⇌811🐾) Annexe 9rm(4⇌5🐾) (10fb) CTV in all bedrooms ® ✖ (ex guide dogs) LDO 6pm
Lic 🍴 23P nc5yrs
Credit Cards 1 3

INN QQQ **Kildare Lodge** 18 Townsend Rd TA24 5RQ
☎(0643) 702009
Built in Edward Lutyens style at the turn of the century, Kildare Lodge offers comfortable and well equipped bedrooms, with an additional six rooms in a converted stable block beside the hotel. The Friar Tuck menu is extensive, ranging from sandwiches to Beef Wellington or Tournedos Rossini, and renowned for the special Sri Lankan meal – 48 hours' notice required. Service is friendly and relaxed.
5⇌🐾 (3fb)✂in 2 bedrooms CTV in all bedrooms ® ✱ sB&B⇌🐾£19.50-£24.50 dB&B⇌🐾£38.50-£49.50 WB&B£142.50 WBDi£202.50 (wkly only Nov-Apr (ex Xmas-New Year)) ✱ Lunch fr£11.50&alc High tea fr£5 Dinner fr£11.50&alc LDO 9.30pm

🍴 CTV 30P
Credit Cards 1 2 3 5

MINSTER LOVELL Oxfordshire Map **04** SP31

FH QQQ Mrs K Brown **Hill Grove** *(SP314115)* OX8 5NA
☎Witney(0993) 703120
Closed Xmas
This modern, Cotswold stone farmhouse is conveniently situated just off the B4047 towards Crawley, and enjoys views over the Windrush valley. The bedrooms are comfortable and nicely equipped, and guests benefit from the friendly and warm atmosphere.
2rm(1⇌🐾) ✂in all bedrooms CTV in all bedrooms ® ✖ (ex guide dogs) dB&B£30-£32 dB&B⇌🐾£36-£38
🍴 CTV 3P 300 acres arable beef mixed £

MOFFAT Dumfries & Galloway *Dumfriesshire* Map **11** NT00

GH QQ **Barnhill Springs Country** DG10 9QS ☎(0683) 20580
Set in a peaceful, rural location but close to the A74 and town centre, this small friendly country house offers unpretentious, tidy accommodation and simple but good food.
6rm(1🐾5hc) (1fb) ® sB&B£14.50-£15.50 dB&B£29-£31 dB&B🐾£34 WB&B£101.50-£108.50 WBDi£160-£167 LDO 3pm
Lic 🍴 CTV 10P £

GH Q **Buchan** Beechgrove DG10 9HG ☎(0683) 20378
This white and stucco house is set in a quiet location on the outskirts of the town. Though undergoing improvements, some rooms with en suite facilities are available for the current season.
7rm(2⇌🐾5hc) (2fb) sB&Bfr£16 dB&Bfr£28 dB&B⇌🐾fr£32 WB&Bfr£98 WBDifr£147 LDO 5pm
🍴 CTV 10P £

SELECTED

GH QQQ **Gilbert House** Beechgrove DG10 9RS
☎(0683) 20050
Situated in a quiet residential area just 5 minutes' walk from the town centre, this well maintained guesthouse offers pleasant, comfortable and reasonably priced accommodation. High-ceilinged, well proportioned rooms are attractively decorated, and everywhere is spotlessly clean. A delicious home-cooked set dinner is offered in the most attractive dining room. Smoking is not permitted in the public rooms.
6rm(4🐾2hc) (3fb) ® sB&B£14-£15 dB&B£28-£30 dB&B⇌🐾£32 WB&B£88-£101 WBDi£144-£160 LDO 5pm
Lic 🍴 CTV 6P
Credit Cards 1 3

GH QQ **St Olaf** Eastgate, Off Dickson St DG10 9AE
☎(0683) 20001
Apr-Oct
Tucked away in a side street just off the High Street, this comfortable, well maintained house offers tranquillity and convenience for the town centre. The bedrooms are bright and cheerful, and the inviting first floor lounge is attractive and comfortable.
7rm(1🐾6hc) (3fb) ® ✱ sB&B£15 dB&B£24 dB&B🐾£26 WB&B£84
🍴 CTV 4P 4🐾 £

MOLD Clwyd Map **07** SJ26

FH QQ Mrs A Brown **Hill** *(SJ263265)* Llong CH7 4JP (on A5118 between Chester and Mold) ☎Buckley(0244) 550415
This large Georgian farmhouse stands on the A5118 in an elevated position, about 2 miles southeast of Mold, at Llong. It is well maintained and provides clean, comfortable accommodation.

3hc (1fb)⊁in all bedrooms ® ✕ (ex guide dogs) sB&B£14.50-£16 dB&B£25-£28
⑭ CTV 5P 300 acres dairy mixed

MOLESWORTH Cambridgeshire Map **04** TL07

INN Ⓠ Ⓠ Ⓠ **Cross Keys** PE18 0QF ☎Bythorn(08014) 283
A good range of bar meals and homemade dishes are prepared by Mrs Bettsworth, the friendly proprietress of this archetypal village inn, set just off the A604. It offers a high standard of accommodation, all with good en suite facilities.
4rm(1⇄3↑) Annexe 5rm(2⇄3↑) (1fb) CTV in all bedrooms ® sB&B⇄↑£18 dB&B⇄↑£28 Lunch £4-£7alc Dinner £4-£8alc LDO 10.30pm
⑭ 30P
Credit Cards ① ③

MONEYDIE Tayside *Perthshire* Map **11** NO02

FH Ⓠ Ⓠ Mrs S Walker *Moneydie Roger (NO054290)* PH1 3JA (on unclass rd signed Methven, off B8063)
☎Almondbank(073883) 239
Apr-29 Sep
This two-storeyed farmhouse is peacefully situated in a secluded position overlooking lovely countryside. It offers attractive, comfortable accommodation, with quite spacious, neatly furnished bedrooms. Genuine hospitality and excellent service are provided by the owner.
3rm(2hc) ⊁in all bedrooms ® ✕
3P nc12yrs 143 acres arable cattle sheep

MONTGOMERY Powys Map **07** SO29

FH Ⓠ Ⓠ Ⓠ Mrs G M Bright **Little Brompton** *(SO244941)* SY15 6HY ☎(0686) 668371
Little Brompton farm is a delightful early eighteenth century farmhouse with timbered walls, beamed ceilings and stone fireplaces. It has very pretty bedrooms, a comfortable lounge and fresh farm food is served in the attractive dining room. Close to Offa's Dyke it is convenient for walkers.
3rm(2↑1hc) (1fb)⊁in 1 bedroom ® sB&B£14-£16 sB&B↑£16-£17.50 dB&B£27-£30 dB&B↑£30-£34 WB&B£98-£119 WBDi£154-£168 LDO 6pm
⑭ CTV 3P 1🏇 ⚯ shooting in season 100 acres arable beef mixed sheep

---

MONTROSE Tayside *Angus* Map **15** NO75

GH Ⓠ Ⓠ *Linksgate* 11 Dorward Rd DD10 8SB ☎(0674) 72273
Close to the golf course and beach, this friendly, family-run guesthouse stands in its own gardens and provides good value holiday accommodation.
9rm(2⇄7hc) (3fb) CTV in 2 bedrooms LDO 6pm
⑭ CTV 9P

FH Ⓠ Ⓠ Mrs A Ruxton *Muirshade of Gallery (NO671634)* DD10 9JU ☎Northwaterbridge(067484) 209
Apr-Oct
Set amid pleasant scenery, 5 miles north west of the town, this cottage style farmhouse provides traditional comforts and good home cooking.
2hc (1fb) ✕ LDO 4pm
CTV 3P 175 acres arable

Street plans of certain towns and cities
will be found in a separate section
at the back of the book.

MORCHARD BISHOP Devon Map **03** SS70

SELECTED

FH Ⓠ Ⓠ Ⓠ Ⓠ Mr & Mrs S Chilcott **Wigham** *(SS757087)* EX17 6RJ ☎(03637) 350
Perched on a hillside in a delightful location overlooking the valley, this 16th-century thatched cottage is part of a small farm, and offers commendable charm, comfort and good food, nicely tempered with genuine hospitality. Sympathetic restoration has resulted in stylish, individual bedrooms, all en suite, and beautifully decorated. The lounge and dining room are equally cosy and full of charm. Fresh produce from the farm is used in the imaginative, home-cooked meals which are eagerly enjoyed at congenial and relaxed dinners. Continued good reports indicate that Wigham is a firm favourite, therefore early bookings are advisable.
5⇄↑ (1fb)⊁in all bedrooms CTV in all bedrooms ® ✕ Lic ⑭ 9P nc10yrs ⌣(heated) ∪ snooker table 31 acres mixed

See advertisement on page 259

MORECAMBE Lancashire Map **07** SD46

GH Ⓠ Ⓠ Ⓠ **Ashley Private Hotel** 371 Marine Rd Promenade East LA4 5AH ☎(0524) 412034
A very well maintained seafront hotel situated close to the town hall. Bedrooms are very well equipped, some with modern private bathrooms, and all have TV, double glazing and tea making facilities. There are fine views over the bay from the first floor lounge.
13rm(3⇄8↑2hc) (3fb) CTV in all bedrooms ® ✕ sB&B£16-£18 sB&B⇄↑£20-£22 dB&B⇄↑£38-£48 WB&B£105-£120 WBDi£140-£160 LDO 3pm
▶

Lic 쀄 5P 1🅿 (charged)
Credit Cards ⓵ ③ ⓔ

GH ⓠⓠ **Beach Mount** 395 Marine Rd East LA4 5AN
☎(0524) 420753
mid Mar-Oct
A family-run seafront hotel with clean, well maintained accommodation. The Beach Mount has a spacious dining room and a sun lounge with views over Morecambe Bay towards the Lake District fells.
26rm(22⇋4hc) (3fb) CTV in 22 bedrooms ® ✼ sB&B£17
sB&B⇋£19.25-£19.75 dB&B£30-£31 dB&B⇋£35.50-£36.50
WB&B£110 WBDifr£149 LDO 7pm
Lic 쀄 CTV 6P
Credit Cards ⓵ ② ③ ⑤

GH ⓠⓠ *Craigwell Hotel* 372 Promenade East LA4 5AH
☎(0524) 410095 & 418399
Closed 20 Dec-10 Jan
This friendly, personally-run small hotel enjoys views over Morecambe Bay's sands. The bedrooms are generally compact but comfortably furnished, well equipped and all have modern en suite facilities. Dinner features a choice of home cooked dishes, including vegetarian items.
13rm(2⇋11🅵) (2fb) CTV in all bedrooms ® LDO 9.30pm
Lic 쀄 4P
Credit Cards ⓵ ③

GH ⓠ **Ellesmere Private Hotel** 44 Westminster Rd LA4 4JD
☎(0524) 411881
A small Victorian terraced house situated in a road of similar properties away from the seafront at the western end of the town. Colour television and tea- making facilities are provided in the bedrooms and there is a cosy, attractive lounge on the ground floor.
6hc (2fb)🅵in 1 bedroom CTV in all bedrooms ®
🐕 (ex guide dogs) ✼ sB&B£11-£12.50 dB&B£22-£25
WB&B£77-£87.50 WBDif£98-£105 LDO 3pm
쀄 CTV
Credit Cards ⓵ ③ ⓔ

GH ⓠⓠ *New Hazelmere Hotel* 391 Promenade East LA4 5AN
☎(0524) 417876
May-29 Nov
The New Hazelmere is a large seafront hotel, with well maintained bedrooms all with en suite facilities. The bar features many items of nautical interest.
20rm(17⇋3🅵) (3fb) CTV in all bedrooms ® LDO 5.30pm
Lic CTV 3P

GH ⓠⓠⓠ **Hotel Prospect** 363 Marine Rd East LA4 5AQ
☎(0524) 417819
Etr-Oct
Situated on the seafront with fine views across the bay, this private hotel provides good accommodation with en suite facilities, colour television and well maintained furnishings and fittings throughout.
14⇋ (9fb) CTV in all bedrooms ® ✼ sB&Bfr£21
sB&B⇋fr£21 dB&B⇋fr£32 WB&Bfr£108 WBDifr£140
LDO 3pm
Lic 쀄 CTV 6P
Credit Cards ⓵ ③ ⓔ

GH ⓠⓠⓠ **Wimslow Private Hotel** 374 Marine Rd East
LA4 5AH ☎(0524) 417804
mid Feb-Nov & Xmas
A very well maintained, friendly seafront property with en suite facilities throughout. The first-floor dining room, the bar lounge and sun lounge offer magnificent views across the bay.
13rm(1⇋12🅵) (2fb) CTV in all bedrooms ®
sB&B⇋🅵fr£19 dB&B⇋🅵fr£38 WB&Bfr£118 WBDifr£149
LDO 4.30pm
Lic 쀄 CTV 3P 6🅿
Credit Cards ⓵ ③ ⓔ

MORETONHAMPSTEAD Devon Map **03** SX78

GH ⓠⓠⓠ **Cookshayes** 33 Court St TQ13 8LG ☎(0647) 40374
mid Mar-Oct
Standing on the edge of Dartmoor, this charming Victorian house is owned and run by Topsy and Doug Harding. Traditionally furnished, it offers a comfortable lounge, well equipped bedrooms, and a bright dining room where Topsy's imaginative cooking is served.
8rm(6🅵2hc) (1fb) CTV in all bedrooms ® ✼ sB&B£18
sB&B🅵£26 dB&B£31 dB&B🅵£36-£39 WB&B£101.50-£119
WBDi£175-£203 LDO 5.30pm
Lic 쀄 CTV 15P nc7yrs putting green
Credit Cards ⓵ ③ ⓔ

GH ⓠⓠⓠ **Moorcote** TQ13 8LS ☎(0647) 40966
Closed Xmas
A Victorian house of character set back off the road, with a small garden. Bedrooms are cosy, comfortable, individually decorated and nicely furnished, combining modern facilities with charm and character. Hearty breakfasts are popular with the numerous Dartmoor National Park walkers and tourists.
6rm(4🅵2hc) CTV in all bedrooms ® 🐕 ✼ dB&B£30
dB&B🅵£32
쀄 CTV 6P nc12yrs

FH ⓠⓠⓠ Mrs M Cuming **Wooston** *(SX764890)* TQ13 8QA
☎(0647) 40367
Mar-Oct
4hc (1fb)🅵in all bedrooms ® ✼ sB&B£13-£15 dB&B£25-£30
WBDi£133-£157.50 LDO 5pm
CTV 6P 280 acres mixed

MORETON-IN-MARSH Gloucestershire Map **04** SP13

GH ⓠⓠ **Moreton House** High St GL56 0LQ ☎(0608) 50747
A large, attractive Cotswold stone house in the town centre, opposite the end of the A44 Evesham road. Bedrooms are comfortable and well equipped, with good en suite facilities. The proprietors and staff are friendly and welcoming, while home cooking is the speciality of the tea rooms which occupy the ground floor.
12rm(5⇋🅵7hc) CTV in all bedrooms ® ✼ sB&B£19-£21
dB&B£35-£40 dB&B⇋🅵£42-£50 LDO 8pm
Lic 쀄 5P
Credit Cards ⓵ ③ ⓔ

MORFA NEFYN Gwynedd Map **06** SH23

GH ⓠ *Erw Goch Hotel* LL53 6BN ☎Nefyn(0758) 720539
Family owned and run, this detached Georgian house stands in its own grounds and provides good home comforts. The facilities provided include a three-quarter size snooker table.
15hc (5fb)
Lic 쀄 CTV 25P
Credit Cards ⓵ ③

MORTEHOE Devon Map **02** SS44

See also Woolacombe

SELECTED

GH ⓠⓠⓠⓠ **Sunnycliffe Hotel** EX34 7EB
☎Woolacombe(0271) 870597
Feb-Nov
A small, cosy hotel in an elevated hillside position, with commanding views across the sandy beach and out to sea. Spotlessly clean and comfortable bedrooms boast the additional benefit of individual videos to complement the excellent range of creature comforts. Public rooms are of a similar standard, with pleasing décor, co-ordinating fabrics and glorous sea views. Good quality, traditional fresh food is served. The hotel is well situated for moorland and coastal
▶

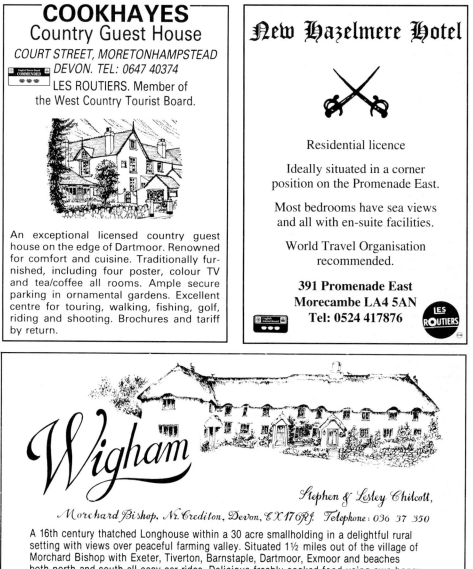

walks, and is a good base for touring North Devon and Cornwall.
8rm(4⇌4♠) ⊠in 4 bedrooms CTV in all bedrooms ® ✗ dB&B⇌♠£46-£58 WB&B£147-£170 WBDi£194-£250 LDO 6pm
Lic ䷀ 10P nc

MOUNT Cornwall & Isles of Scilly Map **02** SX16

GH QQ Mount Pleasant Farm Hotel PL30 4EX ☎Cardinham(020882) 342
Apr-Sep
Peaceful farmland surrounds this remote hotel which enjoys lovely views across the Glyn Valley. Accommodation comprises two lounges, a separate bar and dining-room, plus a choice of bedrooms.
7rm(1⇌5♠1hc) (1fb) ® ✗ ✻ WB&B£90-£125 WBDi£120-£155 LDO 4pm
Lic ䷀ CTV 10P £

MOUSEHOLE Cornwall & Isles of Scilly Map **02** SW42

GH QQQ Tavis Vor TR19 6PR ☎Penzance(0736) 731306
A delightful country house style guesthouse, standing in its own grounds running down to the sea, with commanding and unrestricted views out to St Michaels Mount and across the bay. Bedrooms are bright, cosy and well equipped, and public rooms are comfortable.
8rm(3♠5hc) (1fb) CTV in all bedrooms ® sB&B£20-£22 dB&B£40-£43 dB&B♠£47-£49 WB&B£140-£175 WBDi£206.50-£241.50 LDO 5pm
Lic ䷀ 7P nc5yrs

MUDDIFORD Devon Map **02** SS53

FH QQQ Mrs M Lethaby **Home Park** *(SS553360)* Lower Blakewell EX31 4ET ☎Barnstaple(0271) 42955
Half a mile from the B3230, 3 miles from Barnstaple, this small farmhouse has marvellous views over rolling countryside. The bright bedrooms offer a high standard of modern accommodation, and are fully en suite. The well-kept gardens have a play area and Wendy house.
3rm(2⇌1♠) (2fb) CTV in all bedrooms ® ✗ (ex guide dogs) ✻ sB&B⇌♠£15 dB&B⇌♠£25-£30 WB&B£95 WBDi£120-£130 (wkly only Jul-Aug) LDO 4pm
䷀ CTV 3P ⌂ 70 acres sheep & beef £

MUIR OF ORD Highland *Ross & Cromarty* Map **14** NH55

SELECTED

GH QQQQ The Dower House Highfield IV6 7XN ☎(0463) 870090
Closed 1 wk Oct & 2 wks Feb/Mar
A house party atmosphere prevails at Robyn and Mena Aitchison's delightful cottage home which has been sympathetically converted to create a haven of peaceful relaxation for the touring holidaymaker. Day rooms, though limited in extent, are tastefully appointed and traditionally furnished, with chintzy seating, well filled bookshelves and a welcoming fire in the elegant lounge. Bedrooms are individually decorated and furnished to provide a high standard of comfort, and equipped with thoughtful extras. Robyn is a talented chef who cooks in the modern style, his short fixed-price menu offers dishes which will please the most discerning palates. The wine list is extensive and well chosen.
5rm(4⇌1♠) (1fb) CTV in all bedrooms sB&B⇌♠£45-£70 dB&B⇌♠£90-£100 WB&B£283.50-£441 WBDi£459-£616 LDO 8.30pm
Lic ䷀ 20P
Credit Cards [1] [3]

MULL, ISLE OF Strathclyde *Argyllshire* Map **10**

BUNESSAN Map **10** NM32

GH QQQ ***Ardachy*** PA67 6DR ☎Fionnphort(06817) 505 & 506
The original farmhouse has been tastefully converted and extended to provide accommodation which is modern and comfortable. Just minutes from a fine sandy beach, Ardachy has panoramic views to Jura and the mainland.
8rm(7♠1hc) (2fb) ® LDO 6pm
Lic ䷀ CTV 8P ♪ shooting
Credit Cards [1] [3]

SALEN Map **10** NM54

GH QQQ ***Craig Hotel*** PA72 6JG ☎Aros(0680) 300347 & 300451
Etr-15 Oct
A cosy little roadside hotel on the northern edge of the village, with gardens to the rear and a burn flowing by its side. The lounge, with a wood-burning stove, is equipped with lots of games and books; the small dining room is pine furnished. Bedrooms are neat and comfortable.
6hc LDO 7.15pm
Lic CTV 7P
Credit Cards [1] [3]

MUMBLES West Glamorgan Map **02** SS68

See also Bishopston & Langland Bay
GH QQ Harbour Winds Private Hotel Overland Road, Langland SA3 4LP ☎Swansea(0792) 369298
Situated in an elevated position with good garden and sea views, this spacious hotel, with good comfortable bedrooms, has very friendly and welcoming owners. Good food is served in an attractive, panelled dining room, and the lounge is very relaxing.
8rm(1⇌5♠2hc) (3fb) ® ✻ sB&B⇌♠£21-£25 dB&B£40-£45 dB&B⇌♠£50 WBDi£164-£175 LDO noon
Lic ䷀ CTV 14P nc5yrs
Credit Cards [3] £
See advertisement under SWANSEA

GH Q ***Mumbles Hotel*** 650 Mumbles Rd, SA3 4EA ☎Swansea(0792) 367147
Closed 23 Dec-3 Jan
Situated on the seafront and overlooking Swansea Bay and the harbour, this small guesthouse provides modestly appointed accommodation which is always clean and bright. There is a lounge on the first floor with lovely views, and a popular coffee shop providing meals and snacks all day during the season.
8rm(4♠4hc) (1fb) CTV in all bedrooms ® ✗ LDO 9pm
Lic ䷀ CTV P̸ nc3 yrs
Credit Cards [1] [3]

GH QQQ The Shoreline Hotel 648 Mumbles Road, Southend SA3 4EA ☎Swansea(0792) 366233
This pretty guesthouse is situated opposite the harbour and has good views of the bay. It provides modern and well equipped bedrooms, an attractive restaurant, and an open plan lounge and bar.
14rm(5♠9hc) (1fb) CTV in all bedrooms ® ✻ sB&B£18 sB&B♠£25-£35 dB&B£28-£34 dB&B♠£36-£46 LDO 9.30pm
Lic ䷀ CTV P̸ nc3yrs
Credit Cards [1] £

MUNGRISDALE Cumbria Map **11** NY33

FH QQQ Mr G Weightman ***Near Howe*** *(NY286373)* CA11 0SH (1.5m from the A66) ☎Threlkeld(059683) 678
Mar-Nov
This delightful farmhouse is set in beautiful countryside and moorland. The house is very well appointed and a good standard of food is provided.

7rm(5♠2hc)(3fb)® ✗ LDO 5pm
Lic ♕ CTV 10P snooker 350 acres beef sheep

INN 🇶🇶 *The Mill* CA11 0XR ☎(07687) 79632
*This peaceful, 16th-century inn is on the banks of the River
Glendermakin. Full of character, the bar, with its lovely central
open fire, serves popular snacks cooked by Christine Seal, who also
provides the equally popular residents' meals.*
7rm(2⇌1♠4hc)® LDO 8.30pm
♕ CTV 30P pool table
Credit Cards ③

NAILSWORTH Gloucestershire Map **03** ST89

GH 🇶🇶🇶 Apple Orchard House Orchard Close, Springhill
GL6 0LX ☎(045383) 2503
*Situated close to the town centre, this house offers very comfortable
and well equipped bedrooms, all with en suite or private facilties,
and bright, attractive public areas that include an inviting garden.*
3⇌♠ ⅙in all bedrooms CTV in all bedrooms ® ✲
sB&B⇌♠£18-£20 dB&B⇌♠£27-£28 WB&B£94.50-£98
WBDif£103.50-£107 LDO 10am
♕ CTV 3P ⓔ

NAIRN Highland *Nairnshire* Map **14** NH85

GH 🇶🇶 Ardgour Hotel Seafield St IV12 4HN ☎(0667) 54230
Mar-Oct
*Situated in a quiet residential area not far from the seafront, this
friendly family-run holiday hotel has a friendly atmosphere and
offers traditional services and comforts.*
10hc (2fb) ® sB&Bfr£15 dB&Bfr£26 WB&Bfr£86
WBDifr£119 LDO 5pm
♕ CTV 8P

GH 🇶🇶🇶 Greenlawns 13 Seafield St IV12 4HG
☎(0667) 52738
*This friendly guesthouse is close to the beaches and recreational
facilities. It offers good value holiday accommodation with a
comfortable, quiet lounge and an interesting gallery featuring local
artist's work – including that of Isobel Caldwell, wife of the
proprietor.*
6rm(2⇌♠4hc) CTV in all bedrooms ® ✲ sB&Bfr£17
dB&B£32-£34 dB&B⇌♠£34-£36 WB&B£100-£107
♕ CTV 8P
Credit Cards ①③ⓔ

NANTWICH Cheshire Map **07** SJ65

See also Wybunbury

FH 🇶🇶🇶 Mrs S Allwood *Burland* (*SJ604534*) Wrexham
Rd, Burland CW5 8ND (3m W A534) ☎Faddiley(027074) 210
Closed 19 Dec-1 Jan
*Three miles west of the town on the A534 Wrexham Road, this
attractive house in its mature grounds, has been in the proprietor's
family since it was built 200 years ago.*
3⇌♠ in all bedrooms ® LDO 7pm
♕ 5P nc10yrs bicycles croquet 205 acres arable dairy
Credit Cards ②

NARBOROUGH Norfolk Map **09** TF71

INN 🇶🇶 *Ship* Swaffham Rd PE32 1TE ☎(0760) 337307
*The inn is situated opposite the trout farm on the main A47 King's
Lynn – Norwich road, beside a delightful stream. There is an oak-
panelled lounge bar and a small restaurant serving freshly
prepared and well presented meals.*
6⇌♠ CTV in all bedrooms
50P 3🐾 ♪

Book as early as possible for busy holiday periods.

NEAR SAWREY Cumbria Map **07** SD38

GH 🇶🇶🇶 Buckle Yeat LA22 0LF
☎Hawkshead(09666) 446 & 538
*A charming 200-year-old cottage, illustrated in Beatrix Potter's
'Tale of Tom Kitten'. It is now a very attractive guesthouse, with
log fires, beams and spotless bedrooms and tea-making facilities.
Full of character, there is a very old kitchen stove in the spacious
dining room. There is also a comfortable lounge for residents and
morning coffee and afternoon teas are served. Adequate parking is
provided.*
6rm(2⇌3♠)® ✲ sB&B⇌♠£16-£18 dB&B⇌♠£32-£36
WB&B£224-£250
♕ CTV 10P

SELECTED

GH 🇶🇶🇶🇶 Ees Wyke Country House LA22 0JZ
☎Hawkshead(09666) 393
*A beautiful Georgian country house set in its own grounds
overlooking Esthwaite Water, to which its name Ees Wyke:
'East of the Lake' refers. The house has superb views of the
lake, the nearby fells and, in the distance, Langdale Pike.
Bedrooms are spacious, comfortable and well furnished, all
with views of the surrounding countryside. Beatrix Potter used
to stay here, and the present owners John and Margaret
Williams offer a warm welcome to all their guests.*
8⇌♠ CTV in all bedrooms ® dB&B⇌♠£56-£64
LDO 7.15pm
Lic ♕ 12P nc12yrs
See advertisement under HAWKSHEAD

SELECTED

GH 🇶🇶🇶🇶 *The Garth* LA22 0JZ
☎Hawkshead(09666) 373
Closed Dec & Jan
*This delightful Victorian country house retains the charm and
elegance of its period and is set in its own grounds, with fine
views from the house which overlooks Esthwaite Lake, and is
also close to the village associated with Beatrix Potter.
Bedrooms are attractively furnished, and the charming lounge
has a log fire. Dinner is home cooked using fresh produce and
is served in the dining room.*
7rm(2♠5hc)(1fb) CTV in 4 bedrooms ® LDO 4pm
Lic ♕ CTV 10P nc6yrs ♣
See advertisement under HAWKSHEAD

GH 🇶🇶 High Green Gate LA22 0LF ☎Hawkshead(09666) 296
Mar-Oct rs Xmas & New Year
*An 18th-century farmhouse, converted into a comfortable and
attractive guesthouse, situated in a peaceful hamlet between
Windermere and Esthwaite Water.*
5rm(1⇌2♠2hc) (4fb) sB&B£17-£20 dB&B£46 dB&B⇌♠£52
WB&B£105-£126 WBDif£147.50-£164 LDO 6pm
♕ CTV 7P ♣ⓔ

GH 🇶🇶 Sawrey House Country Hotel LA22 0LF
☎Hawkshead(09666) 387
*An attractive, large house standing in its own grounds of 3 acres,
with magnificent views over Esthwaite Lake and Coniston Fells
beyond. It is very well furnished, and a warm and friendly welcome
is always provided by the resident owner.*
10rm(4⇌3♠3hc) (3fb) ® sB&B£22.50 dB&B£45
dB&B⇌♠£52 WB&B£147-£172 WBDif£217-£241 LDO 4pm
Lic ♕ CTV 15P croquet lawn ⓔ

NEATH West Glamorgan Map **03** SS79

GH 🆀🆀 **Europa Hotel** 32/34 Victoria Gardens SA11 3BH
☎(0639) 635094
Closed Xmas
Standing opposite the Victoria Gardens close to the town centre,
this hotel offers bright bedrooms with modern facilities, and a
relaxing lounge and bar.
12hc (2fb) CTV in all bedrooms ® ✖ (ex guide dogs) ✱
sB&B£15 dB&B£28
Lic 🕮 CTV 3P
Credit Cards 1 3 £

NEATISHEAD Norfolk Map **09** TG32

GH 🆀🆀 **Regency** Neatishead Post Office Stores NR12 8AD
☎Horning(0692) 630233
A 17th century house situated in a popular and picturesque village,
ideal for touring the coast or the Broads. Bedrooms are prettily
decorated, comfortable and well maintained; some en suite
facilities are available.
5rm(1⇆4hc) (2fb) CTV in all bedrooms ® sB&Bfr£19
dB&Bfr£32 dB&B⇆fr£38
CTV 6P £

NEEDHAM MARKET Suffolk Map **05** TM05

SELECTED

GH 🆀🆀🆀🆀 *Pipps Ford* Norwich Rd Rdbt IP6 8LJ
(entrance off rdbt junct A45/A140)
☎Coddenham(044979) 208
Closed Xmas & New Year
A lovely Tudor house set in totally secluded grounds on the
bank of the river Gipping. The bedrooms offer a unique style of
comfort and décor, with handmade soft furnishings; all the
rooms are en suite. This same quality and character is evident
in the public areas: the timbered lounge with an inglenook
fireplace, and either the dining room or conservatory in which
to dine. The house is found by taking the A45/A140
intersection, with access immediately off the roundabout on
the Needham Market side.
3⇆🀆 Annexe 4⇆🀆 ✄in all bedrooms ®
✖ (ex guide dogs) LDO noon
Lic 🕮 CTV 12P nc5yrs ⇨♪(hard)♪

NETLEY Hampshire Map **04** SU40

GH 🆀🆀 **La Casa Blanca** SO3 5DQ
☎Southampton(0703) 453718
Closed Xmas & New Year
Three miles from the centre of Southampton, this friendly
guesthouse has cosy accommodation with pretty, well equipped
bedrooms. It provides bed and breakfast only.
10rm(1🀆9hc) (1fb) CTV in all bedrooms ® ✖ (ex guide dogs)
✱ sB&Bfr£20 sB&B🀆fr£30 dB&Bfr£32 dB&B🀆fr£40
WB&Bfr£112 WBDifr£140 LDO 9.30pm
Lic 🕮 CTV 2P 1🏠
Credit Cards 1 3 £

NETTLEBED Oxfordshire Map **04** SU68

GH 🆀🆀🆀 **Chessall Shaw** Newnham Hill RG9 5TN (2.5m S)
☎(0491) 641311 FAX (0491) 641819
The house is situated along a track on Newham Hill: very detailed
and exact directions are provided by the proprietors, who have
opened their home to guests and offer 2 very comfortable, pretty
and exceptionally well equipped bedrooms. Every comfort for
guests has been considered and provided throughout, and any
additional requirements are met willingly. The house is decorated
with style and flair and enjoys an enviable setting amongst very
pretty coutryside. The establishment is rather difficult to find, and
it is strongly advised to telephone for directions.

2⇆🀆 (2fb) CTV in all bedrooms ® dB&B⇆🀆£35-£44
WB&Bfr£140 WBDifr£230 LDO am
🕮 CTV 6P ⚙ ⇨(heated) ♪(hard) £

NETTLECOMBE Dorset Map **03** SY59

INN 🆀🆀 **The Marquis of Lorne** DT6 3SY
☎Powerstock(030885) 236
Closed Xmas Day
Situated in a rural village surrounded by rolling countryside, this
friendly inn has small cosy bars, one with a log fire and panelling.
There is an à la carte menu offered in the dining room which is
popular with locals. Bedrooms provide some modern facilities:
those in the older part of the house have more character.
6rm(4🀆2hc) (2fb) CTV in 1 bedroom ® ✖ (ex guide dogs)
sB&B£21-£23 sB&B🀆£22-£25 dB&B£41-£46 dB&B🀆£44-£50
WB&B£122.50-£140 WBDi£175-£217 Lunch £13.50-£19.95alc
Dinner £13.50-£19.95alc LDO 9.30pm
CTV 65P
Credit Cards 1 3 £

NETTLETON Wiltshire Map **03** ST87

SELECTED

GH 🆀🆀🆀🆀 **Fosse Farmhouse Country Hotel** Nettleton
Shrub SN14 7NJ ☎Castle Combe(0249) 782286
An old farmhouse lovingly restored by the owner into a very
comfortable guesthouse with an individual style, situated in
Nettleton Shrub in rolling wooded countryside, overlooking
the golf course. Each bedroom is individually furnished and
decorated with simple country furnishings and many
thoughtful extras provided. There are 3 en suite rooms in the
farmhouse, and 3 additional rooms in an adjacent converted
stable block; on the ground floor of the stable block, cream
teas are served daily in an attractive breakfast/tea room. A 3-
course dinner includes a choice of starter and pudding with a
set main course, using fresh local ingredients and garden
herbs.
2⇆🀆 Annexe 3🀆 CTV in all bedrooms ® sB&B⇆🀆£35-
£45 dB&B⇆🀆£65-£95 WB&B£200-£250 WBDi£285-£335
LDO 8.30pm
Lic 🕮 10P ⚙ ♟ 18
Credit Cards 1 2 3 £

NEWARK-ON-TRENT Nottinghamshire
See **Kirton** and **Laxton**

NEWBOLD ON STOUR Warwickshire Map **04** SP24

FH 🆀🆀 Mrs J M Everett **Newbold Nurseries** *(SP253455)*
CV37 8DP ☎(0789) 450285
Mar-29 Oct
A modern farmhouse with a long, pine-lined drive offering
spacious, simply appointed bed and breakfast accommodation.
Convenient for tourists, it is situated half a mile north of the A429
roundabout on the A34.
2rm(1hc) (1fb) CTV in all bedrooms ® dB&Bfr£28
WB&Bfr£90
🕮 CTV 2P 25 acres arable tomato nursery £

NEWBROUGH Northumberland Map **12** NY86

GH 🆀🆀 **The Stanegate** NE47 5AR ☎Hexham(0434) 674241
A well furnished guesthouse and restaurant situated in the centre
of the village on the Stanegate Roman road. The bedrooms have
good facilities, and a wide range of food is available in the
restaurant. Family owned and run, it offers good hospitality.
3⇆ ✄in all bedrooms CTV in all bedrooms ✱ sB&B⇆£31-£40
dB&B⇆£46-£51
🕮 10P
Credit Cards 1 3

NEWBY BRIDGE Cumbria Map **07** SD38

GH Q Q **Furness Fells** LA12 8ND ☎(05395) 31260
Mar-Oct
An attractive, small and friendly guesthouse near the southern outfall of Lake Windermere. Comfortably furnished, it provides good accommodation with an annexe overlooking a large well tended garden.
4hc Annexe 2♠ ® ✹ dB&B£28-£30 dB&B♠£35-£37
Lic ♨ CTV 8P nc3yrs £

NEWCASTLE-UNDER-LYME Staffordshire Map **07** SJ84

GH Q Q Q **Clayton Farmhouse** The Green, Clayton ST5 4AA
☎(0782) 620401
An easy-to-find hotel, just off junction 15 of the M6, half a mile along the A519 to Newcastle. Although alongside the road, the house has a rural setting and a quiet relaxed atmosphere.
5rm(1⇨2♠2hc) (2fb) CTV in all bedrooms ®
✹ (ex guide dogs) sB&B£22.50 sB&B⇨♠£24-£26 dB&B£32
dB&B⇨♠£34-£36 LDO 1pm
♨ CTV 12P
Credit Cards 1 3 £

NEWCASTLE UPON TYNE Tyne & Wear Map **12** NZ26

GH Q Q Q **Chirton House Hotel** 46 Clifton Rd NE4 6XH
☎091-273 0407
A large semi-detached Victorian house situated to the west of the city, near the hospital and the new western by-pass. Bedrooms are spacious, attractively furnished and decorated and very comfortable. The lounges are equally pleasant, and there is a cosy bar.
11rm(2⇨3♠6hc) (3fb) CTV in all bedrooms ® sB&B£22-£24
sB&B⇨♠£32 dB&B£36 dB&B⇨♠£45 WB&B£120-£180
WBDi£150-£250 LDO 5.30pm
Lic ♨ CTV 12P
Credit Cards 1 3 £

GH Q **Clifton Cottage** Dunholme Rd NE4 6XE ☎091-273 7347
A semidetached Victorian house near the Newcastle General hospital and within easy reach of the city centre. The accommodation is simple but comfortable; there is a first-floor lounge, and a small conservatory downstairs overlooking the garden.
6hc (2fb) CTV in all bedrooms ® sB&B£16 dB&B£28
♨ CTV 6P £

NEWDIGATE Surrey Map **04** TQ14

GH Q **Woods Hill Country** Village St RH5 5AD ☎(030677) 437
Compact, functional accommodation is offered here with a choice of modern bedrooms and a breakfast room. Light refreshments are served throughout the day, and car parking facilities can be arranged.
4rm(1⇨1♠2hc) (2fb)✗in all bedrooms CTV in all bedrooms
® ✹ ✹ sB&B£25 dB&B£32 dB&B⇨♠£35
♨ CTV 10P
Credit Cards 1 3

NEWHAVEN East Sussex Map **05** TQ40

GH Q Q **Harbour View** 22 Mount Rd BN9 0LS
☎Brighton(0273) 512096
3hc (2fb)✗in 2 bedrooms CTV in 2 bedrooms TV in 1
bedroom ® ✹ (ex guide dogs) ✹ sB&B£15-£17 dB&B£28-£30
WB&B£84
♨ 3P

GH Q Q Q **Newhaven Marina Yacht Club Hotel** Fort Gate,
Fort Rd BN9 9DR ☎(0273) 513976 FAX (0273) 517990
Closed 3 wks Jan
The Newhaven Marina offers bright, fresh bedrooms with modern furniture and attractive co-ordinated fabrics. The Yacht Club bar is open to residents and an extensive range of bar food is available.

The Riverside Restaurant has an à la carte menu featuring fresh fish. There are views of the docks and marina from the terrace.
7rm(1♠6hc) CTV in all bedrooms ® ✹ ✹ sB&B£28 dB&B£42
dB&B⇨♠£50 WBDi£190 LDO 9.30pm/10.30pm
Lic ♨ 50P Marina facilities
Credit Cards 1 3

NEWLYN EAST Cornwall & Isles of Scilly Map **02** SW85

FH Q Q Q Mrs K Woodley **Degembris** *(SW852568)* TR8 5HY
☎Mitchell(0872) 510555
Etr-Oct
This 17th-century slate hung farmhouse has open country views. Mrs Woodley uses home-grown vegetables in her traditional farmhouse fare, and guests can enjoy the 'country trail' through a beautiful wooded valley. The establishment is 'A Cream of Cornwall' member.
5hc (2fb) CTV in all bedrooms ® ✹ ✹ sB&B£14-£16
dB&B£28-£32 WB&B£98-£112 WBDi£147-£161 LDO 10am
CTV 8P 165 acres arable

NEWMARKET Suffolk Map **05** TL66

See also Kirtling
GH Q Q Q **Live & Let Live** 76 High St, Stetchworth CB8 9TJ
☎(0638) 508153
Closed 20 Dec-3 Jan
This old flintstone inn is now a comfortable guesthouse, situated just over two miles south of Newmarket in the centre of a quiet village. The accommodation is clean and well maintained, each room having its own individual, co-ordinated colour theme. Smoking is not permitted in any area except the TV lounge.
7rm(2⇨♠5hc) (1fb)✗in all bedrooms ® ✹ ✹ sB&B£16-£17
sB&B⇨♠£24 dB&B£30-£32 dB&B⇨♠£34-£36 WB&Bfr£107
WBDifr£154
♨ CTV 5P nc10yrs
Credit Cards 1 3 £

Hill Farm

Kirtling, Nr Newmarket, Suffolk CB8 9HQ
Telephone: (0638) 730253

A 400 year old farmhouse which commands superb views, offers spacious well appointed accommodation. All rooms have tea/coffee facilities and some en suite. Full central heating. Access at all times — own key. Choice of menu with home cooking and special diets catered for by prior arrangement. Fully licensed. Open all year.

NEWPORT Gwent Map **03** ST38

GH 🇶🇶 **Caerleon House Hotel** Caerau Rd NP9 4HJ
☎(0633) 264869
This well maintained guesthouse has been run for many years by the very friendly Powell family, and it is within walking distance of the town centre. The bedrooms are modern and all have private bathrooms. There is a small bar/lounge for residents.
7➪🟤 (1fb) CTV in all bedrooms ® sB&B➪🟤£25-£30 dB&B➪🟤£40-£42 LDO 9pm
Lic 🎮 8P ⓔ

GH 🇶🇶🇶 **Kepe Lodge** 46a Caerau Rd NP9 4HH
☎(0633) 262351
Closed 22-31 Dec
This neat, well maintained house is set back from the road with a tree-lined private drive, and stands away from the town centre. A comfortable lounge is available for residents, and bedrooms are all well furnished and equipped.
8rm(3🟤5hc) CTV in all bedrooms ® ✖ (ex guide dogs) ✳ sB&Bfr£17 sB&B🟤fr£20 dB&B🟤fr£30
🎮 8P ⓔ

GH 🇶🇶 **Knoll** 145 Stow Hill NP9 4FZ ☎(0633) 263557
Situated near the main shopping centre on Stow Hill, this large Victorian house retains many of its original features. It offers comfortable and well equipped bedrooms and a spacious, relaxing guest lounge.
7rm(5➪🟤2hc) (1fb) CTV in all bedrooms ® ✳ sB&Bfr£22 dB&Bfr£34
🎮 6🍴 ⓔ

NEWPORT PAGNELL Buckinghamshire Map **04** SP84

GH 🇶🇶🇶 **Thurstons Private Hotel** 90 High St MK16 8EH
☎(0908) 611377
A substantial town house in the High Street of Newport Pagnell. The bedrooms are simply appointed, well equipped and spotlessly clean. Breakfast is served in an informal restaurant adjacent to a small lounge area.
8rm(2➪6🟤) CTV in all bedrooms ® ✖ (ex guide dogs) ✳ sB&B➪🟤£27-£42 dB&B➪🟤£37-£50
Lic 🎮 14P
Credit Cards 1️⃣ 3️⃣

NEWQUAY Cornwall & Isles of Scilly Map **02** SW86

See **Town Plan Section**
See also **Newlyn East**
GH 🇶🇶 **Aloha** 124 Henver Rd TR7 3EQ ☎(0637) 878366
Closed Dec
Conveniently situated on the A3058 Henver road, this well maintained guesthouse has been skilfully extended, and all bedrooms are modern, each with TV. There is also a TV lounge, separate bar and a well appointed dining room. Home-cooked food is offered on an à la carte menu, and service is friendly and helpful. There are plans to extend the bar lounge with a conservatory, and forecourt car parking is provided.
14rm(6🟤8hc) CTV in all bedrooms ® ✳ sB&B£11-£15 dB&B£22-£30 dB&B🟤£26-£34 WB&B£66-£90 (wkly only Jul & Aug) LDO 6pm
Lic 🎮 CTV 14P
Credit Cards 1️⃣ 3️⃣

GH 🇶🇶 **Arundell Hotel** Mount Wise TR7 2BS
☎(0637) 872481
This very informal, family-run hotel has recently been renovated, and offers excellent indoor facilities. The spacious bar has live entertainment and dancing, and an entertainment programme is provided six nights a week throughout the main season. The bedrooms are slowly being upgraded.

36➪🟤 (8fb) CTV in all bedrooms ® ✳ sB&B➪🟤£17-£31 dB&B➪🟤£34-£56 WB&B£119.70-£194.49 WBDi£140.70-£216.49 LDO 6pm
Lic lift 🎮 CTV 32P 8🍴 🖃(heated) snooker sauna solarium gymnasium
Credit Cards 1️⃣ 2️⃣ 3️⃣

GH 🇶🇶 **Bon-Ami Hotel** 3 Trenance Ln TR7 2HX
☎(0637) 874009
Apr-Sep
This well established family-run guesthouse is set in a very peaceful location overlooking the boating lakes and park. Some bedrooms are rather compact but are furnished in the modern style, and public rooms include a small TV lounge, a bar, sun porch and spacious dining room. Varied menus, extensive service and good value are provided by the friendly and helpful proprietors.
9🟤 ® ✳ sB&B🟤£14-£18 dB&B🟤£28-£36 WB&B£96-£124 WBDi£121-£149 LDO 8pm
Lic 🎮 CTV 9P nc11yrs

GH 🇶🇶🇶 **Copper Beech Hotel** 70 Edgcumbe Av TR7 2NN
☎(0637) 873376
Etr-mid Oct
Mr & Mrs Lentern have run this hotel with care for the past 16 years. Quietly situated opposite Trenance Gardens, it provides well appointed accommodation with bright, airy bedrooms and a very attractive bar lounge.
14rm(3➪11🟤) (3fb) ® ✖ ✳ sB&B➪🟤£17.75-£18.80 dB&B➪🟤£35.50-£37.60 WB&B£123-£131 WBDi£147-£173 (wkly only Jun-Aug) LDO 6pm
Lic 🎮 CTV 14P

GH 🇶🇶 *Fistral Beach Hotel* Esplanade Road, Pentire
TR7 1QA ☎(0637) 850626
Mar-Nov & Xmas
This hotel has been fully modernised and has exceptional views over Fistral Beach. Modern, well equipped bedrooms and a charming dining room make this an ideal holiday retreat.
16rm(5➪11🟤) (2fb) CTV in all bedrooms ® LDO 7.30pm
Lic 🎮 CTV 14P nc4yrs 🖃(heated)
Credit Cards 1️⃣ 2️⃣ 3️⃣

GH 🇶🇶 *Hepworth Hotel* 27 Edgcumbe Av TR7 2NJ
☎(0637) 873686
Apr-Oct
A well maintained guesthouse comprising modern, bright, double-glazed bedrooms, a cosy, comfortable TV lounge, a cheerful dining room and a separate bar. Outside there is a sun lounge and front garden, and cream teas are available on sunny days. This modern family hotel is in a good location set back from the front but still within walking distance of local amenities. Good car parking facilities are available.
13rm(4🟤9hc) (4fb) CTV in all bedrooms ® ✖ (wkly only Jul & Aug) LDO 6.30pm
Lic 🎮 CTV 12P

GH 🇶🇶 *Jonel* 88-90 Crantock St TR7 1JW ☎(0637) 875084
Within easy reach of the town centre and beaches, this family-run property has bright bedrooms, a cosy bar and lounge and an informal dining room which offers a table d'hôte menu.
12hc (1fb) CTV in 11 bedrooms TV in 1 bedroom ® ✖ LDO 4.30pm
Lic CTV 7P

GH 🇶🇶 *Kellsboro Hotel* 12 Henver Rd TR7 3BJ
☎(0637) 874620
Etr-Oct
Well appointed family hotel, close to beaches.
14rm(10➪3🟤1hc) (8fb)✖ in all bedrooms CTV in all bedrooms ® LDO 7pm
Lic 🎮 20P 🖃(heated)

GH ⓆⓆ *Links Hotel* Headland Rd TR7 1HN ☎(0637) 873211
Apr-Oct
Conveniently located on the Towan Headland, within easy reach of the town, beaches and golf course, this hotel has some rooms with views of the golf course and the sea. Bedrooms are simply furnished and equipped, well maintained and bright, with simple décor. The friendly and informal atmosphere is augmented by a lively bar, pool room and reception facilities.
15rm(10⇌3♪2hc) (3fb) CTV in all bedrooms ® (wkly only Jul & Aug) LDO 4pm
Lic ♥♥ CTV ⚘

GH ⓆⓆ *Pendeen Hotel* Alexandra Road, Porth TR7 3ND
☎(0637) 873521
Mar-Nov
A modern, family-run hotel which has been under the same ownership for many years. The accommodation comprises a choice of functional bedrooms, some with very compact showers and en suite facilities. A very small TV lounge augments a cosy bar and alcoved dining room, where a daily roast is provided at dinner. Coin-operated TVs are provided in the bedrooms, and three of the rooms have recently been refurbished. The hotel is in a good location, only 200 yards from Porth beach and bay.
15rm(6⇌9♪) (5fb)⚥in 3 bedrooms CTV in all bedrooms ®
✖ sB&B⇌3♪£15.50-£20 dB&B⇌3♪£30-£38 WB&B£92-£172 WBDi£112-£192 LDO 6pm
Lic ♥♥ CTV 15P
Credit Cards ②ⓔ

GH ⓆⓆⓆ *Porth Enodoc* 4 Esplanade Road, Pentire TR7 1PY
☎(0637) 872372
Apr-Oct

▶

KEPE LODGE

46A Caerau Road, Newport
Gwent NP9 4HH   Tel: (0633) 262351

Comfortable house in quiet residential area within easy walking distance of the town centre (only 5 minutes away from Junction 27 of the M4). Pleasant garden and ample car parking within grounds.
8 rooms – 5 single, 1 double and 2 twins (double & twin rooms have ensuite facilities).
All rooms feature central heating, H&C, shaver point, tea and coffee making facilities, colour TV and radio/alarm. Hair driers and ironing facility available on request.
Good English breakfast a speciality, but most requirements can be catered for.

Non-smoking dining room and guest lounge.

Full fire certificate and smoke alarm in all bedrooms.

Proprietors: Ken and Peggy Long.

WTB – Highly Commended Award

PENDEEN HOTEL
Alexandra Road, Porth, Newquay
Cornwall TR7 3ND
Telephone: (0637) 873521

Tastefully furnished hotel 150 yds from Porth Beach. Personally supervised by the owners who have been resident at the Pendeen for 28 years. A friendly atmosphere always assured.

Fully centrally heated. All bedrooms en suite with colour T.V. and tea/coffee making facilities. Private car park. Mid-week bookings accepted.

Fire certificate. Send stamp for colour brochure.

Proprietors – Mr & Mrs D. Woodfinden.

CAERLEON HOUSE HOTEL
Caerau Road, Newport,
Gwent NP9 4HJ
Telephone: 0633 264869

Small private Hotel situated within ½ mile of the town centre and 1 mile from M4 junction 27.
All bedrooms have full en suite facilities, colour TV and welcome trays etc.
Personally supervised for the past 23 years by the resident owners Wendy and Wally Powell.
Meals available in the bar
Full central heating
Car parking
Open all the year

♚ ♚ ♚   W.T.B.

This elegant property stands in gardens overlooking Fistral Beach. 16 attractive en suite bedrooms are complemented by a quiet lounge and cosy bar, and set meals are served every evening in the relaxed atmosphere of the dining room.
14🛏 Annexe 2rm(1⇌1🛏) (4fb) TV available 🐾
sB&B⇌🛏£19.50-£23.50 dB&B⇌🛏£38-£43 WBDi£125-£165 (wkly only Jun-Sep) LDO 5.30pm
Lic 🍴 CTV 16P £

GH |Q||Q||Q| **Priory Lodge Hotel** Mount Wise TR7 2BH
☎(0637) 874111
Apr-Oct & Xmas rs Mar & Nov
Overlooking the town and the distant sea, this popular family-run hotel has a friendly atmosphere. The bedrooms are decorated and furnished to a high standard, all with direct dial telephones and most with attractive en suite bath/shower rooms. There are attractive surroundings in which to relax, have a drink, enjoy the entertainment or to select a dish from the table d'hôte menu. The outdoor heated pool and patio area are popular with families.
22rm(7⇌13🛏2hc) Annexe 4🛏 (17fb) CTV in all bedrooms ®
sB&B£32-£35 sB&B⇌🛏£35-£38 dB&B£62-£70
dB&B⇌🛏£70-£76 (incl dinner) WB&B£110-£170 WBDi£150-£200 LDO 7.30pm
Lic 🍴 CTV 30P ⊇(heated) sauna solarium pool table video machines £

GH |Q||Q| **Rolling Waves** Alexandra Rd, Porth TR7 3NB
☎(0637) 873236
Etr-Nov Closed 2 days Xmas rs Dec-Etr
Overlooking Porth Beach and the putting green, this bungalow style house has comfortable accommodation and a convivial atmosphere.
10rm(6🛏4hc) (3fb) CTV in all bedrooms ® sB&B£24.61-£31.55 dB&B£50-£63 dB&B🛏£55-£68 (incl dinner) WB&B£115-£156.50 WBDi£145-£186.50 (wkly only Jul & Aug) LDO 6.30pm
Lic CTV 10P
Credit Cards |1||3| £

GH |Q||Q||Q| **Tir Chonaill Lodge** 106 Mount Wise TR7 1QP
☎(0637) 876492
Friendly service and value-for-money holiday accommodation are provided by Mr and Mrs Watts at Tir Chonaill. Bedrooms are bright and simple, with en suite facilities. Public areas are comfortable and the atmosphere is relaxed.
20rm(8⇌12🛏) (9fb) CTV in all bedrooms ® ✳
sB&B⇌🛏£14-£20 dB&B⇌🛏£29-£40 WB&B£98-£130
WBDi£120-£160 (wkly only end Jun-begining Sep) LDO 5pm
Lic 🍴 CTV 20P darts £

GH |Q||Q||Q| **Wheal Treasure Hotel** 72 Edgcumbe Av TR7 2NN
☎(0637) 874136
May-mid Oct
About 10 minutes' walk from the seafront, this detached house set in its small garden offers comfortable bedrooms, and imaginative food is served.
12rm(3⇌8🛏1hc) (3fb) ® ✳ sB&B⇌🛏£16-£22
dB&B⇌🛏£32-£44 WB&B£112-£154 WBDi£140-£172 (wkly only Jun-Aug) LDO 5pm
Lic 🍴 CTV 10P nc3yrs £

GH |Q||Q||Q| **Windward Hotel** Alexandra Road, Porth TR7 3NB
☎(0637) 873185
This small bungalow stands in an elevated position and enjoys views of the distant coastline. Porth Beach is a short walk away. The charming, outgoing owners provide compact, well-equipped bedrooms.
14⇌🛏 (3fb) CTV in all bedrooms ® 🐾 (ex guide dogs)
sB&B⇌🛏£21-£29 dB&B⇌🛏£42-£58 WB&B£132-£192
WBDi£160-£220 (wkly only Jul-Sep) LDO 6pm
Lic 🍴 CTV 14P
Credit Cards |1||3| £

━━━━━━━━━━━━━━━━━

FH |Q||Q||Q| J C Wilson **Manuels** *(SW839601)* Ln
TR8 4NY ☎(0637) 873577
Closed 23 Dec-1 Jan
This delightful 17th-century listed farmhouse stands in a wooded valley 2 miles from Newquay. Alan and Jean Wilson provide ample home cooked meals using home grown produce, and can provide packed lunches.
4hc (2fb)⊁in 3 bedrooms ® 🐾 (ex guide dogs) sB&B£12-£14
dB&B£24-£28 WB&B£84-£98 WBDi£120-£175 (wkly only Spring BH-Aug BH) LDO 4pm
CTV 6P ⚕ 44 acres mixed £

━━━━━━━━━━━━━━━━━

NEW QUAY Dyfed Map **02** SN35

┌─────────────────────────────────────┐
SELECTED

GH |Q||Q||Q||Q| **Park Hall Hotel** Cwmtydu SA44 6LG
☎(0545) 560306
Situated just above the picturesque, wooded valley of Cwmtydu, with lovely views of the sea and countryside, this Victorian house has been carefully restored to provide modern day comforts and facilities. Set in over four acres of attractive grounds, the village is reached from the A487 one mile south of Synod Inn. Bedrooms are individually decorated and furnished, and all are en suite. Some rooms have brass beds, one has a four-poster, and many feature the original fireplaces. There are open fires in the lounge and bar, and a new conservatory restaurant has been added, where good food is offered using fresh local produce.
5⇌🛏 ⊁in 1 bedroom CTV in all bedrooms ®
LDO 7.30pm
Lic 🍴 CTV 20P
Credit Cards |1||2||3||5| £
└─────────────────────────────────────┘

FH |Q||Q||Q| Mr M Kelly **Ty Hen** *(SN365553)* Llwyndafydd
SA44 6BZ (S of Cross Inn, A486) ☎(0545) 560346
This very pleasant farm guesthouse offers well equipped, pine furnished bedrooms, a new leisure centre with a swimming pool, a lounge bar and an attractive restaurant, providing good, imaginatively cooked food.
5🛏 Annexe 2🛏 (2fb)⊁in 5 bedrooms CTV in all bedrooms ®
sB&B🛏£20-£29 dB&B🛏£40-£58 WB&B£120-£190
Lic 🍴 CTV 20P ⊡(heated) sauna solarium gymnasium bowls & skittles 40 acres sheep
Credit Cards |1||3| £

━━━━━━━━━━━━━━━━━

NEWTON Northumberland Map **12** NZ06

FH |Q| Mrs C M Leech **Crookhill** *(NZ056654)* NE43 7UX
☎Stocksfield(0661) 843117
rs Nov-Mar
A stone-built farmhouse set in an elevated position overlooking open countryside, close to the A69. Well furnished and comfortable, it offers friendly service.
3rm(1hc) (1fb)⊁in all bedrooms ® 🐾 ✳ sB&B£12.50-£15
dB&B£25-£30 WB&B£84
🍴 CTV 4P 23 acres beef mixed sheep £

━━━━━━━━━━━━━━━━━

NEWTON ABBOT Devon Map **03** SX87

GH |Q||Q| **Lamorna** Ideford Combe TQ13 0AR (3m N A380)
☎(0626) 65627
Conveniently situated adjacent to the A380 just outside Newton Abbot, this cosy modern guesthouse has pleasant views. Compact, well-equipped bedrooms are available here together with pleasant gardens.
7hc (1fb) CTV in 2 bedrooms TV in 5 bedrooms ®
🐾 (ex guide dogs) LDO 6pm
Lic 🍴 CTV 15P 1🐾 ⊡(heated)

NEWTON STEWART Dumfries & Galloway *Wigtownshire*
Map **10** NX46

GH QQ **Duncree House Hotel** Girvan Rd DG8 6DP
☎(0671) 2001
*This pleasant early Victorian Dower house, former home of the
Earls of Galloway, is peacefully situated in its own grounds just off
the A714 to the north west of the town. Enthusiastic and
welcoming owners are making improvements and the
individually decorated bedrooms enjoy views of the attractive
gardens. Popular with fishing and shooting parties, Duncree House
offers simple accommodation and inexpensive meals.*
6rm(1⇨1♪4hc)(1fb)⅍in 1 bedroom CTV in 4 bedrooms TV
in 1 bedroom ® sB&B£25-£30 sB&B⇨♪£45-£55 dB&B£50-
£60 dB&B⇨♪£60-£75 WB&B£155-£235 WBDi£260-£340
LDO 5.30pm
Lic 15P nc3yrs
Credit Cards ①③ ⑤

NEWTOWN Powys Map **06** SO19

FH QQQ L M & G T Whitticase *Highgate (SO111953)*
SY16 3LF ☎(0686) 625981
Mar-Oct
*15th-century, black and white-timbered farmhouse, in an elevated
position with commanding views over the valley and hills. Rough
shooting, fishing and ponies available.*
3♪ ® ✖ LDO 4.30pm
Lic ♨ CTV P ♪ ∪ shooting 250 acres mixed sheep

NINFIELD East Sussex Map **05** TQ71

FH QQQ Mr & Mrs J B Ive **Moons Hill** *(TQ704120)* The
Green TN33 9LH ☎(0424) 892645
Closed Dec
*This attractive farmhouse provides cosy and comfortable
accommodation with a warm welcome from the friendly owners.
All the bedrooms are individually decorated, and there is a
charming lounge and a small dining room where guests may eat
together or separately as they prefer. There is a large car park.*
4rm(3⇨1hc)(1fb) CTV in 2 bedrooms TV in 2 bedrooms ®
♨ CTV 10P 2🐴 ∪ 10 acres mixed smallholding ⑤

NITON

See **WIGHT, ISLE OF**

NORTHALLERTON North Yorkshire Map **08** SE39

GH QQQ **Porch House** 68 High St DL7 8EG ☎(0609) 779831
*Peter and Shirley Thompson have sympathetically converted this
16th-century listed building to provide cosy accommodation with
well-equipped en suite bedrooms. Wholesome meals are served
around a communal table. Service is very informal and friendly.*
5♪ (1fb) CTV in all bedrooms ® sB&B♪fr£30 dB&B♪fr£42
WB&B£136.50-£195 WBDi£205-£263 LDO 16.00
Lic ♨ CTV 8P ♨
Credit Cards ①③ ⑤

GH QQ **Windsor** 56 South Pde DL7 8SL ☎(0609) 774100
Closed 24 Dec-2 Jan
*Situated within walking distance of the town centre, this small
pleasant guesthouse offers well maintained accommodation,
including a comfortable lounge and small dining room. Two of the
bedrooms now have smart en suite shower rooms and are
particularly comfortable and well decorated.*
6rm(2⇨♪4hc)(1fb) CTV in all bedrooms ® sB&Bfr£19
sB&B⇨♪fr£26 dB&Bfr£29 dB&B⇨♪fr£36 WBDifr£157.50
LDO 3pm
♨ CTV
Credit Cards ①③

NORTHAMPTON Northamptonshire Map 04 SP76

GH ⓠⓠⓠ **Poplars Hotel** Cross Street, Moulton NN3 1RZ
☎(0604) 643983
Closed Xmas wk
A well established and popular hotel located in an attractive village with easy access to Northampton. Rooms improve each year and provide comfortable, well equipped accommodation. There is an attractive dining room and a pleasant TV lounge.
21rm(2⇨13🌂6hc) (4fb) CTV in all bedrooms ® sB&B£16.50-£23.50 sB&B⇨🌂£23.50-£31.50 dB&B⇨🌂£40-£47.50 WB&B£143.50-£186 WBDif£213-£256 LDO 6pm
Lic ⁂ CTV 22P
Credit Cards ①③ⓔ

INN ⓠⓠⓠ *The Fish* Fish St NN1 2AA (Berni/Chef & Brewer)
☎(0604) 234040
Within the town centre, this inn is popular with locals and visitors alike. Rooms are attractively decorated with pine furniture and are exceptionally well equipped. The busy bar has a convivial atmosphere, and there is a small intimate dining room offering good quality pub meals and grills.
12rm(1⇨1🌂10hc) CTV in all bedrooms ® ✖ LDO 10pm
🐾
Credit Cards ①②③⑤

NORTH BERWICK Lothian *East Lothian* Map 12 NT58

GH ⓠ **Cragside** 16 Marine Pde EH39 4LD ☎(0620) 2879
Guests at this seafront guesthouse are sure to receive friendly service.
4hc ® ✖ ✳ sB&Bfr£17 dB&Bfr£34 WB&Bfr£94.50
⁂ CTV 🐾 ⓔ

NORTH DUFFIELD North Yorkshire Map 08 SE63

FH ⓠⓠ Mrs A Arrand *Hall (SE692375)* YO8 7RY
☎Selby(0757) 288301
Etr-Sep
This charming and friendly working farm offers guests spacious and comfortable accommodation. It lies 12 miles south of historic York and a quarter of a mile north east of the village.
3hc (2fb)✖in all bedrooms ✖
⁂ CTV P 170 acres arable sheep

NORTH MOLTON Devon Map 03 SS72

▣◥GH ⓠⓠ **Homedale** EX36 3HL ☎(05984) 206
Etr-Oct
A small, family guesthouse in a restored Victorian house in the centre of the village on the southern edge of Exmoor, well served by the new North Devon link road. The bedrooms are warm and simply styled, there is a bright residents' lounge, and full breakfasts are served in the communal breakfast room.
3rm(1🌂2hc) ✖in all bedrooms TV in 1 bedroom ® sB&B£13-£15 sB&B🌂fr£20 dB&Bfr£26 dB&B🌂fr£30 LDO 5.30pm
⁂ CTV 1P nc3-9yrs ⓔ

NORTH NEWINGTON Oxfordshire Map 04 SP43

INN ⓠⓠⓠ **The Blinking Owl** Main St OX15 6AE
☎Banbury(0295) 730650
This inn, situated in the village, has been extended with the renovation of an adjacent barn which now provides the bedrooms and residents' dining room. Bedrooms are all a reasonable size, comfortably furnished and well equipped, with private bathrooms. The dining room is small and cosy and the public bar areas are a few yards away, for guests wishing to enjoy a lively pub atmosphere.
3rm(1⇨2🌂) CTV in all bedrooms ✖ ✳ sB&B⇨🌂£30-£35 dB&B⇨🌂£50-£55 WB&B£200 WBDif£280-£300 ✳ Lunch £7.95-£10.95&alc Dinner £12-£15&alc LDO 9pm
⁂ 12P nc8yrs ⓔ

NORTH NIBLEY Gloucestershire Map 03 ST79

GH ⓠⓠⓠ **Burrows Court Hotel** Nibley Green, Dursley
GL11 6AZ ☎Dursley(0453) 546230
Situated half a mile from the village centre, this former mill has been carefully modernised to provide a small hotel with modern facilities, whilst retaining many original features. Every bedroom is en suite, and the spacious public areas are comfortable.
10rm(6⇨4🌂) CTV in all bedrooms ® ✖ sB&B⇨🌂£34-£36 dB&B⇨🌂£47-£50 WB&B£133-£140 WBDif£210-£237
LDO 8pm
Lic ⁂ 12P nc5yrs ⌦
Credit Cards ①②③ⓔ

NORTH PERROTT Somerset Map 03 ST40

INN ⓠⓠⓠ **The Manor Arms** TA18 7SG
☎Crewkerne(0460) 72901
A Grade II 16th-century village inn located in North Perrott, a sleepy village renowned for its beautifully situated cricket ground. Lovingly restored and refurbished over the last 2 years by the owners, it offers 3 en suite ground-floor rooms in a converted coach house; a self catering flat is also available. The bars and restaurant are full of character and meals are available in both; all the food is home made and good value for money. There is a car park, beer garden and children's adventure play area at the rear. Smoking is not permitted in bedrooms.
3🌂 ✖in all bedrooms CTV in all bedrooms ®
✖ (ex guide dogs) ✳ sB&B🌂£20-£23 dB&B🌂£34-£40 ✳ Lunch £8-£12alc Dinner £8-£12alc LDO 9.45pm
⁂ P
Credit Cards ①③

NORTH WALSHAM Norfolk Map 09 TG23

GH ⓠⓠⓠ **Beechwood Private Hotel** 20 Cromer Rd NR28 0HD
☎(0692) 403231
Closed 24 Dec-7 Jan
A charming red-brick detached house set in its own acre of beautifully maintained gardens, in a residential area close to the town centre. The Victorian features of the house have been carefully retained, and the décor is light, complementing the spacious accommodation. Many of the bedrooms have private bathrooms, and there are two lounges, one with TV. The emphasis here is firmly on good old fashioned comfort and excellent service.
11rm(3⇨4🌂4hc) (5fb) ® sB&B£21 sB&B⇨🌂£24 dB&B£42 dB&B⇨🌂£48 WB&B£147 WBDif£157-£199 LDO 7pm
Lic ⁂ CTV 12P nc5yrs games room ⓔ

NORTH WOOTTON Somerset Map 03 ST54

FH ⓠⓠⓠ Mrs M White **Barrow** *(ST553416)*
☎Pilton(074989) 245
Closed Dec-Jan
15th-century stone-built farmhouse on edge of village, situated between Wells, Glastonbury and Shepton Mallet.
3hc (1fb) CTV in all bedrooms ® ✖ ✳ sB&B£14-£16 dB&B£24-£26 WB&B£84-£91 WBDif£120-£140 LDO 9am
CTV 4P 150 acres working dairy ⓔ

NORTON FITZWARREN Somerset Map 03 ST12

GH ⓠⓠ **Old Manor Farmhouse** TA2 6RZ
☎Taunton(0823) 289801
On the A361 at the western end of the village, the Old Manor Farmhouse offers seven well equipped bedrooms. There is a small lounge with a bar, and an attractive dining room where both table d'hôte and à la carte menus are available.
7⇨🌂 CTV in all bedrooms ® ✖ (ex guide dogs)
sB&B⇨🌂fr£33 dB&B⇨🌂fr£43 WB&Bfr£144 WBDifr£228 LDO 4pm
Lic ⁂ 12P
Credit Cards ①②③⑤ⓔ

NORWICH Norfolk Map **05** TG20

GH Q Q **Caistor Hall Hotel** Caistor St Edmund NR14 8QN
☎(0603) 624406

*Caistor Hall is less than three miles from the city centre, yet enjoys
a quiet secluded location a short drive off the A140. There has been
a house on the site since the Domesday Book and the building was
enlarged in 1826. Accommodation varies, but all rooms have en
suite facilities and are well equipped. The hotel has a large bar,
restaurant and extensive conference facilities.*

20⇨⋔ (2fb) CTV in all bedrooms ® ✱ sB&B⇨⋔£30-£60
dB&B⇨⋔£45-£75

Lic 250P ௴ croquet putting green

Credit Cards ①③

GH Q Q **Earlham** 147 Earlham Rd NR2 3RG ☎(0603) 54169
*A popular guesthouse situated about 20 minutes walking distance
from the city centre, enthusiastically run by a friendly couple. The
comments in their visitors' book verify that their guests are made
very welcome. Rooms can be compact and are modestly furnished.*

7rm(2⋔5hc) (1fb) CTV in all bedrooms ® sB&B£16-£18
dB&B£29.50-£32 dB&B⋔£32-£35 WB&B£98-£126

⑭ CTV ⅌

Credit Cards ③ ⓔ

GH Q Q Q **Grange Hotel** 230 Thorpe Rd NR1 1TJ
☎(0603) 34734

Closed Xmas wk

*A busy commercial hotel on the Great Yarmouth road, close to the
city centre and railway station. Bedrooms are well equipped, clean
and all with private bathrooms, and public areas have recently been
refurbished. Ample car parking is provided.*

36rm(4⇨32⋔) (1fb) CTV in all bedrooms ® ⋈ ✱
sB&B⇨⋔£30-£35 dB&B⇨⋔£45-£50 WB&Bfr£158
WBDifr£235 LDO 9.45pm

►

Lic ⊮ CTV 40P sauna solarium pool room
Credit Cards ① ② ③ ⑤ ⓔ

GH ⓠⓠ *Marlborough House Hotel* 22 Stracey Road, Thorpe
Rd NR1 1EZ ☎(0603) 628005
*A cheerful and clean family-owned guesthouse situated just off the
Great Yarmouth road, within walking distance of the station and
city centre. Some bedrooms are compact, but they are well
equipped and modestly furnished, with private bathrooms. There is
a small bar/lounge which leads to the dining room.*
12⇨🏿 (2fb) CTV in all bedrooms ⓡ LDO 4.30pm
Lic ⊮ CTV 6P 2🐾

NOTTINGHAM Nottinghamshire Map 08 SK54

GH ⓠⓠ **Crantock Hotel** 480 Mansfield Rd NG5 2EL
☎(0602) 623294
*A large, detached, fully modernised house conveniently set on the
A60 just over a mile from the city centre. Bedrooms are all
furnished with modern amenities, some with private bathrooms.
Ample car parking is available, and the guesthouse is suitable for
tourists and commercial guests alike.*
10rm(1⇨🏿9hc) Annexe 10rm(7⇨🏿3hc) (5fb)✂in 10
bedrooms CTV in all bedrooms ⓡ ✳ sB&B£18-£24
sB&B⇨🏿£27-£35 dB&B£26-£38 dB&B⇨🏿£34-£45
WB&Bfr£105 WBDifr£140 LDO 9pm
Lic ⊮ 70P pool table
Credit Cards ③

GH ⓠⓠ **Grantham Commercial Hotel** 24-26 Radcliffe Rd,
West Bridgford NG2 5FW ☎(0602) 811373
*A commercial guesthouse very close to the Trent Bridge cricket
ground. The rooms are neat and well equipped, and some have en
suite facilities.*
22rm(14🏿8hc) (2fb) CTV in all bedrooms ⓡ ✳ sB&B£20-£22
sB&B🏿£25-£28 dB&B£34-£36 dB&B🏿£38-£44 WB&B£115-
£140
⊮ CTV 8P 2🐾 nc3yrs
Credit Cards ① ③ ⓔ

GH ⓠ **P & J Hotel** 277-279 Derby Rd, Lenton NG7 2DP
☎(0602) 783996
rs 24-29 Dec
*Situated on one of the main roads into the town, this Victorian
guest house caters mainly for bed and breakfast with bar snacks
available in the evening.*
19rm(9🏿10hc) (8fb) CTV in all bedrooms ⓡ sB&B£23-£33
sB&B🏿fr£33 dB&Bfr£38 dB&B🏿fr£46 LDO 9.30pm
Lic ⊮ CTV 12P
Credit Cards ① ② ③ ⑤ ⓔ

GH ⓠⓠ **Park Hotel** 7 Waverley St NG7 4HF
☎(0602) 786299 & 420010
*This period house is set close to the city centre, overlooking a park.
Only street parking is available. The bedrooms are well equipped,
many with en suite facilities.*
27rm(11⇨🏿16hc) (2fb) CTV in all bedrooms ⓡ
✘ (ex guide dogs) sB&B🏿fr£25 sB&B⇨🏿fr£45 dB&Bfr£38
dB&B⇨🏿fr£58 WB&Bfr£160 WBDifr£220 LDO 9.30pm
Lic ⊮ CTV
Credit Cards ① ② ③ ⓔ

GH ⓠⓠⓠ *Royston Hotel* 326 Mansfield Rd NG6 2EF
☎(0602) 622947
*A detached Victorian house on the A60 out of the city, with a
terraced garden and off-street parking. The bedrooms are
individually furnished with care and attention, and include a
selection of creature comforts.*
8rm(6🏿2hc) Annexe 4🏿 (2fb) CTV in all bedrooms ⓡ
✘ (ex guide dogs)
⊮ CTV 16P
Credit Cards ① ② ③ ⑤

NUNEATON Warwickshire Map 04 SP39

GH ⓠⓠⓠ **Drachenfels Hotel** 25 Attleborough Rd CV11 4HZ
☎(0203) 383030
*Situated 10 minutes' walk from the town centre, this imposing
Edwardian house has been well modernised to provide comfortable,
well equipped bedrooms and cosy public areas.*
8rm(2🏿6hc) (2fb) CTV in all bedrooms ⓡ ✳ sB&B£19.50-
£20.50 sB&B🏿£22.50-£23.50 dB&B£29.50-£31.50
dB&B🏿£32.50-£35.50 LDO 8pm
Lic ⊮ 8P
Credit Cards ① ③ ⓔ

NUNNEY Somerset Map 03 ST74

INN ⓠⓠⓠ *George Inn & Restaurant* Church St BA11 4LW
☎(037384) 458 & 565
*A large, busy public house in the centre of the village, opposite the
castle. Bedrooms are spacious, neatly presented and well equipped
with modern facilities. Guests can relax in the comfortable first-
floor lounge away from the busy but cosy bar. There is an
attractive exposed stone restaurant at the rear of the building.*
11rm(7⇨🏿4🏿) (3fb) CTV in all bedrooms ⓡ LDO 9.30pm
⊮ CTV 30P
Credit Cards ① ③

NUTHURST West Sussex Map 04 TQ12

FH ⓠⓠⓠ Mrs S E Martin **Saxtons** *(TQ199274)* RH13 6LG
☎Lower Beeding(0403) 891231
Closed Xmas
*This delightful Georgian farmhouse is situated in an unspoilt rural
area within easy reach of the coast. The generous bedrooms are
individually furnished and there is a combined lounge and dining
room. A friendly, welcoming atmosphere prevails.*
4hc (1fb)✂in all bedrooms CTV in all bedrooms ⓡ
✘ (ex guide dogs) ✳ sB&B£20 dB&B£32 WB&B£112-£140
⊮ CTV 6P 2🐾 100 acres deer sheep goats ⓔ

OAKAMOOR Staffordshire Map 07 SK04

INN ⓠⓠ **Admiral Jervis Inn & Restaurant** Mill Rd ST10 3AG
☎(0538) 702187
*Close to the river Churnett and surrounded by hilly woodland, this
fully modernised inn has many family letting rooms. It is
conveniently situated for Alton Towers.*
6⇨🏿 (4fb)✂in all bedrooms CTV in all bedrooms ⓡ ✘
dB&B⇨🏿£45 LDO 9pm
⊮ 20P
Credit Cards ① ② ③ ⓔ

OAKFORD Devon Map 03 SS92

FH ⓠⓠⓠ Anne Boldry **Newhouse** *(SS892228)* EX16 9JE
☎(03985) 347
Closed Xmas
*Set back off the old South Molton road in 42 acres within a
peaceful valley and bordered by a trout stream, this 17th-century
farmhouse retains much of its charm and character whilst
providing modern comfort. Two en suites have recently been
installed. Home-made soups, pâtés, bread and preserves, as well as
home-produced vegetables can be enjoyed here. The farmhouse is
well sited for touring Devon, together with access to Somerset and
the coast.*
3⇨ (1fb) ⓡ ✘ ✳ sB&B⇨£16-£18 dB&B⇨£29-£32
WB&Bfr£100 WBDifr£150 LDO 4pm
⊮ CTV 3P nc10yrs ✒ 42 acres beef sheep ⓔ

OBAN Strathclyde *Argyllshire* Map 10 NM83

GH ⓠⓠ **Ardblair** Dalriach Rd PA34 5JB ☎(0631) 62668
Apr-Sep rs Etr
*This well-run family guesthouse overlooks the town and bay, and
the residents' lounge enjoys good views. The pleasant owners pay
every attention to their guests.*

15rm(10⇨🌂5hc) (3fb) ® ✖ sB&B£14-£15 sB&B⇨🌂£18-£20
dB&B£28-£30 dB&B⇨🌂£36-£40 WB&B£95-£140
WBDi£140-£162 LDO 5.30pm
🍴 CTV 10P ⓔ

GH **Q** **Q** **Glenburnie Private Hotel** The Esplanade PA34 5AQ
☎(0631) 62089
May-Sep
A solid stone-built period house on the esplanade overlooking the
west bay. Spacious and traditionally furnished, it offers
comfortable bedrooms and neatly appointed public rooms.
9⇨🌂 (1fb) CTV in all bedrooms ® ✖ (ex guide dogs) ✳
sB&B⇨🌂fr£17.50 dB&B⇨🌂£35-£55
🍴 CTV 12P 1🐾 nc4yrs
Credit Cards 1 3

⇔➤ **GH** **Q** **Q** **Roseneath** Dalriach Rd PA34 5EQ
☎(0631) 62929
Closed 24-26 Dec
Attractive sandstone house in terrace on hillside offering views
across bay to Kerrera.
10rm(2🌂8hc) (1fb) CTV in 3 bedrooms ® ✖ sB&B£12-£14.50
dB&B£24-£29 dB&B🌂£30-£36
🍴 CTV 8P

GH **Q** **Q** **Sgeir Mhaol** Soroba Rd PA34 4JF ☎(0631) 62650
A well maintained bungalow on the main A816 road leading out of
Oban going south. Bedrooms are bright and airy, and there is a
cosy lounge and a small attractive dining room.
7hc (3fb) ® ✖ (ex guide dogs) LDO 6pm
🍴 CTV 10P

GH **Q** **Q** **Q** **Wellpark Hotel** Esplanade PA34 5AQ
☎(0631) 62948 FAX (0631) 65808
May-Oct rs Etr
Semi-detached hotel built in granite and sandstone, offering good
standard of accommodation in a seafront location.

▶

17♠ CTV in all bedrooms ® ✱ sB&B♠£28-£30 dB&B♠£46-£56
⋔ 12P nc3yrs
Credit Cards ①③ £

ODDINGTON Gloucestershire Map **04** SP22

INN QQQ *Horse & Groom* Upper Oddington GL56 0XH
☎Cotswold(0451) 30584
Closed 24-27 Dec
5rm(1⇨4♠) Annexe 2hc (1fb) CTV in all bedrooms ®
✻ (ex guide dogs) LDO 9.30pm
⋔ 40P
Credit Cards ①③

OKEHAMPTON Devon Map **02** SX59

FH QQ Mrs K C Heard **Hughslade** *(SX561932)* EX20 4LR
☎(0837) 52883
Closed Xmas
This Devonshire farmhouse on the B3260 has commanding views of Dartmoor. The service here is friendly, and there is the additional feature of a full size snooker table in the games room.
5hc (3fb) ® ✱ sB&B£16-£20 dB&B£32-£40 WB&B£90-£100
WBDi£105-£120 LDO 6pm
CTV 10P ∪ snooker games room horse riding 600 acres beef & sheep £

OLD DALBY Leicestershire Map **08** SK62

FH Q Mr & Mrs S Anderson **Home** *(SK673236)* Church Ln
LE14 3LB ☎Melton Mowbray(0664) 822622
Although mostly Victorian, parts of this ivy and clematis-clad house date back to the 1700s. Set in a small and peaceful village, it provides modest and comfortable accommodation with a wealth of character.
3hc Annexe 2♠ (1fb) CTV in 2 bedrooms ® ✻ (ex guide dogs)
sB&B£20-£25 sB&B♠£25-£30 dB&B£28-£35
⋔ CTV 5P stables for guests horses 1 acre non-working £

OLD SODBURY Avon Map **03** ST78

GH QQ **Dornden** Church Ln BS17 6NB
☎Chipping Sodbury(0454) 313325
Closed Xmas-New Year & 3 wks in Oct
Situated east of the village, off the A432, this former Georgian rectory offers traditional comfort and hospitality. The building retains many original features, and the large gardens are very well maintained.
9rm(2⇨3♠4hc) (4fb) CTV in all bedrooms ✱ sB&Bfr£19.50
sB&B⇨♠£29.50 dB&Bfr£34 dB&B⇨♠£42 LDO 3pm
⋔ 15P ℘(grass) £

ONICH Highland *Inverness-shire* Map **14** NN06

GH QQQ **Cuilcheanna House Hotel** PH33 6SD ☎(08553) 226
Etr-6 Oct
8⇨ (fb) ® dB&B⇨£33-£35 WB&B£210-£235 LDO 7.30pm
Lic ⋔ CTV 10P £

GH QQ *Tigh-A-Righ* PH33 6SE ☎(08553) 255
Closed 22 Dec-7 Jan
This small, hospitable, family-run holiday guesthouse is situated beside the A82 just north of the village. It offers a genuine Highland welcome together with comfortable lounge areas and good home cooking. Bedrooms are compact with modern appointments and are equipped with useful extras.
6rm(1⇨1♠4hc) (3fb) ® LDO 9pm
Lic ⋔ CTV 15P

ORFORD Suffolk Map **05** TM44

INN QQ **Kings Head** Front St IP12 2LW ☎(0394) 450271
This village centre inn dates from the 13th century and has simply furnished well equipped accommodation. The cosy bar offers a good menu, and the restaurant serves imaginative dishes featuring locally caught fish.
6hc (1fb) CTV in all bedrooms ® sB&B£22-£24 dB&B£36-£38
Lunch £5-£20alc Dinner £10-£25alc LDO 9pm
⋔ 50P 1♣ nc8yrs
Credit Cards ⑤ £

OSWESTRY Shropshire Map **07** SJ22

See also Llansilin
GH QQQ *Ashfield Country House* Llwyn-y-Maen, Trefonen
Rd SY10 9DD ☎(0691) 655200
A friendly, personally run small hotel, just 1 mile out of the town, that has a good reputation for home-made food and personal service. Rooms are well equipped and the large lounge has extensive views over the hotel grounds and the Candy Valley. It is found by following signs to Trefonen for about 2 miles.
12rm(6⇨6♠) (2fb) CTV in all bedrooms ® LDO 9pm
Lic ⋔ 50P

OTTERY ST MARY Devon Map **03** SY19

GH QQ *Fluxton Farm Hotel* Fluxton EX11 1RJ
☎(0404) 812818
This 16th-century Devon longhouse is now a small family-run farm hotel in a peaceful setting to the south of the town. The accommodation is neat and cosy, with modestly appointed bedrooms.
12rm(6⇨4♠2hc) (2fb) ® LDO 5.30pm
Lic ⋔ CTV 15P ⚓ putting garden railway

King's Head Inn

FRONT ST.
ORFORD, NR. WOODBRIDGE
Telephone: Orford (0394) 450271

Fresh local seafood is a speciality of this small Inn run by Alistair & Joy Shaw. The 13th century smugglers' Inn with its wealth of old beams and candlelit Dining Room, offers comfortable accommodation in 'olde worlde' bedrooms, and full English breakfast.

Lunches 12.00-2.00pm Daily

Bar meals most evenings

Dinner 7.15-8.45pm Closed Sunday & Thursday evening

WELLPARK HOTEL
ESPLANADE OBAN ARGYLL PA34 5AQ

This seafront hotel has beautiful views of the bay and islands. All bedrooms have
★ Private shower and toilet ★ Central Heating
★ Radio ★ Tea Makers ★ Telephone
★ Colour TV

Bed & full breakfast from £23.00 to £30.00

For tariff and brochure write to
Mr & Mrs R. B. Dickison
Tel (0631) 62948
Fax (0631) 65808

HUGHSLADE FARM
Okehampton, Devon

See how a real Devonshire working farm is run, guests and children are made welcome. Situated on the B3260 with A30 nearby. The farmhouse overlooks Dartmoor which offers excellent walking and horse riding facilities, EXMOOR & CORNWALL are also within easy reach. The farmhouse is comfortably furnished with TV and central heating on the ground floor. Bedrooms have heating, wash basins and tea and coffee making facilities. A large dining room with separate tables serves farmhouse cooking using home produced products. Large games room with full sized snooker table. Bed & Breakfast or Dinner, Bed & Breakfast weekly or nightly. Okehampton town is just 2 miles from the farm and has a superb golf course, tennis courts and a covered swimming pool. Our farmhouse has been offering homely accommodation for a long while with many guests returning.

Terms from MRS K C HEARD, HUGHSLADE FARM, OKEHAMPTON, DEVON EX20 4LR. TELEPHONE: 0837 52883

Connel Village, Nr. Oban, Argyll PA37 1PH
Telephone: 0631-71-400

AA SELECTED   STB ♛♛♛ COMMENDED   LES ROUTIERS

Set in its own grounds in the tranquil village of Connel, 5 miles from Oban. This small first-class hotel, with residential licence and private parking, has recently been fully modernised. All bedrooms are tastefully decorated and furnished, most have private facilities. All bedrooms have: ● Colour TV ● Radio Alarm ● Central Heating ● Tea-making Facilities. Emphasis is placed on food, cleanliness and comfort of guests.

SPECIAL TERMS: 3 or 7 day stays DBB.

OUNDLE Northamptonshire Map **04** TL08

INN Q Q **The Ship Inn** 18-20 West St PE8 4EF
☎(0832) 273918
*A characterful inn in the heart of this attractive market town.
Accommodation is provided in the renovated coach and boat
houses: these rooms are well equipped and attractive. There is a
small lounge and through dining room in another cottage annexe,
but accommodation in this part was not up to AA standards when
inspected. The original inn has a cosy bar which is popular with
locals and residents alike.*
11rm(1⇨10🟊)(1fb) CTV in all bedrooms ® ✳
sB&B⇨🟊fr£27.50 dB&B⇨🟊£45-£55 WB&Bfr£175
WBDif£210-£230 ✳ Lunch £2.50-£7 Dinner £3.95-£8.50
LDO 10pm
🏵 CTV 70P
Credit Cards 1 3

OXFORD Oxfordshire Map **04** SP50

GH Q Q **Acorn** 260 Iffley Rd OX4 1SE ☎(0865) 247998
Closed Xmas-New Year
*A small guesthouse situated on the busy Iffley road, run by the
cheerful resident proprietor. Bedrooms are simple but well
equipped and comfortable. The décor is plain but fresh, and each
room is well maintained, although quite old-fashioned. Breakfast
is served in a small, modestly appointed, bright dining room.*
6hc (3fb) CTV in all bedrooms ® ✕ sB&B£20-£22 dB&B£36-
£40
🏵 5P
Credit Cards 1 3 £

GH Q Q **Bravalla** 242 Iffley Rd OX4 1SE ☎(0865) 241326 &
250511
*A small guesthouse situated along the busy Iffley road,
conveniently located for the city centre. Bedrooms are pretty and
well equipped, although a few are compact, but they are all
comfortable. There is a small parking area at the front of the
house, and the resident proprietor is very informative with regard
to local tourist attractions.*
6rm(4🟊2hc) (2fb) CTV in all bedrooms ® sB&B🟊£25-£35
dB&B£30-£35 dB&B🟊£34-£42
🏵 CTV 6P
Credit Cards 1 3 £

GH Q Q **Brown's** 281 Iffley Rd OX4 4AQ ☎(0865) 246822
*A neat and tidy Victorian property on the Iffley road, a mile away
from the city centre, with some off-street parking. Bedrooms are
well equipped, bright and clean, with showers but no baths. A
cheerful atmosphere prevails in this family-run bed and breakfast
guesthouse.*
6rm(2🟊4hc) (1fb) CTV in all bedrooms ® ✳ sB&B£18-£28
dB&B£30-£40 dB&B🟊£38-£48
🏵 CTV 4P
Credit Cards 1 3 £

GH Q Q Q **Chestnuts** 45 Davenant Rd, off Woodstock Rd
OX2 8BU ☎(0865) 53375
*Conveniently situated along the Woodstock road, just over a mile
from the city centre, this smart, modern guesthouse offers
comfortable and well furnished bedrooms, each en suite, with good
facilities. Public areas are attractive, and breakfast is taken in the
conservatory, which overlooks the well tended garden.*
4🟊 CTV in all bedrooms ® ✕ (ex guide dogs) ✳ sB&B🟊£26-
£30 dB&B🟊£42-£50
🏵 5P nc12yrs £

GH Q Q **Combermere** 11 Polstead Rd OX2 6TW
☎(0865) 56971
*Situated just north of the city centre in a quiet side street, this
guesthouse is gradually being improved by the resident proprietors,
Mr and Mrs Welding – a cheerful couple who enjoy sharing their
home with so many varied visitors to the city. Rooms are nicely*

*decorated and simply furnished and en suite facilities have been
added. Some rooms are a little compact, but certainly adequate.*
9🟊 (2fb) CTV in all bedrooms ® sB&B🟊£25-£35
dB&B🟊£40-£50 WB&B£150-£210
🏵 3P
Credit Cards 1 3

GH Q Q Q **Conifer** 116 The Slade, Headington OX3 7DX
☎(0865) 63055
*Located outside the city centre in Headington, this family-run
guesthouse is spotlessly clean and superbly maintained. Bedrooms
are reasonable in size and well presented, with neat and tidy décor.
There is a small breakfast room/lounge area, and some car parking
is available. In the warmer weather, guests can take advantage of
the outdoor swimming pool.*
8rm(1⇨2🟊)(1fb) CTV in all bedrooms ® ✕ sB&B£22-
£26 sB&B⇨🟊£35-£45 dB&B£34-£38 dB&B⇨🟊£44-£48
🏵 8P ⌒(heated)
Credit Cards 1 3

SELECTED

GH Q Q Q Q **Cotswold House** 363 Banbury Rd OX2 7PL
☎(0865) 310558
*Located north of the city centre, this converted private house
has exceptionally well furnished and tastefully
decorated. Bedrooms are pretty and well equipped with
modern facilities, making the guesthouse an excellent choice
for business people and tourists alike. The en suite facilities
are particularly smart, and housekeeping standards are
excellent throughout. Public areas are rather limited, but the
nicely presented breakfast room provides a quiet reading room
when breakfast service is finished: a meal of particular note,
with pancakes, crumpets and home-made muesli being just a
few of the extra dishes offered. The resident proprietors, Mr
and Mrs O'Kane, assure a warm welcome and helpful,
attentive service in a relaxed, friendly atmosphere.*
6🟊 (2fb)✕in all bedrooms ® ✕
sB&B🟊£30-£33 dB&B🟊£45-£50
🏵 6P nc6yrs

GH Q Q Q **Courtfield Private Hotel** 367 Iffley Rd OX4 4DP
☎(0865) 242991
*A detached house located along the busy Iffley road, in a tree-lined
road close to the Thames, within easy access to the city centre and
colleges. Bedrooms are spacious and well decorated, each with
private bathrooms, and standards of housekeeping are excellent
throughout.*
6rm(1⇨3🟊2hc) (1fb) ✕
🏵 CTV 6P 2⌒ nc3yrs
Credit Cards 1 3

See advertisement on page 277

GH Q Q Q **Dial House** 25 London Rd, Headington OX3 7RE
☎(0865) 69944
Closed Xmas & New Year
*This half-timbered house has been converted into a smart, well
maintained and spotlessly clean guesthouse. It is located along the
busy London road in Headington, and offers a high standard of
accommodation. Bedrooms are freshly decorated and well
furnished, with smart en suite facilities. Public areas are
comfortable and there is a well tended garden at the rear, with car
parking in numbered bays at the front.*
8⇨🟊 (2fb)✕in all bedrooms CTV in all bedrooms ® ✳
dB&B⇨🟊£45-£50
🏵 8P nc6yrs £

See advertisement on page 277

Book as early as possible for busy holiday periods.

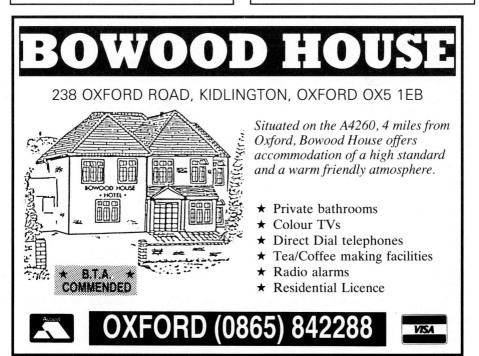

GH |Q||Q| **Earlmont** 322-324 Cowley Rd OX4 2AF
☎(0865) 240236
Closed 24 Dec-1 Jan
A double-fronted house situated along the busy Cowley road to the east of Oxford city centre, with six bedrooms in the main building and the remainder across the road in a small annexe. All bedrooms are regularly redecorated, and have recently been refurbished to ensure that standards remain high. Some of the rooms are fairly compact but comfortable nonetheless. Similarly, public rooms are nicely furnished and decorated if a little limited.
6rm(1⇋1♠4hc) Annexe 7hc (2fb)⊁in 5 bedrooms CTV in all bedrooms ® ✖ sB&B£25-£30 sB&B⇋♠£35-£40 dB&B£36-£40 dB&B⇋♠£45-£48
🎇 CTV 10P 1🐾 nc5yrs

GH |Q||Q||Q| **Falcon Private Hotel** 88-90 Abingdon Rd OX1 4PX
☎(0865) 722995
Situated along the Abingdon road just east of the city, this guesthouse has been created by the conversion of two Victorian houses and carefully refurbished by the new proprietors. Bedrooms are particularly well equipped and comfortable, with excellent en suite facilities. Public areas are comfortable, if a little limited in space. The owners are friendly, helpful and eager to provide for their guests' comfort.
11hc (4fb)⊁in 7 bedrooms CTV in all bedrooms ®
✖ (ex guide dogs) sB&B£26-£28 dB&B£40-£60 LDO 5pm
🎇 CTV 10P jacuzzi
Credit Cards |1| |3| £

GH |Q||Q| **Galaxie Private Hotel** 180 Banbury Rd OX2 7BT
☎(0865) 515688
This popular, privately-run commercial hotel is situated along the busy Banbury road. The guesthouse has gradually been extended and now offers comfortable, well equipped bedrooms, each with a fresh, bright décor. Breakfast only is served in the rear-facing dining room, which leads into a cosy lounge area.
34rm(9⇋8♠17hc) (3fb) CTV in all bedrooms ✳ sB&B£30-£32 sB&B⇋♠£39-£42 dB&B£48-£50 dB&B⇋♠£56-£60
lift 🎇 CTV 25P
Credit Cards |1| |3| £

GH |Q||Q| **Green Gables** 326 Abingdon Rd OX1 4TE
☎(0865) 725870
Closed 20 Dec-6 Jan
Situated just south of the city centre, this Edwardian house is set in a mature garden. The accommodation is comfortable, with some good sized bedrooms. The service is friendly and is under the owner's personal supervision.
8rm(3♠5hc) (2fb) CTV in all bedrooms ® ✖ (ex guide dogs) ✳ sB&B£16-£20 dB&B£30-£40 dB&B♠£38-£40
🎇 CTV 8P
Credit Cards |1| |3| £

GH |Q||Q||Q| **The Palace Hotel** 250 Iffley Rd OX4 1SE
☎(0865) 727627
Closed Dec & Jan
Located on the busy Iffley Road, conveniently close to the centre of town, this privately owned hotel offers nicely presented bedrooms, well equipped with modern facilities. Public areas are limited but comfortable. An evening meal is available on request. Mr and Mrs Parojcic are pleasant, cheery hosts.
8rm(6⇋♠2hc) (2fb) CTV in all bedrooms ® ✳ sB&B⇋♠£25-£28 dB&B⇋♠£40-£45
🎇 6P
Credit Cards |1| |3|

GH |Q||Q||Q| **Pickwicks** 17 London Rd, Headington OX3 7SP
☎(0865) 750487 FAX (0865) 742208
A family-run guesthouse situated on the London road in Headington, just outside the city centre. Two adjacent Victorian houses have been converted to provide comfortable and bright bedrooms, each of which is well equipped, most with their own bathrooms. Public areas are currently being extended, and these too are bright and nicely decorated.

▶

Green Gables
326 Abingdon Road, Oxford
Telephone: Oxford (0865) 725870

Green Gables is an original Edwardian house, set in mature gardens, offering friendly, spacious accommodation.
Situated one mile south of Oxford city centre on the main Abingdon Road (A4144), Green Gables is convenient for visiting historic Oxford, Blenheim Palace, the Cotswolds and also Stratford upon Avon.
All bedrooms have TV, tea and coffee making facilities and many of the rooms also have en-suite bathrooms.
There is also a ground floor bedroom. 🟦 🅰

Galaxie Private Hotel
180 BANBURY ROAD, OXFORD
Telephone: (0865) 515688

This is a small, select, family hotel, run under the personal supervision of the resident proprietors. Situated 1 mile from the city centre, and the colleges. All 30 bedrooms are fully equipped, have full central heating, colour TV, telephone, majority with private facilities. Lift. There is ample car parking. Terms include full English breakfast.

The hotel is open all year round and enjoys international patronage.

9rm(3⇋5♠1hc) Annexe 4rm(2♠2hc) (2fb)⅄in 2 bedrooms
CTV in all bedrooms ® sB&B£20-£45 sB&B⇋♠£30-£50
dB&B£38-£42 dB&B⇋♠£48-£52 (wkly only Nov-Feb)
LDO 1pm
Lic ⑭ CTV 20P
Credit Cards ①③

GH ⓆⓆⓆ **Pine Castle** 290 Iffley Rd OX4 4AE
☎(0865) 241497 & 727230
Closed Xmas
*A small Edwardian house situated along the busy Iffley road, just
east of the city. Public rooms are well decorated and comfortably
furnished, and the bedrooms are modern, comfortable and
reasonably well equipped. Pine Castle is popular with visitors to
the city because of its central location, and also caters for some
commercial guests.*
6hc (3fb) CTV in 5 bedrooms TV in 1 bedroom ® sB&B£19-
£21 dB&B£35-£40 WB&Bfr£75
⑭ CTV 4P
Credit Cards ①③ ⓕ

SELECTED

GH ⓆⓆⓆⓆ **Tilbury Lodge Private Hotel** 5 Tilbury Ln,
Eynsham Rd, Botley OX2 9NB ☎(0865) 862138
*A friendly hotel situated in a residential area, down a quiet
lane about a mile from the city centre. The upgraded
bedrooms are modern, with private bathrooms, TVs and
telephones, and there is a jacuzzi available for guests. The
quiet, well appointed lounge offers a range of local
information, and the freshly cooked breakfast is served in the
informal dining area.*
8⇋♠ (2fb) CTV in all bedrooms ® ✹ sB&B⇋♠£30-£33
dB&B⇋♠£51-£67
⑭ 8P 1🛁 jacuzzi
Credit Cards ①③ ⓕ

GH ⓆⓆⓆ **Westwood Country Hotel** Hinksey Hill Top
OX1 5BG ☎(0865) 735408 FAX (0865) 736536
Closed 22 Dec-2 Jan
*Situated midway along Hinksey Hill, this small family-run hotel
stands in 4 acres of lovely woodland, now designated a nature
reserve. Bedrooms are mostly spacious and well equipped with
modern facilities. The restaurant and bar area have recently been
refurbished: the bar now has a full licence, allowing less restricted
drinking hours. There is a good range of leisure facilities, including
a jacuzzi, sauna and mini-gym.*
26rm(14⇋12♠) (5fb) CTV in all bedrooms ®
✹ (ex guide dogs) sB&B⇋♠£45-£55 dB&B⇋♠£66-£88
LDO 8pm
Lic ⑭ CTV 50P 🛁 sauna jacuzzi mini gym
Credit Cards ①②③⑤ ⓕ

GH ⓆⓆ **Willow Reaches Hotel** 1 Wytham St OX1 4SU
☎(0865) 721545 FAX (0865) 251139
*In a quiet residential area south of the city, Willow Reaches has
been completely refurbished to provide comfortable, well equipped
bedrooms. Public rooms are limited, but the dining room offers a
choice of English and Indian cuisine.*
9rm(3⇋6♠) (1fb) CTV in all bedrooms ® ✹ ✳
sB&B⇋♠£39-£42 dB&B⇋♠£49-£52.80 WB&Bfr£273
WBDifr£378 (wkly only 27 Dec-Feb) LDO 6pm
Lic ⑭ CTV 6P 3🛁
Credit Cards ①②③⑤ ⓕ

OXHILL Warwickshire Map 04 SP34

FH ⓆⓆⓆ Mrs S Hutsby **Nolands Farm & Country
Restaurant** *(SP312470)* CV35 0RJ (1m E of Pillarton Priors on
A422) ☎Kineton(0926) 640309
Closed 15-30 Dec

---

*With the exception of 2 bedrooms and the lounge, all of the
Nolands farm facilities are in carefully restored outbuildings which
house comfortable bedrooms with en suite facilities, a pleasant
dining room and a small comfortable bar area.*
Annexe 9rm(2⇋7♠) (2fb) CTV in all bedrooms ®
✹ (ex guide dogs) sB&B⇋♠fr£25 dB&B⇋♠£30-£40
LDO 6pm
Lic ⑭ 10P 2🛁 nc7yrs ✔ clay pigeon shooting bicycle hire 300
acres arable
Credit Cards ①③

OXWICH West Glamorgan Map 02 SS58

GH ⓆⓆⓆ *Oxwich Bay Hotel* Gower SA3 1LS
☎Swansea(0792) 390329 & 390491 FAX (0792) 391254
Closed 25 Dec
*Right on the beach of this lovely sandy bay, the hotel provides
extensive and comfortable bar and function facilities. The
bedrooms have all been recently refurbished and offer an
abundance of modern comforts.*
13⇋♠ (4fb) CTV in all bedrooms ® ✹ LDO 10.45pm
Lic ⑭ 70P
Credit Cards ①②③⑤

OYNE Grampian *Aberdeenshire* Map 15 NJ62

GH ⓆⓆⓆ *Westhall House* AB5 6RW
☎Old Rayne(04645) 225
*Parts of this fine country mansion house date back to the 13th
century. The bedrooms have private facilities, and guests can enjoy
the other amenities which include a sauna, solarium and a tennis
court.*
12rm(4⇋3♠5hc) (6fb) CTV in all bedrooms ® LDO 7.30pm
Lic ⑭ 50P ♟(hard)✔ sauna solarium
Credit Cards ②

TILBURY LODGE

PRIVATE HOTEL
TEL: (0865) 862138
(Three lines)

Tilbury Lodge is situated in a quiet country lane just two miles west of the city centre and one mile from the railway station. Good bus service available. Botley shopping centre is a few minutes walk away with restaurants, shops, banks, pubs etc.

All rooms en suite with direct dial telephone colour TV, radio, hair dryer and tea & coffee facilities. Jacuzzi. Four poster. Ground floor bedrooms. Central heating, double glazing. Ample parking.

TILBURY LODGE PRIVATE HOTEL
5 TILBURY LANE, EYNSHAM ROAD,
BOTLEY, OXFORD OX2 9NB

Pine Castle Hotel
290 Iffley Road
Oxford
Telephone:
0865 241497
or 727230

A comfortable, family run Edwardian guest house, 1½ miles from the city centre and on an excellent bus route. Very convenient to Post Office, launderette, etc, and also to the lovely River Thames. Well appointed rooms offer Tea/Coffee making facilities and TV and are accessible to guests throughout the day, as is the attractive TV lounge.

Write or telephone for further details to resident proprietors, Peter and Marilyn Morris.

Willow Reaches Hotel
1 Wytham St., Oxford
Tel: Oxford (0865) 721545 Fax: (0865) 251139

English Tourist Board Commended

A private hotel with a high standard of comfort, in a quiet location just a mile south of Oxford city centre.

The hotel is near a fishing lake and a public park with swimming pools and children's boating lake.

Every bedroom has a direct dial telephone, colour television, radio and tea/coffee-making facility; all bathrooms en suite. Bridal suite.

Central Heating throughout. Residents' lounge with teletext TV. Bar, restaurant serving English and Indian meals. A large garden. Children welcome. Parking facilities.

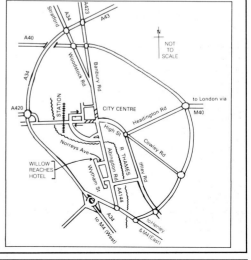

PADSTOW Cornwall & Isles of Scilly Map **02** SW97

See also Little Petherick, St Merryn and Trevone

GH Q|Q| **Alexandra** 30 Dennis Rd PL28 8DE ☎(0841) 532503
Etr-Oct

6hc (2fb) CTV in all bedrooms ® ✸ ✱ sB&B£14-£15
dB&B£28-£30 WB&B£93-£100 WBDi£142-£156 LDO noon
5P nc5yrs

GH Q|Q|Q| *Dower House* Fentonluna Ln PL28 8BA
☎(0841) 532317
Closed Xmas & New Year
A house of character with comfortable bedrooms and friendly service.
8rm(1➪4↾3hc) (3fb) TV available ® LDO 6.30pm
Lic ₪ CTV 9P

PAIGNTON Devon Map **03** SX86

See Town Plan Section

GH Q|Q|Q| **Beresford** 5 Adelphi Rd TQ4 6AW ☎(0803) 551560
Closed Oct, Xmas & New Year
Sound accommodation and personal service is provided by this small, friendly guesthouse. It is close to the town, beach and esplanade.
8↾ (1fb)⤲in 2 bedrooms ® ✸ ✱ dB&B↾fr£38 WB&Bfr£100
WBDifr£125 LDO 10am
Lic ₪ CTV 3P £

🛏🚗 **GH** Q|Q| **Cherra Hotel** 15 Roundham Rd TQ4 6DN
☎(0803) 550723
Mar-Oct
A small private hotel in a quiet residential area a short distance from the town centre, beaches and harbour. The bedrooms are comfortable though some are compact, all have colour television. A colourful garden surrounds the property.
14rm(9↾5hc) (7fb) CTV in all bedrooms ® sB&B£11-£15
dB&B£22-£30 dB&B↾£30-£38 (incl dinner) WB&B£77-£105
WBDi£90-£120 LDO 5.30pm
Lic ₪ CTV 15P putting £

GH Q|Q|Q| *Clennon Valley Hotel* 1 Clennon Rise TQ4 5HG
☎(0803) 550304 & 557736
A modern fronted property with its own car park and a terraced garden, in an elevated position on the Dartmouth road. The bedrooms are brightly decorated and several offer family accommodation all with good facilities. The cosy lounge and bar are comfortably appointed and simple dishes are offered on the menu in the informal dining room.
12rm(1➪9↾2hc) (2fb) CTV in all bedrooms ®
Lic ₪ CTV 12P free access to Torbay leisure centre
Credit Cards 1 3

GH Q|Q|Q| *Danethorpe Hotel* 23 St Andrews Rd TQ4 6HA
☎(0803) 551251
A family run establishment away from the centre of the town but just a brisk walk from the seafront and harbour. Bedrooms are comfortable, though some are compact, and all have colour television. A choice of menu is offered with orders taken in advance.
10rm(4↾6hc) (2fb) CTV in all bedrooms ® ✸
Lic ₪ 10P
Credit Cards 1 2 3

GH Q|Q|Q| **Redcliffe Lodge Hotel** 1 Marine Dr TQ3 2NL
☎(0803) 551394
Apr-mid Nov
A corner plot on Marine Drive, beside the safe, sandy beach and green, and a level walk to the town centre, pier and Festival Theatre. The bedrooms are all en suite with colour television, and the lounge and dining room are cosy and comfortable. The menu offers simple dishes, and a happy, relaxed atmosphere is created by the friendly resident proprietors.

17rm(10➪7↾) (2fb) CTV in all bedrooms ® ✸ ✱
dB&B➪↾£50-£60 (incl dinner) WBDi£168-£198
LDO 6.30pm
Lic ₪ CTV 20P
Credit Cards 1 3

GH Q|Q|Q| **Hotel Retreat** 43 Marine Dr TQ3 2NS
☎(0803) 550596
Etr-Sep
This comfortable private hotel is family owned and set in pleasant grounds in a secluded position on the sea front. The accommodation is comfortable with cosy, bright and well equipped bedrooms.
13rm(5➪8hc) (1fb) CTV in all bedrooms ® ✸ sB&B£16-£20
dB&B£32-£38 dB&B➪£34-£40 WBDi£145-£185 LDO 6pm
Lic CTV 14P
Credit Cards 1 3 £

GH Q|Q|Q| **St Weonard's Private Hotel** 12 Kernou Rd
TQ4 6BA ☎(0803) 558842
An attractive terraced property in a residential street, close to the town centre and only about 100 yards from the seafront. The bedrooms have been brightly decorated and comfortably furnished and the lounge has a home-like feel. A choice of menu promotes home-cooked dishes, and the resident proprietors extend a warm family welcome to guests.
8rm(4↾4hc) (3fb) ® ✸ ✱ sB&B£13.50-£15 sB&B↾£16-£17.50
dB&B£27-£30 dB&B↾£32-£35 WB&B£94.50-£105
WBDi£136.50-£147 LDO 3.30pm
Lic CTV 2P

GH Q|Q| **Sattva Hotel** 29 Esplanade TQ4 6BL ☎(0803) 557820
An attractive end of terrace property on the seafront with a level 2-minute walk to the beach. The bedrooms are simply appointed with good facilities. A lively atmosphere is promoted in the bar lounge where entertainment is provided during the season.
21rm(2➪17↾2hc) (2fb) CTV in all bedrooms ® ✸
sB&B➪↾£22-£28 dB&B£40-£54 dB&B➪↾£45-£58
WB&B£120-£160 WBDi£143-£191 LDO 5pm
Lic lift ₪ CTV 10P
Credit Cards 1 3

See advertisement on page 283

GH Q|Q|Q| **The Sealawn Hotel** Sea Front, 20 Esplanade Rd
TQ4 6BE ☎(0803) 559031
A semidetached 4-storey establishment on the seafront between Paignton Pier and the Festival Hall, affording views across the greens to the sea. The bedrooms are all well equipped and have en suite facilities. The menu offers a choice of simple dishes which should be ordered in advance.
13rm(6➪7↾) (3fb) CTV in all bedrooms ® ✸ sB&B➪↾£23-£29 dB&B➪↾£36-£48 WB&B£119-£196 WBDi£161-£238
LDO 5.30pm
Lic ₪ CTV 13P ⚙ solarium £

GH Q|Q| **Sea Verge Hotel** Marine Dr, Preston TQ3 2NJ
☎(0803) 557795
Closed Dec
A modern building near the beaches, green and town centre with its own car park and small garden. The bedrooms are brightly decorated and a lively atmosphere is created in the public areas by the proprietor's relaxed approach.
12rm(5↾7hc) (2fb) CTV in all bedrooms ® ✸ ✱ dB&B£32-£36 dB&B↾£36-£40 LDO 5pm
Lic ₪ CTV 14P nc9yrs
Credit Cards 1 3

GH Q|Q|Q| **Torbay Sands Hotel** 16 Marine Pde, Preston Sea
Front TQ3 2NU ☎(0803) 525568
Bryan and Fiona Pearsons have created an hospitable atmosphere at their modern hotel which has panoramic views of the bay. The bright, cosy bedrooms are complemented by comfortable and tasteful public rooms.

▶

14rm(9♠5hc) (4fb) CTV in all bedrooms ⓡ ✳ sB&B£13-£16
sB&B♠£14.50-£17.50 dB&B£26-£32 dB&B♠£29-£35
WB&B£85-£105 WBDi£100-£125
Lic ⁣ CTV 5P
Credit Cards ⁣1⁣ ⁣3⁣ ⓔ

PARKMILL (NEAR SWANSEA) West Glamorgan Map **02**
SS58

FH ⬚Q⬚Q Mrs D Edwards *Parc-le-Breos House (SS529896)*
SA3 2HA ☎Swansea(0792) 371636
This early 19th-century farmhouse is situated in the heart of the
Gower and reached by a long, tree-lined farm road. Bedrooms and
lounges are comfortably appointed, and the house still retains
much of its character. There are pleasant grounds, including a well
stocked fish pond, and riding school facilities are available.
8rm(2♠5hc) ✠
⁣ CTV P Ʊ snooker 55 acres mixed

PATELEY BRIDGE North Yorkshire Map **07** SE16

GH ⬚Q⬚Q⬚Q Grassfields Country House Hotel HG3 5HL
☎Harrogate(0423) 711412
Mar-Nov
Set in beautiful grounds in the Nidd Valley, this elegant Georgian
country house has spacious and comfortable en suite bedrooms.
Barbara Garforth provides a warm welcome and prepares
enjoyable meals which are very good value.
9rm(5⇔4♠) Annexe 5rm (3♠1hc) (4fb) CTV in 4 bedrooms
ⓡ sB&B£25 sB&B⇔♠£30 dB&B£45 dB&B⇔♠£50-£54
WB&B£154-£168 WBDi£224-£238 LDO 7pm
Lic ⁣ CTV 24P ⓔ

FH ⬚Q Mrs C E Nelson *Nidderdale Lodge (SE183654)* Felbeck
HG3 5DR ☎Harrogate(0423) 711677
Etr-Oct
This small stone bungalow is high up overlooking beautiful
Nidderdale. The farm is mixed, and guests are welcome to explore.
Bedrooms are simply furnished but clean, and there is a
comfortable lounge.
3hc (1fb)⊁in all bedrooms ⓡ ✠ (ex guide dogs)
⁣ CTV 3P 30 acres mixed

PATRICK BROMPTON North Yorkshire Map **08** SE29

SELECTED

GH ⬚Q⬚Q⬚Q⬚Q Elmfield House Arrathorne DL8 1NE (2m N
unclass towards Catterick Camp) ☎Bedale(0677) 50558 &
50557
This guesthouse is set in an idyllic rural location, yet is
conveniently close to Richmond and Leyburn, with easy access
to the A1. The spacious bedrooms are well equipped and
comfortable, with attractive décor and many thoughtful extras
provided. Inviting public areas include comfortable lounges, a
solarium and a games room. Fresh local produce is used for
the meals which are excellent value, and guests can be assured
of courteous service from the charming resident proprietors.
9rm(4⇔5♠) (2fb) CTV in all bedrooms ⓡ
✠ (ex guide dogs) sB&B⇔♠frf£25 dB&B⇔♠frf£36
WB&Bfrf£126 WBDifrf£189 LDO before noon
Lic ⁣ 12P ♪ solarium games room ⓔ

This is one of many guidebooks pubished by
the AA. The full range is available at any
AA Shop or good bookshop.

PAYHEMBURY Devon Map **03** ST00

SELECTED

GH ⬚Q⬚Q⬚Q⬚Q Colestocks House Colestocks EX14 0JR (1m
N unclass rd) ☎Honiton(0404) 850633
Closed 21 Nov-22 Dec
A charming 16th-century Grade II thatched house attractively
set within 2 acres of mature gardens and surrounded by a high
cob wall. It is conveniently located just two miles north of the
A30 between the villages of Feniton and Payhembury. The
cosy bedrooms are all individually furnished and decorated to
suit the character of the building ; two rooms feature antique
tester beds and one has a four-poster ; they all have private
bathrooms. The lounges are cosy and comfortable, with log
fires. One of the main features is the strong French influence
to the high standard of meals served, with delicious home-
made pâtés, regional French dishes and temptingly rich
sweets, all meals being freshly prepared with top quality
ingredients.
9⇔♠ (1fb) CTV in all bedrooms ⓡ ✠ (ex guide dogs)
sB&B⇔♠£29.50-£35 dB&B⇔♠£49-£55 WBDi£220-£240
LDO 8pm
Lic ⁣ 9P nc10yrs putting green
Credit Cards ⁣1⁣ ⁣3⁣ ⓔ

PEEBLES Borders *Peebleshire* Map **11** NT24

GH ⬚Q⬚Q Lindores Old Town EH45 8JE ☎(0721) 20441
A comfortable house offering spacious accommodation on the main
Glasgow road into the town.
5hc (1fb) ⓡ ✠ (ex guide dogs) dB&B£25-£26
⁣ CTV 3P ⓔ

GH ⬚Q⬚Q⬚Q Whitestone House Innerleithen Rd EH45 8BD
☎(0721) 20337
An impressive converted manse to the east of the town offering
comfortable, neat accommodation and a combined lounge/dining
room.
5hc (2fb) ⓡ ✠ (ex guide dogs) dB&B£24-£25
⁣ CTV 5P ⓔ

FH ⬚Q⬚Q⬚Q Mrs J M Haydock *Winkston (NT244433)*
Edinburgh Rd EH45 8PH ☎(0721) 21264
Etr-Oct
Nicely decorated farmhouse 1.5 miles north of town off Edinburgh
road. Shower room only, no bath.
3hc ⊁in all bedrooms ⓡ ✠ (ex guide dogs)
⁣ CTV 4P 40 acres sheep

PELYNT Cornwall & Isles of Scilly Map **02** SX25

SELECTED

FH ⬚Q⬚Q⬚Q⬚Q Mrs L Tuckett **Trenderway** *(SX214533)*
PL13 2LY ☎Polperro(0503) 72214
Etr-Oct
A mixed, working farm with a cluster of Cornish stone
buildings dating from the 16th century set amid rolling
countryside at the head of Polperro Valley. The
accommodation here is of a superior quality. The 2 bedrooms
in the main farmhouse are very prettily furnished and there is
a barn, recently converted, with lovely colour schemes and
comfortable surroundings. A fourth superior room is currently
being refurbished. Breakfast is served in the sun-filled
conservatory overlooking the lower fields. It is a hearty
traditional meal, with a continental alternative for those with
smaller appetites. Mrs Lynne Tuckett and her family are
welcoming, warm and friendly hosts. Early reservations are
advisable.
2⇔♠ Annexe 2⇔♠ ⊁in all bedrooms CTV in all
bedrooms ⓡ ✠ dB&B⇔♠£23-£25 WB&B£154-£168

ﾙ 2P 2☎ nc10yrs 400 acres arable mixed sheep cattle £

PEMBROKE Dyfed Map **02** SM90

◨◗ **GH** Ⓠ Ⓠ **High Noon** Lower Lamphey Rd SA71 4AB
☎(0646) 683736 & 681232
Just a short walk from the town centre, this busy guesthouse
provides well furnished bedrooms and a comfortable open-plan
lounge and dining room.
9rm(5⇨3 ⌂4hc) (2fb) CTV in 6 bedrooms Ⓡ sB&B£12.50-£15
sB&B⇨⌂£13.50-£15 dB&B£25-£30 dB&B⇨⌂£27-£30
WB&B£84-£101.50 WBDi£118.50-£136 LDO 5pm
Lic ﾙ CTV 9P

PENARTH South Glamorgan Map **03** ST17

GH Ⓠ Ⓠ **Albany Hotel** 14 Victoria Rd CF6 2EF
☎Cardiff(0222) 701598 & 701242 FAX (0222) 701598
This very friendly guesthouse is situated a short walk from the
town centre and railway station. There is a comfortable lounge, a
cosy bar and the bedrooms are all well equipped.
14rm(6⇨3⌂8hc) (4fb)⊬in 2 bedrooms CTV in all bedrooms Ⓡ
❋ sB&B£23 sB&B⇨⌂£29.50 dB&B£40 dB&B⇨⌂£45
LDO 8.30pm
Lic ﾙ CTV 3P
Credit Cards ①②③ £
See advertisement under CARDIFF

PENLEY Clwyd Map **07** SJ44

GH Ⓠ Ⓠ Ⓠ **Bridge House** LL13 0LY
☎Overton-On-Dee(097873) 763
Situated in a quiet rural area only 2 miles north of the village of
Penley is this much extended and considerably modernised former
farmhouse. The impeccably maintained accommodation is equally
suitable for tourists and business people.
3rm(2hc) ⊬in all bedrooms CTV in all bedrooms Ⓡ ✈ ❋
dB&B£30-£36 LDO noon
ﾙ CTV 6P 2☎ nc10yrs £

PENNANT Dyfed Map **02** SN56

GH Ⓠ Ⓠ Ⓠ **Bikerehyd Farm** SY23 5PB ☎Nebo(0974) 272465
Situated just 2 miles from the A487 (signposted to Pennant), this
delightful farmhouse has been carefully converted and now has an
attractive restaurant which is popular with locals and offers a good
selection of food. There are 3 bedrooms in converted outbuildings,
which are comfortably furnished and well equipped.
Annexe 3⌂ (2fb) CTV in all bedrooms Ⓡ ✈ (ex guide dogs) ❋
sB&B⌂fr£25 dB&B⌂fr£45 WB&Bfr£135 LDO 10pm
Lic ﾙ CTV 8P nc5yrs
Credit Cards ①

PENRHYNDEUDRAETH Gwynedd Map **06** SH63

FH Ⓠ Ⓠ Mrs P Bayley **Y Wern** *(SH620421)* LLanfrothen
LL48 6LX (2m N off B4410) ☎(0766) 770556
A large traditional stone-built farmhouse which retains much of its
original character. Y Wern is located in a peaceful area, 2 miles
north of Penrhyndeudraeth, close to the junction of the A4085 and
B4410.
5rm(2⌂3hc) (4fb) Ⓡ ✈ sB&Bfr£21 dB&Bfr£28 dB&B⌂fr£34
WB&Bfr£88 WBDifr£144
ﾙ CTV 6P 110 acres beef sheep £

PENRITH Cumbria Map **12** NY53

See also advertisement on p 285
GH Ⓠ Ⓠ **Brandelhow** 1 Portland Place CA11 7QN
☎(0768) 64470
A comfortable and friendly guesthouse run by the resident owners.
It offers very good value, and is situated in a quiet side road close
to the town centre.

6rm(5hc) (3fb)⊬in 2 bedrooms CTV in all bedrooms Ⓡ ❋
sB&B£14-£16 dB&B£26-£28 WB&B£85-£93
ﾙ CTV 1P £

GH Ⓠ Ⓠ **The Grotto** Yanwath CA10 2LF ☎(0768) 63288
FAX (0768) 63432
Standing in its own secluded, tree-studded gardens next to the west
coast railway line, this traditional, stone residence provides
modernised accommodation with attractive public areas.
6rm(4⌂2hc) (2fb) CTV in all bedrooms Ⓡ ✈ LDO 6pm
Lic ﾙ 12P
Credit Cards ①③

GH Ⓠ Ⓠ **Limes Country Hotel** Redhills, Stainton CA11 0DT
(2m W A66) ☎(0768) 63343
Set in lovely countryside, yet conveniently situated for junction 40
of the M6, this Victorian country house provides friendly service.
6rm(1⇨4⌂1hc) (2fb) Ⓡ ✈ (ex guide dogs) sB&B£15-£17.50
sB&B⇨⌂£18.50-£21 dB&B£28-£32 dB&B⇨⌂£32-£37
WB&B£100-£125 WBDi£157.50-£180 LDO 3pm
Lic ﾙ CTV 7P
Credit Cards ①③ £

GH Ⓠ Ⓠ **Woodland House Hotel** Wordsworth St CA11 7QY
☎(0768) 64177
This elegant Victorian house is built of the local red sandstone, and
is set in a quiet side street close to the town centre. Well furnished,
it offers good all round comforts.
8⇨⌂ (2fb)⊬in all bedrooms CTV in all bedrooms Ⓡ ✈ ❋
sB&B⇨⌂£19 dB&B⇨⌂£36 LDO 4.30pm
Lic ﾙ CTV 10P 1☎ £

Ⓠ is for quality. For a full explanation of this AA quality
award, consult the Contents page.

PENRUDDOCK Cumbria Map **12** NY42

SELECTED

FH Q|Q|Q|Q Mrs S M Smith **Highgate** *(NY444275)*
CA11 0SE ☎Greystoke(07684) 83339
mid Feb-mid Nov

A lovely stone-built farmhouse dated 1730 with a delightful garden, situated on the A66 between Penrith and Keswick. Tastefully decorated throughout, it provides a high standard of comfort and service. Two of the bedrooms feature king-size brass beds, and they all have TV and tea/coffee-making facilities. There is an attractive Victorian-style lounge, and good home-cooking is provided.

3hc CTV in all bedrooms ® ✖ ✱ sB&B£15-£25 dB&B£30-£32 WB&B£90-£95
⅏ 3P nc5yrs 400 acres mixed ⓔ

PENRYN Cornwall & Isles of Scilly Map **02** SW73

GH Q|Q|Q **Bella's Mouse** 8 Shute Ln TR10 8EY
☎Falmouth(0326) 373433
Apr-Sep

A cosy 14th-century cottage with two bedrooms to let, tucked away in a quiet cul-de-sac close to the centre of Penryn. The bedrooms are comfortable and attractive, and there is a pleasant sitting room with a separate study. Breakfast is a feature, with some unusual home-cooked dishes offered, and friendly and relaxed service is provided by Mrs Buchanan-Barbour.

2hc ✖ sB&B£21 dB&B£35
⅏ CTV 2P nc12yrs ⓔ

SELECTED

GH Q|Q|Q|Q **Prospect House** 1 Church Rd TR10 8DA
☎Falmouth(0326) 73198

Previously a Gentleman's residence, built circa 1830, this handsome house retains many original features. Bedrooms are individually furnished and teddy bears are included among the thoughtful extras. The cosy lounge area is full of antiques, and there is a communal table in the pleasant dining room where guests may chat to one another over an enjoyable home-cooked meal. Service is very personal and attentive and the resident proprietors, 2 charming gentlemen, clearly enjoy entertaining guests in their elegant home.

4rm(3⇨↑1hc) TV available sB&B£18-£29.50
dB&B⇨↑£44-£49 WB&B£113.75-£185.50
WBDif£218.75-£290.50 LDO noon
⅏ CTV 4P 1🐾 nc12yrs ⓔ
See advertisement under FALMOUTH

PENSHURST Kent Map **05** TQ54

SELECTED

GH Q|Q|Q|Q **Swale Cottage** Old Swaylands Ln, Off Poundbridge Ln TN11 8AH ☎(0892) 870738

A skilfully converted 18th-century Kentish barn, peacefully located overlooking the Weald of Kent countryside. Bedrooms have all been individually furnished and tastefully decorated by the proprietor, Cynthia Dakin. Breakfast is served at the elegant communal dining table, and there is a comfortable lounge with displays of the proprietor's paintings of the local countryside and places of interest.

3rm(2⇨↑1hc) ✂in all bedrooms CTV in all bedrooms ✖ ✱ sB&B£26-£28 sB&B⇨↑£26-£28 dB&B⇨↑£38-£44
⅏ 5P nc10yrs ⓔ

PENYBONT Powys Map **03** SO16

SELECTED

GH Q|Q|Q|Q **Ffaldau Country House & Restaurant**
LD1 5UD (2m E A44) ☎(059787) 421 due to change to (0597) 851421

An authentic cruck-framed longhouse surrounded by well maintained lawns and gardens in the beautiful Radnor hills, set back off the A44. Bedrooms are cosy and comfortable, and there is a small landing lounge with TV, books and games. The slate-fronted restaurant is very attractive and popular, with fresh local produce much in evidence. Other features include an abundance of beamed ceilings, inglenook fireplaces and roaring fires, together with a cosy bar for a relaxing drink.

3rm(1↑2hc) ® ✖ (ex guide dogs) ✱ sB&B£22 sB&B↑£27 dB&B£34 dB&B↑£39 LDO 9pm
Lic ⅏ CTV 25P nc10yrs ⓔ

PENZANCE Cornwall & Isles of Scilly Map **02** SW43

See Town Plan Section

GH Q|Q|Q **Blue Seas Hotel** 13 Regent Ter TR18 4DW
☎(0736) 64744

This family-run establishment stands near the promenade and town centre. Most of the comfortable bedrooms offer en suite facilities. Home cooked meals are prepared with fresh local produce, and guests receive personal service and a warm welcome.

10rm(2⇨8↑) (3fb) CTV in all bedrooms ® ✖ ✱ sB&B⇨↑£13.50-£33 dB&B⇨↑£27-£33 WB&B£94.50-£115.50 WBDif£154-£175 LDO 6.30pm
Lic ⅏ CTV 12P nc5yrs
Credit Cards 1|3 ⓔ

GH Q|Q **Camilla Hotel** Regent Ter TR18 4DW ☎(0736) 63771

Character Regency residence overlooking seafront promenade with comfortable friendly family atmosphere, positioned close to parks and town centre amenities.

9rm(1⇨4↑4hc) (3fb) CTV in all bedrooms ® sB&B£14-£16 dB&B£28-£32 dB&B⇨↑£30-£36 WB&B£95-£115 WBDif£145-£165 LDO noon
Lic ⅏ CTV 6P
Credit Cards 1|3 ⓔ

See advertisement on page 287

GH Q|Q **Carlton Private Hotel** Promenade TR18 4NW
☎(0736) 62081
Etr-19 Oct rs Mar

This small, modest hotel is positioned right on the seafront and has been personally run by the same family for several years. It offers spotlessly clean, bright and well equipped bedrooms, with commanding views.

10rm(8↑2hc) CTV in all bedrooms ® ✖ (ex guide dogs) ✱ sB&B£15-£16 dB&B£30-£32 dB&B↑£36-£38 WB&B£105-£133
Lic CTV ⨍ nc12yrs ⓔ

GH Q|Q **Dunedin** Alexandra Rd TR18 4LZ
☎(0736) 62652
Closed Xmas rs Jan-Etr

Very comfortable, small, personally-run guesthouse positioned close to seafront.

9rm(1⇨8↑) (4fb) CTV in all bedrooms ® sB&B⇨↑£12.50-£14.50 dB&B⇨↑£25-£29 WB&B£84-£100 WBDif£130-£145 LDO 5pm
Lic ⅏ CTV 1🐾 (£3) nc3yrs

GH Q|Q **Georgian House** 20 Chapel St TR18 4AW
☎(0736) 65664
Closed Xmas rs Nov-Apr

▶

This friendly guesthouse is centrally situated opposite the famous Admiral Benbow Inn and offers good value for money. Bedrooms are well equipped, and there is a popular family restaurant on the ground floor.
12rm(4⇨2♠6hc) (4fb) CTV in all bedrooms ®
✻ (ex guide dogs) ✱ sB&B£18.50-£24 sB&B⇨♠£24 dB&B£30 dB&B⇨♠£40 LDO 8pm
Lic ♚ CTV 11P
Credit Cards ① ② ③ ④

◫➟ GH ◲◲ Kimberley House 10 Morrab Rd TR18 4EZ
☎(0736) 62727
Feb-Nov
Small tastefully furnished residence offering warm and friendly welcome from resident proprietors.
9hc (2fb) CTV in all bedrooms ® ✻ (ex guide dogs) sB&B£13-£15 dB&B£26-£30 WB&B£86-£100 WBDi£133-£147 LDO 5pm
Lic ♚ CTV 4P nc5yrs
Credit Cards ① ③

GH ◲◲◲ Hotel Minalto Alexandra Rd TR18 4LZ
☎(0736) 62923
Closed 18 Dec-3 Jan
11rm(2♠9hc) (1fb) CTV in all bedrooms ® LDO 5.30pm
Lic CTV 10P
Credit Cards ① ③

GH ◲ Mount Royal Hotel Chyandour Cliff TR14 3LQ
☎(0736) 62233
Mar-Oct
Small family hotel facing sea and harbour.
9rm(5⇨4hc) (3fb) CTV in 3 bedrooms ® sB&B£19-£26 sB&B⇨£21-£28 dB&B£38 dB&B⇨£42-£46 WB&B£126-£140 ♚ CTV 6P 4🏕 (£3 per night) ④

GH ◲◲ Penmorvah Hotel Alexandra Rd TR18 4LZ
☎(0736) 63711
Personally-run private hotel with comfortable accommodation.
10rm(5⇨5♠) (4fb) CTV in all bedrooms ® sB&B⇨♠£15-£22 dB&B⇨♠£30-£44 WB&B£92-£135 WBDi£145-£195 LDO 6pm
Lic ♚ ℙ
Credit Cards ① ② ③ ④

GH ◲ Trenant Private Hotel Alexandra Rd TR18 4LX
☎(0736) 62005
Closed Dec-Jan
A stylish Victorian property, conveniently located close to the seafront and local amenities. Personally run, it has spacious public rooms and well furnished bedrooms of varying sizes.
10rm(4⇨5♠6hc) (3fb) CTV in all bedrooms ® ✱ sB&B£14-£16 dB&B£28-£32 dB&B⇨♠£36-£40 WB&B£90-£130 WBDi£135-£180 LDO noon
Lic ♚ CTV ℙ nc5yrs ④

◫➟ GH ◲ Trevelyan Hotel 16 Chapel St TR18 4AW
☎(0736) 62494
17th-century property offering comfortable accommodation within town centre.
8rm(1♠7hc) (4fb) CTV in all bedrooms ® ✻ (ex guide dogs) sB&B£12-£14 dB&B£24-£28 dB&B♠£24-£28 WB&B£80-£85 WBDi£125-£130 LDO am
Lic ♚ CTV 8P ④

◫➟ GH ◲◲ Trewella 18 Mennaye Rd TR18 4NG
☎(0736) 63818
Mar-Oct
Cosy little guesthouse with good home cooking about two minutes from seafront.
8rm(3♠5hc) (2fb) ® sB&B£11.50-£12.50 dB&B£23-£25 dB&B♠£27-£29 WB&B£73-£80 WBDi£109-£116 LDO noon
Lic ♚ CTV ℙ nc5yrs ④

INN ◲ The Yacht The Promenade TR18 4AU ☎(0736) 62787
This inn has uninterrupted views across Mount's Bay. The bar is decorated in Art Deco style, and the bedrooms have recently been refurbished.
6rm (1fb) CTV in all bedrooms ® ✻ (ex guide dogs) LDO 9pm 8P
Credit Cards ② ③

PERRANPORTH Cornwall & Isles of Scilly Map **02** SW75

GH ◲ The Cellar Cove Hotel Droskyn Way TR6 0DS
☎Truro(0872) 572110
This hotel enjoys fine views over the bay and proves good value for family holidays, offering simply appointed accommodation and friendly service.
12rm(2♠10hc) (7fb) CTV in all bedrooms ® sB&B£16-£18 dB&B£32-£36 dB&B♠£37-£41 WB&B£105-£125 WBDi£135-£160 LDO noon
Lic CTV 20P ⌴table tennis pool table
Credit Cards ① ③

GH ◲ Fairview Hotel Tywarnhayle Rd TR6 0DX
☎Truro(0872) 572278
Apr-Oct
Good views from this comfortable family hotel.
15rm(8♠7hc) (6fb)🗲in 2 bedrooms ® ✻ (ex guide dogs) ✱ sB&B£14-£18 dB&B£28-£36 dB&B♠£32-£40 WB&B£98-£115 WBDi£120-£140 LDO 8pm
Lic ♚ CTV 8P 3🏕
Credit Cards ① ③ ④

GH ◲◲ Headland Hotel Cliff Rd TR6 0DR
☎Truro(0872) 573222 FAX (0872) 571003
Enjoying an elevated position overlooking Perranporth's sandy beach and rugged coastline, this family-run hotel is keen to please its guests.
29rm(1⇨11♠17hc) (3fb) CTV in all bedrooms ®
✻ (ex guide dogs) sB&B£15-£20 sB&B⇨♠£18-£23 dB&B£30-£40 dB&B⇨♠£36-£46 WBDi£135-£175 LDO 7pm
Lic ♚ CTV 7P 2🏕
Credit Cards ① ③ ④

GH ◲◲◲ Villa Margarita Country Hotel Bolingey TR6 0AS
☎Truro(0872) 572063
Exceptionally well-appointed colonial style villa in an acre of well-tended gardens. Imaginative table d'hôte menus served by caring owners.
5rm(3♠2hc) Annexe 2♠ (1fb) TV in 1 bedroom ®
✻ (ex guide dogs) sB&B♠£20-£21.50 dB&B♠£40-£43 WB&B£120-£129 WBDi£207-£216 LDO 4pm
Lic CTV 8P nc8yrs ⌴solarium ④

PERTH Tayside *Perthshire* Map **11** NO12

GH ◲◲◲ Ardfern House 15 Pitcullen Crescent PH2 7HT
☎(0738) 22259
3rm(1♠2hc) 🗲in all bedrooms CTV in all bedrooms ® ✱ dB&B£30-£35 dB&B♠£35-£40 (wkly only Sep-Apr) LDO noon
♚ CTV 6P nc5yrs putting green

GH ◲◲◲ Clark Kimberley 57-59 Dunkeld Rd PH1 5RP
☎(0738) 37406
A warm welcome awaits guests at this friendly guesthouse which has convenient access to the city bypass. Mr and Mrs Cattanach are to be congratulated on the high standard of accommodation they offer, most of the rooms having en suite facilities.
8rm(6♠2hc) (5fb) CTV in all bedrooms ® sB&B£14-£16 dB&B♠£28-£32
♚ CTV 12P ④

Visit your local AA Shop.

GH 🅠🅠🅠 *Clunie* 12 Pitcullen Crescent PH2 7HT
☎(0738) 23625
*Situated on the A94 Braemar road a short way from the town
centre, this guesthouse is well furnished in all areas and is mainly
modern in style. The resident owners offer warm and friendly
service and show great concern for their guests' comfort.*
7⇦🌂 (3fb) CTV in all bedrooms ⓡ LDO noon
📺 CTV 8P

GH 🅠🅠🅠 *The Darroch* 9 Pitcullen Crescent PH2 7HT
☎(0738) 36893
*Situated beside the A94 on the northern fringe of the city, this
friendly, family-run guesthouse offers comfortable, well equipped
accommodation to the visiting tourist and businessman alike.*
6rm(3🌂3hc) (2fb) CTV in all bedrooms ⓡ ✠ (ex guide dogs)
LDO 4pm
📺 CTV 10P

GH 🅠🅠 **The Gables** 24-26 Dunkeld Rd PH1 5RW
☎(0738) 24717
*Situated in the western end of the town, this family-run guesthouse
has convenient access to the ring route and to the A9. It has a
friendly atmosphere and offers well-maintained, practical
accommodation.*
8hc (3fb) CTV in all bedrooms ⓡ ✳ sB&B£13-£14 dB&B£24-
£26 WB&B£84-£91 WBDi£124-£133 LDO 4pm
Lic 📺 CTV 8P
Credit Cards 3 £

GH 🅠🅠🅠 **Kinnaird** 5 Marshall Place PH2 8AH
☎(0738) 28021
*Overlooking the South Inch, within easy walking distance of the
town centre, this elegant Georgian terraced house offers tastefully
appointed, comfortable accomodation. Bedrooms, though compact,
are well equipped, and the standard of housekeeping throughout is
commendable.*
6rm(4🌂2hc) CTV in all bedrooms ⓡ ✠ (ex guide dogs)
sB&Bfr£17 dB&Bfr£30 dB&B🌂fr£34 LDO 4pm
📺 2P 4⇦ nc12yrs

GH 🅠🅠🅠 **Lochiel House** 13 Pitcullen Crescent PH2 7HT
☎(0738) 33183
*Guests are warmly welcomed in Rita Buchan's delightful non-
smoking bed and breakfast hotel in a semi-detached Victorian
house on the northern side of town. Bedrooms and bathrooms are
thoughtfully equipped and the lounge, where hearty breakfasts are
served, is cosy, with a real fire.*
3hc CTV in all bedrooms ⓡ ✠ (ex guide dogs) ✳ sB&B£17-
£25 dB&B£30-£32
📺 4P £

GH 🅠🅠 **Ochil View** 7 Kings Place PH2 8AA ☎(0738) 25708
*This semi-detached town house is situated on the eastern fringe of
the city centre overlooking the South Inch. It is tastefully
decorated, well furnished and provides good value bed and
breakfast accommodation.*
5rm(1🌂4hc) (2fb) CTV in all bedrooms ⓡ ✳ sB&B£11-£14
dB&B£22-£26 dB&B🌂£26-£30 WB&B£70-£90
📺 CTV 4P

GH 🅠🅠 **Pitcullen** 17 Pitcullen Crescent PH2 7HT
☎(0738) 26506
*In a residential area beside the A94, this family-run guesthouse is a
popular base for tourists, offering good value accommodation and
an attractive first floor lounge.*
6rm(2🌂4hc) (1fb) CTV in all bedrooms ⓡ ✠ ✳ sB&B£17-£20
sB&B🌂£20-£25 dB&B£30-£36 dB&B🌂£34-£38 LDO 6pm
📺 6P £

See the regional maps of popular holiday
areas at the back of the book.

PETERBOROUGH Cambridgeshire Map **04** TL19

GH 🅠🅠🅠 **Hawthorn House Hotel** 89 Thorpe Rd PE3 6JQ
☎(0733) 340608
*A brick, semidetached Victorian house with some off-street
parking, located on the B1179 opposite the hospital and within ten
minutes' walk from the the city centre and station. Tastefully
converted a few years ago, the house incorporates every modern
facility whilst retaining the original style and elegance of that
period. Bedrooms are well presented and furnished, with a high
standard of cleanliness. A well stocked bar opens into the dining
room and small lounge area.*
8rm(2⇦6🌂) (2fb)⊁in 2 bedrooms CTV in all bedrooms ⓡ ✠
✳ sB&B⇦🌂£36.50-£43.50 dB&B⇦🌂£43.50-£48
WB&B£219-£216 WBDi£267-£309
Lic 📺 CTV 5P
Credit Cards 1 3

PETERSFIELD Hampshire

See **Rogate**

PETHAM Kent Map **05** TR15

GH 🅠🅠🅠 **The Old Poor House** Kake St CT4 5RY (5m S of
Canterbury off B2068) ☎Canterbury(022770) 413
FAX 071-247 1478
4rm(2⇦2🌂) (1fb)⊁in 2 bedrooms CTV in all bedrooms ⓡ ✳
sB&B⇦🌂£30 dB&B⇦🌂£40-£50 WB&Bfr£150 WBDifr£245
LDO 9.45pm
Lic 📺 CTV 45P ♿
Credit Cards 1 3

PEVENSEY East Sussex Map **05** TQ60

GH 🅠🅠 **Napier** The Promenade BN24 6HD
☎Eastbourne(0323) 768875
*Superbly situated on the beach, this well-maintained guesthouse is
ideal for a relaxing holiday away from the crowds, yet convenient
for Eastbourne. Modern functional bedrooms are complemented
by a comfortable sun lounge, small bar, dining room, patio and
friendly efficient service from the proprietors.*
10rm(5🌂5hc) (3fb) CTV in all bedrooms ⓡ ✠ ✳ sB&B🌂£15-
£18 dB&B£28-£34 dB&B🌂£30-£36 WB&B£91-£106
WBDi£118-£134 LDO 4pm
Lic 📺 CTV 7P ✔ £

PICKERING North Yorkshire Map **08** SE88

◪◩ **GH** 🅠🅠🅠 **Bramwood** 19 Hallgarth YO18 7AW
☎(0751) 74066
*In a quiet residential area close to the town centre, this comfortable
guesthouse offers friendly service and excellent home-cooked
dinners. Smoking is not permitted.*
6hc (1fb)⊁in all bedrooms ⓡ ✠ (ex guide dogs) sB&B£12-
£14.50 dB&B£24-£32 WB&B£72-£96 WBDi£128-£152
LDO 2.30pm
CTV 6P nc3yrs
Credit Cards 1 2 3 5 £

PICKHILL North Yorkshire Map **08** SE38

INN 🅠🅠 **Nags Head Country Inn & Restaurant** Pickhill
YO7 4JG (2mE of A1) ☎Thirsk(0845) 567391
*Situated in the heart of the tiny picturesque village, yet only a mile
from the A1, this quaint inn offers well appointed accommodation
and extensive menus.*
8⇦🌂 Annexe 7⇦🌂 ⊁in 3 bedrooms CTV in all bedrooms ⓡ
✳ sB&B⇦🌂£30 dB&B⇦🌂£42 ✳ Lunch £9-£12&alc Dinner
£12.50-£15&alc LDO 9.30pm
📺 CTV 40P
Credit Cards 1 3

PIDDLETRENTHIDE Dorset Map **03** SY79

INN Q Q **The Poachers** DT2 7QX ☎(03004) 358

Bedrooms at the Poachers Inn are mostly purpose-built and grouped around the garden and outdoor swimming pool. They have all the modern facilities and attractive co-ordinating furnishings. There is a large general bar and a separate dining room with a cosy atmosphere.

2⇨♠ Annexe 9⇨♠ (2fb) CTV in all bedrooms ®
sB&B⇨♠£29 dB&B⇨♠£42 WB&B£132 WBDi£200 Lunch
£4-£12&alc Dinner £4-£12&alc LDO 9pm
₩ 40P ⌒(heated) £

PITLOCHRY Tayside *Perthshire* Map **14** NN95

GH Q Q **Adderley Private Hotel** 23 Toberargan Rd PH16 5HG
☎(0796) 2433

Etr-mid Oct

This small family-run guesthouse is situated beside the curling rink, not far from the town centre. It has a friendly atmosphere and offers good value holiday accommodation.

7rm(6⇨♠) (1fb) ✠ (ex guide dogs) sB&B£19-£21
dB&B⇨♠£38-£42 WB&B£139.75-£194.75 WBDi£194.75-£224.25 LDO 5pm
₩ CTV 9P nc6yrs

SELECTED

GH Q Q Q Q **Dundarave House** Strathview Ter PH16 6AT
☎(0796) 3109

Apr-Oct

This charming, late 19th-century house is set in well tended gardens overlooking the town. Tastefully refurbished to retain its original character, it provides a relaxed atmosphere with a high standard of accommodation. Bedrooms are individually decorated and offer a superior level of comfort and facilities. Hearty Scottish breakfasts are served in the attractive dining room.

7rm(5⇨2hc) (1fb) CTV in all bedrooms ® ✱
sB&B£23.90-£26 dB&B⇨£47.80-£52
₩ 7P £

See advertisement on page 291

GH Q Q **Duntrune** 22 East Moulin Rd PH16 5HY
☎(0796) 2172

Feb-Oct

A substantial Victorian house standing in its own grounds in a quiet side road, not far from the town centre. Good value bed and breakfast accommodation is offered.

7rm(5♠2hc) (1fb) CTV in all bedrooms ® ✠ sB&B£16-£18
dB&B♠£32-£36
₩ 8P nc5yrs £

GH Q Q **Fasganeoin Hotel** Perth Rd PH16 5DJ ☎(0796) 2387
15 Apr-12 Oct

A family-run guesthouse set in its own grounds at the southern end of town; it offers a friendly atmosphere and solid Victorian-style accommodation.

9rm(5⇨♠4hc) (3fb) ✠ (ex guide dogs) ✱ sB&B£18-£18.50
dB&B£38-£40 dB&B⇨♠£48-£57 WB&B£123-£196
WBDi£170.25-£265 LDO 7.15pm
Lic ₩ CTV 20P
Credit Cards 1 3 £

GH Q Q **Well House Private Hotel** 11 Toberargan Rd
PH16 5HG ☎(0796) 2239

Mar-Oct

In a residential area, not far from the centre of the town, this friendly family-run guesthouse has a relaxed atmosphere and provides well equipped, comfortably furnished bedrooms and wholesome food.

▶

6➧ (1fb) CTV in all bedrooms ® dB&B➧£30-£33
WB&B£94.50-£103.95 LDO 5.30pm
Lic ⑭ 8P
Credit Cards ①③

PLUCKLEY Kent Map **05** TQ94

FH QQQ Mr & Mrs V Harris **Elvey Farm Country Hotel**
(TQ916457) TN27 0SU ☎(023384) 442 FAX (02384) 726
rs Nov-Mar
*Accommodation is provided in a converted oast house, stable block
and barn at Elvey Farm. Bedrooms are spacious, comfortable and
well equipped, and many have access to a small kitchen area, but
the circular oast house rooms are undoubtedly the most charming.
The typical Kentish dining room is beamed and has long, scrubbed
wooden tables, and the walls are adorned with tools from bygone
years.*
10rm(7➧3➧) (6fb) CTV in all bedrooms ® ✳
dB&B➧➧£49.50-£57 LDO 4pm
Lic ⑭ 40P 75 acres mixed ⓕ

PLYMOUTH Devon Map **02** SX45

See Town Plan Section
GH QQQ *Bowling Green Hotel* 9-10 Osborne Place, Lockyer
St, The Hoe PL1 2PU ☎(0752) 667485
Closed 25-30 Dec
*This terraced Georgian property overlooks Drake's famous
Bowling Green, and is close to the Hoe and the Barbican city
centre. The hotel has been extensively refurbished, and bedrooms
are attractive and well equipped. Full English breakfast is served
in the informal open-plan lounge/dining room, and the
accommodation is spotlessly clean.*
12rm(7➧5hc) (3fb) CTV in all bedrooms ®
⑭ CTV 4🚗 (£2 per night)
Credit Cards ①③

GH QQ **Caraneal Hotel** 12/14 Pier St, West Hoe PL1 3BS
☎(0752) 663589
Closed 20 Dec-2 Jan
*Close to the seafront and within easy reach of The Hoe, Barbican
and city centre, this Georgian terraced house offers en suite
facilities, colour TV, direct dial telephones and tea-making
facilities in all rooms. A set dinner is served in the informal dining
room.*
10rm(6➧4➧) (1fb) CTV in all bedrooms ® ✳ sB&B➧➧£27
dB&B➧➧£38 WB&B£130-£168 WBDif£182-£220
Lic ⑭ 3P
Credit Cards ①③ⓕ

GH QQ **Cranbourne Hotel** 282 Citadel Road, The Hoe
PL1 2PZ ☎(0752) 263858 FAX (0752) 263858
Modern comforts provided in this end of terrace Georgian hotel.
13rm(5➧8hc) (3fb) CTV in all bedrooms ® ✳ sB&B£12-£15
dB&B£24-£30 dB&B➧£30-£35
Lic ⑭ CTV 3🚗
Credit Cards ①②③ⓕ

GH QQQ *Dudley* 42 Sutherland Road, Mutley PL4 6BN
☎(0752) 668322
rs Xmas
*This family Victorian home in a residential area, near the station,
has six simply furnished bedrooms, and there are many personal
pieces throughout the public areas.*
6hc (3fb) CTV in all bedrooms ® LDO 9am
⑭ CTV 🅿
Credit Cards ①③

GH QQQ **Georgian House Hotel** 51 Citadel Rd, The Hoe
PL1 3AU ☎(0752) 663237
Closed 23 Dec-5 Jan rs Sun
*A terraced Georgian house near the famous Hoe and Barbican,
with easy access to the city centre. The bedrooms offer modern,*

---

*simple décor and furnishings, and are well equipped, with en suite
facilities. An à la carte menu offers some imaginative dishes in the
informal 'Four Poster Restaurant' which is adjacent to the small
cocktail bar.*
10rm(4➧6➧) (1fb) CTV in all bedrooms ® 🐾 (ex guide dogs)
✳ sB&B➧➧£27-£29 dB&B➧➧£37-£39 LDO 9pm
Lic ⑭ CTV 2P
Credit Cards ①②③⑤

GH QQ *Lockyer House Hotel* 2 Alfred St, The Hoe PL1 2RP
☎(0752) 665755
Closed Xmas
*Situated in a quiet residential street near to the Hoe and close to
the city centre, Lockyer House provides simple bedrooms, compact
public areas and a relaxed atmosphere.*
6hc (1fb) CTV in all bedrooms 🐾 LDO 10am
Lic ⑭ CTV 🅿 nc3yrs

GH Q **Merville Hotel** 73 Citadel Rd, The Hoe PL1 3AX
☎(0752) 667595
*This terraced property, near the famous Hoe and Barbican is
within easy reach of the city centre. The resident proprietor is on
hand to welcome guests to the comfortable, compact lounge and
dining room, and uncluttered bedrooms.*
10hc (3fb) CTV in all bedrooms ® sB&Bfr£12 dB&Bfr£26
LDO 3pm
Lic ⑭ CTV 2P

GH QQ **Oliver's Hotel & Restaurant** 33 Sutherland Rd
PL4 6BN ☎(0752) 663923
*This end-of-terrace Victorian property, located near the station,
offers six bedrooms which are furnished in a traditional style.
Some interesting dishes are offered on the menu featured in the
attractive restaurant. The resident proprietors extend a warm
welcome to guests.*
6rm(4➧2hc) (1fb) CTV in all bedrooms ® 🐾 sB&B£19
sB&B➧£29 dB&B➧£44 WB&B£127-£195 LDO 8pm
▶

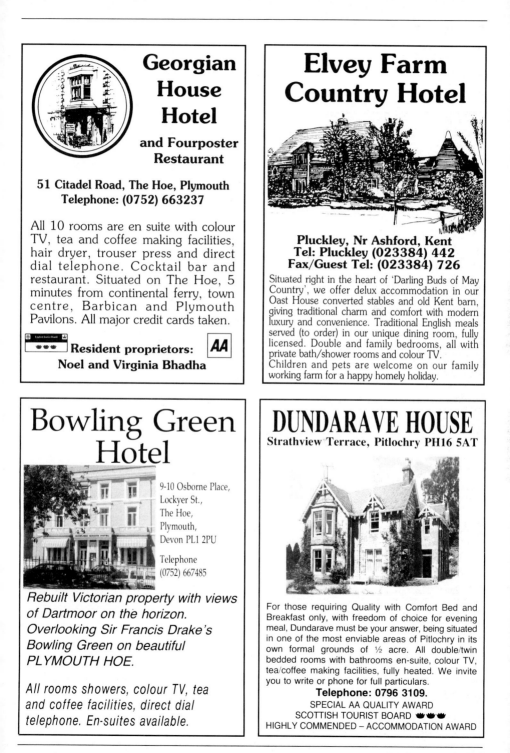

291

Lic 🍴 3P nc11yrs
Credit Cards ①②③⑤

GH 🅀🅀 *Riviera Hotel* 8 Elliott Street, The Hoe PL1 2PP
☎(0752) 667379
Closed Xmas
A family-run hotel, conveniently situated for Plymouth Hoe and the city centre. The public rooms have been recently modernised and extended, providing attractive surroundings. The bedrooms are simply furnished but very well equipped. A choice of menus is offered.
11rm(6⇄5hc) (2fb) CTV in all bedrooms ® LDO 9.30pm
Lic 🍴 ⅌
Credit Cards ①②③⑤

GH 🅀 *Rosaland Hotel* 32 Houndiscombe Rd, Mutley PL4 6HQ
☎(0752) 664749
8rm(2🏠6hc) (2fb) CTV in all bedrooms ® ✗ (ex guide dogs)
✳ sB&B£15-£16 sB&B🏠£19-£20 dB&B£30-£32 LDO 5pm
Lic 🍴 CTV 3P

GH 🅀 *Russell Lodge Hotel* 9 Holyrood Place, The Hoe
PL1 2BQ ☎(0752) 667774
A terraced property in a quiet street close to the Hoe, Barbican and city centre, providing bed and breakfast only. The public rooms promote a family atmosphere and the bedrooms are simply appointed.
9rm(2🏠7hc) (2fb) CTV in all bedrooms ® ✗ (ex guide dogs)
✳ sB&B£18-£20 dB&B£32.50-£34 dB&B🏠£36-£37.50
WB&Bfr£110
🍴 CTV 3P
Credit Cards ①②③⑤ ⓔ

GH 🅀🅀🅀 *St James Hotel* 49 Citadel Rd, The Hoe PL1 3AU
☎(0752) 661950
Closed Xmas
A terraced Victorian property close to Plymouth Hoe and the famous Barbican, yet within easy walking distance of the city centre. The bedrooms have been completely refurbished and offer high standards of modern décor and furnishings. The proprietors personally welcome guests to their family home and meals are available by prior arrangement.
10🏠 (2fb) CTV in all bedrooms ® ✗ (ex guide dogs) ✳
sB&B🏠£30 dB&B🏠£40
Lic 🍴 ⅌ nc6yrs
Credit Cards ①③

POCKLINGTON Humberside Map **08** SE74

FH 🅀 Mr & Mrs Pearson **Meltonby Hall** *(SE800524)*
Meltonby YO4 2PW (2m N unclass) ☎(0759) 303214
Etr-Oct
This large Georgian farmhouse is situated on the edge of the village of Meltonby, 2 miles north of Pocklington. It provides 2 traditionally furnished bedrooms, and an evening meal can be served if advance notice is given.
2rm (1fb) ® ✗
🍴 CTV 4P 118 acres mixed ⓔ

PODIMORE Somerset Map **03** ST52

FH 🅀🅀 Mrs S Crang **Cary Fitzpaine** *(ST549270)* Cary
Fitzpaine BA22 8JB (2m N, take A37 at junc. with A303 for 1 mile then turn rt onto unclass rd)
☎Charlton Mackrell(045822) 3250
Closed 23-26 Dec
One mile north of the A303 Podimore roundabout on the A37, this well kept Georgian farmhouse is surrounded by its own mixed farmland. The cosy dining room for breakfast and comfortable lounge complement the well equipped bedrooms.
3rm(1⇄2hc) (1fb) CTV in all bedrooms ®
✗ (ex guide dogs) sB&B£14 sB&B⇄🏠£18 dB&B£27
dB&B⇄🏠£34 WB&Bfr£90 WBDifr£105
🍴 CTV 6P nc2yrs ✍ 600 acres arable beef horses sheep ⓔ

POLBATHIC Cornwall & Isles of Scilly Map **02** SX35

🛏🚩**GH** 🅀🅀 **The Old Mill** PL11 3HA
☎St Germans(0503) 30596
10rm(7hc) (3fb) ® sB&B£12.50-£14 dB&B£25-£28 WB&B£85-£95 WBDi£150-£175 LDO 8pm
Lic CTV 12P ⓔ

POLMASSICK Cornwall & Isles of Scilly Map **02** SW94

GH 🅀🅀🅀 *Kilbol House Country Hotel* PL26 6HA
☎Mevagissey(0726) 842481
Set amid secluded grounds with a small stream, this 300-year-old cottage has functional bedrooms, 16th-century lounges, bar and an attractive dining room. There is also a peaceful cottage annexe. Early morning tea and home cooking are provided and the small farm is fun for all the family.
8rm(4⇄3hc) (2fb) LDO noon
Lic 🍴 CTV 12P ⇌
Credit Cards ①②③⑤

POLPERRO Cornwall & Isles of Scilly Map **02** SX25

GH 🅀🅀🅀 *Landaviddy Manor* Landaviddy Ln PL13 2RT
☎(0503) 72210
Feb-19 Oct
This charming country manor house dates back over 200 years and is situated down a rural lane, with lovely well kept gardens and distant sea views. Bedrooms are individually decorated, with pretty co-ordinating fabrics and a mixture of antique and modern furniture; many of the rooms have private bathrooms and each is well equipped. Public areas are also attractively appointed and comfortable.
9rm(5🏠4hc) CTV in all bedrooms ® LDO 10am
Lic 🍴 CTV 12P nc5yrs
Credit Cards ①③⑤

POLRUAN Cornwall & Isles of Scilly Map **02** SX15

GH 🅀🅀🅀 *Polmarine* West St PL23 1PL ☎(0726) 870459
Etr-Oct
4rm(1⇄3🏠) ✂in 1 bedroom CTV in 3 bedrooms TV in 1
bedroom ® ✗ dB&B£35-£40
🍴 6⇌ nc10yrs ✍ 2 moorings

POLZEATH Cornwall & Isles of Scilly Map **02** SW97

GH 🅀🅀🅀 **White Lodge Hotel** Old Polzeath PL27 6TJ
☎Trebetherick(020886) 2370
9rm(2⇄🏠7hc) (1fb) CTV in 2 bedrooms ® ✳ dB&B£30-£35
dB&B⇄🏠£48-£56
Lic 🍴 CTV 12P

PONTARDDULAIS West Glamorgan Map **02** SN50

GH 🅀🅀 **Cwmdulais House** Cwmdulais SA4 1NP
☎Swansea(0792) 885008
This is a pleasant family-run guesthouse providing modern facilities. There is a cosy lounge and a comfortable pine-furnished bar. Directions: at Pontlliw traffic lights turn into Clordir road, then turn left at the next junction.
4rm(1🏠3hc) CTV in all bedrooms CTV in all bedrooms ®
sB&B£16-£18 dB&B£31-£34 dB&B🏠fr£34 WB&B£105-£119
WBDi£143.50-£157.50
Lic 🍴 CTV 6P ⓔ

PONTRHYDFENDIGAID Dyfed Map **06** SN76

GH 🅀🅀 *Llysteg* SY25 6BB ☎(09745) 697
This friendly, family-run guesthouse lies in a small village in the heart of the beautiful Welsh countryside. The bedrooms are all pretty, each with a private bathroom, and the public rooms are comfortable.
6⇄🏠 (4fb) ✂in all bedrooms LDO 10.30pm
Lic 🍴 CTV 6P

PONTYPRIDD Mid Glamorgan Map **03** ST09

INN Ⓠ **White Hart Hotel** 1 High St CF37 1BD ☎(0443) 405922
*This busy inn is close to the town centre and its disco bar is popular
with the locals. There is also a small residents' bar on the first floor
and a breakfast room and bright bedrooms.*
6hc (6fb)⤙in 1 bedroom CTV in all bedrooms Ⓡ
✖ (ex guide dogs) ✳ sB&B£20-£25 dB&B£30-£35 ✳
🍴 CTV 15P snooker

POOLE Dorset Map **04** SZ09

See also Bournemouth

GH ⓆⓆ **Avoncourt Private Hotel** 245 Bournemouth Rd,
Parkstone BH14 9HX ☎(0202) 732025
*This small guesthouse is on the main Bournemouth to Poole road,
but has some parking. Bedrooms are compact and neat, and some
have their own bathroom. There is a small well decorated
combined bar and breakfast room, and the resident proprietors
offer a high standard of housekeeping.*
6hc (3fb) CTV in all bedrooms Ⓡ ✖ sB&B£16-£22 dB&B£32-
£40
Lic 🍴 CTV 5P 1🐕
Credit Cards ①③Ⓔ

GH ⓆⓆⓆ **Seacourt** 249 Blandford Rd, Hamworthy
BH15 4AZ ☎(0202) 674995
*A small friendly guesthouse situated on the A350 near the ferry
terminal, with some long-stay parking. Well equipped, modern
bedrooms, some with private bathrooms, and high standards of
décor and housekeeping make this a popular choice for travellers
and business people.*
6rm(2⇆1🛉3hc) (1fb) CTV in all bedrooms Ⓡ
✖ (ex guide dogs) sB&B£15 dB&B£30 dB&B⇆🛉£36
🍴 7P Ⓔ

GH ⓆⓆ **Sheldon Lodge** 22 Forest Rd, Branksome Park
BH13 6DH ☎(0202) 761186
*Sheldon Lodge is in an elevated position in a pleasant residential
area. The bedrooms have many modern facilities and there is a sun
lounge and a three- quarter size snooker table.*
14rm(8⇆6🛉) (1fb)⤙in 4 bedrooms CTV in all bedrooms Ⓡ
sB&B⇆🛉£23-£28 dB&B⇆🛉£46-£50 WBDi£190-£215
LDO 7pm
Lic 🍴 3P solarium Ⓔ

PORLOCK Somerset Map **03** SS84

GH ⓆⓆ *The Gables Hotel* TA24 8LQ ☎(0643) 862552
*Standing in a picturesque garden away from the main street of the
village, this pretty thatched cottage has bedrooms with good views
some which are furnished with antiques. There is also a
comfortable TV lounge and an elegant dining room.*
7rm(1⇆6hc) Ⓡ
Lic 🍴 CTV 🅿 nc8yrs

GH ⓆⓆ **Lorna Doone Hotel** High St TA24 8PS
☎(0643) 862404
*Set in the centre of the village, this house has cosy Victorian sitting
rooms and a smart restaurant which is open to the public. The
bathrooms are simple, and the bedrooms neat and comfortable.*
10rm(3⇆4🛉3hc) CTV in all bedrooms Ⓡ sB&B£17-£19
sB&B⇆🛉£19 dB&B£34 dB&B⇆🛉£38-£42 WB&B£130-£150
LDO 9.15pm
Lic 🍴 CTV 9P
Credit Cards ①③Ⓔ

Every effort is made to provide accurate
information, but details can change after we go to
print. It is advisable to check prices etc. before
you make a firm booking.

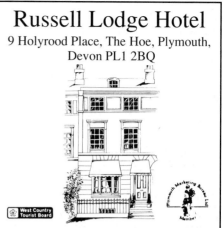

Port Erin - Portnancon

PORT ERIN

See **MAN, ISLE OF**

PORTESHAM Dorset Map **03** SY68

GH Q Q Q **Millmead Country Hotel** Goose Hill DT3 4HE
☎Abbotsbury(0305) 871432
Closed 24-26 Dec
Set in a quiet village, Millmead Hotel offers neat, well kept bedrooms, all with en suite facilities. In addition to the comfortable lounge and dining room there is a small bar and an attractive conservatory restaurant where cream teas are served.
7⇔♪ ✂in all bedrooms CTV in all bedrooms Ⓡ sB&B£21-£23.50 dB&B⇔♪£54-£59 WBDi£223.50-£263.75
LDO 6.30pm
Lic 💷 16P nc10yrs
Credit Cards 1 2 3 £

PORTHCAWL Mid Glamorgan Map **03** SS87

GH Q Q *Collingwood Hotel* 40 Mary St CF36 3YA
☎(0656) 782899
A family-run guesthouse situated close to the shops and seafront, popular with both tourists and business people alike. There is a comfortable, modern lounge, a small bar and pretty bedrooms.
8hc (4fb)✂in all bedrooms CTV in 1 bedroom Ⓡ
✶ (ex guide dogs) LDO 5pm
Lic 💷 CTV ✗

GH Q Q **Heritage** 24 Mary St CF36 3YA ☎(0656) 771881
This completely refurbished hotel is situated close to the seafront and the Grand Pavilion. It offers comfortable, well equipped bedrooms, a small bar and a very well appointed restaurant, where the chef has gained a good local reputation.
5rm(4♪1hc) CTV in all bedrooms Ⓡ ✶ ✶ sB&Bfr£16
sB&B♪fr£26 dB&B♪fr£36 WB&B£108-£116 LDO 9pm
Lic 💷 ✗
Credit Cards 1 3 £

🚗GH Q Q **Minerva Hotel** 52 Esplanade Av CF36 3YU
☎(0656) 782428
This family-run guesthouse is almost on the seafront, yet only a short walk from the town centre. Bedrooms are well equipped and there is a comfortable lounge and small bar for the use of guests.
8rm(2⇔2♪4hc) (3fb) CTV in all bedrooms Ⓡ sB&B£13
sB&B⇔♪£19 dB&B£26 dB&B⇔♪£34 WB&B£80
WBDi£132.50 LDO 6pm
Lic 💷 CTV £

PORTHCOTHAN BAY Cornwall & Isles of Scilly Map **02** SW87

GH Q Q **Bay House** PL28 8LW ☎Padstow(0841) 520472
Apr-Oct
16hc (1fb) ✶ (ex guide dogs) ✶ sB&B£17-£18 dB&B£34-£36
WB&B£119-£126 WBDi£112-£160 LDO 4.30pm
Lic CTV 17P

PORTHMADOG Gwynedd Map **06** SH53

GH Q **Oakleys** The Harbour LL49 9AS ☎(0766) 512482
Apr-Oct
This large, stone-built house dates back to the beginning of the 19th century, and is situated close to the harbour and the Ffestiniog railway terminus. It provides modest but nicely maintained accommodation, and offers very good value. There is also a private car park.
8rm(1⇔2♪5hc) (3fb) ✶ ✶ sB&B£14-£16 dB&B£25-£27
WBDi£120-£130 LDO 5pm
Lic CTV 18P nc5yrs

£ Remember to use the money-off vouchers.

GH Q Q **Owen's Hotel** 71 High St LL49 9EU ☎(0766) 512098
Mar-Oct
This small, family-run hotel provides well maintained accommodation, and many of the bedrooms have en suite facilities. It is situated in the centre of this popular tourist town, and the premises also include a confectionary and coffee shop.
10rm(3⇔4♪3hc) (3fb) CTV in all bedrooms Ⓡ sB&B£15-£16
sB&B⇔♪£20-£22 dB&Bfr£28 dB&B⇔♪£38-£40 WB&B£99-£105
💷 CTV 4P 5🚗
Credit Cards 1 3 £

PORT ISAAC Cornwall & Isles of Scilly Map **02** SW98

GH Q Q Q **Archer Farm Hotel** Trewetha PL29 3RU
☎Bodmin(0208) 880522
Etr-Oct
This rambling Cornish farmhouse has been skilfully converted, and is set in very peaceful and unspoilt rural surroundings. There is a choice of old and new bedrooms, the best being in the modern conversion. Public rooms include a restaurant, bar/lounge and a separate TV lounge. Service is particularly friendly and helpful, and dinner is usually ordered when confirming the booking.
7rm(5⇔♪2hc) (2fb)✂in all bedrooms CTV in 3 bedrooms ✶
sB&B£20-£22 sB&B⇔♪£25.50-£27.50 dB&B£40-£44
dB&B⇔♪£46-£49 WB&B£135-£145 WBDi£210-£220
LDO 8pm
Lic 💷 CTV 8P £

GH Q **Bay Hotel** 1 The Terrace PL29 3SG
☎Bodmin(0208) 880380
Etr-Oct
Double-fronted building in elevated position overlooking sea.
10rm(3⇔♪7hc) (5fb) sB&B£17.50-£21.50 dB&B£35-£43
dB&B⇔♪£44-£52 WB&B£107-£130 WBDi£154-£180
LDO 7pm
Lic CTV 10P

GH Q Q **Old School Hotel** Fore St PL29 3RB
☎Bodmin(0208) 880721
Converted by the present owner 9 years ago, the guesthouse overlooks the picturesque fishing village and harbour. Bedrooms are well equipped, and include 3 self-catering units. Snacks and light meals are available throughout the day, local fish being a speciality. Medieval banquets can be arranged, with prior notice, for groups : costumes may be hired from the hotel. Private parking is available.
13⇔♪ (6fb) CTV in all bedrooms Ⓡ sB&B⇔♪£15.50-£22
dB&B⇔♪£39.50-£73.50 WB&B£140-£185.50 WBDi£200-£245.50 LDO 9.30pm
Lic CTV 20P
Credit Cards 1 3 £

PORTNANCON Highland *Sutherland* Map **14** NC46

GH Q Q **Port-Na-Con House** IV27 4UN
☎Durness(097181) 367
Apr-Oct
Standing on the water's edge with fine views across Loch Eriboll, this former Custom House offers comfortable, compact accommodation. Due to water restraints, only showers may be taken at busy periods. The small à la carte menu, an alternative to the inclusive set dinner, features local sea food.
4hc (2fb) Ⓡ sB&B£22 dB&B£32
Lic 💷 6P nc4yrs
Credit Cards 1 3

Street plans of certain towns and cities
will be found in a separate section
at the back of the book.

PORT OF MENTEITH Central *Perthshire* Map **11** NN50

FH Q Q Mrs C Tough *Collymoon Pendicle (NN591961)*
FK8 3JY ☎Buchlyvie(036085) 222
Apr-Oct
Close to the River Forth and Lake Monteith, this attractive modern bungalow enjoys a secluded location. The service is informal and friendly, and dinner is very good value.
3hc (1fb)⊁in all bedrooms ® ✱ (ex guide dogs) LDO 6pm
🏵 CTV 3P ✔ 500 acres arable mixed

FH Q Q Q Mrs N Erskine **Inchie** *(NN592000)* FK8 3JZ
☎(08775) 233
Apr-Oct
Surrounded by 170 acres of pasture, this modernised stone farmhouse lies close to the shores of Lake Menteith. The bedrooms are modern and the public rooms are traditional in style.
2hc (1fb)⊁in all bedrooms ✱ ✱ sB&B£12-£13
🏵 CTV 2P 170 acres beef sheep £

PORTPATRICK Dumfries & Galloway *Wigtownshire* Map **10** NX05

GH Q Q Q **Blinkbonnie** School Brae DG9 8LG ☎(077681) 282
Mar-Nov Closed Nov-Feb
Set within attractive gardens overlooking the harbour, this small friendly guesthouse has comfortable accommodation (all on one level) and a friendly atmosphere. A choice of dishes is offered in the bright, well-maintained dining room.
6hc (1fb)⊁in all bedrooms ® ✱ dB&B£28-£32
🏵 CTV 10P

PORTREE

See **SKYE, ISLE OF**

PORT ST MARY

See **MAN, ISLE OF**

PORTSMOUTH & SOUTHSEA Hampshire Map **04** SZ69

See **Town Plan Section**
GH Q Q **Abbey Lodge** 30 Waverley Rd PO5 2PW
☎(0705) 828285
This single-fronted Victorian house is quietly situated in a residential area a short walk from the shops and the seafront. The guesthouse is family run and informal, offering bedrooms with tea-making facilities and colour TV. Additional facilities are provided for the benefit of the business person. A lounge is available for guests and street parking is available.
9hc (2fb) CTV in all bedrooms ® ✱ (ex guide dogs) ✱
sB&B£10-£13 dB&B£20-£26 WB&B£70-£91 WBDi£112-£133
LDO 9am
🏵 CTV ✗
Credit Cards ① ② ③ ⑤

GH Q Q Q *Ashwood* 10 St Davids Rd PO5 1QN
☎(0705) 816228
Set in a quiet tree-lined road, yet only 5 minutes by car from the seafront or ferry. The bedrooms are attractively decorated, well equipped and comfortable. The friendly owners, Pat and David Rogers, do all they can to ensure that their guests have an enjoyable and relaxing stay.
7hc CTV in all bedrooms ® ✱ (ex guide dogs) LDO 4pm
🏵 CTV nc

➡➡GH Q Q **Birchwood** 44 Waverley Rd PO5 2PP
☎(0705) 811337
This Victorian terraced house overlooks the grassy municipal garden. The seafront is a 5-minute walk away, and the accommodation is cosy and comfortable.
6rm(3♠3hc) (2fb)⊁in all bedrooms CTV in all bedrooms ®
✱ (ex guide dogs) sB&B£13-£14 sB&B♠£15-£16 dB&B£26-£28 dB&B♠£30-£32 WB&B£81.90-£100.80 WBDi£113.40-£132.30 LDO 3pm

Lic 🏵 CTV ✗
Credit Cards ① ② ③ £

GH Q Q *Bristol Hotel* 55 Clarence Pde PO5 2HX
☎(0705) 821815
Closed Xmas
Attractive, whitewashed Victorian house, dating back to 1851, overlooking the seafront and Southsea Common. The hotel offers simply appointed but fresh bedrooms, with some modern facilities. There is also a comfortable lounge area, a small bar and a prettily decorated basement dining room. Personally run by resident proprietors for the past 15 years, this hotel has a friendly, relaxed atmosphere.
13rm(9♠4hc) (7fb) CTV in 9 bedrooms TV in 4 bedrooms ®
✱ (ex guide dogs)
Lic 🏵 CTV 7P
Credit Cards ① ③
See advertisement on page 297

GH Q Q **Collingham** 89 St Ronans Rd PO4 0PR
☎(0705) 821549
Closed 24-26 Dec
Compact, friendly establishment with comfortable modern bedrooms. Well-maintained accommodation with combined lounge and dining room.
6hc (3fb)⊁in 2 bedrooms CTV in all bedrooms ®
sB&B£13.50-£15 dB&B£27-£30 WB&B£81-£84
🏵 CTV ✗ £

➡➡GH Q **The Elms Hotel** 48 Victoria Rd South PO5 2BT
☎(0705) 823924
6hc (3fb) CTV in all bedrooms ® ✱ (ex guide dogs) sB&B£13-£14 dB&B£24-£26 WB&B£85-£90
Lic 🏵 CTV 2P £

THE OAKLEYS GUEST HOUSE
The Harbour, Porthmadog.
Telephone Porthmadog (0766) 512482

Proprietors: Mr & Mrs A H Biddle.
H&C in bedrooms, electric shaver points. Licensed. Spacious free car park. No undue restrictions. Informal atmosphere. Personal attention.
Comfortable lounge. Interior sprung beds. Tea and snacks obtainable during the day. Excellent facilities for salmon and trout fishing. Also some excellent sea fishing. Comparatively close to an excellent golf course.

GH ⓆⓆ **Gainsborough House** 9 Malvern Rd PO5 2LZ
☎(0705) 822604
Set in a Victorian terrace minutes from the sea, this guesthouse has given visitors a warm, welcome for over twenty years. Bed and breakfast accommodation is provided, with pleasant bedrooms and a comfortable lounge.
7hc (2fb) CTV in all bedrooms ® ✕ sB&B£13.50-£14.50 dB&B£27-£29
⣿ CTV ✗ nc3yrs ⓔ

GH ⓆⓆ **Glencoe** 64 Whitwell Rd PO4 0QS ☎(0705) 737413
This quietly situated terraced guesthouse is family run and has well-maintained comfortable bedrooms. Deceptively spacious, the lounge and attractive dining room are complemented by a colourful courtyard garden. An easy breakfast for those catching ferries or working locally.
7hc (1fb)✗in 1 bedroom CTV in all bedrooms ® ✕ ✳
sB&B£15-£16.50 dB&Bfr£30
⣿ CTV ✗ ⓔ

GH ⓆⓆ **Goodwood House** 1 Taswell Rd PO5 2RG
☎(0705) 824734
Closed 24 Dec-2 Jan
Quietly situated close to all amenities, this guesthouse provides cosy old-fashioned accommodation that is comfortable and well maintained. The lounge/dinning room are combined.
8hc (1fb) TV in all bedrooms ® ✕ (ex guide dogs) ✳
sB&B£12-£15 dB&B£24-£28 WB&B£72-£90 WBDi£108-£126
LDO 5pm
Lic ⣿ ✗ ⓔ

✉️☎️ GH ⓆⓆⓆ **Hamilton House** 95 Victoria Rd North
PO5 1PS ☎(0705) 823502
Deceptively spacious, this Victorian house is in a central residential area. The rooms are comfortable and well equipped, and three new bedrooms have en suite facilities. Handy for the ferry port and local attractions it has a very happy atmosphere.
8rm(3◗5hc) (3fb) CTV in all bedrooms ® ✕ sB&B£13-£15 dB&B£26-£30 dB&B◗£33-£37 WB&B£86-£100 WBDi£120-£135
⣿ CTV ✗ ⓔ

GH ⓆⓆ **Lyndhurst** 8 Festing Grove PO4 9QP ☎(0705) 735239
Quietly situated close the the centre of town and the seafront, this personally run guesthouse has been owned for over 20 years by the charming Mrs Ennever. Bedrooms are simply furnished and comfortable. There is a cosy lounge area and a bright breakfast room. A friendly, relaxed atmosphere prevails and the guesthouse is popular with both commercial and holiday guests.
7hc ® ✳ sB&Bfr£13.50 dB&Bfr£25 LDO noon
⣿ CTV ✗

GH ⓆⓆⓆ **Rock Gardens Hotel** Clarence Rd PO5 2LQ
☎(0705) 833018
Closed Xmas
Friendly, personal service is offered in this quietly located guesthouse which is convenient for the seafront and shops. The modern bedrooms are well equipped, and there is a bar and dining room at the lower ground level.
15rm(8⇨3◗7hc) (3fb)✗in 1 bedroom CTV in all bedrooms ®
✕ (ex guide dogs) ✳ sB&B£16.50-£20 sB&B⇨◗£18.50-£25
dB&B£26-£30 dB&B⇨◗£33-£36 WB&B£95-£115
WBDi£125-£150 LDO 5pm
Lic ⣿ CTV 8P
Credit Cards ①③ⓔ

GH ⓆⓆ **Rydeview** 9 Western Pde PO5 3JF ☎(0705) 820865
Telex no 86626 FAX (0705) 291709
Part of a terrace overlooking the common and the distant sea views, this hotel has well equipped, simply furnished bedrooms on three floors. Breakfast is served in the lower ground floor dining room and bar meals are served in the evening.
14rm(6◗8hc) (6fb) CTV in all bedrooms ® ✕ (ex guide dogs)

Lic ⣿ CTV ✗
Credit Cards ①③⑤

✉️☎️ GH ⓆⓆ **St Andrews Lodge** 65 St Andrew's Rd PO5 1ER
☎(0705) 827079
Closed 21 Dec-3 Jan
Well situated for the shops, this guesthouse has well-equipped, modern bedrooms – some ideal for family use. The ground floor lounge is comfortable and the proprietors offer personal service.
8hc (2fb) CTV in all bedrooms ® ✕ (ex guide dogs) sB&B£13-£18 dB&B£25-£30 WB&B£91-£126 WBDi£126-£161
LDO 5pm
⣿ CTV ✗ ⓔ

GH ⓆⓆⓆ **St David's** 19 St Davids Rd PO5 1QH
☎(0705) 826858
Quietly located in a tree-lined avenue, this semidetached Victorian house is well presented throughout. The bedrooms are spacious, fresh, modestly furnished and comfortable, and there is an elegant residents' lounge.
6hc (2fb)✗in 4 bedrooms CTV in all bedrooms ®
✕ (ex guide dogs) ✳ sB&B£14-£18 dB&B£24-£28 WB&B£165-£195
CTV 1P ⓔ

See advertisement on page 299

GH Ⓠ Ⓠ **Upper Mount House Hotel** The Vale, Clarendon Rd
PO5 2EQ ☎(0705) 820456
Tucked away between the shopping area and the seafront, this listed 3-storey building is set to the rear of a main road in a quiet lane. Public rooms include a comfortable lounge with a separate bar, and the dining room is on the lower ground floor. Bedrooms are simply furnished but well equipped.
▶

12rm(11⇨♪➊1hc) (3fb) CTV in all bedrooms ®
✕ (ex guide dogs) ✱ sB&B£15-£17 sB&B⇨♪➊£17-£26
dB&B⇨♪➊£32-£46 WB&B£105-£154 WBDi£125-£175
LDO 6pm
Lic ∰ CTV 10P
Credit Cards ①③ⓔ

GH ⓠⓠ **Victoria Court** 29 Victoria Rd North PO5 1PL
☎Portsmouth(0705) 820305
7➊ CTV in all bedrooms ® ✕ (ex guide dogs) ✱ sB&B➊fr£23
dB&B➊fr£30
Lic
Credit Cards ①③

POUNDSGATE Devon Map **03** SX77

GH ⓠ **Leusdon Lodge** TQ13 7PE ☎(03643) 304
*A granite-built family-run guesthouse in an elevated position
affording glorious views across Dartmoor. The bedrooms are
conventionally furnished and equipped with many modern
conveniences. There is a wood panelled dining room where a choice
of dishes is served from a small daily changing menu. A popular
resting place for walkers, and an ideal setting from which to
explore Dartmoor.*
9rm(3⇨4➊2hc) (2fb) CTV in 8 bedrooms ® LDO 6.30pm
Lic ∰ CTV 12P
Credit Cards ①②③⑤

PRESTATYN Clwyd Map **06** SJ08

INN ⓠⓠ **Bryn Gwalia** 17 Gronant Rd LL19 9DT
☎(0745) 852442
Closed 24 Dec-1 Jan
*This small, cosy, privately owned and personally run hotel provides
well equipped bedrooms, all of which have en suite facilities. The
hotel is conveniently close to the town centre, and is equally
suitable for tourists and business people alike.*
8⇨➊ (2fb) CTV in all bedrooms ® ✕ (ex guide dogs)
LDO 9pm
∰ 24P
Credit Cards ①③

PRESTON Lancashire Map **07** SD52

GH ⓠ **Fulwood Park Hotel** 49 Watling Street Rd PR2 4EA
☎(0772) 718067
Closed Xmas & Boxing Day
*A large rambling house, converted to a mainly commercial hotel
providing extensive modern facilities. It is situated north of the
town centre, within easy reach of junction 32 of the M6 and exit 1
of the M55.*
20rm(7⇨7➊6hc) (2fb) CTV in all bedrooms ®
✕ (ex guide dogs) LDO 7.15pm
Lic CTV 24P 1🐎 ⚽ pool
Credit Cards ①②③⑤

GH ⓠⓠⓠ **Tulketh Hotel** 209 Tulketh Road, Ashton PR2 1ES
☎(0772) 726250 & 728096
Closed Xmas-New Year
*Off the Blackpool road two miles west of the town, this friendly
family-run commercial hotel in a detached Edwardian house has
well equipped bedrooms, some in a modern extension, a small bar
lounge and a dining room serving freshly cooked meals.*
12rm(11⇨➊1hc) (1fb) CTV in all bedrooms ®
✕ (ex guide dogs) ✱ sB&B£29-£35 sB&B⇨➊£31-£38
dB&B£40-£44 dB&B⇨➊£42-£48 LDO 7.30pm
Lic ∰ CTV 12P
Credit Cards ①③ⓔ

GH ⓠ **Withy Trees** 175 Garstang Road, Fulwood PR2 4LL (2m
N on A6) ☎(0772) 717693
*This mainly commercial guesthouse is situated beside the A6 about
2 miles north of the town centre. Accommodation is modest,
although 2 bedrooms have en suite facilities. There is a
comfortable lounge and a traditional dining room.*
11rm(2➊9hc) (2fb)✗in 5 bedrooms CTV in 6 bedrooms
sB&B£19-£22 sB&B➊£28-£30 dB&B£25-£27 dB&B➊£40-£42
∰ CTV 20P
Credit Cards ①③ⓔ

INN ⓠⓠⓠ **Birley Arms Motel** Bryning Ln, Warton PR4 1TN
☎(0772) 679988 FAX (0772) 679435
16➊ CTV in all bedrooms ® ✕ (ex guide dogs) ✱
sB&B➊£27-£37 dB&B➊£35-£46.50 LDO 9.15pm
∰ P
Credit Cards ①②③⑤

PRESTWICK Strathclyde *Ayrshire* Map **10** NS32

GH ⓠⓠ **Fairways Hotel** 19 Links Rd KA9 1QG
☎(0292) 70396
*This fine semidetached period house with views over the golf course
caters well for devotees of the game ; neatly maintained
throughout, it features a spacious lounge and attractive dining
room.*
6hc (1fb) ® sB&B£17-£18 dB&B£32-£34 WB&B£100-£115
Lic ∰ CTV 8P ⓔ

GH ⓠⓠⓠ **Fernbank** 213 Main St KA9 1SU ☎(0292) 75027
*A spotlessly clean detached house set beside the main road on the
southern side of the town offers thoughtfully maintained
bedrooms – bathrobes being provided in those which do not have en
suite facilities – to compliment a comfortable lounge and a very
attractive dining room.*
7rm(4➊3hc) (1fb) CTV in all bedrooms ® ✕ sB&B£14-£15
dB&B➊£30-£32
∰ CTV 7P nc5yrs ⓔ

GH ⓠⓠⓠ **Golf View Hotel** 17 Links Rd KA9 1QG
☎(0292) 671234 FAX (0292) 671244
*This red sandstone semidetached house overlooks the Prestwick
golf links, home of the first Open Championship in 1860. The hotel
is also convenient for the town centre. Bedrooms are very well
appointed, with those on the first floor enjoying particularly fine
views. The first-floor lounge is comfortably furnished and is just
the spot to watch golfers across the road, likewise the breakfast
room, where a hearty breakfast is served. Dinner is not provided
but the owner can recommend a wide range of local restaurants.*
6rm(5⇨➊) (2fb)✗in 1 bedroom CTV in all bedrooms ® ✕ ✱
sB&B⇨➊£28-£32 dB&B⇨➊£39-£48
Lic ∰ CTV 10P
Credit Cards ①③

GH ⓠⓠ **Kincraig Private Hotel** 39 Ayr Rd KA9 1SY
☎(0292) 79480
*Situated on the main road, this charming detached house has a
comfortable and relaxing lounge. It also has a period dining room
and some well-appointed bedrooms.*
6rm(3➊3hc) (1fb) CTV in all bedrooms ® ✱ sB&B£14
dB&B£28 dB&B➊£34 LDO 5pm
Lic ∰ CTV 8P nc3yrs

RAMSGATE Kent Map **05** TR36

GH ⓠⓠ **St Hilary Private Hotel** 21 Crescent Rd CT11 9QU
☎Thanet(0843) 591427
rs 25-26 Dec
*Cheerful compact bedrooms, basement dining room, situated in
residential area.*
7hc (4fb) ✕ ✱ sB&B£14-£18 dB&B£26-£30 WB&B£60-£75
(wkly only Jul & Aug)
Lic CTV 𝒥 nc4yrs
Credit Cards ①②③ⓔ

RASKELF North Yorkshire Map **08** SE47

RAVENSCAR North Yorkshire Map **08** NZ90

'Selected' establishments, which have the highest quality award, are highlighted by a tinted panel. For a full list of these establishments, consult the Contents page.

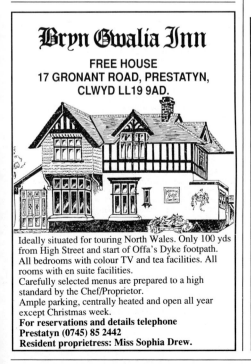

RAVENSTONEDALE Cumbria Map **12** NY70

FH Ⓠ Mrs M Wildman **Ellergill** *(NY737015)* CA17 4LL
☎Newbiggin-on-Lune(05873) 240
Mar-Nov
Situated in a tranquil rural location amid fields, this cosy comfortable farmhouse offers a good standard of accommodation and friendly service. Good home cooking is provided by Mrs Wildman.
3hc (1fb)⊁in all bedrooms ® ✕ (ex guide dogs)
CTV 6P 300 acres dairy sheep ⓔ

READING Berkshire Map **04** SU77

GH ⓆⓆ **Abbey House Hotel** 118 Connaught Rd RG3 2UF
☎(0734) 590549
A friendly, family-run detached period house in a residential road. Bedrooms are on three floors and are well kept and equipped, with bright, simple furnishings; four smarter rooms are outside in a separate building. There is a bright, open-plan dining room with a small bar where a good choice of meals is offered.
20rm(7⇨↑13hc) (1fb) CTV in all bedrooms ®
✕ (ex guide dogs) sB&Bfr£28 sB&B↑fr£40.50 dB&Bfr£44
dB&B⇨↑fr£50.50 LDO 8.30pm
Lic ⫟ CTV 14P
Credit Cards ①②③ⓔ

GH ⓆⓆ **Aeron Private Hotel** 191 Kentwood Hill, Tilehurst
RG3 6JE (3m W off A329) ☎(0734) 424119 FAX (0734) 451953
A small family-run private hotel in a residential area 3 miles west of the town. A new extension provides some en suite bedrooms, and the accommodation is comfortable and well equipped. The dining room is operated separately from the hotel and is currently being extended, a short dinner menu is available.
13rm(4↑9hc) Annexe 10hc (1fb) CTV in all bedrooms ® ✳
sB&B£24.50-£29.50 sB&B↑£38-£43 dB&B£35-£45
dB&B↑£44-£54 LDO 8.15pm
Lic ⫟ CTV 20P
Credit Cards ①③

REDCAR Cleveland Map **08** NZ62

GH Ⓠ *Claxton House Private Hotel* 196 High St TS10 3AW
☎(0642) 486745
Closed 24 Dec-2 Jan
Accommodation here is clean and comfortable and there is an interesting lounge/dining room.
17rm(6↑11hc) (2fb) CTV in 15 bedrooms ®
Lic ⫟ CTV 10P snooker

REDHILL (NEAR BRISTOL) Avon Map **03** ST46

FH ⓆⓆⓆ Mrs M J Hawkings *Hailstones (ST502638)*
BS18 7TG ☎Wrington(0934) 862209
Closed Jan
Set in a peaceful location yet only 1.5 miles from Bristol airport, this charming farmhouse offers comfortable, well-furnished rooms. Mrs Hawkings looks after her guests personally and extends a warm welcome.
4rm(1↑3hc) (2fb)⊁in all bedrooms CTV in 1 bedroom TV in 2 bedrooms ® ✕
⫟ CTV 4P croquet 150 acres dairy mixed sheep

REDHILL Surrey Map **04** TQ25

GH ⓆⓆ **Ashleigh House Hotel** 39 Redstone Hill RH1 4BG
☎(0737) 764763
Closed Xmas
Conveniently situated close to the station and the town centre, this is a well maintained house where Mr and Mrs Warren, renowned for their hospitality, extend a warm welcome. The bedrooms at Ashleigh House are modest, but there is a comfortable lounge for the residents' sole use, and a swimming pool which is open at specific times during the day.

9rm(1↑8hc) (1fb) ✕ (ex guide dogs) ✳ sB&B£25-£27
dB&B£40-£44 dB&B↑£45-£48
⫟ CTV 9P ⇨(heated)
Credit Cards ①

GH ⓆⓆ **Lynwood House** 50 London Rd RH1 1LN
☎(0737) 766894 & 762804
10rm(2↑8hc) (3fb) CTV in all bedrooms ✕ (ex guide dogs) ✳
sB&B£22-£28 dB&B£35-£40 dB&B↑£40-£45
⫟ CTV 8P
Credit Cards ①③

REDMILE Leicestershire Map **08** SK73

GH ⓆⓆ **Peacock Farm Guest House & Restaurant** NG13 NGQ
☎Bottesford(0949) 42475
4hc Annexe 5⇨↑ CTV in 3 bedrooms TV in 2 bedrooms ®
✕ (ex guide dogs) ✳ sB&B£17.50-£22.50 sB&B⇨↑£27
dB&B£30 dB&B⇨↑£37 LDO 8.30pm
Lic ⫟ CTV 30P ♨ ▭snooker solarium
Credit Cards ①

REETH North Yorkshire Map **07** SE09

GH ⓆⓆⓆ **Arkleside Hotel** DL11 6SG
☎Richmond(0748) 84200
Mar-Oct rs Nov-Dec
Set behind the village green with superb views of the Dales, this 17th-century row of cottages is now a small, quality hotel with comfortable, pretty bedrooms and an elegant restaurant and lounge. Good home cooking is served.
8rm(7↑1hc) CTV in all bedrooms ® ✳ sB&B£35-£37.50
sB&B↑fr£37.50 dB&Bfr£50 dB&B↑fr£55 WBDi£172-£186
LDO 7.30pm
Lic ⫟ CTV 6P 2☎ nc12yrs ♪(hard)✈
Credit Cards ①③ⓔ

REIGATE Surrey Map **04** TQ25

GH ⓆⓆⓆ **Cranleigh Hotel** 41 West St RH2 9BL
☎(0737) 223417 FAX (0737) 223734
An elegant town house built in 1870 and retaining many of its original features. The pretty bedrooms offer a high degree of comfort and are exceptionally well equipped. There is a residents' lounge, small bar and attractive dining room where 4-course meals are served. Guests can also use the new conservatory, extensive gardens and outdoor swimming pool.
10rm(6⇨↑3hc) (2fb) CTV in all bedrooms ®
✕ (ex guide dogs) ✳ sB&B£38-£40 sB&B⇨↑£50-£55
dB&B£55-£65 dB&B⇨↑£60-£65 LDO 9pm
Lic ⫟ CTV 6P ⇨(heated)
Credit Cards ①②③⑤ⓔ

RHANDIRMWYN Dyfed Map **03** SN74

INN ⓆⓆ **Royal Oak** SA20 0NY ☎(05506) 201
Reached by a picturesque drive through a wooded valley along the A48 north of Llandovery, this secluded inn has pretty, well-equipped bedrooms and a warm, welcoming bar.
5rm(2⇨↑2hc) (1fb) CTV in 3 bedrooms ® ✳ sB&B£15-£17
dB&B⇨↑£38-£42 LDO 10.30pm
20P pool table clay pigeon wknds
Credit Cards ①③ⓔ

Street plans of certain towns and cities
will be found in a separate section
at the back of the book.

RHOSCOLYN Gwynedd Map **06** SH27

SELECTED

GH ⓠⓠⓠⓠ **The Old Rectory** LL65 2DQ (left off A5 at Valley) ☎Trearddur Bay(0407) 860214
Closed Dec-Jan

A fine Georgian country house, situated in attractive gardens in a peaceful location, with excellent views of the sea and surrounding countryside. The bedrooms are well equipped, and all have modern private bathrooms. The two comfortable lounges cater for both smokers and non-smokers, and meals are served in the dining room on one large table. The house contains many pieces of antique furniture, and is very well preserved and maintained. There is also a self-catering cottage available, sleeping up to eight people.

5rm(3⇨2ﬔ)(2fb) CTV in all bedrooms ®
sB&B⇨ﬔ£27.50 dB&B⇨ﬔ£45 WB&B£138 WBDi£215
LDO 5pm
Lic ⬡ CTV 6P
Credit Cards ①③£

RHOS-ON-SEA Clwyd

See **Colwyn Bay**

RHYL Clwyd Map **06** SJ08

GH ⓠⓠ **Pier Hotel** 23 East Pde LL18 3AL ☎(0745) 350280
Closed Xmas

This small, privately-owned hotel provides well equipped accommodation and many of the bedrooms have en suite facilities. It is located on the promenade, opposite the 'Ocean World' complex. There is a small car park at the rear. ▶

Ashleigh House Hotel

39 Redstone Hill, Redhill, Surrey
Tel: Redhill (0737) 764763

This fine Edwardian residence now run as a family hotel offers a genuine friendly atmosphere with the personal attention of the owners at all times. Our English breakfast is our speciality and value for money.

Colour television ★ Lounge ★ Hairdryers & Shaving points in all rooms ★
★ Full fire certificate ★ Hot & Cold in all rooms ★ Exit Junction 6 & 8 M25 ★ Junction 8 M23.

Gatwick by car 15 minutes by train 10 minutes; London by train 35 minutes.

Cranleigh Hotel

41, West Street,
Reigate RH2 9BL.
Tel:
Reigate 240600 and 223417

This small friendly hotel offers first class accommodation at realistic prices.

All rooms are exquisitely furnished, and there are 2 acres of gardens with heated swimming pool.

Ideally situated for overnight stays, for anyone using Gatwick Airport, which is only 10 minutes away, and M25 one mile.

The Aeron Private Hotel
191 Kentwood Hill, Tilehurst, Reading.
Tel: (0734) 424119 Fax: (0734) 451953

24 bedrooms some en suite, all with colour TV, telephone and tea & coffee making facilities. Full English breakfast. Dinner served Mon-Thurs inclusive except public holidays. Good class accommodation at highly competitive rates.

BUSINESS & PRIVATE.
SPECIAL WEEK END DISCOUNT.

2 miles M4 exit 12. 45 minutes London Airport via M4. 35 minutes London Paddington via BR.

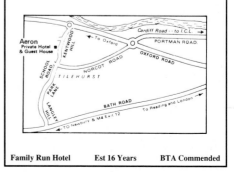

| Family Run Hotel | Est 16 Years | BTA Commended |

9rm(3⇆3🔥3hc) (3fb) CTV in all bedrooms ® ✳ sB&B£13-£14 sB&B⇆🔥£15.50-£17.50 dB&B⇆🔥£31-£35 WB&B£79-£87 WBDif£108-£119 LDO 3pm
Lic 🍴 CTV 2P
Credit Cards ① ③

RICHMOND North Yorkshire Map **07** NZ10

See also Low Row, Reeth and Thwaite
GH 🆀🆀🆀 **Pottergate** 4 Pottergate DL10 4AB ☎(0748) 823826
Standing on the A6108 on its eastern approach to the town, this guesthouse has comfortable well-appointed bedrooms with double glazing, and is very well maintained.
6hc (2fb)⤢in 3 bedrooms CTV in all bedrooms ® ✖ ✳ sB&B£17 dB&B£28 WB&B£98
Lic 🍴 CTV 3P nc2yrs

SELECTED

FH 🆀🆀🆀🆀 Mrs M F Turnbull **Whashton Springs** *(NZ149046)* DL11 7JS (3m W on unclass rd)
☎(0748) 822884
Closed Xmas & New Year
This attractive and unusual stone farmhouse is set in a delightful spot in the Yorkshire Dales, with lovely views over the rolling countryside, yet only 3 miles from the historic town of Richmond. Three spacious bedrooms are provided in the house, and converted outbuildings provide another 5 in the attractive stable courtyard. Most bedrooms have private bathrooms, and are extremely comfortable and attractively decorated, furnished with many thoughtful extras. The owners are charming and hospitable hosts, and guests are treated to a most enjoyable dinner using local produce, followed by substantial Yorkshire breakfasts. Without doubt, this is an excellent example of hospitality at its best.
3rm(2⇆1🔥) Annexe 5rm(2⇆3🔥) (2fb)⤢in 3 bedrooms CTV in all bedrooms ® ✖ (ex guide dogs) sB&B⇆🔥£26 dB&B⇆🔥£38 WB&Bfr£131 WBDifr£194 LDO am
Lic 🍴 10P nc5yrs 600 acres arable beef mixed sheep

RIEVAULX North Yorkshire Map **08** SE58

FH 🆀🆀 Mrs M E Skilbeck **Middle Heads** *(SE584869)*
YO6 5LU ☎Bilsdale(04396) 251
Mar-Nov
This stone farmhouse is in an attractive rural setting, one mile east of the B1257 and three miles west of Helmsley. It offers neat accommodation, with three bedrooms sharing a modern bathroom, and a comfortable lounge.
3rm ⤢in all bedrooms ✖ ✳ dB&Bfr£25
🍴 CTV 6P nc5yrs 170 acres arable beef mixed sheep

RINGWOOD Hampshire Map **04** SU10

SELECTED

GH 🆀🆀🆀🆀 **Little Forest Lodge Hotel** Poulner Hill
BH24 3HS ☎(0425) 478848
An attractive country house set back from the A31 eastbound carriageway from Ringwood, and surrounded by 3 acres of landscaped gardens. Most bedrooms are double glazed and equipped with TV and tea-making facilities, and smoking in bedrooms is discouraged. A four-course dinner is served in the candlelit oak-panelled dining room; a choice is offered at each course, and bar meals can be arranged for late arrivals by prior arrangement. Activities such as fishing, sailing and riding can be arranged, making this an ideal location for touring the area.
5rm(2⇆1🔥2hc) (2fb)⤢in 2 bedrooms CTV in all bedrooms ® ✳ sB&B⇆🔥£31-£35 dB&B⇆🔥£44-£64 WB&B£132-£192 LDO 4pm
Lic 🍴 CTV 10P 2🌸 solarium

Credit Cards ① ③ ⓔ

RIPON North Yorkshire Map **08** SE37

GH 🆀🆀🆀 **Crescent Lodge** 42 North St HG4 1EN
☎(0765) 602331
6 Jan-12 Dec
This Georgian house was reputedly once the town residence of the Archbishop of York. It is situated beside the A61 on the northern approach to the city centre, within easy walking distance of the Market Square and Cathedral. The bedrooms vary in shape and size, but the accommodation is very pleasant and comfortable and well maintained throughout.
10rm(3🔥7hc) (4fb) CTV in all bedrooms ® ✖ sB&B£15 dB&B£24-£36 WB&B£84-£119
Lic 🍴 CTV ✗

ROADWATER Somerset Map **03** ST03

FH 🆀🆀 Mr & Mrs Brewer *Wood Advent (ST037374)*
TA23 0RR ☎Washford(0984) 40920
Set in 350 acres at the foot of the Brendon Hills in Exmoor National Park, this delightful farmhouse has spacious bedrooms, some with en suite facilities and relaxing public rooms. Mrs. Brewer uses home produce whenever possible for the set menu.
5rm(1⇆2🔥1hc) (3fb) ® ✖
Lic 🍴 CTV 10P 2🌸 ♨ ≋(heated) ♪(grass)350 acres arable beef sheep
See advertisement under DUNSTER

ROCHDALE Greater Manchester Map **07** SD81

FH 🆀🆀 Mrs J Neave **Leaches** *(SD835838)* Ashworth Valley
OL11 5UN ☎(0706) 41116 & 41117
Closed 24 Dec-1 Jan
Situated at the end of a rough farm track which is well signposted from the B666 and A680, this farmhouse dating from 1675 enjoys spectacular views over the Manchester plain. Traditional accommodation is offered, with a warm, friendly welcome.
3hc (2fb)⤢in all bedrooms CTV in all bedrooms ✖ (ex guide dogs) ✳ sB&B£19 dB&B£32
🍴 CTV 6P ♪ coarse fishing 140 acres beef sheep ⓔ

ROCHE Cornwall & Isles of Scilly Map **02** SW96

GH 🆀🆀🆀 **Asterisk** Mount Pleasant PL26 8LH
☎St Austell(0726) 890863
A detached stone house, full of character, set back from the A30 east of Roche in its own grounds – home for geese, goats and shetland ponies. Inside there is a friendly welcome, a comfortable sitting room and a cosy bar. Upstairs the bedrooms are bright and clean, and those at the back have views across the fields.
7rm(2🔥5hc) (2fb) ® ✳ sB&B£19.50-£22 dB&B🔥£29.50-£32.50
Lic 🍴 CTV 10P 2🌸
Credit Cards ① ③

ROCHESTER Northumberland Map **12** NY89

FH 🆀🆀 Mrs J M Chapman **Woolaw** *(NY821984)* NE19 1TB
☎Otterburn(0830) 20686
A well furnished and comfortable farmhouse in a lovely rural setting on the edge of the village.
3rm(2🔥) (1fb) TV available ✖ (ex guide dogs) ✳ sB&B🔥£11-£14 dB&B🔥£22-£28 WB&B£84-£90 WBDif£108.50-£120 LDO 7.30pm
🍴 CTV 10P ♪ 740 acres beef sheep

🆀 is for quality. For a full explanation of this AA quality award, consult the Contents page.

ROCK Cornwall & Isles of Scilly Map **02** SW97

GH Q Roskarnon House Hotel PL27 6LD
☎Trebethrick(0208) 862329
Mar-Nov
Standing within an acre of lawns in an elevated position with beautiful views across the Camel Estuary, this detached house has simply appointed bedrooms and an attractive dining room with a table d'hôte menu.
15rm(4⇨2♠9hc) (5fb) CTV in 4 bedrooms TV in 1 bedroom
⊁ ✱ sB&Bfr£20 sB&B⇨♠fr£30 dB&Bfr£40 dB&B⇨♠fr£45
WB&Bfr£140 WBDifr£200 LDO 8pm
Lic CTV 14P 2☎ (£1 per night)

ROEWEN Gwynedd Map **06** SH77

GH Q Q Q Gwern Borter Country Manor Barkers Ln
LL32 8YL ☎Tyn-y-Groes(0492) 650360
Closed 23 Dec-2 Jan
The manor is set in nine acres of grounds at the foot of Talytan Mountain, north of the village. Short breaks are the main business at the manor house which can be enhanced by supervised horse rides. For complete freedom self-catering units are available.
3rm(1⇨2♠) (1fb) CTV in all bedrooms ® ✱ dB&B⇨♠£32-£44 WB&Bfr£110 WBDi£140-£190 (wkly only Jul-Aug)
LDO 4pm
Lic ♨ CTV 10P 4☎ nc3yrs U cycle hire £

ROGART Highland *Sutherland* Map **14** NC70

SELECTED

FH Q Q Q Q Mrs J S R Moodie **Rovie** *(NC716023)*
IV28 3TZ ☎(04084) 209
Apr-Oct
A delightful lodge-style farmhouse, peacefully set in sheltered gardens in the picturesque valley of Strath Fleet. The main lounge with its welcoming peat-burning fire invites peaceful relaxation, while the cosy sun lounge offers board games and TV. The bedrooms are spacious and bright and provide a good standard of comfort. Genuine hospitality, together with traditional comforts and enjoyable home cooking are all part of the appeal of this popular farmhouse, and guests return regularly, so booking is recommended.
6hc (1fb) ✱ sB&B£13.50-£14.50 dB&B£27-£29
LDO 6.30pm
CTV 8P ▶9 ✔ 120 acres beef sheep £

ROGATE West Sussex Map **04** SU82

SELECTED

FH Q Q Q Q Mrs J C Francis **Mizzards** *(SU803228)*
GU31 5HS ☎(0730) 821656
Closed Xmas
Situated in a tranquil rural setting, the house is full of character with attractive, comfortable and well-equipped accommodation. The house is elegant, spacious and has a very comfortable lounge.
3⇨♠ ⊁in all bedrooms CTV in all bedrooms ® ⊁
sB&B⇨♠£26-£32 dB&B⇨♠£38-£42
♨ 10P 2☎ nc6yrs ≋(heated) 13 acres sheep non-working
£

See advertisement on page 305

FH Q Q Q Mrs J Baigent **Trotton** *(SU835225)* GU31 5EN
☎Midhurst(0730) 813618 FAX (0730) 816093
This modern farmhouse is set on a 200-acre working farm, situated 2 miles from Rogate in a tranquil and rural area. The accommodation is well-equipped and maintained with a lounge/games room and family style breakfast room.

▶

Rovie Farm Guest House
Rogart, Sutherland IV28 3TZ
Telephone: (04084) 209

Situated in the picturesque valley of Strathfleet, just 4 miles off the A9, on the A839 Mound - Lairg road. A beef and sheep working farm offering a 'Home from Home' with good home cooking and baking served. All the bedrooms are comfortable and have H & C and heating. Total relaxation or strenuous exercise is available if desired.
Open Easter until November.
Come to Rovie Farm Guest House for Highland Hospitality at its best.

Little Forest Lodge Hotel
Poulner Hill, Ringwood,
Hampshire BH24 3HS
Telephone: Ringwood (0425) 478848

An elegant country house situated on the edge of the New Forest. All bedrooms are elegantly furnished with en suite facilities, including 'The Honeymoon Suite' and 'The Balcony Room' which overlooks the 3 acres of beautiful landscaped gardens where in summer months cream teas are served. A superb buffet followed by traditional English breakfast is served in our oak panelled dining room. Relax in our bar/lounge, with cosy log fire in winter months.
Resident Proprietors: Eric & Jane Martin

3rm(2🛏1hc) ⊬in all bedrooms CTV in 1 bedroom ®
🋘 (ex guide dogs) ✳ sB&B£15-£20 sB&B🛏£25-£30
dB&B🛏£35-£40
🍴 CTV P ✒ table tennis darts 230 acres arable beef
horticulture

ROSLIN Lothian *Midlothian* Map **11** NT26

INN Ⓠ Ⓠ **Olde Original Rosslyn** 4 Main St EH25 9LD
☎031-440 2384
*Early 18th-century inn, full of character, providing a good
standard of modern accommodation. Pleasant, popular bars.*
6🛏🛏 CTV in all bedrooms ® ✳ sB&B🛏🛏£35-£38
dB&B🛏🛏£40-£45 ✳ Lunch £6.50-£10.50&alc Dinner £10-
£15&alc LDO 10pm
🍴 14P
Credit Cards ① ② ③ ④

ROSS-ON-WYE Hereford & Worcester Map **03** SO52

See also St Owen's Cross
GH Ⓠ Ⓠ **The Arches Country House** Walford Rd HR9 5PT
☎(0989) 63348
*A small, popular guesthouse situated on the B4228 to the south of
the town, which is nearby. Bedrooms are well maintained and
comfortable, and all have views of the lawned gardens. There is a
cosy lounge with colour TV and a pleasant dining room.*
7rm(1🛏2🛏4hc) (2fb)⊬in 1 bedroom CTV in all bedrooms ®
🋘 sB&Bfr£15 sB&B🛏🛏fr£20 dB&Bfr£30 dB&B🛏🛏fr£40
WB&B£99.50-£128 WBDi£169.50-£198 LDO 5pm
Lic 🍴 CTV 9P ④

GH Ⓠ Ⓠ **Brookfield House** Ledbury Rd HR9 7AT
☎(0989) 62188
rs Nov-Jan
*This guesthouse is situated within walking distance of the town
centre and has its own car park. Brookfield House is run by Mr
and Mrs Baker who are friendly and helpful.*
8rm(1🛏2🛏5hc) CTV in all bedrooms ® sB&B£15.50
dB&B£30 dB&B🛏🛏£34 WB&B£92-£101
Lic 🍴 10P nc5yrs
Credit Cards ① ③ ④

GH Ⓠ Ⓠ Ⓠ *Edde Cross House* Edde Cross St HR9 7BZ
☎(0989) 65088
Feb-Nov
*Edde Cross House is a Georgian Grade II listed building, once the
summer palace of the Bishops of Hereford, it was also the home of
Sibyl Hathaway, Dame of Sark. Accommodation is comfortable,
attractive and well equipped with some thoughtful extras. Some
rooms have good views across the horseshoe bend of the River
Wye, and there is an attractive small garden from which guests can
also enjoy the view. The proprietors are friendly and welcoming
and work hard to ensure that guests are comfortable. This is a 'no
smoking' house.*
5rm(2🛏3hc) ⊬in all bedrooms CTV in all bedrooms ®
🋘 (ex guide dogs)
🍴 1🍽 (£1 per day) nc10yrs

GH Ⓠ Ⓠ Ⓠ **Ryefield House Hotel** Gloucester Rd HR9 5NA
☎(0989) 63030
*Situated on the outskirts of the town, approximately half a mile
from its centre, this large Victorian house offers comfortable
accommodation. The bedrooms are well equipped and maintained,
and many have en suite facilities. The proprietors' warm and
friendly hospitality contributes much to its popularity.*
8rm(5🛏3hc) (4fb) CTV in all bedrooms ® sB&B£19-£21
dB&B£37-£40 dB&B🛏🛏£47-£52 WB&B£116-£164
WBDi£186-£234 LDO 5pm
Lic 🍴 CTV 10P 1🍽 ④

GH Ⓠ Ⓠ **Sunnymount Hotel** Ryefield Rd HR9 5LU
☎(0989) 63880
Closed Xmas
*Sunnymount is situated in a quiet residential area close to the
town. The accommodation is comfortable and spacious and Mr
and Mrs Williams are welcoming hosts.*
9rm(6🛏3hc) ® 🋘 (ex guide dogs) sB&B£18-£21
sB&B🛏🛏£32 dB&B£36 dB&B🛏🛏£45-£48 WB&B£116.50-
£147.50 WBDi£196-£220 LDO 6.30pm
Lic 🍴 CTV 7P
Credit Cards ① ② ③ ④

ROTHBURY Northumberland Map **12** NU00

GH Ⓠ Ⓠ Ⓠ Ⓠ **Orchard** High St NE65 7TL ☎(0669) 20684
Mar-Nov
*A pleasant stone building set back from the main street, owned
and run by charming hosts who provide a high standard of
accommodation, with many thoughtful extras. A well
produced set dinner is offered each evening, providing
excellent all round value.*
6rm(4🛏2hc) (1fb) CTV in all bedrooms ® 🋘
dB&B£36.50-£38.50 dB&B🛏🛏£41-£42.50 WB&B£127.75-
£148.75 WBDi£199.50-£222 LDO 7pm
Lic 🍴 🐾 ④

ROTHERWICK Hampshire Map **04** SU75

GH Ⓠ Ⓠ Ⓠ **Foresters Oaks** Hook Rd RG27 9BY
☎Basingstoke(0256) 763116
*A modern red-brick detached house on the edge of the village
backing on to private woodland. Bedrooms are exceptionally well
equipped, with hair dryers, trouser presses, remote-control teletext* ▶

TV and individual pay phones, catering specifically for the business person; the lounge/dining room is available for private meetings. An informal buffet breakfast is served or cooked breakfast is available on request; either can be taken in the bedroom.
3⇋↑ CTV in all bedrooms ® ✻ (ex guide dogs) ✲
sB&B⇋↑£22.50-£39 dB&B⇋↑£35-£49
🍴 5P nc3yrs

ROTHLEY Leicestershire Map **08** SK51

GH Q Q Q **The Limes Hotel** 35 Mountsorrel Ln LE7 7PS
☎Leicester(0533) 302531
Closed Xmas
Friendly, efficiently run hotel with comfortable bedrooms and pleasant bars.
12⇋↑ CTV in all bedrooms ® ✻ (ex guide dogs)
sB&B⇋↑£38-£45 dB&B⇋↑£45-£50 LDO 9pm
Lic 🍴 15P nc12yrs
Credit Cards ①②③ ⓔ

ROTTINGDEAN East Sussex Map **05** TQ30

GH Q Q **Braemar House** Steyning Rd BN2 7GA
☎Brighton(0273) 304263
This pleasant family-run hotel combines traditional accommodation, which is very well-maintained, with a comfortable television lounge and a cosy dining room. The hotel is adjacent to the village green and is within easy walking distance of the seafront.
16hc (2fb) sB&B£14-£15 dB&B£28-£30
🍴CTV ⅌ ⓔ

GH Q Q **Corner House** Steyning Rd BN2 7GA
☎Brighton(0273) 304533
This is a rather cosy establishment that is personally run. The accommodation offered is functional and well kept, and breakfast here is taken in a relaxing atmosphere.
6hc (1fb) CTV in 5 bedrooms TV in 1 bedroom ® ✻ sB&B£14-£14.50 dB&B£28-£29
🍴⅌ ⓔ

ROWTON Shropshire Map **07** SJ61

FH Q Mr & Mrs Evans *Church (SJ614198)* TF6 6QY (1m along unclass road, off the A442 Whitchurch to Telford road)
☎High Ercall(0952) 770381
Part of a working farm, this 300-year-old house is 6 miles north of Wellington in a small, peaceful village. The bedrooms are simply furnished and the lounge features an unusual wood panelled inglenook fireplace.
4rm(2↑2hc) (1fb)⅍in all bedrooms ® LDO 5pm
🍴CTV 6P 2🍴 ♨ ♪ 35 acres dairy pigs sheep

ROXTON Bedfordshire Map **04** TL15

FH Q Q Q Mrs J Must *Church (TL153545)* 41 High St
MK44 3EB ☎Bedford(0234) 870234
This attractive farmhouse has a brick façade, with well tended gardens and a patio. The peaceful village setting means a good night's sleep in the two spacious bedrooms, one with grand period furniture. Guests have use of a comfortable lounge with TV and an open fire, and the timbered breakfast room. A warm, friendly atmosphere prevails.
2hc (1fb) ® ✻ sB&B£17-£19 dB&B£28-£30 WB&B£119
🍴CTV 6P 66 acres arable

RUCKHALL Hereford & Worcester Map **03** SO44

SELECTED
INN Q Q Q Q **The Ancient Camp** HR2 9QX
☎Golden Valley(0981) 250449
Situated in an elevated position, with superb views across the River Wye and Golden Valley, the apparent isolation of the inn belies its proximity to Hereford: only 10 minutes' drive away. The accommodation is exceptionally well equipped with every modern convenience. In the bar area, flagged floors and stone walls are warmed by open fires, and a choice of traditional ales is available. The unusual and varied menu is popular with local business people and guests alike.
5rm(2⇋3↑) CTV in all bedrooms ® ✻ (ex guide dogs)
sB&B⇋↑£35-£45 dB&B⇋↑£50-£60 Bar Lunch £3.50-£5.95 Dinner £8.95-£15alc LDO 9.30pm
🍴 30P nc10yrs ♪
Credit Cards ①③

RUFFORTH North Yorkshire Map **08** SE55

GH Q Q **Wellgarth House** Wetherby Rd YO2 3QB
☎(090483) 592 & 595
Closed 25-26 Dec
A large well-appointed modern house on the edge of the village.
8rm(3↑5hc) (1fb) CTV in all bedrooms ® sB&B£16-£20
dB&B£28-£30 dB&B↑£30-£36 LDO 5pm
🍴 CTV 8P nc2yrs
Credit Cards ①③

RUGBY Warwickshire Map **04** SP57

GH Q Q **Avondale** 16 Elsee Rd CV21 3BA ☎(0788) 578639
Quietly situated in a residential area close to the town centre and the famous Rugby School, this guesthouse has the benefit of private parking. The friendly proprietors provide comfortable surroundings.
4rm(1↑3hc) (1fb) CTV in 2 bedrooms ® ✻ sB&B£18-£20
dB&B£32-£34 dB&B↑£38
🍴CTV 6P 2🍴 ⓔ

GH Q *Mound Hotel* 17-19 Lawford Rd CV21 2EB
☎(0788) 543486
Closed Xmas
Formerly three late-Victorian houses, this hotel, situated on the A428 close to the town centre, retains some original features. Although only room and breakfast are provided, there is a good lounge for guests' use.
17rm(6↑11hc) (4fb) CTV in 6 bedrooms TV in 11 bedrooms
✻ (ex guide dogs) LDO 3pm
Lic 🍴CTV 14P
Credit Cards ①

RUISLIP Greater London London plan **4** A5 (pages 000-000)

GH Q Q Q *Barn Hotel* West End Rd HA4 6JB
☎(0895) 636057 Telex no 892514 FAX (0895) 638379
This is a small 'village' of buildings set in pretty landscaped gardens. The reception, bar and 6 executive rooms are housed in converted 17th-century black and white barns, but most of the bedrooms are in 3 modern annexes. Most rooms have en suite facilities and are well equipped, especially for the business user and tour party, who predominate at this busy establishment.
Annexe 66rm(64⇋↑2hc) (1fb)⅍in 4 bedrooms CTV in all bedrooms ® ✻ (ex guide dogs) LDO 9.30pm
Lic 🍴CTV 60P
Credit Cards ①②③⑤

Book as early as possible for busy holiday periods.

RUSHTON SPENCER Staffordshire Map **07** SJ96

FH Q Mrs J Brown **Barnswood** *(SJ945606)* SK11 0RA
☎(0260) 226261
Closed 24 Dec-5 Jan
Smoking is discouraged in the good-sized bedrooms of a homely farmhouse which overlooks Rudyard Lake from its position on the A523 Macclesfield road, approximately five miles from Leek.
4rm(2hc) (2fb) ® ✕ ✳ sB&Bfr£14 dB&Bfr£24 WB&Bfr£77
⑩ CTV 4P 100 acres dairy

RUSTINGTON West Sussex Map **04** TQ00

GH QQQ **Kenmore** Claigmar Rd BN16 2NL ☎(0903) 784634
Quietly located in a residential area, this detached house has recently undergone an extension, and a new lounge has been created. The majority of rooms are en suite, well equipped with colour TV, tea-making facilities and radio alarms. Rooms are attractively co-ordinated. The new dining room is attractive, and three-course dinners are available. Mrs Sylvia Dobbs creates a comfortable atmosphere.
7rm(1⇨5 ♪ 1hc) (2fb) CTV in all bedrooms ® ✳ sB&B£15.25-
£16 sB&B⇨♪£20-£25 dB&B⇨♪£40-£50 WB&B£123.50-
£150 LDO noon
⑩ CTV 7P
Credit Cards ⬚1 ⬚2 ⬚3

RUTHIN Clwyd Map **06** SJ15

SELECTED

GH QQQQ **Eyarth Station** Llanfair Dyffryn Clwyd
LL15 2EE ☎(08242) 3643
This former old railway station, on a disused line, has been tastefully converted into a delightful little guesthouse. It is quietly situated in the picturesque Vale of Clwyd and provides good quality accommodation. Additional facilities include an outdoor swimming pool.
4♪ Annexe 2♪ (2fb) CTV in 1 bedroom ® ✳
sB&B♪£25-£27 dB&B♪£34-£40 LDO 7pm
Lic ⑩ CTV 6P ≋(heated)
Credit Cards ⬚1 ⬚3

FH Q Margaret E Jones **Pencoed** *(SJ107538)* Pwllglas
LL15 2LT ☎Clawdd Newydd(08245) 251
Closed Xmas
A large traditional farmhouse in quite a remote location on a 160-acre beef and sheep-rearing farm. The proprietor is a very successful competitor in sheepdog trials. Situated some four miles south of Ruthin, signed from the A494 at the edge of Pwllglas village, Pencoed Farm offers very cosy accommodation.
2hc (2fb) ✳ sB&B£12-£13 dB&B£24-£25 WB&B£80-£85
⑩ CTV P 160 acres mixed ⓔ

RYDAL Cumbria

See **Ambleside**

RYDE

See **WIGHT, ISLE OF**

RYE East Sussex Map **05** TQ92

SELECTED

GH QQQQ **Holloway House** High St TN31 7JF
☎(0797) 224748
This beautiful Tudor house with its medieval vaulted cellar has an ivy-clad Georgian façade and is situated in the attractive High Street. Bedrooms are tastefully decorated and furnished with traditional and antique furniture, some with four-poster or brass beds, and all with private bathrooms.

There is a cosy lounge with Elizabethan oak panelling and an original Cairn stone fireplace. Dinner is available throughout the summer, and always on request.
7rm(5⇨2♪) (2fb) CTV in all bedrooms ®
✕ (ex guide dogs) sB&B⇨♪£39-£60 dB&B⇨♪£70-£90
LDO 8pm
Lic ⑩ ₽
Credit Cards ⬚1 ⬚3

SELECTED

GH QQQQ **Jeakes House** Mermaid St TN31 7ET
☎(0797) 222828 FAX (0797) 222623
Situated in a picturesque cobbled street, the oldest part of this charming listed building dates back to the 17th century. Bedrooms have been individually furnished and decorated to a high standard; the majority benefit from attractive en suite bathrooms complete with hand-painted Rye tiles. Breakfast is served in the galleried 18th-century chapel which was once a Quaker meeting house, and the owners have recently added a small panelled bar.
12rm(8⇨2♪2hc) (2fb) CTV in all bedrooms ® sB&B£21
dB&B£38 dB&B⇨♪£50 WB&B£266-£350
Lic ⑩ ₽
Credit Cards ⬚1 ⬚2 ⬚3 ⓔ

See advertisement on page 309

GH ||Q||Q||Q|| *Little Saltcote* 22 Military Rd TN31 7NY
☎(0797) 223210
Situated in an elevated position with its own cottage garden, this cosy establishment has well-furnished and maintained bedrooms. Parking is available and the town centre is only 5 minutes' walk away.
6rm(2➤4hc) (2fb) TV in all bedrooms ® ✖
🏵 P

GH ||Q||Q||Q|| *Old Borough Arms* The Strand TN31 7DB
☎(0797) 222128
Built into the medieval town walls, this pleasant guesthouse enjoys an elevated position. The comfortable modern accommodation includes a charming 18th-century dining room and bedrooms with en suite shower rooms.
9➤ (3fb) CTV in all bedrooms ® sB&B➤£20-£25
dB&B➤£40-£55 LDO 8pm
Lic 🏵 CTV 2P
Credit Cards ||1|| ||3|| ⓔ

SELECTED

GH ||Q||Q||Q||Q|| *The Old Vicarage Hotel & Restaurant* 15
East St TN31 7JY ☎(0797) 225131
This listed building has been sympathetically converted into a small elegant hotel, situated just off the High Street. Bedrooms are all individually decorated and furnished in period style, and are well equipped with all modern facilities, each with a private bathroom. The well appointed restaurant offers a varied and interesting menu with reasonably priced wines, and there is a small bar.
4➤➤ (2fb) CTV in all bedrooms ® sB&B➤➤£40-£49
dB&B➤➤£56-£72 WB&B£168-£216 WBDi£234-£282
LDO 9pm
Lic 🏵 ⳨
Credit Cards ||1|| ||3|| ||5|| ⓔ

FH ||Q||Q||Q|| Mrs P Sullivin *Cliff (TQ933237)* Iden Lock
TN31 7QE ☎Iden(07978) 331 due to change to (0797) 280331
Mar-Oct
Quietly situated with views over Romney Marsh, this typical Sussex peg tile farmhouse is over 150 years' old and offers cosy accommodation. Wholesome breakfasts are served in the pretty breakfast room. The general shower room is located on the ground floor.
3hc (1fb) ®
🏵 CTV 6P 6 acres smallholding ⓔ

SAFFRON WALDEN Essex Map **05** TL53

GH ||Q||Q|| *Rowley Hill Lodge* Little Walden CB10 1UZ (2m N on B1052) ☎(0799) 25975 due to change to 525975
2hc ⳨in all bedrooms CTV in 1 bedroom ® ✖ (ex guide dogs)
🏵 CTV 4P

ST AGNES Cornwall & Isles of Scilly Map **02** SW75

GH ||Q|| *Penkerris* Penwinnick Rd TR5 0PA
☎Truro(0872) 552262
Attractive, detached house in lovely gardens on the edge of the village.
5rm(1➤4hc) (3fb) CTV in 3 bedrooms TV in 2 bedrooms ® ✳
sB&B£12-£20 dB&B£22-£30 dB&B➤£25-£35 WB&B£70-£95
WBDi£110-£135 LDO 10am
Lic CTV 8P badminton court childrens swings
Credit Cards ||1|| ||3|| ⓔ

GH ||Q|| *Porthvean Hotel* Churchtown TR5 0QP
☎(0872) 552581
Closed Dec & Mar
Comfortable village centre guesthouse with friendly owners, also Frin's Restaurant with some vegetarian dishes.

6rm(5➤1hc) (3fb) CTV in all bedrooms ® ✖ (ex guide dogs)
LDO 9pm
Lic 🏵 8P
Credit Cards ||1|| ||3||

GH ||Q||Q|| *St Agnes Hotel* Churchtown TR5 0QP
☎(0872) 552307
Centrally situated in this attractive Cornish village endearingly known as 'the Aggie', two character bars here serve traditional bar meals. A separate restaurant operates during the suumer season.
5rm(1➤2➤2hc) (5fb) CTV in 3 bedrooms ® ✳ sB&B£18.50-
£22.50 sB&B➤£22.50-£27.50 dB&B£37-£39 dB&B➤➤£47-
£49 LDO 9pm
Lic CTV 50P
Credit Cards ||1|| ||3|| ⓔ

ST ALBANS Hertfordshire Map **04** TL10

GH ||Q||Q||Q|| *Ardmore House* 54 Lemsford Rd AL1 3PR
☎(0727) 59313 & 861411
Extensive improvements continue at this pleasant commercial hotel, situated in a residential area close to the city centre. Rooms are comfortable, well equipped and very well maintained. The atmosphere here is relaxed and friendly.
26rm(23➤3hc) (2fb) CTV in all bedrooms ® ✳
sB&B£32.90-£37.60 sB&B➤£44.65-£47 dB&B£39.95
dB&B➤£49.35 LDO 8.30pm
Lic 🏵 CTV 30P
Credit Cards ||1|| ||3||

GH ||Q||Q|| *Melford* 24 Woodstock Rd North AL1 4QQ
☎(0727) 53642
An attractive detached house in a pleasant residential area off the A1057, 5 minutes drive from the city centre. Accommodation is well maintained although some single rooms are very compact. The comfortable television lounge overlooks the rear garden and has a small honesty bar.
12rm(4➤8hc) (3fb) ® sB&B£25.15-£43.70 dB&B£36.80-£47
Lic 🏵 CTV 12P

ST ANDREWS Fife Map **12** NO51

GH ||Q||Q|| *Albany Private Hotel* 56 North St KY16 9AH
☎(0334) 77737
Neat and compact terraced house with functional, well-equipped bedrooms.
12rm(5➤7hc) (2fb)⳨in 2 bedrooms CTV in all bedrooms ®
sB&B£20-£27 dB&B£34-£42 dB&B➤£46-£54 WB&B£120-
£190 WBDi£196-£255 LDO 6pm
Lic 🏵 ⳨
Credit Cards ||1|| ||3||

GH ||Q||Q|| *Amberside* 4 Murray Pk KY16 9AW ☎(0334) 74644
Closed end of 1st week Dec-Feb
A compact, modern and well equipped house, part of a tenement row between the town centre and the sea. It is centrally located for all amenities including the golf course.
5rm(4➤1hc) (1fb) CTV in all bedrooms ® ✳ sB&B£17-£21
dB&B➤£34-£42
🏵 CTV ⳨ ⓔ

GH ||Q||Q||Q|| *Argyle Hotel* 127 North St KY16 9AG
☎(0334) 73387
Apr-Oct
A large, private hotel recently upgraded to offer comfortable lounges, well appointed bedrooms and neat, modern bathrooms. Service is friendly and courteous.
19➤ (5fb) CTV in all bedrooms ®
Lic 🏵 CTV ⳨ nc2yrs
Credit Cards ||1|| ||3||

GH Q|Q|Q **Arran House** 5 Murray Park KY16 9AW
☎(0334) 74724 FAX (0334) 72072
A comfortable, tastefully appointed house with spacious, attractive bedrooms.
6rm(3🛇3hc) (4fb) CTV in all bedrooms ® ✕ ✻ sB&B£15-£28 dB&B£30-£40 dB&B🛇£36-£44 WB&B£100-£200
🍴 CTV ⅌

GH Q|Q *Beachway House* 6 Murray Park KY16 9AW
☎(0334) 73319
These 2 adjoining houses in a tenement row have been neatly converted into a guesthouse, between the town centre and the sea. The lounge and dining room are combined.
6rm(5🛇1hc) (2fb) CTV in all bedrooms ®
🍴 ⅌

GH Q|Q **Bell Craig** 8 Murray Park KY16 9AW ☎(0334) 72962
A well maintained house, centrally located for all amenities, particularly the golf course and beach. Cosy accommodation, friendly service and freshly cooked breakfasts are offered.
5rm(3🛇2hc) (3fb) CTV in all bedrooms ® ✻ dB&B£32-£44 dB&B🛇£36-£44 WB&B£240-£280
🍴 CTV ⅌ ⓔ

GH Q|Q **Burness House** Murray Park KY16 9AW
☎(0334) 74314
A well managed establishment offering inviting, comfortable bedrooms and a cosy lounge-dining room.
5🛇 (1fb) CTV in all bedrooms ® ✻ sB&B🛇£16-£21 dB&B🛇£32-£42
🍴 CTV ⅌

⊠ᗡ **GH** Q|Q **Cleveden House** 3 Murray Place KY16 9AP
☎(0334) 74212
Nicely decorated house in side street between town centre and sea.
6rm(4🛇2hc) (2fb) CTV in all bedrooms ✕ (ex guide dogs)
sB&B£13-£18 dB&B🛇£30-£40
🍴 CTV ⅌ ⓔ

GH Q|Q **Craigmore** 3 Murray Park KY16 9AW
☎(0334) 72142 & 77963
Smartly decorated, comfortable guesthouse conveniently situated for town centre and the Old Course.
5rm(1⇋4🛇) (4fb) CTV in all bedrooms ® ✕ dB&B⇋🛇£28-£46 WB&B£180-£300
🍴 CTV ⅌
Credit Cards ①③ⓔ

GH Q|Q **Hazlebank Private Hotel** 28 The Scores KY16 9AS
☎(0334) 72466
Close to the front and with superb views of the coast, Hazelbank has modern bedrooms and a friendly atmosphere
10⇋🛇 (6fb) CTV in all bedrooms ® sB&B⇋🛇£30-£60 dB&B⇋🛇£44-£70
Lic 🍴 CTV ⅌
Credit Cards ①③ⓔ

GH Q|Q|Q **Riverview** Edenside KY16 9ST ☎(0334) 838009
FAX (0334) 838808
A modern, purpose-built extension provides motel-style apartments each with separate access from outside via a glass sliding door. The house is on the A91 west of St Andrews, on the outskirts of Guardbridge, and enjoys a fine open outlook across the Eden estuary. There are three apartments at ground level and four above, with a shared balcony; spacious and nicely appointed, three have bunk beds for family use, and there is a small pine-furnished breakfast room.
(3fb)⅍in all bedrooms CTV in all bedrooms ®
✕ (ex guide dogs) dB&B🛇£44 LDO 5.30pm
🍴 14P
Credit Cards ①③

GH QQ **West Park House** 5 St Mary's Place KY16 9UY
☎(0334) 75933
Mar-Nov
An attractive small detached period town house close to the town centre, with bright, well equipped bedrooms. Dinners are no longer available, but guests can dine by arrangement at the owner's other hotel some five minutes' walk away.
5rm(3♪2hc)(1fb) CTV in all bedrooms ® ✖ (ex guide dogs)
dB&B£33-£36 dB&B♪£37-£40
🏴 ₽

GH QQ **Yorkston Hotel** 68 & 70 Argyle St KY16 9BU
☎(0334) 72019
rs Xmas & New Year
Neatly appointed house on roadside leading into town from west.
10rm(1⇨4♪5hc)(3fb) CTV in all bedrooms ®
✖ (ex guide dogs) sB&B£19-£23 dB&B£36-£44 dB&B⇨♪£45-£54 WB&B£125-£186 WBDi£205.50-£284 LDO 5pm
Lic 🏴

FH QQQ Mrs A E Duncan **Spinks Town** *(NO541144)*
KY16 8PN ☎(0334) 73475
In delightful rural surroundings yet only 2 miles from the town on the picturesque A917 coast road, this very comfortable farmhouse offers most attractive accommodation and substantial breakfasts.
3rm(2⇨♪1hc) ✖in all bedrooms ✖ dB&B£26-£30
dB&B⇨♪£30-£36
🏴 CTV 3P 250 acres arable cattle

ST ASAPH Clwyd Map **06** SJ07

SELECTED

FH QQQQ Mrs A Roberts **Bach-Y-Graig** *(SJ075713)*
Tremeirchion LL17 0UH ☎Trefnant(0745) 730627
Closed Dec
This old farmhouse is set in a remote location and has a wealth of charm and character ; dating back to 1567, it is reputed to be the first brick-built house in Wales. Situated four miles southeast of the village, it is surrounded by 200 acres of land, including 40 acres of ancient woodland with a nature trail. The accommodation is very well equipped and tastefully furnished and decorated, in a style befitting the character of the house. Warm hospitality and good wholesome cooking are provided by the proprietor and her family.
3⇨♪ (1fb)✖in all bedrooms CTV in all bedrooms ® ✖
✱ sB&B⇨♪fr£15 dB&B⇨♪fr£22 WB&Bfr£105
🏴 CTV 3P ✔ woodland trail 200 acres dairy

ST AUBIN

See **JERSEY under CHANNEL ISLANDS**

ST AUSTELL Cornwall & Isles of Scilly Map **02** SX05

GH QQ **Alexandra Hotel** 52-54 Alexandra Rd PL25 4QN
☎(0726) 74242
Closed Xmas
There is a friendly welcome at this comfortable, well maintained, small hotel not far from the town centre. Bedrooms vary in size and are bright and well equipped, with two on the ground floor. There is a comfortable TV lounge, a cosy bar and ample parking outside.
14rm(4♪10hc)(6fb) CTV in all bedrooms ® sB&B♪fr£22
dB&B♪fr£38 WB&B£107-£147 WBDi£148-£167 LDO 5pm
Lic 🏴 CTV 16P
Credit Cards ①②③ ⓔ

INN QQQ *Rashleigh Arms* Quay Rd, Charlestown PL25 3NJ
☎(0726) 73635
Along the A3061 towards Charlestown, this popular inn has a fine selection of real ale on offer. Modern bedrooms are well presented and bright and each has a smart en suite facility. Public areas are numerous, and include a children's room, a choice of two public bars and a restaurant area where an extensive menu is offered.

There is ample car parking available at the rear.
5♪ CTV in all bedrooms ® LDO 10pm
🏴 60P
Credit Cards ①③

ST BRIDES-SUPER-ELY South Glamorgan Map **03** ST17

GH QQQ **Sant-y-Nyll** CF5 6EZ
☎Peterston-Super-Ely(0446) 760209
This elegant country house is situated in the tranquil Vale of Glamorgan, quite near to the Welsh Folk Museum at St Fagans. There are two comfortable lounges and the bedrooms are spacious and well equipped.
6rm(1⇨♪5hc)(1fb) CTV in all bedrooms ® ✱ sB&B£20-£25
dB&B£30-£40 dB&B⇨♪£50-£60 WB&B£120-£180 LDO 6pm
Lic 🏴 20P ⚘ croquet
Credit Cards ② ⓔ
See advertisement under CARDIFF

ST CATHERINE'S Strathclyde *Argyllshire* Map **10** NN10

GH QQQ **Arnish Cottage, Lochside Guest House.** Poll Bay
PA25 8BA ☎Inveray(0499) 2405
This small, comfortable family-run guesthouse is midway between St Catherine's and Strachur, and occupies an idyllic setting by the shore of Loch Fyne, beside Poll Bay. The house has been completely renovated to provide modern comforts and facilities. Bedrooms are compact but comfortable, with private bathrooms. Smoking is not allowed in any part of the house.
3♪ ✖in all bedrooms ® ✖ (ex guide dogs) ✱ sB&B♪£16-£22
dB&B♪£30-£40 WB&B£99-£135 WBDi£170-£200
3P nc16yrs ⓔ

GH QQ **Thistle House** PA25 8AZ ☎Inveraray(0499) 2209
May-mid Oct
This large, detached Victorian house is set in its own gardens beside the A815 and boasts fine views over Loch Fyne and Inveraray. It provides an ideal base from which to tour the beauties of Argyll, being comfortable and well maintained throughout.
5rm(3♪2hc)(1fb) ® sB&Bfr£17.50 sB&B♪fr£20 dB&Bfr£30
dB&B♪fr£35 WB&Bfr£100
🏴 10P nc5yrs ⓔ

ST CLEARS Dyfed Map **02** SN21

INN QQ **Black Lion Hotel** SA33 4AA ☎(0994) 230700
A village inn with neat bedrooms and friendly staff. The characterful bar and pretty restaurant feature an interesting collection of jugs, copper and brass, and a good choice of food is available.
13rm(1⇨3♪9hc)(1fb) CTV in all bedrooms ® ✖ sB&B£18-£20 sB&B⇨♪£25-£27 dB&B£35-£37 dB&B⇨♪£45-£47
WB&B£118-£160 ✖ Lunch £3.50-£5.50alc Dinner £10.25-£12.25alc LDO 9pm
🏴 25P snooker
Credit Cards ①③⑤ ⓔ

ST DAVID'S Dyfed Map **02** SM72

GH QQ **The Ramsey** Lower Moor SA62 6RP ☎(0437) 720321
Run by the friendly Thompson family, this bright, cosy guesthouse lies just outside the town with easy access to the cathedral. It has neat bedrooms and comfortable open-plan lounge and bar areas.
7rm(4♪3hc) ® ✱ sB&B£17.50-£19.50 dB&B£32-£36.30
dB&B♪£37-£41.30 WB&B£112-£144.55 WBDi£160.20-£188.10 LDO 7pm
Lic 🏴 CTV 9P nc12yrs ⓔ

GH QQ **Redcliffe House** 17 New St SA62 6SW
☎(0437) 720389
Apr-Oct
Just a couple of minutes from the cathedral and city centre, this small and cosy guesthouse provides spacious bedrooms and a comfortable lounge.

6hc (2fb) CTV in all bedrooms ® ✱ ✳ dB&Bfr£27
🕮 CTV 2P nc6yrs

GH |Q||Q||Q| **Y** *Glennydd* 51 Nun St SA62 6NU ☎(0437) 720576
Closed Jan-Feb
*A very well maintained small guesthouse within easy walking
distance of the cathedral and shops. Bedrooms are very
comfortable and pretty, and there is a bar and a cosy lounge. Good
value food is served in the restaurant, which is popular locally.*
10rm(3⇔️🟥7hc) (4fb) CTV in all bedrooms ®
✱ (ex guide dogs) ✳ sB&B£15-£25 sB&B⇔️🟥£20-£30
dB&B£30 dB&B⇔️🟥£34 WB&B£105-£120 WBDi£175-£190
LDO 9pm
Lic 🕮 CTV 🅿
Credit Cards |1||3||5|

ST ERME Cornwall & Isles of Scilly Map **02** SW84

FH |Q||Q||Q| Mr & Mrs E Dymond **Trevispian Vean**
(SW850502) TR4 9BL ☎Truro(0872) 79514
Mar-Oct
*Recently extended, this Cornish farmhouse is 4 miles from Truro,
and provides some en suite bedrooms and a choice of lounges.
Home cooked dinners are served in the evening and children are
made very welcome.*
12rm(2⇔️7🟥3hc) (7fb) ✱ (ex guide dogs) ✳ sB&B£12.50-
£14.50 sB&B⇔️🟥fr£14.50 dB&Bfr£25 dB&B⇔️🟥fr£29
WB&B£81-£95 WBDi£117-£131 LDO 4.30pm
Lic 🕮 CTV 20P ⚓ games room 300 acres arable beef pigs
sheep Ⓔ
See advertisement under TRURO

ST HELIER

See JERSEY under CHANNEL ISLANDS

ST HILARY Cornwall & Isles of Scilly Map **02** SW53

FH |Q||Q||Q| S L White **Ennys** *(SW559328)* TR20 9BZ
☎Penzance(0736) 740262
Closed 7-30 Nov
*A beautiful Cornish manor house on a small working farm. The
bedrooms are delightfully furnished with Sanderson and Liberty
décor, patchwork quilts and Laura Ashley cotton bed linen.
Thoughtful touches include Cornish spring water and flowers.
Recently completed, the Hayloft and Nippers stable have been
transformed into family letting rooms in similar style to the house.
Sue White provides worthy home cooking with good use of home-
grown and local produce. Home-baked bread and rich puddings
are daily delights.*
3⇔️🟥 (1fb)✂in all bedrooms CTV in all bedrooms ® ✱
sB&B⇔️🟥fr£20 dB&B⇔️🟥£40-£45 LDO 7.30pm
🕮 CTV P 🐕 ♋ ♟(grass)50 acres arable Ⓔ
See advertisement under PENZANCE

ST IVES Cornwall & Isles of Scilly Map **02** SW54

GH |Q||Q| *Bay View* Headland Road, Carbis Bay TR26 2NX
☎Penzance(0736) 796469
*Extended chalet bungalow in quiet residential area. Friendly
owners provide good home cooking.*
9rm(2🟥7hc) (3fb)✂in all bedrooms ✱ LDO 6pm
Lic CTV 9P 2🐕

GH |Q||Q||Q| *Blue Mist* The Warren TR26 2EA
☎Penzance(0736) 795209
Etr-Oct
*A delightful cottage-style property on the water's edge, affording
beautiful views of the harbour. The bedrooms are cosy and well
equipped, and a choice of home-cooked meals is offered in the
attractive dining room. The resident proprietors, Kathy and Bob
Carr, welcome their guests.*
9rm(8🟥1hc) (1fb) CTV in all bedrooms ® ✱ (ex guide dogs)
LDO 5pm

🕮 4P (£14.50 per wk) nc4yrs
Credit Cards |1||3|

GH |Q||Q| **Channings Hotel** 3 Talland Rd TR26 2DF
☎Penzance(0736) 795681
*Informally run by Mr and Mrs Juggins, this small hotel has a
pleasant, friendly atmosphere. With commanding views over the
town and bay, Channings has brightly decorated bedrooms with
modern en suite facilities, a comfortable bar and dining room*
12rm(2⇔️9🟥1hc) (5fb) ✱ ✳ sB&B£15.50-£22.50
sB&B⇔️🟥£16-£23 dB&B⇔️🟥£31-£45 WB&B£108-£157
WBDi£139-£197 LDO 4pm
Lic 🕮 CTV 12P
Credit Cards |1||3| Ⓔ

🚻➡GH |Q||Q| **Chy-an-Creet Private Hotel** Higher Stennack
TR26 2HA ☎Penzance(0736) 796559
mid Mar-mid Oct rs mid Nov-mid Mar
*Close to the renowned Leach Pottery, this small hotel is run by
jovial proprietors who pride themselves in its friendly atmosphere.
A choice of traditional home cooked meals is offered and there is a
cosy, well-stocked bar for guests.*
10⇔️🟥 (4fb) ® sB&B⇔️🟥£12.50-£20 dB&B⇔️🟥£25-£40
WB&B£87.50-£140 WBDi£120-£185 (wkly only Jul-Sep)
LDO 4pm
Lic 🕮 CTV 16P ♿
Credit Cards |1||3| Ⓔ

GH |Q||Q| *Cottage Hotel* Carbis Bay TR26 2NQ
☎Penzance(0736) 796351 & 795252 FAX (0736) 798636
Apr-Nov
*Set in a wooded location overlooking St Ives Bay, and only 300
yards, from the beach, by private footpaths, this large family hotel
has well-equipped bedrooms and functional public rooms.*
64⇔️ (51fb) CTV in all bedrooms ® LDO 7.30pm ▶

𝒯𝑜𝓇𝒷𝒶𝓃𝓉 𝓕𝒶𝓇𝓂 𝓖𝓊𝑒𝓈𝓉 𝓗𝑜𝓊𝓈𝑒

**Croesgoch, Haverfordwest,
Pembrokeshire, Dyfed SA62 5JN
Telephone: Croesgoch (0348) 831276**

Torbant is a peacefully situated farmhouse on a
working farm near St Davids. 1½ miles from the sea
with beautiful beaches & spectacular scenery. All 6
bedrooms have heaters, tea/coffee makers & H&C —
some en-suite. TV lounge. Spacious fully licensed bar.
Large dining room & useful utility room with picnic
preparation & laundry facilities. Children are welcome
& early suppers available. Also 3 separate fully
equipped s/c apartments available.

Stamp only to Mrs B. A. Charles for brochure.

Lic lift 🏧 CTV 100P ⌒(heated) squash snooker sauna table tennis & pool tables
Credit Cards ①③

GH 🆀🆀🆀 Dean Court Hotel Trelyon Av TR26 2AD
☎Penzance(0736) 796023
Mar-Oct

An attractive Cornish stone house in a commanding position, with glorious and unrestricted views across St Ives Bay. Bedrooms are bright, well decorated and all have modern en suite bathrooms and benefit from the views. The elegant, comfortable lounge and pretty dining room also overlook the bay. Well cooked, traditional fare is provided in pleasant, friendly surroundings. Private car parking is an invaluable asset in this bustling resort.

12⇔↸ (2fb) CTV in all bedrooms ® ✤ ✱ sB&B⇔↸£24-£31 dB&B⇔↸£48-£64 WB&B£140-£180 WBDi£175-£215 LDO 5pm
Lic 🏧 12P nc14yrs ₤

GH 🆀🆀🆀 The Hollies Hotel 4 Talland Rd TR26 2DF
☎Penzance(0736) 796605
The jovial and friendly owner of this well-furnished guesthouse provides good, home-cooked meals. It is the ideal spot for a relaxed holiday in Cornwall.
10⇔↸ (4fb) CTV in all bedrooms ® ✤ ✱ sB&B⇔↸£17.50-£23.50 dB&B⇔↸£35-£47 WB&B£122.50-£164.50 WBDi£155-£195 LDO 9am
Lic 🏧 CTV 12P ₤

GH 🆀🆀 *Island View* 2 Park Av TR26 2DN
☎Penzance(0736) 795111
Mar-Oct
Perched above St Ives and enjoying fine views across the town and harbour, this personally-run Victorian house provides a bright and friendly atmosphere and tasty traditional fare.
10hc (4fb) CTV in all bedrooms ® LDO 6.30pm
🏧 ✗

GH 🆀🆀 Kandahar 11 The Warren TR26 2EA
☎Penzance(0736) 796183
Closed Xmas, New Year & owners hols
A small, charming property with a unique location at the sea's edge, with superb views of the bay and harbour. The bedrooms are compact but cheerful, and they share the views with the lounge and breakfast room. Car parking is prohibited, but arrangements can be made with the guesthouse (payment in season) at a nearby car park.
5rm(2↸3hc) (1fb) CTV in all bedrooms ® ✤ dB&B£30-£35 dB&B↸£35-£39 WB&B£210-£273
🏧 CTV 6P (Apr-Oct) ₤

GH 🆀🆀 *Kynance* The Warren TR26 2EA
☎Penzance(0736) 796636
Closed Nov-Feb
In the heart of the town, yet within sight and sound of the ocean, May and Tony Smith's cosy fishermen's cottage now provides accommodation which is full of character and charm. The garden won an award for 'Best Guesthouse Garden' in St Ives in 1988.
8rm(1↸7hc) (1fb) TV in all bedrooms ® ✤ ✱ sB&B£16-£18 dB&B£32-£36 dB&B↸£36-£42
🏧 CTV ✗ ₤

GH 🆀🆀🆀 Longships Hotel Talland Rd TR26 2DF
☎Penzance(0736) 798180
This holiday hotel enjoys a good position and views over the bay. The bedrooms are well equipped and there is a good choice of meals at dinner.
24rm(5⇔19↸) (7fb) CTV in all bedrooms ®
sB&B⇔↸£15.50-£25 dB&B⇔↸£31-£50 LDO 7pm
Lic 🏧 CTV 17P
Credit Cards ①③₤

GH 🆀🆀🆀 Lyonesse Hotel 5 Talland Rd TR26 2DF
☎Penzance(0736) 796315
Apr-Oct
Set high above the town centre and harbour in a terrace of family-run hotels, the Lyonesse provides well appointed bedrooms and attractive public areas where entertainment is provided on some evenings during the season in a cosy bar. Home-cooked dishes are featured on the menu.
15↸ (4fb) CTV in all bedrooms ® ✤ sB&B↸fr£20 dB&B↸fr£40 LDO 6.30pm
Lic 🏧 CTV 10P pool table

GH 🆀🆀🆀 Monowai Private Hotel Headland Road, Carbis Bay TR26 2NR ☎Penzance(0736) 795733
A family-run, character establishment in an elevated position commanding glorious views across the bay. The brightly decorated bedrooms have been furnished in a cottage style, and a cosy atmosphere is a feature of the bar and lounge. A choice of home-cooked dishes is offered on the table d'hôte menu with vegetarian specialities. A friendly welcome awaits guests.
10rm(6↸4hc) (3fb) ® sB&B£14-£25 dB&B£28-£50 dB&B↸£34-£58 WB&B£95-£190 WBDi£119-£215 LDO 6.30pm
Lic 🏧 CTV 7P nc5yrs ⌒(heated) ₤

GH 🆀🆀🆀 The Old Vicarage Hotel Parc-An-Creet TR26 2ET
☎Penzance(0736) 796124
Mar-Oct
This Victorian rectory has been sympathetically restored and offers every modern convenience whilst retaining its original character. Tucked away from the town, its secluded grounds offer a safe play area for children. The spacious and tastefully furnished accommodation includes an elegant lounge and comfortable dining room and bar, all spotlessly clean.
8rm(4⇔↸4hc) (3fb) CTV in 7 bedrooms TV in 1 bedroom ® sB&B£19-£21 dB&B£34-£38 dB&B⇔↸£40-£44 WB&B£101.50-£110.50 (wkly only Jul & Aug) LDO 6.45pm
Lic 🏧 CTV 12P putting green
Credit Cards ①②③₤

GH 🆀🆀🆀 Pondarosa Hotel 10 Porthminster Ter TR26 2DQ
☎Penzance(0736) 795875
Closed 25th Dec
Standing in a convenient position close to the town and beaches, this guesthouse has a friendly, relaxed atmosphere. Good home cooking is provided by friendly and welcoming Welsh owners.
9rm(1⇔1↸7hc) (4fb) CTV in all bedrooms ®
✤ (ex guide dogs) LDO 4pm
Lic 🏧 CTV 12P nc3yrs ₤

GH 🆀🆀 *Primrose Valley Hotel* Primrose Valley TR26 2ED
☎Penzance(0736) 794939
Closed Jan-Feb
Pleasant, small family hotel ideally positioned about 100 yards from Porthminster beach.
11rm(6⇔↸5hc) (6fb) CTV in all bedrooms ® ✤ (wkly only Jun-Aug)
Lic CTV 12P

GH 🆀🆀 Hotel Rotorua Trencrom Ln, Carbis Bay TR26 2TD
☎Penzance(0736) 795419
Etr-Oct
Purpose-built, in quiet lane just off St Ives Rd, close to Carbis Bay.
13⇔↸ (10fb)⊁in 2 bedrooms ® ✱ sB&B↸£17.50-£23 sB&B⇔↸£17.50-£23 dB&B£35-£46 dB&B⇔↸£35-£46 WB&B£122.50-£161 WBDi£166.50-£203 LDO 5pm
Lic 🏧 CTV 10P ⚲ ⌒ ₤

GH 🆀🆀 *St Merryn Hotel* Trelyon TR26 2PF
☎Penzance(0736) 795767 & 797248
Mar-Nov
Set back off the main road, behind a large garden, this large, detached family hotel is just outside St Ives. It has spacious public rooms and comfortable bedrooms.

19rm(11⇄8hc) (8fb) CTV in all bedrooms ® ✗ LDO 6pm
Lic 쐐 CTV 20P nc4yrs
Credit Cards ① ③

GH QQ **Sunrise** 22 The Warren TR26 2AT
☎Penzance(0736) 795407
Jan-Oct
*This popular cottage guesthouse is still enthusiastically owned and
run by Mrs Vicky Mason, chosen by the AA as one of the top
seaside landladies in 1988, who is now in her 89th year! Compact
but brightly decorated bedrooms, a comfortable lounge and
breakfast room are provided, with assistance from the owner's
daughter, and the outstanding traditional breakfasts are still
produced.*
7rm(4⇄3hc) (2fb) CTV in all bedrooms ® sB&Bfr£20
dB&B£26-£30 dB&B⇄£30-£38
쐐 CTV 4P (£2 day) ⓔ

GH QQ **Thurlestone Private Hotel** St Ives Road, Carbis Bay
TR26 2RT ☎Penzance(0736) 796369
Mar-Sep
*Attractive detached granite house with friendly service and public
rooms of character.*
9rm(1⇄4⯑4hc) (3fb) ® ✗ ✱ sB&B£12-£20 dB&B£24-£40
dB&B⇄⯑£28-£44 WB&B£90-£120 WBDi£125-£155 (wkly
only Jul-Aug) LDO 5pm
Lic 쐐 CTV 6P nc3yrs

GH QQ **Tregorran Hotel** Headland Bay, Carbis Bay
TR26 2NU ☎Penzance(0736) 795889
Apr-Oct
*An attractive outdoor swimming pool and small gym are features
of this small, well-appointed hotel which enjoys a scenic location
overlooking Carbis Bay.*
▶

14rm(12♪2hc) (4fb) ⓇsB&B£17-£26.50 sB&B♪£19-£28.50
dB&B£34-£53 dB&B♪£38-£57 WB&B£119-£185.50
WBDi£154-£224 LDO 3pm
Lic ⑨ CTV 25P ⬚(heated) solarium gymnasium pool table Ⓔ

GH QQ **White House Hotel** The Valley, Carbis Bay TR26 2QY
☎Penzance(0736) 797405
Closed Nov-Feb
*This detached house stands in its own gardens at the foot of a
wooded valley, 150 yards from safe, sandy beaches and one mile
from St Ives. Comfortable bedrooms and cosy public areas are
complemented by home cooked food.*
8⬧♪ Annexe 2⬧♪ (2fb) Ⓡ ♪ sB&B⬧♪£18-£25
dB&B⬧♪£32-£43 WBDi£166.25-£203 LDO 8pm
Lic ⑨ CTV 10P
Credit Cards 1 3

INN QQQ **Queens Tavern** High St TR26 1RR (St Austell
Brewery) ☎(0736) 796468
*A characterful inn right in the heart of this bustling popular seaside
town, amongst shops and close to the harbour. There is a congenial
bar and a simply styled restaurant on the first floor. Due to
significant refurbishment, bedrooms are cosy, bright and well
furnished with pleasing décor and co-ordinating fabrics; each is
well equipped with en suite bathrooms. The inn stocks a good range
of cask and keg beers, but there is no car park on site.*
5♪ (3fb) CTV in all bedrooms Ⓡ ♪ (ex guide dogs) ✱
sB&B♪fr£25 dB&B♪fr£37 LDO 8.15pm
⑨
Credit Cards 1

ST JUST (NEAR LAND'S END) Cornwall & Isles of Scilly
Map **02** SW33

GH QQQ **Boscean Country Hotel** TR19 7QP
☎Penzance(0736) 788748
Mar-Nov
*This interesting house has been tastefully converted to provide
comfortable, en suite accommodation. The wood panelled public
rooms contain unique fitments. Three acres of walled grounds
surround this building, and guests will receive a warm welcome.*
9⬧♪ Annexe 2⬧ (3fb) Ⓡ dB&B⬧♪£34-£36 WB&B£105-
£112 WBDi£167-£175 LDO 7pm
Lic ⑨ CTV 12P ⚿

INN QQQ **Wellington Hotel** Market Square TR19 7HL
☎Penzance(0736) 787319
*Situated right in the heart of the village, this character inn offers a
good range of food and has a cosy bar. Six excellent modern
bedrooms situated in the small courtyard have been recently
added, each offering high standards of comfort, bright en suites
and an extensive range of modern facilities including remote-
control colour TVs, direct dial telephones, trouser presses and tea/
coffee-making facilities combined with quality décor and co-
ordinated furnishings.*
Annexe 6⬧♪ (4fb) CTV in all bedrooms Ⓡ ✱
sB&B⬧♪fr£22 dB&B⬧♪fr£35 ✱ Lunch £5.30-£10&alc
Dinner £5.30-£10&alc LDO 9pm
⑨
Credit Cards 1 3

ST JUST-IN-ROSELAND Cornwall & Isles of Scilly Map **02**
SW83

SELECTED

GH QQQQ **Rose-Da-Mar Hotel** TR2 5JB
☎St Mawes(0326) 270450
mid Mar-mid Oct
*This elegant and tastefully furnished house is peacefully
located along a quiet country lane overlooking the creeks of
Carrick Roads Fal Estuary. The bedrooms all have splendid
views across the water and they are comfortable, nicely*

*appointed and individually decorated. The spacious drawing
room is complemented by a small, cosy bar area and a well
decorated dining room. There is an interesting five-course
table d'hôte menu, and during the summer tea is served on the
sheltered sun terrace. Early reservations are strongly
recommended throughout the year.*
8rm(4⬧1♪3hc) (1fb) Ⓡ sB&B£38.95 dB&B£71.30-£73.50
dB&B⬧♪£77.90-£83.50 (incl dinner) WB&B£144.35-
£185.95 WBDi£243.30-£285 LDO 6.30pm
Lic ⑨ CTV 9P nc11yrs Ⓔ

ST KEYNE Cornwall & Isles of Scilly Map **02** SX26

GH QQQ **Old Rectory Country House Hotel** PL14 4RL
☎Liskeard(0579) 42617
*This secluded former Rectory dating from the 16th century, is
peacefully situated in over 3 acres of gardens and woodland, 3
miles from Liskeard. Mr and Mrs Wolfe provide a short à la carte
menu, served between 7pm and 8pm, and pre-dinner drinks are
available from the bar on an 'honesty' system. No smoking in the
dining room. After dinner, coffee is provided in the elegantly
furnished lounge. Bedrooms are comfortable; each is individually
furnished and decorated and some have four-poster beds.*
8rm(4⬧3♪1hc) CTV in all bedrooms Ⓡ LDO 7pm
Lic ⑨ 20P
Credit Cards 1 3

ST MARTINS

See **GUERNSEY under CHANNEL ISLANDS**

ST MARY'S

See **SCILLY, ISLES OF**

ST MARY'S LOCH Borders *Selkirkshire* Map **11** NT22

INN QQQ *Tibbie Shiels* TD7 5NE
☎Capercleuch(0750) 42231
rs Mon Nov-Feb
*Situated on the shores of St Mary's Loch, this historic inn has been
welcoming guests since 1824, and is named after one of the first
inhabitants. Gradually extended, it now offers good
accommodation in 5 neat ground floor rooms, in most attractive
surroundings. A good range of bar meals is available, with high
teas a speciality. A popular haunt for fishermen, birdwatchers and
walkers, it is closed on Mondays in winter.*
5hc (1fb) Ⓡ ♪ (ex guide dogs) LDO 8.30pm
⑨ CTV 30P ✓
Credit Cards 1 3

ST MAWGAN Cornwall & Isles of Scilly Map **02** SW86

INN QQ **The Falcon** TR8 4EP ☎Newquay(0637) 860225
3rm(2♪1hc) CTV in all bedrooms Ⓡ ♪ (ex guide dogs) ✱
dB&B£30 dB&B♪£37 ✱ Lunch £3.35-£11.15alc Dinner £4.70-
£13.05alc LDO 10pm
⑨ 20P nc14yrs
Credit Cards 1 3

ST MERRYN Cornwall & Isles of Scilly Map **02** SW87

INN QQQ *Farmers Arms* PL28 8NP (St Austell Brewery)
☎Padstow(0841) 520303
*Recently renovated, this village pub offers well-equipped bedrooms
which are prettily decorated and have limed oak furniture. An
extensive bar menu is available and the separate restaurant has a
carvery. A salad counter is open through the summer.*
4♪ CTV in all bedrooms Ⓡ LDO 9.30pm
⑨ 100P
Credit Cards 1 2 3

ST NEOTS Cambridgeshire Map **04** TL16

INN Q Q *The Old Falcon Hotel* Market Square, Huntingdon
PE1 2AW ☎Huntingdon(0480) 72749
*This inn, facing the market place and backing on to the River
Great Ouse, provides comfortable and very well equipped
accommodation. There is also a popular, convivial bar, and a coffee
shop where hot and cold meals are available all day.*
8rm(4⇨3♠1hc) CTV in all bedrooms ® ✕ (ex guide dogs)
LDO 9.30pm
10P
Credit Cards ⓵ ⓶ ⓷ ⓹

ST OWEN'S CROSS Hereford & Worcester Map **03** SO52

FH Q Q Mrs F Davies **Aberhall** *(SO529242)* HR2 8LL
☎Harewood End(098987) 256
Mar-Nov
*Set in the beautiful Wye Valley with some superb views, this 17th
century farmhouse is 5 miles from Ross-on-Wye. Energetic visitors
can use the hard tennis court or enjoy table tennis, darts and pool
in the basement games room.*
3rm(1♠2hc) ✕in all bedrooms ® ✕ (ex guide dogs)
sB&B£18.50-£20 sB&B♠fr£25 dB&B£27-£29 dB&B♠£30-£32
🍴 CTV 3P nc10yrs ℘(hard) pool & table tennis 132 acres
arable beef mixed ⓺

ST PETER PORT

See **GUERNSEY** under **CHANNEL ISLANDS**

ST SAMPSON

See **GUERNSEY** under **CHANNEL ISLANDS**

SALCOMBE Devon Map **03** SX73

Telephone numbers are liable to change during the currency of
this guide.

GH Q Q Bay View Hotel Bennett Rd TQ8 8JJ ☎(054884) 2238
Mar-Sep
*The magnificent views of the estuary are a memorable part of this
small privately owned bed and breakfast establishment. The
bedrooms are simply appointed but comfortable and the public
areas are situated at various levels of the 5-storey building. The
resident proprietors have a very relaxed attitude.*
5rm(2⇨♠3hc) (2fb) ® ✕ dB&B£40-£50 dB&B⇨♠£48-£54
WB&B£140-£189
Lic 🍴 CTV 6P
Credit Cards ⓵ ⓷

GH Q Q Q Devon Tor Hotel Devon Rd TQ8 8HJ
☎(054884) 3106
8rm(4⇨♠4hc) (2fb) ✕in all bedrooms CTV in 4 bedrooms TV
in 4 bedrooms ® ✕ ✳ sB&B£18-£20 dB&B£37-£40
dB&B⇨♠£40-£46 WB&B£112-£145 WBDi£169-£215
LDO 4.30pm
Lic 🍴 CTV 5P nc9yrs
Credit Cards ⓵ ⓷

GH Q Q Q Lyndhurst Hotel Bonaventure Rd TQ8 8BG
☎(054884) 2481
Closed Dec
*Views over Salcombe bay and estuary are one of the greatest
assets of this efficiently run, friendly guesthouse. Bedrooms are
prettily decorated with many modern facilities, and some have
good en suite showers. Mrs Sharp, the proprietoress, is a keen cook
and dinner is served in a compact but elegant dining room.*
8♠ (1fb)✕in all bedrooms CTV in all bedrooms ® ✕
dB&B♠£37-£46 WB&B£126-£157.50 WBDi£199.50-£238
LDO 4.30pm
Lic 🍴 4P nc7yrs

GH Q Q Q Torre View Hotel Devon Rd TQ8 8HJ
☎(054884) 2633 due to change t o (0548) 842633
Feb-Oct
*A small, family-run licensed hotel in a quiet residential area, in an
elevated position with some lovely views of the estuary. The
bedrooms are clean and bright, and some offer en suite facilities.
There is a cosy lounge and a more spacious and recently
refurbished bar lounge. A choice of home-cooked dishes is
available on the blackboard menu in the informal dining room.*
8⇨♠ (2fb) CTV in 2 bedrooms ® ✕ ✳ sB&B⇨♠£24-£30
dB&B⇨♠£43-£51 WB&B£140-£160 WBDi£200-£225
LDO 6pm
Lic 🍴 CTV 4P nc4yrs
Credit Cards ⓵ ⓷ ⓺

GH Q Q Trennels Private Hotel Herbert Rd TQ8 8HR
☎(054884) 2500
Mar-Nov
*A privately managed licensed hotel, conveniently situated for the
town centre and harbour, yet in a quiet, elevated position
commanding glorious views of the estuary. Bedrooms are bright
and comfortable, and a set evening meal is provided in the dining
room.*
7rm(1⇨4♠2hc) (1fb)✕in all bedrooms CTV in 5 bedrooms ®
✕ ✳ sB&B£16.50-£18.50 dB&B£33-£37 dB&B⇨♠£36-£42
WB&B£115.50-£140 WBDi£171.50-£196 LDO 10am
Lic 🍴 CTV 8P nc4yrs ⓺

SALEN

See **MULL, ISLE OF**

SALFORD Bedfordshire Map **04** SP93

INN Q Q *Red Lion Country Hotel* Wavendon Rd MK17 8AZ
☎Milton Keynes(0908) 583117
*A small village inn with a rural setting. The cosy half-panelled bar
has an open fire, and the cheerful breakfast room is furnished with
pine tables and Victorian memorabilia. Bedrooms are well
equipped but vary in size and decoration and are scattered around
the building : three are in a converted barn, and three without en
suites reach their bathroom though the residents' sitting area.*
10rm(6⇨4hc) CTV in all bedrooms ® ✕ LDO 9.30pm
🍴 40P nc3yrs putting course petanque
Credit Cards ⓵ ⓶ ⓷ ⓹

SALFORD Greater Manchester Map **07** SJ89

GH Q Q Q Hazeldean Hotel 467 Bury New Rd M7 0NX
☎061-792 6667 FAX 061-792 6668
Closed 4 days Xmas
*Set back from the A56, 2.5 miles from the centre of Manchester
and convenient for the M62, this privately owned and run hotel
offers comfortable and particularly well equipped bedrooms. There
is a comfortable lounge, an attractive bar and a small, good
restaurant which is open to the public as well as the residents.*
21rm(17⇨4♠4hc) Annexe 3rm(2⇨♠1hc) (2fb) CTV in all
bedrooms ® ✳ sB&B£44.65 sB&B⇨♠£52.87
dB&B⇨♠£68.15 LDO 9pm
Lic 🍴 CTV 21P
Credit Cards ⓵ ⓶ ⓷ ⓹ ⓺

SALHOUSE Norfolk Map **09** TG31

GH Q Q Q *Brooksbank Hotel* Lower St NR13 6RW
☎Norwich(0603) 720420
*This lovely guesthouse is set in the centre of the village, and is run
by the friendly proprietors, Mr and Mrs Coe. The row of white
18th-century cottages retains its appeal, and is surrounded by well
tended gardens. The accommodation is of a good quality with the
emphasis on comfort. All rooms are en suite.*
3rm(2⇨1♠) (1fb) CTV in all bedrooms ®
🍴 CTV 3P

315

SALISBURY Wiltshire Map **04** SU12

See also Downton (6.5m S off A338)

GH QQ Byways House 31 Fowlers Rd SP1 2QP
☎(0722) 328364 FAX (0722) 322146

A large Victorian house in a central position, Byways has been extended and updated over the years and new prorietors, Mr and Mrs Arthey, have continued that process in the 2 years of their ownership. Some bedrooms are more spacious than others but they are all well equipped and comforable, and some now have pretty co-ordinated décor and furnishings.

23rm(19⇌↱4hc) (5fb) CTV in all bedrooms ® sB&Bfr£20 sB&B⇌↱fr£26.50 dB&Bfr£31 dB&B⇌↱£37-£47 WB&B£105-£164.50 WBDi£164.50-£224 LDO 6.30pm
Lic ▥ 15P ⌂
Credit Cards [1] [3] (£)

GH QQQ Cricket Field Cottage Skew Bridge, Wilton Rd SP2 7NS ☎(0722) 322595

On the western edge of the city on the road to Wilton, the cottage overlooks extensive playing fields. Here 2 cottages have been joined and extended to provide modern, well decorated and clean bedrooms, together with a convivial dining room.

5rm(1⇌4↱) (2fb) CTV in all bedrooms ® ✗ (ex guide dogs) * sB&B⇌↱£22 dB&B⇌↱£38
▥ 8P (£)

GH QQ Glen Lyn 6 Bellamy Ln, Milford Hill SP1 2SP
☎(0722) 327880

A large, well positioned Victorian house, close to the centre of Salisbury but in a quiet area away from the hubbub of the town. Bedrooms are comfortable, without fuss, and equipped with some modern conveniences. The charm of the place is undoubtedly the friendly, caring proprietors, Mr and Mrs Poat. This is a no smoking establishment.

9rm(2⇌2↱5hc) (1fb)⊬in all bedrooms CTV in all bedrooms ® ✗ (ex guide dogs) * sB&B£18-£24 dB&B£32-£34 dB&B⇌↱£36-£40
▥ 7P nc12yrs (£)

GH QQ Hayburn Wyke 72 Castle Rd SP1 3RL
☎(0722) 412627

This small, family-run guesthouse is situated on the busy Castle Road, just a short distance from the centre of Salisbury, but with the advantage of a public park nearby. Bedrooms here are comfortably furnished and nicely decorated, and there is a friendly, informal atmosphere which, combined with the location, makes it a popular choice.

6rm(2↱4hc) (2fb) CTV in all bedrooms ® ✗ (ex guide dogs) sB&B£20-£25 dB&B£29-£33 dB&B↱£34-£38
▥ CTV 5P 1🚗 (£)

GH Q Holmhurst Downton Rd SP2 8AR ☎(0722) 323164
Mar-Oct

A detached private house with its own car park, within walking distance of the city centre, on the A338 signed to Ringwood. The inexpensive accommodation comprises neat well kept bedrooms, a television lounge and a separate dining room.

8rm(5↱3hc) (2fb)⊬in 1 bedroom ✗ sB&B£16-£28 sB&B↱£25-£30 dB&B£28 dB&B↱£32
▥ CTV 8P nc5yrs

GH QQ Leena's 50 Castle Rd SP1 3RL ☎(0722) 335419

A small guesthouse on the main road leading into Salisbury town centre, with a friendly, relaxed atmosphere. Bedrooms are prettily decorated with good modern facilities. Public areas are comfortable and have many personal touches. A family-run establishment where the family is much in evidence.

6rm(3↱3hc) (1fb)⊬in all bedrooms CTV in all bedrooms ® ✗ (ex guide dogs) * sB&B£16-£18 sB&B↱£17-£20 dB&B£30-£34 dB&B↱£32-£35
▥ CTV 6P (£)

GH QQQ The Old House 161 Wilton Rd SP2 7JQ
☎(0722) 333433

Personally run by Mrs Hilary Maidment, this delightful private hotel stands on the edge of town, along the busy Wilton Road. The charming house has been decorated with style and flair; each of the six bedrooms has individual décor and all are nicely equipped. There is also a cosy feel to the public areas. A home- cooked meal is offered and is produced using fine, fresh produce.

6rm(1⇌4↱) (2fb)⊬in all bedrooms CTV in all bedrooms ® ✗ (ex guide dogs) * sB&B⇌↱£18-£20 dB&B⇌↱£30-£32
▥ CTV 10P

GH Q *Roman House* 49 Roman Rd SP2 9BJ ☎(0722) 414633

Set in a quiet residential area, this detached Edwardian house is simply furnished, comfortable and well equipped. The bedrooms and breakfast room are of a good size and the house has a relaxed, friendly atmosphere.

5rm(1⇌1↱3hc) (1fb) CTV in all bedrooms ® ✗ (ex guide dogs)
▥ 5P
Credit Cards [1]

INN QQ Old Bell 2 St Anne St SP1 2DN ☎(0722) 327958 FAX (0722) 411485

This small 14th-century inn is ideally situated close to the cathedral, opposite St Ann's Gate. Each of the bedrooms is comfortable, well decorated and tastefully furnished: many have beams and low ceilings, and 2 house splendid 4-poster beds. The dining room is bright and cheerful and contains an impressive antique mirror and a piano, and the public bar area has a lively atmosphere, with log fires.

7rm(1⇌6↱) ® ✗ * sB&B⇌↱£55-£60 dB&B⇌↱£55-£65
▥ CTV ⊘P nc12yrs solarium
Credit Cards [1] [2] [3] [5]

SANDBACH Cheshire Map **07** SJ76

GH QQ *Poplar Mount* 2 Station Rd, Elworth CW11 9JG
☎Crewe(0270) 761268

A fully modernised house reached via a steep drive. It is situated almost opposite the railway station in Elworth, a suburb of Sandbach.

5rm(2↱3hc) (1fb) LDO 7.45pm
▥ CTV 7P
Credit Cards [1] [3]

SANDOWN

See **WIGHT, ISLE OF**

SANDPLACE Cornwall & Isles of Scilly Map **02** SX25

GH QQQ *Polraen Country House Hotel* PL13 1PJ
☎Looe(05036) 3956

Dating back to 1742, this attractive granite country house is set in two acres of pretty, well kept gardens. The spacious bedrooms are well appointed, freshly decorated and comfortable. Public areas are well furnished and cosy, and the proprietress is a warm and welcoming hostess.

5rm(1⇌4↱) (2fb) CTV in all bedrooms ® LDO 8pm
Lic ▥ 21P
Credit Cards [1] [3]

SANDWICH Kent Map **05** TR35

INN QQQ St Crispin The Street CT14 0DF
☎Dover(0304) 612081

A charming inn dating back to 1426, refurbished, yet retaining its original character, Crispin's Inn is set in a picturesque village and offers a good selection of cask conditioned beers, and a fine choice of food. The bedrooms are well equipped.

4rm(2⇌2↱) Annexe 3⇌ (2fb) CTV in all bedrooms ® * sB&B⇌↱fr£30 dB&B⇌↱fr£45 LDO 9.30pm
▥ 30P
Credit Cards [1] [3]

SARISBURY GREEN Hampshire Map **04** SU50

GH Q Q Q **Dormy House Hotel** 21 Barnes Ln SO3 6DA
☎Locks Heath(0489) 572626
6 Jan-18 Dec
*Mollie and Eddie Rees provide friendly caring service at their
quietly situated guesthouse which has well equipped, very
comfortable bedrooms. Home prepared food is served from the
open plan kitchen. Dormy is convenient for Southampton,
Portsmouth and Hamble.*
10rm(8♠2hc) (1fb) CTV in all bedrooms ® ✕ (ex guide dogs)
sB&Bfr£23.50 sB&B♠fr£36.50 dB&Bfr£45.80
dB&B♠fr£49.50 LDO 5pmn
ㅰ CTV 18P
Credit Cards ③ ⓔ

SAUNDERSFOOT Dyfed Map **02** SN10

GH Q Q **Jalna Hotel** Stammers Rd SA69 9HH ☎(0834) 812282
Mar-Oct
*Just above the harbour and seafront, this family-run hotel provides
modern, quite spacious accommodation. The well equipped
bedrooms are all en suite, there is a comfortable lounge and a large
bar in the basement.*
14rm(8⇔6♠) CTV in all bedrooms ® ✳ sB&B⇔♠£22-
£23.50 dB&B⇔♠£37.50-£39 WB&B£120-£139 WBDi£160-
£189 LDO 6.30pm
Lic ㅰ CTV 14P solarium
Credit Cards ① ③

GH Q Q Q **The Sandy Hill** Sandy Hill Road/Tenby Rd
SA69 9DR ☎(0834) 813165
Mar-Sep
*This delightful small guesthouse, once a farm, is alongside the
A478 before the Tenby roundabout. Bedrooms are pretty and
comfortabale, and there is a cosy lounge and bar. Good value home
cooking is provided, and a swimming pool in the garden for warm
days.*
5hc (3fb) CTV in all bedrooms ® sB&B£14-£20 WB&B£98
WBDi£133-£140 (wkly only Jul-Aug)
Lic ㅰ 7P nc3yrs ➾ ⓔ

GH Q Q Q **Vine Farm** The Ridgeway SA69 9LA
☎(0834) 813543
Apr-Oct
*This old farmhouse, dating back in parts to the early 19th-century,
is now a very pleasant family-run guesthouse, set in well-kept
lawns and gardens. There is an attractive timbered dining room, a
spacious lounge with an open fire, and pretty, well furnished and
equipped bedrooms.*
5⇔♠ (1fb) CTV in all bedrooms ® ✳ dB&B⇔♠£35-£38
WBDi£150-£179 LDO 6pm
Lic ㅰ 10P nc2yrs

SAWLEY Lancashire Map **07** SD74

GH Q Q Q **Spread Eagle Hotel** BB7 4NH
☎Clitheroe(0200) 41202 FAX (0200) 41973
*Ten modern and very well equipped bedrooms, all with private
bathrooms, are located in a converted barn beside the nicely
situated Spread Eagle hotel. Full English breakfasts are served in
the bedrooms; main meals can be taken in the hotel if required.*
10rm(7⇔3♠) (2fb) CTV in all bedrooms ® ✕ (ex guide dogs)
✳ sB&B⇔♠£39-£54 dB&B⇔♠£59-£65 LDO 9pm
Lic ㅰ 80P
Credit Cards ① ② ③ ⑤

Street plans of certain towns and cities
will be found in a separate section
at the back of the book.

10 minutes drive from Salisbury.
Come to the quiet, unspoilt
village of Downton for a
comfortable bed and delicious
breakfast at

THE
WARREN

HIGH STREET,
DOWNTON,
SALISBURY, WILTS.

A modernised Georgian house of
great antiquity and character
offering pleasant English fare
and homely high-class
accommodation.

Tel: Downton (0725) 20263

2 MILES FROM THE NEW
FOREST.

HOLMHURST
GUEST
HOUSE

**Downton Road, Salisbury,
Wiltshire**
Tel: (0722) 323164

A well-appointed
guest house a few
minutes walk from
Salisbury Cathed-
ral, city centre and
pleasant riverside
and country walks.
All rooms centrally
heated, hot and cold, most have showers
and toilets en-suite. Colour TV and free
parking in grounds. Reasonable rates.

SAXELBY Leicestershire Map **08** SK62

FH 🔲🔲 Mrs M A Morris **Manor House** *(SK701208)*
LE14 3PA 🏠Melton Mowbray(0664) 812269
Etr-Oct

The manor house, parts of which date back to the 12th and 15th centuries, is situated on the edge of the village, 5 miles from Melton Mowbray.

3rm(1🟊2hc) (2fb) CTV in all bedrooms ® ✘ (ex guide dogs)
✱ sB&Bfr£20 dB&Bfr£30 dB&Bfr£38 WB&Bfr£100
WBDifr£150 LDO noon
🍴 CTV 6P 125 acres dairy sheep

SCARBOROUGH North Yorkshire Map **08** TA08

See Town Plan Section

GH 🔲 **Avoncroft Hotel** 5-7 Crown Ter YO11 2BL
🏠(0723) 372737

Part of an attractive Georgian terrace overlooking Crown Gardens, Avoncroft is a friendly guesthouse, simply furnished.

34rm(1⇔20🟊13hc) (13fb) CTV in all bedrooms ®
sB&Bfr£17.40-£19.40 sB&B⇔🟊£21-£23 dB&B£34.80-£38.80
dB&B⇔🟊£42-£46 WB&B£122-£136 WBDif£150-£163
LDO 6.15pm
Lic 🍴 CTV 🎱 games room pool table ⓔ

GH 🔲🔲 **Bay & Premier Hotels** 67 Esplanade, South Cliff
YO11 2UZ 🏠(0723) 501038 & 501062
Mar-Nov

These elegant Victorian hotels, situated next door to each other and under the same ownership, command fine views overlooking the South Bay, the picturesque harbour and the ruins of Scarborough Castle. Bedrooms in both hotels have en suite facilities, colour TV and tea-making equipment. Both are licensed, each hotel having its own bar lounge as well as comfortable residential lounges and well appointed dining rooms.

18rm(2⇔16🟊) Annexe 20rm(17⇔3🟊) (2fb) CTV in all
bedrooms ® sB&B⇔🟊£30-£42 dB&B⇔🟊£54-£64
WB&B£189-£224 WBDif£231-£266 LDO 6pm
Lic lift 🍴 10P
Credit Cards 🔲🔲 ⓔ

GH 🔲🔲🔲 **Burghcliffe Hotel** 28 Esplanade, South Cliff
YO11 2AQ 🏠(0723) 361524

A friendly family-run hotel with bright, comfortable, well equipped bedrooms, each with a private bathroom. Sitauted in an elevated position, the hotel enjoys panoramic views of the South Bay harbour. Public rooms include a cosy cocktail bar, a relaxing lounge and spacious dining room, where the proprietor offers freshly cooked food.

12rm(4⇔8🟊) (6fb) CTV in all bedrooms ® ✘ ✱
sB&B⇔🟊£25-£30 dB&B⇔🟊£43-£51 WB&B£143.50-£171.50
WBDif£210-£238 LDO 4pm
Lic 🍴 CTV 🎱
Credit Cards 🔲🔲 ⓔ

GH 🔲🔲 *Dolphin Hotel* 151 Columbus Ravine YO12 7QZ
🏠(0723) 374217

A small terraced house close to North Bay, the cricket ground and Peasholm Park. Bedrooms are particularly well equipped, each with a private bathroom, and home-cooked dinners are served by the friendly resident owners.

6⇔🟊 (2fb) CTV in all bedrooms ® ✘ LDO 8.30pm
Lic 🍴 CTV 🎱 nc5yrs
Credit Cards 🔲🔲

GH 🔲🔲 *Geldenhuis Hotel* 145-147 Queens Pde YO12 7HU
🏠(0723) 361677
Etr-end Oct

Terraced houses on sea front overlooking North Bay with comfortable lounge and separate bar lounge.

30rm(3⇔6🟊21hc) (6fb) ✘ (ex guide dogs) LDO 6pm
Lic 🍴 CTV 24P nc5yrs

GH 🔲🔲 **Manor Heath Hotel** 67 Northstead Manor Dr
YO12 6AF 🏠(0723) 365720
Closed 24-25 Dec

A detached 1930's house with gardens to the front and parking to the rear. Situated close to the North Bay and Peasholm Park, it enjoys pleasant open views of the surrounding area. Most bedrooms have private bathrooms, and the accommodation is pleasing and modern. There is a cosy bar, and a comfortable lounge with sea views from the bay window.

16rm(2⇔9🟊5hc) (5fb) CTV in all bedrooms ® ✘
sB&B£15.50-£17.50 sB&B⇔🟊£17.50-£19.50 dB&B£31-£35
dB&B⇔🟊£35-£39 WB&B£108.50-£136.50 WBDif£133-£164
LDO 4.30pm
Lic 🍴 CTV 16P ⓔ

GH 🔲🔲🔲 **Paragon Hotel** 123 Queens Pde YO12 7HU
🏠(0723) 372676

This very well furnished and comfortable small hotel occupies one of the best positions overlooking the North Bay. Personally owned and run, the hotel offers excellent value for money.

14rm(3⇔11🟊) (5fb) CTV in all bedrooms ® sB&B⇔🟊£25-
£27 dB&B⇔🟊£36-£40 WB&B£126-£140 WBDif£161-£189
LDO 6.30pm
Lic 🍴
Credit Cards 🔲🔲

GH 🔲🔲 **Parmelia Hotel** 17 West St YO11 2QN
🏠(0723) 361914
Apr-1 Nov

This private, family-run hotel is situated on the South Cliff, not far from the Esplanade. It offers pleasant, well maintained accommodation, including two lounges, one with a bar, and dinners are excellent value.

15rm(1⇔10🟊4hc) (4fb) CTV in all bedrooms ®
✘ (ex guide dogs) LDO 4pm
Lic 🍴 CTV ⓔ

GH 🔲🔲🔲 **Riviera Hotel** St Nicholas Cliff YO11 2ES
🏠(0723) 372277
Closed Xmas & New Year

20rm(15⇔5🟊) (6fb) CTV in all bedrooms ®
✘ (ex guide dogs) sB&B⇔🟊£26-£30 dB&B⇔🟊£52-£60
WB&Bfr£170 WBDifr£240 LDO 7pm
Lic lift 🍴 🎱
Credit Cards 🔲🔲

GH 🔲 **Sefton Hotel** 18 Prince of Wales Ter YO11 2AL
🏠(0723) 372310
Mar-Oct

Victorian town house with spacious public rooms and some charming bedrooms.

14rm(6⇔8hc) (2fb)⚲in 6 bedrooms ✘ (ex guide dogs)
sB&B£17-£17.50 dB&B£34-£35 dB&B⇔£38-£39 (incl dinner)
WB&B£119-£121 WBDif£140-£152 LDO 6pm
Lic lift 🍴 CTV nc12yrs ⓔ

GH 🔲🔲 **West Lodge Private Hotel** 38 West St YO11 2QP
🏠(0723) 500754

Close to the South Cliff and town centre, this comfortable hotel has modestly furnished and equipped bedrooms, and serves home cooked evening meals. A small bar offers a choice of drinks.

7rm(1🟊6hc) (4fb) CTV in all bedrooms ® ✘ ✱ sB&Bfr£12
dB&Bfr£24 dB&B🟊fr£28 WB&Bfr£84 WBDifr£112
LDO 10am
Lic 🍴 CTV ⓔ

'Selected' establishments, which have the highest
quality award, are highlighted by a tinted panel.
For a full list of these establishments, consult the
Contents page.

SCILLY, ISLES OF No map

ST MARY'S

SELECTED

GH QQQQ **Brantwood Hotel** Rocky Hill TR21 0NW
☎Scillonia(0720) 22531 Telex no 45117
Jun-Aug
A single-storey guesthouse with pretty gardens, in a rural location, yet just 20 minutes' walk from the town and beaches. It offers 4 comfortable and individually styled bedrooms, spotlessly clean and well equipped, with private bathrooms. There is a cosy lounge and an attractive dining room where wholesome traditional English breakfasts are served.
4♪ CTV in all bedrooms ® ✗ (ex guide dogs) ✳
sB&B♪£38 dB&B♪£76 (incl dinner) WB&B£266
Lic ⑭ ⫙ nc10yrs croquet
Credit Cards ①②③ ⓔ

SELECTED

GH QQQQ **Carnwethers Country House** Carnwethers,
Pelistry Bay TR21 0NX ☎Scillonia(0720) 22415
11 Apr-10 Oct
A pretty house standing in its own grounds which include a croquet lawn, gardens and a small swimming pool, situated above the beautiful secluded Pelistry Bay, just over 2 miles from Hugh Town. The accommodation comprises prettily decorated, spotlessly clean, well equipped bedrooms of varying sizes; most rooms have en suite facilities, and many also boast glorious sea views. Wholesome, good quality home cooking is provided in the cheerful dining room.
9rm(8⇨♪1hc) Annexe 1♪ (2fb) CTV in all bedrooms ®
✗ (ex guide dogs) sB&B£32-£40 sB&B⇨♪£37.50-£47.50
dB&B⇨♪£60-£92 (incl dinner) LDO 6.30pm
Lic ⑭ CTV 4P nc7yrs ⌷(heated) sauna pool table croquet
lawn library

SCOTCH CORNER North Yorkshire Map **08** NZ20

SELECTED

INN QQQQ **Vintage Hotel** DL10 6NP
☎Richmond(0748) 824424 & 822961
Closed Xmas Day & New Years Day rs Jan & Feb
A popular hotel situated on the A66, just a few yards from the A1. Bedrooms are compact but neat and cosy and well appointed. The rustic-style lounge and bar feature chunky stone and wood, and are comfortable and inviting. The extensive menus in both bar and restaurant offer freshly cooked food at realistic prices, and light snacks, tea and coffee are also available. Service is friendly and courteous.
8rm(5⇨♪3hc) CTV in all bedrooms ® ✗ (ex guide dogs)
✳ sB&B£23.50-£28.50 sB&B⇨♪£28.50-£33.50 dB&B£30-
£40 dB&B⇨♪£36-£46 WB&B£120-£200 WBDi£200-£300
✳ Lunch £9-£11.50 Dinner £12.50-£14.50&alc
LDO 9.15pm
⑭ 50P
Credit Cards ①③ ⓔ

This is one of many guidebooks pubished by
the AA. The full range is available at any
AA Shop or good bookshop.

SEAFORD East Sussex Map **05** TV49

GH QQQ **Avondale Hotel** 4-5 Avondale Rd BN25 1RJ
☎(0323) 890008
Extensively modernised, this conveniently situated and well-run hotel has bedrooms with generous facilities and a combined lounge and dining room. The extensive service is personally supervised by Mr and Mrs Jenkins.
16rm(4♪12hc) (8fb)⊬in 6 bedrooms CTV in all bedrooms ®
✗ (ex guide dogs) ✳ sB&B£14-£17.50 dB&B£28-£32
dB&B♪£35 WB&B£105-£122.50 WBDi£150.50-£168
LDO 2pm
lift ⑭ CTV
Credit Cards ①③

SEASCALE Cumbria Map **06** NY00

GH QQQ **Cottage** Black How CA20 1LQ ☎(09467) 28416
Well furnished modern accommodation is available at this small guesthouse at the end of a quiet lane near the village. The bedrooms have very good facilities and the resident owners provide friendly and attentive service.
8rm(7⇨♪1♪) (1fb) CTV in all bedrooms ® ✗ ✳ sB&B⇨♪£22
dB&B⇨♪£35
⑭ CTV 10P

SEATON (NEAR LOOE; 7M) Cornwall & Isles of Scilly
Map **02** SX35

GH QQQ **Blue Haven Hotel** PL11 3JQ
☎Downderry(05035) 310
6rm(5♪1hc) (3fb) CTV in 2 bedrooms TV in 2 bedrooms ®
sB&B£15-£18 dB&B♪£30-£36 WB&B£96-£115 WBDi£152-
£171 LDO 8pm
Lic CTV 6P
Credit Cards ①③ ⓔ

SEATON Devon Map **03** SY29

GH 🔲🔲 **Harbourside** 2 Trevelyan Rd EX12 2NL
☎(0297) 20085
Mar-Oct
This small, family-run guesthouse is situated in a quiet residential area close to the town centre and overlooking the harbour. Bedrooms are comfortable and clean, and set home-cooked meals are served in the lounge/dining area.
4rm(1🐾3hc) (2fb) CTV in all bedrooms ® ✳ sB&B£12-£13 dB&B£24-£26 WB&B£78-£84 WBDi£128 LDO 9pm
Lic 🍴 CTV 8P

GH 🔲🔲🔲 *Mariners Hotel* Esplanade EX12 2NP
☎(0297) 20560
Mar-Dec
A small, private hotel on the seafront with some glorious views. The bedrooms are well equipped and comfortably decorated and furnished, and the lounges have a relaxed, friendly atmosphere. Home-cooked evening meals are available in the dining room.
10rm(3🔄7🐾) (1fb) CTV in all bedrooms ®
Lic 🍴 CTV 10P
Credit Cards 🔲

SEAVIEW
See **WIGHT, ISLE OF**

SEDBERGH Cumbria Map **07** SD69

GH 🔲🔲 **Cross Keys Hotel** LA10 5NE ☎(05396) 20284
Etr, Apr-Dec & New Year
A small 18th-century stone-built house situated in open countryside. Owned by the National Trust, it is now unlicensed and there is no TV. Low ceilings, beams, flagged floors and open fires make up the character of this old inn, and a good standard of home cooking is provided, together with friendly service. Smoking is not permitted.
5rm(1🔄🐾4hc) ✂in all bedrooms ® ✖ (ex guide dogs)
sB&B£22 dB&B£44 dB&B🔄🐾£51 WB&B£154-£178.50 WBDi£248.50-£273 LDO 24hr notice
9P ⓔ

SEDGEFIELD Co Durham Map **08** NZ32

INN 🔲🔲🔲 *Dun Cow* High St TS21 3AT ☎(0740) 20894
A charming village inn near the popular Sedgefield racecourse. Full of character and atmosphere, it is renowned for its excellent standard of cuisine, with a wide range of bar meals and an appetising à la carte menu in the very pretty restaurant. There are six spacious, well appointed bedrooms, all equipped with TV and tea and coffee making facilities.
6hc CTV in all bedrooms ® LDO 10pm
🍴 25P
Credit Cards 🔲🔲🔲🔲

SELBY North Yorkshire Map **08** SE63

GH 🔲 **Hazeldene** 32-34 Brook St, Doncaster Rd YO8 0AR
(A19) ☎(0757) 704809
Closed Xmas wk
Friendly guesthouse near the town centre with comfortable accommodation. There is a TV lounge and a separate breakfast room.
7hc (2fb)✂in all bedrooms TV in all bedrooms ® ✖ sB&B£15-£17 dB&B£30-£34
CTV 5P

Street plans of certain towns and cities
will be found in a separate section
at the back of the book.

SELKIRK Borders *Selkirkshire* Map **12** NT42

GH 🔲🔲🔲 **Hillholm** 36 Hillside Ter TD7 4ND ☎(0750) 21293
Mar-Sep
This immaculate semidetached Victorian villa has a small front garden and stands on the A7, south of the town. It offers attractive, well maintained accommodation and delightful service from the friendly proprietors.
3hc ® ✖ ✳ sB&Bfr£18 dB&Bfr£30
🍴 CTV ✗ nc10yrs

SEMLEY Wiltshire Map **03** ST82

INN 🔲🔲 *Benett Arms* SP7 9AS ☎East Knoyle(0747) 830221
Closed 25 & 26 Dec
This country inn is situated in a quiet village between Tisbury and East Knoyle. There is a popular bar menu, complemented by daily specials; visitors may choose to eat in the public bars or in a pretty restaurant area. Bedrooms are well equipped and comfortable: 3 are located in a rear annexe, adjacent to the inn, the other 2 are older in style and located in the main building. Public areas are lively, with many local business people and visitors enjoying the hospitality of the resident proprietors.
2rm(1🔄1🐾) Annexe 3🐾 CTV in all bedrooms ®
LDO 9.45pm
🍴 30P
Credit Cards 🔲🔲🔲🔲

SENNEN Cornwall & Isles of Scilly Map **02** SW32

GH 🔲 **The Old Manor** TR19 7AD ☎(0736) 871280
Closed 23-28 Dec
8rm(5🐾3hc) (3fb)✂in 1 bedroom CTV in 7 bedrooms ® ✖ sB&B£14-£26 sB&B🐾£23-£26 dB&B£32-£42 dB&B🐾£36-£42 WB&B£63-£126 WBDi£115-£213.50 LDO 6.30pm
Lic 🍴 CTV 50P putting green
Credit Cards 🔲🔲🔲ⓔ

📶🍺 GH 🔲🔲 **Sunny Bank Hotel** Sea View Hill TR19 7AR
☎(0736) 871278
Closed Dec
An attractive Cornish stone-built detached house in a rural position just outside the village. It offers clean, simple family accommodation complemented by commanding views over the sea and countryside. En route to Lands End, it provides a good base for touring the south west peninsula.
11hc (2fb) ® ✖ (ex guide dogs) sB&B£13-£17 dB&B£26-£34 WB&B£91-£119 WBDi£120-£144 LDO 7.30pm
Lic 🍴 CTV 12P

SENNYBRIDGE Powys Map **03** SN92

See also Trecastle

SELECTED

FH 🔲🔲🔲🔲 Mrs M C Adams **Brynfedwen** *(SN963297)*
Trallong Common LD3 8HW ☎(0874) 636505
Closed Jan & Feb
This very friendly farmhouse, tucked away in the Brecon Beacons and overlooking the Usk Valley, is reached by taking the second turning for Trallong off the A40. Genuinely warm hospitality is matched by good home cooking, and the two pine-furnished rooms in the main building are supplemented by a converted granary making excellent provision for disabled guests.
2🔄🐾 Annexe 1🐾 (2fb) CTV in 1 bedroom ®
✖ (ex guide dogs) sB&B🔄🐾£14-£15 dB&B🔄🐾£28-£29 WB&B£98-£105 WBDi£147-£154 LDO 6.30pm
🍴 CTV 6P 150 acres sheep cattle horses ⓔ

SETTLE North Yorkshire Map **07** SD86

GH Q Q Liverpool House Chapel Square BD24 9HR
☎(0729) 822247
Closed 21 Dec-Jan
Charming 200-year-old house of great character, in quiet part of town.
7hc ⊁in all bedrooms ® ✖ sB&B£16-£18.50 dB&B£32-£37
WB&Bfr£112 WBDifr£206.50 LDO 10am
Lic CTV 8P nc3yrs
Credit Cards [1] [3] £

SEVENOAKS Kent

See **Wrotham**

SHALDON Devon

See **Teignmouth**

SHANKLIN

See **WIGHT, ISLE OF**

SHAP Cumbria Map **12** NY51

GH Q Q Q Brookfield CA10 3PZ ☎(09316) 397
Closed 20 Dec-Jan
Situated on the A6 at the southern end of the village, this warm and comfortable guesthouse has a pretty front garden, and offers good hospitality and home-cooked food. Housekeeping and maintenance are of a high standard throughout.
6hc (3fb) CTV in all bedrooms ® ✖ ✻ sB&B£15-£16.50
dB&B£30-£33 LDO 8.15pm
Lic ♨ CTV 30P 6🍴 £

⟦⟧ FH Q E & S Hodgson **Green Farm** *(NY565143)*
CA10 3PW ☎(09316) 619
Etr-Sep
A typical Cumbrian farmhouse which dates back to 1703 and is situated on the A6, set back from the road, on the south side of the village. It offers good value for money and a friendly atmosphere.
3rm(2hc) (2fb) ® ✖ sB&Bfr£13 dB&Bfr£26
CTV 4P 200 acres mixed

SHAWBURY Shropshire Map **07** SJ52

FH Q Mrs S J Clarkson **Longley** *(SJ602228)* Stanton Heath
SY4 4HE ☎(0939) 250289
Closed Xmas
An extended family-run farmhouse with a long drive, surrounded by 15 acres. The house is around 250 years old, and is located in the village of Stanton Heath, just off the A53 Shrewsbury-Newcastle road.
2hc Annexe 1⇆ ®
♨ CTV 4P 15 acres arable sheep

FH Q Q Q G C Evans **New** *(SJ586215)* TF6 6RJ
☎(0939) 250358
This extended and modernised farmhouse is situated to the north east of Shrewsbury, and is reached via the A53. It is well-maintained throughout, many of the well-equipped bedrooms having en suite facilities.
4rm(3🌓1hc) CTV in all bedrooms ® ✖ sB&B£15-£18
dB&B🌓£30-£36 WB&B£95-£110
♨ CTV 10P nc3yrs 70 acres arable sheep £

SHEARSBY Leicestershire Map **04** SP69

FH Q Q Q Mrs A T Hutchinson **Knaptoft House Farm & The Greenway** *(SP619894)* Bruntingthorpe Rd LE17 6PR
☎Leicester(0533) 478388
Closed Xmas
Situated one mile from the village of Shearsby towards Bruntingthorpe, this family farm offers accommodation and separate public areas in adjoining houses. Surrounded by beautiful open countryside and well-tended gardens with well-stocked carp ponds, the accommodation is thoughtfully furnished with guests' comfort foremost in mind, the majority of bedrooms having en suite shower rooms. A high standard is maintained throughout.
3hc Annexe 3hc (1fb) ® ✻ sB&Bfr£15 dB&Bfr£30
♨ CTV 10P nc3yrs ⏀ stabling 145 acres mixed £

FH Q Q Mrs S E Timms **Wheathill** *(SP622911)* Church Ln
LE17 6PG ☎Leicester(0533) 478663
Closed Xmas
Old brick-built farmhouse retaining original beams and inglenook fireplaces.
4rm(3hc) (1fb)⊁in all bedrooms ® ✖ (ex guide dogs) LDO am
♨ CTV 3P 133 acres dairy

SHEFFIELD South Yorkshire Map **08** SK38

GH Q Q Lindum Hotel 91 Montgomery Rd S7 1LP
☎(0742) 552356
Closed Xmas
This semidetached, stone-built house is situated in the residential suburb of Nether Edge, a mile southwest of the city centre. It provides simple but modern accommodation and has a small car park.
12rm(1⇆11hc) (1fb) CTV in 11 bedrooms TV in 1 bedroom ®
LDO 6pm
Lic ♨ CTV 6P £

GH Q Q Millingtons 70 Broomgrove Rd S10 2NA (off A625
Eccleshall Rd) ☎(0742) 669549
A small friendly guesthouse, 1.5 miles south west of the city centre via the A625, opposite the polytechnic buildings in a tree-lined side road. It provides simple but sound modern accommodation and is popular with commercial visitors. There is a small car park at the front of the house.

▶

6rm(2🐾4hc) CTV in all bedrooms ® ✘ (ex guide dogs) ✳
sB&B£21-£23 dB&B£41 dB&B🐾£44
🍴 CTV 4P nc12yrs

SHEPTON MALLET Somerset Map **03** ST64

INN Q Q *Kings Arms* Leg Square BA4 5LN ☎(0749) 343781
Closed Xmas rs Sun evenings
*An attractive 17th-century inn in the older part of the town offers
two warm and cosy bars with a small dining room. Bedrooms are
fresh and bright, with some modern facilities, and there is a clean,
well-kept bathroom.*
3🐾 CTV in all bedrooms ® ✘ (ex guide dogs) LDO 9.30pm
🍴 6P nc10yrs games room
Credit Cards [1]

SHEPTON MONTAGUE Somerset Map **03** ST63

INN Q *Montague* BA9 8JW ☎Bruton(0749) 813213
*Just 3 miles from Wincanton, this small roadside inn has ample
space for cars. The bedrooms all have en suite facilities and the
bar/lounge has an informal atmosphere in which to enjoy home
cooked food and speciality real ales.*
3🐾 TV in all bedrooms ® LDO 8pm
🍴 24P nc14yrs
Credit Cards [1] [3]

SHERBORNE Dorset

See **Halstock**

SHERBOURNE Warwickshire

See **Warwick**

SHERIFF HUTTON North Yorkshire Map **08** SE66

GH Q Q Q *Rangers House* Sheriff Hutton Park YO6 1RH
☎(03477) 397
*This interesting and unusual house is peacefully located within
attractive gardens. The oak-beamed bedrooms are cosy and the
lounge features a minstrels' gallery. Guests will enjoy a high
standard of cooking.*
6rm(2⇨2🐾2hc) (1fb) ® ✘ sB&B£27-£30 sB&B⇨🐾£29.80-
£32 dB&B£54-£60 dB&B⇨🐾£57.60-£64 WB&B£189-£201.60
WBDi£315-£327.60 LDO 9.30pm
Lic 🍴 CTV 30P

SHERINGHAM Norfolk Map **09** TG14

GH Q Q Q *Beacon Hotel* Nelson Rd NR26 8BT
☎(0263) 822019
May-Sep
*Beacon Hotel is perched atop Beeston Hill, to the east of the town,
a minute from the sea. It is a particularly well cared for
establishment with light, fresh décor and furnishings, and a
comfortable lounge and dining room.*
6rm(3🐾3hc) ⅙in all bedrooms ® ✘ sB&B£27 dB&B🐾£58
(incl dinner) WBDi£170-£182
Lic 🍴 CTV 5P nc14yrs
Credit Cards [1] [3] £

GH Q Q Q *Fairlawns* 26 Hooks Hill NR26 8NL
☎(0263) 824717
Etr-Oct
*Fairlawns is situated in a quiet residential cul-de-sac just off the
Holt road. The well proportioned rooms are comfortably furnished,
colour TVs have recently been installed, and there are excellent en
suite facilities providing each room with a bath and shower.
Evening meals are freshly prepared and the premises are licensed.*
5⇨🐾 CTV in all bedrooms ® ✘ (ex guide dogs)
dB&B⇨🐾£36-£39 WB&Bfr£115 LDO noon
Lic 🍴 CTV 6P nc12yrs £

GH Q Q Q *Melrose Hotel* 9 Holway Rd NR26 8HN
☎(0263) 823299
*Conveniently situated for the town centre, this is a cheerful
guesthouse with very well equipped accommodation and a
comfortable lounge. The dining room has a bar at one end.*
10rm(5🐾5hc) (1fb) CTV in 5 bedrooms ® sB&B£16-£17
sB&B🐾£20-£22 dB&B£32-£34 dB&B🐾£40-£44 WB&B£105-
£126 WBDi£150-£175 LDO 9am
Lic 🍴 CTV 10P cycle hire dinghy hire & tuition
Credit Cards [1] [2] [3]

SHETLAND Map **16**

LERWICK Map **16** HU44

GH Q Q Q *Glen Orchy* 20 Knab Rd ZE1 0AX
☎Shetland(0595) 2031
*Sitting high above the town centre, this guesthouse has bright, airy
bedrooms together with a combined lounge/dining room.*
6rm(1🐾5hc) (1fb) CTV in all bedrooms ®
🍴 CTV ▶9

SHIFNAL Shropshire Map **07** SJ70

GH Q Q *Village Farm Lodge* Sherriffhales TF11 8RD
☎Telford(0952) 462763
*This former farm building has been cleverly converted to provide
modern, well equipped accommodation with en suite bathrooms. It
is located on the B4379 on the northern edge of the village, about
three miles north of Shifnal. Telford town centre and business
areas are within a few minutes' drive, and the guesthouse is
understandably popular with commercial visitors.*
8🐾 (3fb) CTV in all bedrooms ® ✳ sB&B🐾£25-£28.50
dB&B🐾£35-£39.50
Lic 🍴 CTV 12P
Credit Cards [1] [2] [3]

SHIPBOURNE Kent Map **05** TQ55

INN Q Q Q *The Chaser* Stumble Hill TN11 9PE
☎Plaxtol(0732) 810630 FAX (0732) 810941
15⇨🐾 (1fb) CTV in all bedrooms ® sB&B⇨🐾£45
dB&B⇨🐾£50 WB&B£175-£315 ✳ Lunch £12.50 Dinner
£19.75-£23&alc LDO 9.30pm
🍴 30P
Credit Cards [1] [2] [3]

SHIRENEWTON Gwent Map **03** ST49

FH Q Q Q Mrs G Powell *Parsons Grove* (*ST452943*)
Earlswood NP6 6RD ☎(02917) 382
Closed 20-31 Dec
*Run by the friendly Powell family, this very comfortable
farmhouse has good bedrooms and a spacious lounge. All rooms
are fully en suite and the annexe room is suitable for disabled
guests. A swimming pool and self catering flats are also available.*
2⇨🐾 Annexe 1⇨🐾 CTV in 1 bedroom ® ✘ (ex guide dogs)
✳ dB&B⇨🐾£30-£32 WB&B£95-£105
🍴 CTV 10P ⌷(heated) 20 acres vineyards £

SHOTTLE Derbyshire Map **08** SK34

GH Q Q *Shottle Hall Farm* DE5 2EB
☎Cowers Lane(077389) 276 & 203
Closed Xmas
*Guests are assured of a warm welcome at this large family home.
Surrounded by 3 acres of grounds and a large farm, this is the
ideal spot for a relaxing holiday.*
9rm(1⇨8hc) (3fb)⅙in all bedrooms ® LDO 6pm
Lic 🍴 CTV 30P
See advertisement under BELPER

SELECTED

FH 🅠🅠🅠🅠 Mrs J L Slack **Dannah** *(SK314502)*
Bowmans Ln DE5 2DR ☎Cowers Lane(077389) 273 & 630
FAX (077389) 590
Closed Xmas
This Derbyshire farmhouse is full of character and has been extensively and tastefully restored to provide quality bedrooms and comfortable lounge facilities. An outbuilding has been converted to a restaurant where local produce is used.
7rm(6⇔🏿1hc) (1fb)⊬in all bedrooms CTV in all bedrooms ® 🏿 (ex guide dogs) sB&B⇔🏿£27.50-£29.50 dB&B£45-£50 dB&B⇔🏿£50-£55 WB&B£150-£175 LDO 9.15pm
Lic 🍺 CTV 20P 128 acres mixed
Credit Cards 🗌🗌🗌Ⓔ
See advertisement under DERBY

SHREWLEY Warwickshire Map **04** SP26

SELECTED

GH 🅠🅠🅠🅠 **Shrewley House** CV35 7AT
☎Claverdon(092684) 2549
Set in 1.5 acres of well tended gardens in open countryside, this Grade II listed Georgian farmhouse provides comfortable and well equipped accommodation. There are some bedrooms in the spacious main house, with deluxe rooms and king-size draped 4-poster beds, and more compact rooms in annexe cottages, which are also available to let for self catering; the standards and quality are the same throughout, and all have modern en suite bathrooms. Light meals or suppers can be arranged with Mrs Green, but formal meals are no longer available.
3⇔🏿 Annexe 6⇔🏿 (1fb) CTV in 5 bedrooms ®
sB&B⇔🏿£29-£41 dB&B⇔🏿£41-£52
🍺 CTV 15P 2🏌 ♿
Credit Cards 🗌🗌
See advertisement under WARWICK

SHREWSBURY Shropshire Map **07** SJ41

GH 🅠 *Cannock House Private Hotel* 182 Abbey Foregate
SY2 6AH ☎(0743) 356043
Closed Xmas
This small guesthouse stands on the main road, opposite Shrewsbury's famous abbey. The owners provide a friendly and informal service to complement the modest but well-maintained accommodation.
7hc (1fb)
🍺 CTV 5P

GH 🅠🅠🅠 **Fieldside Hotel** 38 London Rd SY2 5NX
☎(0743) 353143
Closed 18 Dec-18 Jan
Easily accessible from both the A49 and the A5, this large, beautifully maintained Victorian house stands on the A5112, east of the town centre. The well-equipped accommodation is of good quality and suitable for business guests and tourists.
9rm(1⇔5🏿3hc) ⊬in 7 bedrooms CTV in all bedrooms ® 🏿
✳ sB&B£18-£30 sB&B⇔🏿£30 dB&B⇔🏿£40-£45
Lic 🍺 10P 2🏌 nc9yrs
Credit Cards 🗌🗌🗌

GH 🅠🅠🅠 **Sandford House Hotel** St Julians Friars SY1 1XL
☎(0743) 343829
A well run family hotel on the edge of the town, close to the English bridge. Parking can be a problem, but there is a public car park near by. There is an elegant lounge overlooking the rear gardens and a pretty restaurant where breakfast is served.

10rm(5⇔🏿5hc) (2fb) CTV in all bedrooms ® sB&Bfr£21 sB&B⇔🏿fr£27.50 dB&Bfr£35 dB&B⇔🏿fr£42
Lic 🍺 CTV 3P Ⓔ

GH 🅠🅠🅠 **Sydney House Hotel** Coton Crescent, Coton Hill
SY1 2LJ ☎(0743) 354681
Closed 24-30 Dec
A smart, friendly and well run Victorian house with facilities that benefit both the tourist and the business person. It is situated on the northern edge of town, just off the A528 to Ellesmere.
7rm(3🏿4hc) (4fb) CTV in all bedrooms ® 🏿 (ex guide dogs) sB&B£32 sB&B🏿£32-£40 dB&B£38 dB&B🏿£52 WB&B£120-£252 WBDi£172.50-£353.50 LDO 8.30pm
Lic 🍺 7P 1🏌 (£2.50 per night)
Credit Cards 🗌🗌🗌Ⓔ
See advertisement on page 325

FH 🅠🅠 Mrs P A Roberts *The Day House* *(SJ465104)*
Nobold SY5 8NL (2.5m SW between A488 & A49)
☎(0743) 860212
Closed Xmas & New Year
Mostly built in the 1840s, this rambling farmhouse is surrounded by attractive gardens in a peaceful area 2.5 miles south south west of the town centre and provides spacious accommodation.
3rm(1⇔1🏿1hc) (3fb) CTV in all bedrooms ®
🏿 (ex guide dogs)
🍺 CTV 10P 1🏌 ⌁ rough & game shooting 400 acres arable dairy

FH 🅠🅠 Mrs J M Jones **Grove** *(SJ537249)* Preston
Brockhurst SY4 5QA ☎Clive(093928) 223
Closed Xmas & New Year
This 17th-century farmhouse with Victorian modifications provides well-maintained, traditional accommodation. Situated in the village of Preston Brockhurst it is just 8.5 miles north of the historic county town of Shrewsbury.

▶

3hc (1fb)⊁in all bedrooms CTV in 1 bedroom ®
✖ (ex guide dogs) sB&Bfr£14 dB&Bfr£29
🏻 CTV 4P 320 acres arable mixed

SIDMOUTH Devon Map **03** SY18

GH Ⓠ Ⓠ Ⓠ **Canterbury** Salcombe Rd EX10 8PR
☎(0395) 513373
Mar-Nov
A period house in a residential area close to the river and park, and only a short walk from the town centre and sea front. The bedrooms are well appointed and many have good en suite facilities. The resident proprietors provide a set home-cooked dinner.
8rm(7⇔3♠1hc) (4fb) CTV in all bedrooms ® sB&B£16.50-£19.50 sB&B⇔3♠£19.50 dB&B£33 dB&B⇔3♠£39
WB&B£122-£134 WBDi£158-£180 LDO 4.30pm
Lic CTV 6P ⓔ

GH Ⓠ Ⓠ **Mariners** 69 Sidford High St EX10 9SH
☎(0395) 515876
Closed Nov & Dec
The family home of the resident proprietors, set in well kept grounds in the small village of Sidford, just 1.5 miles from the seafront. The bedrooms are modern and brightly decorated and the lounge cosy. Evening meals are available in the relaxed atmosphere of the dining room.
8♠ (2fb) CTV in all bedrooms ® ✱ sB&B♠£15.50-£16.50
dB&B♠£31-£33 WB&B£98-£108 WBDi£105-£150 LDO 10am
🏻 CTV 8P

GH Ⓠ **Ryton House** 52-54 Winslade Rd EX10 9EX
☎(0395) 513981
This semidetached property has its own garden and is located away from the town centre, but still within easy reach of all local amenities. The recently refurbished lounge complements the bright bedrooms and the informal dining room.
9rm(3♠6hc) (3fb) ® ✱ sB&Bfr£14 dB&B£27-£31 dB&B♠£32-£36 WB&B£89-£109 WBDi£125-£145 (wkly only 1-19 Aug)
LDO 4.30pm
Lic 🏻 CTV 9P ⓔ

SILLOTH Cumbria Map **11** NY15

GH Ⓠ Ⓠ *Nith View* 1 Pine Ter CA5 4DT ☎(06973) 31542
Well run with a friendly atmosphere, this guesthouse is in a delightful location overlooking the Solway Firth. Well-furnished, comfortable accommodation is offered.
8rm(4♠4hc) (4fb) CTV in 2 bedrooms TV in 1 bedroom ®
LDO 4pm
Lic 🏻 CTV 8P 1🏖

SILVERSTONE Northamptonshire

See **Whittlebury**

SIMONSBATH Somerset Map **03** SS73

FH Ⓠ Ⓠ Ⓠ Mrs A R Brown **Emmett Grange** *(SS753369)*
TA24 7LD (2.5m SW unclass towards Brayford)
☎Exford(064383) 282
Mar-Oct
A large Victorian farmhouse approached by an attractive drive situated in unspoilt moorland within Exmoor National Park, with superb views. Bedrooms are comfortable and well equipped, complete with TV and hairdryers. Guests return regularly for the owner's cooking, which comprises four-course dinners using local produce, and hearty breakfasts. Self-catering cottages are also available.
4rm(2⇔2hc) CTV in all bedrooms ® ✱ sB&B£19-£22
sB&B⇔£22 dB&B£38-£44 dB&B⇔£44 (incl dinner)
WB&B£115-£135 WBDi£190-£210 LDO 6.30pm
Lic 🏻 6P 1200 acres hill stock ⓔ

SKEGNESS Lincolnshire Map **09** TF56

GH Ⓠ Ⓠ **Crawford Hotel** South Pde PE25 3HR ☎(0754) 4215
due to change to 764215
Situated south of the town centre on the seafront, the Crawford has a particularly high level of cleanliness and hospitality. The varied range of facilities and public areas attracts the holiday-making family in season and the commercial users at other times.
20rm(10⇔7♠3hc) (8fb) CTV in all bedrooms ® ✱
sB&B⇔♠fr£34.55 dB&B⇔♠fr£59.22 WB&B£129.54-£148.05 LDO 5pm
Lic lift 🏻 CTV 8P 🖾(heated) jacuzzi games room
Credit Cards ① ③

GH Ⓠ Ⓠ *Northdale* 12 Firbeck Av PE25 3JY ☎(0754) 610554
South of the town and two blocks from the seafront, this nicely maintained guesthouse continually improves its comfort and facilities, and is an ideal place for those seeking a quiet relaxing stay. Good en suite facilities are provided.
11rm(2⇔1♠8hc) (3fb) CTV in 1 bedroom TV in 4 bedrooms
® LDO 5.30pm
Lic CTV 8P ♨

SKIPTON North Yorkshire Map **07** SD95

GH Ⓠ Ⓠ **Craven House** 56 Keighley Rd BD23 2NB
☎(0756) 794657
Closed 24 Dec-31 Dec
The Rushtons provide a welcome at their guesthouse, situated on the main Keighley road and a short walk from the town centre. The comfortable accommodation gives good value, and there is a pleasant dining room and a relaxing lounge.
7rm(2⇔1♠4hc) CTV in all bedrooms ® sB&B£16-£20
dB&B£32-£34 dB&B⇔♠£36-£38
Lic 🏻 CTV 3P ⓔ

GH Ⓠ Ⓠ **Highfield Hotel** 58 Keighley Rd BD23 2NB
☎(0756) 793182
Closed 6-20 Jan rs 24-30 Dec
A cosy bar, lounge and dining room are available at this comfortable guesthouse, which has easy access to the town centre. The rooms have excellent facilities including hairdryers and trouser presses.
10rm(3⇔6♠1hc) (2fb) CTV in all bedrooms ® ✱
sB&B£18.50-£19.50 dB&B£37-£38 dB&B⇔♠£37-£38
WB&B£94.50-£101.50 LDO 5pm
Lic 🏻 CTV ♪
Credit Cards ① ③ ⓔ

INN Ⓠ Ⓠ *Red Lion Hotel* High St BD23 1DT ☎(0756) 790718
Cosy, well-furnished inn (the oldest building in Skipton).
3⇔♠ (1fb) CTV in all bedrooms ® ✖
🏻 4P
Credit Cards ① ③

SKYE, ISLE OF Highland *Inverness-shire* Map **13**

DUNVEGAN Map **13** NG24

GH Ⓠ *Roskhill* Roskhill IV55 8ZD (3m S A863) ☎(047022) 317
An attractive whitewashed house situated just off the A863, three miles south of Dunvegan. The bedrooms are small, but there is a pleasant beamed dining room with exposed stone walls, and the friendly new owners plan to make improvements.
5hc (2fb) ® LDO 5pm
Lic 🏻 CTV 6P

See advertisement on page 327

PORTREE Map **13** NG44

GH Ⓠ *Bosville Hotel* Bosville Ter IV51 9DG ☎(0478) 2846
Closed Jan
Bedrooms at this long-established tourist restaurant, situated in the centre of town, are generally compact, simply furnished but
▶

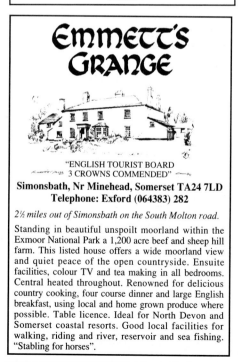

clean and well maintained. Three more spacious rooms are now available in a separate house next to the restaurant and these have the use of their own lounge.
16rm(9♠7hc) Annexe 3♠ CTV in all bedrooms ® *
sB&Bfr£20 sB&B♠fr£25 dB&Bfr£34 dB&B♠fr£49
WB&Bfr£119 WBDifr£182 LDO 8pm
Lic ♨ CTV 10P
Credit Cards ① ③

GH ⓠⓠⓠ **Craiglockhart** Beaumont Crescent IV51 9DF
☎(0478) 2233
Closed Dec
This pleasant, friendly bed and breakfast establishment is attractively situated by the water's edge overlooking the harbour. Bedrooms vary in size, but all are comfortably furnished and everywhere is well maintained and spotlessly clean. There is a pleasant lounge and neat dining room, where guests may have to share tables at breakfast time.
10rm(3♠7hc) CTV in 9 bedrooms ® * sB&B£14-£15
dB&B£30-£32 dB&B♠£34-£40
♨ CTV 4P

GH ⓠⓠⓠ **Quiraing** Viewfield Rd IV51 9ES ☎(0478) 2870
A modern extended bungalow situated on the southern approach to the town offering a good standard of accommodation in well maintained surroundings. There is a comfortable lounge and separate spacious breakfast room.
6rm(2♠4hc) (3fb)⊁in all bedrooms CTV in all bedrooms ® *
sB&B£15 dB&B£30 dB&B♠£34
♨ CTV 8P

FH ⓠⓠ Mrs M Bruce **Cruachanlea** *(NG513373)* Braes
IV51 9LJ ☎Sligachan(047852) 233
Closed 20 Dec-10 Jan
Cruachanlea is situated beside the B883 in the small community of Braes, six miles south of Portree. It is a modern house, part of a smallholding, offering neat and clean accommodation. Two of the bedrooms have particularly fine views of the Isle of Raasay.
4hc (2fb) sB&Bfr£15 dB&Bfr£26
♨ CTV 6P 15 acres sheep ⓔ

SLAIDBURN Lancashire Map 07 SD75

SELECTED

GH ⓠⓠⓠⓠ **Parrock Head Farm House Hotel**
Woodhouse Ln BB7 3AH ☎(02006) 614
Closed Xmas
Situated in unspoilt rolling countryside, one mile northwest of the village, this former farmhouse is now a small luxurious country house hotel. Excellent English cuisine is provided in the attractive beamed dining room, which was formerly the farm milking parlour. Originally a 17th-century longhouse, it features a cosy low-timbered bar, an elegant lounge with antiques and comfortable seating, and a charming timbered library, converted from the old hay loft. There are three delightful bedrooms in the farmhouse and seven in cottages in the grounds, all with full en suite and tea-making facilities. The attractive and well appointed restaurant serves freshly cooked local produce complemented by a well chosen wine list.
3⇔♠ Annexe 6⇔♠ (1fb) CTV in all bedrooms ® *
sB&B⇔♠£35.75-£37.50 dB&B⇔♠£53-£59 LDO 8.30pm
Lic ♨ 20P
Credit Cards ① ② ③ ⓔ

SLEAFORD Lincolnshire Map 08 TF04

INN ⓠⓠ *Carre Arms Hotel* Mareham Ln NG34 7JP
☎(0529) 303156
A large Victorian public house just off the town centre near the railway station. The bedrooms are well equipped, comfortable and clean. Service is friendly and there is a choice of meals from the restaurant or the bar.

14rm(3⇔11hc) CTV in all bedrooms ® LDO 9pm
♨ CTV 50P
Credit Cards ① ③

SLEDMERE Humberside Map 08 SE96

INN ⓠ **Triton** YO25 0XQ ☎Driffield(0377) 86644
Good value accommodation in this attractive estate village.
7rm(3⇔2♠2hc) (1fb) CTV in all bedrooms ® * sB&Bfr£19
sB&B⇔♠fr£25 dB&Bfr£38 dB&B⇔♠fr£50 * Lunch £2.95-
£6.95alc Dinner £3.50-£6.95alc LDO 9pm
♨ CTV 30P
Credit Cards ① ③ ⑤ ⓔ

SLOUGH Berkshire Map 04 SU97

GH ⓠ **Colnbrook Lodge** Bath Rd, Colnbrook SL3 0NZ (3m E
A4) ☎(0753) 685958
Closed 24-25 Dec
A family-run guesthouse located in a residential area of Slough, this detached villa is a convenient stop to or from Heathrow airport. The bedrooms are modest but well maintained, clean and comfortable. There is a warm, friendly atmosphere, the owners, Mr and Mrs Cuniff, are both welcoming and hospitable.
8rm(3⇔♠5hc) (2fb) CTV in all bedrooms ®
✖ (ex guide dogs) sB&B£30-£35 sB&B⇔♠£38-£42 dB&B£38-
£46 dB&B⇔♠£45-£55 WB&B£150-£200 WBDi£185-£235
LDO 7pm
Lic ♨ CTV 12P
Credit Cards ① ③ ⓔ

GH ⓠⓠ **Eton Lodge** 26 Albert St SL1 2BU ☎(0753) 520133
FAX (0628) 781831
A modern detached house set back from a main residential route, not far from the M4. It is a small guesthouse offering bed and breakfast, with limited public space and only a few bedrooms, but these are neat and tidy and all have en suite shower rooms.
5♠ (3fb)⊁in all bedrooms TV in all bedrooms ®
✖ (ex guide dogs) sB&B♠£30-£35 dB&B♠£40-£45
WB&B£161-£196
♨ 10P nc5yrs
Credit Cards ① ③ ⓔ

SOLVA Dyfed Map 02 SM82

See also **Llandeloy**

SELECTED

FH ⓠⓠⓠⓠ Mrs M Jones **Lochmeyler** *(SM855275)*
SA62 6LL (4m N on unclass rd) ☎Croesgoch(0348) 837724
This large 16th-century farmhouse is situated on a 220-acre dairy farm and is quite remotely located, some six miles east of St Davids and three miles north of Solva. It has been extensively renovated by Mr and Mrs Jones to provide spacious, modern and very well equipped accommodation, which is complemented by very friendly hospitality.
6⇔ (5fb)⊁in all bedrooms CTV in all bedrooms ®
sB&B⇔£22.50 dB&B⇔£35 WB&B£120 WBDi£165 (wkly only wkly only Whitsun-early Sep) LDO 6pm
Lic ♨ CTV P nc10yrs 220 acres dairy
Credit Cards ① ③ ⓔ

SOMERTON Somerset Map 03 ST42

GH ⓠⓠⓠ *Church Farm* School Lane, Compton Dandon
TA11 6PE ☎(0458) 72927
Jan-3 wk Dec Closed Xmas & New Year
Most of the comfortable, thoughtfully equipped accommodation is in the annexe of this charming cottage. A warm welcome is assured and the new owners personally supervise the running of Church Farm.

2rm(1⇔1♪) Annexe 5rm(2⇔2♪1hc) (1fb) CTV in 6 bedrooms ® LDO 5.30pm
Lic ♨ 6P nc4yrs

SELECTED

GH Ⓠ Ⓠ Ⓠ Ⓠ **The Lynch Country House** 4 Behind Berry
TA11 7PD ☎(0458) 72316
A delightful Grade II listed property set in its own peaceful and well kept grounds on the edge of the village. There are over 2 acres of gardens containing an abundance of trees, shrubs and flowers, and a host of wild birds, including black swans, have made a home on the ornamental lake. The house has been lovingly restored and tastefully decorated and furnished, with many antiques. The bedrooms boast 4-poster and brass beds, and are equipped with modern facilities and thoughtful extras. Drinks are served in the comfortable lounge, and breakfast is provided in the elegant breakfast room.
5⇔♪ CTV in all bedrooms ® ✱ sB&B⇔♪£30-£60 dB&B⇔♪£35-£75 WB&B£210-£420
Lic ♨ 15P

SOPWORTH Wiltshire Map **03** ST88

FH Ⓠ Mrs D M Barker **Manor** *(ST826865)* SN14 6PR
☎Didmarton(045423) 676
Etr-Oct
2rm(1♪) (2fb) ✗ (ex guide dogs) sB&B♪fr£14 dB&B♪fr£25 dB&B♪fr£25 WB&B♪fr£75
♨ TV 5P 300 acres arable beef horses sheep ⓔ

SOUTHAMPTON Hampshire Map **04** SU41

See **Town Plan Section**
GH Ⓠ Ⓠ **Banister House Hotel** Banister Rd SO9 2JJ
☎(0703) 221279
Closed 25-27 Dec
Private hotel with warm and friendly atmosphere. Popular bar meals and dining room.
23rm(9⇔♪14hc) (3fb) CTV in all bedrooms ® sB&B£21.50-£27.50 sB&B⇔♪£24.50-£27.50 dB&B£30-£35 dB&B⇔♪£35 LDO 7.45pm
Lic ♨ 14P
Credit Cards ①②③ⓔ

GH Ⓠ Ⓠ **Capri** 52 Archers Rd SO1 2LU ☎(0703) 632800
Centrally positioned for all of Southampton's amenities, this detached Victorian property has recently been refurbished. The bedrooms vary in size, and the dining room is compact but is understood to be extended. Good car parking space is available around landscaped gardens. Room 15 has a water bed!
14rm(9♪5hc) (2fb) CTV in all bedrooms ® sB&B♪fr£15 sB&B♪£18 dB&B♪fr£30 dB&B♪£36 LDO 1pm
CTV 14P nc2yrs steam room
Credit Cards ①③ⓔ

GH Ⓠ **Hill Lodge Hotel** 126-128 Hill Ln, Shirley SO1 5DD
☎(0703) 223071
This detached Edwardian hotel enjoys a quiet position, yet is conveniently situated for all the city's amenities. Accommodation is currently being upgraded, and some rooms are nicely furnished with pine. Guests here receive friendly family service, and have the advantage of a large car park.
19rm(16⇔♪3hc) (3fb)✗in 3 bedrooms CTV in all bedrooms ® ✗ (ex guide dogs) LDO 6pm
♨ CTV 20P

GH Ⓠ Ⓠ Ⓠ **Hunters Lodge Hotel** 25 Landguard Rd, Shirley
SO1 5DL ☎(0703) 227919 FAX (0703) 230913
Closed 17 Dec-7 Jan

With a good bar, well-maintained and equipped rooms and a small lounge, this friendly, family-managed hotel enjoys a quiet situation with parking and garaging facilities.
18rm(8⇔4♪6hc) (2fb)✗in 1 bedroom CTV in all bedrooms ®
✱ sB&B£20-£23.50 sB&B⇔♪£22.50-£33.49 dB&B£37.50-£52.29 dB&B⇔♪£44.50-£52.29 WB&B£117.50 WBDi£178.75 LDO 6pm
Lic ♨ CTV 16P 4🅿 (75p per night)
Credit Cards ①②③

GH Ⓠ Ⓠ **Landguard Lodge** 21 Landguard Rd SO1 5DL
☎(0703) 636904
Landguard Lodge is a quietly located semidetached property in a residential area. The accommodation has recently been refurbished throughout. This bed and breakfast establishment offers simple yet well-equipped bedrooms and an attractive pine furnished breakfast room.
13rm(4♪9hc) (1fb) CTV in all bedrooms ® ✗ (ex guide dogs) sB&B£15-£20 sB&B♪£20 dB&B♪£40 WB&B£105-£140
♨ CTV 4P nc5yrs
Credit Cards ①②③ⓔ

GH Ⓠ Ⓠ **Linden** 51-53 The Polygon SO1 2BP ☎(0703) 225653
Closed Xmas
This double-fronted house stands in the city centre and provides neat, bright and comfortable accommodation. Mr and Mrs Hutchins have run this guesthouse for many years and provide pleasant, efficient service and a well cooked breakfast.
12hc (4fb) CTV in all bedrooms ® ✗ ✱ sB&B£13.50-£14.50 dB&B£27-£29
♨ CTV 7P ⓔ

Southampton - Southport

GH |Q||Q| **Lodge** 1 Winn Rd, The Avenue SO2 1EH
☎(0703) 557537
Closed Xmas-New Year
A Tudor-style detached house on the outskirts of the city centre offering simple accommodation at competitive prices, popular with students and business people. The bedrooms vary in size, but all are well equipped with modern facilities. There is a small bar, comfortable lounge area and dining room, with evening meals cooked by the proprietor.
14rm(2⇄4♠8hc) (2fb) CTV in all bedrooms ® ✱
sB&Bfr£20.95 sB&B⇄♠fr£29.95 dB&Bfr£34 dB&B⇄♠fr£40
LDO 9pm
Lic � CTV 10P
Credit Cards |1| |3| £

GH |Q| **Madison House** 137 Hill Ln SO1 5AF ☎(0703) 333374
FAX (0703) 772264
rs 23 Dec-2 Jan
A cosy, simple and well-maintained guesthouse, this is set in a residential area giving easy access to the city centre and the docks. There are facilities for guests to make tea and coffee at any time.
9rm(3♠6hc) (2fb) CTV in all bedrooms ® ✖ sB&B£14.50-£16.50 sB&B♠£16-£18.50 dB&B£28-£32 dB&B♠£30.50-£35
♨ CTV 7P £

SOUTH BRENT Devon Map 03 SX66

FH |Q| M E Slade *Great Aish (SX689603)* TQ10 9JG
☎(0364) 72238
Closed Dec
A Devonshire welcome awaits guests at this Victorian farmhouse, close to Dartmoor National Park in an elevated position, commanding views of the surrounding countryside. Bedrooms are spacious and the lounge and dining rooms are well cared for.
5hc (3fb) ® ✖ (ex guide dogs)
CTV 8P 60 acres beef dairy mixed

SOUTHEND-ON-SEA Essex Map 05 TQ88

GH |Q||Q| **Argyle Hotel** 12 Clifftown Pde SS1 1DP
☎(0702) 339483
Closed Xmas
A small, comfortable hotel situated in an ideal position overlooking the bandstand and seafront, within walking distance of the town. The accommodation is simple, clean and comfortable.
11hc (3fb) CTV in all bedrooms ® ✖ sB&B£18-£20 dB&B£36
Lic ♨ CTV ✗ nc5yrs £

GH |Q||Q||Q| **Cobham Lodge Hotel** 2 Cobham Rd, Westcliff On Sea SS0 8EA ☎(0702) 346438
A substantial and attractive guesthouse located in a peaceful residential area a few minute's walk from the sea. Accommodation is clean, well equipped and comfortable, and public rooms include a choice of lounges, a well stocked bar and a large dining room providing a table d'hôte menu.
30rm(9⇄13♠8hc) (3fb) CTV in all bedrooms ® ✖ ✱
sB&B£20-£29.50 sB&B⇄♠fr£29.50 dB&B⇄♠fr£38
WB&B£100-£147.50 WBDi£150-£170 LDO 7pm
Lic ♨ CTV ✗ snooker
Credit Cards |1| |3| |5|

SELECTED

GH |Q||Q||Q||Q| **Ilfracombe House Hotel** 11-13 Wilson Rd
SS1 1HG ☎(0702) 351000
Situated within walking distance of the seafront, this hotel has been tastefully refurbished to create an elegant and comfortable guesthouse. Bedrooms offer well equipped and freshly decorated accommodation, and there is a comfortable open-plan bar; home-cooked English fare can be enjoyed in the dining room.

14⇄♠ (2fb) CTV in all bedrooms ® ✖ sB&B⇄♠£30-£38 dB&B⇄♠£40-£48 WB&B£240 WBDi£295
LDO 7.30pm
Lic ♨ CTV ✗ ◑
Credit Cards |1| |2| |3| |5| £

GH |Q||Q| **Marine View** 4 Trinity Av, Westcliff on Sea SS0 7PU
☎(0702) 344104
An Edwardian terraced house ideally located between the town centre and the seafront, providing simply furnished and well equipped accommodation.
6hc (1fb) CTV in all bedrooms ® ✖ (ex guide dogs) ✱
sB&B£15-£16 dB&B£28-£30 WB&B£80-£87.50
♨ CTV ✗

GH |Q||Q| **Mayflower Hotel** 5-6 Royal Ter SS1 1DY
☎(0702) 340489
Closed Xmas
This grade II Regency house is part of the Royal terrace, and in summer the wrought iron balconies are festooned with wonderful flowers by the charming proprietors. Bedrooms are on 4 floors, simply furnished, clean and well maintained. The front rooms have sea views, as does the lounge which also offers a pool table.
23rm(4♠19hc) (3fb) CTV in all bedrooms ® sB&Bfr£19
sB&B♠£28-£30 dB&Bfr£30 dB&B♠£38-£40
♨ CTV 2P pool table

GH |Q||Q| **Terrace Hotel** 8 Royal Ter SS1 1DY ☎(0702) 348143
A most attractive villa-style house built around the end of the 18th century. Situated above the cliff, some bedrooms have excellent sea views, and the accommodation is clean and comfortable.
9rm(3♠6hc) (3fb) CTV in all bedrooms ® ✱ sB&Bfr£17
dB&Bfr£28 dB&B♠fr£35
Lic ♨ ✗ nc5yrs £

GH |Q||Q||Q| **Tower Hotel** 146 Alexandra Rd SS1 1HE
☎(0702) 348635
A fully modernised house situated in a quiet residential area a few yards from the cliff. Most bedrooms are en suite and some are located in the annexe; they are generally more spacious. The accommodation is well furnished and equipped.
16rm(14⇄♠2hc) Annexe 16rm(3⇄13♠) (6fb) CTV in all bedrooms ® ✱ sB&B£33-£36 sB&B⇄♠£36-£39.50
dB&B⇄♠£45-£55 LDO 9pm
Lic ♨ CTV 2P residents membership of near by sports club
Credit Cards |1| |2| |3| |5| £

GH |Q||Q||Q| **West Park Private Hotel** 11 Park Road, Westcliff-on-Sea SS0 7PQ ☎(0702) 330729 & 334252 FAX (0702) 338162
A large, well managed guesthouse, centrally located. Accommodation is clean, tidy and well equipped, with spacious annexe rooms, an attractive dining room and a well stocked bar.
21rm(13⇄3♠5hc) CTV in all bedrooms ® ✖ sB&Bfr£32
sB&B⇄♠£34-£41 dB&B£45-£51 dB&B⇄♠£45-£51
LDO 6.30pm
Lic ♨ CTV 16P
Credit Cards |1| |3| £

SOUTHPORT Merseyside Map 07 SD31

See **Town Plan Section**
GH |Q||Q||Q| **Ambassador Private Hotel** 13 Bath St PR9 0DP
☎(0704) 543998 & 530459 FAX (0704) 536269
Closed 20 Dec-7 Jan
Situated between fashionable Lord Street and the Promenade, this small hotel offers comfort with well-appointed bedrooms. Fresh, seasonal produce is used for the dishes offered at dinner.
8♠ (4fb)⤢in 2 bedrooms CTV in all bedrooms ® ✱
sB&B♠£30-£33 dB&B♠£46-£50 WB&Bfr£140 WBDifr£175
LDO 7pm
Lic ♨ 6P nc5yrs
Credit Cards |1| |3|

GH QQ **Crimond Hotel** 28 Knowsley Rd PR9 0HN
☎(0704) 536456 FAX (0704) 548643
Situated in a quiet residential area, this family-run hotel offers well equipped bedrooms which are gradually being upgraded and the modern conference and leisure facilities are popular with businessmen.
16➾⊓ (2fb) CTV in all bedrooms ® sB&B➾⊓£42-£45 dB&B➾⊓£64-£70 LDO 8.30pm
Lic ♨ 20P ⊠(heated) sauna
Credit Cards ① ② ③ ⑤ ⑤

GH QQ **Fairway Private Hotel** 106 Leyland Rd PR9 0JQ
☎(0704) 542069
Mar-Nov
Situated in a peaceful residential area close to the Municipal Golf Course, this privately owned, small hotel offers traditionally furnished bedrooms and comfortable public rooms including a small lounge bar.
9rm(4⊓5hc) (4fb) CTV in 8 bedrooms ® ✕ (ex guide dogs) ✳ sB&B£17-£18 dB&B£34-£36 dB&B⊓£38-£40 (incl dinner) WB&B£105-£112 WBDi£122-£189 LDO 6pm
Lic CTV 10P

GH QQQ **The Gables Private Hotel** 110 Leyland Rd PR9 0JE
☎(0704) 535554
Apr-Oct
Quietly situated off the northern promenade, this pleasantly appointed and well maintained guesthouse offers comfortable accommodation for a relaxing holiday with good home cooking being served in the charming dining room.
9rm(2➾6⊓1hc) CTV in all bedrooms ® ✕ LDO 3pm
Lic ♨ CTV 9P nc12yrs

GH Q **Lake Hotel** 55-56 The Promenade PR9 0DY
☎(0704) 530996
Close to the theatre on the promenade, Lake Hotel provides comfortable accommodation and a friendly atmosphere. The bedrooms vary in size, but all are equipped to the same standard, with en suite showers.
20⊓ (5fb) CTV in all bedrooms ® ✳ sB&B⊓£22-£23 dB&B⊓£41-£43 WB&B£130.50-£141 WBDi£166-£175 LDO 4.30pm
Lic ♨ CTV 14P
Credit Cards ③

GH Q **Lyndhurst** 101 King St PR8 1LQ ☎(0704) 537520
This terraced property is situated in a side street close to the town centre, and offers modestly appointed and compact accommodation.
7hc CTV in all bedrooms ® ✕ (ex guide dogs) LDO 12pm
Lic ♨ CTV 2P nc5yrs

GH QQQ **Oakwood Private Hotel** 7 Portland St PR8 1LJ
☎(0704) 531858
Etr-Nov
This friendly, long-established guesthouse is conveniently situated close to the centre of town and offers well maintained and comfortable accommodation which is appreciated by the more mature holidaymaker.
7rm(4⊓3hc) ⅙in all bedrooms CTV in all bedrooms ® ✕ ✳ dB&B⊓frf40
Lic ♨ CTV 8P nc5yrs

GH QQ **Rosedale Hotel** 11 Talbot St PR8 1HP
☎(0704) 530604
This friendly, family-run guesthouse, close to the town centre, has compact and modestly furnished bedrooms, but a comfortable lounge and a small bar in which to relax.
10rm(6⊓4hc) (2fb) CTV in all bedrooms ® ✕ (ex guide dogs)
✳ sB&B£18-£20 sB&B⊓£21-£23 dB&B£36-£40 dB&B⊓£42-£46 LDO 4pm
Lic ♨ 8P

GH QQQ **Sunningdale Hotel** 85 Leyland Rd PR9 0NJ
☎(0704) 538673
Situated in a quiet residential road, near the golf course and Hesketh park, this personally run hotel offers guests particularly well equipped bedrooms. There is a comfortable television lounge and a spacious lounge-bar, with snooker and darts available for guests.
14rm(1➾11⊓2hc) (4fb) CTV in all bedrooms ® sB&B£21 sB&B➾⊓£23 dB&B➾⊓£44 WB&B£140-£154 WBDi£196-£210 LDO 4.30pm
Lic ♨ CTV 10P half size snooker table dart board
Credit Cards ① ③

GH QQ **The White Lodge Private Hotel** 12 Talbot St PR8 1HP
☎(0704) 536320
A long-established, family-run guesthouse situated close to the town centre and offering pleasant, fresh accommodation. Bedrooms are fairly compact but well maintained, as are the attractive and comfortable public areas.
9rm(1➾4⊓4hc) (3fb) CTV in 4 bedrooms ®
✕ (ex guide dogs) sB&B£14-£18 sB&B➾⊓£16-£20 dB&B£28-£36 dB&B➾⊓£32-£40 WB&B£95-£120 WBDi£110-£150 LDO 6pm
Lic CTV 6P ๗ ⑤

GH QQ **Windsor Lodge Hotel** 37 Saunders St PR9 0HJ
☎(0704) 530070
A small hotel situated close to the promenade and marine lake. The enthusiastic new owners plan to make improvements to the clean though modest accommodation. It is well decorated throughout, and in addition to a comfortable lounge, offers a pleasant basement bar and games room.
12rm(1➾⊓11hc) (1fb) CTV in all bedrooms ®
✕ (ex guide dogs) LDO noon
Lic ♨ CTV 9P pool table

SOUTHSEA Hampshire

See **Portsmouth & Southsea**

SOUTHWELL Nottinghamshire Map **08** SK75

GH 🅠🅠🅠 **The Old Forge** 2 Burgage Ln NG25 0ER
☎(0636) 812809

*A personally run guesthouse just on the edge of the town centre.
The bedrooms are well equipped and pretty. There is a car park
and a secluded patio to the rear of the house. Smoking is not
permitted.*

3rm(2⇨1♠) Annexe 2♠ ⊁in all bedrooms CTV in all
bedrooms ® sB&B⇨♠£30-£33 dB&B⇨♠£40-£45
WB&B£198-£210
♨ 5P

Credit Cards ①③ ⓔ

SOUTH ZEAL Devon Map **02** SX69

GH 🅠🅠🅠 **Poltimore** EX20 2PD ☎Okehampton(0837) 840209

*This pretty thatched cottage stands in its gardens on the fringe of
Dartmoor. The bedrooms are simply furnished and comfortable,
and there are two lounges. Home produced vegetables are used
whenever possible in the home cooked meals.*

7rm(2⇨2♠3hc) CTV in all bedrooms ® sB&B£16-£22
sB&B⇨♠£20-£26 dB&B£32-£44 dB&B⇨♠£36-£48
WB&B£96-£145 WBDi£166-£215 LDO 9pm
Lic ♨ CTV 25P nc8yrs

Credit Cards ①②③ ⓔ

SPEAN BRIDGE Highland *Inverness-shire* Map **14** NN28

GH 🅠🅠 **Coire Glas** PH34 4EU ☎(039781) 272

Closed Nov-Dec

*This family-run, licensed guesthouse is a modern bungalow with its
own garden situated 50 yards from the A86, on the eastern edge of
the village and overlooking the Ben Nevis mountain range. It has a
friendly atmosphere and offers good value holiday
accommodation.*

14rm(8♠6hc) (2fb) ® sB&B£15.50-£16 dB&B£25-£26
dB&B♠£31-£32 LDO 8pm
Lic CTV 20P ⓔ

▒▒ GH 🅠🅠 **Inverour** PH34 4EU ☎(039781) 218

Apr-Oct

*This friendly and well maintained family-run holiday guesthouse is
conveniently situated near the junction of the A86/A82. The
attractive lounge, with its welcoming open fire, invites easy
relaxation and the new dining room has been furnished to a good
standard. Bedrooms, though mostly compact, are cosy and
comfortable.*

7rm(3♠4hc) TV in all bedrooms ® sB&Bfr£13 dB&Bfr£26
dB&B♠fr£30 WB&Bfr£86.45 WBDifr£149.45 LDO 6pm
♨ 7P

STAFFORD Staffordshire Map **07** SJ92

GH 🅠🅠 **Leonards Croft Hotel** 80 Lichfield Rd ST17 4LP
☎(0785) 223676

Closed Xmas

*Friendly hosts ensure that guests feel at home here in a large
detached house with extensive and well-tended rear gardens which
stands on the edge of the town.*

12hc (2fb) ® sB&B£17 dB&Bfr£34 LDO 9pm
Lic ♨ CTV 10P

Every effort is made to provide accurate
information, but details can change after we go to
print. It is advisable to check prices etc. before
you make a firm booking.

STAMFORD BRIDGE Humberside

See **Low Catton & High Catton**

STANSTED Essex Map **04** SP43

GH 🅠🅠 **The Laurels** 84 St Johns Rd CM24 8JS
☎(0279) 913023

*A family-run guesthouse just off the main route running through
the village. It offers simply furnished, well equipped bedrooms of
varying sizes, a cheerful lounge and parking at the front.*

STANTON WICK Avon Map **03** ST66

GH 🅠🅠🅠 **Carpenters Arms** BS18 4BX
☎Compton Dando(0761) 490202

12⇨♠ CTV in all bedrooms ® ✖ (ex guide dogs)
sB&B⇨♠fr£42.50 dB&B⇨♠fr£49.50 LDO 10pm
Lic ♨

Credit Cards ①③

STAPLETON Leicestershire Map **04** SP49

GH 🅠🅠 **Woodside Farm** Ashby Rd LE9 8JE
☎Market Bosworth(0455) 291929

*A Georgian farmhouse in 16 acres of grounds, situated one mile
north of the village of Stapleton and three miles from Hinckley.
Bedrooms are clean and quite well equipped, and there is a good
choice of menus in the restaurant, which is popular with locals.*

6rm(2♠4hc) ⊁in 1 bedroom CTV in all bedrooms ® ✖
✳ sB&Bfr£17.50 sB&B♠fr£20.50 dB&Bfr£33 dB&B♠fr£35
LDO 9.30pm
Lic ♨ CTV 20P 2🏫

Credit Cards ①③

STARBOTTON North Yorkshire Map **07** SD97

SELECTED

GH 🅠🅠🅠🅠 **Hilltop Country** BD23 5HY
☎Kettlewell(075676) 321

mid Mar-mid Nov

*A charming little guesthouse most hospitably run by Tim and
Marie Louise Rathmell. The house was built for the family in
the 17th century, and displays a wealth of character and
original features. The attractive dining room contains an
authentic 'beef loft' and inglenook fireplace, and there is a
cosy lounge with an open fire and a tiny bar. Bedrooms are
pretty and all have private bathrooms: one room is located in
the converted barn next to the house. Dinner is a very
enjoyable experience, with a high standard of home cooking.
Walkers enjoying this beautiful part of the Yorkshire Dales
National Park are well catered for, with full drying facilities
available.*

4rm(1⇨3♠) Annexe 1♠ (1fb)⊁in 4 bedrooms CTV in all
bedrooms ® ✖ (ex guide dogs) dB&B⇨♠fr£50 (incl
dinner) LDO 6pm
Lic ♨ 6P ⓔ

STEEPLE ASTON Oxfordshire Map **04** SP42

GH 🅠🅠 **Westfield Farm Motel** The Fenway OX5 3SS
☎(0869) 40591

*This motel was created by converting farm buildings and is set in a
peaceful rural location on the edge of the village. The six
comfortable bedrooms are well equipped, with private bathrooms,
and are accessible from the car park. Breakfast only is served in an
adjacent dining room.*

7♠ (1fb) CTV in all bedrooms ® sB&B♠£28-£38
dB&B♠£38-£48 WB&B£176-£240
Lic ♨ CTV 12P ↺

Credit Cards ①③ ⓔ

STEPASIDE Dyfed Map **02** SN10

GH **Q** **Q** **Bay View Hotel** Pleasant Valley SA67 8LR
☎Saundersfoot(0834) 813417
Apr-Sep
A modern hotel situated in a secluded position in a lovely wooded valley convenient for many fine beaches. Accommodation is simple but clean and bright : there is a large residents' bar, a small TV lounge and an outdoor pool for the summer.
12rm(7↑5hc) (4fb) ® ✳ ✖ (ex guide dogs) ✳ sB&B£13-£15.50
dB&B£26-£31 dB&Bↂ£28.90-£33.90 WB&B£91-£118.65
WBDi£120-£150 (wkly only mid Jun-Aug) LDO 5pm
Lic ﷽ CTV 14P ⋔ ⇌(heated)

STEVENTON Oxfordshire Map **04** SU49

GH **Q** **Q** **Steventon House Hotel** Milton Hill OX13 6AB
☎Abingdon(0235) 831223 FAX (0235) 831223
A detached property with its own attractive grounds which include a heated outdoor pool. Some of the 23 bedrooms are in a converted stable block accessible from the garden ; they are all well equipped and have en suite facilities. There is a residents' bar and two dining areas, where a simple à la carte menu is available.
8rm(3⇌5ↂ) Annexe 15⇌ↂ (2fb) CTV in all bedrooms ®
✖ (ex guide dogs) ✳ sB&B⇌ↂ£52-£60 dB&B⇌ↂ£62-£75
LDO 8.30pm
Lic ﷽ 50P ⇌(heated)
Credit Cards ① ② ③ ⑤

STEWARTON Strathclyde *Ayrshire*

See **Dunlop**

STEYNING West Sussex Map **04** TQ11

GH **Q** **Q** **Nash Hotel** Horsham Rd BN4 3AA ☎(0903) 814988
Set in a peaceful spot off a country road, the Nash Hotel provides modest yet comfortable accommodation. The public areas are spacious and are tastefully furnished with co-ordinating soft furnishings. The house is surrounded by its own vineyard and samplings are held in the wine-tasting room.
4rm(1⇌3hc) (2fb)✖in 1 bedroom CTV in all bedrooms ® ✳
sB&B£25-£30 dB&B£43 dB&B⇌£45 LDO 7pm
Lic ﷽ CTV 18P ⇌ ℙ(hard)wildfowl lake vineyard ℒ

GH **Q** **Q** **Q** **Springwells Hotel** 9 High St BN44 3GG
☎(0903) 812446 & 812043
Closed 1 wk Xmas
Two of the bedrooms at this friendly hotel have four-poster beds. The comfortable accommodation includes a pleasant lounge, pretty dining room and an appealing conservatory-style bar/lounge. Springwells enjoys a central location and has an outdoor swimming pool.
10rm(6⇌4hc) (1fb) CTV in all bedrooms ® ✳ sB&B£30-£49
sB&B⇌£38-£43 dB&Bfr£53 dB&B⇌£59-£79 WB&Bfr£228
Lic ﷽ CTV 6P ⇌(heated) sauna
Credit Cards ① ② ③ ⑤ ⑭
See advertisement on p 333

STIPERSTONES Shropshire Map **07** SJ30

⌂⊌ **GH** **Q** **Q** **Tankerville Lodge** SY5 0NB
☎Shrewsbury(0743) 791401
Set in a lovely area this hotel is found off the A488 near Minsterley from the north, and from the south you should follow signs via Shelve and Pennerley. Guests will be well rewarded with comfortable and relaxing accommodation.
4hc ® sB&B£13-£15 dB&B£26 WB&B£81.90-£95.90
WBDi£134.40-£148.40 LDO 4pm
Lic ﷽ CTV 4P ℒ

This guide is updated annually – make sure you
use an up-to-date edition.

🏰 The Castle Hotel

The Street, Bramber, West Sussex
Telephone: (0903) 812102

Situated in the delightful historical village of Bramber in West Sussex, ten miles from Brighton, four from Shoreham and seven miles from Worthing. A village Inn where the accommodation has been converted to a high standard, the restaurant has a full á la carte menu and a wide variety of bar snacks, ample car parking and conveniently situated for a multitude of outdoor activities and picturesque walks.
For further information see gazetteer entry under Bramber.

Struther Farmhouse
Newmill Road, Dunlop, Ayrshire KA3 4BA
Telephone: 0560 84946

In a beautiful country setting in an acre of garden . . .

Come and taste Scottish food at its best . . .
Super menus, best of Scottish fare, freshly cooked and served to perfection. All bedrooms are large and comfortable. Situated 20 minutes from the famous Burrell Collection and within easy reach of the superb Ayrshire coast, golf courses and the Burns Country. Dinner, bed & breakfast £160 per person per week. Bed & breakfast £90 per person per week.

331

STIRLING Central *Stirlingshire* Map **11** NS79

See also **Denny**

GH Q Q Q *Castlecroft* Ballengeich Rd FK3 1TN
☎(0786) 74933

Closed Xmas & New Year

Situated in an elevated position under Stirling Castle, with panoramic views of the surrounding hills, this family-run guesthouse is an ideal base for the tourist. It has a friendly atmosphere and offers well equipped bedrooms, all with private bathrooms. Facilities for disabled guests are also available.

6♠ (1fb) CTV in all bedrooms ®
lift ♛ 6P

STOCKBRIDGE Hampshire Map **04** SU33

GH Q Q Q *Carbery* Salisbury Hill SO20 6EZ
☎Andover(0264) 810771

Closed 2 wks Xmas

An attractive Georgian house situated at the west end of the main street, very close to the River Test, set in an acre of well tended landscaped gardens, with lovely views. The guesthouse has been owned and run by Ann and Phillip Hooper since 1965. Bedrooms are individually furnished and decorated, and all are well equipped.

11rm(2⇔6♠3hc) (2fb) CTV in all bedrooms ® ✖
sB&B£18.80 sB&B⇔♠£26.65 dB&B£37.60 dB&B⇔♠£43.48 WB&B£197-£245 WBDi£261.40-£309 LDO 6pm
Lic ♛ 14P ⌂(heated) badminton pool table

GH Q Q Q *Old Three Cups Private Hotel* High St SO20 6HB
☎Andover(0264) 810527

24 Dec-early Jan rs Jan

A former 15th-century coaching inn situated in the main street. The young proprietors provide friendly service, and meals are available throughout the day. Bedrooms are simple but comfortable; there are very low beams in places: please note!

8rm(3⇔♠5hc) (2fb) CTV in all bedrooms ✖ (ex guide dogs)
LDO 9.30pm
Lic ♛ 12P
Credit Cards 1 3

STOCKPORT Greater Manchester Map **07** SJ98

GH Q Q Q *Ascot House Hotel* 195 Wellington Rd North, Heaton Norris SK4 2PB ☎061-432 2380 Telex no 666514 FAX 061-443 1936

Closed 2 wks Xmas

This large detached Victorian house with a friendly atmosphere is set back from the A6 to the north of the town, and is particularly suited to the businessman. Bedrooms in the rear extension are more spacious but all are well equipped and particularly clean and warm.

18rm(16⇔♠2hc) (1fb) CTV in all bedrooms ®
✖ (ex guide dogs) sB&B£20-£40 sB&B⇔♠£33-£40 dB&B£35 dB&B⇔♠£40-£45 LDO 7.15pm
Lic ♛ CTV 20P 1⌂ sauna
Credit Cards 1 3

STOCKTON-ON-TEES Cleveland Map **08** NZ41

GH Q Q *The Court Private Hotel* 49 Yarm Rd TS18 3PE
☎(0642) 604483

Three-storeyed, mid-terrace property near the town centre with small dining room and comfortable sitting room.

9hc (3fb) CTV in all bedrooms ® ✖ (ex guide dogs) LDO 6pm
Lic ♛ CTV ✗ nc2yrs

GH Q Q Q *The Edwardian Hotel* 72 Yarm Rd TS18 3PQ
☎(0642) 615655

A late-Victorian terraced house situated on the A135 west of the town centre, about one mile from its junction with the A61. Bedrooms are very well equipped, and there is secure car parking.

6rm(4♠) (3fb) CTV in all bedrooms ® ✖ (ex guide dogs)
LDO 7pm
Lic ♛ CTV 8P
Credit Cards 1

STOKE-BY-NAYLAND Suffolk Map **05** TL93

INN Q Q Q **The Angel Inn** Polstead St CO6 4SA
☎Nayland(0206) 263245

Closed 25-26 Dec & 1 Jan

A popular and at times very busy inn dating from the 16th-century, situated in one of Suffolk's most interesting villages and surrounded by lovely countryside, has been totally restored and refurbished whilst retaining such original features as exposed brickwork, beams, two large open fireplaces in the bars and the gallery overlooking the high ceilinged dining room. Individually decorated and furnished bedrooms of a high standard are provided with good modern en suite facilities. The restaurant serves the same dishes as are listed on the daily blackboard bar-meals menu – both bars and restaurant being much frequented by local customers.

5⇔♠ Annexe 1⇔♠ CTV in all bedrooms ®
✖ (ex guide dogs) ✳ sB&B⇔♠£38.50 dB&B⇔♠£51.25 ✳
Lunch £16.70-£24.50alc Dinner £10.65-£24.50alc LDO 9pm
♛ 25P nc8yrs
Credit Cards 1 2 3 5

STOKE HOLY CROSS Norfolk Map **05** TG20

FH Q Q Mrs Harrold **Salamanca** *(TG235022)* NR14 8QJ
☎Framlingham Earl(05086) 2322

Closed 15 Dec-15 Jan & Etr

This large farmhouse is set in the heart of a picturesque village and dates back to the 16th century. Surrounded by well tended gardens, it offers traditional, comfortable accommodation and a pleasant lounge.

3hc Annexe 1⇔ ✖ sB&B£15-£18 sB&B⇔£15-£20 dB&B£28-£32 dB&B⇔£32-£36
♛ CTV 7P nc6yrs 175 acres dairy mixed ⓔ
See advertisement under **NORWICH**

STOKE-ON-TRENT Staffordshire Map **07** SJ84

GH Q Q Q *White Gables Hotel* Trentham Rd, Blurton ST3 3DT ☎(0782) 324882

Closed 2 wks Xmas & New Year

A large, fully modernised house in extensive grounds with a rural outlook, set on the A5035 on the outskirts of the city. The rooms are spacious, well equipped and distinctively decorated. Additional facilities include a basement games room.

8rm(3⇔3♠2hc) (2fb) CTV in all bedrooms ®
✖ (ex guide dogs) LDO 7.30pm
Lic ♛ CTV 12P 2⌂ ♪(hard)games room
Credit Cards 1 3

GH Q Q *The White House* Stone Rd, Trent Vale ST4 6SP
☎(0782) 642460 or 657189

Closed Xmas & New Year

Extended and modernised, this Victorian house is run by friendly hosts who ensure their guests of an enjoyable stay and maintain the good reputation of The White House.

8hc Annexe 2♠ (2fb) CTV in 9 bedrooms ® ✖ (ex guide dogs)
sB&B£22-£35 dB&B£36-£40 dB&B♠£44-£48 WB&B£154-£280 WBDi£210-£340 LDO 6pm
Lic ♛ CTV 10P
Credit Cards 1 2 3 ⓔ

STOKE ST GREGORY Somerset Map **03** ST32

GH Q Q *Jays Nest* TA3 6HZ ☎North Curry(0823) 490250

Conference facilities are available at this cottage style property which has its own sunny garden. Three of the bright and comfortable bedrooms have en suite facilities and the recently extended public areas are tastefully furnished and decorated.

6rm(1⇔2🌂3hc) (2fb)✗in 2 bedrooms Ⓡ ✳ sB&B£16–£20
sB&B⇔🌂£18–£22 dB&B£32–£36 dB&B⇔🌂£36–£40
WB&B£105–£115 WBDi£150–£175 LDO 9pm
Lic ⫟ CTV 15P 2🐾 nc12yrs
Credit Cards ②ⓔ

STORNOWAY

See **LEWIS, ISLE OF**

STOURBRIDGE West Midlands Map **07** SO98

GH Ⓠ Ⓠ **Limes Hotel** 260 Hagley Rd, Pedmore DY9 0RW
☎Hagley(0562) 882689
*This guesthouse is situated 1.5 miles from Stourbridge in a
pleasant residential area. The rooms are well kept although some
are quite compact. This is a friendly household which is
particularly popular with commercial travellers.*
11rm(2🌂8hc) (1fb) CTV in 8 bedrooms Ⓡ ✳ sB&Bfr£28.25
sB&B🌂fr£32.50 dB&Bfr£35.25 dB&B🌂fr£40.50
WB&Bfr£197.75 WBDifr£225.35 LDO 7.30pm
Lic ⫟ CTV 12P
Credit Cards ①②③ⓔ

STOW-ON-THE-WOLD Gloucestershire Map **04** SP12

GH Ⓠ Ⓠ **Limes** Evesham Rd GL54 1EJ
☎Cotswold(0451) 30034
Closed 23 Dec–1 Jan
*Large gabled house within walking distance from town centre
offering friendly family service.*
3rm(2🌂1hc) Annexe 1🌂 (1fb) CTV in all bedrooms Ⓡ
dB&B£28–£29 dB&B🌂£32–£35
⫟ CTV 6P

The Topps

*Fintry Road, Denny,
Stirlingshire FK6 5JF
Telephone: 0324 822471*

Eight bedroomed, modern
bungalow with tastefully
appointed rooms. Situated in
beautiful countryside, 4 miles
west of Denny on the B818.

See gazetteer under Denny.

Domvilles Farm

Barthomley Road, Audley,
Nr Stoke on Trent, Staffordshire ST7 8HT
Tel: Stoke on Trent (0782) 720 378

18th century
listed farmhouse
with oak beams
and stair case,
set in land-
scaped garden
on a 120 acre
dairy farm. Ideal
for families with lots of animals to see. All rooms
have wash basins, tea/coffee tray and colour TV
with four rooms en suite. Two rooms have Victorian mahogany four poster beds and two rooms,
two poster Victorian brass beds. Ideally situated
3 minutes from junc 16 of M6 motorway and
within easy reach of Potteries, Bridgemere
Gardens, Stapeley Water Gardens and Alton
Towers. Closed Xmas.
Proprietor: Mrs E E Oulton

Springwells Hotel

STEYNING, WEST SUSSEX (Nr. Brighton)
Telephone: 0903-812446
Once a Georgian merchant's town house
now an elegant ten-bedroomed bed &
breakfast hotel. All rooms have telephones
& colour TV and most have private
facilties.
Tea/coffee making facilities if required.
Some four-poster beds. Lovely walled
gardens, outdoor swimming pool. Victorian
style conservatory. Half hour from
Gatwick/Newhaven. £30-£79 per room.

GH Q|Q **Royalist Hotel** Digbeth St GL54 1BN
☎Cotswold(0451) 30670
13rm(8➪5👤) (3fb) CTV in all bedrooms ® sB&B➪👤£25-£40
dB&B➪👤£40-£66 WB&B£120-£396
Lic ♔ 12P
Credit Cards ①②③ £

FH Q|Q Mr R Smith **Corsham Field** *(SP217249)* Bledington
Rd GL54 1JH ☎Cotswold(0451) 31750
Closed 25-26 Dec
*Newly constructed, Cotswold-stone farmhouse incorporating many
traditional features.*
3rm(1➪2hc) (1fb) CTV in all bedrooms ® ✳ sB&B£12-£20
sB&B➪£15-£25 dB&B£22-£30 dB&B➪£26-£33 WB&B£84-
£115
♔ CTV 10P 100 acres arable beef sheep

STRATFORD-UPON-AVON Warwickshire Map **04** SP25

See **Town Plan Section**

GH Q|Q **Ambleside** 41 Grove Rd CV37 6PB ☎(0789) 297239 &
295670 FAX (0789) 295670
Closed Xmas
*On the Evesham road close to the town centre, this hotel has the
benefit of a spacious car park. Facilities are constantly being
improved, and Ambleside offers good value for money.*
7rm(3👤4hc) (3fb)✂in 3 bedrooms CTV in all bedrooms ® ✳
sB&B£15-£17 dB&B£30-£34 dB&B👤£32-£40
♔ CTV 15P 1🐾 (50p per night)
Credit Cards ①③ £

GH Q|Q **Avon View Hotel** 121 Shipston Rd CV37 7LW
☎(0789) 297542 (0789) 294550
*This small private hotel has the benefit of its own car park and is a
short walk from the town centre. Recent improvements have given
all the bedrooms en suite facilities. Light meals and snacks can be
served in the evening upon request.*
9➪👤 (1fb)✂in all bedrooms CTV in all bedrooms ® ✖
sB&B➪👤£22-£32 dB&B➪👤£40-£54 WB&B£126-£175
WBDi£196-£304 LDO 4pm
Lic ♔ CTV 16P nc12yrs
Credit Cards ①②③⑤ £

GH Q|Q|Q **Brook Lodge** 192 Alcester Rd CV37 9DR
☎(0789) 295988
Closed Xmas
*Close to Anne Hathaway's cottage on the Alcester Road, this
recently modernised hotel has comfortable, well-equipped
bedrooms and good public area facilities.*
7rm(5👤2hc) (2fb) CTV in all bedrooms ® dB&B£32-£36
dB&B👤£34-£38 WB&B£96-£114
♔ CTV 10P
Credit Cards ①②③ £

GH Q|Q **Courtland Hotel** 12 Guild St CV37 6RE
☎(0789) 292401
*The Courtland Hotel is a comfortable Georgian Grade II listed
building situated in the town centre behind Shakespeare's
birthplace. Mrs Johnson's friendly manner helps to create a
relaxed and informal atmosphere.*
7rm(1➪1👤5hc) (1fb) CTV in all bedrooms ® sB&B£15-
£16.50 sB&B➪👤£28-£34 dB&B£30-£34 dB&B➪👤£38-£44
♔ CTV 2P 1🐾 £

GH Q|Q|Q **Craig Cleeve House** 67-69 Shipston Rd CV37 7LW
☎(0789) 296573 FAX (0789) 299452
*Situated 100 yards from Clopton Bride, this large Edwardian
house has been totally refurbished to provide very comfortable
accommodation. Terry and Margarita Palmer are charming hosts
and Margarita's Spanish origin is very much in evidence with lots
of ornaments and attractive ceramic tiling.*
15rm(9👤6hc) CTV in all bedrooms ® sB&B£17.50-£29
sB&B👤£30-£40 dB&B£35-£40 dB&B👤£41-£50
WB&B£122.50-£175

Lic ♔ 15P
Credit Cards ①③⑤ £

GH Q|Q **The Croft** 49 Shipston Rd CV37 7LN ☎(0789) 293419
*Situated 100 yards from Clopton Bridge, on Shipston road, this
guesthouse has direct access to the ornamental gardens and the
theatre from the rear entrance.*
9rm(3👤6hc) (5fb) CTV in all bedrooms ® sB&B£17.50-£28
sB&B👤£26-£34 dB&B£31-£35 dB&B👤£38-£42
WB&B£103.50-£142 WBDi£159.50-£198 LDO noon
Lic ♔ 4P ⚙
Credit Cards ①③ £

GH Q|Q|Q **Eastnor House Hotel** Shipston Rd CV37 7LN
☎(0789) 268115
Closed Xmas
*Attentive, friendly service at this comfortable Victorian house close
to centre.*
9➪👤 (3fb) CTV in all bedrooms ® dB&B➪👤£40-£54
Lic ♔ 9P
Credit Cards ①③ £

GH Q|Q **Eversley Bears** 37 Grove Rd CV37 6PB
☎(0789) 292334
*Close to the town centre, this well-appointed family-run guesthouse
has a friendly atmosphere. Mrs. Thomas has a large collection of
teddy bears for guests to admire.*
6hc (2fb) ® ✖ (ex guide dogs) ✳ sB&B£16-£20 dB&B£32-£40
WB&B£110-£126
♔ CTV 3🐾 (50p) nc14yrs £

GH Q|Q **Hardwick House** 1 Avenue Rd CV37 6UY
☎(0789) 204307 FAX (0789) 296760
Closed Xmas

▶

A spacious, detached Victorian house situated off the Warwick road, within walking distance of the river and the Memorial Theatre. Bedrooms are comfortable and well equipped, some with private bathrooms.
14rm(7⇨🏠7hc) (3fb) CTV in all bedrooms ®
🏶 (ex guide dogs) sB&B£16-£21 dB&B£32-£42 dB&B⇨🏠£40-£53
🅿 12P
Credit Cards ①②③ ⓔ

GH ⓠⓠⓠ **Highcroft** Banbury Rd CV37 7NF ☎(0789) 296293
A large, red-brick country house situated two miles south on the A422 Banbury road. There is one bedroom in the main house, and one with a separate direct entrance ; both have either antique or pine furniture and are well equipped with modern, en suite facilities. In addition to the comfortable bedrooms, there is a spacious lounge/dining room and a tennis court.
1⇨🏠 Annexe 1⇨🏠 (1fb) CTV in 1 bedroom TV in 1 bedroom ® ✱ dB&B⇨🏠£30
🅿 5P ♪(hard) ⓔ

GH ⓠⓠⓠⓠ **Hollies** 'The Hollies', 16 Evesham Place CV37 6HQ
☎(0789) 266857
Mrs Morgan is a very amiable host and is anxious for guest to feel at home in this pleasant guesthouse. Hollies stands close to the town centre and has its own car park.
6rm(1🏠5hc) (2fb) CTV in all bedrooms ® ✱ dB&B£30 dB&B🏠£37
🅿 CTV 6P

GH ⓠⓠ **Hunters Moon** 150 Alcester Rd CV37 9DR
☎(0789) 292888
Standing on the Alcester Road, this hotel offers simple public areas and comfortable bedrooms, most of which have private facilities.
7rm(5🏠2hc) (5fb) CTV in all bedrooms ® sB&B£17.50-£20 dB&B£30-£34 dB&B🏠£33-£45 WB&B£110-£130
🅿 CTV 6P
Credit Cards ①②③ ⓔ

GH ⓠⓠ *Kawartha House* 39 Grove Rd CV37 6PB
☎(0789) 204469
Semidetached house not far from the town centre, pleasantly situated opposite a small park and with family atmosphere.
6rm(3🏠3hc) (2fb) CTV in 4 bedrooms ®
🅿 CTV 4🏠

GH ⓠⓠ **Marlyn** 3 Chestnut Walk CV37 6HG ☎(0789) 293752
Closed Xmas
Situated in a Chestnut tree lined, town centre lane, this spacious terraced house offers comfortable bed and breakfast accommodation, with well-equipped traditional style bedrooms.
8hc (1fb) ® 🏶 (ex guide dogs) sB&Bfr£17 dB&Bfr£32
🅿 CTV

GH ⓠⓠ **Melita Private Hotel** 37 Shipston Rd CV37 7LN
☎(0789) 292432
Closed Xmas
This attractive Victorian house stands on the A34 close to the town centre and its major attractions. En suite bedrooms are comfortably furnished providing up-to-date facilities in this friendly, family-run guesthouse.
12⇨🏠 (3fb)✂in 8 bedrooms CTV in all bedrooms ®
sB&B⇨🏠£30-£42 dB&B⇨🏠£45-£59
Lic 🅿 CTV 12P
Credit Cards ①②③ ⓔ

GH ⓠⓠⓠ **Moonraker House** 40 Alcester Rd CV37 9DB
☎(0789) 299346 FAX (0789) 295504
Situated half a mile from the town centre this establishment offers good bed and breakfast accommodation which is spread over 4 buildings. Bedrooms vary in size and all have en suite facilities, modern fitted furniture and tasteful colour schemes.
6🏠 Annexe 9⇨🏠 (1fb)✂in 4 bedrooms CTV in all bedrooms
® sB&B⇨🏠£28-£32 dB&B⇨🏠£36-£54 WB&B£126-£196

🅿 12P 3🏠 (£1 per night)
Credit Cards ①②③ ⓔ
See advertisement on page 339 and in colour supplement

GH ⓠⓠ **Nando's** 18-19 Evesham Place CV37 6HT
☎(0789) 204907
A double-fronted Edwardian house situated close to the centre of Stratford. It offers pretty, comfortable bedrooms, some with modern en suite facilities, and an attractive dining room.
21rm(1⇨6🏠14hc) (10fb) CTV in all bedrooms ✱ sB&B£16-£18 sB&B⇨🏠£25-£35 dB&B£26-£32 dB&B⇨🏠£37-£40
🅿 CTV 8P
Credit Cards ①②③ ⓔ

GH ⓠⓠ **Parkfield** 3 Broad Walk CV37 6HS ☎(0789) 293313
Friendly, attentive services and excellent breakfasts have earned proprietress Pauline Rush a good reputation at this spacious corner house situated just five minutes' walk from the town centre. It also offers well equipped, comfortable bedrooms and a good private car park.
7rm(3🏠4hc) (1fb) CTV in all bedrooms ® sB&B£15-£17 dB&B£30-£34 dB&B🏠£36-£40
🅿 8P nc7yrs
Credit Cards ① ③ ⓔ

GH ⓠⓠⓠ **The Payton Hotel** 6 John St CV37 6UB
☎(0789) 266442
Situated in the Georgian part of what is affectionately known as 'new town', this corner terraced house has been tastefully converted by John and June Rickett into a quality bed and breakfast hotel with cosy bedrooms and an imaginative breakfast menu.
5rm(4🏠1hc) (1fb) CTV in all bedrooms ® 🏶 (ex guide dogs)
✱ sB&B🏠£32-£36 dB&B🏠£40-£50
🅿 ♪ nc1-8yrs
Credit Cards ② ⓔ

Kawartha House is a well appointed town house with a friendly atmosphere overlooking the 'old town' park. It is located just a few minutes walk from the town centre and ideal for visiting the places of historic interest. Private parking is available as are evening meals by arrangement. With pretty en suite bedrooms and quality food these are the ingredients for a memorable stay.

39 Grove Rd, Stratford-Upon-Avon CV37 6PB Tel: (0789) 204469

Our delightful Victorian Building dating from 1887, set within a tree-lined Avenue, has been skilfully converted to Guest House Accommodation of the highest calibre. Quiet home comforts, pleasant surroundings and only a short walk from all the major attractions of this historic town.

1 Avenue Road, Stratford-upon-Avon, Warwickshire CV37 6UY
Telephone: (0789) 204307

Ample Parking

HUNTERS MOON

GUEST HOUSE

150 ALCESTER ROAD STRATFORD-ON-AVON WARWICKSHIRE CV37 9DR
Reservations: (0789) 292888   Guests: (0789) 204101

SAVE MONEY, BOOK MIDWEEK, GENEROUS PRICE REDUCTIONS

Hunters Moon has been operated by the same family for over 30 years and has recently been completely modernised and refurbished. We can now offer hotel-type accommodation at Guest House prices. Single, double, twin and family rooms are now offered, with private facilities, fitted hair dryers, and colour TV. Orthopaedic beds available on request. There are tea and coffee making facilities in all rooms, TV lounge, free parking for cars and coaches. Arrangements can be made for coach parties at reduced rates. Single night bookings accepted. Children half price.

Visa, Access, American Express and J.C.B. Cards accepted

AA LISTED

English Tourist Board

Recommended by Arthur Frommer

GH QQ **Penryn House** 126 Alcester Rd CV37 9DP
☎(0789) 293718
*This semidetached house on Alcester Road, one mile from the town
centre, has small but attractive public areas, well-equipped
bedrooms, including one in a former garden chalet, and offers good
private car parking facilities.*
7rm(1⇌4♠2hc) Annexe 1♠ (3fb) CTV in all bedrooms ®
sB&B£17.50-£25 dB&B£28-£40 dB&B⇌♠£30-£45
WB&B£100-£120
⊯ 9P
Credit Cards ① ② ③

GH QQ **Penshurst** 34 Evesham Place CV37 6HT
☎(0789) 205259
*This guesthouse is personally run by the friendly proprietors who
provide sound accommodation. A good breakfast is served in the
pleasant, Victorian-decorated dining room.*
7rm(2♠5hc) (2fb) CTV in all bedrooms ® ✖ (ex guide dogs)
sB&B£16-£18 dB&B£30-£36 dB&B♠£36-£48 WB&B£90-£125
WBDi£140-£175 LDO 6pm
Lic ⊯ ⊬
Credit Cards ① ③ ⓔ

GH QQ **Ravenhurst** 2 Broad Walk CV37 6HS ☎(0789) 292515
Closed Xmas
*Situated in a quiet road, just five minutes' walk from the centre of
the town, this spacious Victorian house offers well equipped,
comfortable bedroom accommodation and an attractive dining
room.*
7rm(1⇌2♠4hc) (2fb) CTV in all bedrooms ® ✖ ✖ sB&B£20-
£35 dB&B£30-£34 dB&B⇌♠£34-£40 WB&B£110-£130
⊯
Credit Cards ① ② ③ ⑤

GH Q **Salamander** 40 Grove Rd CV37 6PB
☎(0789) 205728
*This Victorian terraced house stands on the Evesham Road and
provides simply appointed accommodation and good public areas.*
7rm(2♠5hc) (3fb) ® sB&B£12.50-£16 dB&B£25-£36
dB&B♠£30-£40 WB&B£87.50-£105 WBDi£129-£150
LDO 6.30pm
⊯ CTV 4P 2⊞

GH QQQ *Sequoia House Private Hotel* 51-53 Shipston Rd
CV37 7LN ☎(0789) 268852 FAX (0789) 414559
Closed 24-25 Dec
*This warm and spacious Victorian house is run by friendly
proprietors who pride themselves in offering high quality
breakfasts, which prove popular with guests. The bedrooms here
are well appointed.*
16rm(2⇌10♠4hc) Annexe 5♠ (4fb) CTV in all bedrooms ®
✖ LDO 4pm
Lic ⊯ CTV 26P nc5yrs
Credit Cards ① ② ③ ⑤

See advertisement on page 341

GH Q **Stretton House Hotel** 38 Grove Rd CV37 6PB
☎(0789) 268647
*Stretton House is situated to the north west of the town centre
close to the Information Centre. Mr and Mrs Machin provide good
value room and breakfast accommodation in simply appointed
bedrooms which are equipped with central heating and colour
television.*
6hc (2fb) CTV in all bedrooms ® ✱ sB&B£12-£17 dB&B£24-
£32 dB&B£34-£40 LDO 4pm
⊯ 3P 1⊞

GH QQQ **Twelfth Night** Evesham Place CV37 6HT
☎Stratford(0789) 414595
*Friendly proprietors John and Margaret Harvard offer a warm
welcome to guests and provide a good standard of accommodation.
All bedrooms (no-smoking) are individually decorated, and are
very clean and well maintained. The public rooms have been
tastefully refurbished to offer quality and comfort.*

7rm(6♠1hc) (1fb)⊬in all bedrooms CTV in all bedrooms ® ✖
sB&B£17-£30 dB&B♠£34-£48
⊯ 3P 4⊞ nc5yrs

GH QQQ *Victoria Spa Lodge* Bishopton Ln CV37 9QY
☎(0789) 267985 & 204728
*Once a popular 'spa' hotel (there are still 17 springs in the area)
this house is beautifully situated and affords a high standard of
accommodation with well- equipped bedrooms with a Victorian air.
Substantial breakfasts are served.*
7rm(1⇌3♠3hc) (3fb) CTV in all bedrooms ® ✖ LDO 4pm
⊯ 12P
Credit Cards ① ③

GH QQQ **Virginia Lodge** 12 Evesham Place CV37 6HT
☎(0789) 292157
*The friendly proprietor takes great pride in the garden and
hanging baskets surrounding this guesthouse. The well-appointed
bedrooms are equally pleasing, with lovely soft furnishings
matching the individual decor.*
7rm(4♠3hc) (1fb)⊬in 2 bedrooms CTV in all bedrooms ®
sB&B£13-£16 dB&B£26-£32 dB&B♠£30-£40 WB&Bfr£105
Lic ⊯ CTV 7P 2⊞

See advertisement on page 341

FH QQ Mrs R M Meadows **Monk's Barn** *(SP206516)*
Shipston Rd CV37 8NA ☎(0789) 293714
Closed 25-26 Dec
*The farm is on the A34, just two miles from Stratford towards
Shipton on Stour. A warm welcome is offered by Mr and Mrs
Meadows, who make every effort to meet guests' needs, making a
comfortable and friendly stay.*
4rm(2♠2hc) (1fb)⊬in all bedrooms CTV in 1 bedroom TV in
1 bedroom ® ✖ (ex guide dogs) sB&Bfr£13.50
sB&B♠fr£15.50 dB&Bfr£24 dB&B♠fr£28
⊯ CTV 5P 75 acres mixed

FH QQQ Mr & Mrs R Evans **Oxstalls** *(SP217566)*
Warwick Rd CV37 4NR ☎(0789) 205277
5hc Annexe 13rm(3⇌8🏠2hc) (5fb)⊁in all bedrooms CTV in
2 bedrooms TV in 1 bedroom ® ✖ (ex guide dogs) ✱
sB&B£14-£22 dB&Bfr£28 dB&B⇌🏠fr£44
🍴 CTV P ▶18 ✔ 70 acres stud farm

STRATHAVEN Strathclyde *Lanarkshire* Map **11** NS74

GH QQ **Springvale Hotel** 18 Letham Rd ML10 6AD
☎(0357) 21131
Closed 26-27 Dec & 1-3 Jan
*This converted and extended house in a residential area offers
modern, well equipped bedrooms, traditional lounge and bright,
cheery dining room overlooking the garden and playing fields.
Personal and friendly service is provided by the owners, and home
cooking is a feature of the popular high teas. Some long-stay
residents are accommodated.*
14rm(1⇌10🏠3hc) (1fb) CTV in all bedrooms ® ✱
sB&B⇌🏠£22-£24 dB&B⇌🏠£32-£34 LDO 6.45pm
Lic 🍴 CTV 8P

STRATHYRE Central *Perthshire* Map **11** NN51

GH QQQ **Auchtubhmor House** Balquidder FK19 8NZ
☎(08774) 632
*This delightful country house is an ideal base for the holidaymaker
seeking relaxation. Comfortably appointed, each of the bedrooms
has magnificent views across countryside. Prime Scottish produce
is used in the imaginative dinner menu.*
5rm(3⇌2hc) (1fb) ® sB&B£20-£25 sB&B⇌£22-£27
dB&B£30-£32 dB&B⇌£32-£34 WB&B£90-£100 WBDi£146-
£167 LDO 6pm
🍴 CTV 6P
Credit Cards 1 2 3 £

STRETTON Leicestershire Map **08** SK91

INN QQ **The Shires Hotel** LE15 7QT
☎Castle Bytham(078081) 332
*Situated on the A1 Great North Road north of Stratford, this
stone-built Georgian inn has pleasant public areas and
comfortable, simple bedrooms.*
5rm(4hc) (3fb) CTV in all bedrooms ® LDO 10.30pm
🍴 100P
Credit Cards 1 3

STROUD Gloucestershire Map **03** SO80

GH QQ **Downfield Hotel** 134 Cainscross Rd GL5 4HN
☎(0453) 764496
Closed 2 wks from 25 Dec
*Situated west of the town centre on the A419, this extended
Victorian house offers comfortable bed and breakfast
accommodation, with spacious open-plan public areas.*
21rm(5⇌8🏠8hc) (4fb) CTV in 15 bedrooms ® ✱ sB&Bfr£20
sB&B⇌🏠fr£32 dB&B£34-£38 dB&B⇌🏠fr£43 LDO 8pm
Lic 🍴 CTV 25P
Credit Cards 1 3 £

STUDLAND Dorset Map **04** SZ08

GH QQ **Studholme Hotel** Ferry Rd BH19 3AQ ☎(092944) 271
mid Mar-mid Oct
*A pleasant detached hotel situated close to Studland Beach in its
own gardens, offering good home cooking and an informal
atmosphere.*
6rm(4⇌🏠2hc) (2fb) CTV in all bedrooms ® ✖ ✱ sB&Bfr£23
dB&Bfr£46 dB&B⇌🏠fr£50 WBDifr£200 LDO 6pm
Lic CTV 6P nc3yrs

STURMINSTER NEWTON Dorset Map **03** ST71

FH QQ Mrs S Wingate-Saul **Holebrook** *(ST743117)*
Lydlinch DT10 2JB ☎Hazelbury Bryan(0258) 817348
Closed Xmas Day & New Years Day rs Nov-Mar
*A farm 3 miles west of the A357 Stalbridge road with attractive
converted stable bedroom suites. The lounge is in the main house,
and breakfast is served in the kitchen. Leisure facilities include fly
fishing, clay-pigeon shooting and a small outdoor swimming pool.*
2rm(1hc) Annexe 4rm(3🏠) CTV in 4 bedrooms ®
✖ (ex guide dogs) ✱ sB&B£17-£18 dB&Bf🏠£34-£36 LDO 4pm
🍴 CTV 12P ⌯clay pigeon shooting games room 126 acres
mixed £

STURTON BY STOW Lincolnshire Map **08** SK88

FH QQQ Mrs Brenda Williams **Gallows Dale** *(SK874809)*
Stow Park Rd LN1 2AH ☎Gainsborough(0427) 788387
Closed Xmas
*A detached 18th-century red-brick farmhouse situated a mile from
the village on the A1500 towards Gainsborough. Recently
extended and modernised in keeping with its period, the house now
provides comfortable, attractive bedrooms. There is a choice of
lounges with one permitting smoking, otherwise smoking is not
allowed.*
3rm(2hc) (1fb)⊁in all bedrooms ® ✖ ✱ sB&B£13-£15
dB&B£26-£30
🍴 CTV 3P nc6yrs 33 acres cattle £

SELECTED

FH QQQQ Mrs S Bradshaw **The Village** *(SK889807)*
LN1 2AE ☎Gainsborough(0427) 788309
Apr-Oct
*A long-established charming farmhouse set in the centre of the
village amongst the well tended gardens and outbuildings.
Mrs Bradshaw is a warm and caring host which is reflected in* ▶

DOWNFIELD HOTEL
134 Cainscross Road, Stroud, Glos GL5 4HN
Telephone: Stroud (0453) 764496

An ideal hotel for stopping over on your journey from
the north to Devon or Cornwall or as a base for
touring the Cotswolds. Situated 5 miles from the M5
motorway — junction 13. Majority of the rooms have
private bathroom with most having TV and direct dial
telephone and all with tea/coffee facilities. Bed &
breakfast available with evening meal optional.
Ample parking. Families and pets welcome. Under
the personal supervision of the proprietors, Mr & Mrs
D. J. R. Spandler. Access/Visa accepted.

B & B from £20.00 per person

Virginia Lodge

PRIVATE CAR PARK

Virginia Lodge is a lovely spacious Victorian House in the centre of Stratford-upon-Avon in easy walking distance of the Theatre.

All the bedrooms are luxuriously furnished and have colour T.V. and Tea/Coffee making facilities.

Most rooms have their own bathrooms and all are individually styled.

- Four Poster Room
- Blue Shalimar Room
- Country Manor Room
- Laura Ashley Room
- Cottage Style Room
- Satellite Television in all Rooms
- Hair Dryer in all Rooms

FIRST CLASS ACCOMODATION

Virginia Lodge, 12 Evesham Place, Stratford-upon-Avon, Warwickshire CV37 6HT. Telephone: (0789) 292157

We have an elegant Lounge and Dining Room where you can enjoy an English Breakfast served with Real Coffee.

SEQUOIA HOUSE

HOTEL, RESTAURANT & CONFERENCE CENTRE

51 Shipston Road Stratford-upon-Avon CV37 7LN
Telephone (0789) 268852   Fax (0789) 414559

Large private car park and beautifully mature gardens in which stands the "Sequoia" tree that gives the house its name – a delightful garden walk leads to the theatre. Riverside gardens, Shakespeare Properties, Shops and Leisure complex.

- Bed and Breakfast
- Licensed Bar
- Private Car Park
- Cottage Annexe
- Air Conditioned Restaurant

Superbly situated across the River Avon opposite the Theatre – recently restored and modernized to a high standard – offers beautifully appointed private hotel accommodation with friendly personal attention of resident proprietors. Residential lounge with licensed bar and open Victorian fireplace. All 21 bedrooms have colour television; tea/coffee facilities, H&C, shaver point, central heating and direct dial telephone. Most bedrooms have private bathroom/showers/wc.

the care and attention placed in providing attractively furnished and comfortable rooms. There is also a lovely elegant lounge and dining room.
3rm(1⇨3♠2hc) ⊁in all bedrooms ℝ ✖ sB&B£14-£16 dB&B£28-£32 dB&B⇨♠£32-£36 WB&B£86-£100 LDO day before
▦ CTV 6P nc9yrs ♫(hard)➤ 400 acres arable beef sheep
£

SURBITON Greater London London plan **4** B1 (pages 221-227)

GHℚ **Warwick** 321 Ewell Rd KT6 7BX ☎081-399 5837 & 2405
This small guesthouse, convenient for the A3, is run by a cheerful proprietress. Bedrooms are simply furnished and best suited for single guests. Public areas are limited.
9rm(1⇨8hc)(1fb) CTV in all bedrooms ℝ ✱ sB&B£28-£30 sB&B⇨£34-£36 dB&B£38-£40 dB&B⇨£44-£46 WB&B£160-£170 WBDi£195-£205 LDO 2pm
▦ CTV 8P
Credit Cards ①③£

SUTTON Greater London London plan **4** C1 (pages 221-227)

GHℚℚℚ **Ashling Tara Hotel** 50 Rosehill SM1 3EU
☎081-641 6142 FAX 081-644 7872
Closed Xmas Day
Two detached houses have been converted to make up this hotel on a residential road to the north of Sutton. Various improvements are taking place, which will leave the bar and dining room in one building with some bedrooms, and the remaining bedrooms will be a few doors away. All bedrooms are well maintained and equipped.
10rm(2⇨5♠3hc) Annexe 5rm(3♠2hc) (2fb) CTV in 14 bedrooms ℝ ✖ sB&B£27.50-£56 sB&B⇨♠£56 dB&Bfr£50 dB&B⇨♠fr£60 WB&Bfr£175 WBDifr£250 LDO 9pm
Lic ▦ CTV 10P nc4yrs
Credit Cards ①③

GHℚ **Dene Hotel** 39 Cheam Rd SM1 2AT ☎081-642 3170
Conveniently situated near the centre of Sutton with its own car park, the Dene is a personally run bed and breakfast hotel. The bedrooms vary in size, are clean and well equipped, though some have narrow beds.
28rm(8⇨4♠16hc) (3fb) CTV in all bedrooms ℝ
✖ (ex guide dogs) sB&B£21.15-£32.90 sB&B⇨♠£39.95-£49.35 dB&B£42.30-£51.70 dB&B⇨♠£58.75-£61.10
▦ 18P£

GHℚℚ **Eaton Court Hotel** 49 Eaton Rd SM2 5ED
☎081-643 6766
Closed 1 wk Xmas
A converted Victorian house located in a quiet residential area which offers functional but well equipped accommodation. There is a spacious lounge where guests may relax.
14rm(2♠12hc) Annexe 7rm(1⇨6♠) (3fb) CTV in all bedrooms ℝ ✖ sB&B£28-£32 sB&B⇨♠£38-£42 dB&B£36-£40 dB&B⇨♠£48-£52
Lic ▦ CTV 10P
Credit Cards ①②③£

GHℚℚ **Thatched House Hotel** 135 Cheam Rd SM1 2BN
☎081-642 3131 FAX 081-770 0684
An extended and modernised thatched house offering comfortable accommodation. Several of the bedrooms, on the ground and first floor, overlook the garden and pond ; some are more recently redecorated than others and all are well equipped. Mr and Mrs Wells have been here many years and are always making improvements.
27rm(19⇨♠8hc) CTV in all bedrooms ℝ sB&Bfr£37.50 sB&B⇨♠£52.50-£55 dB&B£49.50 dB&B⇨♠£57.50-£65 LDO 8.45pm

---

Lic ▦ CTV 24P
Credit Cards ①③£

SUTTON West Sussex Map **04** SU91

> **SELECTED**
>
> **INN**ℚℚℚℚ **The White Horse** RH20 1PS ☎(07987) 221 FAX (07987) 291
> *This inn dates back to 1746 and is situated in the picturesque village at the edge of the downs. Bedrooms are tastefully furnished to a high standard with all modern amenities and a few thoughtful extras. The bar is popular with locals, offering a selection of real ales and freshly cooked meals and snacks ; cosy in the winter with two log fires, in summer drinks can be taken outside to the patio and garden.*
> 4⇨ CTV in all bedrooms ℝ ✖ sB&B⇨£38 dB&B⇨£48 WB&B£120-£190 WBDi£204-£294 ✱ Lunch £9.40-£18alc High tea £2-£4alc Dinner £9.40-£18alc LDO 9.30pm
> ▦ 10P
> Credit Cards ①③

SUTTON COLDFIELD West Midlands Map **07** SP19

GHℚ **Standbridge Hotel** 138 Birmingham Rd B72 1LY
☎021-354 3007
Conveniently situated for access to the Midlands' motorway network, Birmingham and Sutton Coldfield, this hotel has some compact, but well-kept rooms. There is a comfortable lounge and an attractive rear garden.
8hc Annexe 1hc CTV in all bedrooms ℝ ✱ sB&Bfr£18.50 sB&Bfr£23 dB&Bfr£30 LDO 6pm
Lic ▦ CTV 11P nc5yrs jacuzzi
Credit Cards ①③£
See advertisement under BIRMINGHAM

SWAFFHAM Norfolk Map **05** TF80

GHℚℚℚ **Corfield House** PE32 2EA ☎(0760) 23636
mid Mar-mid Dec
A delightful red-brick farmhouse in the village of Sporle, close to Swaffham and well situated for touring north west Norfolk. Bedrooms are individually furnished with good pine furniture and co-ordinated Laura Ashley fabrics and décor, and all have modern en suite facilities. There is a comfortable lounge which is no smoking, and a set four-course dinner is served in the cosy dining room.
5rm(2⇨3♠) ⊁in all bedrooms CTV in all bedrooms ℝ sB&B⇨♠fr£18.50 dB&B⇨♠£33-£37 WB&B£115-£129.50 WBDi£170-£185 LDO 6pm
Lic ▦ 5P
Credit Cards ①③

SWANAGE Dorset Map **04** SZ07

GHℚℚℚ **Bella Vista Hotel** 14 Burlington Rd BH19 1LS
☎(0929) 422873
Mar-Oct
A small house in an excellent location on the cliff top, by a path leading to the beach, and within easy reach of the town centre. Neat, clean and well decorated bedrooms are complemented by a nicely furnished lounge and a breakfast room.
6rm(5♠1hc) (4fb) ℝ ✖ ✱ dB&B£33-£35 dB&B♠£36-£39 WB&B£95-£125 (wkly only Jul & Aug)
Lic ▦ CTV 6P nc4yrs

GHℚℚ **Burlington House Hotel** 7 Highcliffe Rd BH19 1LW
☎(0929) 422422
11 Apr-Oct

A small, comfortably appointed hotel with a cliff-top garden overlooking the sea and town. Public rooms include a cosy bar with a piano, and a comfortable lounge. The bedrooms are in the process of being redecorated and modernised.
9rm(7⇨↱2hc) (5fb) CTV in 8 bedrooms TV in 1 bedroom ® ✗ sB&B£13.50-£16.20 dB&B£30-£36 dB&B⇨↱£32.50-£39.50 WB&B£100-£120 WBDi£140-£160 (wkly only mid Jun-mid Sep) LDO 5pm
Lic 🍽 CTV 9P musical evenings £

GH QQQ Chines Hotel 9 Burlington Rd BH19 1LR
☎(0929) 422457
24 Apr-Sep rs Mar-Oct
Neat 2-storeyed house in quiet road near beach and town.
13rm(6↱7hc) (3fb) ⊁in all bedrooms CTV in all bedrooms ® ✗ (wkly only Jul-Aug) LDO 4pm
Lic 🍽 CTV 9P ⌂ £

GH QQ *Eversden Private Hotel* Victoria Rd BH19 1LY
☎(0929) 423276
Mar-Nov
A cheerful family house with a bright dining room and a bar as well as a television lounge. The bedrooms are generally of a good size, if modestly furnished.
12rm(2⇨3↱7hc) (3fb) ⊁in 2 bedrooms CTV in 1 bedroom TV in 1 bedroom ® ✗ LDO 6pm
Lic 🍽 CTV 12P

GH QQ Firswood Hotel 29 Kings Rd BH19 1HF
☎(0929) 422306
Closed Xmas
A small family-run guesthouse close to the town centre and steam railway. Bedrooms are well maintained and provide modern facilities. The resident proprietors provide a warm welcome.
6rm(1⇨1↱4hc) (3fb) CTV in 5 bedrooms ® ✗ ✱ sB&B£13.50-£15 dB&B£27-£30 dB&B⇨↱fr£30 LDO 4.30pm
🍽 CTV 7P nc5yrs

GH QQ *Gillan Hotel* 5 Northbrook Rd BH19 1PN
☎(0929) 424548
A small hotel with clean, simply furnished bedrooms, complemented by a smartly decorated restaurant and bar. The restaurant is open to non-residents for its Sunday carvery and fresh fish dishes.
10⇨↱ (4fb) CTV in all bedrooms ® ✗ LDO 5.30pm
Lic 14P nc4yrs ⛆(heated)
Credit Cards 1 2 3

GH QQ Glenlee Hotel 6 Cauldon Av BH19 1PQ
☎(0929) 425794
Closed Nov-Feb
This small and friendly private hotel has modern, well-equipped bedrooms. It is conveniently situated, close to the seafront and shops, overlooking tennis courts.
8⇨↱ (2fb) CTV in all bedrooms ® ✗ (ex guide dogs) sB&B⇨↱fr£21 dB&B⇨↱fr£42 WB&Bfr£141 WBDifr£194 LDO 5.30pm
Lic 🍽 CTV 7P 2🚗 nc4yrs
Credit Cards 1 3

GH QQQ *Havenhurst Hotel* 3 Cranbourne Rd BH19 1EA
☎(0929) 424224
A popular holiday hotel run by resident proprietors Pat Cherrett and Nicola Robson. Since taking over here, they have redecorated and upgraded almost throughout to a well co-ordinated modern standard. The dining room provides fresh food wherever possible, including home-made bread rolls and fresh fish, meat and vegetables. There is a smart bar lounge sometimes used by outside parties and a warm friendly atmosphere prevails.
17rm(6⇨11↱) (4fb) ® ✗ (ex guide dogs) (wkly only Jun-Aug) LDO 7pm
Lic 🍽 CTV 17P

See advertisement on page 345

GH ⓠⓠ **Hotel Monsal** 32/34 Victoria Av BH19 1AP
☎(0929) 422805
This family-run hotel stands in a prime position, 350 yards from the seafront and town centre. Bedrooms are simply furnished and decorated, but each is well equipped with modern facilities. There is an adjacent annexe with three bedrooms, two of which have smart new en suite bathrooms. Public areas are cosy and the atmosphere is friendly and informal. An evening meal is offered, home cooked by a member of the family.
8rm(4⇋3♠4hc) (2fb) CTV in all bedrooms ® ✱ sB&B£13.60-£18.80 sB&B⇋♠£18.20-£23.50 dB&B£27.20-£37.60 dB&B⇋♠£31.81-£43.48 WB&B£89.01-£124.55 WBDi£123.63-£164.50 LDO 6.30pm
Lic ⁗ CTV 12P solarium gymnasium
Credit Cards ①③

GH ⓠⓠⓠ **Oxford Hotel** 3 & 5 Park Rd BH19 2AA
☎(0929) 422247
Located on the rise of hill leading from town centre and seafront.
14rm(7⇋5♠7hc) (4fb) CTV in 12 bedrooms TV in 2 bedrooms ® ✘ sB&B£18-£19 sB&B⇋♠£40-£45 dB&B£36-£40 dB&B⇋♠£44-£48 WB&B£180-£200 WBDi£236-£256 LDO 4.30pm
Lic ⁗ CTV nc3yrs

GH ⓠⓠⓠ **St Michael Hotel** 31 Kings Rd BH9 1HF
☎(0929) 422064
Feb-Nov
Well placed for both the town centre and the steam railway, this pleasant family house has a comfortable lounge and separate dining room. The bedrooms are freshly decorated and provide modern facilities.
6rm(3♠3hc) (4fb) CTV in all bedrooms ® dB&B£28.50-£30.50 dB&B♠£30.50-£34.50 WB&B£90-£115 WBDi£139-£164 LDO 2pm
Lic ⁗ 5P nc5yrs

GH ⓠⓠⓠ **Sandringham Hotel** 20 Durlston Rd BH19 2HX
☎(0929) 423076
Mar-Nov rs Dec-Mar
Comfortable, well-maintained accommodation is offered at this small, private hotel. Situated in a quiet residential area close to the sea, Sandringham Hotel is personally supervised by owners Mr & Mrs Ward, and has a warm, friendly atmosphere.
11rm(9♠2hc) (5fb) ® ✘ (ex guide dogs) ✱ sB&B£20-£24 dB&B♠£40-£48 WB&B£120-£144 WBDi£174-£198 LDO 6.30pm
Lic ⁗ CTV 8P

GH ⓠⓠⓠ **Seychelles Private Hotel** 7 Burlington Rd BH19 1LR ☎(0929) 422794
May-Oct
Personally supervised by the proprietors, Mr and Mrs Fisher, this small hotel which has its own private beach has been tastefully refurbished to provide comfortable accommodation.
9rm(2⇋5♠6♠1hc) (4fb) CTV in all bedrooms ® ✘ sB&B£16.50-£22 sB&B⇋♠£19.50-£25 dB&B£33-£44 dB&B⇋♠£36-£47 WB&B£90-£120 WBDi£141-£170
Lic ⁗ 10P

SWANSEA West Glamorgan Map 03 SS69
See also Bishopston, Langland Bay and Mumbles
GH ⓠ **Alexander Hotel** 3 Sketty Road, Uplands, Sketty SA2 0EU ☎(0792) 470045 & 476012
Closed Xmas
Close to the busy Uplands Shopping Centre, this friendly hotel provides a comfortable lounge and bar, and modern, well-equipped bedrooms. There is also a basement games room.
7rm(6⇋3♠1hc) (3fb) CTV in all bedrooms ® ✘ ✱ sB&B£20-£22 sB&B⇋♠£30-£32 dB&B⇋♠£42-£45 WB&B£126-£165 Lic ⁗ ✗ nc2yrs games room
Credit Cards ①②③⑤ ⓔ

GH ⓠⓠⓠ **Cefn Bryn** 6 Uplands Crescent SA2 0PB
☎(0792) 466687
Closed Xmas
This very well maintained family run hotel is situated close to the Uplands shopping centre and is also convenient for the city centre. There is a very comfortable resident's lounge and an attractive dining room. Bedrooms are spacious, spotlessly clean and well furnished and equipped, most with private bathrooms.
6♠ (2fb) CTV in all bedrooms ® ✘ ✱ sB&B♠£20 dB&B♠£40 WB&B£99
CTV ✗

GH ⓠⓠ **Channel View** 17 Bryn Rd, Brynmill SA2 0AR
☎(0792) 466834
This bright family-run guesthouse overlooks the St Helens rugby and cricket grounds, and the rear bedrooms provide grandstand views. Furnishings are modest but the accommodation is spotlessly clean, and the Parr family offer a warm welcome.
6hc (1fb)⤵in all bedrooms CTV in all bedrooms ® ✱ sB&B£12-£15 dB&B£24-£30 WB&B£76-£84 LDO 10am
⁗ CTV ⓕ

GH ⓠⓠ **Crescent** 132 Eaton Crescent, Uplands SA1 4QR
☎(0792) 466814
Closed Xmas & New Year
Convenient for the Uplands shopping centre and not too far from the town and the Gower, this friendly, family-run hotel is in a quiet residential area and provides bright, comfortable accommodation.
7rm(1♠6hc) (1fb) TV in all bedrooms ® ✱ sB&B£15 sB&B♠£20 dB&B£30 dB&B♠£30 WB&B£100-£125 WBDi£140-£175
⁗ CTV 4P

GH ⓠⓠ **The Guest House** 2/4 Bryn Rd SA2 0AR
☎(0792) 466947
This cosy guesthouse is opposite the St Helens cricket and rugby ground. The bedrooms are comfortable and pretty, with an additional seven en suite rooms added recently by the friendly owners. There is a small bar and a choice of two comfortable lounges for visitors.
14rm(6♠8hc) (2fb)⤵in 7 bedrooms ✘ (ex guide dogs) ✱ sB&B£13-£20 dB&B£26-£34 dB&B♠£34-£40 WB&B£88-£110 LDO 1pm
Lic ⁗ CTV ✗ nc9yrs
Credit Cards ①②③

GH ⓠⓠⓠⓠ **Tredilion House Hotel** 26 Uplands Crescent, Uplands SA2 0PB ☎(0792) 470766
rs Xmas
This Victorian town house, situated near the Uplands shopping centre, has been very carefully modernised to provide comfortable and well equipped bedrooms. There is a relaxing lounge and a small bar for residents.
7⇋3♠ (1fb) CTV in all bedrooms ® ✘ (ex guide dogs) ✱ sB&B⇋3♠£34-£39 dB&B⇋3♠£50-£54 WB&B£157.50-£246 WBDi£237-£325 LDO noon
Lic ⁗ 8P 1🐾
Credit Cards ①③ ⓔ

GH ⓠ **Tregare Hotel** 9 Sketty Rd, Uplands SA2 0EU
☎(0792) 470608 & 456612
Conveniently situated for the shops, this family-run guesthouse has comfortable, well-equipped bedrooms.
10rm(3⇋6♠1hc) (3fb) CTV in all bedrooms ® LDO 4pm
Lic ⁗ CTV 5P snooker
Credit Cards ①③

SWINDERBY Lincolnshire Map **08** SK86

GH Q Q Q **Halfway Farm Motel & Guest House** A46
LN6 9HN (8m N of Newark on A46, 8m SW Lincoln)
☎(052286) 749 due to change to 8749
*Aptly named, as it lies on the A46 midway between Lincoln and
Newark. A very well kept 18th-century farmhouse with motel-style
accommodation in the nicely converted brick and pantile
outbuildings. These offer particularly good comfort and good en
suite facilities.*
7rm(3♠4hc) Annexe 10♠ (4fb) CTV in all bedrooms ®
✖ (ex guide dogs) sB&Bf18 sB&Bf♠£24-£28 dB&B£34-£36
dB&Bf♠£38-£42
ᵐ CTV 20P nc2yrs
Credit Cards ① ② ③
See advertisement under LINCOLN

GH Q *The Lodge* Sheep Walk, Newark Rd LN6 9PU
☎(052286) 651
*Well positioned on the A46 adjacent to RAF Swinderby, The
Lodge is small and very friendly with a warm atmosphere, offering
simple, clean accommodation, a comfortable television lounge and
good car park. Rooms are double- glazed.*
6rm(5hc) (2fb) ®
Lic CTV 10P

SWINDON Wiltshire Map **04** SU18

GH Q Q **Grove Lodge** 108 Swindon Rd SN3 4PT
☎(0793) 825343
*North of Swindon, this prominently positioned terraced guesthouse
offers well- equipped, simple bedrooms, each with an easy chair,
and caters mainly for the commercial sector.*
10➪♠ (1fb) CTV in all bedrooms ® ✱ sB&B➪♠£25-£30
dB&B➪♠£35-£42 WB&Bfr£140 WBDifr£182 LDO 6pm
ᵐ 12P ⓔ

SYMONDS YAT (EAST) Hereford & Worcester Map **03**
SO51

GH Q Q Q **Garth Cottage Hotel** HR9 6JL ☎(0600) 890364
*This small hotel enjoys an enviable location at the edge of the River
Wye. The accommodation is very well maintained, and all rooms
have superb views. Public areas include a sun lounge, small cosy
bar and pine fitted dining room.*
4♠ ® ✖ (ex guide dogs) dB&Bf♠£44 WB&B£140
WBDi£234.50 LDO 3pm
Lic ᵐ CTV 9P nc12yrs ✒
Credit Cards ① ③

INN Q Q *Saracens Head* HR9 6JL ☎(0600) 890435
*This half-timbered inn stands on the bank of the river Wye and
offers modern, well equipped accommodation. A small first floor
lounge area is available for guests, in addition to the bar areas;
there is also a separate restaurant.*
10rm(7♠3hc) (1fb) ® ✖ LDO 9.30pm
ᵐ CTV 60P ✒
Credit Cards ① ② ③ ⑤

SYMONDS YAT (WEST) (NEAR ROSS-ON-WYE)
Hereford & Worcester Map **03** SO51

GH Q Q **Woodlea Hotel** HR9 6BL
☎Symonds Yat(0600) 890206
Closed Jan-13 Feb
*With lovely views across the valley to wooded hills, this pleasant
and cosy house is quietly situated at the end of a narrow lane above
the Wye rapids. Many of the bedrooms have en suite facilities and
the amenities include a pleasant bar.*
9rm(6➪♠3hc) (2fb) ® sB&Bfr£21.50 dB&Bfr£43
dB&B➪♠fr£52 WBDi£195-£225 LDO 6.30pm
Lic ᵐ CTV 9P
Credit Cards ① ② ③ ⓔ

TADCASTER North Yorkshire Map **08** SE44

GH Q Q **Shann House** 47 Kirkgate LS24 9AQ ☎(0937) 833931
*This 3-storeyed Georgian house, situated in the town centre, offers
consistently high standards. The well-equipped, spacious
accommodation is complemented by a warm dining room and an
elegant lounge, with marble fireplace and Chesterfield sofa.*
8➪♠ (1fb) CTV in all bedrooms ® ✱ sB&B➪♠£20.50-£25
dB&B➪♠£31-£36 WB&B£140.50
Lic ᵐ 8P
Credit Cards ① ③ ⓔ

TALGARTH Powys Map **03** SO13

FH Q Q Mrs B Prosser **Upper Genffordd** *(SO171304)*
LD3 0EN ☎(0874) 711360
*Just off the A479 and 3 miles south of Talgarth, these 16th-century
farm buildings have been converted to provide farmhouse
accommodation. The proprietors provide pretty bedrooms and a
lounge with character. A cheerful welcome awaits guests.*
2➪♠ (1fb) CTV in all bedrooms ® ✱ dB&B➪♠£25-£28
WB&B£87.50-£98 LDO 5pm
ᵐ CTV 4P 200 acres dairy mixed sheep ⓔ

TAL-Y-LLYN Gwynedd Map **06** SH60

GH Q Q Q **Dolffanog Fawr** LL36 9AJ ☎Corris(0654) 761247
FAX (0654) 761480
*This delightful old house, fronted by a beautiful, well tended
garden, is surrounded by magnificent mountain scenery and is close
to the edge of the lake. The accommodation is attractive and
comfortable and there is a choice of lounges for smokers and non-
smokers. Dolffanog Fawr is personally run in a very friendly
manner by Joy Ashby.*
3hc ✖in all bedrooms CTV in all bedrooms ® ✖ ✱ dB&B£30-
£32 WB&B£98-£105 WBDi£182-£189 LDO 5pm
ᵐ CTV 8P nc

TAUNTON Somerset Map **03** ST22

GH Q Q Q **Brookfield** 16 Wellington Rd TA1 4EQ
☎(0823) 272786
*A friendly, family-run hotel standing beside the A38 near the town
centre provides accommodation in bedrooms with some modern
facilities.*
8hc (2fb) ® ✱ sB&B£13-£18 dB&B£25-£30 LDO 2.30pm
Lic ᵐ CTV 8P ⓔ

SELECTED

GH Q Q Q Q **Meryan House Hotel** Bishop's Hull
TA1 5EG ☎(0823) 337445
*Quietly tucked away in Bishops Hull, yet only a mile from the
centre of Taunton, this hotel is personally run by Nick and
Cher Clark and family. It is a charming house, over 300 years
old, with 12 individually furnished and decorated bedrooms,
all very well equipped. Public areas are comfortable with
period furnishings and 3 inglenook fireplaces – the kitchen has
a well in it. Dinner is available with a choice of 4 dishes at
each course; there is a free newspaper at breakfast. Book
early to avoid disappointment.*
12➪♠ (3fb)✖in 4 bedrooms CTV in all bedrooms ®
LDO 6.30pm
Lic ᵐ CTV 17P solarium tennis net croquet
Credit Cards ① ③

TAVISTOCK Devon Map **02** SX47

GH Q Q Q **Old Coach House Hotel** Ottery PL19 8NS (2mW)
☎(0822) 617515
*This former coach house to the adjacent farm has been recently
restored and converted into a small hotel of character, situated in
the hamlet of Ottery. The three bedrooms on the ground floor are
en suite and comfortably furnished. Both the cosy lounge and the*

intimate restaurant have access to the patio and a set evening dinner is available. Resident proprietors extend a warm welcome to guests.

3⇨ ® ✗ (ex guide dogs) sB&B⇨£27 dB&B⇨£54
WB&B£170 WBDi£210 LDO 2pm
Lic ⑭ CTV 8P nc10yrs
Credit Cards [1] [3]

TEBAY Cumbria Map **12** NY60

GH ◨◨◨ **Carmel House** Mount Pleasant CA10 3TH
☎Orton(05874) 651
Closed 23 Dec-3 Jan
A delightful little guesthouse situated in the village centre next to the Post Office. The bedrooms are very comfortable, with good facilities, and service is very friendly.
5♠ (1fb) CTV in all bedrooms ® ✗ (ex guide dogs) ✳
sB&B♠£15.50-£18 dB&B♠£31-£36
⑭ CTV 6P
Credit Cards [1] [3]

TEIGNMOUTH Devon Map **03** SX97

GH ◨◨◨ **Fonthill** Torquay Rd, Shaldon TQ14 0AX
☎Shaldon(0626) 872344
Closed Jan & Feb
3rm(1⇨♠2hc) ✍in all bedrooms ® sB&B£21-£25
dB&B£33-£35 dB&B⇨♠£37-£39
⑭ CTV 6P ♪(hard)

GH ◨◨ **Glen Devon Hotel** 3 Carlton Place TQ14 8AB
☎(0626) 772895
Compact, brightly decorated bedrooms and comfortable public areas are offered at this simply appointed, family-run hotel, which is in a road just off the seafront, close to the town centre. ▶

7rm(2⇌2↑3hc) (4fb) ® ✱ ✱ dB&B£24-£28 dB&B⇌↑£28-£32 LDO 5pm
Lic ⁜ CTV 6P £

GH Q Q **Hill Rise Hotel** Winterbourne Rd TQ14 8JT
☎(0626) 773108
*Bright, well-equipped bedrooms and good, comfortable public
areas are provided by a large detached Edwardian house located
in a residential area.*
8rm(2↑6hc) (3fb)⊁in all bedrooms CTV in 2 bedrooms ®
✱ (ex guide dogs)
Lic ⁜ CTV 4P 1⇞ ⚲

GH Q Q Q **Lyme Bay House Hotel** Den Promenade TQ14 8SZ
☎(0626) 772953
Apr-Oct
*A large Victorian house, standing on the Promenade close to the
town centre, provides spaciously comfortable public rooms and
well-equipped, individually styled bedrooms.*
9rm(3↑6hc) (1fb) ®
Lic lift ⁜ CTV ⊁ £

⊠✈ **GH** Q Q **Rathlin House Hotel** Upper Hermosa Rd
TQ14 9JW ☎(0626) 774473
Closed Xmas
10rm(4↑6hc) (4fb) CTV in 2 bedrooms ® sB&B£13-£16
sB&B↑£15.50-£18.50 dB&B£26-£32 dB&B↑£31-£37
WB&B£85-£105 WBDi£110-£130 LDO 6.15pm
Lic CTV 12P £

SELECTED

GH Q Q Q Q **Thomas Luny House** Teign St TQ14 8EG
☎(0626) 772976
Closed mid Dec-mid Jan
*Built in the 1800s by marine artist Thomas Luny, this quietly
situated house retains the elegance of its past and is a worthy
winner of the Best Newcomer award for 1991 for the western
region. The four spacious bedrooms are equipped with every
facility and guests may browse through the many books in the
comfortable lounge. John and Alison Allan join guests for
drinks before serving excellent meals, which are taken around
the table in the attractive dining room.*
4rm(3⇌1↑) CTV in all bedrooms ✱ (ex guide dogs) ✱
sB&B⇌↑£27.50 dB&B⇌↑£55 WB&B£154 WBDi£231
LDO 8pm
Lic ⁜ 8P nc12yrs

TELFORD Shropshire Map **07** SJ60

See also Rowton

GH Q Q Q **Broseley** The Square TF12 5EW ☎(0952) 882043
*A comfortable guesthouse in the centre of the town with adjacent
public car park. The rooms are well equipped and have all the
facilities required by the business or private visitor.*
6⇌↑ CTV in all bedrooms ® sB&B⇌↑£27.50-£32
dB&B⇌↑£42-£46 LDO by arrangement
Lic ⁜
Credit Cards 1 3 £

GH Q Q Q **Church Farm** Wrockwardine, Wellington TF6 5DG
☎(0952) 244917
*Adjacent to the church in the heart of the village, this 200-year-old
listed farmhouse has charming gardens and buildings with some
animals roaming freely. The hospitable hosts are keen to make
their guests welcome.*
5rm(2⇌3hc) Annexe 1↑ (1fb) CTV in all bedrooms ® ✱
sB&Bfr£25 sB&B⇌↑fr£30 dB&Bfr£38 dB&B⇌↑fr£46
LDO 9am
⁜ CTV 10P ⚲ £

GH Q Q Q **West Ridge** TF11 9LB ☎(0952) 581223
*A much extended, privately owned and personally run guesthouse
set in large gardens, situated on the A4169 close to its junction
with the B4379. The accommodation is very well equipped, and all
rooms have private bathrooms. Its location close to the A54 and
the nearby Halesfield industrial estate in Telford make it popular
with business people ; however it is equally suitable for tourists
wishing to visit the historic town of Ironbridge.*
5⇌↑ CTV in all bedrooms ® ✱ (ex guide dogs) ✱
sB&B⇌↑£46-£62 dB&B⇌↑£51-£67 LDO 9pm
Lic ⁜ CTV 10P nc10yrs
Credit Cards 1 2 3

INN Q Q Q **Cock Hotel** 148 Holyhead Rd, Wellington TF1 2ED
☎(0952) 244954
*This roadside inn stands on the outskirts of Wellington. The
bedrooms are well equipped, though without en suite facilities, and
breakfast is taken in an oak panelled room. All meals are prepared
by the host, Mr Miles.*
7hc (1fb) CTV in all bedrooms ® ✱ LDO 9pm
⁜ 30P 4⇞

INN Q Q Q **Swan Hotel** Watling St, Wellington TF1 2NH
☎(0952) 223781
*This red brick hotel has comfortable modern bars and a restaurant
serving a good range of food. The bedrooms are pleasant and
bright. The Swan stands alongside historic Watling Street (now
the A5) at Wellington.*
12rm(7↑5hc) (2fb) CTV in all bedrooms ® ✱ sB&B£25
sB&B↑£39 dB&B£35 dB&B↑£49 ✱ Lunch £6.95&alc Dinner
£2.25-£6.95&alc LDO 10pm
⁜ 150P ⥤ 18
Credit Cards 1 2 3

TEMPLE CLOUD Avon Map **03** ST65

FH Q Q **Mr & Mrs Wyatt Temple Bridge** *(ST627575)*
BS18 5AA ☎(0761) 52377 due to change to 452377
Mar-Oct
*This 17th-century white farmhouse with mullion windows and oak
beams also has a large garden available to guests. The house is
situated south of the village and set back from the A37 road. It is
within easy distance of Bath, Wells and Bristol. Simple
accommodation is provided in comfortable rooms.*
2hc (2fb) ® ✱ ✱ sB&B£14.50-£16.50 dB&B£28-£32
⁜ CTV 2P 1⇞ nc2yrs 250 acres beef arable £

TENBY Dyfed Map **02** SN10

GH Q Q **Castle View Private Hotel** The Norton SA70 8AA
☎(0834) 2666
Mar-Oct
*A family-run hotel ideally situated overlooking the harbour and
North Beach. The first-floor lounge and several bedrooms have
lovely views of the beach and harbour, and all the rooms are well
equipped and en suite.*
10rm(7⇌3↑) (4fb) CTV in all bedrooms ® ✱
sB&B⇌↑£22.50 dB&B⇌↑£45 WB&B£157.50
WBDi£206.50 LDO 6.30pm
Lic CTV 7P
Credit Cards 3 £

GH Q Q **Clareston House Hotel** Warren St SA70 7AL
☎(0834) 4148
rs Nov-Feb
*A cosy guesthouse situated near the railway station and just a
short walk from the sandy beaches and town centre. It is well
maintained and provides a comfortable lounge, a basement bar and
restaurant and bright bedrooms.*
6hc (5fb) CTV in all bedrooms ® ✱ ✱ sB&B£12-£15
dB&B£24-£30 WB&B£84-£105 WBDi£115-£140 (wkly only
Jun-Aug) LDO 11am
Lic ⁜ CTV 4P £

GH Q Q *Gumfreston Private Hotel* Culver Park SA70 7ED
☎(0834) 2871
Closed Nov
Bright and friendly, this small hotel is a few yards from the south beach and close to the shops. It has modern bedrooms and comfortable public rooms and features excellent displays of flowers and hanging baskets.
11rm(1⇨10♠) (5fb) ® ✕ LDO 4pm
Lic ♥ CTV ⨍
Credit Cards 3

GH Q Q *Hildebrand Hotel* Victoria St SA70 7DY
☎(0834) 2403 due to change to 842403
Apr-Oct rs Jan-Mar & Nov
Just off the seafront and a short walk from the town centre, this holiday guesthouse is decorated with an abundance of floral baskets and displays. The bedrooms are all well equipped and there is a cosy basement bar.
11rm(3⇨5♠3hc) (6fb) CTV in all bedrooms ® sB&B£14-£19 sB&B⇨♠£16-£23 dB&B£26-£34 dB&B⇨♠£32-£42 WB&B£100-£133 WBDi£160-£193 LDO 4pm
Lic ♥ ⨍
Credit Cards 1 2 3 5 £

GH Q Q Q *Myrtle House Hotel* St Mary's St SA70 7HW
☎(0834) 2508
Mar-Nov
Situated within the walls of the old town and a few yards from the seafront and shopping centre, this well maintained guesthouse provides well equipped facilities. Smoking is not permitted here.
8rm(7⇨♠1hc) (3fb)✕in all bedrooms CTV in all bedrooms ® ✕ (ex guide dogs) ✳ sB&B£19 sB&B⇨♠£22 dB&B£30 dB&B⇨♠£36 WB&B£100-£115 WBDi£140-£150 (wkly only Jun-Aug) LDO 4pm
Lic ♥ ⨍
Credit Cards 1 3

GH Q Q *Ripley St Marys Hotel* St Mary's St SA70 7HN
☎(0834) 2837
Apr-Oct rs Feb-Mar & Nov
A warm welcome is assured at Ripley St Marys, a cosy guesthouse tucked away in the old part of the town, conveniently situated with the seafront and the shopping centre near by.
14rm(8⇨♠6hc) (6fb) CTV in all bedrooms ® sB&B£17-£20 sB&B⇨♠£18.50-£24 dB&B£34-£40 dB&B⇨♠£37-£44 WB&B£112-£150 WBDi£160-£200 LDO 5.30pm
Lic CTV ⨍
Credit Cards 1 3 £

GH Q Q *Sea Breezes Hotel* 18 The Norton SA70 8AA
☎(0834) 2753
Jun-Sep rs Mar-May & Oct-Nov
Situated a few yards from the North Beach and 2 minutes from the town centre, this small family-run hotel provides comfortable bedrooms and a combined lounge and small bar.
11rm(5⇨1♠5hc) (3fb)✕in 6 bedrooms CTV in 6 bedrooms TV in 5 bedrooms ® ✕ (ex guide dogs) LDO 4.30pm
Lic ♥ CTV ⨍

GH Q Q Q *Tall Ships Hotel* 34 Victoria St SA70 7DY
☎(0834) 2055
Mar-Oct
A bright, spotlessly clean guesthouse located a few yards from the south beach. A short walk from the town centre. Bedrooms are all pretty and well equipped and there is a comfortable residents' lounge and a cosy basement bar.
9rm(5♠4hc) (6fb) CTV in all bedrooms ® ✕ (ex guide dogs) ✳ sB&B£15-£18 sB&B♠£17.50-£20.50 dB&B£26-£32 dB&B♠£31-£37 WB&B£87-£125 WBDi£125-£166 LDO 5pm
Lic CTV ⨍
Credit Cards 1 3 £

TETBURY Gloucestershire Map 03 ST89

INN Q Q Q *Priory* London Rd GL8 8JJ ☎(0666) 502251
Friendly and attentive services are provided by hosts Pat and Paul Gregory and their staff at this inn, located on the edge of the village. The well-equipped bedrooms complement the imaginative food served in the bar and formal restaurant.
3hc (1fb) CTV in all bedrooms ® LDO 10pm
♥ 100P
Credit Cards 1 3

Visit your local AA Shop.

TEWKESBURY Gloucestershire Map **03** SO83

GH Q Q **The Abbey Hotel** 67 Church St GL20 5RX
☎(0684) 294247
Situated opposite the Abbey gardens, this fine Georgian terraced town house has been converted into a hotel of character, with comfortable, well equipped bedrooms and pleasant public areas, including an intimate bar and a new extended restaurant.
16rm(7⇨7♠2hc) (3fb) CTV in all bedrooms ⓇＸ sB&B£30-£38 sB&B⇨♠£35-£40 dB&B£40-£45 dB&B⇨♠£45-£55 WB&B£190-£250 WBDi£240-£300 LDO 9.30pm
Lic ∰ 11P
Credit Cards ① ② ③ ⓔ

FH Q Q Q Mick & Anne Meadows *Home (SO933390)*
Bredons Norton GL20 7HA ☎Bredon(0684) 72322
Closed Dec
Situated 100 yards up the lane beside the village school, this 300-year-old farmhouse is set in 150 acres of land with mixed sheep, cattle and poultry. Home Farm has been tastefully improved to provide pretty and comfortable bedrooms with en suite or private facilities.
3rm(2⇨1hc) (1fb) Ⓡ
6P ⚘

THAME Oxfordshire Map **04** SP70

GH Q Q Q **Essex House** Chinnor Rd OX9 3LS
☎(084421) 7567 FAX (084421) 6420
Originally a station hotel, this guesthouse stands on the bend of the Chinnor road, between Thame and Chinnor. Bedrooms are well equipped and comfortably furnished; there is also an annexe providing bright, modern rooms which are 'no smoking'. The public rooms are comfortable, with a small bar area; ample parking is available.
10rm(1⇨6♠3hc) Annexe 6rm(3⇨3♠) (2fb)⤢in 5 bedrooms CTV in all bedrooms Ⓡ Ｘ (ex guide dogs) Ｘ sB&Bfr£31 sB&B⇨♠fr£41 dB&B⇨♠fr£56 LDO 7pm
Lic ∰ CTV 20P
Credit Cards ① ③ ⓔ

SELECTED

FH Q Q Q Q Mrs M Aitken **Upper Green** *(SP736053)*
Manor Rd, Towersey OX9 3QR (1.5m E unclass rd)
☎(084421) 2496
Closed Xmas & New Year
This 15th-century, thatched, whitewashed farmhouse is situated in a quiet country lane, surrounded by 7 acres of lovely countryside. The majority of bedrooms are located in a barn opposite the main house: this has been splendidly renovated and offers a spacious lounge; breakfast is also served here. Bedrooms are individual in style and décor, furnished with antiques and bric-a-brac. The farmhouse serves breakfast only, in the beamed dining room, over in the 'Paradise' barn; children and pets are not accepted and smoking is not permitted. Otherwise, the atmosphere is relaxed, warm and informal.
3rm(1♠1hc) Annexe 6⇨♠ ⤢in all bedrooms CTV in 7 bedrooms TV in 2 bedrooms Ⓡ Ｘ sB&B£17 sB&B⇨♠£28 dB&B£33 dB&B⇨♠£35-£50
∰ CTV 11P nc16yrs 7 acres poultry sheep

THAXTED Essex Map **05** TL63

INN Q Q Q *Farmhouse* Monk St CM6 2NR ☎(0371) 830864 FAX (0371) 831196
This attractively extended inn has 16th-century origins and is situated in picturesque Monk Street, 1 mile south of Thaxted off the B184. There is a freehouse bar with local beers, snacks and a pool table. Bedrooms are well equipped and have good en suite facilities.

11⇨♠ ⤢in 4 bedrooms CTV in all bedrooms Ｘ (ex guide dogs) LDO 9.30pm
∰ 48P
Credit Cards ① ② ③

THIRLMERE Cumbria Map **11** NY31

FH Q Q Mr & Mrs J Hodgson **Stybeck** *(NY319188)* CA12 4TN
☎Keswick(07687) 73232
Closed 25 Dec
A pleasant lakeland farmhouse set back from the road in open countryside. It is well furnished, with bedrooms of a good standard, and service is friendly and welcoming.
3hc (1fb) Ⓡ Ｘ Ｘ sB&B£15-£16 dB&B£30-£32
∰ CTV 4P nc5yrs 200 acres dairy mixed sheep working

THORGANBY North Yorkshire Map **08** SE64

INN Q Q **Jefferson Arms** Main St YO4 6DB
☎Wheldrake(0904) 448316 FAX (0904) 448837
A charming 300-year-old beamed inn with an old-world atmosphere. Good food is served in the Poachers Restaurant, and the bedrooms have good facilities and thoughtful extras.
3⇨ Annexe 3rm(2⇨1hc) (1fb)⤢in 3 bedrooms CTV in 5 bedrooms Ｘ sB&B⇨£51-£63 dB&B⇨£68-£81 Ｘ Lunch fr£8.50&alc High tea fr£5.50 Dinner fr£16.50&alc LDO 9.30pm
∰ 60P
Credit Cards ① ② ③ ⑤ ⓔ
See advertisement under YORK

THORNEY Cambridgeshire Map **04** TF20

FH Q Q Mrs Y G Baker **Oversley Lodge** *(TF269041)* The Causeway PE6 0QH ☎Peterborough(0733) 270321
A modern detached house on an arable farm, a few miles east of Peterborough on the A47 towards Wisbech. Bedrooms are large, comfortable and well equipped, and the dining room combines as a pleasant lounge. Nicely maintained and decorated, this is an ideal location for tourists and commercial guests alike.
3hc (1fb)⤢in all bedrooms CTV in all bedrooms Ⓡ Ｘ sB&B£18-£22 dB&B£30-£40 LDO 7pm
∰ CTV P 260 acres arable ⓔ

THORNTON Lancashire Map **07** SD34

SELECTED

GH Q Q Q Q **The Victorian House** Trunnah Rd FY5 4HF
☎Blackpool(0253) 860619 FAX (0253) 865350
A charming Victorian house set in its own grounds and gardens close to the A5268. There are just 3 bedrooms, all well equipped and sumptuously furnished and decorated in period style, one with a 4-poster. Throughout the house are objets d'art, paintings, fresh flowers and antiques. There is a cosy bar, a beautiful parlour and a most elegant restaurant, all splendidly Victorian, with a more modern conservatory. The hotel is owned by Louis and Didier Guerin, and M. Guerin's excellent cooking is decidedly French.
3⇨♠ CTV in all bedrooms Ⓡ sB&B⇨♠£39.50 dB&B⇨♠£65-£69.50 LDO 9.30pm
Lic ∰ 20P nc6yrs
Credit Cards ① ③

THORNTON DALE North Yorkshire Map **08** SE88

GH Q Q **Easthill** Wilton Rd YO18 7QP
☎Pickering(0751) 74561
Mar-Dec
This tastefully appointed house is situated on the eastern edge of the village, set back from the A170. It offers a tranquil and relaxing atmosphere, with over 2 acres of delightful garden to the rear.

8rm(4⇌4↾) (2fb) TV in 1 bedroom ⋊ ✳ sB&B⇌↾fr£18
dB&B⇌↾£31-£35 WB&B£101.50-£115.50 WBDi£150.50-
£164.50 LDO noon
Lic ♨ CTV 12P ⚿ ♪(grass)crazy golf games room

THORPE BAY Essex

See **Southend-on-Sea**

THORPENESS Suffolk Map **05** TM45

INN Ⓠ **Dolphin Hotel** IP16 4NB ☎Aldeburgh(0728) 452681

*Located just north of Aldeburgh in an interesting setting, a leisure
village built with Tudor timbered façades in the 1920s, now mostly
privately owned. The accommodation is simply furnished, with
some en suite facilities. There is a nicely appointed restaurant with
a bar, and a residents' lounge.*

18rm(5⇌1↾↾12hc) (3fb) CTV in all bedrooms Ⓡ LDO 9pm
♨ ⚼

Credit Cards 1 2 3

THRAPSTON Northamptonshire Map **04** SP97

INN Ⓠ **Court House Hotel** NN14 4NF ☎(08012) 3618

*Court House was built in 1858 as a courthouse, police station and
lock-up cells, and was converted 15 years ago to an inn providing
simple, old-fashioned accommodation. The restaurant was the
original courtroom, and has a remarkable hammer-beam ceiling
together with court bric-a-brac including a life-size dummy in
police uniform.*

7rm(2⇌1↾4hc) TV in all bedrooms Ⓡ ⋊ (ex guide dogs) ✳
sB&B£18-£25 sB&B⇌↾£25 dB&B£30-£36 dB&B⇌↾£36
WB&B£126-£175 WBDi£161-£210 ✳ Lunch £4.90-£15&alc
Dinner £4.90-£15&alc LDO 9.30pm
♨ 5P

Credit Cards 1 3 ⓔ

THE ABBEY HOTEL

Featuring Abbots restaurant.
Centrally situated in a conservation area.

**This warm family run hotel offers private and
business accommodation at reasonable cost.**

**The hotel has a residents car park and all
rooms have a colour TV and Telephone.**

**There is a Resident's Bar and Abbots
restaurant is open Monday to Saturday.**

67 Church Street, Tewkesbury, Glos GL20 5RX
Telephone: (0684) 294247 & 294097

Stybeck Farm

Thirlmere, Nr. Keswick, Cumbria CA12 4TN
Tel: Keswick 73232

Proprietors:
Joey & Jean Hodgson

A working farm with mixed animals, set in the lovely Thirlmere Valley. Offering excellent accommodation. Bed & breakfast with optional dinner, at moderate rates. Central for walking, touring or fishing on Lake Thirlmere.

AA
QQQQ
Selected

Tavern House

English Tourist Board
HIGHLY COMMENDED

Willesley, Nr Tetbury, Gloucestershire GL8 8QU
Telephone: (066688) 444
due to change (0666880) 444

Delightfully situated 17th century former Cotswold coaching house, set in idyllic countryside close to the Arboretum, yet convenient for Bath and Cirencester and providing easy motorway access to Bristol, Cheltenham and the Midlands.

All rooms en suite with direct dial telephone, colour TV, tea maker, central heating etc. Charming secluded garden. A combination of the standards of an excellent hotel with the warmth and welcome of a country house.

THREE COCKS Powys Map **03** SO13

GH 🔘🔘🔘 *Old Gwernyfed Country Manor* Felindre LD3 0SU
☎Glasbury(04974) 376
mid Mar-mid Nov
*This Elizabethan manor house lies in several acres of parkland,
and has many notable features including a minstrel's gallery, an
oak-panelled banqueting hall, a mast from the Spanish Armada, a
secret code carved by Shakespeare and a priest's hole. The
accommodation is comfortable, with most of the bedrooms en suite,
and there is a good range of home-cooked meals.*
11rm(7⇔2♠2hc) (4fb) LDO 7.30pm
Lic 15P croquet

THREE LEGGED CROSS Dorset Map **04** SU00

FH 🔘🔘 Mr & Mrs B Gent **Homeacres** *(SU096054)*
Homelands Farm BH21 6QZ ☎Verwood(0202) 822422
*A modern-style farmhouse on the main road between Three
Legged Cross and Ashley Heath, close to but not dominated by
Ashley Heath Industrial Park. The bedrooms are fairly spacious
and reasonably equipped, and there are two lounges, both well laid
out, the most comfortable being on the ground floor.*
6rm(4⇔2♠2hc) (2fb) ® sB&Bfr£17 sB&B⇔♠£19.50
dB&B£28-£33 dB&B⇔♠£34-£39 WB&B£98-£105
🍴 CTV 5P 3🎱 games room 270 acres beef

THRESHFIELD North Yorkshire Map **07** SD96

GH 🔘🔘🔘 **Greenways** Wharfeside Av BD23 5BS
☎Skipton(0756) 752598
Apr-Oct
*A family residence situated on the banks of the River Wharfe with
the dining room and some bedrooms overlooking one of the most
spectacular stretches of the river. Greenways is located in
Threshfield; from the Skipton direction, turn left at the school and
follow the road to the bottom.*
5hc (1fb) ® ✱ sB&B£19-£24 dB&Bfr£38 WB&B£119.70-
£144.70 WBDif£189-£214 LDO 5pm
Lic 🍴 CTV 8P nc7yrs
See advertisement under GRASSINGTON

THRINGSTONE Leicestershire Map **08** SK41

FH 🔘 Miss F E White **Talbot House** *(SK423173)* LE6 4NQ
☎Coalville(0530) 222233
*Mostly built in Victorian times, around a much earlier building,
this large, rambling farmhouse provides simple, old-fashioned and
comfortable accommodation. It stands on the B587, 4.5m W of
M1 junction 23.*
4rm (1fb) CTV in 1 bedroom TV in 1 bedroom
✖ (ex guide dogs) ✱ sB&B£14-£15 dB&Bfr£26 WB&Bfr£94.50
WBDifr£136.50 LDO noon
🍴 CTV 6P croquet 150 acres dairy

THURNING Norfolk Map **09** TG02

🛏🔽 FH 🔘🔘 Mrs A M Fisher **Rookery** *(TG078307)*
NR24 2JP ☎Melton Constable(0263) 860357
Closed Dec-Jan
*A 17th-century detached red brick farmhouse in a rural, secluded
setting, surrounded by well tended gardens. The traditionally
furnished accommodation is spacious and comfortable, and there is
an attractive lounge/dining room with an open fire. Guests are
advised to obtain directions from the proprietor, Mrs. Fisher.*
3rm(1♠) (1fb) ® ✖ sB&B£12 dB&B£24 dB&B♠£27
CTV P 400 acres arable

THURSBY Cumbria Map **11** NY35

🛏🔽 FH 🔘🔘 Mrs M G Swainson **How End** *(NY316497)*
CA5 6PX ☎Wigton(06973) 42487
*A typical Cumbrian farmhouse situated on the main A595 between
Carlisle and Wigton. It offers good value for money with friendly
service provided by the resident owner.*

3rm (2fb)⚡in all bedrooms ✖ (ex guide dogs) sB&B£12-£14
dB&B£24-£28 WB&B£80-£95
🍴 CTV 4P 200 acres dairy mixed

THWAITE North Yorkshire Map **07** SD89

GH 🔘🔘 **Kearton** DL11 5DR
☎Richmond (North Yorks)(0748) 86277
Mar-Dec
*Set in the heart of this pretty village, this comfortable guesthouse
has a delightful, spacious restaurant, which provides quality
morning coffee, lunch, afternoon tea and dinner.*
13hc (2fb) ® ✖ (ex guide dogs) sB&B£22-£23.50 dB&B£44-
£47 (incl dinner) WB&Bfr£119 WBDifr£154 LDO 6.30pm
Lic 🍴 50P
Credit Cards 1 3 £

TIDEFORD Cornwall & Isles of Scilly Map **02** SX35

FH 🔘🔘 Mrs B A Turner **Kilna House** *(SX353600)* PL12 5AD
☎Landrake(0752) 851236
Closed Xmas & New Year
*This small, stone-built farmhouse is set in a large pleasant garden
and overlooks the River Tiddy Valley; it is situated along the busy
A38 between Liskeard and Plymouth, just outside the village.
Bedrooms are well appointed and comfortable and the public areas
simple but neat, with a relaxed atmosphere. The proprietors have
run it for the past 20 years and, having made gradual
improvements, now enjoy a returning clientèle.*
5hc (2fb) CTV in all bedrooms ® ✱ sB&B£15-£17 dB&B£28-
£32 WB&B£84-£98
🍴 CTV 6P 12 acres arable pasture £

TILSTON Cheshire Map **07** SJ45

FH 🔘🔘🔘 Mrs K M Ritchie **Tilston Lodge** *(SJ463511)*
SY14 7DR ☎(0829) 250223
3rm(2⇔1hc) (1fb) CTV in 2 bedrooms ® ✖ (ex guide dogs)
sB&B£15-£20 dB&B⇔£32-£40
🍴 CTV 10P 12 acres cattle poultry sheep £

TIMSBURY Avon Map **03** ST65

GH 🔘🔘 **Old Malt House Hotel & Licensed Restaurant**
Radford BA3 1QF ☎(0761) 70106
Closed Xmas
*On the outskirts of the village. This former malting house has been
renovated to provide spacious public areas and well-equipped
bedrooms which all have en suite facilities. The Holder family also
operate a shire horse stud adjacent to the house.*
10⇔♠ (2fb) CTV in all bedrooms ® ✖ sB&B⇔♠£28.50-£33
dB&B⇔♠£47-£58 WB&Bfr£164.50 WBDifr£243.25
LDO 8.30pm
Lic 🍴 40P nc3yrs
Credit Cards 1 2 3 5 £

TINTAGEL Cornwall & Isles of Scilly Map **02** SX08

GH 🔘🔘 **Belvoir** Tregatta PL34 0DY
☎Camelford(0840) 770265
Closed Xmas
*Mrs Martin provides a warm welcome here. The house is cottage-
like in style, with a sun lounge in addition to another cosy lounge.
The bedrooms are comfortable, and most contain en suite facilities.*
7rm(1⇔4♠2hc) (1fb) CTV in 6 bedrooms TV in 1 bedroom ®
✱ sB&B£12.50-£13.50 dB&B£25-£27 dB&B⇔♠£27-£29
WB&B£82-£96 WBDif£118.75-£132.75 LDO 5.30pm
Lic CTV 12P nc1yr £

🔘 is for quality. For a full explanation of this AA quality
award, consult the Contents page.

GH QQQ **Castle Villa** Molesworth St PL34 0BZ
☎Camelford(0840) 770373 & 770203
This small cottage of Cornish stone provides neat bedrooms,
equipped with tea and coffee-making facilities. There is a cosy
lounge with stone fireplaces, and a conservatory dining room.
Fresh homemade food and home brewed beer are on offer.
5rm(1⇨4hc) ✗in all bedrooms CTV in all bedrooms ®
sB&B£11.50-£13.50 dB&B£23-£27 dB&B⇨£30-£34
WB&B£72.50-£85 WBDi£132.30-£148 LDO 10am
Lic ங CTV 6P
Credit Cards 1 3 ⓔ

GH QQQ **Trebrea Lodge** Trenale PL34 0HR
☎Camelford(0840) 770410
A fine 14th-century stone-built country house in a rural setting
with panoramic views over the surrounding countryside and
coastline. The well equipped bedrooms have recently been
upgraded, and the interior, including an elegant first-floor drawing
room, is tastefully furnished. There is an honesty bar in the ground
floor snug, and good home-cooked set dinners are served using
local produce.
6⇨3🮑 (1fb)✗in all bedrooms CTV in all bedrooms ®
sB&B⇨🮑£40-£52 dB&B⇨🮑£50-£75 WB&B£150-£230
WBDi£260-£330 LDO 8pm
Lic ங 20P
Credit Cards 1 2 3 ⓔ

GH QQ **The Trevervan Hotel** Trewarmett PL34 0ES
☎Camelford(0840) 770486
In the village of Trewarmett, this is a detached house with fine sea
views. It is personally run by the resident proprietors and offers a
warm welcome, together with neat and well-kept accommodation.
6hc (3fb)✗in 2 bedrooms ® sB&B£13.50-£14.50 dB&B£27-£29
WB&B£89-£96 WBDi£133-£140 LDO 7pm
Lic ங CTV 6P
Credit Cards 1 2 3 ⓔ

"BELVOIR HOUSE"

The small friendly guest house, with all the
comfort you want. Situated away from the
crowds, 3 mins walk to coastal path. Seven
bedrooms, five en suite, all with tea makers,
T.V., heaters, etc. Lovely gardens, parking for
12 cars. Cordon Bleu cooking, log fires,
personal attention to those little extras.
Weekday bookings. Pets by arrangement.

B&B from £13.50, Dinner £6.50
Reductions for children.

Ring Joyce Martin for brochure
(0840) 770265
Tregatta, Tintagel, Cornwall PL34 0DY

CASTLE VILLA GUEST HOUSE
Molesworth Street, Tintagel, Cornwall.
Telephone: (0840) 770373/203

A charming old stone cottage, Castle Villa is
situated in the picturesque village of Tintagel. All
bedrooms have tea & coffee making facilities, wash
basin, shaver points and colour television. A full
Cornish breakfast is served and a varied dinner
menu is available if required. Pets welcome.

Write or phone for brochure.

Proprietors Karen & Andrew Hill.

Old Gwernyfed Country Manor

FELINDRE, THREE COCKS, BRECON, POWYS
Telephone: 04974 (Glasbury) 376

Elizabethan Manor House set in 12 acres isolation of
foothills of Black Mountains (12 miles NE Brecon).
Lovely unspoilt rooms (some with 4 posters; all en
suite) have superb views. Panelled Banqueting Hall,
Minstrel's Gallery, Armada Mast, Escape Hatch,
Secret Code make it a very interesting small hotel.
Food is interesting and fresh, service personal and
friendly. See gazetteer for further information.

GH Q Q Q **Trewarmett Lodge** PL34 0ET
☎Camelford(0840) 770460
Closed Nov rs Dec-Etr
Trewarmett Lodge is located in a small hamlet a mile from Tintagel with distant coastal views. The Pig Sty Bistro serves a wide range of meals to suit all pockets, and features a pottery pig collection. Bedrooms are light, airy and well presented – all are non-smoking.
6rm(1↑5hc)(2fb)⊬in all bedrooms ® ✹ sB&B£16.50-£19 dB&B£32-£39 dB&B↑£36-£40 WB&B£109-£122 WBDi£155-£169 LDO 9pm
Lic ⅏ CTV 10P
Credit Cards 1 3 £

INN Q Q Q **Tintagel Arms Hotel** Fore St PL34 0BD
☎Camelford(0840) 770780
Situated in the centre of the town, this fully licensed free house has been tastefully restored, and offers well equipped, modern bedrooms with very generous en suite facilities. The restaurant has a strong Greek influence and bar meals are very popular, along with the real ales and well stocked cellar. The standard of service, hospitality and general housekeeping is commendable.
7⇔↑ CTV in all bedrooms ® ✕ (ex guide dogs) ✹ sB&B⇔↑£25 dB&B⇔↑£42-£50 ✹ Bar Lunch £1.10-£4 Dinner £9.50-£16alc LDO 9.30pm
⅏ 8P
Credit Cards 1 3 £

TINTERN Gwent Map **03** SO50

GH Q Q **Valley House** Raglan Rd NP6 6TH ☎(0291) 689652
Set in a tranquil valley, this Georgian house has en suite, well-equipped bedrooms and a comfortable residents' lounge. Valley House is half a mile from the A466.
3⇔↑ ⊬in 2 bedrooms CTV in all bedrooms ® ✹ sB&B⇔↑£22-£25 dB&B⇔↑£32-£35 WB&B£100-£110 WBDi£180-£190 LDO 7.30pm
⅏ 7P £
See advertisement under CHEPSTOW

INN Q **Fountain** Trellech Grange NP6 6QW ☎(0291) 689303
This 17th-century inn is situated two miles west of the village (turn at the Royal George hotel). There is a cosy beamed bar and an attractive restaurant offering a wide range of good value food.
5hc (2fb) CTV in 4 bedrooms TV in 1 bedroom ® sB&Bfr£17 dB&Bfr£28 WB&B£91-£105 WBDifr£151 Lunch fr£9 Dinner fr£9&alc LDO 10.30pm
⅏ 40P
Credit Cards 1 3 £

TISSINGTON Derbyshire Map **07** SK15

FH Q Q Q **Mrs B Herridge Bent** *(SK187523)* DE6 1RD
☎Parwich(033525) 214
Etr-Oct
Part of a country estate within the Peak District National Park, this stone-built house is part of a working farm. Guests will enjoy comfortable accommodation and a charming country garden.
4rm(2⇔2hc)(1fb) ® ✕ (ex guide dogs) sB&B£16 dB&B£24 dB&B⇔£30 WB&B£84 WBDi£126 LDO 5pm
⅏ CTV 6P nc5yrs 280 acres beef dairy mixed sheep

TIVERTON Devon Map **03** SS91

GH Q Q Q **Bridge** 23 Angel Hill EX16 6PE ☎(0884) 252804
This large Victorian house stands on the river-bank close to the town centre. The house retains many original features and is traditionally furnished. Guests can enjoy private fishing from the river garden.
10rm(2↑8hc)(2fb) TV in all bedrooms ® LDO 6.30pm
Lic ⅏ CTV 6P 1🏕 ⊿ riverside tea garden

FH Q **Barbara & Len Fullilove Lodge Hill** *(SS945112)*
Ashley EX16 5PA ☎(0884) 252907
A simply appointed, family-run Devonshire farmhouse near the centre of Tiverton, within easy reach of the M5; it is open all year round for bed and breakfast.
8rm(6↑2hc)(2fb) CTV in 4 bedrooms ® ✹ sB&Bfr£13 sB&B↑fr£15 dB&Bfr£26 dB&B↑fr£30 WB&B£80-£90
Lic ⅏ CTV 12P 2🏕 (£1 per night) 10 acres poultry sheep horses
Credit Cards 3 £

FH Q Q Q Q **Mrs R Olive Lower Collipriest** *(SS953117)*
EX16 4PT ☎(0884) 252321
Etr-Oct
Peacefully situated in the beautiful Exe Valley yet close to Tiverton, Lower Collipriest is a thatched Devon farmhouse of character and charm looking out over open pastureland. The 2 traditionally styled bedrooms are spacious and comfortable, with a feel of quality which extends into the guests' lounge with its magnificent inglenook fireplace, where log fires blaze on chilly evenings. Home-cooked dishes are offered from a set menu, and are served at a large communal table in the dining room, where a maximum of 4 guests can enjoy the friendly services of Mrs Olive who welcomes visitors to her home.
2⇔↑ ⊬in all bedrooms ® ✕ (ex guide dogs) sB&B⇔↑£24-£26 dB&B⇔↑£48-£52 (incl dinner) WB&B£126-£130 WBDi£160-£170 LDO noon
⅏ CTV 2P 2🏕 nc16yrs ⊿ 220 acres beef dairy £

TIVETSHALL ST MARY Norfolk Map **05** TM18

INN Q Q Q **Old Ram Coaching Inn** Ipswich Rd NR15 2DE
☎Pulham Market(0379) 676794 FAX (0379) 608399
5⇔↑ (1fb)⊬in 3 bedrooms CTV in all bedrooms ® ✹ sB&B⇔↑£40-£45 dB&B⇔↑£60-£65 WB&B£200 LDO 10pm
⅏ 120P
Credit Cards 1 3

TORBAY Devon
See **Brixham, Paignton and Torquay**

TORQUAY Devon Map **03** SX96
See **Town Plan Section**
GH Q Q **Avron Hotel** 70 Windsor Rd TQ1 1SZ
☎(0803) 294182
May-Sep
14rm(6↑8hc)(1fb) TV in all bedrooms ® (wkly only Jun-Aug) CTV 8P

GH Q Q Q **Barn Hayes Country Hotel** Brim Hill, Maidencombe TQ1 4TR ☎(0803) 327980
rs Nov-Feb
Set in a peaceful valley 2 miles from the centre of Torquay, this most attractive property stands in its own well-tended gardens with a swimming pool and some lovely sea views. Some of the bedrooms offer en suite facilities, and the lounges and dining room are tastefully decorated. A simple menu offers home cooked dishes.
10rm(6↑4hc) Annexe 3rm(2⇔1↑)(2fb) CTV in 3 bedrooms ® sB&B£17-£20 sB&B⇔↑£21-£24 dB&B£34-£40 dB&B⇔↑£38-£44 WB&B£112-£161 WBDi£170-£220
Lic ⅏ CTV 16P ⊇
Credit Cards 1 3 £

GH Q Q Q **The Berburry Hotel** 64 Bampfylde Rd TQ2 5AY
☎(0803) 297494
Closed 3 wks during Dec-Jan
An attractive detached house, close to the English Riviera Leisure Centre and overlooking the Torre valley sports ground. The bedrooms have recently been decorated and furnished to a high

standard, with many thoughtful touches provided. A choice of home-cooked dishes make up the table d'hôte menu, and the service offered by the residential proprietors is friendly and attentive.

10⇨🏐 (3fb) CTV in all bedrooms ® ✕ ✳ sB&B⇨🏐£19-£24
dB&B⇨🏐£38-£48 WB&B£100-£160 WBDi£160-£220
LDO 5pm
Lic ♔ CTV 10P nc7yrs
Credit Cards [1] [3] (£)

GH Q|Q|Q Braddon Hall Hotel Braddons Hill Rd East
TQ1 1HF ☎(0803) 293908
Within easy reach of the harbour and beaches, this quietly set hotel has en suite facilities and public areas of a high standard. The resident proprietors provide a choice of menu and a warm welcome.
11⇨🏐 (3fb) CTV in all bedrooms ® LDO 5pm
Lic ♔ 8P

GH Q|Q|Q Burley Court Hotel Wheatridge Lane, Livermead
TQ2 6RA ☎(0803) 607879
mid Mar-mid Nov
Situated in an elevated position overlooking Livermead Beach, Burley Court has well-equipped bedrooms with en suite facilities. An indoor leisure complex has a plunge pool, solarium, mini gym and games room. There is a heated swimming pool outside as well.
21rm(1⇨20🏐) (7fb) CTV in all bedrooms ®
✕ (ex guide dogs) sB&B⇨🏐£27-£32 dB&B⇨🏐£54-£64 (incl dinner) WB&B£125-£142 WBDi£170-£192 (wkly only Jul-Aug)
LDO 6.30pm
Lic ♔ 25P ▣(heated) ♨(heated) solarium gymnasium (£)

GH Q|Q|Q Chesterfield Hotel 62 Belgrave Rd TQ2 5HY
☎(0803) 292318
This charming Victorian house is part of a terrace close to the seafront. The bedrooms are tastefully furnished and the public rooms still have their original carved ceilings.
11rm(7🏐4hc) (4fb) CTV in all bedrooms ® sB&B£12-£18 sB&B🏐£15-£21 dB&B£22-£30 dB&B🏐£28-£37 WB&B£68-£125 WBDi£99-£160 LDO 4pm
Lic ♔ CTV 3P
Credit Cards [1] [3] (£)

GH Q|Q|Q Hotel Concorde 26 Newton Rd TQ2 5BZ
☎(0803) 292330
Standing on the outskirts of town, this guesthouse has been well modernised and offers spacious public rooms, well-equipped bedrooms and a sheltered swimming pool.
22rm(14⇨🏐8hc) (7fb) CTV in all bedrooms ® LDO 6pm
Lic ♔ CTV 18P ♨(heated)
Credit Cards [1] [3]

GH Q|Q|Q Craig Court Hotel 10 Ash Hill Rd, Castle Circus
TQ1 3HZ ☎(0803) 294400
Etr-Oct
Spacious and detached, an early Victorian house in a quiet road close to the shopping centre offers large, comfortable bedrooms and a choice of two lounges.
10rm(5🏐5hc) (2fb) ® ✕ (ex guide dogs) sB&B£15-£18 sB&B🏐£18-£21 dB&B£30-£36 dB&B🏐£36-£42 WB&B£105-£126 WBDi£143.50-£182 LDO noon
Lic CTV 8P model railway in garden (£)

See advertisement on page 357

GH Q|Q|Q Cranborne Hotel 58 Belgrave Rd TQ2 5HY
☎(0803) 298046
Closed Dec
This fine Victorian house has been carefully modernised by Mr and Mrs Dawkins, and has very well-equipped bedrooms, most of which have en suite facilities, and good public areas. The small front garden is a past winner of the 'Devon in Bloom' competition.
12rm(11⇨🏐1hc) (6fb) CTV in all bedrooms ® ✕
sB&B£14.50-£16.50 dB&B⇨🏐£35-£39 WB&B£89-£119
WBDi£109-£143 LDO 3pm
▶

Lic CTV 3P
Credit Cards 1 3 £

GH ◻◻◻ Cranmore 89 Avenue Rd TQ2 5LH
☎(0803) 298488
*Ken and Margaret Silver have totally refurbished their attractive
semi-detached house. The open plan public areas have a Tudor
theme and the bedrooms are well equipped with orthopaedic beds.
Little personal touches make guests feel at home.*
9rm(5⇆4hc) (2fb) CTV in all bedrooms ®
✗ (ex guide dogs) sB&B£11-£13 dB&B£22-£26 dB&B⇆ £26-
£30 WB&B£77-£91 WBDi£115.50-£129.50 LDO 5pm
⚑ CTV 4P
Credit Cards 1 2 3 £

GH ◻◻◻ Daphne Court Hotel Lower Warberry Rd TQ1 1QS
☎(0803) 212011
mid-Mar-mid-Oct
*This Victorian villa has a heated swimming pool in its gardens. All
bedrooms have colour TV and are tastefully furnished. Simple
dishes are served in the relaxed dining room and Geoff and Jenny
Langley create a welcoming atmosphere.*
16rm(2⇆14) (8fb) CTV in all bedrooms ®
✗ (ex guide dogs) sB&B⇆ £27-£33 dB&B⇆ £54-£60 (incl
dinner) WB&B£125-£165 WBDi£170-£230 LDO 7.30pm
Lic ⚑ CTV 15P ⌂(heated) games room
Credit Cards 1 3 £

GH ◻◻ Devon Court Hotel Croft Rd TQ2 5UE
☎(0803) 293603
Etr-Oct
*The public rooms of a large Victorian house close to the Riviera
Centre retain many original features, and some of its comfortable
bedrooms have good en suite facilities.*
13rm(8 5hc) (3fb) CTV in all bedrooms ® ✗ ✳ sB&B£11.30-
£21.45 sB&B£13.40-£23.55 dB&B£22.60-£42.90
dB&B£26.80-£47.10 WB&B£79-£136.50 WBDi£100-£157.50
LDO 4.30pm
Lic ⚑ CTV 14P ⌂(heated)
Credit Cards 1 3 £

GH ◻◻◻ Elmdene Rathmore Rd TQ2 6NZ ☎(0803) 294940
rs Nov-Feb
*Situated near the cricket field and convenient for the station, this
spacious detached Victorian house retains many original features
in the public areas and in the modern and comfortable bedrooms.*
12rm(2⇆5 5hc) (3fb) CTV in 13 bedrooms ® ✳ sB&B£16-
£22 sB&B⇆ £22-£28 dB&B£32-£44 dB&B⇆ £38-£50
WB&B£112-£123 WBDi£161-£181 LDO 5pm
Lic ⚑ CTV 12P nc5yrs
Credit Cards 1 3 £

GH ◻◻ Exmouth View Hotel St Albans Rd, Babbacombe
Down TQ1 3LG ☎(0803) 327307
*A large detached family hotel, converted from two buildings,
enjoying a commanding view overlooking Babbacombe Downs.
Rooms are comfortable, well equipped and regularly decorated.
Various public rooms include an open-plan lounge area, complete
with dance floor. A simple home-cooked menu is offered with a
choice of dishes, and the service is friendly and helpful.*
32rm(19⇆ 13hc) (9fb) CTV in all bedrooms ® sB&B£15.90-
£28.80 sB&B⇆ £17.90-£30.80 dB&B£31.80-£57.60
dB&B⇆ £35.80-£61.60 (incl dinner) WB&B£87.50-£176.75
WBDi£101.50-£208.75 LDO 6.30pm
Lic ⚑ CTV 25P
Credit Cards 1 3 £

This is one of many guidebooks pubished by
the AA. The full range is available at any
AA Shop or good bookshop.

SELECTED

GH ◻◻◻◻ Glenorleigh Hotel 26 Cleveland Rd
TQ2 5BE ☎(0803) 292135
6 Jan-14 Oct & Xmas
*A friendly, family hotel in a quiet residential area, with south-
facing gardens, complete with a heated swimming pool and
Spanish style patio. The bedrooms are modern, freshly
decorated and beautifully kept, and some bathrooms have
whirlpool baths. There is an elegant, quiet lounge, whilst the
more lively bar lounge has a dance floor and live
entertainment during the season. Home-cooked meals are
served in the intimate lower ground floor dining room, and the
social atmosphere and efforts of the friendly proprietors have
resulted in the hotel being a regular award winner.*
16rm(9 7hc) (5fb) ® ✗ (ex guide dogs) ✳ WB&B£90-
£140 WBDi£115-£173 (wkly only Jul-Aug & Xmas)
LDO 6pm
Lic ⚑ CTV 10P ⌂(heated) solarium pool table £
See advertisement in colour supplement

GH ◻◻ Ingoldsby Hotel 1 Chelston Rd TQ2 6PT
☎(0803) 607497
*Standing in its own grounds away from the town centre, this hotel
is run by friendly, welcoming proprietors. Most of the bedrooms
have en suite facilities and there are comfortable, simple public
areas. A table d'hôte menu is offered.*
15rm(3⇆9 3hc) (5fb) ® ✗ (ex guide dogs) ✳ sB&B£17.85-
£24 dB&B£35.50-£48 dB&B⇆ £38.50-£54 WB&B£112.25-
£114.25 WBDi£116.50-£156.50 LDO 7pm
Lic ⚑ CTV 15P
Credit Cards 1 3

GH ◻ Jesmond Dene Private Hotel 85 Abbey Rd TQ2 5NN
☎(0803) 293062
rs Oct-Apr
*Located within walking distance of the town centre, this pleasant
guesthouse offers comfortable accommodation that is ideal for the
family. During the summer months, evening dinners are available
for guests.*
11hc (3fb) ® LDO noon
⚑ CTV 3P

GH ◻ Lindum Hotel Abbey Rd TQ2 5NP ☎(0803) 292795
Mar-Nov
*Close to the promenade and town centre, this spacious Victorian
house has well-furnished bedrooms and public rooms plus a cosy
bar.*
20rm(1⇆10 9hc) (3fb) CTV in all bedrooms ® LDO 7.15pm
Lic ⚑ CTV 14P

GH ◻◻◻ Mapleton Hotel St Lukes Rd North TQ2 5PD
☎(0803) 292389
Mar-15 Nov
*Surrounded by its own grounds, with glorious views across the bay,
this hotel extends a warm welcome to its guests and provides
attractive and comfortable rooms. A choice of home cooked dishes
is available from the table d'hôte menu.*
10rm(1⇆6 3hc) (3fb) CTV in all bedrooms ®
✗ (ex guide dogs) sB&B£19-£23 dB&B£38-£46 dB&B⇆ £43-
£53 (incl dinner) WB&B£95-£130 WBDi£125-£175
LDO 6.30pm
Lic ⚑ 10P nc5yrs
Credit Cards 1 3

GH ◻◻◻ Olivia Court Upper Braddons Hill Rd TQ1 1HD
☎(0803) 292595
*This picturesque property is in a quiet residential area close to the
town centre. The bedrooms are tastefully decorated, while the
lounge and bar offer a warm, relaxed atmosphere. Meals are
served in the elegant dining room.*

16rm(9⇨3♠7hc) (2fb)✗in 4 bedrooms CTV in all bedrooms ®
sB&B£17.50-£26.10 dB&B£31-£38.50 dB&B⇨♠£35-£42.50
WB&B£107-£135 WBDi£151-£180 LDO 4pm
Lic ♛ CTV 4P
Credit Cards 1 3 £

GH Q Q Q *Pencarrow Hotel* 64 Windsor Rd TQ1 1SZ
☎(0803) 293080
13rm(8♠5hc) (2fb) CTV in all bedrooms ® (wkly only Jul &
Aug) LDO 6pm
Lic CTV 8P games room

GH Q Q The Porthcressa Hotel 28 Perinville Road,
Babbacombe TQ1 3NZ ☎(0803) 327268
*This family-run hotel is located in a quiet, residential part of the
town and provides bright bedrooms with attractive soft furnishings
and colour televisions. The public areas are comfortable, and a
lively bar proves popular with guests.*
13rm(2♠11hc) (3fb) TV in 12 bedrooms ® ✻ (ex guide dogs)
✳ sB&B£15 sB&B♠£16.50 dB&B£30 dB&B♠£33 WBDi£95-
£130 (wkly only Jul-Aug) LDO 8pm
Lic ♛ CTV 6P

GH Q Q Q Rawlyn House Hotel Rawlyn Road, Chelston
TQ2 6PL ☎(0803) 605208
Apr-Oct & Xmas
17rm(2⇨10♠5hc) (3fb) CTV in all bedrooms ® ✻
sB&B⇨♠£22-£26 dB&B⇨♠£42-£52 (incl dinner)
WBDi£180-£212 LDO 7.15pm
Lic ♛ CTV 15P ⩬(heated) games room badminton £

GH Q Q Q Richwood Hotel 20 Newton Rd TQ2 5BZ
☎(0803) 293729
*Open all year round, this hotel is ideal for families, with cosy
bedrooms that are brightly decorated and furnished. It has an
attractive bar and an elegant lounge, with meals available in the
relaxed dining room.*
21rm(3⇨15♠3hc) (9fb) CTV in all bedrooms ® ✳ sB&B£12-
£22 sB&B⇨♠£12-£26 dB&B£24-£48 dB&B⇨♠£28-£52
WB&B£70-£130 WBDi£96-£179 (wkly only mid summer)
LDO 6.30pm
Lic ♛ CTV 14P ⩬(heated) pool table games room
Credit Cards 1 3 £

GH Q Q Q *Seaway Hotel* Chelston Rd TQ2 6PU
☎(0803) 605320
*A Victorian residence standing in its own gardens with easy access
to the town centre and the railway station. The bedrooms, some in
a more modern wing, have been tastefully decorated and furnished
and most have views of the bay. The public rooms have also been
upgraded, but retain their aura of spacious comfort.*
14rm(1⇨6♠7hc) (3fb) sB&B⇨♠£20-£27 dB&B£36-£50
dB&B⇨♠£40-£54 (incl dinner) WB&B£117-£170 WBDi£120-
£170 LDO 7pm
Lic ♛ CTV 15P
Credit Cards 1 3 £

GH Q Q Q *Sevens Hotel* 27 Morgan Av TQ2 5RR
☎(0803) 293523
*Supervised by resident proprietors, this small hotel is in a quiet
avenue within walking distance of the town and seafront. The
simply appointed bedrooms are comfortable, and there is a
spacious bar where guests can play pool and darts.*
12rm(3♠9hc) (3fb) ✻ LDO 4.30pm
Lic ♛ CTV 10P

GH Q Q Skerries Private Hotel 25 Morgan Av TQ2 5RR
☎(0803) 293618
*Family run, this cosy private hotel has comfortable public rooms
and well-maintained, compact bedrooms. It is conveniently close
to the town centre and has parking facilities.*
12rm(2♠10hc) (3fb) CTV in all bedrooms ® ✳ sB&B£12-£16
dB&B£24-£30 dB&B♠£31-£37 WB&B£80-£108 WBDi£110-
£129.50 LDO 2pm
Lic ♛ CTV 7P £

GH Q *Torbay Rise* Old Mill Rd TQ2 6HL ☎(0803) 605541
Apr-Oct
15rm(9⇨5♠1hc) (2fb) CTV in all bedrooms ® (wkly only Jul
& Aug) LDO 11am
Lic 8P ⩬(heated)
Credit Cards 1 3

GH Q Q Q *Villa Marina Hotel* Cockington Ln, Livermead
TQ2 6QU ☎(0803) 605440
Apr-Oct
*In Cockington Lane close to Livermead Beach, this modern hotel
offers well-equipped bedrooms and open plan public areas. Ideally
suited to the lively holidaymaker, there is also a good outdoor
heated swimming pool with a sunbathing area.*
26rm(20⇨4♠2hc) (6fb) CTV in all bedrooms ® LDO 6.45pm
Lic ♛ CTV 20P
Credit Cards 1 3

GH Q Q Westgate Hotel Falkland Rd TQ2 5JP
☎(0803) 295350
*This large, detached Victorian house is well situated amongst
many tourist attractions, including the English Riviera Leisure
Centre and Torre Abbey. The hotel is continually being upgraded
and renovated to improve standards, and the bedrooms are well
equipped and nicely decorated. Home-cooked dishes and fresh
produce are offered by the proprietor in an atmosphere that
succeeds in being both relaxed and friendly.*
13♠ (2fb) CTV in all bedrooms ® ✻ sB&B♠£18-£21
dB&B♠£36-£42 WB&B£130-£150 WBDi£180-£200 LDO 8pm
Lic CTV 14P nc5yrs games room pool table
Credit Cards 1 3 £

See advertisement on page 359

TORRINGTON, GREAT Devon Map **02** SS42

GH QQ Smytham Manor EX38 8PU (2m S A386)
☎Torrington(0805) 22110
Mar-Oct
A campsite and self-catering cabins stand in the 15 acres surrounding this manor house. The bedrooms are simply appointed and public areas, which are also enjoyed by those using the campsite, include a TV lounge and bar lounge.
6rm(3⇨1🚿2hc) ® LDO 9pm
Lic 🍽 CTV 14P ⛹(heated) snooker croquet mini golf table tennis games room
Credit Cards [1] [3] £

FH Q Mrs E J Watkins **Lower Hollam** *(SS501161)* Little Torrington EX38 8QS (on unclass rd 3m S of Torrington off A386) ☎(0805) 23253
Mar-Oct
Historic house situated in a peaceful, picturesque position, offering good play facilities for children.
3hc (1fb)⊬in all bedrooms ® ✗ (ex guide dogs) ✱ sB&B£10.50-£12 dB&B£21-£24 WBDi£87.50-£96 LDO 5pm
CTV 3P rough shooting 220 acres beef cereal sheep £

TOTLAND BAY

See **WIGHT, ISLE OF**

TOTNES Devon Map **03** SX86

SELECTED

GH QQQQ Lyssers Hotel 4 Chapel Ln, Bridgetown TQ9 5AF ☎(0803) 866513
A little difficult to find, but well worth the effort, this charming little hotel and restaurant is tucked away close to the River Dart in Chapel Lane. Originally a rope works, when hemp boats used to discharge their cargoes in the port of Totnes, it is now transformed into a cosy retreat with spotlessly clean and bright bedrooms, well furnished and comfortable. Food is another of the hotel's strengths, where good use is made of quality fresh produce.
6rm(4⇨🚿2hc) Annexe 1🚿 (1fb)⊬in all bedrooms CTV in all bedrooms ® ✱ sB&B£25 sB&B⇨🚿£30 dB&B£40 dB&B⇨🚿£45 LDO 9pm
Lic 🍽 20P
Credit Cards [1] [3]

SELECTED

GH QQQQ The Old Forge Seymour Place TQ9 5AY ☎(0803) 862174
rs Xmas wk
Dating back over 600 years, The Old Forge is within walking distance of the town and makes an ideal base for touring south Devon. Bedrooms, although compact, have been very well equipped and many thoughtful extras have been carefully provided. Two rooms have access to the pretty walled gardens, which are also open for cream teas in the summer. Breakfast only is served in the Tudor style dining room, and an extensive menu is offered. The cosy lounge area is licensed, but smoking is not permitted in the house. The proprietor runs the smithy/workshop, and many of his creations are for sale.
10rm(6⇨🚿4hc) (4fb)⊬in all bedrooms CTV in all bedrooms ® ✗ (ex guide dogs) ✱ sB&Bfr£30 sB&B⇨🚿fr£40 dB&B£36-£40 dB&B⇨🚿£46-£50
Lic 🍽 CTV 8P 🏠 putting
Credit Cards [1] [3] £

TOTTENHILL Norfolk Map **09** TF61

GH QQ Oakwood House Private Hotel PE33 0RH ☎Kings Lynn(0553) 810256
This fine, detached, family-run hotel is situated on the A10 midway between King's Lynn and Downham Market, and is set in 2 acres of very attractive grounds. The accommodation varies: some rooms have been refurbished by the present owners and are comfortable and well furnished, with good en suite facilities. Evening meals are served.
7rm(5⇨🚿2hc) Annexe 3⇨🚿 CTV in all bedrooms ® sB&B£21 sB&B⇨🚿£36-£38 dB&B£26 dB&B⇨🚿£46-£48 WBDi£224 LDO 8.30pm
Lic 🍽 20P 🏠
Credit Cards [1] [3]

TREARDDUR BAY Gwynedd Map **06** SH27

GH QQ Highground Off Ravenspoint Rd LL65 2YY ☎(0407) 860078
Closed 15 Dec-6 Jan
A small, privately owned hotel enjoying a superb location overlooking the sea. The bedrooms are quite well equipped, and have private bathrooms.
3rm(2⇨1🚿) (1fb) CTV in all bedrooms ® ✗ ✱ sB&B⇨🚿£25.50-£35 dB&B⇨🚿£43-£46 WB&B£150.50
🍽 3P nc2yrs
Credit Cards [1] [3] £

GH QQ Moranedd Trearddur Rd LL65 2UE ☎(0407) 860324
This large, well furnished house is farmily run and stands in its own delightful spacious gardens. It is situated in a quiet road, conveniently close to the beach. Good home cooking is provided.
6hc (1fb) ® sB&B£12-£14 dB&B£24-£28 WB&B£84-£98
Lic 🍽 CTV 10P £

TRECASTLE Powys Map **03** SN82

INN QQQ Castle Hotel LD3 8UH ☎Sennybridge(0874) 636354
A very pleasant inn situated centrally in the village, which is on the A40. The Castle Hotel provides very pretty and well equipped bedrooms. There is a good choice of food, a character bar and a small cosy lounge for residents.
10rm(3⇨2🚿5hc) (2fb) CTV in all bedrooms ® ✱ sB&B£25-£27.50 sB&B⇨🚿£32.50-£35 dB&B£36-£40 dB&B⇨🚿£45-£48 ✱ Bar Lunch £2.50-£10alc Dinner £5-£17.50alc LDO 9pm
🍽 30P
Credit Cards [1] [3] £

TREGARON Dyfed Map **03** SN65

FH QQ Mrs M J Cutter **Neuadd Las Farm Country Guest House** *(SN663620)* SY25 6LG ☎(0974) 298905 & 298965
This well maintained guesthouse is set in its own grounds a short distance from the Teifi River, with panoramic views of the Cambrian mountains. Situated just 1 mile from the town, off the Aberystwyth road, it offers bright and comfortable accommodation. Private fishing is available, and the Cors Caron Nature Reserve is nearby.
4rm(3⇨1hc) (2fb) CTV in 1 bedroom ® sB&B£15-£18 sB&B⇨£17-£20 dB&B£30-£36 dB&B⇨£34-£40 WB&B£105-£140 WBDi£154-£189 LDO 9pm
🍽 CTV 10P 🏠 ✓ 25 acres mixed £

TRENEAR (NEAR HELSTON) Cornwall & Isles of Scilly Map **02** SW63

FH Q Mrs G Lawrance **Longstone** *(SW662319)* TR13 0HG ☎Helston(0326) 572483
Mar-Nov
Well-appointed farmhouse set in beautiful countryside. Facilities include a playroom and sun lounge.

5hc (2fb) sB&B£12-£14 dB&B£24-£28 WB&B£84-£95 WBDi£115-£130 LDO 4pm
⑾ CTV 6P 62 acres dairy Ⓔ

TREVONE Cornwall & Isles of Scilly Map **02** SW87

GH QQ Coimbatore Hotel West View PL28 8RD
☎Padstow(0841) 520390
Set in its own gardens at the end of a cul-de-sac, this comfortable hotel is just 150 yards from Trevone beach.
10rm(7⌐3hc) (1fb) Ⓡ ✱ sB&B⌐£17.50 dB&B⌐£35 WB&B£122.50 WBDi£189 LDO 4.30pm
Lic CTV 4P 6🚘
Credit Cards [1] [3] Ⓔ

GH QQQ Green Waves Private Hotel PL28 8RD
☎Padstow(0841) 520114
Etr-Oct
In a quiet residential area, only a few minutes from two beaches, one of which has a natural bathing pool, this hotel has well-equipped, comfortable rooms, some with lovely coastal views. There is a small bar for residents, a very comfortable lounge and a billiard room. Mrs Chellew supervises the kitchen, and has a good reputation for her meals and homemade bread. A selective wine list complements her cooking skills.
20rm(15⌐5hc) (4fb) CTV in all bedrooms Ⓡ sB&B£18-£32 sB&B⌐£21-£32 dB&B£36-£64 dB&B⌐£42-£64 WBDi£141-£170 LDO 7pm
Lic ⑾ 17P nc4yrs half size snooker table
See advertisement under PADSTOW

TRINITY

See **JERSEY under CHANNEL ISLANDS**

TROON Cornwall & Isles of Scilly Map **02** SW63

GH Q Sea View TR14 9JH ☎Praze(0209) 831260
Closed Dec
7hc (3fb)⊬in all bedrooms Ⓡ dB&B£24-£32 WB&B£75-£90 WBDi£131-£146 LDO 6pm
⑾ CTV 8P ⩯(heated) Ⓔ

TROTTON West Sussex Map **04** SU82

FH QQ Mrs J R Field **Mill** *(SU832224)* GU31 5EL
☎Midhurst(0730) 813080
This 1930s farmhouse, situated on a working farm in a slightly elevated position, overlooks attractive open countryside. The house has a comfortable family atmosphere, with open fires and an elegant lounge. The bedrooms are cosy and well equipped.
2hc (1fb)⊬in all bedrooms CTV in all bedrooms Ⓡ
✗ (ex guide dogs) sB&B£15-£25 dB&B£26-£36 WB&B£91-£154
⑾ CTV 8P ℘(grass)15 acres sheep beef Ⓔ

TROUTBECK (NEAR KESWICK) Cumbria Map **11** NY32

FH QQ Mr & Mrs A F Bew **Lane Head** *(NY375271)*
CA11 0SY ☎Threlkeld(07687) 79220
Situated just off the A66 between Penrith and Keswick, this pleasant farmhouse dates back to 1752 and features original beams, with a good standard of accommodation and service.
7rm(3⇌1⌐3hc) (1fb) CTV in 6 bedrooms Ⓡ
✗ (ex guide dogs) sB&B£18-£20 sB&B⇌⌐£21-£23 dB&B£34-£36 dB&B⇌⌐£42-£44 WB&B£116-£150 WBDi£200-£235 LDO 10.30am
Lic ⑾ CTV 10P ∪ 110 acres non-working Ⓔ

TRURO Cornwall & Isles of Scilly Map **02** SW84

GH QQQ Lands Vue Lands Vue, Three Burrows TR4 8JA
☎(0872) 560242
Closed Xmas & New Year
An attractive country house in a peaceful setting, with 2 acres of gardens and fine views. The breakfast room enjoys these views, and

▶

there is a cosy lounge with an open fire. Bedrooms are compact and prettily decorated; one is in an annexe cottage. To find the house from the A30, take the A390, then the first left turn signposted to Tregevathen; stay on that road and Lands Vue is on the left – do not follow further signs to Tregevathen.

3rm(1🔥2hc) Annexe 1🔥 CTV in 1 bedroom ®
🇽 (ex guide dogs) ✻ sB&B£12-£15 dB&B£24-£30 dB&B🔥£28-£34 WB&B£84-£98 WBDi£136.50-£154 LDO 4pm
🍴 CTV 6P nc8 yrs ≙croquet ©

TUNBRIDGE WELLS (ROYAL) Kent Map **05** TQ53

SELECTED

GH ℚℚℚℚ **Danehurst House** 41 Lower Green Rd, Rusthall TN4 8TW ☎(0892) 27739
A charming house situated in a peaceful residential area of this historic town. Bedrooms are all individually decorated and furnished and offer a good standard of comfort and most modern facilities; there is a no-smoking policy throughout. Dinner is available by prior arrangement or alternatively a light supper can be arranged. Breakfast is ordered the previous evening and is served in the sunny conservatory.
6rm(4⇨🔥2hc) (1fb)⚤ in all bedrooms CTV in all bedrooms ® 🇽 sB&B£25-£39.50 sB&B⇨🔥£39.50 dB&B£36 dB&B⇨🔥£48 WB&B£175-£276.50 WBDi£307.86-£409.36 LDO 6pm
Lic 🍴 CTV 6P
Credit Cards 1 3

TWO BRIDGES Devon Map **02** SX67

GH ℚℚℚ **Cherrybrook Hotel** PL20 6SP
☎Tavistock(0822) 88260
Closed 20 Dec-4 Jan
With panoramic views across the moors, this secluded house has an attractive, comfortable bar lounge. A television is available in the bedrooms on request. There is a good choice of well cooked dishes and a fine selection of local cheeses.
7rm(6🔥1hc) (2fb) CTV in all bedrooms ® sB&B🔥£23-£25.50 dB&B🔥£46-£51 WB&B£162 WBDi£233 LDO 7.15pm
Lic 🍴 12P ©

TWYNHOLM Dumfries & Galloway *Kirkcudbrightshire* Map **11** NX65

SELECTED

GH ℚℚℚℚ **Fresh Fields** DG6 4PB ☎(05576) 221
Feb-Oct
Situated in this relatively unspoilt and undiscovered region of Scotland, which offers the visitor a wealth of varying interests and activities, this charming house stands within its own grounds. Spotlessly clean and tastefully decorated and furnished throughout, the accommodation has been thoughtfully equipped with many extras. Mouth-watering home-cooked dinners include home-made bread and ice creams, and guests are assured of a warm welcome.
5🔥 ⚤in 2 bedrooms ® sB&B🔥£35 dB&B🔥£70 (incl dinner) LDO 5.30pm
Lic 🍴 CTV 10P

TYNEMOUTH Tyne & Wear Map **12** NZ36

GH ℚℚℚ **Hope House** 47 Percy Gardens NE30 4HH
☎091-257 1989
An elegantly furnished and decorated Victorian end-of-terrace house overlooking the sea and sandy beach, yet only 30 minutes by car from Newcastle city centre. The bedrooms and public rooms are commodious with stylish antique furniture and fittings. Meals are served at one large table in the handsome dining room.

3rm(1⇨2🔥) (1fb) CTV in all bedrooms ® 🇽 (ex guide dogs) sB&B⇨🔥£32.50-£40 dB&B⇨🔥£37.50-£45 WB&B£131.25-£157.50 WBDi£186-£231 LDO 9pm
Lic 🍴 3P 3🍽 (£1.50 per night) ♨
Credit Cards 1 2 3 ©

TYWARDREATH Cornwall & Isles of Scilly Map **02** SX05

GH ℚℚℚ **Elmswood** Tehidy Rd PL24 2QD
☎(Par(072681) 4221
Home cooking and friendly service are provided by the proprietor of this comfortable guesthouse, which is an easy car ride from secluded Cornish beaches. Tastefully appointed public areas complement the bedrooms, some of which have en suite facilities.
7rm(1⇨3🔥3hc) (2fb) CTV in all bedrooms ®
🇽 (ex guide dogs) ✻ sB&B£15-£19.50 sB&B⇨🔥£20 dB&B£30-£34 dB&B⇨🔥£34-£40 WB&B£105-£119 WBDi£154-£168 LDO noon
Lic 🍴 CTV 8P

UCKFIELD East Sussex Map **05** TQ41

SELECTED

GH ℚℚℚℚ **Hooke Hall** 250 High St TN22 1EN
☎(0825) 761578 FAX (0825) 768025
Closed Xmas
An attractive Queen Anne house at the top of the High Street with an atmosphere of warmth and elegance. The 6 bedrooms are beautifully decorated and furnished with antiques, benefitting from the owner's skill as an interior designer. Each room, named after a famous mistress or lover, has its own individuality and charm and is equipped with many extras such as mini bars, trouser presses and ducks for the bath. There is a very smart panelled lounge and an elegant spacious restaurant which is available for residents by prior arrangement, and also open to the public on Friday and Saturday evenings.
6rm(5⇨1hc) CTV in all bedrooms ® 🇽 sB&Bfr£30 sB&B⇨🔥£35-£65 dB&Bfr£50 dB&B⇨£57.50-£95 LDO 8.30pm
Lic 🍴 6P nc10yrs
Credit Cards 1 3

SELECTED

GH ℚℚℚℚ **South Paddock** Maresfield Park TN22 2HA
☎(0825) 762335
Major and Mrs Allt and family provide a warm welcome for guests at their country home, peacefully situated on a private road in 3.5 acres of delightful, well tended gardens. Bedrooms are south-facing, comfortable, tastefully decorated and well equipped. There is an attractive lounge, and an antique-furnished dining room with one large table where guests enjoy a splendid cooked breakfast with home-made preserves.
2hc CTV in all bedrooms ® 🇽 (ex guide dogs) sB&B£23-£30 dB&B£40-£45 WB&Bfr£140
🍴 CTV 6P nc5yrs croquet ©

UFFCULME Devon Map **03** ST01

FH ℚℚ Mrs M D Farley *Houndaller* (*ST058138*) EX15 3ET
☎Craddock(0884) 40246
The Farley family's farmhouse stands on the A38, a few hundred yards from Junction 27 of the M5. Comfortable bedrooms are complemented by spacious public areas, and guests are treated as part of the family.
3hc (2fb) ® LDO 6pm
CTV 3P 1🍽 176 acres arable beef dairy sheep
Credit Cards 1 2 3 5

ULLINGSWICK Hereford & Worcester Map **03** SO54

SELECTED

GH ⓆⓆⓆⓆ **The Steppes** HR1 3JG
☎Hereford(0432) 820424
Closed 2 wks before Xmas & 2 wks after New Year
A charming small hotel peacefully situated in a quiet hamlet,
yet close to the A417. The house is delightful, beautifully
furnished and has a wealth of charm and character. The well
appointed dining room is the perfect setting in which to enjoy
the imaginative cuisine, which includes an appetising gourmet
menu which changes daily, as well as an à la carte menu. The
cellar bar has been converted from the former cider cellar and
dairy. Accommodation is well furnished, with an exceptional
range of facilities provided. There are rooms at present in both
the main house and courtyard cottages; work is underway to
introduce further courtyard rooms. Breakfast includes an
amazing number of unusual items, and is well worth
attending.
3🛏 Annexe 2⇨🛏 (1fb) CTV in all bedrooms ® ✳
dB&B⇨🛏£75-£92 (incl dinner) WBDifr£275
LDO 6.30pm
Lic ⊯ 8P nc10yrs
Credit Cards ① ③ ⓔ

UNDERBARROW Cumbria Map **07** SD49

FH ⓆⓆⓆ Mrs D M Swindlehurst **Tranthwaite Hall**
(SD469930) LA8 8HG ☎Crosthwaite(04488) 285
A delightfully furnished farmhouse situated at the end of a long
farm track in a lovely rural location. The old beamed house, which
dates back to the 16th century, is full of character. Good
accommodation and friendly service is provided.
2hc (1fb) ® ✖ (ex guide dogs) ✳ sB&B£15-£16 dB&B£28-£30
⊯ CTV 2P 200 acres dairy sheep ⓔ

UPTON PYNE Devon Map **03** SX99

🚐🍽 **FH** ⓆⓆ Mrs Y M Taverner **Pierce's** *(SX910977)*
EX5 5JA ☎Exeter(0392) 841252
Etr-Sep
Set in the centre of the village between Exeter and Crediton,
Pierce's Farm has two bedrooms which have wash basins and share
a bathroom. The attractive lounge and dining room are tastefully
furnished, and Mrs Taverner is a very friendly host.
2rm(1🛏1hc) (1fb) ® ✖ sB&Bfr£12 sB&B🛏fr£14 dB&Bfr£24
dB&B🛏fr£28 WB&B£75-£90
⊯ CTV 2P 300 acres mixed

UPTON UPON SEVERN Hereford & Worcester Map **03**
SO84

GH ⓆⓆⓆ **Pool House** WR8 0PA ☎(0684) 592151
Closed Xmas
Pool House is a lovely Queen Anne residence situated close to
Upton-upon-Severn. The gardens area delightful and lead down to
the River Severn. Accommodation is attractive, well furnished and
spacious.
9rm(3⇨3🛏3hc) (2fb)⥤in all bedrooms CTV in 1 bedroom ®
✖
Lic CTV 20P ✦
Credit Cards ① ③ ⓔ

USK Gwent Map **03** SO30

INN ⓆⓆ **Casey's Court** Chepstow Rd, Llangeview NP5 1EN
(2m E on unclass rd off B4235) ☎(02913) 2047
rs Mon
Annexe 3⇨🛏 CTV in all bedrooms ® ✖ (ex guide dogs)
sB&B⇨🛏fr£32 dB&B⇨🛏fr£45 Bar Lunch £2.50-£3.50
Dinner £6.50-£14.40 LDO 10pm
⊯ 33P ✦

UTTOXETER Staffordshire Map **07** SK03

GH ⓠⓠⓠ *Hillcrest* 3 Leighton Rd ST14 8BL ☎(0889) 564627
Closed Xmas Day
Perched on a hill on the edge of town, this friendly family-run hotel has well- equipped accommodation, some rooms having en suite facilities.
7⇔🟊 (6fb) CTV in all bedrooms ® ✹ (ex guide dogs) ✱
sB&B⇔🟊£25-£26 dB&B⇔🟊£34-£36 LDO 4pm
Lic ⁗ CTV 10P 2🏵
Credit Cards ①②③ⓔ

VENN OTTERY Devon Map **03** SY09

GH ⓠⓠⓠ *Venn Ottery Barton Country Hotel* EX11 1RZ
☎Ottery St Mary(040481) 2733
Situated in the centre of this charming village, this hotel, parts of which date back to 1530, retains some original features while providing modernised, well- equipped bedrooms.
16rm(5⇔🟊 5hc) (3fb) ® ✱ sB&B£19.50-£21.50
sB&B⇔🟊£23.50-£25.50 dB&B£35-£39 dB&B⇔🟊£43-£47
WBDi£175.50-£189 LDO 7.30pm
Lic ⁗ CTV 20P 🎱 large games room
Credit Cards ①③
See advertisement under OTTERY ST MARY

VENTNOR

See **WIGHT, ISLE OF**

VOWCHURCH Hereford & Worcester Map **03** SO33

SELECTED

GH ⓠⓠⓠⓠ *The Croft Country House* HR2 0QE
☎Golden Valley(0981) 550226
A delightful small country house hotel situated in the centre of the beautiful Golden Valley on the B4348, about 10 miles southwest of Hereford. Dating from the 18th century, the house has been furnished with comfort in mind. There is a charming lounge area overlooking the gardens with views of the Black Mountains, and the lovely grounds are a feature, with a summerhouse, grass tennis court and lily pond. The dining room includes a conservatory, and there is a choice of menus, with freshly prepared food and generous portions. Bedrooms are individually furnished with a mixture of modern and period furniture, and all have private bathrooms. Smoking is discouraged throughout the house.
4⇔🟊 Annexe 3⇔🟊 (1fb)⚊in all bedrooms CTV in all bedrooms ® ✹ (ex guide dogs) LDO 9pm
Lic ⁗ 15P 2🏵 nc10yrs croquet lawn
Credit Cards ①③

WADEBRIDGE Cornwall & Isles of Scilly Map **02** SW97

INN ⓠⓠⓠ *Swan Hotel* PL27 7DD (St Austell Brewery)
☎(0208) 812526
Situated in the town centre, the inn has recently been renovated and offers a spacious and comfortable bar with bar snacks in addition to the daily special dish. A choice of table d'hôte and à la carte menus are available. The well decorated bedrooms are of a very high standard with good quality furniture. All bedrooms are en suite and have modern facilities.
6⇔ (1fb) CTV in all bedrooms ® ✹ (ex guide dogs)
6P
Credit Cards ①②③

WANSFORD Cambridgeshire Map **04** TL09

INN ⓠ *Cross Keys* PE8 6JD ☎Stamford(0780) 782266
2hc Annexe 5hc (2fb) CTV in all bedrooms ® ✹ sB&B£20-£23
dB&B£36-£40 LDO 9.30pm
⁗ pool table

WARE Hertfordshire Map **05** TL31

INN ⓠⓠⓠ *Feathers Hotel* Wadesmill SG1 2TN
☎(0920) 462606
This coaching inn is situated on the A10 just outside Ware. An adjacent modern accommodation block offers attractive cottage style rooms with an excellent array of modern facilities. There is a breakfast room within the accommodation block in addition to the inn's dining room which provides a popular carvery.
Annexe 22rm(11⇔4🟊7hc) CTV in all bedrooms ®
✹ (ex guide dogs) LDO 10.30pm
⁗ 100P
Credit Cards ①②③⑤

WAREHAM Dorset Map **03** SY98

FH ⓠⓠ L S Barnes *Luckford Wood* (SY873865) East Stoke
BH20 6AW ☎Bindon Abbey(0929) 463098
5rm(1🟊2hc) (3fb)⚊in 1 bedroom CTV in 4 bedrooms TV in 1
bedroom ® ✱ sB&B£16-£20 dB&Bfr£30 dB&B🟊fr£32
WB&Bfr£84
⁗ CTV 5P 167 acres dairy ⓔ

SELECTED

FH ⓠⓠⓠⓠ Mrs J Barnes *Redcliffe* (SY932866)
BH20 5BE ☎(0929) 552225
Closed Xmas
This well established, small modern farmhouse has wonderful views over the River Frome to Wareham and the yacht club. Three very comfortable bedrooms share a modern bathroom, and are freshly decorated and well maintained. There is a communal table in the dining room, although breakfast can also be served on the patio. A sun lounge overlooking the garden complements a family lounge with TV. Two of the bedrooms have a sunny balcony. To find the farm from the centre of Wareham, take the B3075 towards Stoborough; after crossing the river bridge take 3 successive left turns.
4rm(1⇔1🟊2hc) ⚊in 3 bedrooms ✹ (ex guide dogs)
⁗ CTV 4P 250 acres dairy mixed ⓔ

WARREN STREET (NEAR LENHAM) Kent Map **05** TQ95

INN ⓠⓠⓠ *Harrow* ME17 2ED ☎Maidstone(0622) 858727
Enjoying a good local reputation for its homemade food in the well-appointed restaurant and spacious bar, this establishment also has very well-equipped accommodation, which is furnished in the modern style.
7rm(2⇔4🟊1hc) (1fb) ® ✹ LDO 10pm
⁗ CTV 40P
Credit Cards ①③

WARRINGTON Cheshire Map **07** SJ68

GH ⓠⓠⓠ *Kenilworth Hotel* 2 Victoria Rd, Grappenhall
WA4 2EN ☎(0925) 62323 due to change to 262323
A deceptively large hotel on the A50, close to the swing bridge. The bedrooms are warm and nicely decorated, with most of the facilities expected at a classified hotel.
17rm(16🟊1hc) (2fb) CTV in all bedrooms ® ✱ sB&B🟊£21-
£30 dB&B🟊£36-£42
⁗ CTV 18P
Credit Cards ①③

WARSASH Hampshire Map **04** SU40

GH ⓠⓠⓠ *Solent View Private Hotel* 33-35 Newtown Rd
SO3 6FY ☎Locks Heath(0489) 572300
Ideally situated for leisure and commercial guests, a friendly and relaxed atmosphere is generated by the owners Anne and Roy Mills. Solent View is situated in the village centre, within short walking distance of the River Hamble. The bedrooms are comfortable and well equipped. A lounge is available for guests,

*and good freshly cooked breakfasts are served in the dining room/
bar.*
6rm(1⇨5🛏) CTV in all bedrooms ® ✳ sB&B⇨🛏fr£33
dB&B⇨🛏fr£46 WB&Bfr£230 WBDifr£266 LDO noon
Lic ⁇ CTV 8P
Credit Cards 1 3 ©

WARWICK Warwickshire Map 04 SP26

See also Lighthorne
GH QQ *Austin House* 96 Emscote Rd CV34 5QJ
☎(0926) 493583
*Derick and Daphne Edwards offer a modest but well-maintained
establishment. Most bedrooms have en suite showers and all have
colour televisions. The comfortable ground floor lounge also offers
the use of a large colour television.*
6rm(4🛏2hc) (3fb) CTV in all bedrooms ®
⁇ CTV 8P 2🏕

GH QQ *Avon* 7 Emscote Rd CV34 4PH ☎(0926) 491367
*A large Victorian terraced house half a mile from the town centre
on the Leamington road, offering clean and simply appointed bed
and breakfast accommodation close to amenities and with the
advantage of a good car park.*
7hc Annexe 3hc (4fb) ® 🐾 sB&B£13 dB&B£25-£26
WB&B£126 WBDi£168 LDO 8pm
Lic ⁇ CTV 6P 1🏕
Credit Cards 3 ©

GH QQ *Cambridge Villa Private Hotel* 20A Emscote Rd
CV34 4PL ☎(0926) 491169
*A double-fronted Victorian terraced house, 1/2 mile east of the
town centre on the Leamington Spa road, offering simply appointed
bedrooms and a bright basement dining room where the
enthusiastic Italian owner offers specialities from her homeland.*
16rm(4🛏12hc) (2fb) CTV in all bedrooms ® LDO 10pm
Lic ⁇ CTV 28P ⚿
Credit Cards 1 3

GH QQQ *The Old Rectory* Vicarage Ln, Sherbourne
CV35 8AB (off A46 2m SW)
☎Barford (Warwicks)(0926) 624562
Closed 24-27 Dec
*Tastefully restored house offering very comfortable
accommodation and home cooked food.*
7rm(1⇨6🛏) Annexe 7⇨🛏 (2fb) CTV in all bedrooms ® ✳
sB&B⇨🛏£27.50-£35 dB&B⇨🛏£39.50-£47 LDO 3pm
Lic ⁇ CTV 10P
Credit Cards 1 2 3 ©

See advertisement on page 365

INN QQ *Tudor House* West St CV34 6AW ☎(0926) 495447
FAX (0926) 492948
*This scheduled Tudor house, still retaining much wattle and daub
and timbers, was built in 1472. The bedrooms are of a cosy nature,
being equipped with good en suite facilities. Its attractive public
rooms are complemented by traditional wholesome food.*
11rm(8⇨🛏3hc) (1fb) CTV in all bedrooms ®
🐾 (ex guide dogs) sB&B£24-£25 sB&B⇨🛏£38-£42
dB&B⇨🛏£54-£60 Lunch £10-£15alc High tea £1.95-£4alc
Dinner £10-£20alc LDO 10.30pm
⁇ 5P ⚿
Credit Cards 1 2 3 5

See advertisement on page 364

WASHFORD Somerset Map 03 ST04

INN QQQ *Washford* TA23 0PP ☎(0984) 40256
*The Quantock and Brendon Hills are easily reached from this
roadside inn which is just 6 miles from Minehead. The tastefully
modernised bedrooms offer good facilities and a bar menu is
available in the busy, attractive public bar.* ▶

8⚫ CTV in all bedrooms ⓡ ✻ (ex guide dogs) ✱ dB&Bⁿ£38-£42 ✱ Bar Lunch £3.25-£4.75alc Dinner £4.25-£10.25alc LDO 9pm
🍴 30P nc12yrs
Credit Cards ① ② ③ ⑤ ⓔ

WATERHOUSES Staffordshire Map **07** SK05

GH Ⓠ Ⓠ **Croft House Farm** Waterfall ST10 3HZ (1m NW unclass) ☎(0538) 308553
The compact, but well-equipped, cheerful bedrooms enhance the warm and friendly atmosphere at this stone-built house, which lies, surrounded by farmland, in the moorland village of Waterfall.
6hc (2fb) CTV in all bedrooms ⓡ ✻ ✱ dB&Bfr£34 LDO 8pm
Lic 🍴 CTV 15P

INN Ⓠ **Ye Olde Crown** ST10 3HL ☎(0538) 308204
Dating back in parts to the 17th century, this popular village inn is easily accessable alongside the A523. Bedrooms are modern and there are two characterful bars which are popular with locals.
7rm(5⇨ⁿ2hc) (1fb) CTV in all bedrooms ⓡ
✻ (ex guide dogs) sB&B£14 sB&B⇨ⁿ£21.50 dB&B£33 dB&B⇨ⁿ£33 Lunch £5-£14alc Dinner £5-£14alc LDO 10pm
🍴 50P
See advertisement under ASHBOURNE

WATERROW Somerset Map **03** ST02

INN Ⓠ Ⓠ **The Rock** TA4 2AX ☎Wiveliscombe(0984) 23293
A character inn with low beams and open fireplaces offering good value, clean and tidy accommodation. The proprietor has gradually improved the establishment over the last 5 years, and while bedrooms vary in size and comfort, most now have en suite facilities and modern equipment. There is a small dining area, set away from the public bar, and the food is home- prepared, simple and wholesome.
6rm(4⇨ⁿ1hc) (1fb) CTV in all bedrooms ✱ sB&B£19-£21 sB&B⇨ⁿ£19-£21 dB&B£38-£42 dB&B⇨ⁿ£38-£42 ✱ Lunch £3.95-£10alc Dinner £3.95-£10alc LDO 10pm
🍴 CTV 20P
Credit Cards ① ③
See advertisement under TAUNTON

WEETON Lancashire Map **07** SD33

FH Ⓠ Mr & Mrs J Colligan **High Moor** *(SD388365)* PR4 3JJ
☎Blackpool(0253) 836273
Closed Xmas & New Year
A comfortable and hospitable farmhouse, situated on the B5260, near the Military Camp.
2rm (1fb) CTV in all bedrooms ⓡ ✻ ✱ dB&Bfr£24
🍴 CTV 10P 7 acres non-working

WELCOMBE Devon Map **02** SS21

FH Ⓠ Ⓠ Ⓠ Mrs P Tunnicliffe **Henaford Manor** *(SS249187)*
EX39 6HE ☎Morwenstow(028883) 252
Built in the 13th century, this farmhouse has an elegant dining room and comfortable lounge. One of the nicely appointed bedrooms has en suite facilities and all are equipped to modern standards. There is also a self- catering cottage next to the house.
3rm(1⇨2hc) (1fb) CTV in all bedrooms ⓡ ✻ ✱ dB&Bfr£30 dB&B⇨fr£32 LDO 6pm
🍴 CTV 6P 226 acres dairy mixed
See advertisement under BIDEFORD

'Selected' establishments, which have the highest quality award, are highlighted by a tinted panel. For a full list of these establishments, consult the Contents page.

WELLINGBOROUGH Northamptonshire Map **04** SP86

GH Ⓠ Ⓠ Ⓠ **Oak House Private Hotel** 8-11 Broad Green
NN8 4LE ☎(0933) 271133
Closed Xmas
A well established private hotel standing on the former village green, close to the town centre. Bedrooms can be compact, but are well equipped and most have en suite showers. Home-cooked meals are served in the split-level dining room.
16rm(15ⁿ1hc) (1fb) CTV in all bedrooms ⓡ ✱ sB&Bⁿ£28-£32 dB&B£38 dB&Bⁿ£42 WB&B£133-£224 WBDi£192.50-£283.50 LDO noon
Lic 🍴 CTV 12P
Credit Cards ① ③ ⓔ

See advertisement on page 367

WELLINGTON Shropshire

See **Telford**

WELLINGTON Somerset Map **03** ST12🌿

GH Ⓠ **Blue Mantle Hotel** 2 Mantle St TA21 8AW
☎(0823) 662000
This small, bow-fronted privately owned guesthouse was originally 4 Elizabethan cottages and is situated just off the town centre. The accommodation is comfortable and well maintained : bedrooms are simple, each with TV and tea-making facilities. Traditional English cuisine is served in the dining room ; smoking is not permitted here at breakfast. There is a plunge pool available for guests in the neat back garden.
8hc (1fb) CTV in all bedrooms ⓡ sB&B£21 dB&B£35 LDO 8.30pm
Lic 🍴 CTV ✗ nc3yrs ⌿
Credit Cards ① ② ③ ⓔ

Tudor House Inn

West Street, Warwick
Telephone: (0926) 495447
Fax: (0926) 492948

A privately owned building of great charm and character. Dating from 1472 it still has a wealth of timbers many used in old warships. Situated almost opposite Warwick Castle and convenient for Stratford, National Exhibition Centre, National Agricultural Centre, M1, M5, M6 and M40 motorways. Some rooms have private bathroom and all have central heating, shaving point, radio and television. A warm welcome, comfortable accommodation and good food awaits the guests.

REDLANDS FARM

Banbury Road, Lighthorne,
Nr Warwick
Telephone:
Leamington Spa (0926) 651241

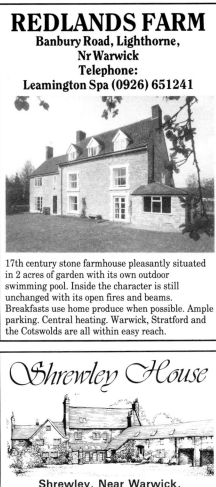

17th century stone farmhouse pleasantly situated in 2 acres of garden with its own outdoor swimming pool. Inside the character is still unchanged with its open fires and beams. Breakfasts use home produce when possible. Ample parking. Central heating. Warwick, Stratford and the Cotswolds are all within easy reach.

THE OLD RECTORY

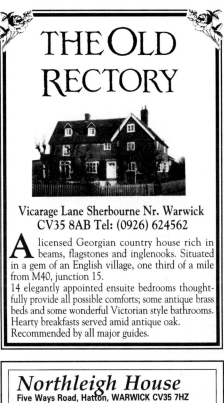

Vicarage Lane Sherbourne Nr. Warwick CV35 8AB Tel: (0926) 624562

A licensed Georgian country house rich in beams, flagstones and inglenooks. Situated in a gem of an English village, one third of a mile from M40, junction 15.
14 elegantly appointed ensuite bedrooms thoughtfully provide all possible comforts; some antique brass beds and some wonderful Victorian style bathrooms. Hearty breakfasts served amid antique oak. Recommended by all major guides.

Shrewley House

Shrewley, Near Warwick,
Warwickshire CV35 7AT
Telephone: (092684) 2549

Surrounded by the beautiful Warwickshire countryside, Shrewley House is a grade II listed Georgian farmhouse and home, part of which dates back to the 17th century. The elegant drawing room opens onto the 1½ acres of lawned gardens, making an ideal setting for small meetings or conferences. The delightfully furnished bedrooms, some with king size four poster beds, all have en suite bathroom and shower, direct dial telephone, colour television, clock radio, hair dryer and tea/coffee making facilities, fresh fruit and complimentary bar.

AA Best Newcomer Award 1990-91
English Tourist Board – HIGHLY COMMENDED

See gazetteer entry under Shrewley

Northleigh House

Five Ways Road, Hatton, WARWICK CV35 7HZ
Telephone Warwick (0926) 484203

The personal welcome, the exceptionally beautiful rooms each with co-ordinated furnishings, linen and toiletries, en-suite bath or shower rooms, remote control TV, easy chairs, writing table, tea/coffee/chocolate making facilities and many thoughtful extras make this small exclusive guest house a haven of peace and comfort.

Northleigh House is set in the heart of the countryside yet near some excellent pubs and restaurants and handy for Midlands historic towns, villages and exhibition centres.

AA selected since 1987

See gazetteer under Hatton

For brochures please call Sylvia Fenwick (proprietor)

FH QQQ Mrs Howe **Gamlins** *(ST082194)* Greenham
TA21 0LZ ☎Greenham(0823) 672596
Closed Xmas
A well presented farmhouse set on the Somerset/Devon borders
offering good value for money. Facilities include a heated covered
swimming pool, rough shooting and coarse fishing available on site,
and there are three self-catering cottages. There is a selection of
local pub and restaurant menus on view in the lounge for dinner.
4rm(1⇨3🐾3hc) (1fb) CTV in 2 bedrooms TV in 2 bedrooms ®
🐾 ✱ sB&B£15-£20 dB&B£26-£32 dB&B⇨🐾£27-£32
WB&B£87.50-£98
🍴 CTV 6P nc2yrs ⊇(heated) ✔ 116 acres poultry

FH QQQ Mrs N Ash **Pinksmoor Mill House** *(ST109198)*
Pinksmoor TA21 0HO (3m W off A38 at Beam Bridge Hotel)
☎Greenham(0823) 672361
Closed 23-29 Dec
Part 13th-century property, 3 miles west of Wellington, with neat
comfortable accommodation. Original mill house on site.
3rm(2⇨🐾1hc) (1fb)⊁in all bedrooms CTV in all bedrooms ®
sB&Bfr£18.50 sB&B⇨🐾fr£18.50 dB&Bfr£32 dB&B⇨🐾fr£32
WB&B£105-£122.50 WBDi£178-£195.50 LDO 4pm
🍴 CTV 6P 98 acres dairy sheep Ⓔ

WELLS Somerset Map 03 ST54

GH QQQ **Bekynton House** 7 St Thomas St BA5 2UU
☎(0749) 672222
Closed Xmas & New Year
Comfortable, well appointed accommodation is provided at this
well-maintained guesthouse which stands on the fringe of the city
centre.
9rm(3🐾6hc) (2fb)⊁in all bedrooms CTV in all bedrooms ® 🐾
✱ sB&B£19-£23 dB&B£34-£37 dB&B🐾£37-£43
🍴 6P nc5yrs
Credit Cards ①③ Ⓔ

SELECTED

GH QQQQ **Coach House** Stoberry Park BA5 3AA
☎(0749) 676535
Closed 24-31Dec
This converted coach house stands in 6 acres of parkland and
has spectacular views of the city across to Glastonbury Tor.
The bedrooms are spacious and comfortable, each with private
bathrooms. The vast open lounge has various seating areas
and an open-plan staircase. Bed and breakfast only are
provided, but the 'kind' breakfast includes local bacon and
sausages from free range pigs. Smoking is not permitted in
bedrooms.
3⇨ ⊁in all bedrooms ® ✱ dB&B⇨£34-£36 WB&B£112
Lic 🍴 CTV 6P nc3yrs Ⓔ

GH QQ **Tor** 20 Tor St BA5 2US ☎(0749) 672322
This charming 17th-century house, close to the cathedral, is being
thoughtfully restored to provide comfortable accommodation and
yet maintain the house's character. The owners offer a warm
welcome to their guests.
7rm(2🐾5hc) (2fb) CTV in all bedrooms ® ✱ sB&B£16-£25
dB&B£32-£34 dB&B🐾£38-£44 WB&B£210-£225 LDO 10am
🍴 CTV 11P 1🐾 Ⓔ

FH QQ Mrs P Higgs **Home** *(ST538442)* Stoppers Ln, Upper
Coxley BA5 1QS (2m SW off A39) ☎(0749) 672434
Closed 2wks Xmas
Situated off the A39, 1.5 miles south west from the city, this
farmhouse offers a friendly welcome from the proprietor, Mrs
Higgs. The comfortable, attractively decorated bedrooms are
adequately equipped and furnished.

7hc (1fb) ® ✱ sB&B£13.50-£15.50 dB&B£27-£31
WB&B£94.50-£108.50
Lic 🍴 CTV 12P 15 acres pigs

FH QQQ Mr & Mrs Gnoyke **Littlewell** *(ST536445)* Coxley
BA5 1QP (2 miles SW on A39) ☎(0749) 677914
Closed Jan
4rm(1⇨3🐾) CTV in 5 bedrooms ® ✖ (ex guide dogs)
sB&B⇨🐾£19.50-£22 dB&B⇨🐾£29-£38
Lic 🍴 4P 4🐾 nc10yrs 2 acres non-working

FH QQQ Mrs J Gould **Manor** *(ST546474)* Old Bristol Rd,
Upper Milton BA5 3AH (1m W A39 towards Bristol, 200 yds
beyond rdbt) ☎(0749) 673394
Closed Xmas
Part of a large beef farm, this charming house offers traditional
informal hospitality and a relaxing atmosphere together with
comfortable accommodation.
3hc (1fb) ® ✖ (ex guide dogs) ✱ sB&B£15-£16 dB&B£25-£27
WB&B£85-£90
🍴 CTV 6P 130 acres beef

FH QQQ Mr & Mrs Frost **Southway** *(ST516423)* Polsham
BA5 1RW (3m SW off A39) ☎(0749) 673396
A warm and cosy atmosphere is found at this charming Georgian
farmhouse. The bedrooms are attractively decorated and well
furnished, and the public rooms are comfortably appointed.
Further upgrading is in progress.
3hc ✖ (ex guide dogs)
🍴 CTV 5P 170 acres dairy

See the regional maps of popular holiday
areas at the back of the book.

LITTLEWELL FARM
Coxley, Wells, Somerset BA5 1QP
Telephone: (0749) 677914

Littlewell Farm is about 200 years old
and enjoys extensive rural views of
beautiful countryside. The Farm is a small
guesthouse with comfortable and attractive
accommodation with all bedrooms having
their own bathroom or shower, television,
tea & coffee making facilities. The house
is centrally heated and offers excellent
cuisine for dinner. Winter bargain breaks
from Mid-November to March.
German and Spanish spoken.
BTA COMMENDED.

HOME FARM

**Wells, Somerset Farmhouse accommodation
Details and terms, Mrs Pat Higgs,
Home Farm, Stoppers Lane, Coxley, Wells,
Somerset BA5 1QS.
Tel: Wells 0749 72434**

Pat Higgs offers a relaxed holiday, long or short stay, in a peaceful spot just 1½ miles from the City of Wells, slightly off the A39, with extensive views of the Mendip Hills.

Somerset offers a varied type of holiday, with the popular city of Bath only ½ hour ride, there are National Trust properties, Cheddar Gorge, The Fleet Air Arm Museum, Wookey Hole Caves, also many other attractions.

We have all facilities including a shower. Bed & Breakfast only.

Many good restaurants and pubs within easy reach.

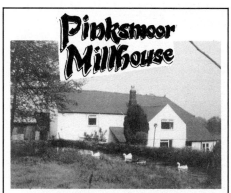

**PINKSMOOR, WELLINGTON,
SOMERSET TA21 0HD**

Take a stroll along the old millstream, the haunt of kingfisher, snipe and mallard; go badger watching, or just wander where you please around this family run dairy farm. Period millhouse, cosy lounges with log fire, spacious ensuite bedrooms. Farmhouse cooking and personal service.
Just 10 minutes junc 26—M5.

Mrs Nancy K. M. Ash
Tel: 0823 672361

COMMENDED
English Tourist Board

Tor Guest House

**20 Tor Street, Wells, Somerset BA5 2US
Telephone: Wells (0749) 72322**

Delightful 17th century family run guest house set in attractive grounds overlooking Wells Cathedral/Bishop's Palace and borders National Trust woodland. Comfortable, centrally heated and tastefully furnished rooms (some en suite) enjoying fine views and equipped with beverage making facilities. Excellent home cooking including vegetarian cuisine. 3 minute walk alongside Palace moat to town centre. Large car park. Open all year. Ideal centre for touring Somerset with Bath and Bristol 30 minutes by car.
Resident Proprietors: Adrian and Letitia Trowell

Oak House Private Hotel

A small licensed private hotel

ALL BEDROOMS EN-SUITE
with Colour TV Radio/Alarm
Tea making facilities Double glazed
throughout Centrally heated
Comfortable residents lounge Car park
**8/11 BROAD GREEN, WELLINGBOROUGH
NORTHANTS NN8 4LE
Tel: Wellingborough (0933) 271133**
Registered with the English Tourist Board

WELLS-NEXT-THE-SEA Norfolk Map **09** TF94

GH QQQ Scarborough House Clubbs Ln NR23 1DP ☎Fakenham(0328) 710309 & 711661

This is a popular guesthouse, quietly situated a few minutes from the quay. A Victorian detached house, it is furnished comfortably and attractively with antiques and collectables of the era. There are some en suite facilities, and a delightful lounge and carvery restaurant. There are immediate plans to extend the accommodation.

10rm(1⇌5⛉4hc) (2fb) CTV in all bedrooms ® sB&B£23-£26 sB&B⇌⛉£23-£26 dB&B£36 dB&B⇌⛉£42 WB&B£115-£136 WBDi£190-£211 LDO 8.30pm

Lic 🍽 CTV 10P nc7yrs

Credit Cards 1 2 3 £

WELSHPOOL Powys Map **07** SJ20

FH QQQ Mrs E Jones **Gungrog House** *(SJ235089)* Rhallt SY21 9HS (1m NE off A458) ☎(0938) 553381

Apr-Oct

Providing good quality bedrooms and public rooms this guesthouse has superb views from its elevated position over the Severn Valley. It is reached via a country lane opposite to the junction of the A483 and A458.

3rm(2⛉1hc) ✗ ✱ sB&B£16 sB&B⛉£16 dB&B⛉£30 WB&B£100 WBDi£150 LDO 5pm

🍽 CTV 6P 21 acres mixed

FH QQ Mr & Mrs M C Payne **Heath Cottage** *(SJ239023)* Kingswood, Forden SY21 8LX (3m S off A490) ☎Forden(093876) 453

Etr-Oct

This former country pub, just yards away from Offa's Dyke, is run by the friendly Payne family. There is a comfortable lounge available for guests, and the bedrooms have recently been improved with all rooms now having en suite facilities.

3⇌⛉ (1fb) ® ✗ sB&B⇌⛉£15 dB&B⇌⛉£30 WB&B£100 WBDi£150

🍽 CTV 4P 6 acres poultry sheep £

FH QQQ Mr & Mrs G Jones **Lower Trelydan** *(SJ225105)* Lower Trelydan, Guilsfield SY21 9PH (3.5m N off A490) ☎(0938) 553105

3rm(2⇌1⛉) (1fb) ✱ sB&B⇌⛉£16 dB&B⇌⛉£30 WB&B£95 WBDi£145 LDO 5pm

Lic CTV P 108 acres beef dairy sheep

FH QQQ Mr & Mrs W Jones **Moat** *(SJ214042)* SY21 8SE ☎(0938) 553179

Apr-Oct rs Feb, Mar & Nov

One mile south of Welshpool, this working farm dates back to the 16th century and provides comfortable accommodation. The Jones family are welcoming and a tennis court and pool table are available. The River Severn runs through the grounds.

3⇌⛉ (1fb)⚟in all bedrooms CTV in all bedrooms ® ✗ ✱ dB&B⇌⛉£48-£52 WB&B£112-£119 WBDi£168-£182 LDO 2pm

🍽 3P 🎾(grass)pool table 260 acres dairy £

FH QQQ Mrs F Emberton **Tynllwyn** *(SJ215085)* SY21 9BW ☎(0938) 553175

Providing good comfortable bedrooms and spacious lounge this large eighteenth century farmhouse is situated off the A490 North of Welshpool with good rural views.

6hc (3fb) CTV in all bedrooms ® ✗ sB&Bfr£12.50 dB&Bfr£25 WB&Bfr£84 WBDifr£120 LDO 6.30pm

Lic 🍽 CTV 20P 150 acres mixed £

This guide is updated annually – make sure you use an up-to-date edition.

WEM Shropshire Map **07** SJ53

FH QQQ Mrs A P Ashton **Soulton Hall** *(SJ543303)* Soulton SY4 5RS ☎(0939) 32786

Steeped in history and standing on a site mentioned in the Domesday Book, this 16th-century manor house features a pillared courtyard, walled garden and 50 acres of woodland together with 2 miles of fishing. All bedrooms are spacious and comfortable with interesting features.

3rm(2⇌1hc) Annexe 2⇌⛉ (2fb)⚟in 1 bedroom CTV in all bedrooms ® ✱ sB&B£24.25-£30.25 sB&B⇌⛉£28.50-£34.50 dB&B£47.50 dB&B⇌⛉£56 WB&B£150-£176.50 WBDi£235-£268 LDO 9pm

Lic 🍽 10P 2🚗 ⛳ ✓ U 560 acres mixed

Credit Cards 1 3 £

See advertisement under SHREWSBURY

WEST BAGBOROUGH Somerset Map **03** ST13

GH QQQ *Higher House* TA4 3EF ☎Bishops Lydeard(0823) 432996

Closed Xmas rs Dec-Mar

Nestling on the slopes of the Quantocks, this 17th-century farmhouse has been converted by William and Jo Beaumont to offer 6 attractive bedrooms with good facilities. A three quarter sized snooker table is provided, as well as an outdoor pool. A set meal is served around a large antique table.

6rm(3⇌1⛉2hc) (1fb) CTV in all bedrooms ® LDO 4.30pm

Lic 🍽 CTV 13P ⛱(heated) three quarter snooker table

Credit Cards 1 3

INN QQQ *Rising Sun* TA 4 3EF ☎Bishops Lydeard(0823) 432575 Telex no 94013345

In a peaceful village at the foot of the Quantocks, this inn is within easy reach of motorway routes. The tasteful bedrooms are en suite and provide modern amenities. There is also a bar lounge with log fire and a relaxed atmosphere.

Annexe 4⛉ (1fb) CTV in all bedrooms ® ✗ LDO 9.30pm

🍽 6P

WEST BUCKLAND Devon Map **03** SS63

FH QQ Mrs J Payne **Huxtable** *(SS666308)* EX32 0SR ☎Filleigh(05986) 254

Closed 25 Dec

An unmade road opposite the school leads to a peaceful valley, the setting for this medieval long house. The living areas are full of character with exposed beams, flagstone floors and inglenook fireplaces. Bedrooms are brightly decorated and some are in recently converted barn annexes. Guests share a large table in the wood-panelled dining room, and Mrs Payne extends a warm welcome to visitors to her delightful home.

3hc Annexe 3⇌⛉ (2fb) CTV in 2 bedrooms ® ✗ (ex guide dogs) ✱ sB&B⇌⛉£17-£22 dB&B⇌⛉£32-£38 LDO 6pm

🍽 CTV 8P ⛳ sauna games room 80 acres mixed sheep

Credit Cards 2 £

WEST CHILTINGTON West Sussex Map **04** TQ01

FH QQQ Mrs A M Steele ***New House*** *(TQ091185)* Broadford Bridge Rd RH20 2LA ☎(0798) 812215

Closed Dec

A charming character farmhouse which dates back to 1450. The bedrooms are tastefully furnished in the traditional style and offer a good standard of comfort. Log fires burn in the cosy sitting room and in the dining room where breakfast is served at a communal table. The welcoming atmosphere is completed by the friendly owners, Mr and Mrs Steele.

3⇌⛉ (2fb) CTV in all bedrooms ® ✗

CTV 4P 2🚗 nc9yrs 50 acres mixed

WESTCLIFF-ON-SEA Essex

See **Southend-on-Sea**

WEST COKER Somerset Map **03** ST51

GH Q *The Old Rectory* Church St BA22 9BD (off A30)
☎(093586) 2048
Built of Ham stone in the 17th century, this house is in a peaceful setting and has a warm atmosphere. The modestly appointed accommodation is spacious and has interesting furnishings.
4hc (4fb) CTV in 2 bedrooms TV in 1 bedroom ® ⵗ
CTV 6P

WEST DOWN Devon Map **02** SS54

SELECTED

GH Q Q Q Q The Long House EX34 8NF
☎Ilfracombe(0271) 863242
mid Mar-mid Nov
This former village post office and forge is now a cottage-style hotel and tea shop, offering a high standard of accommodation, cuisine and hospitality in a peaceful location, 10 miles from Barnstaple. The four bedrooms have been individually decorated and furnished with co-ordinating colour schemes and many thoughtful extras. The lounge is full of character, featuring an inglenook fireplace and bread oven; drinks are served in an adjacent, snug lounge. The dining room doubles as the tea room during the day, and a range of home-made cakes and scones are served. The dinner menu offers unusual dishes and delicious puddings.
4rm(3⤻1↑) ⵗin 1 bedroom CTV in all bedrooms ®
ⵗ (ex guide dogs) dB&B⤻↑£47 (incl dinner)
WBDi£227.50 LDO 8pm
Lic ⵉⵉ CTV ⚬⚬
Credit Cards ① ⓔ

GH Q Q Sunnymeade Country House Hotel Dean Cross
EX34 8NT (1m W on A361) ☎Ilfracombe(0271) 863668
Feb-Nov
A family-run detached property within easy reach of Ilfracombe and Woolacombe. Bedrooms are simply appointed, all with colour television and most with en suite facilities, and the public areas have a 'lived-in' feel about them.
10rm(8↑2hc) (2fb) CTV in all bedrooms ® ⵗ sB&Bfr£15
dB&Bfr£30 dB&B↑£37 WBDi£147-£158 LDO 6pm
Lic ⵉⵉ CTV 14P
Credit Cards ① ② ③ ⑤

WEST GRAFTON Wiltshire Map **04** SU26

FH Q Q Q Mrs A Orssich **Mayfield** *(SU246598)* SN8 3BY
☎Marlborough(0672) 810339
Closed Xmas & 2 wks July
3rm ⵗin all bedrooms ⵗ sB&B£22-£25 dB&B£35-£38
ⵉⵉ CTV 6P ⚬⚬ ⚫(heated) 8 acres

WEST LINTON Borders *Peebleshire* Map **11** NT15

SELECTED

GH Q Q Q Q Medwyn House Medwyn Rd EH46 7HB
☎(0968) 60542 & 60816 FAX (0968) 60005
Closed mid Jan-mid Mar
An impressive country house in 30 acres of gardens and woodlands adjoining the golf course. Guests are welcomed into a fine panelled reception room where an open fire burns in winter. Bedrooms and bathrooms are very spacious and attractively decorated and fitted, with many thoughtful extras provided. Anne and Mike Waterston are charming hosts who

clearly enjoy caring for their guests. It is Anne who produces the interesting, freshly cooked dinners.
3⤻ ⵗin all bedrooms TV available ® ✳ dB&B⤻£60-£68
LDO noon
ⵉⵉ CTV 12P 2⚫ nc12yrs sauna ⓔ

WESTON-SUPER-MARE Avon Map **03** ST36

See **Town Plan Section**

GH Q Q *Almond Lodge* 42 Clevedon Rd BS23 1DQ
☎(0934) 625113
In a road opposite the Tropicana Centre, this Edwardian house offers good accommodation with simply appointed, well-equipped rooms. Kathleen and Dennis Hall provide friendly service.
4hc (2fb) CTV in all bedrooms ® ⵗ
CTV

GH Q Q Q *Ashcombe Court* 17 Milton Rd BS23 2SH
☎(0934) 625104
A short drive from the seafront and town, this attractive property offers good accommodation with some thoughtful extras. Guests will find a hospitable atmosphere here.
6rm(1⤻5↑) (1fb)ⵗin all bedrooms CTV in all bedrooms ®
ⵗ (ex guide dogs) ✳ sB&B⤻↑£17 dB&B⤻↑£34-£36
WB&B£110 WBDi£131-£139 LDO 6pm
ⵉⵉ CTV 9P
Credit Cards ② ⓔ

GH Q Q *Baymead Hotel* Longton Grove Rd BS23 1LS
☎(0934) 622951
Closed Jan & Feb
This large, family-run hotel is close to the amenities and has a popular bar and upgraded bedrooms with modern facilities.
33rm(28⤻↑3hc) (3fb) CTV in all bedrooms ® sB&B£15-£18
sB&B⤻↑£18-£24 dB&B⤻↑£35-£40 WB&B£100-£140
WBDi£125-£170 LDO 6.30pm
Lic lift ⵉⵉ CTV 4P

GH Q Q *Kara* Hewish BS24 6RQ (1m E of junc 21 M5 on
A370) ☎Yatton(0934) 834442
Alongside the A370 some 3 miles from the resort, on the Bristol side of its junction with the M5 (junction 21), this is a family-run guesthouse set in pleasant secluded lawns and gardens. Bedrooms are bright and cosy and there is a comfortable lounge/diner with a log fire in cooler weather.
6rm(2⤻↑4hc) (3fb) CTV in all bedrooms ® ✳ sB&B£14.50-
£16 dB&B£29 dB&B⤻↑£32 WB&B£96-£110 LDO 3pm
Lic ⵉⵉ CTV 5P small putting green swing seesaw

GH Q Q Q *Milton Lodge* 15 Milton Rd BS23 2SH
☎(0934) 623161
Apr-Sep
Adrienne and Les Cox have totally refurbished this charming Victorian house to provide comfortable public rooms and spacious, well-equipped bedrooms with modern en suite facilities. It stands on the town's outskirts, yet is close to the amenities.
6rm(3⤻3↑) CTV in all bedrooms ® ⵗ dB&B⤻↑£32-£34
WB&B£95-£105 WBDi£130-£140 (wkly only 23 May-12 Sep)
LDO 10am
ⵉⵉ CTV nc9yrs ⓔ

GH Q Q *Newton House* 79 Locking Rd BS23 3DW
☎(0934) 629331
East of the seafront and town centre, this friendly guesthouse has comfortable, well-maintained rooms. The public rooms include a cosy lounge, separate bar and dining room.
8rm(5⤻↑3hc) (4fb) CTV in all bedrooms ® ✳ sB&Bfr£15
sB&B⤻↑frf£18 dB&B£31 dB&B⤻↑£36 WB&B£97.65-
£113.40 WBDi£144.90-£160.65 LDO 2pm
Lic ⵉⵉ CTV 9P
Credit Cards ① ② ③ ⑤ ⓔ

GH |Q||Q||Q| **Wychwood Hotel** 148 Milton Rd BS23 2UZ
☎(0934) 627793
*Located on the outskirts of the town, this recently renovated
Victorian house offers an outside heated swimming pool, in
addition to the well-equipped, modern bedrooms, many of which
have en suite facilities.*
11rm(1⇌7♠3hc) (1fb) CTV in all bedrooms ®
✖ (ex guide dogs) ✱ sB&B£19-£20 sB&B⇌♠£22-£23
dB&B⇌♠£41-£43 WB&B£150-£154 WBDi£198-£205
LDO 6.30pm
Lic ♉ 14P ⇌(heated)
Credit Cards [1][3] ⓔ

FH |Q||Q| Mrs T G Moore **Purn House** *(ST331571)* Bleadon
BS24 0QE ☎Bleadon(0934) 812324
Feb-Nov
*Some 3 miles from Weston, this creeper-clad, part 17th-century
farmhouse is situated in the village of Bleadon. Bedrooms are
bright and mostly spacious, and there is a panelled dining room
and a cosy lounge. This is very much a working farm and fishing
and pony trekking are available in addition to the usual farm
activities.*
6rm(3⇌♠3hc) (3fb)⊁in all bedrooms CTV in 2 bedrooms ®
✖ (ex guide dogs) sB&B£16-£18 dB&B£28-£32 dB&B⇌♠£36-
£42 WB&B£80-£85 WBDi£120-£128 LDO 10am
♉ CTV 10P ✔ 450 acres arable dairy

WEST PENNARD Somerset Map 03 ST53

INN |Q||Q||Q| *Red Lion* Newton BA6 8NN
☎Glastonbury(0458) 32941
*Standing on the A361 between Glastonbury and Shepton Mallet
this inn has its bedrooms in a converted barn, all equipped to a
high, modern standard, yet retaining character. The main building
houses the bar and several eating areas.*
Annexe 7⇌ CTV in all bedrooms ® ✖ (ex guide dogs)
LDO 9.45pm
♉ 50P 2☎
Credit Cards [1][2][3]

WEST STOUR Dorset Map 03 ST72

INN |Q||Q| **The Ship** SP8 5RP ☎East Stour(074785) 640
*This inn was built in 1750 and has fine views of Blackmore Vale. A
series of cosy bars have log fires and there is an extensive range of
bar food available. The attractive dining room features a working
hand pump for the well. Bedrooms are light and fresh with pretty
soft furnishings; some have old fireplaces and they all have modern
facilities such as double glazing.*
6⇌♠ (2fb) CTV in all bedrooms ® ✖ (ex guide dogs) ✱
sB&B⇌♠£28-£30 dB&B⇌♠£38-£42 ✱ Bar Lunch £8-£12
Dinner £8-£12&alc LDO 9.30pm
♉ CTV 50P ✔
Credit Cards [1][3]

WESTWARD HO! Devon Map 02 SS42

GH |Q||Q||Q| **The Buckleigh Lodge** 135 Bayview Rd EX39 1BJ
☎Bideford(0237) 475988
*Standing on the edge of the village, this spacious Victorian house
has tastefully furnished bedrooms and good public areas, retaining
original features.*
6rm(3⇌♠3hc) (1fb) CTV in all bedrooms ®
✖ (ex guide dogs) sB&B£15-£17 sB&B⇌♠frf17 dB&Bfr£30
dB&B⇌♠fr£34 WB&B£100-£114 WBDi£154-£168 LDO 4pm
Lic ♉ CTV 8P ⓔ

WETHERBY West Yorkshire Map 08 SE44

GH |Q| **Prospect House** 8 Caxton St LS22 4RU ☎(0937) 582428
*Situated on the corner of a quiet side road, this guesthouse is only a
short walk from the town centre. The resident owners offer good
value for money, together with friendly service and comfortable
accommodation.*

6hc (1fb) CTV in 1 bedroom ✱ sB&B£15-£15.50 dB&B£30-£31
WB&B£105-£108.50
♉ CTV 6P ⓔ

WEYBRIDGE Surrey London plan 4 A1 (pages 000-000)

GH |Q||Q||Q| **Warbeck House Hotel** 46 Queens Rd KT13 0AR
☎(0932) 848764 FAX (0932) 847290
*An attractive Edwardian house in a residential area close to the
town centre. The bedrooms are functional, but comfortable and
well maintained. Breakfast is served in the Barclay Room which
retains many of its original features with the addition of a new
conservatory overlooking the beautiful landscaped gardens. There
is a small bar and ample car parking at the front of the house.*
10rm(1♠9hc) (1fb) CTV in all bedrooms ® ✖ ✱ sB&B£32.90-
£34.08 sB&B♠£36.43 dB&B£45.83 dB&B♠£49.35
Lic ♉ CTV 20P

WEYMOUTH Dorset Map 03 SY67

◄►GH |Q||Q| **Hazeldene** 16 Abbotsbury Rd, Westham
DT4 0AE ☎(0305) 782579
*Typical seaside family holiday accommodation is provided here,
with bright, cheerfully decorated bedrooms, which tend to be
compact but are clean and well kept. There is a television lounge as
well as a dining room.*
7hc (4fb) ® ✖ sB&B£13-£14 dB&B£26-£28 WB&B£75-£99
WBDi£80-£125 LDO noon
Lic ♉ CTV 7P 1☎ nc5yrs ⓔ

GH |Q||Q||Q| **Kenora** 5 Stavordale Rd DT4 0AB ☎(0305) 771215
Etr & 9 May-4 Oct
*A Victorian house in a quiet cul-de-sac with views of the harbour
from rear rooms. Bedrooms vary in size but are neat and clean.
Public rooms include a bar lounge and a spacious dining room
where a traditional English menu is served. Guests can relax in the
award-winning garden, which also has a children's play area.*
15rm(4⇌9♠2hc) (5fb) ® ✖ (ex guide dogs) sB&B£18-£21.50
sB&B⇌♠£20-£24 dB&B⇌♠£40-£48 WB&B£121-£142
WBDi£146-£170 (wkly only Jun-Aug) LDO 4.30pm
Lic ♉ CTV 20P
Credit Cards [1][3]

GH |Q||Q| **Kings Acre Hotel** 140 The Esplanade DT4 7NH
☎(0305) 782534
Closed 15 Dec-5 Jan rs Oct, Nov & Dec
Terraced Georgian hotel on seafront.
13rm(5♠8hc) (4fb) CTV in all bedrooms ® ✖ sB&B£17-£22
sB&B♠£23-£34 dB&B£29-£34 dB&B♠£34-£46 WB&B£112-
£138 WBDi£120-£180 LDO 4.30pm
Lic ♉ CTV 9P
Credit Cards [1][3]

GH |Q||Q||Q| **Sou'west Lodge Hotel** Rodwell Rd DT4 8QT
☎(0305) 783749
Closed 21 Dec-1 Jan
*A small family-run hotel situated above the Old Quay, a short
distance from the seafront and town centre. Bedrooms are well
maintained and many have en suite facilities. There is a
comfortable lounge and bar.*
9rm(2⇌4♠3hc) (2fb) CTV in all bedrooms ® sB&B£16.50-
£18 sB&B⇌♠£18.50-£21 dB&B£33-£36 dB&B⇌♠£37-£42
WB&B£97-£130 WBDi£139-£175 LDO 3pm
Lic ♉ CTV 14P ⓔ

GH |Q||Q||Q| **Sunningdale Private Hotel** 52 Preston Rd,
Overcombe DT3 6QD ☎(0305) 832179
Mar-Oct
*A family holiday hotel set back from the main Preston road, in an
elevated position. Public areas are smartly furnished and include a
comfortable lounge and well appointed dining room. The freshly
decorated bedrooms vary in size, and many have private
bathrooms. The garden contains an outdoor pool with seating, and
a putting green.*

20rm(5⇔2♠13hc) (8fb) CTV in 12 bedrooms TV in 2 bedrooms ® sB&B£19-£24 sB&B⇔♠£24.25-£28.25 dB&B£38-£48 dB&B⇔♠£43.25-£53.25 WB&B£124-£154 WBDi£154-£191 LDO 6.30pm
Lic CTV 20P ➔(heated) putting green table tennis pool table games room
Credit Cards 1 3 £

GH Q Q Q Tamarisk Hotel 12 Stavordale Rd, Westham DT4 0AB ☎(0305) 786514
Mar-Oct
A Victorian house in a quiet cul-de-sac close to the harbour, a short walk from the town centre. Bedrooms are freshly decorated and well maintained, many with private bathrooms, and there is an attractive and spacious dining room and a comfortable bar lounge.
16rm(4⇔8♠4hc) (7fb) CTV in 6 bedrooms ® ✶ sB&B£15-£18 sB&B⇔♠£17.50-£20.50 dB&B£30-£36 dB&B⇔♠£35-£41 WB&B£90-£115 WBDi£120-£145 (wkly only Jul-Aug) LDO 2pm
Lic ♨ CTV 19P £

GH Q Q *The Westwey* 62 Abbotsbury Rd DT4 0BJ ☎(0305) 784564
A small, friendly, family-run hotel offering comfortable accommodation: most bedrooms have private bathrooms and TV, although they vary in size.
11rm(1⇔8♠2hc) (2fb) CTV in all bedrooms ® ✶ (wkly only Jul-Aug) LDO 6.30pm
Lic ♨ CTV 10P nc6yrs

WHADDON Buckinghamshire Map **04** SP83

INN Q Q Q Lowndes Arms & Motel 4 High St MK17 0NA ☎Milton Keynes(0908) 501706 FAX (0908) 504185
A country inn of character, enjoying a quiet rural setting in the centre of the village. Eleven extremely well equipped bedrooms have been tastefully decorated and furnished in a converted stable annexe around the car park. Simple steak meals are offered on the limited à la carte menu served in the bars.
Annexe 11♠ CTV in all bedrooms ® ✖ (ex guide dogs) LDO 9.30pm
♨ 30P nc14yrs
Credit Cards 1 3 5
See advertisement under MILTON KEYNES

WHAPLODE Lincolnshire Map **08** TF32

FH Q Q Q Mrs A Thompson **Guy Wells** *(TF337241)* Eastgate PE12 6TZ ☎Holbeach(0406) 22239
Closed 20-31 Dec
Situated in the heart of the countryside just a mile off the A151 Holbeach- Spalding road, this is a splendid period house surrounded by beautiful gardens. The interior is harmoniously furnished with an attractive lounge and inglenook fireplace, and all the rooms are spacious, light and comfortable. Mrs Thompson is a friendly and informative host.
3hc (1fb)✂in all bedrooms TV in 1 bedroom ®
✖ (ex guide dogs) sB&B£19-£21 dB&B£30-£32
♨ CTV 4P nc10yrs 85 acres arable flowers

WHEDDON CROSS Somerset Map **03** SS93

GH Q Q Q The Higherley TA24 7EB ☎Timberscombe(0643) 841582
Higherley is an attractive modern detached building standing in pleasant gardens alongside 6 acres of smallholding. Well-appointed rooms enjoy superb country views.
6hc (1fb) CTV in 2 bedrooms LDO 9pm
Lic ♨ CTV 25P 6🐾 nc3mths
Credit Cards 1 3 £

WHIMPLE Devon Map **03** SY09

GH Q Q Q Down House EX5 2QR ☎(0404) 822860
Apr-Sep
Alan and Vicky Jiggins provide a warm welcome at their beautiful Edwardian house, very much a home with many personal pieces in evidence about the place. The Down House is set in five acres of paddocks and gardens, and offers easy access to the A30, Honiton and Exeter. The bedrooms are spacious, comfortable and brightly decorated; there is a lounge for families and a quieter room with patio doors to the gardens. Guests can share the set evening meal with the proprietors at the large dining room table, where country house party style is a speciality.
4rm(2♠2hc) (1fb) CTV in 2 bedrooms TV in 2 bedrooms ®
✖ (ex guide dogs) ✶ sB&Bfr£17 dB&Bfr£34 dB&B♠fr£40 WB&Bfr£95 WBDifr£160 LDO 4.30pm
♨ CTV 8P games lounge £

WHITBY North Yorkshire Map **08** NZ81

7⇌⬉ (2fb) CTV in all bedrooms ® * sB&B⇌⬉£35-£45 dB&B⇌⬉£60-£68 WB&B£205-£230 LDO 6pm
Lic 🍽 10P ⊡(heated) ℛ(hard)snooker gymnasium croquet putting green
Credit Cards [1] [3] (£)

GH QQQ Europa Private Hotel 20 Hudson St YO21 3EP ☎(0947) 602251
mid Jan-mid Nov
This friendly hotel is situated on West Cliff and provides comfortable and attractive accommodation throughout. The bedrooms all have colour TV and tea and coffee making facilities. There is a relaxing lounge on the first floor, and a separate dining room with individual tables downstairs.
9rm(2⬉7hc) (1fb) CTV in all bedrooms ® ✗ * sB&Bfr£13 dB&Bfr£24 dB&B⬉£28-£30 LDO 11am
🍽 CTV nc2yrs

GH Q Glendale 16 Crescent Av YO21 3ED ☎(0947) 604242
Apr-Oct
Glendale is a very comfortable and friendly guesthouse with neat bedrooms. It offers very good value for money.
6rm(3⬉3hc) (3fb) CTV in all bedrooms ® sB&B£14.50-£15 dB&B£29-£30 dB&B⬉£32-£34 WB&B£95-£100 WBDi£135-£140 LDO 4.15pm
Lic CTV 6P (£)

GH QQ Haven 4 East Crescent YO21 3HD ☎(0947) 603842
Feb-Oct
Sitting high on the west cliff, this comfortable guesthouse has some fine views over the harbour and sea. A substantial home-cooked dinner is provided, and there is a comprehensive breakfast menu.
8rm(4⇌⬉4hc) (1fb) CTV in all bedrooms ® ✗ * sB&B£15-£16 dB&B£28-£31 dB&B⇌⬉£31-£37 WB&B£98-£125 WBDi£147-£175 LDO 4pm
Lic 🍽 CTV nc5yrs (£)

GH QQQ Seacliffe Hotel North Promenade, West Cliff YO21 3JX ☎(0947) 603139
A charming small hotel, Seacliffe overlooks the sea and offers guests a warm welcome. All bedrooms are en suite and have telephones and colour TV. A cosy bar and comfortable lounge complement the 'Candlelight' restaurant where an extensive à la carte menu is served.
19⇌⬉ (4fb) CTV in all bedrooms ® * sB&B⇌⬉£30-£46 dB&B⇌⬉£49-£51 WB&B£170-£179 LDO 8.45pm
Lic 🍽 CTV 8P
Credit Cards [1] [2] [3] [5]

GH QQQ Waverley Private Hotel 17 Crescent Av YO21 3ED ☎(0947) 604389
Mar-Oct
A friendly guesthouse offering comfortable bedrooms, a spacious lounge, cosy bar and home-cooked meals served in the attractive dining room.
6rm(5⬉1hc) (4fb) CTV in all bedrooms ® ✗ sB&Bfr£13.50 dB&Bfr£27 dB&B⬉fr£31 WB&Bfr£86 WBDi£121.50-£135.50 LDO 5.45pm
Lic 🍽 CTV nc3yrs

WHITCHURCH Hereford & Worcester Map 03 SO51

GH QQ Portland HR9 6DB ☎Symonds Yat(0600) 890757
Closed Jan rs Nov-Mar
The Portland guest house is ideal for touring as it is close to Ross-on-Wye, Goodrich, and Symonds Yat situated in the village centre. The rooms are well equipped and modestly furnished.
8hc (2fb) CTV in all bedrooms ® * sB&B£16-£18 dB&B£31-£34 WB&B£105-£120 WBDi£145-£165 LDO 6pm
Lic 🍽 CTV 7P (£)

INN Q Crown Hotel HR9 6DB ☎Symonds Yat(0600) 890234
Closed Xmas Day & Boxing Day
Situated in the centre of the village, and close to the A40, this large inn offers character, and modest but well-equipped bedrooms. A range of bar meals is available, both at lunchtime and in the evening.
5rm(1⇌4⬉) (3fb) CTV in all bedrooms ® * sB&B⇌⬉£25-£28 dB&B⇌⬉£43-£45 WB&B£130-£145 WBDi£170-£175 * Lunch £6-£8&alc Dinner £8-£12&alc LDO 9pm
🍽 CTV 40P skittle alley pool room
Credit Cards [1] [2] [3] [5] (£)
See advertisement under ROSS-ON-WYE

WHITCHURCH Shropshire Map 07 SJ54

FH QQ Mrs M H Mulliner **Bradeley Green** *(SJ537449)* Waterfowl Sanctuary, Tarporley Rd SY13 4HD ☎(0948) 3442
Closed Xmas
This is an interesting place to stay in, the farm being surrounded by a wildfowl sanctuary. In addition to the well-equipped bedrooms in the house, there is a self-catering cottage available to let.
3⬉ 🚭in all bedrooms ® ✗ (ex guide dogs) * sB&B⬉£18-£20 dB&B⬉£30-£35 WB&B£95-£105 WBDi£130-£140 LDO 9am
🍽 CTV 6P ᒍ water gardens 180 acres dairy waterfowl fish farming (£)

WHITESTONE Devon Map 03 SX89

FH QQ Mrs S K Lee **Rowhorne House** *(SX880948)* EX4 2LQ ☎Exeter(0392) 74675
Farmhouse set in attractive gardens and lawns.
3hc (2fb) CTV in 1 bedroom TV in 1 bedroom ✗ * sB&B£12 dB&B£24 WB&B£84 WBDi£122.50
CTV 6P 103 acres dairy
Credit Cards [1] [2] [3] [5] (£)

WHITEWELL Lancashire Map 07 SD64

INN QQ *The Inn at Whitewell* BB7 3AT ☎Dunsop Bridge(02008) 222
A traditional old inn, full of character and atmosphere, beautifully situated in the picturesque Forest of Bonland. The bedrooms are generally spacious, many having been upgraded, but still contain fine antique furniture and paintings. Real ale is served in the bar, together with home-made bar lunches and suppers. Dinner served in the restaurant offers a house menu or à la carte.
11rm(6⇌5hc) (4fb) CTV in 6 bedrooms LDO 9.30pm
🍽 CTV 60P ᒍ clay pigeon shooting by arrangement
Credit Cards [1] [2] [3] [5]

WHITHORN Dumfries & Galloway *Wigtownshire* Map 10 NX44

FH QQ Mrs E C Forsyth ***Baltier*** *(NX466429)* DG8 8HA ☎Garlieston(09886) 241
Mar-Nov
With fine views of the surrounding countryside, this stone-built farmhouse has modern extensions and offers comfortable accommodation. Meals are taken around the traditional farmhouse table.
2hc (1fb) ® ✗
🍽 CTV 4P 220 acres dairy sheep

WHITLAND Dyfed Map 02 SN21

FH QQ C M & I A Lewis ***Cilpost*** *(SN191184)* SA34 0RP ☎(0994) 240280
Apr-Sep
Pleasant accommodation is provided on this working farm by the Lewis family. The spacious dining room offers imaginative and enjoyable food, and the comfortable public areas include an excellent snooker room and an indoor swimming pool.
7rm(3⇌3⬉1hc) (3fb) ✗
Lic 🍽 12P ⊡(heated) ᒍ snooker 160 acres dairy

WHITLEY BAY Tyne & Wear Map **12** NZ37

GH Q Q **Lindisfarne Hotel** 11 Holly Av NE26 1EB
☎091-251 3954 & 091-297 0579
A small, friendly terraced guesthouse situated in a quiet part of the town, yet within easy reach of the sea and shops. Bedrooms are bright and fresh, with attractive fabrics, and there is an attractive dining room, complemented by friendly service.
9rm(2♠7hc) (1fb) CTV in all bedrooms ® ✠ sB&B£14-£15
sB&B♠£20-£22 dB&B£28-£30 dB&B♠£32-£34 WB&B£91-
£105 WBDi£133-£154 LDO 9am
Lic ♥♥♥ CTV ⚡
Credit Cards ① ③ ⓔ

GH Q Q Q **Marlborough Hotel** 20-21 East Pde, Central
Promenade NE26 1AP ☎091-251 3628
In a fine position overlooking the sea, this comfortable well maintained private hotel welcomes both business and leisure visitors. Many of the front bedrooms enjoy sea views.
15rm(9⇨6hc) (4fb) CTV in 17 bedrooms ® sB&Bfr£20
sB&B⇨♠£26 dB&B⇨♠£40 LDO noon
Lic CTV 7P
Credit Cards ① ③

GH Q Q **White Surf** 8 South Pde NE26 2RG ☎091-253 0103
A brightly painted, terraced house conveniently situated between the town and the seafront. The bedrooms are bright and fresh with modern furnishings and all have TV. There is a comfortable lounge and an attractive dining room, and a forecourt car park is available.
7hc (2fb)⚡in 8 bedrooms CTV in all bedrooms ®
✠ (ex guide dogs) sB&B£14.50-£16.50 dB&B£29-£33
WB&B£99-£115.50 WBDi£141-£157.50 LDO 6pm
♥♥♥ CTV 7P 2🅿 satellite TV ⚡

GH Q Q Q **York House Hotel** 30 Park Pde NE26 1DX
☎091-252 8313 & 091-251 3953
A small family-run hotel, part of an attractive terrace, conveniently located for both shops and beaches. Bedrooms are nicely decorated and very well equipped ; seven of the rooms have private bathrooms. There is also a ground floor room with special facilities for disabled guests.
8rm(7♠1hc) (2fb) CTV in all bedrooms ® ✱ sB&B£20-£21.50
sB&B♠£21.50-£24 dB&B♠£33-£35 WB&Bfr£140
WBDifr£189 LDO 7pm
Lic ♥♥♥ CTV 2P
Credit Cards ① ② ③ ⓔ

WHITNEY-ON-WYE Hereford & Worcester Map **03** SO24

SELECTED

INN Q Q Q Q **The Rhydspence** HR3 6EU (2m W A438)
☎Clifford(04973) 262
This black and white timbered inn stands in its own delightful gardens and dates back from the 14th century. It is set in a lovely location on the A438 exactly on the border between England and Wales. The accommodation has been completely modernised and is attractive and well equipped, each room with an en suite bath or shower room. The convivial bars are popular with locals and tourists alike, with a patio for summer use, overlooking a stream. There is a beautifully appointed restaurant offering extensive and interesting menus which make full use of local produce.
5rm(4⇨1♠) CTV in all bedrooms ® ✠ ✱ sB&B⇨♠£25-
£30 dB&B⇨♠£50-£60 ✱ Lunch £10-£25alc Dinner £10-
£25alc LDO 9.30pm
♥♥♥ 60P
Credit Cards ① ② ③

WHITTINGTON Shropshire Map **07** SJ33

FH 🅀🅀🅀 Mrs H M Ward *Perry (SJ348303)* SY11 4PF
☎Oswestry(0691) 662330
Mar-Oct
*A large early 19th century farmhouse, full of character and
atmosphere. Guests are encouraged to dine with the family and
view the daily running of the farm. There are also 2 self catering
cottages available to let. It is situated on the B5009, 1 mile east of
the A5 ; follow the sign to the village and just over a mile turn right
into Berghill Lane and follow the signs.*
2hc ⌑in all bedrooms ® ⊁ LDO am
ᵐ CTV P ↲ cycle hire 750 acres arable beef dairy mixed

WHITTLEBURY Northants Map **04** SP64

GH 🅀🅀🅀 *Linden Cottage* 12 High St, NN12 8XJ
☎Silverstone(0327) 857672
*This guesthouse is conveniently situated close to the motor racing
circuit at Silverstone, and offers attractive accommodation with
antique furniture and pretty, co-ordinating soft furnishings. All
rooms have excellent en suite facilities. There is a cosy lounge in
addition to the dining room where a communal dining table ensures
that the convivial informal atmosphere is maintained. The
proprietors are friendly and helpful, and guests are made very
welcome.*
4⇨🄵 (1fb) CTV in 5 bedrooms ® LDO 5pm
Lic ᵐ 10P
Credit Cards ⊡ ② ③

WIDDINGTON Essex Map **05** TL53

FH 🅀🅀🅀 Mrs L Vernon *Thistley Hall (TL556311)* CB11 3ST
☎Saffron Walden(0799) 40388
Apr-Oct
*A drive lined with chestnut trees leads guests to this friendly 17th-
century farmhouse, surrounded by lovely gardens, working
pastureland and quiet countryside. The three bedrooms are
spacious, traditionally furnished and very clean. Downstairs in the
breakfast room there is a communal table for eating, some
armchairs and a television. The atmosphere here is warm and the
proprietors are charming.*
3rm(2hc) ⌑in 2 bedrooms ® ⊁ (ex guide dogs) dB&B£30-£32
ᵐ CTV 4P nc8yrs 30 acres mixed working £

WIDEGATES Cornwall & Isles of Scilly Map **02** SX25

GH 🅀🅀🅀 *Coombe Farm* PL13 1QN ☎(05034) 223
Mar-Oct
*This attractive 1920s house has superb views and offers large,
comfortable family bedrooms. There is a cosy lounge and the
dining room is furnished with antiques.*
8hc Annexe 1🄵 (4fb) CTV in 7 bedrooms ® ⊁ (ex guide dogs)
sB&B£16.80-£18.90 sB&B🄵£18.80-£21 dB&B£33.60-£37.80
dB&B🄵£33.60-£41.80 WB&B£117.60-£132.30 WBDi£177.80-
£190 LDO 7pm
Lic ᵐ CTV 12P nc5yrs ⇌(heated) games room croquet £
See advertisement under LOOE

WIDEMOUTH BAY Cornwall & Isles of Scilly Map **02** SS20

GH 🅀 *Beach House Hotel* EX23 0AW ☎(0288) 361256
Etr-Sep
13rm(8🄵5hc) (5fb) ® ⊁ LDO 7pm
Lic CTV 20P games room childrens play area
See advertisement under BUDE

GH 🅀🅀 *Trelawny Hotel* Marine Dr EX23 0AH
☎(0288) 361328
Etr-Oct
10🄵 (3fb) CTV in all bedrooms ® ✳ sB&B🄵£20 dB&B🄵£40
WBDi£160-£185 LDO 7pm
Lic 12P
Credit Cards ⊡ ③ £

WIGAN Greater Manchester Map **07** SD50

GH 🅀🅀 *Aalton Court* 23 Upper Dicconson St WN1 2AG
☎(0942) 322220
*Situated close to the centre of town and convenient for the rugby
ground, this Victorian terraced house offers well equipped but
compact bedrooms, a neat dining room and comfortable lounge
bar.*
6rm(2⇨4🄵) (1fb) CTV in all bedrooms ® ⊁ LDO 2pm
Lic ᵐ CTV 11P

WIGHT, ISLE OF Map **04**

FRESHWATER Map **04** SZ38

GH 🅀🅀🅀 *Blenheim House* Gate Ln PO40 9QD
☎(0983) 752858
May-Sep
*An attractive Victorian house a few hundred yards from
Freshwater Bay. Inside is a lounge with comfortable red
chesterfields, a cosy bar and a warm welcome. The bedrooms are
clean, well kept and all have en suite showers. Pause on the landing
to admire the grandfather clock made by one of Mrs Shakeshaft's
forebears ; and note the bramley espallier by the outdoor pool – the
apples are probably on the menu.*
8🄵 (4fb) CTV in all bedrooms ® ⊁ ✳ WB&B£147
WBDi£196 LDO noon
Lic ᵐ 6P nc10yrs ⇌(heated) table tennis billards darts

NITON Map **04** SZ57

GH 🅀🅀🅀 *Pine Ridge Country House* Niton Undercliff
PO38 2LY ☎(0983) 730802
*A country house style hotel in a prime location, set in well kept,
spacious grounds, with good views over the sea, close to the main
road but in a peaceful setting. The bedrooms and public areas are
comfortably furnished throughout, and each bedroom is well
equipped with modern facilities. Service is friendly and relaxed,
the proprietors being actively involved.*
9rm(6⇨3hc) (2fb) CTV in all bedrooms ® sB&Bfr£26
dB&B⇨🄵£56 WB&B£188 WBDi£256 LDO 9pm
Lic ᵐ CTV 10P ⚗
Credit Cards ⊡ ③ £

RYDE Map **04** SZ59

GH 🅀 *Dorset Hotel* 31 Dover St PO33 2BW ☎(0983) 64327
*A small privately owned hotel, the Dorset has a warm and friendly
atmosphere and on some evenings provides entertainment. The
bedrooms are nicely appointed.*
25rm(15🄵) (4fb) CTV in all bedrooms ®
Lic CTV 25P ⇌ ▸

GH 🅀🅀🅀 *Teneriffe Hotel* 36 The Strand PO33 1JF
☎(0983) 63841
Closed Jan-Feb
*This long established holiday hotel is well managed and provides
modern en suite rooms, now serviced by a lift. There are generous
public rooms, a licensed function room and an attractive dining
room, and the service is friendly and helpful.*
50rm(26⇨24🄵) (7fb) CTV in all bedrooms ®
⊁ (ex guide dogs) sB&B⇨🄵£17.75-£20 dB&B⇨🄵£35.25-£40
WB&B£124.25-£140 WBDi£164.50-£189 LDO 7pm
Lic lift ᵐ CTV 9P
Credit Cards ⊡ ③ £

Every effort is made to provide accurate
information, but details can change after we go to
print. It is advisable to check prices etc. before
you make a firm booking.

SANDOWN Map **04** SZ58

SELECTED

GH 🔾🔾🔾🔾 *Braemar Hotel* 5 Broadway PO36 9DG
☎(0983) 403358 & 407913
Dating back to the Victorian era, this hotel has been refurbished and renovated to a high standard of décor and comfort. Public areas include an attractive, spacious dining room which overlooks a well tended rear garden, a cosy bar area and a very elegant and quiet lounge. Bedrooms are individually furnished in a style well suited to the era of the building; most are good sizes, with high ceilings, and they are all well equipped with modern facilities. There is also a honeymoon suite with a mahogany four-poster bed and a jacuzzi bath. The resident proprietors are young and enthusiastic, providing guests with a small choice, home-made evening meal, together with cheerful service.
14rm(5⇄9♠) (5fb) CTV in all bedrooms ® ✖
LDO 7.30pm
Lic ⁹⁹⁹ 12P
Credit Cards 1️⃣2️⃣3️⃣5️⃣

GH 🔾 **Chester Lodge Hotel** Beachfield Rd PO36 8NA
☎(0983) 402773
mid Jan-mid Dec rs Oct
Conveniently situated within easy reach of the shops and Cliff Walk, this guesthouse has modernised, well-equipped bedrooms, some of which are on the ground floor. A bar-lounge and separate dining room complete the accommodation.
20rm(2⇄10♠8hc) (4fb)✖in all bedrooms CTV in all bedrooms ® dB&B⇄♠£47.50-£51.50 WBDi£164-£169.50 (wkly only Jul-Aug)
Lic ⁹⁹⁹ CTV 19P Ⓔ

GH 🔾🔾 **Culver Lodge Hotel** Albert Rd PO36 8AW
☎(0983) 403819 & 402902
Apr-Oct Closed Nov-Mar
Situated conveniently close to the centre of town, the hotel offers comfortable and nicely presented public areas and bright, well equipped bedrooms. There is a first-floor guest laundry which is popular, and a games room on the ground floor with a pool table and games machines. The staff are friendly and helpful.
21rm(20⇄♠1hc) (2fb) CTV in all bedrooms ® ✖ sB&B£18-£21.50 sB&B⇄♠£18-£21.50 dB&B⇄♠£36-£43 WB&B£119-£144 WBDi£163-£187 LDO 7pm
Lic ⁹⁹⁹ CTV 20P pool room darts video games
Credit Cards 1️⃣2️⃣3️⃣Ⓔ

GH 🔾🔾 **Rose Bank Hotel** 6 High St PO36 3DA
☎(0983) 403854
A small cottage-style hotel – the oldest property in the town. Peace and tranquillity are offered here, along with comfortable, neat bedrooms and public rooms with views out to sea and across the well kept gardens. The resident proprietors enjoy welcoming guests into their home and ensure a good standard of service.
6rm(1⇄5hc) Annexe 2⇄ (2fb) ® ✱ sB&B£12-£14 sB&B⇄£15-£16 dB&B£24-£26 dB&B⇄£28-£30 WB&B£70-£80 WBDi£96-£102 LDO 7pm
Lic ⁹⁹⁹ CTV ✗ nc6yrs

SELECTED

GH 🔾🔾🔾🔾 **St Catherine's Hotel** 1 Winchester Park Rd
PO36 8HJ ☎(0983) 402392
Closed 24 Dec-2 Jan rs Nov
This Purbeck stone house was built in 1860 and has a modern extension; well situated, it is only a short walk from the beach and pier. Bedrooms are prettily and tasefully decorated and well equipped with good modern facilities. There is a cosy bar area and a comfortably appointed separate lounge. Home-

cooked meals are served in the spacious, well presented dining room; there is a choice of three of four dishes for each course.
19⇄♠ (3fb) CTV in all bedrooms ® ✖ sB&B⇄♠£18-£21 dB&B⇄♠♠£36-£42 WB&B£117-£136.50
WBDi£172.25-£198.25 LDO 7pm
Lic ⁹⁹⁹ CTV 8P
Credit Cards 1️⃣3️⃣Ⓔ

GH 🔾 **Seacourt** Cliff Path PO36 8PN ☎(0983) 403759
FAX (0983) 7815
A small family-run hotel in a secluded setting along the cliff path, which is being refurbished. The bedrooms are reasonable in size and are very well equipped with modern facilities. Public areas include a games room and a small bar.
12rm(11⇄1hc) Annexe 9rm(8⇄1♠) CTV in all bedrooms ® sB&B⇄♠£32-£38.65 dB&B⇄♠£60-£73 (incl dinner) WB&B£126-£162 WBDi£180-£220 LDO 7pm
Lic ⁹⁹⁹ 25P ⌷(heated) snooker sauna solarium pool table tennis petanque hydro spa multi-gym
Credit Cards 1️⃣2️⃣3️⃣Ⓔ

SEAVIEW Map **04** SZ69

GH 🔾 **Northbank Hotel** Circular Rd PO34 5ET
☎(0983) 612227
Etr-Sep
Northbank is an old Victorian house with a garden sloping down to the seashore. Splendid views are enjoyed from the traditional lounge, the cosy bar crammed with memorabilia, and many of the bedrooms. The latter vary in size, some have fine old furniture, but most are fairly simple.
18hc (6fb) CTV in 3 bedrooms ® LDO 8pm
Lic ⁹⁹⁹ CTV 8P 4🍴 ♨ ♪ snooker

St. Catherine's Hotel

1 Winchester Park Road
(off The Broadway)
Sandown Tel: 0983 402392

Holiday and business hotel open all year, except Christmas and New Year. Your bedroom has private en suite facilities and telephone, colour television, radio and free tea/coffee making facilities. Tastefully decorated. Five course evening meal and full English breakfast with excellent friendly service. Car parking and ground floor rooms available. Licensed bar and restful lounge. Only five minutes walk to shops, seafront, pier complex and leisure centre.
Phone for brochure.

SHANKLIN Map **04** SZ58

See **Town Plan Section**

GH QQQ **Apse Manor Country House** Apse Manor Rd
PO37 7PN ☎(0983) 866651

Set in countryside 1.5 miles from the town, this 15th-century manor stands in 2 acres of grounds. A choice of dishes is offered in the dining room and the bedrooms are comfortable.

7⇄ (2fb) CTV in all bedrooms ® dB&B⇄£68-£72 (incl dinner) WB&B£168-£180 WBDi£230-£240 LDO 7.30pm
Lic ⁜ 10P nc6yrs
Credit Cards ① ③

GH QQQ **Aqua Hotel** The Esplanade PO37 6BN
☎(0983) 863024

Etr-5 Nov

A friendly, modern hotel situated on the Esplanade, in a prime position directly on the seafront. Bedrooms are modern and comfortable, simply furnished and well presented ; the sizes vary, but each is well equipped with facilities and six of the front-facing rooms have balconies. Public areas enjoy sea views and Boaters restaurant offers a choice of table d'hôte or à la carte menus. There is a bar/lounge area and a smaller, quiet lounge with TV. Long-term improvements are planned to further upgrade the hotel.

22⇄↑ (4fb) CTV in all bedrooms ® ✸ sB&B⇄↑£20-£30 dB&B⇄↑£40-£60 WB&B£140-£154 WBDi£145-£190 (wkly only Jul & Aug) LDO 4.30pm
Lic ⁜ 2P
Credit Cards ① ② ③ ⓔ

GH QQQ **Bay House Hotel** 8 Chine Av, Off Keats Green, PO36 6AN ☎(0983) 863180 FAX (0983) 866604

On the edge of Keats Green with superb views far out to sea, this family-run hotel offers a relaxed and friendly atmosphere. Bedrooms are simply decorated and appointed, and each is equipped with modern facilities. Public areas include a spacious open-plan dining room and bar area, a quiet lounge and a smart indoor heated swimming pool, sauna and solarium.

22rm(21⇄↑1hc) CTV in all bedrooms ✸ sB&B£26-£34.70 sB&B⇄↑£26-£34.70 dB&B£52-£69.40 dB&B⇄↑£52-£69.40 (incl dinner) WB&B£154-£207.20 WBDi£170.50-£224.80 LDO 7pm
Lic ⁜ 16P ⌷(heated) sauna solarium
Credit Cards ① ② ③

GH QQQ **Carlton Hotel** 9 Park Rd PO37 6AY
☎(0983) 862517

The spacious lounge takes full advantage of the hotel's cliff top situation. All except 2 single rooms are en suite and the well-equipped accommodation is complemented by good home cooking.

12rm(7⇄5↑) (1fb) CTV in all bedrooms ® ✖ (ex guide dogs) sB&B⇄↑£24-£28 dB&B⇄↑£48-£56 (incl dinner) WB&B£140-£168 WBDi£160-£190 LDO 6.30pm
Lic ⁜ CTV 10P
Credit Cards ① ③ ⓔ

SELECTED

GH QQQQ **Chine Lodge** East Cliff Rd PO37 6AA
☎(0983) 862358

Closed Xmas & New Year

An early Victorian house in pretty gardens with beautiful countryside views which may be enjoyed from the verandah. Bedrooms are individually decorated and are pretty and welcoming, indeed the whole house has an air of comfort and charm, invoked, no doubt, by the proprietors Mr and Mrs May. Chine Lodge was the Duke of Hamilton's birthplace, and 2 smugglers' tunnels still remain.

7⇄↑ CTV in all bedrooms ® ✖ ✸ sB&B⇄£20.50-£26.50 dB&B⇄£41-£53
Lic ⁜ 7P nc ⓔ

GH QQ **Culham Lodge** 31 Landguard Manor Rd
PO37 7HZ ☎(0983) 862880

Apr-Oct

Set in a quiet tree-lined residential street, this detached redbrick private hotel offers clean and well maintained bedrooms, a comfortable no-smoking lounge, a small garden room with pond and subtropical plants and, in the secluded garden, a heated swimming pool.

10rm(1⇄7↑2hc) ® ✖ (ex guide dogs) sB&B£13-£14.50 dB&B£26-£29 dB&B⇄↑£31-£34 WB&B£90-£100 WBDi£125-£140 LDO 4pm
⁜ CTV 8P nc12yrs ⌷(heated) solarium

GH QQ **Curraghmore Hotel** 22 Hope Rd PO37 6EA
☎(0983) 862605

Mar-Oct

A well equipped modern hotel situated in a residential area, surrounded by similar, holiday-style hotels. Family run, it offers simple, nicely presented bedrooms and spacious public areas, including a popular bar area, dance floor and a nicely appointed dining room, together with comfortable lounges. A varied home-cooked evening meal is also offered by the friendly proprietors.

26rm(10⇄8↑8hc) (9fb) CTV in all bedrooms ® ✸ sB&B£19-£24 sB&B⇄↑£21-£26 dB&B£38-£48 dB&B⇄↑£42-£52 WB&B£114-£154 WBDi£149-£189 LDO 6pm
Lic CTV 20P putting

GH QQ **Edgecliffe Hotel** Clarence Garden PO37 6HA
☎(0983) 866199 Telex no 869441

Closed Nov-Dec

A traditional guesthouse, personally run by resident proprietors, quietly situated away from the town centre, close to the sea. Bedrooms are well decorated and comfortably furnished ; the dining room and lounge enjoy views of the small, well tended garden and benefit from the morning and afternoon sunshine. The hotel does not permit smoking ; vegetarian and special requirement diets are well catered for, with prior notice.

10rm(2⇄4↑4hc) (2fb) ✖in all bedrooms CTV in all bedrooms ® ✖ sB&B£15-£19.50 dB&B£30-£39 dB&B⇄↑£39-£46 WB&B£90-£130 WBDi£150-£185 LDO 6.30pm
Lic ⁜ 3P nc5yrs cycles for hire
Credit Cards ① ② ③ ⓔ

GH QQQ **Hambledon Hotel** Queens Rd PO37 6AW
☎(0983) 862403 & 863651

Children are especially catered for at this hotel which provides a baby listening service. The bedrooms are comfortable and well equipped and there is a licensed bar and a comfortable lounge. The Hambledon provides easy access to local amenities.

11↑ (4fb) CTV in all bedrooms ® ✸ sB&B↑£18-£21 dB&B↑£36-£42 WB&B£110-£139 WBDi£175-£175 LDO 6pm
Lic ⁜ CTV 8P ♻
Credit Cards ① ② ③ ⓔ

GH QQQ **Havelock Hotel** 2 Queens Rd PO37 6AN
☎(0983) 862747

Mar-Oct rs Xmas

Situated only yards from Keats Green and the seafront, this nicely presented private hotel offers comfortably appointed bedrooms with good modern facilities. Public areas are nicely decorated and there is a simple evening menu on offer to guests wishing to dine in. An outdoor pool area and well tended front garden are also offered at this informally run and relaxed hotel.

22⇄↑ (6fb) CTV in all bedrooms ® ✖ (ex guide dogs) ✸ sB&B⇄↑£21.50-£29.50 dB&B⇄↑£43-£59 (incl dinner) WBDi£140-£196 LDO 6.30pm
Lic ⁜ CTV 14P ⌷(heated) snooker sauna solarium
Credit Cards ① ③

ⓔ Remember to use the money-off vouchers.

GH QQ **Kenbury Private Hotel** Clarence Rd PO37 7BN
☎(0983) 862085
Etr-Oct
A large red-brick Victorian house with a well kept garden, the public areas are spacious and include a comfortable lounge overlooking the garden, and a characterful bar. Bedrooms, on ground and first-floor levels, are functional, clean and well maintained.
18rm(15⇨🏠3hc) (3fb)✂in 3 bedrooms CTV in all bedrooms
® 🏃 (ex guide dogs) ✻ sB&B£15-£17 sB&B⇨🏠£17-£19
dB&B£30-£34 dB&B⇨🏠£34-£38 WB&B£100-£129
WBDi£135-£169 LDO 6.30pm
Lic 🍺 CTV 8P nc3yrs
Credit Cards [1][3] £

SELECTED

GH QQQQ **Osborne House** Esplanade PO37 6BN
☎(0983) 862501
Jan-24 Oct
A gabled Victorian house dating back to 1850, complete with veranda and sun terrace, overlooking the Esplanade below and with panoramic views far out to sea. Proprietors for over 20 years, Mike and Liz Hogarth enjoy a returning clientèle and a local following for Mike's cooking. An extensive hot and cold buffet is served from late May to September, and for the other months a six-course, candlelit dinner is offered. Bedrooms are simply but prettily furnished, with good modern facilities and equipment, and public areas benefit from an abundance of pot plants and fresh flowers.
12⇨🏠 CTV in all bedrooms ® 🏃 ✻ sB&B⇨🏠fr£31
dB&B⇨🏠fr£62 LDO 8pm
Lic 🍺 ✗ nc13yrs
Credit Cards [1][3]

✉�"🅿 **GH** QQQ **Soraba Private Hotel** 2 Paddock Rd
PO37 6NZ ☎(0983) 862367
Closed Dec-Jan
Within easy reach of the beach, shops and amenities, this Victorian house has simply furnished bedrooms and offers excellent value for money. Mr and Mrs Wynn Davies provide wholesome evening meals and friendly service.
6rm(3🏠3hc) (1fb) CTV in 3 bedrooms TV in 1 bedroom
sB&B£13-£15.50 dB&B£26-£31 dB&B🏠£32-£37 WB&B£85-£123 WBDi£105-£145 LDO 3pm
Lic 🍺 CTV 4P nc3yrs

TOTLAND BAY Map **04** SZ38

GH QQQ *Hermitage Hotel* Cliff Rd PO39 0EW
☎(0983) 752518
Mar-Nov
Quietly situated in its own well kept sheltered gardens overlooking the sea, this country hotel offers bright, fresh and well presented bedrooms with traditional, comfortable public areas. There is a piano and an organ available for guests' use, and sound English cooking is offered using fresh local produce. There is a children's outdoor play area, and pets are very welcome here.
12rm(2⇨4🏠6hc) (3fb) LDO 7pm
Lic 🍺 CTV 12P 1🎾 ⋒ ⌣
Credit Cards [1][3]
See advertisement on page 379

GH QQ **Lismore Private Hotel** 23 The Avenue PO39 0DH
☎(0983) 752025
Closed Nov-Dec
This villa dates back to 1896 and has been lovingly modernised by the resident proprietors. Bedrooms are functional and simple in décor and design; each is well equipped with modern facilities and spotlessly clean. A changing daily menu offers four courses of traditional fare, using fresh produce. Personally run for the past 16

▶

years by Mr and Mrs Nolson, this simple hotel enjoys a regular following of returning clientèle.
7rm(5♪2hc) (3fb) CTV in all bedrooms ® ✱ (ex guide dogs)
dB&B♪£52-£54 (incl dinner) WBDi£144-£162 LDO 3pm
Lic ♔ 8P nc5yrs ⓔ

GH 🔲🔲 **The Nodes Country Hotel** Alum Bay Old Rd
PO39 0HZ ☎(0983) 752859 FAX (0705) 201621
A Victorian country house set in a peaceful rural location, backing on to Tennyson Down, with over 2 acres of grounds. The wood-panelled, cosy courtyard bar is the hub of the hotel, with a warm and lively atmosphere. Bedrooms are simply decorated and furnished in a comfortable manner, and public areas are traditional in design. Young families are especially welcome, with facilities such as cots, highchairs, high teas and a baby listening service readliy provided. The traditional English country cooking uses fresh local produce to great effect.
11rm(3⇔6♪2hc) (5fb) CTV in all bedrooms ® sB&B£16.50-£29.50 sB&B⇔♪£29.50-£34.50 dB&B£53-£59 dB&B⇔♪£59-£69 (incl dinner) WB&B£115.50-£135.50 WBDi£175-£225 LDO 3pm
Lic ♔ CTV 15P badminton table tennis

GH 🔲🔲🔲 **Sandford Lodge Hotel** 61 The Avenue PO39 0DN
☎(0983) 753478
rs Nov-Dec
This Edwardian house is situated in a quiet residential street and is well kept and nicely presented. Bedrooms are pretty and comfortable, with modern facilities. There are two comfortable lounges at this exclusively non-smoking hotel.
6rm(3⇔2♪1hc) (2fb)⤡in all bedrooms ® ✱ (ex guide dogs)
✱ sB&B£17-£19 sB&B⇔♪£19-£23 dB&B£28-£31
dB&B⇔♪£32-£39 WB&B£115-£155 WBDi£160-£210 LDO 4pm
Lic ♔ CTV 6P ⓔ

GH 🔲🔲🔲 *Westgrange Country Hotel* Alum Bay Old Rd
PO39 0HZ ☎(0983) 752227
Mar-Oct
Situated in a quiet country lane with super views across the rolling meadows, this small, friendly hotel offers comfortable bedrooms, with fresh décor and modern facilities. The public rooms are pretty and cosy and include a small bar, a simple dinng room and a smart lounge.
13rm(2⇔7♪4hc) (11fb) TV available ® LDO 7.30pm
Lic ♔ CTV 30P

VENTNOR Map **04** SZ57

GH 🔲🔲 **Channel View Hotel** Hambrough Rd PO38 1SQ
☎(0983) 852230
Apr-19 Oct rs Mar
This family-run hotel enjoys a prominent position overlooking the sea, and offers simply appointed accommodation, with freshly decorated and well presented bedrooms. The public areas are sunny and bright, with pleasant sea views; there is a cosy bar and a nicely appointed restaurant where evening meals are served.
14rm(2♪12hc) (6fb) ® ✱ (ex guide dogs) LDO 8pm
Lic CTV 🅿
Credit Cards 1 3

GH 🔲🔲🔲 **Glen Islay Hotel** St Boniface Rd PO38 1NP
☎(0983) 854095
Mar-Oct
A late-Victorian house in a quiet residential area with a hillside rear garden, close to the town. The modern bedrooms are neatly presented and furnished, and public areas include a small residents' bar, equipped with a pool table, dart board and games machine. In addition to a traditional English breakfast, an evening meal is also offered at this friendly, family-run hotel.

Visit your local AA Centre.

10rm(1⇔8♪1hc) (8fb) CTV in all bedrooms ®
✱ (ex guide dogs) sB&B£21-£22 sB&B⇔♪£22-£25
dB&B⇔♪£44-£50 (incl dinner) WB&B£145-£154 WBDi£154-£175
Lic ♔ CTV 6P ⓔ

GH 🔲🔲🔲 **Hillside Private Hotel** Mitchell Av PO38 1DR
☎(0983) 852271
This thatched house was built in 1801 and enjoys en elevated position high above the town, with spectacular views across the bay; it is surrounded by 2 acres of wooded grounds. The spacious bedrooms are modern and smartly decorated, with pretty co-ordinating fabrics and good facilities. The bright, sunny dining room leads into an airy conservatory, where guests can relax and enjoy drinks from the small bar.
11rm(4⇔7♪) (2fb) CTV in all bedrooms ® sB&B⇔♪£25-£28
dB&B⇔♪£50-£56 (incl dinner) WB&B£122.50-£136.50
WBDi£175-£196 LDO 4.30pm
Lic ♔ 16P nc5yrs
Credit Cards 1 2 3

GH 🔲🔲🔲 **Lake Hotel** Shore Rd, Bonchurch PO38 1RF
☎(0983) 852613
Mar-Oct
This family-run hotel is quietly situated in over an acre of lovely terraced gardens, in the village of Bonchurch. Bedrooms are prettily and tastefully decorated in co-ordinated Laura Ashley prints, and many have en suite facilities. The public areas include 2 sunny conservatory-style lounges, a TV lounge and a comfortably appointed larger seating area; there is also a cosy bar area with a range of bar games.
11rm(9⇔♪2hc) Annexe 10⇔♪ (7fb) ® sB&B£16-£18
sB&B⇔♪£16-£18 dB&B£32-£36 dB&B⇔♪£32-£36
WB&B£119 WBDi£157.50-£169.75 LDO 6.30pm
Lic ♔ CTV 20P nc3yrs

GH 🔲🔲🔲 **Llynfi Hotel** 23 Spring Hill PO38 1PF
☎(0983) 852202
Etr-Oct
A well maintained and nicely presented private hotel in a residential street behind the centre of town. The bedrooms are bright, nicely decorated and offer good facilities, and there are lounges for non-smokers, a dining room and a separate bar. The cooking is of a good standard, enjoyed by many guests who return year after year.
10rm(7♪3hc) (2fb) CTV in all bedrooms ® ✱ (ex guide dogs)
✱ sB&B£15-£21 dB&B£30-£42 dB&B♪£36-£50 WBDi£140-£175 LDO 6.30pm
Lic CTV 7P
Credit Cards 1 3 ⓔ

GH 🔲🔲🔲 **Hotel Picardie** Esplanade PO38 1JX
☎(0983) 852647
Mar-Oct
This hotel enjoys a prime location directly facing the seafront on the Esplanade. Bedrooms are simply and comfortably furnished : some are small but they are all well equipped and neatly presented. In addition to a comfortable, sunny lounge overlooking the seafront, there is also a small, bright bar area – the only room where smoking is allowed – and a simply appointed dining room where evening meals are offered as well as a traditional English breakfast.
10⇔♪ (3fb)⤡in all bedrooms CTV in all bedrooms ®
sB&B⇔♪£16.50 dB&B⇔♪£31 WB&B£110 WBDi£153
LDO 4.30pm
Lic CTV
Credit Cards 1 3

GH 🔲🔲 **St Martins Hotel** The Esplanade PO38 1SX
☎(0983) 852345
Apr-Nov
This small, privately owned hotel occupies a prime position on the seafront, and the sea-facing terrace allows guests to sit and watch the world go by. Bedrooms are bright and fresh, furnished in a

simple modern style. Public areas are limited in size but are sunny and comfortable. A home-cooked evening meal is offered.

7rm(4⇩3hc) (1fb) CTV in all bedrooms ® ⋈ ✱ sB&B£15-£20 dB&B£30-£40 dB&B⇩£34-£56 WB&B£100-£185 WBDi£140-£225 LDO 8.30pm

Lic ⁗ nc9yrs

Credit Cards ⊡ ② ③ ⑤

GH ⓆⓆⓆ St Maur Hotel Castle Rd PO38 1LG
☎(0983) 852570

Feb-Nov

Peacefully situated on a hillside, overlooking the park, this private hotel offers bright and freshly decorated bedrooms with simple, modern furniture. The public rooms are comfortable and traditional in style, with a cosy bar area complementing the spacious lounge and dining room. The well managed service is personally supervised by the proprietor.

14rm(13⇩⋔1hc) (4fb) ® sB&B£22-£23 sB&B⇩⋔£26-£27 dB&B⇩⋔£52-£54 (incl dinner) WBDi£182-£189 (wkly only Feb-May & Nov) LDO 7pm

Lic ⁗ CTV 12P nc3yrs

Credit Cards ⊡ ③ Ⓔ

WIGMORE Hereford & Worcester Map **07** SO46

INN Ⓠ *Compasses Hotel* HR6 9UN ☎(056886) 203

Set in a pleasant village close to the Herefordshire/Shropshire border, this ivy-clad hotel is popular with walkers exploring the beautiful countryside of this area, and provides simple accommodation.

3hc (1fb) CTV in all bedrooms ® LDO 9.30pm
⁗ 70P

Credit Cards ⊡ ② ③ ⑤

WILBERFOSS Humberside Map **08** SE75

FH Ⓠ Mrs J M Liversidge *Cuckoo Nest (SE717510)*
☎(07595) 365

Closed Xmas

This small traditional farmhouse, with a pantiled roof, dates back some 200 years. It is a mixed farm on the A1079, close to the village of Wilberfoss. The accommodation is simple but well maintained.

2hc (1fb)⊬in all bedrooms ⋈
⁗ CTV P nc2yrs 150 acres arable beef dairy mixed sheep

WILLAND Devon Map **03** ST01

FH ⓆⓆ Mrs J M Granger *Doctors (ST015117)* Halberton Rd EX15 2QQ ☎Tiverton(0884) 820525

Mar-Oct

Parts of this farmhouse date back to the 15th century. Peacefully set in 90 acres and with well-kept gardens, it has 2 comfortable bedrooms which share a bathroom, and the public rooms are full of character. This is a bed and breakfast establishment only.

2rm (1fb)⊬in all bedrooms ® ⋈
CTV 6P ✔ 95 acres dairy

WILLERSEY Gloucestershire Map **04** SP13

SELECTED

GH ⓆⓆⓆⓆ Old Rectory Church St WR12 7PN
☎Broadway(0386) 853729

Closed Xmas

Situated in the heart of this pretty Cotswold village, opposite the Norman church, this 17th-century stone house with its beautiful walled garden has been successfully converted by the proprietors into a small hotel of quality. Bedrooms are spacious, very comfortable and well equipped, and there is a large oak-beamed dining room and a bright, comfortable sitting room. Although they only provide bed and breakfast,

the owners will offer useful advice on local restaurants, and also provide a personal chauffeur service.

6rm(4⇩2⋔) ⊬in all bedrooms CTV in all bedrooms ® ⋈ sB&B⇩⋔£39-£49 dB&B⇩⋔£59-£95

⁗ CTV 10P 2☂ nc9yrs

Credit Cards ⊡ ③

See advertisement under BROADWAY

WILLEY Warwickshire Map **04** SP48

FH ⓆⓆⓆ Mrs Helen Sharpe **Manor** *(SP496849)* CV23 0SH
☎Lutterworth(0455) 553143

A traditional 18th-century red-brick farmhouse set in a peaceful location overlooking pastureland in an unspoilt village, yet within five miles of the M1, M6 and M69 and very close to the A5. The bedrooms are all thoughtfully furnished with co-ordinated décor and soft furnishings. Guests have the use of a large lounge with an open fire, and breakfast is taken around a communal table in the adjacent dining room. Smoking is not permitted.

3rm(1⋔2hc) ⊬in all bedrooms ® ⋈ (ex guide dogs) ✱ sB&B£16-£20 dB&B£30 dB&B⋔£36 WB&B£112-£140 WBDi£182-£210

⁗ CTV 3P 93 acres sheep

WILMSLOW Cheshire Map **07** SJ88

GH ⓆⓆⓆ Fernbank 188 Wilmslow Rd, Handforth SK9 3JX
☎(0625) 523729 & 539515

This large Victorian house, situated near to the airport, has been tastefully restored to provide comfortable bedrooms and warm hospitality. Residential weekend ceramics courses are a feature of this guesthouse.

3⇩⋔ (1fb) CTV in all bedrooms ® ✱ sB&B⇩⋔£27.50-£33 dB&B⇩⋔£28.50-£44 LDO 4pm

⁗ CTV 3P china restoration and weekend leisure courses

WILTON Wiltshire Map **04** SU03

INN QQ **The Swan** Stoford SP2 0PR (3m N off A36)
☎Salisbury(0722) 790236
*This 300-year-old inn, alongside the A36 and the River Wylye, has
well appointed, comfortable bedrooms and a popular skittle alley.
The bar and restaurant serve a good range of food, including
home-made specials and vegetarian dishes.*
8rm(5♠3hc) (3fb) CTV in all bedrooms ® ✖ (ex guide dogs)
✳ sB&B£18-£20 sB&B♠£18-£20 dB&B£36-£40 dB&B♠£36-
£40 WB&B£126-£140 ✳ Lunch £3.50-£7alc Dinner £7-£12alc
LDO 10.30pm
💷 CTV 100P ♪ skittle alley pool table ⓔ

WIMBORNE MINSTER Dorset Map **04** SZ09

SELECTED

GH QQQQ **Beechleas** 17 Poole Rd BH21 1QA
☎(0202) 841684
Feb-24 Dec
*An attractive Georgian house close to the town centre, with
ample parking. Bedrooms are varied and luxurious, with very
well equipped bathrooms; they are all comfortable and well
furnished with attractive co-ordinated fabrics. Public rooms
include a small but smart drawing room where drinks are
served, and a spacious dining room leading to a conservatory;
both have open fires with period fireplaces. There is a small
menu of interesting English dishes using naturally reared
produce from a local farm. The whole hotel is spotlessly clean
and immaculately maintained, proving popular with tourists
and business people alike who enjoy its quiet good taste.*
5⇨♠ Annexe 2⇨♠ CTV in all bedrooms ✖ ✳
sB&B⇨♠£43-£60 dB&B⇨♠£50-£70 LDO 9pm
Lic 💷 9P
Credit Cards ① ③

GH Q **Riversdale** 33 Poole Rd BH21 1QB ☎(0202) 884528
Closed Xmas rs Nov-Feb
*A detached guesthouse on the edge of town with simply furnished
bedrooms complemented by a comfortable lounge and dining room.
Well established by the resident proprietors for 16 years, the hotel
is popular with tourists, walkers and business people.*
8rm(1♠7hc) (3fb) CTV in all bedrooms ® ✳ sB&B£12-£24
dB&B£24-£48 dB&B♠£30-£50 LDO 10am
💷 CTV 5P nc3yrs
Credit Cards ① ③

GH QQ **Stour Lodge** 21 Julian's Rd BH21 1EF
☎(0202) 888003
Closed 20 Dec-5 Jan
*Stour Lodge is located on the A31 Dorchester Road within easy
walking distance of the town centre, but with views of open
countryside. An early Victorian house with spacious and very well
equipped bedrooms together with a comfortable lounge and
conservatory. Meals are served at one large table in the dining
room, dinners are available by prior arrangement.*
3rm(1⇨2hc) (2fb) CTV in all bedrooms ® ✳ sB&B£25-£30
sB&B⇨£25-£30 dB&B£50-£60 dB&B⇨£50-£60 WB&B£150-
£180 WBDif£200-£220 LDO 9pm
Lic 💷 CTV 4P croquet ⓔ

WIMPSTONE Warwickshire Map **04** SP24

FH QQ Mrs J E James **Whitchurch** *(SP222485)* CV37 8NS
☎Alderminster(0789) 450275
*A lovely Georgian farmhouse built 1750, very much part of a
working farm, situated a few miles south of Stratford-on-Avon.
Bedrooms have recently been improved, with good en suite
facilities added. There is a small but comfortable lounge with a
collection of toys for children.*

3rm(2♠1hc) (2fb) ® ✖ sB&B£15-£16 dB&B£24-£26
dB&B♠£30-£32 LDO 6.30pm
💷 CTV 6P 220 acres arable beef sheep ⓔ

WINCANTON Somerset Map **03** ST72

FH QQQ Mrs A Teague **Lower Church** *(ST721302)* Rectory
Ln, Charlton Musgrove BA9 8ES ☎(0963) 32307
Closed Xmas & New Year
*18th-century, brick built farmhouse with inglenook fireplace and
beams.*
3rm(2♠1hc) ✂in all bedrooms ® ✳ dB&B♠fr£27
WB&Bfr£90
💷 CTV 3P nc6yrs 60 acres dairy sheep

WINCHELSEA East Sussex Map **05** TQ91

SELECTED

GH QQQQ **The Country House at Winchelsea** Hastings
Rd TN36 4AD ☎Rye(0797) 226669
Closed Xmas
*Formerly a farmhouse dating back to the 17th century, this
delightful guesthouse is set in 2 acres of well kept grounds.
Bedrooms have been individually and tastefully furnished with
comfort in mind, and each has a private bathroom and lovely
garden views. There is a cosy lounge and an elegant dining
room where guests can enjoy the natural hospitality and good
home cooking of the proprietors. A new bar/lounge is being
added to extend the public areas available for guests.*
4rm(2♠2hc) CTV in all bedrooms ® ✖ ✳ dB&B♠fr£39
LDO 7.30pm
Lic 💷 3P 3🐾 nc9yrs

GH QQQ **The Strand House** TN36 4JT ☎Rye(0797) 226276
*Dating from the 15th century with beams, low ceilings and
doorways, the house has been sympathetically modernised
retaining all the original architectural features and inglenook
fireplaces. There is a comfortable and elegant lounge, hospitality
bar and a good breakfast. Bedrooms vary, and the en suite showers
are confined. Service is helpful and there is a pleasant garden and
ample parking.*
10rm(2⇨6♠2hc) (1fb) CTV in all bedrooms ® sB&B⇨♠£20-
£32 dB&B⇨♠£28-£42
Lic 💷 12P nc5yrs

WINCHESTER Hampshire Map **04** SU52

GH QQQ **Aerie** 142 Teg Down Meads, (off Dean Lane)
SO22 5NS ☎(0962) 862519
*Situated in a quiet residential area, this detached property, with
far reaching views, offers immaculate rooms which are light, airy
and well equipped, and is popular with tourists and commercial
guests. Parking is available on the premises, and there is a 'no
smoking' policy throughout.*
4hc (1fb)✂in all bedrooms CTV in all bedrooms ® ✖ ✳
sB&B£15 dB&Bfr£29
💷 6P nc10yrs

GH QQ *Harestock Lodge Hotel* Harestock Rd SO22 6NX
(situated 2m N of the city on the B3420) ☎(0962) 881870
Closed 24 Dec-3 Jan
*A mainly commercial hotel with two conference/function rooms.
The spacious public areas have been refurbished. The bedrooms
are functional and well equipped.*
20rm(9♠11hc) (5fb) CTV in all bedrooms ®
✖ (ex guide dogs) LDO 9.15pm
Lic 💷 CTV 20P ⇨spa pool
Credit Cards ① ② ③

GH QQQ **Markland** 44 St Cross St SO23 9PS
☎(0962) 854901
A red-brick Victorian house in a residential area of the city.
Bedrooms are comfortable and well equipped, and include a
ground floor suite for the disabled. Parking is available at the rear,
and a friendly, relaxed atmosphere prevails.
4♠ (1fb) CTV in all bedrooms ® ✱ sB&B♠fr£26
dB&B♠fr£37
🍴 CTV 4P
Credit Cards 1 3

SELECTED

INN QQQQ **The Wykeham Arms** 73 Kingsgate St
SO23 9PE ☎(0962) 853834 FAX (0962) 854411
This historic coaching inn located close to the Cathedral
features a popular choice of bars, with real ales and
blackboard menus. The standard of cooking is good, with
attentive service. The interior is tastefully furnished, and
bedrooms are particularly well equipped.
7⇄♠ CTV in all bedrooms ® ✱ sB&B⇄♠£59.50-£65.80
dB&B⇄♠£69.50-£75 ✱ Lunch £9.50-£18.50 Dinner £14-
£20alc LDO 8.45pm
🍴 14P nc14yrs sauna

WINCLE Cheshire Map **07** SJ96

GH QQ **Four Ways Diner Motel** Cleulow Cross SK11 0QL (1m
N of A45) ☎(0260) 227228
rs Oct-Mar
A small family-run motel situated in the National Peak Park, with
fine views over the Dane valley, on the A54 Congleton-Buxton
road. The accommodation is well equipped, with en suite
bathrooms. The small restaurant is popular for Sunday lunches.
6rm(1⇄5♠) Annexe 5♠ (2fb) CTV in all bedrooms ®
LDO 8pm

▶

Lic 🛏 50P
Credit Cards [1] [3]

WINDERMERE Cumbria Map **07** SD49

See **Town Plan Section** During the currency of this publication Windermere telephone numbers are liable to change.

GH 🔲🔲 **Aaron Slack** 48 Ellerthwaite Rd LA23 2BS
☎(05394) 44649

This cosy little guesthouse – part of a Victorian terrace – provides clean, brightly decorated accommodation equipped with colour television, tea-making facilities and private shower/bathroom facilities ; smoking is not permitted on the premises and pets cannot be accepted.

3rm(1➪♠2hc) ⊁in all bedrooms CTV in all bedrooms ® ⊁
✳ sB&B➪♠£17-£18 dB&B➪♠£28-£30 WB&B£93-£120 WBDi£135-£162 LDO noon
🛏 nc12yrs

Credit Cards [1] [3]

GH 🔲🔲🔲 **Applegarth Hotel** College Rd LA23 3AE
☎(09662) 3206 due to change to (05394) 43206

A spacious and well furnished Victorian hotel close to the town centre and railway station, in a quiet side road. Some of the comfortable bedrooms have four-poster beds, and many have views towards the lake and fells ; they all have en suite facilities.

15♠ (4fb) CTV in all bedrooms ® sB&B♠£20-£30 dB&B♠£32-£60 WB&B£112-£210
Lic 🛏 CTV 20P

Credit Cards [1] [2] [3]

GH 🔲🔲🔲 **Archway Country** College Rd LA23 1BY
☎(09662) 5613

A charming Victorian terrace house with period décor enhanced by antiques, paintings, prints, flowers and good books, plus all the modern accessories. Guests are captivated by the fine English cooking – breakfast is a gastronomic delight – home-made yoghurt, freshly squeezed fruit and vegetable juices, traditional farmhouse grill, poached kippers, home-made preserves, fresh filtered coffee and a choice of tea blends.

6rm(5♠1hc) ⊁in all bedrooms CTV in all bedrooms ® ⊁
sB&B£16-£17 dB&B♠£40-£50 WB&B£135-£160 LDO 3pm
Lic 🛏 3P nc12yrs Ⓔ

GH 🔲🔲🔲 **Belsfield House** 4 Belsfield Ter LA23 3EQ
☎(09662) 5823

A pleasant Victorian house situated in the centre of Bowness village and close to the lake. Bedrooms are especially well furnished and decorated, with good facilities. A pleasant lounge is available for guests.

9♠ (4fb) CTV in all bedrooms ⊁ (ex guide dogs)
sB&B♠£19.50-£22 dB&B♠£36-£43
🛏 ⨓ ⒺⒺ

GH 🔲🔲🔲 **Blenheim Lodge** Brantfell Rd, Bowness on Windermere LA23 3AE ☎(09662) 3440

This well furnished house in a quiet backwater of Bowness enjoys fine lakeland views from its elevated position. The comfortable bedrooms have good facilities and the home-cooked meals are of notable standard.

11rm(10➪♠1hc) (1fb)⊁in all bedrooms CTV in all bedrooms
® ⊁ ✳ sB&B£21.50-£25 sB&B➪♠£23-£27 dB&B➪♠£40-£54 WB&B£133-£180 WBDi£203-£250 LDO 7pm
Lic 🛏 12P 2❁ nc6yrs

⌐redit Cards [1] [3] ⒺⒺ

GH 🔲🔲🔲 **Brendan Chase** 1&3 College Rd LA23 1BU
☎(09662) 5638 due to change to (05395) 45638

A delightful family-owned and run guest house in a quiet side road just off the town centre, furnished and decorated throughout to a very pleasing standard. Bedrooms have good facilities and there is a comfortable lounge for guest's use.

8rm(4♠4hc) (4fb)⊁in 1 bedroom CTV in all bedrooms ® ✳
sB&B£12.50-£22 sB&B♠£15-£22 dB&B£25-£44 dB&B♠£30-£44 WB&B£87-£300
🛏 8P ⨓ ⒺⒺ

GH 🔲🔲🔲 **Brooklands** Ferry View, Bowness LA23 3JB
☎(05394) 42344

A delightful, small, family-owned and run guesthouse situated south of Bowness at the junction of the B5284 and A5074. In a rural setting with views of the lake, it is comfortable and very well maintained and offers a good standard of accommodation and car parking facilities alongside the hotel.

6rm(3➪♠2hc) (1fb) CTV in all bedrooms ® sB&B£18-£20 dB&B£32-£34 dB&B♠£36-£38
Lic 🛏 CTV 6P ⒺⒺ

GH 🔲🔲🔲 **Clifton House** 28 Ellerthwaite Rd LA23 2AH
☎(09662) 4968

A pleasant little terraced house situated in a quiet side road off New Road, near the village centre. Bedrooms are attractive and well equipped, and there is a cosy lounge. The friendly proprietors offer amiable service.

5rm(1➪♠4hc) (1fb) CTV in all bedrooms ® ⊁ ✳ sB&B£12-£17 dB&B£27-£28 dB&B➪♠£30-£34
🛏 CTV 5P nc5yrs

GH 🔲🔲🔲 **Cranleigh Hotel** Kendal Road, Bowness LA23 3EW
☎(09662) 3293 due to change to (05394) 43293
Mar-Oct

This charming stone-built Victorian house is furnished to a high standard and situated just a short distance from Bowness and Lake Windermere. The bedrooms have good facilities, and there are two comfortable lounges, one of which is for non-smokers.

9➪♠ Annexe 6➪♠ (1fb) CTV in all bedrooms ®
⊁ (ex guide dogs) ✳ dB&B➪♠£46-£50 WB&B£154-£168 LDO 7pm
Lic 🛏 CTV 15P ⨓

Credit Cards [1] [3] ⒺⒺ

GH 🔲🔲🔲 **Fir Trees** Lake Rd LA23 2EQ ☎(09662) 2272 due to change to (05394) 42272

Midway between Windermere and Bowness villages, this warm and friendly small hotel offers a good standard of accommodation, with very well furnished bedrooms and caring service from the resident owners.

7➪♠ (2fb) CTV in all bedrooms ⊁ sB&B➪♠£22.50-£29 dB&B➪♠£35-£48 WB&B£115-£160
🛏 8P

Credit Cards [1] [2] [3] ⒺⒺ

GH 🔲🔲🔲 **Glenburn** New Rd LA23 2EE ☎(05394) 42649 FAX (05394) 88998

This delightful guesthouse offers a high standard of comfort and service. The bedrooms are very well appointed and home cooked meals are served in the pleasant dining room.

16➪♠ (3fb)⊁in 4 bedrooms CTV in all bedrooms ®
⊁ (ex guide dogs) ✳ dB&B➪♠£40-£60 WB&B£129-£189 WBDi£205-£265 LDO 5.30pm
Lic 🛏 CTV 16P nc5yrs solarium

Credit Cards [1] [3] ⒺⒺ

GH 🔲🔲🔲 *Glencree Private Hotel* Lake Rd LA23 2EQ
☎(09662) 5822
Mar-Dec rs Feb

A small Lakeland stone building situated between Bowness and Windermere. It is well furnished and comfortable, with well equipped bedrooms and a charming lounge.

5rm(3➪♠2♠) CTV in all bedrooms ® ⊁
Lic 🛏 8P nc9yrs

Credit Cards [1] [3]

See advertisement on page 385

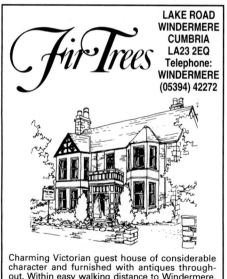

Windermere

GH ⓠⓠⓠ **Glenville Hotel** Lake Rd LA23 2EQ
☎(09662) 3371. Due to change to (05394) 43371
Feb-Nov
A pleasant family-run guesthouse situated between Bowness and Windermere. Bedrooms are well furnished, and there is a comfortable lounge for guests.
9rm(1⇨8♠)(1fb)✻in 2 bedrooms CTV in all bedrooms ⓡ ✖
✱ sB&B⇨♠£17.50-£22 dB&B⇨♠£35-£44 WB&B£152-£154
LDO 2pm
Lic ♔ 12P ⓔ

⌨▶GH ⓠⓠⓠ **Green Gables** 37 Broad St LA23 2AB
☎(09662) 3886 due to change to (05394) 43886
Closed Xmas & New Year
Well furnished and comfortable, this family-owned and run guesthouse in a side road just off the town centre represents very good value for money; bedrooms have good facilities, and there is a cosy lounge for guests' use.
6rm(2♠4hc)(2fb)✻in 3 bedrooms CTV in all bedrooms ⓡ
✖ (ex guide dogs) sB&B£12-£15 dB&B£23-£30 dB&B♠£30-£40 WB&B£77-£126
♔ CTV 2P ⓔ

⌨▶GH ⓠⓠⓠ **Greenriggs** 8 Upper Oak St LA23 2LB
☎(09662) 2265. Due to change to (05394) 42265
This attractive family-owned and run guesthouse has recently been completely refurbished to a very high standard. Set in a quiet and peaceful side road close to the town centre, it offers very friendly and attentive service.
7rm(4♠2hc)(1fb) CTV in all bedrooms ⓡ sB&B£13-£14
dB&B£27-£28 dB&B♠£29-£34 WB&Bfr£86 WBDi£134-£160
LDO noon
♔ CTV 4P nc5yrs ⓔ

GH ⓠⓠ *Haisthorpe* Holly Rd LA23 2AF ☎(09662) 3445
Mar-Oct
This pleasant and comfortable house stands in a quiet side road close to the town and lake, and provides friendly family service.
6rm(1♠5hc)(3fb)✻in all bedrooms ⓡ ✖ (ex guide dogs)
♔ CTV ✗

SELECTED

GH ⓠⓠⓠⓠ **The Hawksmoor** Lake Rd LA23 2EQ
☎(09662) 2110. Due to change to (05394) 42110
Feb-Nov
A delightful small hotel situated midway between Bowness and Windermere. The bedrooms are beautifully furnished, with matching wallpaper and fabrics, two have four-poster beds, and all have en suite bathrooms, TV and tea-making facilities. A very good standard of cooking is provided in the charming restaurant, and the lounge is comfortably furnished. Barbara and Bob Tyson offer friendly and personal service in a quiet and peaceful atmosphere.
10⇨♠ (3fb)✻in 3 bedrooms CTV in all bedrooms ⓡ
✖ (ex guide dogs) sB&B⇨♠£25-£30 dB&B⇨♠£37-£55
WB&B£135-£165 WBDi£195-£230 LDO 5pm
Lic ♔ 12P nc6yrs ⓔ
See advertisement in COLOUR SUPPLEMENT

GH ⓠ **Holly Lodge** 6 College Rd LA23 1BX ☎(05394) 43873
This detached Victorian house is situated in a quiet side road, close to the village centre. A good standard of accommodation is offered, with cosy bedrooms and a comfortable lounge, and service is friendly.
10rm(3♠7hc)(3fb) CTV in all bedrooms ⓡ ✖ (ex guide dogs)
sB&B£15-£17 dB&B£30-£34 dB&B♠£36-£40 WB&B£105-£115.50 WBDi£164.50-£175 LDO 10am
Lic ♔ 7P ⓔ

GH ⓠⓠⓠ **Holly Park House** 1 Park Rd LA23 2AW
☎(09662) 2107
Mar-Oct
Built of lakeland stone, this attractive house stands on the corner of a quiet side road. Resident owners provide well-furnished bedrooms and friendly service.
6⇨♠ (4fb) CTV in all bedrooms ⓡ ✖ (ex guide dogs)
sB&B⇨♠£20-£27.50 dB&B⇨♠£29-£40 WB&B£94-£130
Lic ♔ 4P ⓔ

GH ⓠⓠ **Kenilworth** Holly Rd LA23 2AF ☎(09662) 4004
In a quiet side road a short walk from Windermere village, this charming little guesthouse is caringly run by its friendly owners and provides a good standard of accommodation.
6rm(3♠3hc)(2fb)✻in 3 bedrooms ⓡ ✖ (ex guide dogs)
sB&B£13.50-£15 dB&B£27-£30 dB&B♠£33-£36 WB&B£90-£116
♔ CTV ✗ ⓔ

GH ⓠⓠⓠ **Kirkwood** Prince's Rd LA23 2DD ☎(09662) 3907
due to change to (05394) 43907
Situated in a quiet side road between Windermere and Bowness, this comfortable and friendly guesthouse has bedrooms with good facilities and a cosy lounge.
7rm(4♠3hc)(6fb) CTV in all bedrooms ⓡ ✱ dB&B£28-£36
dB&B♠£32-£44 WB&B£95-£150
♔ 1P
Credit Cards ①③ ⓔ

GH ⓠⓠⓠ **Latimer House** Lake Rd LA23 2JJ ☎(09662) 6888 due to change to (05394) 46888
A Victorian house of Lakeland slate on the main approach to Bowness, close to the shops and only a few minutes' drive from the lake. Exclusively for non- smokers, there is no dining room, but cooked breakfasts are served in bedrooms each morning. There is a garden where guests may relax, and car parking facilities are available.
6hc (1fb)✻in all bedrooms CTV in all bedrooms ⓡ ✖
dB&B£24-£44 WB&B£98-£115
♔ CTV 4P 2⊕ nc8yrs ⓔ

GH ⓠⓠⓠ **Laurel Cottage** Saint Martins Square LA23 3EF
☎(09662) 5594 due to change to (05394) 45594
A charming cottage with a neat garden in the centre of Bowness-on-Windermere, providing a high standard of accommodation including 4 fully en suite bedrooms which are most attractively decorated and furnished. The oak beams in the cosy lounge and dining room are characteristic of the 17th century when part of the building was a grammar school.
16rm(6♠10hc)(2fb) ⓡ ✖ (ex guide dogs) ✱ sB&B£18-£21
dB&B£33-£40 dB&B♠£44-£48 WB&B£105-£142
♔ CTV 8P ⓔ

See advertisement on page 387

⌨▶GH ⓠⓠⓠ **Lynwood** Broad St LA23 2AB ☎(09662) 2550
due to change to (05394) 42550
Close to the town centre in a quiet side road, this well furnished, comfortable guesthouse is family owned and run, and offers a friendly welcome.
9rm(4♠5hc)(4fb)✻in all bedrooms CTV in all bedrooms ⓡ
✖ (ex guide dogs) sB&B£12.50-£16.50 dB&B♠£15-£22
dB&B£22-£30 dB&B♠£30-£44 WB&B£73.50-£154
♔ 2P 2⊕ nc5yrs ⓔ

See advertisement on page 387

GH ⓠⓠⓠ **Meadfoot** New Rd LA23 2LA
☎(09662) 2610. Due to change to (05394) 42610
Feb-Nov
This is a well-furnished and comfortable modern house with an attractive garden. The bedrooms are very pleasant and there is a lounge with a relaxed atmosphere. The owners offer a warm, friendly welcome to all.

▶

8rm(4🐾4hc) (1fb) CTV in all bedrooms ® ✖ (ex guide dogs) ✳ sB&B£15-£20 dB&B£30-£35 dB&B🐾£35-£40 WB&B£98-£133
🍴 9P nc3yrs ⓔ

GH Ⓠ Ⓠ **Mylne Bridge House** Brookside, Lake Rd LA23 2BX ☎(09662) 3314
Mar-Oct
Situated in a quiet side road, this comfortable family-run guesthouse has well- furnished bedrooms with good facilities.
10rm(7🐾3hc) (1fb) CTV in all bedrooms ® ✳ sB&B£14-£16 sB&B🐾£16-£18 dB&B£28-£32 dB&B🐾£32-£36
Lic 🍴 10P ⓔ

GH Ⓠ *Oakthorpe Hotel* High St LA23 1HF ☎(09662) 3547
Closed 25 Dec-24 Jan
Family owned and run, this hotel stands in the centre of Windermere.
18rm(4🔄3🐾11hc) (4fb) ® LDO 8.15pm
Lic 🍴 CTV 18P
Credit Cards ①③

GH Ⓠ Ⓠ Ⓠ **Oldfield House** Oldfield Rd LA23 2BY ☎(05394) 88445
Situated in a quiet side road close to the village, this guesthouse offers very good standards of comfort and service. Bedrooms are well furnished and delightfully decorated, with good facilities.
7rm(1🔄3🐾3hc)🔄in 2 bedrooms CTV in all bedrooms ® ✖ (ex guide dogs) sB&B£15-£19 sB&B🔄🐾£17-£21 dB&B£30-£36 dB&B🔄🐾£34-£40 WB&B£94.50-£132.30
🍴 CTV 7P nc2yrs free membership to leisure club
Credit Cards ①③ⓔ

GH Ⓠ Ⓠ Ⓠ **Parson Wyke Country House** Glebe Rd LA23 3HB ☎(09662) 2837
An old rectory, parts of which are said to date from 1450, with other areas of 16th-century origin. It is set in a peaceful location, in its own grounds and gardens, only a short distance from Bowness Pier and the marina. Beams, antiques and many other features of its era abound, and several of the well equipped bedrooms have been furnished in character.
3rm(2🔄1🐾) (1fb) CTV in all bedrooms ® ✖ (ex guide dogs) ✳ sB&B🔄🐾£25-£32 dB&B🔄🐾£40-£55
🍴 CTV 9P

GH Ⓠ Ⓠ Ⓠ **Rosemount** Lake Rd LA23 2EQ
☎(09662) 3739. Due to change to (05394) 43739
A well furnished, comfortable and friendly small hotel, situated midway between Windermere and Bowness. Bedrooms are well furnished and pretty at this non-smoking establishment. A nice place in which to stay and relax when visiting the Lake District.
8rm(5🐾3hc) 🔄in all bedrooms CTV in all bedrooms ® ✖ sB&B🐾£17.50-£22 dB&B🐾£35-£44 WB&B£116-£146
Lic 🍴 6P 2🛵
Credit Cards ①③ⓔ

GH Ⓠ Ⓠ Ⓠ **St Johns Lodge** Lake Rd LA23 2EQ ☎(09662) 3078 due to change to (05394) 43078
Closed Dec
This comfortable private hotel is situated midway between Bowness and Windermere. Bedrooms are well furnished and attractive, with good facilities. There is a pleasant lounge and friendly, helpful service is provided by the resident owners.
14rm(1🔄13🐾) (3fb) CTV in all bedrooms ® ✖ sB&B£16.50-£22 sB&B🔄🐾£20-£25 dB&B🔄🐾£33-£45 WB&B£112-£130 WBDi£178-£210 LDO 6pm
Lic 🍴 11P nc3yrs
See advertisement in COLOUR SUPPLEMENT

GH Ⓠ **Thornleigh** Thornbarrow Rd LA23 2EW ☎(05394) 4203
Feb-Nov
This friendly and comfortable guesthouse stands in a quiet side road between Bowness and Windermere.

6hc (4fb) CTV in 5 bedrooms ® ✖ (ex guide dogs) sB&B£14-£17.50 dB&B£28-£35
🍴 CTV 5P
Credit Cards ①③ⓔ

See advertisement on page 389

GH Ⓠ Ⓠ Ⓠ **Westlake** Lake Rd LA23 2EQ ☎(09662) 3020 due to change to (05394) 43020
This small, friendly family-run guesthouse offers a very high standard of comfort and helpfulness.
8🔄🐾 (2fb) CTV in all bedrooms ® ✖ sB&B🔄🐾£17-£21 dB&B🔄🐾£34-£42 WB&B£119-£147 WBDi£205 LDO 3.30am
Lic 🍴 CTV 8P ⓔ

See advertisement on page 389

GH Ⓠ Ⓠ Ⓠ **White Lodge Hotel** Lake Rd LA23 2JJ ☎(09662) 3624 due to change t o (05394)43624
Mar-Nov
Attractively furnished and comfortable, this guesthouse offers good, all round service and a friendly atmosphere. It is close to all amenities in Bowness.
12🔄🐾 (3fb) CTV in all bedrooms ® ✖ (ex guide dogs) sB&B🔄🐾£24-£28 dB&B🔄🐾£44-£50 WB&B£150-£160 WBDi£210-£220 LDO 6.30pm
Lic 🍴 CTV 14P
Credit Cards ①③

See advertisement on page 389

GH Ⓠ Ⓠ Ⓠ **Winbrook** 30 Ellerthwaite Rd LA23 2AH ☎(09662) 4932
Mar-Nov & Xmas
Situated in a quiet side road close to the village, this pleasant guesthouse offers good home comforts and well equipped bedrooms, with a comfortable lounge for guests.
6rm(1🔄2🐾3hc) 🔄in all bedrooms CTV in all bedrooms ®
🍴 CTV 7P nc6yrs

GH QQQ ***Woodlands*** New Rd LA23 2EE ☎(09662) 3915
Very comfortable and well furnished, this guesthouse offers friendly service and attention from the resident owners. It stands half way between Windermere and Bowness.
11rm(9🚿2hc) (2fb)⊘in 2 bedrooms CTV in all bedrooms ®
✗ (ex guide dogs) LDO 3pm
Lic 📺 11P nc5yrs
Credit Cards [1] [3]

WINDSOR Berkshire Map **04** SU97

GH QQQ ***Melrose House*** 53 Frances Rd SL4 3AQ
☎(0753) 865328
This elegant detached Victorian house is located about five minutes from the castle and town centre. The accommodation is comfortable, clean and well maintained. Bedrooms are bright and cheerful in pink and green and the shower rooms are smartly tiled. Downstairs there is a spacious breakfast room, a mirrored entrance hall and a cosy television lounge.
9🛁🚿 (2fb)⊘in 2 bedrooms CTV in all bedrooms ®
📺 CTV 10P

WINDYGATES Fife *Kirkcaldy* Map **12** NO30

GH QQ **Greenfield** Cameron Bridge KY8 5RW
☎Buckhaven(0592) 713301
This fine Victorian house has been attractively converted, and offers a comfortable lounge and a bright, cheerful dining room. The house is situated off the A915: approaching from the south, turn left at the first roundabout then left again.
3hc TV in all bedrooms ✱ sB&B£18-£25 dB&B£30-£35 dB&Bfr£36 WBDi£136
📺 CTV 15P (£)

WINSTER Derbyshire Map **08** SK26

GH QQQ **The Dower House** Main St DE4 2DH
☎(062988) 213 due to change to (0629) 650213
Mar-Oct
This Elizabethan country house with its walled garden stands in the heart of the Peak District village. It has spacious bedrooms and a lounge with a log fire. Breakfast is served 'en famille'.
3hc CTV in all bedrooms ® sB&B£16-£32 dB&B£32
Lic 📺 4P nc10yrs

WINTERBOURNE ABBAS Dorset Map **03** SY69

GH QQ **Churchview** DT2 9LS ☎Martinstown(0305) 889296
rs Nov-Feb
An attractive 17th-century roadside flint cottage which provides an ideal base for touring the area. Bedrooms tend to be small: some are newly decorated, with modern furnishings, while others have a rather dated charm; the private bathrooms are modern and well maintained. There are two lounges, one is non smoking and both have colour TV, and the cosy dining room has polished tables, open fires and country bric-a-brac.
10rm(2🛁2🚿6hc) (1fb) ® ✱ sB&B£16-£20 sB&B🛁🚿£20-£24 dB&B£32-£36 dB&B🛁🚿£40-£44 WB&B£112-£140 WBDi£168-£180 LDO 7pm
Lic 📺 CTV 9P 1🚗 nc3yrs (£)
See advertisement under DORCHESTER

WISBECH Cambridgeshire Map **05** TF40

FH QQQ Mrs S M King **Stratton** *(TF495140)* West Drove North, Walton Highway PE14 7DP ☎(0945) 880162
A modern bungalow-style farmhouse set within 22 acres of grazing; it is situated four miles north east of Wisbech and eight miles from Kings Lynn; take the first left after the village of Wallon Highway from the A47. A superior style of accommodation is offered: bedrooms are spacious, well equipped and decorated with pretty co-ordinating soft furnishings, and all are en suite. There is also a covered, heated swimming pool and a small lake for fishing.

3🛁🚿 ⊘in all bedrooms CTV in all bedrooms ®
✗ (ex guide dogs) sB&B🛁🚿£18-£20 dB&B🛁🚿£36-£40 WB&B£126
📺 CTV 6P nc5yrs ≈(heated) ♩ 22 acres beef dairy pigs (£)

WITHERIDGE Devon Map **03** SS81

INN QQQ **Thelbridge Cross** Thelbridge EX17 4SQ On the B3042 ☎Tiverton(0884) 860316
rs 25 & 26 Dec
Tucked away just north of Crediton, this inn has cosy, pleasant bars and restaurant, together with a new complex of bright bedrooms equipped with colour TV, direct dial telephones and tea facilities. Home cooked meals are available with prompt, friendly service.
8🛁🚿 (1fb) CTV in all bedrooms ® ✗ (ex guide dogs) sB&B🛁🚿£35-£45 dB&B🛁🚿£52-£65 WB&Bfr£175 WBDifr£250 Lunch £6-£12&alc Dinner £8-£15alc LDO 9pm
📺 CTV 50P
Credit Cards [1] [3] (£)

WITHLEIGH Devon Map **03** SS91

FH QQQ Mrs S Hann **Great Bradley** *(SS908135)* EX16 8JL
☎Tiverton(0884) 256946
Etr-Oct
A beautiful Devonshire longhouse on a 155-acre farm dating back to the 16th century. Set in an elevated position, the farmhouse affords uninterrupted views of glorious countryside, yet it is only five miles from the North Devon link road and 10 miles from Junction 27 of the M5. The bedrooms have private bathrooms across the corridor and are tastefully decorated with co-ordinating colour schemes. Full of character with exposed beams and fireplaces and original wood panelling, the farmhouse offers bed and breakfast only, but snacks are available if requested. ▸

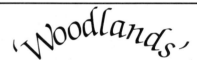

2hc ⚡in all bedrooms ® ✗ ✻ dB&B£27-£32 WB&Bfr£94.50
🍴 CTV 4P nc7yrs 155 acres dairy

WITNEY Oxfordshire Map 04 SP30

INN 🅀🅀🅀 **The Bird in Hand** White Oak Green, Hailey
OX8 8LP (1.75m N on B4022) ☎(0993) 868321 & 868811
16⊸🎓 (2fb) CTV in all bedrooms ® ✗ (ex guide dogs) ✻
sB&B⊸🎓£39.95 dB&B⊸🎓£49.50 WB&B£173.25-£279.65
WBDi£215-£304.15 ✻ Lunch £6.15-£20alc Dinner £6.15-
£20alc LDO 9.45pm
🍴 30P
Credit Cards ①③
See advertisement under BURFORD

WIVELISCOMBE Somerset Map 03 ST02

GH 🅀🅀 **Deepleigh Country Hotel** Langley Marsh TA4 2UU
☎(0984) 23379
6⊸🎓 (2fb) CTV in all bedrooms ® ✗ (ex guide dogs) ✻
dB&B⊸🎓£42-£46 WB&Bfr£140 WBDifr£224 LDO noon
Lic 🍴 5P ♨ ♬(hard)◡ ⓔ

WIX Essex Map 05 TM12

FH 🅀🅀🅀 Mrs H P Mitchell **New Farm House** (TM165289)
CO11 2UJ (0.5m N off Wix-Bradfield road) ☎(0255) 870365
*A modern farmhouse with an annexe, surrounded by 50 acres of
arable farmland. Family run, it caters well for children, and there
are limited facilities for disabled guests. Bedrooms are nicely
furnished and adequately equipped, and public rooms are
comfortable.*
6rm(1🎓5hc) Annexe 6🎓 (5fb)⚡in 10 bedrooms CTV in all
bedrooms ® sB&Bfr£18 sB&B🎓fr£20 dB&Bfr£33
dB&B🎓fr£38 WB&B£113.40-£126 WBDi£172.50-£185.50
LDO 5.30pm
🍴 CTV 12P ♨ 52 acres arable non-working
Credit Cards ①③ⓔ

WOKING Surrey Map 04 TQ05

GH 🅀🅀🅀 **Glencourt** St Johsn Hill Rd GU21 1RQ
☎(0483) 764154
*One-and-a-half acres of secluded gardens and woodland surround
this attractive house. The traditionally furnished accommodation
is particularly well equipped and à la carte meals are served in the
adjoining Fountain Restaurant which specialises in flambé
cookery. Service is very friendly and supervised by the proprietor
Zelda Lewis.*
9rm(6⊸3🎓) Annexe 2⊸ (1fb) CTV in all bedrooms ® ✻
sB&B⊸🎓£47 dB&B⊸🎓£63.45 LDO 10pm
Lic 🍴 29P table tennis
Credit Cards ①③ⓔ

WOODBRIDGE Suffolk Map 05 TM24

GH 🅀🅀 **Grove House** 39 Grove Rd IP12 4LG ☎(0394) 382202
*Mr and Mrs Kelly are friendly hosts at this hotel which is set back
from the A12 with car parking to the front. The well-kept and
equipped accommodation has some en suite facilities, and a small
menu is offered.*
9rm(5🎓4hc) (1fb) CTV in all bedrooms ® sB&B£18-£20
dB&B£34-£38 dB&B🎓£38.50-£42 WB&B£106-£120
WBDi£160-£180 LDO 6.30pm
Lic 🍴 CTV 12P
Credit Cards ①③ⓔ

WOODY BAY Devon Map 03 SS64

GH 🅀🅀 *The Red House* EX31 4QX ☎Parracombe(05983) 255
Apr-Oct
*Detached house in lovely elevated position, set in wooded valley,
offering friendly, personal services, comfort, and good home
cooking.*

6rm(3⊸1🎓2hc) (1fb) CTV in all bedrooms ® LDO 6.30pm
Lic 🍴 CTV 8P nc4yrs

WOOKEY HOLE Somerset Map 03 ST54

GH 🅀🅀 **Glencot House** Glencot Ln BA5 1BH
☎Wells(0749) 677160 FAX (0749) 670210
Closed 25-28 Dec
*This splendid Grade II listed mansion stands in 18 acres of
parkland; including river frontage with trout fishing. Two
bedrooms have four-poster beds and in addition to the comfortable
public rooms there are hairdressing facilities, a sauna, jet stream
pool and a snooker table.*
10rm(3⊸7🎓) (3fb) CTV in all bedrooms ® ✻ sB&B⊸🎓£40-
£45 dB&B⊸🎓£52-£75 WB&B£280-£305 WBDi£380-£445
LDO 9pm
Lic 🍴 CTV 21P ⊠(heated) ♪ snooker sauna solarium
Credit Cards ①③

WOOLACOMBE Devon Map 02 SS44

See also Mortehoe
GH 🅀🅀 *Camberley Hotel* Beach Rd EX34 7AA
☎(0271) 870231
*In an elevated position with some lovely views, this family-run hotel
offers a warm welcome and well equipped accommodation. A
choice of menu is available and orders for dinner are taken after
breakfast.*
6⊸🎓 (3fb) CTV in all bedrooms ® LDO 6.30pm
Lic CTV 6P

GH 🅀🅀🅀 **The Castle** The Esplanade EX34 7DJ
☎(0271) 870788
Apr-Oct
*Built of local stone in 1897, and set in its own gardens, this house
overlooks the beach and Woolacombe Bay. Tastefully converted to
provide hotel accommodation, some original features have been
retained in the public areas, and the establishment is owned and
personally managed by John and June Frazier.*
8🎓 (2fb) ® ✗ (ex guide dogs) ✻ dB&B🎓£49-£54 (incl dinner)
WB&B£115-£136.50 WBDi£160-£180 LDO 6pm
Lic 🍴 CTV 8P nc5yrs

GH 🅀🅀🅀 *Combe Ridge Hotel* The Esplanade EX34 7DJ
☎(0271) 870321
Mar-Oct
*A family-run hotel, just away from the centre of the village, with
beautiful views of Morte Point and Woolacombe Bay. The
bedrooms are simply appointed and spotlessly clean, some with en
suite facilities. There is a comfortable residents' lounge, and a set
evening meal is available.*
8rm(4🎓4hc) (4fb) CTV in 7 bedrooms ® (wkly only Jul-Aug)
LDO 5pm
Lic 🍴 CTV 7P

GH 🅀🅀🅀 **Holmesdale Hotel** Bay View Rd EX34 7DQ
☎(0271) 870335
Closed Feb
*Many guests return regularly to this well-equipped holiday hotel
with its friendly and outgoing Spanish proprietors. The Gema
restaurant offers an extensive menu and features interesting
Basque dishes.*
15🎓 (10fb) CTV in all bedrooms ® ✻ sB&B🎓£20-£26
WBDi£150-£200 (wkly only high season) LDO 8.30pm
Lic 🍴 CTV 14P
Credit Cards ①③ⓔ

GH 🅀🅀🅀 *Pebbles Hotel & Restaurant* Combesgate Beach,
Mortehoe EX34 7EA ☎(0271) 870426
Closed Jan
*A stone's throw away from sandy Combesgate beach, this elevated
terraced property has superb views of the Devon coastline. A
carvery and separate restaurant offer a comprehensive choice of
meals with seafood a speciality. The bedrooms are well equipped.*

12rm(11⇨1hc) (5fb) CTV in all bedrooms ® LDO 9.30pm
Lic 25P 1🏌
Credit Cards ① ③

WOOLHOPE Hereford & Worcester Map **03** SO63

INN Q Q *Butchers Arms* HR1 4RF ☎Fownhope(043277) 281
due to change to (0432) 860281
*Located just outside the rural village, and close to Hereford, this
inn has extensive bar and restaurant menus, with some unusual
choices. The bar areas are 'old world' in style, with beamed ceilings
and traditional country inn hospitality.*
3hc TV in all bedrooms ® ✕ (ex guide dogs) LDO 8.30pm
🍴 80P nc14yrs

WOOLSTONE Oxfordshire Map **04** SU28

SELECTED

INN Q Q Q *The White Horse* SN7 7QL
☎Uffington(036782) 566 & 726
*Part of 'Tom Brown's Schooldays' is said to have been written
in this 16th-century inn. Six modern, en suite, well-equipped
bedrooms surround a courtyard and the public rooms retain
the original character of the building. Ray and Maureen
Batty offer an extensive à la carte menu accompanied by a
wide selection of wines.*
Annexe 6⇨♠ CTV in all bedrooms ® ✕ (ex guide dogs)
LDO 10pm
🍴 60P
Credit Cards ① ② ③ ⑤

WORCESTER Hereford & Worcester Map **03** SO85

See also Leigh
GH Q Q Q *40 Britannia Square* WR1 3DN ☎(0905) 611920
FAX (0905) 27152
*A beautiful Georgian house situated on the north side of Brittania
Square, near the city centre. Two rooms are self-contained units
with comfortable seating areas and separate kitchenettes, and one
room is inside the house. The owner runs courses on paint finishes,
and her artistic flair is evident throughout the house.*
1⇨♠ Annexe 2⇨♠ (2fb)✂in 1 bedroom CTV in all
bedrooms ® ✕ ✱ sB&B⇨♠£30 dB&B⇨♠£45-£55
🍴 CTV P

GH Q *Wyatt* 40 Barbourne Rd WR1 1HY ☎(0905) 26311
*A Victorian house situated on a busy main road close to the city
centre. Modest accommodation is provided in simply appointed
rooms, and it is popular with a mainly commercial clientèle.*
8rm(4♠4hc) (4fb) CTV in all bedrooms ® ✱ sB&B£16-£18
dB&B£26-£28 dB&B♠£28-£30 LDO 5.30pm
🍴 CTV
Credit Cards ① ③ ⑤

WORKINGTON Cumbria Map **11** NX92

GH Q Q *Morven Hotel* Siddick Rd CA14 1LE
☎(0900) 602118 & 602002
*On the Maryport road north of the town, this pleasantly furnished
hotel, offers good value for money and is personally supervised by
resident owners.*
6rm(4♠2hc) (1fb) CTV in all bedrooms ® ✱ sB&B£18-£20
sB&B⇨£20-£26 dB&B£30-£34 dB&B⇨£34-£40 LDO 4pm
Lic 🍴 CTV 20P

Street plans of certain towns and cities
will be found in a separate section
at the back of the book.

WORTHING West Sussex Map **04** TQ10 During the currency
of this publication Worthing telephone numbers are liable to
change.

GH Q Q Q **Blair House** 11 St Georges Rd BN11 2DS
☎(0903) 34071 due to change to 234071
*Close to the seafront, Beach House Park and bowling greens, this
hotel offers a warm, friendly welcome. A comfortable, well-
appointed lounge complements the modern bedrooms. The
proprietors offer personal service and good home cooked meals.*
7rm(2⇨4♠1hc) (1fb) CTV in all bedrooms ®
✕ (ex guide dogs) ✱ sB&B£18.50-£19.50 sB&B⇨♠£18.50-£20
dB&B£30-£35 dB&B⇨♠£35-£40 WB&B£129.50-£136.50
WBDi£182-£189 (wkly only Xmas) LDO 6.30pm
Lic 🍴 3P 1🏌 (£5 per day)
Credit Cards ① ② ③ ⑤

GH Q Q Q **Delmar Hotel** 1-2 New Pde BN11 2BQ
☎(0903) 211834 FAX (0903) 850249
*Ideally situated on the seafront, this small family-run hotel offers
comfortable accommodation and a friendly informal atmosphere.
Bedrooms are compact but well equipped, and basic English
cooking is well prepared, using fresh local produce.*
13rm(10⇨♠3hc) (2fb)✂in all bedrooms CTV in all bedrooms
® ✕ (ex guide dogs) ✱ sB&B£22.33 sB&B⇨♠£24.68
dB&B⇨♠£40-£49.36 WB&B£140.68-£155.49 WBDi£217.86-
£236.88 (wkly only Oct-May) LDO noon
Lic 🍴 CTV 5P 1🏌
Credit Cards ① ③ ⑤

GH Q Q Q **Heene House** 140 Heene Rd BN11 4PJ
☎(0903) 33213 & 210804
*This charming detached house, in Victorian style, offers
comfortable, well- equipped bedroom accommodation. There is a
delightful conservatory which overlooks the garden, a comfortable
lounge with a small bar and a nicely appointed dining room.*

▶

DELMAR HOTEL
1/2 New Parade, Worthing
West Sussex BN11 2BQ
Tel: (0903) 211834 Fax: (0903) 850249

A licensed family hotel in quiet location
overlooking sea and gardens, convenient
for all local amenities. Bedrooms have colour TV/video, telephone/radio, tea making
facilities/mini bar, hair dryer and hot & cold
water. En suite facilities, sun balcony,
ground floor rooms and four poster bed
available. Lounge, conservatory bar and
roof garden. Ample car parking, full central
heating. Open all year.

15rm(3⇨8♠♦4hc) (3fb) CTV in all bedrooms ® ✱
sB&B⇨♠£22-£33.50 dB&B⇨♠£37-£52 LDO 8pm
Lic ♥ 7P
Credit Cards ①②③⑤

GH ◯◯◯ *Moorings* 4 Selden Rd BN11 2LL ☎(0903) 208882
This is a comfortable and welcoming guesthouse, with well-appointed bedrooms. There is a very pleasing lounge and attractive dining room where a good selection of home cooking is offered. The restaurant is open to non-residents by prior arrangement.
8rm(2⇨6♠) (2fb) CTV in all bedrooms ® ✖ LDO noon
Lic ♥ 5P
Credit Cards ①③

GH ◯ *Osborne* 175 Brighton Rd BN11 2EX ☎(0903) 35771
Situated in a prime position overlooking the sea, this guesthouse offers a pleasant patio to the front where guests can sit out during the summer months. The bedrooms are fairly basic but offer adequate comfort. Snacks are available throughout the day.
8rm(2♠6hc) (4fb) CTV in all bedrooms ®
Lic ♥ CTV ✗ nc9yrs
Credit Cards ①②③

GH ◯◯◯ South Dene 41 Warwick Gardens BN11 1PF
☎(0903) 32909
This bright and cheerful, end-of-terrace house is set in a quiet cul-de-sac away from the seafront. It has been tastefully modernised and furnished, creating a warm and friendly atmosphere.
6rm(1♠5hc) (1fb) CTV in 3 bedrooms ® ✖ ✱ sB&B£16-£18
dB&B£32-£36 dB&B♠£36-£38 WB&B£106-£120 WBDi£148-£162 LDO 3pm
Lic ♥ CTV ✗ nc9yrs ⓔ

GH ◯◯ South Dene 41 Warwick Gardens BN11 2EX

GH ◯◯ Wolsey Hotel 179-181 Brighton Rd BN11 2EX
☎(0903) 36149
Closed mid-end Dec
Commanding a good seafront position, this family-run guesthouse offers simple but comfortable accommodation. There is a residents' lounge with adjoining bar, and dinner is served by arrangement.
13rm(3♠10hc) (2fb) CTV in all bedrooms ® sB&B£18.50
sB&B♠£26 dB&B£35 dB&B♠£50 LDO 6.30pm
Lic ♥ CTV ✗
Credit Cards ①②③ⓔ

WREXHAM Clwyd

See **Hanmer & Penley**

WROTHAM Kent Map **05** TQ65

INN ◯◯ The Bull Hotel Bull Ln TN15 7RF
☎Borough Green(0732) 885522
This 14th-century inn first accommodated pilgrims to Canterbury and retains much of its early character while providing well-equipped rooms. Freshly prepared meals are offered in the restaurant and an extensive bar menu is available. Mrs Elaine Dunnell provides helpful service.
10rm(6⇨4hc) (1fb) CTV in all bedrooms ® ✱ sB&Bfr£35
sB&B⇨£40 dB&Bfr£45 dB&B⇨£50 ✱ LDO 10pm
♥ 50P
Credit Cards ①②③⑤ⓔ

WYBUNBURY Cheshire Map **07** SJ64

FH ◯◯ Mrs Jean E Callwood Lea *(SJ717489)* Wrinehill Rd
CW5 7NS ☎Crewe(0270) 841429
Lea Farm is a modern house with country views from all rooms and peacocks meandering around the charming gardens. The comfortable lounge has a small snooker table for guests' use.
3rm(1♠2hc) (1fb) CTV in all bedrooms ® ✱ sB&B£13-£15
sB&B♠£14-£15 dB&B£24-£26 dB&B♠£26-£28 WB&B£80-£90 WBDi£120-£130 LDO 5pm
CTV 22P ♪ snooker & pool tables 150 acres dairy ⓔ

WYE Kent Map **05** TR04

INN ◯◯ New Flying Horse Upper Bridge St TN25 5AN
☎(0233) 812297
Ownership has now reverted to the brewery, and this long-established, popular little village inn is scheduled for a complete refurbishment with more bedrooms being added. Bar meals chosen from the blackboard are still a feature, and the daily specials are recommended. There is also an attractive beer garden, and ample car parking is available. Service, supervised by Mr and Mrs Evans, is friendly and helpful.
4hc Annexe 4⇨ (1fb) CTV in all bedrooms ® ✱ sB&B£31-£36
sB&B⇨£36 dB&Bfr£41 dB&B⇨£46 ✱ Lunch £4.50-£9.50
Dinner £4.50-£9.50 LDO 9.30pm
♥ 20P
Credit Cards ①②③

YARMOUTH, GREAT Norfolk Map **05** TG50

GH ◯◯ Balmoral Private Hotel 65 Avondale Rd NR31 6DJ
☎(0493) 662538
Situated on a quiet street adjacent to the seafront, this modest accommodation is cheerfully decorated and furnished and some bedrooms have en suite facilities.
7rm(2♠5hc) (1fb) CTV in all bedrooms ® sB&B£14-£18
sB&B♠£17-£21 dB&B£28-£36 dB&B♠£34-£42 WB&B£85-£121 WBDi£105-£145 LDO 4pm
Lic ♥ CTV ✗

GH ◯ Frandor 120 Lowertoft Rd NR31 6ND (2m S off A12)
☎(0493) 662112
Situated on a busy road close to the town centre and with off street parking. This accommodation is spacious, simply furnished and has a friendly atmosphere. The evening meal is freshly prepared with a choice of main courses.
6rm(2♠4hc) (3fb)⑤in 4 bedrooms CTV in all bedrooms ®
(wkly only mid May-Sep) LDO 6.30pm
Lic ♥ CTV 12P
Credit Cards ①③

GH ◯◯ Georgian House NR30 4EW ☎(0493) 842623
Closed Xmas-Feb rs Nov-Etr
Situated on the seafront on the quieter north side of the town centre. This family-run hotel has modestly furnished rooms with some en suite facilities and sea views. The hotel offers good value for money.
19rm(11⇨6♠2hc) (1fb) CTV in all bedrooms ® ✖ dB&B£30-£35 dB&B⇨♠£35-£45 WB&B£95-£125 (wkly only end Jun-Sep)
Lic ♥ 18P nc5yrs

GH ◯ Helm House 2 Trafalgar Rd NR30 2LD
☎(0493) 843385
Situated between the sea front and the town centre Helm House has quite compact rooms which are attractively furnished and decorated in bright fresh shades and have good facilities.
11hc (5fb) CTV in all bedrooms ® ✖ (ex guide dogs)
LDO 5pm
♥ CTV ✗

GH ◯ Jennis Lodge 63 Avondale Rd NR31 6DJ (2m S off A12)
☎(0493) 662840
Adjacent to the seafront and within easy walking from the shops this establishment is modestly furnished with cheerful, tidy rooms. The evening meal is freshly prepared and there is a small bar next to the dining room.
11hc (4fb) CTV in all bedrooms ® LDO 4pm
Lic ♥ CTV ✗

GH ◯◯ Palm Court Hotel NR30 1EF ☎(0493) 844568
Closed Jan
47rm(35⇨♠12hc) (6fb) CTV in all bedrooms ® sB&B£25-£35
sB&B⇨♠£40-£50 dB&B£40-£50 dB&B⇨♠£52-£68
WB&B£120-£190 WBDi£150-£225 LDO 8pm

Lic lift 📺 CTV 47P 🖾(heated) sauna solarium gymnasium pool table
Credit Cards ①②③

GH ◗◗ Squirrels Nest 71 Avondale Rd NR31 6DJ
☎(0493) 662746
Situated at Gorleston, on the edge of the seafront. Mr and Mrs Squirrel work hard to offer modern facilities and a warm welcome: an attitude which is particularly appreciated by families.
9rm(1⇨8✎) (1fb) CTV in all bedrooms ® sB&B⇨✎£25-£35 dB&B⇨✎£50-£70 WB&B£160-£220 WBDi£195-£245 LDO 9.30pm
Lic 📺 CTV 5P
Credit Cards ①②③ ⓔ

YEALAND CONYERS Lancashire Map **07** SD57

GH ◗◗ The Bower LA5 9SF ☎Carnforth(0524) 734585
A family house set in delightful gardens on the edge of this attractive village. There are two very comfortable bedrooms, a period-style dining room with a communal table, and the owners' drawing room which guests may share. Breakfast is served at the large kitchen table. Dinner by prior arrangement.
2⇨✎ (1fb)✂in all bedrooms CTV in all bedrooms ®
✖ (ex guide dogs) sB&B⇨✎£27.50-£31.50 dB&B⇨✎£40-£48 WB&B£125-£200 WBDi£219.50-£294.50 LDO noon
📺 6P nc12yrs croquet lawn ⓔ

GH ◗◗ Holmere Hall Hotel LA5 9SN
☎Carnforth(0524) 735353 FAX (0524) 734860
A small hotel, parts of which date from the 17th century, located alongside the A6, two miles from junction 35 of the M6, making it a convenient base for touring southern Lakeland or for breaking an overnight journey. Morning coffee, bar lunches, afternoon teas and evening meals are served in the attractive dining room or comfortable lounge bar.
8rm(2⇨6hc) (2fb) CTV in all bedrooms ® LDO 10pm
Lic 📺 20P
Credit Cards ①③⑤

YEALMPTON Devon Map **02** SX55

FH ◗◗◗ Mrs A German Broadmoor *(SX574498)* PL8 2NE
☎Plymouth(0752) 880407
This attractive 16th-century stone-built house is to be found on the Yealmpton to Newton Ferrers road. Retaining many original features, the farmhouse offers comfortable open plan public areas and spacious bedrooms.
3hc CTV in 2 bedrooms TV in 1 bedroom ® ✖ ✳ sB&Bfr£12 dB&Bfr£24
P nc7yrs 200 acres mixed

YELVERTON Devon Map **02** SX56

GH ◗◗◗ Harrabeer Country House Hotel Harrowbeer Ln PL20 6EA ☎(0822) 853302
Closed Xmas
This small, family-run and characterful hotel, situated on the edge of Dartmoor, is an easy drive from the centre of Plymouth. The bedrooms offer good facilities and are well maintained, and the public areas are comfortably furnished with a lively atmosphere in the bar. Home-cooked dishes from a predominently set menu are served in the attractive beamed restaurant.
7rm(5⇨✎2hc) (2fb) CTV in all bedrooms ® ✖ ✳ sB&Bfr£23 dB&B£46 dB&B⇨✎£51 WB&B£149-£159.50 WBDi£220-£238 LDO 7.30pm
Lic 📺 CTV 10P ⌂
Credit Cards ①②③⑤
See advertisement under PLYMOUTH

GH ◗◗ Waverley 5 Greenbank Ter PL20 6DR
☎(0822) 854617
This terraced family home, situated in the village of Yelverton on the edge of Dartmoor, offers clean, bright bedrooms and a

comfortable lounge. Dinner is available in the evening if booked in advance, and a relaxed atmosphere is created by the resident proprietors.
5hc (2fb) CTV in all bedrooms ® sB&B£15-£16 dB&B£30-£32 WB&B£105-£112 WBDi£154-£161 LDO 10am
📺 CTV 2P ⓔ

YEOVIL Somerset Map **03** ST51

See also Halstock

FH ◗◗◗ Mrs M Tucker Carents *(ST546188)* Yeovil Marsh BA21 3QE (2m N of Yeovil off A37) ☎(0935) 76622
Feb-Nov
Charm and character abound in this mellow 16th-century stone farmhouse, which is set in a quiet location. A hearty cooked breakfast is served in the attractive dining room, while the large, comfortable lounge has an open fireplace.
3hc ✂in all bedrooms ® ✖ ✳ sB&Bfr£15 dB&B£29-£30 CTV 6P 350 acres arable beef

YORK North Yorkshire Map **08** SE65

See also Acaster Malbis, Copmanthorpe & Rufforth

GH ◗◗ Abbingdon 60 Bootham Crescent YO3 7AH
☎(0904) 621761
A well furnished and comfortable small guesthouse situated in a quiet side road a short walk from the city centre, near the town's football ground. Bedrooms have good facilities and there is an attractive lounge and cosy dining room.
8rm(5✎3hc) (3fb) CTV in all bedrooms ® ✖ (ex guide dogs)
📺 CTV

GH ◗◗ Aberford Hotel 35 East Mount Rd YO2 2BD
☎(0904) 622694
Aberford House is a pleasantly appointed, family-run establishment situated close to the city centre, with comfortable, well-equipped bedrooms. There is a cosy cellar bar for guests' use, and breakfast is served in the pretty dining room.
12rm(2⇨10hc) (1fb)✂in 6 bedrooms CTV in all bedrooms ® ✖ (ex guide dogs) ✳ sB&B£17-£20 sB&B⇨✎£21-£24 dB&B£32-£38 dB&B⇨✎£40-£46 WB&B£107-£126
Lic 📺 CTV 7P 1🚗
Credit Cards ①②③ ⓔ
See advertisement on page 395

GH ◗◗◗ Acer Hotel 52 Scarcroft Hill, The Mount YO2 1DE
☎(0904) 653839 & 628046
A comfortable house offering compact but well appointed bedrooms, a very good value dinner menu with a good choice of dishes and friendly service from the proprietors.
6rm(1⇨4✎1hc) (1fb) CTV in all bedrooms ® LDO 6.30pm
Lic 📺 CTV 4P 1🚗
Credit Cards ①③
See advertisement on page 395

GH ◗ Acomb Road 128 Acomb Rd YO2 4HA ☎(0904) 792321
The simple accommodation at this guesthouse is good value for money. It is about one mile from the city centre.
12rm(6✎6hc) (3fb) CTV in all bedrooms ® LDO 7.30pm
Lic CTV 20P

GH ◗◗ Adams House Hotel 5 Main Street, Fulford YO1 4HJ
☎(0904) 655413
Closed Xmas
Conveniently situated in a pleasant area, one mile south of the town centre, this comfortable hotel offers well appointed bedrooms, a spacious lounge and friendly proprietors. There is also a car park for guests.
7rm(2⇨4✎1hc) (2fb) CTV in all bedrooms ®
Lic 📺 8P
See advertisement on page 395

York

GH **QQ** *Alcuin Lodge* 15 Sycamore Place, Bootham YO3 7DW
☎(0904) 632222
Feb-Nov
*This three-storeyed, Edwardian mid-terraced guesthouse is quietly
located in a cul-de-sac close to the town centre, and offers neat,
well maintained accommodation.*
6rm(2♠4hc)(1fb) CTV in all bedrooms ® ✖ (ex guide dogs)
💷 2P nc5yrs

GH **QQQ** *Alfreda* 61 Heslington Ln, Fulford YO1 4HN
☎(0904) 631698
*A pair of Edwardian houses in Regency style, surrounded by
spacious, attractive gardens in a quiet location, with easy access to
the town centre. Bedrooms are pleasant and comfortable with
modern equipment and several extras, and there is an impressive
dining room.*
10rm(8♠2hc)(4fb) CTV in all bedrooms ® dB&B£25-£35
dB&B♠£38-£45 WB&B£120-£150
💷 CTV 20P 2🏀 (£2 per night)
Credit Cards 1 3 £

GH **QQ** *Ambleside* 62 Bootham Crescent YO3 7AH
☎(0904) 637165
*A comfortable, well maintained house offering neat, modern
bedrooms, a pleasant lounge, attractive beamed dining room and
friendly service.*
7rm(4♠3hc) CTV in all bedrooms ® ✖ ✳ dB&Bfr£26
dB&B♠fr£34
💷 CTV ✗ nc9yrs

GH **QQQ** *Arndale Hotel* 290 Tadcaster Rd YO2 2ET
☎(0904) 702424
Closed Xmas & New Year
*This elegant Victorian house overlooks the racecourse and has
spacious bedrooms with en suite facilites. Several rooms have half-
tester or four-poster beds. Every modern facility is provided by
David and Gillian Reynard, together with ample parking space
and splendid gardens.*
10⇔♠ (1fb) CTV in all bedrooms ® ✖ (ex guide dogs)
dB&B⇔♠£39-£59 WB&B£129.50-£199.50 LDO noon
Lic 💷 15P nc5yrs £

🚻🖵 GH **QQ** *Arnot House* 17 Grosvenor Ter, Bootham
YO3 7AG ☎(0904) 641966
Closed Dec-Jan
*This spacious and pleasant guesthouse is personally run, and is
situated within easy walking distance of the city centre. The large
bedrooms retain many of their original features, and the charming
owners have added a number of personal touches. Those with
musical interests will particularly enjoy the extensive collection of
Wagnerian memorabilia.*
6hc (2fb) CTV in all bedrooms ® ✖ sB&B£12-£15 dB&B£24-
£30 WB&B£84-£105 LDO 1pm
Lic 💷 2P nc5yrs £

GH **QQ** *Ascot House* 80 East Pde YO3 7YH ☎(0904) 426826
*Attractive Victorian house with unusual oriel staircase window.
Bedrooms have modern fittings.*
9rm(2⇔7♠) (2fb) CTV in all bedrooms ® LDO 6pm
💷 CTV 10P 1🏀 sauna solarium

GH **QQQ** *Ashbourne House* 139 Fulford Rd YO1 4HG
☎(0904) 639912
*High standards are maintained at this guesthouse, which is one
mile from the city centre on the A19, and has off-street parking.
The rooms are well furnished and equipped, and some have en suite
facilities.*
6rm(1⇔5♠)(1fb) CTV in all bedrooms ® sB&B⇔♠fr£25
dB&B⇔♠£40-£48 LDO 7pm
Lic 💷 CTV 5P 1🏀
Credit Cards 1 3 £

See advertisement on page 397

395

GH Q *Avenue* 6 The Avenue, Clifton YO3 6AS
☎(0904) 620575
Feb-Oct
*This three-storeyed, late-Victorian house is situated in a quiet,
tree-lined street near the city centre. It offers simple but neat
accommodation, with an attractive small forecourt garden.*
6rm(2♠4hc) (2fb) CTV in 2 bedrooms TV in 4 bedrooms
♥ CTV ⚡ nc4yrs

GH QQ **The Beckett** 58 Bootham Crescent YO3 7AH
☎(0904) 644728
Closed 15 Dec-13 Jan
*A privately owned terraced Victorian property situated in a quiet
residential road off the A19 and convenient for the city centre.
Although some bedrooms are fairly compact, they are pleasantly
furnished and well maintained. There is also a comfortable lounge
and a small breakfast room.*
7rm(5♠2hc) (2fb) CTV in all bedrooms ® ♥ (ex guide dogs)
✳ sB&B£14-£15.50 dB&B£26-£32 dB&B♠£28-£36 WB&B£98-
£126
♥ CTV 3P

GH QQQ *Bedford* 108/110 Bootham YO3 7DG
☎(0904) 624412
*This turn-of-the-century building situated very close to the town
centre features outstanding architectural decoration. The
accommodation is all tastefully decorated and furnished, and the
resident proprietors offer attentive service. There is also a spacious
car park.*
14rm(3⇨11♠) (3fb) CTV in all bedrooms ®
♥ (ex guide dogs) LDO 1pm
Lic ♥ CTV 14P
Credit Cards 1 3

GH QQQ **Beech House** 6-7 Longfield Terrace, Bootham
YO3 7DJ ☎(0904) 634581 & 630951
Closed Xmas & New Year
*An attractive converted Victorian terraced house. Well furnished,
it provides excellent facilities in the bedrooms, and offers very good
value. It is family owned and run, and is conveniently located
within walking distance of the city centre.*
9♠ CTV in all bedrooms ® ♥ ✳ sB&B♠£18-£23
dB&B♠£34-£46 LDO breakfast
♥ 5P nc10yrs ©

GH QQ **Bootham Bar Hotel** 4 High Petergate YO1 2EH
☎(0904) 658516
Closed 7-13 Jan
*This delightful 18th-century house is just inside one of the fortified
gateways to the city. It is well-furnished with good facilities and a
Victorian Parlour tea room which is open all day.*
9rm(1⇨8♠) (2fb) CTV in all bedrooms ® ♥ (ex guide dogs)
dB&B⇨♠£44-£58 LDO 7.30pm
Lic ♥ ⚡
Credit Cards 1 3 ©
See advertisement on page 399

GH QQ **Brontë House** 22 Grosvenor Terrace, Bootham
YO3 7AG ☎(0904) 621066
Closed 25 Dec
*Just 5 minutes' walk from the city, this Victorian town house
provides simple and comfortable accommodation. The bedrooms
are rather compact, but nicely decorated. Providing friendly
family-run accommodation, the guesthouse has a pleasant dining
room and combined lounge.*
8rm(5♠3hc) (1fb) CTV in all bedrooms ® ♥ (ex guide dogs)
✳ sB&B£10-£16 dB&B£20-£30 dB&B♠£24-£36
♥ CTV 3P
Credit Cards 1 2 3 ©

GH QQQ *Byron House Hotel* The Mount YO2 2DD
☎(0904) 632525 FAX (0904) 613174
Closed 25 Dec-4 Jan

*Close to the city centre on the A1036, this attractive building
features elegant rooms with high ceilings. The bedrooms are
mostly en suite and of generous proportions, well equipped and very
comfortable. There is also an attractive lounge and dining room.*
10rm(7⇨3♠3hc) (4fb) CTV in all bedrooms ®
♥ (ex guide dogs) LDO noon
Lic ♥ 7P
Credit Cards 1 2 3 5

GH QQQ **Cavalier Private Hotel** 39 Monkgate YO3 7PB
☎(0904) 636615
*An early Georgian listed building which has recently been
completely refurbished. Family owned and run, it offers warm and
comfortable accommodation together with friendly service.*
10rm(2⇨5♠3hc) (4fb) CTV in all bedrooms ®
♥ (ex guide dogs) sB&B£18.50 dB&B£34-£37
dB&B⇨♠£37-£40 LDO 3.30pm
Lic ♥ CTV 4P sauna

GH QQ **City** 68 Monkgate YO3 7PF ☎(0904) 622483
*Centrally situated, this small guesthouse is just a few minutes from
the Minster and City Walls. A totally non-smoking establishment
it provides compact, nicely decorated bedrooms, a small lounge and
well-appointed dining room.*
8rm(4♠3hc) in all bedrooms CTV in all bedrooms ® ♥
✳ sB&Bfr£10 sB&B♠£15-£20 dB&B£26-£36 dB&B♠£28-£38
WB&B£70-£140
♥ 6P 1🚗 nc5yrs
Credit Cards 1 3 ©

GH QQ **Clifton Green Hotel** 8 Clifton Green, Clifton
YO3 6LH ☎(0904) 623597
*On the A19 opposite the green, this attractive little guesthouse is
light and airy, with a comfy lounge bar and cosy dining room.
Ideal bed and breakfast accommodation is provided with
attractive, compact bedrooms.*
▶

A small Private Hotel open all year and offering every modern comfort in a beautiful old building only a 100 yards from the ancient city walls and five minutes from the Minster and City centre.

Bed and Breakfast-evening meals available – colour TVs, coffee and tea facilities in all rooms – Central Heating – Sauna, some rooms with Private Bath/Shower.

John and Edna Taylor
The Cavalier Private Hotel,
39 Monkgate, York YO3 7PB
Telephone: (0904) 636615

Beech House

6-7 Longfield Terrace, Bootham, York
Tel: (0904) 634581

Beech House is family run and situated in a quiet tree lined street, less than ten minutes' walk from York Minster and the city centre.
● All rooms have ensuite shower and toilet
● Colour TV and clock radio in all rooms
● Direct dial telephone
● Tea & coffee making facilities
● Central heating & double glazing in all bedrooms
● Full English breakfast

Bed & breakfast, ensuite £17-24
according to season

Proprietors: Bill and Sheila Stratton

BYRON HOUSE HOTEL

PERIOD ELEGANCE AND CHARM FOR THE DISCERNING VISITOR

Friendly personal service in a pleasant atmosphere and surroundings. Excellent cuisine, good wines and licensed bar. Spacious rooms with en-suite facilities, colour TV and telephone. Ideal situation for historic York centre and for visiting Yorkshire's beautiful countryside. Private car park. Tariff from £29.00 per night including full English breakfast.

Please write or telephone for brochure and tariff.

The Mount, York YO2 2DD
Tel: York (0904) 632525 Fax: York (0904) 613174

Ashbourne House Hotel

139 Fulford Road
York
YO1 4HG
Tel: 0904 639912

Lovely family run hotel. Close York city. On-site parking. Convenient for the University and close to Fulford International Golf Course. Evening meals available. Licensed lounge bar. Full central heating. All rooms have wash hand basins, shaver point, colour TV, tea/coffee trays. All en-suite. Open all year. Reductions for children. Bargain Winter/Spring Breaks. Major credit cards accepted.

8rm(2↱6hc) CTV in all bedrooms ® ✗ (ex guide dogs) sB&Bfr£20 dB&Bfr£35 dB&B↱fr£45
Lic ♨ CTV P 5🚗 (£)

GH QQQ Coach House Hotel Marygate YO3 7BH
☎(0904) 652780

The interior of this hotel, with its exposed beams and brickwork, is most attractive and complements the accommodation which includes an appealing restaurant. Situated in Marygate off the A19, it is a short walk from the Minster.

13rm(5⇨6↱2hc) ® ✗ (ex guide dogs) sB&Bfr£22 sB&B⇨↱fr£24.50 dB&Bfr£44 dB&B⇨↱fr£49 WB&B£150-£165 WBDi£210-£230 LDO 9.30pm
Lic ♨ CTV 13P
Credit Cards [1] [3]

GH QQQ Collingwood Hotel 163 Holgate Rd YO2 4DF
☎(0904) 783333

Set back from the A59 within easy reach of the city centre, this fine Georgian house dates back to 1745 and has been sympathetically restored and retains many period features. It offers comfortable, well maintained accommodation including a lounge bar, separate television room and a small attractive dining room.

10rm(4⇨6↱) (2fb) CTV in all bedrooms ® ✗ (ex guide dogs) dB&B⇨↱£42-£50 WB&B£147-£175 LDO 10am
Lic ♨ CTV 10P
Credit Cards [1] [2] [3] [5] (£)

GH Q Coppers Lodge 15 Alma Terrace, Fulford Rd YO1 4DQ
☎(0904) 639871

Simple, good value accommodation in a former police HQ (and gaol) one mile from the town centre.

8rm(1⇨↱7hc) (5fb) CTV in all bedrooms ® ✱ sB&B£13-£16 dB&B£24-£30 dB&B⇨↱£30-£32 (wkly only Nov-Feb) LDO 2pm
♨ CTV 2P (£)

GH QQ Crescent 77 Bootham YO3 7DQ ☎(0904) 623216

This attractive 18th-century house is close to Bootham Bar and the Minster, and has been carefully converted to offer well-appointed accommodation. All rooms are prettily decorated and there is also a cosy lounge.

10rm(6⇨↱4hc) (5fb) CTV in all bedrooms ® ✗ sB&B£14.50-£17.50 sB&B⇨↱£17.50-£25 dB&B£28-£35 dB&B⇨↱£35-£45 WB&B£98-£157.50 WBDi£143-£202.50 LDO noon
Lic ♨ 3P 1🚗 beauty salon
Credit Cards [1] [2] [3] [5] (£)

GH QQ Crossways 23 Wiggington Rd YO3 7HJ
☎(0904) 637250

A Victorian end-of-terrace house on the A1363 signed Helmsley, just a 10 minute walk from the Minster. All rooms have en suite facilities as well as colour TV and tea-making facilities. There is also an attractive breakfast room.

6⇨↱ CTV in all bedrooms ® ✗ (ex guide dogs) ✱ dB&B⇨↱£27-£30
♨ 3🚗

GH QQQ Curzon Lodge and Stable Cottages 23 Tadcaster Rd, Dringhouses YO2 2QG ☎(0904) 703157
Closed Xmas-New Year

A most attractive white-washed listed building surrounded by its own well tended gardens, standing close to the race course on the main route into the city. The bedrooms feature stripped pine furniture and antique beds, and some in a converted stable block have the original beams.

5rm(3⇨2↱) Annexe 5rm(3⇨2↱) (1fb) CTV in all bedrooms ® ✗ sB&B⇨↱£30-£36 dB&B⇨↱£44-£54
♨ 15P nc7yrs (£)

Book as early as possible for busy holiday periods.

GH QQ Dray Lodge Hotel Moor Ln, Murton YO1 3UH (3m E off A166) ☎(0904) 489591 FAX (0904) 488587

Converted from a 19th-century carriage works, Dray Lodge is in a small village on the eastern edge of the city. The Mortimer family create a cosy, welcoming atmosphere. Most of the well-equipped bedrooms are en suite.

10⇨↱ (1fb) CTV in all bedrooms ® ✗ (ex guide dogs) ✱ sB&B⇨↱£27.05-£29.90 dB&B⇨↱£42.30-£46 LDO 8pm
Lic ♨ CTV 15P gymnasium fitness training room
Credit Cards [1] [2] [3] (£)

GH QQQ *Field House Hotel* 2 St George's Place YO2 2DR
☎(0904) 639572
Closed Xmas

Beautiful gardens surround this carefully refurbished late 19th-century building situated close to the racecourse. The fine Victorian exterior blankets a superb mix of modern styles and comfort inside, including a tasteful spacious ground floor lounge and separate lounge bar. On the lower ground floor there is an elegant and charming dining room.

17rm(1⇨10↱6hc) CTV in all bedrooms ® ✗ (ex guide dogs) LDO 7pm
Lic ♨ 20P
Credit Cards [1] [2] [3]

See advertisement on page 401

GH QQQ Four Poster Lodge 68-70 Heslington Rd, off Barbican Rd YO1 5AU ☎(0904) 651170

Attractive and very well appointed, this guesthouse stands by the city walls. Judith Jones and her family offer a warm welcome and provide cosy, well-equipped bedrooms, mostly en suite and with four-poster beds. Dinner is available.

10rm(8↱2hc) (2fb) CTV in all bedrooms ® ✱ sB&B↱£22-£30 dB&B£38-£42 dB&B↱£47-£56 WB&B£132-£189 WBDi£200-£260 LDO 6pm

▶

Bootham Bar Hotel

4 High Petergate
York YO1 2EH
Tel. (0904) 658516

One of the best locations in York. This 18th century building is situated only 100 yards from York Minster, adjacent to the city walls.

All York's other tourist attractions, shopping streets, restaurants and the theatre are within easy walking distance.

All our bedrooms are very comfortably furnished. Each room has private facilities, colour TV, radio with alarm and tea making facilities.

Our Victorian tearoom is open from Monday to Saturday for light refreshments 10-30 a.m. — 5-30 p.m.

Telephone or write to the resident proprietors: Mr. & Mrs. J. Dearnley for further details.

Lic 🍷 5P 3🛏
Credit Cards 1 3 £

GH Q Q **Four Seasons Hotel** 7 St Peters Grove, Clifton
YO3 6AQ ☎(0904) 622621 FAX (0904) 430565
A handsome house situated in a tree-lined Victorian cul-de-sac just off the A19 on the outskirts of the city centre offers spacious, well maintained bedrooms, a comfortable lounge, and friendly service from its proprietors.
5rm(3🖪2hc) (2fb) CTV in all bedrooms ® ✗ (ex guide dogs) ✱ dB&B£33-£37 dB&B🖪£37-£41
Lic 🍷 CTV 6P
Credit Cards 1 3

SELECTED

GH Q Q Q Q **Grasmead House Hotel** 1 Scarcroft Hill, The Mount YO2 1DF ☎(0904) 629996
Situated within walking distance of the city centre, this delightful guesthouse offers impressive accommodation. The comfortable bedrooms all have 4-poster beds, each one different, a most inviting lounge with a small bar and a spacious dining room. The charming proprietors give courteous, attentive service, and specialise in assisting guests with detailed information on the city and surrounding area.
6🖪🖪 (2fb)✒in 3 bedrooms CTV in all bedrooms ® ✗
dB&B🖪🖪£48-£54 WB&B£150-£170
Lic 🍷 CTV 1P
Credit Cards 1 3 £

🅱🖉 GH Q Q **Greenside** 124 Clifton YO3 6BQ
☎(0904) 623631
This pleasant detached house is situated beside the A19 overlooking Clifton Green, about a mile from the city centre. Family-owned and run, it offers a sound standard of accommodation and personal service.
6rm(3🖪3hc) (2fb) CTV in all bedrooms sB&Bfr£13
dB&Bfr£25 dB&B🖪fr£28
Lic 🍷 CTV 5P 1🛏 ⏸ £

GH Q *Heworth* 126 East Pde YO3 7YG ☎(0904) 426384
This small, comfortable establishment has recently been tastefully redecorated with Laura Ashley colour coordinated furnishings. Mr and Mrs Cooper pride themselves in providing a wide range of breakfasts – including full continental, vegetarian and vegan – and real value for money.
6hc CTV in all bedrooms ®
Lic 🍷 1P 1🛏

GH Q Q Q **Hobbits Hotel** 9 St Peters Grove, Clifton YO3 6AQ
☎(0904) 624538
Closed 24-26 Dec
A large Victorian house in a pleasant, quiet road with its own garden and close to the town centre. It offers spacious, comfortable accommodation, with interesting, well equipped bedrooms.
5🖪🖪 (2fb)✒in all bedrooms CTV in all bedrooms ®
sB&B🖪🖪£22.50-£25 dB&B🖪🖪£45-£50
Lic 🍷 CTV 6P
Credit Cards 1 3 £

GH Q Q **The Hollies** 141 Fulford Rd YO1 4HG
☎(0904) 634279
Closed Xmas
The Hollies is a comfortable family-run guesthouse, a mile or so from the city centre, providing a warm and friendly atmosphere. The comfortable bedrooms are attractively decorated. A lounge is available for guests, and breakfast is served in a small dining room.
5rm(2🖪3hc) (3fb) CTV in all bedrooms ® sB&B£16-£22
sB&B🖪£18-£26 dB&B£26-£40 dB&B🖪£30-£44
🍷 CTV 5P
Credit Cards 1 3 £

GH Q Q Q **Holmwood House Hotel** 112-114 Holgate Rd
YO2 4BB ☎(0904) 626183
Two large terraced houses now provide attractive, well-appointed and elegant accommodation, conveniently situated on the A59, close to the town centre. Bedrooms are comfortable and well equipped; some are reserved for non-smokers. The inviting lounge and spacious dining room are nicely appointed.
10🖪🖪 (1fb)✒in 6 bedrooms CTV in all bedrooms ®
sB&B🖪🖪£38-£40 dB&B🖪🖪£48-£55 WB&B£160-£180
WBDi£230-£245 LDO 7pm
Lic 🍷 10P 1🛏 (£2 per night) nc8yrs
Credit Cards 1 3 £

GH Q Q Q **Inglewood** 7 Clifton Green YO3 6LH
☎(0904) 653523
A commendable hotel overlooking Clifton Green offering very good all round standards. Service from the resident proprietors is warm and friendly.
7rm(3🖪4hc) (2fb) CTV in all bedrooms ✗ sB&Bfr£20
dB&Bfr£35 dB&B🖪fr£45
🍷 CTV 1🛏 £

See advertisement on page 403

GH Q Q **Limes** 135 Fulford Rd YO1 4HE ☎(0904) 624548
A comfortable hotel managed by its friendly resident proprietor provides spacious modern bedrooms, an inviting lounge with bar, and an attractive dining room. Conveniently situated in a residential area south of York, it offers easy access to the ring road and city.
10rm(9🖪1hc) (2fb)✒in all bedrooms CTV in all bedrooms ®
✗ ✱ sB&B£16-£45 sB&B🖪£16-£45 dB&B£22-£40
dB&B🖪£26-£45 WB&B£80-£225 LDO 6.30pm
Lic 🍷 14P
Credit Cards 1 3 £

See advertisement on page 403

401

GH ⓠⓠ **Linden Lodge Hotel** Nunthorpe Avenue, Scarcroft Rd YO2 1PF ☎(0904) 620107

Closed 23 Dec-9 Jan

This attractive, detached Victorian house is located within walking distance of the city centre. Mr and Mrs Wharton provide comfortable accommodation that is well equipped. There are two comfortable lounges available for guests' use.

12rm(4🛏8hc) (3fb) CTV in 4 bedrooms ® ✠ sB&B£16-£20 sB&B🛏£20-£25 dB&B£28-£30 dB&B🛏£35-£40 WB&B£105-£115 LDO noon

Lic ⁿⁿ CTV 🅿

Credit Cards ① ③ ⓔ

GH ⓠⓠⓠ **Midway House Hotel** 145 Fulford Rd YO1 4HG ☎(0904) 659272

This detached Victorian house has been tastefully modernised to offer well appointed and comfortable accommodation and an attractive dining room where a choice of menus is available offering reasonably priced dinners.

12rm(11🛏1hc) (2fb)⚕in 10 bedrooms CTV in all bedrooms ® ✠ (ex guide dogs) sB&B🛏£20-£40 dB&B£30-£40 dB&B🛏£33-£48 WB&B£140-£280 WBDi£199-£239 LDO 7pm

Lic ⁿⁿ 14P

Credit Cards ① ② ③ ⑤ ⓔ

GH ⓠ **Minster View** 2 Grosvenor Ter YO3 7AG ☎(0904) 655034

This tall, Victorian terraced house is situated close to the town centre and offers neat, clean bedrooms and a most attractive dining room.

8rm(3🛏1🛏4hc) (4fb) CTV in all bedrooms ® ✱ sB&B£12-£16 dB&B£24-£30 dB&B🛏£26-£36 WB&B£84-£100 WBDi£140-£168 LDO 5.30pm

Lic ⁿⁿ CTV 6P ⓔ

GH ⓠ **Moat Hotel** Nunnery Ln YO2 1AA ☎(0904) 652926

Benefitting from its own car park, this well furnished hotel is close to the city walls, and is an ideal base from which to tour the city.

9rm(6🛏3hc) (1fb) CTV in all bedrooms ® ✠ (ex guide dogs)

Lic ⁿⁿ CTV 10P ⚓

Credit Cards ① ② ③ ⑤

GH ⓠⓠ **Monkgate Lodge** 51 Monkgate YO3 7PB ☎(0904) 631501

This small family-run guesthouse is conveniently situated close to the city centre. There are two well furnished bedrooms and a good breakfast is served in the attractive dining room.

2🛏3🛏 (1fb)⚕in all bedrooms CTV in all bedrooms ® ✠ ✱ dB&B🛏3🛏£36-£38 WB&B£115-£125

ⁿⁿ CTV nc5yrs ⓔ

GH ⓠⓠⓠ **Orchard Court Hotel** 4 St Peters Grove YO3 6AQ ☎(0904) 653964

A large, impressive Victorian house set within its own garden in a tree-lined avenue, close to the town centre. The accommodation is generally spacious; bedrooms are well appointed and the lofty public rooms are tastefully decorated.

11rm(8🛏🛏3hc) (4fb) CTV in all bedrooms ®
✠ (ex guide dogs) sB&B£20-£30 dB&B🛏🛏£44-£58 LDO 7.30pm

Lic ⁿⁿ CTV 12P

Credit Cards ① ③

GH ⓠⓠⓠ **Le Petit Hotel & Restaurant Français** 103 Mount Rd YO2 2AX ☎(0904) 647339

Conveniently situated between the town centre and racecourse, this small guesthouse has neat accommodation and the resident proprietor gives guests a warm welcome.

6🛏 (1fb) CTV in all bedrooms ® ✠ ✱ sB&B🛏£35-£40 dB&B🛏£60-£65 WB&B£205-£210 WBDi£255-£260 (wkly only all year) LDO 7pm

Lic ⁿⁿ CTV 1🚐

Credit Cards ① ② ③ ⓔ

GH ⓠⓠ **Priory Hotel** 126 Fulford Rd YO1 4BE ☎(0904) 625280

Closed Xmas

A pair of large double-fronted Victorian town houses have been converted into a very comfortable hotel with rear gardens, and situated near the city centre. Bedrooms are neat and well appointed, and menus are interesting, extensive and good value.

20🛏🛏 (5fb) CTV in all bedrooms ® ✠ (ex guide dogs) ✱ sB&B🛏3🛏£25-£35 dB&B🛏3🛏£45-£50 (wkly only Nov-Mar) LDO 9.15pm

Lic ⁿⁿ CTV 25P

Credit Cards ① ② ③ ⑤ ⓔ

See advertisement on page 405

GH ⓠⓠⓠ **St Denys Hotel** St Denys Rd YO1 1DQ ☎(0904) 622207

Closed 2wks Xmas

Former vicarage offers comfortable spacious accommodation and cosy lounge.

11rm(7🛏4🛏) (4fb) CTV in all bedrooms ® ✱ sB&B🛏3🛏£32-£42 dB&B🛏3🛏£40-£46 WB&B£224-£294 WBDi£283.50-£353.50 LDO noon

Lic ⁿⁿ CTV 9P

Credit Cards ① ③ ⓔ

GH ⓠⓠ **St Raphael** 44 Queen Anne's Rd, Bootham YO3 7AF ☎(0904) 645028

Improvements continue to be made at this three-storey mock Tudor town house situated in a quiet road off the A19 and within walking distance of the city centre. Bedrooms are comfortable, some having modern en suite shower rooms, and although there is no lounge, there is a neat breakfast room.

8rm(2🛏6hc) (2fb) CTV in all bedrooms ® sB&B£14.50-£17.50 dB&B£26-£32 dB&B🛏£29-£37 WB&B£101.50-£122.50 WBDi£150.50-£171.50 (wkly only Nov-Mar) LDO 4pm

▶

📺 CTV 🏳
Credit Cards 1 3

GH Q Q Q **Scarcroft Hotel** 61 Wentworth Rd, The Mount
YO2 1DG ☎(0904) 633386
*A very well furnished and comfortable hotel situated in a quiet side
road, notable for its fine home comforts and hospitality.*
7rm(1⇨6🏠) ⊁in all bedrooms CTV in all bedrooms ®
✻ (ex guide dogs) sB&B⇨🏠£22-£25 dB&B⇨🏠£44-£48
WB&B£150-£170
Lic 📺 CTV £

GH Q Q **Sycamore** 19 Sycamore Place YO3 7DW
☎(0904) 624712
Closed Dec
*Situated at the head of a quiet cul-de-sac close to the town centre,
this small family-run guesthouse offers cosy accommodation and
friendly service.*
6rm(3🏠3hc) (1fb) CTV in all bedrooms ® ✻
📺 3P nc5yrs

GH Q Q **Tower** 2 Feversham Crescent, Wigginton Rd
YO3 7HQ ☎(0904) 655571 & 635924
Closed 25 Dec-Jan
*An attractive house with a corner position outside York, but with
convenient access to the city centre. The bedrooms are very well
equipped and friendly service is provided by the resident owner.*
6⇨🏠 (4fb) CTV in all bedrooms ® ✻ (ex guide dogs)
dB&B⇨🏠£32-£42 LDO 10.30am
📺 6P
Credit Cards 1 3 £

YOULGREAVE Derbyshire Map **08** SK26

INN Q Q **The Bulls Head** Church St DE4 1UR
☎(0629) 636307
4hc (2fb) CTV in all bedrooms ® ✻ dB&B£24 Lunch £3-£9alc
Dinner £3-£9alc LDO 8.30pm
8P nc5yrs
Credit Cards 3 £

ZELAH Cornwall & Isles of Scilly Map **02** SW85

GH Q Q Q **Nanteague Farm** Marazanvose TR4 9DH
☎(0872) 540351
Etr-Oct
*A modernised and extended 300-year-old farmhouse, peacefully
positioned amid its own land yet with access from the A30, with
well equipped, co-ordinated bedrooms. The friendly young owners
specialise in home cooking and provide a substantial breakfast.
There is a man-made lake for water sports, a nine-hole golf course
and a solar heated swimming pool.*
4🏠 (3fb) CTV in all bedrooms ® ✻ (ex guide dogs)
sB&B🏠£13.50-£16.50 dB&B🏠£27-£33 WB&B£94.50-£115.50
WBDi£147-£168
Lic 📺 CTV 8P ⚬ ≋(heated) 🏌9 ⚓ solarium canoeing
windsurfing private beach
Credit Cards 1 3 £

The Priory Hotel, York

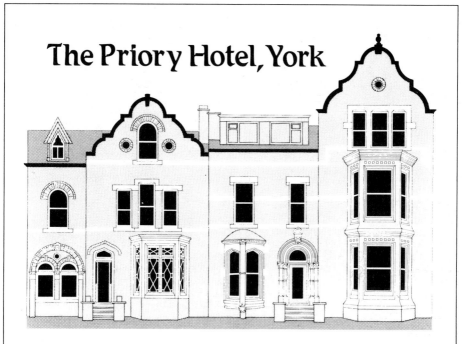

The Priory offers comfortable accommodation with full English breakfast, and is situated 600 yards south of York's medieval city walls, within easy direct reach of the nearby inner and outer ring roads. The city centre can be reached by a pleasant riverside walk.

The 20 bedrooms, all equipped with colour TV and tea/coffee making facilities, include single, double and family accommodation, all with en suite shower and toilet facilities.

The Hotel is AA listed, and has full central heating, a licensed bar and restaurant. The pleasant garden leads to the large private car-park.

Reductions are available for children sharing accommodation with their parents. Please send for brochure and tariff.

Proprietors:
George and Barbara Jackson
The Priory Hotel
Fulford Road
York YO1 4BE
Telephone York (0904) 625280

Useful information - IRELAND

In most instances, the details for establishments in the Irish section are as outlined in *'Your stay - what you need to know'* on page 29, the explanation of *Symbols and Abbreviations* and the *'How to use the Guide'* section on page 31

1 *Town and Country* In the Republic of Ireland establishments classified as Town & Country Houses are indicated by the abbreviation T&C. Because of statutory regulations regarding operation, these properties cannot be officially classified as Guesthouses although their facilities are similar.

2 *Prices* In the Republic of Ireland prices are quoted in Punts, indicated by the symbol IR£. The rates of exchange between Pounds Sterling and Punts is liable to fluctuate.

In the Republic of Ireland, as part of the registration scheme operated by 'Bord Failte', establishments must display tariffs; these are usually shown in bedrooms or reception. The application of VAT and service charges varies, but all prices quoted must be inclusive of VAT.

3 *Telephone Numbers* The area codes shown against the numbers in the Republic of Ireland are applicable within the Republic only. Similarly, the area codes shown for entries in Great Britain and Northern Ireland. Check your Telephone Directory for details.

4 *Fire Precautions* In Northern Ireland the Fire Precautions Act 1971 does not apply. The Fire Services (NI) Order 1984 covers hotel and boarding houses providing sleeping accommodation for more than six persons, which must have a fire certificate issued by the Northern Ireland Fire Authority. Properties that sleep less must satisfy the Authority that they have adequate exits. In the Republic of Ireland AA officials inspect emergency notices, fire-fighting machinery and fire exits, although fire safety regulations are a matter for local authority fire services. You are strongly urged to read and understand emergency notices for your own and other people's safety.

5 *Licensing Regulations* In Northern Ireland public houses open 11.30-23.00 Monday-Saturday, 12.30-14.30 and 19.00-22.00 Sunday. Also Christmas Day 12.30-22.00. Hotels can serve residents seven days a week without restriction. On Sundays non-residents may be served 12.00-14.30 and 19.00-22.00, and on Christmas Day 12.30-22.00. Children under 18 not allowed in the bar area of licensed premises, neither can they buy or consume liquor in hotels.

In the Republic of Ireland general licensing hours under present legislation are 10.30-23.00 Monday-Saturday winter and 10.30-23.30 summer. On Sundays and St Patrick's Day 12.30-14.00 and 16.00-23.00. No service on Christmas Day and Good Friday.

AA

BUDGET GUIDE
BRITAIN

In this new series, the AA's Budget Guide Britain breaks entirely fresh ground. Practical budgeting advice on planning your holiday is combined with a voyage of discovery.

The book covers eight regions, from the Scottish Highlands in the north to the Cornish penninsula in the far South-west. Insider information reveals unusual places to visit as well as familiar tourist attractions such as the Shakespeare country of the Midlands and the Georgian elegance of Bath.

Good value accomodation and eating out, money-saving tips, getting around by bus and train, local specialities and events, specially drawn location maps - all these and more are included in this wide-ranging guide which gives you all the information you need to plan and enjoy a stay in Britain.

Available at good bookshops and AA shops.

Another great guide from the AA

ACHILL ISLAND Co Mayo Map **01** A4

GH Gray's Dugort ☎(098) 43244 & 43315
Mar-7 Oct
8hc Annexe 7rm(5♠2hc) ✕ ✱ dB&BfrIR£31 dB&B♠frIR£35
WBDiIR£170-IR£185 LDO 6pm
🍴 CTV 18P table tennis pool table

ADARE Co Limerick Map **01** B3

T&C Coatesland House Killarney Rd, Graigue
☎Limerick(061) 396372
Closed 25 Dec
*Coatesland House, situated on the main Killarney road (N21) five
minutes from Adare village, is a very well appointed house with
attractive bedrooms, all en suite. Proprietors Florence and Donal
Hogan are welcoming and friendly and give superb attention to
detail. Dinner is available. Nearby activities include hunting,
fishing, golf and there is also an equestrian centre.*
5♠ (3fb) CTV in 1 bedroom ✕ (ex guide dogs)
sB&B♠IR£14.50-IR£19.50 dB&B♠IR£29 WB&BIR£95
WBDiIR£165 LDO noon
Lic 🍴 CTV 25P ♨
Credit Cards ② ③

ANNAMOE Co Wicklow Map **01** D3

T&C Carmel's ☎(0404) 45297
Etr-Oct
*Modern bungalow with nice gardens situated in scenic touring area
of Co. Wicklow on R755 route. Easy access to all areas of local
interest.*
4hc (2fb) ✕ sB&BfrIR£16 dB&BfrIR£24 LDO noon
🍴 CTV P

ARDARA Co Donegal Map **01** B5

T&C Bay View House Portnoo Rd ☎(075) 41145
Mar-7 Nov
7rm(1⇨6♠) (3fb) ✕ LDO noon
🍴 CTV 10P

ARDEE Co Louth Map **01** C4

GH The Gables House Dundalk Rd ☎Drogheda(041) 53789
Closed first 2wks in Jun & Nov
*Smart, comfortable house with a historic past. Very fully equipped
bedrooms and a popular restaurant offering excellent food.*
5rm(2⇨1♠2hc) (2fb) CTV in all bedrooms ®
✕ (ex guide dogs) ✱ sB&B⇨♠IR£25 dB&B⇨♠IR£35
LDO 9.30pm
Lic 🍴 20P
Credit Cards ① ② ③ ⑤

ARKLOW Co Wicklow Map **01** D3

FH M T Bourke **Killinskyduff** ☎(0402) 32185
Jun-Sep
3hc (3fb)✕in 2 bedrooms ✕ sB&BIR£15-IR£18 dB&BIR£30-
IR£35 WB&BfrIR£99 LDO 4pm
🍴 CTV 20P 2🐎 nc12yrs 165 acres hens tillage
Credit Cards ① ② ③ ⑤

ATHLONE Co Westmeath Map **01** C4

T&C Rocwal The Beeches, Coosan ☎(0902) 75640
Apr-Oct
4rm(2♠2hc) (1fb) ® ✕ (ex guide dogs) ✱ sB&BIR£15
sB&B♠IR£16 dB&BIR£26 dB&B♠IR£28 (incl dinner)
WB&BIR£90
🍴 CTV 6P

AVOCA Co Wicklow Map **01** D3

🖂📠**T&C Ashdene** Knockanree Lower ☎Arklow(0402) 35327
Apr-Oct
5rm(4♠1hc) (1fb)✕in all bedrooms ✕ sB&BIR£12-IR£16
sB&B♠IR£14-IR£18 dB&BIR£24 dB&B♠IR£28
WB&BIR£84 WBDiIR£160 LDO noon
🍴 CTV 5P ♪(grass)

T&C Riverview House ☎Arklow(0402) 35181
Apr-Oct
5hc (1fb) ✱ sB&BfrIR£15 dB&BfrIR£24
CTV 8P 1🐎

BALLINA Co Mayo Map **01** B4

T&C Whitestream House (N57) Foxford Rd ☎(096) 21582
6rm(5♠1hc) (2fb) ® ✕ ✱ sB&BfrIR£14.50
sB&B♠frIR£15.50 dB&BfrIR£24 dB&B♠frIR£26 LDO 4pm
🍴 CTV 10P
Credit Cards ③

BALLINADEE Co Cork Map **01** B2

T&C Glebe House ☎(021) 778294 FAX (021) 778456
Closed Xmas
3rm(2⇨1♠) (2fb) CTV in 1 bedroom ® ✕ (ex guide dogs)
sB&B⇨♠frIR£25 dB&B⇨♠frIR£40 WB&BfrIR£140
WBDifrIR£255.50 LDO noon
Lic 🍴 30P croquet lawn

BALLINHASSIG Co Cork Map **01** B2

T&C Blanchfield House Rigsdale ☎Cork(021) 885167
Mar-Oct rs Nov-Feb
6rm(2⇨♠4hc) (2fb) ✕ (ex guide dogs) ✱ sB&BIR£19
sB&B⇨♠IR£24 dB&BIR£30-IR£35 dB&B⇨♠IR£35-IR£40
LDO 9pm
Lic 🍴 CTV 20P
Credit Cards ① ② ③ ⑤

BALLINSKELLIGS Co Kerry Map **01** A2

GH Sigerson Arms ☎(0667) 9104 & 9106
May-Sep
10hc (2fb) ® ✕ (ex guide dogs) LDO 10pm
Lic 🍴 CTV 80P sauna
Credit Cards ① ③

BALLYBUNION Co Kerry Map **01** A3

T&C The Country House Rahavanig, Car Ferry Rd
☎(068) 27103
4rm(3♠1hc) (1fb) CTV in 1 bedroom ✕ (ex guide dogs) ✱
sB&BfrIR£15 sB&B♠frIR£16.50 dB&BfrIR£24
dB&B♠frIR£27 WB&BfrIR£84
🍴 CTV 5P ♨
Credit Cards ①

GH Eagle Lodge ☎(068) 27224 & 27403
Mar-Nov
8♠ ✱ sB&B♠frIR£20 dB&B♠frIR£30 LDO 9pm
Lic 🍴 CTV P

BALLYCASTLE Co Antrim Map **01** D6

🖂📠**GH Q Hilsea** 28 Quay Hill BT54 6BH ☎(02657) 62385
*An extended Victorian house overlooking the harbour and bay,
with fine views of Rathlin island and the Mull of Kintyre. Family-
owned and run, the public areas offer plenty of character, but
bedrooms are modestly appointed.*
19hc (4fb) sB&B£11-£13 dB&B£22-£25 WB&B£75-£85
WBDif£105-£130 LDO 7.30pm
🍴 CTV 70P
Credit Cards ① ② ③ ⓔ

BALLYMACARBRY Co Waterford Map **01** C2

GH Clonanav Farm Nire Valley ☎Clonmel(052) 36141
FAX (052) 36141
Feb-Nov
10♠ (1fb) ✕ (ex guide dogs) ✻ sB&B♠IR£25 dB&B♠IR£36
WB&BIR£120 WBDiIR£200
Lic ♨ CTV 10P ♫(grass)♪ ∪

BALLYMURN Co Wexford Map **01** D3

FH Mr & Mrs J Maher **Ballinkeele House** ☎(053) 38105
FAX (053) 38468
Apr-12 Nov
*Built in 1840, designed by Daniel Robertson and standing in 360
acres. This classical house has been lovingly restored by owners
John and Margaret Maher, completely retaining its ambience
while providing today's comforts. Lovely drawing and dining room.
Very comfortable bedrooms with decanter sherry to welcome you.*
4♠ ✕ (ex guide dogs) sB&B♠IR£29-IR£31 dB&B♠IR£50-
IR£54 LDO noon
Lic ♨ 20P nc3yrs ♫(hard)snooker 350 acres arable
Credit Cards ①③

BALLYVAUGHAN Co Clare Map **01** B3

T&C Rusheen Lodge ☎(065) 77092
15 Mar-Oct
*A charming house nestling in the valley of the Burren Limestone
mountains, an area famous for its arctic and alpine plants in spring
and summer. The McCann family were founders of the famous
Aillwee Caves and are a fund of local folklore. Bedrooms are
excellently appointed.*
6⇨♠ (2fb) CTV in all bedrooms ® ✕ (ex guide dogs)
sB&B⇨♠IR£18-IR£20 dB&B⇨♠IR£30-IR£35 (wkly only
Mar-Apr & Sep-Oct)
♨ CTV 10P

BANSHA Co Tipperary Map **01** B3

FH J & M Marnane **Bansha House** ☎(062) 54194 & 54245
Closed Xmas
7rm(4♠3hc) (1fb) ✕ (ex guide dogs) ✻ sB&BIR£13-IR£14
dB&BIR£25-IR£30 dB&B♠IR£30 WB&BIR£80-IR£90
WBDifrIR£160 LDO 7pm
♨ CTV 10P ♪ 100 acres mixed

BANTRY Co Cork Map **01** A2

T&C Shangri-La Glengarriff Rd ☎(027) 50244
FAX (027) 51417
May-Sep
7rm(4⇨♠3hc) (1fb) ® ✕ ✻ sB&BIR£18 dB&BIR£26
dB&B⇨♠IR£30 WB&BIR£85
Lic ♨ CTV 12P
Credit Cards ①③

BELFAST Map **01** D5

GH Ⓠ Camera 44 Wellington Park BT9 6DP
☎(0232) 660026 & 667856
*A double-fronted end-of-terrace Victorian house with a neat front
garden, situated just off the A1 Lisburn road, not far from the
university, Windsor Park football ground and the hospital.
Accommodation is simple but adequate.*
11rm(2♠9hc) (2fb) CTV in all bedrooms ✕ (ex guide dogs)
LDO 9am
♨ CTV
Credit Cards ③

Book as early as possible for busy holiday periods.

BLARNEY Co Cork Map **01** B2

T&C Casa Della Rosa Carrigrohane ☎(021) 385279
May-Oct
4rm(1⇨3hc) (2fb)⤝in 1 bedroom ✕ (ex guide dogs) ✻
sB&BIR£14 dB&BIR£23 WB&BIR£130 WBDiIR£180
LDO 4pm
♨ CTV 6P

BOYLE Co Roscommon Map **01** B4

FH Rushfield Croghan ☎(079) 62276
Mar-Oct
4hc (2fb) ✻ sB&BIR£11 dB&BIR£22
♨ CTV 10P 80 acres dairy sheep

BUNCRANA Co Donegal Map **01** C6

T&C St Bridget's Cockhill Rd ☎(077) 61319
4hc (3fb) ✕ (ex guide dogs) ✻ sB&BIR£12 dB&BIR£20-IR£24
♨ CTV 6P

BUSHMILLS Co Antrim Map **01** C6

SELECTED

GH ⓆⓆⓆⓆ White Gables 83 Dunluce Rd BT57 8SJ
☎(02657) 31611
Apr-Sep Closed Oct-Mar
*A modern villa situated in its own well maintained grounds
beside the A2 and enjoying dramatic views over the lovely
Antrim coastline. The house is attractively decorated and
furnished, with a particularly comfortable lounge where a
powerful telescope enables guests to pinpoint details along the
coast or across the sea to the isles of Islay. Pleasant bedrooms
also have fine views and are thoughtfully equipped. The
Johnstons are most hospitable hosts, and Mrs Johnston
produces excellent home-cooked meals, including an award-
winning Irish breakfast to set guests up for exploring the many
local places of interest. It is little wonder that visitors from all
over the world return to this delightful spot – but it does mean
that reservations should be made well in advance.*
4rm(3♠1hc) (1fb)⤝in all bedrooms ® ✕ sB&B£17.50-£20
dB&B♠£35 WB&B£115-£122.50 WBDi£180-£192.50
LDO 2pm
♨ CTV 10P 2🐾 nc5yrs Ⓔ

CAHIR Co Tipperary Map **01** C2

FH Mrs H O'Gorman **Lissava House** Lissava
☎Clonmel(052) 41117
May-Sep
5rm(3⇨♠2hc) (2fb) ✕ (ex guide dogs) ✻ sB&BIR£15-IR£17
sB&B⇨♠IR£17 dB&BIR£24 dB&B⇨♠IR£28
WB&BfrIR£80 WBDifrIR£150 LDO noon
♨ CTV 12P ♣ 140 acres beef horses sheep

CAHIRCIVEEN Co Kerry Map **01** A2

FH T Sugrue **Valentia View** ☎(0667) 2227
Mar-Oct
6rm(5♠1hc) (2fb) sB&BIR£15 sB&B♠IR£16 dB&BIR£24
dB&B♠IR£26 WB&BIR£91 WBDiIR£150 LDO 7pm
Lic ♨ CTV 20P ♣ 38 acres mixed

CAPPOQUIN Co Waterford Map **01** C2

GH Richmond House ☎(058) 54278
Feb-Oct
9rm(5⇨4♠) (2fb) ® ✕ sB&B⇨♠IR£21-IR£25
dB&B⇨♠IR£38-IR£44 WB&BIR£120-IR£140
WBDiIR£190-IR£210 LDO 8pm
Lic ♨ CTV 15P 2🐾
Credit Cards ③

CARLOW Co Carlow Map **01** C3

T&C Dolmen House Brownshill ☎(0503) 42444
Jul-Sep
6hc Ⓡ 🐕 sB&BIR£14 dB&BIR£24 WB&BfrIR£80
♨ CTV 8P

CARRICK-ON-SHANNON Co Leitrim & Co Roscommon Map **01** B4

FH C McDermott **Scregg House** ☎(078) 20210
Mar-Nov
4rm(1🚿3hc) (2fb) 🐕 (ex guide dogs) ✱ sB&BfrIR£15 dB&BfrIR£24 dB&B🚿frIR£24 LDO 4pm
♨ CTV 8P snooker games room 40 acres beef

CARRIGALINE Co Cork Map **01** B2

T&C Beaver Lodge ☎(021) 372595
Closed Xmas
An old ivy-clad house in own grounds off main street.
6rm(2🛁2🚿2hc) (5fb)🚭in 1 bedroom CTV in all bedrooms Ⓡ 🐕 (ex guide dogs) ✱ sB&BIR£12 sB&B🛁🚿IR£13.50 dB&BIR£22 dB&B🛁🚿IR£25 LDO 4pm
♨ CTV 14P
Credit Cards 1 2 3

CARRIGANS Co Donegal Map **01** C6

T&C Mount Royd Country Home Dunmore ☎Letterkenny(074) 40163
Situated off N.13, N.14 and A40 a large attractive creeper-clad house surrounded by a well tended garden. Very well appointed bedrooms and excellent home cooking. Caters for tourist and business guests.
4rm(2🚿2hc) (3fb) CTV in 1 bedroom 🐕 (ex guide dogs) sB&BIR£12 sB&B🚿IR£12 dB&BIR£24 dB&B🚿IR£24 LDO noon
♨ CTV 6P 1🚗

CASHEL Co Tipperary Map **01** C3

FH E O'Brien **Knock-Saint-Lour House** ☎(062) 61172
Apr-Oct
8rm(4🛁🚿4hc) (2fb) CTV in 1 bedroom 🐕 (ex guide dogs) sB&BIR£14 sB&B🛁🚿IR£20 dB&BfrIR£25 dB&B🛁🚿IR£29
♨ CTV 20P 30 acres mixed

CASTLEDERMOT Co Kildare Map **01** C3

T&C *Woodcourte* Castledermot ☎Athy(0507) 24167
7rm(3🛁🚿4hc) (2fb) Ⓡ 🐕 (ex guide dogs) LDO 8.45pm
Lic ♨ CTV 25P ✿ snooker
Credit Cards 3

CASTLEFINN Co Donegal Map **01** C5

FH D Taylor **Gortfad** ☎(074) 46135
Closed Nov-Feb
5rm(2🚿3hc) (3fb) CTV in 2 bedrooms 🐕 (ex guide dogs) sB&BfrIR£14 sB&B🚿frIR£15 dB&BfrIR£28 dB&B🚿frIR£28 WB&BfrIR£98 WBDifrIR£150 LDO 4pm
♨ CTV P 140 acres mixed

CASTLEGREGORY Co Kerry Map **01** A2

FH Mrs C Griffin **Griffin's** Goulane ☎(066) 39147
Apr-Oct
8rm(4🛁4🚿) (3fb)🚭in all bedrooms ✱ sB&BfrIR£15 sB&B🛁🚿frIR£17 dB&BfrIR£24 dB&B🛁🚿frIR£28 WB&BfrIR£98 WBDifrIR£189 LDO 5pm
♨ CTV 10P 150 acres dairy sheep

CLIFDEN Co Galway Map **01** A4

T&C Failte Ardbear, Ballyconneely Rd ☎(095) 21159
Apr-Oct
Modern bungalow in scenic location on edge of Clifden. Excellent standards of comfort and welcoming hosts. Ideal touring centre.
6rm(2🚿4hc) (2fb) 🐕 (ex guide dogs) sB&BIR£12 dB&BIR£24 dB&B🚿IR£28 WBDiIR£77
♨ CTV 15P
Credit Cards 1 3

T&C Kingstown House Bridge St ☎(095) 21470
Family-run street-side house. Ideal touring centre.
8rm(6🚿2hc) (3fb) 🐕 (ex guide dogs) ✱ dB&BfrIR£23 dB&B🚿frIR£26 WB&BfrIR£77
♨ CTV
Credit Cards 1 3

CLIFFONY Co Sligo Map **01** B5

T&C Villa Rosa Bunduff ☎Sligo(071) 66173
May-Sep rs Oct, Nov & Mar-Apr
6rm(2🛁🚿4hc) (2fb) 🐕 (ex guide dogs) sB&BIR£12 dB&BIR£24 dB&B🛁🚿IR£28 WB&BIR£75 WBDiIR£153 LDO noon
♨ CTV 30P 1🚗
Credit Cards 1 2 3

CLONAKILTY Co Cork Map **01** B2

FH D Jennings **Desert House** Ring Rd ☎Bandon(023) 33331 FAX (023) 33048
5rm(4🛁🚿1hc) Annexe 3hc (3fb) CTV in 3 bedrooms Ⓡ sB&BIR£16.50 sB&B🛁🚿IR£18.50 dB&BIR£24 dB&B🛁🚿IR£28 WB&BIR£80 WBDiIR£154 LDO 5pm
♨ CTV P 100 acres dairy mixed
Credit Cards 1 3

FH Mrs B Helen **Hillside** Kilgarriffe ☎Bandon(023) 33139
Mar-Oct
4rm(2🚿2hc) (3fb) CTV in 1 bedroom Ⓡ 🐕 (ex guide dogs) ✱ dB&BIR£28 dB&B🚿IR£34 WB&BIR£105 WBDiIR£147
P ✿ 150 acres arable dairy mixed

FH Mrs P Beechinor **Liscubba** Liscubba, Rossmore ☎Bandon(023) 38679
6hc (3fb) ✱ sB&BIR£11.50 dB&BIR£23 WB&BfrIR£73.50 WBDiIR£140
♨ CTV P 🚗 180 acres beef
Credit Cards 1

CLONBUR Co Galway Map **01** B4

GH Fairhill ☎Galway(092) 46176
Etr-19 Oct
10hc (1fb) CTV in 1 bedroom Ⓡ 🐕 (ex guide dogs) ✱ sB&BIR£11-IR£13 dB&BIR£22-IR£26 WB&BIR£73.50-IR£91 WBDiIR£147-IR£164 LDO 8pm
Lic CTV 10P outdoor pursuit centre pitch & putt

CORK Co Cork Map **01** D4

T&C Antoine House Western Rd ☎(021) 273494
7🚿 CTV in all bedrooms Ⓡ sB&B🚿IR£25 dB&B🚿IR£30 WB&BIR£150
♨ CTV 8P
Credit Cards 1 2 3 5

GH Garnish House 1 Aldergrove, Western Rd ☎(021) 275111 FAX (021) 273872
15rm(10🚿5hc) (1fb) CTV in all bedrooms Ⓡ 🐕 (ex guide dogs) ✱ sB&BIR£25-IR£30 sB&B🚿IR£32-IR£35 dB&BIR£35-IR£40 dB&B🚿IR£40-IR£45
♨ CTV 10P
Credit Cards 1 2 3 5

T&C Killarney House Western Rd ☎(021) 270179 & 270290
Closed 25-26 Dec
19rm(8♠11hc)(3fb) CTV in all bedrooms ®
✠ (ex guide dogs) ✱ dB&BIR£30-IR£50 dB&B♠IR£30-
IR£60
⁋ CTV 20P
Credit Cards ①②③⑤

GH Lotamore House Tivoli ☎(021) 822344 FAX (021) 822219
21⇔♠ (7fb) CTV in all bedrooms ✱ sB&B⇔♠IR£26
dB&B⇔♠IR£46
⁋ CTV 40P ♨
Credit Cards ①②③

COROFIN Co Clare Map 01 B3

FH Mary Kelleher **Fergus View** Kilnaboy
☎Limerick(065) 27606
Etr-Sep
6rm(5♠1hc) (4fb)✄in all bedrooms ✠ LDO noon
⁋ CTV 8P 17 acres non-working

FH Mrs B Kelleher **Inchiquin View** Kilnaboy ☎(065) 27731
Apr-Sep
5rm(3♠2hc) (2fb) ✠ (ex guide dogs) ✱ sB&BIR£12
sB&B♠IR£14 dB&BIR£24 dB&B♠IR£28 WB&BIR£75
WBDiIR£140 LDO 5pm
⁋ CTV 8P 15 acres beef mixed

CROSSHAVEN Co Cork Map 01 B2

GH *Whispering Pines* ☎Cork(021) 831448 & 831843
Apr-Oct rs Nov & Feb
15rm(11⇔4♠) (6fb) ✠ LDO 9.30pm
Lic ⁋ CTV 40P

CRUSHEEN Co Clare Map 01 B3

FH Dilly Griffey *Lahardan* Lahardan ☎Ennis(065) 27128 &
27319
rs Nov-17 Mar
8rm(6⇔2♠) (4fb) LDO 3pm
Lic ⁋ CTV P 230 acres beef
Credit Cards ②③

DINGLE Co Kerry Map 01 A2

GH Alpine Mail Rd ☎(066) 51250
15♠ (4fb) ✠ ✱ dB&B♠IR£27-IR£29
⁋ CTV 20P
Credit Cards ①③

T&C Cleevaun Lady's Cross, Milltown ☎(066) 51108
mid Mar-mid Nov
5rm(4♠1hc) (2fb) ✠ (ex guide dogs) sB&B♠IR£18
dB&BIR£29
⁋ CTV 7P nc3yrs

GH Doyles Town House 4 John St ☎Tralee(066) 51174
mid Mar-mid Nov
8⇔♠ CTV in all bedrooms ✠ (ex guide dogs) ✱
sB&B⇔♠IR£35 dB&B⇔♠IR£55 LDO 9pm
Lic ⁋
Credit Cards ①③⑤

GH Milltown House Milltown ☎Tralee(066) 51372
Etr-Oct
7rm(2⇔5♠) (3fb) ✠ (ex guide dogs) ✱ sB&B⇔♠IR£20-
IR£22 dB&B⇔♠IR£26-IR£30
⁋ CTV 10P nc5yrs mini golf
Credit Cards ①③

DONEGAL Co Donegal Map 01 B5

T&C Ardeevin Lough Eske, Barnesmore ☎(073) 21790
Apr-Oct
5⇔♠ (2fb) ® ✠ ✱ sB&BIR£16 dB&B⇔♠IR£26 LDO noon
⁋ CTV 8P 2🛋 nc9yrs

DOOLIN Co Clare Map 01 B3

FH J Moloney **Horse Shoe** ☎(065) 74006 FAX (065) 74421
Closed Dec
5♠ ✠ (ex guide dogs) ✱ dB&B♠frIR£25
⁋ CTV P boat trips 20 acres dairy
Credit Cards ③

DOWNPATRICK Co Down Map 01 D5

FH ❑❑❑ Mrs Macauley *Havine* 51 Bally Donnel Rd
☎Ballykinlar(0396) 85242
Closed Xmas wk
*A modernised farmhouse dating back 200 years in parts, situated
3.5 miles southwest of Downpatrick, off the A25. Take the
Ballykibeg road signed Tyrella past the Ramblers Inn, and the
farm is about a mile further, on the left. Bedrooms are well
furnished, with many thoughtful extras, including dressing gowns,
sewing materials and radios.*
4hc (1fb) ® LDO 4.40pm
⁋ CTV 10P 2🛋 125 acres arable

DUBLIN Co Dublin Map 01 D4

T&C Aaronmor House 1c Sandymount Av ☎(01) 687972
FAX (01) 682377
6rm(5♠1hc) (2fb) CTV in 1 bedroom TV in 1 bedroom ® ✠
✱ sB&B♠frIR£20 dB&B♠frIR£34 LDO 10am
⁋ CTV 8P nc5yrs
Credit Cards ①③

GH Aberdeen Lodge 53/55 Park Av ☎(01) 2838155
FAX (01) 2837877
*An old Victorian house built in 1870 and carefully refurbished to
the highest guesthouse standards. Sitauted on a tree-lined avenue
close to the Royal Dublin Society showgrounds and Lansdowne
Road rugby grounds.*
16⇔♠ (8fb)✄in 2 bedrooms CTV in all bedrooms ✠
Lic ⁋ CTV 16P
Credit Cards ①②③⑤

GH Ariel House 52 Lansdowne Rd ☎(01) 685512
FAX (01) 685845
*A luxurious Victorian mansion built in 1850, situated beside
Lansdowne Rugby grounds. Charming proprietors ensure guests
every comfort. Attractive bedrooms with authentic antiques of the
period.*
22⇔♠ CTV in all bedrooms ✠ sB&B⇔♠IR£20-IR£50
dB&B⇔♠IR£35-IR£70
⁋ CTV 18P nc5yrs
Credit Cards ①②③

T&C *Bective House* 2 Eglinton Ter, Donnybrook ☎(01) 692983
Closed 24-25 Dec
*Comfortable streetside tarraced house overlooking Bective Rugby
grounds, situated 1.5 miles from the city centre.*
6rm(4♠2hc) ✠ (ex guide dogs)
⁋ CTV

GH Beddington 181 Rathgar Rd ☎(01) 978047
FAX (01) 978275
Closed 23 Dec-13 Jan
14♠ (1fb) CTV in all bedrooms ® ✠ sB&B♠IR£33
dB&B♠IR£50
Lic ⁋ CTV 10P
Credit Cards ①③

T&C Darren House 7 Pembroke Rd ☎(01) 606126
Closed Xmas
Large Georgian house situated a short distance from Lansdowne Rugby grounds and the Royal Dublin Society.
6♠ (1fb) CTV in 4 bedrooms ® ✙ ✱ sB&B♠IR£30 dB&B♠IR£38-IR£40 LDO 10am
⅏ CTV 8P nc5yrs
Credit Cards ① ③

GH Egan's 7/9 Iona Park, Glasnevin ☎(01) 303611 & 303818
FAX (01) 303312
25♠ (4fb) CTV in all bedrooms ® ✱ sB&B♠IR£23.75-IR£31.35 dB&B♠IR£40-IR£51.50 LDO 8pm
Lic ⅏ 8P
Credit Cards ① ③

GH The Fitzwilliam 41 Upper Fitzwilliam St ☎(01) 600199
FAX 767488
5 Jan-15 Dec
12rm(2⇨10♠) (1fb) CTV in all bedrooms ✱ sB&B⇨♠IR£31.90-IR£39.60 dB&B⇨♠IR£48.40-IR£64.90 WB&BIR£154-IR£225 LDO 10.30pm
Lic ⅏ CTV 4P
Credit Cards ① ② ③ ⑤

GH Georgian House 20 Baggot St Lower ☎(01) 618832
FAX (01) 618834
Large Georgian house on streetside, situated close to city centre. Catering for tourists and commercials.
18♠ (10fb) CTV in all bedrooms ✙ (ex guide dogs) sB&B♠IR£38.50-IR£49.50 dB&B♠IR£52.80-IR£69.90 LDO 10.30pm
Lic ⅏ 18P
Credit Cards ① ② ③ ⑤

GH Iona House 5 Iona Park ☎(01) 306217 & 306855
FAX (01) 306732
Closed Dec-15 Jan
14rm(12♠2hc) (1fb) CTV in 11 bedrooms ✱ sB&BIR£24-IR£25.50 dB&B♠IR£48-IR£51
⅏ nc3yrs
Credit Cards ① ③

T&C Marelle 92 Rathfarnham Rd, Terenure ☎(01) 904690
6rm(5♠1hc) (1fb) CTV in 5 bedrooms TV in 1 bedroom ✙ ✱ sB&BfrIR£25 sB&B♠frIR£25 dB&B♠frIR£40 LDO 10am
⅏ CTV 8P nc5yrs
Credit Cards ① ③

GH Mount Herbert 7 Herbert Rd ☎(01) 684321
Telex no 92173 FAX (01) 607077
144rm(122⇨3♠19hc) (9fb) CTV in all bedrooms ✙ (ex guide dogs) ✱ sB&BIR£18-IR£35 sB&B⇨♠IR£30-IR£50 dB&BIR£35-IR£55 dB&B⇨♠IR£42-IR£60 LDO 9.30pm
Lic lift ⅏ CTV 80P ☍ sauna solarium gymnasium
Credit Cards ① ② ③ ⑤

GH St Aiden's 32 Brighton Rd, Rathgar ☎(01) 902011 & 906178
10rm(2⇨5♠3hc) (3fb)✂in 1 bedroom CTV in all bedrooms ✙ ✱ sB&BIR£18-IR£20 sB&B⇨♠IR£25-IR£28 dB&B⇨♠IR£40-IR£50
Lic ⅏ CTV 8P
Credit Cards ① ② ③

DUNCORMICK Co Wexford Map **01** C2
⌂ ✈ FH E Burrell **Ingleside** The Hill ☎(051) 63154
Mar-Oct
6hc (3fb) ® ✙ (ex guide dogs) sB&BfrIR£13 dB&BfrIR£24 WB&BfrIR£75 WBDifrIR£130 LDO 8.30pm
⅏ CTV 8P 90 acres mixed

DUNGARVAN Co Waterford Map **01** C2
⌂ ✈ FH Miss B Lynch **Killineen House** N 25, Waterford Rd ☎Waterford(051) 91294
5rm(3♠2hc) (3fb)✂in 2 bedrooms ® sB&BfrIR£13 dB&B♠frIR£26 WB&BfrIR£91 WBDifrIR£145 LDO 5pm
⅏ CTV 10P 50 acres grass

DUN LAOGHAIRE Co Dublin Map **01** D3
T&C Ferry 15 Clarinda Park North ☎(01) 808301
Closed 20-31 Dec
6rm(2♠4hc) (2fb) CTV in all bedrooms ✙ (ex guide dogs) dB&BIR£28-IR£30 dB&B♠IR£35-IR£37
⅏ CTV
Credit Cards ① ③

T&C Tara Hall 24 Sandycove Rd, Sandycove ☎(01) 805120
6rm(1♠5hc) (2fb) ®
⅏ CTV 4P

FERNS Co Wexford Map **01** D3
FH Mrs B Breen **Clone House** ☎Enniscorthy(054) 66113
Mar-Oct
5rm(4⇨♠1hc) (4fb)✂in all bedrooms CTV in 1 bedroom TV in 2 bedrooms ✙ (ex guide dogs) ✱ sB&BfrIR£17 sB&B⇨♠frIR£19 dB&B⇨♠frIR£30 WB&BIR£98-IR£90 WBDiIR£150-IR£164 LDO 4pm
⅏ CTV P ☍ ♪(hard)✈ 280 acres mixed

FOULKESMILL Co Wexford Map **01** C2
FH Mrs J Crosbie **Crosbie's** ☎Waterford(051) 63616
Mar-Oct
10hc (3fb) ✙ ✱ WBDifrIR£140 LDO 3pm
CTV 150 acres mixed

92 Rathfarnham Road, Terenure, Dublin
Telephone: (01) 904690

Old style residence, beautifully appointed.
Just 15 minutes from city centre. Linked to
N4, N7 and N81 routes from car ferry.
Plenty of private car space. All rooms are en
suite and have TV, tea making facilities
available. Golf courses and parks nearby.

FH Mrs Vera Young **Horetown House**
☎Waterford(051) 63633 & 63706
Mar-mid Jan (ex Xmas day)
12hc (10fb) ✱ sB&BIR£16.50 dB&BIR£30 WBDifrIR£180
LDO 9pm
Lic ⑪ CTV 15P ∪ all weather indoor riding arena outdoor
riding 214 acres beef dairy mixed

GALWAY Co Galway Map **01** B3

T&C Bay View Gentian Hill, Upper Salthill ☎(091) 22116
Feb-Nov
6rm(5🏠1hc) (2fb)⚡in 5 bedrooms ✖
⑪ CTV 6P nc5yrs

T&C Fortaleza Circular Rd, Dangan ☎(091) 22845
Jun-Aug
4hc (1fb) TV available ® ✖ (ex guide dogs) ✱ sB&BIR£15-
IR£17 dB&BIR£24-IR£28 WB&BIR£77-IR£84 LDO noon
⑪ CTV 20P

T&C Inishmore House 109 Fr. Griffin Rd, Lower Salthill
☎(091) 62639
Closed Xmas wk
8rm(5🏠3hc) (3fb) CTV in 6 bedrooms TV in 2 bedrooms ® ✱
dB&BIR£24-IR£28 dB&B🏠IR£26-IR£30
8P

GH Knockrea House 55 Lower Salthill ☎(091) 21794
9hc (2fb) ✖ (ex guide dogs) sB&BfrIR£14 dB&BfrIR£25
⑪ CTV 10P nc4yrs

[♿🍴] **T&C Roncalli House** 24 Whitesand Av, Lower Salthill
☎(091) 64159
6🏠 (1fb) ✖ sB&B🏠IR£13-IR£19 dB&B🏠frIR£26
⑪ CTV 5P

GLENEALY Co Wicklow Map **01** D3

FH Mrs Mary Byrne **Ballyknocken House**
☎Wicklow(0404) 44627 & 44614
Closed 21 Dec-1 Feb
8🏠 (1fb) ✖ sB&B🏠frIR£17.50 dB&B🏠frIR£27
WB&BfrIR£94.50 WBDifrIR£165 LDO 5pm
Lic ⑪ CTV 10P ♪(hard)200 acres dairy sheep
Credit Cards ①

GOREY Co Wexford Map **01** D3

FH P O'Sullivan **Woodlands** Killinieril ☎Arklow(0402) 37125
*Georgian-style residence 1.5 km off the N.11. Excellent
accommodation, three rooms have balcony. Charming dining room
run by chef Gara, daughter of the proprietor, Mrs O'Sullivan. All
fresh produce assured. Award winning gardens enhance the house
where relaxation is the priority of the family.*
6🏠 (3fb) CTV in all bedrooms ✖ (ex guide dogs) ✱
sB&B🏠frIR£20 dB&B🏠frIR£32 WBDifrIR£175 LDO 8pm
Lic ⑪ CTV 6P 🐎 play room pony rides 8 acres beef (non-
working)

HOLYWOOD Co Down Map **01** D5

SELECTED

GH ⓠⓠⓠⓠ *Tudor Guest Lodge* 60 Demesne Rd
BT18 9EX ☎(02317) 5859
*A large, detached Victorian house situated in an elevated
position overlooking its own well tended grounds towards
Belfast Lough. It is situated about five miles east of Belfast, in
a pleasant and quiet residential area at the back of the town,
just east of Jacksons Road and Old Holywood Road off the
A2 dual carriageway. The property is very well maintained,
with well equipped bedrooms, all with modern en suite
facilities, TV and a provision for making tea. There is a*

*spacious and very comfortable lounge, and a charming dining
room.*
8⇨ (8fb) CTV in all bedrooms ®
⑪ CTV P

INISTIOGE Co Kilkenny Map **01** C3

T&C Ashville Kilmacshane ☎(056) 58460
Mar-Oct
5rm(3🏠2hc) (1fb) TV in 1 bedroom ✖ (ex guide dogs) ✱
sB&BfrIR£11 dB&BfrIR£22 dB&B🏠frIR£27 WB&BfrIR£75
WBDifrIR£130 LDO 8pm
⑪ CTV 5P
Credit Cards ①③

KANTURK Co Cork Map **01** B2

GH Assolas Country House ☎(029) 50015 FAX (029) 50795
13 Mar-1 Nov
6⇨🏠 Annexe 3⇨🏠 (3fb) ✖ (ex guide dogs)
sB&B⇨🏠IR£49-IR£60 dB&B⇨🏠IR£74-IR£140
LDO 8.30pm
Lic ⑪ 20P ♪(grass)⚲ croquet clock golf boating
Credit Cards ①③⑤

KENMARE Co Kerry Map **01** A2

T&C Ceann Mara ☎Killarney(064) 41220
Etr-Oct rs Mar & Nov
6rm(1⇨3🏠2hc) (2fb) ® ✱ dB&BfrIR£24 dB&B⇨🏠frIR£28
WBDifrIR£152
⑪ CTV P ♪(grass)

GH Foleys Shamrock Henry St ☎(064) 41361
FAX (064) 41799
*Town-centre guesthouse over pub/restaurant. All bedrooms have
been recently refurbished and are very comfortable. A good food
service is available via the bar and restaurant.*
10⇨🏠 CTV in all bedrooms ✖ (ex guide dogs)
sB&B⇨🏠frIR£20 dB&B⇨🏠frIR£36
Lic ⑪ CTV
Credit Cards ①③

FH M P O'Sullivan **Sea Shore** Tubrid ☎(064) 41270
May-Sep
4🏠 (3fb) ✖ (ex guide dogs) sB&B🏠IR£17 dB&B🏠IR£26
WBDiIR£175 LDO 3pm
⑪ CTV 12P 🐎 32 acres dairy

FH Mrs R Doran **Templenoe House** Greenane ☎(064) 41538
Etr-Oct
5rm(2🏠3hc) (2fb) ✖ (ex guide dogs) ✱ dB&BfrIR£28
dB&B🏠frIR£32 LDO 3pm
CTV 8P 50 acres dairy

KILCULLEN Co Kildare Map **01** C3

FH B O'Sullivan **Chapel View** Gormanstown
☎Curragh(045) 81325
May-Dec
6🏠 (2fb) sB&B🏠IR£17-IR£20 dB&B🏠IR£30
WB&BfrIR£105 WBDifrIR£161 LDO 4pm
⑪ CTV 20P 22 acres beef
Credit Cards ①③

KILGARVAN Co Kerry Map **01** A2

FH E Dineen **Glanlea** ☎(064) 85314
Feb-Oct
8rm(3🏠5hc) (3fb) ® ✖ (ex guide dogs) ✱ sB&BfrIR£13
LDO 3pm
Lic ⑪ CTV 6P 4🐎 nc10yrs 500 acres

FH K Dineen **Hawthorn** ☎(064) 85326
Apr-15 Oct
6rm(3↱3hc) (2fb) ✗ (ex guide dogs) sB&B↱frIR£26
dB&BfrIR£28 dB&B↱frIR£28 WBDifrIR£147 LDO 4pm
𝍖 CTV 12P 87 acres sheep

KILKENNY Co Kilkenny Map **01** C3

GH Lacken House Dublin Rd ☎(056) 61085 & 65611
FAX (056) 62435
8rm(1⇌7↱) CTV in all bedrooms ® ✗ (ex guide dogs) ✱
sB&B⇌↱IR£30.80-IR£33 dB&B⇌↱IR£48.40-IR£55
WB&BfrIR£169 LDO 10pm
Lic 𝍖 CTV 30P
Credit Cards [1] [2] [3] [5]

KILLAMASTER Co Carlow Map **01** C3

FH M Walsh **Killamaster House** ☎Carlow(0503) 63654
Apr-Oct
3rm(2↱1hc) Annexe 1↱ (1fb) ® ✱ sB&BfrIR£14.50
sB&B↱frIR£15.50 dB&BfrIR£24 dB&B↱frIR£26 LDO 2pm
𝍖 CTV 8P 120 acres arable beet

KILLARNEY Co Kerry Map **01** A2

T&C Avignon Cork Rd ☎(064) 31229
17 Mar-Nov
7rm(4↱3hc) (2fb) ✗ (ex guide dogs) ✱ sB&BfrIR£15
dB&BfrIR£26 dB&B↱frIR£30 LDO noon
𝍖 CTV
Credit Cards [1] [2] [3]

GH Glena House Muckross Rd ☎(064) 32705
Mar-Nov
18rm(3⇌15↱) (3fb) ✱ sB&B⇌↱IR£18-IR£20
dB&B⇌↱IR£30-IR£33 WB&BIR£105 WBDiIR£175
LDO 8.30pm
Lic 𝍖 CTV 25P ⌂
Credit Cards [1] [3] [5]

T&C Glendale House Dromadessart, Tralee Rd ☎(064) 32152
Mar-15 Dec
5⇌↱ (2fb) ✗ (ex guide dogs) ✱ dB&B⇌↱IR£26-IR£27
WB&BIR£85-IR£95 LDO 4pm
𝍖 CTV 8P
Credit Cards [3]

T&C Green Acres Fossa ☎(064) 31454
Closed Xmas
8rm(6⇌↱2hc) (2fb) ✗ ✱ sB&BfrIR£16 sB&B⇌↱frIR£18
dB&BfrIR£24 dB&B⇌↱frIR£28
𝍖 CTV 12P

GH Kathleen's Country House Tralee Rd ☎(064) 32810
FAX (064) 32340
17 Mar-5 Nov
16⇌↱ (2fb)⊬in 3 bedrooms CTV in all bedrooms ® ✗ ✱
sB&B⇌↱IR£30-IR£40 dB&B⇌↱IR£40-IR£50
WB&BIR£130-IR£168 WBDiIR£225-IR£245 LDO 6pm
Lic 𝍖 20P nc4yrs lawn croquet

T&C Killarney Villa Cork-Waterford Rd (N72) ☎(064) 31878
Mar-Oct
11⇌↱ (1fb) sB&BIR£14-IR£16 sB&B⇌↱IR£18-IR£20
dB&BIR£25-IR£28 dB&B⇌↱IR£29 WB&BIR£98
WBDiIR£161-IR£165 LDO 6.30pm
𝍖 CTV 20P nc6yrs
Credit Cards [1] [2] [3]

GH Loch Lein Golf Course Rd, Fossa ☎(064) 31260
17 Mar-Sep
A bungalow on the shores of the Lower Lake. Well maintained lawns and flower beds. Situated in a very quiet and peaceful location.
15rm(2⇌10↱2hc) (5fb)⊬in 2 bedrooms ✗ ✱ sB&BIR£15-IR£17 sB&B⇌↱IR£20-IR£22 dB&BIR£24-IR£26
dB&B⇌↱IR£30-IR£32
𝍖 CTV 15P nc⚲(hard)

T&C Mulberry House Ballycasheen Rd ☎(064) 34112 & 32534
Closed Xmas & New Year
4rm(2⇌2↱) (1fb) ✗ ✱ sB&B⇌↱IR£18-IR£20
dB&B⇌↱IR£28-IR£35
𝍖 CTV 7P ⚲(grass)

T&C Purple Heather Gap of Dunloe ☎(064) 44266
Etr-Sep
6rm(4↱2hc) (1fb)⊬in 2 bedrooms ® ✱ sB&BIR£12-IR£16
WB&BIR£84-IR£87.50
𝍖 CTV 6P ⚲(hard)

T&C St Rita's Villa Mill Rd ☎(064) 31517
Feb-8 Dec
6rm(4↱2hc) (2fb) ✱ sB&BIR£14 sB&B↱IR£15
dB&BIR£23.50 dB&B↱IR£26.50
𝍖 CTV 6P

T&C Shraheen House Ballycasheen ☎(064) 31286
Closed Xmas & New Year
6rm(2⇌4↱) (2fb) ✗ ✱ sB&B⇌↱IR£18.50-IR£20.50
dB&B⇌↱IR£27-IR£31
𝍖 CTV 8P

KILLEAGH Co Cork Map **01** B2

T&C Tattans Main St ☎(024) 95173
Mar-Oct
Very comfortable bedrooms are a feature of Tattans Town House on the main Cork-Rosslare road, N25. There is a TV room, large attractive gardens, a hard tennis court and an adjoining bar where snacks are available all day. Evening meals are served to residents. Mrs Tattan takes pride in running the hotel, is very welcoming and serves good food.
5rm(4↱1hc) (3fb) ✗ ✱ sB&BfrIR£16 sB&B↱frIR£16
dB&BfrIR£28 dB&B↱frIR£28 WB&BfrIR£84
WBDifrIR£156 LDO 10pm
Lic 𝍖 CTV 8P ⚲(hard)

KILLESHANDRA Co Cavan Map **01** C4

FH K H Locher **Derreskit** ☎(049) 34156 & 34154
7rm(1↱6hc) ✗ ✱ sB&BIR£12 dB&B↱IR£22 WB&BIR£70
WBDiIR£126 LDO 8pm
Lic 𝍖 TV 5P 1🚘 161 acres beef mixed sheep

KILLORGLIN Co Kerry Map **01** A2

T&C *Torine House* Sunhill Rd ☎(066) 61352
6↱ (6fb) ® ✗
𝍖 CTV 10P

KILMALLOCK Co Limerick Map **01** B2

FH Mrs Imelda Sheedy King **Flemingstown House**
☎(063) 98093
Mar-Oct
6rm(3↱3hc) (2fb) CTV in 2 bedrooms ® ✗ (ex guide dogs) ✱
sB&BfrIR£15 dB&BfrIR£26 dB&B↱frIR£26 WB&BfrIR£95
WBDifrIR£150 LDO 8pm
Lic 𝍖 CTV P ▶18 ⚲(hard&grass)⤶ squash Ʊ gymnasium
102 acres dairy
Credit Cards [3]

Street plans of certain towns and cities
will be found in a separate section
at the back of the book.

KILMEADEN Co Waterford Map **01** C2

T&C Hillview Lodge Adamstown ☎(051) 84230
Mar-Oct
5rm(1♪4hc) (2fb) CTV in 1 bedroom ✖ (ex guide dogs)
sB&BIR£15 dB&BIR£24 dB&B♪IR£26 WB&BfrIR£84
WBDifrIR£150 LDO 10am
⊞ CTV 10P

KILMEENA Co Mayo

[⇔♥] **FH** M O'Malley **Seapoint House** ☎Westport(098) 41254
Apr-Oct
7rm(3⇔2♪2hc) (4fb) CTV in 2 bedrooms ® ✖
sB&BIR£12.50-IR£13 sB&B⇔♪IR£18-IR£20 dB&BIR£24-
IR£26 dB&B⇔♪IR£26-IR£30 WB&BIR£80-IR£100
WBDiIR£175-IR£180
sea angling 40 acres mixed

KILRANE Co Wexford Map **01** D2

FH K O'Leary **O'Leary's** Killilane, St Helen's Bay
☎(053) 33134
10rm(7♪3hc) (3fb) ✱ sB&BIR£13.50 dB&BIR£22
dB&B♪IR£25 LDO noon
⊞ CTV P 97 acres arable

KINSALEBEG Co Waterford Map **01** C2

T&C Blackwater House ☎(024) 92543
5hc (3fb) ✖ (ex guide dogs) LDO 6pm
⊞ CTV 6P ▶ 18

T&C Gables Rath ☎Cork(024) 92739
May-Oct
5rm(1♪4hc) (1fb) ✖ (ex guide dogs) ✱ sB&BfrIR£15
dB&BfrIR£23 dB&B♪IR£25 WB&BfrIR£78
WBDifrIR£140 LDO 6pm
⊞ CTV 8P ♪(hard)
Credit Cards ①

KNOCKFERRY Co Galway Map **01** B4

FH D & M Moran **Knockferry Lodge** ☎Galway(091) 80122
FAX (091) 80328
May-Sep
10⇔♪ (1fb) ✖ (ex guide dogs) sB&B⇔♪IR£25
dB&B⇔♪IR£40 WB&BIR£140 WBDiIR£175 LDO 8pm
Lic ⊞ CTV 12P boats for hire games room pool table 35 acres
mixed
Credit Cards ① ② ③ ⑤

KNOCKNAREA Co Sligo Map **01** B5

FH E & M Carter **Primrose Grange** ☎Sligo(071) 62005
rs Dec-Jan
8rm(2♪6hc) (3fb) ✖ (ex guide dogs) ✱ sB&BIR£17
dB&BIR£28 dB&B♪IR£31 WB&BIR£95 WBDiIR£154
LDO 3pm
Lic ⊞ CTV 10P 55 acres dairy

LARAGH Co Wicklow Map **01** D3

T&C Laragh Trekking Centre Glendalough ☎(0404) 45282
Run by husband and wife team Noreen and David McCallion.
Their joint skills, Noreen's experience in the hotel industry and
David's love and knowledge of horses, combine to make a holiday
spent with them a memorable occasion. David personally leads the
rides around 600 acres of mountains and forests of Co. Wicklow.
4rm(1♪3hc) (1fb)⊁in 2 bedrooms CTV in all bedrooms ®
LDO noon
⊞ CTV 10P 2🐴 ⚶ ♪ ∪

LARNE Co Antrim Map **01** D5

GH 🅠🅠 **Derrin** 2 Prince's Gardens BT40 1RQ
☎(0574) 273269 & 273762
Situated in a residential road close to the town centre, this spacious
well maintained detached house offers friendly service and
spotlessly clean, comfortable accommodation.
7rm(2♪5hc) (2fb) dB&Bfr£23 dB&B♪fr£27
⊞ CTV 3P 2🐴

LETTERKENNY Co Donegal Map **01** C5

T&C Hill Crest House Lurgybrack, Sligo Rd ☎(074) 22300 &
25137
rs Xmas wk
6rm(4♪2hc) (2fb) ✖ (ex guide dogs) sB&BIR£14-IR£17.50
dB&BfrIR£24 dB&B♪frIR£27
⊞ CTV 10P 1🐴
Credit Cards ① ② ③

LISBURN Co Antrim Map **01** D5

FH 🅠🅠🅠🅠 Mrs D Moore **Brook Lodge** 79 Old
Ballynahinch Rd, Cargacroy BT27 6TH
☎Bailliesmills(0846) 638454
This modern farmhouse is peacefully situated in a rural
position just off the A49, three miles south of junction 6 of the
M1. It offers comfortable accommodation including a
pleasant lounge with particularly good views of the
surrounding countryside. Bedrooms are compact but prettily
decorated and well furnished. The farmhouse offers excellent
value for money, and Mrs Moore is a most friendly and
hospitable host and provides guests with good home-cooked
meals.
5rm(1♪4hc) ✖ (ex guide dogs) sB&Bfr£13.50 dB&Bfr£27
dB&B♪fr£28 WB&Bfr£94.50 WBDifr£133
⊞ CTV 10P 65 acres mixed ©

LISDOONVARNA Co Clare Map **01** B3

GH *Ballinalacken Castle* ☎(065) 74025
Jun-Oct
6rm(1⇔3♪2hc) (3fb) ✖ (ex guide dogs) LDO 7.45pm
Lic CTV

T&C Sunville off Doolin Rd ☎(065) 74065
5♪ (3fb) ✖ (ex guide dogs) ✱ sB&B♪frIR£16
dB&B♪frIR£24 WB&BfrIR£80 LDO noon
⊞ CTV 10P
Credit Cards ①

LISTOWEL Co Kerry Map **01** A2

[⇔♥] **T&C North County** 67 Church St ☎(068) 21238
8rm(2♪6hc) (2fb) ✖ (ex guide dogs) sB&BIR£11-IR£15
dB&BfrIR£22-IR£30 dB&B♪IR£26-IR£34 LDO noon
⊞ CTV
Credit Cards ①

MILFORD Co Carlow Map **01** D3

T&C Goleen Country House ☎(0503) 46132
Closed Dec-1 Jan
6rm(4♪2hc) ⊁in 2 bedrooms CTV in all bedrooms ® ✖ ✱
sB&BIR£15 dB&B♪IR£30 WB&BIR£84
⊞ CTV 12P
Credit Cards ① ③

Visit your local AA Shop.

MOYARD Co Galway Map **01** A4

FH Mrs M O'Toole **Rose Cottage** Rockfield ☎(095) 41082
May-Sep
6🐾 (2fb) ® ✠ (ex guide dogs) ✱ dB&B🐾frIR£28 LDO 3pm
🍴 CTV 10P 36 acres mixed

NAAS Co Kildare Map **01** C3

FH Mrs J McLoughlin **Setanta** Castlekeely, Caragh
☎(045) 76481
Mar-Oct
5rm(3🐾) (4fb) ® ✠ (ex guide dogs) ✱ sB&BfrIR£13
sB&B🐾frIR£17 dB&B🐾IR£28 WB&BfrIR£95 LDO noon
🍴 CTV 4P 2🐾 43 acres dry stock

FH M & E Nolan **Westown** Johnstown ☎(045) 97006
Closed 16 Dec-Jan
5hc (3fb) ✠ ✱ sB&BfrIR£15 dB&BIR£26-IR£28 LDO noon
🍴 CTV 9P 92 acres arable mixed

NAVAN (AN UAIMH) Co Meath Map **01** C4

FH E McCormack **Balreask House** ☎Drogheda(046) 21155
Apr-Oct
4rm(3hc) (2fb) ✠ ✱ sB&BfrIR£16 dB&BfrIR£24
4P 200 acres mixed

NEW ROSS Co Wexford Map **01** C2

T&C Inishross House 96 Mary St ☎Waterford(051) 21335
6hc (2fb) ® ✠ (ex guide dogs) sB&BIR£14.50 dB&BIR£23
LDO 6pm
🍴 CTV 6P 2🐾

NINE MILE HOUSE Co Tipperary Map **01** C3

T&C Grand Inn ☎(051) 47035
5rm(2🐾3hc) (3fb) ✱ sB&BfrIR£15 sB&B🐾frIR£17
dB&BfrIR£23 dB&B🐾frIR£27 WB&BIR£80.50
WBDifrIR£136.50 LDO 7pm
🍴 CTV 5P

OGONNELLOE Co Clare Map **01** B3

T&C Lantern House ☎Scarriff(0619) 23034 & 23123
mid Feb-Oct & Dec
6🐾🐾 (2fb) ✠ (ex guide dogs) ✱ sB&B🐾IR£18
dB&B🐾🐾IR£30 WB&BIR£91 WBDiIR£175 LDO 9.30pm
Lic 🍴 CTV 25P
Credit Cards ①②③⑤

OVENS Co Cork Map **01** B2

T&C Milestone ☎(021) 872562
5hc (3fb)🚭in 2 bedrooms ✠ ✱ sB&BIR£15 dB&BIR£24
WB&BIR£77 WBDiIR£140 LDO noon
🍴 CTV 20P

PORTLAOISE Co Laoise Map **01** C3

T&C Aspen House Rock of Dunamase
☎Portlaois(0502) 25405
Mar-Oct
4rm(1🚭2🐾1hc) (2fb)🚭in all bedrooms ✠ (ex guide dogs)
sB&BfrIR£16.50 sB&B🚭🐾frIR£19 dB&BfrIR£25
dB&B🚭🐾frIR£29 WB&BIR£85-IR£95
🍴 CTV 10P
Credit Cards ①③

🚗🚛**T&C Knockmay Town House** Marian Av ☎(0502) 22509
Closed 20-30 Dec
6hc (1fb)🚭in all bedrooms CTV in 1 bedroom ✠
sB&BfrIR£12.50 dB&BfrIR£23 WB&BfrIR£87 (wkly only
Nov-Mar)
🍴 CTV 10P

T&C O'Sullivan 8 Kelly Ville Park ☎(0502) 22774
6🚭 (1fb) ✠ (ex guide dogs) sB&B🚭IR£16.50 dB&B🚭IR£28
WB&BIR£98
🍴 CTV 6P

T&C Vicarstown Inn Vicarstown ☎(0502) 25189
17 Mar-Oct
8rm(2🚭🐾6hc) Annexe 3hc (3fb) ® ✠ (ex guide dogs) ✱
sB&BIR£16 sB&B🚭🐾IR£16 dB&BIR£25 dB&B🚭🐾IR£30
WB&BIR£85 WBDiIR£150 LDO noon
Lic 🍴 CTV P
Credit Cards ③

PROSPEROUS Co Kildare Map **01** C4

FH Mrs K Phelan **Silverspring House** Firmount
☎Naas(045) 68481
Mar-Nov
4hc (2fb)🚭in all bedrooms ® ✠ ✱ sB&BIR£15-IR£16
dB&BIR£25-IR£26 (wkly only Mar-Nov) LDO 10am
🍴 CTV 12P 12 acres cattle sheep

RATHDRUM Co Wicklow Map **01** D3

T&C Abhainn Mor House Corballis ☎(0404) 46330
Feb-13 Nov
6🚭 (2fb) ® ✠ ✱ sB&B🚭frIR£25 dB&B🚭frIR£30
LDO noon
🍴 CTV 10P 𝒫(grass)

GH Avonbrae House ☎Wicklow(0404) 46198
15 Mar-15 Nov
6🐾 (2fb) ® ✱ sB&B🐾IR£21 dB&B🐾IR£34 WB&BfrIR£105
WBDifrIR£180 LDO noon
Lic 🍴 CTV 6P 🏊(heated) 𝒫(grass)solarium games room
Credit Cards ①②③

T&C St Bridget's Corballis ☎Wicklow(0404) 46477
Closed 23-31 Dec
3hc (2fb) ✠ sB&BfrIR£16 dB&BfrIR£24 WB&BfrIR£84
WBDifrIR£140 LDO noon
🍴 CTV 10P 🏓 18 squash ⛳ snooker

ROSSDUFF Co Waterford Map **01** C2

FH Mrs J Richardson **Elton Lodge** ☎(051) 82117
Jun-Sep
5🚭🐾 (1fb) ✠ ✱ dB&B🚭🐾frIR£28 WBDifrIR£150
LDO 3pm
🍴 CTV P 200 acres dairy

ROSSNOWLAGH Co Donegal Map **01** B5

T&C Ardeelan Manor ☎Bundoran(072) 51578
Jun-Aug
5rm(4hc) (3fb)🚭in all bedrooms ✱ sB&BfrIR£16
dB&BfrIR£25 WB&BfrIR£87.50
🍴 P stabling available
Credit Cards ①

SHANAGARRY Co Cork Map **01** B2

GH Ballymaloe House ☎Cork(021) 652531 Telex no 75208
Closed 24-26 Dec
18rm(14🚭4🐾) Annexe 12rm(11🚭1🐾) (1fb)
✠ (ex guide dogs) LDO 9.30pm
Lic 🍴 CTV P 🏊(heated) 🏓9 𝒫(hard)
Credit Cards ①②③⑤

SKERRIES Co Dublin Map **01** D4

T&C Teresa's 9 Thomas Hand St ☎(01) 491411
Mar-Sep
4rm(1🐾3hc) ✠ ✱ sB&BfrIR£15 dB&BIR£25
🍴 CTV

SKIBBEREEN Co Cork Map **01** B2

FH Mrs M McCarthy **Abbeystrewery** Abbey ☎(028) 21713
Jun-Sep
4hc (2fb) ✕ (ex guide dogs) ✳ dB&BfrIR£22 LDO am
TV P 20 acres dairy
Credit Cards ①

SLIGO Co Sligo Map **01** B5

T&C Aisling Cairns Hill ☎(071) 60704
6rm(3�3hc) (2fb) ✕ ✳ sB&BIR£17 sB&B🌢IR£18.50
dB&BIR£24 dB&B🌢IR£27
🕮 CTV 6P nc6yrs

T&C Tree Tops Cleveragh Rd ☎(071) 60160
6rm(4🌢2hc) (2fb) ✕ ✳ sB&BfrIR£16 sB&B🌢frIR£18
dB&BfrIR£24 dB&B🌢frIR£27
🕮 CTV 6P

FH Mrs E Stuart **Hillside** Glencar Rd ☎(071) 42808
Apr-Oct
Situated in the heart of Yeats Country on the Sligo/Enniskillen
road (N.16) offering comfortable accommodation. Pony and
donkey for children.
4rm(2🌢2hc) (4fb)⚡in all bedrooms ✕ (ex guide dogs) ✳
sB&BIR£15 sB&B🌢IR£20 dB&BIR£26 dB&B🌢IR£30
WB&BIR£91-IR£80 WBDifrIR£145 LDO 3pm
🕮 CTV 8P 3🏊 70 acres beef dairy

SPIDDAL Co Galway Map **01** B3

🚐🛁**T&C Ard Aoibhinn** Cnocan-Glas ☎Galway(091) 83179
6🌢 (3fb) ✕ (ex guide dogs) sB&B🌢IR£12-IR£14
dB&B🌢IR£24-IR£28 WB&BIR£84-IR£98 LDO noon
🕮 CTV 6P

T&C Ardmor Greenhill ☎Galway(091) 83145
Mar-Nov
8rm(2⇨6🌢) (4fb)⚡in 7 bedrooms ✕ (ex guide dogs) ✳
sB&B⇨🌢frIR£18 dB&B⇨🌢frIR£28 WB&BfrIR£90
🕮 CTV 20P
Credit Cards ③

STREAMSTOWN Co Westmeath Map **01** C4

FH Mrs M Maxwell **Woodlands** ☎Mullinngar(044) 26414
Mar-Oct
6rm(2🌢4hc) (2fb) ✳ sB&BIR£15 dB&BfrIR£24
dB&B🌢IR£28 WB&BfrIR£75 WBDifrIR£140 LDO 3pm
🕮 CTV P 120 acres mixed
Credit Cards ③

SUMMERHILL Co Meath Map **01** C4

FH Mrs J Hughes **Cherryfield** Dangan ☎(0405) 57034
Apr-Oct
4rm(2🌢2hc) (2fb) ✕ (ex guide dogs) ✳ sB&BIR£14.50
dB&B🌢IR£26 WB&BfrIR£69 WBDiIR£138 LDO noon
🕮 CTV P ⚙ 75 acres dairy

TAGOAT Co Wexford Map **01** D2

FH Mrs E Doyle **Orchard Park** Rosslare
☎Wexford(053) 32182
8hc (2fb) ✳ sB&BIR£14-IR£16 dB&BIR£26-IR£30
WB&BIR£85-IR£100 WBDiIR£155-IR£180 LDO am
CTV 15P 🎾(hard)⚓ trampoline 80 acres arable

TAHILLA Co Kerry Map **01** A2

GH Tahilla Cove ☎Killarney(064) 45204
Etr-Oct
3⇨ Annexe 6rm(4⇨2🌢) (4fb) ✳ sB&B⇨🌢IR£30
dB&B⇨🌢IR£55 WBDiIR£260-IR£275 LDO 10am

Lic 🕮 CTV 10P
Credit Cards ①②③⑤

THE ROWER Co Kilkenny Map **01** C3

T&C Hillcrest ☎(051) 23722
4⇨🌢 (2fb)⚡in 1 bedroom CTV in 1 bedroom TV in 1
bedroom ® ✕ (ex guide dogs) sB&B⇨🌢frIR£14
dB&B⇨🌢frIR£24 WB&BfrIR£70 WBDifrIR£120
LDO 10.30pm
🕮 CTV 6P 2🏊

FH Mrs J Prendergast **Garranavabby House**
☎Waterford(051) 23613
Apr-Oct
3hc (2fb) ✳ dB&BIR£28 WB&BIR£98 WBDiIR£182
LDO noon
🕮 CTV P 84 acres sheep

TIPPERARY Co Tipperary Map **01** B3

GH Ach-na-Sheen Clonmel Rd ☎(062) 51298
Closed 23-31 Dec
10rm(2⇨2🌢6hc) (2fb) ✳ sB&BIR£13-IR£14 dB&BIR£26-
IR£28 dB&B⇨🌢IR£28-IR£30 LDO 3pm
🕮 CTV 10P
Credit Cards ③

TOBERCURRY Co Sligo Map **01** B4

T&C Cruckawn House Ballymote/Boyle Rd ☎(071) 85188
5rm(4🌢1hc) (1fb)⚡in 2 bedrooms CTV in all bedrooms
✕ (ex guide dogs) ✳ sB&BfrIR£15 sB&B🌢frIR£17
dB&B🌢IR£26-IR£27 WB&BfrIR£85 WBDifrIR£160
LDO 6pm
🕮 CTV 8P ▶9 🎾(hard)squash snooker sauna gymnasium
Credit Cards ①③

TRALEE Co Kerry Map **01** A2

T&C Cnoc Mhuire Oakpark Rd ☎(066) 26027
5rm(3⇨🌢2hc) (5fb) ✳ sB&B⇨🌢frIR£15 dB&BfrIR£24
dB&B⇨🌢frIR£25 WB&BfrIR£70
🕮 CTV P
Credit Cards ①②③

TRAMORE Co Waterford Map **01** C2

T&C Rushmere House Branch Rd ☎Waterford(051) 81041
Closed Xmas & New Year
6rm(3🌢3hc) (2fb) ® ✕ (ex guide dogs) ✳ sB&BfrIR£16
dB&BfrIR£23 dB&B🌢frIR£27
🕮 CTV

TULLAMORE Co Offaly Map **01** C3

GH Moorhill Country House Moorhill, Clara Rd (N80)
☎(0506) 21395 FAX (0506) 52424
4⇨🌢 Annexe 8⇨🌢 (1fb) CTV in all bedrooms ® ✳
sB&B⇨🌢IR£25 dB&B⇨🌢IR£45 LDO 9.30pm
Lic 🕮 CTV 50P 🎾(grass)
Credit Cards ①②③⑤

VALLEYMOUNT Co Wicklow Map **01** C3

T&C Escombe Lockstown ☎Naas(045) 67157
Mar-Oct
6rm(4🌢2hc) (4fb) ✕ ✳ sB&B🌢IR£18 dB&BIR£24
dB&B🌢IR£28 WB&BIR£72 LDO 6.30pm
Lic 🕮 CTV 1P

£ Remember to use the money-off vouchers.

WATERFORD Co Waterford Map **01** C2

GH Diamond Hill Diamond Hill, Slieverne ☎(051) 32855 & 32254
A two storey house in its own well maintained grounds with well tended flower beds and lawns. Situated on Waterford/Wexford Road.
10rm(9⇔↑1hc) (2fb) ⑱ ✖ (ex guide dogs) ✳ sB&BfrIR£15 sB&B⇔↑frIR£16 dB&B⇔↑IR£30-IR£32
20P
Credit Cards ①③

T&C Dunroven Ballinaneesagh, 25 Cork Rd ☎(051) 74743
Closed 24-26 Dec
7rm(4↑3hc) (2fb) ✖ (ex guide dogs) ✳ sB&BfrIR£12 sB&B↑frIR£17 dB&BfrIR£22 dB&B↑frIR£25
WBDifrIR£140 LDO noon
🍴 CTV 7P

T&C Knockboy House Dunmore Rd ☎(051) 73484
Closed Dec-Jan
6rm(2↑4hc) (1fb) ✖ sB&BfrIR£17 sB&B↑frIR£19 dB&BfrIR£24 dB&B↑frIR£28 WB&BIR£84-IR£98
WBDiIR£150-IR£165
🍴 CTV 12P nc3yrs

FH Mrs A Forrest **Ashbourne House** Slieverue ☎(051) 32037
Apr-Oct
7rm(6↑1hc) (5fb) ✳ sB&BIR£12.50-IR£15.50 sB&B↑IR£15.50 dB&BIR£22 dB&B↑IR£25 WB&BIR£75
WBDiIR£137 LDO 3pm
CTV 8P ♻ 20 acres mixed

WATERVILLE Co Kerry Map **01** A2

GH Smugglers Inn Cliff Rd ☎(0667) 4330 & 4422
Mar-14 Dec
10rm(3⇔7↑) (4fb) ✖ (ex guide dogs) ✳ sB&B⇔↑IR£22-IR£28 dB&B⇔↑IR£30-IR£52 WB&BfrIR£126
WBDiIR£220-IR£270 LDO 9.30pm
Lic 🍴 CTV 40P ▶ 18
Credit Cards ①②③⑤

WESTPORT Co Mayo Map **01** A4

FH Mrs M O'Brien **Rath-a-Rosa** Rossbeg ☎(098) 25348
Mar-Oct
6rm(3⇔3hc) (2fb) ✖ (ex guide dogs) sB&BIR£17 sB&B⇔↑IR£20 dB&BIR£24 dB&B⇔↑IR£30 LDO 11am
🍴 CTV 6P 20 acres mixed
Credit Cards ③

WEXFORD Co Wexford Map **01** D2

T&C Arduagh Spawell Rd ☎(053) 23194
5⇔↑ (2fb) ⑱ ✖ (ex guide dogs) ✳ sB&BfrIR£17 dB&B⇔↑frIR£30
🍴 CTV 10P
Credit Cards ①③

GH Faythe Swan View ☎(053) 22249
Closed 23 Dec-4 Jan
Fine old house in quiet part of town. Modest comfort and pleasant atmosphere.
11rm(1↑10hc) (4fb) CTV in 1 bedroom ✖ (ex guide dogs) sB&BIR£15 sB&B↑IR£20 dB&BIR£28 dB&B↑IR£34 WB&BIR£98 WBDiIR£198 LDO 7.30pm
Lic 🍴 CTV 30P ♨ snooker
Credit Cards ①②③⑤

T&C *Rathaspeck Manor* Rathaspeck ☎(053) 42661 & 45148
Jun-Oct
7↑ CTV in all bedrooms ✖ LDO noon
Lic CTV 12P ▶ 18 ♟(hard)

T&C Tara Villa Larkins Cross, Barntown ☎(053) 45119
May-10 Nov
Situated on main Wexford/New Ross route (N.25) go past the sign for Barntown, continue on main road until a large pink house is reached where a warm welcome awaits the traveller from proprietors Mr and Mrs Whitty.
5⇔↑ (3fb) ✖ (ex guide dogs) ✳ dB&B⇔↑IR£25-IR£30 LDO 8pm
Lic 🍴 CTV 10P 3🛖
Credit Cards ①③

GH Whitford House New Lime Rd ☎(053) 43444 & 43845
Closed 20 Dec-8 Jan
27⇔↑ (10fb) CTV in all bedrooms ✖ (ex guide dogs) ✳ sB&B⇔↑IR£22-IR£24 dB&B⇔↑IR£42-IR£46
WBDiIR£210 (wkly only Jul & Aug) LDO 8pm
Lic 🍴 CTV 100P
Credit Cards ①③

WICKLOW Co Wicklow Map **01** D3

GH The Old Rectory Country House & Restaurant
☎(0404) 67048 FAX (0404) 69181
Etr-mid Oct
5⇔↑ (1fb) CTV in all bedrooms ⑱ ✖ sB&B⇔↑IR£55 dB&B⇔↑IR£78 WB&BIR£203-IR£217 WBDiIR£329-IR£350 LDO 8pm
Lic 🍴 12P
Credit Cards ①②③⑤

T&C Thomond House St Patrick's Rd Upper ☎(0404) 67940
Mar-Oct
5rm(2↑3hc) (1fb) ✖ (ex guide dogs) ✳ sB&BIR£16-IR£16.50 dB&BIR£24-IR£25 dB&B↑IR£28-IR£29 WB&BIR£82-IR£100 WBDiIR£150-IR£160 LDO noon

▶

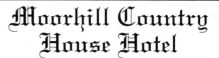

🛏 CTV 5P
Credit Cards 1

FH Mrs P Klaue **Lissadell House** Ashtown Ln ☎(0404) 67458
Mar-Dec
4rm(1⇄1🛏2hc)(1fb) ✗ ✱ dB&BfrIR£28 dB&B⇄🛏frIR£32
LDO noon
🛏 CTV P 285 acres mixed

YOUGHAL Co Cork Map **01** C2

📧▼ **T&C Carriglea** Ballyvergan East, Summerfield
☎(024) 92520
Jun-Sep
Well appointed modern bungalow situated on the outskirts of

Youghal on the N.25 overlooking the sea. Mr and Mrs Walsh are a hospitable friendly couple who will ensure your every comfort.
4hc sB&BIR£13 dB&BIR£22 WB&BIR£70
🛏 CTV 8P

T&C Devon View Pearse Square ☎(024) 92298
6rm(3⇄🛏3hc)(2fb) CTV in all bedrooms ® ✱ sB&BIR£15
dB&B⇄🛏IR£26 WB&BIR£90 WBDiIR£125 LDO 5pm
🛏 CTV 8P
Credit Cards 1 3

FH Mrs E Long **Cherrymount** ☎(024) 97110
5hc (2fb) ✱ sB&BIR£12 dB&BIR£20 WB&BfrIR£70
LDO 5pm
🛏 CTV 10P ▶ 18 ♪(hard)70 acres dairy
Credit Cards 1 2 3

Index of Town Plans

Key to Town Plans

▬▬▬ Recommended Route	⒤ Tourist Information	❻ Guesthouse, inn, etc.
⌇ ▬ Other Routes	Centre	◀▭ₘ Distance to guesthouses,
▪▪ ⌇▬ Restricted Roads	AA AA Centre	etc, from edge of plan
✝ Churches	P Car Parking ASHFORD 16m	Mileage to town from
		edge of plan

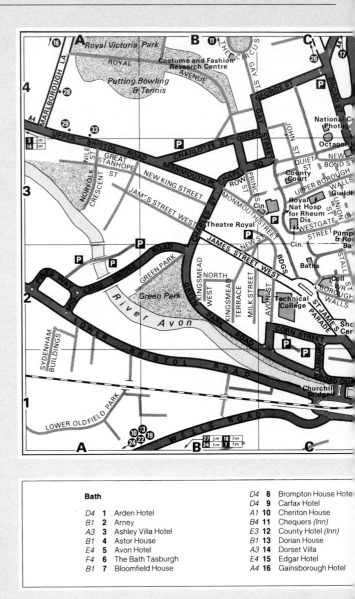

Bath

			D4	**8**	Brompton House Hotel
			D4	**9**	Carfax Hotel
D4	**1**	Arden Hotel	A1	**10**	Cheriton House
B1	**2**	Arney	B4	**11**	Chequers (Inn)
A3	**3**	Ashley Villa Hotel	E3	**12**	County Hotel (Inn)
B1	**4**	Astor House	B1	**13**	Dorian House
E4	**5**	Avon Hotel	A3	**14**	Dorset Villa
F4	**6**	The Bath Tasburgh	E4	**15**	Edgar Hotel
B1	**7**	Bloomfield House	A4	**16**	Gainsborough Hotel

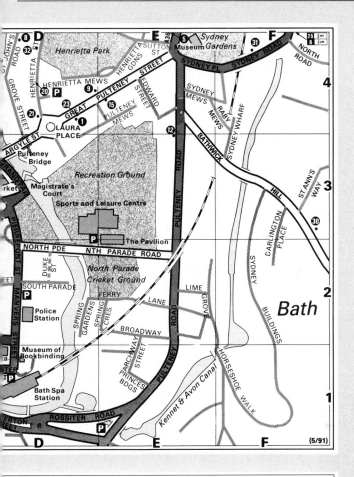

17	Grove Lodge	*C4* **26**	Oxford Private Hotel
18	Haydon House	*B1* **27**	Paradise House Hotel
19	Highways House	*A4* **28**	Parkside
20	Kennard Hotel	*A4* **29**	Hotel St Clair
21	Laura Place Hotel	*F3* **30**	Somerset House
22	Leighton House	*F4* **31**	Sydney Gardens Hotel
23	Millers Hotel	*D4* **32**	Villa Magdala Private Hotel
24	Oldfields	*A4* **33**	Waltons
25	Orchard House Hotel	*B1* **34**	Wentworth House Hotel

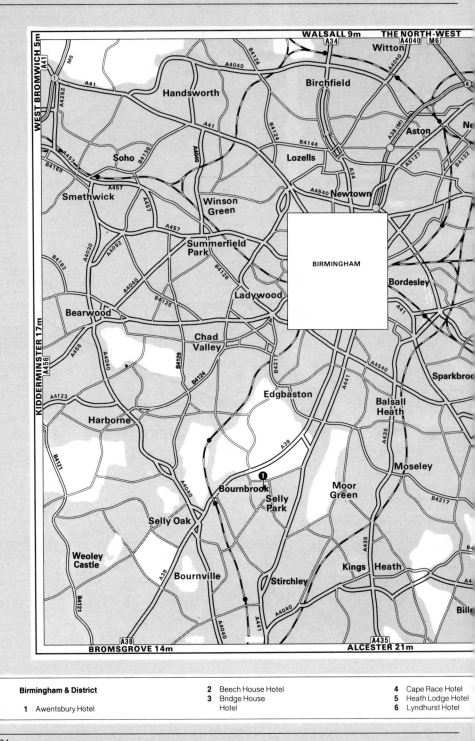

BIRMINGHAM

Birmingham & District

1 Awentsbury Hotel

2 Beech House Hotel
3 Bridge House
   Hotel

4 Cape Race Hotel
5 Heath Lodge Hotel
6 Lyndhurst Hotel

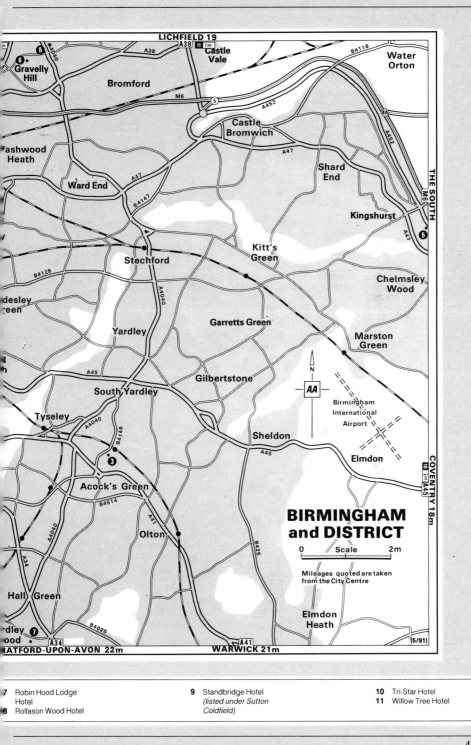

BIRMINGHAM and DISTRICT

Birmingham International Airport

0 Scale 2m

Mileages quoted are taken
from the City Centre

(5/91)

LICHFIELD 19
Castle Vale
Water Orton
Bromford
Castle Bromwich
Gravelly Hill
ashwood Heath
Ward End
Shard End
Kingshurst
Kitt's Green
Stechford
Chelmsley Wood
desley reen
Yardley
Garretts Green
Marston Green
Gilbertstone
South Yardley
Tyseley
Sheldon
Elmdon
Acock's Green
Olton
Hall Green
Elmdon Heath
rdley ood
RATFORD-UPON-AVON 22m
WARWICK 21m
THE SOUTH M6
COVENTRY 18m

7 Robin Hood Lodge
  Hotel
8 Rollason Wood Hotel

9 Standbridge Hotel
  *(listed under Sutton
  Coldfield)*

10 Tri-Star Hotel
11 Willow Tree Hotel

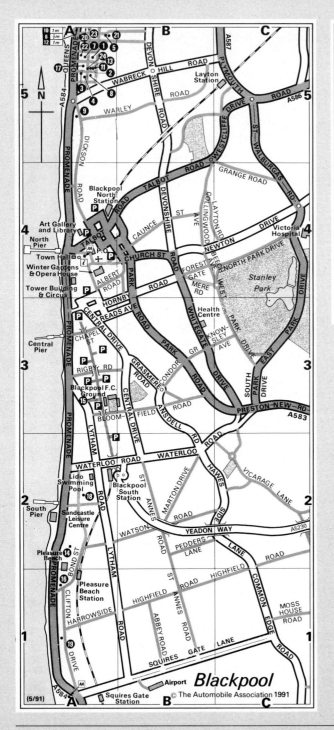

Blackpool

A5	1	Arosa Hotel
A5	2	Ashcroft Private Hotel
A5	3	Berwick Private Hotel
A5	4	Brooklands Hotel
A5	5	Burlees Hotel
A5	6	Cliff Head Hotel
A5	7	Cliftonville Hotel
A5	8	Denely Private Hotel
A5	9	Derwent Private Hotel
A5	10	The Garville Hotel
A5	11	Hartshead Hotel
A5	12	Inglewood Hotel
A5	13	Lynstead Private Hotel
A2	14	Lynwood
A3	15	Hotel Mimosa
A1	16	The New Esplanade Hotel
A5	17	North Mount Private Hotel
A2	18	The Old Coach House
A1	19	Rewa Private Hotel
A5	20	Sunny Cliff
A5	21	Sunray Private Hotel
A5	22	Surrey House Hotel
A5	23	Westmorland Hotel
A5	24	Woodleigh Private Hotel

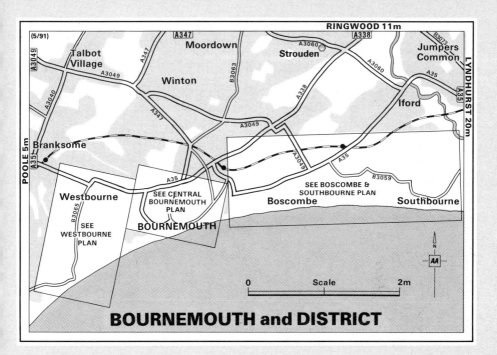

BOURNEMOUTH and DISTRICT

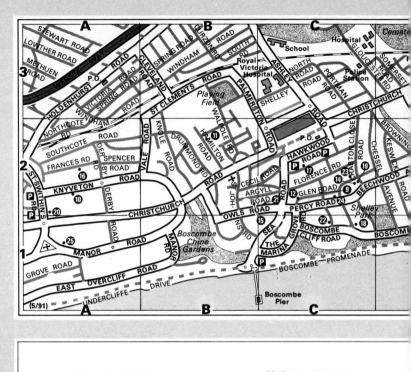

Boscombe & Southbourne

E3	**8**	Amitie
C2	**9**	Braemar Private Hotel
A2	**10**	Cransley Private Hotel
B2	**11**	Derwent House
C2	**12**	Hawaiian Hotel
F2	**13**	Kelmor Lodge
C2	**14**	Linwood House Hotel
B2	**15**	Lynthwaite Hotel
A2	**16**	Mayfield Private Hotel

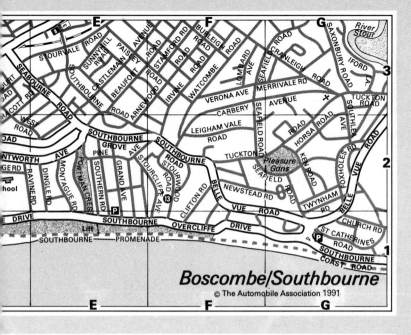

Boscombe/Southbourne

© The Automobile Association 1991

C2	**17**	Naseby-Nye Hotel
C1	**18**	Norland Private Hotel
C2	**19**	Oak Hall Private Hotel
A2	**20**	St John's Lodge Hotel
C2	**21**	Hotel Sorrento
C1	**22**	Valberg Hotel
C2	**23**	Weavers Hotel
C2	**24**	Woodlands Hotel
A1	**25**	Wood Lodge Hotel

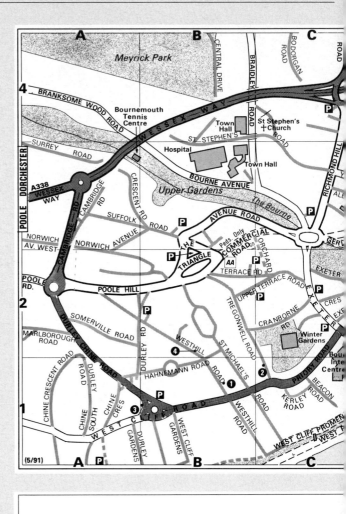

Central Bournemouth

B1 **1** Albemarle Private Hotel

C1 **2** Carisbrooke Hotel
B1 **3** Croham Hurst Hotel

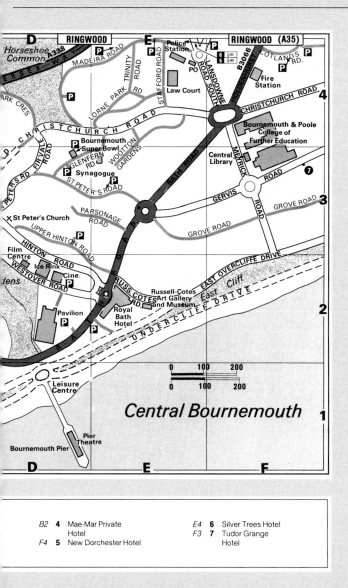

Central Bournemouth

B2	4	Mae-Mar Private Hotel	E4	6	Silver Trees Hotel
F4	5	New Dorchester Hotel	F3	7	Tudor Grange Hotel

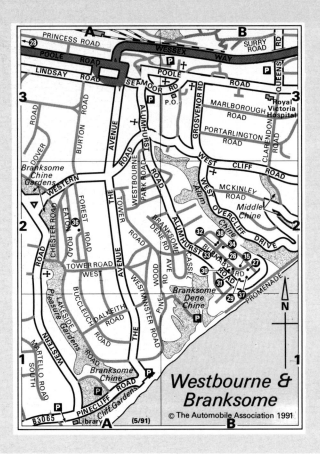

Westbourne & Branksome

B2 **26**	Alum Bay Hotel	
B2 **27**	Alum Grange Hotel	
A3 **28**	Avoncourt Private Hotel *(listed under Poole)*	

B2 **29**	Cliff House Hotel	
B2 **30**	Golden Sands Hotel	
B2 **31**	Highclere Hotel	
B2 **32**	Holmcroft Hotel	
B2 **33**	Newfield Private Hotel	
B2 **34**	Northover Private Hotel	

B2 **35**	Sea-Dene Hotel	
A2 **36**	Sheldon Lodge *(listed under Poole)*	
B2 **37**	West Dene Private Hotel	
B2 **38**	Woodford Court Hotel	

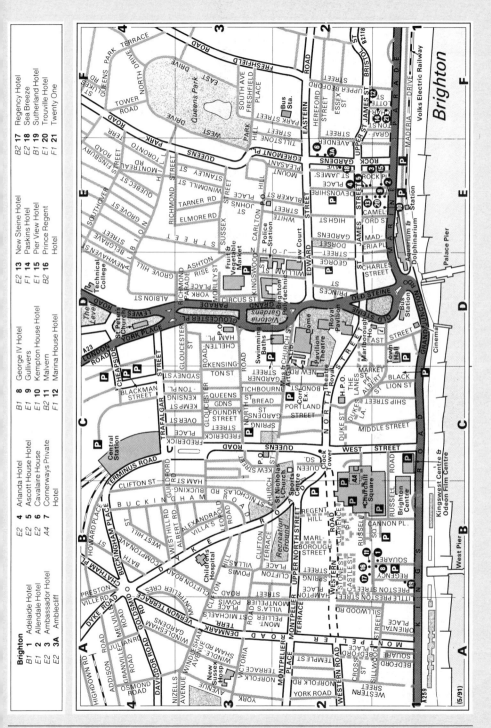

Brighton

B1 **1**	Adelaide Hotel	
E1 **2**	Allendale Hotel	
E2 **3**	Ambassador Hotel	
E2 **3A**	Amblecliff	
E2 **4**	Arlanda Hotel	
E2 **5**	Ascott House Hotel	
E2 **6**	Cavalaire House	
A4 **7**	Cornerways Private Hotel	
B1 **8**	George IV Hotel	
E1 **9**	Gullivers	
E1 **10**	Kempton House Hotel	
B2 **11**	Malvern	
F1 **12**	Marina House Hotel	
E2 **13**	New Steine Hotel	
F1 **14**	Paskins Hotel	
E1 **15**	Pier View Hotel	
B2 **16**	Prince Regent Hotel	
B2 **17**	Regency Hotel	
E2 **18**	Sea Breeze	
B1 **19**	Sutherland Hotel	
E1 **20**	Trouville Hotel	
F1 **21**	Twenty One	

Brighton

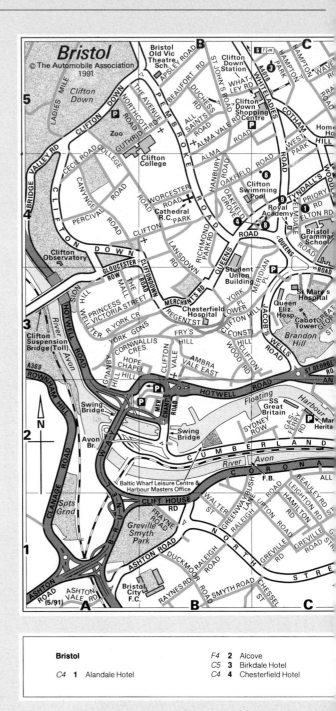

Bristol

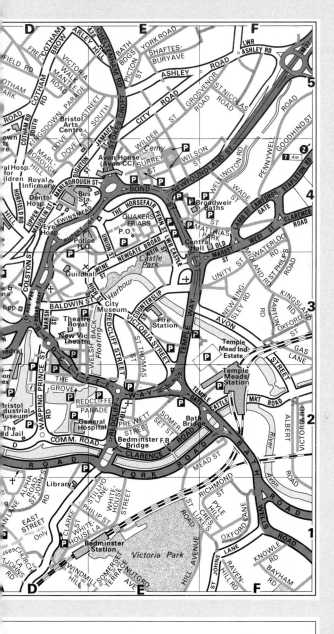

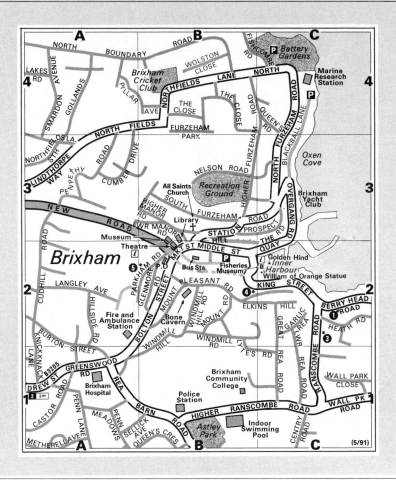

Brixham

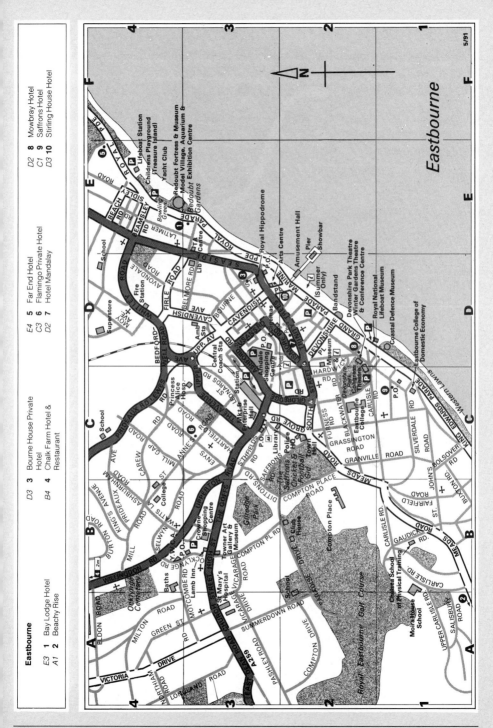

Eastbourne

E3	1	Bay Lodge Hotel
A1	2	Beachy Rise
D3	3	Bourne House Private Hotel
B4	4	Chalk Farm Hotel & Restaurant
E4	5	Far End Hotel
C3	6	Flamingo Private Hotel
D2	7	Hotel Mandalay
D2	8	Mowbray Hotel
C1	9	Saffrons Hotel
D3	10	Stirling House Hotel

Eastbourne

5/91

Edinburgh

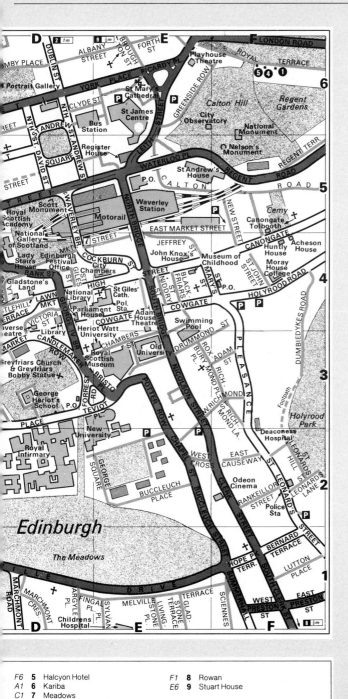

Edinburgh

F6	5	Halcyon Hotel
A1	6	Kariba
C1	7	Meadows

F1	8	Rowan
E6	9	Stuart House

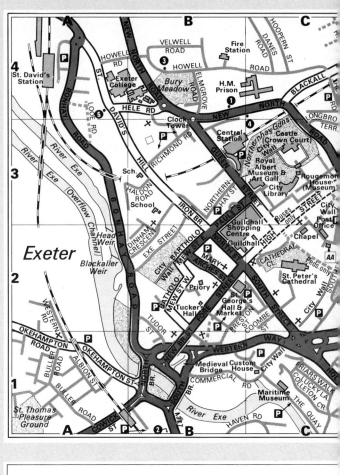

Exeter

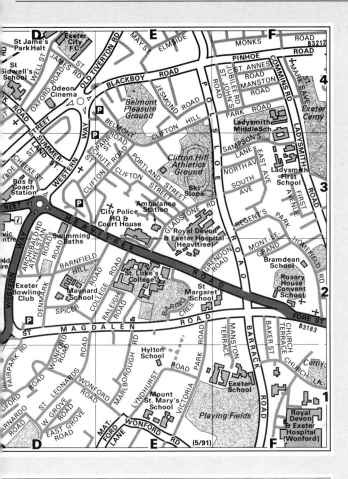

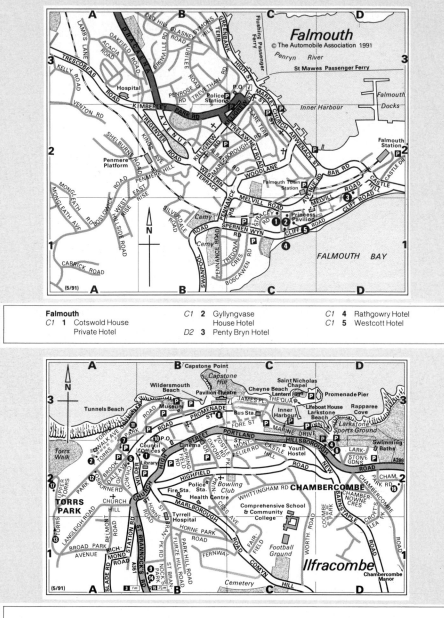

Falmouth

C1	1	Cotswold House Private Hotel	C1	2	Gyllyngvase House Hotel	
			D2	3	Penty Bryn Hotel	
C1	4	Rathgowry Hotel				
C1	5	Westcott Hotel				

Ilfracombe

B2	1	Avenue Private Hotel	D2	6	Collingdale Hotel	A1	13	South Tor Hotel
A2	2	Avoncourt Hotel	A2	7	Cresta Private Hotel	B1	14	Strathmore Private Hotel
A1	3	Cairngorm Hotel	B3	8	Dèdès Hotel	B1	15	Sunnymeade County House Hotel *(listed under West Down)*
D2	4	Cavendish Hotel	B1	9	Earlsdale Hotel			
A2	5	Chalfont Private Hotel	B2	10	Lympstone Private Hotel	D2	16	Varley House
			A3	11	Merlin Court Hotel	A2	17	Westwell Hall Hotel
			A2	12	Southcliffe Hotel			

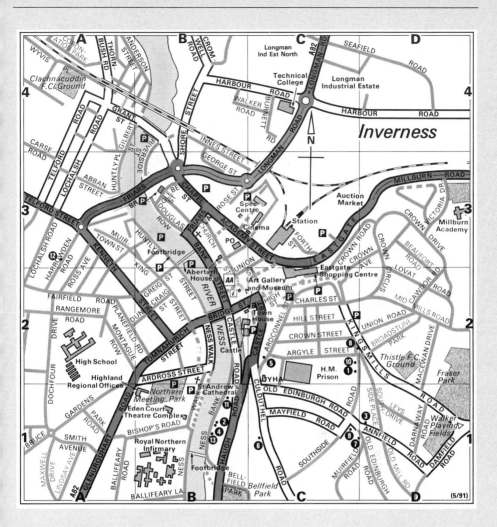

Inverness

		B1	**4** Brae Ness Hotel	*C1*	**9**	Leinster Lodge
		C2	**5** Craigside	*C2*	**10**	The Old Rectory
C2	**1** Aberfeldy Lodge	*C1*	**6** Culduthel Lodge	*B1*	**11**	Riverside House Hotel
B1	**2** Ardmuir House	*C1*	**7** Four Winds	*A3*	**12**	St Ann's Hotel
D1	**3** Ardnacoille House	*C2*	**8** Heathmount	*B1*	**13**	Windsor House Hotel

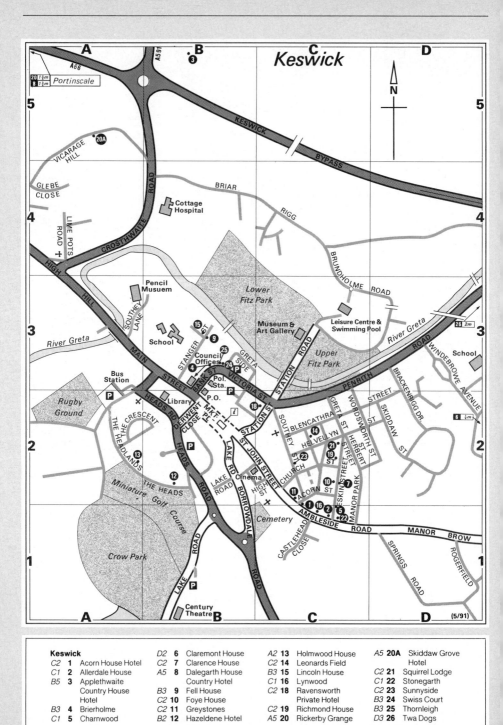

Keswick

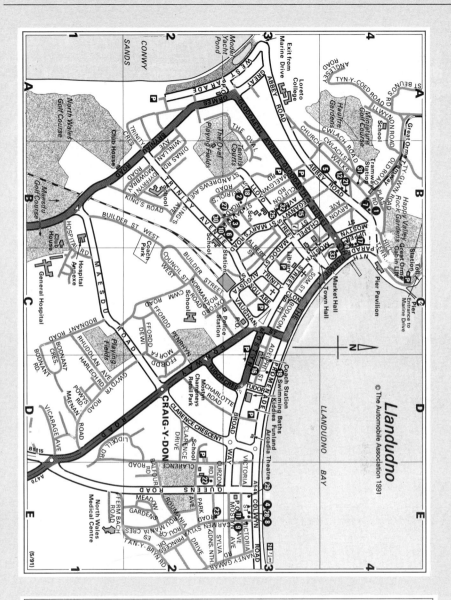

© The Automobile Association 1991

Llandudno

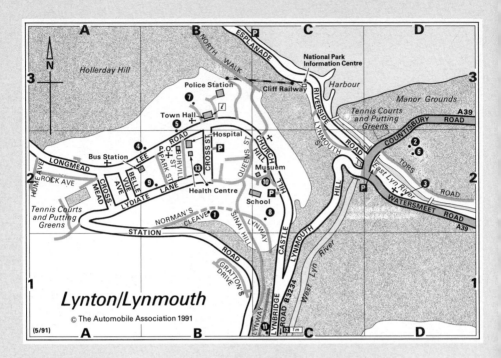

Lynton/Lynmouth

© The Automobile Association 1991

(5/91)

Lynton & Lynmouth

B2	**1**	Alford House Hotel *(see under Lynton)*
D2	**2**	Countisbury Lodge Hotel *(see under Lynmouth)*
D2	**3**	East Lyn House *(see under Lynmouth)*
B2	**4**	Gable Lodge *(see under Lynton)*
B2	**5**	Hazeldene *(see under Lynton)*
D2	**6**	The Heatherville *(see under Lynmouth)*
B3	**7**	Ingleside Hotel *(see under Lynton)*
C2	**8**	Mayfair Hotel *(see under Lynton)*
B2	**9**	Retreat *(see under Lynton)*
C2	**10**	St Vincent *(see under Lynton)*
C1	**11**	Valley House Hotel *(see under Lynton)*
C1	**12**	The Village Inn *(see under Lynmouth)*
B2	**13**	Waterloo House Hotel *(see under Lynton)*

446

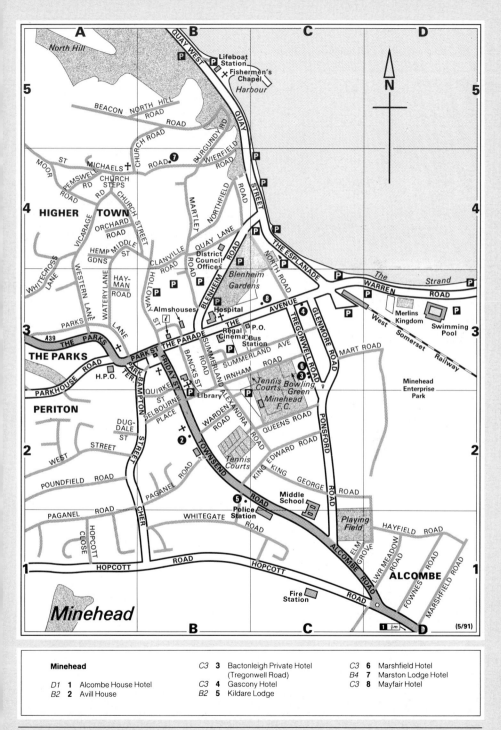

Minehead

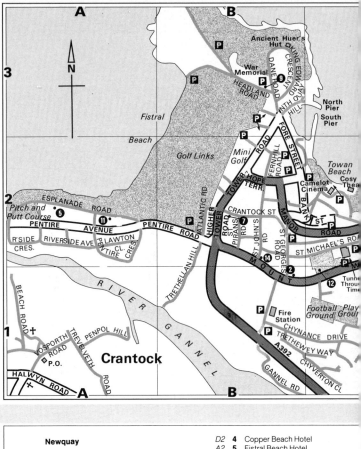

Newquay

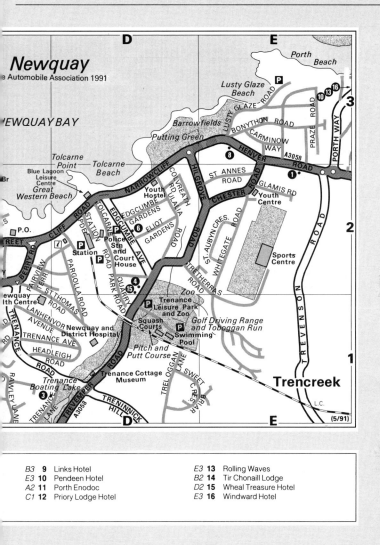

Newquay

The Automobile Association 1991

B3	**9**	Links Hotel
E3	**10**	Pendeen Hotel
A2	**11**	Porth Enodoc
C1	**12**	Priory Lodge Hotel
E3	**13**	Rolling Waves
B2	**14**	Tir Chonaill Lodge
D2	**15**	Wheal Treasure Hotel
E3	**16**	Windward Hotel

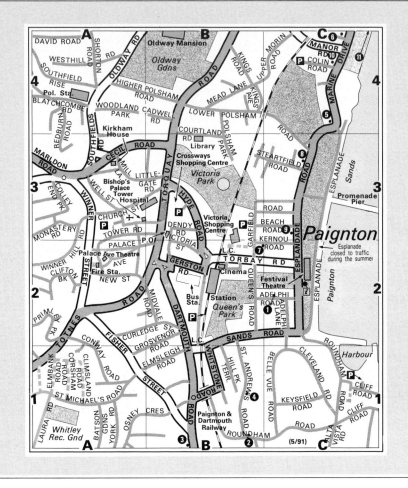

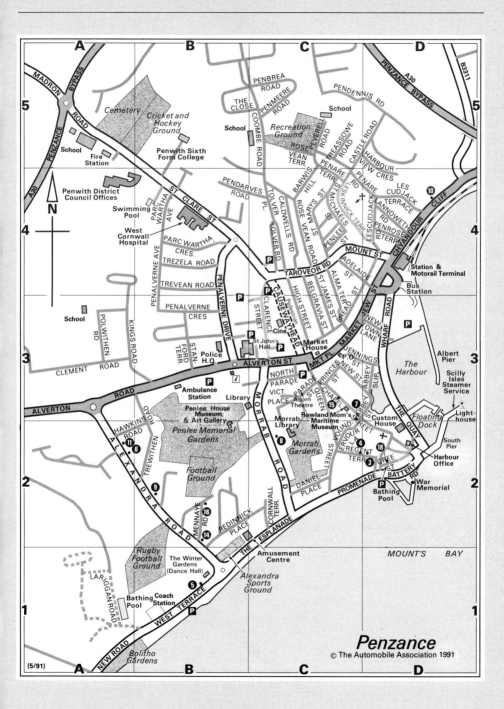

Penzance
© The Automobile Association 1991

(5/91)

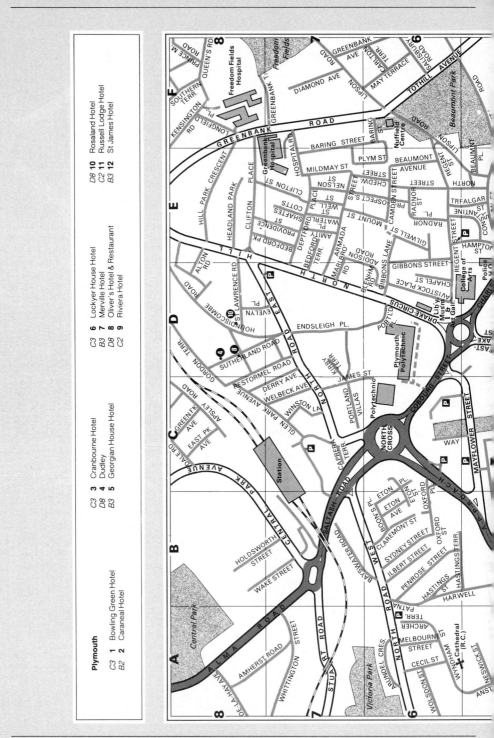

Plymouth

C3	**1**	Bowling Green Hotel
B2	**2**	Caraneal Hotel
C3	**3**	Cranbourne Hotel
D8	**4**	Dudley
B3	**5**	Georgian House Hotel
C3	**6**	Lockyer House Hotel
B3	**7**	Merville Hotel
D8	**8**	Oliver's Hotel & Restaurant
C2	**9**	Riviera Hotel
D8	**10**	Rosaland Hotel
C2	**11**	Russell Lodge Hotel
B3	**12**	St James Hotel

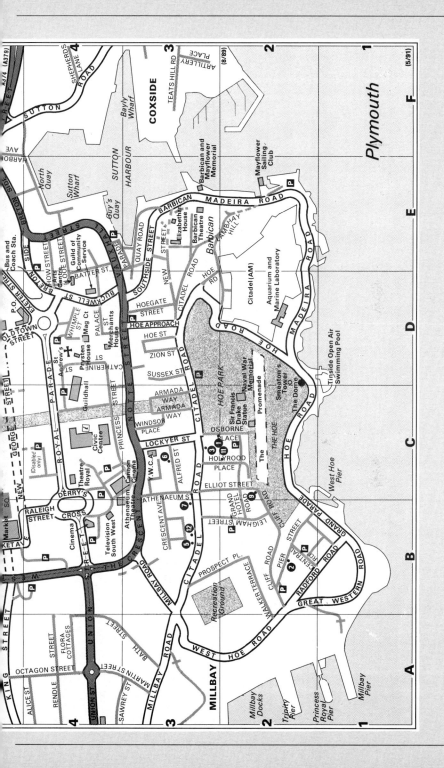

Plymouth

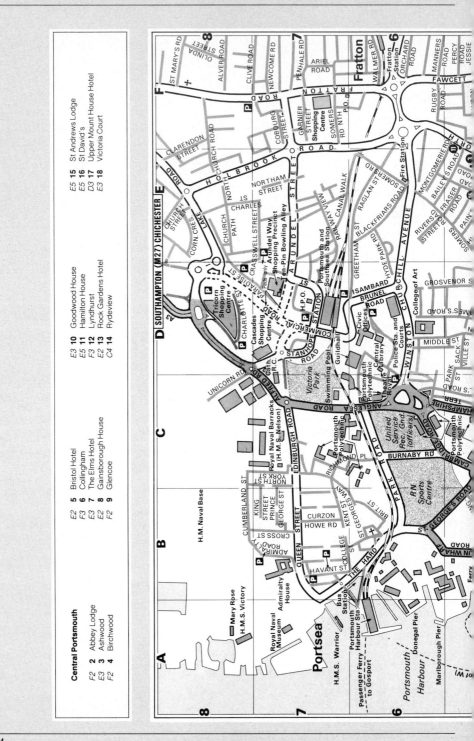

Central Portsmouth

F2	**2**	Abbey Lodge	
E3	**3**	Ashwood	
F2	**4**	Birchwood	

E2	**5**	Bristol Hotel	
F3	**6**	Collingham	
E3	**7**	The Elms Hotel	
E2	**8**	Gainsborough House	
F2	**9**	Glencoe	

E3	**10**	Goodwood House	
E5	**11**	Hamilton House	
F3	**12**	Lyndhurst	
E2	**13**	Rock Gardens Hotel	
C4	**14**	Rydeview	

E5	**15**	St Andrews Lodge	
E5	**16**	St David's	
D3	**17**	Upper Mount House Hotel	
E3	**18**	Victoria Court	

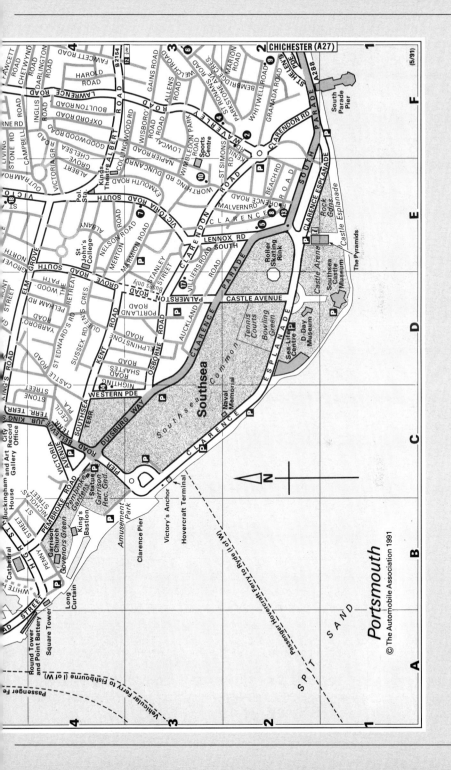

Portsmouth

© The Automobile Association 1991

CHICHESTER (A27)

South Parade Pier

(5/91)

455

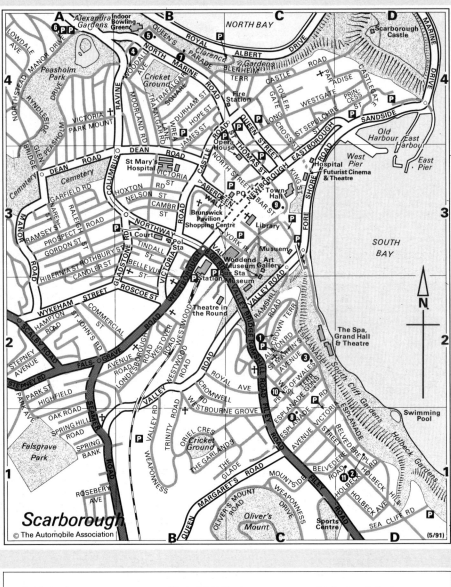

Scarborough
© The Automobile Association

(5/91)

Scarborough		
C2	**1**	Avoncroft Hotel
D1	**2**	Bay & Premier Hotels
C2	**3**	Burghcliffe Hotel
B4	**4**	Dolphin Hotel
B4	**5**	Geldenhuis Hotel
A4	**6**	Manor Heath Hotel
B4	**7**	Paragon Hotel
C1	**8**	Parmelia Hotel
C3	**9**	Riveria Hotel
C2	**10**	Sefton Hotel
D1	**11**	West Lodge Private Hotel

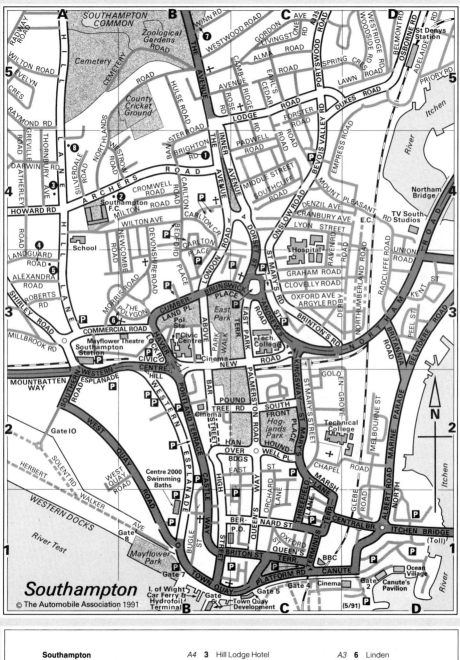

Southampton

© The Automobile Association 1991

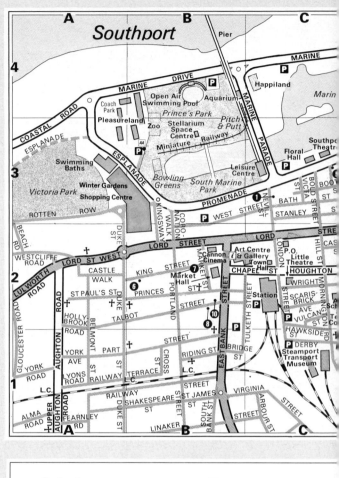

Southport

C3 **1** Ambassador Private Hotel
D3 **2** Crimond Hotel

D3 **3** Fairway Private Hotel
D3 **4** The Gables Private Hotel
C3 **5** Lake Hotel

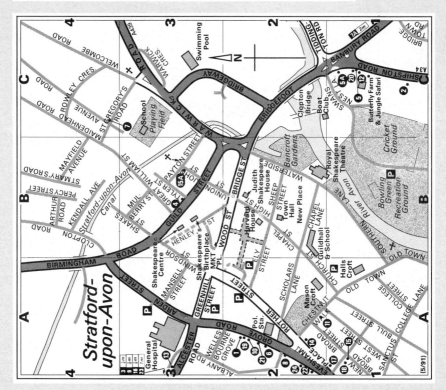

Stratford-upon-Avon

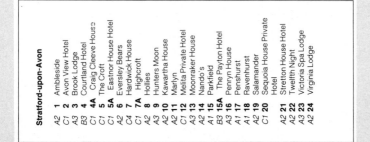

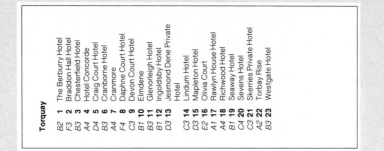

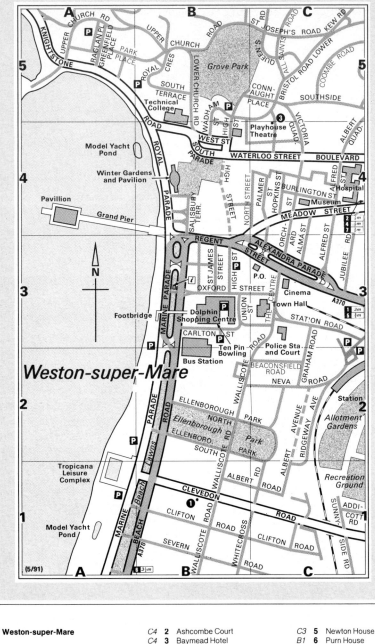

Weston-super-Mare

B1	**1**	Almond Lodge				

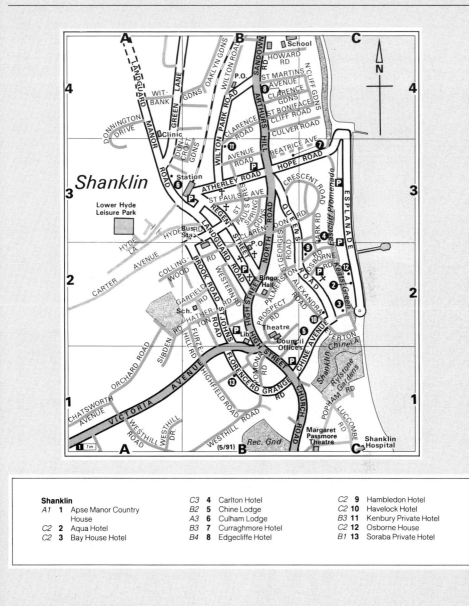

Shanklin

A1	1	Apse Manor Country House
C2	2	Aqua Hotel
C2	3	Bay House Hotel
C3	4	Carlton Hotel
B2	5	Chine Lodge
A3	6	Culham Lodge
B3	7	Curraghmore Hotel
B4	8	Edgecliffe Hotel
C2	9	Hambledon Hotel
C2	10	Havelock Hotel
B3	11	Kenbury Private Hotel
C2	12	Osborne House
B1	13	Soraba Private Hotel

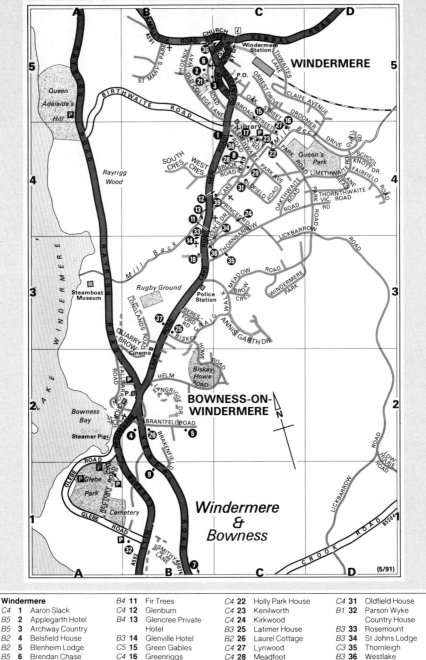

Windermere & Bowness

WINDERMERE

BOWNESS-ON-WINDERMERE

Windermere		*B4* **11** Fir Trees		*C4* **22** Holly Park House		*C4* **31** Oldfield House
C4 **1** Aaron Slack		*C4* **12** Glenburn		*C4* **23** Kenilworth		*B1* **32** Parson Wyke
B5 **2** Applegarth Hotel		*B4* **13** Glencree Private		*C4* **24** Kirkwood		Country House
B5 **3** Archway Country		Hotel		*B3* **25** Latimer House		*B3* **33** Rosemount
B2 **4** Belsfield House		*B3* **14** Glenville Hotel		*B2* **26** Laurel Cottage		*B3* **34** St Johns Lodge
B2 **5** Blenheim Lodge		*C5* **15** Green Gables		*C4* **27** Lynwood		*C3* **35** Thornleigh
B5 **6** Brendan Chase		*C4* **16** Greenriggs		*C4* **28** Meadfoot		*B3* **36** Westlake
B1 **7** Brooklands		*C4* **17** Haisthorpe		*C4* **29** Mylne Bridge		*B3* **37** White Lodge Hotel
C4 **8** Clifton House		*B3* **18** The Hawksmoor		House		*C4* **38** Winbrook
B1 **9** Cranleigh Hotel		*B5* **21** Holly Lodge		*C5* **30** Oakthorpe Hotel		*C4* **39** Woodlands

464

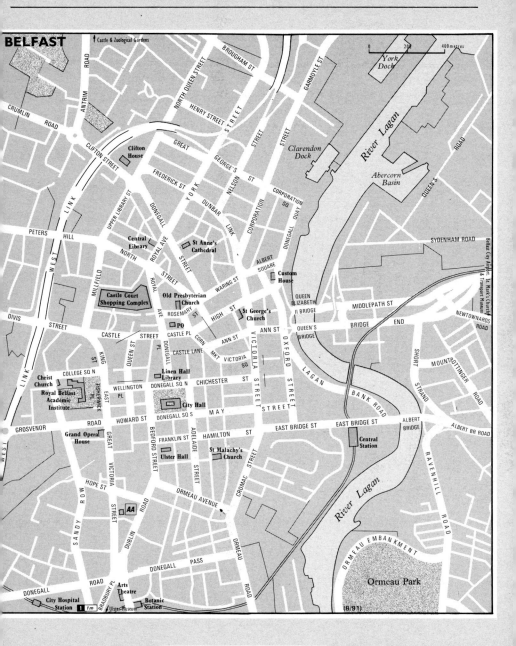

BELFAST

Belfast

1 Camera

Dublin

1 Ariel House
2 The Fitzwilliam
3 Georgian House

Index of Regional Maps

Follow the Country Code

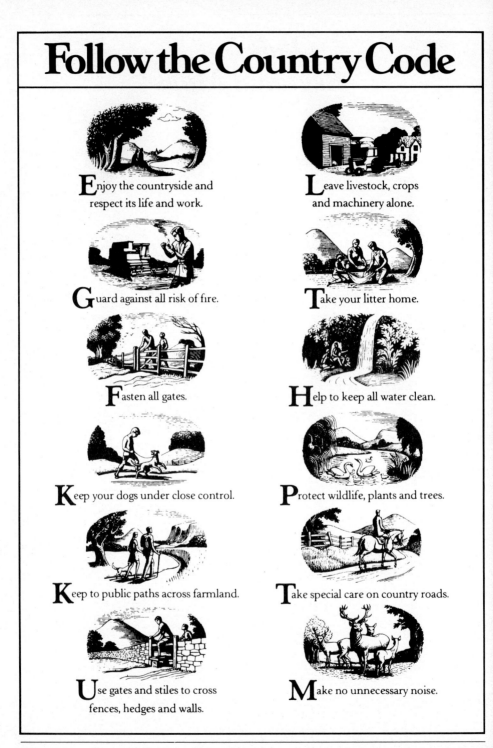

Enjoy the countryside and respect its life and work.

Leave livestock, crops and machinery alone.

Guard against all risk of fire.

Take your litter home.

Fasten all gates.

Help to keep all water clean.

Keep your dogs under close control.

Protect wildlife, plants and trees.

Keep to public paths across farmland.

Take special care on country roads.

Use gates and stiles to cross fences, hedges and walls.

Make no unnecessary noise.

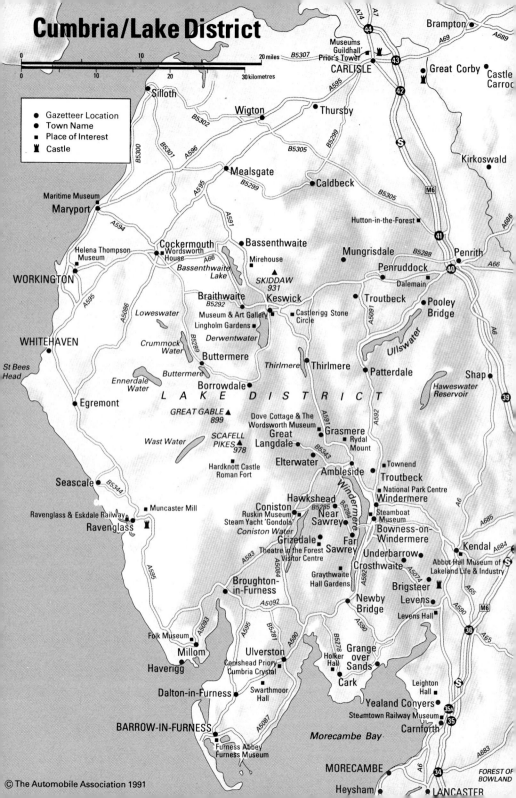

Cumbria/Lake District

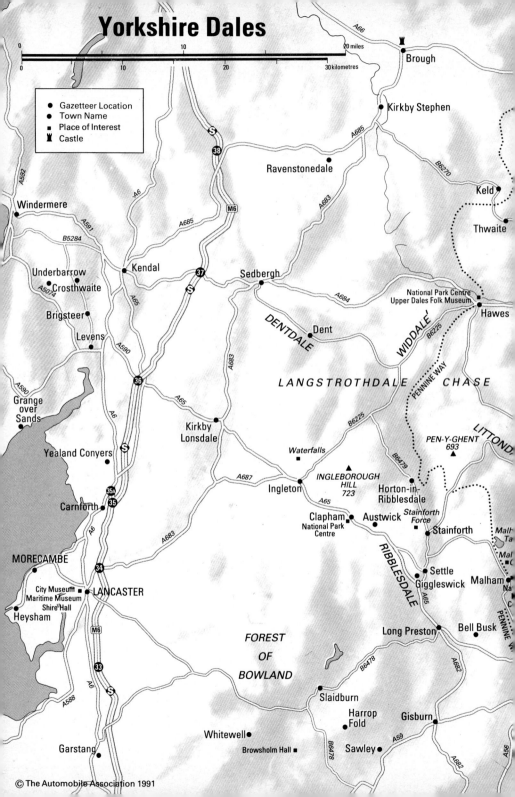

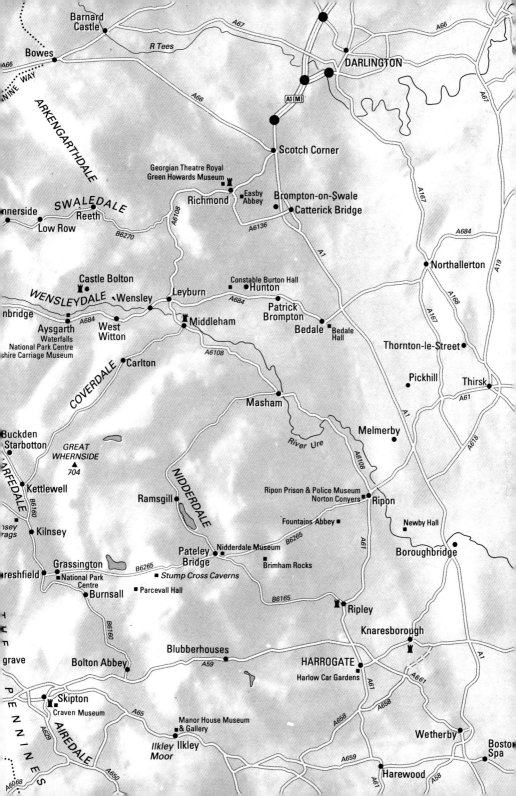

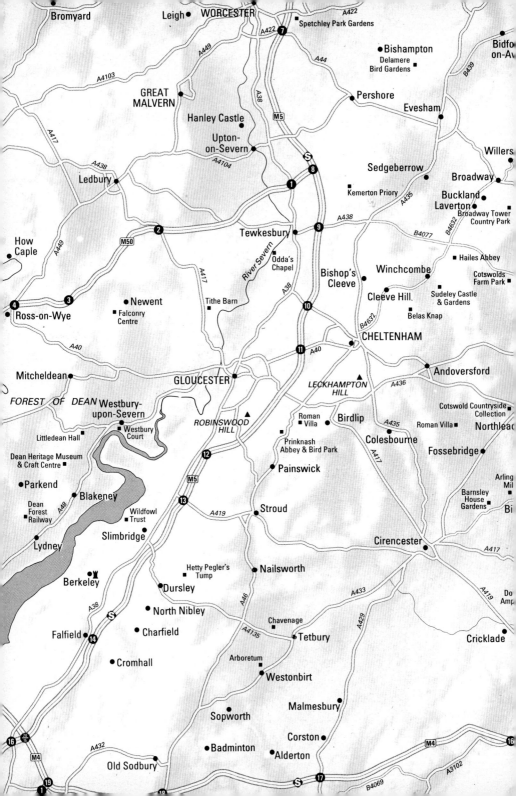

Cotswolds and Forest of Dean

0   10   20 miles

0   10   20   30 kilometres

- ● Gazetteer Location
- ● Town Name
- ■ Place of Interest
- ♜ Castle

© The Automobile Association 1991

Somerset, Avon, Wiltshire and Dorset

Rhoose · BARRY
Welsh Hawking Centre

WESTON-SUPER-MARE

International Helicopter Museum

Bridgwater Bay

Burnham-on-Sea

Minehead
Dunster
Old Dovecote
Cleeve Abbey
Roadwater
Washford
Watchet
Kilve
Nether Stowey
Coleridge Cottage

Combe Sydenham Hall
Gauldon Manor

BRENDON HILLS
Wimbleball Lake

Wiveliscombe
Waterrow

QUANTOCK HILLS

West Bagborough
BRIDGWATER
Hestercombe Gardens
Burrowbridge
Stoke St Gregory

Norton Fitzwarren
TAUNTON
Sheppeys Cider
Wellington
Poundisford Park

MONUMENT

Uffculme
Willand
Cullompton

Payhembury
Whimple
Honiton

Ottery St Mary
Venn Ottery

EXMOUTH
Budleigh Salterton
Sidmouth
Beer
Seaton
Colyton
Colyford
Charmouth
Lyme Regis

Redhill
Stanton Wick
CHEW VALLEY LAKE

Blagdon
MENDIP HILLS
Temple Cloud
Axbridge
Cheddar
Cheddar Gorge & Caves
Wookey Hole Caves & Mill
Wookey Hole
Wells
Sheptor Malle
Bishops Palace
Wootton Vineyard
North Wootton
Glastonbury
Shoe Museum
Street
West Pennard
Butleigh

KING'S SEDGE MOOR
Somerton
Langport
Lytes Cary
Podimore
Fleet Air Arm & Concorde
Ilchester
Muchelney Abbey
East Lambrook Manor
Tintinhull House
Stoke-sub-Hamdon Priory
Montacute House
Chiselborough
Brympton d' Evercy
YEOVIL
West Coker
Coker Court

Stoke St Gregory
Beercrocombe
Barrington Court

Crewkerne
Clapton Court Gardens
North Perrott
Halstock

Chard
Forde Abbey
Cricket St Thomas Wildlife Park & Country Life Museum

Bettiscombe
Axminster
Parnham
Beaminster
Mapperton
Nettlecombe
Eversho
Bridport
Winterb Abba
Chideock
Burton Bradstock
Abbotsbury
Swan Sub-tro Gard
Lyme Bay
Chesil

Legend

- Gazetteer Location
- Town Name
- Place of Interest
- Castle

0 ___ 10 ___ 20 miles
0 ___ 10 ___ 20 ___ 30 kilometres

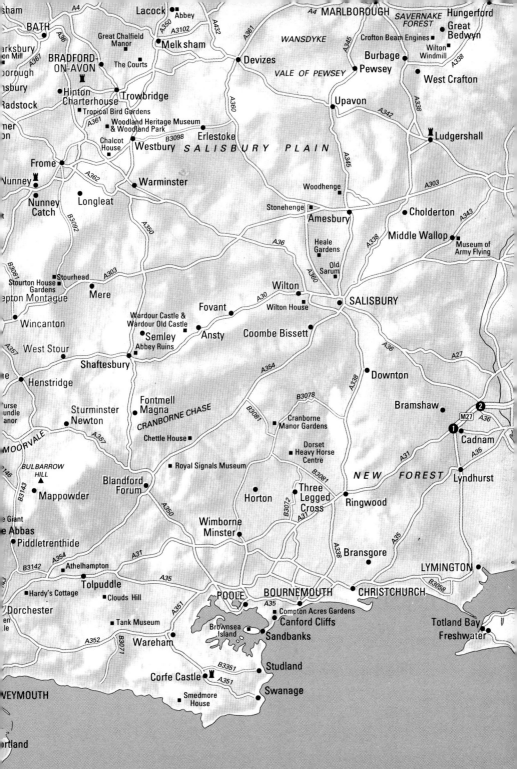

Devon and Cornwall

Hartland Point

Hart

Welcomb

Bude
Bude
Bay

Widemouth Bay

Crackington
Haven

Boscastle

Hallwo

Tintagel

B3263

Port Isaac

Polzeath

Trevone   Rock

St Merryn   Padstow

Little Petherick   Pencarrow

Porthcothan   Tropical Bird
Gardens   Wadebridge

BODMIN   MOC

Collifo
Lake

BODMIN

B3276

Mawgan Porth   BODMIN

Mount   Do

Newquay   St Mawgan   Dobwalls

A30

A392   A390   Liske

Newlyn   Roche   Lostwithiel   St Keyne

East

A391   Sandp

Wheal Martyn
Museum   Lanlivery

Perranporth   Pelynt

St Agnes   Zelah   ST   Fowey

Leisure   St   AUSTELL   Tywardreath

Park   Erme   A3058   Trewithen   Polruan   Pol

B3285   Charlestown Shipwreck
& Heritage Museum

B3277   Truro   Grampound

Polmassick   Mevagissey

St Ives   *St Ives*   Redruth   Gorran
Bay   Camborne   Haven

Troon   St Just-in-Roseland

Lelant

Ludgvan   Paradise Park   Penryn

St Just   Penzance   St Hilary   Trenear   Falmouth

A394   Seal   Constantine
Sanctuary

St Michael's   Helston
Mount

*Land's
End*   Flambards
Theme Park

Lands   Sennen   Mousehole
End

A3083

Lizard

Lizard Point

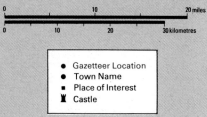

- ● Gazetteer Location
- ● Town Name
- ■ Place of Interest
- ♜ Castle

0   10   *20 miles*

0   10   20   *30 kilometres*

© The Automobile Association 1991

Opening doors to the World of books

Book Tokens

Book Tokens can be bought and exchanged at most bookshops

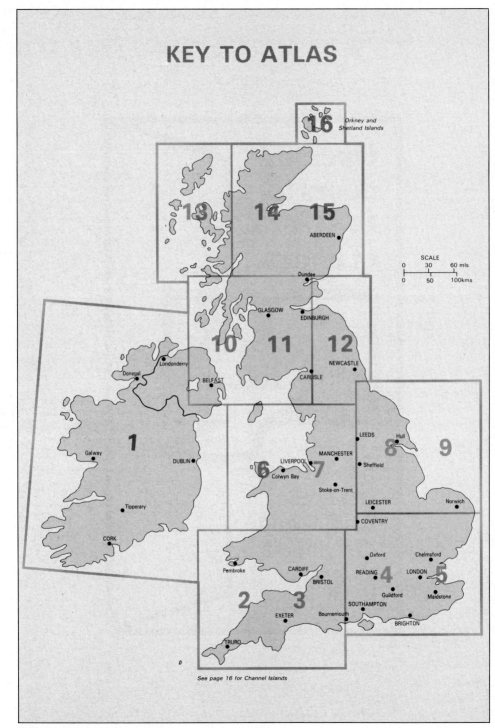

KEY TO ATLAS

Orkney and Shetland Islands

SCALE

| 0 | 30 | 60 mls |
| 0 | 50 | 100kms |

See page 16 for Channel Islands

© The Automobile Association 1991.

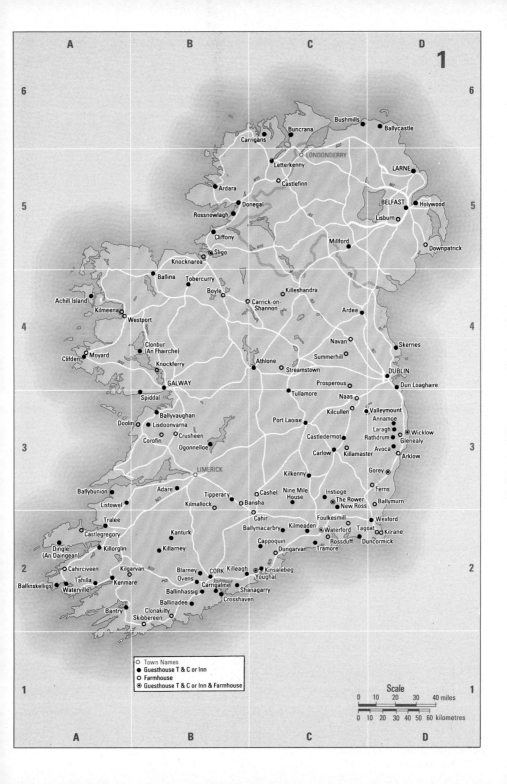

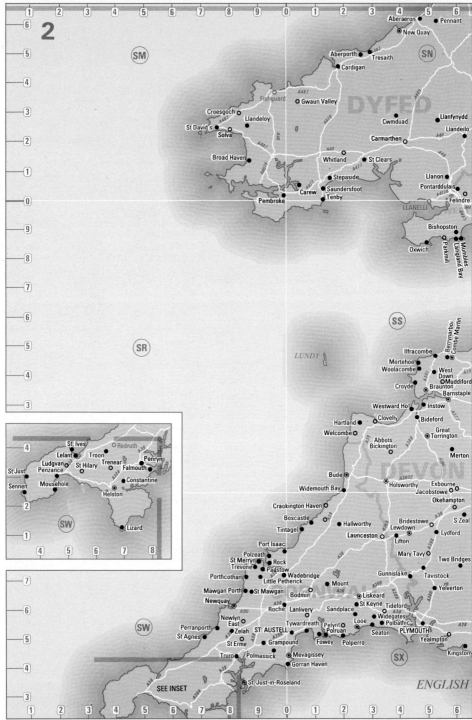

2

SM · SN · SR · SS · SW · SX

DYFED

Aberaeron · Pennant · New Quay · Aberporth · Tresaith · Cardigan · Croesgoch · Cwmduad · Llanfynydd · St David's · Llandeloy · Llandeilo · Solva · Carmarthen · Broad Haven · Whitland · St Clears · Llanon · Stepaside · Pontarddulais · Carew · Saundersfoot · Felindre · Pembroke · Tenby · LLANELLI · Bishopston · Oxwich · Parkmill · Mumbles · Langland Bay

LUNDY

Berrynarbor · Combe Martin · Ilfracombe · Mortehoe · Woolacombe · West Down · Muddiford · Croyde · Braunton · Barnstaple · Westward Ho! · Instow · Hartland · Clovelly · Bideford · Welcombe · Great Torrington · Abbots Bickington · Merton · Bude · Exbourne · Jacobstowe · Widemouth Bay · Holsworthy · Okehampton · Crackington Haven · S Zeal · Boscastle · Bridestowe · Lewdown · Tintagel · Hallworthy · Lifton · Lydford · Launceston · Mary Tavy · Two Bridges · Port Isaac · Gunnislake · Tavistock · Polzeath · Yelverton · St Merryn · Rock · Trevone · Padstow · Porthcothan · Wadebridge · Mount · Mawgan Porth · Little Petherick · Liskeard · St Mawgan · Bodmin · St Keyne · Tideford · Newquay · Roche · Lanlivery · Sandplace · Looe · Widegates · Polbathic · PLYMOUTH · Newlyn East · Tywardreath · Pelynt · Polruan · Seaton · Yealmpton · Perranporth · Zelah · ST AUSTELL · Fowey · Polperro · St Agnes · St Erme · Grampound · Polmassick · Mevagissey · Kingston · Truro · Gorran Haven · St Just-in-Roseland

DEVON

CORNWALL

ENGLISH

SEE INSET

Inset:
St Ives · Lelant · Troon · Penryn · Redruth · Ludgvan · Penzance · St Hilary · Trenear · Falmouth · St Just · Constantine · Sennen · Mousehole · Helston · Lizard

For continuation pages refer to numbered arrows

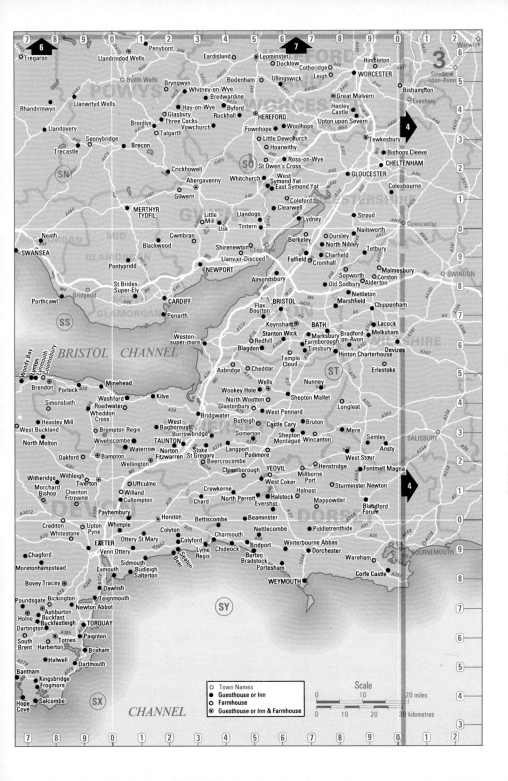

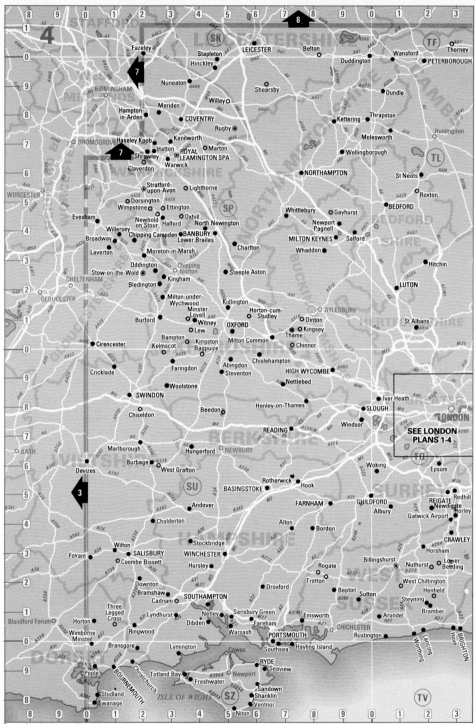

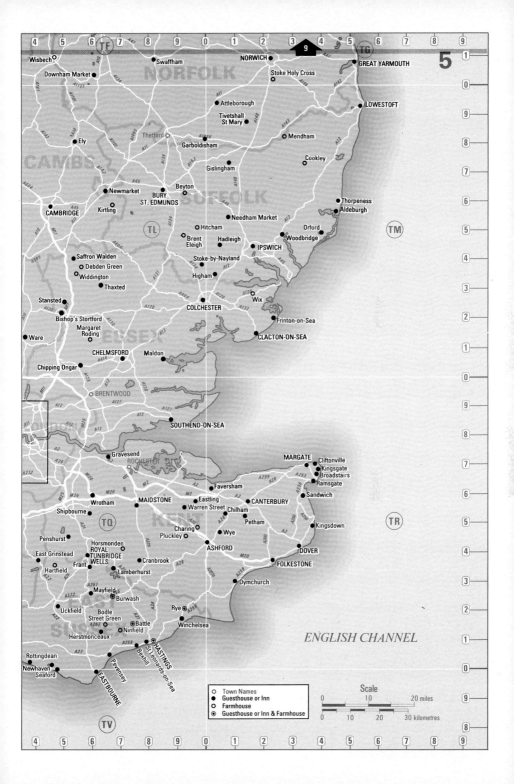

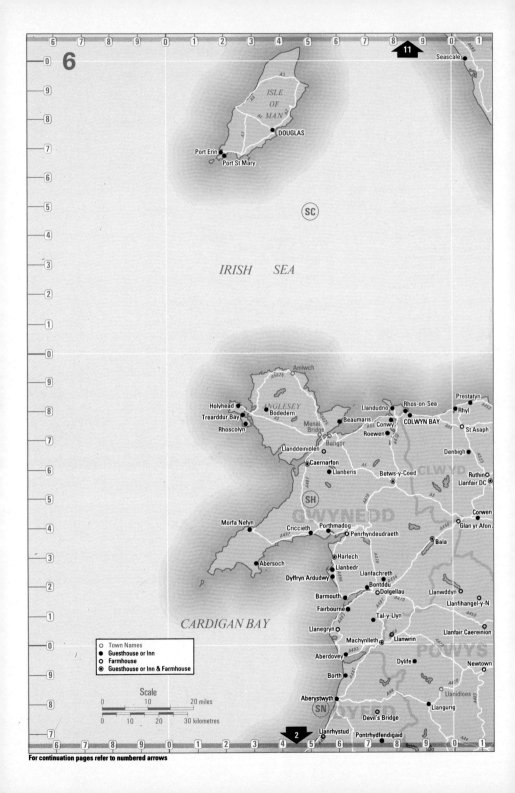

IRISH SEA

ISLE OF MAN

DOUGLAS

Port Erin

Port St Mary

SC

Seascale

11

Amlwch

ANGLESEY

Holyhead
Trearddur Bay
Rhoscolyn

Bodedern

Menai Bridge

Bangor

Llanddeiniolen

Caernarfon

Llanberis

SH

Llandudno
Rhos-on-Sea
Prestatyn

Beaumaris
Conwy
COLWYN BAY
Rhyl

Roewen

St Asaph

Denbigh

Betws-y-Coed

CLWYD

Ruthin
Llanfair DC

GWYNEDD

Morfa Nefyn

Criccieth
Porthmadog
Penrhyndeudraeth

Bala

Corwen
Glan yr Afon

Abersoch

Harlech
Llanbedr
Llanfachreth

Dyffryn Ardudwy

Bontddu

Barmouth

Dolgellau

Fairbourne

Tal-y-Llyn

Llanegryn

Machynlleth

Llanwrin

POWYS

Llanwddyn

Llanfihangel-y-N

Llanfair Caereinion

Newtown

Aberdovey

Dylife

Borth

Aberystwyth

SN

DYFED

Llanidloes

Llangurig

Devil's Bridge

Llanrhystud

2

Pontrhydfendigaid

CARDIGAN BAY

Town Names
Guesthouse or Inn
Farmhouse
Guesthouse or Inn & Farmhouse

Scale

0   10   20 miles

0   10   20   30 kilometres

For continuation pages refer to numbered arrows

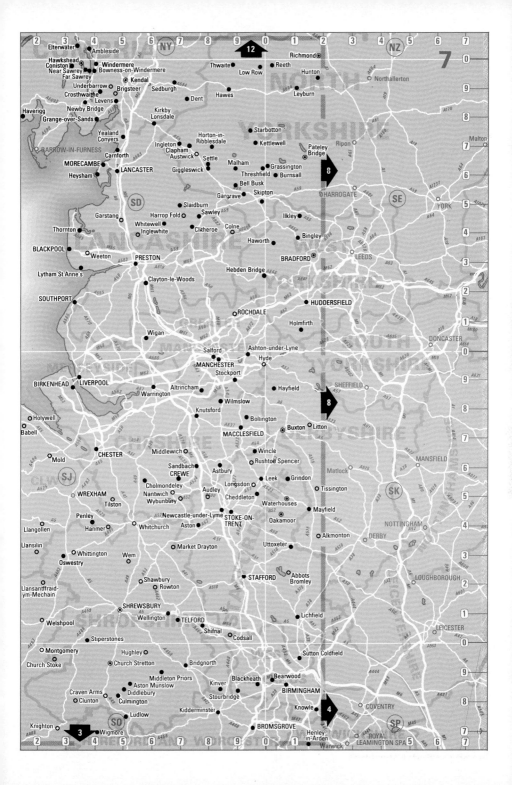

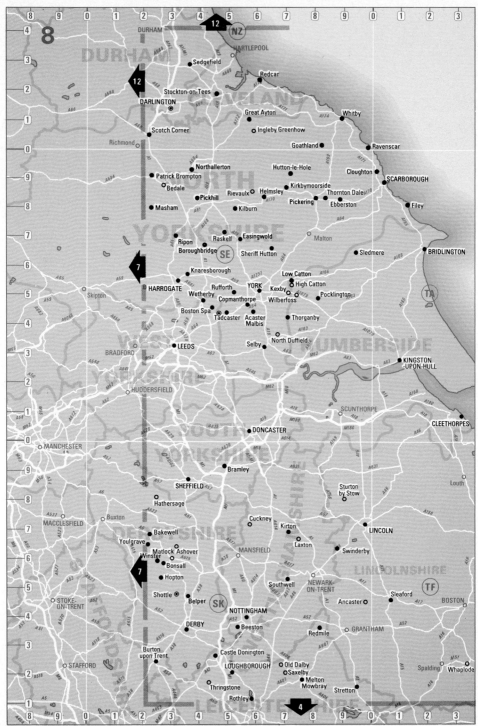

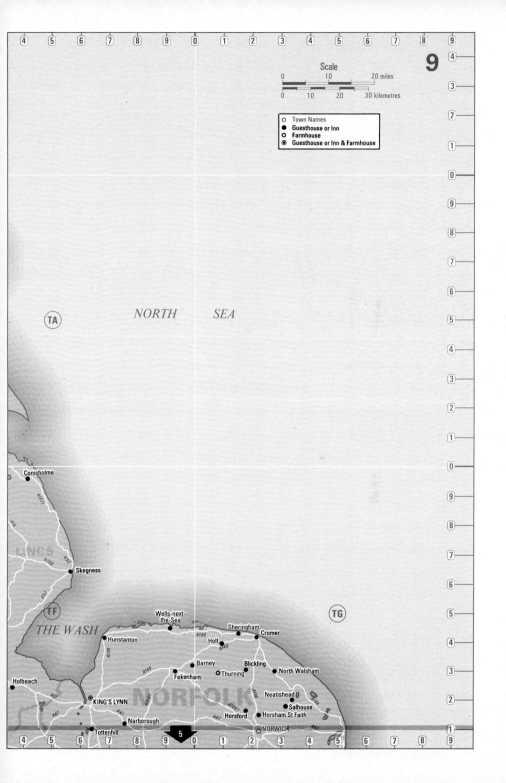

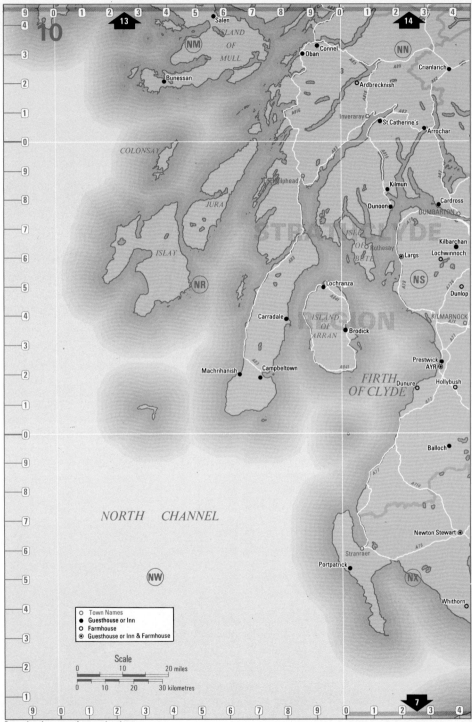

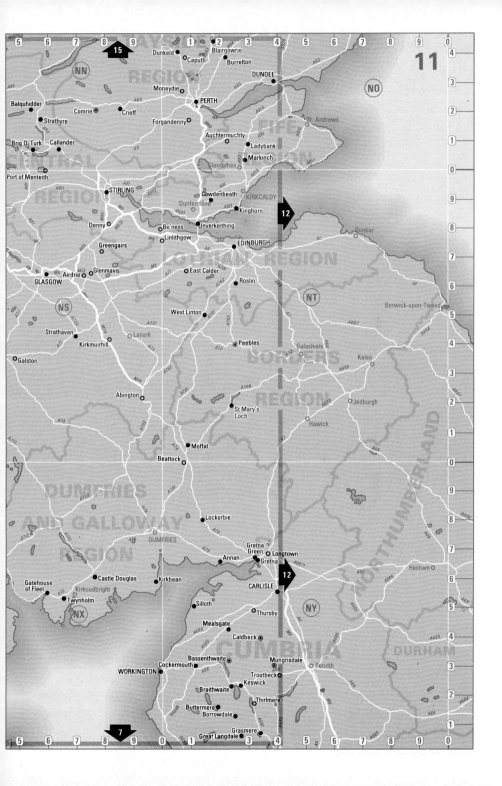

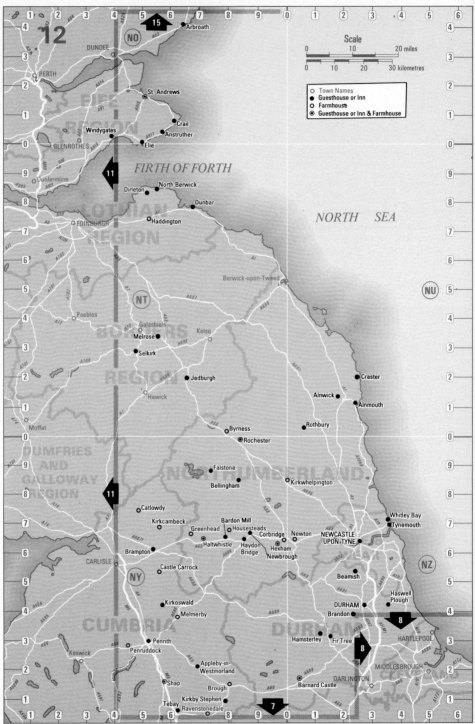

12

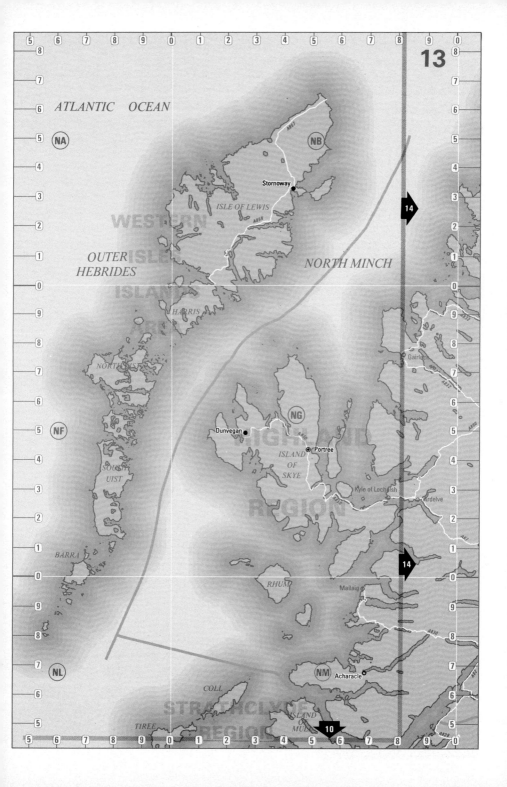

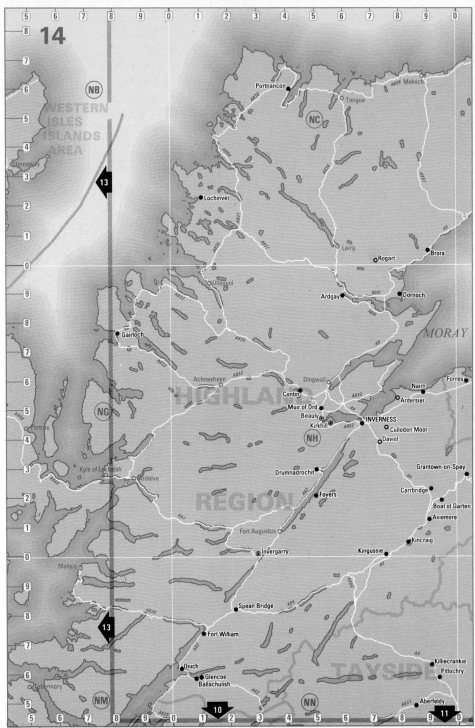

NB

WESTERN
ISLES
ISLANDS
AREA

Stornoway

13

NC

Portnancon

A838 Melvich

Tongue

Lochinver

Lairg

Rogart

Brora

Ullapool

Ardgay

A949

Dornoch

MORAY

Gairloch

Achnasheen

A832

Dingwall

Forres

NG

Contin

A832

Nairn

Portree

Muir of Ord

Beauly

Ardersier

Kirkhill

INVERNESS

NH

Culloden Moor

Daviot

Kyle of Lochalsh

Ardelve

Drumnadrochit

Grantown-on-Spey

REGION

Foyers

Carrbridge

Boat of Garten

Fort Augustus

Aviemore

Invergarry

Kincraig

Kingussie

Mallaig

Spean Bridge

13

Fort William

Tobermory

NM

Onich

Glencoe

Ballachulish

A82

A9

Killiecrankie

Pitlochry

TAYSIDE

NN

Aberfeldy

10

11

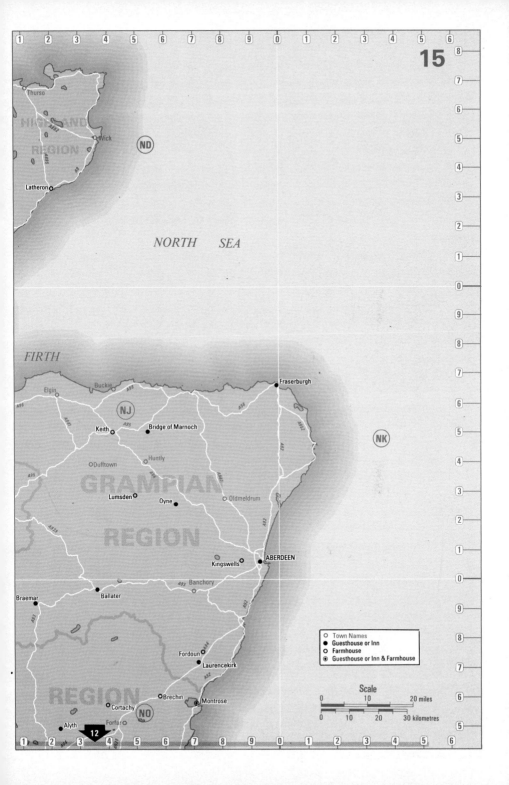

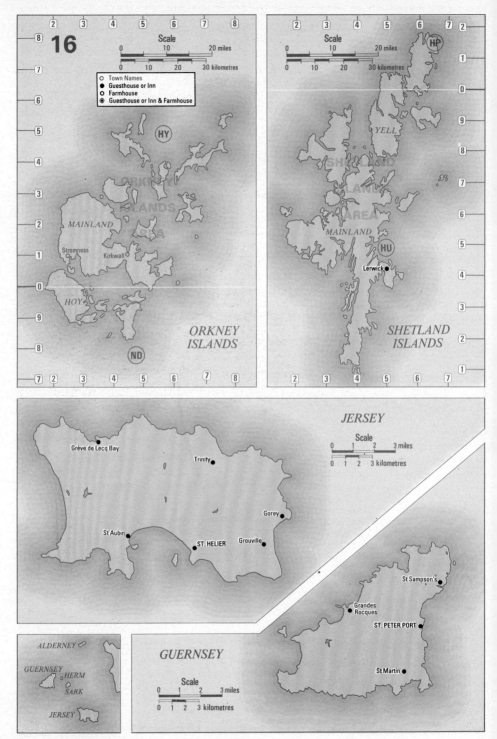

16

Scale
0   10   20 miles
0 10 20 30 kilometres

Town Names
Guesthouse or Inn
Farmhouse
Guesthouse or Inn & Farmhouse

HY

ORKNEY
ISLANDS
AREA

MAINLAND

Stromness
Kirkwall

HOY

ND

ORKNEY
ISLANDS

Scale
0   10   20 miles
0 10 20 30 kilometres

HP

YELL

SHETLAND
ISLAND
AREA

MAINLAND

HU

Lerwick

SHETLAND
ISLANDS

JERSEY

Grève de Lecq Bay

Trinity

Scale
0   1   2   3 miles
0 1 2 3 kilometres

Gorey

St Aubin

ST. HELIER
Grouville

St Sampson's

Grandes
Rocques

ST. PETER PORT

St Martin

ALDERNEY

GUERNSEY
HERM
SARK

JERSEY

GUERNSEY

Scale
0   1   2   3 miles
0 1 2 3 kilometres